OXFORD READER'S COMPANION TO GEORGE ELIOT

OXFORD READER'S COMPANION TO

George Eliot

Edited by John Rignall

OXFORD

UNIVERSITY PRESS

OXFORD
UNIVERSITY PRESS

Great Clarendon Street, Oxford OX2 6DP

Oxford University Press is a department of the University of Oxford.
It furthers the University's objective of excellence in research, scholarship,
and education by publishing worldwide in

Oxford New York

Athens Auckland Bangkok Bogotá Buenos Aires Calcutta
Cape Town Chennai Dar es Salaam Delhi Florence Hong Kong Istanbul
Karachi Kuala Lumpur Madrid Melbourne Mexico City Mumbai
Nairobi Paris São Paulo Singapore Shanghai Taipei Tokyo Toronto Warsaw
and associated companies in Berlin Ibadan

Oxford is a registered trade mark of Oxford University Press
in the UK and in certain other countries

Published in the United States
by Oxford University Press Inc., New York

© Oxford University Press 2000

Database right Oxford University Press (maker)

First published 2000

British Library Cataloguing in Publication Data
Data available

Library of Congress Cataloging in Publication Data
Data available

ISBN 0–19–860099–2

1 3 5 7 9 10 8 6 4 2

Typeset in Minion
by Alliance Phototypesetters, Pondicherry, India
Printed in Great Britain
on acid-free paper by
T. J. International Ltd
Padstow, Cornwall

10020 24903

ACKNOWLEDGEMENTS

M ANY hands and minds have played their part in the production of this volume, which could never have been created by a single individual. As General Editor I am conscious of a large debt of gratitude. First I would like to thank the contributors who gave so generously of their expertise for small reward, and the Consultant Editors, Gillian Beer and Elizabeth Deeds Ermarth, who provided invaluable advice and assistance. Needless to say, responsibility for the final form of the volume and for all errors and omissions remains mine alone.

I am particularly grateful to Graham Handley and Ruth Harris for taking on extra entries as the deadline for submission approached, and to Margaret Harris for undertaking to write such a large proportion of the text. She, together with Judith Johnston and Cambridge University Press, provided precious assistance by allowing me to see proofs of *The Journals of George Eliot*, which facilitated the composition of many entries. My thanks go also to Kathleen and Bill Adams of the George Eliot Fellowship for their help with finding illustrations, for composing George Eliot's family tree, and for their readiness to loan books and answer queries. I am grateful, too, to the staff of the Warwick University library for their efficient service, and to Rachel Parkins and Pauline Wilson for their computing expertise and advice. The efficiency and courtesy of the staff at Oxford University Press made my task less onerous, and I would like to express my thanks to Michael Cox, Pam Coote, Alison Jones, Wendy Tuckey, and Rebecca Collins, and to Rowena Anketell for her meticulous and expert copy-editing. My greatest debt of gratitude is to Athena Economides, without whose unfailingly cheerful and competent editorial assistance the text would never have reached a presentable final form. Finally I would like to thank my wife Ann for her invaluable moral support and practical assistance.

JOHN RIGNALL

PREFACE

A NY attempt to compile a comprehensive work about George Eliot is inevitably haunted by the grey figure of Mr Casaubon and his fruitless labours to create a 'Key to all Mythologies'. Casaubon, numbing his young wife with a pedantic recitation of received opinion when confronted by the artistic riches of Rome, defines in his person and his project all that a *Companion* should not be: 'a lifeless embalmment of knowledge'. What this volume aspires to, by contrast, is comprehensiveness and accuracy combined with the vitality that comes from lucid writing, critical insight, and a variety of different minds and voices. Not pedantry but professional scholarship made accessible to the general reader as well as the academic.

In aiming for comprehensiveness *The Oxford Reader's Companion to George Eliot* provides detailed information about her life and work, with a long entry which surveys her life, and entries on her family, friends, and acquaintances; on the places she lived in and the countries she visited; on her novels, stories, and poetry, and on the thematic and formal features of her fiction; on her letters and journals, notebooks and manuscripts; and on the different aspects of her career as a writer, which included translation and journalism as well as writing fiction. What it does not offer is an annotation of the novels, which is left to the many editions that are now readily available.

The particular challenge for a *Companion* to George Eliot, the most formidably erudite of English novelists, is to do justice to the extraordinary range and depth of her intellectual life and to the wide interests she brought to bear on the world of provincial England that was the principal subject of her fiction. Thus entries on general topics such as philosophy and science, music and the visual arts, history and society, France and Germany, theatre and tragedy, Judaism and evangelicalism, are cross-referenced to a large number of entries on the individual writers, thinkers, artists, and composers from different cultures whose work she knew. The aim is to situate her work in the broad intellectual and cultural context of the 19th century; and, as is particularly appropriate for a writer who had a reading knowledge of seven languages besides English and whose interests were never narrowly national, the cast of contributors to this volume is an international one. Unlike Mr Casaubon's work, this volume is informed by a knowledge of German and other languages. It also aims to be contemporary as well as comprehensive, and the entry on modern criticism, for instance, surveys current critical approaches to George Eliot which draw on recent developments in the theory and criticism of literature. Altogether the *Oxford Reader's Companion to George Eliot* aspires to be a lively, up-to-date, informative, and wide-ranging reference work that will serve the interests of specialists and general readers alike. In eschewing the example of Casaubon, it seeks, rather, to emulate that of Dorothea and to be 'incalculably diffusive' in its effect on the many readers of George Eliot.

JOHN RIGNALL

Coventry, July 1999

CONTENTS

MAPS

EDITORS AND CONTRIBUTORS

General Editor

JOHN RIGNALL, Senior Lecturer in the Department of English and Comparative Literary Studies at the University of Warwick. He is the author of *Realist Fiction and the Strolling Spectator* (1992) and the editor of *George Eliot and Europe* (1997), to which he also contributed. He has edited *Daniel Deronda* for Everyman Paperbacks (1999) and is co-editor of the *George Eliot Review*.

Consultant Editors

GILLIAN BEER, King Edward VII Professor of English at the University of Cambridge and President of Clare Hall College. Among her books are *Darwin's Plots* (1983), *George Eliot* (1986), *Arguing with the Past* (1989), *Virginia Woolf: The Common Ground* (1996), and *Open Fields: Science in Cultural Encounter* (1996). Dame Gillian is a Fellow of the British Academy and was Vice-President from 1994 to 1996. She was Chair of the Booker Judges in 1997 and is a Trustee of the British Museum.

ELIZABETH DEEDS ERMARTH, Saintsbury Professor of English Literature at Edinburgh University. She writes on various interdisciplinary topics, including George Eliot, feminist theory, the discursive conditions of modernity and of postmodernity, rethinking historical conventions and democratic institutions; she has published many essays and articles and four books: *Realism and Consensus: Time, Space, Narrative* (1983, 1998), *George Eliot* (1985), *Sequel to History: Postmodernism and the Crisis of Representational Time* (1992), *The Novel in History: 1840–1895* (1997). She is currently writing a book on the implications of postmodernity for democratic institutions.

Contributors

KA KATHLEEN ADAMS, secretary of the George Eliot Fellowship since 1968. Her publications include *George Eliot: a Brief Biography, George Eliot Country, The Little Sister*, and *Those of Us Who Loved Her: The Men in George Eliot's Life* (1980).

RA ROSEMARY ASHTON, Professor of English at University College London. She is the author of critical biographies of Coleridge (1996), G. H. Lewes (1991), and George Eliot (1996), and of two books on Anglo-German relations in the 19th century. She has edited *Middlemarch* (Penguin, 1994) and *Selected Critical Writings of George Eliot* (World's Classics, 1992).

WB WILLIAM BAKER, Professor of English at Northern Illinois University. He edits *George Eliot–George Henry Lewes Studies*. Publications include *George Eliot and Judaism* (1975), *Some George Eliot Notebooks* (1976–1985), *The Libraries of George Eliot and George Henry Lewes* (1981), *The Letters of George Henry Lewes*, vols. i–ii (1995) and vol. iii. *With New Letters by George Eliot* (1999). He is joint editor of *The Letters of Wilkie Collins* (1999), and the Broadview edition of *Felix Holt, the Radical* (forthcoming).

DB DOROTHEA BARRETT, who teaches English and Italian literature at Syracuse University in Florence. She is the author of *Vocation and Desire: George Eliot's Heroines* (1989) and various articles on literature of the 19th and 20th centuries. Her edition of George Eliot's *Romola* was published by Penguin Classics in 1996.

GB GILLIAN BEER, Consultant Editor.

MB MICHAEL BELL, Professor of English at the University of Warwick. His books include *Primitivism* (1972), *The Sentiment of Reality: Truth of Feeling in the European Novel* (1983), *D. H. Lawrence: Language and Being* (1991), *Gabriel García Márquez: Solitude and Solidarity* (1993), and *Literature, Modernism and Myth: Belief and Responsibility in the Twentieth Century* (1997).

FB FELICIA BONAPARTE, Professor of English at The City University of New York. Her publications include *Will and Destiny* (1975), *The Triptych and the Cross* (1979), and *The Gypsy-Bachelor of Manchester*

Editors and Contributors

(1992). At present, she is completing two volumes: *The Making of Victorian Fiction: The Aesthetics of Poesis* and *Written in Invisible Ink: The Metafictions of the Victorians.*

TCC TERENCE CAVE, Professor of French Literature in the University of Oxford and Fellow of St John's College, Oxford. He is also a Fellow of the British Academy. His publications include *Devotional Poetry in France 1570–1613* (1969), *The Cornucopian Text: Problems of Writing in the French Renaissance* (1979), and *Recognitions: A Study in Poetics* (1988). He has edited *Daniel Deronda* for Penguin Classics (1995) and *Silas Marner* for Oxford World's Classics (1996).

KC KAREN CHASE, Professor of English Literature at the University of Virginia. She is the author of *Eros and Psyche: The Representation of Personality in Charlotte Brontë, Charles Dickens, George Eliot* (1984), a book on *Middlemarch* (1991), and with Michael Levenson, *The Spectacle of Intimacy: Victorian Family Life on the Public Stage.*

KKC K. K. COLLINS, Associate Professor of English at Southern Illinois University, Carbondale, is the co-author of *The Cumulated Dickens Checklist 1970–1979*. He has published essays on Dickens, George Eliot, G. H. Lewes, and other Victorian figures. He is now writing a book entitled *George Eliot's Life and Death in the American Press.*

VC VALENTINE CUNNINGHAM, Professor of English at Oxford University and Fellow and Tutor in English Literature at Corpus Christi College. He has edited *Adam Bede* (Oxford World's Classics, 1996) and is the author of *Everywhere Spoken Against: Dissent in the Victorian Novel* (1975), *British Writers of the Thirties* (1988), and *In the Reading Gaol: Postmodernity, Texts, and History* (1994).

DdSC DELIA DA SOUSA CORREA, Lecturer in the Literature Department at the Open University. She is completing a book on music in Victorian literary culture. She has written on Eliot and German Romanticism in *George Eliot and Europe* (1997), on music and memory in Eliot's novels (*Nineteenth-Century Contexts*), and on Ruskin and music.

AE ATHENA ECONOMIDES, who has worked as a research student in the English Department at the University of Warwick.

EDE ELIZABETH DEEDS ERMARTH, Consultant Editor.

GF GILL FRITH, Lecturer in English at the University of Warwick and the author of *Dreams of Difference: Women and Fantasy* (1991). She is currently completing a book about female friendship and national identity in novels by 19th- and 20th-century British women writers.

SG STEPHEN GILL, Professor of English Literature at Oxford University and a Fellow and Tutor of Lincoln College. His principal publications are *William Wordsworth: A Life* (1989) and *Wordsworth and the Victorians* (1998). He has also published editions of Wordsworth's poems and of a number of Victorian novels, including *Adam Bede.*

SAG SOPHIE GILMARTIN, Lecturer in English Literature at Royal Holloway, University of London. She is the author of *Ancestry and Narrative in Nineteenth-Century British Literature* (1998) and has published articles on 19th-century literature and culture. She is currently working on an edition of Anthony Trollope's *The Last Chronicle of Barset* and a book on widowhood.

BG BERYL GRAY, who teaches for the Faculty of Continuing Education, Birkbeck College. She is the author of *George Eliot and Music* (1989), and has edited several of George Eliot's works including *The Mill on the Floss* (1996).

GRH GRAHAM HANDLEY, the editor of *Daniel Deronda* (Clarendon and World's Classics), *The Mill on the Floss* (Macmillan), and *Scenes of Clerical Life* (Everyman). He has also written *George Eliot: The State of the Art* (1990) and *George Eliot's Midlands* (1991). He is series editor of the Everyman Gaskell, and has edited seven Trollope novels: he published *Trollope the Traveller* in 1993, and has contributed to *The Oxford Reader's Companion to Anthony Trollope.*

MH MALCOLM HARDMAN, Senior Lecturer, Department of English and Comparative Literary Studies, University of Warwick. He has written *Ruskin and Bradford* (1986), *Six Victorian Thinkers* (1991), *A Kingdom in two Parishes: Religious Writers and Monarchy 1521–1689* (1998).

BH BARBARA HARDY, Professor Emeritus, University of London; Hon. Professor, University College of Swansea; Hon. Fellow, Birkbeck College and Royal Holloway College; Hon. Member Modern Languages Association; Member of Welsh Academy; Fellow Royal Society of Literature. Books include work on theory

Editors and Contributors

of narrative and lyric; pioneering analysis of George Eliot's art, starting with *The Novels of George Eliot* (1959); close readings of Jane Austen, Thackeray, Dickens, Eliot, Hardy, etc. Recent publications include *Swansea Girl: A Memoir* (1994), *London Lovers* (novel, winner of Sagittarius prize), *Henry James: The Later Writing*, and *Shakespeare's Storytellers*.

MAH MARGARET HARRIS, Professor of English Literature at the University of Sydney. She has edited, with Judith Johnston, *The Journals of George Eliot* (1998) and the Everyman Paperback *Middlemarch* (1997). Her other publications in Victorian literature include *The Notebooks of George Meredith*, with Gillian Beer.

RMH RUTH M. HARRIS, a vice-president of the George Eliot Fellowship and a former English teacher in Edinburgh and Coventry. For 23 years she was a part-time tutor in Literature for the Workers' Educational Association, and she has lectured on 19th-century authors, especially George Eliot. She is a regular contributor to the *George Eliot Review*.

NEH NANCY HENRY, Assistant Professor of English at the State University of New York at Binghamton. She is the editor of *Impressions of Theophrastus Such* (1994) and the author of several articles on George Eliot.

NH NEIL HERTZ, who teaches in the Humanities Center of Johns Hopkins University, Baltimore. He is the author of *The End of the Line: Essays on Psychoanalysis and the Sublime* (1985).

PH PAM HIRSCH, Senior Research Associate at Homerton College and a member of both the English and the Education Faculties of the University of Cambridge. She has written on Mary Wollstonecraft, George Sand, Charlotte Brontë, Elizabeth Barrett Browning, and George Eliot. She is the author of *Barbara Leigh Smith Bodichon: Feminist, Artist and Rebel* (1998).

AJ ANNE JANOWITZ, Professor of English at Queen Mary and Westfield College, London. She is the author of *England's Ruins: Poetic Purpose and the National Landscape* (1990) and *Labour and Lyric in the Romantic Tradition* (1998).

RHAJ RICHARD JENKYNS, Reader in Classical Languages and Literature at the University of Oxford and a Fellow of Lady Margaret Hall.

JJ JUDITH JOHNSTON, Arts Faculty Teaching and Research Fellow at the Department of English, University of Western Australia. She is the author of *Anna Jameson: Victorian, feminist, woman of letters* (1997) and editor, with Margaret Harris, of *The Journals of George Eliot*.

CJ CHARLOTTE JOLLES, Professor Emeritus, London University. She taught German at Birkbeck College, specializing in 19th- and 20th-century literature and the work of Theodor Fontane in particular.

HL HAO LI, Assistant Professor in the English Department at the University of Toronto where she teaches 19th-century literature and thought. Her book on memory and history in George Eliot is forthcoming from Macmillan. She is currently working on a study of George Eliot and 19th-century theories of language.

SL SCOTT LEWIS, editor of *The Brownings' Correspondence*, and author of several articles on the Brownings and their circle.

GM GAIL MARSHALL, lecturer in Victorian literature at the University of Leeds. She has published on George Eliot, Ibsen, and actresses in the late Victorian period, and is the author of *Actresses on the Victorian Stage: Feminine Performance and the Galatea Myth* (1998). She is currently working on a study of Shakespeare and Victorian women.

JM JOSEPHINE MCDONAGH, who teaches English and humanities at Birkbeck College, University of London. She is author of *De Quincey's Disciplines* (1994) and *George Eliot* (1997).

BSM BONNIE SHANNON MCMULLEN, who lives in Oxford, where she teaches English and American literature. She holds degrees from Bryn Mawr College, the University of Pittsburgh, and the University of Toronto, where she completed a doctoral thesis on George Eliot. She has published articles on George Eliot and Edgar Allan Poe.

WM WILLIAM MYERS, Professor of English at Leicester University. His B.Litt. thesis (1964) was on mental and social evolution in George Eliot's novels. He has published *The Teaching of George Eliot* (1984) and an essay on *Daniel Deronda* is included in *The Presence of Persons* (1998).

KMN K. M. NEWTON, Professor of English at the University of Dundee and the author of *George Eliot: Romantic Humanist* (1981) and editor of the Longman Critical Reader, *George Eliot* (1991). Among his most recent articles are 'Sutherland's Puzzles: The Case of *Daniel Deronda*', *Essays in Criticism*

Editors and Contributors

(1998) and 'George Eliot as Proto-Modernist', *Cambridge Quarterly* (1998).

LO   LEONEE ORMOND, Professor of Victorian Studies at King's College, London University. She has published widely on Victorian and Edwardian literature and fine art, with books on George du Maurier, J. M. Barrie, and Tennyson. She is the author, with Richard Ormond, of a critical biography of Frederic, Lord Leighton, and was one of the organizers of the 1996 Royal Academy Leighton Centenary Exhibition.

SP   SIMON PETCH, Senior Lecturer in the Department of English, University of Sydney.

LP   LEAH PRICE, Research Fellow in English at Girton College, Cambridge. She has recently finished a Ph.D. dissertation in Comparative Literature at Yale University, 'Compiling Authority: Anthologies and Narrative Form in Modern Britain', and has published articles on Elizabeth Gaskell, on Samuel Richardson, on bowdlerized Shakespeare, on legal narrative in pre-revolutionary France, and on the politics of pornography.

MR   MARGARET REYNOLDS, Research Fellow at Clare Hall, Cambridge. She has taught English at the University of Birmingham and has produced a critical edition of Elizabeth Barrett Browning's *Aurora Leigh* (1992) and, with Angela Leighton, has edited an anthology of Victorian Women Poets (1995). Her book on the influence of Sappho's poetry is scheduled for publication in 1999.

JMR   JOHN RIGNALL, General Editor.

JMS   JAN-MELISSA SCHRAMM, a lawyer with a Ph.D. in English Literature, currently employed as a research fellow at Lucy Cavendish College, University of Cambridge. Her book *Testimony and Advocacy in Victorian Law, Literature, and Theology* is currently in production with Cambridge University Press.

HUS   HANS ULRICH SEEBER, Professor of English Literature at Stuttgart University. His publications include a book on the utopian novel (1970) and one on Edward Thomas (1979). He is editor of a standard history of English literature in German, *Englische Literaturgeschichte* (1991, 3rd edn. forthcoming), and the author of the sections on the 19th and early 20th centuries.

SAS   SALLY SHUTTLEWORTH, Professor of Modern Literature at the University of Sheffield. She is the author of *George Eliot and Nineteenth Century Science* (1984) and *Charlotte Brontë and Victorian Psychology* (1996), and co-editor, with Jenny Bourne Taylor, of *Embodied Slaves: An Anthology of Psychological Texts 1830–1890* (1998).

SS   SUSANNE STARK, Research Fellow at the University of Leeds. She is the author of *'Behind Inverted Commas': Translation and Anglo-German Cultural Relations in the Nineteenth Century* (1999) and the editor of a volume of articles on the novel in Anglo-German context. Her research interests include translation studies, interdisciplinary 19th-century studies, as well as 19th- and 20th-century women writers.

JS   JOHN STOKES, Professor of English in the Department of English, King's College London. He has written widely on the relations between the English and the French theatre and is co-author of *Bernhardt, Terry, Duse: The Actress in Her Time* (1988) and *Three Tragic Actresses: Siddons, Rachel, Ristori* (1996).

MWT   MARK TURNER, Senior Lecturer in English at Roehampton Institute London. He is author of *Trollope and the Magazines*, co-editor of *From Author to Text: Re-reading George Eliot's Romola* (1998), and has written articles and chapters on Victorian serialization and cultural production. He also co-edits the interdisciplinary journal *Media History*.

AvdB   A. G. VAN DEN BROEK, Head of English at Forest School, London. He has published a number of articles on George Eliot, and edited *Felix Holt, the Radical* (Everyman Paperbacks, 1997).

TW   TIM WATSON, who teaches in the English Department at Montclair State University in New Jersey.

JW   JOANNE WILKES, who teaches at Auckland University (New Zealand). She studied English and French at Sydney University, and did her doctorate at Oxford, focusing on George Eliot. She has published on Scott and Austen as well as Eliot, and edited Geraldine Jewsbury's *The Half Sisters* for World's Classics.

TJW   TOM WINNIFRITH, who taught at Eton College and the University of Warwick between 1961 and 1998. He has published extensively on 19th-century literature, especially on the Brontës, including *The Brontës and their Background* (1973) and *A New Life of Charlotte Brontë* (1987). He also contributed to *George Eliot and Europe* (1997).

CLASSIFIED CONTENTS LIST

[entries are arranged alphabetically by headword beneath the topic headings]

Classified Contents List

Classified Contents List

myth
names in George Eliot's fiction
narration
nationhood
natural world
politics
poverty and wealth
radicalism
realism
renunciation
secrecy
settings, original basis of
society
style
symbolism
sympathy
tragedy
vocation
voice, representation of
woman question, the
women, education of

The Literary and Artistic Context

Writers before George Eliot
Addison, Joseph
Aeschylus
Aristotle
Austen, Jane
Bunyan, John
Burke, Edmund
Byron
Cervantes Saavedra, Miguel de
Chaucer, Geoffrey
classical literature
Coleridge, Samuel Taylor
Cowper, William
Dante Alighieri
Edgeworth, Maria
Euripides
Fielding, Henry
French literature
German literature
Gibbon, Edward
Goethe, Johann Wolfgang
Goldsmith, Oliver
Hoffman, E. T. A.
Homer
Horace
influence of other writers on George Eliot
Johnson, Samuel
Keats, John
Lessing, Gotthold Ephraim
Milton, John
Novalis
Pascal, Blaise
Plato
Pope, Alexander

Richardson, Samuel
Romanticism
Rousseau, Jean-Jacques
Schiller, Friedrich
Scott, Walter
Shakespeare, William
Shelley, Percy Bysshe
Sophocles
Staël, Mme (Germaine) de
Sterne, Laurence
Swift, Jonathan
Taylor, Jeremy
Virgil
Voltaire
Wollstonecraft, Mary
Wordsworth, William
Young, Edward

Writers in George Eliot's lifetime
Arnold, Matthew
Balzac, Honoré de
Braddon, Mary Elizabeth
Bremer, Fredrika
Bronte, Charlotte, Emily, and Anne
Browning, Elizabeth Barrett and Robert
Bulwer-Lytton, Edward George
Carlyle, Jane Welsh and Thomas
Clough, Arthur Hugh
Collins, Wilkie
Dickens, Charles
Dickinson, Emily
Disraeli, Benjamin
Emerson, Ralph Waldo
Flaubert, Gustave
Fontane, Theodor
Forster, John
French literature
Froude, J. A.
Fuller, Margaret
Gaskell, Elizabeth Cleghorn
German literature
Grand, Sarah
Hardy, Thomas
Hawthorne, Nathaniel
Heine, Heinrich
Hugo, Victor
James, Henry
Jameson, Anna
Jewsbury, Geraldine
Keller, Gottfried
Kingsley, Charles
Linton, Eliza Lynn
Lytton, Edward George Bulwer-
Manzoni, Alessandro
Martineau, Harriet
Meredith, George
Newman, John Henry
Oliphant, Margaret

Classified Contents List

Classified Contents List

Beethoven, Ludwig van
Bellini, Vincenzo
Donizetti, Gaetano
Gluck, Christoph Willibald
Gurney, Edmund
Handel, George Frideric
Haydn, Joseph
Joachim, Joseph
Lehmann, Frederick and Nina
Lind, Jenny
Liszt, Franz
'Liszt, Wagner, and Weimar'
Mendelssohn (-Bartholdy), Felix
Meyerbeer, Giacomo
Mozart, Wolfgang Amadeus
opera
Palestrina, Giovanni
piano
Piatti, Carlo Alfredo
Purcell, Henry
Rossini, Gioachino
Rubinstein, Anton
Schubert, Franz
Schumann, Clara Josephine (Wieck)
Sully, James
Verdi, Giuseppe
violin
voice, representation of
Wagner, Richard

Theatre
theatre
Aeschylus
'*Antigone* and its Moral, The'
Bernhardt, Sarah
classical literature
Euripedes
French literature
German literature
Goethe, Johann Wolfgang
Hugo, Victor
Lessing, Gotthold Ephraim
Rachel
Reade, Charles
Schiller, Friedrich
Shakespeare, William
Sophocles
theatrical adaptations
tragedy

Other Contexts

Feminism and the woman question
feminism
criticism, modern: feminist approaches
woman question, the
Beauvoir, Simone de
Bodichon, Barbara Leigh Smith
Davies, Emily

education
English Woman's Journal, The
France
Fuller, Margaret
Grand, Sarah
Hill, Octavia
history, George Eliot's view of
Jameson, Anna
Jewsbury, Geraldine
Linton, Eliza Lynn
Mansfield, Katherine
'Margaret Fuller and Mary Wollstonecraft'
Martineau, Harriet
Nightingale, Florence
Parkes, Bessie (Elizabeth) Rayner
Sand, George
'Silly Novels by Lady Novelists'
Simcox, Edith
Staël, Mme (Germaine) de
Stowe, Harriet Beecher
vocation
Ward, Mrs Humphry
Wollstone craft, Mary
'Woman in France: Madame de Sablé'
Woolf, Virginia

History, politics and society
history, George Eliot's view of
politics
society
'Address to Working Men, by Felix Holt'
American civil war
anti-Semitism
Beaconsfield, Lord, *see* Disraeli Benjamin
Chartism
colonialism
Corn Laws
Crimean war
education
Empire, British
Franco-Prussian war
Garibaldi, Giuseppe
Gladstone, William Ewart
Higher Criticism, The
industrialism
law
Marx, Karl
Mazzini, Giuseppe
medicine and health
Napoleon III (Louis Napoleon Bonaparte)
nationalism
'Natural History of German Life, The'
poverty and wealth
progress, idea of
race
radicalism
Reform Acts (1832 and 1867)
revolutions of 1848

Classified Contents List

Classified Contents List

Reception and Aftermath

LIST OF ABBREVIATIONS

AB   *Adam Bede*

BJ   'Brother Jacob'

CH   *George Eliot: The Critical Heritage*, ed.
          David Carroll (1971)

Cross   J. W. Cross (ed.), *George Eliot's Life as
          Related in her Letters and Journals*, 3
          vols. (1885; new edn. with additions,
          1886) (unless otherwise stated,
          references are to the 1st edn. of
          1885)

DD   *Daniel Deronda*

Essays   *Essays of George Eliot*, ed. Thomas
          Pinney (1963)

FH   *Felix Holt, the Radical*

Journals *The Journals of George Eliot*, ed.
          Margaret Harris and Judith Johnston
          (1998)

L   *The George Eliot Letters*, ed. Gordon
          S. Haight, 9 vols. (1954–78)

LV   'The Lifted Veil'

MF   *The Mill on the Floss*

MM   *Middlemarch: A Study of Provincial
          Life*

RO   *Romola*

SC1   'The Sad Fortunes of the Reverend
          Amos Barton', in *Scenes of Clerical
          Life*

SC2   'Mr Gilfil's Love-Story', in *Scenes of
          Clerical Life*

SC3   'Janet's Repentance', in *Scenes of
          Clerical Life*

SG   *The Spanish Gypsy*

SM   *Silas Marner: The Weaver of Raveloe*

TS   *Impressions of Theophrastus Such*

See also A Note to the Reader, p. xxv.

GEORGE ELIOT FAMILY TREE

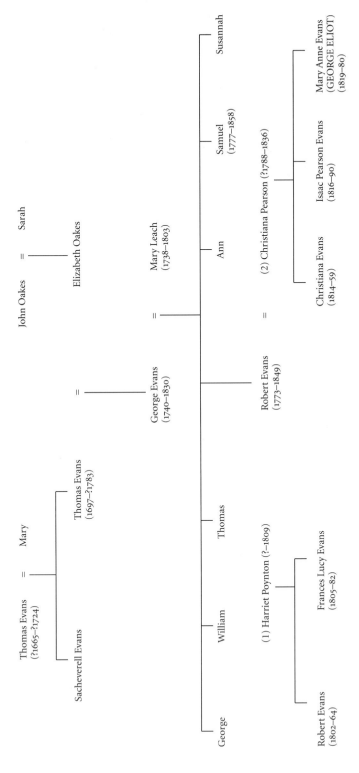

A NOTE TO THE READER

ENTRIES in this *Companion* are arranged alphabetically under headwords. These refer to people George Eliot knew, and to writers she read or with whom she may be compared; to all her novels and short stories, to her poetry (treated in a single entry), and to her more important essays; to thematic and formal features of her fiction, and to its reception by critics from her own day up to the present; to places she was familiar with and countries she visited; to different aspects of her career as a writer, and to a large number of topics relating to the social, historical, intellectual, literary, and artistic contexts in which she lived and worked. Cross-references are indicated either by an asterisk in front of a word, indicating that it has its own entry (e.g. 'George Eliot's commitment to *realism'), or by the use of 'see' or 'see also', followed by the headword in small capitals. Of George Eliot's works, only the essays she published in journals are cross-referenced with an asterisk, since, unlike the novels and short stories, they cannot all be assumed to have a separate entry.

Readers seeking a survey of her life should turn to **life of George Eliot**. The critical response to her work is divided between three entries: **reception** covers her lifetime; **reputation, critical** covers the period from her death to the 1970s, while **criticism, modern** discusses contemporary approaches to her work under separate subheadings (e.g. 'feminist approaches'). General entries, such as **philosophy**, **music**, or **visual arts**, refer to thinkers or artists whose individual entries may be consulted for more detailed information.

The entries on the novels and short stories follow the same format, with sections on composition, publication, illustrations, reception, plot outline, and critical approaches. These and other substantial entries are followed by a list of works for further reading. Works cited in these bibliographical lists simply by author or editor and date can be found in their full form in the General Bibliography at the end of the volume.

References to *The George Eliot Letters*, ed. Gordon S. Haight (1954–78) are by volume and page number, preceded by *L*: '*L* iii. 218' indicates volume iii, p. 218. Quotations from the novels and short stories are identified by chapter only ('*MM* 66' indicates *Middlemarch*, chapter 66), or in the case of *The Mill on the Floss*, by book and chapter ('*MF* 4.3' indicates book 4, chapter 3). For quotations from critical or biographical works references are to page numbers: 'Haight 1968: 66' indicates Gordon S. Haight, *George Eliot: A Biography* (1968), p. 66. For a list of abbreviations see p. xxii.

In the case of George Eliot names are a particular problem, and not only because she adopted a pseudonym. Her own real name underwent many metamorphoses. Baptized Mary Anne Evans, but referred to as Mary Ann in her father's diary on the day of her birth, she signed herself Mary Ann in her teens and then called herself Marian as an adult. At the same time she used nicknames, such as Pollian or Polly, and was Mutter to Lewes's sons and sometimes Madonna to Lewes. When she began to live with Lewes she called herself Marian Evans Lewes, and, since she regarded herself as

A Note to the Reader

his wife even though they were unable to marry, she insisted on being addressed as Mrs Lewes. The entry on her life follows the standard biographer's practice of changing her first name as she changed it herself in the different stages of her life. Other entries concerned with her family relationships or close friendships also often refer to her as Mary Ann or Marian rather than George Eliot. Practice also differs with respect to her pseudonym: it was once customary to refer to her always as George Eliot, but more recently many scholars and critics have taken to treating her in the same way as male writers and contracting her name to Eliot. Both practices are to be found in this volume and no attempt has been made to impose uniformity, beyond ensuring that the first mention in each entry is to the full George Eliot.

Acton, Lord. See DALBERG-ACTON, JOHN.

Adam Bede (*see page 2*)

Addison, Joseph (1672–1719), English essayist of *Tatler* and *Spectator* celebrity but also the author of a few noteworthy hymns. George Eliot mentions him twice in letters to Maria *Lewis in 1839, once describing her current reading as 'morsels of Addison and Bacon' (*L* i. 29), and once feeling herself 'like Addison's ass between two bundles of hay' (*L* i. 34). Eighteen years later she writes to Sara *Hennell that Charles *Bray's face is 'a great centre of content radiating cheerfulness to all the planets that around him shine' (*L* ii. 302), the last phrase echoing one of Addison's hymns. On 21 June 1863 she tells Charles Lee Lewes (see LEWES FAMILY) of Thackeray's somewhat distorted 'estimate of Swift and Addison' in his *Lectures on the English Humourists* (*L* iv. 91). GRH

'Address to Working Men, by Felix Holt'.
This essay by George Eliot was aimed at educating newly enfranchised voters about reform objectives. She resurrected Felix Holt to speak for her since he had espoused similar views throughout *Felix Holt*, especially in chapter 30. The essay was published in January 1868 in *Blackwood's Edinburgh Magazine*, also known as 'Maga' (repr. in *Essays*).

The Second Reform Bill (see REFORM ACTS) of 15 August 1867 enfranchised mainly middle-class men from the counties and a large majority of working-class men from towns and cities. Altogether, it added 938,000 voters to the existing list of 1,057,000 in England and Wales. This extension of suffrage, introduced by the 14th Earl of Derby's Conservative government, followed reform agitation that had gathered significant momentum in the years immediately before 1867. The Reform League, founded in 1865, had called for manhood suffrage and had organized huge rallies in Hyde Park, London. During meetings in July 1866 and May 1867, disturbances, which some described as riots, broke out. Meanwhile, the more moderate Reform Union, founded in the 1860s, had peacefully campaigned for household suffrage with broad support from many Conservative, Liberal, and Radical MPs.

As it turned out, the Bill that was eventually agreed on protected Conservative interests. But many conservatively minded people remained nervous about what they saw as a large number of poor and disgruntled voters interfering, or worse, with the status quo. Nearly 500,000 working-class men were enfranchised, and many in the Establishment became very anxious about ballot-box democracy. Thomas *Carlyle likened the attainment of 'completed Democracy' to 'the Niagara

leap' and prophesied a calamitous end for everyone ('Shooting Niagara: and After?', 1867). Other, more moderate observers, like Eliot's publisher, John *Blackwood, felt that what the new voters needed was instruction on how best to exercise their civic responsibilities.

Blackwood wrote to Eliot suggesting that she might write an instructive address to working men for 'Maga', his monthly magazine, and sign it 'Felix Holt'. At first, Eliot demurred, saying, 'Felix Holt is immensely tempted by your suggestion, but George Eliot is severely admonished by his domestic critic [G. H. *Lewes] not to scatter his energies' (*L* iv. 396–7). She changed her mind, however, and began the 'Address' on 22 November 1867, sending it to Blackwood on 4 December. With the return of the proof, she urged Blackwood to write a preliminary note to the 'Address' in which he could distance himself from 'any overtrenchant statements on the part of the well-meaning Radical' (*L* iv. 403–4). Blackwood did not write an introduction, and the 'Address' was published in the January 1868 edition of 'Maga'.

The message of the 'Address' is not substantially different from the one Felix Holt gives in Duffield on Nomination Day (*FH* 30), except that, here, he keeps his temper. He assumes he is again addressing a 'mixed assembly of workmen' and develops at greater length the idea that working-men's suffrage is an opportunity for furthering the common good, not for insisting on change for change's sake. He ends by urging right moral conduct, acknowledging his avoidance of 'special questions'. Since he earlier refers to trade unions and their reasons for existing, he presumably has in mind hotly debated questions concerning the Master and Servant Acts, which were eventually replaced by the Employers and Workmen Act in 1875; and the Act of Combinations of 1800 and the Friendly
(*cont. on page* 9)

G

EORGE ELIOT's first full-length novel, published 1 February 1859.

Composition

Adam Bede was begun at Richmond on 22 October 1857, five days after the proof of 'Janet's Repentance' (the last of the *Scenes of Clerical Life*) had been returned to John *Blackwood. Before she and G. H. *Lewes left for *Germany in early April 1858, the publisher had been given the manuscript of the first volume. During their five months' absence George Eliot worked on her novel whenever their 'wandering' (*L* ii. 475) permitted, making slow headway in *Munich, where the second volume was begun, but progressing uninterruptedly in *Dresden, where it was almost completed. The final chapter of this volume, and the whole of the third volume, were written after her return to Richmond. The last of the manuscript was dispatched on 16 November, and on 30 November George Eliot set down in her journal her brief 'History of *Adam Bede*' (*L* ii. 502–5).

As this 'History' records, the 'germ' of *Adam Bede* was an anecdote her Methodist Aunt Samuel (the wife of her father's younger brother Samuel *Evans) had told her about Mary Voce, a young woman condemned to death for infanticide in 1802, but who had refused to confess. Aunt Samuel had visited the young woman in prison, and had stayed with her throughout the night, praying, until at last the girl cried, and admitted her guilt. Afterwards, Aunt Samuel went with her in the cart to the gallows (see EVANS, MRS SAMUEL).

George Eliot had recounted this anecdote to Lewes, who thought 'that the scene in the prison would make a fine element in a story' (*L* ii. 502), which, blended with 'some other recollections of my aunt [and] . . . some points in my father's early life and character', George Eliot originally intended to develop as one of the *Scenes*. But, as she informed Blackwood, she found that she instead 'inclined to take a large canvas . . . and write a novel' (*L* ii. 381). It was to be 'a country story—full of the breath of cows and the scent of hay' (*L* ii. 387).

Publication

Adam Bede was originally intended as a serial for *Blackwood's Edinburgh Magazine* ('Maga'), but Blackwood's reservations about the suitability of some elements of the story (or storytelling) prompted George Eliot to propose forgoing monthly publication and await the printing of the book in three volumes (*L* viii. 202). In this form it duly first appeared (price 31s. 6d.) bound in orange-brown cloth. Two impressions of a second edition in the same form were issued in April, but for the two-volume (12s.) edition that was printed in June, George Eliot submitted an alteration to the scene in chapter 4 where Adam is alone in his workshop at night, making a coffin. He hears a rap 'as if with a willow wand' at the house door, and remembers 'how often his mother had told him of just such a sound coming as a sign when someone was dying'. Described as 'at once penetrating and credulous', he is unable to help believing in this 'traditional superstition', which in the morning appears to be ratified with the discovery that his father has drowned. But George Eliot felt that 'Some readers seem not to have understood what I meant, namely—that it was in Adam's peasant blood and nurture to believe in this [omen]' (*L* iii. 60). Accordingly, where (after Adam's common sense has been exemplified) the first edition reads: 'yet he believed in dreams and prognostics, and you see he shuddered at the idea of the stroke with the willow wand', this and subsequent editions read: 'yet he believed in dreams and prognostics, and to his dying day he bated his breath a little when he told the story of the willow wand. I tell it as he told it, not attempting to reduce it to its natural elements: in our eagerness to explain impressions, we often lose our hold of the sympathy that comprehends them'.

George Eliot 'shuddered not a little' (*L* iii. 184) at the misprints she found in this first two-volume edition, and—using what Gordon S. *Haight has identified as this edition's fifth impression (*L* viii. 291 n), and the two-volume New Edition (1860) of *The Mill on the Floss*—George Eliot 'read carefully all through' (*L* viii. 291) both novels before the publication of the one-volume, 6*s*. editions (*AB* 1861; *MF* 1862), marking all the errata she could find. As Haight notes, 'This careful reading renders the 6/- edition important in establishing the text' (*L* viii. 291 n) of these novels.

The manuscript is in the British Library (Additional MSS 34020–2). Bound in red Russia leather, the flyleaf is inscribed: 'To my dear husband, George Henry Lewes, I give this M.S. of a work which would never have been written but for the happiness which his love has conferred on my life. Marian Lewes March 23. 1859'. Under the inscription, George Eliot briefly describes the circumstances of the novel's composition.

Illustrations

Adam Bede (followed by *The Mill on the Floss, Silas Marner, Scenes of Clerical Life*, and *Felix Holt, the Radical*) was the first in a series of George Eliot's works that were issued—with illustrations—in thirty monthly sixpenny numbers between 1867 and 1869, before each work was bound as a single volume to sell as the Stereotyped Edition, with prices ranging from 2*s*. 6*d*. to 3*s*. 6*d*. (*Adam Bede* sold for 3*s*. 6*d*.). The six full-page plates for *Adam Bede* (numbers 1–7) were designed by William Small (1843–1929). As Blackwood clearly anticipated ('Some of the illustrations will, I doubt not, give you "a turn"' (*L* iv. 352)), George Eliot was quite unable to be enthusiastic about them, finding them at best 'endurable to a mind well accustomed to resignation', while the 'unctuousness' of the depiction of Adam making love to Dinah enraged her to the extent of declaring that she 'would gladly pay something to be rid of it' (*L* vi. 335). Small was not used for the remaining numbers. The vignette for the series title-page, however, she found 'perfect—almost exactly as I saw the Hall Farm eight years ago in my mind's eye' (*L* iv. 366), and the same artist—Edmund Morison Wimperis (1835–1900), whose signature, EMW, is just discernible in each case—provided the vignettes for the remaining volumes in the series as it was so far planned. The illustrations for all thirty parts (five volumes), including the vignettes, were engraved by James Cooper (1825–1904).

The striking wrapper design for the sixpenny numbers is by John Leighton ('Luke Limner'). Each wrapper bears within a decorative frame the general title, *The Novels & Tales of George Eliot*, and the title of the individual work. The inscription 'Illustrations by J. D. Cooper' and John Leighton's name (centred) are set in the bottom of the frame. In the corners of the frame are roundels relating in turn to each work in the series, with the exception of *Felix Holt*. The same designs were used for the gilt medallions on the front covers of the bound volumes.

Reception

Although some reservations were expressed, the general response to *Adam Bede* was overwhelmingly laudatory. Writing in the *Athenaeum* (26 February 1859), Geraldine *Jewsbury, for example, described it as 'a work of true genius', and E. S. *Dallas (*The*

Times, 12 April 1859) declared it 'a first-rate novel' whose 'author takes rank at once among the masters of the art' (*CH 77*). The *Saturday Review* (26 February 1859; repr. in *CH 73–6*) was alert to many of the novel's qualities, especially to the ability of the author (assumed to be a country clergyman) to awaken new feelings, and to his originality and powers of observation. This reviewer's appreciation of George Eliot's *realism was nevertheless limited: the charting of the stages of Hetty Sorrel's pregnancy was found to be deplorably explicit, and the attention devoted to the apparent horrors of rustic reality altogether objectionable. The criticism of the author's recourse in the novel's third volume to the arbitrary melodrama of trials, scaffolds, and pardons, has proved to be more enduring.

For Jane *Carlyle, on the other hand, reading the book 'was as good as *going into the country for one's health*' (*L* iii. 17); but perhaps the most satisfying accolade came from Charles *Dickens, who, through Blackwood, wrote on 10 July 1859 revealing his conviction that the author was a woman, and generously praising the work as having

taken its place among the actual experiences and endurances of my life. . . . The conception of Hetty's character is so extraordinarily subtle and true, that I laid the book down fifty times, to shut my eyes and think about it. I know nothing so skilful, determined, and uncompromising. . . . if you should ever have the freedom and inclination to be a fellow labourer with me, it would yield me a pleasure that I have never known yet and can never know otherwise. (*L* iii. 114–15)

Dickens was not the only early reader of *Adam Bede* to guess that its author was a woman. In a searching review article for the July 1859 issue of Bentley's *Quarterly Review* (repr. in *CH 86–103*), Anne Mozley expressed her suspicion that it was from a female pen.

The time is past for any felicity, force, or freedom of expression to divert our suspicions on this head; if women will write under certain conditions, . . . it is proved that a wide range of human nature lies open to their comprehension; so that if things in this novel seem to be observed from a woman's point of view, we need not discard the notion because it is well and ably done.

Although sharing the belief of many of her contemporaries 'that there are subjects and passions which will always continue man's inalienable field of inquiry', Mozley absolves George Eliot of encroachment. She is convinced 'that the knowledge of female nature is feminine . . . in its whole tone of feeling; that so is the full, close scrutiny of observation exercised in scanning every feature of a bounded field of inquiry; . . . that the position of the writer towards every point in discussion is a woman's position, that is, from a stand of observation rather than more active participation' (*CH 90*). George Eliot's friend Barbara *Bodichon was quite certain she knew who the author was, ecstatically exclaiming on 26 April that reading one long extract in a review had made her 'internally exclaim that is written by Marian Evans, there is her great big head and heart and her wise wide views' (*L* iii. 56).

The novel's popularity was reflected in the gathering momentum of the sales. Only six weeks after publication, Blackwood realized that a second three-volume edition was required, which itself needed to be reprinted before a two-volume edition was issued in June. The pace kept up, and Lewes announced that 'they' were 'becoming quite European celebrities' (*L* iii. 274) as the novel was translated into Russian, Hungarian, German, French, and Dutch.

George Eliot felt no exultation in the success of *Adam Bede*, telling Barbara Bodichon—'the first heart that has recognized me in a book that has come from my heart of hearts' (*L* iii. 63)—that 'these last months have been sadder than usual to me' (*L* iii. 64). Neither the (at this stage, amusing) rumour that a Joseph *Liggins had written her books, nor the undermining of her incognito by John *Chapman's and Herbert *Spencer's combined indiscretions concerning it, accounted for this sadness, which was the sort, explained Lewes, that 'lies near joy' (*L* iii. 36); but in the background was the distressing news (24 February 1859) of her sister Chrissey's illness (see EVANS, CHRISTIANA), and subsequently of her death on 15 March—just six weeks after *Adam Bede*'s publication. The bound volume of the manuscript was delivered the day after Chrissey's funeral.

Plot

Adam Bede, the stalwart carpenter-hero, is reverently in love with pretty, orphaned, penniless Hetty Sorrel, who has been taken in by her uncle and aunt, the Poysers of Hall Farm, and brought up as a domestic help. The Poysers hope that their niece and Adam will marry, but, although the self-absorbed Hetty exploits her power over her suitor, she has little feeling for him, or for any creature—until her passion is aroused by the young squire Arthur Donnithorne, a captain in the Loamshire militia.

Meanwhile, Adam's Methodist brother Seth is in love with the Poysers' other niece, Dinah Morris. An unselfconsciously beautiful and inspired Wesleyan preacher, Dinah has elected to live and work among the impoverished inhabitants of Snowfield in Stonyshire. She refuses Seth's marriage proposal in the belief that it is God's will that she should devote herself to her vocation. Sensing that Hetty does not truly love Adam, and is in danger of going astray, Dinah tries to warn her, promising her sanctuary if ever she should need it. But Hetty is indifferent: she is sure that Captain Donnithorne loves her very much and intends to marry her.

Unable to resist Hetty's coquettish appeal, Arthur tenderly seduces her. Adam, who has not yet proposed to her, interprets the symptoms of her infatuation with Arthur as signs that she reciprocates his own love, and is bitterly disillusioned when he comes upon Hetty and Arthur about to kiss. It is clear that there have been many such meetings. After challenging Arthur, Adam knocks him out in a fight, but is afterwards contrite. Arthur assures the credulous Adam that Hetty's honour is intact. At Adam's insistence, Arthur writes to her ending the relationship. Conscience-stricken, he joins his regiment at Windsor.

Concealing her misery from the Poysers, Hetty carries on with her work while adjusting her mind to the idea of marrying Adam after all. He duly proposes, but Hetty discovers she is pregnant by Arthur. Rejecting the idea of drowning herself, she sets off for Windsor to find him under the pretext of visiting Dinah (who has returned to Snowfield). She arrives exhausted, only to discover that his regiment has left for Ireland. Despairing and now fundless, Hetty retraces her journey after pawning the trinkets Arthur had given her; but can muster the resolution neither to seek refuge with Dinah, nor to drown herself.

Anxious for her return, Adam goes to Snowfield to fetch her. After finding that she has not been heard of there, he confides in Arthur's mentor, Mr Irwine, who, realizing with horror that Arthur is the father of Hetty's child, is obliged to inform Adam that she is in Stoniton prison charged with infanticide. Irwine takes the distraught Adam to Stoniton, but leaves him there. After breaking the news to the Poysers, Irwine returns to his parsonage, where he learns that the old squire has died: the estate now belongs to Arthur, who has been recalled from Ireland.

Now tended by his friend and teacher Bartle Massey, Adam applies to visit Hetty, who refuses to see him. Massey attends the opening of her trial, and reports that the evidence weighs heavily against her. Adam resolves to 'stand by' her in court; but, already cast off by her kin, Hetty is found guilty and sentenced to death.

Dinah visits Hetty in prison. Eventually, Hetty clings to her and confesses. She asks Adam to forgive her before she dies, and is comforted by Dinah on the way to the gallows. At the very last moment Arthur gallops up with her reprieve. She is transported.

Moved by Arthur's repentant anguish, Adam forgives him. Arthur goes abroad; Dinah stays at the Hall Farm while the Poyser family recovers from its shame. It gradually emerges that Adam and Dinah are deeply drawn to each other. Eventually they marry and prosper. The chastened Arthur returns to his estate, but Hetty has died while still in exile.

Critical Approaches

Adam Bede was not neglected during the first wave of revived critical interest in George Eliot's works that began in the late 1940s (see REPUTATION, CRITICAL). Important discussions of the novel, focusing significantly on George Eliot's artistry, are to be found, for example, in Joan Bennett's *George Eliot: Her Mind and Her Art* (1948); in Dorothy Van Ghent's *The English Novel: Form and Function* (1953); and in Barbara Hardy's *The Novels of George Eliot* (1959). Hardy argues that 'Adam's growth is the growth of sensibility . . . and he begins with an initial ability to move away from particulars, as Hetty Sorrel does not. . . . At the beginning, Adam has as much to learn, in his terms, as Lear' (36–7).

However, by 1964 U. C. Knoepflmacher was able to claim that recent George Eliot scholarship had been singularly one-sided. Critics had either concentrated on a close scrutiny of George Eliot's art by focusing on form and thus ignored the ideological purposes which shape the formal features of her novels; or, conversely, aware of George Eliot as a Victorian thinker, they had reconstructed her ideology in the light of Charles *Darwin, T. H. *Huxley, Auguste *Comte, John Stuart *Mill, Spencer, Lewes, Charles Christian *Hennell, D. F. *Strauss, or Ludwig *Feuerbach. This second category is represented by articles such as George Levine's 'Determinism and Responsibility in the Works of George Eliot' (*PMLA* 77, 1962) and Bernard J. Paris's 'George Eliot's Religion of Humanity' (*ELH* 29, 1962).

To exemplify the criticism he believes is needed Knoepflmacher goes to *Adam Bede* and Feuerbach, suggesting that only through a combination of the methods he has described 'can we get at the full meaning of the symbology used in *Adam Bede* and thus penetrate George Eliot's artistic and "philosophic" intentions in her portrayal of Adam's development' (1964: 80). With Adam unequivocally perceived as the protagonist, his development, Knoepflmacher persuasively argues, is depicted 'through a series of symbolic suppers which ultimately lead to a Feuerbachian "religion of suffering"' (82).

His development notwithstanding, neither Adam's suffering, nor his physical and moral uprightness, nor his commitment to good workmanship, unfailingly win the reader's sympathy. On the other hand, Hetty, who is denied the capacity to develop, is increasingly seen as a victim—not only of circumstances, but also of the fictitiously male narrator. As Gillian Beer notes in *George Eliot* (1986), her presentation is considered by many critics to be 'ungenerous and rebuffing in its insistence on her small scope, her paucity of love, her vanity' (69). However, as Beer goes on to point out, 'the treatment of Hetty is also a radical challenge to the stereotypical portrayals of virgins and fallen women'. But the prevailing view is that she is sacrificed—'annihilated' as Jennifer Uglow puts it in her *George Eliot* (1987); 'banished for ever so that the slow process of [Adam's] rebirth can begin and he can rejoin the wider community through his "better and more precious love" for Dinah' (113).

John Sutherland develops the theme of Hetty's sacrifice in 'Why doesn't the Reverend Irwine speak up for Hetty?'. Sutherland suggests that, from an instinct to protect the young squire from scandal and preserve the 'old order', the Revd Irwine neither takes nor encourages any action that would increase the chances of Arthur returning from Ireland in time to give evidence in court. 'Had the full story of Arthur's seduction, mendacity, and abandonment come out—particularly if it had been reiterated in court by Irwine, Adam, and Arthur himself', Sutherland argues, '[Hetty] might have won a full pardon, or at least a light custodial sentence in England. What actually happens to her is politically necessary (if one shares Irwine's politics) but horribly unjust.' Going on to point out that the transported Hetty would be subject to sexual molestation, and that female convicts had virtually no chance of redeeming themselves, Sutherland flourishingly concludes his indictment with 'Thank you, Reverend Irwine, thank you, Captain Donnithorne' (1997: 125).

The critical attention accorded Hetty's (mis)treatment indicates that her realization continues to claim the imagination as effectively as it claimed Dickens's, though his emphasis was on the subtlety and uncompromising truthfulness he discerned in her presentation, rather than on her victimization. This subtlety extends to the position in which she is placed at Hall Farm. While her skill as a 'butter-maker' (*AB* 9) makes the dairy her particular setting, her status is that of kin (she is Mr Poyser's blood relation), and should not be confused, as it frequently—even usually—is, with that of dairymaid. It is Nancy who expressly (*AB* 22) occupies that position. To assign the role to Hetty is to impose on her the stereotype her author eschews—an imposition that, in the first place, takes no account of the fact that a crucial aspect of the consequence of her seduction is the shame the Poysers feel to be visited on them. A dairymaid's fall, on the other hand, would not have been perceived as family dishonour. It also takes little account either of Arthur's awareness that Hetty is a respected tenant farmer's niece, or of the conflict within him between his belief in his own integrity and capacity for self-restraint, and his passion. As the authorial analysis makes clear, his greatest capacity is for self-deception. It is this inherent weakness that is compounded when he chooses against his own better judgement to disguise his growing obsession by describing Hetty to Mr Irwine as a 'perfect Hebe' (*AB* 9)—the goddess of youth and spring; cupbearer (until usurped by Ganymede) of Olympus. In thus deceiving his classicist mentor by mythologizing and depersonalizing—stereotyping—Hetty, Arthur denies both his feelings concerning her, and the living girl herself.

What the continued, charted process from enflamed desire and flattered hope to yielding and despair restores to the squire–dairymaid literary (and pictorial) cliché that the story subverts, is the actuality of individual human experience. But the sense that the narrator is ultimately unjust to Hetty is abiding. As Raymond Williams puts it, 'Hetty is a subject to that last moment on the road before she abandons her baby; but after that moment she is an object of confession and conversion—of *attitudes* to suffering' (173). To whatever extent this is held to be true, however, the harrowing confession itself remains one of the most effectively sustained, sympathetic, and memorable passages in the book. If Hetty is now displaced as the object of the narrative, it is her child—with its crying haunting her and penetrating the reader—that, with its claim to life heard and de-nied, becomes the usurping subject.

Dinah's destiny as Adam's non-preaching wife, and mother of his children, is now also regarded by many critics as a form of sacrifice, with her final image, according to Dorothea Barrett in *Vocation and Desire: George Eliot's Heroines* (1989), 'diminished, eclipsed, in discouraging contrast to our first view of her' (36). As Gillian Beer puts it, she is safely 'contained within the family, back in the conventional ordering' (1986: 73).

In thus containing Dinah, and reuniting Arthur with his community, the novel's clos-ure appears to leave the social order restored, and to promise its continuity. While this deemed compliance on the part of the narrator is often deplored, the representation of the weaknesses and injustices inherent in the hierarchical system tends to be overlooked. Yet these weaknesses and injustices are exposed through the flaws of those who are both privileged and in authority. In the exploitative tyranny of old Squire Donnithorne, the pastoral idleness and partiality of the otherwise essentially decent rector, the aristocratic presumptuousness of his mother, and the dishonourable capabilities of his protégé, the fallibility of the system is clearly embodied.

With the village of Hayslope at its heart, the main setting is Loamshire, an idyllic, richly fertile, imaginary region which nostalgically (but not sentimentally) conjures the Warwickshire of George Eliot's own childhood, though the novel opens twenty years before she was born. The unequivocal passion that imbues the narrative is often under-stood as exaltation. W. J. Keith—who recognizes that George Eliot 'was feeling towards that sense of regional consciousness which is so important and neglected a development of the Victorian period'—speaks for many when he suggests that modern readers 'are likely to consider the idyllic aspects overstressed. Accustomed to Hardy's Wessex and the dark vision so congenial to the modern mind, we tend to find the landscape of "Loamshire" too idealized and simplistic; where, we feel obliged to ask, is the grinding poverty which social historians assure us was widespread?' (Keith, 80). The answer is, if not in Loamshire, then in the neighbouring district of Stonyshire. With its 'hungry' (*AB* 38) land, Stonyshire presents its own, very different rural face, as well as providing a lo-cation for the grim, grey, unsheltered town of Snowfield and its ugly cotton mill, where Dinah gets her living.

That Stonyshire contrasts with Loamshire, and the dismal town with the pretty village, is self-evident. But while the contrast enhances the 'Eden-like peace and loveliness' (*AB* 4) with which Loamshire is blessed, it also comments on the attitudes of those who live, sow, and reap there. It is true that the Loamshire way of life is in visual—and auditory—harmony with nature. The reader is made intimately familiar with the features of both lovingly (re-)created landscape and domestic interior, and with the sounds—of a scythe being whetted, of hedgerow birds and farmyard creatures, of the 'light music of the drop-ping whey' (*AB* 20), or the click of Mrs Poyser's iron—that give them immediacy. But, concealed within this quickened pictorialism, between the clusters of golden ricks, the corn, the meadow grass, and 'pretty confusion of trees and thatch and dark-red tiles' (*AB* 2), is what Creeger has properly identified as 'a core of hardness' (1956:227). Unlike Dinah, whose travels arterially connect the localities of plenty and want, the sympathet-ically portrayed inhabitants of the beguiling Hall Farm, for example, themselves lack broad sympathy. It is their 'land of Goshen' that is bountiful, not the Poysers themselves, who are complacent as well as comfortable. They acknowledge no natural association between their fertile terrain and the barren hills lying to the north-west, on whose 'rugged, tall' (*AB* 2) protection their yield, and the sleekness of their cattle (a favourite subject of Victorian painting), depends. Instead, they express only pitying contempt for the wretched hill dwellers, most of whose land, Mr Poyser assesses, 'isna worth ten shillings an acre, rent and profits' (*AB* 49), and whose deprivation Mrs Poyser can dismiss in one of her aphorisms: 'Them as ha' never had a cushion don't miss it' (*AB* 49), she assures Dinah. George Eliot intended the reader to recognize this hardness. She defends it no more than she defends the abuse of social and economic power, while neither the celebratory 'Harvest Supper' (*AB* 53), nor the 'Marriage Bells' (*AB* 55), mitigate it. If Hetty is banished from the picture, George Eliot refrains from negating or dismissing her suffering, rather allowing the elegiac mood that permeates the whole story to intensify as it draws towards closure. Conceived when the author was feeling 'a greater capacity for moral and intellectual enjoyment' (Cross, i. 389) than she had ever before experienced, it is as the evocative, sensory 'country story' she intended it to be that *Adam Bede* unequivocally triumphs. But the sadness that 'lies near joy', which—as Lewes reported—she was to experience with the success of the novel, is already apparent in the dying fall of the Epilogue, its mood anticipated early in the story. At the end of chapter 2, as the stranger rides away from the green where Dinah has been preaching, 'the voices of the Methodists reached him, rising and falling in that strange blending of exultation and sadness which belongs to the cadence of a hymn'.   BG

Carroll, David, '*Adam Bede*: Pastoral Theodicies', in *Carroll* (1992).

Creeger, George R., 'An Interpretation of Adam Bede', *ELH* 23 (1956).

Cunningham, Valentine, *Everywhere Spoken Against: Dissent in the Victorian Novel* (1975).

Goode, John, '*Adam Bede*', in Hardy (1970).

Keith, W. J., 'The Land in Victorian Literature', in G. E. Mingay (ed.), *The Rural Idyll* (1989).

Knoepflmacher, U. C., 'George Eliot, Feuerbach, and the Question of Criticism', *Victorian Studies*, 7 (1964).

—— (1968).

Sutherland, John, 'Why doesn't the Reverend Irwine speak up for Hetty?', in *Can Jane Eyre Be Happy? More Puzzles in Classic Fiction* (1997).

Williams, Raymond, *The Country and the City* (1973).

Societies Act of 1855, which had made trade unions illegal and were not fully abolished until 1871. See also CLASS; POLITICS; SOCIETY; TRADE UNIONS.

                                                                          AvdB

Aeschylus (525/4–456 BC), Greek tragic dramatist. His trilogy, the *Oresteia,* is concerned with a family curse worked out across three generations, and displays one killing leading to others in a sequence of vengeance and counter-vengeance. George Eliot interpreted this in psychological terms (see TRAGEDY), seeing it as an expression of love and hatred intertwined in family relationships, and of the moral truth that 'Our deeds carry their terrible consequences . . . consequences that are hardly ever confined to ourselves' (*AB* 16). She handles Aeschylus again in very similar terms in *Felix Holt, the Radical* (*FH* 48, 49). She is thinking of Aeschylus also when she writes in *Adam Bede*, 'Family likeness has often a deep sadness in it. Nature, that great tragic dramatist, knits us together by bone and muscle, and divides us by . . . our brains; blends yearning and repulsion; and ties us by our heart-strings to the beings that jar us' (*AB* 5). A pattern of allusions runs through *Adam Bede*: Arthur Donnithorne finds Parson Irwine at breakfast reading Aeschylus, and Aeschylus later appears as a spectre at the feast which marks Arthur's coming of age, when Irwine quotes him as a warning against the dangers of love misapplied (*AB* 16, 22). When Arthur finds Adam standing before him 'like a terrible fate' and feels Nemesis tormenting him, George Eliot is again applying an Aeschylean colour (*AB* 28, 29).

Prometheus Bound, now widely thought by scholars not to be by Aeschylus, was beloved by radicals. It was Karl *Marx's favourite play, and *Goethe, *Shelley, and *Byron were among those who developed the story of the Titan who was chained and tortured for defying the supreme god Zeus in order to benefit mankind. George Eliot exploits these associations in *Daniel Deronda*, comparing the suffering of Mordecai, visionary in his aims but politically impotent, to 'the cry of Prometheus ... whose chained anguish seems a greater energy than the sea and sky he invokes', and even suggesting that his tragedy is deeper than Prometheus', because poverty and disease prevent him from heroic action (*DD* 16, 38). The pattern of allusion is continued when a member of Mordecai's circle quotes Shelley's *Prometheus Unbound* (*DD* 42). See also CLASSICAL LITERATURE.

RHAJ

'Agatha'. See POETRY OF GEORGE ELIOT.

America did not draw from George Eliot unqualified praise. In 1853 she admitted 'profound interest' in the United States as a 'cradle of the future', but confessed near loathing for 'the *common* American type of character' (*L* ii. 85). Pleasantly surprised to meet an American she liked—as when she met Ralph Waldo *Emerson—or to hear of one who had acted admirably (*L* ii. 21; iv. 23), she maintained a dedicated aversion to 'impertinent' American behaviour: requests for her autograph or photograph, 'impudent romancing' about her in the newspapers, social blunders by the 'travelling society' she and G. H. *Lewes instinctively fled (*L* vii. 193; vi. 246; iii. 295). 'Some one told me on oracular authority that if I had to be born again,' she wrote to Sara *Hennell in 1862, 'I ought to pray to God to be born an American. I should sooner pray to be born a Turk or an Arab' (*L* iv. 72). All the same, her investments in US bonds, railways, and public utilities later swelled her capital rapidly (Haight 1968:458). She never visited America, though invited by Harriet Beecher *Stowe, among others.

George Eliot's essays and reviews contain occasional references to American eccentricities (*Essays*, 247, 320), but she made few comments upon the American character or American literature generally. In Margaret *Fuller she found 'a sort of vague spiritualism and grandiloquence which belong to all but the very best American writers' (*Essays*, 200). H. D. *Thoreau's *Walden*, in contrast, showed 'that energetic, yet calm spirit of innovation, that practical as well as theoretic independence of formulæ, which is peculiar to some of the finer American minds' (*Westminster Review*, 65: 302). George Eliot's impact upon 19th-century American literature, and especially upon American *realism, is often taken for granted but rarely spelled out—understandably so, since the nature and formal coherence of literary realism in the USA have remained matters of intense critical debate. William Dean Howells, who waged his 'Realism War' in the 1880s, consistently praised George Eliot; Mark Twain consistently abused her

(Michael Davitt Bell, *The Problem of American Realism* (1993), 45). Insofar as American novelists wanted George Eliot's considerable cultural authority for certain practices—a loving though not credulous view of the ordinary, a rigorous analysis of character and motive, a sense of pluralistic truth balanced with the assertion of individual morality, a vision of the ideal within the particularities of common life and familiar landscape—she helped form, defend, and sustain part of a functional concept of realism that operated decisively in late 19th-century American literature.

Beyond debate is George Eliot's enormous American popularity. Readers and critics admired her dignified treatments of humble family life, her moral precision, and her complication of character. As a later member of Harper and Brothers, her American publisher, pointed out, she appealed 'to the great world of novel readers', not only 'to the thoughtful few' (J. Henry Harper, *The House of Harper* (1912), 388). Both *Adam Bede* and *Silas Marner* were best sellers in the USA, with *Middlemarch* and *Daniel Deronda* probably falling just short of that level (Frank Luther Mott, *Golden Multitudes* (1947), 136). At the beginning of her career, George Eliot declared American publishers 'very narrow-necked jars indeed'; at the end, she acknowledged that Harper had 'behaved most handsomely' (*L* ii. 508; vii. 119). She had received £3,630 for the initial American rights for six of her novels (see EARNINGS; PUBLISHERS). As Cate suggests, the difference between the £30 which Harper gave her for *Adam Bede* and the £1,700 she received for *Deronda* illustrates the growth and magnitude of her *reputation (69).

George Eliot's death occasioned extensive coverage by the American press. Memorial columns were reserved for the special Saturday Christmas newspapers that year, a few with portraits and sketches (very hard to come by). There were sermons about her the next day and, around New Year, commemorative recitals, concerts, and speeches in clubs and book societies. Then the periodicals—literary, family, women's—added their more extensive essays and assessments. Numerous editorials, articles, and letters from readers reveal that many Americans felt as if they had lost one of their own.

KKC

Bamlett, Steve, 'The Scene of a Great Future: George Eliot, America and Political Economy', in Neil Taylor (ed.), *America in English Literature* (1980).

Cate, Hollis L., 'The Initial Publication of George Eliot's Novels in America', *Forum*, 10 (1969).

Griffith, George V., 'George Eliot's American Reception, 1858–1881: A Bibliography', *Bulletin of Bibliography*, 44 (1987).

Weisbuch, Robert, *Atlantic Double-Cross: American Literature and British Influence in the Age of Emerson* (1986).

American civil war (1861–5), in which the industrial and commercial states of the North (abolition of slavery their aim) eventually defeated the agricultural states of the South. George Eliot's initial response, expressed to Mrs *Congreve (*L* iii. 460) was one of concern for the poor cotton weavers (dependent on trade with the South). Late in 1861, after the Trent incident involving the removal of Southern envoys from the British ship by Northern forces, G. H. *Lewes felt that Anthony *Trollope's book on North America would sell well despite anti-British feeling (*L* iii. 470), and early in 1862 Eliot wrote to Barbara *Bodichon of her continued anxiety and disgust, regarding the war as revealing 'evidence of the low moral conditions—the barbarism of feeling made all the more hideous by the pretension to advancement—which discloses itself in the acts and writings of the Americans' (*L* iv. 13). Eliot sympathized with the North, rejoiced in their successes, but 'with that check which attends all joy in a war not absolutely ended' (*L* iv. 139). See also AMERICA.   GRH

'Amos Barton'. See SCENES OF CLERICAL LIFE.

Anglicanism. George Eliot was born into a family of loyal members of the Church of England, the church established by law as the national religion of England, and was brought up to be a practising Anglican Christian. About half of all churchgoers in England were revealed on Census Sunday 1851 to be attending an Anglican place of divine worship (the rest of the practising Christians were at Dissenting churches—Methodist, Baptist, Congregational, Quaker, Unitarian, and so on—or Roman Catholic churches). George Eliot was baptized in her parish church at *Chilvers Coton. Her father was a conservative High Churchman. Her very influential first close friend, Maria *Lewis, was an evangelical or Low Church Anglican (see EVANGELICALISM). The Anglican evangelicals were on friendly terms with evangelical Dissenters; High Churchmen and -women were not. In Coventry George Eliot and her brother Isaac (see Evans, Isaac) attended Trinity church. When she abandoned her Christian faith and momentously refused to continue attending church on Sunday 2 January 1842, it was Coventry's Trinity church which was the place of her refusal. But for all her own backsliding from it, England's state religion, its congregations, its clergymen, its doctrines and practices, and the question of its future, were preoccupying staples of her writing. She cut her teeth as a critic with powerful satirical attacks on Anglican Christianity (in *'Worldliness and Other-Worldliness: The Poet Young'); with memorable satirical reflections on the literature of its enthusiasts (in *'Silly Novels by Lady Novelists' and her review of Charles *Kingsley's *Westward Ho!* in the

Westminster Review in July 1856); and with support for the literature of its opponents (like J. A. *Froude's *The Nemesis of Faith*, which she reviewed in the *Coventry *Herald and Observer* in March 1849). And the Church of England subject propelled her into fiction. She began her career as a novelist with *Scenes of Clerical Life*, three fictions about Anglican clergymen, remarkable for a sympathy no one would have predicted from encountering the hostile and ribald tones of the critical prose. And this interest in the Anglican subject continued, most notably in her first full-length novel *Adam Bede*, and in *Middlemarch*, the great novel of her maturity. But nowhere in her novels set in England is the national church entirely absent as a factor in her kept-up investigations of the future prospects for religion.

The authorial attitude in these writings runs the gamut from dry mock, through a measured tolerance, to social and moral hostility. The novels particularly recognize the intimate bond between the national church and its rural parishioners—the political and economic dependence of farmers and other agricultural workers on the squire who is not neutrally their landlord but is also the patron of the local parish church and expects loyalty to it and to the minister in his pay, and, more than this, the subtle internalized compliances in which the parishioner is bonded into a cycle of ritualized local religious observances. Mrs Poyser in *Adam Bede* stands for the rural Anglican, happy with the religion of 'the Catechism and the Prayer-book' (*AB* 6), the provider of religious significance at all life's key turning points. The burial service for Adam's father (*AB* 18) illustrates the sociologist George Eliot's profound recognition of the way the rural Church of England provided 'good words' and meanings for human endurance at such times. *Adam Bede*'s plot of moral failure, involving the downfall of Hetty Sorrel, is a strong critique, of course, of the inability of the Established Church (as of all churches in George Eliot's work) to provide in the end proper moral sustenance for people's actual living.

In *Silas Marner*, 'Raveloe theology'—the bunch of religious notions with which the good Anglican Dolly Winthrop seeks to console Silas Marner—is little distinguishable from a vague pantheism. George Eliot is not all unkindly disposed to this brand of mere religiose paganism as the cement of illiterate peasant existences. Dolly is kind and loving and a true friend of the lonely outcast Marner. And of course George Eliot's group of tolerant rural clergymen, like Irwine in *Adam Bede* and Farebrother in *Middlemarch*, are condoned in their struggles with the more strictly orthodox and righteous, because like all approved Anglicans in her work, such as Adam Bede and the Garths, their rather undogmatic theology can be read as the *religion of humanity (see also FEUERBACH, LUDWIG). What really offends in her novels is excessive Anglican strictness and partisanship, exemplified by the Dissent-hating and wife-beating Dempster in 'Janet's Repentance' (*SC* 3), and the pious but crooked, and finally murderous, banker Bulstrode in *Middlemarch*—an intolerance which denies common humanity. Only an Anglicanism flattened out doctrinally and rejigged as sympathy and human kindness has any future in George Eliot's vision. Dorothea's refusal to carry on her clergyman husband's mythological researches, her marrying the man Bulstrode wronged financially, her settling finally for small-scale humanist good works, are all offered as indictments of the Established Church's great intellectual and social as well as great moral limitations. See also METHODISM; MORAL VALUES; RELIGION; ROMAN CATHOLICISM.

VC

animals. Ranging from the generic to the specific, animal allusion is extensive and purposeful in George Eliot, and crucial to her moral purpose. In the early 'Mr Gilfil's Love-Story', for example, a pattern of images of animal types—principally of a songbird and a little black-eyed monkey—is used to emphasize the dilemma of the story's passionate, inwardly suffering Italian heroine, Caterina Sarti, who is perceived and treated as a kind of pet-entertainer by her English adoptive society. Conversely, actual pets, like Dame Fripp's privileged, never-to-be-eaten (but unsentimentalized), indispensable pig companion, are individualized and permitted their idiosyncratic satisfactions and responses.

The profound interest in natural history George Eliot shared with G. H. *Lewes, and which she had applied to her important 1856 *Westminster Review* article on the German cultural historian Wilhelm von Riehl, 'The *Natural History of German Life', is transmitted in many ways to *The Mill on the Floss*. This novel abounds in animal analogy and animal metaphor. Even the young Maggie Tulliver's speculations concerning the family intercourse and social embarrassments of spiders, or her stories about the creatures the children come upon, are informed by the close scrutiny of a naturalist. The social organism of St Ogg's, and many of the novel's human characters—including the 'emmet-like' (*MF* 4.2) Dodsons and Tullivers—are compared to or identified with other species, or with particular beasts. Thus Mrs Tulliver is likened to an ineducable goldfish, a protective sheep, a waterfowl, or a foolish hen taking to stratagem, while Mr Stelling, Tom's unadaptable schoolmaster, is represented by the naturalist W. J. Broderip's deluded beaver, instinctively

constructing his dam as earnestly 'in a room up three pair of stairs in London, as if he had been laying his foundation in a stream or lake in Upper Canada' (*MF* 2.1). In boyhood, animals are the crucial adjunct of Tom's self-image: poignantly destined to struggle stoically with the commercial world in order to regain his family's honour, his thwarted ambition is to be master of many dogs and horses, and to make a figure on a fine hunter. His father is almost invariably an equestrian figure when outdoors. As the narrative progresses, Mr Tulliver's moods are registered through his relationship with his psychologically indispensable horse, to or through whom he transmits all his nuances of feeling, whether of severity, tenderness, triumph, or anger. Perceived by the narrator as one of those animals 'to which tenacity of position is a law of life—they can never flourish again, after a single wrench' (*MF* 3.1), he perceives himself after his downfall as a yoked horse galled by his harness. The final stage of his decline is signified when he is unable to remount after ignominiously and vengefully thrashing his defenceless enemy, Mr Wakem.

Between them, the Leweses owned a series of pet dogs (see PETS). Lewes, who described his bulldog Ben as 'a synthesis of love and ugliness, and gentleness, and spoiled-childishness!' (*L* viii. 366), told Elma Stuart that dogs were his passion (*L* v. 377). George Eliot clearly shared his pleasure in them, on 29 July 1859 celebrating the arrival of John Blackwood's gift of a pug with the single entry in her diary, 'Pug came!' (*Journals*, 79). Described by Lewes as 'a great beauty, though not wise' (*L* iii. 124 n.), and fondly by George Eliot as their 'very slow child' (*L* iii. 304), the indulged Pug was lost about eighteen months after his acquisition. He was memorialized by a china pug Blackwood sent to her on New Year's Day, 1862.

Given this background, it is unsurprising that dogs receive considerable attention in George Eliot. Farm dogs, guard dogs, and figurative dogs animate her works throughout; but there is also an extensive family of individuals who are significant members of their fictive worlds, and who are often the interpreters, representatives, judges, or victims of their human associates. To be shown to interpret, they must themselves be interpreted, a process which inevitably involves a degree of anthropomorphism. However, while they are frequently invested with complex interior lives and human anxieties, the success of their depictions is the result of accurate, intrinsically sympathetic, observation. Each dog—including Jet in 'Amos Barton'; Rupert and Ponto in 'Mr Gilfil's Love-Story'; Gyp and Vixen in *Adam Bede*; Yap, Minny, and Mumps in the *Mill*; Monk in *Middlemarch*; Fluff and Fetch in *Daniel Deronda*—has a distinctive role. Accorded its own claims and susceptibilities (and gender), it may either provide the acceptable alternative to human society, or be an important agent in the narrative. George Eliot's works teem with references to animals of all kinds, exotic and familiar; but the dog is pre-eminent.

BG

Ashton (1990).
Gray, Beryl, '"Animated Nature": The Mill on the Floss', in Rignall (1997).
Hardy (1959).
Lodge, David, introduction to George Eliot, Scenes of Clerical Life (1973).

anti-Semitism. In her early adult life George Eliot showed some symptoms of the anti-Semitism that was rife in 19th-century Europe; subsequently her attitudes underwent radical transformation. In England literary stereotypes of Jews were found in Charles *Dickens's *Oliver Twist*, and in Anthony *Trollope's and Edmund Yates's novels—to give only three examples from many. Until the second half of the century, Jews were barred from sitting in Parliament or gaining University degrees until they had affirmed allegiance to the Church of England. Frequently Benjamin *Disraeli, the most prominent of politicians of Jewish descent, was attacked because of his origins rather than for the policies he advocated. Eliot herself was guilty of this and of such anti-Semitic reflexes as 'everything *specifically* Jewish is of a low grade' (*L* i. 246). In her maturity she turned against such prejudices, developing a sympathetic interest in Judaism and attacking racial intolerance (but see also COLONIALISM).

Daniel Deronda and 'The Modern Hep! Hep! Hep!' chapter in *Impressions of Theophrastus Such* (*TS* 18), named after the series of anti-Jewish riots which broke out in Germany in 1819, contain Eliot's fullest treatment of anti-Semitism. Her letter to Harriet Beecher *Stowe in October 1876 succinctly explains her motivation in *Daniel Deronda*.

There is nothing I should more care to do, if it were possible, than to rouse the imagination of men and women to a vision of those human claims in those races of their fellow-men who most differ from them in customs and beliefs . . . not only towards the Jews, but towards all oriental peoples with whom we English come in contact, a spirit of arrogance and contemptuous dictatorialness is observable which has become a national disgrace. (*L* vi. 301–2)

See also NATIONALISM; RACE; RELIGION.   WB

Baker, William, *George Eliot and Judaism* (1975).
Cheyette, Brian, *Constructions of 'the Jew' in English Literature and Society: Racial Representations, 1875–1945* (1993).
Klein, Charlotte, 'The Jew in Modern English Literature', *Patterns of Prejudice*, 5 (1971).

Ragussis, Michael, *Figures of Conversion: The Jewish Question & English National Identity* (1995).

'*Antigone* and its Moral, The'. This essay by George Eliot, notionally a review of a school edition of *Sophocles' *Antigone*, appeared in the *Leader* in March 1856 (repr. in *Essays*). Though derivative and undistinguished, it is of considerable interest for the light it sheds on her attitude to the inclusion of tragic elements in modern fiction (see TRAGEDY). She gives an extensive synopsis of the play, in which Antigone defies the command of Creon, the new king of Thebes, and gives ritual burial to her dead brother, the traitor Polynices; this act leads to the death of Antigone herself and the deaths of Creon's wife and son. George Eliot adopts the interpretation, drawn by her from the German classicist August Böckh though today chiefly associated with Hegel, which sees the dispute between Antigone and Creon as a clash of two just and compelling moral imperatives—the well-being of the state and the demands of family duty—and she explicitly rejects the view (which most modern scholars would accept) that Creon behaves tyrannically: 'Coarse contrasts like this are not the materials handled by great dramatists'. The principles informing her own fiction are seen in her depiction of both Creon and Antigone as psychologically complex, and alike conscious of just blame for transgressing one principle in following out another. She also insists that the 'antagonism of valid principles' is not peculiar to polytheism; rather, the play is timeless as a representation of the clash between the outer life of man and his inward needs and in the way in which it explores the truth that martyrs and reformers 'are never fighting against evil only; they are also placing themselves in opposition to a good' (*Essays*, 264). This analysis is of particular relevance to the depiction of Dorothea in *Middlemarch* as a modern Antigone. See also CLASSICAL LITERATURE.   RHAJ

appearance, personal. The question that is implicit in many descriptions of George Eliot in person is whether she was merely plain, or actually ugly. Who better to express the complex nuance of such a question than Henry *James? After his first meeting with George Eliot he wrote to his father:

To begin with she is magnificently ugly—deliciously hideous. She has a low forehead, a dull grey eye, a vast pendulous nose, a huge mouth, full of uneven teeth and a chin and jaw-bone *qui n'en finessent* [sic] *pas* . . . Now in this vast ugliness resides a most powerful beauty which, in a very few minutes steals forth and charms the mind, so that you end as I ended, in falling in love with her. Yes behold me literally in love with this great horse-faced

Photograph of George Eliot by Mayall in 1858, which her friend Bessie Rayner Parkes (1829–1924), later Belloc, found not favourable but 'the only real indication left to us of the true shape of the head, and of George Eliot's smile and general bearing'.

blue-stocking. I don't know in what the charm lies, but it is thoroughly potent. An admirable physiognomy—a delightful expression, a voice soft and rich as that of a counselling angel (10 May 1869, *Henry James Letters*, ed. Leon Edel, i. (1974), 116–17).

Generally, accounts of her physical appearance are consistent in their factual descriptions, but not in their subjective responses. Leslie *Stephen provides a benchmark: 'Her features were strongly marked, with a rather large mouth and jaw; her eyes a grey-blue, with very variable expression; her hands were finely formed; her voice low and very musical . . . the whole appearance expressive of a singular combination of power with intense sensibility' (*George Eliot* (1902), 145). There are recurrent elements in the descriptions—for instance, her hair, sometimes light, or golden, in her later years streaked with grey, is always 'abundant' (however, George Eliot herself confessed: 'I have all my life wished it were possible for me to have my hair cut short that I might wash it every day' (*L* vii. 334). John Walter Cross described her manner as 'sincere, cordial, grave' (iii. 337), and these adjectives, along with 'gentle', 'simple', 'earnest', are frequently used. Then there is the voice. A nursery governess to Charles Lewes's daughters commented: 'I do not quite recall her features, but what I can remember was that you forgot everything else when she *spoke*. Her voice had a wonderfully sweet tone. It was more like music than a speaking voice' (Arthur Paterson, *George Eliot's Family Life and Letters* (1928), 252). Later accounts tend to come from visitors to The *Priory, coloured by the reverent atmosphere and preoccupied with whether her appearance is masculine, but some are at pains to make the point that though her demeanour was often serious, she had a sense of fun, a wonderful smile, and a merry laugh. Bessie *Parkes testified that the photograph taken by the fashionable photographer Mayall in 1858 gives 'the only real indication left to us of the true shape of the head and of George Eliot's smile and general bearing' (Haight 1968: 102).

George Eliot seems to have been self-deprecatory about her appearance, unless Oscar *Browning's report in his *Life of George Eliot* (1890) that she told him 'that her right hand was broader than her left from the amount of butter which she had made in her youth' is a boast (20). She rarely mentions dress in letters or journals, but told Maria Congreve: 'you would perhaps have been amused to see an affectionate but dowdy friend of yours, splendid in a grey moire antique—the consequence of a severe lecture from Owen Jones on her general neglect of personal adornment' (28 November 1863, *L* iv. 116). To Elma Stuart, the recipient of many intimacies, George Eliot described

herself with the instruction to 'Imagine a first cousin of the old Dante's—rather smoke-dried—a face with lines in it that seem a map of sorrows' (17 September 1873, *L* v. 437); comparisons with Dante, and with Savonarola, were made also by others. See also PORTRAITS; VOICE OF GEORGE ELIOT.   MAH

Aristotle (384–322 BC), Greek philosopher and scientist whose works George Eliot read closely, inscribing passages from them in Greek in her *notebooks and referring to them in her *letters and fiction. The *Poetics* was particularly important: she knew it well, reading it for the first time in 1856, the year she began writing fiction, again in 1865, and for a third time in 1873. In the context of Tom Tulliver's education (*MF* 2.1) she alludes to Aristotle's praise of metaphorical speech as a sign of high intelligence (see METAPHOR), but it is his ideas on *tragedy that have the most important bearing on her fiction. As Darrell Mansell has shown, she has them clearly in mind when she writes of 'pity and terror' in relation to tragedy in the Introduction to *Felix Holt, the Radical* and when, echoing Aristotle's definition of the tragic hero, she writes in a letter of her concern with 'the truthful presentation of a character essentially noble but liable to great error' (*L* iii. 318). She does not follow Aristotle systematically (Mansell, 155), and her conception of tragedy may in the end be more Hegelian than Aristotelian, but just as his notion of hamartia, or error, is pertinent to her presentation of mixed and erring humanity, so her plots make central use of the peripeteia or sudden reversal of fortune, such as befalls Mr Tulliver in *The Mill on the Floss* when he loses his lawsuit, Silas Marner when his money is stolen, and Harold Transome when he discovers that Jermyn is his father (*FH* 47). The structural principle of the *Mill* can be seen as a series of such reversals (Swann, 205).   JMR

Holtze, Elizabeth, 'Aristotle and George Eliot: Hamartia in *Adam Bede*', in Donald Stump et al. (edd.), *Hamartia: The Concept of Error in the Western Tradition* (1983).

Mansell, Darrell Jun., 'George Eliot's Conception of Tragedy', *Nineteenth-Century Fiction*, 22 (1967–8).

Swann, Brian, '*The Mill on the Floss* and the Form of Tragedy', *English Miscellany*, 24 (1974).

'Armgart', a verse drama written in 1870–1 while George Eliot was working on *Middlemarch*. It was published in the *Legend of Jubal and Other Poems* in 1874 and its story of the opera singer Armgart and the loss of her voice reflects upon the problem of women's *vocation, which is taken up both in *Middlemarch* and the later *Daniel Deronda*. See POETRY OF GEORGE ELIOT.   MR

Arnold, Matthew (1824–88), English critic, poet, essayist, educationalist. There is only one recorded meeting between Matthew Arnold and George Eliot—on Boxing Day 1876 (noted in her letters, *L* ix. 184 n. 2)—but her *notebooks, *journals, and journalism show that she was familiar with his writing, and parallels can be seen between her views on culture and *politics and his, although she does not share his lofty detachment and always stresses the individual's involvement in the cultural process. Eliot's '*Middlemarch*' *Notebooks*, edited by J. C. Pratt and V. A. Neufeldt (1979), reveal her reading Arnold's 'The Scholar-Gypsy', 'Thyrsis', and 'Stanzas from the Grand Chartreuse'. In a journal entry, 6 February 1869, she writes of 'looking through Matthew Arnold's poems' (*L* v. 11). She took notes from her reading of Arnold's conclusion to *Literature and Dogma: An Essay towards a Better Apprehension of the Bible* (1871–3) and noted Arnold's conclusion: 'For Science, God is the "Stream of tendency whereby all things fulfil the law of their being"—for Religion, i.e. "Morality heightened by emotion". He may be most adequately conceived as "the Eternal Power, not ourselves, which makes for righteousness"' (*Some Notebooks*, ed. Baker, iii. 73). Similarly she noted Arnold's 'God is really here, at bottom, a deeply moved way of saying *Conduct* or righteousness' and 'When we say that culture is *To know the best that has been said & thought in the world*, we imply that, for culture, a system directly tending to this end is necessary to our reading. . . . Our reading being so without purpose as it is, nothing can be truer than what Butler says, that really in general, no true part of our time is more idly spent than the time spent in reading' (*Some Notebooks*, ed. Baker, iii. 21). In her article in the 'Belles Lettres' section in the *Westminster Review* (July 1855), Eliot reviews Arnold's *Poems Second Series* (1855), especially commending lines from 'Empedocles' and his 'Resignation'.

In November 1874 G. H. *Lewes wrote to Mrs Elma *Stuart asking whether she had seen 'Mat Arnold's papers in the October and November numbers' of the *Contemporary Review*. His letter conveys views that he shares with George Eliot:

Much that he says on Religion we both think very good, and likely to have *a yeasty* effect on that strange fluid Public Opinion. I, myself cannot see how the Bible 'makes for righteousness' though I profoundly agree with him that righteousness is salvation—and it is not to be sought in metaphysical refinements about a 'personal God' but is to be found in our idealization of human relations and human needs. (*L* vi. 86–7)

Lines from Arnold's 'God and the Bible: A Review of Objections to "Literature and Dogma"', from the January 1875 *Contemporary Review*, are in Eliot's notebooks.

Arnold's translation from Italian of the 'Hymn of St Francis' in his 'Pagan and Christian Religious Sentiment', *Cornhill Magazine* (April 1864) and included in *Essays in Criticism* (1865), also find their way into Eliot's notebooks (*Some Notebooks*, ed. Baker, iv. 116): ideas fictionally transmitted in the figure of Mordecai in *Daniel Deronda* who, like St Francis, is 'living an intense life in an invisible past and future, careless of his personal lot' (*DD* 42). Arnold emphasizes bodily loss 'transfigured by the power of a spiritual emotion' (*Cornhill*, 9: 431), providing a medieval Christian mystical counterpart to Mordecai's search for Deronda to whom he can transmit his views.

Arnold is not used as a source for Eliot's epigraphs in her writings. References to Arnold in her letters are far from extensive. From the evidence so far available neither she nor G. H. Lewes appear to have written to Arnold or received letters from him. Nevertheless they had interests in common. Eliot's 1855–6 essays on Heine appeared seven years before Arnold's more well-known 1863 *Cornhill* assessment. On the other hand Arnold's elegiac 'The Scholar-Gypsy' (1853), with its central figure of the dreaming rootless wanderer, predates Eliot's lengthy dramatic poem *The Spanish Gypsy*, set in post-medieval Spain.

Arnold, Eliot, Lewes, amongst other Victorians, were fascinated by *Rachel, the great French tragic actress. Arnold wrote three sonnets in her memory, five years after her death in 1863. Arnold, like Lewes in his reviews of her performances, stressed her Jewish origins yet universal appeal. Eliot's Princess and Gwendolen in *Deronda* are both actresses owing something to the great French tragedian. Eliot and Arnold were both interested in *Sophocles' *Antigone*. In his 1853 Preface to *Poems* Arnold questioned the modern relevance of the *Antigone* story, and attempts to come to terms with it in his poem 'Fragment of an Antigone' in *The Strayed Reveller and Other Poems* (1849). Eliot, in 'The *Antigone* and its Moral', *Leader* (March 1856), finds interest in the tragic drama and draws upon it for *Romola*, *Middlemarch* and *Daniel Deronda* (see for instance *DD* 32).

Both Eliot and Arnold were concerned with religion and culture in an increasingly secular age. U. C. Knoepflmacher observes that Eliot's 'ethical humanism finds its most immediate counterpart in the religious thought of Matthew Arnold. Basic for this similarity is their identical redefinition of culture' (1965: 62). Arnoldian elements have been noted in *Felix Holt, the Radical*: for instance, ideas in the novel relating to democracy, culture, and the issue of working-class representation parallel those in the Arnold essays which became *Culture* and *Anarchy* (1869). In *Felix Holt, the Radical* Eliot marginalizes politics; in *Culture and Anarchy* Arnold observes: 'everything in our political life tends to hide from us that there is anything wiser than our ordinary selves' (1966 edn., ed. Dover Wilson, 117–18). *Felix Holt* should be placed within the context of 1860s writings about representation such as, for instance, Arnold's essays. Eliot's narrative voice in *Felix Holt*, as Pykett indicates, echoes Arnold's: 'the ironic tone of the Arnoldian essayist is employed whenever the provincial world is anatomized, and it is usually the vehicle of an Arnoldian class analysis' (231). In short, given their similarities, it is surprising that they refer to each other's works so rarely.   WB

Some George Eliot Notebooks, ed. William Baker, 4 vols. (1976–85).

George Eliot's 'Middlemarch' Notebooks: A Transcription, ed. John Clark Pratt and Victor Neufeldt (1979).

Gallagher, Catherine, 'The Politics of Culture and the Debate over Representation', *Representations*, 5 (1984).

Knoepflmacher, U. C., *Religious Humanism and the Victorian Novel: George Eliot, Walter Pater, and Samuel Butler* (1965).

Pykett, Lyn, 'George Eliot and Arnold: The Narrator's Voice and Ideology in *Felix Holt The Radical*', *Literature and History*, 11 (1985).

art is the subject of a famous definition by George Eliot in her 1856 essay on 'The *Natural History of German Life*': 'Art is the nearest thing to life; it is a mode of amplifying experience and extending our contact with our fellow-men beyond the bounds of our personal lot' (*Essays*, 271). This idea that art has the moral and social function of extending our sympathies is one that informs her fiction, and in the early work it gives rise to that *realism of the ordinary life that is celebrated in chapter 17 of *Adam Bede*, where the narrator turns willingly away from the grand conventional subjects of art—'cloud-borne angels, prophets, sybils, and heroic warriors'—to focus on the humbler subjects of Dutch painting. Such realistic art may serve to overcome class divisions, but not all art serves that end or works in that way. The artistic treasures of Rome are experienced by Dorothea in *Middlemarch* as merely oppressive, as remnants of an alien world that check the flow of her emotion (*MM* 20). But the example of Will Ladislaw, whose imagination is stimulated by these fragments of former ages into being constructive (*MM* 22), indicates how these artistic forms may also be seen to demand an extension of sympathy, though of a different kind. As Eliot puts it in a review of John *Ruskin's *Modern Painters* in 1856: 'in learning how to estimate the artistic products of a particular age according to the mental attitude and external life of that age, we are widening our sympathy,

and deepening the basis of our tolerance and charity' (*Westminster Review*, 70: 626). The exercise of the historical imagination is another mode of amplifying experience; and although Eliot's later pronouncements on art in *'Notes on Form in Art' and 'Leaves from a Notebook' differ from her 1856 definition, she never dissents from the notion that the value of art lies in its capacity to arouse our attention to what is apart from ourselves (*Essays*, 270). The function of art is a moral one, and she has no time for aestheticism, referring ironically to 'that softening influence of the fine arts which makes other people's hardships picturesque' (*MM* 39). See also music; theatre; visual arts.

JMR

Myers (1984).

Wiesenfarth, Joseph, '*Middlemarch*: The Language of Art', *PMLA* 97 (1982).

Witemeyer (1979).

atheism. From 1842, when she lost her faith in Christianity, George Eliot did not believe in God, yet she was more of an agnostic (to use the term that T. H.*Huxley was to coin for himself in 1869) than an outright atheist. As she put it in a review of Harriet *Martineau's *Letters* in the *Leader* in March 1851, 'as it is confessed we cannot have direct immediate knowledge of God, so neither can we know that he is not' (Ashton 1996: 83). Moreover, the term atheism suggests a more militant hostility to religious faith than she was inclined to show. From *Scenes of Clerical Life* onwards clergymen and their beliefs were treated sympathetically, and readers and reviewers of this first work, and of *Adam Bede* which followed, tended to assume that the author was himself a gentleman and a member of the clergy. When the true identity of George Eliot became known, 'her teaching had been dubbed clerical, and it was too late in the day to turn upon her and call her an atheist', as the critic Richard Simpson remarked in 1863 (*CH* 225). He was uncomfortable with what he saw as her atheism, though conceded that her sensible ethics outweighed 'the negative evil of her atheistic theology', which most readers would not in any case discern (*CH* 249–50). Her lack of religious faith became more obvious to later reviewers, like W. H. Mallock who in an 1879 review of *Impressions of Theophastus Such* described her as 'the first great *godless* writer that has appeared in England' (*CH* 453); and after the publication of John Walter *Cross's *Life* in 1885 it could no longer be overlooked (see reputation, critical). She herself had no intention of undermining anyone else's religious faith with her writing, as she insisted to her friend Barbara *Bodichon in November 1862: 'I have too profound a conviction of the efficacy that lies in all sincere faith, and the spiritual blight that comes with No-faith to have any negative propagandism in me' (*L* iv. 64). She went on to say that she had very little sympathy with freethinkers as a class. In her fiction the clearest example of atheism is Silas Marner's loss of faith when he is unjustly expelled from Lantern Yard, declaiming in his despair that 'there is no just God that governs the earth righteously' (*SM* 1). However, he finds his way back to a religious sense of the mystery of life—'there's dealings with us—there's dealings'—and a *Feuerbachian sense of the goodness of humanity: 'There's good i' this world—I've a feeling o' that now' (*SM* 16). See also CHRISTIANITY; RELIGION; RELIGION OF HUMANITY.   JMR

Ashton (1996).

Myers (1984).

Auber, Daniel-François-Esprit (1782–1871), French opera composer. In *Berlin, December 1854, George Eliot saw his *Masaniello, ou La muette de Portici* (1828). In *The Mill on the Floss* (6. 7), Maggie is profoundly affected by Stephen's singing during his rendition with Philip of a stirring duet from the opera. See also MUSIC.   BG

Austen, Jane (1775–1817), English novelist, mentioned by G. H. *Lewes in his initial letter to John *Blackwood defining the content of his 'friend's' work by emphasizing that since *The Vicar of Wakefield* and the work of Miss Austen no writer of stories had represented 'the clergy like any other class with the humours, sorrows, and troubles of other men' (*L* ii. 269). Lewes's admiration for Austen is somewhat fulsomely attested in an article in the *Westminster Review* (July 1852) by which time George Eliot was the effective if unacknowledged editor of that journal. He calls Austen 'the greatest artist that has ever written', while reading her 'is like an actual experience of life: you know the people as if you had lived with them' (*Westminster Review*, 58: 134). In the same year he adapted a one-act farce from the French called *Taking by Storm*, adopting the pseudonym of Frank Churchill, a self-mocking allusion to the self-indulgent 'hero' of *Emma* (1816). His enthusiasm and evaluation were certainly shared by George Eliot. Between February and June 1857, they read all the novels aloud with the possible exception of *Pride and Prejudice* (1813). *Northanger Abbey* (1818) and *Persuasion* (1818) were enjoyed in the Scillys as Eliot finished 'Mr Gilfil's Love-Story' and began 'Janet's Repentance', *Emma* and *Sense and Sensibility* (1811) in May/June in Jersey. Interestingly in July 1859 Lewes published an article on Austen in *Blackwood's Edinburgh Magazine* which was less enthusiastic than his earlier one: perhaps he now felt that Eliot was already a more complete, greater artist. John Blackwood, who was an Austen

devotee, wrote to her from Sponden on 25 May 1859 that 'This place realises Miss Austen's pictures of an English village and would have afforded rich materials to her or to George Eliot' (*L* iii. 73).

Thereafter references in the letters are sparse but suggest continuing familiarity, as when Eliot writes to Mrs Congreve, 'I did not promise, like Mr Collins, that you should receive a letter of thanks for your kind entertainment of me' (*L* iv. 182), a neat glance at chapter 22 of *Pride and Prejudice*. The Leweses read *Persuasion* aloud in September 1874, *Mansfield Park* in June of the same year, *Emma* in September and October 1875. For Eliot Jane Austen is a major influence. The reading aloud which was their domestic practice would also convey the truth by ear of the dialogue, indicating how interested Eliot was in establishing the psychological realism of what was said as well as maintaining a complementary commentary on character, another Austen strength. They share an abiding concern for presenting accurately the manners and mores of a particular society at a particular time, and, in Eliot's early fiction at least, a comic spirit which is perfectly captured through the use of chorus and casual gossip (see HUMOUR). Lady Catherine de Bourgh and Aunt Glegg occupy different positions in the social scale but in terms of domestic intransigence they have similiarities, Lady Catherine the inheritance of birth, Aunt Glegg the command of economic shrewdness, to back their autocracies. Lewes wrote of Austen that she would appeal to 'a small circle of cultivated minds'; Eliot extends the range of appeal by a concomitant extension of the social mores. Claire Tomalin, like many before her, feels that Eliot is indebted to Austen in the first part of *Middlemarch* (*Jane Austen: A Life*, 1997). This may be true, but the fact is that Eliot's *irony is of a different texture. Sisters Dorothea and Celia have no circumstantial connection with Elinor and Marianne, and the cutting edge with which Mrs Bennett is carved is more epigrammatically serrated in the case of Mrs Cadwallader. Austen's egoists like Wickham and Willoughby (or Isabella Thorpe and Mary Crawford) show a limited capacity for development within the narrative frame, but Eliot's egoists, like Arthur Donnithorne and Tito, develop in their various ways, in the case of the first through a strongly moral conscience, in the second through the need to survive at all costs in the worlds of practical politics and lies. The psychology of character is superbly done in Austen: the moving reticence of Colonel Brandon; the gradual self-discoveries of Emma; the sufferings of Fanny which lead to fine steel replacing the vapours; the self-recognitions of Darcy and Elizabeth. Eliot's concerns in this area are comparable but different: the investigation of Lydgate, for example, or of Gwendolen, where retrospective narrative on character tends to extend or expand psychological coherence. In 'The Sad Fortunes of the Reverend Amos Barton' the Countess Czerlaski excites the kind of speculation which is raised in Catherine Morland's mind about General Tilney, the irony in each case effectively deflationary in its simple truth.

It is tempting to link *Mansfield Park* with 'Mr Gilfil's Love-Story', which was being written (in February 1857) as Eliot and Lewes read the novel, but Wybrow lacks the seductive animation of Henry Crawford, and the historical tone and perspective are different in motivation and effect. There is nothing in Austen to compare with the desiccations of Mrs Transome and Transome Court, though both novelists throughout their fiction are intent on the interiors in which their characters have their particularized existence. The initially ironic presentation of Dorothea and Gwendolen does have connectives with that of Emma, though Eliot's irony becomes more compassionate and tolerant or is subsumed in natural character development. The marriageability of daughters (or wards) is certainly a theme omnipresent in Austen, and central in Eliot's final novels. Eliot's treatment has all the sombreness of realism: contrast the balding and do-nothing absolutist Grandcourt with the pent but impassioned Darcy, where Austen's character fulfils, though not without a comic awareness, the contrivance of romance. Austen and Eliot share comic flair, accuracy of description, exactness in choice of word and phrase, an acute sensitivity to the nuances of language, an ear for truthful dialogue, a moral omniscience (occasionally in the use of narrative voice, more often in situation, dilemma, consequences), and a sense of high art which enhances their chosen genre. George Eliot recognized in Austen a great practitioner in the medium she had chosen to adopt.   GRH

Carroll, David R., 'Mansfield Park, Daniel Deronda, and Ordination', *Modern Philology*, 62 (1964–5).

Lerner, Laurence, *The Truthtellers: Jane Austen, George Eliot, D. H. Lawrence* (1967).

Moers, Ellen, *Literary Women* (1976).

B

Bach, Johann Sebastian (1685–1750), German composer. Although George Eliot refers to Bach infrequently, he features in her poem 'Stradivarius'. She approved of the Bach Choir of London (founded in 1875 by Jenny *Lind's husband, Otto Goldschmidt), enjoying the spectacle of fashionable people—with Jenny Lind in the middle of them—'taking pains to sing fine music in tune and time' (*L* vi. 321). See also MUSIC.   BG

Balzac, Honoré de (1799–1850), French novelist whose work George Eliot knew well, referring to it or quoting from it at intervals throughout her writing life. It was the provincial novels in his *Comédie humaine* that she admired most, praising him in 1856 alongside Jane Austen for his high standards in 'the delineation of quiet provincial life' (*Westminster Review*, 65: 638) and choosing to reread one such delineation, *Eugénie Grandet*, on her honeymoon in 1880. Her response to his Parisian novels was more critical. In a journal entry for 25 October 1859, she condemned *Le Père Goriot* as a 'hateful book' (Cross, ii. 139)—a judgement which may owe something to its theme of filial ingratitude, but also reveals her general distaste for the moral squalor of Balzac's Parisian world and the way in which it is presented.

In her fullest discussion of the relationship between morality and the novel, her essay on 'The *Morality of Wilhelm Meister*' of 1855, where she insists that not 'all fact is a fit subject for art', she singles out Balzac as a writer who goes beyond the limit of what is morally acceptable: 'Balzac, perhaps the most wonderful writer of fiction the world has ever seen, has in many novels overstepped this limit. He drags one by his magic force through scene after scene of unmitigated vice, till the effect of walking among this human carrion is a moral nausea' (*Essays*, 146). In thus castigating Balzac she shares a view earlier expressed by G. H.

*Lewes in articles on Balzac in the *Monthly Magazine* (May 1842) and the *Foreign Quarterly Review* (July 1844). She is also implicitly defining a difference between English and French literary culture and their traditions of fiction: writing to her publisher John *Blackwood in 1858 she claimed that the story of Walter *Scott's *Heart of Midlothian* 'told by a Balzacian French writer would probably have made a book that no young person could read without injury' (*L* viii. 201). This remark, unwittingly anticipating Charles *Dickens's Mr Podsnap, suggests a fundamental difference of outlook, but its censorious tone is noticeably absent from her later remarks on Balzac, which show her valuing him as a fellow craftsman.

When François *D'Albert Durade was translating *The Mill on the Floss* into French in 1861 and having difficulty in rendering different shades of style determined by character and social position, she observed that she had 'discerned such shading very strikingly rendered in Balzac', who 'dares to be thoroughly colloquial in spite of French strait-lacing' (*L* iii. 374). When her poem *The Spanish Gypsy* received some critical reviews in 1868, she reminded her publisher of Balzac's remark: 'when I want the world to praise my novels, I write a drama; when I want them to praise my drama, I write a novel' (*L* iv. 464). And in her later years she more than once used the image of the shrinking skin from *La Peau de chagrin* to convey the sense of her own ebbing life (*L* iii. 475). The subtitle of *Middlemarch*, 'A Study of Provincial Life', echoes the terms Balzac uses for one section of his *Comédie humaine*, 'Études de mœurs: Scènes de la vie de province'; and in that novel she suggests like Balzac an affinity between the practice of the novelist and that of the scientist. And when in *Daniel Deronda* she eventually came to write about the kind of society found in Balzac's Parisian novels, the fashionable world of the wealthy and the aristocratic, she made gambling a central motif in a way that is reminiscent of *La Peau de chagrin* and other Balzac novels. The opening scene of *Deronda* around the gaming tables also works in a typically Balzacian fashion, implying at the outset in one detail of the social scene the nature of the whole society that is to be explored. Her last novel, with its sharp social criticism and moments of melodramatic intensity, suggests that George Eliot found more in Balzac than mere grounds for moral disapproval. See also REALISM.   JMR

Couch (1967).

Kendrick, Walter M., 'Balzac and British Realism: Mid-Victorian Theories of the Novel', *Victorian Studies*, 20 (1976).

Rignall, John, 'George Eliot, Balzac and Proust', in Rignall (1997).

Beaconsfield, Lord. See DISRAELI, BENJAMIN.

Beauvoir, Simone de (1908–86), French theorist of the politics of the Other, essayist, feminist, novelist. Best known for her seminal post-war study of the condition of women, the two-volume *The Second Sex* (1949), and her narrative mapping of the existentialist moment, *The Mandarins* (1954), she is also noted for her frank autobiography, in the first volume of which, *Memoirs of a Dutiful Daughter* (1958), she refers to her telling contacts with George Eliot's fiction. A precocious and voracious reader from the start, her schoolgirl reading material was sternly scrutinized by her respectable Catholic family. Eliot's initial impact was to complicate de Beauvoir's relationships with her parents:

Paradoxically, it was through reading a 'permitted' book that I was launched upon the dread paths of deception. . . . Before going on holiday, my mother had bought me a copy of *Adam Bede*. Sitting under the poplars in the 'landscape garden' I had been patiently plodding my way through a slow, rather dull story. Suddenly, after a walk through a wood, the heroine—who was not married—found herself with child. My heart began to pound: heaven forbid that Mama should read this book!

It is at this juncture that de Beauvoir seems to have had her first intimation of 'the gaze'—something that became a key concept in the existentialist analysis of the fabrication of the identity of the Self in terms of the Other: 'If they had been able to read my thoughts, my parents would have condemned me; instead of protecting me as once it did, their gaze held all kinds of dangers for me' (*Memoirs*, ed. James Kirkup (1963 edn.), 111).

Soon after, in the midst of her adolescent crisis of faith, still confused by the torments of doubt and pubescent mystification, she credits Eliot's insights with engaging her directly in significant debate, furthering self-discovery, and with releasing the potential of the narrative mode of expression: 'About this time I read a novel which seemed to me to translate my spiritual exile into words: George Eliot's *The Mill on the Floss* . . . I read it in English . . . Maggie Tulliver, like myself, was torn between others and herself: I recognized myself in her.' Maggie's sorrows tried the young de Beauvoir's judgement.

It was when she went back to the old mill, when she was misunderstood, calumniated, and abandoned by everyone that I felt my heart blaze with sympathy for her. . . . I resembled her and henceforth I saw my isolation not as proof of infamy but as a sign of my uniqueness. I couldn't see myself dying of solitude. Through the heroine, I identified myself with the author: one day other adolescents would bathe with their tears a novel in which I would tell my own sad story. (*Memoirs*, 140)

For all de Beauvoir's self-mockery, Eliot made a lasting impression and she is mentioned as instrumental in later philosophical exchanges. Maggie Tulliver features several times in arguments in *The Second Sex*, where, too, de Beauvoir, attuned to Virginia *Woolf's provisos, finds *Middlemarch* splendid but wanting (see also CRITICISM, MODERN: FEMINIST APPROACHES). In this same volume, G. H. *Lewes, in a passage outlining emancipated conjugal relations, is cited as an illustration of the traditional situation reversed.

Simone de Beauvoir went on to become a woman of considerable intellectual substance, with global resonances, and during her lifelong partnership with Jean-Paul Sartre, an icon of the French left. AE

Fullbrook, Kate and Edward, *Simone de Beauvoir and Jean-Paul Sartre: The Remaking of a Twentieth Century Legend* (1993).

Moi, Toril, *Feminist Theory and Simone de Beauvoir* (1989).

Showalter, Elaine, 'The Greening of Sister George', *Nineteenth Century Fiction*, 35 (1980–1).

Beesly, Edward Spencer (1831–1915), professor of Latin and positivist, who joined the circle of scientific and literary men around George Eliot and G. H. *Lewes after writing an article for the *Fortnightly Review* in 1865. He helped translate Auguste *Comte's *Système de Politique Positive* (1866), which Eliot admired. In 1867 he risked his professorship and the headship of University College by supporting unionism, threats Eliot termed persecution (*L* iv. 374). While she did not always sympathize with him, he was one of a select group informed of her forthcoming marriage to John Walter *Cross on 6 May 1880. JJ

Beethoven, Ludwig van (1770–1827), arguably George Eliot's favourite composer, and the one most frequently mentioned in her letters and diaries. In *Weimar in 1854, after abandoning a performance of *Wagner's *Lohengrin*—an opera which she had ultimately found monotonous, and which G. H. *Lewes, who was with her, did not have the patience to sit through—she was restored by hearing an exquisite rendition of one of Beethoven's quartets (*Essays*, 103). In *Berlin the same year, after hearing Luise Köster acquit herself well as the titular heroine of Beethoven's only opera, *Fidelio*, she wrote: 'Wonderful is that prison scene with the recognition—Ich—Du!' (*Journals*, 251). Later, in the early 1870s, she has the singer Armgart in the poem of that name aspire to sing the part of Fidelio (see POETRY OF GEORGE ELIOT). She and Lewes went to many concerts that included 'glorious Beethoven music' (*Journals*, 127); she liked both to play and listen to his piano sonatas, which she knew well; and she collected arrangements of his symphonies. In September 1860 she told Cara Bray that she and Charles Lee Lewes—'quite a passionate musician . . . play Beethoven duets with increasing appetite every evening' (*L* iii. 346). A Beethoven night celebrated the arrival of her new Broadwood piano in October 1861; it was Beethoven she chose to study when she wanted to improve her skills as an accompanist, and Beethoven and Mozart she enjoyed playing with the amateur violinist Frederick *Lehmann.

George Eliot was much moved by Beethoven's songs, having discovered with delight his 'Per pietà non dirmi addio' ('Ah, perfido!'), which, after consulting Charles, she caused Mirah to sing in *Daniel Deronda* (*DD* 32). His 'Adelaide' she found exquisite and described it as 'that ne plus ultra of passionate song' (*L* iii. 365), and expressly wished Charles to learn it. It was this passionate, searching quality in Beethoven that most abidingly appealed to George Eliot. See also MUSIC.

BG

beginnings of novels. From *Scenes of Clerical Life* onwards the openings of George Eliot's fiction show her ability to raise narrative expectation through an immediate focus on places or people, sometimes both, and, from *Romola* to *Middlemarch,* a measured, elevated omniscience which is part of her mature aesthetic and artistic structure. 'The Sad Fortunes of the Reverend Amos Barton' opens with the leisurely description of Shepperton Church, with time past, as so often in Eliot, about to be re-created; 'Mr Gilfil's Love-Story' takes the reader back thirty years in the first sentence, and soon beyond that; 'Janet's Repentance' opens with the graphic present of people and place—Dempster and others in the Red Lion at Milby—the story unfolding with dramatic immediacy despite the fact that it is set in the past, a variant of the technique. *Adam Bede* starts with the unusual, intriguing 'With a single drop of ink for a mirror, the Egyptian sorcerer undertakes to reveal . . . far-reaching visions of the past' (a reference explained by Eliot in *L* iii. 301), while *The Mill on the Floss* evokes the past through a dream in which the narrator is 'standing on the bridge in front of Dorlcote Mill . . . many years ago'. Modes of unlocking the past continue with *Silas Marner*, cottage weaving at the turn of the century preceding the description of Silas in Raveloe and then a brief retrospect in the same chapter going back another fifteen years. With *Romola* comes the more elaborate, sophisticated beginning, the Proem (prelude) invoking 'the spirit of a Florentine citizen' in the spring of 1492 as a means of atmospherically entering historical time. *Felix Holt, the Radical* has the variant of a leisurely introduction (called that) beginning 'Five-and-thirty years ago' (i.e. 1831) on

the edge of the First Reform Bill, while in *Middlemarch* the Prelude (neatly balancing the Finale) introduces St Theresa of Avila and, without naming her, Dorothea, as 'foundress of nothing' by way of contrast. The past—1829–32—is not here explicitly mentioned. In *Daniel Deronda* there is the move to near contemporary time (in fact 1865) with its arresting question 'Was she beautiful or not beautiful? and what was the secret of form or expression which gave the dynamic quality to her glance?' in the specific gambling location of Leubronn (Homburg). The first chapter epigraph signals this 'make-believe of a beginning' reflecting her creative self-consciousness, while starting with the thoughts of an unidentified character anticipates modernism. In 1859 Eliot had written to Barbara *Bodichon, 'at present my mind works with the most freedom and the keenest sense of poetry in my remotest past' (*L* iii. 128–9). It is not always 'my' past: sometimes it is a past beyond her living experience. The openings reflect Eliot's deep affiliation with the past : they arouse narrative interest variously through historical and social authenticity, thus accentuating the *realism of her characters in a medium of identified time. See also ENDINGS OF NOVELS; HISTORY; NARRATION.

GRH

Belgium was the first country George Eliot reached on the journey to *Weimar with G. H. *Lewes in July 1854 that marked the crucial turning point in her life. On 10 July she had written to Sara *Hennell that she was preparing to go to 'Labassecour' (*L* ii. 165), Charlotte *Brontë's term for Belgium in *Villette* (1855), but the country was never to be as important in her life as it was for Brontë, or to feature in her fiction. Her diary entry for 20 July describes the dawn breaking over the estuary of the Scheldt and the first sight of land as the sun rose, lighting up 'the sleepy shores of Belgium with their fringe of long grass, their rows of poplars, their church spires and farm buildings' (*Journals*, 14). The moment was a profoundly important one, the dawn of a new life with Lewes (see *Journals*, 9). The couple spent just over a week in the country, stopping at Antwerp, Brussels, Namur, and Liège on the way to Cologne, which they reached on 29 July. The record of the visit in Eliot's diary is one of diligent and contented sightseeing. In Antwerp she was particularly impressed by the *Rubens paintings in the cathedral and the museum, but also noted details of dress—women's caps and bonnets—and commented on the cleanliness of the population, 'the most wholesome-looking I have ever seen' (*Journals*, 14). They toured Brussels on foot in the midsummer heat, admiring the picturesque Basse Ville, which they strolled through by starlight, but finding the smells in the streets sickening. On the train to Namur they had to share a carriage with 'some disgustingly coarse Belgians with baboonish children' and heard soldiers singing in a hideous howl which was typical of all the attempts at vocal music they had heard in the country (*Journals*, 16–17). Liège, however, they found so entrancingly beautiful, with 'the rich green everywhere breaking the lines of the picturesque houses', that they stayed an extra day (*Journals*, 17). In general Belgium seems to have made a positive impression on George Eliot, coloured by the happiness of her union with Lewes. Twelve years later in June 1866 the couple returned on a two-month tour of Belgium, Holland, and the Rhine provinces of *Germany, revisiting some of the scenes of the first journey, in particular Antwerp, where they admired the Rubens paintings again and attended an impressive mystery play of Christ's life and death performed by the people of Oberammergau (*L* iv. 270–1).   JMR

Bellini, Vincenzo (1801–35), Italian opera composer. One of the first operas George Eliot saw after she had shed the piety that precluded delight in *music was Bellini's *I puritani* (1835), which she pronounced 'a perfect treat' (*L* i. 233) the day after she had attended a performance of it at Her Majesty's Theatre, London. In May 1852 she saw (Giulia) Grisi in *Norma* (1831), and in April 1871 (Adelina) Patti in *La sonnambula* (1831). In *The Mill on the Floss*, Maggie is significantly 'touched, not thrilled' (*MF* 6. 7) by Philip's rendition of Elvino's lament from this opera, 'Ah! perché non posso odiarti?'.   BG

Belloc, Mme Louis. See PARKES, BESSIE (ELIZABETH) RAYNER.

Bennett, Arnold (1867–1931), English novelist who referred slightingly to George Eliot but followed her example by writing novels about life in the English Midlands. He secured his reputation with novels such as *Anna of the Five Towns* (1902) and *Clayhanger* (1910), set in the Five Towns of the Potteries region of Staffordshire.

Like many of his contemporaries, Bennett turned his back on English 19th-century novelists and claimed allegiance to the French naturalists, notably Maupassant and Zola, and to Russian writers, especially *Turgenev and Chekhov. George Eliot provided a benchmark: 'About a year ago, from idle curiosity, I picked up *The Old Curiosity Shop*, & of all the rotten vulgar un-literary writing . . . [*sic*]! Worse than George Eliot!' (6 February 1898, *Letters of Arnold Bennett*, ii. 104). Reading *Adam Bede*, he declared that George Eliot's style 'is downright aggressive, sometimes rude . . . feminine in its lack of restraint, its wordiness, and

the utter absence of feeling for form which characterizes it' (13 May 1896, *Journals of Arnold Bennett*, 5–6).

Yet Bennett's main claim to fame is as a provincial novelist, and his fiction demonstrates more affinities than he might allow with that of the author of *Middlemarch: A Study of Provincial Life*. Indeed, the emphasis in the Finale of *Middlemarch* on the significance of 'unhistoric acts' and the effects of 'the conditions of an imperfect social state', particularly for women, is similar to Bennett's commitment in his finest works, like *The Old Wives' Tale* (1908), to showing the extraordinary in the ordinary.   MAH

The Journals of Arnold Bennett 1896–1910, ed. Newman Flower (1932).
Letters of Arnold Bennett, ed. James Hepburn, 4 vols. (1966–86).

Berlin, capital city of Prussia, where George Eliot and G. H. *Lewes spent four months in the winter of 1854–5 on their first visit to *Germany at the beginning of their life together. She wrote up their experiences in 'Recollections of Berlin 1854–1855' (*Journals*, 243–58). They travelled to Berlin from *Weimar, arriving on 4 November 1854, and took lodgings at 62 Dorotheenstrasse. They found Berlin to be as everyone described it, 'an uninteresting modern city, with broad monotonous streets' (*Journals*, 243), but their time there was anything but dull. On their first morning they met Karl August *Varnhagen von Ense, an old acquaintance of Lewes's, by chance on the street and he invited them to two parties and showed them his autographs and portraits of *Goethe and his circle. They led an active social life, meeting scholars like Adolf Stahr and Otto Friedrich Gruppe, whose books Eliot was later to review (see 'FUTURE OF GERMAN PHILOSOPHY'); writers like the novelist Fanny Lewald, whom Stahr was soon to marry; and artists, like the sculptor Rauch, whom they considered to be the most distinguished man they met in Germany after *Liszt. They also enjoyed the cultural life of the city, attending the opera (see MUSIC), seeing plays by G. E. *Lessing among others, and frequenting the museums and art galleries (see VISUAL ARTS). At the same time they read intensively, particularly Goethe, *Shakespeare, and Heinrich *Heine, and continued to write: George Eliot translated Baruch *Spinoza's *Ethics* and Lewes worked on his life of Goethe. The four months in Berlin were full and happy, despite the cold; and the journal describes how they would battle their way home from dining at the Hôtel de l'Europe against the wind and snow to spend the long evenings reading contentedly in their well-heated room (*Journals*, 255). It was on one of those evenings that she read to Lewes an introductory chapter of descriptive prose which she had once written and which first suggested to him that she might be able to write a novel (see 'HOW I CAME TO WRITE FICTION').

They left Berlin on 11 March 1855, returning again in the summer of 1867 when they were 're-visiting the scenes of cherished memories' (*Journals*, 130), and for a longer stay in March and April 1870, when they were lionized as celebrities. They remarked on how much the city had grown and on the increase of luxury in all its forms (*L* v. 87). George Eliot's dramatic poem *'Armgart' (see POETRY), which appeared the following year, appears to be set in Berlin although the setting is of little significance. JMR

Bernhardt, Sarah (1844–1923), French actress whom George Eliot and G. H. *Lewes probably saw perform only once. This was in Paris in 1876 and the play was *L'Etrangère* by Dumas fils. Lewes said that it was 'a most interesting and engrossing piece and the acting very fine' (*L* vi. 264). His enthusiasm shows that his theories of natural acting were sufficiently flexible to appreciate Bernhardt's innovatory style. She played 'The Stranger', American mistress of a bankrupt aristocrat determined to find her lover a rich bride; although in the event her own husband saves the situation by murdering him. Dumas's point was that divorce laws would prevent such tragedies, though Eliot and Lewes were probably unmoved by the practical implications. There is no record of Eliot having seen Bernhardt's London début in 1879, no way of knowing if she would have concurred with Matthew *Arnold who made comparisons with *Rachel to Bernhardt's disadvantage, and with Henry *James who disliked the actress's use of publicity; or whether she would have acknowledged, like many other women, that here was a genuinely erotic personality. See also THEATRE.
JS

Bible, The. George Eliot first acquired her thorough knowledge of the Bible as a young girl, when she went to Mrs Wallington's boarding school in *Nuneaton in 1828. In her four years there she read it over and over again, and that reading was to leave its mark on her mature writing: Gordon S. *Haight can claim with justification that 'the vigorous prose of George Eliot is based on a thorough familiarity with the King James version' (1968: 9). In her evangelical phase her letters to her Methodist aunt and uncle, Mr and Mrs Samuel *Evans, parade her piety in biblical phrasing and quotation: 'I desire to be entirely submissive and without care for the morrow ... I earnestly desire a spirit of childlike humility that shall make me willing to be lightly esteemed among men' (*L* i. 73). After her abandonment of *Christianity in 1842

the Bible continues to colour the prose of her letters, as when she refers in 1849 to 'the rushing mighty wind' of Rousseau's inspiration (*L* i. 277); and the index to Haight's edition of the *letters shows how consistently she drew on her biblical knowledge throughout her life (*L* ix. 377–8). In 1861 she praised the 'simple pregnant, rhythmical English' of the Prayer Book and the Bible (*L* iii. 442), and that phrase is echoed in the fiction in 'the pregnancy of Marner's simple words' when he angers Godfrey Cass by describing his closeness to Eppie: 'we eat o' the same bit, and drink o' the same cup' (*SM* 19). In *Adam Bede* she also uses such English for the Methodist preacher Dinah Morris, whose speech is a tissue of biblical references and quotations. In *Felix Holt*, on the other hand, Rufus Lyon's failings as a preacher are illustrated by his insensitivity to the beauty of biblical prose when he truncates a text he is preaching on and omits all the rich poetry of one of the psalms (Sheets, 152).

George Eliot's loss of faith (see ATHEISM) and reading of Charles Christian *Hennell led her to see the Old and New Testaments as 'histories consisting of mingled truth and fiction' (*L* i. 128), but even her long immersion in the biblical criticism of D. F. *Strauss as his translator (see TRANSLATIONS BY GEORGE ELIOT) did not diminish her respect for the stories of the Bible as powerful and moving accounts of human experience. Translating Strauss's dissection of 'the beautiful story of the crucifixion' reportedly made her ill (*L* i. 206). In her fiction she alludes to and adapts biblical stories for her own ends. In *Adam Bede* the story of Jacob and Rachel (Genesis 29) is mentioned in relation to Adam's love for Hetty (*AB* 3) and is the subject of a needlework screen for which he makes a frame (*AB* 21). In the Genesis story Jacob works seven years for Rachel and then is given her elder sister Leah instead by the trickery of their father Laban; and, in order to secure Rachel as a second wife, he has to agree to serve Laban for another seven years. In the novel Adam works long to win Hetty but ends up wooing and marrying Dinah. However, Dinah is not Leah but rather his true Rachel; and if he has been deceived it is by his own feelings. The biblical story of the patient suitor is given a psychological inflection. In *Silas Marner*, a novel which can be seen as sharing the *realism and economy of Old Testament narratives (Fisch, 343–60), the stories of the afflictions of Job, whose 'days are swifter than a weaver's shuttle, and are spent without hope' (Job 7: 6), and of Lot's rescue from the city of destruction (Genesis 19) are adapted to yield a secular meaning, revealing the redemptive power of human love and community. In *Daniel Deronda* Mordecai's visionary discourse is informed by the language and cadences of the

Old Testament, while the narrator's interjections in that last novel and in *Middlemarch* can be seen sometimes to resemble the gnomic form of biblical proverbs (Bloomfield, 28). See also LANGUAGE; NAMES; STYLE.   JMR

Bloomfield, Morton W., 'The Tradition and Style of Biblical Wisdom Literature', in David H. Hirsch and Nehama Aschkenazy (edd.), *Biblical Patterns in Modern Literature* (1984).

Carroll (1992).

Fisch, Harold, 'Biblical Realism in *Silas Marner*', in Mark H. Gelber (ed.), *Identity and Ethos* (1986).

Sheets, Robin, '*Felix Holt*: Language, the Bible, and the Problematics of Meaning', *Nineteenth-Century Fiction*, 37 (1982–3).

Wiesenfarth (1977).

Bildungsroman, German term for the novel of personal growth and development whose prototype is generally considered to be *Goethe's Wilhelm Meister's Apprenticeship* (1795–6), a novel which George Eliot knew well and discussed in her 1855 essay 'The *Morality of Wilhelm Meister*'. Goethe's novel is more abstract, playfully ironic, and overtly self-conscious than works in the mode of *realism to which George Eliot was committed, but the term *Bildungsroman* is often used rather loosely for novels in that mode which trace a young man's progress through his formative years up to the point where he adopts a serious role in society. Of all Eliot's novels *Daniel Deronda* is the one that comes closest to this model: the Goethean phrase 'apprenticeship to life' is explicitly used in relation to Deronda (*DD* 16), and like Goethe's hero he has mentors like Mordecai who guide his steps towards the discovery of his vocation. Where the central character of a novel is a woman, as in *The Mill on the Floss*, this pattern of privileged experimentation and final accommodation to the demands of the social world becomes problematic; and it has led to critical debate in recent years about the female *Bildungsroman* (Fraiman, 136–50). See also GENRES.   JMR

Buckley, Jerome H., 'George Eliot's Double Life: *The Mill on the Floss* as a *Bildungsroman*', in Samuel Mintz et al. (edd.), *From Smollett to James* (1981).

Fraiman, Susan, '*The Mill on the Floss*, the Critics, and the *Bildungsroman*', *PMLA* 108 (1993).

Redfield, Marc, *Phantom Formations: Aesthetic Ideology and the Bildungsroman* (1996).

Biographical History of Philosophy, A, G. H. *Lewes's popular account of the history of Western philosophy, which was first published in 1845–6, and then underwent significant revisions over the course of his career, reflecting his changing interests and eventually dropping the 'Biographical' from its title (2nd edn, 1857; 3rd edn, *A History of Philosophy*, 1867; 4th edn, 1871).   NEH

biographies of George Eliot. The biography of George Eliot from which others take their bearings is *George Eliot's Life as related in her letters and journals, arranged and edited by her husband J. W. Cross* (1885). As the standard Victorian 'Life and Letters' prepared by a surviving spouse, it has particular authority. During her lifetime George Eliot consistently and courteously refused requests for biographical information, declaring herself 'thoroughly opposed in principle . . . to the system of *contemporary* biography', which offers trivial details to 'the mass of the public' (*L* vi. 67). Her position was clear: 'Biographies generally are a disease of English literature' (*L* vii. 230), and in the particular case of a biography of an author, can distract attention from that person's own writings as well as being invasive. In an author who distanced her private from her public self by adopting a *pseudonym, the distinction is piquant, especially as George Eliot professed herself antipathetic to reading criticism of her work.

She had reservations also about autobiography: 'It was impossible for her to write an autobiography, but she wished that somebody else could do it, it might be useful—or, that she could do it herself. She could do it better than any one else, because she could do it impartially, judging herself, and showing how wrong *she* was' (Emily *Davies to Jane Crow, 21 August [1869], *L* viii. 465). John Walter *Cross was perhaps responding (unconsciously?) to these views when he declared *George Eliot's Life* to be autobiography:

With the materials in my hands I have endeavoured to form an *autobiography* (if the term may be permitted) of George Eliot. The life has been allowed to write itself in extracts from her letters and journals. Free from the obtrusion of any mind but her own, this method serves, I think, better than any other open to me, to show the development of her intellect and character (Cross, vol. i, p. v).

So far, so good: but Cross goes on to state that in arranging the documentary material at his disposal into sequence, he has in fact intervened. 'Each letter has been pruned of everything that seemed to me irrelevant to my purpose—of everything that I thought my wife would have wished to be omitted' (Cross, vol. i, p. vii). The image of George Eliot that Cross felt bound to uphold was very much the public figure, for all his protestations about his 'desire to make known the woman, as well as the author' (Cross, vol. i, p. v). It is a life of the mind that George Eliot is allowed to lead in Cross's account: some bodily ailments (see HEALTH) are admitted (it would have been difficult to exclude them entirely from the record), but not such sensuous pleasures as a picnic near *Weimar with G. H. *Lewes in 1854 (*Journals*,

227–8). However cordial the relationship of the two men during Lewes's life, the challenge of writing about the common law union of the two Georges was a peculiarly demanding one which Cross handled by omitting reference to Lewes wherever possible. Similarly, the part played in Eliot's emotional life by other men such as John *Chapman and Herbert *Spencer is muted, as, for that matter, is the part played in her emotional life by her friendships with women. The *Life* concentrates on the production of her novels, and on her intellectual and cultural activities.

Subsequent research, especially that of Gordon S. *Haight, has demonstrated the extent of Cross's manipulation of his sources: he conflates passages from separate letters, and sections of diary with letters, as well as editing out unseemly locutions ('When she wrote "It is raining horribly here—raining blue devils," he pruned the "blue devils"', *L*, vol. i, p. xiii). As a result, Cross's biography has been largely discounted, but as Ruby Redinger points out, students of George Eliot have reason to be grateful for Cross's persistence in the task of assembling the primary material that others have restored and reinterpreted (*George Eliot: The Emergent Self* (1975), 5). Almost immediately after her death, Cross began to shoulder the burden represented by the memorial task of writing his wife's biography, gaining the important approval of Isaac *Evans (who wrote on 22 January 1881, 'I think you are the right person to write her biography and I hope no one else will attempt it', Nuneaton Central Library), and the support of others who lent him letters and shared memories. Throughout the process he was concerned not to give offence, taking advice from Lord Acton (see DALBERG-ACTON, JOHN), for example, on the treatment of her religious beliefs and of her relationship with Lewes, as well as from Herbert Spencer who was selfishly concerned about the way he was to appear in the biography.

Cross's caution had unfortunate consequences. Alice James reacted vehemently: 'What a lifeless, diseased, self-conscious being she must have been! not one burst of joy, not one ray of humour, not one living breath in one of her letters or journals' (*The Death and Letters of Alice James*, ed. Ruth Bernard Yeazell (1981), 25). More temperately, W. E. *Gladstone declared, 'It is not a Life at all. It is a Reticence in three volumes' (*L*, vol. i, p. xiv), while William Hale *White was sufficiently moved to write to the *Athenaeum* to express the 'hope that . . . in some future work, the salt and spice will be restored to the records of George Eliot's entirely unconventional life' (28 November 1885).

Cross was anticipated by Mathilde *Blind's *George Eliot* ('Eminent Women' Series, 1883). Blind, a poet and journalist, also sought out

friends and relations, and incorporated their recollections in her study, which is both searching and sensitive especially on the subjects of George Eliot's embracing *sympathy, and the mutual dependence in her all-important relationship with George Lewes. Other contemporaries published reminiscences, mostly in journals, or in their own memoirs (for instance, Charles *Bray's *Phases of Opinion and Experience during a Long Life: An Autobiography*, 1885), though Oscar *Browning in *Life of George Eliot* (1890) inserts his own anecdotes into copious quotation from Cross.

In many respects, the most intimate and enlightening biographical account of George Eliot by someone who knew her is Edith *Simcox's 'The Autobiography of a Shirt Maker' (consisting of a diary kept from 1876 to 1900, with two-thirds of the entries relating to 1876–81: published in part in 1961 in K. A. McKenzie's *Edith Simcox and George Eliot*, but not published complete until 1998, edited by Constance M. Fulmer and Margaret E. Barfield). Edith's jealous passion attuned her to the intimacy of 'the fatal Johnny' (*L* ix. 212) with George Eliot before anyone else—possibly including Eliot herself—was quite aware of what was happening. The devotion of Edith, who inscribed a copy of her *Natural Law* (1877) to George Eliot 'with idolatrous love' (*L* ix. 203 n), is the most fully documented of the attractions between George Eliot and younger women, including Elma *Stuart, Maria *Congreve, and Georgiana *Burne-Jones. It is as difficult to gauge the homoeroticism of these relationships as it was for Edith to accept that her idol had 'never in all her life cared very much for women' (*L* ix. 203).

Leslie *Stephen's *George Eliot* (1902) in the 'English Men of Letters' series attends rather to 'George Eliot' the novelist than to the life of Mary Ann Evans Lewes Cross, though he proceeds from the view that her fiction is 'implicit autobiography' (201), seeing a fairly simplistic transcription of childhood experience and family history in those novels he considers successful. Consciously psychoanalytic biographies develop more sophisticated versions of the relation of George Eliot's life and art. Anne Fremantle (1933) drew on Chapman's diaries in one of the first Freudian readings of George Eliot as rebel, but not until Ruby V. Redinger's psychobiography *George Eliot: The Emergent Self* (1975) is a more discriminating and illuminating psychoanalytic approach developed (see CRITICISM, MODERN: PSYCHOANALYTIC APPROACHES). The focus of Redinger's genuinely analytic study is on the evolution of George Eliot's writing self. She identifies Mary Ann's relationship with her brother and playfellow Isaac as the source of her motivation, and builds a complex reading of Eliot's need to discipline the disturbing capacities of imagination before she could rework her life experiences through the writing of fiction. In the nature of her argument, Redinger's account of Eliot's life after the publication of *Scenes of Clerical Life* in 1857 is summary.

There was a hiatus in the production of orthodox biographies in the first decades of the 20th century, with the decline of George Eliot's critical *reputation. However, Lewes's granddaughters, especially Elinor (Mrs Ouvry), were instrumental in the production by Arthur Paterson of *George Eliot's Family Life and Letters* (1928), which by bringing into the public domain much family correspondence makes some redress for Cross's downplaying of Lewes. Family co-operation was also extended to Anna T. Kitchel during preparation of *George Lewes and George Eliot: A Review of Records* (1933), which concentrates on Lewes, using his diaries and letters, while acknowledging that 'no small part of his accomplishment was his share in the perfecting of [George Eliot's] abilities' (289).

There is a different emphasis in Pierre Bourl'honne's *George Eliot: Essai de Biographie intellectuelle et morale 1819–1854* (1933), the first systematic examination of '*Influences anglaises et étrangères*' on her intellectual formation, providing extended analysis of her engagement with the work of Spencer, Auguste *Comte and Lewes, *Spinoza and *Feuerbach. Bourl'honne delineates successive mental phases, discerning a turn from idealism to realism in 1849–50 consequent on her going into the world after her father's death. Valerie A. Dodd is a recent successor to Bourl'honne: *George Eliot: An Intellectual Life* (1990) engages particularly with George Eliot in the context of philosophical debate in England in the 19th century, and with the concept of George Eliot as 'an intellectual turned novelist' (1).

The entry of Gordon S. Haight on the scene overshadowed earlier works. His first major contribution to George Eliot studies was *George Eliot and John Chapman, with Chapman's Diaries* (1940), a work already dominated by his reading of George Eliot in terms of Charles Bray's summation of a phrenological analysis of her character: 'She was not fitted to stand alone'. Haight's monumental edition of *The George Eliot Letters* (1954–78) is in itself a documentary biography, including not only letters by Eliot and Lewes, but letters to and about them, and extracts from their journals (see JOURNALS; LETTERS). This edition has underpinned all subsequent scholarly and critical work on George Eliot, and Haight's *George Eliot: A Biography* (1968) is essentially a continuous narrative version of its text and apparatus, abridged.

The strength of Rosemary Ashton's authoritative critical biography, *George Eliot: A Life* (1996), is that it positions Eliot in the context of the 19th-century British and European literary and intellectual scenes. Ashton sees the union with Lewes as decisive in enabling George Eliot's literary career, and is briskly matter-of-fact in reaction to lubricious speculation about Eliot's sexuality either in the affair with Chapman, or the marriage to Cross. Ashton's George Eliot is accorded both admiration and respect, nowhere more tellingly than in the earlier sections on the provincial making good in London.

Eliot herself observed that 'The best history of a writer is contained in his writings—these are his chief actions' (*L* vii. 230). Alison Booth, in *Greatness Engendered: George Eliot and Virginia Woolf* (1992), describes how 'I fell out of love with my vision of Marian Evans Lewes/"George Eliot"... Yet the textual George Eliot that I recreate as I read the writings published during her lifetime—a creature distinct from that rather depressing Victorian woman—still convinces me of greatness and wisdom' (p. x). Some of the most subtle and searching biography of George Eliot is of just that 'textual self', in Rosemarie Bodenheimer's *The Real Life of Mary Ann Evans: George Eliot Her Letters and Fiction* (1994). Bodenheimer's inspiration was 'to suggest that a "best history" of George Eliot may be told by reading her letters in conjunction with her novels, stories and poems'. From this reading, she elucidates 'two related patterns of consciousness... The first is a moral and emotional pattern in which acts of assertion, satire or rebellion are followed by remorse or retreat. The second is George Eliot's peculiarly intense consciousness of audience, which caught her between scorn and defiance of public opinion and a strong dependence on it' (pp. xiv–xv). Thus Bodenheimer draws attention to such matters as symmetries between her transgressions in taking up with Lewes and in marrying Cross, so that 'George Eliot' emerges in a devious complexity denied her by more literal readings. See also OBITUARIES.

MAH

Nadel, Ira Bruce, 'George Eliot and her Biographers', in Gordon S. Haight and Rosemary T. Van Arsdel (edd.), *George Eliot: A Centenary Tribute* (1982).

Blackwood, John (1818–79). See BLACKWOOD, WILLIAM AND SONS.

Blackwood, William (Major) (1810–61). See BLACKWOOD, WILLIAM AND SONS.

Blackwood, William (Willie) (1836–1912). See BLACKWOOD, WILLIAM AND SONS.

Blackwood, William and Sons, George Eliot's primary publisher and an important publisher in the 19th century. Founded in 1804 by William Blackwood, the Edinburgh firm became

John Blackwood (1818–79), George Eliot's principal publisher and patient, encouraging friend, from a portrait of 1857.

increasingly prominent after the publication of *Blackwood's Edinburgh Magazine* in 1817. 'Maga', as the monthly periodical was known, was initially devised as a challenge to the dominance of the Whig *Edinburgh Review*, one of the great quarterlies of the 19th century. After a slow start, 'Maga' caused a stir, largely due to the liveliness of the two editors, John Gibson Lockhart and John Wilson. Among the notable early series in the magazine is the conversational 'Noctes Ambrosianae', in which characters based on real people meet to discuss topical events and gossip.

William Maginn, who later went on to found *Fraser's Magazine*, helped to secure many of the most important writers of the day for the magazine and the firm's book list. The popular poet Felicia Hemans, for example, was published largely by Blackwood's, and *Coleridge wrote a number of occasional papers for 'Maga'.

After William Blackwood's death in 1834, his sons Alexander and Robert took charge of editorial and business arrangements. Another son, John, was apprenticed in the book trade in London for several years, until the death of his brother. In 1845, John became editor of 'Maga' and head of the firm, and it is with John and his brother Major William Blackwood that George Eliot had her closest dealings.

George Eliot's relationship with the Blackwood's firm began when G. H. *Lewes sent the manuscript of 'The Sad Fortunes of the Reverend Amos Barton' to John Blackwood for publication in *Blackwood's Edinburgh Magazine*. Lewes had been a contributor to 'Maga' and had known Blackwood in London. In submitting 'Amos Barton' as the first in a series about clerical life to the publisher, Lewes appeared simply to be acting on an anonymous friend's behalf, as he suggests in a letter to Blackwood, maintaining that the proposed series 'will consist of tales and sketches illustrative of the actual life of our country clergy about a quarter of a century ago; but solely in its *human* and *not at all* in its *theological* aspect' (*L* ii. 269).

Blackwood generally approved of 'Amos Barton' as 'unquestionably very pleasant reading', although he suggested that 'the author falls into the error of trying too much to explain the characters of his actors by descriptions instead of allowing them to evolve in the action of the story' (*L* ii. 272). Such criticisms discouraged George Eliot, as Lewes reported to Blackwood, but the publisher explained that he was merely exercising caution in publishing an unknown author, which reassurance 'has greatly restored the shaken confidence of my friend, who is unusually sensitive, and unlike most writers is more anxious about *excellence* than about appearing in print' (*L* ii. 276). It was agreed that 'Amos Barton' would be published in 'Maga'

in January and February 1857. Blackwood continued to be a sharp critic in reading the subsequent *Scenes of Clerical Life*. He objected to the third in the series, 'Janet's Repentance', which is one reason she ended the series (*L* ii. 409–10). But Blackwood recognized the power of her fiction and had a way of easing George Eliot's pain through his high praise of her work generally. On the whole, her relations with John Blackwood were strong, and although she also dealt with Major William, 'an unaffected agreeable man' (*L* ii. 405), he was always cooler towards her than his brother John.

It was not until February 1858 that George Eliot's real identity was revealed to her publisher, although Blackwood had no doubt already guessed who Lewes's friend really was. George Eliot recorded the lifting of her veil of anonymity in her journal:

On Sunday the 28th Mr. John Blackwood called on us, having come to London for a few days only. He talked a good deal about the 'Clerical Scenes' and George Eliot, and at last asked, 'Well, am I to see George Eliot this time?' G. said, 'Do you wish to see him?' 'As he likes—I wish it to be quite spontaneous.' I left the room, and G. following me a moment, I told him he might reveal me. Blackwood was kind, came back when he found he was too late for the train, and said he would come to Richmond again. He came on the following Friday, and chatted very pleasantly—told us that Thackeray spoke highly of the 'Scenes' and said *they were not written by a woman*. Mrs. Blackwood is *sure* they are not written by a woman. Mrs. Oliphant, the novelist, is confident on the same side. (*L* ii. 435)

Blackwood was acutely aware of the need to maintain George Eliot's anonymity, given the unconventional relationship between Lewes and Marian Evans, and the fact that her identity was made known to him attests to the high regard in which he was held by them both. As Blackwood writes to his wife,

this is to be kept a profound secret, and on all accounts it is desirable, as you will readily imagine. She is a most intelligent pleasant woman, with a face like a man, but a good expression. I am not to tell Langford the secret even. . . . Lewes says he would do ten times the work for me that he would do for any other man, and he does not think any other editor in the world would have been able to induce George Eliot to go on. (*L* ii. 436)

Blackwood decided not to serialize *Adam Bede*, George Eliot's next work of fiction and her first novel, in 'Maga', partly due to the sensitive nature of the material which treats subjects such as the fallen woman and matricide. He asked to see an overall outline of the story, which George Eliot refused absolutely, arguing that she would not have the novel 'judged apart from my *treatment*' (*L* ii. 503–4). Despite some reservations, particularly by Major William, who wrote to John that 'I don't like the story and don't think it fulfills the promise which the finely written opening holds out' (Haight 1968: 297), the firm published the novel in volume form and it was an extraordinary success (see RECEPTION). So popular and highly acclaimed was *Adam Bede* that Blackwood was unsure that he could afford George Eliot's work in the future, given the tremendous sums which were being offered to other novelists. After some wrangling and hurt feelings, George Eliot accepted the sum of £2,000 for *The Mill on the Floss*. There was some uncertainty whether serialization was necessary with *The Mill*, given the extreme success of *Adam Bede*, and the novel was published directly in volume form partly to capitalize on the popularity of the author. *The Mill* was well received, although less well than *Adam Bede*.

Blackwood continued to publish George Eliot until the lure of the market tempted her away to George *Smith, publisher of the *Cornhill Magazine*, who offered her £10,000 for *Romola*, an unprecedented sum for a novel in the 19th century. Blackwood's was never a publisher that paid very high sums to its magazine contributors or its book list authors. George Smith, by contrast, had a great deal of money to lavish on authors, and his generosity in payments was well known. Like a true friend, Blackwood did not begrudge George Eliot's move to another publisher:

I am of course sorry that your new Novel is not to come out under the old colours but I am glad to hear that you have made so satisfactory an arrangement. Hearing of the wild sums that were being offered to writers of much inferior mark to you, I thought it highly probable that offers would be made to you, and I can readily imagine that you are to receive such a price as I could not make remunerative by any machinery that I could resort to. (*L* iv. 35–6)

The split between George Eliot and the publisher who had so nurtured and assisted her was an amicable and temporary one.

As it happened, *Romola* was not the success George Smith had hoped, and it did not distinguish itself in sales. George Eliot returned to Blackwood's with *Felix Holt, the Radical* in 1866, and she remained with them for *Middlemarch* and *Daniel Deronda* in the 1870s. In a letter to George Eliot in 1867, Blackwood suggests that in 'our next adventure, I think, we must try some innovation in form of publication' (*L* iv. 353). Partly, the need for innovation was a way of getting round the financial dominance of the circulating libraries

who insisted on the three-volume novels which were most lucrative to their business. That innovation came in *Middlemarch* which appeared in six bimonthly parts and two monthly parts. This gave the author more time to write and longer serial instalments, which suited her writing better than the deadlines and page requirements of magazine serial fiction (see SERIALIZATION). Blackwood continued to be a supportive editor and publisher, and his support and praise of her writing, from *Scenes of Clerical Life* to the mature final novels, was constant and helped her to maintain her confidence. As Lewes recounted to Blackwood, 'she who needs encouragement so much . . . relies on you, and takes comfort from you to an extent you can hardly imagine' (*L* v. 201). John Blackwood died in October 1879, at which time George Eliot wrote to Lewes's son Charles that John 'has been bound up with what I most cared for in my life for more than twenty years and his good qualities have made many things easy to me that without him would often have been difficult' (*L* vii. 217). It was an honest and sincere description of her relationship with the figure who, after Lewes, was most important in the publication of her fiction. After John's death, with Major William having died many years earlier, the firm was led by John's nephew William (Willie), who had long been involved with the firm and the publishing of George Eliot's works.

See also PUBLISHERS, NEGOTIATIONS WITH.

MWT

Porter, Mrs Gerald, *Annals of a Publishing House: John Blackwood* (1898).

Blackwood's Edinburgh Magazine, monthly magazine which published George Eliot's first fiction, *Scenes of Clerical Life*, in 1857. Founded in 1817 by William Blackwood, 'Maga', as *Blackwood's* was commonly known, was a consistently Tory-leaning miscellany particularly known for introducing foreign literature to its audience. G. H. *Lewes had been a contributor since 1843, and in 1856 his *'Sea-side Studies' were appearing. It was at this time that he submitted anonymously George Eliot's story 'The Sad Fortunes of the Reverend Amos Barton' to the editor John *Blackwood, who agreed to publish in January–February 1857 as the first story in the *Scenes* series. The other two stories, 'Mr Gilfil's Love-Story' and 'Janet's Repentance', appeared later in the same year. The publication of *Scenes of Clerical Life* in 'Maga' established the Blackwood's firm (see BLACKWOOD, WILLIAM AND SONS) as the most important publisher of Eliot's fiction during her lifetime. Although Blackwood was a supportive reader, he was also a perceptive editor and George Eliot remained extremely sensitive to his criticisms of her work. Her identity was kept from her publisher/editor until 1859, when his firm published *Adam Bede*, which was intended to be serialized in 'Maga' but was brought out in volume form. *Blackwood's* also published her short story 'The Lifted Veil' (July 1859), which she described as 'not a *jeu d'esprit*, but a *jeu de mélancolie*' (*L* iii. 41), and *'Address to Working Men, by Felix Holt' (January 1868), an appeal to the working classes to use restraint in exercising their power after the introduction of the ballot. Her verse story adapted from Boccaccio's *Decameron*, 'How Lisa Loved the King' (see POETRY), appeared in May 1869 and it was her last contribution to 'Maga'. See also PUBLISHERS.   MWT

Blind, Mathilde (1841–96), George Eliot's first biographer, who was born in Mannheim but came to England in 1852. She greatly admired Eliot and, by a strange irony, translated Strauss's last work *The Old Faith and the New* (1873). Her *George Eliot* (1883) appeared in the 'Eminent Women' series. It is uneven, tailing off towards the end but noteworthy for quoting Eliot's whimsical self-mocking letter about the 'German Dryasdust' (not printed until *L* viii. 12–15). There is sound evaluation of the essays and the early fiction, though the later works are felt to be flawed: Blind summarizes 'Jermola the Potter' by the Polish novelist J. I. Kraszewski, establishing similarities with Silas Marner while allowing that Eliot may not have seen it.   GRH

Bodichon, Barbara Leigh Smith (1827–91), the woman most of her contemporaries regarded as George Eliot's closest woman friend. Barbara was a professional artist, an educationist, and the acknowledged leader of the feminist activists known as the Langham Place Group. Through her friendship with Barbara, Marian (as George Eliot was always known to her) gained an intimate knowledge of the women's movement (see WOMAN QUESTION). She was first introduced to Barbara in June 1852 by Bessie *Parkes, whose father, Joseph *Parkes, had commissioned the translation of D. F. *Strauss's *Das Leben Jesu*. Marian's Coventry friend, Sara *Hennell, had been a governess to the Bonham Carter family (1837–42) and had maintained a friendship with the eldest girl, Hilary Bonham Carter, who was a first cousin of Barbara's. However, Barbara's father Benjamin Smith (1783–1860), MP for Norwich, from a powerful Unitarian family, one of the first families of Dissent, had never married Barbara's mother, who was a miller's daughter from Derbyshire. As a consequence, as Mrs *Gaskell wrote, 'some of the legitimate don't acknowledge her' (*The Letters of Mrs Gaskell*, ed. J. A. V. Chapple and Arthur Pollard (1966), 606–7). After meeting Hilary Bonham Carter at one of John *Chapman's soirées at 142

Strand, Marian wrote to Sara, 'I am far more agreeably impressed with Barbara Smith—one of the *tabooed* family' (*L* ii. 45). Marian belonged to the newly emerging class of intellectuals and neither she nor Barbara fitted comfortably into genteel English family life.

Barbara's first political act was to publish a pamphlet, *A Brief Summary of the Laws in England concerning Women* (1854). She then formed a committee to collect signatures for a petition to support a Married Women's Property Bill in order to safeguard the property and earnings of married women. Barbara sent Marian a copy of the petition for her to sign and pass on. Marian signed and passed it on to Sara Hennell, who in turn passed it on to Eleanor Cash, of the Coventry ribbon factory family. Marian wrote to Sara, 'I am glad you have taken up the cause, for I do think, with proper provisos and safeguards, the proposed law would help to raise the position and character of women. It is one round of a long ladder stretching far beyond our lives' (*L* ii. 227). Marian recognized that this was the first step in Barbara's long campaign to achieve legal autonomy and full status as citizens for women.

Both exceptional women, Marian and Barbara looked for partnerships with men who regarded them as equals. When Marian 'eloped' with Lewes, many women repudiated her. Barbara's own background inclined her towards sympathy with anyone who was 'tabooed' from genteel society, and she wrote to Marian on her return from *Germany assuring her of her loyal friendship. Marian sent this letter on to Sara Hennell, saying that it was 'a manifestation of her strong noble nature. Burn it when you have read it' (*L* ii. 211). Another thing that drew the two women together were their respective involvements with John Chapman. In June 1854, the Chapmans rented a house at 43 Blandford Square, conveniently near Benjamin Smith's house at 5 Blandford Square. John Chapman, already married, laid siege to Barbara, suggesting that they should have an extramarital relationship. There seems more than a suspicion that Chapman was interested in Barbara's money, because the *Westminster Review* creditors were pushing him hard at this time. Barbara's decision to resist Chapman's seductions caused her much pain and Marian wrote to comfort her: 'I shall say nothing of sorrows and renunciations, but I understand what you must have to do and bear' (*L* ii. 255). Bessie Parkes wrote that 'it was an open secret' that Barbara 'suggested the conception of *Romola* to George Eliot' (Bessie Rayner Parkes Belloc, *A Passing World* (1897), 21). In that case, the representation of the philandering Tito may be seen (among other things) as a fictional revenge on the man who had grieved both women.

Bodichon, Barbara Leigh Smith

In 1857 Barbara wrote a pamphlet called *Women and Work* in which she stressed the value of work for every human being regardless of gender or class. She quoted from a letter from Marian within the pamphlet: 'Ill-done work seems to me the plague of human society. People are grasping after some grandiose task, something "worthy" of their powers, when the only proof of capacity they give is to do small things badly.' In much of her fiction Marian criticized a society which, although accepting work as its highest good for men, systematically prevented middle-class women from claiming this good. In 1858 Barbara became the major shareholder in the *English Woman's Journal* founded to serve working women. Although sympathetic with its aim, Marian thought that the standard of the literature reviewing was poor. She expressed this view plainly to Barbara, which influenced Barbara's withdrawal from the journal in 1863.

Barbara told Marian her favourite tale from the *Arabian Nights*, the story of Perie-zadeh, who succeeded in a quest where her brothers had failed. Barbara wrote, 'I never forgot some of the stories and Marian Lewes felt them through me' (William Smith Papers, Cambridge University Library). This myth served as a talisman to validate their ambitions.

Following her marriage to a French physician resident in Algiers in 1857 Barbara spent the winter months abroad. On 26 April 1859, after reading a review in an English newspaper of *Adam Bede*, containing an extract, Barbara wrote from Algiers to Marian to tell 'my dear George Eliot' of her delight 'That YOU *that you* whom they spit at should do it' (*L* iii. 56). This act of recognition formed a bond between them which was never broken. Marian wrote to Barbara, 'you are the first friend who has given any symptom of knowing me—the first heart that has recognized me in a book which has come from my heart of hearts'(*L* iii. 63). Barbara wrote to her Aunt Patty that she had immediately recognized *Adam Bede* as Marian's work 'for in it I saw her peculiar and surpassing tenderness and wisdom. I know no one so learned and so delicate and tender' (Haight 1968: 381). One unfortunate result of the pseudonym was that authorship was attributed to a certain Joseph *Liggins of Attleborough. Marian was cheered by Barbara sending her a cartoon drawn by her sister, Nannie Leigh Smith, called 'Popular Idea of George Eliott [*sic*] in the act of composing "Adam Bede"' (Beinecke Library, Yale University).

The other picture sent by Nannie was a drawing of Perie-zadeh, which Marian hung over her desk. When Marian was at work on *The Mill on the Floss* (1860) she wrote to Barbara, 'Perizade has a mysterious resemblance for me, to the heroine of the book I am writing. It is not a formal resemblance, but an inward affinity felt through the attitude of Perizade and the expression of her face' (*L* iii. 172). Maggie Tulliver had some resemblance to Barbara's mother, a miller's daughter, who had run off with a gentleman, failed to get married to him, and borne the social disgrace. Barbara wrote to Marian, 'I think so much of your Mill that I do not like to put it in one sentence. I find it more interesting than AB even ... probably because it touches our private experience' (Beinecke Library, Yale University). The two women also shared the sadness of incurring the disapproval of their respective brothers, though in both cases, reconciliations eventually took place.

When the Second Reform Bill was in the process of increasing male suffrage, Marian in *Felix Holt, the Radical* pondered whether working-class men should have the vote before middle-class women. Barbara, at the same time, was organizing a campaign to persuade Parliament to enfranchise women property holders. The petition of 'Barbara L. S. Bodichon and others' containing the signatures of 1,499 women was presented to Parliament by John Stuart *Mill on 7 June 1866. Marian described her role as a novelist as 'the rousing of the nobler emotions, which make mankind desire the social right, not the prescribing of special measures' (*L* vii. 44). Barbara was herself a political activist but she believed that her friend's novels helped to orchestrate a sympathetic climate for feminist reforms.

Barbara worked with Emily *Davies to found the first university college for women in England, Girton College, Cambridge. Barbara sought Marian's support, both financially and emotionally. Marian assured Barbara that 'the better Education of women is one of the objects about which I have *no doubt*, and I shall rejoice if this idea of a college can be carried out' (*L* iv. 399). She offered £50 from 'the author of Romola' and sent some books from her library to help establish a college library. It was a hard struggle to establish the College and after one rather depressing Executive Committee meeting Barbara wrote to Marian in January 1873, 'I am very grateful to you ... for that book and I know it will help us, in fact when some of our Council were very down I felt hopeful partly because of the last few pages of Middlemarch' (Beinecke Library, Yale University).

Barbara introduced her protégée, a young Jewish woman called Hertha Marks, to Marian in 1873, because she was persuading her friends to give to a fund to pay for Hertha to go to Girton College. Marian was impressed both by the young woman's intellect and because she looked after a semi-invalid sister. At the time of their meeting Marian was planning her novel *Daniel Deronda* (1876).

The structure of *Daniel Deronda* relies on two entwined themes, the progress of women in society and the progress of the Jewish people towards a homeland. Marian retained a strong interest in Hertha's progress and achievements.

In 1877 Barbara suffered a stroke and retired to her house in Sussex. Marian wrote to her:

I miss so much the hope I always used to have of seeing you in London and talking over everything just as we used to do—in the way that will never exactly come with anyone else. How unspeakably the lengthening of memories in common endears old friends! The new are comparatively like foreigners, with whom one's talk is hemmed in by mutual ignorance. The one cannot express, the other cannot divine (*L* vii. 71).

When Lewes died Barbara invited Marian to live with her and Dr Bodichon, an offer which was declined. She wrote to Barbara, 'Bless you for all your goodness to me, but I am a bruised creature, and shrink even from the tenderest touch (*L* vi. 93). Marian wanted to found a George Henry Lewes Studentship trust fund 'to supply an income to a young man who is qualified and eager to carry on physiological research' (*L* vii. 128). Barbara visited Marian in June 1879 and persuaded her to change the wording so that 'persons of either sex' would be eligible for the scholarship. In May 1880 Barbara was astonished to read in *The Times* that Marian had married John Walter *Cross. Nevertheless, she wrote immediately: 'Tell Johnny Cross I should have done exactly what he has done if you would have let me and I had been a man. You see I know all love is so different that I do not see it unnatural to love in new ways' (*L* vii. 273).

In November 1880 Marian wrote to tell Barbara that she had been unwell but that 'Mr Cross had nursed me as if he had been a wife nursing a husband'; she also enquired after Hertha's welfare (*L* vii. 332). This was her last letter to Barbara before her death. Earlier, Barbara had told her niece that when she was with 'thoroughly great people' like Marian Lewes 'I feel that the intellect is not the quality which strikes me most, it is the power of being truthful & having a soul which is pure & active' (Girton College). PH

Burton, Hester, *Barbara Bodichon* (1949).

Herstein, Sheila, *A Mid-Victorian Feminist, Barbara Leigh Smith Bodichon* (1985).

Hirsch, Pam, *Barbara Leigh Smith Bodichon: Feminist, Artist and Rebel* (1998).

Brabant, Elizabeth Rebecca (Rufa) (1811–98), widow of Charles Christian *Hennell, married Wathen Mark Wilks Call (1817–90) on 23 July 1857. Although little correspondence between the two women has survived, Rufa was one of George Eliot's earliest, most enduring friends. They met at Rosehill in 1842, and Rufa joined in various excursions Eliot made with the *Brays in 1843. Eliot appears to have been prepared to dislike her but told Sara *Hennell her first unfavourable impression was 'unjust' and that Rufa's 'tender seriousness' and other qualities made her 'almost worthy of Mr. Hennell' (Haight 1968: 47–8). Eliot was bridesmaid when Rufa married Charles Hennell in November 1843, the marriage having originally been opposed by Dr *Brabant because of Hennell's weak lungs. After the wedding, Eliot went to Devizes with Dr Brabant 'to fill the place of his daughter' (Haight 1968: 49). Rufa attributed the subsequent misunderstandings to 'simplicity' and 'ignorance' on Eliot's part (*L*, vol. i, p. lvii).

Rufa had undertaken the translation of Strauss's *Das Leben Jesu* but in 1844 offered it to Eliot. During 1851 Rufa called regularly at 142 The Strand as John *Chapman's diary shows, and Eliot reported back to the Brays on Rufa's state of mind, Charles Hennell having died in September 1850. It was Rufa who corrected the proofs of Eliot's essay *'Woman in France: Madame de Sablé', her request to Chapman that *Miss* Hennell do the work having been mistaken as *Mrs.* Nevertheless, Eliot told Sara she was indebted to Rufa for the trouble she had taken (*L* ii. 188).

On the return of Eliot and G. H. *Lewes from *Germany in 1855, Rufa was the first woman to call, a visit Eliot did not neglect to report to Bray and Chapman, telling both 'I respect her for it' (*L* ii. 198, 199). On Rufa's remarriage in 1857, Eliot and Lewes were among the first invited to dine, Eliot telling Sara that Call, who was already known to Lewes, 'is a man one really cares to talk to', but more importantly, how much she felt Rufa's 'graceful as well as kind behaviour to me' (*L* ii. 389). To Chapman she recommended Call in strong terms as a contributor to the *Westminster Review* and Call became a long-term writer for the journal (*L* viii. 177). The two couples exchanged regular visits until the Calls moved to Lymington in 1858. Two years on Eliot still regards this move as 'quite a loss to us' (*L* iii. 359). In 1870 Eliot expresses sympathetic anxiety for Rufa who was troubled about the future of her son Frank Hennell, and when the Calls moved to Italy in 1871, Eliot was able to engage Rufa's servants, her own having suddenly resigned after ten years. On their return to England in 1877 regular intercourse was resumed and these visits, as Eliot's 1880 diary shows, continued until the end of Eliot's life. JJ

Haight (1940).

The Letters of George Henry Lewes, ed. William Baker (1995).

Brabant, Dr Robert Herbert (1781?–1866), physician practising in Devizes, whose interests included German *Higher Criticism, and whose daughter Rufa *Brabant was one of George Eliot's earliest friends. He had been 'engaged for years upon a great work', which remained unfinished, showing the absence of the supernatural in Christianity (*L*, vol. i, p. lvi). Gordon S. *Haight consistently assigns Brabant as the original of Casaubon in *Middlemarch* (Haight 1940: 25; Haight 1968: 449; *L* v. 39). Eliot met Brabant in 1843 and after his daughter's wedding the same year was invited on a visit to his home to be a daughter to him. She describes herself as 'in a little heaven here, Dr Brabant being its archangel' (*L* i. 165), assuring Cara *Bray he 'really is a finer character than you think' (*L* i. 167). Eliot was suddenly asked to leave, apparently because she and Brabant spent too much time together, but suggestions that the blind Mrs Brabant's sister, in advising Eliot on her homeward route, was hinting for her early departure, seem fanciful (Haight 1968: 50), Eliot's letter only revealing a consultation on what she feared would be a 'formidable' journey (*L* i. 166). Further suggestions of sexual impropriety in Haight's *Life* are mostly based on an account of the incident in John *Chapman's 1851 diary, told to him by Rufa Brabant eight years after the event. Chapman's paraphrased version of Rufa's conversation, full of sexual innuendo that appears to be his own contribution, makes much of Brabant's 'unmanliness' (Haight 1940: 186) in attributing all the blame to Eliot. Eliot herself writes only of her 'grief at parting with my precious friends here' (*L* i. 167), interpreted by Haight as 'effusive language' to cover 'the unpleasant episode' (*L* i. 168). Eliot herself three years later asserts that she 'offered incense' to Brabant because she 'wanted some kind of worship pour passer le temps' and claims she 'laughed at him in my sleeve' (*L* i. 225). Occasional jibes at Brabant exchanged between Eliot and Sara *Hennell do not actually begin until after Sara's trip to Germany with him and his sister-in-law in 1844.

In 1851 Brabant was nevertheless a regular visitor at 142 The Strand escorting Eliot to the theatre and the Crystal Palace, and offering Chapman £800 towards the *Westminster Review*, Charles *Bray reassuring George Combe, 'he is a regular old screw, with more money than he knows what to do with' (*L* viii. 30). Eliot too is less than kind, writing to Cara that the 'house is only just exorcized of Dr Brabant' (*L* i. 363) and calling him 'fatuous' (*L* ii. 10). Whatever the facts of the case, it is certain that in her particular circle, Brabant became a figure of fun. However, travelling with Lewes to Weimar in 1854, they by chance met Brabant en route and he 'kindly exerted himself' (*L* ii. 171) to arrange a meeting for her with D. F. *Strauss whose *Das Leben Jesu* Eliot had translated

and published in 1846. Eliot and Brabant appear to have had little subsequent contact.　　　　JJ
Haight (1940).

Braddon, Mary Elizabeth (1837–1915), author who rose to prominence as a writer of sensational fiction especially with the publication of *Lady Audley's Secret* (1862). She does not appear to have met George Eliot, but there was some symmetry in their personal lives: both women lived with men who were not free to marry, though Braddon and her publisher John Maxwell were able to wed in 1874 after the death of his first wife in an asylum. Braddon, who was very widely read in contemporary fiction both English and French, knew George Eliot's work well: however, she held Charlotte *Brontë to be 'the only *genius* the weaker sex can point to in literature', whereas George Eliot was 'somewhat passionless', with 'a fine mind cultured to the highest point' (Wolff, 234).

George Eliot regarded herself as being in a different league from Braddon: G. H. *Lewes wrote querulously to John *Blackwood in 1877, 'While Mrs. Henry Wood, Miss Braddon, Wilkie Collins etc. sell their novels at 6/- surely G. E. may expect a public?' (*L* vi. 345). Yet particular analogies between Braddon's writing and George Eliot's have been proposed, such as the influence of Braddon's *The Doctor's Wife* (1865), itself based on Gustave *Flaubert's *Madame Bovary*, in the evolution of both major plots of *Middlemarch* (Wolff, 167). And recent feminist criticism shows such texts as *Lady Audley's Secret* to offer in their subversive way as serious an examination of woman's lot as *Romola* or *Middlemarch*.　　　　MAH

Wolff, Robert Lee, *Sensational Victorian: The Life and Fiction of Mary Elizabeth Braddon* (1979)

Bray, Caroline (Cara) (1814–1905), friend and correspondent of George Eliot. In April 1836 Charles *Bray, a ribbon manufacturer in Coventry, married Caroline Hennell, a refined young woman of 21 whose reticence contrasted with his candour: 'She was exceedingly reserved, I too open,' he wrote, calling himself '*a leaky fool* as George Eliot calls Mr. Brooke in *Middlemarch*' (Bray, 47). The daughter of devout Unitarian parents, she was deeply disturbed when he tried to overturn her faith on their wedding tour. She applied for reassurance to her elder brother Charles who re-examined the biblical evidence in his *Inquiry into the Origins of Christianity* (1838) and found his own beliefs challenged. Although Cara's Commonplace Book suggests a lasting interest in spiritual questions, the Brays soon discontinued regular churchgoing.

Their religious position was therefore similar to that of Mary Ann Evans, the future George Eliot, when she visited Rosehill in November 1841:

already questioning, she bought Charles Christian *Hennell's *Inquiry*, and her refusal to attend church followed in January 1842. Cara sympathized deeply with Mary Ann in her 'Holy War' (see LIFE OF GEORGE ELIOT): 'not one of her family seems to care what becomes of her' (*L* i. 130). It was a new, comforting family that Mary Ann found at Rosehill, and a 'mother' in Caroline. Together the two young women studied *Schiller, G. E. *Lessing, and *Goethe, enjoyed musical evenings, helped in Bray's infant school, and shared other charitable concerns. In September 1842 Cara completed a watercolour painting of Mary Ann which she presented to the National Portrait Gallery in 1899 (see PORTRAITS). Mary Ann's letters to her new friend are warmly affectionate, more natural than her correspondence with Maria *Lewis, less intellectual than her letters to Cara's sister, Sara *Hennell. Cara's comments to Sara are sympathetic but light in tone: 'so vexed about poor Mary Ann . . . but on Tuesday morning she came with a face about two inches shorter, and said all was right again' (*L* i. 156). Cara pitied her in her headaches, her struggles with translating D. F. *Strauss, and her anxiety over her father's illness: 'the poor thing looks as thin as a poker' (*L* i. 259).

The Brays became holiday companions for her: in summer 1843, she accompanied them to the West Country and Wales, in 1844 to the Lake District, in 1845 to Scotland; in 1849 they escorted her to *Geneva. The long letters she wrote to them from Switzerland reveal her deep if sometimes possessive affection for old friends and also an ease of relationship that allowed her creative energies to flower: her lively, satirical interest in new acquaintances suggests a novelist in the making. When she was working in London, she found Rosehill a place of refuge and convalescence. Presents ranging from books to beetroot and from music to fig puddings sustained her in exile.

Although Cara was her 'Heart's Ease', the Brays' marriage had its problems. According to John *Chapman's Diary, Rufa *Brabant told him that Cara had been for years in love with Edward Noel, a relationship that her husband accepted with the proviso that in return she tried to advance his happiness in any way he wished. Since Cara was childless, she apparently accepted his liaison with another woman who is said to have borne him six children. In 1845 she wrote in her diary, 'Brought home Elinor Mary'. This was Bray's baby daughter known as Nelly whom Cara tended as lovingly as if she were her own. When Nelly died at 19 in 1865, George Eliot as her 'affectionate Auntie Pollian' wrote to Cara: 'There is no such thing as consolation when we have made the lot of another our own as you did Nelly's' (*L* iv. 183). When Thornie

Lewes (see LEWES FAMILY) died in 1869, she valued Cara's letter 'which came in the first hours of our trouble' (*L* v. 68). Foster-parents are sympathetic figures in her life and fiction.

The irregularities in the Brays' marriage make it harder to understand Cara's coolness over Marian's elopement with G. H. *Lewes in 1854. Fearing the sisters' disapproval, Marian had trusted Charles to break the news of her liaison with a man they disliked, and her inability to confide in them was felt as a betrayal of friendship. After one letter of protest (now lost) Cara kept silent for a year although Marian assured Sara that she, Cara, and Chrissey were 'the three women . . . tied to my heart by a cord which can never be broken' (*L* ii. 182). It was Cara who received in September 1855 Marian's famous defence of her union with Lewes. Correspondence was resumed but it was more reserved, and Marian declined several invitations to revisit Coventry. She would never return to Rosehill which the Brays, in straitened circumstances, left in 1857 for Ivy Cottage, moving in 1861 to humbler accommodation in Barr's Hill Terrace. Yet the old affection was not forgotten. A recently discovered letter, undated but marked 1856 on the envelope, suggests that an earlier letter from Cara had prompted an affectionate response in which Marian maintained that her happiness with Lewes drew her closer in understanding to her friend. She valued these links.

When the Brays visited London in 1859, Marian and Cara met after nearly six years' separation, and she revealed her authorship of *Adam Bede*. She appreciated Cara's comment that the novel would help people. In return, she was pleased to learn of the success of Cara's *Physiology for Common Schools* (1860), a helpful guide to health. She advised with the publication of *The British Empire* (1863), a geography textbook for children, and recommended *Our Duty to Animals* (1871), an attractively illustrated book that foreshadows Cara's founding of the Coventry Society for the Prevention of Cruelty to Animals. In 1873 Marian outlined a theme for a children's story on animals, sent Cara £50, and helped with the printing of *Paul Bradley*.

Cara gave her blessing to Marian's union with John Walter Cross and was left an annuity of £100 in George Eliot's will, a sum which must have eased the remaining years of her long life.   RMH

Bodenheimer (1994).
Bray, Charles, *Phases of Opinion and Experience during a Long Life: An Autobiography* (1884).
Redinger (1975).

Bray, Charles (1811–84), Coventry ribbon-manufacturer, writer, philanthropist, and friend of George Eliot throughout her adult life. In

Charles Bray (1811–84), the freethinking Coventry ribbon-manufacturer and philanthropist, as he was when George Eliot first met him in the 1840s, beginning a friendship that was to last a lifetime.

November 1841 Mary Ann Evans, as she then was known, was welcomed into the circle of Charles Bray's family and friends at Rosehill, *Coventry, where the atmosphere of approval, the willingness to debate, and the wider intellectual interests liberated and excited her. The Brays were blamed for a loss of faith that had already started before she met them, but delight in new friends reinforced her rebellion. Charles Bray was a handsome, self-confident man with ideas and enthusiasms who pleased her so much that they were soon walking affectionately, arm-in-arm, discussing 'all subjects in heaven or earth'. Despite their 'quarrels' and her times of depression, he found her 'a delightful companion' who 'knew everything' but was, he claimed, 'not fitted to stand alone' (Bray, *Phases of Opinion*, 73, 75). He noted her cultured speech and affectionate disposition, her lack of self-esteem, the intellectual nature of her approach to character, and the impartiality of her judgements. For her part, she valued his cheerful zest, his idealism, his social and humanitarian concerns. Her own organization at Griff of a clothing club to help the families of out-of-work ribbon weavers must have ensured her sympathy with his attempt to introduce Robert Owen's ideals of equality and profit-sharing into his silk-ribbon factory. Although the attempt failed, as Dorothea's plans in *Middlemarch* for a self-supporting community also came to nothing, Bray continued to believe in co-operative movements that could transform society. In Coventry he helped to establish a weavers' garden club that failed to work, a co-operative store that went bankrupt, a working men's club with a reading-room that failed to tempt men away from the public house, and an infant school open to Dissenters that succeeded. His involvement in local issues as well as wider philosophical theories, his concern for the welfare of the poor, for better medical care and sanitation, and his readiness to pay for his failures make his attraction for Mary Ann understandable.

In 1846 Bray purchased the *Coventry *Herald and Observer*, a radical newspaper which soon gave her the opportunity to publish sketches and reviews. Bray himself had already written *The Education of the Body* (1837) and *The Education of the Feelings* (1838). In *The Philosophy of Necessity* (1841) he maintained that the laws of mind were as fixed as the laws of matter. Despite its crudity, such a claim had its attraction for Mary Ann since it offered her after the loss of her faith 'something definite to believe . . . as fixed and determinate as the laws of the physical world' (Bray, *Phases of Opinion*, 54). She soon came to realize that mental phenomena were far more complex than physical, the causes of human behaviour more complicated and abstract explanations more suspect, but at the

time his assertion that man could not act against his own nature was likely to appeal: it encouraged tolerance and eliminated extravagant expectations since it would be unrealistic to expect 'from the cat-nature the generous unselfishness of the dog' (Bray, *Phases of Opinion*, 55). His stress on the irrevocable seemed to echo her own belief in the duty of 'unembittered resignation to the inevitable' (Bray, *Phases of Opinion*, 74). Moreover, Bray dealt with themes that interested her and that she would afterwards handle with greater subtlety and rigour: the need for tolerance, the question of accountability, the corrective nature of pain, the inexorable law of consequences. Later Bray felt confident that he had 'laid down the base of that philosophy which she afterwards retained' (*Phases of Opinion*, 73). Both were inspired by the ethical idealism of Baruch *Spinoza whom she read at 17 and whom she was soon to translate. His delight in *mesmerism she treated with caution, but his passion for *phrenology persuaded her into having a cast made of her head. Analysing bumps sounds bizarre today, but the deterministic nature of phrenology appealed to a young woman who needed to explain and at times exonerate human behaviour.

It is likely that Mary Ann knew of Charles Bray's liaison with one 'Hannah Steane' who is said to have borne him six illegitimate children (Adams 1980: 52–5). If so, she had the chance to study unconventional relationships at Rosehill and be prepared for the unorthodox households of John *Chapman and G. H. *Lewes. More significantly, friendship with the Brays introduced her to many enlightened people who sat under the acacia tree overlooking the spires of Coventry: visitors included Robert Owen, Dr John Conolly, Richard Cobden, J. A. *Froude, Herbert *Spencer, Ralph Waldo *Emerson, Rufa *Brabant, and Chapman himself. Her future was unfolding.

The Brays proved congenial holiday companions. In 1854 she confided her liaison with Lewes only to Charles Bray and the Chapmans. He continued to be a helpful friend, visiting her and advising her on business matters. His experiences first as a candidate encountering hostility in a local election and secondly as a long-standing member of the Provident Dispensary's board in Coventry (Ashton 1996: 321) probably influenced the composition of political and medical scenes in *Middlemarch*.

Fluctuations in the sale of ribbons led to Bray's resignation (1856), the relinquishing of Rosehill (1857), and subsequent moves to humbler accommodation. He faced reduced circumstances with characteristic buoyancy, even building a house at Sydenham—an unwise speculation. When the Labourers' and Citizens' Co-operative Society failed in 1860, he retired from public life with the surprisingly sharp comment that no one had ever thanked him. A reviewer of his *On Force—its Mental Correlates* (1866) remarked, 'Fitly art thou called Bray, my worthy friend!' Although she outgrew him, George Eliot never lost 'the sympathy that comes from memory' (*L* iii. 391). When he was fined £150 for libel, she immediately volunteered to lend him £100, and offers of financial help with Cara's books also show her concern for old friends with whom she corresponded until her death. Perhaps Charles Bray remained for her as he had been in the past, 'the dearest, oldest, stupidest, tiresomest, delightfullest, and never-to-be-forgottenest of friends to me' (*L* ii. 82).   RMH

Bray, Charles, *Phases of Opinion and Experience during a Long Life: An Autobiography* (1884).

Adams (1980).

Ashton (1996).

Dodd (1990).

Bremer, Fredrika (1801–65), Swedish novelist and women's rights' activist. George Eliot first met her at John *Chapman's house in the Strand in October 1851 where Bremer stayed on her homeward journey after two years in America. Eliot's initial impression is harsh, 'she is old—extremely ugly, and deformed—. . . . Her eyes are sore—her teeth horrid' (*L* i. 365), but later she repented her repugnance (*L* i. 367), praising Bremer's skill as an artist and recounting their conversations to her friends. From 1843 Bremer's novels and travel writings had been translated into English by Mary Howitt, thus assuring Bremer's popularity both in England and America, an enthusiasm Eliot never shared, remarking as early as 1847 that she had more pleasure from Samuel *Richardson than 'all the Swedish novels together' (*L* i. 240). In 1856 Eliot reviewed Bremer's novel *Hertha* in the *Westminster Review*, remarking on her sudden popularity in the 1840s and equally sudden decline. Eliot suggests *Hertha* explains this decline, lacking 'attention to detail' and 'humorous realism', qualities needed in a novel written 'with the object of advocating the liberation of woman', rather than an inappropriate sentimentality Eliot dismisses as the 'pink haze of visions and romance' (*Essays*, 332).   JJ

Brontë, Charlotte (1816–55), **Emily** (1818–48), and **Anne** (1820–49). The Brontë sisters were almost the contemporaries of George Eliot, but by the time Eliot came to write fiction all three had died. Charlotte's *The Professor* was published posthumously in 1857 at the same time as Mrs Gaskell's *Life of Charlotte Brontë*, a work which Eliot read while engaged on *Scenes of Clerical Life*. Charlotte's other novels *Jane Eyre*, *Shirley*, and *Villette* were published in 1847, 1849, and 1853 respectively;

Anne's *Agnes Grey* and *The Tenant of Wildfell Hall* in 1847 and 1848; and Emily's *Wuthering Heights* in 1847. For Eliot as for most Victorians Charlotte was the main Brontë, although she and G. H. *Lewes read *Wuthering Heights* aloud in the evenings at *Munich in 1858.

In July 1851 Eliot wrote to John *Chapman about Miss Bronty (*sic*) being an unsuitable person to write an article on modern novelists on the grounds that she would have to omit Currer Bell (Charlotte Brontë's pseudonym) 'who is perhaps the best of them all' (*L* i. 355). So Eliot clearly admired Brontë, although sometimes this admiration is a little ambivalent. Five years later in *'Silly Novels by Lady Novelists' she herself wrote such an article, in which Currer Bell is praised, and her inferior imitators castigated, but there is the faint suggestion that Brontë is partly responsible for this flood of foolish female authors.

As early as 1848, before he had met Eliot, Lewes had been in correspondence with Charlotte Brontë. He had reviewed *Jane Eyre* in generally favourable terms while Charlotte had responded with surprising enthusiasm to Lewes's early novels. The two authors compared notes on Jane *Austen and George *Sand. In 1850 Brontë met Lewes and said that his appearance reminded her of Emily. She had reacted angrily to a review of *Shirley* in 1850. Lewes also reviewed *Wuthering Heights* and *Agnes Grey* in December 1850 and was to review *Villette* twice in 1853. So after Lewes met Eliot in 1851 he would have been able to tell her a good deal about Miss Bronty, whose name she still misspells in a letter to Chapman of July 1852.

In June 1848 Eliot had read *Jane Eyre*. Long before she had done what Jane Eyre does not do, namely run away with a married man, she raises an anxiety which modern readers feel: 'All self-sacrifice is good—but one would like it to be in a somewhat nobler cause than that of a diabolical law which chains a man soul and body to a putrefying carcass' (*L* i. 268). She also blames the characters for speaking like the heroes and heroines of police reports. In February 1853 she praises *Villette* as a still more wonderful book than *Jane Eyre*. She was disappointed that Lewes in his review of *Ruth* and *Villette* devoted more attention to Mrs Gaskell's novel.

At the time of the publication of *Adam Bede* in 1859 both Lewes and Eliot seem to have used the fortunes of *Jane Eyre* as a kind of barometer in charting the success of Eliot's first major novel. They comforted themselves with the thought that sales of *Jane Eyre* took a little time to get off the ground. It was felt, particularly by Lewes, that it was a disadvantage to betray the sex of the author. This seems to contradict the views of Eliot's 1856 article in which she says that the supposedly masculine Currer Bell had been more harshly treated than her foolish female successors. It does, however, seem in line with Lewes's review of *Shirley* which annoyed Charlotte Brontë because it treated her as a woman rather than as an author. Eliot was angry to find that the same Newby who had so mishandled the publication of Emily's and Anne's novels was also trying to promote an 'Adam Bede Junior'.

While engaged on *Scenes of Clerical Life* in 1857 Eliot and Lewes read Mrs Gaskell's *Life of Charlotte Brontë*. She was deeply moved by the book. Her one criticism is interesting, although in fact unjustified. She says that the fall from grace of Branwell is too sudden when it is obvious that 'the germs of vice had sprouted and shot up long before' (*L* ii. 319). In fact Mrs Gaskell is likely to have exaggerated and anticipated Branwell's wickedness before 1845 as a smokescreen to explain Charlotte's unhappiness because of her own love affair with Monsieur Héger, her married teacher in Belgium. The interest in Branwell may have borne fruit, however, not only in the immediate portrait of drunkenness in 'Janet's Repentance', but also in the succession of male characters slowly succumbing to the germs of vice in Eliot's major novels. Arthur Donnithorne, Godfrey Cass, and Tito Melema all, like Branwell Brontë, promised much and meant well, but ended badly. Similarly Charlotte in Mrs Gaskell's account appeared at any rate in Eliot's eyes as giving 'a lesson in duty and self reliance' (*L* ii. 320). Modern biographers of the Brontës may not agree, but we do see here the forerunner of Romola and Dorothea Brooke.

Eliot's preference for *Villette* over *Jane Eyre* and her perception of Mrs Gaskell's biography as a moving story, as good as any of the novels, show her astuteness as a literary critic. In contrast Lewes's reviews and remarks seem rather clumsy and tasteless. The lives of the Brontës were very different from that of Eliot, although there were superficial resemblances. All four novelists were brought up in the stern doctrines of evangelical Christianity, but the Brontës though rejecting low churchmanship did not desert Christianity entirely. Maria Brontë and Christiana Evans played little part in their daughters' lives, while Patrick Brontë and Robert Evans were strong characters, Tory in politics, suspicious of Catholics and Dissenters. Again Eliot would seem to have been the more rebellious. All the novelists achieved astonishing successes in spite of the obstacles placed in the way of female advancement. But the Brontës, except for the foray by Charlotte and Emily to the Continent and a few journeys by Charlotte away from Haworth when she was a successful novelist, remained firmly attached to their home. In contrast Eliot travelled very widely indeed (see TRAVELS), home being the one place that she could not really visit. This was because, unlike Charlotte Brontë and Monsieur Héger and unlike Jane Eyre and Mr Rochester, she and Lewes had offended against social propriety by setting up house together when Lewes was already married.

This fact rendered her an outcast in Victorian society, although curiously Eliot seems to have managed Victorian society a good deal better than the Brontës, whose reputation was unblemished but who were crippled by shyness. It is perhaps unfair to compare Charlotte Brontë's dealings with George *Smith and Eliot's relations with the same publisher. By the time Smith met Eliot he was rich, married, and successful, and there were no dangers of any amorous entanglement. Comparisons of Eliot novels with Brontë novels are equally unfair. The critic F. R. *Leavis put Eliot firmly at the centre of the Great Tradition, and was only grudgingly prepared to allow some kind of praise to one Brontë, namely Emily. Popular taste laps up the Brontës, and finds Eliot hard going, craving for the melodrama which the critics despise. Oddly, Eliot in spite of her sojourns in Europe seems solidly English, while the Brontës, always popular on the Continent, are not very deft for instance in their handling of the English class system. It is part of the greatness of Eliot to admire the Brontës. One wonders, since Charlotte Brontë in writing to Lewes dismissed Jane *Austen as narrowly boring, what any Brontë would have said of Eliot, whose reading was so much deeper and wider than theirs. See also BELGIUM; WOMAN QUESTION.   TJW

Barker, Juliet, *The Brontës* (1994).

Swinburne, Algernon Charles, *A Note on Charlotte Brontë* (1887).

'Brother and Sister' Sonnets, a sonnet sequence published in 1874. It probably draws upon George Eliot's own memories of her relationship with her brother Isaac (see EVANS, ISAAC), and it certainly can be read as a parallel to *The Mill on the Floss* (see POETRY OF GEORGE ELIOT).   MR

'Brother Jacob' (*see page 40*)

brothers and sisters of George Eliot. From her father's first marriage she had a half-brother Robert (1802–64) and a half-sister Frances Lucy, known as Fanny (1805–82). Her elder sister Christiana (Chrissey) was born in 1816 and her brother Isaac in 1814 (see EVANS, CHRISTIANA and EVANS, ISAAC). Younger twin brothers William and Thomas died ten days after birth in 1821.   JMR

Browning, Elizabeth Barrett (1806–61) and **Robert** (1812–89), poets whose works George Eliot knew and reviewed. She first mentioned Elizabeth Barrett Browning in a letter to Sara Hennell in November 1856: 'You must read *Aurora* (*cont. on page 41*)

'Brother Jacob'

A HUMOROUS, fabular novella by George Eliot in three chapters, narrated in the third person.

Composition and Publication
Written at Holly Lodge, Wandsworth (see HOMES), in August 1860—that is, five months after the completion of *The Mill on the Floss*—'Brother Jacob' was not published until July 1864, when it appeared anonymously in George *Smith's *Cornhill Magazine*. George Eliot and G. H. *Lewes had returned from *Italy on 1 July 1860, where, in *Florence, the idea for the novel that was to become *Romola*—serialized in *Cornhill* July 1862–August 1863—was conceived; but, in London, George Eliot found herself instead writing *Silas Marner: The Weaver of Raveloe*. Since this novel had, as George Eliot recorded, 'thrust itself between' her and *Romola* (*Journals*, 87), it is noteworthy that 'Brother Jacob' (originally 'Mr David Faux, Confectioner') had already interposed itself between her decision to write the Italian novel and the composition of *Silas Marner*. The story was offered to Sampson Low for £250 as 'The Idiot Brother', but was not accepted. Early in 1862, Smith offered the author 250 guineas for it; but, after *Romola* had failed to bolster the sale of his magazine (the subscription to the 1863 three-volume edition was also disappointing), George Eliot made a highly appreciated gift of it to him.

Along with her only other short story, 'The Lifted Veil', John *Blackwood (her principal publisher) chose in 1866 to exclude 'Brother Jacob' from the recognized series of her works, finding both stories 'as clever as can be', but with 'a painful want of light about them' (*L* iv. 322). Despite Blackwood's preference for printing *Silas Marner*—'such a perfect thing' (*L* vi. 340)—by itself, George Eliot's wish to 'fatten the volume' (*L* vi. 336) by adding 'The Lifted Veil' and 'Brother Jacob' prevailed when the three works were harnessed together in the Cabinet Edition (1878). The manuscript is at Yale.

Illustrations
The *Cornhill* depicted two scenes from the story: one as a full-page plate; the other embellishing the initial letter. Both were designed by Charles Samuel Keene (1823–91) and engraved by Joseph Swain (1820–1909).

Reception
Reviewing 'The Lifted Veil' and 'Brother Jacob' for the *Nation* when they were printed in the Cabinet Edition, Henry James considered the latter 'extremely clever' and 'much the better' of the two, though 'a little injured, perhaps, by an air of effort. . . . The minor touches are very brilliant, and the story is, generally, excellent reading' (Haight 1968: 131). This judgement notwithstanding, several decades were to elapse before critics offered anything of comparable substance—or anything at all—concerning 'Brother Jacob'.

Plot
Dissatisfied with his trade and social status, the spiritually and physically unprepossessing confectioner David Faux decides to emigrate to the West Indies, where he hopes to be wooed by a princess. To fund himself he steals his mother's savings of 20 guineas, which he hides in the ground. The hoard is discovered by his sweet-toothed, youngest brother, the idiot Jacob, whom David beguiles into secrecy with sugary yellow lozenges—ostensibly transmogrified golden guineas. With his booty, David escapes to an unimpressed Jamaica. Six years later he returns, settles in Grimworth as Mr Edward Freely,

and—prospering as a confectioner after all—pretends to be well connected in order to win the hand of the socially superior Penny Palfrey. Forced to reveal his position when he claims a small legacy, he is unmasked when Jacob, lured to his brother's shop by the prospect of unlimited delicacies, publicly and ecstatically greets him.

Critical approaches

Although interest in 'Brother Jacob' has increased during the last two decades, few critics have found it, like James, 'generally, excellent reading'. Dismissed by W. J. Harvey in *The Art of George Eliot* (1961) as 'that tedious tale' (212), for example, or considered (more respectfully) to be 'rather cheerless and austere as a comedy' (Knoepflmacher 1968: 224), even James's notice of it has been judged 'gracefully superficial'—this commentator's own view being that 'Brother Jacob' is an embarrassing, 'bitter, thoroughly nasty piece of work' (Dessner, 266). While there is a growing tendency both to relate the story to the circumstances of George Eliot's life—in particular the Joseph *Liggins affair (see Bodenheimer 1994)—when she wrote it, and to examine it in the light of its discerned political discourse (see CRITICISM, MODERN: POSTCOLONIAL APPROACHES), the evidence suggests that this in fact adroit and exuberant tale remains relatively unappreciated.

BG

Bodenheimer (1994).

Dessner, Lawrence Jay, 'The Autobiographical Matrix of *Silas Marner*', *Studies in the Novel*, 11 (Fall 1979).

Gray, Beryl, Afterword to 'Brother Jacob' (1989).

James, Henry, '"The Lifted Veil" and "Brother Jacob"' in Haight (1965).

Knoepflmacher (1968).

Sola Rodstein, Susan de, 'Sweetness and Dark: George Eliot's "Brother Jacob"', *Modern Language Quarterly*, 52 (1991).

Leigh. I wish I had seen Mrs. Browning, as you have, for I love to have a distinct human being in my mind, as the medium of great and beautiful things' (*L* ii. 278). A month later, she again praised the poem, remarking that 'such books are among the great blessings of life' (*L* ii. 282). Reading it for the third time, she claimed it gave her 'a deeper sense of communion with a large as well as beautiful mind' (*L* ii. 342), and in the *Westminster Review* of January 1857 she applauded Elizabeth Barrett Browning as 'the first woman who has produced a work which exhibits all the peculiar powers without the negation of her sex', noting that she 'has shown herself all the greater poet because she is intensely a poetess'. None the less, Eliot was disappointed that Elizabeth Barrett Browning had imitated 'the catastrophe in "Jane Eyre," by smiting her hero with blindness', a device which, she claimed, diminished 'tragic effect' (*Westminster Review*, 67: 306). While preparing to write *Romola*, George Eliot reread Elizabeth Barrett Browning's political poem *Casa Guidi Windows* (1851), finding in it 'the true relation of the religious mind to the Past' (*L* iv. 15).

Elizabeth Barrett Browning's comments on Eliot's novels, scattered sparsely throughout her correspondence of 1859 to 1861, are as informative as they are rare. Writing to her sister Arabella in July 1860, she expressed her preference for *The Mill on the Floss* over *Adam Bede*. Describing the former as 'vivid throughout to the senses of my mind', she referred to the opening of *Adam Bede* as heavy (MS: Gordon Moulton-Barrett).

Despite familiarity with each other's work, George Eliot and Elizabeth Barrett Browning never met, although their paths almost crossed. In a letter to Arabella of June 1860, the poet expressed the hope of meeting Eliot and G. H. *Lewes while they were in *Italy: 'The author has been here with her Lewes—& will return I believe—in which case I must see her. There is great good in that woman, I am certain—in spite of everything. Great good, besides the great genius' (MS: Berg Collection, New York Public Library). As the letter shows, Elizabeth Barrett Browning was characteristically uncensorious of Eliot's union with Lewes. In June 1860, she wrote: 'I admire her books so much, that certainly I shall not refuse to receive her' (*Letters of Elizabeth Barrett Browning*, ii. 400), noting a month later: 'Yes,—the writer lives with a man who is not her husband—but the more unhappy she! for certainly she is not an "immoral woman" in the way of loving evil & ensuing it' (MS: Gordon Moulton-Barrett).

Years later, Robert Browning expressed similar views. When conversation at a dinner party turned to the question of Eliot's relationship with Lewes, and Browning was asked if 'he thought great genius entitled a man or woman to overstep the bounds of conventionality', he laughed, replying that the question was '"a poser for a poet. You would have lost the world some interesting people," said he, "if that excuse could not be urged"' (*The Sunday Inter-Ocean*, 13 April 1890, 17).

After Elizabeth Barrett Browning's death in 1861, Browning returned to London, where his social activities included visits to The *Priory, the first falling in December 1862. Following a visit in October 1865, Eliot and Lewes accompanied Browning home, where he showed them his wife's memorabilia: 'her chair, tables, books, etc. . . . her Hebrew Bible with notes in her handwriting, and several copies of the Greek dramatists with her annotations' (*L* iv. 205). Browning's association with the couple is documented in his correspondence with Isa Blagden, which includes numerous references to Eliot's work. In August 1863, he reported that she was 'much annoyed by criticisms on her "Romola"' (*Dearest Isa*, 173), a work which, in a letter to Eliot herself, he described as 'the noblest and most heroic prose-poem that I have ever read' (*L* iv. 96). However, after finishing the final volume, Browning wrote in November 1863: 'My impression of the great style and high tone remain, of course,—but as a work of art, I want much' (*Dearest Isa*, 178).

Although she admired Browning's poetry, George Eliot, like other critics, complained that his writing was obscure. Reviewing *Men and Women* (1855) for the *Westminster Review* of January 1856, she noted that Browning's incomprehensibility was 'like the obscurity of the stars, dependent simply on the feebleness of men's vision' (65: 291). 'The greatest deficiency . . . in his poetry', she felt, 'is its want of music' (295). Writing to Frederic *Harrison in November 1867 she confessed that 'my conscience made me a little unhappy after I had been speaking of Browning on Sunday. . . . I do not find him unintelligible, but only peculiar and original' (*L* iv. 395–6). Browning may not have been deaf to her criticism. Although there is no evidence to support the assertion, Nicoll and Wise (i. 377) have made the widely accepted claim that, at George Eliot's suggestion, and to improve the clarity of the poem, Browning added three stanzas to 'Gold Hair' (*Dramatis Personae*, 1864).

Browning summed up his friendship with George Eliot in a letter to Mary Gladstone in December 1878: 'deeply impressed by her genius I could not fail to be and some particular acts of personal kindness, beside a general extreme cordiality, endeared her much to me' (*Some Hawarden Letters*, 44). At Eliot's invitation, he attended Lewes's funeral, and he was to be one of the mourners at her burial in Highgate Cemetery. See also POETRY.   SL

Dearest Isa: The Letters of Robert Browning to Isabella Blagden, ed. Edward C. McAleer (1951).

The Letters of Elizabeth Barrett Browning, ed. Frederic G. Kenyon, 2 vols. (1897).

W. Robertson Nicoll and Thomas J. Wise (edd.), *Literary Anecdotes of the Nineteenth Century*, 2 vols. (1895–6).

Some Hawarden Letters, ed. Lisle March-Phillips and Bertram Christian (1917).

Browning, Oscar (1837–1923), schoolmaster, fellow of King's College Cambridge, and historian. When he was introduced to George Eliot and G. H. *Lewes in 1866, he was a housemaster at Eton, his old school, where they paid him a visit in June 1867. George Eliot commented to him that 'The getting older brings some new satisfactions, and among these I find the growth of a maternal feeling towards both men and women who are much younger than myself' (*L* v. 5), and it was a considerable satisfaction to Browning, evidently drawn to celebrities, to see himself as one of that group.

He was dismissed from Eton in 1875 on suspicion of making homosexual advances to pupils, though ostensibly because of disagreement with the headmaster over Browning's challenges to the classical curriculum and to the cult of sport. He then returned to *Cambridge where he took an active role in the life of the University at large and King's College in particular, urging that more modern history be taught, and he wrote a number of historical works during his retirement in Italy. His *Life of George Eliot* (1890) draws heavily on that of John Walter *Cross but also includes some personal anecdotes: 'I asked her once what struck her as the most salient difference between the society of the two universities, and she replied that at Cambridge they all seemed to speak well of each other, whereas at *Oxford they all criticized each other' (99). Browning's commentary on George Eliot's works is distinguished by his admiration for *Daniel Deronda*, in which he anticipates later readers by seeing it as 'one step further upwards' (140). However, his claim to be the original of Lydgate is understandably questioned by Haight, who suggests that Ladislaw may be a closer fit (1968: 448).

Henry James wrote to his sister Alice on 30 January 1881: 'Browning has a theory that she "went back" on Lewes after his death: i.e. made discoveries among his papers which caused her to wish to sink him in oblivion. But this, I think, is

Browningish and fabulous' (*Henry James Letters*, ed. Leon Edel, ii (1975), 337). The rumour has not always been dismissed so unequivocally.   MAH

Browning, Oscar, *Life of George Eliot* (1890).

Bulwer-Lytton Edward George (1803–73), English novelist, playwright, essayist, poet, and politician. More properly 'Edward Bulwer' until 1843, 'Edward Bulwer-Lytton' upon inheriting the family estate in that year, and 'Lord Lytton' from 1866, when he became 1st Baron Lytton of Knebworth. In early letters George Eliot refers to the eagerness with which readers wait for 'Bulwer's last' and remembers 'a very amiable atheist depicted by Bulwer in Devereux' (*L* i. 37, 45). She sent Bulwer's autograph to Sara *Hennell in June 1855, and in April 1857 John *Blackwood informed G. H. *Lewes that Bulwer was suspected of writing *Scenes of Clerical Life*. Bulwer himself praised the series. In April 1858 Eliot wrote to Sara Hennell, having seen a photograph of him, 'Bulwer looks more of a sham even than his novels' (*L* ii. 439). *Adam Bede* was delayed because of Bulwer's *What Will He do With It?*, but when it did appear Bulwer wrote a generous tribute to John Blackwood which Eliot copied into her journal. Blackwood brought about their meeting. Bulwer did not like the dialect in *Adam Bede* and objected to Adam's marriage to Dinah. Eliot observed, 'I would have my teeth drawn rather than give up either' (*L* iii. 264). Although he placed *The Mill on the Floss* above *Adam Bede* he found that it contained some unconscious imitation of Charles *Dickens, that Maggie was made to appear too passive in the Red Deeps, that the tragedy was inadequately prepared and that Maggie's relationship with Stephen Guest was flawed (*L* iii. 314–15). Eliot's response allowed the weakness of her third volume, but unequivocally defended Maggie's position towards Stephen. She asserted that she knew her own heroine's feelings and added that the 'ethics of art' must accommodate 'the truthful presentation of a character essentially noble but liable to great error—error that is anguish to its own nobleness' (*L* iii. 317–18). Bulwer admired *Felix Holt* though he found the Mrs Transome plot painful. Eliot maintained her interest in him, noting the success of *The Coming Race* in 1871: when he died in 1873 she recorded her reaction to his final novel, *Kenelm Chillingly*, referring to 'the purity and elevation of its tone—its catholic views of life, free from all snobbishness or bitterness of partisanship' and feeling that it was completely 'harmonious with the closing epoch of a long career' (*L* v. 402–3).   GRH

Bunyan, John (1628–88), major Nonconformist religious writer and preacher who was imprisoned for his beliefs. *The Pilgrim's Progress* (1678–84), second only to the *Bible in popularity for many years, was present in the Evans's household just as it was in the Tullivers'. References to it are speckled throughout George Eliot's work, perhaps the most impressive and weighted being used as epigraph to chapter 85 of *Middlemarch*, where the list of the jury trying Christian and Faithful are given in all their varied bias. Eliot's love for Bunyan was strong, and she recorded in her journal in 1859 that she was reading him again and appreciating 'the true genius manifested in the simple, vigorous, rhythmic style' (*Journals*, 82).   GRH

Burke, Edmund (1729–97), Irish-born English statesman and philosopher. Like George Eliot in her younger years, he memorized passages of Edward *Young's *Night Thoughts*. Twice in 1852–3 she quotes his 'self-interest well understood' from *Reflections on the Revolution in France*, repeating the phrase later to John *Blackwood in 1860 (*L* iii. 312). Oliver *Goldsmith's satire on Burke in *Retaliation* is also quoted (*L* v. 169). In *The Mill on the Floss* (*MF* 4.3) there is a reference to Burke's 'grand dirge' over 'the days of chivalry', in *Felix Holt, the Radical* (*FH* 23) the Revd Augustus Debarry threatens to quote a telling passage from Burke on the Dissenters, while in *Middlemarch* (*MM* 46) Mr Brooke wishes he had a pocket borough to give to Ladislaw, there having been always one available for Burke when he wanted to re-enter Parliament.
      GRH

Burne-Jones, Edward Coley (1833–98), *Pre-Raphaelite painter, created baronet 1894, and his wife **Georgiana** (1840–1920). George Eliot's friendship with both began in February 1868 but focuses on Georgiana, called 'Mignon' by the Leweses, although Eliot also uses the familiar 'Georgie'. From 1869 Edward was having an affair with Mary Zambaco which continued for some years and there has been some speculation as to what extent Georgiana confided in Eliot, Haight claiming that confidences included 'her marital difficulties' (*L*, vol. viii, p. x) although as Ashton points out, there is no way of knowing how detailed such confidences were (1996: 306). The affair was painfully public as Dante Gabriel *Rossetti's letter to Madox Brown indicates (Henderson, 125). Speculations regarding G. H. *Lewes's possible infidelities, linked to information from Edward, cannot be substantiated. What we can be certain of is Eliot's fondness for Georgiana, pressing her in a series of letters to holiday with them at Whitby in 1870, 'It will be a real joy to have you and the chicks' (*L* v. 103–4), and representing herself and Lewes as 'two grandparents' (*L* v. 105); asking her advice about suitable dress for *Oxford and *Cambridge (*L* vi. 365); spending Fridays regularly together; and after Lewes's death allowing Georgiana to call while telling older friends like Cara Bray

'I see no visitors yet' (*L* vii. 124). On the eve of Eliot's marriage to John Walter *Cross, Georgiana was one of the few informed of the 'great momentous change' (*L* vii. 269).

Eliot admired Edward Burne-Jones's art as her letter of 1873 testifies: 'I write in gratitude to tell you that your work makes life larger and more beautiful to us' (*L* v. 391); he responded that her praise was important to him (*L* ix. 85). She remarks, a little drily perhaps, to Emelia Pattison in 1876 that 'Burne Jones goes on transcending himself and is rising into the inconvenient celebrity which is made up of echoes as well as voices' (*L* vi. 229). In 1896 Edward says of Eliot that 'there will always be times when her books will be studied. But ladies never give us any fighting—they only give us magnificent sentiments' (Lago, 94).   JJ

Burne-Jones Talking: His conversations 1895–1898, ed. Mary Lago (1982).
Burne-Jones, Georgiana, *Memorials of Edward Burne-Jones* (1904).
Ashton (1996).
Henderson, Philip, *William Morris: His Life, Work and Friends* (1967).

Burton, Frederic (1816–1900), painter, born in Ireland, where his artistic ability was early recognized (he was elected to the Royal Hibernian Academy at 23). His preferred medium was watercolour, and he specialized in portraiture, making two portraits of the actress Helen *Faucit (one standing, as Antigone) before he left Dublin for Munich in 1851. George Eliot's later acquaintance with Faucit was facilitated by Burton.

Eliot and Lewes met Burton in *Munich in 1858, when she described him as 'the English artist . . . an agreeable man with a little English glazing of shyness' (*Journals*, 314; *L* iii. 128 n. 7) After his move to London in the early 1860s, he became a close friend and frequent guest, nicknamed 'the Maestro'. On the spur of the moment, Eliot and Lewes accompanied Burton on his first visit to *Italy in May–June 1864, described by Eliot in a staccato journal account of the trip. While both acknowledged the benefit of Burton's expertise in developing their appreciation especially of the art and architecture of *Venice, at times Lewes rested or went shopping while Burton and George Eliot ('the best man of the three', *Letters of George Henry Lewes*, ii. 62) voraciously continued on to another gallery.

On their return to London, Burton began to paint a portrait of George Eliot for which there were numerous sittings between 29 June 1864 and 22 July 1865 (possibly Burton made several versions). It was exhibited at the Royal Academy in 1867, and given to the National Portrait Gallery in 1883 (see PORTRAITS). When Lewes first saw the portrait, he 'was in raptures with it, whereupon Mr. Burton told him it was *his* (George's). I don't know myself whether it is good or not' (*L* viii. 321). Lewes hung it over the mantel in his study.

Burton's appointment as Director of the National Gallery London in 1874 was not widely predicted, but during his twenty years' tenure of the position he displayed 'discretion founded upon sound knowledge' (*DNB*). His purchases included significant Italian Renaissance works such as Leonardo da Vinci's *Virgin of the Rocks*, but also the gallery's first painting by Vermeer, *Young Woman standing at a Virginal*, and Velásquez's *Philip IV in Brown and Silver*. He was knighted on his retirement in 1894, and never married. See also VISUAL ARTS.   MAH

The Letters of George Henry Lewes, ed. William Baker, 2 vols. (1995).

Byron (1788–1824), Romantic poet. Although George Eliot is most associated with William *Wordsworth among Romantic poets, George Gordon Byron may have had a more significant effect on her writing, despite the fact that she clearly had little sympathy for Byronic attitudes and characteristics. In a letter she wrote that Byron 'seems to me the most *vulgar-minded* genius that ever produced a great effect in literature' (*L* v. 57). Yet Byronic characters are a strong presence in her novels and *poetry. In the poetry they are presented in a particularly graphic fashion. In 'The Legend of Jubal', a poem that shows an awareness of Byron's *Cain*, the major conflict is between the different responses to death by the Byronic Tubal-Cain and Jubal, the one constructing a philosophy based on will and power and the other creating music to unite humanity in fellowship. 'Armgart', a poem about an opera singer who exults in the power of her ego and values self-realization above all things, is another attack on the Byronic. This character re-emerges as Deronda's mother, the Princess Halm-Eberstein, in *Daniel Deronda*. But the major Byronic figure in the poetry is Don Silva, in the dramatic poem *The Spanish Gypsy*:

You may divide the universe with God,
Keeping your will unbent, and hold a world
Where He is not supreme.

In both the poems and the novels characters who elevate the ego in this way eventually have to acknowledge defeat, as can be seen in the fates of such characters as Mrs Transome in *Felix Holt* and Deronda's mother. Byronic influence is strongest in *Daniel Deronda*. In addition to the Princess, Gwendolen Harleth is clearly Byronic—indeed the character was suggested by Byron's grand-niece whom George Eliot saw gambling at Bad Homburg—and Mirah probably derives from the heroine of Byron's *Sardanapalus*, Myrrha. See also ROMANTICISM.   KMN

Cabinet Edition. In February 1877 G. H. *Lewes suggested to John *Blackwood that a uniform edition of George Eliot's novels was desirable. In April Blackwood was considering a 19–20-volume set, details being finalized in July. In January 1878 publication began with volume i of *Romola*, one volume of the works being added per month, though *Middlemarch* and *Daniel Deronda* were probably issued in December 1878. In 1879 the poetry (2 volumes), in 1880 *Impressions of Theophrastus Such* were added, making 20 volumes. Eliot made a number of corrections and alterations. The original binding was olive green cloth, brown later: there were no illustrations. See also PUBLISHERS, NEGOTIATIONS WITH.   GRH

Call, Mrs W. M. W. See BRABANT, ELIZABETH REBECCA (RUFA).

Cambridge, university town visited by George Eliot and G. H. *Lewes in the 1860s and 1870s. Journal entries include mention of an enjoyable visit to Cambridge in February 1868 and another one nine years later in June which was 'delightful'. On 19 May 1873 they visited F. W. H. *Myers, enjoyed talking with him and some Trinity men, watched a boat race, and had the company of, among others, Henry *Sidgwick and Edmund *Gurney. Myers recalled the occasion with telling emphasis. She probably drew on this visit and the breakfast at Trinity that Myers arranged when she wrote her poem 'A College Breakfast-Party' the following year; and in her next novel Daniel Deronda is said to have studied for a short time at Cambridge. After Lewes's death Eliot founded the George Henry Lewes Studentship in Physiology at Cambridge, £5,000 being made over by her to the Trustees. The first student was C. S. Roy: several later distinguished scientists were to follow him. See also BROWNING, OSCAR.   GRH

Carlyle, Jane Welsh (1801–66) and **Thomas** (1795–1881). Thomas Carlyle was the admired historical writer and sage of the early Victorian era, and his early work provided intellectual stimulus for George Eliot. His wife Jane (they married in 1826) was among the first to recognize the moral and intellectual status of Eliot's fiction, and became a source of personal encouragement.

Like Eliot, Thomas Carlyle was intellectually awakened by Jean-Jacques *Rousseau's *Confessions*, a philosophic source of the French Revolution. Eliot's response was in essence affirmative, Carlyle's negative (Karl 1995: 98). His *French Revolution: A History* (1837) expressed the progressivist scorn of 'shams' in politics and religion that Eliot shared with G. H. *Lewes. They disliked, however, the authoritarianism behind his *On Heroes, Hero-*

Worship and the Heroic in History (1841); and Eliot's notes from Carlyle's *Oliver Cromwell's Letters and Speeches* (1845) suggest personal empathy rather than political approval (*Writer's Notebook*, ed. Wiesenfarth, 23). Craving emotional reassurance as well as intellectual challenge, the younger Eliot read into Carlyle's earlier writings a kindliness many readers did not find there. By December 1841, she dubbed him 'a grand favourite of mine'; and was recommending *Sartor Resartus* (1833–4) to Martha *Jackson as a specimen of the 'brightest and purest philanthropy', though she added that the work was 'not orthodox' (*L* i. 122–3). *Sartor*, a medley of fantasy novel, metaphysical autobiography, and cultural satire, charts the journey of its hero, Diogenes Teufelsdröckh, from orthodoxy towards nihilistic despair, and (most important for Eliot) his rescue from the latter by a personally intuited conviction of the 'Everlasting Yea' at the heart of things. Eliot was currently revising her evangelical doctrines under the influence of Mr and Mrs Charles *Bray, and she was also beginning to study German Higher Criticism, with its radical reappraisal of the historical basis of Christianity. Carlyle's reclaiming, in *Sartor*, of inner convictions in favour of right action and compassionate feeling, despite the absence of dogmatic beliefs, came as a great boon for her. In his *Past and Present* (1843), Carlyle argued for a revival, in modern terms, of the Catholic principles of spiritual power, organic community, and personal responsibility. Current 'Dilettantism' and inaction must be replaced by deeds of social and moral leadership undertaken by a 'Working Aristocracy' (book 3, chapters 3 and 9). By the time Eliot began work on *Middlemarch*, she would have rejected Carlyle's authoritarianism, but the challenge she had welcomed in *Sartor* and *Past and Present* (Hardman, 77) would be transmuted into the useful life of Dorothea, reviving, not the

Catholic doctrines of St Theresa, but her 'passionate, ideal' (and practical) goodness in modern form and in partnership with Ladislaw: 'Our sense of duty must often wait for some work which shall take the place of dilettantism—make us feel that the quality of our action is not a matter of indifference' (*MM* 46).

In 1841, Eliot was reading *Chartism* (1840), in which Carlyle raised the 'Condition-of-England Question' (*L* i. 71). She particularly admired the last paragraph of chapter 4, in which he denounced the 'liquid Madness' of gin and its demoralizing effects on the masses, and she continued to share a Carlylean mixture of angry pity and moralistic condescension towards the working classes (see also CHARTISM; CLASS). In 1867, as Carlyle was denouncing the coming of the working-class vote, Eliot would issue an *'Address to Working Men' in the persona of the eponymous hero of *Felix Holt*. Far more generous in her attitude to the coming democracy than Carlyle, she retained elements of his conservatism and (as in the novel itself) of his middle-class incomprehension and disdain of dangerous elements, maddened (to quote the 'Address') on 'drugged beer and gin' (see POLITICS).

Eliot's intellectual sympathies were expanding during the 1850s and 1860s, as Carlyle's were contracting. In reviewing his *Life of John Sterling* (1851) for the *Westminster Review* of January 1852 (*Essays*, 46–51), Eliot expressed regret for the 'threatenings and slaughter' of his reactionary *Latter-Day Pamphlets* (1850); and she privately confessed her sense of Carlyle's egoism when she wrote to Sara *Hennell and the Brays that it was not the explicit 'presentation of Sterling'—a figure who epitomized 19th-century religious and philosophic dilemmas—that made the book pleasurable, but its implicit presentation of Carlyle (*L* i. 370). In her review, she makes Carlyle the hero of his own narrative, and dubs him a 'Teufelsdröckh still, but humanized by a Blumine worthy of him'. In *Sartor*, the hero fails to win Blumine, but in real life Carlyle was fortunate to win the hand of Jane Welsh, to whom Eliot now turned for the kind of moral support Carlyle himself denied. Although an early friend and mentor of Lewes, he was ambiguous, even offensive, in 1854, in his attitude to his former protégé's embarking on an unconventional ménage with Eliot, whom he dubbed the 'strong minded woman' (*L* ii. 177 n.). Her review of Thomas Ballantyne's selections from Carlyle in the *Leader* of 27 October 1855 (*Essays*, 212–15) acknowledges Carlyle's influence on the superior and active minds of a generation; but confesses it is 'several years now since we read a work of Carlyle's *seriatim*'. When in 1858 Eliot sent copies of *Scenes of Clerical Life* to nine respected persons,

the copy for the Carlyle household was directed to Mrs, not Mr, Carlyle.

Jane's reaction was enthusiastic. Writing on 8 January 1858, she assured the author she had enjoyed 'a surprise, a pleasure, and a—*consolation* (!) all in one Book!' Better 'than the most sympathetic helpful friend', the book had supported her through one of her many nights of pain. More than just another new novel, *Scenes* was a work of humanity, of 'pathos without a scrap of sentimentality, of sense without dogmatism, of earnestness without twaddle'. To read it was to become '*friends*, at once and for always with the man or woman who wrote it'. The terms of her appreciation are significant: they provide the first reading of an Eliot novel that assigns the author the status of Victorian sage, an intellectual and moral successor to Carlyle himself, a view corroborated by 20th-century critics. Unsurprisingly, the reactions of Mr and Mrs Carlyle to *Adam Bede* would be very different (Haight 1968: 273–4). Wilfully misreading Wiry Ben's joke about 'leaving the panels out o' th' door' (*AB* 1), Thomas threw the book down as mere 'woman's writing—she supposed that in making a door, you last of all put in the *panels!*' The incident was symptomatic of the 'shallow, undiscriminating scorn' Eliot would increasingly deplore in Carlyle (*L* v. 422). At least one cabinet-maker wrote to congratulate Eliot on her technical accuracy. Jane Carlyle wrote warmly, 20 February 1859 (*L* iii. 17–19): 'It was as good as *going into the country for one's health*, the reading of that Book was! ... a beautiful most *human* book!' In his dedication of 1625 to his *Essays*, Francis Bacon had written of them as having 'come home, to Mens Businesse, and Bosoms'. Deploying allusion to accord *Adam Bede* a status approaching the work of the great empirical philosopher, Mrs Carlyle assured Eliot that 'Every *Dog* in it, not to say every woman and child in it, is brought home to one's "business and bosom", as an individual fellow-creature'. Fully aware of the compliment, Eliot begged John *Blackwood to thank Mrs Carlyle and to say the 'effect she declares herself to have felt ... is just what I desire to produce'. Mrs Carlyle's enthusiasm was communicated to her friend Geraldine *Jewsbury, who reviewed *Adam Bede* in the *Athenaeum* as 'a work of true genius ... a novel of the highest class' (Haight 1968: 276).

Eliot and Lewes remained on polite terms with both Thomas and Jane Carlyle. The four made a party to see *Hamlet* in London on 26 July 1861, for example (*L* iii. 441–2). Eliot and Lewes continued to admire and read Carlyle's *French Revolution* (Haight 1968: 430); and when, in 1875, a testimonial was arranged from Carlyle's literary friends, Eliot was anxious to be included, though the intensity of her feelings made her spoil several papers before she could produce a fair signature (*L* ix. 167). It would seem that Jane anticipated the terms on which Eliot would be valued in the 20th century, while Thomas turned away in pursuit of the Prussian values of the eponymous hero of his *Frederick the Great* (1858–65), the dominant military presence of the 18th century in which he was born, and the epitome of the strongman theory of history that Eliot privately found so 'painful' (*L* iii. 23) and that *Daniel Deronda* was in part written to oppose. MH

Thomas Carlyle: Selected Writings, ed. Alan Shelston (1986).
George Eliot: A Writer's Notebook 1854–1879, ed. Joseph Wiesenfarth (1981).
Clubbe, John (ed.), Carlyle and His Contemporaries (1976).
Hardman, Malcolm, Six Victorian Thinkers (1991).
Holloway, John, The Victorian Sage (1953).
Karl (1995).

Cash, Mrs John. See SIBREE, MARY.

Cervantes Saavedra, Miguel de (1547–1616), Spanish author of *Don Quixote* (1605, 1615) and other fiction, plays, and poems. He was read in English, French, and Spanish by George Eliot intermittently over a period of forty years, but his influence on her work is difficult to assess. In 1839, Eliot included *Quixote* in a list of works of fiction acceptable to an evangelical reader, but did not read it until 1840, finding it 'full of philosophical wit' (*L* i. 60). Eliot read *Quixote* aloud to Lewes and translated it while learning Spanish in 1864. She also read 'La Gitanella,' one of the *Novelas ejemplares* (1613), while working on *The Spanish Gypsy*. It 'promises well . . . but falls into sad commonplace towards the end' (*L* v. 33), she wrote. Lewes's annotated copy is in Dr Williams's Library, along with Emile Chasles's *Michel de Cervantes, sa vie, son temps, son œuvre, politique et littéraire* (1866), with Eliot's marginal notes.

There are two notes from Cervantes in Eliot's notebook for 1854–79 taken from the French translation by Louis Viardot (*Writer's Notebook*, ed. Wiesenfarth, 20, 36). Another passage, in Spanish, is copied in the Folger notebook, which reflects Eliot's reading for *Middlemarch* ('*Middlemarch*' Notebooks, ed. Pratt and Neufeldt, 93). The epigraph, in Spanish and English, for chapter 2 of *Middlemarch* is from *Quixote*. Contrasting illusion with reality, it implicitly likens the idealistic Dorothea and the commonsensical Celia to the knight and his squire.

Cervantes's pervasive influence on European literature makes it hard to ascertain how much his effect on Eliot was direct, and to what extent it was mediated by earlier writers. Cervantes and Eliot share a preoccupation with the conflict between the ideal and the real, which, in Eliot, culminates in *Daniel Deronda*, where the 'knight errant' hero seizes the opportunity to act on his book-fed idealism and right the wrong done to an entire people.

Eliot was reading *Don Quixote* in Alexander James Duffield's translation in December 1880, shortly before her death. BSM

George Eliot's 'Middlemarch Notebooks': A Transcription, ed. John Clark Pratt and Victor A. Neufeldt (1979).
George Eliot: A Writer's Notebook 1854–1879, and Uncollected Writings, ed. Joseph Wiesenfarth (1981).

Chapman, John (1821–94), publisher, author, editor, physician, and friend of George Eliot, who played a crucial part in her life during her first years in London in the early 1850s. The son of a Nottingham druggist, he was apprenticed to a watchmaker in Worksop, but, endowed with striking good looks that earned him the nickname of Byron, and a lively, enquiring mind, he had larger ambitions. Abandoning his apprenticeship he travelled widely, getting as far as Australia and spending some time in Paris, where he later claimed to have studied medicine. He was practising as an unlicensed surgeon in Derby when he married a wealthy older woman, Susanna Brewitt, on 27 June 1843. Fourteen years his senior, she had been left a comfortable fortune by her father, a Nottingham lace manufacturer, which, after they had moved to London, enabled Chapman to set himself up as a publisher by buying J. H. Green's bookselling and publishing business. Living in Clapton, the Chapmans entertained regularly, including Herbert *Spencer and Sara *Hennell among their acquaintances, and they also took in boarders, one of whom was Eliza Lynn, later *Linton. In 1844 Chapman began to publish Ralph Waldo *Emerson's works and in 1846, during a short-lived partnership with his brother Thomas, he published George Eliot's anonymous translation of D. F. *Strauss's *Das Leben Jesu*. He then moved his business and his family to 142 Strand, where he and his wife continued to offer board and lodging and to give Friday evening parties for writers and intellectuals of a liberal or radical persuasion. The house was a convenient base for visitors to London and popular with Americans: Emerson stayed there for nearly three months in 1848.

It is likely that George Eliot, Mary Ann Evans as she then was, first met Chapman in 1846 when she went to stay with Sara Hennell in Clapton shortly after finishing the translation of Strauss. A letter of the following February clearly implies that she had met him and was not immediately susceptible to the attractions of his handsome appearance and self-confident, expansive personality. 'Mr

Chapman', she writes to Sara Hennell, 'was always too much of the *interesting* gentleman to please us. Men must not attempt to be interesting on any lower terms than a fine poetical genius' (*L* i. 231). But he remained important to her as a bookseller and publisher. She bought books from him and in March 1849 wrote to him to ask whether he would consider publishing a translation of Baruch *Spinoza's *Tractatus Theologico-Politicus* which she had started to work on. He gave his tentative agreement, but the translation was abandoned after her father's death when she went to the Continent. On her return from *Geneva in 1850, she was staying at Rosehill in *Coventry with the *Brays when Chapman came to visit in the summer and again in October, this time accompanied by Robert William Mackay, whose *The Progress of the Intellect* he had just published. They suggested that she should write a review of the book for the *Westminster Review* and she agreed. Her review, published in January 1851, was the first of the many articles she was to write for that periodical, which Chapman purchased in the following September. Deciding to move to *London to make her living as a writer, she went to stay with the Chapmans in the Strand for a trial fortnight in November 1850. It was there, at one of the regular parties, that she met Eliza Lynn for the first time—a meeting that is unflatteringly recorded in the latter's memoirs. The trial was apparently successful, for on 8 January 1851 she returned to London and moved in as a permanent boarder at 142 Strand.

Her presence added a further complication to Chapman's already complicated household, which included not only his wife and children but a so-called governess, Elisabeth Tilley, who was also his mistress. Although his diary frankly records the complexities of his private life, it offers no insight into how he reconciled keeping a mistress with 'the lofty morality he seemed quite sincerely to profess' (Haight 1969: 18), and which prompted him, for instance, to withdraw from publishing Eliza Lynn's novel *Realities* because it contained a too graphic love scene. What his diary does make clear, however, is how soon and how bitterly his wife and his mistress came to resent the attention he was paying to the new boarder, visiting her room to hear her play the piano and getting her to teach him German. By 24 January he was writing that 'Elisabeth has not spoken kindly to me since Thursday evening,—on account of Miss Evans' (Haight 1969: 137). By 18 February Susanna found him holding Marian's hand, and wife and mistress had concluded that he and Marian were 'completely in love with each other' (Haight 1969: 141–2). Although the diary evidence is inconclusive, Chapman and Marian Evans may have had a brief sexual relationship in January (Ashton 1996:

84–5). At any rate by late March the situation had become so difficult that Marian agreed to leave and to return to the Brays at Rosehill. Chapman's diary records the apparent state of her feelings as he accompanied her to the station to catch the train to Coventry:

She was very sad, and hence made me feel so.—She pressed me for some intimation of the state of my feelings,—[*struck through*: I told her that I felt great affection for her, but that I loved E. and S. also, though each in a different way.] At this avowal she burst into tears. I tried to comfort her, and reminded [her] of the dear friends and pleasant home she was returning to,—but the train whirled her away very very sad. (Haight 1969: 147)

What for Chapman was probably only a passing flirtation had clearly aroused far deeper emotions in the future novelist.

At the beginning of May 1851 he entered into an agreement to buy the *Westminster Review* from W. E. Hickson and at once began to consider how he could arrange for Marian Evans to return to London to help him manage the new venture. On 27 May he went to Coventry to stay with the Brays in order to approach her, and found her 'shy, calm, and affectionate' (Haight 1969: 30). She agreed to write the regular articles he was planning on foreign literature and helped him write the prospectus for the new version of the periodical. The still delicate state of her feelings and his own blithe tactlessness are revealed by a diary entry recounting a visit to Kenilworth castle during his stay:

As we rested on the grass, I remarked on the wonderful and mysterious embodiment of all the elements characteristics and beauties of nature which man and woman jointly present. I dwelt also on the incomprehensible mystery and witchery of beauty. My words jarred upon her and put an end to her enjoyment. Was it from a consciousness of her own want of beauty. She wept bitterly. (Haight 1969: 172)

While admiring her intellect and ability, which he was already coming to rely upon, Chapman was clearly not offering any deeper relationship, and Marian seems to have sensibly resigned herself to that fact. A few days later he records that 'during our walk we made a solemn and holy vow which henceforth will bind us to the right. She is a noble being' (Haight 1969: 175). The difficulty remained of persuading the other two women to accept her back into the house, but eventually Chapman succeeded and on 29 September 1851 she took up residence again at 142 Strand, where she was to remain for the next two years.

A week later Chapman completed the purchase of the *Westminster Review* and began to prepare the first number for January 1852. Although he was the nominal editor, it was Marian Evans who did the real editorial work for the first ten numbers up to April 1854, as well as writing the reviews and *essays that established her as a writer and prepared the ground for the novelist she was to become (see JOURNALIST). She firmly steered him away from his idea of contributing articles to the *Westminster* himself and proved far more adept than he could ever have been at dealing tactfully with contributors and their sensitivities. What she gained in return for her self-effacing work was contact with leading figures in the literary and intellectual life of London, and indeed of Europe, since refugees from the failed *revolutions of 1848 like Louis Blanc and Giuseppe *Mazzini were drawn to the premises of the influential radical periodical that seemed now to have regained the importance it had formerly had under the editorship of John Stuart *Mill.

The *Westminster*, which paid contributors generously, lost money from the outset and Chapman was constantly in financial difficulty and dependent on wealthy backers. Somehow he managed to keep his various businesses going, moving to cheaper premises at 43 Blandford Square in June 1854. In July 1854 he published George Eliot's translation of Ludwig *Feuerbach, *The Essence of Christianity*, the only one of her works to bear her real name of Marian Evans. In the same month she left for Germany with G. H. *Lewes, and it is a testimony of the closeness of Chapman's friendship with her at this time that he and Charles Bray were the only people to whom she had confided the truth about her relations with Lewes. He never betrayed that confidence. He also gave them valuable assistance after their elopement by continuing to commission articles and reviews from Marian for which he paid well. His own private life remained complicated. In the summer of 1854 he began a year-long affair with George Eliot's friend Barbara Leigh Smith (see BODICHON, BARBARA), with whom he planned to live openly in an extramarital union, until her father and family intervened and arranged for her to go off to Algiers, where she met her future husband Dr Bodichon. Professionally his life took a new turn when he decided to take up medicine again, while continuing with his other businesses and his editorship of the *Westminster*. In May 1857 he took his MD from St Andrews and later became a member of the Royal College of Physicians and the Royal College of Surgeons. Since his principal treatment for everything from epilepsy to cholera seems to have been the application of an ice-bag to the spine, it is hard to disagree with Haight's judgement that 'Chapman's career as a physician is open to strong suspicion of quackery' (1969: 113). Never-

theless, he continued to practise medicine until his death.

What put an end to his friendship with the novelist was her desire to remain anonymous as an author of fiction and his inquisitive attempts to penetrate her secret. After the publication of *Scenes of Clerical Life* in 1858 he asked Herbert Spencer, the only friend apart from Lewes who had been entrusted with the secret of George Eliot's identity, whether she had written the stories. Learning of this on 5 November, she wrote to him at once with a denial to put an end to the gossip and was hurt by his long delay in replying. After the publication of *Adam Bede* in February 1859 he once again taxed Spencer on the subject and was met with equivocation and silence. Lewes then intervened and wrote a letter of emphatic denial. Although the truth became generally known later that year, the breach with Chapman was never repaired. When he wrote to her in January 1860 with a proposal to republish her articles from the *Westminster*, Lewes replied on her behalf to reject the idea.

In 1874 he moved to Paris to practise as a physician in the British community, leaving his wife Susanna behind. In 1879 he took a second wife, Hannah Hughes MacDonald. He continued to edit the *Westminster* until his death in Paris on 25 November 1894 and was buried near to George Eliot in Highgate Cemetery.   JMR

Ashton (1996).

Haight, Gordon S., *George Eliot and John Chapman: with Chapman's Diaries*, 2nd edn. (1969).

characterization. The vivid characters that delighted Victorian readers and reviewers in George Eliot's fiction define themselves through their own idiosyncratic utterances, like Mrs Poyser in *Adam Bede* with her sharp-tongued lecturing and earthy epigrams: 'Ay, it's ill livin' in a hen roost for them as doesn't like fleas' (*AB* 14). This form of characterization through self-revealing speech may be more marked in the early novels but it runs throughout her work and can be seen in the amiably meandering Mr Brooke in *Middlemarch* and the musician Klesmer in *Daniel Deronda* with his distinct German inflection. However, the presentation of the central characters in the novels involves more complex procedures in order to disclose and assess what lies behind the surface of speech: either the agency of a reflective and analytical narrative voice combining sympathy and irony in varying proportions, or the use of free indirect style, which moves unobtrusively between the character's own thoughts and the evaluative discourse of the narrator. Thus Dorothea's state of mind when she is contemplating marriage to Casaubon is presented in a way which reveals her earnest idealism and naivety, defines her inner needs, and passes judgement on the inadequate preparation for life afforded by a woman's education: 'What could she do, what ought she to do?—she hardly more than a budding woman, but yet with an active conscience and a great mental need, not to be satisfied by girlish instruction comparable to the nibblings and judgments of a discursive mouse' (*MM* 3). Characteristically, Eliot indicates here a connection between the inner life of the individual and its social context, for character in her novels is always subject to the determining pressure of social conditions and it was the habit of her imagination 'to strive after as full a vision of the medium in which a character moves as of the character itself' (*L* iv. 96–7). At the same time a margin of mobility and freedom remains. 'Character is not cut in marble—it is not something solid and unalterable' (*MM* 72), as Camden Farebrother points out in *Middlemarch*, and its flexibility is demonstrated at those moments when Eliot has her characters act in surprising and unexpected ways: Mrs Glegg taking Maggie's side when she returns from the boat journey with Stephen Guest to face social disgrace (*MF* 7.3); or Rosamond Vincy dropping her habitual selfishness to tell Dorothea of Ladislaw's feelings for her (*MM* 81).

The inclination of her first readers to take her characters as portraits of real people was something Eliot deplored and vigorously resisted, insisting, for instance, that '*There is not a single portrait in Adam Bede*' (*L* iii. 155); and her later work shows her awareness of the problematic nature of literary character and of the complex processes involved in its creation. The detailed account of Lydgate's past life in *Middlemarch* is prefaced by the narrator's intention to make him better known to the reader than he could be to his fellow citizens, thereby drawing attention to the transparency that fiction can achieve; at the same time a man like Lydgate can, we are told, remain virtually unknown in his own community, 'known merely as a cluster of signs for his neighbours' false suppositions' (*MM* 15). Character is a construct, and if it is, too, 'a process and an unfolding' as the narrator also maintains (*MM* 15), the changes it undergoes involve changes in the way that it is perceived. The story of Lydgate is that of a man 'altering with the double change of self and beholder' (*MM* 11), and, as a recent study has shown, the novel charts the complex construction of his character both in the minds of others and in his own perception of himself (Wright 1991: 40–1). In *Middlemarch* Eliot questions the idea of character as a stable entity that seems to be implied in figures like Mrs Poyser and explores the fluid nature of identity, while in the enigmatically evil figure of Grandcourt in *Daniel Deronda* she shows how character may resist understanding and remain puzzlingly opaque. In these late works her characterization tests the limits of realist practice and invites comparison with modernism and postmodernism. See also CHARACTERS, ORIGINALS OF; LANGUAGE.   JMR

Hardy (1959).
Wright (1991).

characters, originals of. George Eliot was always impatient with readers who looked for portraits of real people in her fiction, insisting to Charles *Bray in September 1859 with italicized exasperation that '*There is not a single portrait in Adam Bede*', and maintaining that everything from description of scenery to characters and dialogue was 'a combination from widely sundered elements of experience' (*L* iii. 155). When members of her Aunt Samuel's family (see EVANS, MRS SAMUEL) saw a good portrait of her in Dinah Morris, she did concede, however, that it was not surprising that 'simple men and women without pretension to enlightened discrimination should think a generic resemblance constitutes a portrait' (*L* iii. 176). Generic resemblance probably best defines the relationship between characters in her fiction and their possible originals, and she only ever admitted to two portraits, both in *Scenes of Clerical Life*: Amos Barton, who she claimed was a much better man than his original, the Revd John Gwyther, curate of *Chilvers Coton, whose wife Emma died young like the fictional Milly; and the lawyer Dempster, who was the Nuneaton lawyer James William Buchanan (1792–1846). This has not prevented readers from finding models for other characters, and some of the most frequently cited originals are listed below, with the reservation that all such suggestions are open to the charge of being what G. H. *Lewes called 'foolish identifications' (*L* iii. 159–60), and that generic resemblance is the most that should be claimed for nearly all of them after *Scenes of Clerical Life*.

In that first work the Oldinports are the *Newdigate family, thinly disguised, and Sir Christopher Cheverel (*SC* 2) is based on what George Eliot had heard of Sir Roger Newdigate (1719–1806), who had undertaken the Gothic transformation of Arbury Hall. Mr Gilfil (*SC* 2) is modelled on the Revd Bernard Gilpin Ebdell, who had baptized her. Janet Dempster (*SC* 3) is drawn from Mrs Nancy Wallington Buchanan, the daughter of the Mrs Wallington whose boarding school in Nuneaton the novelist attended, though she died of illness a week before her husband suffered the accident that is used in the story—and from which he recovered—and there is no evidence that their marriage was unhappy (Haight 1992: 6). Mr Tryan (*SC* 3) is derived from the Revd John Edwin Jones, the earnestly evangelical curate of Stockingford.

In *Adam Bede*, apart from drawing on her Aunt Samuel's account of comforting a condemned girl, Mary Voce, in Nottingham gaol, Eliot used some of what she had heard about her father Robert *Evans's early experience in creating Adam himself. The schoolteacher Bartle Massey is named after the teacher in her father's village. In *The Mill on the Floss* her brother Isaac *Evans lies behind the character of Tom Tulliver, and Maggie Tulliver's relationship with him as a child resembles her own with Isaac described in the 'Brother and Sister' Sonnets (see POETRY). The Dodson sisters are based on her Pearson aunts on her mother's side of the family. Her sister Chrissey (see EVANS, CHRISTIANA) has been seen as the model for Lucy Deane and for the very different figure of Mr Tulliver's sister Gritty Moss, while the Swiss artist François *D'Albert Durade has been cited as the original for Philip Wakem.

In *Romola* Mme Belloc (see PARKES, BESSIE) saw in the heroine a portrait of the form and bearing of Barbara Leigh Smith *Bodichon. In *Felix Holt* Rufus Lyon has been likened to the Baptist minister in Coventry, Francis Franklin, the father of the Misses Franklin whose school Eliot attended. It has been claimed that Felix himself is modelled on Gerald Massey (1828–1907), a self-educated socialist and poet, though Haight (1992) sees a closer affinity with John *Chapman. In *Middlemarch* Margaret *Fuller has been cited as a model for Dorothea, while Lydgate may owe something to Eliot's brother-in-law Dr Edward *Clarke, and Caleb Garth to her father Robert Evans. Casaubon has been identified with Dr *Brabant, and more improbably Mark *Pattison; however, on two occasions when asked where she had derived his character, she is reported to have pointed to herself. In *Daniel Deronda* Mordecai has affinities in his life and death with her friend Emanuel *Deutsch, while Klesmer has been likened to both *Liszt and Anton *Rubinstein. Deronda himself was claimed by Leslie *Stephen to be modelled on Edmund *Gurney. Haight (1992) mentions other possible models for Deronda and for other characters in the fiction. See also CHARACTERIZATION; SETTINGS; VISUAL ARTS.

JMR

Ellmann, Richard, *Golden Codgers: Biographical Speculations* (1976).

Haight, Gordon S., *George Eliot's Originals and Contemporaries*, ed. Hugh Witemeyer (1992).

Chartism, a national though fundamentally eclectic movement, comprising mainly urban working-class societies engaged in trade and industry. They joined forces to sign 'the People's Charter' in 1838—five or six years after the times in which *Felix Holt, the Radical* and *Middlemarch* are set. In George Eliot's most political novel, *Felix Holt*, some of the Charter's demands are heard (*FH* 30).

Chartists called for (i) annual parliaments, (ii) universal male suffrage, (iii) equal electoral districts, (iv) the abolition of property qualification for MPs, (v) the secret ballot, and (vi) salaries for MPs. They petitioned Parliament in 1839, 1842, and 1848; but on each occasion their charter was rejected. By 1839 the movement had its own newspaper, the *Northern Star*, with a circulation of almost 50,000 per week. The first parliamentary petition had 1,200,000 signatures, the second over 3,000,000. What united the Chartists was widespread hunger and starvation throughout England, Scotland, and Wales; anger at dangerous and unfair working conditions; and, above all, discontent with the limited male suffrage extended in the Great *Reform Act of 1832.

By 1850, Chartism had largely dissipated as its leaders, though not its rank and file, became less concerned with political reform and more with social revolution. The movement had been able to unite on political issues, but the disparate backgrounds of Chartists meant that they could not agree on social ones. Some Chartists surfaced again in the reform agitation that prefaced the Second Reform Bill of 1867. Meanwhile, from 1850 onwards, smaller trade unions gradually took over where Chartism had left off. These unions involved skilled men asking for improved working conditions specific to their jobs.

The unnamed public speaker in Duffield's market place on Nomination Day repeats four of the Charter's six demands: 'we must have universal suffrage, and annual Parliaments, and the vote by ballot, and electoral districts.' Felix responds to him by saying that before men decide on such specifics it is necessary to engender a 'ruling belief in society about what is right and what is wrong, what is honourable and what is shameful' (*FH* 30). See also POLITICS.

AvdB

Chaucer, Geoffrey (before 1346–1400), Middle English poet famous for *The Canterbury Tales*. Eliot's notebooks and journals reveal her long and scholarly interest in Chaucer, in common with other Victorian writers and artists. In 1855 reviewing Bell's edition of Chaucer for the *Westminster Review*, she writes that 'our modern school of poets are more obviously the lineal descendants of the Father of English poetry than many poets who were nearer to him chronologically' (64: 299). Engaged on her dramatic poem *The Spanish Gypsy* she records in 1866 that she is 'reading Chaucer to study English' (*Journals*, p. 129). Four epigraphs in *Middlemarch* are from *The Canterbury Tales*, which Eliot notes in three separate workbooks. In her bereavement after Lewes's death, Eliot writes, into her 1879 diary, these lines from Chaucer's *Book of the Duchess* (*c*. 1370), 'Whoso seeth me first on morrow I May sayne he hath met with sorrow I For I am sorrow and sorrow is I.' To the end she still turns to Chaucer, reading the 'Prologue' to *The Canterbury Tales* to while away a 'dark' January day in 1880.   JJ

childhood, portrayal of. An early review of *The Mill on the Floss* in the *Spectator* in April 1861 drew a contrast between the naturalness of the children in George Eliot's fiction and the oddity of those in Dickens's—'Her children are healthy with flesh-and-blood rosiness, not sickly or queer' (*CH* 109)—and the figures of children in her cameos of affectionate family life, from the Bartons in *Scenes of Clerical Life* to the Garths in *Middlemarch*, could be cited as examples. But her fullest portrayal of childhood, in the first two books of *The Mill on the Floss*, is more penetrating, going beyond the simple appearance of naturalness to examine the often painful emotional and social reality of the child's world. Eliot was drawing here on her own early experience, in particular her companionship with her brother Isaac (see EVANS, ISAAC), which was later commemorated in the directly autobiographical 'Brother and Sister' Sonnets (see POETRY), where she presents herself as her brother's happy and loving subordinate and sees childhood in Wordsworthian terms as 'the seed to all my after good', 'the primal passionate store, I Whose shaping impulses make manhood whole' (sonnet 5).

In *The Mill on the Floss* the narrator adopts a similar stance, maintaining that the thoughts and loves of their early years would always be a part of Maggie's and Tom's lives, and reflecting on childhood in idealizing terms that approach the sentimental: 'We could never have loved the earth so well if we had had no childhood in it,—if it were not the earth where the same flowers come up again every spring that we used to gather with our tiny fingers as we sat lisping to ourselves on the grass' (*MF* 1.5). Although this vision of lisping innocence matches some of Eliot's earlier child figures, such as Mrs Poyser's insufferably ingratiating Totty in *Adam Bede*, it bears little relation to the actual experiences of Maggie in the novel. Set apart by her intelligence, her looks, and her temperament, she is a child not comfortably at home in the world but painfully at odds with it; and unhappiness is her most common emotion. George Eliot's ability to enter into the child's mental processes, which the *Spectator* review praised, can be seen in her grasp of the complex mechanisms of Maggie's reaction to this unhappiness: retreating, for instance, to the attic where she frets out all her ill humours talking aloud to the floors, shelves,

and rafters, and where she keeps the wooden doll that she punishes for her own misfortunes by driving nails into its head (*MF* 1.4). Her defiant acts of cutting off her hair and running away to the gypsies are further impulsive attempts to compensate for unhappiness and humiliation.

This psychological insight into unconscious mechanisms of defence and compensation is accompanied by an understanding of how childhood is shaped by the pressures and prejudices of the adult world it anticipates. Maggie's subordinate role as the younger sister of a domineering brother defines her lasting predicament in a male-dominated society where, in the brutal words of lawyer Wakem, 'We don't ask what a woman does—we ask who she belongs to' (*MF* 6.8). Even Tom's feelings of brotherly affection are ironically exposed as assuming her perpetual subservience: 'Still, he was very fond of his sister, and meant always to take care of her, make her his housekeeper, and punish her when she did wrong' (*MF* 1.5). The astringency of this kind of ironic insight qualifies the idealizing reflections of the narrator and makes this novel George Eliot's most searching portrayal of childhood. See also FAMILY LIFE, PORTRAYAL OF.   JMR

Coveney, Peter, *The Image of Childhood* (1967).

Chilvers Coton, Nuneaton, is 'Shepperton' in *Scenes of Clerical Life*. Mary Ann Evans was born in the parish and baptized in November 1819 by Revd Ebdell (the model for Mr Gilfil). The 1830s curate Revd Gwyther was the original of Revd Amos Barton.

George Eliot's first words of published fiction are 'Shepperton Church'. She worshipped there until she was 21 and described it fully in *Scenes*.

Her parents, infant brothers, and her brother Isaac are buried in the churchyard. The 13th-century church was bombed in 1941 and rebuilt in 1946–7; the tower, with 'its intelligent eye, the clock' (*SC* 1.1) survived, however.   KA

Christianity was the faith George Eliot grew up in and then rejected, while continuing to respect its ethical teaching and cultural importance. In her adolescence she was an ardent evangelical Christian, practising asceticism, despising worldly pleasures, and wanting to live only for eternity (*L* i. 7). But by the age of 22 she had come to question this early faith, and in January 1842 she refused to accompany her father to church because she no longer believed in the basis of Christianity. Her reading of biblical criticism like that of Charles Christian *Hennell led her to see the Bible not as divine revelation but as mingled truth and fiction, a view that was reinforced by her translation of D. F. *Strauss's *Das Leben Jesu* as *The Life of Jesus* (1846). Her later reading of Ludwig *Feuerbach, whose *Das Wesen des Christenthums* she translated as *The Essence of Christianity* (1854), encouraged her in an anthropological view of the Christian religion as a projection of what is highest in human nature. 'The idea of God', as she was later to write, 'is the idea of a goodness entirely human' (*L* vi. 98). In her 1855 essay *'Evangelical Teaching: Dr Cumming' she was scathing about the absence of genuine charity in the evangelical version of Christianity, and she was always critical of any doctrine, such as the idea of personal immortality, which turned attention away from the needs and suffering of one's fellow men (Paris 1965: 112). By 1859, however, she could claim that she had lost all antagonism to religious faith and that, although she had not returned to Christianity, she valued it highly: 'I see in it the highest expression of the religious sentiment that has yet found its place in the history of mankind, and I have the profoundest interest in the inward life of sincere Christians in all ages' (*L* iii. 231). She was then writing *The Mill on the Floss* where that interest can be seen in the inspiration Maggie Tulliver finds in Thomas à *Kempis, whose *The Imitation of Christ* is described as 'a lasting record of human needs and human consolations' (*MF* 4.3). It was for such records that she treated all the great religions as 'objects of deep reverence and sympathy' (*L* v. 447–8). See also ANGLICANISM; EVANGELICALISM; METHODISM; RELIGION; ROMAN CATHOLICISM; UNITARIANISM.   JMR

Paris (1965).

Church of England. See ANGLICANISM.

Clark, Andrew (1826–93), Scottish physician recommended to George Eliot and G. H. *Lewes by his friend John Walter *Cross, first called to examine them in December 1873. Clark was in the Royal Navy (1846–53), then at London Hospital, and was admitted to the Royal College of Physicians in 1854. In 1866 he became Gladstone's doctor, acquiring other celebrated patients, and in 1867 moved his large practice to Cavendish Square. Eliot first described him as one 'who ministers to all the brain-workers' (*L* vi. 23) and by May 1874 Lewes was calling him 'St. Andrew' (*L* vi. 50). When Eliot suffered a series of painful 'renal' attacks from 1874 on, both valued his attention, which included instructing Lewes on his methods of examination (*L* vi. 355). They met him socially as well at the Cross family home. Asking him to call on Lewes, Eliot assured him that even 'if there is no prescription but patience, the sight of you and the sound of your voice will strengthen the patience', addressing him as an 'angel of Mercy' (*L* xi. 186). On 22 December 1880 her 'dear Physician' (*L* ix. 268) was with her at 6p.m. She died four hours later. See also HEALTH.   JJ

Clarke, Edward (1809–52), surgeon who married George Eliot's sister Chrissey (see EVANS, CHRISTIANA) in 1837. Like Lydgate in *Middlemarch* he experienced difficulties as a newcomer in the local medical profession, starting a small practice at Meriden near Coventry which never flourished. He was declared bankrupt in 1845 and died in 1852 leaving his wife with six children and little money to support them.   JMR

Clarke, Mrs Edward. See EVANS, CHRISTIANA.

class, as a theme. George Eliot's view of the function of art as the extension of sympathy, set out in her essay on 'The *Natural History of German Life', implies that fiction should seek to overcome class divisions by 'linking the higher classes with the lower' (*Essays*, 270) rather than explore their dramatic potential. The appeal for sympathy tends to obscure the real differences between the classes (Dentith 1986: 52–3), which are not a central concern of her fiction. Class conflict is not a subject congenial to her imagination and when she deals with it directly, as in *Felix Holt, the Radical*, her treatment is evasive. Felix himself is presented as superior to, and remote from, the working class he is supposed to represent, while that class as a whole is only ever seen in its collective action as a mob. The effect is to assimilate Felix to the middle class and to abandon larger questions of class relationship in favour of the resolution of private problems. The novel comes down against radical political reform, and its essential conservatism is spelt out in the subsequent *'Address to Working Men, by Felix Holt', which argues that society cannot be improved by 'any attempt to do away directly with the actually existing class divisions and advantages' (*Essays*, 421).

Class tensions and conflicts are more effectively dramatized in those novels where they are not the central issue but arise out of intense personal relationships and rivalries. In *Adam Bede* Adam's fist fight with Arthur Donnithorne over his relationship with Hetty Sorrel brings to the surface and challenges the class hierarchy of Hayslope. Adam's words after the fight—'I don't forget what's owing to you as a gentleman, but in this thing we're man and man, and I can't give up' (*AB* 28)—are more appropriate than he realizes, for he has in one sense just given Arthur what is owing to him as an irresponsible gentleman, one who has exploited his class position to seduce Hetty. It is the psychology of Arthur's class that has allowed him to treat her casually, on the firm assumption that 'No gentleman, out of a ballad, could marry a farmer's niece' (*AB* 13). In *Silas Marner* Godfrey Cass's attempt to redeem his past neglect by adopting Eppie from Silas leads to another confrontation of classes in which the assumptions and irresponsibility of the gentry are exposed and challenged. Godfrey's fear that Eppie might marry 'some low working man' is met by her robust defence of the class she has grown up in: 'I like the working-folks and their victuals, and their ways. And . . . I'm promised to marry a working-man, as 'll live with father, and help me to take care of him' (*SM* 19).

Despite these moments of dramatic confrontation, Eliot's early novels tend to naturalize and universalize the values of the middle class and consolidate middle-class hegemony (Homans, 156). Adam Bede the carpenter develops unobtrusively into the owner of a business and the manager of an estate, and the Epilogue presents a tableau of his and Dinah's prosperous domesticity that can be read as an image of the Victorian 'middle-class family triumphant' projected back on to 1807 (Homans, 158). Nevertheless, there are always occasions, even in the early work, when Eliot ironically exposes the limitations of middle-class attitudes to class and gives a glimpse of a world her fiction rarely enters. In 'Amos Barton' the troublesome district that is Amos's parish is seen from his limited perspective as one where, 'over and above the rustic stupidity furnished by the farm-labourers, the miners brought obstreporous animalism, and the weavers an acrid Radicalism and Dissent': but this view is qualified by a glimpse through the window of every other cottage, 'where you might see a pale, sickly-looking man or woman pressing a narrow chest against a board, and doing a sort of treadmill work with legs and arms' (*SC* 1.2). In *Middlemarch* Dorothea Brooke looks out from her luxurious shelter at emblematic figures of labour and endurance from whom she can draw strength and inspiration, but at the same time this glimpse of the rural poor defines the limits and the privileges of her own position (*MM* 80). And in *Daniel Deronda*, which presents a scathing indictment of upper-class arrogance in the figure of Grandcourt, even Deronda himself is shown up in an ironic aside as the beneficiary of class privilege when he indulges in his characteristic contemplation: he is one of those 'young men in whom the unproductive labour of questioning is sustained by three or five per cent on capital which somebody else has battled for' (*DD* 17). Such moments of insight give a sharper critical edge to a fiction that is not centrally concerned with class relationships. See also POLITICS; SOCIETY.   JMR

Dentith (1986).
Eagleton, Mary, and Pierce, David, *Attitudes to Class in the English Novel* (1979).
Homans, Margaret, 'Dinah's Blush, Maggie's Arm: Class, Gender and Sexuality in George Eliot's Early Novels', *Victorian Studies*, 36 (1993).

classical literature. Debarred by her sex from 'the Eleusinian mysteries of a University education' (*SC* 1.2), George Eliot was essentially self-taught in the classical languages—a formidable achievement (see LANGUAGES). The Romantic age, followed by the Victorian, had shifted the focus of attention on the ancient world from Rome to Greece, and she inherited that taste: Latin literature seems to have meant little to her, but Greek was a lifelong passion. *Silas Marner* is the only one of her novels which can be printed without the use of a Greek font. Her keenest engagement was with the tragic playwrights *Aeschylus, *Sophocles (her favourite), and *Euripides (see TRAGEDY). Many of her allusions to Greek tragedies in her novels express her understanding of them as psychological dramas depicting the way in which the actions of human beings are shaped both by their own past actions and by the compelling pressures exerted on them by the society around them. She also recurrently used references to Greek tragedy as a means of both likening and contrasting her own subject matter, the everyday joys and sorrows of ordinary people, with the glamour of heroic drama. Thus in *The Mill on the Floss* Aristotle's discussion of tragedy is used to cast a light both humorous and poignant on the passions of Maggie Tulliver as a little girl (*MF* 1.10)

After the tragedians, her greatest interest was in *Homer. She considered the *Iliad* a 'semi-savage poem' (*L* iv. 424), and supported the German scholar F. A. Wolf's argument that the Homeric epics were the products of many authors against the belief that each was the work of a single man. This scholarly debate is broadly parodied in the account of the harvest supper in *Adam Bede* (*AB* 53). This scene, like that in *Middlemarch* in which a yokel 'shouted a defiance which he did not know to be Homeric' (*MM* 56), owes something also to the Homeric burlesques in Henry *Fielding's *Tom Jones*. There is a serious side to this, though; as with her allusions to tragedy, George Eliot is comparing and contrasting high poetry with everyday life. Similarly, the Introduction to *Felix Holt, the Radical* speaks of 'enough stories of English life . . . to make episodes for a modern Odyssey'.

Classical scholarship is a frequent subject in the novels, most conspicuously in *Romola* and *Middlemarch*. *The Mill on the Floss* gives a wittily ironic account of Tom Tulliver's classical education (*MF* 2.1). See also HORACE; VIRGIL.   RHAJ

Jenkyns, Richard, *The Victorians and Ancient Greece* (1980).
McClure, Laura, 'On Knowing Greek: George Eliot and the Classical Tradition', *Classical and Modern Literature*, 13 (1993).

Clough, Arthur Hugh (1819–61), poet with whom George Eliot was acquainted, although she came to know his wife Blanche far better following his early death. G. H. *Lewes, in an article on Clough in the *Contemporary Review* (1862) after his death, took the conventional, imperceptive view of him as a man of high promise who achieved little, and he singled out an indifferent poem, 'Qua Cursum Ventus', as an example of his best work, although conceding that there was considerable promise in *The Bothie of Tober-na-Vuolich* (1848). Whether George Eliot appreciated *The Bothie* and Clough's other great poem 'Amours de Voyage' (1858), is open to doubt, since the classical metres in which they are written were something she expressly objected to when she reviewed his friend Matthew *Arnold's poetry in the *Westminster Review*. Nevertheless there were unperceived affinities between her and Clough, who was her exact contemporary. Both writers responded enthusiastically to the *revolutions of 1848, Eliot from a distance in Coventry while Clough was able to see things at first hand, in Paris in the summer of 1848 and in Rome the following year. Subsequently both of them took up a stance that can best be described as realistic in acknowledging the recalcitrance of existing conditions and of the writer's obligation to uncomfortable and unflattering truth—a draft passage to that effect at the end of 'Amours de Voyage' closely resembles the observations on artistic truthfulness made by the narrator of *Adam Bede* (*AB* 17).

JMR

Coleridge, Samuel Taylor (1772–1834), Romantic poet and critic. Coleridge's most obvious influence on George Eliot is through his poem 'The Rime of the Ancient Mariner'. There is clearly a connection between the eponymous hero of *Silas Marner* and Coleridge's Mariner as the name suggests. Marner is associated with 'wandering men': 'the remnants of a disinherited race . . . one of these alien-looking men' who 'rarely stirred abroad without that mysterious burden' (*SM* 1). But though such imagery links Marner with Wandering Jew figures such as the Ancient Mariner, George Eliot makes it clear that her character has firm social roots. Marner's 'mysterious burden' is not the consequence of some sin committed in the past but contains the materials for practising his trade as a weaver. The language and symbols of early Romanticism thus express the dehumanizing effect of the Industrial Revolution. In *Adam Bede* also George Eliot draws on Coleridge's poem in describing Hetty Sorrel's wanderings after she has abandoned her baby. E. S. Shaffer has argued that George Eliot is part of a wider Coleridgean mythological tradition of writing. See also ROMANTICISM.

KMN

Shaffer (1975).

Collins, Wilkie (1824–89), English novelist. In a journal entry of 10 November 1858 (*Journals*, 75) George Eliot records her approval of Collins's 'sturdy uprightness'. He dined with her and G. H. *Lewes (and others) in October 1859 (*L* iii. 178) at a time when Charles *Dickens was trying to persuade her to contribute a novel to *All the Year Round*. This was just prior to the serial run of *The Woman in White* (November 1859–August 1860). Catherine Peters, in *The King of Inventors: A Life of Wilkie Collins* (1991), suggests that Marian Halcombe in Collins's novel may derive physically from Eliot (217). Collins was on good terms with Eliot and Lewes, frequently attending their Saturday evenings, and on one occasion told Eliot a story about Edward *Bulwer-Lytton's *A Strange Story* (1861–2) which she retailed to Sara *Hennell (*L* iii. 468). Lewes and Eliot found *No Name* (1862–3) somewhat depressing when they read it aloud as it appeared. Lewes told John *Blackwood in June 1866 that when they went abroad they overheard a fellow passenger saying how much she liked Wilkie Collins, but deplored the fact that Adam Bede had gone into politics (a glancing reference to *Felix Holt*). There is a practical note from Lewes to Blackwood in May 1877 which mentions Collins among others as selling his novels at 6 shillings, and suggesting that surely Eliot therefore may expect to do the same.

GRH

colonialism. There is a marked ambivalence in George Eliot's views on British colonial expansion and the imperialist discourses that were increasingly necessary to underwrite British colonialism as the 19th century wore on. On the one hand, in her letters and essays George Eliot was occasionally highly critical of British claims to superiority over other peoples. For example, in her well-known letter of 29 October 1876 to Harriet Beecher *Stowe, she said that the British 'spirit of arrogance and contemptuous dictatorialness' towards 'all oriental peoples . . . has become a national disgrace to us' (*L* vi. 301). On the other hand, she maintained a conspicuous silence at key moments of imperial crisis, even when the majority of her fellow intellectuals in Britain were roused to action. This was most notable during the so-called Indian Mutiny of 1857 and the controversy over Governor Eyre's suppression of the Morant Bay rebellion in Jamaica in 1865—the latter example is all the more striking because at the time of the debate George Eliot was engaged in an extended correspondence with Frederic *Harrison over the legal plot of *Felix Holt* while Harrison was simultaneously one of the leading activists on the Jamaica Committee set up by John Stuart *Mill to prosecute Eyre for 'high crimes and misdemeanours'. Silence and complacency about the empire were of course characteristic marks of Victorian Britain (at least until the 1880s), but the fact that George Eliot had remarkably little to say even about these instances of imperial excess might be read as evidence of her tacit approval of the British 'civilizing mission'.

Her ambivalence receives its clearest expression in *Daniel Deronda* and in 'The Modern Hep! Hep! Hep!' (*TS* 18). *Deronda* counters European persecution of the Jews—an 'oriental people', for George Eliot—by endorsing the establishment of a Jewish nation in Palestine (see JUDAISM); but it can only do this by envisioning Israel on the model of European colonial projects, with 'the total absence of any thought about the actual inhabitants of the East, Palestine in particular' (Said, 65). In 'The Modern Hep!', Theophrastus applauds the 'brave and steadfast men of Jewish race who fought and died . . . to resist the oppression and corrupting influences of foreign tyrants' (*TS* 18); and the characterization of the English as 'a colonizing people . . . who have punished others' raises the possibility of sympathy for the colonized who would likely see the English as 'foreign tyrants'. However, Theophrastus never goes this far, despite a passing reference to 'the Hindoos' who 'have doubtless had their rancours against us'. Instead, the anti-imperial resistance of the Jews is assimilated to the tradition of English liberalism: the brave and steadfast Jews who resisted foreign tyranny turn out to be the political and spiritual forebears of the valiant Englishmen 'who resisted the oppressive acts of our native kings, and by resisting rescued or won for us the best part of our civil and religious liberties'. Ultimately, and paradoxically, George Eliot takes Theophrastus' romantic Jewish anti-colonialism and makes it an integral part of a liberal English tradition that relied, economically and socially, on British colonialism for its success. See also CRITICISM, MODERN: POSTCOLONIAL APPROACHES; NATIONALISM; RACE.

TW

Said, Edward W., *The Question of Palestine* (1980).

Combe, George (1788–1858), phrenologist who had a particular interest in penal reform and education (see PHRENOLOGY). He first met George Eliot at the home of Charles *Bray in 1851. He considered her extraordinary, examined her head, finding that she had 'a very large brain; the anterior lobe is remarkable for length, breadth, and height'. He thought she looked 40 (she was in fact 32), noted her delicate health, but felt she had 'great analytic power and an instinctive soundness of judgment'. He added, 'she appeared to me the ablest woman whom I have seen' (*L* viii. 27). Eliot's correspondence with Combe and his wife during the period of their friendship reveals her

editorial astuteness as practical editor for the *Westminster Review*: on the personal level she confides in them and appears to enjoy their invitations and trust. Combe felt that John *Chapman was an unreliable businessman, and this calls forth Eliot's tact and diplomacy. Combe's reaction when he learned that she was living with G. H. *Lewes was one of horror. A tetchy correspondence with Charles Bray culminates in his suspecting insanity in her family, for him the only explanation of her conduct, which had defied the definitions of phrenology.

GRH

composition, method of. On a typical working day George Eliot wrote in the mornings, taking a walk in the afternoons, reading—sometimes aloud to G. H. *Lewes—in the evenings. Many of her statements about her working habits emphasize the need for careful preparation: according to Emily *Davies, writing on 21 August 1869:

Whatever she has done, she has studied for. Before she began to write the Mill on the Floss, she had it all in her mind, and read about the Trent to make sure that the physical conditions of some English river were such as to make the inundation possible, and assured herself that the population in its neighbourhood was such as to justify her picture. (*L* viii. 466)

This statement demonstrably applies to most of George Eliot's writing, though her use of *The Mill on the Floss* as her example is a little disingenuous given the extent to which she was drawing on childhood memories and family history in that work as she had done in *Scenes of Clerical Life* and *Adam Bede* (the composition of these two works is described in *'How I came to write Fiction' and 'History of "Adam Bede"'). Certainly she undertook prodigious research for *Romola*; but she also consulted with Frederic *Harrison about points of law in *Felix Holt, the Radical*, and studied the history of medicine and Reform Bill politics for *Middlemarch*, and Jewish matters for *Daniel Deronda*. Her working *notebooks show how she developed plot outlines and otherwise premeditated her fiction. She also commented in 1859, '*Re*writing is an excellent process frequently both for the book and its author' (*L* iii. 53); other letters bear out her belief in the need to revise.

Yet George Eliot espoused an essentially Romantic concept of artistic creation as dependent on imagination and the unconscious (see ROMANTICISM). Through his work on the process of composition of *Middlemarch*, especially the planning and execution of chapter 81, Jerome Beaty definitively tested her claims to write best in a state of inspiration or possession. He traces her hesitations about the point at which to introduce the momentous scene between Dorothea and Rosamond, and about the actual content of that scene, as well as tracking her emendations while writing, rereading, and proofing: 'She changed a word, a phrase, a sentence, or a passage. She added passages on the backs of pages. She re-wrote whole pages, groups of consecutive pages. She made changes in every stage of writing and of almost ever possible extent' in 'a process of evolution and discovery' (122–3). Even a brief study of plans, manuscripts (see MANUSCRIPT COLLECTIONS), and printed versions of other works supports the extension of these conclusions: George Eliot modified her original conception in numerous ways in the process of writing.

George Eliot's frequent ailments, except perhaps for headaches, were not generally attributable to the physical process of writing, for which she sometimes used a writing board on her lap. It is not clear whether the facility attributed to her in 1851 by Herbert *Spencer lasted into later life: 'I remember being struck with her great rapidity in writing—far exceeding my own. She wrote at that time a very much larger and more masculine hand than that given as a sample in Mr. Cross's life of her: a hand of something like double the size and more sweeping in character' (*An Autobiography*, 2 vols. (1904), i. 393).   MAH

Beaty, Jerome, *'Middlemarch' from Notebook to Novel: A Study of George Eliot's Creative Method* (1960).

Comte, Auguste (1798–1857) French philosopher, founder of *positivism. G. H. *Lewes and John Stuart *Mill were among his earliest English supporters, and George Eliot read his work in the early 1850s. Comte was an atheist, basing his philosophy initially on strictly scientific principles. Later, however, under the influence of Clotilde de Vaux, with whom he was idealistically in love, he endorsed 'the subjective method' and proposed a positivist social order of a distinctly conservative character linked to an internationally organized *religion of humanity.

Lewes met and corresponded with Comte in the 1840s, addressing him as '*Mon cher maître*', and fervently endorsing his reactionary views on women (Wright 1986: 52). In Lewes's *A Biographical History of Philosophy* (1846), Comte is described as seeing 'the causes of our intellectual anarchy, and . . . the cure' (245). Lewes's *Comte's Philosophy of the Sciences* (1853) is cooler about the social doctrine, which is also rejected in the 1857 edition of the *Biographical History*. Later George Eliot encouraged Lewes to treat Comte's 'polity' 'as a utopia, presenting hypotheses rather than doctrines' (*Fortnightly Review*, NS 3 (1866), 404). The updated history of 1867 is entitled *The History

of Philosophy from Thales to Comte*, and the posthumous *Problems of Life and Mind*, edited by George Eliot, is 'permeated with Positivism' (Wright 1986: 58).

There is disagreement about Comte's influence on George Eliot herself. An early anonymous account of her work, *George Eliot Moralist and Thinker* (1884), analyses Comte's influence in detail, along with that of *Spencer and others. John *Morley agreed (*Critical Miscellanies* (1886), iii. 107); and the subsequent decline in her reputation had much to do with her alleged adherence to outmoded ideas such as positivism. The restoration of her standing saw a downplaying of Comte's influence, notably by F. R. *Leavis and Gordon S. *Haight.

She was already familiar with Comte's leading ideas when she reviewed R. W. Mackay's *The Progress of the Intellect* for the *Westminster Review* in 1851. In 1852 she served as trustee of the fund for publishing Harriet *Martineau's version of *The Positivist Philosophy* (1853). She conceded positivism might be 'one-sided; but Comte was a great thinker, nevertheless' (*L* iii. 439). She quoted him as an authority to Sara *Hennell in 1852 and 1853 (*L* ii. 54, 129). The *Politique positive* was among the 'deep draughts' of her reading in December 1863 (*L* iv. 119). She assured Frederic *Harrison in 1866 that in *Romola* she had tried to represent 'some out of the normal relations'—an explicitly Comtist formulation (*L* iv. 300); and she wrote to Maria *Congreve of her gratitude for 'the illumination Comte has contributed to my life' (*L* iv. 333). Between 1868 and 1871 she recorded reading Comte's *Lettres . . . à M. Valat*, and his *Système de politique positive* in her diary (*Jounals*, 141, 133) and transcribed the positivist liturgical calendar in a notebook. Another notebook (see *Some Notebooks*, ed. Baker, iii (1984)) contains notes on the English translation of the *Système* (1875–7), which she and John Walter *Cross read aloud together in 1880. The record is of sustained and independent interest in Comte's thought.   WM

Some George Eliot Notebooks, ed. William Baker, 4 vols. (1976–85).

Wright, T. R., *The Religion of Humanity: The Impact of Comtean Positivism in Victorian Britain* (1986).

Congreve, Richard (1818–99) and **Maria** (1846–1915), positivists. The close friendship that developed between the Congreves and George Eliot in 1859 continued to her death. When Eliot and G. H. *Lewes moved to Wandsworth in February 1859 (see HOMES), their landlord assured them that Mr Richard Congreve who lived nearby was 'a gentleman who visited with no one in the neighbourhood—which eccentric course we had declared our intention of following' (*L* iii. 16).

However, the Congreves varied their practice and called, possibly because Maria was aware that during her Coventry girlhood she had memorably met Mary Ann Evans: Maria was a daughter of John Bury, the surgeon who treated Robert *Evans during his last illness.

The Congreves had married in 1856. Richard, educated at Rugby and Oxford, resigned his Wadham fellowship in 1854 as a consequence of his conversion to *positivism and moved to London to set up a positivist community. He also studied medicine to provide an additional means of support. Dedicated to the point of fanaticism, when in 1878 Lafitte was chosen titular head of the movement Congreve split the English positivists in a quarrel with Frederic *Harrison and other leading figures.

Positivism was only one of the subjects discussed by Eliot and Lewes with the Congreves. Their familiarity is nicely conveyed in Eliot's report that 'The delightful relief of having got through the medical examination has made a young man again of *Dr.* Congreve' (10 August 1866, *L* iv. 298); and her request to Maria as *Middlemarch* took shape, 'to get me some information about provincial Hospitals, which is necessary to my imagining the conditions of my hero' (21 September 1869, *Journals*, 138).

Maria Congreve poured out her intense attraction to George Eliot in a letter from Dieppe on 1 May 1859: 'you do make such a difference to me in my rising up and lying down and in all my ways—now that I actually know you, and that you will let me love you and even give me some love too' (Haight 1968: 300). George Eliot wrote warmly in reply, noting in her journal: 'This new friend whom I have gained by coming to Wandsworth, is the chief charm of the place to me. Her friendship has the same date as the success of Adam Bede—two good things in my lot' (3 May 1859, *Journals*, 77). In July 1859, while Lewes went to visit his sons (see LEWES FAMILY) at Hofwyl, George Eliot stayed in Lucerne with the Congreves, and confided to them the secret of her authorship. Yet despite twenty years of intimacy, Eliot found herself unable to tell Maria of her impending marriage, writing on 5 May 1880: 'A great, momentous change is going to take place in my life . . . Charles [Lewes] will call on you and tell you what he can on Saturday' (*L* vii. 270)—a task Charles told Edith *Simcox he dreaded (*L* ix. 308). The next week, George Eliot wrote to Charles, 'my chief anxiety is to know that my dear Mrs. Congreve is not too much pained' (*L* vii. 277), a concern that can hardly have been due only to her awareness of Maria's adherence to the positivist position of 'perpetual widowhood', which precluded second marriages. She noted receipt of 'a loving though brief letter' on 28

May (*L* vii. 288), to which she responded—though not until 10 June—with one of the fullest explanations of her marriage that she vouchsafed: 'The whole history is something like a miracle-legend. But instead of any former affection being displaced in my mind, I seem to have recovered the loving sympathy that I was in danger of losing' (*L* vii. 296). Rosemarie Bodenheimer persuasively argues that out of her mourning George Eliot was constructing a fable of renewal akin to Silas Marner's (1994: 111–18).

The apparent guilt on Eliot's part, and hurt on Maria's, caused no estrangement. The Congreves lunched in Cheyne Walk during Eliot's brief residence there. After Eliot's death, Edith Simcox learned from Maria 'with a sort of pleasure that she had loved my Darling lover-wise too' (18 January 1881, Haight 1968: 495). See also COMTE.

MAH

Bodenheimer (1994).

Corn Laws. George Eliot probably first heard of these from her father, Robert *Evans, who, as an estate manager, would have harvested and sold grain for his employers. A staunch conservative who generally accepted the views of landowners (Haight 1968: 33), he no doubt supported the Laws. Much later, Eliot recalled them in her fiction.

The Laws were protective measures introduced by Parliament in 1815, following the cessation of the Napoleonic wars, limiting the importation of cheap, surplus European grain and thus stabilizing the price of English grain. They prevented foreign grain being sold until domestic grain reached 80 shillings a quarter. Widespread hunger and starvation, due to high costs and fluctuating annual yields, forced a modification of the Laws in 1828. A sliding-scale tariff was then introduced: imported grain could be bought once home grain reached 52 shillings, but only at a high rate of duty, which fell once the price of English grain rose.

In 1838 the Anti-Corn Law League was founded in Manchester, the result of scattered agitation by various groups interested in promoting universal free trade. One of the League's primary objectives was the repeal of the Corn Laws. A middle-class alternative to working-class Chartism, the League gave lectures, sent petitions and pamphlets, and, in 1843, helped establish *The Economist*, a weekly financial and commercial review. The League, then, played a part in the process of repealing the Laws. Its pressure, however, coincided with the reduced availability of European grain as well as improved farming methods in Britain, which meant that the Laws were no longer necessary to protect home interests. Consequently, in the autumn of 1845, when the potato blight in Ireland threatened famine, Parliament suspended the Laws. It repealed them in 1846.

In *Felix Holt, the Radical* and *Middlemarch*, Eliot remembers how poor grain yields, high prices, and the devastating effects of the Corn Laws on ordinary people contributed to demands for political reform. There are references to disturbances or riots involving rick-burning and machine breaking in *Felix Holt* (Introduction) and *Middlemarch* (3), acts of protest usually perpetrated by hungry or starving people. Eliot's notebook, the so-called 'Quarry for Felix Holt', also contains entries on riots in Bolton and Bristol and the state of agriculture in 1831–2, particularly corn yields in Lancaster, Leicestershire, and Northamptonshire (Yale University Library). However, as the daughter of Robert Evans, she could also look beyond the Corn Laws for related causes of misery. In chapter 3 of *Silas Marner*, for instance, the narrator makes ironic reference to 'that glorious war time' before 'the fall of [corn] prices'. Farmers' 'extravagant habits and bad husbandry' also contributed to the collapse in grain prices once war ended. The 'bad husbandry' she had in mind probably refers to the practice of enclosing 'open' fields or common land with hedgerows, which occurred a great deal between 1800 and 1815. The practice was designed to increase corn production but often succeeded in only wasting land. That particular criticism is certainly heard in *Felix Holt*: 'But everywhere the bushy hedgerows wasted the land ... shrouded the grassy borders of pastures ... tossed their long blackberry branches on the cornfields' (Introduction). See also POLITICS.

AvdB

Cornhill Magazine, The, shilling monthly which serialized *Romola* (July 1862–August 1863) and published 'Brother Jacob' (July 1864). *Cornhill* was the first phenomenally successful shilling monthly, with early circulation figures above 100,000. Edited initially by the novelist William Makepeace *Thackeray, whose prominence attracted contributors and readers, the magazine was noted for including two serial novels in each issue, with accompanying high quality woodcut illustrations. *Romola*, impressively illustrated by Frederic *Leighton, overlapped with serials by Thackeray and Anthony *Trollope (see ILLUSTRATIONS; SERIALIZATION). The publisher George *Smith of Smith, Elder & Co. was generous in payments to contributors and George Eliot was initially offered a staggering £10,000 for *Romola*, later receiving £7,000, still far above the payments received for most serial novels. *Romola* did not succeed in attracting large numbers of readers, and partly in recognition of this fact, George Eliot later gave Smith 'Brother Jacob' as a gesture of good

will. She offered Smith *Felix Holt, the Radical*, but he declined and it was published by Blackwood in 1866. G. H. *Lewes, whose series 'Studies in Animal Life' appeared in *Cornhill* (January–June 1860), served on the editorial committee after Thackeray's death in 1863. *Cornhill's* early success spawned several less substantial imitators all clamouring for the middle-class magazine reader, causing a boom in shilling monthlies in the 1860s. See also PUBLISHERS, NEGOTIATIONS WITH. MWT

Coventry played an important part in the intellectual development of George Eliot. From the age of 13 to 16 (1832–5) she was a pupil at the school in Warwick Row run by Mary and Rebecca Franklin, daughters of Revd Francis Franklin (thought to be the model for Rufus Lyon in *Felix Holt, the Radical*), minister of Cow Lane Baptist Chapel. At the school she excelled at English, French, and music.

In March 1841, at the age of 21, she moved with her newly retired father to a semi-detached house, Bird Grove, in Foleshill Road, Coventry (now in George Eliot Road and with an interior inaccessible to her admirers). Through her neighbour, Elizabeth Pears, Mary Ann was introduced to Charles and Caroline *Bray at his house, Rosehill, in Radford Road. The Brays gathered around them an intellectual circle where she met such people as Robert Owen, Dr John Conolly, James Simpson, George Dawson, W. J. Fox, George *Combe, Ralph Waldo *Emerson, and John *Chapman, bringing her from provincial isolation into a world previously unknown to her.

The stimulus at Rosehill resolved her already gnawing religious doubts and she refused to continue attending Holy Trinity church with her father (see EVANS, ROBERT) in what is known as her 'Holy War'.

When her father died in 1849 it was necessary to supplement her small income from his estate. She had written reviews and essays for the *Coventry Herald and Observer* owned by Bray; earning her living by her pen was an inevitable choice. She began a literary life in London, returning only infrequently. But she had absorbed enough of life in the city to set *Middlemarch* partially there—not in its buildings but in events such as the coming of the railway and the need for a fever hospital. She also set the trial in *Adam Bede* in St Mary's Guildhall. KA

Lynes, Alice, *George Eliot's Coventry: A Provincial Town in the 1830s and 1840s* (1970).

Coventry *Herald and Observer*, a weekly newspaper purchased by George Eliot's friend Charles *Bray in June 1846 to promote his projects for reform (Haight 1968: 61). She wrote a number of anonymous reviews for it in the autumn of 1846 (*Essays*, 452), and from December 1846 to February

Rosehill, the Coventry home of the Brays, where George Eliot was a frequent visitor until 1854 and where many eminent intellectuals were entertained in the 1840s and early 1850s.

1847 published in it her first efforts as an essayist, *'Poetry and Prose, from the Notebook of an Eccentric'. In March 1849 she reviewed J. A. *Froude's novel *The Nemesis of Faith*. JMR

Cowper, William (1731–1800), English poet, read by George Eliot at the Misses Franklin's school and greatly admired by her. In February 1839 she quotes one of the Olney Hymns (1779) ''Tis my happiness below' (*L* i. 17). After the removal to Coventry she misses 'the prolixity of shade', a phrase of his she recalled, and she later says that she carries fragments of Cowper's poetry in her mind. Another Olney Hymn, 'Walking with God', is referred to in her article on 'Evangelical Teaching: Dr Cumming' in October 1855, while in her essay on Edward *Young in the *Westminster Review* in January 1857, she refers to Cowper, by way of contrast with Young, as presenting the everyday common things of life 'truthfully and lovingly'. *The Task* (1785) is much referred to: in 'Amos Barton' 'the cups that cheer but not inebriate' is quoted, *The Mill on the Floss* (2.2) cites 'in unrecumbent sadness', and *Table Talk* gets a mention in her article 'A *Word for the Germans' in the *Pall Mall Gazette* (7 March 1865). *Impressions of Theophrastus Such* has a reference to John Gilpin (*TS* 18), and in *Daniel Deronda* there is the charming incident, via Grandcourt's dog Fetch, of Cowper's spaniel Beau retrieving a water-lily (*DD* 37). This anecdote from the much-loved poet's letters marks Cowper as having a special place in her affections. GRH

crime features in George Eliot's fiction more often as an unresolved question of intent than as actual breaking of the law. An early instance, in 'Mr Gilfil's Love-Story', is Caterina Sarti's impassioned charge towards Anthony Wybrow, dagger in hand, intent on revenge for the falsehood he has told about her, only to find him already lying dead from a heart attack. Her spirit is as completely broken as if she were indeed guilty of murdering him. A considerably more complex instance occurs in *Daniel Deronda*, when Gwendolen, who has actually secreted a knife with the intention of killing her husband Henleigh Grandcourt because of his mental cruelty, fails to save him from drowning. 'I did kill him in my thoughts . . . I saw my wish outside me' (*DD* 56), she confesses to Deronda, whose rescue of Mirah earlier in the novel when she attempts suicide by drowning provides an ironic parallel to Grandcourt's death.

George Eliot's awareness of the complexities of motivation generates many intense studies of equivocal situations where moral rather than legal guilt is at issue, especially in relation to allegations of murder. For all that Hetty Sorrel is convicted of the murder of her child by Arthur Donnithorne, the narrative does not permit easy acquiescence in the 'guilty' verdict. An analogous case is that of Felix Holt, who is convicted of manslaughter, assault, and inciting a mob to riot, though he had been trying to defuse the violence of the mob; he is eventually pardoned because of the power of the testimony of Esther Lyon to his character and motivation. In 'The Lifted Veil', Latimer foresees Bertha's intention to poison him—which is thwarted. *Middlemarch* poses the question whether Nicholas Bulstrode is guilty of the murder of Raffles, as well as of robbing Will Ladislaw of his inheritance. In Lydgate's earlier life, he has heard the actress Laure's account of murdering her husband: later, he bitterly addresses his wife Rosamond: 'He once called her his basil plant; and when she asked for an explanation, said that basil was a plant which had flourished wonderfully on a murdered man's brains' (*MM* Finale). Middlemarch is relatively speaking a hotbed of crime, ranging from blackmail (Bulstrode by Raffles, Lydgate by Bulstrode) to poaching.

Theft is the crime most often presented in the novels, and poetic justice is usually done. So after Silas Marner is falsely accused of theft by the congregation in Lantern Yard, he leaves to make a new life in the country, where Dunstan Cass steals his gold but the golden-haired Eppie materializes to bring the miserly weaver back to the warmth of community. The motif of gold coins and Nemesis appears also in 'Brother Jacob': David Faux steals from his mother but is finally brought down after many years when he is recognized by his idiot brother who associates him with golden lozenges and coins. The criminality of Tito Melema's misappropriation of the prize possessions both of his foster-father Baldassarre (gems), and of his father-in-law Bardo (library), is secondary to the moral guilt of his disloyal actions. See also LAW; MORAL VALUES; SECRECY. MAH

Welsh (1985).

Crimean war (1853–56). This arose from Russia's expansionist threat to Turkey which the latter, Britain, and France resisted. George Eliot initially refers flippantly to the situation, wishing her unpleasant cough on the Russian Emperor Nicholas (*L* ii. 143), but she wrote to John *Chapman from *Berlin in December 1854 (war had been declared on 28 March) expressing anxiety about it but adding that 'The sympathies of the people here seem to be entirely with the Allies' and taking some pride in the truthfulness of English reportage of the campaign (L viii. 132). From Dover she wrote to Charles *Bray in April 1855 deploring the effects of the conjunction of the war and the severe winter on trade for the Coventry workers (*L* ii. 197). Her *Ilfracombe journal includes an account of the peace celebrations there a month after the conclusion of peace on 29 April 1856 (*L* ii. 248). The span of the war coincides with the major change in Eliot's life, her cohabitation with G. H. *Lewes and the attendant personal fulfilment which facilitated her development.   GRH

criticism, modern. The critical reappraisal of George Eliot that began in the late 1940s with the work of Joan Bennett and F. R. *Leavis (see REPU-TATION, CRITICAL) concentrated mainly on the moral vision of her novels and their thematic and formal coherence. Amidst these demonstrations and celebrations of unity and moral purpose a dissonant note was struck by critics whose approach was influenced by Marxism. From Arnold Kettle in his *Introduction to the English Novel* (1951), through Raymond Williams in *Culture and Society* (1958), *The English Novel from Dickens to Lawrence* (1970), and *The Country and the City* (1973), to Terry Eagleton's *Criticism and Ideology* (1976), such criticism directed its attention to the contradictions and discontinuities in the fiction relating them to the predicament and the limitations of the bourgeois writer. For Kettle, analysing *Middlemarch* in terms of antitheses that fail to be dialectically related, Eliot is a mechanistic thinker who can see no possibility of changing society and thus takes refuge in idealism. Williams, despite his admiration for the seriousness of Eliot's purpose and the force of her intelligence, identifies a contradiction in the form of the novel as she received and developed it: its moral emphasis on individual conduct is at odds with its representation of social life, creating a break in the texture of the novel, a discontinuity between the analytic idiom of the novelist and the language of her characters, and a narrowing focus on isolated individuals separate from society at large. For Eagleton Eliot's fiction seeks to resolve a conflict between two forms of Victorian ideology: a Romantic individualist ideology of the free spirit on the one hand, and the corporate ideologies of Feuerbachian humanism and scientific rationalism on the other. This intractable conflict is not confronted directly but repressed and recast into ideologically resolvable terms, so that the problem of history in *Middlemarch* is reduced to an ethical problem of egoism and its overcoming, while in *Daniel Deronda* resolution of the ideological contradiction is only achieved by magical means that transcend *realism.

Eagleton's analysis in particular is predicated on a dismissive notion of the bourgeois writer and conducted at a level of theoretical abstraction that inevitably elides much of the complexity and interest of the fictional texts. The best criticism on Marxist lines, like Williams's or John Goode's

essay on *Adam Bede* in Hardy (1970), which argues that the novel transforms historical realities into ideological fable, combines ideological analysis with detailed textual insight. Goode's later article on '"The Affections Clad with Knowledge": Woman's Duty and the Public Life', in *Literature and History*, 9 (1983), indicates a general trend of recent criticism by pursuing the political and ideological implications of the fiction into the realm of sexual politics. In the last twenty years the concern with ideology that was once the province of Marxist criticism has been taken up by feminist, gender-oriented, new historicist, and post-colonial approaches to George Eliot (see below).

The new theoretical impulses that have invigorated criticism in recent years have found in her fiction a rich vein of material to exploit. The psychological and emotional complexity of her work invites scrutiny in psychoanalytic terms; its engagement with the advanced thinking of her day makes it particularly responsive to new historicist analyses of discourse and intertextuality; while Eliot's sophisticated self-consciousness about language and form anticipates post-structuralist theory and acts as a stimulus to deconstruction. In the words of the narrator of *Middlemarch*, 'interpretations are illimitable' (*MM* 3), and the range and variety of interpretations opened up by recent modern criticism are indicated in the following surveys of different critical approaches. These approaches do not, of course, cover the whole range of George Eliot criticism, and there are important general studies, such as Myers (1984) and Carroll (1992), as well as specialized studies of topics like *music and the *visual arts, that do not fit into any of these categories.   JMR

Newton (1991).
Hutchinson (1996), vol. iv.

Deconstruction

Modern critical theory has tended to take a negative view of the realist novel. Roland Barthes, the most famous structuralist critic, believed that, like scientific discourse, the realist novel treated language as if it could represent reality transparently and neutrally and was thus complicit with dominant ideologies which he believed literature should seek to undermine. The classic realist in his view was Honoré de *Balzac and Barthes's work was very influential on certain British critics for whom the classic realist in the English tradition was George Eliot (see REALISM). But while British post-structuralist critics identified George Eliot with the 'classic realist text', American deconstructive criticism took a different view. Deconstruction called into question Barthes's distinction between 'readerly' texts by writers such as Balzac which limit the plurality of language and 'writerly' texts in which language functions as a play of signifiers, part of deconstruction's strategy being to problematize such oppositions. A brief characterization of deconstruction is that 'it proceeds by the careful teasing out of the warring forces of signification within the text itself' (Barbara Johnson, *The Critical Difference* (1980), 5). The leading American practitioner of deconstructive criticism, J. Hillis Miller, showed how this approach to texts could be applied to George Eliot's fiction.

Remarks such as the following from her *'Notes on Form in Art' that 'form is unlikeness ... every difference is form' (*Essays*, 422–3) and the narrator's comment in *The Mill on the Floss* that Aristotle should have lamented 'that intelligence so rarely shows itself in speech without metaphor— that we can seldom declare what a thing is, except by saying it is something else' (*MF* 2.1), suggest that she anticipates deconstructive thinking. In contrast to her British critics, Miller argues that a novel like *Middlemarch* deconstructs classic realism. In his essay 'Narrative and History', he discusses the novel's treatment of history. He contrasts George Eliot with Henry *James in relation to how they view narrative and *history. Whereas James stated that a novelist must regard himself 'as an historian and his narrative as history' (Miller 1974: 458), George Eliot in *Middlemarch* questions the 'logocentric' tradition in Western thinking which regards unity and teleology as intrinsic to narrative, whether fictional or historical. Miller states that 'The notions of narrative, of character, and of formal unity in fiction are all congruent with the system of concepts making up the Western idea of history' (1974: 461) but argues that certain novels such as *Middlemarch* which operate within the realist tradition obliquely put into question that system of concepts:

the novel, so to speak, pulls the rug from under itself and deprives itself of that solid ground without which, if Henry James is right, it is 'nowhere'. Her fiction deprives itself of its ground in history by demonstrating that ground to be a fiction too, a figure, a myth, a lie, like Dorothea's interpretation of Casaubon or Bulstrode's reading of his religious destiny. (1974: 467)

Miller's best-known essay on George Eliot, 'Optic and Semiotic in *Middlemarch*', admits that a totalizing impulse informs the novel but he argues that this impulse is destabilized in the text. For example, the pier-glass analogy which begins chapter 27 and suggests that the mind orders an essentially unordered world in the way that a candle imposes pattern on the scratches on a mirror has implications for narration. He concludes: 'This incoherent, heterogeneous, "unreadable", or non-synthesizable quality of the text of *Middlemarch*

jeopardizes the narrator's effort at totalization. It suggests that one gets a different kind of totality depending on what metaphorical model is used' (1975: 144). He believes, however, that George Eliot collaborates with the novel's deconstruction, referring to her 'insight into the dismaying dangers of metaphor' and 'her recognition of the deconstructive powers of figurative language' (see METAPHOR).

Miller's view of George Eliot as proto-deconstructionist is not shared by all deconstructive critics, however. Cynthia Chase believes George Eliot refuses to acknowledge the 'warring forces of signification' in her text. Chase argues that *Daniel Deronda* seeks to cover up a contradiction in its realistic narrative in the interests of sustaining a plot committed to the 'triumph of idealism over irony' (1978: 215). The novel's plot, she claims, is undermined since Deronda's discovery and acceptance of his Jewish identity cannot be reconciled with the demands of realism which require that he be circumcised, and if he were circumcised he would already know that he had been born a Jew, which cannot be reconciled with the plot. This argument can be objected to, however, on the grounds that it assumes that circumcision is an unambiguous sign of Jewishness, a view which fails to take account of George Eliot's position—one which is easily reconcilable with deconstructive thinking—that signs are always open to interpretation. As the narrator puts it in *Middlemarch*: 'Signs are small measurable things, but interpretations are illimitable' (*MM* 3). In Deronda's context, believing as he does that he is almost certainly Sir Hugo's illegitimate son, circumcision would not be an unambiguous sign of Jewishness.

George Eliot's connections with deconstructive thinking can be linked to her interest in 19th-century ideas which anticipate deconstruction, notably Romantic irony (see ROMANTICISM) and neo-Kantian philosophy (see PHILOSOPHY). In *Daniel Deronda*, a novel in which virtually all the main characters have Romantic aspects, Hans Meyrick is a Romantic ironist who is both idealist and sceptic, with neither position subverting the other. George Eliot's partner, G. H. *Lewes, had affinities with neo-Kantian thinking as can be seen, for example, in the view he expresses in the second volume of his *Problems of Life and Mind* that the atom, though indispensable to physicists, may not actually exist as it is 'only an artifice, by which we introduce congruity into our symbols' (*Foundations of a Creed* (1875), 317). George Eliot's connection with such thinking is suggested by the comment in the epigraph to the first chapter of *Daniel Deronda* that 'Even Science, the strict measurer, is obliged to start with a make-believe unit'.   KMN

Chase, Cynthia, 'The Decomposition of the Elephants: Double-Reading *Daniel Deronda*', *PMLA* 93 (1978).

Miller, J. Hillis, 'Narrative and History', *ELH* 41 (1974).

—— 'Optic and Semiotic in *Middlemarch*', in Jerome H. Buckley (ed.), *The Worlds of Victorian Fiction* (1975).

Feminist Approaches

The emergence of contemporary feminist criticism in the early 1970s immediately led to an encounter with George Eliot, who stood out as a luminous icon, recognized both by male critics who had constructed the 'great tradition' of the novel and by female scholars intent to revise the literary history they inherited. If she was an inevitable magnet of attention, George Eliot proved to be as much a vexing problem as a large opportunity. The changing course of feminist criticism in the last third of the 20th century is marked by strong revisions in the approach to her work.

Early feminist readings, in pursuing new enquiries into dominant literary texts and identifying new disturbances within them, asked one simple and central question that the work of George Eliot was not likely to satisfy: did the fiction participate in the broad movement of liberation that linked the courageous precursors of the mid-19th century to those who reasserted and radicalized their claim over a century later? On initial appraisal, the answer seemed no. The heroines of the novels not only failed to commit themselves to the political challenges of an emerging feminism; still more strikingly, they failed to sustain any public vocations that would free them from the tight constraints of the domestic sphere. Dinah Morris gives up her preaching; Maggie Tulliver drowns in a flood; Esther Lyon meekly submits to Felix Holt; Dorothea Brooke puts her greatness to the service of her second husband's career; and Gwendolen Harleth returns home in a spirit of resigned endurance.

A sense of betrayal can be detected in the first wave of feminist evaluation. Kate Millet regrets that Dorothea's gifts, her 'fine mind', do not lead to a proper occupation and that the claim of *Middlemarch* 'goes no further than petition' (*Sexual Politics* (1970), 139). Lee R. Edwards wrote of her painful escape from an adolescent fantasy of the novel to an understanding of the strict limits it placed on the aspirations of women. 'Angered, puzzled, and finally depressed', she deplored George Eliot's refusal to follow narrative possibilities that are broached and then abandoned: 'Madame Laure's history without her husband, the story of Dorothea as a social force, the tale of Rosamond as a political novel' ('Women, Energy and *Middlemarch*', *Massachusetts Review*, 13 (1972),

238). Millet and Edwards look for ratifying exemplars and inspiring models and find instead narratives that refuse the vision they excite, that recede from their own best insights.

Much of the frustration turned on the distance between what was seen as the revolution of George Eliot's life and the conservatism of her fiction. One who had dared to ignore the ceremonies of propriety, living with G. H. *Lewes outside marriage and therefore inside the most spectacular taboo, one who had assumed the strenuous vocation of *novelist, essayist (see JOURNALIST, GEORGE ELIOT AS), and poet (see POETRY), gave no such opportunity to her female characters. The example of her life was thus undone by the example of her fiction. Many critics pointed to this as a fateful contradiction, the charge being that the author cruelly denied not only her female characters but also the women in her audience the chances that she herself enjoyed. 'What is fatally hampering to George Eliot's heroines', wrote Patricia Beer, 'is not society, not even provincial society, but their own lack of creativity, which includes creative intellectual powers . . . George Eliot herself triumphed over greater handicaps than any of her women characters are faced with' (*Reader, I Married Him* (1974), 181). Millett had objected to the fact that George Eliot 'lived the revolution', but 'refused to write of it' (*Sexual Politics* (1970), 139). Ellen Moers represented her as fundamentally unconcerned with 'the lives of ordinary women', the problem of their inhibited lives, and the need to widen their choices (*Literary Women* (1976), 194).

Even the biographic case raised sharp difficulties. Victorian contemporaries such as Eliza Lynn *Linton and Margaret *Oliphant had complained of the dully dominating aura of the acclaimed author, who, in Oliphant's words, 'took herself with tremendous seriousness' and 'was always on duty', and in Linton's phrase, 'was so consciously George Eliot' (in Showalter 1980: 295, 294). In Elaine Showalter's characterization, the provocation of the life was that 'Eliot was reserved, inaccessible, and opaque', that in 'avoiding close friendships with other women writers' she 'violated the values of sisterly communion', that she made so much money, that she got away with the flouting of respectability, in short, that she attained a depressing superiority (1977: 107). The image inherited by modern feminist critics was thus only partly that of the marital revolutionary; it also included this older picture of the lofty sibyl, the strenuous moralist, guarded, remote, unaccommodating. Despite her personal ties to leading activists, George Eliot seemed to lack the courage of her transgressions, keeping herself aloof from the legal struggles of the 1850s and 1860s, and rather than affirm the radicalism of her romantic life, she insisted on treating it as a marriage in all but letter and on being called Mrs Lewes.

One of the consequences of ongoing feminist criticism, however, was a renewed biographical precision, a reconsideration of the life stories that had congealed into legend. The publication of the letters and the biographies by Gordon S. *Haight and Redinger unsettled the forbidding image of George Eliot as the cold male impersonator, eager to affirm her mastery of knowledge and her moral elevation. The recovery of the ardour and the anguish of the early life—the family struggles, the religious crisis, the romantic upheavals with John *Chapman and Herbert *Spencer—allowed the apparent stiffness of the late years to find its place within a far more subtle context: the sibyl of The *Priory was the late invention of a woman who had experienced passionate turbulence and who was making her choices within a limited repertoire and with few useful precedents.

Here, as in so many other areas, feminist criticism looked back to Virginia *Woolf, who in her centenary essay of 1919 had disregarded the clichés encrusting George Eliot's reputation and in a few evocative paragraphs had opened the complexity of the life and work. From the standpoint of a polemical modernism, the novels had been taken as the ponderous, unwanted legacy of an awkward age. Thus Ford Madox *Ford spoke of George Eliot as emanating the heaviness of 'a great figure' who 'dilated upon sin and its results, and so found the easy success of the popular preacher who deals in horrors'. She sought to be an influence, complained Ford, and 'cared in her heart very little whether or no she would be considered an artist' (*The Critical Attitude* (1911), 56). In the face of such characteristic dismissal, Woolf briskly satirized the masculine desire for the charming literary woman: 'George Eliot was not charming; she was not strongly feminine; she had none of those eccentricities and inqualities of temper which give to so many artists the endearing simplicity of children.' Against the modernist confidence in its summary judgements, Woolf places the tonic of bafflement: 'To read George Eliot attentively is to become aware how little one knows about her.' In the course of a few deft pages Woolf dissolves the simplicity of the portrait and retrieves the stress of life behind the composed image. George Eliot looked past the 'burden and complexity of womanhood' toward the 'strange bright fruits of art and knowledge', and yet 'she would not renounce her own inheritance—the difference of view, the difference of standard—nor accept an inappropriate reward' ('George Eliot', *Times Literary Supplement*, 20 November 1919; repr. in *Virginia Woolf: Women and Writing*, ed. Michele Barrett (1979), 152, 150, 160). Here Woolf not only recovers the fierce and strenuous labour of George Eliot's life, but she also establishes her as a necessary precursor, an indispensable ally in the invention of a female literary tradition.

Showalter began her essay on 'The Greening of George Eliot' (1980) by recalling Woolf's discussion sixty years earlier, and in celebrating Woolf's ability 'to get over all this malice, rivalry and cant, and to encounter Eliot freshly as a novelist and a woman' (295) she pointed to a clearly marked second phase in the contemporary feminist approach. She referred to an essay by Zelda Austen called 'Why Feminist Critics are Angry with George Eliot' (*College English*, 1976), which could now be recognized as a beginning of the turn. Austen had taken biting issue with the assumptions governing the earlier interpretations that asked literature 'to provide better models for women' (551); and she had called on feminist critics to pay attention to style and structure, insisting that they ought to admire and to love George Eliot's achievement, not resent it. Acknowledging what a difficult case George Eliot had made for feminists of the 1970s, Showalter endorses Austen's rebuttal of the 'polemics of this early phase'. Much as Woolf contested the reputation of the dull and stagnating sibyl, so contemporary critics should mark a comparable change of view: 'No longer a distant and powerful mother, she has been brought closer by time as an imperfect, impulsive, and attractive sister whose conflicts and choices prefigure modern women's emergent selves' (Showalter 1980: 309, 299). Guided by the example of modern novelists who have seen George Eliot as a living presence, critics should recognize that 'her demystification as the superior woman, above pain, conflict, and compromise, has led to a firmer acceptance of her sisterhood with all other women'.

The influential readings offered by Sandra M. Gilbert and Susan Gubar in *The Madwoman in the Attic* (1979) suggest how this second phase of feminist demystification came to inform the tasks of ambitious interpretation. 'We are unaccustomed to think of Eliot exploring the secret, self-enclosed, and ravaged place of her own self', note Gilbert and Gubar, as they develop elaborate arguments for the place of self-division, frustration, and rage within the fiction. To the significant extent that George Eliot internalized patriarchal values and accepted prevailing conventions, she experienced the contradictions of a self-loathing that could only be resolved by narrative violence. Behind the 'insistent rhetoric of renunciation', the novels perform such aggressive actions as Hetty's infanticide, Baldassarre's murder of Tito, or Mirah's attempted suicide, and even for characters kept free from such violence (such as Romola, Dorothea, Gwendolen), the author recruits the power of

Nemesis to destroy the male oppressors (Gilbert and Gubar 1979: 477, 498).

Once seen as the great celebrant of female *renunciation, George Eliot now appears as a turbulent and contradictory figure, whose renouncing heroines often incite fantasies of revolt that guide the plot of her novels from their subterranean position. Gilbert and Gubar show how resistance to men threads its way through the oeuvre, from the cry in 'Janet's Repentance'—'You knew what brutes men could be'—to Mrs Transome's assertion that 'men are selfish and cruel', to Gwendolen Harleth's despairing claim that 'all men are bad, and I hate them'. Without denying the prominence of the renouncing women, *The Madwoman in the Attic* seeks to demonstrate that self-submission conceals a far more complex set of attitudes: 'Eliot does not countenance female renunciation because she believes it to be appropriately feminine, but because she is intensely aware of the destructive potential of female rage. Thus she simultaneously demonstrates the necessity of renouncing anger and the absolute impossibility of doing so' (Gilbert and Gubar 1979: 513). In this view, the moralizing energies of the novel, traditionally seen as the mark of a conservatism or even a complacency, now appear as defensive reactions to transgressive emotions.

In the period since the revisions marked by Showalter and the speculative challenge mounted by Gilbert and Gubar, feminist criticism of George Eliot has insisted on the radically complex character of the novels, their bracingly subtle legacy, and their resistance to simple critical judgement. Gillian Beer notes pointedly that any theories 'which result in blame for the most creatively achieving of women' must themselves be questioned. Beer's emphasis falls on the novelist's refusal to follow a feminist model which 'so overvalued aspiration as misleadingly to set aside difficulty'. The priority of the myth of Antigone, suggests Beer, demonstrates the intractable force of the problem, for 'Antigone like George Eliot, is a law-breaker with a profound respect for law' (1986: 6, 48, 43).

The high regard for traditional forms in George Eliot's fiction has not been ignored in the more recent work; rather it has been placed in dynamic relationship to resisting tones and unaccommodated emotions such as anger, ambition, revolt. In *The Real Life of Mary Ann Evans* Rosemary Bodenheimer has pointed out how certain literary contexts, such as the poems, allow for more 'direct expression' of 'volcanic feeling', and while the larger structure of the novels never follows 'positively feminist principles', the texts contain resonant moments when challenges can be strongly uttered. The 'feminist voice may be clearly heard', writes Bodenheimer, 'when it opposes a voiced

and represented patriarchal argument' (1994: 182, 181); her examples are the Prelude in *Middlemarch* and the educational critique in *The Mill on the Floss*.

The burden of the last decade of feminist criticism has been to defer judgement and to engage the irresolution that George Eliot herself felt on the *woman question. Gillian Beer notes that the value of experience for her characters 'is measured by the power to sustain puzzlement and to acknowledge passionate feeling' (1986: 38), and that the narrative goal was not to resolve dilemmas but to persist in an endless questioning of women's fate. It can be said that the unfolding history of feminist criticism has been precisely the history of a puzzlement, a refusal to accept the settled judgements of an earlier stage of thought, and a willingness to live up to the agitations of the fiction. KC

Beer (1986).
Bodenheimer (1994).
Gilbert and Gubar (1979).
Showalter (1977).
—— 'The Greening of Sister George', *Nineteenth-Century Fiction*, 35 (1980).

Gender Studies

Since the start of her writing life George Eliot has engaged the gender-awareness of critics, from those who try to make her into a figure who is 'either irredeemably, charmingly "feminine" or transcendently without sex or gender' (David, 172) to those who try to enlist her in the service of either sexual radicalism or conservatism. Though the term *'gender' itself only received a fully theorized critical status relatively recently, the differentiations of a gendered way of thinking are present in the earliest responses to Eliot's life and work. Eliot's obituaries are particularly concerned to examine the gender implications of a woman who could produce work of such intellectual and moral authority. Mrs *Oliphant responded in 1885 by trying to restore a corrective gender balance by suggesting that G. H. *Lewes was primarily responsible for initiating Eliot's fictional writing: 'Would she have carried her genius like an unlighted lamp to the grave with her had not her little Sultan struck the spark that was to throw its light over half a world?' (*Edinburgh Review*, 161: 540).

The legacy of such thinking can be seen in Haight who reiterates 19th-century thinking about Eliot's perpetually needing someone stronger to lean on. More recent feminist critics have been quick to take issue with the suppositions underlying such responses, and have been concerned to separate George Eliot the woman from George Eliot the writer (see Ashton, *George Eliot: A Life*, 1996), seeking for her work an independent space free from, or at least not entirely fettered by, some of the gender considerations which determined women's lives in the Victorian period.

Modern responses to Eliot are determined in large part by the sense that, as a writer, she is enabled to interrogate, as well as partially to be defined by, her society's gender beliefs. As Gillian Beer puts it, 'In the case of George Eliot we have a striking example of a writer who sought to slough off the contextuality of her own name and enter a neutral space for her writing' (1986: 25). The very act of choosing her pseudonym is itself an acknowledgement of her 'ambivalent and anxious relationship to patriarchal authority' (Boumelha, 16), and its maintenance alongside the range of other names by which Eliot was known means that the reader is perpetually confronted with the difficulties of Eliot's position as a woman writer at the time.

Beer suggests that although Eliot writes as a woman, her writing takes the 'full measure of human experience' and that a refusal to be bound solely to women's issues is an assertion of the scope and authority of Eliot's writing persona (1986: 17–18). Simon Dentith similarly interrogates the connotations of Eliot's adopting male narrators in some of her early works (see NARRATION), connotations which, taken alongside her *pseudonym, seem deliberately to set out to confound her society's expectations of the woman writer (Dentith 1986: 113). As Gilbert and Gubar note, in *The Madwoman in the Attic* (1979: 523), 'the narrator presents her/himself as so far above and beyond the ordinary classifications of our culture that s/he transcends gender distinctions'.

The figure of the artist in Eliot's work, and the gender implications of characters such as Armgart (see POETRY OF GEORGE ELIOT) and Alcharisi in *Daniel Deronda* have been central topics of much gender-based criticism of Eliot in recent years. In these figures, Eliot investigates the lures of performance for women who seek glory and acclaim rather than give in to the demand that they should marry, and who, in Alcharisi's case, use art to 'defend the "right" of her talent against the ghost of the father she defied' (Bodenheimer 1990: 2). Through them, critics such as Bonnie J. Lisle suggest, we can see something of Eliot's own sense of her own 'peculiar struggle' as both an artist and a woman (Lisle, 275). In Eliot's work, however, the arts are not a resource which serve the cause of gender-rebels, whose rebellions end in defeat. Rather Eliot advocates an artistry which defies such egoism. Mirah Cohen in *Deronda* is Eliot's exemplary female artist, using her voice as a link to unite generations, in the process of which she herself becomes submissive to her art.

The redemption of such submission has been a difficult aspect of Eliot's work for many modern critics who see the matrimonial destinies of such heroines as Dinah Morris, Esther Lyon, and Dorothea Brooke, and Maggie Tulliver's death, as disappointing finales to lives which seemed to promise to evade and to show up the inadequacies of women's contemporary lot. Dorothea Barrett suggests, however, that George Eliot's 'rarely [showing] her heroines making sincere attempts to actualize their yearning for something better' (1989: 54) may maintain an edge of protest which a fulfilled longing cannot do. In Barrett's reading, the gap between the realization of Eliot's own *vocation as expressed in her novels and their subject matter of the lack of realizable vocations for her heroines itself acts as a critique of women's situation. In the case of Eliot's last hero, Daniel Deronda, we might also, as Simon Dentith suggests, be alert to the ways in which he demonstrates a marked capacity for 'female values' (1986: 121) and thus further interrogates contemporary gender-qualifications for public life.   GM

Barrett (1989).

Beer (1986).

Bodenheimer, Rosemarie, 'Ambition and its Audiences: George Eliot's Performing Figures', *Victorian Studies*, 34 (1990).

Boumelha, Penny, 'George Eliot and the End of Realism', in Sue Roe (ed.), *Women Reading Women's Writing* (1987).

David, Deirdre, *Intellectual Women and Victorian Patriarchy: Harriet Martineau, Elizabeth Barrett Browning, George Eliot* (1987).

Dentith (1986).

Lisle, Bonnie J., 'Art and Egoism in George Eliot's Poetry', *Victorian Poetry*, 22 (1984).

New Historicist Approaches

New historicist approaches emerged in the 1980s predominantly in North America, as a response to post-structuralist developments in literary criticism, and they have been fruitfully applied to George Eliot's work. New historicism eschewed the perceived dehistoricizing tendencies of deconstruction, but at the same time drew on its critical methodologies—in particular, its close analysis of textual details, and its belief in the power of texts to construct and interrogate social realities rather than merely reflect them. Crucial to the development of new historicism was the work of the French historian Michel Foucault, especially his insights into the complicitous relations between knowledge and power, his development of the idea of 'discourse', and his distinctive notion of power, which he defined not as a repressive force, inflicted from the top down in hierarchical social relations, but as something that proliferates and which is operative in every kind of social situation, from the most public practices of governments, to the most private acts and intimacies of the bedroom.

'Discourse' is broadly understood as a set of textual operations that define a subject matter and produce power relationships to which we are all subjected. At any particular historical moment, many discourses can be seen to circulate and interact, establishing an economy of power which defines the shape of the society and the relationships which constitute it. For new historicists, literature is just one form of discourse that circulates alongside others. Moreover, they insist on the fictionality of all discourses, even the non-literary, so that all can be subjected to the same critical analysis. New historicist work is characteristically interdisciplinary, drawing heavily on non-literary documents—for instance, diaries and letters, as well as legal records, parliamentary papers, medical treatises, bank balances, street maps, and fashion designs. It is often anecdotal, using snippets of seemingly random evidence to exemplify larger cultural trends. In its methodologies, it draws on the approaches of critical anthropology, especially the work of Clifford Geertz, and in its aims and objectives as well as style, it is often closer to cultural history than conventional literary criticism.

New historicism was developed initially by scholars working on the Renaissance, but one of its defining practitioners was the critic Catherine Gallagher, whose studies of 19th-century literature and culture, including essays on *Felix Holt* and *Daniel Deronda*, have demonstrated the potential of new historicist methodologies for readings of Victorian culture. This work has been central to a revisionary account of 19th-century literature, based on a new examination of the relationships between literary texts, particularly the novel, and contemporary knowledge, in particular of *science, *medicine, the *law, and economics. Although such works tend to be thematic in approach, rather than author-based, George Eliot's work has provided fruitful material for new historicist critics on, for instance, legal and financial systems (e.g. Alexander Welsh, *George Eliot and Blackmail*, 1985), and medicine. In relation to the latter, of particular interest are Miriam Bailin's *The Sickroom in Victorian Fiction: the Art of Being Ill* (1994), Jill L. Matus's *Unstable Bodies: Victorian Representations of Sexuality and Maternity* (1995), and Lawrence's Rothfeld's *Vital Signs: Medical Realism in Nineteenth-Century Fiction* (1992), all of which present elucidating accounts of Eliot's incorporation of, and intervention in, debates in contemporary medicine.

Historicist readings of Eliot, however, are prefigured by the historical concerns of her own literary work. Eliot's overriding preoccupation with questions of historicism was part of a broad cultural interest in history witnessed during the first half of the 19th century, led by German philosophers, such as G. W. F. *Hegel, in whom Eliot had a deep interest. Indeed, her first published work, the translation of D. F. *Strauss's *Das Leben Jesu* (*The Life of Jesus*), was a landmark of historicism, in its reading of the *Bible as a historically and culturally rooted text. Although *Romola* and *The Spanish Gypsy* are alone among Eliot's works in being set in the remote past, all her works are historical works in the sense that they attempt to achieve an accurate reconstruction of a past society through a representation of the material details of the past, and in their efforts to come to terms with moments of historical change (see HISTORY). Her works typically focus on such moments of change, for example, the time of the First Reform Bill of 1832, which provides the setting for both *Felix Holt* and *Middlemarch*. Eliot uses fiction to explore not only the mechanisms for change, which are identified beyond the narrowly political sphere, but also its broad social and cultural effects. In Eliot's fiction, change is understood as a complex blend of cultural, scientific, economic, and political factors—all of which have their bearing on the social.

The dominant trend of George Eliot criticism has been historicist since the publication of Gordon S. *Haight's biography in 1968. In emphasizing the seriousness and breadth of Eliot's intellectual interests, and the social and cultural networks to which she belonged, Haight's work shifted critical attention from Leavisite concerns about the presentation of enduring moral truths, and recast Eliot as a novelist of ideas rather than of feeling. In the light of this, the most influential critical works on Eliot in recent years have examined her interactions with contemporary cultural, intellectual, and political movements, such as evolutionary science (see DARWINISM), *positivism, and the early stages of the women's movement (see WOMAN QUESTION). Although not necessarily 'new historicist' as such, many of these works share the concerns of new historicism, and its theoretical sophistication. Eliot's engagement with scientific thought has provided one of the most fruitful areas of investigation. Gillian Beer's *Darwin's Plots* (1983); George Levine's 'George Eliot's Hypothesis of Reality', *Nineteenth-Century Fiction*, 25 (1980); and Sally Shuttleworth's *George Eliot and Nineteenth-Century Science* (1984) have substantially reconfigured the understanding of Eliot's fiction, taking account of its investment not only in scientific argument but also in the social contexts of science. Like the new historicists, these critics underline the extent to which Eliot's works demonstrate the embeddedness of forms of knowledge—literary, scientific, and other—in its social contexts.   JM

Beer (1983).

Gallagher, Catherine, *The Industrial Reformation of English Fiction: Social Discourse and Narrative Form* (1985).
—— 'George Eliot and Daniel Deronda: The Prostitute and the Jewish Question, in Ruth Bernard Yeazell (ed.), *Sex, Politics, and Science in the Nineteenth-Century Novel* (1986).
Hamilton, Paul, *Historicism* (1996).

Post-colonial Approaches

Post-colonial approaches to George Eliot's work have been striking in their scarcity, despite the flood of critical analyses of other British 19th-century novelists since Edward Said's *Orientalism* (1978) inaugurated the loosely organized field of 'post-colonial studies'. The neglect of George Eliot by post-colonial critics is perhaps not altogether surprising: with the notable exception of *Daniel Deronda*, the works that still receive the bulk of critical attention (especially *Middlemarch* and *The Mill on the Floss*) seem particularly resistant to interpretations that seek to recover the (often unspoken) relationship between imperial and national histories in the 19th century. Narrative elements such as Mrs Tulliver's characterization of Maggie as a 'mulatter' in *The Mill* (*MF* 1.2) have for the most part not provided critics with the kinds of material they need to provide the type of wide-ranging, revisionary interpretations that have characterized recent readings of *Jane Eyre* and *Wuthering Heights*, for instance—although Susan Meyer has provided an interesting, if not entirely successful, analysis of the connection between female rebellion and sympathy for non-white racial groups in *The Mill on the Floss*. Faced with George Eliot's oeuvre, post-colonial critics appear to be in something of a double bind: one can point to the general absence of imperial references in the novels as evidence of the fact that the Empire was so overwhelmingly central to Victorian Britain that it barely needed to be mentioned; however, this very absence seems to rule out the possibility of moving beyond this general point by analysis of particular examples culled from George Eliot's writings. In general, then, critics have not turned to George Eliot in their various attempts to flesh out Said's thesis in *Culture and Imperialism* that 'the novel, as a cultural artefact of bourgeois society, and imperialism are unthinkable without each other' (1993: 70–1).

Daniel Deronda is the exception to this generalization, and here again it is Edward Said's work that opened up this field of enquiry. In *The Question of Palestine*, Said makes a reading of George Eliot's last novel the centrepiece of his critique of the blind spots of most contemporary understandings of the history of Zionism. Noting that *Deronda* has been frequently praised for the prophetic vision of its resolution (in which Daniel

and Mirah sail for Palestine to help build a Jewish homeland there), Said contends that such a reading is dependent on an evasion of the colonial nature of that project, such that 'Eliot cannot sustain her admiration of Zionism except by seeing it as a method for transforming the East into the West' (1980: 65); an East 'for whose people—as people having wishes, values, aspirations—Eliot expresses the complete indifference of absolute silence' (63). Said's brief comments on *Daniel Deronda* have encouraged critics radically to rethink the so-called 'Jewish half' of the novel.

Susan Meyer, for example, in the best post-colonial reading of *Deronda*, has emphasized the ways in which the novel incorporates the (European) Jews into the project of British colonialism, while at the same time symbolically expelling them from the British nation state. For Meyer, *Deronda* is a novel saturated with imperial questions and anxieties. It becomes important that Gwendolen's lost family fortune came from Caribbean slave plantations; the decline of Britain's West Indian colonies surfaces again in the vision of Grandcourt as a potential governor of 'a difficult colony, [where] he … would have understood that it was safer to exterminate than to cajole superseded proprietors' (*DD* 48), surely a reference to Governor Eyre's brutal suppression of the uprising in Jamaica in 1865 and the bitter controversy that followed it. Thus the decline of English aristocratic and imperial life, represented by Gwendolen's miserable subjection to Grandcourt 'like a galley-slave' (*DD* 56), can only be redeemed by a new, spiritually rejuvenated, colonial force; Daniel tells Gwendolen at the end of the novel that his task will be '"restoring a political existence to my people, making them a nation again, giving them a national centre, such as the English have, though they too are scattered over the face of the globe"'(*DD* 69).

This analysis of *Deronda* suggests some possible future directions for post-colonial criticism of George Eliot, which might take the form of re-evaluation of her relatively neglected works. Susan de Sola Rodstein provides a subtle and suggestive reading of 'Brother Jacob' in terms of the place of sugar in mid-19th-century Britain: David Faux spends six years in the Caribbean, and then returns to England to corrupt provincial society by selling sweets. Sugar here yokes together the dangers of an emerging British consumer economy and its roots in an older, rapacious form of colonial commerce based on slavery. Rodstein's work might be extended and amplified by turning to *Felix Holt*, which also revolves around the return of a central character from striking it rich overseas—the novel begins with Harold Transome arriving home from Smyrna to take over Transome

Court. Harold's shallow and self-serving politics, his new-found dislike of independent-minded English women, and his taste for spicy food all signal the social and spiritual dangers associated by George Eliot with foreign and colonial trade. (Turkey was not exactly a British colony, but it was central to the so-called 'Eastern Question', and Britain sought to develop its influence in the region to counter Russian advances and to safeguard the route to India.) Harold also returns with a son and heir, Harry, whose mother 'had been a slave—was bought, in fact' (*FH* 43), as Harold tells Esther, thus stopping instantly any chance of a relationship between the two of them. Three-year-old Harry is 'savage' and 'gypsy-like'; Transome Court ultimately passes to him, but by so doing, it ceases to be the central concern of the story (despite the elaborately designed inheritance plot that dominates so much of the novel). A post-colonial approach to *Felix Holt* might therefore emphasize the way in which—in contrast to the final movement beyond England in *Deronda*—George Eliot discovers a possible source of English renewal in Felix's artisanal, Arnoldian politics by stressing the negative consequences of the importation of 'modern', imperial ideas and foreign blood into the provincial heartland of England.   TW

Meyer, Susan, *Imperialism at Home: Race and Victorian Women's Fiction* (1996).

Rodstein, Susan de Sola, 'Sweetness and Dark: George Eliot's "Brother Jacob" ', *Modern Language Quarterly*, 52 (1991).

Said, Edward W., *Culture and Imperialism* (1993).

—— *The Question of Palestine* (1980).

Psychoanalytic Approaches

Although psychoanalysis has been turning its intense gaze on literary works for over a century—ever since 1897, when Sigmund *Freud worked his way to his formulation of the Oedipus complex by thinking about *Oedipus Rex* and *Hamlet*—it is only in the last twenty-five years that a body of criticism informed by the writings of Freud and his followers has accumulated around the works of George Eliot. Two books from the middle 1970s may be singled out, not as initiating sources of that criticism but as indicative of the energies driving it and the directions it would take. One is Ruby V. Redinger's *George Eliot: The Emergent Self* (1975), a subtle psychobiographical exploration of what it meant for Mary Ann Evans to be born a woman and to become an admired and successful writer; the other is Leo Bersani's *A Future for Astyanax: Character and Desire in Literature* (1976) which, although it only devotes a few pages to Eliot in a chapter entitled 'Realism and the Fear of Desire', nevertheless represents an important turning in Anglo-American psychoanalytic criticism and in discussions of realist fiction.

Redinger's biography rarely mentions Freud, but its interpretation of the childhood sources of the conflicts that both enabled and inhibited George Eliot's career as a novelist is informed by a tactful psychoanalytic perceptiveness. Along with Sandra M. Gilbert and Susan Gubar's *The Madwoman in the Attic: The Woman Writer and the Nineteenth-Century Literary Imagination* (1979)—which devoted a hundred pages to George Eliot—it appeared at a moment when Freudian understandings of psychic struggle were being mobilized in the interest of a feminist rewriting of the literary history of women in patriarchal societies.

Both Redinger's and Gilbert and Gubar's books focus on the drama of authorship, Redinger concerned to describe that provokingly composite figure Evans/Eliot, Gilbert and Gubar reading poems and novels to discern the unconscious debts of filiation and acts of creative disavowal produced by a sequence—a canon—of women writers. The psyche being analysed in each case is the author's, as it is in many of Freud's own writings on literary works. Bersani's chapter is less concerned with the vicissitudes of an authorial psyche than it is with the forces that produced the characteristic traits of 19th-century *realism, forces best examined by rhetorically tracking the signs of desire in novelists' language. He is drawing on a different side of Freud, one made available to him through the works of contemporary French theorists like Jacques Lacan, Jean Laplanche, and J.-B. Pontalis, Parisian analysts whose writings were beginning to circulate in England and America in the 1970s. It was this work, along with the deconstructive account of Freud that Jacques Derrida was elaborating, that combined with feminism to foster an energetic outpouring of psychoanalytically inflected criticism in the decades that followed.

Two discussions of George Eliot stand out in the early 1980s: D. A. Miller's chapter on *Middlemarch* in *Narrative and its Discontents* (1981) and Dianne F. Sadoff's investigation of father–daughter relations in *Monsters of Affection: Dickens, Eliot & Brontë on Fatherhood* (1982). Miller's book, whose title alludes to Freud's *Civilization and its Discontents* (1930), is more formal in its emphasis, Sadoff's more thematic and biographical, but both draw attention to a twofold strangeness in Eliot's fictions—on the one hand, the distortions that the demands of narrative produce in the depicted world of personal relations, and on the other, the odd performances that the world depicted would seem to exact of its narrators. Both take the narrative surface of the novels as anything but a transparent medium but rather see it as a sort of psyche, a field in which one can discern the struggles of a culture's desires and its inhibitions.

But what were the desires of Victorian culture? And—of particular concern to George Eliot and her readers—how, and where, were women to locate themselves in that field? One central issue has been what to make of repeated instances in Eliot's fiction of a woman's aggression, or even her ambition—overt or surreptitious—earning her some decisive punishment in the narrative's outcome: think of Maggie Tulliver's death, of Gwendolen Harleth's final breakdown. Some of the strongest feminist readings have drawn on Freud's and Lacan's understandings of sexual difference to take up such questions: see, for example, Jacqueline Rose's chapter 'George Eliot and the Spectacle of the Woman', in *Sexuality in the Field of Vision* (1986). But psychoanalysis has never been an unequivocal resource for feminists; rather it has served as a provocation, seeming at once an instrument with which to loosen the strictures of patriarchy and one capable of enforcing those very constraints. Books like Margaret Homans's *Bearing the Word* (1986) and Mary Jacobus's *Reading Woman* (1986) display their authors grappling with this theoretical issue while shifting attention to less frequently discussed works of Eliot's—*Romola*, 'The Lifted Veil', or the autobiographical sonnet sequence 'Brother and Sister' (see POETRY).

Both Homans and Jacobus have found the writings of the French philosopher Luce Irigaray—*Speculum of the Other Woman* (1985); *This Sex Which Is Not One* (1985)—useful in taking some distance from both Freudian and Lacanian accounts of femininity. More recently, Irigaray has served as the lens with which Kathryn Bond Stockton has brought Victorian culture—its investments in work, in sexuality, and in spirituality—into focus in a powerfully argued and wide-ranging book, *God between their Lips: Desire between Women in Irigaray, Brontë, and Eliot* (1994).

Finally, as a reminder that some of the most nuanced contemporary criticism—of Victorian culture and of George Eliot—can be informed by psychoanalysis without being, strictly speaking, 'psychoanalytic criticism', one should turn to the chapter on *Daniel Deronda* in Garrett Stewart's *Dear Reader: The Conscripted Audience in Nineteenth-Century British Fiction* (1996).   NH

Brooks, Peter, *Psychoanalysis and Storytelling* (1994).
Koffman, Sarah, *The Childhood of Art: an Interpretation of Freud's Aesthetics* (1988).
Newton (1991) (contains excerpts from some of the studies mentioned above).

Cross, John Walter (1840–1924) and the **Cross family.** 'Married this day at 10.15 to John Walter Cross, at St. George's, Hanover Square. Present, Charles, who gave me away, Mr. and Mrs. Druce, Mr. Hall, Willie, Mary, Eleanor, and Florence'

(*Journals*, 203): George Eliot's diary entry for 6 May 1880 not only states the fact of her marriage, but declares her entry into the Cross family. John's sister Florence Nightingale Cross (1857–1915; married Henry Weston Eve) expressed the warmth of the family's embrace in a letter to the bride the day after the wedding, writing of Johnnie's having 'the sort of happiness one had dreamed of for him' (Beinecke Library, Yale University). On the same day, she wrote to the groom, 'I had such a vision of her beautiful, radiant face this morning, as she came up that aisle in her elegant robes looking like a queen, bless her' (Beinecke Library). Apart from Charles Lewes (see LEWES FAMILY), those named in George Eliot's journal were sisters, brothers, and brothers-in-law of the groom. Of Cross's surviving siblings, only one brother, Richmond James (1845–1917), a banker in New York, and one sister, Emily Helen (1848–1907), who married Francis Otter in 1875 and had illness in the family at the time of the wedding, were not in attendance. The children of his sister Anna Bowling Buchanan, Mrs Albert Druce (1841–1921), became John Cross's heirs: Miss Elsie Druce is said to have destroyed some of the vast quantity of letters and other papers left at his death, apparently because they gave a different version of some events from that in *George Eliot's Life.*

John Cross was twenty years younger than his bride. Born at St Michael's Mount, Aigburth, Liverpool, he was the second son, and the third of the ten children of William and Anna Chalmers Wood Cross (1813–78). His father was a partner in the banking house of Cross and Dennistoun, into which John followed him from Rugby School. He was based in New York from 1857 to 1869, then in London, where in 1875 he set up his own firm, Cross, Benson and Company, commission agents. In the course of business he spent several months in Australia in 1872, from where he wrote to his family lively letters critical of the colonial society of which he was temporarily part. In one of them he reveals the extent to which George Eliot was already integral to his world-view, describing an encounter with W. P. Wilson, Professor of Mathematics at the University of Melbourne, 'to whom Macmillan gave me a letter. He seems a clever little fellow, but he could not get through "Romola", and his idea of a good novel is "the Bramleighs of Bishop's Folly" [by Charles Lever], so that we have not a bond of union in leeterature' (13 April 1872, Beinecke Library). Cross had a reputation for his sporting activities, and also nurtured literary inclinations: his essay 'Social New York' appeared in *Macmillan's Magazine* in June 1872 and earned favourable comment from George Eliot, who 'read his paper on New York with much interest and satisfaction' (*L* v. 302). Naturally, she expressed

John Walter Cross (1840–1924) seated on the right with hand in pocket. George Eliot's husband for the last few months of her life, his biography of her was described by Gladstone as 'a Reticence in three volumes' (date of photograph unknown).

even deeper approbation after their marriage, for instance when she proudly described her husband to Charles *Bray: 'you would be satisfied with his coronal arch which finishes a figure six feet high. If his head does not indicate fine moral qualities, it must be phrenology that is in fault' (4 December 1880, L vii. 342).

The acquaintance of the Cross family with George Eliot and G. H. *Lewes began in 1867, developing particularly after a chance encounter in *Rome in 1869—when John Cross and George Eliot met for the first time. Visits followed to the widowed Mrs Cross, and to the eldest daughter Elizabeth (1836–69) and her husband William Henry Bullock (later Bullock Hall). Elizabeth, who published *An Old Story and other poems* in 1867, died in childbirth. George Eliot was particularly attached to the unmarried sisters Mary Finlay (1843–1902), Eleanor (1847–95), and Florence, who lived with their mother, brother William (1838–1916), and John. Mary had claims to authorship, publishing stories and sketches in *Macmillan's*, collected in *Railway Sketches* (1899). During the *Franco-Prussian war, she and William joined Henry Bullock, who was a correspondent for the *Daily News*, in setting up a soup kitchen at Sedan to relieve the suffering of non-combatant victims of the fighting.

From the early 1870s, John Cross made time to provide advice on investments to the Leweses. He also assisted their long search for a country house, finding for them The Heights, Witley, not far from his mother's home at Weybridge (see HOMES). He taught them to play tennis and badminton, as well as organizing visits of various kinds, including one to the Bank of England. Both Eliot and Lewes addressed him as 'nephew': Rosemarie Bodenheimer points out that the Cross family at large gave Eliot respite from her sibylline persona, and conjectures that 'the special charm of "Nephew Johnnie" was that he could be teased, confided in, and depended on' (1994: 256). Edith *Simcox in her jealous devotion was almost alone in detecting the intensification of George Eliot's partiality for him after Lewes's death.

Cross, whose mother died on 9 December 1878, shortly after Lewes, was the first person outside her household and family received by the bereaved George Eliot, though not until 23 February 1879. By this time she was already hard at work on Lewes's papers, and was dealing with both household and business matters, drawing heavily on the assistance of Charles Lewes as well as Cross. Bodenheimer speculates that the practical necessity to provide for the management of her own literary remains was part of her motivation for marrying Cross (1994: 115). Certainly such conventional explanations of the marriage as Eliot's emotional

dependence, or 'the pleasurable guilt of another socially dubious attachment' (114), or her essential conservatism yearning for an orthodox union at last, lack the conviction of Bodenheimer's argument through analysis of Eliot's letters of the significant change in her self-representation, her abrogation of 'the power and pride of choice' (115), in favour of allowing Cross to make a heroic and sacrificial choice on her account.

The wedding tour proceeded from *London to *Paris, and thence to *Italy. The letters of both bride and groom exude happiness, and imply a reversal of the trope of a husband's initiation of his wife on a European honeymoon as George Eliot instructed Cross in the beauties of their itinerary. But in *Venice in the middle of June, Cross broke down, and threw himself from their hotel room into the Grand Canal. He blamed the foul waters of the Venetian canals, and the languor of the tourist's life: 'The effect of this continual bad air, and the complete and sudden deprivation of all bodily exercise, made me thoroughly ill' (Cross, iii. 407–8). Willie Cross came post-haste to provide support. John was well enough to travel within a relatively short period of time, and resumed normal activities (including tree-felling, *Journals*, 212) on their return to England towards the end of July. He appears to have been subject to bouts of depression, and it is plausible to conjecture that his self-esteem was diminished by his wife's fame, her age, and her intellect. Henry *James confided to his sister Alice on 30 January 1881: 'my private impression is that if she had not died, she would have killed him. He couldn't keep up the intellectual pace—all Dante and Goethe, Cervantes and the Greek tragedians. As he said himself, it was a cart-horse yoked to a racer' (*Henry James Letters*, ed. Leon Edel, ii (1975), 337).

Cross had a brief married life, and a long widowhood. He disposed of the house in Cheyne Walk 'we meant to be so happy in' (L vii. 351), and lived with his sisters in London and in Tunbridge Wells. Within weeks of George Eliot's death, he turned to the duty of preparing her biography. Well-schooled in such family responsibilities, he solicitously consulted the Evanses, with conspicuous deference especially to Isaac *Evans. This labour over, he seems to have spent his time in travel, family duties, and writing. He was not involved in the celebrations of the centenary of George Eliot's birth in *Coventry and *Nuneaton in 1919.

He published two more books after *George Eliot's Life as related in her letters and journals, arranged and edited by her husband J. W. Cross* (3 vols., 1885), both with William *Blackwood and Sons, both collections of his periodical publications: *Impressions of Dante and of the New World*

(1893) and *The Rake's Progress in Finance* (1905). His introduction to the former includes the poignant admission that 'The real reason for these republications is ... a desire on the part of the writer to leave some print of his footsteps, however shallow, on the sands of time' (pp. v–vi). The depth of the print may be gauged from *The Times* obituary: 'a well-known and interesting figure in the London world of the 'eighties and 'nineties, with a wide circle of friends among the men and women of that day, many of whom he outlived, died on Sunday at the age of 84'. See also BIOGRAPHIES.   MAH

Bodenheimer (1994).

Dalberg-Acton, John (1834–1902), liberal Catholic apologist and distinguished historian, author of the famous dictum 'Power tends to corrupt, and absolute power corrupts absolutely', created 1st Baron Acton in 1869. He met George Eliot and G. H. *Lewes at Lord Houghton's in May 1872, and was present at one or two gatherings with them in the last year of Lewes's life. His admiration for Eliot is seen in his letters, where he refers to her as being 'capable of reaching those whom no Christian could possibly touch' (*Selections from the Correspondence of the first Lord Acton*, ed. J. N. Figgis and R. V. Lawrence, 1917, i. 291). But it is in his review of John Walter *Cross's *Life* in the *Nineteenth Century* in March 1885 (17: 464–85) that the quality of his appraisal and of his own prose is evident: he asserts that Eliot is her own most interesting character, describing her emergence in early womanhood as moving 'from earnest piety to explicit negation'. The translation of D. F. *Strauss, he feels, 'is an episode not an epoch'; she adhered to 'a rule of life in place of her rejected creeds', it being 'the problem of her age to reconcile the practical ethics of belief and unbelief, to save virtue and happiness when dogmas and authorities decay'. He elevates her learning and achievements though she occasionally lacked invention, believes that her major theme is retribution, links this with Baruch *Spinoza's ethics and Strauss's belief, and defines her creed as being 'altruism and the reign of the dead'. For Acton all her work was ethical: she reconciled science and art, her truths were timeless, to read her was to be ennobled. When she died he felt that the sun had gone out. This founding historian at *Cambridge, who had opposed authoritarianism in the Catholic Church, whose reputation for probity was international, whose creed was liberty, felt that by living with Lewes outside matrimony she had sacrificed 'the foremost rank among the women of her time, and a tomb in Westminster Abbey'.　　　　GRH

D'Albert Durade, François (1804–86) and **Julie** (1800–80), Swiss artist and his wife in whose house in *Geneva George Eliot stayed as a boarder for five months in 1849–50 on her first visit to continental Europe after her father's death, and with whom she remained lifelong friends. François had first studied to be an evangelical minister before turning to painting and becoming a portrait painter. From 1857 until his death he was curator of the permanent exhibition of the Athénée Museum (*L*, vol. i, p. lxiv). At the age of 30 he married another artist, Julie Covelle, who specialized in painting flowers. On 9 October 1849 the future novelist Mary Ann Evans began to board with them at their house in Geneva and soon felt comfortably at home with a host who was kindly and

thoughtful and a motherly hostess who was an excellent cook. A letter to her friends the *Brays, in which she claims to love M. D'Albert like both a father and a brother, paints a vivid portrait of him:

You must know that he is not more than four feet high with a deformed spine—the result of an accident in his boyhood—but on this little body is placed a finely formed head, full in every direction. The face is plain with small features, and rather haggard looking, but all the lines and the wavy grey hair indicate the temperament of the artist. I have not heard a word or seen a gesture of his yet that was not perfectly in harmony with an exquisite moral refinement—indeed one feels a better person always when he is present. (*L* i. 316)

The deformity and the artistic temperament have led some people, beginning with the Brays, to see him as a model for Philip Wakem in *The Mill on the Floss*. She was no less fond of Mme D'Albert, who took great care of her, anticipating all her wants and treating her so like one of her own children that Mary Ann ended up calling her 'Maman'. She profited, too, from meeting the D'Alberts' circle of cultivated friends, who gathered at their house on Monday evenings to play music, or on some occasions to act comedies and recite verses (Haight 1968: 76). In February 1850 she sat for a portrait by him at his request, which now hangs in Coventry City Libraries with a copy in the National Portrait Gallery (see PORTRAITS).

When the time came for her to return home she was very sad to leave the D'Alberts, and it is a measure of their protective concern for her that François took it upon himself to accompany her all the way to England. They left Geneva on 18 March 1850 and a week later she left D'Albert sightseeing in London while she returned to her friends the Brays at Rosehill in *Coventry. He stayed two months in England, visiting her at

François D'Albert Durade's (1804–86) portrait of George Eliot, painted in February 1850 when she was staying as a boarder with him and his wife in Geneva.

Rosehill for a few days in early May when she took him to Kenilworth and Warwick. After his departure they kept in touch by letter. Her early letters to him were written in French and, since she had obtained Mme D'Albert's permission to *tutoyer* him, addressed him in the familiar form. He later burnt them, fearing, as he explained to John Walter *Cross, that aftercomers might misinterpret the familiarity (Haight 1968: 79).

They met only once more, ten years later, but the correspondence continued at intervals until her death. In October 1859 she wrote to him to tell him of her 'marriage', of her transformation into the novelist George Eliot, and of the success of *Adam Bede*. His reply revealed that he had already read *Scenes of Clerical Life* and had felt that he would like to translate it into French. When she asked him in her next letter about possible translators for *Adam Bede*, he offered to translate it himself and received her permission to do so (see TRANSLATIONS OF GEORGE ELIOT'S WORKS). His translation was published in 1861, and he later translated *The Mill on the Floss* (1863), *Silas Marner* (1863), *Romola* (1878), and *Scenes of Clerical Life* (1884).

Returning from their visit to *Italy in 1860, George Eliot and G. H. *Lewes went to Hofwyl in Switzerland to collect Lewes's eldest son Charles from his school there (see LEWES FAMILY). Being close to Geneva, Eliot made a point of visiting the D'Alberts and introducing them to Lewes and his son. The reunion was a happy one, and Lewes was delighted to see how the D'Alberts loved and valued his companion. François read some of his translation of *Adam Bede* and received permission to translate *The Mill* (Haight 1968: 332). This was the last time they saw each other. George Eliot intended to visit the D'Alberts again during a holiday in France and Germany in the summer of 1873, since she knew Mme D'Albert's health was failing, but a combination of heat, fatigue, and the prospect of a long railway journey deterred her. Their correspondence, however, continued. A month before her own death she wrote her last letter to M. D'Albert to commiserate with him on the death of 'Maman'.   JMR

Dallas, E. S. (1828–79), journalist who did much to promote George Eliot's fame by his discerning and elevating reviews in *The Times*. He also contributed to the *Saturday Review* and by the mid-1860s he and his wife were on visiting terms with Eliot and G. H. *Lewes. He was present at the housewarming and coming-of-age party for Charles Lee Lewes on 24 November 1863. His notice of *Adam Bede* set the seal on approval and recognition and, according to John *Blackwood, he was one of the first to disbelieve the *Liggins

rumours. He wrote a favourable review of *The Mill on the Floss*, a 'long discriminating review' of *Silas Marner*, and a highly laudatory one of *Felix Holt*. This last opens with the words 'Hitherto Miss Austen has had the honour of the first place among our lady novelists, but a greater than she has now arisen' (*L* viii. 379). Friendship, however, was wont to colour his continuing praise: he wrote of *The Spanish Gypsy* that its author was not only 'a great writer' but 'a true poet'.   GRH

Daniel Deronda (*see page 78*)

Dante Alighieri (1265–1321), the Italian poet of *La Divina Commedia*, was a major influence on George Eliot: she read the *Commedia* many times over the course of her life and could recite several passages from memory. She spent an entire year (1879–80) reading and discussing *Inferno* and *Purgatorio* with John Walter *Cross, who later wrote, 'The divine poet took us into a new world. It was a renovation of life' (Cross, iii. 359). In her only extant love letter to him (October 1879), she assumed the name of the beloved in Dante's *Vita Nuova* and *Commedia*, signing herself 'thy tender Beatrice' (*L* vii. 211–2).

She often described her state of mind in Dantean terms, as in this letter of 1874: 'I am no longer one of those whom Dante found in a Hell-border because they had been sad under the blessed daylight' (*L* vi. 70). The image stayed with her, and she used it again in another letter five years later (*L* vii. 169). George Eliot's intensely personal relation to Dante was not only to the poetry but also to the poet himself: in her 'Recollections of Italy 1860' she wrote, 'I used to feel my heart swell a little at the sight of the inscription on Dante's tomb— "Onorate l'altissimo poeta"' (*Journals*, 356).

Her later novels include frequent allusions to Dante. This comes as no surprise in her Renaissance Florentine novel *Romola* or in the chapters of *Middlemarch* and *Daniel Deronda* that are set in Italy; but the use of images from the *Commedia* on other occasions shows that Dante's influence on her was not simply associated with things Italian.

Dante allusions in *Romola* form part of its rich intertextual backdrop and are balanced by references to the secular satirical writings of Boccaccio and Luigi Pulci. The novel's opening scene is set outside Dante's birthplace; the Malebolge of *Inferno*, xviii–xxx are mentioned in chapter 29; and chapter 45 contains two references to *Inferno* (xx. 7–15 and iv. 20–1). *Purgatorio*, xxxiii. 130–2 was to be the *epigraph (later discarded) for chapter 2; *Purgatorio*, xxi. 104 is quoted in chapter 6; and *Purgatorio*, xxi. 37–8 in chapter 13. The most revealing Dante reference in *Romola*, however, is in a passage deleted from chapter 21 of the

(*cont. on page 86*)

G EORGE ELIOT's last novel, published in eight monthly parts between February and September 1876. With its near contemporary setting and sympathetic presentation of Jewish life, it represents a bold new departure by a novelist at the height of her powers.

Composition

The origins of the opening scene of the novel around the roulette table at Leubronn can be traced back to the visit George Eliot and G. H. *Lewes made to the German spa of Bad Homburg in September 1872, where she wrote the Finale to *Middlemarch*. There she caught sight of a young Englishwoman, 'Miss Leigh, Byron's greatniece', gambling compulsively in the casino, her fresh young face standing out from the ugly and stupid ones around her in a setting for which 'Hell' seemed to be the only appropriate name (*L* v. 312, 314). The seeds of Gwendolen Harleth's character, the central motif of gambling, and the nature of life in fashionable, affluent society appear to have been planted there. During this visit the couple also bought a collection of stories about Jewish life in the ghetto, which was later to form part of Eliot's extensive reading in preparation for the novel. Her interest in *Judaism, however, went back much further. Although as a young woman she had shown signs of conventional *anti-Semitism, maintaining in 1848 that 'Everything *specifically* Jewish is of a low grade' (*L* i. 247), her views had radically changed during her life with Lewes. She had, for instance, come to know and write sympathetically about the work of the German-Jewish poet Heinrich *Heine in the 1850s; and in 1866 she had attended a synagogue in Amsterdam and been deeply moved by the chanting and the swaying bodies, 'the faint symbolism of a religion of sublime far-off memories' (*L* iv. 298). More importantly, she and Lewes had made friends of a Jewish scholar working at the British Museum, Emanuel *Deutsch, from whom she had taken lessons in Hebrew and acquired a deeper knowledge of Judaism. The advocate of a Jewish national homeland, he had travelled to Palestine, and in 1873, although terminally ill with cancer, he set off again for the Near East, dying in Alexandria in May. It is his views and his fatal illness that lie behind the figure of Mordecai in the novel.

The first mention of the novel comes in Lewes's diary, shortly after Deutsch's death, on 29 June 1873, when he refers to a discussion of projects for 'a novel & play Deronda' (*L* v. 425 n.). The couple were on holiday in Fontainebleau and soon went on to Frankfurt, where they bought books on Jewish subjects and attended the synagogue, doing the same later in Mainz and Homburg. By 5 November 1873 she could tell her publisher John *Blackwood that she was 'slowly simmering towards another big book' (*L* v. 454). The first sketches towards the new novel were made in January and February 1874 (Haight 1968: 472), and she worked on the first volume that summer at Earlswood Common in Surrey and during the following winter, finally delivering it to Blackwood on 19 May 1875. In the autumn of 1874 she and Lewes went to Salisbury in search of topographical details and to Lacock Abbey in Wiltshire, which provided the basis for Sir Hugo Mallinger's Topping Abbey. In February they walked along the Thames from Kew to Richmond to find a spot for the meeting of Deronda and Mirah. The summer of 1875 was again spent writing in seclusion, this time at Rickmansworth, and the second volume and much of the third were completed. However, when publication began on 1 February 1876 the novel was still unfinished, and she finally finished Book 8 on 8 June 1876.

Publication

After the success of *Middlemarch* a similar pattern of serial publication was adopted for *Deronda*, though with the difference that the eight parts, corresponding to the eight books, appeared in grey wrappers, price 5*s.*, at monthly rather than two-monthly intervals. Harper's secured the American rights for £1,700, and the novel was published in their monthly magazine as the parts appeared in Britain (although continuing until October, since Book 2 was divided between the March and April issues). Christian Bernhard *Tauchnitz produced the continental reprint, for which he paid £250, and the novel was also published serially in the *Australasian*. Words ending in -*ize* in the manuscript were changed to -*ise* in the first and subsequent editions to conform to Blackwood's house style. The manuscript, in four volumes bound in maroon leather, is in the British Library (Add. MSS 34039–42). On the first page it is inscribed 'To my dear Husband George Henry Lewes, October, 1876', followed by lines from Shakespeare's Sonnet 29.

At the end of August 1876 the unsold parts were bound up into four volumes octavo, in maroon cloth with gold lettering, price £2. 2*s.* (two guineas). In December 1876 there was a cheaper reprint of this four-volume edition, price 21*s.* (one guinea). A new edition in one volume, bound in brown cloth with gold lettering, was published in October 1877, price 7*s.* 6*d.* There were a few corrections made for this edition; and for the *Cabinet Edition, published in three volumes in December 1878, Eliot made a few alterations mainly to the Jewish sections of the novel. For these and a full publishing history, see the Clarendon Edition, ed. Graham Handley (1984).

Illustrations

The one-volume edition of 1877 has a title-page vignette engraved by Charles Jeens.

Reception

The first instalments of *Daniel Deronda* were well received, sales were strong, and reviews approving. Henry James, in an unsigned notice in the *Nation* in February 1876, looked forward to the intellectual luxury of reading the novel month by month (*CH* 362). Noting in her journal on 12 April 1876 the public's strong and increasing interest in the novel, Eliot nevertheless expressed reservations about the reception of the later books: 'The Jewish element seems to me likely to satisfy nobody' (*L* vi. 238). Although sales did not fall off, reviews of the completed novel tended to confirm her fears. The *Saturday Review* in September 1876 declared that the Jewish characters were 'personages outside our interest' and their 'world completely foreign to us' (*CH* 377). George Saintsbury in the *Academy* in the same month criticized the figure of Deronda, finding him both dislikeable and impossible to believe in, and judged Mordecai's views too provincial to arouse any fellow feeling (*CH* 373–5). Henry James in his conversation between three characters has one of them praise Gwendolen and Grandcourt but find the Jewish part of the story wearisome and the characters hardly more than shadows (*CH* 422). Such reactions were typical but not universal, for the presentation of Jewish life had its defenders. James Picciotto in the *Gentleman's Magazine* in November 1876 welcomed the novel as 'the vindication of a long maligned race against ignorant misrepresentation', claiming that George Eliot had done more for the cause of toleration and enlightenment than any amount of legislation (*CH* 416). Jewish readers were naturally enthusiastic, and Eliot received many appreciative letters from Jews both in Britain and abroad, including the Deputy Chief Rabbi, the editor of the *Jewish Chronicle*, and another prominent member of the London Jewish community, Chaim Guedalla, who sent her a translation into Hebrew of the scene in the 'Hand and Banner' (*DD* 42) which he had published in a newspaper in Lemberg. From Budapest she received a long commentary on the novel in German by David Kaufmann, which was translated into English and published by Blackwood in 1878 as *George Eliot and Judaism*. She also had a letter from Harriet Beecher *Stowe in reply to which she explained her intentions in dealing with Jewish life in the novel: she wished to counter the 'spirit of arrogance and contemptuous dictatorialness' which marked the English attitude to the Jews and other oriental races, and 'to rouse the imagination of men and women to a vision of human claims in those races of their fellow-men who most differ from them in custom and belief' (*L* vi. 301).

R. H. *Hutton, one of George Eliot's most perceptive reviewers, writing in the *Spectator* in September 1876, compared *Deronda* to *Middlemarch*, finding it more unequal though rising above its great predecessor at certain moments, like the scene in which Deronda's mother tells him of her life, and the parting interview between Deronda and Gwendolen. He still found the hero laboured and took exception to the 'ostentatious humility' of Mirah, but was impressed by the powerful construction of the plot. Criticism of Deronda was widespread, Robert Louis Stevenson memorably calling him 'the Prince of Prigs' (*CH* 33), though E. S. *Dallas in the *Contemporary Review* in February 1877 went to some lengths to defend him as a creature of flesh and blood rather than a pallid shadow (*CH* 441–2). Lewes wrote to thank him for his deep insight and sympathy. Another sympathetic review by R. E. Francillon in the *Gentleman's Magazine* in October 1876 was exceptional in arguing that George Eliot was attempting something new in this novel, forsaking her customary uncompromising realism for romance, with its elevation of the universal and essential over the accidental and transitory (*CH* 395). That move beyond realism has become the focus of much modern criticism.

Plot

There are two distinct, though related, strands to the narrative: the story of the beautiful, spirited, but spoilt Gwendolen Harleth and her disastrous marriage, and the story of Daniel Deronda's discovery of his true identity and his vocation. The novel opens in a German spa, where Deronda is struck by the sight of Gwendolen gambling and she is disturbed by his measuring gaze. She is summoned home to her mother by the news that her family has been ruined by the failure of a bank. The narrative then moves back in time to relate how Gwendolen came to be in Germany. Courted by the coldly impressive aristocrat Grandcourt, she had been expecting a proposal and then had discovered that he already had a mistress, Lydia Glasher, who had borne him children and whom he ought to marry now that her husband was dead. Gwendolen had then fled to the Continent. Now, reduced to genteel poverty, she is more susceptible to the wealthy Grandcourt's attentions and, having had her musical ambitions ridiculed by the musician Klesmer, she eventually chooses to marry him rather than go to work as a governess.

Deronda has been raised by his guardian, Sir Hugo Mallinger, as an upper-class Englishman, but knows nothing about his family background and suspects he might be Sir Hugo's illegitimate son. Uncertain what to do with his life, he abandons his studies at Cambridge to widen his horizons through travel. Rowing on the Thames he sees a poorly dressed but beautiful young woman, Mirah, prevents her from drowning herself, and finds lodgings for her with his friends, the artistic and intellectual Meyrick family. Through Mirah he begins to get interested in Judaism and meets a Jewish pawnbroker

Ezra Cohen, and the Cohen's lodger Mordecai, a consumptive scholar and visionary who sees in Deronda the friend and disciple he has been waiting for. Deronda realizes that Mordecai must be Mirah's lost brother and reunites them.

Gwendolen's marriage makes her the victim of Grandcourt's tyrannical will, and she sees Deronda as the only person she can turn to in her misery. Grandcourt decides to go yachting with her in the Mediterranean, while Deronda receives from Sir Hugo a letter from his unknown mother, Princess Halm-Eberstein, asking him to meet her in Genoa. There she tells him that he is of Jewish blood and how she delivered him from the bondage of being a Jew by having him raised by Sir Hugo, while she made a career as the famous singer Alcharisi. Fatally ill, she says farewell. Grandcourt and Gwendolen also arrive in Genoa. Sailing in a small boat Grandcourt is drowned and Gwendolen rescued. She confesses her feelings of guilt to Deronda at not having tried to save her husband and he comforts her; but, in love with Mirah, he cannot give her the commitment she would like. On the way home, in a discussion with his grandfather's friend Kalonymos in Mainz, he announces his vocation to serve the Jewish people. He eventually marries Mirah, informing Gwendolen beforehand in a painful interview. On his wedding day he receives a dignified letter from her saying that it shall be better with her for having known him. He determines to travel to the East with Mirah and Mordecai, but before they can set out Mordecai dies.

Critical Approaches

The critical distinction drawn by many of the early reviewers between the Gwendolen story and the Jewish part of the novel was taken to an extreme by F. R. *Leavis in *The Great Tradition* (1948) in what has become the most notorious pronouncement on the novel: his proposal that the bad Jewish part should be cut away and *Gwendolen Harleth* published as a separate work (122). By an interesting irony, precisely the opposite procedure had been advocated by a Jewish critic nearly fifty years earlier, and the early Hebrew translations of the novel omitted or reduced the Gentile sections of the novel (Werses 1976: 35). Eliot herself was impatient with 'readers who cut the book into scraps and talk of nothing in it but Gwendolen', and she insisted that she 'meant everything in the book to be related to everything else there' (*L* vi. 290). Certainly the two parts are inseparable, as Leavis later acknowledged, and Eliot creates a web of interconnected motifs, images, parallels, and intertextual allusions to hold the elements of the novel together. Her ambition to relate everything to everything else invites comparison with Joyce's in *Ulysses* and indicates the radical demands the complexity of *Deronda* makes on its readers. In its attempt to 'widen the English vision a little', as she put it in a letter to Blackwood (*L* vi. 304), it is a challenging experiment in form as well as a challenge to racial prejudice and complacent notions of national superiority. This last novel is a dark and daring assault on convention.

The opening paragraph, which plunges directly into the mind of an as-yet-unidentified figure, is an arresting departure from the usual procedures of 19th-century realist fiction and anticipates the practice of later writers like Marcel *Proust and Virginia *Woolf. Similarly, the preceding *epigraph, which reflects on the 'make-believe of a beginning', reveals a degree of self-consciousness that is more readily associated with modernist than with Victorian fiction. And the use of flashback, allowing the encounter between Deronda and Gwendolen to be dramatically highlighted in the opening pages as a seminal moment, is another move that shows a willingness to experiment with narrative forms other than the straightforward chronology common to *realism. Beginning with a series of questions—'Was she beautiful or not beautiful?'—this novel is marked by its capacity for interrogation, both of its own premises and practice and of the values of the social world and the moral behaviour of its inhabitants. For instance, while creating powerful characters like Grandcourt, it also suggests, with a strategically placed epigraph, that character may be ultimately unfathomable, merely a matter for conjecture (see CHARACTERIZATION). The chapter in which he first appears is headed by the motto 'The beginning of an acquaintance whether with persons or things is to get a definite outline for our ignorance' (*DD* 11). Reducing character to an outline for ignorance questions the very power to penetrate and understand that the novel appears to be exercising. And with the figure of the humane and sensitive Deronda himself, Eliot seems to be testing the qualities of sympathy and understanding that characterize her own typical narrator (see NARRATION), asking how they might function in real living relationships. At the culmination of her career she is in a position to reflect upon her own past practice.

She is also able to confront directly what she described as 'the intellectual narrowness—in plain English, the stupidity which is still the average mark of our culture' (*L* vi. 302), by presenting an unsparing vision of that culture, and in particular its ruling class, then at the height of its imperial power (see COLONIALISM). For the first time in her novels she dispenses with the security of historical distance (see HISTORY) and writes about a period—the 1860s—so nearly contemporary that her social criticism can only be read as applying to the present in which she was writing. Fashionable affluent *society is shown to have a spiritual emptiness at its heart, most obvious in the figure of Grandcourt but also visible in the opening scene around the roulette tables, where all the players have 'a certain uniform negativeness of expression which had the effect of a mask—as if they had all eaten of some root that for the time compelled the brains of each to the same narrow monotony of action' (*DD* 1). By contrast there is a warmth and vitality in the scenes of Jewish life, like the picturesque sabbath witnessed by Deronda at the Cohens with their 'Venetian glow of colouring' (*DD* 34), a contrast pointed up by the juxtaposition of this celebration of a living faith with the Christmas party at Sir Hugo's in the next chapter, where the guests are taken to see a Gothic chapel that has been converted into stables (*DD* 35).

However, such contrasts are not the only strategy Eliot employs, for she is careful to offer some differentiation in her presentation of Jewish life. Mirah and Mordecai may be idealized but they are accompanied by their feckless father, the wheedling light-fingered Lapidoth. Deronda's visit to the synagogue in Frankfurt, where he is deeply moved by the *music and the liturgy, is preceded by 'certain ugly little incidents' which reveal the mercenary side of life in the ghetto (*DD* 32). Eliot's strategy involves acknowledging the grounds for vulgar prejudice and then soliciting interest in, and sympathy for, Jewish life by analogies with the more familiar foreign culture of *Italy. The music of the synagogue is likened to that of Allegri and Palestrina, and Italian Renaissance painting is used to define the foreign appearance of faces without resorting to racial stereotypes: Deronda, for instance, puts Mrs Davilow 'in mind of Italian paintings' and is described in terms of portraits by *Titian (see VISUAL ARTS). The cause of a Jewish national homeland is also served by an implied analogy with the struggle for Italian unity, a popular cause at the time (see RISORGIMENTO), and by references to Giacomo Leopardi's poetry and Giuseppe *Mazzini's political career. With these allusions Eliot seeks to bring Jewish life into the common framework of European culture without relying solely on the *Bible.

Jewish culture is nevertheless itself subject to questioning scrutiny in the testimony of Deronda's mother. The historical continuity and sense of community he finds in it have been for her merely oppressive. The 'endless discoursing about Our People' which he finds so inspiring in Mordecai has been 'a thunder without meaning' in her ears (*DD* 51). For a sceptical individualist and a woman, Jewishness was a bondage she had to escape. Thus although the novel suggests parallels between Jews and women as victims of discrimination, it ironically qualifies both that affinity and Deronda's idealistic vision of Judaism by stressing the subordinate role of women in Jewish life.

This subordination is one of those parallels that links the two parts of the novel, for it is, of course, also Gwendolen's fate. Her vulnerability as an attractive ummarried woman is brought out at the beginning by the way that she is examined and discussed in the casino, with her physical features—her eyes, her neck, her mouth—each receiving appraisal. Anatomized as a sexual object, likened later by Lord Brackenshaw to a high-mettled racehorse, she is little more than a commodity on the marriage market; and when she is eventually purchased by Grandcourt, he treats her like one of his material possessions, looking at her on their fateful yachting holiday 'with his narrow immovable gaze, as if she were part of the complete yacht' (*DD* 54). The victimization she suffers in the painted, gilded prison of her *marriage confirms the terror she felt earlier when listening to Lydia Glasher, Grandcourt's discarded mistress, by the Whispering Stones, 'as if some ghastly vision had come to her in a dream and said, "I am a woman's life"' (*DD* 14). In the sadistic pyschological cruelty of this marriage, the predicament of women that George Eliot had explored in *The Mill on the Floss* and *Middlemarch* is given a new, melodramatic intensity (see WOMAN QUESTION).

With Grandcourt, too, Eliot breaks new ground, creating a figure whose inscrutable evil cannot be understood in terms of the rapacious self-interest that motivates villainous characters in her earlier novels, like Dunstan Cass in *Silas Marner*, Tito in *Romola*, and Bulstrode in *Middlemarch*. Grandcourt's embodiment of a tyrannical will without purpose beyond its own exercise may owe something to her reading of Arthur *Schopenhauer, and it certainly implies a darkening view of human capacities. Whereas understanding customarily generates *sympathy in George Eliot's world, Grandcourt's understanding of his wife simply feeds his cruelty: 'indeed, he had a surprising acuteness in detecting that situation of feeling in Gwendolen which made her proud and rebellious spirit dumb and helpless before him'. His insight enables his inexorable will, 'like that of a crab or a boa-constrictor which goes on pinching or crushing without alarm or thunder' (*DD* 35), to press Gwendolen where it hurts most, forcing her to wear the diamonds that are tainted with her horror at having betrayed Lydia Glasher. Although there is a suggestion of sexual sadism in the repeated images of horses, reins, whips, and bridles used to define Grandcourt's subjection of Gwendolen, his evil power over her seems to transcend the personal, and recent criticism has come to relate his oppression to the class he represents and its role in the institution of empire (see CRITICISM, MODERN: POST-COLONIAL APPROACHES).

Published in the year that Queen *Victoria was declared Empress of India, *Daniel Deronda* makes frequent reference to Britain's imperial possessions. The fortune of Gwendolen's family was made in the West Indies; when she rejects her cousin Rex's love, he thinks of emigrating to the colonies; Grandcourt and Deronda define their opposite moral natures by their reactions to the rebellion in Jamaica brutally suppressed by Governor Eyre; and Grandcourt himself, who takes the side of Eyre, is described in his tyrannical treatment of his wife as maintaining 'an empire of fear' (*DD* 35), and as a man who, if he 'had been sent to govern a difficult colony, . . . might have won reputation among his contemporaries' (*DD* 48). The drama of oppression and rebellion played out in the Grandcourts' marriage is related to the exercise of power on the larger stage of empire, and with this parallel the novel implies, even if it does not state, a critique of imperialism.

Post-colonial criticism has, however, also defined the limits of *Deronda*'s liberal, enlightened vision. Edward Said has pointed out how Mordecai's idea of creating a Jewish homeland by redeeming the 'soil from debauched and paupered conquerors' (the Turks), and bringing the 'brightness of Western freedom' to the East, passes over in silence the actual inhabitants of the East and of Palestine in particular. Eliot's blindness to the historical reality of the vaguely defined East is one that she shares with her contemporaries (and it also anticipates the assumptions of Zionism), but, however much it is the unexceptional product of her culture, it must qualify any reading of the novel as a critique of imperialism. Indeed, Deronda's escape from a leisured and aimless existence by discovering a mission to play a role of 'social captainship' in the Jewish cause abroad is uncomfortably close to the imperial adventurism common among Englishmen of his time and class, who go off to the colonies to find a role and make a reputation. Such awkward parallels, like that between Deronda's mother and Gwendolen, testify to this novel's power to question and disturb even its own affirmations.

The figure of Deronda and his story have been from the outset a frequent target of criticism. The dramatic appeal of the novel lies with Gwendolen and the often melodramatic intensity of her suffering and mental anguish, which are repeatedly described in terms of terror, dread, and despair. Deronda's experience is tame by comparison, and the disparity between them has been interpreted as undermining the moral superiority that is claimed for him. Not only is he a pallid fictional creation by the side of the 'splendid Gwendolen', he is also her moral inferior because while his dilemmas are simply abstractions, she is engaged in real ones, confronting the social, economic, and familial pressures of an actual environment (Robinson, 288). This difference can be seen as one of fictional mode. The realism that characterizes the portrayal of Gwendolen and her world does not fully extend to Deronda, for he is presented with an approving earnestness that contrasts sharply with the critical and ironic scrutiny to which she is subjected. In one respect, with his longing to have 'the sort of apprenticeship to life which would not shape him too definitely' (*DD* 16), he invites comparison with the hero of *Goethe's *Wilhelm Meister's Apprenticeship* and is treated with the moral leniency characteristic of that kind of *Bildungsroman*. But the web of cultural and literary allusions woven around him make him a strangely overdetermined figure: he is not only a kind of Wilhelm Meister, but, among other things, a Moses or Daniel of the Diaspora wanting to lead his people home; a knight errant like Rinaldo, a Christian prince in *Jerusalem Delivered*, Tasso's epic poem of the First Crusade; and a hero of romance like Prince Camaralzaman in the *Arabian Nights*. With these associations the novel strains against the bounds of realism, invoking patterns of myth and romance to create possibilities of allegorical interpretation that are left, like the narrative itself, open-ended.

There is altogether something experimental about Deronda, as though Eliot is essaying a new kind of hero, one endowed with all the privileges of a man of wealth and standing yet who, at the same time, challenges conventional distinctions of *gender by displaying a feminine quality of sensitivity and understanding. In his last interview with his mother 'it seemed that all the woman lacking in her was present in him' (*DD* 53); and later he sobs over her life 'with perhaps more than a woman's acuteness of compassion' (*DD* 55). His peculiar sensibility is related to the novel's psychological probing, its exploration of what the narrator refers to as the 'unmapped country within us' (*DD* 24). The motto to the chapter in which his early life is recounted refers to 'the hidden pathways of feeling and thought which lead up to every moment of action' (*DD* 16), and it is this hidden territory of the mind that determines the course of the characters' lives in this novel. There are no moments of moral decision like Dorothea's in *Middlemarch* (*MM* 80): Gwendolen feels herself to be 'only drifted towards the tremendous decision' to marry Grandcourt (*DD* 27), while Deronda's *vocation bursts upon him in response to the challenge of a question from his grandfather's friend Kalonymos (*DD* 60). The resolution is prepared in the unconscious rather than arrived at by conscious reflection; and it is to this unconscious region of the mind that Deronda seems to respond when he acts as confidant and confessor to Gwendolen. As she pours out her feelings of guilt, 'not clearly distinguishing between what she said and what she only had an inward vision of', his readiness to 'let her mind follow its own need' anticipates the insights of psychoanalysis and the practice of the therapist. In her last novel Eliot enters the territory that was to be explored by Sigmund *Freud.

Opening out on to a wider world (see SPAIN) than her previous novels—Judaism, empire, the American civil war, the rise of Prussia, the lives of the cosmopolitan rich— and penetrating deeper into problematic areas of the psyche, *Daniel Deronda* leaves behind the stabilities of the earlier fiction. Although the narrator famously proclaims that 'a human life . . . should be well rooted is some spot of a native land' (*DD* 3), there are no Garths or Poysers here who are so rooted, while the land is simply a capital asset for landowners like Sir Hugo and Grandcourt to trade. In presenting the common condition of life in terms of rootlessness and exile the novel looks forward to modernism, although its most immediate successor is Henry James's study of Americans in voluntary exile in Europe, *The Portrait of a Lady* (1881), which owes a clear debt to the story of Gwendolen and her marriage. Yet, however rootless the lives of the characters are in a social sense, the novel, with its dense network of allusions, roots them for the reader in a culture stretching back to classical Greece and the Old Testament. It has been described as a novel about boundaries—of nationality, gender, custom, self (Uglow 1987: 221–2)—and one of the boundaries it is testing with its extraordinary range of reference is the boundary of the English tradition of fiction in the 19th century (Shaffer 1975: 233–4). The work of an astonishingly encompassing imagination with a lifetime's erudition at its service, it belongs in a European tradition with Dante and Goethe, bearing comparison with *Wilhelm Meister* in one direction, and Joyce's *Ulysses*, with *its* Jewish hero and manifest ambition to relate everything to everything else, in another. Like *Ulysses* it ranges from the mundane to the mythical and ends on a note of openness, with Deronda and Mirah about to set off for an unknown world and Gwendolen facing an uncertain future. George Eliot's refusal to offer here the kind of knowledge of fates and futures that rounds off *Middlemarch* (see ENDINGS) is the final move in a novel which consistently questions and disturbs.   JMR

George Eliot's 'Daniel Deronda' Notebooks, ed. Jane Irwin (1996).

Barrett (1989).

Beer (1986).

David, Deirdre, *Fictions of Resolution in Three Victorian Novels* (1981).

Linehan, Katherine Bailey, 'Mixed Politics: The Critique of Imperialism in *Daniel Deronda*', *Texas Studies in Literature and Language*, 34 (1992).

Robinson, Carole, 'The Severe Angel: A Study of *Daniel Deronda*', *ELH* 31 (1964).

Said, Edward W., 'Zionism from the Standpoint of its Victims', *Social Text*, 1 (1979).

Shaffer, Elinor, '*Daniel Deronda* and the Conventions of Fiction', in Shaffer (1975).

Uglow (1987).

Werses, Shmuel, 'The Jewish Reception of *Daniel Deronda*', in Alice Shalvi (ed.), *Daniel Deronda: A Centenary Symposium* (1976).

manuscript: 'The greatest of Italian poets recorded in his vitriolic verse his hope of a deliverer for Italy'. Here she alludes to *Paradiso* xxx. 137–8, and her comment provides a succinct and striking insight into her attitude towards Dante. Even though she considered him the 'greatest of Italian poets', his poetry could be summed up in that incisive pejorative, 'vitriolic verse'. She had no illusions about her literary influences and recognized a clear distinction between being influenced by another writer and sharing that writer's opinions, as she herself explained in a letter of 1849 (*L* i. 276–8).

In the 'Author's Introduction' to *Felix Holt*, we are told that the coach-driver knew the names of sites and people 'as well as the shade of Virgil in a more memorable journey'. This suggests that the novel will on some level be a guided tour of hell after the manner of *Inferno*. The idea resurfaces in the closing paragraph of the Introduction: 'The poets have told us of a dolorous enchanted forest in the under world'. The poets are *Virgil (*Aeneid*, iii) and Dante (*Inferno*, xiii). In Dante's 'enchanted forest', the trees contain the souls of the suicides, and a branch, when broken, bleeds and causes pain to the soul trapped within. Here George Eliot borrows the image to foreshadow the story of Mrs Transome, whose secret past is the cause of her present silent suffering. In his introduction to the 1972 Penguin edition, Peter Coveney claims that this Dantean tree imagery is 'central to the imagination of the work' (36).

The epigraph to chapter 19 of *Middlemarch* is from *Purgatorio*, vii. 107–8, and it serves to introduce the four chapters set in Italy. *Daniel Deronda*, however, makes a much more pervasive use of the *Commedia*. It contains several quotations from *Inferno*: canto v. 121–3 in chapter 17; canto iv. 112 in chapter 36; canto xxix. 43–4 in chapter 50; and canto vi. 106–8 is the epigraph to chapter 55. The story of La Pia from *Purgatorio*, v. 133–6 is alluded to in chapter 54. Genoa is described as 'a circle of punishment' at the beginning of chapter 64, but this hell-image is mitigated by the epigraph to that chapter (*Purgatorio*, iv. 88–90), which suggests that Gwendolen's life, after her husband's equi-

vocal death, will be one of (albeit secularized) repentance and eventual salvation.

When George Eliot died in 1880, Cross had a quotation from the *Inferno* (i. 79–80) inscribed on her coffin (Cross, iii. 438). The lines are voiced by Dante and addressed to Virgil, describing him as, 'Quella fonte | Che spande di parlar si largo fiume' ('that source | Which pours forth so wide a river of song'). See also FLORENCE; ITALY.   DB

Coveney, Peter, Introduction to *Felix Holt, the Radical* (1972).

Toynbee, Paget, *Britain's Tribute to Dante in Literature and Art* (1921).

Darwin, Charles (1809–82), English naturalist whose theory of evolution by natural selection in *On the Origin of Species*, published in 1859, created the major impact on Victorian thought (see DARWINISM). On 23 November 1859 George Eliot recorded in her journal: 'We began Darwin's work on "The Origin of Species" tonight. It seems to be not well written: though full of interesting matter, it is not impressive, from want of luminous and orderly presentation' (*Journals*, 82). But with the publication in 1860 of G. H. *Lewes's *Studies in Animal Life*, which is largely supportive of Darwin's theories, and his later series in the *Fortnightly Review* on Darwin, the early reactions gave way to broad acceptance. The Leweses were on visiting terms with the Darwins, who also attended a seance which disgusted the Leweses in 1874 (see SPIRITUALISM). After Lewes's death the Darwins continued to visit Eliot (*Journals*, 130).

Eliot's individual response to the importance of Darwin's discovery despite her reservations about its mode of expression was swift. Two days after her observations she wrote to Charles *Bray that she and Lewes were reading 'Darwin's Book on Species . . . It is an elaborate exposition of the evidence in favour of the Development Theory, and so, makes an epoch' (*L* iii. 214). And on 5 December she repeated her praise and reservations to Barbara *Bodichon, predicting that Darwin would make an indelible mark on the scientific world, commending his integrity and dedication but adding, 'to me the Development theory and all other explanations of processes by which things came to be, produce a feeble impression compared with the mystery that lies under the processes' (*L* iii. 227). Writing to George *Smith in July 1867 (*L* iv. 377) Eliot observes that 'natural selection is not always good, and depends (see Darwin) on many caprices of very foolish animals'. Ten years on the later Viscount Esher recorded in his journal that Eliot adored Charles Darwin because of his humility (*L* vi. 381). Lewes corresponded with Darwin, who obviously respected him as a scientist, and valued his friendship with them both. Lewes's articles on Darwin set him in the centre of the great controversy of the day and elevated him as a scientist in the eyes of some contemporaries, thus providing Eliot with the assurance of the wider recognition of his work which she coveted for him. See also SCIENCE. GRH

Darwinism. George Eliot greeted the publication of Charles *Darwin's *On the Origin of Species* as the making of an 'epoch' (*L* iii. 227). She and G. H. *Lewes had eagerly commenced reading this work 'after long expectation' on the very eve of its publication date, 24 November 1859. For Eliot it was not a startling work, but rather a thorough scientific exposition of the evidence supporting the 'Doctrine of Development', which would open up discussion of a topic 'about which people have hitherto felt timid. So the world gets on step by step towards brave clearness and honesty!' (*L* iii. 227). Eliot was already familiar with the ideas of evolution from the work of J. B. Lamarck (*Histoire naturelle des animaux sans vertèbres*, 1815), and Robert Chambers's popular work *Vestiges of the Natural History of Creation* (1844) and clearly did not at this stage note the distinguishing characteristic of Darwin's work: his identification of the *mechanism* of change in the processes of natural selection.

George Eliot was at this point in time a third of the way through *The Mill on the Floss*, a novel that displays a thorough preoccupation with issues of breeding, development, and survival. It is important to note that many of the issues crystallized by Darwin were already current in the cultural and scientific discourse of the era, discourses from which both writers drew inspiration. In considering 'Darwinism', therefore, we need to look at a cultural nexus of ideas which extends well beyond Darwin's own particular contribution. Although Eliot's reading of the *Origin* undoubtedly influenced her writing of *The Mill*, its framework was already 'Darwinian' in conception. Maggie Tulliver, who has the misfortune to be an intelligent female, is ironically introduced as 'a small mistake of nature', an unfortunate product of the 'crossing o' breeds' (*MF* 1.1). Human behaviour is repeat-

edly compared to that of animal life, from goldfish to beavers (see ANIMALS). Eliot draws on emerging anthropological theories of human development, but usually to stress the *lack* of real improvement, as in the comic contrast between the behaviour of Mrs Pullet, 'a fashionably dressed woman in grief' and that of a Hottentot. Where direct reference is made to the evolutionary distance between human and animal life, the gains seem of questionable nature. Tom early displays that 'desire for mastery over the inferior animals, wild and domestic, including cockchafers, neighbours' dogs and small sisters, which in all ages has been an attribute of so much promise for the fortunes of our race' (*MF* 1.9). Maggie, on the other hand, is differentiated from animal life by her 'superior power of misery' which places the human being 'at a proud distance from the most melancholy chimpanzee' (*MF* 1.6).

Darwin draws attention in his work to the sheer wasteful prodigality of nature, and Eliot, in a passage written shortly after she had read the *Origin*, likewise captures this sense of waste. Moving into direct authorial comment she suggests that St Ogg's is like the

narrow, angular skeletons of villages on the Rhone [which] oppress me with the feeling that human life—very much of it—is a narrow, ugly grovelling existence . . . I have a cruel conviction that the lives these ruins are the traces of, were part of a gross sum of obscure vitality, that will be swept into obscure oblivion with the generations of ants and beavers. (*MF* 4.1)

Darwin in his work was torn between the desire to celebrate the fecundity of nature, the wonderful adaptations, and progress towards perfection, and his sense of the unpleasantness of the 'war, famine and death' which underpinned the struggle for survival. Eliot registers a similar ambivalence. While noting the 'grovelling' nature of St Ogg's life, she none the less wishes to tie it to a vision of the 'onward tendency of human things' made possible by natural science, 'for does not science tell us that its highest striving is after the ascertainment of a unity which shall bind the smallest things with the greatest?' (*MF* 4.1). Darwin, in his theory, tied all of organic life into a single theory of adaptation and evolution. Eliot similarly seeks to bind her heroine's life into a larger vision of onward *progress. Her final emphasis falls, however, on the individual casualties of this process. Maggie is too finely formed to survive amidst the coarse community of St Ogg's; although highly developed she is none the less maladapted to her surroundings. Eliot's friend Herbert *Spencer had celebrated in his 1851 work *Social Statics* the 'state of universal warfare' in nature which would lead to the 'purifying' of stock, and hence to the development of 'a constitution completely adapted to surrounding conditions, and therefore most productive of happiness' (322). Eliot early on registers that the 'survival of the fittest' (a phrase Darwin drew from Spencer) is not necessarily that of the best.

The major difference between Darwin's theory and that of his predecessor Lamarck lay in the emphasis he placed on natural selection as the primary agency of change. Lamarck had outlined a theory of inheritance of 'acquired characteristics' which suggested that any efforts made towards improvement could be passed on to offspring. It was a theory that could be neatly encompassed within Victorian ideologies of self-improvement and moral effort. Darwin, by contrast, suggested that improvement could not be striven for; random individual variations occurred at birth, and it was a matter of chance whether these might lead to greater adaptation. It is unlikely that Eliot fully grasped the implications of Darwin's theory of natural selection initially; certainly her partner, G. H. Lewes, seems not to have come to terms with this aspect of the work until his series of articles 'Mr Darwin's Hypothesis' in the *Fortnightly Review* in 1868. His *Physiology of Common Life* (1859–60) is firmly committed to a theory of acquired characteristics, while his *Studies in Animal Life* (1862) draws on Darwin to celebrate the wondrous unity of Nature, at the same time as registering real doubts as to the underlying theory.

To some extent Eliot and Lewes's failure to register the full implications of natural selection can be linked to the uncertainties of Darwin's own text. Two models of development can be traced in the *Origin*. The first is progressive, celebrating the development of 'exquisite adaptations' of a plumed seed wafted by the gentlest breeze, or a beetle diving through water (51). Darwin notes in the conclusion that 'as natural selection works solely by and for the good of each being, all corporeal and mental endowments will tend to progress towards perfection' (395). Yet against this model of onward development one must set his statements elsewhere, that adaptation is relative: perfect adaptation at one moment could become maladaptation at another if the climate changes, or new competitors emerge. This latter model is the one subsequently associated with social Darwinism, where the elements of competitive struggle for scarce resources are emphasized. In place of evolving perfection we are given chance, warfare, and extermination. These two very different visions of *history are held in tension in Darwin's work, offering different possibilities for literary appropriation.

Early literary responses to Darwin tended to pick up on his celebration of the complex networks of connections and interdependencies that bind organic life, an idea that, as Beer (1983) and Levine (1988) point out, was itself already part of the literary culture of the era. All Eliot's novels display a fascination with the webs of interdependence that bind social life, and the workings of inheritance which extend that interdependence back into history. In *Middlemarch* Eliot foregrounds these relations of interdependence in her use of an organizing metaphor of the web (Beer 1983: ch. 5). Dorothea is introduced in Darwinian terms as a test case for the 'limits of variation'. The novel explores whether Dorothea, with her spiritual aspirations, and Lydgate, with his medical ideals, can survive in the uncongenial environment of Middling England. Like Darwin, Eliot is torn between her desire to celebrate the complex webs of interdependence which make up social life, and her despairing sense of the predatory basis of much of that interconnection. Hence Middlemarch 'counted on swallowing Lydgate, and assimilating him very comfortably'. In a strikingly Darwinian passage, Eliot outlines the struggle for survival which ensues when environmental stability is threatened by new settlers who come 'from distant counties, some with an alarming novelty of skill, others with an offensive advantage in cunning' (*MM* 11). Lydgate, for all his advantages in skill, is defeated by the environment of Middlemarch, while Dorothea seems to survive by moving away.

Humanity occupied a conspicuously absent role in *The Origin*. All the outcry about man's descent from the animal chain was based on extrapolation. In many ways Darwin had been exceedingly successful, leading his readers to reach his own conclusions, without ever stating the case. In 1871 he published *The Descent of Man and Selection in Relation to Sex*, openly discussing for the first time the implications of his theories for human life. As the title suggests, Darwin here focuses on another form of selection that had been only briefly touched upon in the *Origin*: sexual selection. This form of selection occurs in two ways: either the males compete for the females, and the strongest, victorious males become the most successful breeders, or, females choose male breeding partners according to aesthetic criteria: a bird's song, or brilliant plumage, for example. Darwin was clearly deeply troubled by the implications of the latter theory which gave to females a power of agency conspicuously lacking in Victorian culture. He is at pains to stress that in human life it is primarily females who are selected for their beauty, and not the other way round.

In *Daniel Deronda* (1876) Eliot directly addresses the issue of sexual selection. Following Gwendolen Harleth's dismissive thoughts on her ugly rival, Juliet Fenn, 'whose receding brow resembl[ed] that of the more intelligent fishes', the narrator intervenes to warn English males to 'look at themselves dispassionately in the glass, since their natural selection of a mate prettier than themselves is not certain to bar the effect of their own ugliness' (*DD* 11). It is a deliberate dig at the male-dominated marriage market in England, and a sly reminder that control cannot be exerted over inheritance and the forms of offspring. The realm Gwendolen inhabits seems to belong, despite its apparent sophistication, to the lower reaches of evolution. Grandcourt is repeatedly depicted as a form of reptilean or insect life, while the crowd round the gaming table in the opening scene seem to have shrunk into a form of automated, sub-human life. Through Gwendolen, Eliot reveals the illusion of choice: Gwendolen believes she is free to make her own sexual selection, but her experience reveals, crushingly, her actual powerlessness. Her world is a Darwinian one, characterized by chance (as epitomized by the gaming tables, and her family's losses on the stock market) and struggle. Yet, set alongside this negative picture, Eliot offers an alternate Darwinian vision: a realm of hope and potentiality, grounded in the workings of inheritance. Hebrew culture is 'an inheritance that has never ceased to quiver in millions of human frames'. The Jews are a nation, the visionary Mordecai proclaims, whose 'religion and law and moral life [have] mingled as the stream of blood in the heart and made one growth' (*DD* 42). Eliot is here drawing on the evolutionary psychology developed by both Herbert Spencer (*Principles of Psychology*, 1870–2) and her own partner, G. H. Lewes (*Problems of Life and Mind*, 1st ser, 1874–5) to offer a model of social progression based on both cultural and biological inheritance. It is significant, however, that Gwendolen is excluded from Deronda's forward march within the sweep of Jewish history.

In many ways the divisions within this final novel mirror the internal conflicts within Darwin's own work: a negative vision of a world dominated by chance and conflict is set alongside a positive vision of historical progress grounded in the workings of inheritance. 'Darwinism', for Darwin as much as his interpreters, was a complex, 'tangled bank' of ideas. See also NATURAL WORLD; SCIENCE. SAS

Darwin, Charles, *On the Origin of Species*, ed. Gillian Beer (1996).
Beer (1983).
Levine, George, *Darwin and the Novelists: Patterns of Science in Victorian Fiction* (1988).

Davies, Emily (1830–1921), campaigner for women's education, employment, and suffrage. It is from an 1869 letter by Davies that we know of George Eliot's pronouncement that *The Mill on the Floss* represents a collision between older and higher states of culture (*L* viii. 465). Eliot invited Davies to discuss her plans for the foundation of a women's college, subsequently subscribing £50 to what was to become Girton College (*L* iv. 399). She remained closely interested in the project, and keen that Davies should write a book on the subject of women's education (*L* iv. 401, 425). Davies's *The Higher Education of Women* (1866) provides a useful account of debates over women's education during the 19th century. (See also her *Thoughts on Some Questions relating to Women, 1860–1908*, 1910).

Frequently quoted in discussions of Eliot's equivocal attitude towards woman's nature is the letter to Davies in which she writes of her concern that 'there lies just that kernel of truth in the vulgar alarm of men lest women should be "unsexed"' and suggests that woman's possible maternity conferred qualities of gentleness, tenderness, and affectionateness which society cannot afford to lose (*L* iv. 468). The best defence of improved *education for women, she suggests, is 'to point out that complete union and sympathy' between the sexes 'can only come by women having opened to them the same store of acquired truth or beliefs as men have' (*L* iv. 468). See also WOMAN QUESTION. DdSC

death, as a theme. In George Eliot's first story, 'The Sad Fortunes of the Reverend Amos Barton', the death of the angelic Milly Barton, stroking the fair heads and kissing the tear-stained cheeks of her children in her final hours, is patently designed to create pathos, but this conventionally sentimental deathbed scene is an exception in the novelist's work. Even in the next two *Scenes of Clerical Life* the early deaths of Caterina and Tryan are handled more discreetly, while Captain Wybrow's sudden death from a heart attack, just before Caterina can reach him with her dagger, is the first in a series of providential deaths that are to be a feature of the novels. Such opportune deaths, like Casaubon's in *Middlemarch* moments before Dorothea is due to promise to honour his wishes after he has gone, may be more fully prepared than Wybrow's, but their timely convenience may seem to run counter to the stern insistence on the law of consequences that marks Eliot's *realism. The device has been criticized on these grounds and as a means of eliminating the need for aggression in characters like Dorothea and thus limiting their heroic and tragic potential (Christ, 130–40). But even though the providential death may be liberating, it still leaves moral dilemmas and consequences in its train that have to be faced. Dorothea may not be bound by a promise, but Casaubon's will still impugns her integrity and constricts her freedom of action by its insinuations; the death of Raffles in the same novel frees Bulstrode from blackmail but its suspicious convenience ultimately brings about his disgrace; in *Silas Marner* the death of Godfrey Cass's secret wife leaves him free but he still has to accept or shirk responsibility for his child; and in *Daniel Deronda* Grandcourt's death by drowning puts an end to Gwendolen's marital oppression but leaves her struggling with a desperate sense of guilt at having wished him dead. In a review article in the *Westminster Review* in January 1857, when she was writing *Scenes of Clerical Life*, George Eliot remarked ironically on the way that deaths in novels always happen opportunely, and her own recourse to that convention should be seen not as a regrettable lapse into romance but as a considered move in her exploration of moral behaviour. The sudden and violent deaths of overbearing husbands like Grandcourt, or like Dempster in 'Janet's Repentance' dying as a result of a drunken road accident, or Tito in *Romola* killed by Baldassare whom he had betrayed, are forms of poetic justice, but they all leave a woman who, like Dorothea, still has a life to lead and responsibilities to assume. Only in *The Mill on the Floss* does death provide a tragic resolution, but even the problematic embrace of Maggie and Tom in their *Liebestod* does not stop the issues raised by their diverging lives from continuing to reverberate. Although some characters are shown facing up to the prospect of death, as when Casaubon 'suddenly found himself on the dark river-brink and heard the plash of the oncoming oar' (*MM* 42), the strangest and most powerful contemplation of death is in the opening of 'The Lifted Veil' where the clairvoyant Latimer foresees in vivid detail how he soon will die in an agony of pain and suffocation, entirely alone and untended by his household.   JMR

Beer (1986).
Christ, Carol, 'Aggression and Providential Death in George Eliot's Fiction', *Novel*, 9 (1975–6).

deconstruction. See CRITICISM, MODERN: DE-CONSTRUCTION.

determinism is a term which (like *positivism, morality, and other such generics) has been often used in discussion of George Eliot's work in a way which obscures the distinctive nature of her ideas. In the case of determinism, she advanced the treatment of the term well beyond conventional understanding of it. This, however, was unfortunately not grasped at all by one of her contemporaries, F. W. H. *Myers, whose simple and thus memorable but ill-informed summary of her opinions misled several generations of readers (see Ermarth 1974: 274).

It is important, therefore, to begin by understanding what George Eliot does not mean by determinism. It does not mean that cultural life—the life of human consciousness and value—operates according to universal laws of the kind ascribed to the natural and material world. She was well acquainted with scientific knowledge and respected it for its power to silence 'preconceived notions' (*Essays*, 413). But through her entire career, George Eliot makes a point of separating the realm of culture—'the realm of light and speech'—from the regularities of material nature. She in no way assimilated her view of cultural and conscious life into a general realm of natural necessity. About the term 'necessitarianism', she wrote: 'I hate the ugly word' (*L* iv. 166).

Without a full sense of the whole of George Eliot's work—of all her fiction but also of her essays and translations—it is easy to mistake her strong sense of human freedom by assimilating it to the very deterministic models that she considered outworn. Her novels do emphasize the power of conditions and the weight of those conditions on individual choice: but only for the reason that those conditions—and not some imaginary ones—constitute the raw material of choice and action. It is the human condition which is precisely a realm apart from the calm determinism of nature which knows nothing of meaning or value, but only of physical mechanism.

This separate cultural realm consists of individual choice and responsibility, but also of tradition. Tradition is the name for that raw material of choice and action. While tradition is not single but multiple and contradictory, it is not chaotic; it is the cumulative result of lives lived, choices made, and actions taken long before any individual is born. For better or worse, these conditions are 'determinate' in the sense that they exist; in all their contradictoriness and finitude, they nevertheless constitute that 'hard, unaccommodating Actual' (*DD* 33) into which all individuals are born, and with reference to which all choices must be made and actions taken.

But 'determinate' is not at all the same thing as 'determined'. The hard unaccommodating Actual is only the starting point for choice and action; it is 'hard' and 'unaccommodating' because it is not subject to wish or caprice; whatever has already been thought and done and said, it governs invisibly the conditions in which real freedom can be exercised. When George Eliot says in an early book review, summarizing the author's point, that the 'undeviating law in the material and moral world . . . can alone give value to experience and render education in the true sense possible', she is claiming that the 'moral' world (in the French sense of *vie morale* or 'conscious life') contains principles of order, just as the material world does; she most decidedly is not claiming that they are the same principles as those found in the material world.

So, when she emphasizes the 'far reaching consequences of every action' (*L* iv. 286–9), as she often does in her writing, George Eliot is not suggesting that moral or cultural existence is 'determined for us' (as one of her weaker characters complains) but, on the contrary, insisting that it matters what we do: precisely because cultural conditions are pluralized and every action involves choice between different possibilities.

When she speaks of moral 'law' she is not referring moral life to the kind of single, systematic laws that govern the material universe. George Eliot's moral 'law' is diverse, not singular. This in itself might seem to be nothing new in the 19th century—the doctrine of the plurality of worlds had troubled astronomers and theologians since the early 17th century—but George Eliot's use of relativism moves further toward controversial outcomes of a kind more familiar in the late 20th century. Compared to material laws of the kind described by physical sciences, where the particulars exist as representatives and constituents of general laws, George Eliot's moral laws are the constituent elements, each a cumulative result of long-prepared actions. Every person, every book, every political protocol is in her sense a 'law': a determinate condition, irreducible and finite. The sum total of cultural embodiments, however described, constitutes the sum total of moral 'laws' in this sense. There is no single set, or system that unifies and rationalizes them all; they, like Ludwig *Feuerbach's individual persons, are unified only in aggregate. The impulse behind this thinking is closer to Camus's 'I rebel, therefore we exist' (*The Rebel*) than it is to Enlightenment rationality.

These 'laws' of culture, unlike those of nature, are embodied ideas, intentional objects produced for better or worse by human intention and imagination, or the lack of them. It is precisely because cultural objects are intentional in this sense, the resolved consequences of human effort, that they cannot meaningfully be systematized. When in *Middlemarch* Will Ladislaw famously tells Dorothea, 'you are a poem', he might as well have said, 'you are a moral "law"'. Dorothea's aspirations and limitations are themselves the resolved consequences of choices made by those who went before her—parents and legislators who, for instance, did not educate women, or who observed laws of primogeniture, or who removed politics from the hands of divine kings—and at the same time Dorothea is herself a 'law' or determinate condition influencing the lives of others. George Eliot's moral 'law' therefore is irreducibly diverse and

finite, but a 'law' none the less by virtue of being determinate and irreducible and not subject to caprice. See also MORAL VALUES; NATURAL WORLD; PHILOSOPHY. EDE

Beer, Gillian, 'Beyond Determinism: George Eliot and Virginia Woolf', in M. Jacobus (ed.), *Women Writing and Writing about Women* (1979).

Ermarth, Elizabeth, 'Incarnations: George Eliot's Conception of "Undeviating Law"', *Nineteenth-Century Fiction*, 29 (1974).

Levine, George, 'Determinism and Responsibility', *PMLA* 77 (1962).

Deutsch, Emanuel (1829–73), orientalist, Hebrew and Semitic scholar, popularizer into English of the Talmud and Midrash, known personally to George Eliot and G. H. *Lewes. He is the probable model for Mordecai in *Daniel Deronda*. Deutsch came to London from Prussian Silesia and found a position in 1855 at the British Museum. He wrote for *Chambers Encyclopedia*, Smith's *Dictionary of the Bible*, and other Victorian reference works. His October 1867 *Quarterly Review* article on 'The Talmud' aroused widespread attention. Writers such as Robert *Browning and Wilkie *Collins consulted him. Deutsch had socially well-connected patrons such as Sir A. H. Layard, the archaeologist. After his death in Alexandria, Emily Viscountess Strangford edited *The Literary Remains of the Late Emanuel Deutsch with a Brief Memoir* (1874). This contains nineteen of his essays ranging in topics from 'The Talmud' and 'Islam' to 'Early Arabic Poetry' and 'Arabic Poetry in Spain and Sicily'.

Eliot's friendship with Deutsch seems to have been particularly close in the years between 1867 and his death. Her letters to him reveal her awareness of his professional difficulties and personal desires. She wrote, 'we never *shall* be rosy and comfortable, and our good is to be got by weary struggle, and by that alone . . . This is not to tell you what you don't know already, O Rabbi.' Eliot's comments are 'simply the discourse of a fellow Houynhym! who is bearing the yoke with you' (Baker 1975: 132).

Deutsch visited Palestine in March 1869 writing to Lady Strangford: 'The East . . . all my wild yearnings fulfilled at last' (*Literary Remains*, p. xi). On his return in May 1869 he visited Eliot and Lewes giving them a full report of his impressions of Jerusalem and the Holy Land. In spite of ill health—cancer—he set out again in the autumn of 1872. He died on route before reaching the promised land.

Deutsch's articles on 'The Talmud', the Midrasch, the 'Targums', and medieval Jewish culture, are noted in Eliot's notebooks. Deutsch's personal experience, his physical suffering, yearning for a Jewish homeland, scholarship, desire to transmit his ideas and knowledge to others, all find poetic expression in *The Spanish Gypsy*, and fictional transformation, especially in the character of Mordecai, in *Daniel Deronda*. During his visits to The *Priory he answered Eliot's questions relating to Jewish history, *Judaism, and the significance of the land of Israel. As her letters reveal, he also gave Eliot Hebrew lessons (*L* v. 73).   WB

> *Some George Eliot Notebooks*, ed. William Baker, 4 vols. (1976–85).
> Baker (1975).
> Temple, Mary Kay, 'Emanuel Deutsch's Literary Remains: A New Source for George Eliot's *Daniel Deronda*', *South Atlantic Review*, 54 (1989).

Dickens, Charles (1812–70), English novelist who was at the height of his powers and popularity when George Eliot began writing fiction and who both admired her early work and sensed that it was written by a woman. She first saw Dickens, in May 1852, when he chaired a protest meeting against the price-fixing of the Booksellers' Association held at John *Chapman's premises in the Strand, where she was working on the *Westminster Review*. While praising his conduct of the meeting in a letter to Charles *Bray, she found his appearance disappointingly undistinguished, showing none of the benevolence she had seemingly expected (*L* ii. 23–4). A few weeks earlier she had commented ironically on the luxury in which this sympathizer with the suffering classes was known to live (*L* ii. 17–18). Her critical estimation of his work in this period can be seen in her essay on 'The *Natural History of German Life' in July 1856. Finding fault with sentimental and heroic representations of peasants and workers, she clearly refers to Dickens, without naming him, when she writes of 'one great novelist who is gifted with the utmost power of rendering the external traits of our town population', and who would make the greatest contribution to the awakening of social sympathies if he could give their psychological character as well (*Essays*, 271). In this criticism of Dickens for presenting characters only in terms of outward appearance, idiom, and manners, she may fail to understand his achievement but she is indicating in advance the direction in which her own fiction is to go when, in the following weeks, she begins to write *Scenes of Clerical Life*. Her implied principles are those of a *realism that refuses to sentimentalize ordinary life by creating 'preternaturally virtuous poor children and artisans' and suggesting that 'high morality and refined sentiment can grow out of harsh social relations, ignorance, and want' (*Essays*, 271–2). One may question whether her own fiction is always as far from Dickens's in this respect as her criticism would imply, but she clearly differs from him in

the way in which she explores and analyses the complex inner lives of her characters (see CHARACTERIZATION). The Dickens novel she clearly has in mind in the *Westminster Review* essay is *Little Dorrit*, and it has been suggested that *Middlemarch* many years later can be seen as an unconscious revision of that novel (Booth, 199). Comparison can certainly be made between Dorothea in Rome and Little Dorrit in Italy (Leavis, 423–8), and both heroines are finally shown proceeding to a modest life of usefulness and happiness through marriage.

When *Scenes of Clerical Life* appeared in book form she had a presentation copy sent to Dickens. After reading the first two stories, Dickens wrote to George Eliot in January 1858 praising the 'exquisite truth and delicacy, both of the humour and the pathos' in them and maintaining that the masculine name of the author on the title-page failed to convince him: 'If they originated with no woman, I believe that no man ever before had the art of making himself, mentally, so like a woman, since the world began' (*L* ii. 423–4). The letter moved her deeply and she was unhappy that the 'iron mask' of her incognito prevented her from writing to him to express her appreciation (*L* ii. 424). When Dickens launched his new weekly *All the Year Round* in the following year, he had his manager invite George Eliot to write for it. It was only after she had dropped the mask of her incognito that she replied, expressing her interest. Dickens then wrote to her directly in July 1859 announcing his pleasure at being able to write to her as a woman and praising *Adam Bede* warmly. He also delicately repeated the suggestion that she might like to write for *All the Year Round*, maintaining that no other form of publication would be so profitable to her, and expressed his desire to meet her (*L* iii. 115). Their first meeting took place on 10 November when Dickens dined with her and G. H. *Lewes—whom he had known for years—at their home in Wandsworth. Four days later Dickens wrote to Lewes about the possibility of her producing a new novel for *All the Year Round*, retaining copyright for herself and choosing her own publisher for the completed novel after serialization. She was by this time writing *The Mill on the Floss*, but Dickens wanted to sign up her next novel, to begin appearing in July 1860. On 18 November she declined his proposal on account of the pressure of time (Cross, ii. 142). Nevertheless, she had been impressed by meeting him, describing him as 'a man one can thoroughly enjoy talking to—there is a strain of real seriousness along with his keenness and humour' (*L* iii. 200); and they remained on friendly terms, meeting socially from time to time. He was the one person to whom she sent a presentation copy of *The Mill on the Floss*.

In the last months of his life he visited The *Priory on several occasions, lunching there for the last time on 6 March 1870 when he entertained the company with the story of Lincoln having a premonition on the day of his death that something momentous was about to happen (*L* v. 81). Dickens looked 'dreadfully shattered' himself and his own death came only three months later. The following year Eliot was reading John *Forster's *Life*, finding particular interest in its information about Dickens's childhood and in his letters from America but criticizing the 'keepsakey' portrait by Daniel Maclise with its 'odious . . . beautification' and preferring a photo of the young Dickens which she had acquired and which corresponded to the older Dickens whom she had known (*L* v. 226). She later remarked on the melancholy aspect of his latter years with their feverish pursuit of loud effects and money.

After his death she was indisputably the greatest living English novelist for the ten years that were left to her. Although Edward *Bulwer-Lytton found in The Mill on the Floss 'a little unconscious imitation of Dickens' (*CH* 120), and although there may be distant echoes of *Little Dorrit* in *Middlemarch*, their writing has little in common. In the *Fortnightly Review* in February 1872 Lewes published a fine article on 'Dickens in Relation to Criticism' which was the first to examine the psychological aspects of Dickens's imagination, famously asserting that 'in no other perfectly sane mind have I observed vividness of imagination approaching so closely to hallucination' (144); but when he points to what is missing in Dickens's work, he seems to imply a comparison with a very different kind of novelist: 'Thought is strangely absent from his work . . . one sees no indication of the past life of humanity having ever occupied him; keenly as he observes the objects before him, he never connects his objects into a general expression, never seems interested in general relations of things' (151). Power of thought, understanding of the history of humanity, and a sure grasp of the general relations of things: in defining Dickens's failings Lewes indicates some of George Eliot's strengths.   JMR

Booth, Alison, 'Little Dorrit and Dorothea Brooke: Interpreting the Heroines of History', *Nineteenth-Century Fiction*, 41 (1986–7).

Leavis, Q. D., 'A Note on Literary Indebtedness: Dickens, George Eliot, Henry James', *Hudson Review*, 8 (1955).

Dickinson, Emily (1830–86), American poet whose ardent interest in '*my* George Eliot' (*Letters of Emily Dickinson*, iii. 700) lasted from *c*.1862, when she acquired *The Mill on the Floss*, until her death. Dickinson's correspondence reveals a highly personal, often passionate, engagement with George Eliot's life and works. '"What do I think of *Middlemarch*?"' she replied to friends who had asked: 'What do I think of glory—' (*Letters of Emily Dickinson*, ii. 506). Reading *Daniel Deronda*, she described George Eliot as 'the Lane to the Indes, Columbus was looking for', later recommending it as a 'wise and tender Book . . . full of sad (high) nourishment' (*Letters of Emily Dickinson* ii. 551; iii. 865)—though her niece reported that Dickinson called Grandcourt's drowning 'a cheap way out' (Martha Dickinson Bianchi, *Emily Dickinson Face to Face* (1932), 170). In April 1883 Mathilde Blind's biography led Dickinson to characterize George Eliot's life as 'a Doom of Fruit without the Bloom, like the Niger Fig' (*Letters of Emily Dickinson*, iii. 769) and to write a commemorative poem in vindication: 'Her Losses make our Gains ashamed—| She bore Life's empty Pack | As gallantly as if the East | Were swinging at her Back. | Life's empty Pack is heaviest, | As every Porter knows— | In vain to punish Honey— | It only sweeter grows' (*Poems*, no. 1562). January 1885 saw Dickinson, curiosity unslaked, 'watching like a vulture' for Cross's biography (*Letters of Emily Dickinson*, iii. 856). Critics have noted similarities in George Eliot's and Dickinson's religious crises and in their imagery, satire, and social criticism. Probably *The Mill* was especially influential; Dickinson's poem beginning 'Me prove it now— Whoever doubt' (*Poems*, no. 537, *c*.1862) may be a revision of Maggie's drowning in which Maggie is thinking of Stephen Guest, not her brother Tom.

KKC

The Letters of Emily Dickinson, ed. Thomas H. Johnson (1958).

The Poems of Emily Dickinson, ed. Thomas H. Johnson (1955).

Cary, Cecile W., '*The Mill on the Floss* as an Influence on Emily Dickinson', *Dickinson Studies*, 36 (1979).

Phillips, Elizabeth, *Emily Dickinson: Personae and Performance* (1988).

Disraeli, Benjamin, (1804–81), novelist, statesman, politician, Prime Minister (1868, 1874–80), created first Earl of Beaconsfield (1876). George Eliot and Disraeli seem not to have personally met but she knew his work well and her attitude both to his writing and to his political career seems to have changed from that of hostility to sympathy and admiration. Eliot comments on her reading of *Sybil* (1845) in a letter to Charles *Bray in May 1845: 'I am not utterly disgusted with D'Israeli . . . The man hath good veins . . . but there is not enough blood in them' (*L* i. 192–3). Two years later she accuses Disraeli in a letter to Mary *Sibree of May 1847 of 'writing himself much more detestable stuff than ever came from a French pen'. Disraeli 'can do nothing better to bamboozle the unfortunates who are seduced into reading his

Tancred than speak superciliously of all other men and things' (*L* i. 235–6). Her response to *Tancred*, *Coningsby*, and *Sybil*, and to Disraeli's political stance of 'Young Englandism'—a form of egalitarian élitism—are found at length in a letter of February 1848 to John *Sibree: *Tancred* she found 'thin and inferior' to the other novels, 'Young Englandism . . . almost as remote from my sympathies as Jacobitism as far as its form is concerned'. Disraeli 'is unquestionably an able man' and she enjoys 'his tirades against liberal principles as opposed to *popular* principles'. His racial theories, however, have not a leg to stand on, and 'The fellowship of race, to which D'Israeli exultingly refers the munificence of Sidonia, is so evidently an inferior impulse which must ultimately be superseded that I wonder even he, Jew as he is, dares to boast of it. My Gentile nature kicks most resolutely against any assumption of superiority in the Jews.' She ends her diatribe: 'Everything *specifically* Jewish is of a low grade' (*L* i. 246–7).

In November 1852 she draws Mr and Mrs Charles Bray's attention to a 'sample of plagiarism by Disraeli' (*L* ii. 69). However, her explorations into the areas of political radicalism, class conflict, and the consequences of industrialism—found for instance in *Felix Holt, the Radical*; her review article 'The *Natural History of German Life' in the *Westminster Review*, 1856; and *'Address to Working Men, by Felix Holt'—have much in common with ideas found in *Sybil*. Unlike Disraeli she doesn't create a union between the ruling class—the aristocracy—and the people, in order to regenerate England. For Eliot the everyday, common life will be the source for the regeneration of society.

Her last completed novel, *Daniel Deronda*, and parts of *The Spanish Gypsy*, show a change of opinion in that they share similar concerns with notions of *nationalism, *race, blood, inheritance, orientalism, and the return to Zion, to those found in Disraeli's *Tancred*, *Coningsby*, and his early novels in which his heroes embark on voyages of self-realization, especially *Alroy* (1833), and *Henrietta Temple* (1837). In the latter novel the central character, Ferdinand Armine, is found to be, rather like Daniel Deronda, the scion of an 'illustrious and fallen race'.

A passage from *Tancred* concerning the lack of leadership on the part of English bishops in relation to the condition of England is found in Eliot's late notebooks. She does not draw upon Disraeli for *epigraphs in her novels and there is hardly any direct mention of him in her later letters. In February 1876, during the serialization of *Daniel Deronda*, she wrote to John *Blackwood: 'Doubtless the wider public of novel-readers must feel more interest in Sidonia than in Mordecai. But

then, I was not born to paint Sidonia' (*L* vi. 223), the enigmatic Jewish hero of *Coningsby*. Eliot's ideas in *Deronda* are more eclectic and cosmopolitan than Disraeli's. Her intention, as she told Harriet Beecher *Stowe in an October 1876 letter, is 'to rouse the imagination of men and women to a vision of human claims in those races of their fellow-men who most differ from them in customs and beliefs' (*L* vi. 301), not to assert with Disraeli Jewish superiority over the Gentiles. There is little doubt that she is engaging in a dialogue with his ideas on race, history, and inheritance in her essays 'Shadows of the Coming Race' and 'The Modern Hep! Hep! Hep!' (*TS* 17, 18).

Edith *Simcox records in her *Autobiography*, 26 December 1879, that Eliot vigorously defended Disraeli. She was 'disgusted with the venom of' parliamentary attacks on him. He was no fool, 'he must care for a place in history and how could he expect to win that by doing harm?' (*L* ix. 282). It is Lewes who makes the most references to Disraeli and these are tinged with a degree of irony. His review of the fifth edition of *Coningsby* in the *British Quarterly* (August 1849) is hostile to the novel and to Disraeli's politics, personality, and ideas. A 9 October 1877 letter to John Blackwood retells an anecdote told by Jowett: 'When Ignetieff was with Lord Salisbury he was talking of D'Israeli & said in his soft feline manner, "There are several points on which your prime minister & myself are not agreed; but on *one* point we are thoroughly agreed & that is—the love of truth!"' (*Letters of Lewes*, ed. Baker, ii. 236). Eliot and Lewes were close to Disraeli's Indian Viceroy Edward Robert Bulwer-Lytton. Their correspondence has scant reference to Disraeli and his administration, dwelling rather on literary and family matters. For his part Disraeli seems to have been too busy in office to react to *Daniel Deronda* (*L* vi. 282). See also ANTI-SEMITISM; JUDAISM.   WB

Brantlinger, Patrick, 'Nations and Novels: Disraeli, George Eliot, and Orientalism', *Victorian Studies*, 35 (1992).

Guy, Josephine M., *The Victorian Social-Problem Novel* (1996).

The Letters of George Henry Lewes, ed. William Baker (1995).

Ragussis, Michael, *Figures of Conversion: 'The Jewish Question' and English National Identity* (1995).

Donizetti, Gaetano (1797–1848), Italian opera composer. Donizetti's *La Favorite* (1840) was the first opera George Eliot saw (*L* iv. 145). She saw *Les Martyrs* (a revised [1839] version of *Poliuto* [1838]) in April 1852, and *L'elisir d'amore* (1832) in London in July 1863 and in Turin on 8 May 1864. In July 1857 she saw Giulia Grisi—'still lovely and impassioned', G. H. *Lewes recorded (*L* ii. 370 n.)—in *Lucrezia Borgia* (1833). In *Daniel Deronda*, the artist Hans Meyrick asserts that Grandcourt 'has the sort of handsome physique that the duke ought to have in *Lucrezia Borgia*—if it could go with a fine baritone, which it can't' (*DD* 45). See also MUSIC.   BG

Dowden, Edward (1843–1913), Professor of English Literature, University of Dublin, who wrote an article on George Eliot which was published in the *Contemporary Review* (August 1872). G. H. *Lewes wrote to him that it displayed 'a deep sympathetic insight' into 'one who is more than life to me' (*L* v. 299): it moved him to tears and later he read some of it aloud to a 'touched' Eliot. Ever promotional, he suggested to Dowden that the essay be expanded into book form as *George Eliot: A Critical Study* (*L* vi. 255): Eliot thought Dowden 'worthy of attention and regard' (*L* vi. 266) but could not comment on the proposal to write about her. According to Dowden, pressure of work precluded his writing a critical study of Eliot, but he told John *Blackwood that he was pleased to have had his say about *Daniel Deronda* (*L* vi. 333) in the *Contemporary Review* (January 1877). Both essays were reprinted in Dowden's *Studies in Literature 1789–1877* (1877): they are an example of early detailed criticism, particularly the second, which defines the interrelationship of *Middlemarch* and *Daniel Deronda*, the latter existing on 'a higher plane of thought and feeling than any other work of its author'.   GRH

Dresden, the capital of the German state of Saxony, was described by George Eliot in 1856, before she had ever been there, as 'one of the most interesting capitals in the world' (*Saturday Review,* 2: 424). The reality did not disappoint her. On their second visit to *Germany she and G. H. *Lewes spent six happy weeks there in July and August 1858, finding it, in Lewes's words, 'one of the most habitable of German towns' (*L* ii. 469). The sound of birds and the perpetual sight of green foliage made a refreshing change from the prospect of tall blank houses they had experienced in *Munich. Settled in a large apartment and undisturbed by visitors, they were able to work quietly and steadily, and during their stay Eliot completed the latter half of the second volume of *Adam Bede*. For relaxation they would visit the picture gallery three times a week, where the most sublime painting to their eyes was *Raphael's *Sistine Madonna*, which they returned to again and again and found harder and harder to leave. In the rich collection they also admired paintings by Holbein and *Titian and portraits by *Rembrandt (*Journals*, 325–6). Dresden also offered them open-air concerts, theatres, and walks into the open country outside the town, 'all helping to make an agreeable fringe to the quiet working time' (*Journals*, 326). The stay was so happy and rewarding that they chose to return to Dresden in 1867 when they were, as she wrote in her journal, 'revisiting the scenes of cherished memories' (*Journals*, 130). On that occasion George Eliot was working on *The Spanish Gypsy* and she rewrote the scene between Fedalma and Zarca. See also VISUAL ARTS.   JMR

E

earnings of George Eliot. George Eliot's first earnings were £20 for her translation of D. F. *Strauss's Das Leben Jesu*, published in 1846 (and 25 copies of the book). Her later translation of Ludwig *Feuerbach was hardly more lucrative: she earned 2s. a page, about £30 in all. She was in the fortunate position of having a small income of about £90 annually from her father's estate, so that when she went to *London in 1851 she was not entirely dependent on her earnings. Her work as editor of the *Westminster Review* appears to have been unpaid, though she received the usual contributors' rate for articles. From 1855, the details of payments received were methodically entered in her journal and later in an account book. She tallied in her journal her earnings for 1855: £119. 8s. 0d., and then £192. 11s. 0d. for 1856: she was getting a guinea for a review in the *Leader*, twelve guineas for 'Belles Lettres' in the *Westminster Review*, and sums ranging between twelve and twenty pounds for major essays.

Her first earnings from fiction were £52.10s. 0d. for 'Amos Barton' in *Blackwood's Edinburgh Magazine*, the serial publication bringing her £263 in all, and the first edition £180. With the success of *Adam Bede*, her income began to increase markedly, and she earned £1,705 from it, the bulk from William *Blackwood and Sons, but with payments of £30 for an American edition, £50 from a *Tauchnitz edition, and £25 from a German translation. *The Mill on the Floss* earned £3,685 in the year of publication, 1860, including such additional fees as £300 for the American reprint and £100 for the German; the following year, the one-volume *Silas Marner* made £5,345, again including fees for reprints. Such figures put in perspective the splendour of George *Smith's offer for the entire copyright of *Romola*, initially £10,000, and eventually £7,000 for twelve monthly instalments in the *Cornhill Magazine* (she needed fourteen),

with the copyright reverting to George Eliot after six years. Blackwood paid his returning prodigal £5,000 for *Felix Holt*. Late in 1879, George Eliot tallied her total earnings from *Middlemarch* at a figure approaching £9,000, and over £9,000 for *Daniel Deronda*. Her own calculation of her career earnings came to more than £45,000. By contrast, G. H. *Lewes earned more than £1,000 only in those years in the 1860s when he had income as editor of the *Fortnightly Review* and the *Pall Mall Gazette*; and his total income in the 1870s was hardly more than £1,000.

Anthony *Trollope, a much more prolific writer than George Eliot, in the closing chapter of *An Autobiography* (1883) reported a tally up to 1879 of £68,959. 17s. 5d.: he earned around £2,500 to £3,000 for most of his three-volume novels, £3,525 for *Can You Forgive Her?* (1864) being the top price fetched by one of his works. Dickens, famously the most entrepreneurial of the great Victorian novelists, earned around £80,000 from his novels alone (including part publication). See also PUBLISHERS, NEGOTIATIONS WITH.   MAH

Edgeworth, Maria (1767–1849), Irish novelist who is best remembered for her tales of Irish social life and children's stories. When a schoolgirl at the Misses Franklin's George Eliot had to translate pages from Maria Edgeworth into French, as a result of which she received a prize of *Pascal's *Pensées*. The experience remained with her. As late as 5 September 1879 (*L* vii. 197) when she is recommending a school friend for translation work to Major William *Blackwood she says, 'We sat side by side on the same form translating Miss Edgeworth into French when we were girls'.   GRH

editor, George Eliot as. See JOURNALIST, GEORGE ELIOT AS.

education in a broad sense is of crucial importance for individual and social development in George Eliot's fiction, whilst English formal education and its institutions are a frequent target of ironic criticism. In the first of the *Scenes of Clerical Life* the Revd Amos Barton, despite having 'gone through the Eleusinian mysteries of a University education' (*SC* 1.2), is ignorant of Greek and Hebrew and cannot even write English correctly. The uncompleted university education lavished on Fred Vincy in *Middlemarch* is similarly ineffective, preparing him for nothing but a career in the Church to which he is entirely unsuited. His real education comes from working on the land with Caleb Garth. Daniel Deronda in Eliot's last novel leaves Cambridge without completing his university education since he wants to be rid of a 'merely English attitude in studies' and to come to understand other points of view by studying abroad (*DD* 16). In *Middlemarch* the best educated characters, Lydgate and Ladislaw, have done just that, studying in *Paris and Heidelberg, while Casaubon's researches are hampered by the merely English attitude that has left him ignorant of German. The example of Christy Garth suggests that Scottish universities offer a better education that English ones (*MM* 57).

The narrowness of conventional English education—which George Eliot and *G. H. Lewes sought to avoid for Lewes's sons by sending them to school in *Switzerland (see LEWES FAMILY)—is most dramatically illustrated in the rigid and pointless instruction in 'the Eton grammar and Euclid' that Tom Tulliver receives from Mr Stelling in *The Mill on the Floss* (*MF* 2.1); while the fact that Maggie is excluded from even this rudimentary schooling emphasizes the much narrower educational opportunities available to women. Women's education is the object of Eliot's most scathing ironies, for it seems to be predicated on the prejudiced assumptions of men like Stelling that girls are quick and shallow: 'They can pick up a little of everything . . . but they couldn't go far into anything' (*MF* 2.1). Thus Dorothea's education in *Middlemarch* has been both narrow and promiscuous, leaving her with 'a great mental need, not to be satisfied by a girlish instruction comparable to the nibblings and judgements of a discursive mouse' (*MM* 3). It is 'that toy-box history of the world' (*MM* 10) imparted to her as the main element in her education that is responsible for making Casaubon and his researches seem impressive. The shallowness of conventional female education is epitomized by the school of which Rosamond Vincy is the flower, Mrs Lemon's academy, 'where the teaching included all that was demanded in the accomplished female—even to extras, such as the getting in and out of a carriage' (*MM* 10). This is not attributable simply to the setting of the novel in the 1830s, for in the near contemporary *Daniel Deronda* Gwendolen has had a similarly shallow education (*DD* 4). It is not surprising that George Eliot lent support to the founding of Girton College at Cambridge (see WOMAN QUESTION).

It is the less formal education offered by Bartle Massey's night school in *Adam Bede* that is sympathetically portrayed, stirring in Adam a fellow-feeling 'as he looked at the rough men painfully holding pen or pencil with their cramped hands, or humbly labouring through their reading lesson' (*AB* 21). This is an example of men exerting themselves to break the yoke of ignorance such as Eliot urges on the working class in the *'Address to Working Men, by Felix Holt'. Education in this sense is seen as vital to the cohesion and develop-

ment of society, while the informal education that a character like Deronda undergoes in his contacts with Mordecai, Gwendolen, and Mirah is more valuable than his formal schooling. In her 1855 essay on Carlyle, George Eliot maintained that the highest aim in education was 'to obtain not results but *powers*', and that the most effective educator is one 'who does not seek to make his pupils moral by enjoining particular courses of action, but by bringing into activity the feelings and sympathies that must issue in noble action' (*Essays*, 213). In her last novel it is that kind of education that Deronda receives in his apprenticeship to life, and it is that kind of educator he becomes in his relationship with Gwendolen. See also BILDUNGS-ROMAN; SOCIETY.   JMR

Robertson, Linda K., *The Power of Knowledge: George Eliot and Education* (1997).

Spittles (1993).

'Edward Neville' is the first surviving attempt at fiction by Mary Ann Evans, the future George Eliot. It is a fragment of an historical story about the English civil war, written when she was 14 and contained in a school notebook dated 16 March 1834 and bearing the name Marianne Evans. This version of her name may reflect her recent introduction to French (Haight 1968: 552), and might be seen as a bid for the dignity that befits an aspiring author. In the fragment, Edward Neville, a young supporter of Parliament who is fleeing from Royalist forces after a military defeat, rides into Chepstow on an autumn morning in 1650 to see his uncle Henry Marten, confined for life in the castle. Surprising his irascible uncle by his appearance, he tells of his recent adventures and of the existence of a traitor in the parliamentary ranks. Then after an account of Edward's background and upbringing, and his love for Mary Mordaunt, the story breaks off. The fragment was first published in Haight's biography and it was Haight who gave it the title of 'Edward Neville' (1968: 554–60). There is also a recent annotated edition by Juliet McMaster. The manuscript is in the Beinecke Library at Yale University.

The choice of a historical subject indicates the influence of Walter *Scott, the favourite author of her early years; and like Scott she combines fictional characters such as Edward Neville with historical figures like Henry Marten, one of the judges at the trial of Charles I and later imprisoned for regicide. Edward Neville's determined and haughty character may owe something to Cleveland in Scott's *The Pirate* (McMaster, et al., pp. vi–vii). The beginning of the story seems to be modelled on the work of another historical novelist with which she was familiar, G. P. R. James. The figure of the solitary horseman is James's characteristic opening device (McMaster, et al., p. vii), and it is one that George Eliot was later to use again herself at the beginning of *Adam Bede*, where an elderly unnamed traveller on horseback serves to provide an outsider's view of Adam, Hayslope, and Dinah Morris's sermon on the Green. The description of the historical Henry Marten also prefigures in some respects the characterization of the historical Savonarola in chapter 15 of *Romola* (McMaster, et al., p. ix). The historical orientation of this early fragment was to remain a central aspect of Eliot's fiction, and in *Romola*, the only one of her works that is a historical novel in the same sense as Scott's, she focuses on another period of civil and religious strife like the English civil war, but this time in 15th-century *Florence. 'Edward Neville' is interesting as apprentice work which, with the benefit of hindsight, can be seen to give some indication of the career to come. That the aspiring author did not continue with her effort at fiction may be attributed in part to the period of evangelical zeal that she was about to enter. A few years later she was to consider 'all novels and romances pernicious' (*L* i. 23). See also HISTORY.

JMR

Edward Neville by Marianne Evans (George Eliot), ed. Juliet McMaster et al. (1995).

Eliot, T. S. (1888–1965), poet, literary and social critic, dramatist. T. S. Eliot's most memorable pronouncement on George Eliot occurs in a work he later disavowed, *After Strange Gods: A Primer of Modern Heresy* (1934), the published version of three lectures given at the University of Virginia in 1933. Acknowledged as symptomatic of acute anxiety, the book is an acerbic critique of the decayed condition of the civilized world as he saw it, with its endemic liberalisms and self-indulgent deviations. His arguments are interlaced with damning illustrations drawn from a wide-ranging tradition of writers modern and previous whom he regarded as aberrant and contributing to disintegration. Of 19th-century writers, including Jane *Austen, Charles *Dickens, and William Makepeace *Thackeray, but excepting Gustave *Flaubert, he asserted:

They are orthodox enough according to the light of their day: the first suspicion of heresy creeps in with a writer who, at her best, had much profounder moral insight and passion than these, but who unfortunately combined it with the dreary rationalism of the epoch of which she is one of the most colossal monuments: George Eliot. George Eliot seems to me of the same tribe as all the serious and eccentric moralists we have had since: we must respect her for being a serious moralist, but deplore her individualistic morals. (*After Strange Gods*, 54)

T. S. Eliot did not refer to George Eliot extensively. There is, however, one further noteworthy aside, in 'The Three Voices of Poetry' (1953), from *On Poetry and Poets* (1957). Here T. S. Eliot, ever preoccupied with the filiations of good and evil, examining the generation of character and the insinuations of language, murmurs, '(And I am quite sure that Rosamond Vincy, in *Middlemarch*, frightens me far more than Goneril or Regan.)'— something of a coup for George Eliot, whatever the circumstances.   AE

Ackroyd, Peter, *T. S. Eliot* (1984).
Ricks, Christopher, *T. S. Eliot and Prejudice* (1994).
Tamplin, Ronald, *A Preface to T. S. Eliot* (1988).

Emerson, Ralph Waldo (1803–82), American philosophical essayist, poet, and lecturer whom George Eliot described, after their meeting in July 1848, as 'the first *man* I have ever seen'; Emerson, in turn, praised her calm, serious soul (*L* i. 270–1). In 1843 Mary *Sibree noticed Emersonian leanings in George Eliot's view of the *Bible (*L* i. 162), but references to Emerson in the letters do not specify the precise grounds on which his thought interested her. She read *Man the Reformer* (1841) for her spiritual good and found in *Society and Solitude* (1870) enough gospel to serve one for a year (*L* iii. 337; v. 93). On New Year's Day 1877, contemplating her rickety body and the prospect of the great parting, she recalled Emerson's poem 'Days' (1857), in which the lingering years offer gifts—but she admitted that Emerson was perhaps thinking of the something good rather than the many things evil (*L* vi. 327). After Emerson's death, an essay in *Century Magazine* (23: 619–21) contrasted his joy to George Eliot's melancholy. Recently Emerson's *The American Scholar* (1837) has been cited as a source of her treatment of uncreative scholarship in *Romola*. One might add that in *The American Scholar* Emerson also expressed an intellectual commitment that would characterize George Eliot's early fiction: 'I embrace the common, I explore and sit at the feet of the familiar, the low' (*Collected Works*, i. ed. Alfred R. Ferguson and Robert E. Spiller (1971), 67). Emerson's papers contain a reference to *The Spanish Gypsy*, which he considered manufactured, not natural poetry (*Journals and Miscellaneous Notebooks*, xvi. ed. Ronald A. Bosco and Glen M. Johnson (1982), 105). See also AMERICA; ROUSSEAU, JEAN-JACQUES.

KKC

Fontana, Ernest, 'George Eliot's *Romola* and Emerson's "The American Scholar"', *English Language Notes*, 32 (1995).

Empire, British. See COLONIALISM.

endings of novels. George Eliot recognized the make-believe of endings, as she did of beginnings, but her own treatment reflects the realist's love of narrative and historical continuity, as well as her command of the arts of narrative. Endings of all her fictions are constructed in generic categories (see GENRES) and conventions of form and theme: *tragedy and comedy, *death and *marriage, openness and closure.

Her inherited culture was Christian and humanist, inclining her to create didactic and meliorist—often optimistic—conclusions. In *Scenes of Clerical Life* the three important characters die significant deaths, Milly Barton of pregnancies, miscarriages, and family strain, Caterina of deprivation and pregnancy, Tryan of tuberculosis and overwork; Milly is the domestic martyr, Caterina the poor orphan destroyed by patronage, Tryan the seducer converted to good clerical social worker. Sacrificial death is redeemed by significant survival: Milly's happy family, Tina's good vicar-husband, the reformed noble Janet. The endings are morally optimistic, mutedly tragic, closed, marked by Eliot's habit of bringing the historically retrospective novel up to date: in 'Amos Barton' we dip into the future to see a professionally successful son, and a maiden daughter keeping up traditions of family martyrdom. Such endings, like those of *Silas Marner* and *The Mill on the Floss*—and most Dickens novels—show life going on after the story's end to catch up with the reader's time. *Middlemarch*'s Finale juxtaposes conventional plot projections with historical openings.

Moral endings stress loss and gain, rewarding altruists and punishing egoists: Hetty's and Arthur's losses, Adam and Dinah's gain, Maggie and Tom's drowning, and reunion in love and vision; vastation and horror in 'The Lifted Veil' where a perverted creative narrator is enabled, by dexterous fantasy, to conclude his own death; Godfrey and Nancy's loss, Marner's paternal content, Tito's and Savonarola's destructions, Romola's sublimation, the Transomes' tragedy, Esther's and Felix's union, the fine intricate web of *Middlemarch*, the isolation of Gwendolen, the *vocation and marriage of Deronda. The emphasis is on moral discovery, sadness companioned, often alleviated, by ethical joy. Eliot used fiction to praise life without opiate, imagining failure and success—not ahistorically.

Fundamental to her art is an evolving historical consciousness (see HISTORY). Her endings are often politically analytic, conclusively summing up private story in a public context (see SOCIETY). *Adam Bede* ends with Dinah the preacher kept at home—by history. The first edition of *Middlemarch* strongly stressed social causes at the end; though revision muted this political summing-up, it preserved the many well-wishers ahistorically lamenting Dorothea's absorption into a domestic lot, to provoke the narrator's insistence on history,

'no one stated exactly what else was in her power she ought rather to have done'. It kept an emphasis on unideal achievement, too, modifying the idealizing strain and simplification in her earlier work.

Even the earlier novels are sophisticatedly time-conscious. They emphasize artifice by concluding time-marks: dates, brilliantly formalized in 'The Lifted Veil' and *Adam Bede*; quotations, ends echoing beginnings in *The Mill on the Floss* and *Daniel Deronda*; and in *Silas Marner* as well as *Middlemarch*, Shakespeare's great trick of making people at the end of a story retell, or anticipate another retelling of, the story. Eliot is sharply aware of endings as she ends.

Middlemarch opens out from its fiction to the knowledge of history with which it began, reflecting on its genre and theme, as it pluralizes—many Dorotheas—to admit that it aspires to be history as well as fiction. Though an open ending was not invented by Eliot but tried by Charlotte Brontë and Disraeli before her, Eliot's departure from the convention of closure is startling.

Daniel Deronda's open end is aptly 'grand and vague' (Major William *Blackwood's words) since Daniel's political future is morally, not historically, definable as he hopes for Zionist separateness with communication, an internationalist ideal for a projected nation state. Openness frees heroine and novel from a conventional limit and definition of happy family ending, and the liminal hint of a bond for Gwendolen with Rex gives security and social norm but opens to the unacted possibilities permeating lives.

The open end of *Deronda*'s action—though not of its settled morality—is more conspicuous than the generalizing expansion in the close of *Middlemarch*, but that earlier Finale is more experimental in artistic reflexivity, more bravely uncertain and tentative in its sense of history and morality. George Eliot's late innovative endings revise the consolatory wish-fulfilling closures of her earlier work. Even there she was no simple-minded conservative realist but cleverly emphasized her linked beginnings and endings, announcing and compounding function and artifice by mottoes, and by labels like Conclusion—in 'Amos Barton', *The Mill on the Floss*, and *Silas Marner*—and Epilogue—in 'Mr Gilfil's Love-Story' and *Romola*. But it is the last two novels whose bold conclusions anticipate the structural dislocations, doubts, and vastations of modernists like Joyce, T. S. *Eliot, Virginia *Woolf, and Samuel Beckett. See also BEGINNINGS OF NOVELS; NARRATION; REALISM.

BH

English Woman's Journal, The, feminist magazine founded in 1858 by Bessie *Parkes with funds from Barbara *Bodichon. George Eliot was asked to contribute to this important groundbreaking periodical but never did. Among other feminist concerns, the *English Woman's Journal* focused on employment rights and married women's property rights. See also WOMAN QUESTION.   MWT

epigraphs. The practice of using novel epigraphs or chapter epigraphs pre-dates George Eliot. Sir Walter *Scott, for example, whom she greatly admired, included hundreds in his Waverley novels. Graham Tulloch in *The Language of Walter Scott* (1980) argues that Scott probably quotes more often than any English novelist of equal stature and that his great love and enormous knowledge of history, particularly of the Renaissance and medieval periods, meant he remembered lines or phrases from *Shakespeare and others, which often gave expression to his own thoughts and ideas. In his introduction to *Chronicles of the Canongate* (1827), Scott himself wrote that he also made up his own epigraphs because he found it 'too troublesome to turn to the collection of the British poets to discover apposite mottoes'. Eliot also relied on a wide range of writers for her novel—and chapter—epigraphs; and she, too, created her own. She began with novel epigraphs: the ones to *Adam Bede, The Mill on the Floss, Silas Marner*, 'The Lifted Veil,' 'Brother Jacob', *Felix Holt, the Radical*, and *Impressions of Theophrastus Such* are taken from other writers, but *Daniel Deronda*'s is unascribed, probably her own. These epigraphs broadly suggest the ideas inspiring her stories. *Adam Bede*'s epigraph, for instance, is taken from *Wordsworth's the 'Churchyard among the Mountains' (book 6 of *The Excursion*) and points to strong thematic similarities between the novel and poem. The out-of-the-way Hayslope resembles the remote Enclosure visited by The Vicar, The Author, The Solitary, and The Wanderer; and just as Wordsworth's poem dwells on the trials and tribulations of people variously tainted by sin and weakness or blessed with patience and the strength of their faith and will to endure, so does Eliot's novel. Similarly, *Silas Marner*'s epigraph, from Wordsworth's *Michael* (lines 146–8) describing Luke's rejuvenating effect on his old father, draws attention to the tremendous influence that Eppie eventually has on Silas.

During the early stages of writing *Romola*, Eliot began to experiment with chapter epigraphs. Various critics have shown that she selected extracts from Italian and Latin authors, left spaces for epigraphs while writing her chapters, but that she later incorporated the few epigraphs already selected in *Romola*'s text. (For a detailed account, see Andrew Sanders's Penguin edition of *Romola*, 'Appendix B: The Unused Epigraphs to Romola.')

Why she abandoned the idea of epigraphs in *Romola* is not known. Sanders and others suggest that serializing *Romola* in the *Cornhill Magazine* may have posed problems; or perhaps Eliot, increasingly conscious of the 'burden of erudition' already placed on readers of *Romola*, tried to lighten their load as much as possible.

The use of chapter epigraphs in *Felix Holt, Middlemarch*, and *Daniel Deronda* was an important development in Eliot's fiction. In these wide-ranging novels, with their multiple plots and huge galleries of characters, the many epigraphs variously comment on people and events, and also create structural and thematic unities with the past and present. J. R. Tye says that Eliot's unascribed epigraphs, or mottoes as she preferred to call them, were, in fact, her own creations, and that she wrote them whenever she failed to find another writer's words to 'convey the particular aspect of truth and experience she wished to convey' (235–49).

David Leon Higdon notes that all the epigraphs—her own and those borrowed—serve specific purposes. He argues that Eliot primarily used them to create structural allusions, abstractions, ironic refractions, and metaphoric evaluations. Sometimes, he says, they also describe characters, indicating their unconscious thoughts and arguing for realistic presentations, although those are fewer in number. Structural allusion epigraphs encourage comparisons of a theme of some work with Eliot's or offer an indication of the genesis of her characters. The epigraph to chapter 2 of *Middlemarch*, for instance, comes from *Don Quixote* (1605, 1615) and recalls that novel's hero mistaking a brass basin for a golden helmet; in *Middlemarch*, it serves to indicate Dorothea's quixotic evaluation of Casaubon's supposed greatness. Epigraphs of abstraction involve allegorical figures to make abstractions concrete. *Daniel Deronda*'s novel epigraph is a case in point. In a Miltonic tone of voice, the epigraph justifies man's ways to man by pointing out that 'vengeance' and 'pestilence' lurk in souls driven by 'hurrying desires'. Epigraphs involving ironic refraction rely on discrepancies to create *irony, as is the case in chapter 6 of *Felix Holt*, for example, when Rufus Lyon is humorously compared to Marlowe's Tamberlaine. Metaphoric epigraphs, meanwhile, provide sketches of things or people subsequently fleshed out in the novel or chapter. The epigraph to chapter 43 of *Middlemarch* asks readers to look carefully at a figure of rare beauty, though it has 'nought modish in it'; and in the chapter the reader compares Dorothea with Rosamond—the one full of 'grace and dignity,' the other an 'expensive substitute for simplicity'. It is worth noting, however, that Eliot's epigraphs often serve more than one function: a structural allusion epigraph can also be metaphoric as well as ironic. Higdon thus concludes that all the epigraphs are part of a 'consistent aesthetic purpose': 'The frequent quotations used to create ironies, stress abstract content, evaluate metaphorically, and maintain an authorial stance, suggest relationships between epigraph and chapter and between epigraph and novel' (127–51).

Exactly when the epigraphs were written is often difficult to determine. Eliot usually included them in finished drafts once the manuscripts were otherwise completed. In the case of *Felix Holt*, she added chapter epigraphs to the proofs less than a month before the novel went on sale in June 1866. But as Higdon points out, in the case of 'The Lifted Veil,' she waited a full seven years after the story's publication before including its epigraph (see also *L* v. 380). She copied almost 60 mottoes used in *Felix Holt*, *Middlemarch*, and *Daniel Deronda* into one of the Yale *notebooks. See also BEGINNINGS OF NOVELS; COMPOSITION; DANTE; NARRATION.

AvdB

Higdon, David Leon, 'George Eliot and the Art of the Epigraph', *Nineteenth-Century Fiction*, 25 (1970).
Tye, J. R., 'George Eliot's Unascribed Mottoes', *Nineteenth-Century Fiction*, 22 (1967).

essays. George Eliot, or Marian Evans as she then was, was an essayist before she became a novelist, and it is likely that, had she never written a line of fiction, her essays together with her *translations would have assured her a significant if minor place in the intellectual history of 19th-century Britain. Most of her articles are review essays, and they show the formidable scope of her reading and knowledge as she ranges across disciplines and cultures with incisive analytical power, firm judgement, and exuberant, sometimes devastating, wit.

Her first essays, *'Poetry and Prose, from the Notebook of an Eccentric', published in the *Coventry *Herald and Observer* in 1846–7, were written before she left the Midlands for London, as was her first review essay for the *Westminster Review*, 'The *Progress of the Intellect' (1851). The great majority of the essays were written between 1854 and 1857 after she had left her editorial position at the *Westminster* and they were a vital source of income in her first years with G. H. *Lewes. In that period she wrote further substantial articles for the *Westminster*, two long essays for *Fraser's Magazine* arising from her stay in *Germany with Lewes, and shorter essays and reviews for the *Leader* and the *Saturday Review*. Later in her career, in 1865, she wrote four articles for the new *Pall Mall Gazette* where Lewes was an adviser, and two for the first number of the *Fortnightly Review*, which he was editing, including

'The *Influence of Rationalism'. In 1868 she published the *'Address to Working Men, by Felix Holt' in *Blackwood's Edinburgh Magazine*. Her last work, *Impressions of Theophrastus Such* is of an essayistic nature, though Theophrastus' reflections should not be read as essays in Eliot's own voice.

The essays of the 1850s reveal the interests and values of the novelist she was to become: her understanding of *society and *art in 'The *Natural History of German Life'; her views on conventional women's fiction, mockingly dissected with scathing wit in *'Silly Novels by Lady Novelists', and on women's position in the world in *'Woman in France: Madame de Sablé', and *'Margaret Fuller and Mary Wollstonecraft'; her discriminating moral sense in 'The *Morality of *Wilhelm Meister' and in the withering attack on an evangelical minister in *'Evangelical Teaching: Dr Cumming'; and her conviction of the importance of sympathy and the danger of abstraction in *'Worldliness and Other-Worldliness: The Poet Young'. These and other essays, like the important *'German Wit: Heinrich Heine', are discussed in detail in the entries under their titles, while Eliot's reviews of the work of other writers, like Charles *Kingsley, Geraldine *Jewsbury, Harriet Beecher *Stowe, and *Tennyson, are considered in the entries under their names.

The authorized edition of the essays, which she selected and revised, was edited by Charles Lee Lewes (see LEWES FAMILY) and published after her death as *Essays and Leaves from a Notebook* (1884). It contains, however, only eight articles from what was a much larger output. Since nearly all of this was unsigned (in the articles in the *Pall Mall Gazette* she used the pseudonym 'Saccharissa', and her contributions to the *Fortnightly* were the only articles she signed 'George Eliot'), there has been some uncertainty about what is definitely her work. This has been largely dispelled by Thomas Pinney's authoritative edition, *Essays of George Eliot* (1963), which lists the essays and reviews that can definitely be attributed to her (452–5), as well as mistaken attributions (456–9). He also indicates where areas of doubt still remain (452), and lists earlier published collections of the essays, all of them selective (460–1). His own edition reprints the most important essays, and others that he omits can be found in the collections edited by Wiesenfarth, Ashton, and Byatt and Warren listed below. See also JOURNALIST, GEORGE ELIOT AS.

JMR

George Eliot: Selected Critical Writings, ed. Rosemary Ashton (1992).
George Eliot: Selected Essays, Poems and Other Writings, ed. A. S. Byatt and Nicholas Warren (1990).
Essays of George Eliot, ed. Thomas Pinney (1963).

George Eliot: A Writer's Notebook 1854–1879, and Uncollected Writings, ed. Joseph Wiesenfarth (1981).

Collins, K. K., 'Questions of Method: Some Unpublished Late Essays of George Eliot', *Nineteenth-Century Fiction*, 35 (1980–1).

Myers, William, 'George Eliot's Essays and Reviews 1849–1857', *Prose Studies 1800–1900*, 1 (1978).

Stange, G. Robert, 'The Voices of the Essayist', *Nineteenth-Century Fiction*, 35 (1980–1).

Essence of Christianity, The. George Eliot's translation of Ludwig *Feuerbach's *Das Wesen des Christenthums* (1841), published under her real name of Marian Evans by John *Chapman in 1854. See TRANSLATOR, GEORGE ELIOT AS.   JMR

Euripides (*c.*485–*c.*406 BC), Greek tragic dramatist. Allusions to his *Medea* appear in three of George Eliot's novels. In *Adam Bede* the description of Hetty as a woman spinning a light web of folly and vain hopes which will turn into a rancorous poisoned garment echoes Euripides' picture of the innocently vain Glauce, Medea's rival in love, whom she murders by means of a poisoned bridal dress (*AB* 22). In *Daniel Deronda* an observer compares Grandcourt between two fiery women to the struggle between Medea and her rival, and though he is thinking of an Italian play, the author herself evidently has Euripides in mind (*DD* 36). Gwendolen Harleth is in the rival's position; George Eliot hints by dramatic *irony that she will suffer dreadfully for supplanting another in Grandcourt's life. *Felix Holt, the Radical* includes her most extended use of a classical theme. Mrs Transome's passionate character and her relationship with her maid Denner are modelled on Medea and her nurse, and several scenes parallel parts of the Greek play. Mrs Transome is also compared to another of Euripides' heroines when she is called a dishevelled Hecuba-like woman (*FH* 39). Medea is abandoned by her husband Jason; Mrs Transome would not seem to be in the same case, but here George Eliot has a fine irony in store, for Jermyn (the name is carefully chosen) proves to have been her lover, to be the father of her child, and to have cast her off for the sake of worldly advantage, in all these respects taking Jason's role. See also CLASSICAL LITERATURE, TRAGEDY.   RHAJ

'Evangelical Teaching: Dr Cumming' was the second of George Eliot's eight major essays in the *Westminster Review*, where it appeared in October 1855 (repr. in *Essays*). She was paid £15 for it.

Charles Lewes (see LEWES FAMILY) recalled that 'it was after reading this article that his father was prompted to say to George Eliot, whilst walking one day with her in Richmond Park, that it convinced him of the true genius in her writing . . . Up to this time he had not been quite sure of anything beyond great talent in her productions' (Cross, i.

384–5). She was not keen that the author should be known to be a woman, however (*L* ii. 218).

Dr John Cumming (1807–81) was the minister of the Scottish National Church in Crown Court, Covent Garden, London, from 1832 to 1879. He wrote prolifically on biblical prophecy: eight of his works published between 1847 and 1854, of which the most recent were *The Church before the Flood* and *The Finger of God* (both 1853) and *Signs of the Times* (1854), are listed at the head of the article. The essay is not in the narrow sense a review, however: as Pinney comments, George Eliot's major essays serve as occasions to deliver herself of something she really wants to say (*Essays*, 2). All her reading in historical criticism, and the experience of translating Feuerbach, issue in this comprehensive attack on an evangelical position she had once entertained (see EVANGELICALISM).

'Evangelical Teaching: Dr Cumming' opens by characterizing the evangelical preacher as intellectually mediocre, bigoted, and hypocritical, abusing the authority of the pulpit by 'riot[ing] in gratuitous assertions, confident that no man will contradict him' (*Essays*, 161). She turns to Cumming as a particular instance, and—disavowing personal knowledge of the man—savages his published works. For a start, 'his productions are essentially ephemeral' (164); among their 'most striking characteristics . . . is *unscrupulosity of statement*' (165). She goes on to deplore (in detail) 'the *absence of genuine charity*' (179) and '*perverted moral judgment*' (184), moving in her closing pages from demolition into demonstration of the logic and appeal of an alternative position: 'The idea of God is really moral in its influence—it really cherishes all that is best and loveliest in man—only when God is contemplated as sympathizing with the pure elements of human feeling, as possessing infinitely all those attributes which we recognize to be moral in humanity' (187). She closes by quoting *In Memoriam* in support of the claim that 'The fundamental faith for man is faith in the result of a brave, honest, and steady use of all his faculties' (189).

William Myers accords George Eliot, in spite of her Anglican background, 'a place in the great tradition of provincial dissent', identifying the basis of her disgust with Cumming in his occupation of 'a metropolitan pulpit' and absorption in fashionable pursuits, and his corresponding remoteness from provincial contexts (1984: 24–5).

The review (with some omissions) was included in *Essays and Leaves from a Note-Book*, ed. Charles Lee Lewes (1884).   MAH

Myers (1984).

evangelicalism. Victorian evangelicalism was a set of beliefs and practices uniting Christians across a wide spectrum of Protestant denominations and sects—in the Church of England (see ANGLICANISM), in the large number of Methodist denominations, among Baptists and Congregationalists. The newer Victorian sects, such as the Plymouth Brethren, the Salvation Army, and the Derby Faith Folk to which George Eliot's Uncle and Aunt Samuel belonged (see METHODISM), as well as the adherents of the numerous tin tabernacles and upper rooms spawning with great vigour across the towns of England (like the Lantern Yard community in *Silas Marner*) were usually entirely evangelical. Breakaway nonconformist groups were formed precisely to be more evangelical than their parent bodies. The general religious impetus came from the so-called Evangelical Revival of the mid-18th century, which began in the Church of England and was carried outside it by Methodism in particular. The movement was biblicist, believing in the literal truth of Scripture and in the *Bible as a completely sufficient guide of faith and morals; salvationist, insisting on the need to be saved from sin by faith in the redemptive death of Jesus Christ; sometimes Calvinist, holding like the Anglicans and Baptists that salvation was only for the predestined few; sometimes Arminian, holding like the Methodists that salvation was open to all believers; pietistic, defining the world and worldliness (theatregoing, gambling, card-playing, etc.) as sinful because distracting from seriousness; evangelistic, with a strong emphasis on mission to the unchurched and the heathen in foreign parts; second-adventist, believing that Christ would soon return to consummate time and usher in the eternal kingdom of true believers. For most Anglican evangelicals their pot of beliefs included a great emphasis on social reform, and evangelicals were prominent in all the 19th-century reform movements.

George Eliot was early on a characteristic and fervent evangelical Anglican—Calvinist in theology, serious in every practical way, self-scrutinizing as to all thought and behaviour, devoted to reading the Bible (measuring her life by it, finding constant tropes in it to figure her life by) and to perusing volumes of Church history, biblical exegesis, and pietistic guides to living. She was in every way 'methodistical', the sneering epithet constantly directed at evangelicals in her fiction by worldlier critics. Her correspondence with her former schoolteacher Maria *Lewis is intensely evangelical (see LETTERS), to a degree that strikes the modern reader as religiously over-precious and hectic to the point of neurosis (see the letter of 30 March 1840, *L* i. 46). And her revulsion from *Christianity at the end of 1841 was a revulsion from the evangelical forms of that faith. It was evangelicalism that particularly obsessed her as a

post-Christian critic and novelist. As the translator of D. F. *Strauss she produced the English version of one of the 19th century's most hurtful anti-evangelical manifestos, which struck right into the heart of the evangelical faith in biblical unity, veracity, and historicity (see TRANSLATIONS BY GEORGE ELIOT). Her attack on the self-serving Christianity of the 18th-century poet Edward *Young was given a title to arrest precisely the evangelical attention: *'Worldliness and Other-Worldliness: The Poet Young'. Her violent attack on the apocalyptic preacher Dr John Cumming for intellectual mediocrity and for mendacious distortions of the biblical text (see 'EVANGELICAL TEACHING: DR CUMMING'), offered him as a representative of his religious kind: all 'Evangelical Teaching' was in the dock with Dr Cumming. Her scathing assault in *'Silly Novels by Lady Novelists' singled out evangelical Anglican love stories for particular scorn. But this critique also signalled George Eliot's recognition of the potential value of evangelicalism as a fictional subject:

The real drama of Evangelicalism—and it has abundance of fine drama for any one who has genius enough to discern and reproduce it—lies among the middle and lower classes . . . Why can we not have pictures of religious life among the industrial classes in England, as interesting as Mrs Stowe's pictures of religious life among the negroes? (*Essays*, 318–19)

It was a *cri de cœur* that led straight to *Scenes of Clerical Life*, particularly 'Janet's Repentance'. It led straight, too, to the inside story of the working-class evangelical preacher Dinah Morris in *Adam Bede*; to the satirized early life of Silas Marner in his narrow predestinarian upper room, and above all to *Middlemarch*, with Dorothea Brooke, the high-minded evangelical Anglican, and banker Nicholas Bulstrode, the less high-minded corrupt one. Here indeed are the real dramas of evangelical individuals and communities.

The drift of George Eliot's scepticism and her hostility to everything evangelical is clear. Mrs Poyser's rebuking vision of Dinah Morris getting her own way by following religious feelings or leadings, segues acutely into the case of Bulstrode, easily construing his own crooked wishes and greeds as God's will for his life. And yet even Bulstrode is not presented as some merely vulgar hypocrite to be dismissed out of hand in Dickensian style. The story of his long fall from grace, his Faustian moral decline, is one of the great fictional portraits of moral corruption. George Eliot's sympathies as a presenter of character are with the selves whose evangelical selfhood she wants to reclaim, rewrite, redefine. Bulstrode is too bad to be redeemable, but Dorothea is not. Greatly mocked for her religious inconsistency in the matter of her mother's jewels; greatly sympathized with in her mistaken admiration for the studious biblicism of Casaubon and in her bruising encounter with Catholic Europe and the city of *Rome, Dorothea is saved for the truly moral life denied by Dr Cumming, Bulstrode, and Casaubon. By the end of the novel she is a post-Christian philanthropist, effectively another illustration of Ludwig *Feuerbach's 'Essence of Christianity' (see RELIGION OF HUMANITY). What George Eliot does with all her good Christians, but not least her evangelicals, is to translate what she saw as the good of the Gospels (its emphasis on love, *sympathy, duty) into humanized, humanist, secular versions of itself, and all according to the post-Christian gospel of Feuerbach. It was what she had done in her own life, after all, transmuting her Christian morality into mere morality, and what she did throughout her fiction—rewriting the key tropes of evangelicalism as the necessities of humanist plot-making, so that, for example, the doctrine of predestination turns into her repeatedly re-enacted law of moral consequences (see DETERMINISM). See also MORAL VALUES; RELIGION.   VC

Cunningham (1975).

Evans, Christiana (Chrissey) (1814–59), George Eliot's elder sister, born at Arbury (now South) Farm on the Arbury estate. When the family moved to Griff House Chrissey attended Miss Lathom's school in nearby Attleborough but little is known about her schooldays.

After her mother's death in 1836 Chrissey and Mary Ann kept house for their father until, in 1837, Chrissey married Edward *Clarke and joined her husband at Meriden near Coventry where he had a small medical practice. Mary Ann was her bridesmaid and Robert *Evans gave his daughter a wedding gift of £1,000, a sum she was to need as her family grew. Chrissey bore nine children between 1838 and 1851, five of whom died in childhood.

The family income was irregular. Dr Clarke was competing for patients in a small village with a more successful practitioner, Dr Kittermaster. Robert Evans bought them a small house in Attleborough for £250 to help them through financial difficulties. When her father died in 1849 her brother Isaac inherited the house. Chrissey inherited £1,000 from Robert's estate and the family struggled on.

In 1852 Edward died, leaving Chrissey with six children between 15 months and 15 years and little money. When Edward's practice was sold, she had an annual income of about £100 for the seven of them.

Isaac, now head of the family, is likely to have had little sympathy for his unsuccessful brother-in-law but he tried to help Chrissey by allowing the family to live rent-free in the Attleborough house. Marian was also helping by sending money from London to her beloved sister. Isaac was now managing Chrissey's affairs but, it appears, not too helpfully. She wrote to him, 'I shall be very thankful if you will be so kind as advance me the £100 as soon as you conveniently can for I have *not any money* and I should be glad to pay the bills and get that trouble off my mind'. Later, she wrote again:

My dear Brother,
I should much prefer settling my bills myself—but as you do not approve of it I will send the accounts to you as soon as I can . . . Edward is well but I am in a constant state of anxiety about him. My cough and breathing are very bad I hope the weather is the cause. I was 45 on Monday—only 2 yrs younger than my Mother when she died.

Edward, her 21-year-old son, was to be a thorn in the side of the Evans family for many years. In 1877 Isaac was to write to him that, on his return from America, he would not be welcome and if he wished to contact the family it must be by letter only.

In 1857, when news of Marian's relationship with G. H. *Lewes was revealed to her family, Isaac rejected her. She hoped that Chrissey would be able to accept her situation. Sadly, at her brother's insistence, her sister wrote only to break off all communication with her.

In 1859 Chrissey became ill with tuberculosis, and, fearing she might have little time left, she wrote to Marian, regretting the break with her sister who had been so kind to her and the children. Marian decided to go immediately to Attleborough but Chrissey's daughter wrote to say that her mother feared that the excitment of a reunion would be too much for her. On 15 March Chrissey died. Marian does not appear to have attended the burial in Meriden churchyard.

Chrissey, much prettier than her younger sister, is thought to be the original of both Lucy Deane in *The Mill on the Floss* and Celia Brooke in *Middlemarch*. When George Eliot was writing *Scenes of Clerical Life* in the mid-1850s, Chrissey's plight with her young family may have been in her mind as she described the ailing Milly Barton and her six small children in 'The Sad Fortunes of the Reverend Amos Barton'.

In a letter to her Coventry friend, Sara Hennell, in 1854, Marian had written, 'Cara, you and my own sister are the three women who are tied to my heart by a cord which can never be broken'. Despite Isaac's efforts to sever her from the family,

Thought to be George Eliot's elder sister Chrissey (1814–59) about the age of 20.

Chrissey's letter in 1859 showed that the cord between the sisters had not been broken.　　KA

Evans, Isaac (1816–90), George Eliot's brother, to whom she was very close as a child but who refused all contact with her while she was living with G. H. *Lewes and only relented in the last year of her life when he learned of her marriage to John Walter *Cross. Three years older than his famous sister, he was the dominant but much-loved companion of her early childhood. Their relationship is reflected in Maggie's and Tom's childhood in *The Mill on the Floss* and fondly recalled in the 'Brother and Sister' Sonnets that she wrote in 1869 (see POETRY). There she describes herself following him 'puppy-like' through the meadows and woods, fishing with him in the canal, admiring his knowledge of the natural world, enjoying his protection and guidance, and sharing in his feelings: 'His sorrow was my sorrow, and his joy | Sent little leaps and laughs through all my frame.' In 1824 their constant companionship came to an end when he was sent away to school at Foleshill and she to Miss Lathom's at Attleborough.

Steadily they grew apart. When Isaac was given a pony of his own, he spent all his time riding it and had none to spare for Mary Ann (Haight 1968: 6). At about the age of 16 he was sent to a private tutor, Mr Docker, in Birmingham where he absorbed High Church views which further distanced him from his earnest evangelical sister, who was always trying to reform his behaviour. As she later admitted: 'I used to go about like an owl to the great disgust of my brother, and I would have denied him what I now see to have been quite lawful amusements' (Cross, i. 157). When they visited *London together in the summer of 1838, she refused to go to the *theatre with him on the grounds that she disapproved of such idle entertainment. His interests, too, were practical rather than intellectual, and his father began to train him in his own business of estate management (see EVANS, ROBERT).

In 1841 his father decided to retire, handing over the management of the Arbury estate to Isaac along with *Griff House. In June 1841 Isaac married Sarah Rawlins, the daughter of a Birmingham hide and leather merchant, and the couple set up house at Griff. When Mary Ann fell out with her father over her refusal to attend church in 1842, Isaac and Sarah offered her a sympathetic retreat at Griff and helped to bring about the eventual truce. Nevertheless, Isaac disapproved of her friendship with the radical freethinking *Brays, believing that it was interfering with her chances of finding a husband. His view of Charles Bray as a 'leader of mobs' who could only ever introduce her to 'Chartists and Radicals' (Haight 1968: 48)

suggests the extent to which Isaac had taken over his father's conservative views as well as his job. He was not a man to have much sympathy with the liberal intellectual circles his sister was to frequent when she moved to London after their father's death.

Conducting his business as successfully as his father before him and on good terms with the local gentry, Isaac was becoming well established in local society. As head of the family he exercised power and expected deference. When his younger sister started to live with Lewes she refrained from telling him, or any other member of her family, for nearly three years, fearful of offending their sensibilities. When she finally wrote to him on 26 May 1857 from Jersey to say that she had changed her name and to ask him to pay her income from the money left in trust to her by her father into Lewes's account (L ii. 331–2), he had his solicitor reply to her seeking details of when and where they were married. Her immediate reply (L ii. 349–50), announcing that she and Lewes were not, and could not be, legally married, was forwarded to Isaac and never directly answered, although he made his sisters Fanny and Chrissey write to Marian that very day to break off all communication with her (Haight 1968: 233).

His disapproving silence lasted 23 years, although his wife Sarah wrote a letter of sympathy to her on Lewes's death. Shortly after he had resigned from managing the Arbury estate in April 1880 he learned from his solicitor of Marian's marriage to John Walter Cross. After a delay of several days he wrote a stiff letter of congratulation on 17 May, addressing her as 'my dear sister' and taking 'much pleasure in availing myself of the present opportunity to break the long silence which has existed between us' (L vii. 280). The offer of reconciliation was swiftly accepted and she wrote to him as 'my dear brother' to express her great joy at his words of sympathy, affirming that 'our long silence has never broken the affection for you which began when we were little ones' (L vii. 287). She signed herself Mary Ann Cross, reverting to the Christian names of the childhood to which she had alluded. But they were never to meet again. When Cross wrote to inform him of her death on 22 December, his reply expressed real grief and echoed the words and sentiments of her own earlier letter: 'although we have seen so little of each other for many years the old feeling of affection between us has not died out and I shall feel all this very deeply now she is gone' (Adams 1980: 37). Although it is unlikely that he felt any remorse at his own part in their long estrangement, his sorrow seems genuine, and he made the journey to London in the depth of winter to attend her funeral. He outlived her by ten years, but his enduring memorial is the figure

of Tom Tulliver in *The Mill on the Floss*: practical, enterprising, and energetic, but at the same time overbearing and unbendingly self-righteous. See also LIFE OF GEORGE ELIOT.   JMR
  Adams (1980).

Evans, Mrs Samuel (1766–1849), George Eliot's Methodist aunt who told her the story that was to be the germ of *Adam Bede*. Born Elizabeth Tomlinson, she married the younger brother of the novelist's father. He had converted to *Methodism as a young man and she was one of the significant body of women preachers in the early Methodist Church. Early in 1839 she stayed with the Evans's at *Griff House for two or three weeks and had debates with her adolescent niece, then earnestly evangelical and Calvinist in outlook, about predestination. In later life the novelist recalled with admiration her gentle aunt's superior tolerance and understanding (L iii. 173). During that visit Aunt Samuel, as she was known, told the story of how she had ministered to a young woman, Mary Voce, in Nottingham gaol on the night before her execution for infanticide. After praying all night with the prisoner and bringing her to confess her guilt, she accompanied her in the prison-cart to the place of execution. George Eliot's recollection of this anecdote seventeen years later provided the initial inspiration for *Adam Bede* (see 'The History of Adam Bede', L ii. 502–5), in which novel the figure of the Methodist preacher Dinah Morris owes much to memories of her aunt.   JMR

Evans, Robert (1773–1849), George Eliot's father. Born at Roston Common in Derbyshire, he was the fourth son of the village carpenter. After receiving a basic education at the village school run by Bartle Massey, whose name is later given to the schoolmaster in *Adam Bede*, he was apprenticed to his father's trade. He then established his own carpentry business in the neighbouring village of Ellastone, Staffordshire, and was employed by a local landowner, Francis Parker, who thought so highly of him that in 1802 he invited him to manage an estate he had inherited at Kirk Hallam in Derbyshire. In 1801 Robert had married a servant of the Parker family, Harriet Poynton, who bore two children, Robert in 1802 and Frances Lucy in 1805. In his four years as agent at Kirk Hallam he applied himself to the study of modern agricultural methods, introducing crop rotation and the selective breeding of sheep on the estate (Adams 1980: 8). In 1806, on the death of Sir Roger Newdigate (see NEWDIGATE FAMILY), Francis Parker inherited the Arbury estate near Nuneaton in Wawickshire and once again turned to Robert Evans to manage it. The Evans family moved to Arbury farm which Robert ran while overseeing work on the 7,000 acres of the whole estate. He

was a man of legendary physical strength (Cross, i. 12–13), great practical ability, and unimpeachable honesty. His knowledge and integrity were so widely respected that he was often called upon as a valuer and as an arbitrator in disputes (Cross, i. 11), while his advice on estate management was often sought by other local landowners. Having prospered in the service of the aristocracy he shared their political outlook and remained a lifelong conservative, opposing, for instance, the repeal of the *Corn Laws.
  In 1809 Harriet died after the birth of a third child which barely survived her. In 1813 Robert Evans married again. His second wife Christiana, the daughter of a local farmer, Isaac Pearson of Astley, gave birth to a daughter Christiana (Chrissey) in 1814 and a son Isaac in 1816 (see EVANS, CHRISTIANA and EVANS, ISAAC). On 22 November 1819 a second daughter, the future novelist, was born and christened Mary Anne. A few months later Robert and his family moved to *Griff House where Mary Ann (as he wrote her name in his diary) grew up. As a child she used to accompany her father on his business and she seems to have been far closer to him than to her mother. After her mother's death in 1836 she became indispensable to him, helping to run the home, mending his clothes, and reading Walter *Scott's novels to him in the evening. After Chrissey's marriage in May 1837 she ran the house on her own and drew even closer to her father, who encouraged his clever daughter's intellectual development, buying her any book that she wanted and arranging for her to have tuition in Italian and German from a local language teacher (see LANGUAGES).
  In 1841 Robert Evans decided to retire, handing over his job and Griff House to Isaac whilst he and Mary Ann moved to Coventry. On 17 March 1841 father and daughter took up residence at Bird Grove, Foleshill, on the outskirts of the town. The move to Coventry brought Mary Ann into contact with the radical freethinking circle of Charles and Cara *Bray and helped bring about a period of painful estrangement from her father when, in January 1842, she announced that she could no longer believe in Christianity as practised in the Church of England and refused to accompany him to church. Although he was not apparently a deeply religious man, that refusal outraged his conservative sense of propriety and threatened him with a grave social embarrassment. She would not bend to his will and he would not discuss her religious scruples with her, despite an eloquent letter explaining her position (L i. 128–30). After several weeks of cold silence and tension, during which he started to plan to move to a cottage on his own and she went to stay with Isaac, a truce was arranged in this 'Holy War': she would

Robert Evans (1773–1849), George Eliot's father, from a miniature by Carlisle, painted in 1842 after he had moved to Coventry with her.

accompany him to church on the understanding that she could think what she liked about religion. In the last year of her life she maintained, according to John Walter *Cross, that 'few things had occasioned her more regret than this temporary collision with her father, which might, she thought, have been avoided by a little management' (Cross, i. 113).

They continued to live together at Foleshill and she continued to associate with the freethinking Brays. In 1845 he broke his leg and his health began to decline. As he became increasingly infirm, she took him on visits to the seaside to restore him and nursed him assiduously when he developed a heart condition. By the autumn of 1848 it was clear that he had not long to live, and he made his will, leaving Mary Ann £2,000 in trust and £100 cash. Financially his three daughters were treated equally, but it is curious that the edition of Scott's novels which Mary Ann had read to him for years was left to her half-sister Fanny. In the last months of his life Mary Ann devoted herself to his care, writing to Charles Bray that 'these will ever be the happiest days of my life. The one deep strong love I have ever known has now its highest exercise and fullest reward' (L i. 283–4). As he lay dying she wondered desperately what would become of her without him and expressed her lurid fears: 'I had a horrid vision of myself last night becoming earthly sensual and devilish for want of that purifying restraining influence' (L i. 284). He died on 31 May 1849.

He was the most important figure in the novelist's early life, inspiring love and yet provoking her equally strong character into rebellion. Unsurprisingly, the relationship of father and daughter plays an important part in her fiction, particularly *The Mill on the Floss* and *Romola* (see FAMILY LIFE, PORTRAYAL OF). She remained proud of his achievement. In 1859 she reprimanded Charles Bray for having referred to him as a mere farmer and set the record straight in terms that reveal her pride and admiration:

Now my Father did not raise himself from being an artizan to be a farmer: he raised himself from being an artizan to be a man whose extensive knowledge in very varied practical departments made his services valued through several counties. He had large knowledge of building, of mines, of plantation, of various branches of valuation and measurement—of all that is essential to the management of large estates. He was held by those competent to judge as *unique* amongst land-agents for his manifold knowledge and experience. (L iii. 168)

Some of his qualities are visible in Adam Bede and in Caleb Garth in *Middlemarch*, while his political views in particular are portrayed in Theophrastus's father in *Impressions of Theophrastus Such* (*TS* 2). See also LIFE OF GEORGE ELIOT.   JMR

Adams (1980).
Ashton (1996).
Redinger (1975).

Evans, Samuel (1777–1858), George Eliot's uncle, the younger brother of her father Robert. He converted to Methodism as a young man and his wife Elizabeth was a Methodist preacher, one of whose anecdotes provided the germ for *Adam Bede* (see EVANS, MRS SAMUEL).   JMR

evolution, theory of. See DARWINISM; SPENCER, HERBERT.

F

family life, portrayal of. The family occupies a central position in George Eliot's fiction, representing on the one hand an ideal of how people can live together in love and sympathy (McDonagh 1997: 50), and, on the other, displaying the powerful tensions and contradictions that generate dramatic action and invite the scrutiny of the realist. Adam and Dinah and their children briefly glimpsed in the epilogue to *Adam Bede*, Romola with Tessa and her children at the end of *Romola*, and the Garths in *Middlemarch*, are all exemplary families that offer a model of relations for society as a whole. By contrast the Tulliver family in *The Mill on the Floss* is riven by the pressures and prejudices of society at large and is examined with a sympathetic but unsentimental eye that refuses to idealize. When Tom Tulliver refrains from telling his father about the money he is making with his small enterprises, he is said to be driven by 'that disinclination to confidence which is seen between near kindred—that family repulsion which spoils the most sacred relations of our lives' (*MF* 5.3). Such strong, sacred, contradictory relations have the seeds of *tragedy in them, as the narrator of *Adam Bede* observes:

Family likeness has often a deep sadness in it. Nature, that great tragic dramatist, knits us together by bone and muscle, and divides us by the subtler web of our brains; blends yearning and repulsion; and ties us by our heartstrings to the beings that jar us at every moment. (*AB* 4)

That complex intertwining of affinity and difference is something that Eliot knew from her own relationships with her father and brother (see EVANS, ROBERT and EVANS, ISAAC), and in the story of the Tullivers she realizes its tragic potential. *The Mill on the Floss* is a tragedy of family life in which the relations between parents and children and the relations between the children

themselves are all involved (see CHILDHOOD, PORTRAYAL OF).

Although the narrator of 'Janet's Repentance' sings the praises of motherhood—'Mighty is the force of motherhood!' (*SC* 3.13)—and the angelic Milly Barton is an exemplary mother in the first of the *Scenes of Clerical Life*, the figure of the natural mother tends to play a minor role in Eliot's fiction. Mrs Bede and Mrs Tulliver are querulous, complaining, and ineffectual; Tessa in *Romola* remains mentally a child; Mrs Davilow in *Daniel Deronda* is affectionate and well meaning but subordinate to her daughter Gwendolen's will, while Deronda's mother has abandoned motherhood in favour of a career. Mrs Poyser in *Adam Bede* and Mrs Garth in *Middlemarch* are the rare mothers who combine authority with affection, but they remain marginal figures, and only Mrs Transome, as the tragic embodiment of motherhood, is for half of *Felix Holt, the Radical* a central figure. Yet mothering is of central importance and not confined to biological mothers, nor even to women. The childless Romola plays mother to a whole community when she tends the inhabitants of the plague village, and Silas Marner is both mother and father to the orphan Eppie. Moreover, when the narrator of *Adam Bede* describes the 'mother's yearning' as 'that completest type of the life in another life which is the essence of real human love' (*AB* 43), it is in relation to Adam's feelings for Hetty as she goes on trial. Similar terms are used in *Felix Holt* when the three years that Rufus Lyon spends tending the dying Annette are described as 'a period of such self-suppression and life in another as few men know' (*FH* 6). The implication is that maternal love is the exemplary form of human love in general, an ideal which transcends both biology and gender (McDonagh 1997: 44).

The father is a more important figure in the novels up to and including *Romola*, but the authority traditionally invested in him in patriarchal culture never goes unchallenged. Thias Bede is a drunkard; Mr Tulliver is reduced to bankruptcy and early death; Godfrey Cass is humiliated by being rejected by his own daughter; and in *Romola* father figures are subject to betrayal and violent death. The fate of the father can be related to George Eliot's own project and narrative practice: he is humbled so that she, in the form of the narrator, can assume his authority. The first-person narrator in the first chapter of *The Mill on the Floss*, who wakes from a dream 'pressing my elbows on the arm of my chair', has usurped the position of the enfeebled Mr Tulliver, 'resting his elbows on the arm-chair, and looking on the ground as if in search of something' (*MF* 3.8). In *The Mill* the father's strongest relationship is with the daughter, as it is with Silas Marner and the adopted Eppie, and Bardo and Romola, whose loyalty to her father contrasts with the betrayal he feels he has suffered from his son's abandonment of scholarship for religious extremism. In Romola's strong but ambivalent feelings for Bardo, where sympathy, 'which had made all the passion and religion of her young years', mixes with impatience and inner rebelliousness (*RO* 27), there is a reminder of Eliot's relationship with her own father; but more important is the seed these feelings contain of her later development away from male authority. In this novel where sons betray fathers, it is Romola who, after the deaths of father, godfather, and spiritual father Savonarola, inherits the authority of these displaced paternal figures, playing the role of didactic father as well as nurturing mother to Tito's children in the Epilogue. In *Romola* family relationships are brought into the realm of sexual politics, and, although the novel may owe much to *positivism, it challenges the implied assumption of male superiority in Auguste *Comte's view of women's mission by making Romola an independent-minded, educated woman (Uglow 1987: 172–4). As a mother figure she has moved far beyond the docile domesticity of a Milly Barton with her 'soothing, unspeakable charm of gentle womanhood! which supersedes all acquisitions, all accomplishments' (*SC* 1.2).

After the killing-off of fathers in *Romola*, they play only a minor role in the later novels. In *Middlemarch* and *Daniel Deronda* family relationships in general are of secondary importance, while issues of *vocation and *marriage provide the main focus of interest. See also SOCIETY.   JMR

Ashton (1990).

Chase, Karen, 'The Modern Family and the Ancient Image in *Romola*', *Dickens Studies Annual*, 14 (1985).

McDonagh (1997).

Sadoff, Diane F., *Monsters of Affection: Dickens, Eliot, and Brontë on Fatherhood* (1982).

Faucit, Helen (1817–98), actress, whom George Eliot first met at a soirée in 1853, writing, 'I fell in love with Helen Faucit. She is the most poetic woman I have seen' (*L* ii. 98). Faucit played the British stage for four decades, marrying, in 1851, Theodore Martin, a fellow journalist with G. H. *Lewes since the 1840s. Martin drove Lewes home after William Makepeace *Thackeray's funeral in December 1863, meeting Eliot for the first time (Haight 1968: 374), later dining with them, and subsequently calling with Helen. Lewes proposed that Eliot write a play for Faucit, sketching a five-act plot, but nothing eventuated (Haight 1968: 375). In 1865 Lewes reviewed Faucit's performance of Rosalind in *As You Like It* complaining of over-elaboration (*Pall Mall Gazette* (10 March 1865), 10) and offending the Martins, but for Eliot the per-

formance produced heartfelt joy (*L* iv. 181). The Martins continued to call, and the four travelled from Calais to Brussels together in 1867 (*L* iv. 383). Eliot remained an admirer, telling Faucit in 1874 that her performance as Lady Teazle had filled her with gratitude, creating 'that deep benefit which comes from seeing a high type of womanly grace, to shame away false ideas' (*L* vi. 25). See also THEATRE.   JJ

Felix Holt, the Radical (*see page 112*)

Félix, Rachel. See RACHEL.

feminism. See WOMAN QUESTION.

feminist approaches. See CRITICISM, MODERN: FEMINIST APPROACHES.

Feuerbach, Ludwig (1804–72), German philosopher. A key text for understanding George Eliot's original conception of human freedom was Feuerbach's groundbreaking *Das Wesen des Christenthums* (1841), translated by her under her real name as Marian Evans as *The Essence of Christianity* and published in 1854 (see TRANSLATIONS BY GEORGE ELIOT). Hers remains the definitive English translation. Of the vast reading that informs her writing, this work ranks with Baruch *Spinoza's *Ethics* as one of the most influential.

Feuerbach's work belongs to the German theological movement, known as the Higher Criticism, which created explosive effects across Europe by historicizing and thus relativizing religious dogma, especially Christian dogma. For many in her generation, and certainly including the Mary Ann Evans who had once devoted herself to charting the universal history of *Christianity, this anthropological approach to religion reversed the pernicious effects of dogmatic factionalism and opened more humane ways to interpret religion.

This revolution in metaphysics and theology sustains the perception, often found in George Eliot's work, that absolute authorities of any kind encourage passivity and actually destroy morality. Eliot finds in Feuerbach, as she found in Spinoza, a philosopher of freedom who attacks dogmatic certainty; but more than that, in Feuerbach she found a philosopher intent upon reducing transcendent explanations, and one who consequently refused to separate ideas and things. This gesture, as George Eliot says in her essay on 'The *Future of German Philosophy', goes against the entire movement of Western philosophy from Parmenides to Kant and returns the interpreter from absolutes like Truth and The Word back to the finite systems of human meaning and value. The implications of this step are still being explored by philosophers and cultural critics in the late 20th century (see PHILOSOPHY).

(*cont. on page 118*)

G EORGE ELIOT's sixth novel, published in three volumes on 14 June 1866.

Composition

On 29 March 1865, when Eliot wrote in her journal, 'I have begun a Novel' (Haight 1968: 381), she had put aside *The Spanish Gypsy* for *Felix Holt*. Throughout 1865 progress was steady, particularly in the last quarter of the year, but the writing slowed down by late December and during the early months of 1866, largely because of her difficulties resolving the legal aspects of the Transome inheritance. Having already written the first volume, she turned to Frederic *Harrison, a friend and Chancery barrister, for help with the intricate questions surrounding the law of entail and statutes of limitation. During frequent meetings and in lengthy correspondence, Harrison gave her detailed advice. Encouraged, she continued writing with more and more confidence and speed. In April, according to George *Smith, of *Smith, Elder & Co., who had published *Romola*, G. H. *Lewes sent him the first two volumes, asking £5,000 for the copyright. However, Smith rejected *Felix Holt*, no doubt because *Romola* had done badly for him and he was unwilling to take another risk. Leonard Huxley quotes him as having said, 'I read the MS. to my wife, and we came to the conclusion it would not be a profitable venture and I declined it' (cited in *L* iv. 240).

On 18 April 1866, and without telling Eliot about Smith's rejection, Lewes offered *Felix Holt* to John *Blackwood, Eliot's earlier publisher, who asked to see 'a volume or so'. Having read a little beyond the Introduction and the first two chapters, Blackwood wrote enthusiastically to Lewes about Eliot's artistic skills; and within days of receiving the first two volumes he formally offered £5,000 for the copyright for five years from the date of publication (*L* iv. 240–3). Eliot accepted Blackwood's offer on 25 April 1866. On 17 May 1866, Eliot recorded, 'Did nothing but write mottoes to my proofs' (*Journals*, 128). Chapter *epigraphs, or mottoes, for *Felix Holt* were later copied out in another notebook, and the motto for the novel itself, taken from Michael Drayton's 'Poly-Olbion' (1612; 1622), the Thirteenth Song, lines 1–2, 8–12, is recorded in her 'Commonplace Book'. Volume iii was completed in approximately six weeks: and on 31 May 1866 Eliot wrote in her diary, 'Finished Felix Holt' (*Journals*, 128). Harrison continued to assist throughout by helping her check the proofs for legal errors that might have crept back in and by giving her a number of suggestions for the trial scene. Blackwood sent the final proof in early June, and the novel went on sale on the 14th of that month.

The manuscript of *Felix Holt* is in the British Library (Add. MSS 34030–2), dedicated to Lewes: 'From George Eliot (otherwise Polly) to her dear Husband, this thirteenth year of their united life, in which the deepening sense of her own imperfectness has the consolation of their deepening love. August 4, 1866'.

Publication

The first edition of June 1866 (Edinburgh and London: William Blackwood and Sons, 3 vols.) comprised 5,252 copies, priced 31*s*. 6*d*. bound in marble effect covers and an orange-brown leather spine. It is the only edition for which Eliot is known to have read proofs. Despite the largely favourable reviews, by late 1873 Blackwood still had 374 unsold copies. In December 1866, 2,100 copies of a second edition in two volumes went on sale at 12*s*. It contained several significant revisions, which were made in the text of the first edition but not in the proofs; and by 1876 Blackwood still had 1,274 copies on hand. Because of the sluggish sales, Blackwood reluctantly sold the rights in 1867 to a rival German publisher, Christian Bernhard *Tauchnitz, whose reprints of British authors competed with English editions. There were two other cheaper editions published by Blackwood in Eliot's lifetime: the one-volume Stereotyped Edition, priced 3s. 6d., which went on sale in January 1869, and the two-volume Cabinet Edition, priced 10s., which appeared during October–November 1878. The textual variants of the two cheaper editions from the first and second editions are minor. For these and a full publishing history see the Clarendon Edition, ed. Fred C. Thomson (1980).

Illustrations

The Stereotyped Edition carried a title-page vignette of Little Treby showing a stage-coach in the distance, and six illustrations (see ILLUSTRATIONS).

Reception

Most critics welcomed *Felix Holt*: its subject matter was familiar and accessible, while *Romola's* had been remote and difficult. After reading only a part of the manuscript, John Blackwood praised it for being unlike an ordinary novel: 'it is like looking on at a series of panoramas where human beings speak and act before us. There is hardly a page where there is not some turn of expression, witty or wise or both which one loves to dwell upon' (*L* iv. 240–1). John *Morley, in his article for the *Saturday Review*, dated 16 June 1866, praised Eliot for her fine portrayals of comic provincial characters in *Adam Bede, The Mill on the Floss, Silas Marner*, and *Felix Holt*, but added that her art consists of more than just 'brilliant comedy': beneath the surface of every book she has written there is also a 'profound pathos' and a 'comprehensive discernment of the proportion between the different elements of human life,' which help to enlarge her 'consciousness of the puzzle which surrounds human existence' (*CH* 252–5). E. S. *Dallas, in his unsigned review for *The Times*, dated 16 June 1866, also praised Eliot's characterization and anticipated many later critics by singling out Mrs Transome for special mention. She is, he said, 'in some respects, the most striking character of the novel'. Her scenes of suffering towards the end of the novel 'are given with remarkable power, and show how perfectly George Eliot can master the difficulties of a strong situation and follow the movements of strong passion' (*CH* 267–9).

However, Felix Holt came in for immediate criticism. In his unsigned review for the *Spectator*, dated 23 June 1866, R. H. *Hutton praised the novel's 'vivid intellectual insight and humour' but added, despite his nobility 'Felix Holt seems a grand *stump* of a character in an impressive but fixed attitude'. Compared with, say, the 'beautifully delineated Rufus Lyon', Felix appears incomplete, a 'mutilated statue of massive mould . . . [among] a group of others less grand in build, but finished and of finer symmetry' (*CH* 258–9). Henry *James agreed. Writing in the *Nation*, on 16 August 1866, James called Felix 'a fragment', because 'he and his principles play so brief a part and are so often absent from the scene'. He added that Felix is certainly sincere, full of integrity and intelligence, but 'there is nothing in his figure to *thrill* the reader'.

Plot

The novel is set in and around Treby Magna, loosely based on *Nuneaton and perhaps *Coventry, shortly after the Great Reform Bill of 1832. It spans the period 1 September 1832 to 'One April day' in 1833. Chapter 1 sees Mrs Transome awaiting the return of her son, Harold, who has been abroad for many years and is now heir to the Transome estates. He shocks everyone by intending to stand as a Radical MP, using Matthew Jermyn, the family solicitor, as his electioneering agent.

At about the same time, Felix Holt also returns home. He shocks his mother by refusing to sell his family's quack medicines, preferring instead to live among the poor. Through his mother, Felix meets Rufus Lyon, the Dissenting Minister of Malthouse Yard, and his adopted daughter, Esther.

During the political campaign, Felix finds evidence of election bribery and, on Nomination Day, makes an impassioned speech in the market place, urging political caution and responsibility. However, Jermyn's campaign of dirty tricks eventually spawns a riot on Election Day. Felix tries to steer the rioters clear of trouble but is subsequently arrested, charged with assault, manslaughter (a constable dies in the riot), and leading a riot. Meanwhile, Harold Transome learns that Esther has a legal claim on his estates. He tries to woo her but stops when he discovers that he is, in fact, illegitimate.

At Felix's trial Esther pleads on his behalf and moves influential people to seek a pardon when he is found guilty. She relinquishes her claims on Transome Court in favour of Harold and returns home to Rufus Lyon, hoping that Felix will not be transported. The Transomes, now the legal owners, nevertheless leave Transome Court in disgrace but return at an unspecified later date. In April 1833, Felix is released from prison and soon afterwards marries Esther. They move away from Treby Magna, taking Rufus Lyon with them.

Critical Approaches

When the 20th century's revaluation of George Eliot's art began with Joan Bennett's *George Eliot: Her Mind and Her Art* (1948) and F. R. *Leavis's *The Great Tradition* (1948), the general line of criticism of *Felix Holt* remained much the same as in early reviews (see REPUTATION, CRITICAL). In her consideration of *Felix Holt*, Bennett argued that the novel's political theme is, in fact, 'subordinate to the human theme', that political reform has no real 'bearing on human happiness', despite the detailed and 'convincing picture of electioneering methods in 1830 [sic]'. She also identified Mrs Transome and Esther as the main characters in the novel's moral theme, dealing with the sort of conduct necessary to secure happiness. The two women, Bennett suggests, are 'almost allegorical simplifications', and it is the juxtapositioning of the two that helps bring out the moral theme, the treatment of which is very subtle and serious precisely because Mrs Transome's character is so complex. Nevertheless, Bennett argued, *Felix Holt* fails to rank with Eliot's best work because 'the total composition is too schematic, too much the illustration of preconceived ideas'. For his part, Leavis placed Eliot in his pantheon of great writers who further the 'great tradition' of English literature, although where *Felix Holt* is concerned he only considered the part of the novel dealing with Mrs Transome as evidence of creative genius. That tragic portrayal, he considered, is never sentimental but wholly objective, never titillating but poignantly sympathetic. Eliot's morality never obtrudes, he added; instead, she demonstrates 'a great novelist's psychological insight and fineness of human valuation'.

Eliot as formal artist is the focus of Barbara Hardy's *The Novels of George Eliot: A Study in Form* (1959). In this still influential and detailed examination of Eliot's imaginative insight into and presentations of character, plot, and imagery, Hardy argues that Eliot's compositions rival those of Henry James, Marcel *Proust, or James Joyce in terms of complexity and subtlety, although they tend to be 'less conspicuous because of the engrossing realistic interest of her human and social delineation'. Analysing *Felix Holt's* double plot, Hardy notes that the action consists of roughly three connecting episodes 'in which Harold and Felix exist in opposition': first there are the separate accounts of the two men rebelling against their mothers; then comes the electioneering story, bringing them together briefly and then only to emphasize their moral contrast; and finally there is the story of their rivalry for Esther, told without the two men being brought together. This process of comparing and contrasting two characters, with one usually absent, leads to different levels of *irony: Harold loses Esther but gains the Transome estates, mainly because of Felix's influence on Esther; Felix is imprisoned, largely because of Harold's failure to control the orchestrated dirty tricks campaign which helped cause the riot. If the novel's only really successful character is Mrs Transome, because 'she is certainly the only one presented with the weight of time behind her', Hardy argues, *Felix Holt* is, nevertheless, an interesting experiment in form, anticipating the more successful forms of *Middlemarch* and *Daniel Deronda*.

Unevenness in the novel's form has also been noted by Fred C. Thomson, who has argued that Eliot probably began *Felix Holt* as a tragedy about Mrs Transome and only later decided on the political plot. Pointing out that Eliot had been rereading *Aristotle's *Poetics* and plays by *Aeschylus and *Sophocles, Thomson argues that the Transome plot contains traces of Greek *tragedy, since 'the plot and outcome of the action hinge upon events outside the boundaries of the story itself'. He goes on to say that if she was aiming for a Greek-style drama, she fell short: 'The total impression left . . . is rather of Elizabethan luxuriance, with an injection too, one fears, of grand opera' (Thomson, 89–90).

Yet another aspect of *Felix Holt's* aesthetic purpose that has often come in for criticism is the legal plot (see LAW). It is usually condemned for being too complex and, therefore, very difficult to follow. The story of ownership (the estates were originally entailed to the Transomes and left in remainder to the Bycliffes but, in fact, fell into the hands of the Durfeys, who later called themselves Transomes) is mainly designed to create opportunities for reversals of fortune. And those reversals fit in with some of the novel's central concerns: the idea that present conditions of things, whether public or private, are often founded on histories ignored at one's peril. Harold's story illustrates the point. His tenure at Transome Court is conditional, only possible because of John Justus Transome's will and a set of circumstances and events stretching back to the early part of the 18th century (*FH* 29). Harold's brand of extreme *radicalism, his tendency to brush aside all conservative values and thoughts, however, sets into motion a series of events leading to the revelation that Esther is the legal owner of Transome Court; worse, that he is altogether illegitimate. Put simply, his disregard for *history triggers his downfall. The moral behind Esther's rejection of her sudden changed circumstances is similar: wise people do not turn their backs on the past in the hope or expectation that the greatest good lies just over the horizon. That is essentially Felix's message to the crowd on Nomination Day (*FH* 30) and Eliot's in her *'Address to Working Men, by Felix Holt'. The complicated legal twists and turns, then, are justified, driving the novel's plot and serving a thematic purpose. Nevertheless, they take a long time to unfold, and the reader is often left hard at work putting all the information together. For that reason, most modern editions of *Felix Holt* provide appendices explaining or outlining the machinations.

Eliot's treatment of women has also posed a number of difficulties for feminist critics (see CRITICISM, MODERN: FEMINIST APPROACHES). They note her radical insight into the plight of women but also point out that her conservative instincts are never far away. At best, Eliot is ambivalent when it comes to saying what the roles for women should be and what needs to be done to achieve those ends; at worst, she is evasive. Gillian Beer and Jennifer Uglow note Eliot's ambivalence. Beer argues that in terms of conviction and strength of feelings, Mrs Transome is the most radical person in *Felix Holt*. Her compelling story, giving the novel so much of its interest, succeeds in challenging Victorian attitudes towards women and sex far more than Felix Holt's 'political ideas and practice of the time'. And yet she is notably absent throughout the middle part of the novel (Beer 1986: 133–6). Jennifer Uglow refers to Felix, Esther, and their son as '*banished* to a good life in some nameless town' (my emphasis), and adds that the novel's enduring image is not of Felix and Esther supposedly finding happiness in love but of Esther and Mrs Transome 'comforting each other for the pain they experience on behalf of the men they love' (1987: 175–92). Kristin Brady is more critical, arguing that just as Eliot is evasive in the political plot of *Felix Holt* about how to accomplish change, she is evasive in the gender plot about how women may improve their lot. The major subplot, involving Mrs Transome, says Brady, 'constantly interrogates the premises of the romance plot' involving Esther, Harold, and Felix. Nevertheless, although Esther is free to choose between two suitors, she remains 'a passive agent enabling masculine success', since she ends up subordinating her life and furthering Felix's cause (Brady 1992: 136–8).

Felix Holt's narrator tells us that 'there is no private life which has not been determined by a wider public life' (*FH* 3), and, hence, the novel should be read against the political, social, and economic conditions in England, which constituted that wider public life. Those conditions had their roots in the past and gave rise to many and complex reform debates that had been rumbling along ever since the last two decades of the 18th century and were still topical at the time of the novel's publication. The Second *Reform Act of 1867 was just over the horizon.

The 'Quarry for *Felix Holt*' (Yale University Library) contains numerous entries on various reform issues and concerns, economic and political theories and proposals, all relevant to 1832 and beyond. These entries are both fascinating and revealing, including as they do information on wheat yields and prices in Lancashire, Leicestershire, and Northamptonshire; reports from newspapers and Parliament on how voting procedures were sometimes abused immediately before and after the passing of the Great Reform Bill; notes on how the Church and State fought or co-operated with each other from medieval times onwards; arguments for and against electoral enfranchisement by political commentators and philosophers; assessments of how the House of Commons had been affected by the Great Reform Bill; entries on how the courts had dealt with 'Offences against the Riot Act' in the 1830s, as well as entries dealing with quack medicines and medical theories.

The last two sets of entries point to Eliot's thoughts concerning Felix Holt's punishment for his role in the riot (*FH* 46) and the account of his family, who hoped to be supported by 'Holt's Cathartic Lozenges and Holt's Restorative Elixir' (*FH* 3). The other entries point to her appreciation of more complex ideas. Wheat yields and prices, for instance, were, apart from anything else, political indicators. Hunger and starvation helped influence the speed and direction of the reform process. The social unrest and rioting, seen in a number of towns and villages throughout England in the first half of the 19th century, often came about because of fluctuations in wheat yields and prices made worse by the unfair *Corn Laws. The various entries, then, indicate that Eliot saw political reform as part of a chorus of demands and counter-demands made by people from all walks of life variously determined to protect or change an array of social, economic, and religious prejudices, convictions, ideologies, and beliefs (see POLITICS). And human nature being what it is, she saw that otherwise sensible people sometimes contradict themselves trying to protect and change what they hold dear.

The Revd John Lingon, Harold Transome's uncle, is a comic case in point. A confirmed Tory all his life, he quickly welcomes his nephew's plan to stand as a Radical candidate (*FH* 2), and his hasty return to the safety of Conservative numbers, after Harold loses the election, is equally smooth (*FH* 43). Likewise, Felix Holt. Also plagued by inconsistency, he is not the idealistically conceived spokesman for Eliot that some critics say he is (see Kettle (1970), and Jerome Thale's *The Novels of George Eliot* (1959), 94–5). When he urges the Duffield crowd to consider 'what is right and what is wrong, what is honourable and what is shameful' (*FH* 30) instead of making ill-considered political demands, he voices any reasonable person's sentiments. The point about him is, however, that he is not always so reasonable. Behind his impatient attitude towards Esther's vanities lie his own pride and arrogance, which are felt in the hectoring tone of voice that he frequently adopts when they converse. Similarly, pride and arrogance shape his decision to remain poor. Staying poor means he may not vote—and yet he seeks some kind of political role. The riot he is caught up in is the inevitable outcome of political mischief-making, very like the election riots Eliot witnessed in Nuneaton in December 1832. But the riot also gives Eliot an opportunity for presenting the noble Felix at his most foolhardy.

Insight into people caught up in the demands and counter-demands of personal and public issues is often achieved with the help of chapter epigraphs, or mottoes as Eliot preferred to call them. The nobility and foolhardiness in Felix Holt's nature, for instance, is effectively created with allusions to *Shakespeare's *Coriolanus*. The epigraph to chapter 27 consists of five lines (II. iii. 116–20) from a scene in which Coriolanus voices contempt for the quaint Roman custom that demands he wear a 'wolfish toge' and plead for 'needless vouches' from the populace when the Senate has already elected him consul. In the chapter Felix mirrors some of Coriolanus' extreme impatience and irritability when he tells Esther about his hopes and aspirations for the workers he plans to live among—and his absolute refusal to debase himself in the process. Similarly, chapter 30 is prefaced with a lament by Menenius about Coriolanus' inability to seek diplomatic solutions to disagreements (cf. III. i. 253–8). Coriolanus has just infuriated the Tribunes with an uncompromising analysis of who does and does not rule Rome; and the rioting of the fickle crowd in Rome does, of course, lend some credence to his autocratic views. The same is true of Felix Holt: his cautionary approach to extending the franchise, which he voices in Duffield, appears justified when the Treby Magna riot breaks out shortly afterwards. Nevertheless, if politics is the art of compromise, then in both play and novel we see men with much to learn.

Both men are, of course, very different and are dealt with differently: they have different ranks, and Shakespeare's hero dies while Eliot's is redeemed. Nevertheless, the similarities and differences create opportunities for structural and ironic comparisons, which, above all else, are meant to remind readers that people are part of a historical continuum. The reasons behind their prejudices, convictions, ideologies, and beliefs have not changed over the ages, Eliot suggests, only the circumstances in which these come to light.

The use of chapter epigraphs in *Felix Holt* was a new and important development in Eliot's fiction. She had, in fact, experimented with it in *Romola* but then abandoned the idea, absorbing the few epigraphs already selected in that novel's text. David Leon Higdon has convincingly shown that epigraphic allusions and references to texts, characters, or allegorical figures (such as Love, Rumour, and Mischief) are part of Eliot's consistent aesthetic purpose. Noting that literature as well as *realism influenced her fiction, Higdon argues for the complex relationships between epigraph and chapter and between chapter and novel.

To varying extents, all of Eliot's novels engage with and respond to ideas and customs handed down through literature, philosophy, science, or other disciplines. But beginning with *Felix Holt*, Eliot introduced a concentrated and sophisticated reworking of inherited material, designed to spin and eventually weave together multiple plot strands involving an enormous number and variety of characters. *Felix Holt* has something approaching a hundred characters, many very minor, some so minor that they are only ever reported on by the narrator or other characters. But all help to convey the surges, as it were, of a multifarious *society at times dimly aware, at other times totally oblivious, to its place in history. Struggles for awareness, beginning with self-awareness, are what the novel charts. The apotheosis of this phase in Eliot's writing was, of course, *Middlemarch*, and it has been the fate of *Felix Holt* to lie in the shadow of that great novel—which is a pity because *Felix Holt* deserves more than just the occasional honourable mention.

AvdB

Beer (1986).
Brady (1992).
Carroll, David, '*Felix Holt*: Society as Protagonist', in Creeger (1970).
Gallagher, Catherine, 'The Failure of Realism: *Felix Holt*', in Newton (1991).
Hardy (1959).
Kettle, Arnold, 'Felix Holt the Radical', in Hardy (1970).
Sandler, Florence, 'The Unity of *Felix Holt*', in Gordon S. Haight and Rosemary T. Van Arsdel (edd.), *George Eliot: A Centenary Tribute* (1985).
Thomson, Fred C., '*Felix Holt* as Classical Tragedy', *Nineteenth-Century Fiction*, 16 (1961).
—— 'The Genesis of *Felix Holt*,' *PMLA* 74 (1959).
Uglow (1987).

Feuerbach's work is most radical in its methodology, which was to reduce what he called the false or theological essence of *religion and to emphasize instead the true or anthropological essence of religion. Religion is an activity of spirit that is entirely human, not supernatural or foreign. The new philosophy can no longer, like the old Catholic and modern Protestant scholasticism, fall into the temptation to prove its agreement with religion by its agreement with religious dogmas. True religion lies elsewhere. Religion is not maintained by institutional theologies, but instead by human activity. God or the Trinity are not foreign but native mysteries, the mysteries of human nature (part 1, chapter 4).

What is most radical about Feuerbach's method is his inversion of familiar Christian doctrines, which he claims are only projections of human aspiration, or need, or fear, or even cowardice. For example, the incarnation of God in Jesus Christ is not to be understood as a positive event but rather as a way of recognizing and expressing the divinity of human nature. The incarnation functions as an expression of the human nature of God: 'Is not the love of God to man—the basis and central point of religion—the love of man to himself made an object . . . ?' (part 1, chapter 4). George Eliot echoes this sentiment in a letter to a friend, where she says that 'the idea of God, so far as it has been a high spiritual influence, is the Ideal of a goodness entirely human (i.e. an exaltation of the human' (*L* iv. 98). This affirmative understanding of human possibilities helps to explain why George Eliot chose to translate and publish this text.

Feuerbach makes much of the power of anthropological religion to sustain humanity's recognition of itself as a species. This has importance to Feuerbach because it simultaneously encourages human aspiration and shrinks human egoism. Early Christianity cared nothing for the species, and had only the individual in its eye and mind (part 1, chapter 16). The consequence of this was to reduce difference among individuals who are seen as being all alike in sin. Truly spiritual life, however, depends upon the mutually accepted differences among individuals; the 'I' exists only in conjunction with 'Thou', to use the Feuerbachian terms that have been so broadly used in the 20th century by existential theologians and others. Everyone makes a difference, by definition; but that individual uniqueness depends upon its differential function within the whole collectivity, the whole of human possibility. Subordinate factionalism of any kind is a malignancy that curbs human possibilities and reinforces dogmatic, theological principles at the expense of humanistic and anthropological principles. Productive knowledge of personal limitation can only be learned within a social group that is at once holistic and entirely differentiated.

This species-awareness distinguishes George Eliot's work, and suggests why she found Feuerbach's writing so congenial. It maintains a deeply social definition of identity, a rare recognition that 'I' and 'Thou' or Self and Other, are born together in Western philosophy and that each thrives on that difference. In *The Essence of Christianity* Feuerbach writes what is in effect a monologue of Human Nature speaking to itself. Human consciousness is by definition species-consciousness, awareness of one's identity as a member of the total group. Each individual is both finite and representative, at once I and Thou. Individuals aware of that perpetual boundary of difference are by definition aware of the species and of themselves as unique constituents of that species. In George Eliot's work, likewise, it is possible to consider her much-discussed narrator as a representation of the self-awareness of the human species (see NARRATION).

While Feuerbach does not explicitly address the problem of defining the social or cultural universe separate from nature, his separation of the two supports George Eliot's orchestration of her distinction of the free human universe of choice and action. As George Eliot develops it, this specifically human arena negotiates not with matter and motion but with tradition: with the incarnate aspirations bequeathed from one generation to another. The problem is then how to use that tradition as material for renewing, and not just repeating what is traditional. See also DETERMINISM; RELIGION OF HUMANITY.   EDE

Feuerbach, *The Essence of Christianity*, trans. Marian Evans (George Eliot) (1854).
Ermarth (1985).

Fielding, Henry (1707–54), English dramatist and novelist whose fiction George Eliot knew well, and whose practice as a narrator in *The History of*

Tom Jones (1749) is the subject of a famous contrast with her own in chapter 15 of *Middlemarch*. There may be a suggestion of ironic hyperbole in her allusion to him at the beginning of that chapter as a 'great historian, as he insisted on calling himself', and as one of the 'colossi whose huge legs our living pettiness is observed to walk under', but the point of the comparison is not to mock Fielding but to define her own place in that tradition of the English novel to which he and she both belong. His copious observations and digressions as a narrator, when 'he seems to bring his arm-chair to the proscenium and chat with us in all the lusty ease of his fine English', are an example that cannot be followed, she argues, in the different conditions of her own century. The role of the fictional historian has changed. The mind that seeks, like the narrator of *Middlemarch*, to unravel certain human lots by 'concentrating all the light I can command . . . on this particular web', is closer to the scientist with his microscope than to the 18th-century English gentleman like Fielding with a traditional classical education; and chapter 15 of *Middlemarch* is expressly concerned with the education of a gentleman, Lydgate, who abandons classics for science. The confident assumption implied in Fielding's expansive narration that the educated English gentleman is in a position to pronounce authoritatively on 'that tempting range of relevancies called the universe' is called into question by a more exacting and less insular view of knowledge. Lydgate has to go to Paris for an up-to-date knowledge of medical science, while the research of the English gentleman scholar Casaubon is fatally flawed by his ignorance of German. Authority, it is implied, has to be worked for and is not the privilege of any one class, or gender.

This contrast with Fielding also implies Eliot's concern with particularities and distrust of generalizations, her 'instinctive repugnance to the men of maxims', as she puts it in *The Mill on the Floss* (7.2), a novel in which the narrator's armchair in the opening chapter dissolves into the details of the Tullivers' world and is never brought to the proscenium again. Her critical distance from the narrative manner of *Tom Jones* may have been encouraged by G. H. *Lewes, who ten years earlier, in March 1860, had written an article in *Blackwood's Edinburgh Magazine* challenging the idea that Fielding's novel was a masterpiece of comic fiction. He considered Fielding's knowledge to be mere knowingness and found it 'impossible to ascribe a profound knowledge of human nature to one so utterly without seriousness' (87: 337). The less assured and knowing manner of Fielding's last novel *Amelia* (1751) may have made it more congenial to Eliot. She once planned to use a passage from it as an epigraph to *Scenes of Clerical Life*, and refers to it respectfully in *Adam Bede*, when Seth's contribution to the housework is defended as no more unmanly than Fielding's Colonel Bath making gruel for his invalid sister (*AB* 50). The blurring of gender roles here is very different from the patrician authoritativeness of the narrator of *Tom Jones*. See also CLASSICAL LITERATURE; NARRATION.   JMR

Doody, Margaret Anne, 'George Eliot and the Eighteenth-Century Novel', *Nineteenth-Century Fiction*, 35 (1980–1).

films. In the early days of the movies, there were a number of film versions of George Eliot's novels or parts of them. After Lillian Gish played Romola in 1924, and the advent of the 'talkies' later in the 1920s, there have been relatively few: indeed, very few by comparison with adaptations of works by other 19th-century novelists such as Jane *Austen and Thomas *Hardy. This entry may not include all film versions of Eliot's novels: some adaptations may have appeared under a title different from the one Eliot gave her text, and film bibliographies vary in their accuracy and comprehensiveness. In many cases there is no known copy of the film extant.

Silas Marner, the first of George Eliot's works to be adapted, has continued to be the most frequently filmed. D. W. Griffith directed a version called *A Fair Exchange* in 1909 (adaptation by Frank E. Woods). It was followed by a version in 1911 (directed by Theodore Marsten), another in 1913 directed by Charles J. Brabin, and yet another in 1916 directed by Ernest C. Warde (presumably the same version that starred Frederick Warde as Silas). An animated version directed by Alison de Vere came out in 1983. In 1985 BBC and Arts and Entertainment Network made *Silas Marner: The Weaver of Raveloe*, putting paid to any assumption that a film 'made-for-television' is an inherently inferior genre. The scriptwriters, Giles Foster (who also directed) and Louis Marks (who also produced), acknowledged that at many points a problem in production was solved by recourse to George Eliot's text. Their intelligent filmcraft, especially in flashbacks and close-ups and in the palette of the film, should also be acknowledged, together with the sensitive characterization of Silas, played by Ben Kingsley. *A Simple Twist of Fate* (1994, dir. Gillies MacKinnon, written by Steve Martin, USA) was loosely based on *Silas Marner*.

There have also been several versions of *The Mill on the Floss*. The earliest was a British production in 1913, directed (apparently) by Charles Calvert; followed in 1915 by an American version, directed by Eugene Moore, adapted by Philip Lonergan, produced by Thanhouser Film Corporation, and distributed by Mutual Film Corporation,

in which Mignon Anderson played Maggie Tulliver, and Harris Gordon, Tom. A 1937 version starred Geraldine Fitzgerald as Maggie, and was directed by Tim Whelan, written by John Drinkwater, Austin Melford, and Tim Whelan (presumably the first George Eliot 'talkie'). Graham Theakston directed a 'made-for-television' version in 1997, adapted by Hugh Stoddart, produced by UGC DA International/Canal + Productions/ Carnival Films.

All the other major works of fiction except *Middlemarch* have been adapted for film at least once. There appears to have been only one attempt at *Scenes of Clerical Life*—a 1920 version of the second 'scene', 'Mr Gilfil's Love-Story' (script by Eliot Stannard, directed by A. V. Bramble, distributed by Ideal, with Maynard Gilfil played by R. Henderson Bland)—and at *Felix Holt, the Radical* (directed by Travers Vale, USA, 1915). Vale also directed *Adam Bede* in the same year; there was another, British version of this novel directed by Maurice Elvey in 1918. In 1992 there was a BBC TV film adapted by Maggie Wardley, produced by Peter Goodchild and directed by Giles Foster, which restructured the narrative to begin with Hetty's trial scene, and paid considerable attention to authenticity in settings and dialect. *Daniel Deronda* has also been made in both an American version (as *Gwendolyn*, a Biograph film, 1914) and a British version (directed by W. C. Rowden, 1921).

Finally, there are two versions of *Romola*, one made in 1915 (Cines, ITL). The 1924 *Romola*, directed by Henry King, adaptation by Don Bartlett, Jules Furthman, and Will M. Ritchey, produced by Inspiration Pictures and distributed by Metro-Goldwyn Corporation, is second only to the 1985 *Silas Marner* as the best-known film of a George Eliot novel. There are some modifications to George Eliot's text: for instance, political and moral complexities are ironed out, so that the subtleties of Florentine politics are reduced to an opposition of freedom and tyranny. Again, the motifs of rescues and drowning are redeployed so that early on Tito (William Powell) rescues Romola (Lillian Gish) and her father from death by water, and in the end Tessa (Dorothy Gish) drowns. Ronald Colman plays Carlo, a young artist who combines the functions of Romola's uncle Bernardo and Piero di Cosimo, and remains Romola's faithful suitor at the end of the novel. The performance of Lillian Gish—who also had significant responsibility for the editing—was praised for its authority and dramatic intensity. See also TELEVISION ADAPTATIONS; THEATRICAL ADAPTATIONS.   MAH

Flaubert, Gustave (1821–80), French novelist who was writing at the same time as George Eliot and whose fiction is comparable to hers in intelligence, subtlety, and psychological insight, while presenting a radically different understanding of life. There is no record of the two writers having read each other's work—although Eliot would almost certainly have seen George Meredith's review of *Madame Bovary* in the *Westminster Review* in October 1857—and if they had it seems unlikely that it would have been with approval. Although both can be termed realists, their *realism takes very different forms. For Flaubert it involves the pursuit of impersonality, with the author withdrawing from his work and trying to endow it with the pitiless precision of the physical sciences. For George Eliot, on the other hand, a scientific understanding of the world, although just as important, leads to sympathy not detachment (Chase 1991: 25–6). Where *art for Eliot serves the moral purpose of extending our sympathies with our fellow men, as she famously maintains in her essay on 'The *Natural History of German Life', for Flaubert it is its own justification, and his impersonal aesthetic stance can be seen to have nihilistic implications. This led F. R. *Leavis (1948) to see him as representing the opposite pole to the 'great tradition' of the English novel, to which George Eliot belongs and which is characterized by its reverent openness towards life and a marked moral intensity. The contrast between the two novelists is one of narrative method as well as moral vision. Flaubert for the most part practises narrative indirection, with a characteristic use of free indirect style and only occasional recourse to the voice of the kind of narrator who is a constant controlling presence in George Eliot's fiction (see NARRATION).

In spite of this contrast in moral vision and narrative method there are points of affinity. Both writers make extensive use of *irony, although Eliot's is less corrosive and pervasive than Flaubert's. Flaubert's most famous novel, *Madame Bovary* (1857), has been compared to *Middlemarch* as a treatment of a woman's predicament in the context of provincial life. Indeed it has been suggested that a novel loosely based on *Madame Bovary*, Mary Elizabeth *Braddon's *The Doctor's Wife* (1865), influenced the two main plots of *Middlemarch* (Heywood, 184–5). The evidence for Flaubert's influence via Braddon is thin, but there are some similarities of character and theme. Aspects of Emma Bovary's personality and situation are echoed in the two principal female figures in *Middlemarch*: Dorothea bears some resemblance to her as a victim of romantic illusions and marriage to an inadequate man, while Rosamond, as well as being a doctor's wife, matches her in shallowness, accumulation of debts, and apparent readiness for extramarital affairs. Although Doro-

thea's altruistic idealism has little in common with Emma's romantic fantasies, there is a quixotic dimension to both characters' readiness to live out their dreams, which is spelt out in *Middlemarch*, when Dorothea is first taken with Casaubon, by a chapter *epigraph from *Cervantes's novel, relating how Don Quixote takes a barber's basin to be the helmet of Mambrino (*MM* 2). However, whereas Eliot treats her quixotic heroine with a sympathetic understanding tempered by irony, Flaubert presents Emma with an irony so unsparing that it may sometimes generate the very sympathy that it seems designed to deny her. The contrast between the two novels emerges clearly in their conclusions. Flaubert ends with an accumulation of uncompromising negations, whilst in *Middlemarch* the waste of Lydgate's life and energy is counterbalanced by the modest, muted achievement of Dorothea, and Fred and Mary.

There are also affinities between other novels. George Eliot's laborious reconstruction of Renaissance Florence in *Romola*, which, she claimed, turned her from a young woman into an old one, can be compared to Flaubert's exactly contemporary attempt to resuscitate Carthage in *Salammbô* (1862), and the sadness he maintained was involved in such writing. The contrast between the two writers emerges again in their very different treatments of a young man's sentimental education in *Éducation sentimental* (1869) and *Daniel Deronda*. The life of Eliot's aimlessly drifting hero is given direction by his chance encounter with Mirah on the Thames, whilst Frédéric Moreau's meeting with Mme Arnoux on the Seine is simply the prelude to a life that continues to drift and is finally wasted by unfulfilled love and persistent procrastination. The kind of idealism evinced by Daniel Deronda is the target of Flaubert's destructive irony, while the idle emptiness of an existence like Frédéric's is the object of Eliot's moral scorn in the figure of Grandcourt. Flaubert's ironic and aesthetic vision make him a very different writer from George Eliot, but not one who is superior to her in the art of fiction, as was once maintained (Steiner, 262–79). If their novels invite comparison, it is not only for their subject matter but by virtue of the creative intelligence and sophistication that they have in common.

JMR

Garrett, Peter K., *Scene and Symbol from George Eliot to James Joyce* (1969).

Heywood, Christopher, 'A Source for Middlemarch: Miss Braddon's The Doctor's Wife and Madame Bovary', *Revue de littérature comparée*, 44 (1970).

Redfield, Marc, *Phantom Formations: Aesthetic Ideology and the Bildungsroman* (1996).

Smalley, Barbara, *George Eliot and Flaubert: Pioneers of the Modern Novel* (1974).

Steiner, George, 'A Preface to Middlemarch', *Nineteenth-Century Fiction*, 9 (1955).

Florence. George Eliot and G. H. *Lewes spent a fortnight in Florence on their first visit in 1860, during which they made the acquaintance of Thomas *Trollope and other resident expatriates, and took many drives in the vicinity and a day trip to Siena. Eliot's account in 'Recollections of Italy. 1860' gives rhapsodic descriptions both of the natural beauty of the surrounding countryside, and of the art and architecture of Florence, saturated with her consciousness of associations with *Dante, Michaelangelo, and Girolamo *Savonarola, all 'a living part of *Risorgimento* mythology', as Andrew Thompson points out (1998: 45). It is, however, to Lewes's journal that we need to turn to find the record of the inception of *Romola*, in his suggestion of 'an historical romance' based on Savonarola (*L* iii. 295), though Eliot hinted in a letter to Major William *Blackwood: 'There has been a crescendo of enjoyment in our travels, for Florence, from its relation to the history of modern art, has roused a keener interest in us even than Rome, and has stimulated me to entertain rather an ambitious project' (*L* iii. 300).

A second visit from April to June 1861 was undertaken with the particular intention of getting up Florentine background for *Romola*, though they had begun to collect material already in 1860. George Eliot recommended to Blackwood their procedure of travelling by carriage from Toulon, 'the most delightful (and the most expensive) journey we have ever had' (*L* iii. 410). But it was a time of dedicated study, despite influenza which afflicted them both. Lewes regaled Charles with an account of their routine once settled in lodgings:

we trot out, visit a church or two, or a picture gallery, look over bookstalls, and poke into the curiosities of old Florence. Then we go to the Magliabecchian Library . . . where with great facility we get what books we desire, and read them in peace and comfort. You should see the Mutter turning over the old books with love! (*L* iii. 414)

He visited again on George Eliot's behalf parts of the convent of San Marco to which women were not admitted. Their stay was extended when Tom Trollope persuaded them to 'witness the great national festival of regenerated Italy on Sunday [2 June]' (*L* ii. 421), a celebration of the unification of Italy under Victor Emmanuel II. They also undertook a demanding four-day trip on horseback to the monasteries of Camoldi and La Vernia (the latter built by Francis of Assisi in the 13th century).

During a third visit to *Italy in 1869, the Leweses stayed in Florence from 20 to 25 March and again 23 to 27 April, both times with Tom Trollope

and his second wife, the former Frances Eleanor Ternan, whom he had married in 1866 following the death of the first Mrs Trollope (*née* Theodosia Garrow, 1825–65). They dined with the American ambassador, George Perkins Marsh, and his invalid wife, but missed meeting Longfellow, so strictly did their hosts respect their preference for privacy.

Henry *James wrote inimitably to John Walter *Cross from Florence, conveying 'very friendly sympathy on the occasion' of his marriage: 'I wish I could fold into this sheet a glimpse of the yellow Arno, the blue-grey hills, the old brown city, which your wife knows so well and which she has helped to make me know' (14 May 1880, *L* ix. 309).

MAH

Thompson (1998).

Fontane, Theodor (1819–98), German poet, journalist, and novelist. Fontane seems to have been struck by George Eliot's anonymous article 'The *Natural History of German Life' in the *Westminster Review* (July 1856). He read it, when he was a journalist in London, sitting in Simpsons Café Divan on the Strand, a favourite haunt. 'Read review of Riehl's books in the *Westminster Review*' is his entry in his diary (1 July 1856). As short as his entry is, it is of some significance as Fontane himself had a few years earlier set out his own views on the concept of realism in his essay *Unsere lyrische und epische Poesie seit 1848*. Both authors state in these articles their aesthetic aims before they themselves had embarked on their careers as novelists.

Their reflections on realism were corroborated by their reading of John *Ruskin. In the summer of 1857 Fontane visited the great Art Exhibition in Manchester. His letters to the German newspaper *Die Zeit* were later included in his book *Aus England*. According to his diary, Fontane read Ruskin's pamphlet on the *Pre-Raphaelites and his writing on Turner. He sees in the new school of the Pre-Raphaelites a germ for the future and perhaps a new possibility for the arts. He may also have read Eliot's reviews of Ruskin's *Modern Painters*, in the *Westminster Review*. Both authors were influenced by Ruskin's concept of truth and beauty. Fontane speaks later of 'Wahrheit und Verklärung'.

Eliot as well as Fontane started to write fiction comparatively late. Both were attracted early in life by each other's country, George Eliot by German intellectual life (see GERMANY) which led her to translate D. F. *Strauss and Ludwig *Feuerbach (see TRANSLATIONS), whilst Fontane was fascinated by English literature, especially *Shakespeare and old ballads which he translated. This difference in their interest is significant for the difference in their mental constitution, Eliot the intellectual and philosophical, Fontane the poetic and empiric mind. This also becomes evident in their fiction.

George Eliot visited Germany frequently, while Fontane worked in London from 1855 to 1859 as a journalist attached to the Prussian Embassy. They never met. Fontane took an interest in Eliot as soon as her novels came out. She died too early to be able to take notice of Fontane's development as a novelist.

We can assume that Fontane knew some of Eliot's novels. In June 1862 Fontane's wife Emilie wrote to him about *The Mill on the Floss*, maintaining that the description of details deprived the reader of a clear vision of the whole, and that an excess of detail was the general failing of contemporary English novels. Fontane answered:

What you say about the modern English novels is correct, but there are some exceptions, and among these exceptions are more or less the novels by Eliot. What she lacks is something else. Whilst others have really nothing but details, she (already more artistic than the others) has detail *and* composition; she only errs in the degree. It is not true that she forgets the composition on account of the details; the details only take up too much room. Nothing can be said about the quality of the whole, only the *quantity* of the observations and single descriptions has an oppressive effect. It [the book] is a decently, properly and cleanly dressed lady who indeed wears her jewellery in all the right places; she only has the idiosyncrasy to hang on one earring yet another one and so on until the half dozen is complete.

These words are significant for Fontane's own concept of a good novel, indicating the importance of that artistry in which his novels excel. What he in this letter calls 'the earring' he later calls 'finesse'.   CJ

Klieneberger, H. R., *The Novel in England and Germany* (1979).

Malcolm, David, 'Contemporary and Radical Themes in George Eliot's and Theodor Fontane's Fictions', Ph.D. thesis (London, 1981).

Wittig-Davis, Gabriele A., *Novel Associations: Theodor Fontane in the Context of Nineteenth Century Realism* (1983).

Ford, Ford Madox (1873–1939, formerly Ford Hermann Hueffer), English novelist and editor, whose best-known novel, *The Good Soldier* (1915), brilliantly demonstrates the impressionist technique that he vigorously espoused also in his critical pronouncements. He celebrated the work of Henry *James, Stephen Crane, and Joseph Conrad in memoirs and idiosyncratic studies such as *The March of Literature from Confucius' Day to our own* (1938), in which only Dickens among the Victorians warrants attention.

In *The Critical Attitude* (1911), however, Ford attacked George Eliot with gusto. He acknowledged that in her day she appealed both to 'the great multitude and the austere critic'. No longer: 'George Eliot has become a writer unreadable in herself and negligible as a critical illustration. Her character-drawing appears to be singularly wooden: her books without any form, her style entirely pedestrian and her solemnity intolerable' (55). Such criticisms were by this time fairly standard (see REPUTATION, CRITICAL). Ford, however, uniquely valorizes Anthony *Trollope in comparison, who by his personal honesty, humility, and conscientiousness, 'helps us to live in a real world, . . . affords us real experiences' (57); declares George Eliot to be 'another Frankenstein' (56); and proceeds to even more bizarrely provocative claims:

she has as an artist no existence whatever. Having studied 'Das Leben Jesu,' she became inflated by the idea of the writer as prophet, she evolved monstrous works which contained her endless comments upon Victorian philosophy, forgetting that our Lord, Who was the supreme influence, because He was the supreme artist, limited Himself in His recorded fiction to the barest statement of fact, to the merest citation of instance. (57)   MAH

Forster, E. M. (1879–1970), novelist who repudiated George Eliot's work along with much else that he found uncongenial in the 'Immediate Past' (*Aspects of the Novel*, 126), while at the same time taking his bearings from the realist literary tradition in which she wrote, and from liberal humanist philosophies compatible with hers. The motif 'only connect' that so insistently resonates through such of his novels as *Howards End* (1910) and *A Passage to India* (1924) appears in different registers also in George Eliot's.

Forster's most sustained reflections on fiction are in his 1927 Clark Lectures, which illustrate his belief that English fiction pales beside the explorations of the human soul and psyche offered by great Russian and French novelists (*Aspects of the Novel*, 3–4); hence *Adam Bede* suffers by comparison with *The Brothers Karamazov* (*Aspects*, 87–93). Though he disclaims possession of 'critical equipment' (101), Forster aligns himself with a Jamesian criterion of total relevance, by which George Eliot's novels appear to him shapeless, dependent on 'massiveness', and lacking in 'nicety of style' (89).

It may be that Forster was exposed to George Eliot's work at too tender an age. His Christmas gift to his mother in 1888 was *Scenes of Clerical Life*, a book whose appearance in a Penguin edition he welcomed in 1938.   MAH

Forster, E. M., *Aspects of the Novel and Related Writings*, ed. Oliver Stallybrass (1974).
—— *Selected Letters of E. M. Forster*, ed. Mary Lago and P. N. Furbank, 2 vols. (1983, 1985).

Forster, John (1812–76), biographer and critic who reviewed *Adam Bede* in the *Edinburgh Review* (July 1859), although George Eliot did not appreciate his laudatory remarks, telling Charles *Bray, 'Praise is so much less sweet than comprehension and sympathy' (*L* iii. 148). John *Blackwood considered him an 'unfriend', and reported him as saying that he could not read *The Mill on the Floss* again; later Forster revealed that he could not stand *The Spanish Gypsy*. The first volume of his *Life of Dickens* was published on 4 December 1871, and Eliot advised Sara *Hennell to get it for the account of Charles *Dickens's childhood and his development in America, but added that it was 'ill-organized, stuffed with criticism and other matter which would be better in limbo' (*L* v. 226). Reading the third volume caused her to remark on the painful revelations in it, and she told John Blackwood that she thought Lockhart's life of Walter *Scott 'a perfect biography. How different from another we know of!' (*L* v. 379). Her views may owe something to the hostility between G. H. *Lewes and Forster over the former's 'Dickens in Relation to Criticism' (*Fortnightly Review*, February 1872) to which Forster responded with a personal attack in the third volume of *The Life of Dickens*. GRH

Fortnightly Review, The, pioneering periodical established in 1865 by a group of independent investors, including Anthony *Trollope, who persuaded G. H. *Lewes to become the first editor. Modelled on the French *Revue des Deux Mondes*, it broke with the tradition of anonymity for contributors and contained a mixture of reviews, stories, serious articles, and poems. George Eliot assisted Lewes by contributing two articles, including 'The *Influence of Rationalism', to the first issue in May 1865, and these were her only pieces of journalism to be signed 'George Eliot'. The early issues were not a commercial success and in November 1866 the *Fortnightly* became a monthly. In the same month Lewes's failing health led him to resign the editorship, which was taken over by John *Morley. At the end of that year the original investors made over the copyright to the publishers Chapman and Hall. The *Fortnightly* went on to become a successful and highly regarded publication, continuing under its original title until 1934. JMR

France was the first foreign country whose literature George Eliot read in the original, and through her wide reading and frequent visits she came to know the country and its culture well. She started to learn French at the age of 13 when she entered the Misses Franklin's school in Coventry, and at the end of her first year she was awarded a copy of Blaise *Pascal's *Pensées* as a prize for her progress. In her adult life, after spending the winter of 1849–50 in Geneva with the *D'Albert Durades, she wrote them long letters in French, which unfortunately have not survived; and although there is no direct evidence of how well she spoke the language, she must have attained a level of competence in associating with them and their circle. She took pleasure in reading *French literature throughout her life, naming different writers as her favourites at different times. After the labour of translating D. F. *Strauss in 1846, she found relief from German biblical scholarship in French sensibility, reading Jean-Jacques *Rousseau and George *Sand with excitement at the new perceptions they awakened in her. A few years later she referred to them as writers who had profoundly influenced her, not by their opinions, from which she made a point of distancing herself, but by their power to quicken her faculties (*L* i. 277–8).

In the late 1840s French politics, too, were a source of excitement. She responded with enthusiasm to news of the February revolution in Paris in 1848 (see REVOLUTIONS OF 1848), praising her friend John Sibree in a letter of 8 March for thinking as she did about 'la grande nation' and being 'sansculottish' and rash in his support for the revolution (*L* i. 252–3). In her republican fervour she mocks monarchs and sees the French people as far superior to the British working classes by virtue of their intellectual vitality: 'In France, the *mind* of the people is highly electrified—they are full of ideas on social subjects—they really desire social reform', while the revolutionary spirit fired the whole nation not just the artisans of the towns (*L* i. 254). These confident generalizations had no basis in first-hand experience and can only have been derived from the reading of newspapers; but they reveal a positive image of France and the intellectual energy of its culture which is evident again in her 1854 essay on *'Woman in France: Madame de Sablé' for the *Westminster Review*. Reflecting on the delightful women of France who shone so brightly in the literary and political history of the 17th and 18th centuries, she again pronounces admiringly on the country, using the same image of electricity: 'in France alone woman has had a vital influence on the development of literature; in France alone the mind of woman has passed like an electric current through the language, making crisp and definite what is elsewhere heavy and blurred'. The electric current connecting France, women, and language suggests the stimulus she found as a woman writer in the culture of a country which she saw as having 'presented the highest examples of womanly achievement in almost every department' (*Essays*, 54). Since what made the women of France superior was their access to a common fund of ideas with men, the implications for contemporary culture were clear, and the essay closes with an appeal for the whole field of reality to be laid open to women as well as men. At the outset of George Eliot's career as a writer France thus offered an inspiring model of intellectual freedom and equality.

This essay was written during her first visit to *Germany with G. H. *Lewes, and although she continued to draw on French ideas—Auguste *Comte's *positivism was particularly important—it was German culture, now associated with the emotional and intellectual fulfilment of life with Lewes, that henceforth assumed greater importance. One of her later detractors, Edmund *Gosse, claimed in his *Aspects and Impressions* (1922) that this turn to Germany was unfortunate for her genius, leading to excessive erudition and pedantry; and he wondered what a little more Paris and a little less Berlin might have done for her. As it is, she spent far more time in Germany than in France and engaged more deeply with its life and culture. She had none of the personal contacts and acquaintances in France that enlivened her visits to Germany, and she made little effort to acquire them. A visit to Paris in January 1866 where she and Lewes met writers and intellectuals at Mme Mohl's, including the critic Edmond Scherer and the historian Ernest *Renan, was an exception (Couch 1967: 186).

She first visited France on her first journey abroad in 1849, when her friends the *Brays took her on a continental tour after her father's death. Her initial impressions of the country were probably coloured by her depressed and morbid state of mind, and the description in *The Mill on the Floss* of the ruined villages on the banks of the Rhône and the oppressive feeling of an ugly, narrow existence which they arouse (*MF* 4.1), is doubtless a legacy of the boat journey down the river she made on that first tour. Even *Paris seems not to have appealed to her at first, and she later spoke of having initially detested the city (*L* viii. 333). Although she visited the country on many occasions and became particularly fond of the South (Couch 1967: 186), Paris and France were often passed through en route to or from other destinations, like *Italy on three occasions in the early 1860s and *Spain in 1866–7. It was not until January 1865 that she and Lewes crossed the Channel specifically to visit Paris, where they spent ten days sightseeing and attending the theatre. In August and September of that year they returned to France to spend a month touring Normandy and Brittany. Her journals record appreciative and attentive visits to churches and cathedrals, including Chartres with its 'transcendent' stained glass, and her pleasure in the beauty of the countryside and the neighbourly politeness of the people to each other (*Journals*, 380–90). Provincial France proved attractive, welcoming, and restful, while Paris at the end of the tour offered the pleasures of galleries and theatres and the aesthetic delight of mass at the Russian church.

In spite of this enjoyment of France under the Second Empire, when the *Franco-Prussian war broke out in 1870, Eliot's and Lewes's sympathies were initially with the Germans, whom she saw as repelling France's effort to invade and divide them (*L* v. 113). She expressed sympathy for the sufferings of the French people, drawn into war by an iniquitous government, but at the same time found fault with French pride and vanity as if these moral failings were receiving their due punishment. After the battle of Sedan in September the balance of sympathy began to shift: by December she could be moved to tears by an article of Frederic *Harrison's defending the French as progressive republicans deserving British support, and during the commune she lamented the fate of the country to D'Albert Durade and expressed her love for it: 'Unhappy France, alas, poor country! I love the French and am grateful to them for what they have contributed to the mind of Europe, feeling that the Good outweighs the Evil' (*L* v. 141). Even so her next journey abroad with Lewes was to Germany in the autumn of 1872, and when they returned via Paris, still scarred by the war, they soon fled the city, comparing it unfavourably with the provincial Germany they had just left (*L* v. 318). Later visits to France and Paris were happier, and in the mid-1870s Eliot followed political events in France with close interest, expressing dismay at the possibility of the Second Empire being restored, since she found the traditions of both First and Second Empires bad (*L* vi. 57). It is a measure of how far her political views had changed since 1848 that she could claim to find the prospect of a restoration of the monarchy more acceptable. Her interest in the political fate of France was a recognition of its central role in western civilization, whose future, she declared in 1877, was more critically involved in the maintenance of the French republic than in the Bulgarian struggle (*L* vi. 409).

In spite of this interest in France, it hardly features in her fiction. Paris is the setting for Lydgate's student experiences in *Middlemarch* (*MM* 15), but the city is not represented in any substantial detail. The Rhône landscape in *The Mill on the Floss* is more specific but it serves simply to illustrate a view of *history rather than playing a part in the action of the novel. More significant than the absence of France from the fiction is the absence of a stereotyped image of the French and the moral laxity so often associated with them in Victorian Britain (Couch 1967: 188). Only the sketchy figure of the actress Laure in *Middlemarch*, with whom Lydgate is infatuated and who murders her husband, owes anything to caricature. Esther Lyon's French mother in *Felix Holt*, the delicate angelic-faced Annette with her love of flowers, music, dancing, and her handsome first husband (*FH* 6), is an alien creature in her lack of Protestant energy and earnestness, but her virtue is beyond reproach. In *Daniel Deronda* Mrs Meyrick's combination of French and Scottish blood simply makes for liveliness and 'a pretty articulateness of speech that seemed to make daylight in her hearer's understanding' (*DD* 18). In both cases Frenchness makes for a difference that is presented without prejudice.

This lack of prejudice does not appear to have helped endear George Eliot to her early French readers, for, although her novels were soon translated into French (see TRANSLATIONS OF GEORGE ELIOT'S WORKS), they made little impact at first. After the translation of *Adam Bede* had appeared she saw little prospect of it appealing to French readers, observing that her mind must be 'one of those most remote from the French standard' (*L* iii. 362). Late in life, in 1877, she wrote to her friend and translator D'Albert Durade about how she often received letters from French men and women asking permission to translate her works, as though they were ignorant of the existing translations. Her conclusion was that her French public must be small (*L* vi. 428). That was indeed the case despite sympathetic and intelligent reviews of, and articles on, her work by the critics Emile Montégut and Edmond Scherer (Couch 1967: 51–85). It was only after her death that the conservative critic Ferdinand Brunetière, starting in 1881, began to change things by championing her work in his campaign against Zola's naturalism. George Eliot's novels, while using some of the methods of the naturalists, retained the traditional moral values that he saw Zola as attacking and thus served as a model for Brunetière of what the French novel should aspire to. The central feature of her work, which distinguished it from French naturalism with its attempt at scientific objectivity, was the role of *sympathy in the process of literary creation, and this sympathy was the source of the psychological depth, the metaphysical solidity, and the breadth of moral vision that he found in her work (Couch 1967: 96). In the wake of Brunetière's 1881 article in the *Revue bleue*, reprinted with some modifications in 1892 and 1897, George Eliot's novels became more widely known and their sales increased, reaching a peak in the late 1880s and early 1890s (Couch 1967: 86–7). Brunetière considered her the greatest English novelist of the 19th century and he played a decisive part in establishing her reputation in France, a reputation that was later to be enhanced by the admiration of French writers such as Marcel *Proust, André Gide, and Simone de *Beauvoir. JMR

Brunetière, Ferdinand, 'Le Naturalisme anglais: Étude sur George Eliot', in *Le Roman naturaliste* (1897).
Couch (1967).

Franco-Prussian war (1870–1), a focus of concern to George Eliot, who was initially pro-German but whose attitudes, always humanitarian, changed as the brutality of the conflict emerged. Through Bismarck's cunning release of the Ems telegram, France, fearing German control of the Spanish throne, declared war, whereupon an invading German army defeated Napoleon III at Sedan (1 September 1870). Napoleon was overthrown, the Third Republic set up (4 September), the Prussians besieged Paris, which suffered horrifically before yielding, and by the treaty of Frankfurt France ceded Alsace and Lorraine to the Prussians (1871). The war had begun on 15 July. Eliot believed that the French had lied, that their government had caused the war, that they would invade Germany, and on 15 September confessed to reading *The Times* and the *Daily News* each day. By 18 October she was expressing her doubts (to Oscar *Browning) about the German cause, on 2 December she wrote to Mrs *Congreve that she had wept over Frederic *Harrison's article on Bismarckism in the *Fortnightly Review*, which urged British support for the French. Her journal entry for 31 December mentioned *Paris, 'where our fellow-men are suffering and inflicting horrors' (*L* v. 127). Two days later she referred to the brutalizing effect of protracted fighting on everybody, and on 24 January she wrote to Colonel Edward Bruce *Hamley congratulating him on his letter to *The Times* which condemned Prussian ruthlessness in France, following this with a letter on the 27th to François *D'Albert Durade about the French families she knows who have been ruined: by 25 April she could tell him that she loved the French, that she valued their contributions to the culture of Europe and feared for the indignities they were about to suffer. Her feelings throughout the conflict are torn. See also FRANCE; GERMANY. GRH

Fraser's Magazine, monthly magazine which published two articles by George Eliot on *Weimar. Founded in 1830 by William Maginn to rival *Blackwood's Edinburgh Magazine*, *Fraser's* was a successful periodical, initially known for its acerbic humour. It was relaunched in 1849 under William John Parkes, with a more sober outlook.

Eliot's 'Three Months in Weimar' (June 1855) and *'Liszt, Wagner, and Weimar' (July 1855), were based on her 'Recollections of Weimar 1854' in her *journal. Both articles demonstrate her appreciation of German thought and culture (see GERMANY). See also JOURNALIST, GEORGE ELIOT AS.

MWT

French literature was for George Eliot one of the three greatest literatures of the world, together with English and German (*Essays*, 390). Her knowledge of it, acquired through a lifetime's reading, was unrivalled among English writers of her time. As a 14-year-old, at the end of her first year of learning French, she was awarded Blaise *Pascal's *Pensées* as a prize for her progress, and in later life she claimed to have continually returned to them for their wisdom. She took pleasure in reading French writers throughout her life: after the labour of translating D. F. *Strauss's *Life of Jesus* she found relief from German biblical scholarship in French sensibility, responding enthusiastically to the new perceptions awakened in her by her reading of Jean-Jacques *Rousseau and George *Sand. Later she could refer to Molière (1622–73) as a great favourite and his *Le Misanthrope* (1666) as the finest production of its kind in the world (*L* iii. 227); and she ranked him alongside *Shakespeare as a writer who united in his mind both wit and humour in the highest degree (*Essays*, 220). Her essays reveal her knowledge of Montaigne (1533–92) and *Voltaire; among contemporary novelists she read Dumas *père* (1802–70) and Victor *Hugo. In her 1854 essay *'Woman in France: Madame de Sablé', she maintains that French literature is the only one on whose development women have had a vital influence, and she cites Mme de Sévigné (1626–96) and Mme de *Staël as well as George Sand as examples of the power of women's writing in French literary culture. La Bruyère (1643–96) and his Theophrastan *Caractères* were important for *Impressions of Theophrastus Such*. Her own fiction has invited comparison with that of her contemporary Gustave *Flaubert, and was seen by French critics as a salutary alternative to the naturalism of Émile Zola (Couch 1967: 86 ff.). She was also admired by later French writers, including Marcel *Proust and Simone de *Beauvoir. See also FRANCE.   JMR

Couch (1967).

Freud, Sigmund (1856–1939), Austrian neurologist and psychiatrist, founder of psychoanalysis, and (among many other things) an admiring reader of George Eliot's fiction. His letters to his fiancée in 1882 testify to his special fondness for *Middlemarch* and to his astonishment, typical of Jewish readers of *Daniel Deronda* shortly after it appeared, at the accuracy of Eliot's portrayal of Jewish life.

Had Freud been unaware of George Eliot's writings, he would still have a claim to be included in this volume. He often remarked that the insights of psychoanalysis were not news, that a long line of literary figures—from *Sophocles to *Shakespeare, Diderot, *Goethe, and Dostoevsky—had anticipated his theories of unconscious motivation. George Eliot may be added to that list, and indeed many 20th-century readers have found in her works striking instantiations of such key psychoanalytic notions as narcissism (in Rosamond Vincy, or in the bleaker variety exemplified by Mr Casaubon) or the compulsion to repeat (e.g. in Gwendolen Harleth's obsessive replayings of the scene of her husband's drowning (see CRITICISM, MODERN: PSYCHOANALYTIC APPROACHES)).

Such readings avoid the accusation of anachronism because, as recent scholarship has demonstrated, 19th-century novelists, psychologists, and philosophers were alike engaged in the post-Enlightenment reassessment of the place of reason in human affairs, and questioning the limits of consciousness was an important aspect of that project. The final chapters of Alexander Welsh's *George Eliot and Blackmail* (1985) offer an account of that shared intellectual milieu, arguing that both the dramatizing of psychology in novels like *Daniel Deronda* and Freud's own narratives of the struggles of conscious and unconscious impulses constitute responses to the pressures of modern societies increasingly threatened by proliferating quantities of information.   NH

Ellenberger, Henri F., *The Discovery of the Unconscious: The History and Evolution of Dynamic Psychiatry* (1970).

Rieff, Philip, *Freud: The Mind of the Moralist* (1959).

Froude, J. A. (1818–94), English historian, biographer, authority on Thomas *Carlyle. He was elected Fellow of Exeter College Oxford in 1842. Initially influenced by John Henry *Newman, he published *The Nemesis of Faith* (1849), a novel which expressed his religious doubts but also caused a storm through its related theme of adultery. It was reviewed by George Eliot in the *Coventry Herald and Observer* in March; the book was publically burned in Oxford and Froude lost his Fellowship, though after a distinguished writing career he returned to Oxford as Professor of Modern History in 1892. Eliot obtained her copy of the heterodox sensation and sent a letter of thanks to Froude from 'The Translator of Strauss', her review having styled Froude as 'a bright particular star' and praised his 'hints as to the necessity of recasting the currency of our religion'. They met on 7 June 1849, the day after Robert *Evans's funeral:

Charles *Bray arranged for Froude to accompany them abroad, but Froude, after initially agreeing, withdrew at the last moment because he was planning to marry.

Eliot effectively ran the *Westminster Review for the first ten numbers beginning in January 1852, her professional association with Froude rubber-stamping his radical articles on the Tudors (later a major book), and feeling that he was with others 'amongst the world's vanguard' who should be afforded 'every facility for speaking out' (24 July 1852, L ii. 49). Her valuation of him is seen in the fact that she asked for a copy of *Scenes of Clerical Life* to be sent to him when it was issued in two volumes in January 1858. He responded with delight. Speaking of the pleasure he and his wife felt in it, he added, 'I do not know whether I am addressing a young man or an old—a clergyman or a layman' (*Journals*, 294), following this with a letter in September which refers to 'the George Eliot who has touched me so keenly' (296). Later she sent him *Adam Bede*, and his response conveyed his passionate fascination with the novel. Thereafter references are sparse: in 1870 she read his *History of England*, in 1878 he was at the dinner given for the Leweses by the Goschens on 31 May and sat next to Lewes. His path and Eliot's crossed in the early years when the intellectual doubts of both are perhaps summarized in the belief of his character Markham Sutherland in *The Nemesis of Faith* who preferred 'the religion of Christ' to 'the Christian religion'. See also ATHEISM; CHRISTIANITY; RELIGION; RELIGION OF HUMANITY.   GRH

Fuller, Margaret (1810–50), American feminist whose *Memoirs* George Eliot reviewed in the *Westminster Review in April 1852. Subsequently, Eliot wrote an essay on *'Margaret Fuller and Mary Wollstonecraft' for the *Leader (October 1855).

In her review of the *Memoirs of Margaret Fuller Ossoli*, Eliot describes the remarkable influence which Fuller exerted on her contemporaries which makes it difficult to judge whether she was the parent or child of New England transcendentalism. She extols Fuller's conversational brilliance, comparing her with *Coleridge, Sterling, and Thomas *Carlyle and attributing her with the inspired powers of a pythoness. Fuller, she declares, was rescued from the temptation to despise others by a sympathy as boundless as her self-esteem, a telling comment on Eliot's own sense of the responsibilities conferred by female genius (*Westminster Review*, 57: 665).

In her *Leader* essay Eliot asserts that Fuller's *Woman in the Nineteenth Century* has been unduly overlooked. She finds Fuller's work invaluable despite certain defects of taste and a sort of vague

spiritualism and grandiloquence which belong to all but the very best American writers (*Essays*, 200). In Eliot's view, Fuller avoids exaggeration of woman's moral excellence or intellectual capabilities or arguments about her capacity to perform roles dominated by men in favour of 'a calm plea for the removal of unjust laws and artificial restrictions, so that the possibilities of her nature may have room for full development' (*Essays*, 200). Eliot's many portrayals in her fiction of frustrated female talent evince her sympathy for this aspect of Fuller's thought.

Aspects of Fuller's appearance and character, including her reforming aspirations, have led her to be seen as a specific model for Dorothea Brooke. See also WOMAN QUESTION.   DdSC

Derry, Patricia, 'Margaret Fuller and Dorothea Brooke', *Review of English Studies*, 36 (1985).

'Future of German Philosophy, The', a review by George Eliot in the *Leader in July 1855 (repr. in *Essays*) of a book on the present and future of *philosophy in Germany, *Gegenwart und Zukunft der Philosophie in Deutschland* (1855) by Otto Friedrich Gruppe, whom she and G. H. *Lewes had met in *Berlin on their first visit to *Germany together in 1854–5. She praises him here for his versatility, pointing out that he had published a good book on Greek drama and another on the cosmic system of the Greeks as well as being a philosopher and a poet. The particular appeal for Eliot of the book under review was that it turns against the construction of philosophic systems so characteristic of German philosophy, proclaiming that the age of systems has passed and that the future of philosophy lies in investigation, for which a reform of logic—the method of philosophical enquiry—is needed. Gruppe sees the fundamental error of philosophy from Parmenides onwards as the severing of '*ideas* from *things*' (*Essays*, 150), citing Immanuel *Kant's notion of a priori ideas as a further elaboration of this error. To elevate abstract ideas above experience is 'an attempt to poise the universe on one's head' (151), and George Eliot's agreement with Gruppe on this point defines a central element in the thinking that is to inform her novels. Ideas cannot be separated from experience; they are not prior to judgement but stem from judgement, so that 'from the simple act of judgement we ascend to the formation of ideas, to their modification, and their generalization' (152). Abstract ideas are thus properly derived from concrete particulars. Gruppe's argument is familiar enough in England, she maintains, but what is less familiar is to find it advanced by a German professor; and the only criticism she makes of this unusual ally is his failure fully to understand and appreciate John Stuart *Mill's work on logic.

The conclusion that Gruppe draws for the future of philosophy is that it must renounce metaphysics and abandon efforts to devise a theory of the universe, turning its logical method instead to the investigation of fields such as psychology, aesthetics, ethics, and jurisprudence. This renunciation of 'the attempt to climb to heaven by the rainbow bridge' of the a priori road is seen by George Eliot as the main point of interest for her readers, and she gives Gruppe credit for being content to tread the uphill a posteriori path which leads not to heaven but to a terrestrial eminence from which 'we may see very bright and blessed things on earth' (*Essays*, 153). It is such a vantage point that she will seek to occupy in her fiction. See also PHILOSOPHY.   JMR

G

independence. George Eliot's reference to him in April 1860 (*L* iii. 288) in a letter to Mrs *Congreve from *Rome passingly engages with the effects of his recent coup. In May she writes to John *Blackwood that she is more concerned about G. H. *Lewes's health than 'Garibaldi and the Tuscan filibusters' (*L* iii. 294). In *L* v. 383 she mentions Mrs Schwabe, who had nursed the wounded Garibaldi at Caprera, and although Thornton Lewes (see LEWES FAMILY) waxes lyrical about Garibaldi to his father (*L* viii. 217), Eliot's journal entry for 18 April 1864 merely registers, 'We went to the Crystal Palace to see Garibaldi' (*Journals*, 120) where he received a deputation in his red shirt. See also MAZZINI, GIUSEPPE; NATIONALISM; RISORGIMENTO.   GRH

Gainsborough, a town in Lincolnshire which George Eliot drew on in writing *The Mill on the Floss*. She began planning the novel in January 1859, but progress was fitful, hindered by a variety of anxieties, including the need to find an actual location that would authenticate the imaginary setting for the novel, and allow for its tragic denouement. Crucial to this location was a tidal river. Having eventually decided that, with its history of flooding, the River Trent was a promising Floss, on 26 September 1859 George Eliot and G. H. *Lewes set off for Gainsborough (Lincolnshire) in quest of an appropriate site for the novel's St Ogg's.

At Gainsborough, which lies on the Trent, Lewes hired a boat and rowed George Eliot downstream as far as the river's confluence with the Idle at Stockwith—like Gainsborough, one of the best points to see the tidal bore that forces its way up the Humber estuary. The river, and the features of the landscape through which it flowed, answered George Eliot's imaginative purpose perfectly. Gainsborough's local history informs St Ogg's' local history, while Gainsborough itself presented the broad-gabled, ancient wharf buildings with 'fluted' (pantile) roofs that influence the fictive town's description in the novel's opening chapter. Gainsborough's magnificent Old Hall, a late medieval manor house of which the centre is an impressive, timber-framed Great Hall, is undoubtedly the inspiration and model for St Ogg's' 'fine old hall' by the riverside with its 'ancient half-timbered body' and 'oak-roofed banqueting-hall' (*MF* 1.12)—the setting for 'Charity in Full Dress' (*MF* 6.9). As George Eliot recorded (*Journals*, 80), she had found what she was looking for. See also SETTINGS.   BG

Garibaldi, Giuseppe (1807–82), Italian patriot, charismatic figure in the struggle for Italian independence.

Gaskell, Elizabeth Cleghorn (1810–65), English novelist, story-writer, and biographer of Charlotte *Brontë. As George Eliot's contemporary she was curious to the point of gossip about Eliot's identity but generous in recognition and praise of her writing. John *Blackwood sent her *Adam Bede* in March 1859 and she was quick to respond to the authenticity of place: she had been educated at the Misses Byerley's school at Barford, then Stratford-on-Avon 1821–6, and recognized the *Warwickshire locations delightedly. On 3 June she wrote to Eliot (addressed as Gilbert Elliott) saying that she was flattered to be suspected of having written the novel and generously praising it together with 'Amos Barton' and 'Janet's Repentance'. Her sincerity is unquestionable and her whimsical wit temporarily masks her anxiety about the author's identity. By August she is writing to her publisher George *Smith seeking reassurance that Miss Evans is not responsible, though she allows, 'It is a noble grand book, whoever wrote it' (*The Letters of Mrs Gaskell*, ed. Chapple and Pollard (1966), 566). By the beginning of October she is caught up on the *Liggins side of the myth, at the end of the month she puts herself down by saying, 'it is hardly worth trying to write while there are such books as *Adam Bede* & *Scenes from* [*sic*] *Clerical Life*'—I set *Janet's Repentance* above all, still.—' (581). But soon she is convinced that the author is Miss Evans and writes to Harriet *Martineau damning Liggins in a letter with some facts and not a little fiction and the wish that Miss Evans had never seen Mr G. H. *Lewes (586), whom she obviously judges on his (past) reputation. On 10 November comes the abandonment of rumour in the form of a moving recantation to Eliot which the latter describes as 'A very beautiful letter—beautiful in feeling—Very sweet and noble words they are' (*L* iii. 199) but which also contains the wistful 'I wish you were Mrs Lewes' (*L* iii. 197). Gaskell, fascinated and critically insightful, never allowed the gossip to undermine her generosity of spirit and warm integrity: she takes the direct course of writing to Eliot with humility and with open recognition of her greatness.

The first significant mention by Eliot of Gaskell is on 18 January 1856, when she notes that Gaskell is one of the signatories of Barbara Leigh Smith *Bodichon's petition to Parliament about married women having the legal right to retain what they earn. Her reaction to Gaskell's first letter, which she describes as very pleasant, is to indulge herself to Major William *Blackwood by saying, 'I hope the inaccuracy with which she writes my name is not characteristic of a genius for fiction' (L iii. 76), but her most moving letter to Gaskell is in response to the warm letter noted above. Her own warmth, her joy in the fact that Gaskell had written her such unselfish encouragement, is followed by her expressed admiration for *Cranford* (1853) read in March 1857, and parts of *Mary Barton* (1848) read in April 1858. She had already been deeply moved by *The Life of Charlotte Brontë* (1857), praised Gaskell's care and attention to her material, but deplored the emphasis on Branwell's remorse (before Mrs Gaskell was forced to withdraw the libellous passages about his relationship with Mrs Robinson), and both she and Lewes cried over a book they much admired. They read it aloud in Jersey in 1857. Her critique of *Ruth* (1853) in a letter of 1 February 1853 praises the style and the courage, the little graphic touches of description, but doubts whether it will endure because Mrs Gaskell is intent on contrasts and not with 'the subdued colouring—the half tints of real life' (L ii. 86), an early indication of some of her own concerns when she came to write fiction herself. At the same time Eliot cannot help loving her as she reads her books. (Ironically Lewes, in the *Westminster Review* for April 1853, gave *Ruth* fuller treatment than *Villette* (1853), of which Eliot thought highly.) *Sylvia's Lovers* (1863) is also praised in a letter to George Smith of March 1863 for its emotional and structural content (L iv. 79).

Eliot and Mrs Gaskell never met, though Lewes had visited her, intent on seeing Charlotte Brontë, when he lectured in Manchester in 1849. Mrs Gaskell disliked him initially but found that he improved on acquaintance on this visit. He lent her letters Charlotte Brontë had written him for her biography, and wrote to her in April 1857 praising it but asking for her emphasis in regard to his earlier review of *Shirley* to be adjusted in future editions so that he was not thought to be discriminating against women authors. This she carried out in a somewhat muted way. It is quite obvious from her correspondence with Harriet Martineau at the time of the Liggins controversy (Sara *Hennell exercised a kind of mediating influence on it

since she had learned that her Marian was George Eliot) that Lewes's earlier reputation was against him, that Mrs Gaskell disapproved of the extramarital relationship, but that, despite herself, she felt that *Scenes* and *Adam Bede* were so emblematic of goodness that she could not criticize Mrs Lewes but only praise her. The warmth she expresses is a reflection of her own humanity, her acknowledgement of Eliot's moral concerns which were contiguous to her own and, although she wrote that we must not judge others, her own Christian morality, derived from her Unitarian faith, meant that she did judge but set aside that judgement in her assurance of a literary and human greatness beyond creed. Her death in 1865 is merely noted by Eliot, who had grown in stature and status. Mrs Gaskell's familial concerns (she brought up four daughters) and Eliot's *homes being in or near *London perhaps ensured that they did not meet, though they each undertook Italian journeys and certainly shared the sympathetic ambience of *Florence. GRH

Hardy, Barbara, 'Mrs Gaskell and George Eliot', in Arthur Pollard (ed.), *History of Literature in the English Language*, vi. *The Victorians* (1970).

Uglow, Jenny, *Elizabeth Gaskell: A Habit of Stories* (1993).

—— 'George Eliot and Elizabeth Gaskell', *George Eliot Review*, 23 (1992).

gender derives from the Latin 'genus' meaning type, a root which has also given us 'genre', and which thus facilitates a mode of classification based on differences, either essential or perceived. It is this distinction between essence and perception that has given rise to contemporary notions of gender, which have informed much recent criticism of George Eliot's work. Ideas of gender identity and gender politics have developed as a result of feminist critiques of theories of biological determinism and essentialism. The latter are based in extrapolations from the perception of differently sexed physical bodies. Empirical differences were thought to correlate directly to differences in essence, for instance in the areas of creativity, intelligence, and aspirations. The decision of George Eliot and the *Brontës to write under male *pseudonyms is a good example of the way in which the perceived implications of the biologically female body could act as a highly influential factor in determining the lives of even the most gifted women.

The new wave of feminist criticism and political agitation in the late 1970s suggested that the implications of biological identity were far from inevitable and 'given', rather that they were themselves socially constructed. Specifically, the body itself was not a given, predetermined factor, but its implications were derived from a range of politically and socially determined interests. The body that resulted was a product of its time, and was not a 'God-given' entity. In the 19th century, for instance, the popular prejudice that too much intellectual work would unfit a woman for reproduction was a direct result of contemporary fears and prejudices, and not of medical research.

We can see in Eliot's work a profound understanding of the ways in which *society conspired to entrap the young girl or aspiring female artist in webs spun from the connotations of female bodies. Maggie Tulliver in *The Mill on the Floss* falls victim to Mr Riley and Mr Stelling's views on the inappropriateness of young girls' being educated (see EDUCATION); while Armgart (see POETRY) and Alcharisi in *Daniel Deronda* struggle with the dictates of a society which regards their emphatically desirable bodies as more appropriate to childbearing than to the satisfying of their artistic ambitions in public performance. Eliot also more playfully toys with her society's notions of the appropriate gender roles of the author at the end of *Middlemarch*, when she writes of the canny society of that town's ascribing Mary Vincy's *Stories of Great Men, taken from Plutarch* to her husband, and his agricultural treatise to her. See also CRITICISM, MODERN: GENDER STUDIES; WOMAN QUESTION.   GM

Butler, Judith, *Gender Trouble: Feminism and the Subversion of Identity* (1990).
Levine, Caroline, and Turner, Mark (edd.), *Gender, Genre and George Eliot* (1996). (*Women's Writing*, 3/2, special issue.)
Showalter, Elaine (ed.), *Speaking of Gender* (1989).

gender studies. See CRITICISM, MODERN: GENDER STUDIES.

Geneva was the scene of George Eliot's first extended stay abroad in 1849–50. In May 1848 she referred to the Swiss city as the kind of romantic continental town she would find it bliss to spend a year in, reading and reflecting in some high attic (*L* i. 261). The following year she did just that, choosing to spend nearly eight months in Geneva from late July, at the end of the continental tour she was taken on by the *Brays after her father's death. On 25 July 1849 she took up residence in a pension, the Campagne Plongeon, just outside the city, and her letters to her friends in Coventry describe the other boarders, and their comings and goings, with the acutely observant eye of the future novelist. It was in Geneva, too, that she began to keep a journal, the early years of which, up to 1854, John Walter *Cross used for his *Life* (see BIOGRAPHIES) and then destroyed (see JOURNALS). She was enthusiastic about the beauty of the city and its setting: 'the lake, the town, the campagnes with their stately trees and pretty houses, the glorious mountains in the distance—one can hardly

believe one's self on earth' (*L* i. 302). She was to draw on this experience later in 'The Lifted Veil' (see also ROUSSEAU, JEAN-JACQUES), where Latimer enjoys his one period of happiness in Geneva and finds his first sight of the Alps on descending the Jura 'like an entrance into heaven' (LV 1). On 9 October she moved into the town for the winter, taking up lodgings with the painter François *D'Albert Durade and his wife Julie, who became lifelong friends. In their apartment in the Rue des Chanoines she found something close to the high attic she had dreamed of: 'one feels in a downy nest high up in a good old tree' (*L* i. 320). She stayed until 18 March 1850. Ten years later, in June 1860, she returned with G. H. *Lewes to introduce him to the D'Albert Durades, which was another happy occasion. In 1875 on hearing from D'Albert of the changes that the city had undergone, she observed that 'We old people cannot help regretting the beautiful old Geneva, enclosed in its harmless fortifications' (*L* vi. 174).   JMR

genres. Clearly thinking of a genre not as a formal structure only but as a substantive point of view, George Eliot regularly incorporates major genres into her fictions, translating them into modern terms.

The epic is among her favourites, providing, in its looser sense, an appropriate size and scope for her encompassing conceptions and, in the stricter, a form in which she can focus her attention not only on individual characters but on the story of a people. *Romola*, in which mythic symbolism expands a series of events occurring in 15th-century *Florence into an epic that examines the Christian, Greek, and Roman legacies in the progress of the West, puts the epic to new uses that anticipate developments in 20th-century writers like Joyce. And *Daniel Deronda*, whose titular hero is a Jew brought up as a Christian, offers a similar epical enquiry into Judaeo-Christian traditions.

Eliot's sense that human beings must function, in the absence of God, in an indifferent universe interjects a tragic element into nearly all her fictions, but several come close to actual tragedies: *The Spanish Gypsy*, which fulfils some of the genre's more formal requirements but is not, for that reason perhaps, fully successful as a work of 19th-century literature; *Felix Holt, the Radical* in connection especially with the nemesis of Mrs Transome; and *The Mill on the Floss*, in which Aristotelian tragic criteria are completely redefined (see TRAGEDY).

Taking a genre to be an expression of the conceptual universe of the age that engendered it, Eliot frequently uses genres to stand for the different epistemologies of the major historical periods. In *Middlemarch*, which demonstrates her most intricate handling of genres, different characters are presented as living in different generic frames: Dorothea and Ladislaw (his very name derived from St Ladislaus, patron of the chivalric spirit) re-enact a chivalric romance as they bring to modern history the passionate spiritual quest of the medieval form; Mary and Fred, a Daphnis and Chloë (*MM* 86), recreate a pastoral idyll, Fred to the point of playing the flute (*MM* 11); and Sir James and Celia Brooke blunder through an ironic version of 17th-century sonnet sequences, ironic since, having no sonnets to write (*MM* 6), Sir James is a sonneteer manqué and Celia, although endowed with a name often chosen by sonneteers for its etymological meaning, is not, as the more worldly sister, an appropriate embodiment of their heavenly ideal. Used in this manner, genres become those experiments in life Eliot conducted in her fictions (*L* vi. 216–17) as well as a means of examining what, in the Prelude of *Middlemarch*, she describes as the history of man under the experiments of Time.

Ironic invocations of genres, as in the case of Sir James and Celia, are not unusual in Eliot. In *Adam Bede* both the pastoral and the romance are interrogated as rustic simplicity proves to be a deadly rather than innocent state and Arthurian chivalry deconstructs in Arthur Donnithorne's unchivalric conduct towards Hetty.

Eliot's self-conscious use of genres leads sometimes to astounding results. *The Mill on the Floss*, by assigning its characters conventional operatic voices and by allowing them to sing *music appropriate to their roles, weaves many kinds of musical works, from oratorios to folksongs, into a single continuous opera that comments on and sometimes questions the action of the fictional text.   FB

Marotta, Kenny, '*Middlemarch*: The Home Epic', *Genre*, 15 (1982).

Rowe, Margaret Moan, 'Melting Outlines in *Daniel Deronda*', *Studies in the Novel*, 22/1 (1990).

Thornton, Bruce S., 'A Rural Singing Match: Pastoral and Georgic in *Adam Bede*', *Victorian Newsletter*, 74 (1988).

George Eliot Birthday Book, The. See MAIN, ALEXANDER.

George Eliot Fellowship.
The Fellowship exists to honour George Eliot, to promote interest in her life and works, and to gather together admirers of the novelist, to encourage the collection of books, manuscripts, letters, portraits, etc. for public display.

The annual programme includes, among other events, a programme of readings from her novels, essays, and letters, wreath-laying ceremonies in the George Eliot Memorial Garden in *Nuneaton

and in Poets' Corner in Westminster Abbey, a Memorial Lecture and a Birthday Luncheon in November.

The Fellowship was founded in 1930 in Nuneaton and has a membership of approximately 500 in twenty countries. Annual and life membership is open to individuals and annual membership to corporate bodies.

In 1980, the centenary of George Eliot's death, the Fellowship, as a result of a public appeal, placed a memorial stone in Poets' Corner, Westminster Abbey, and in 1986 erected a bronze statue in the centre of her native Nuneaton.

Four quarterly newsletters and an annual magazine, *The George Eliot Review*, are free to members.

An annual prize is awarded for an essay on George Eliot's novels, life, family, or friends together with guaranteed publication in *The George Eliot Review*.   KA

George Eliot–George Henry Lewes Studies
was first issued as the *George Eliot–George Henry Lewes Newsletter* in September 1982. Founded by William Baker, the journal's current editor, the *Newsletter* was published twice a year at the English Division, West Midlands College, for the mutual benefit of those interested and actively engaged in working with either George Eliot, George Henry Lewes, or the relationship between them and their circle.

The eighth number of April 1986 was a fourteen-page tribute to the great George Eliot scholar Gordon S. *Haight who died in December 1985. This was the first number from the new editorial address at Clifton College, Bristol. With the September 1989 issue, nos. 14–15, the *Newsletter* moved to its present location, Northern Illinois University, became a double issue published once a year, and received an ISBN (0953–0754). The subsequent issue had an Advisory Board of distinguished international Eliot–Lewes scholars. In September 1992 with a 110-page issue, nos. 20–1, the journal's name changed to *George Eliot–George Henry Lewes Studies*. Kenneth Womack became associate editor with nos. 28–9 of September 1995. From humble beginnings, *Studies* now has subscribers from individuals and libraries throughout the world, and also may be found on-line with a world wide web page containing a listing of the contents of previous issues, subscription information, and other details: see http://www.personal. psu.edu/faculty/k/a/kaw16/Eliot.htm.   WB

George Eliot Review, The,
journal of the *George Eliot Fellowship, published annually in August. It carries articles and notes on aspects of George Eliot's life and works, publishes newly discovered letters and documents, contains book reviews, and records the activities of the Fellowship,

including the text of the annual memorial lecture in *Nuneaton and of the addresses delivered at the other memorial events during the year. The journal was launched in 1970 as *The George Eliot Fellowship Review*, edited by Kathleen Adams, the Secretary of the Fellowship. In 1992 it changed to its present title. The current editors are Beryl Gray and John Rignall, and the appointment of an Advisory Board is planned. Back numbers, where available, may be obtained from the Secretary of the Fellowship, 71 Stepping Stones Road, Coventry CV5 8JT, UK. JMR

German literature was for George Eliot one of the three greatest literatures of the world, together with English and French (*Essays*, 390). She began reading it in the original in 1840, when she started learning German, and was soon reading *Schiller's *Maria Stuart* (1801). Schiller was her favourite German author in her early years but was later supplanted by *Goethe, particularly after 1854 when she began to live with G. H. *Lewes and collaborated with him on his *Life of Goethe* (1855). She knew Goethe's work intimately, praising its wisdom and large tolerance in her 1855 essay on 'The *Morality of *Wilhelm Meister*', and it was of central importance in her own creative life. Another early favourite was the humorist Jean Paul (1763–1825), whose work she continued to read on occasions throughout her life, although she was critical of the lack of measure and tact in his humour that made it frequently tiresome (*Essays*, 221). What he lacked was the wit that she admired in the poetry and prose of Heinrich *Heine, about whom she wrote four articles, including the important *'German Wit: Heinrich Heine' of 1856. Wit was also a feature of another admired figure G. E. *Lessing, whose comedy *Minna von Barnhelm* (1767) she found charming and whose prose style in his aesthetic treatise *Laokoon* (1766) she praised for its un-German lucidity. The absence of comic or satirical writing in German that could rank with the best in Europe was something she remarked upon (*Essays*, 222). Goethe is the only German novelist about whom she wrote, although she helped Lewes with the preparation of his article on 'Realism in Art: Recent German Fiction' for the *Westminster Review* in October 1858, and may have shared his view that 'German novels are, for the most part, dreary afflictions' on account of their lack of *realism (*Westminster Review*, 70: 518). An exception for Lewes was Gottfried *Keller, and Eliot certainly read his short fiction, which has some thematic parallels with her own work. She also met another contemporary writer Paul Heyse (1830–1914) in Munich and read his *Novellen*. She was altogether more widely and deeply read in German than any other English writer of

the mid-19th century and her work alludes frequently to German writers, including the Romantics E. T. A *Hoffmann and *Novalis, as well as those mentioned above. See also GERMANY; ROMANTICISM. JMR

Ashton (1980).
McCobb (1982).

'German Wit: Heinrich Heine', the second and longest of four articles George Eliot wrote on the German poet Heinrich *Heine. It was published in the *Westminster Review* in January 1856 (repr. in *Essays*). A sympathetic and well-informed appreciation of Heine's work, it helped establish his reputation in the English-speaking world as probably the best-known German lyric poet after *Goethe. The article begins by distinguishing acutely between humour and wit: the former is diffuse and follows its own fantastic will, whereas the latter is 'brief and sudden, and sharply defined as a crystal' (*Essays*, 218). *German literature has little of either before the 19th century. Heine is thus a unique example of German wit, 'who holds in his mighty hand the most searching lightnings of satire' and at the same time is 'a humourist, who touches leaden folly with the magic wand of his fancy' (223). He is also an even greater master of German prose than Goethe and, most importantly, a surpassing lyric poet. Eliot draws on her thorough knowledge of Heine's writing to give a full account of his life and work, illustrated by lengthy quotations, chiefly from his prose, in her own translation. She defends him against charges of venality and lack of patriotism, and praises his constant attachment to the principles of freedom, but admits to his occasional coarseness and scurrility. Although she does full justice to the range and versatility of his work, she is clearly uncomfortable with his self-conscious irony, and in acclaiming him as above all a lyric poet 'whose greatest power . . . lies in his simple pathos' (248), she underestimates the characteristic ironic temper of his verse. On the other hand she aptly defines and illustrates the lightness and vigour of his prose, from which 'you might imagine that German was pre-eminently the language of wit, so flexible, so subtle, so piquant does it become under his management' (251). Her appreciation of Heine's wit and mastery of language, despite her unease at his moral stance and sometimes baffling irony, is a measure of her intellectual emancipation at the beginning of the year in which she was to begin to write fiction. See also GERMANY. JMR

Germany was the foreign country George Eliot visited most often and spent most time in on her extensive European *travels with G. H. *Lewes. It was to Germany that the couple went when they first began to live together in 1854, and the happiness of those early months together in *Weimar and *Berlin seems to have coloured her feelings about the country, which remained warm. What struck her particularly in that first visit was the Germans' capacity for enjoying life, their 'freedom from gnawing cares and ambitions, contentment in inexpensive pleasures with no suspicion that happiness is a vice which we must not only not indulge in ourselves but as far as possible restrain others from giving way to' (*L* ii. 185). Germany was both liberated and liberating. She liked, too, the simplicity with which Germans entertained their friends, with no concern about appearances or grand dinners but instead just 'heartiness and intelligence' (*L* ii. 189). She and Lewes were well received and made many friends so that, later in life at the time of the Franco-Prussian war, she could write that 'whenever we have been in Germany we have been treated with warm friendliness, and for this reason among many others we cherish a great love for Germany and the Germans, both North and South' (*L* v. 159).

Among the other reasons for liking Germany were the achievements of German culture and scholarship, which she lists in her essay *'German Wit: Heinrich Heine' in the *Westminster Review* in January 1856: 'She [Germany] has fought the hardest fight for freedom of thought, has produced the grandest inventions, has made magnificent contributions to science, has given us some of the divinest poetry, and quite the divinest music in the world' (*Essays*, 222–3). These achievements she had encountered long before visiting the country. As an accomplished pianist she was familiar with German *music from an early age. She began learning German together with Italian in 1840 and was soon reading *Schiller's *Maria Stuart* and *Goethe's *Tasso*, finding that her mind had a greater affinity with German than with Italian (*L* i. 69). She came to know the language thoroughly and probably spoke it quite accurately though with an indifferent accent (see LANGUAGES). Her intellectual interest in German culture was deepened by her friendship with the *Brays and *Hennells, whom she met in 1841 after moving with her father to Foleshill, Coventry. Through them she came into contact with German Higher Criticism of the Bible and took on the task of translating D. F. *Strauss's *Das Leben Jesu* (*The Life of Jesus*). While labouring on the translation she continued to read German literature, particularly Schiller but also Goethe and Jean Paul (see GERMAN LITERATURE). When she moved to London in 1852, editing the *Westminster Review* involved her in bringing to the notice of the British public important new works of German philosophy and theology. It was under her editorship, for

instance, that Oxenford's pioneering essay on Arthur *Schopenhauer appeared, and in the same period she produced her translation of Ludwig *Feuerbach's *Das Wesen des Christenthums* (*The Essence of Christianity*, 1854). When she met Lewes he was working on his biography of Goethe and it was this project that took them to Germany in 1854. Lewes had visited the country at least twice before, while for her it was primarily associated with the life of the mind. When her friend John Sibree wrote to say that he was going to Germany in 1848, she thought of the 'bliss of having a very high attic in a romantic continental town . . . far away from the morning callers, dinners and decencies' (*L* i. 261), where she could pause for a year and think about things. The town she named as an example was *Geneva, where she was to stay for several months the following year, but it was significantly the mention of Germany that prompted this dream of study and escape. For her and Lewes that was to be the reality Germany offered them in 1854 and throughout their life together. In all they made eight extended visits to the country.

On 20 July they left London for Weimar, arriving on 2 August and staying until 3 November when they left to spend the winter in Berlin, returning to England via Cologne and Brussels on 14 March. The professional purpose of the journey was research for Lewes's biography of Goethe, in which the future George Eliot assisted. This first visit was their longest and most amply recorded. In Berlin she wrote up her diary record of Weimar into an essay 'Recollections of Weimar 1854' (*Journals*, 215–40), which was later recast into two articles published in *Fraser's Magazine* in June and July 1855: 'Three Months in Weimar' (see WEIMAR), and *'Liszt, Wagner and Weimar' (both repr. in *Essays*). Weimar seemed small and dull at first but they warmed to its charm under the influence of its associations with Goethe and Schiller. Particularly memorable was the experience of hearing *Liszt, resident Kapellmeister at the Weimar court, play the piano. He proved friendly, inviting them to parties and introducing them to Clara *Schumann and Anton *Rubinstein, often taken to be the model for Klesmer in *Daniel Deronda*. Berlin they found an ugly modern city but much enjoyed their time there, reading intensively, visiting museums and art galleries, and meeting scholars and intellectuals, including Karl August *Varnhagen von Ense and Professor Otto Friedrich Gruppe, whose book was to be the subject of Eliot's review essay 'The *Future of German Philosophy', published in the *Leader* the following July. The four months passed quickly: 'the day seems too short for our happiness', she wrote at the time, 'and we both of us feel that we have

A photograph of George Eliot by Sophus Williams taken in Berlin on her first visit to
Germany in 1854–5.

begun life afresh—with new ambition and new powers' (*L* viii. 134). Back in England in March 1855 and writing up her experiences in 'Recollections of Berlin' (*Journals*, 243–58), she was glad to have returned to the comfort and good food of an English inn, but concluded that 'Germany is no bad place to live in'; and if Germans lacked taste and politeness, they were at least free from the bigotry and exclusiveness of more refined people. Her final wish was to return: 'I even long to be among them again—to see Dresden and Munich and Nürnberg [Nuremberg] and the Rhine country. May the day soon come' (*Journals*, 258).

It was three years before it did, although in that period her journalism revealed the continuing impact of the German visit: of the 34 reviews and notices she wrote, half were on German subjects (McCobb 1982: 43), including her important essays for the *Westminster Review* on Goethe and *Heine, 'The *Morality of Wilhelm Meister*' and *'German Wit: Heinrich Heine'. On 7 April 1858, after completing the first volume of *Adam Bede*, she left with Lewes for Munich. Once again Germany was the place for study and escape—this time escape from speculation about the identity of George Eliot after the publication of *Scenes of Clerical Life*. While she continued with *Adam Bede*, Lewes undertook research for his *Physiology of Common Life*. On their way South they visited Nuremberg, which she found far more picturesque than she had expected, and her journal records detailed and delighted description of the architecture of the town, with its different-coloured façades and bright red or rich purple tiles, and its air of cleanliness and well-being (*Journals*, 306–9). In *Munich they met the scientists von Seebold and von Liebig and the writers Geibel and Heyse, and took pleasure in the art galleries and the distant view of the snow-capped Alps. But although they liked the people, they found the city architecturally unattractive and its climate depressing and were quite glad to leave on 6 July. They travelled through the Tyrol and via *Vienna and *Prague to *Dresden, where they took a large apartment and kept their own company for six weeks 'as happy as princes' (Cross, ii. 57), working and writing steadily and visiting the picture gallery three times a week. They returned to Richmond at the beginning of September with Eliot having written nearly all of the second volume of *Adam Bede* during their stay in Germany.

George Eliot's interest in German culture seems to have declined between 1859 and the couple's next journey to Germany in 1866 (McCobb 1982: 60), the first of three successive summer visits. In June 1866, shortly after the completion of *Felix Holt, the Radical* the couple travelled down the Rhine to Schwalbach and spent twelve days at the spa of Schlangenbad before returning via Holland and Belgium. Their visit coincided with the outbreak of war between Prussia and Austria over Schleswig-Holstein, which had the effect of scaring away other tourists (*L* iv. 284). At the end of July 1867, when both of them were in poor health and in need of recuperation, they set out to revisit 'the scenes of cherished memories' (*Journals*, 130), returning to some of the German towns they had stayed in thirteen years before and spending two weeks near Weimar at Ilmenau, where Eliot wrote some scenes of *The Spanish Gypsy*. In late May 1868, the day after the verse drama had finally been published, they set off for another two months in Germany and Switzerland, spending some time in the Black Forest, which provided material for the poem 'Agatha'. After a two-year interval, they returned to Germany again in March and April 1870, seeking to improve Lewes's health after the distressing death of his son Thornton (see LEWES FAMILY). They spent several weeks in Berlin moving in illustrious social circles, meeting the historian Mommsen, the chemist Bunsen, and 'Princes, Professors, Ambassadors, and persons covered with stars and decorations', as Lewes put it (*L* v. 83). Eliot, however, was suffering from a permanent cold which made the social round something of an ordeal. When they moved on to Vienna they were similarly received, before returning home via Salzburg and Munich.

Given their affection for Germany, it is not surprising that, at the outbreak of the *Franco-Prussian war later that summer, the couple's sympathies were at first firmly on the side of the Germans 'in their grand repulse of the French project to invade and divide them' (*L* v. 113). Seeing the war as a conflict between two differing forms of civilization, Eliot indicated where her own loyalties lay by insisting on 'the great contributions which the German energies have made in all sorts of ways to the common treasure of mankind'. But as the war dragged on she began to feel more sympathy for the defeated French, realizing by January 1871 during the siege of Paris that 'no people can carry on a long fierce war without being brutalized by it, more or less' (*L* v. 131–2).

In their later visits to Germany Eliot and Lewes tended to spend most of their time in quiet watering places, ministering to their failing health. In September and October 1872 they stayed three weeks at Bad Homburg, a spa near Frankfurt, where Eliot wrote the Finale of *Middlemarch* and witnessed Augusta Leigh, Byron's great-niece, gambling in the casino—an experience that was to inspire the opening scene of *Daniel Deronda*. In July and August 1873 they spent three and a half weeks in Germany, staying at Homburg again for ten days and visiting Mainz and Frankfurt to view

Germany

Jewish locations for use in *Deronda*. Their last journey abroad together, in the summer of 1876 shortly after the completion of *Deronda*, was chiefly to *Switzerland, though they did stay for a time in the Black Forest towards the end of their holiday. On their way home from Homburg in 1872 they stopped in Paris, still bearing the scars of war, and in a letter from Boulogne-sur-mer, to which they had soon fled, Eliot described their distaste for the modern metropolis in comparison with the 'old Germany' they had just left, maintaining that 'we have an affinity for what the world calls "dull places" and always prosper best in them' (*L* v. 318). It was precisely the old Germany of small spas and picturesque old towns, of slow provincial life, that they preferred in these last visits, rather than the new Germany of growing industrial and military power, united by Bismarck into the second German Empire. Their Germany, almost a second home to them, was the land of poets and thinkers, scientists and scholars, intellectually advanced but, to the eyes of mid-Victorian travellers, still materially and economically rather backward. Eliot had the foresight to see that the Franco-Prussian war marked the beginning of 'The period of German ascendancy' (*L* v. 112), but about that new ascendant power she was silent.

Following *Coleridge and Thomas *Carlyle, she was the most important disseminator of German ideas in mid-19th-century Britain. Her knowledge of German thought and culture was unrivalled in its depth and range, and she repeatedly alerted her readership to the leading role played by German scholarship in nearly every field of intellectual enquiry. In a review in the *Leader* in June 1855 she pointed out that the Germans were 'the purveyors of the raw material of learning for all Europe', while in 'A*Word for the Germans' in 1865 she maintained that 'no one in this day really studies any subject without having recourse to German books' (*Essays*, 389), and 'if anyone can be called cultivated who dispenses with a knowledge of German, it is because the other two greatest literatures of the world are impregnated with the results of German labour and German genius' (*Essays*, 390). As Will Ladislaw points out to Dorothea in *Middlemarch*, Casaubon's work as a scholar is fatally flawed by his ignorance of German and German research (*MM* 21). Ladislaw himself, to Casaubon's disapproval, has studied at Heidelberg, and his breadth of understanding is attributable in some measure to his German education.

There are few such direct references to Germany in George Eliot's fiction before her last novel *Daniel Deronda*. In *The Mill on the Floss* the narrator's reflections on history at the beginning of Book 4 exploit the romantic associations of the Rhine, where ruined castles form an organic part of the landscape and recall a medieval past that was 'a day of romance . . . a time of colour, when the sunlight fell on glancing steel and floating banners; a time of adventure and fierce struggle—nay, of living, religious art and religious enthusiasm' (*MF* 4.1). Here the German landscape thrills the narrator with 'a sense of poetry', and it is in Eliot's poetry that Germany again provides some of the settings: a German city, probably Berlin, for 'Armgart' and the Black Forest around Sankt Märgen for 'Agatha' (see POETRY OF GEORGE ELIOT). But it is in *Daniel Deronda* that Germany plays the most substantial role. The action begins in a German spa, Leubronn, which is based on her experience of Bad Homburg in particular, but also of other spa towns like Baden-Baden; and Deronda later returns to Germany, visiting the Jewish quarter and synagogue in Frankfurt (*DD* 32) and his grandfather's friend Kalonymos in Mainz (*DD* 60). The subject of Judaism necessarily involved for Eliot an engagement with Germany, where the Jewish population of 600,000 was ten times greater than in Britain, and where G. E. *Lessing's play *Nathan der Weise*, which she saw in Berlin in 1854, had presented the figure of a nobly enlightened Jew and thrilled her with its advocacy of religious tolerance.

As their later visits to Germany made clear—especially the Berlin trip of 1870—both Eliot and Lewes were well known and much respected in that country. Although her fiction never enjoyed the popularity among Germans of Walter *Scott and Charles *Dickens, her works were quickly translated and widely read. Baron Christian Bernhard *Tauchnitz, whom she first met in Leipzig in 1858, secured the rights for the continental reprint of the novels in English (except for *Middlemarch* which went to Asher in Berlin), and published them soon after their appearance in Britain. There were German translations of *Adam Bede* (1860), *Silas Marner* (1861), *The Mill on the Floss* (1861), *Romola* (1864), *Felix Holt* (1867), *Middlemarch* (1873), and *Daniel Deronda* (1876). The combination of realism and moral idealism appealed to her German audience and her reputation did not suffer the sharp decline after her death that occurred in Britain (see REPUTATION, CRITICAL). Ernst von Wolzogen published a positive biographical and critical study in 1885, and there were other appreciative critical and academic studies in that decade and into the 20th century, while translations continued to appear: *The Spanish Gypsy* (1885), 'The Lifted Veil' (1897), and new versions of *Romola* (1909) and *Daniel Deronda* (1918). *Deronda* was received with particular enthusiasm by the Jewish community in Germany and generally met with greater understanding than in Britain. However, it was *Silas Marner* that remained the most popular of her works in Germany, and there were new versions published in 1902 and 1925 and an abridged edition for schools in 1912 (Wiebel, 199–216).

Her final visit to Germany took place at the end of her honeymoon with John Walter *Cross in the summer of 1880. Cross had been taken ill in *Venice, suffering some form of breakdown and throwing himself into the Grand Canal, and it was to Austria and Germany that the couple retreated. After a few days in Innsbruck, they travelled via Munich and Stuttgart to Wildbad in the Black Forest, where Cross was pleased to linger for a week or more, restoring his health in the quiet surroundings and the sweet air. Her letters to Lewes's son Charles from their German resting places speak of her own good *health and contentment after the anxiety of Venice, and dwell appreciatively on the beauty of the landscape. Once again, and for the last time, Germany was a place of refuge and recuperation for George Eliot and her partner. See also MUSIC; VISUAL ARTS.   JMR

Argyle, Gisela, *German Elements in the Fiction of George Eliot, Gissing, and Meredith* (1979).
Ashton (1980).
McCobb (1982).
Pfeiffer, Sibilla, *George Eliots Beziehungen zu Deutschland* (1926).
Wiebel, Jane, *George Eliot: The Reception of her Works and her Personal Standing during and after her Lifetime* (Diss. Hamburg, 1971).

Gibbon, Edward (1737–94), English historian. George Eliot mentions him in relation to her translation of D. F. *Strauss when she is feeling discouraged, saying that she can't do what Gibbon did, 'put my work in the fire and begin again' (*L* i. 187), a reference to his (supposedly) burning the pages of his *History of the Liberty of the Swiss* after criticism from friends. Eleven years later, again to Sara *Hennell, Eliot copies a note from *The Decline and Fall of the Roman Empire* that 'The signification of Islam, therefore, is to make peace, or to obtain immunity', and in *The Mill on the Floss* (2.1) Maggie reads out the title of that work. She read Gibbon on the revival of Greek learning in July 1861, and in August 1878 Eliot and G. H. *Lewes read J. Cotter Morrison's *Gibbon* in the 'English Men of Letters' series.   GRH

Gladstone, William Ewart (1809–98), English Liberal politician and Prime Minister. As early as May 1852 George Eliot is referring to Gladstone's support for the campaign against the price-fixing by booksellers which John *Chapman was orchestrating. John *Blackwood frequently criticizes Gladstone, but it is not until February 1874 that Eliot herself, in a letter to Barbara *Bodichon,

refers to Benjamin *Disraeli's triumph over his rival by saying, 'Do you mind about the Conservative majority? I don't' (*L* vi. 14). In the same month she accuses Gladstone (though without naming him) of 'putting on a fool's cap instead of laurels' and debasing his high office by 'turning the Shield of Achilles into doggrel of this sort' (*L* vi. 22). The reference here is to Gladstone's 'The Shield of Achilles' in the *Contemporary Review* (February 1874). Other references show her critical of his Eastern policy (August 1878), admiring of his longevity (sadly compared to Lewes's death at 'sixty-one and a half', *L* vii. 231), and critical of the venom of his speeches in 1879.   GRH

Gluck, Christoph Willibald (Ritter von) (1714–87), German composer, who, according to G. H. *Lewes, was among the composers he and George Eliot were created to respond to—the others being *Schubert, *Beethoven, *Mozart, and 'even Verdi' (*L* v. 85). In Berlin in January 1855, the Leweses had heard Richard *Wagner's niece, the soprano Johanna Jachmann Wagner (1828–94), perform the role of Orpheus in Gluck's opera. This work evidently made a deep impression on George Eliot. In 'Mr Gilfil's Love-Story' in *Scenes of Clerical Life* she causes the passionate, love-lorn Caterina to sing Orpheus' tragic aria 'Che farò senza Euridice?', and the role is triumphantly performed by the protagonist of her poetic drama 'Armgart' (see POETRY), whose salon exhibits mounted busts of Gluck and Beethoven. Declaring that the immortal Gluck had sung through her singing, Armgart crowns his bust with her own wreath. George Eliot comments on Frederic *Leighton's depiction of the fine moment in the opera, 'where Eurydice, not knowing the command that Orpheus is not to look at her, clings to him in pained wondering entreaty, while he turns his head away in anguish' (*L* iv. 143).

After attending *Orpheus* in Berlin, Lewes and George Eliot heard Gluck's 'operatic treat' *Iphigenia in Aulis* (*Journals*, 251), with Luise Köster in the title role. In 1870 they heard his *Armide*. See also MUSIC.   BG

Goethe, Johann Wolfgang (1749–1832), German poet, dramatist, novelist, and man of letters, whose work was of central importance to George Eliot. She read it intensively and repeatedly, referring to it and quoting from it throughout her writing life. Although *Schiller was her first enthusiasm among German writers, there is evidence that she also read Goethe during her early study of German in Coventry in the 1840s (see GERMANY). The diary of her friend Cara *Bray, with whom she studied the language, suggests that she read at least *Wilhelm Meisters Lehrjahre* (1795–6), *Die Wahlverwandtschaften* (*Elective Affinities*, 1809), and *Egmont*

(1788) in that period, while a letter to another friend Mary *Sibree records their reading of *Faust* (1808, 1832) together in 1845 (*L* viii. 10). After she had moved to London following her father's death, she wrote to her Coventry friends the Brays in 1852 asking them to send on her Goethe, along with *Shakespeare, *Byron, and *Wordsworth; and in the following year she referred to Goethe as one of her companions in her London life. However, her most intensive engagement with Goethe came when she began to live with G. H. *Lewes, leaving London with him in July 1854 to spend eight months in Germany helping him with the preparation of his *Life and Works of Goethe* (1855). She was an active collaborator in that project, translating many of the prose passages from Goethe's work cited in Lewes's book, and the association of Goethe with the happiness and fulfilment of her relationship with Lewes gave him an enduring importance in her life (Shaffer 1996: 4). In *Weimar they visited Goethe's house, and in her account of their stay, 'Three Months in Weimar', she relates how she was moved to tears by the sight of his simple study and dark little bedroom. Her journals indicate that she read most of Goethe's work during these months in Weimar and later *Berlin; and she and Lewes also met Goethe's friend Karl August *Varnhagen von Ense and his secretary Johann Peter Eckermann. She drew on that intense period of study in the following years, but also continued to read and reread Goethe. In December 1870 her journal records reading aloud 'Wilhelm Meister again!' (*L* v. 124); and in the last months of her life she read the first part of *Faust* with her husband John Walter *Cross, who claimed in his *Life* of the novelist that 'nothing in all literature moved her more than the pathetic situation and the whole character of Gretchen. It touched her more than anything in Shakespeare' (Cross, iii. 421).

The qualities that she admired in Goethe emerged in the essays which she wrote on her return from Germany, in particular 'The *Morality of *Wilhelm Meister*' (1855), where, in defending the novel against the charge of being an immoral book, she praised Goethe's large tolerance, his avoidance of overt moralizing, and his presentation of human character as 'mixed and erring, and self-deluding' (*Essays*, 146), but never without some redeeming feature. The true morality of Goethe's works, which 'has a grander orbit than any which can be measured by the calculations of the pulpit' (144) lies in his understanding that there is no sharp dividing line between the virtuous and the vicious. Her own fiction was to share this generous view of humanity (see MORAL VALUES), which is both morally discriminating and essentially secular, unsupported by any religious faith. Like Auguste *Comte and Ludwig

*Feuerbach, Goethe was one of those thinkers who appealed to Eliot by secularizing religious feeling and directing it into human relationships. In 'The *Natural History of German Life' (1856) she again praised his breadth of vision, describing him as 'eminently the man who helps us rise to a lofty point of observation, so that we may see things in their relative proportions' (*Essays*, 297). That lofty vantage point entailed holding himself aloof from the turbulent stream of historical events, and in 1870 she referred to him approvingly when claiming to Sara *Hennell that, in order to continue with intellectual work, it was necessary to withdraw from the disturbing reality of the *Franco-Prussian war and its barbarism: 'You remember Goethe's contempt for the Revolution of '30, compared with the researches in the Vertebrate Structure of the skull?' (*L* v. 122–3).

When she began to write fiction some of her readers and reviewers immediately recognized affinities with Goethe and drew comparisons with his work, showing an awareness of the European dimension of her novels which is only now beginning to be recovered. Crabb Robinson found a parallel between the 'Confessions of a Beautiful Soul' in *Wilhelm Meister* and the portrayal of evangelicalism in *Scenes of Clerical Life*, seeing both writers as having the ability to write wisely and beautifully about something they did not believe in themselves (Ashton 1980: 173). R. H. *Hutton compared Goethe's 'beautiful soul' with Dinah Morris in *Adam Bede*, finding the latter superior as a fully realized character (Ashton 1980: 173), while, in one of the most searching contemporary analyses of Eliot's fiction, Richard Simpson in *The Home and Foreign Review* in October 1863 maintained that the principles of Goethe's writing as elucidated by Lewes were the 'guiding stars of George Eliot' (*CH* 245–7). Like Goethe she dwells on the pathos of common life, focuses on realities as opposed to ideals, distrusts logic, and seeks to encompass the rich variety of life, holding that its complexity is not to be embraced by maxims. Simpson goes so far as to claim that the story of *Adam Bede* is only a modification of *Faust*, and she certainly heard Radziwill's music to *Faust* and was deeply moved by Gretchen's second song whilst she was writing the second volume of the novel in *Munich (*Journals*, 315). But Simpson's claim reduces Goethe's work to the seduction of Gretchen and its tragic consequences. He is on firmer ground when he claims that Goethe's moral and religious principles are also those of Lewes and George Eliot, singling out the doctrine of *renunciation and self-sacrifice for the benefit of others as a central concern of both writers, whether presented symbolically as in *Faust* or expressed in clear aphorism.

The influence that Simpson seems to be implying is always hard to establish, but it is clear that Goethe's example was important for George Eliot in a general way as she developed her own distinctive form of realistic fiction, one that does not shrink from a use of *symbolism comparable to Goethe's, as E. S. Shaffer has argued (1996: 15). There are also specific and acknowledged debts. The title of one chapter in *The Mill on the Floss*, 'Illustrating the Laws of Attraction' (6.6), is a direct reference to the chemical laws of elective affinity that Goethe uses in *Die Wahlverwandtschaften*, and the presence of that novel can be felt behind the last two books of Eliot's. In the chapter in question Maggie and Stephen Guest are drawn to each other despite their respective commitments to Philip and Lucy, rather as the quartet of characters in Goethe's novel—the married couple Charlotte and Eduard and their guests the Hauptmann and Ottilie—are attracted into adulterous relationships. Adultery is not the issue in *The Mill* but rather loyalty to obligations entered into in the past—'If the past is not to bind us, where can duty lie?' (*MF* 6.14). However, in both novels the conflict between duty and passion raises questions of free will and imposes the necessity of choice. When Charlotte finally agrees to divorce Eduard, Ottilie refuses to marry him and wastes away to death. Similarly, Maggie resists Stephen's passionate appeals for her hand in marriage and prefers to remain true to her conscience. In Goethe's novel the accidental drowning of Charlotte's and Eduard's child, who slips from Ottilie's hands into a lake, precipitates the final events, whilst *The Mill* ends, of course, with the death of Maggie and Tom by drowning. Interestingly, George Eliot had defended the denouement of *Die Wahlverwandtschaften* in a discussion in Berlin on the grounds that it followed naturally from the characters of the respective actors and that denouements in real life were very often unreasonable (McCobb 1982: 168). Her own ending has always attracted criticism without eliciting a similar defence, but it remains, like Goethe's, challenging and unsettling, refusing to offer that speciously moral distribution of rewards and punishments that she had criticized in 'The Morality of *Wilhelm Meister*'. In spite of the affinities between Goethe's novel and the last two books of Eliot's, the mode of narration that each adopts remains very different. Goethe refrains from comment while the narrator of *The Mill* maintains a commentary on the action and the characters. However, when that commentary comes to reflect on the 'shifting relations between passion and duty', it refuses to resolve the issue neatly, maintaining that 'we have no master key that will fit all cases' (*MF* 7.2). The final effect may thus be similar to Goethe's, achieving openness and ambiguity not by his elusive ironic indirection but by explicit comment and emphasis.

A central concern of *The Mill on the Floss* and a subject of narrative comment is the value of renunciation—the renunciation which Maggie first practises without understanding its true implications, which Philip criticizes, and which she finally embraces in a way that brings experience of its real pain and sorrow. Renunciation (*Entsagung*) is an important issue for Goethe, too, though he emphasizes less its cost than its value as a form of self-restriction, one that is necessary for the full development of the individual and the social group to which he or she belongs. This is the lesson that Wilhelm Meister has to learn in his apprenticeship to life, and it has echoes in George Eliot's novels, most notably in *Middlemarch* and *Daniel Deronda*, where the development of the central character is not cut short as it is in *The Mill*. When Dorothea renounces, as she thinks, her love for Will Ladislaw and, stifling her own pain, sets out to help her friends (*MM* 80, 81), she is performing just such an act of renunciation. When Deronda decides to marry Mirah, he is taking an important step in defining his identity as a Jew, but his decision entails his painful renunciation of his relationship with Gwendolen. Development involves a concomitant restriction and the sacrifice of one loving relationship for another. These reminders of *Wilhelm Meister* have led to *Middlemarch* and *Deronda*, and even *The Mill*, being described as *Bildungsromane*, novels of education and development on the Goethean model, but the term needs to be used with caution, since Eliot's mode of narration and representation of a dense and complex social world have little in common with Goethe's more abstract, playfully ironic, and self-conscious procedures.

Goethe's work is an informing presence in *Middlemarch*, where the study of English provincial life is set in a larger European frame. Dorothea's experience in Rome has some resemblance to Goethe's own as recorded in his *Italian Journey*, insofar as it involves the initiation of a Protestant sensibility into a wider and richer life (Wiesenfarth 1982: 101). Lydgate's search for the hypothetical primitive tissue echoes Goethe's quest for the *Urpflanze*, the original ideal plant (Argyle, 41). When the German artist Naumann responds to the sight of Dorothea in the Vatican museum by describing her as 'a sort of Christian Antigone—sensuous force controlled by spiritual passion' (*MM* 19), that combination of classical form and contemporary spirit is reminiscent of the heroine of Goethe's *Iphigenie auf Tauris*, who, in the words of Lewes's *Life of Goethe*, 'has the high, noble, tender, delicate soul of a Christian maiden' (bk. 5, ch. 2), and like Dorothea does good by the mild influence of her exemplary humanity. The moral climax of Dorothea's development is marked, however, by an allusion not to Iphigenie but to Faust: chapter 81, in which Dorothea acts on the resolution she makes after her sleepless night of mental anguish and goes to help the Lydgates, has as its epigraph lines from the beginning of the second part of *Faust*. Awaking from his healing sleep, Faust resolves henceforth to strive continually towards the highest form of existence, 'zum höchsten Dasein immerfort zu streben'. Goethe's sense of reawakening life and determination is set at sunrise, and that motif is taken up in the title of Book 8 of *Middlemarch*, 'Sunset and Sunrise', in which this chapter is located. Yet the Faustian parallel has its obvious limits: Dorothea may share Faust's determination to strive upwards and harbour Faustian plans of draining land and founding a colony, but her striving is a moral struggle for the good, untainted by any Faustian urge for power or boundless experience. Significantly, he comes to his resolution through the oblivion granted by sleep, whereas Dorothea's is the product of a wakefulness which indicates *Middlemarch*'s distinctive moral inflection of the Faustian motif. Eliot never allows her characters to bury the past as Goethe permits Faust to do with his healing sleep, for accepting responsibility for past actions is a necessary step towards the achievement of moral maturity. George Eliot may share Goethe's large tolerance in many respects, but not to the extent of granting her characters convenient oblivion of their past wrongdoings.

The figure of Will Ladislaw, with his wide and initially unfocused interests and his concern for 'self-culture' (*MM* 46), bears some resemblance to Goethe's Wilhelm Meister. Although he appears at first to be something of a dilettante, Eliot sympathetically interprets that dilettantism as many-sidedness (a term associated with Goethe himself) and a mark of potential, treating him with the moral leniency that is characteristic of Goethe's *Bildungsroman*. Events work out in his favour as they do for Wilhelm, and when he and Dorothea are finally brought together by a flash of lightning in a convenient thunderstorm (*MM* 83), Eliot's benignly ironic handling of her characters and self-conscious use of romantic cliché invite comparison with Goethe (Ashton 1993: 113). However, Will Ladislaw remains a peripheral figure, and it is in Daniel Deronda that the echo of Wilhelm Meister is strongest. Deronda is a privileged character, and although he enjoys somewhat earnest authorial approval rather than Goethe's genial irony, his early aspirations are presented in terms that allude directly to the Goethean model: 'He longed now to have the sort of apprenticeship to life which would not shape him too definitely, and rob him of that

choice that might come from a free growth' (*DD* 16). He is, indeed, granted the freedom to grow, guided like Wilhelm by mentors in the figures of Mordecai and his grandfather's friend Kalonymos; and the narrative of his apprenticeship to life resembles Eliot's own description of Goethe's in 'The Morality of *Wilhelm Meister*' in that it 'quietly follows the stream of fact and of life; and waits patiently for the moral processes of nature as we all do for her material processes' (*Essays*, 146–7). The metaphor of the stream is taken literally in the scene on the Thames in which Deronda drifts into his encounter with Mirah (*DD* 17), and his development as a whole seems to be entrusted to the moral processes of nature, which do not fail him.

The contrast with Gwendolen's experience in the same novel is striking, and the echoes of Goethe in her half of the narrative have a significantly different source, drawing on *Faust* rather than *Wilhelm Meister*. Goethe's 'Prologue in Heaven' is alluded to in the epigraph to the first chapter, and the Faustian context has immediate implications both in the hellish atmosphere of the opening scene around the gaming tables and in Deronda's question as to whether the 'good or evil genius' is dominant in Gwendolen's glance. Although Gwendolen later quotes a line by Mephistopheles (*DD* 5) and adopts a façade of cynical worldliness, she is less the tempter than the tempted, whether in the casino or in the marriage market, where she is faced with Grandcourt's materially attractive but morally tainted offer. Proud, frustrated by narrow circumstances, and seeking escape through a reckless compact with an evil and manipulative man, her experience has some parallels with Faust's (Röder-Bolton, 110); but she is a Faust rendered powerless by her gender and in thrall to a Mephistopheles whose negating spirit is that of a strangely inert and reptilian upper-class Englishman. Evil is here rooted in the privileges of class and gender which feed the appetite of a monstrously overbearing ego.

The impact of Goethe thus extends to George Eliot's last novel, as it does to the last years of her life. After Lewes's death she included two poems by Goethe in the collection of grieving verse she inscribed in her diary in January 1879, and in May she relived the past by reading again Lewes's *Life and Works of Goethe* 'with great admiration and delight' (*Journals*, 174). In December 1880, the final month of her life, she is reading Goethe's epic poem *Hermann und Dorothea*. From the happiness of her first months with Lewes in Weimar in 1854, Goethe held a special and central place in her life, and she found in his work a wisdom and tolerance, a breadth and profundity that were an enduring source of inspiration. Her early reviewers were right to compare her work to his, for it is in such company that she properly belongs.   JMR

Argyle, Gisela, *German Elements in the Fiction of George Eliot, Gissing, and Meredith* (1979).

Ashton (1980).

——, 'Mixed and Erring Humanity: George Eliot, G. H. Lewes and Goethe', *George Eliot–George Henry Lewes Studies*, 24–5 (1993).

McCobb (1982).

Röder-Bolton, Gerlinde, *George Eliot and Goethe: An Elective Affinity* (1998).

Shaffer, E. S., 'George Eliot and Goethe: "Hearing the Grass Grow"', *Publications of the English Goethe Society*, 66 (1996).

Wiesenfarth, Joseph, 'The Greeks, the Germans and George Eliot', *Browning Institute Studies*, 10 (1982).

Goldsmith, Oliver (1728–74), Irish novelist, playwright, and poet, much loved by George Eliot. The first important mention of him with regard to her comes in G. H. *Lewes's letter to John *Blackwood signalling *Scenes of Clerical Life* (6 November 1856) where he refers to 'such humour, pathos, vivid presentation and nice observation have not been exhibited (in this style) since "The Vicar of Wakefield"' (*L* ii. 269). Blackwood himself strengthened the analogy by quoting a friend ('it reminds me in its tender simplicity of the Vicar of Wakefield', *L* ii. 300). Eliot responded warmly: 'Dear old "Goldie" is one of my earliest and warmest admirations and I don't desire a better fate than to lie side by side with him in people's memories' (*L* ii. 303). She repeats the analogy and 'tender simplicity' in *'How I came to write Fiction' (*L* ii. 409). In *The Mill on the Floss* (1.3) Maggie refers indirectly to Goldsmith's *A History of the Earth and Animated Nature* (1774), and in *Middlemarch* there are a cluster of mentions in chapters 14, 29 (an epigraph from *The Vicar of Wakefield*), 57 (with Mary Garth speaking of Dr Primrose and Mr Farebrother in the same breath), and 63 (the epigraph from *The Traveller*, 1764).

Eliot told Blackwood in 1871 that she felt she was liable to parody 'dear Goldsmith's satire on Burke, and think of refining when novel readers only think of skipping' (*L* v. 169), a reflection of her familiarity with Goldsmith's *Retaliation* (1774), 35–6: 'Who, too deep for his hearers, still went on refining | And thought of convincing while they thought of dining'. The early attraction remains. Writing to Blackwood in 1867 about a cheap illustrated edition of her works (see ILLUSTRATIONS) she refers nostalgically to 'my own childish happiness in a frightfully illustrated cheap copy of the Vicar of Wakefield' adding that 'illustrations may be a great good relatively' (*L* iv. 354).   GRH

Gosse, Edmund (1849–1928), the pre-eminent late Victorian, Edwardian, and Georgian man of letters despite what Henry *James called his 'genius for inaccuracy' (Thwaite, 2) and whose criticism of George Eliot was influential. He is best known now for his biographical *Father and Son: A Study of Two Temperaments* (1907): his father was Philip Gosse, zoologist and Christian fundamentalist, whose studies of marine life were pored over by G. H. *Lewes in his *'Sea-side Studies' phase.

Gosse damningly articulated the posthumous reaction against George Eliot. Allowing that she dominated English fiction in the decade from Dickens's death in 1870 to her own, he declared her a 'partial and accidental failure' because she turned away from the 'felicity of expressed reminiscence' in the early novels to 'a strenuous exercise of intellect', and compared her unflatteringly with 'that mighty woman, the full-bosomed' George Sand (*Aspects and Impressions*, 4). He never met George Eliot though he reported glimpses of her, and remarked of *Middlemarch*, 'Look narrowly at it and you will see Lydgate is herself' (Thwaite, 171). See also REPUTATION, CRITICAL.   MAH

Gosse, Edmund, *Aspects and Impressions* (1922).

Thwaite, Ann, *Edmund Gosse: A Literary Landscape 1849–1928* (1984).

Grand, Sarah (pseudonym of Frances Bellenden McFall, née Clarke, 1854–1943), one of the pioneering 'New Woman' novelists of the 1880s and 1890s and an energetic lecturer and political campaigner, active in the Women Writers' Suffrage League and the National Union of Women's Suffrage Societies. The story of Grand's early years, including her unhappy marriage at the age of 16 and her struggle to succeed as a writer, is told in the largely autobiographical *The Beth Book* (1897), in which the representation of the rebellious and idealistic heroine owes a clear debt to that of Maggie Tulliver in George Eliot's *The Mill on the Floss*. In *The Beth Book* and in her other fiction, most notably *Ideala: A Study from Life* (1888) and the best-selling *The Heavenly Twins* (1893), Grand engaged, often controversially, with the feminist issues of her day: the sexual double standard, the impact of the Contagious Diseases Acts and the Married Women's Property Acts, and the constraints upon women's education and achievement (see WOMAN QUESTION).

Grand's final years, which included a six-year spell as Mayoress of Bath, were of impeccable sobriety and respectability. This is not such a reversal as it might seem. Although her novels frequently depict women crushed within marriages to syphilitic, abusive, and overbearing men, struggling for financial and artistic independence, Grand was of the more conservative 'purity school' of turn-of-the-century feminism, which

An engraving in Cross's *Life* of Griff House, where George Eliot grew up, living there from a few months after her birth until the age of 21.

advocated temperance, men's need for reform, and women's right to autonomy within existing social structures. In *The Beth Book*, Beth evokes the 'serener spirit' of George Eliot in support of her refutation of the 'passion' of George *Sand: 'I believe it is only those who renounce the ruinous riot of the senses, and find their strength and inspiration in contemplation, who reach the full fruition of their powers' (471). GF

Grand, Sarah, *The Beth Book: Being a Study of the Life of Elizabeth Caldwell Maclure, A Woman of Genius* (1897; repr. 1980).

Kersley, Gillian, *Darling Madame: Sarah Grand and Devoted Friend* (1983).

Griff House, George Eliot's home, 1820–41. When Mary Anne was 4–5 months old, the Evans family moved from South Farm to Griff, a spacious, comfortable, red-brick farmhouse, dating mainly from the 18th century, also on the Arbury estate. Griff's Round Pool, 4-acre gardens, dairy, and attics are reflected in her writings; so are Griff Hollows, Arbury Mill, and the Coventry canal close by. Fields and farmyard, stables and orchard nourished her love of rural concerns while neighbouring coal-pits and quarries fostered her understanding of industrial life. From the age of 17 she combined academic studies with farmhouse management. The loss of Griff when her father retired proved very painful. In later life she referred to it

affectionately as 'my old, old home' (*L* iii. 224), and in May 1874 when she was given a photograph of the house by her niece, she wrote how 'Dear old Griff still smiles at me . . . and I seem to feel the air through the window of the attic above the dining room', from which she used to think the view rather sublime (*L* vi. 45–6). The house still stands, with modern extensions, on the road between *Nuneaton and *Coventry. It is now a Beefeater restaurant. RMH

Gurney, Edmund (1847–88), Fellow of Trinity College, Cambridge, and friend of George Eliot. Gurney trained in medicine and the law in addition to writing a substantial work of musicology, *The Power of Sound* (1880). In the 1870s he became interested in psychic phenomena. Together with Myers and Sidgwick, Gurney became a founding member of the Society for Psychical Research (1882). He undertook research into telepathy and hypnotism. Gurney's work on hallucination and hypnosis make him a forerunner of modern experimental psychology. Leslie Stephen saw him as the probable model for the character of Deronda (*L* vi. 140). Moments of heightened sympathetic communion in *Daniel Deronda* (*DD* 4) might certainly suggest affinities with the way in which Gurney's work challenged the limits of materialist *science. See also SPIRITUALISM. DdSC

H

Haight, Gordon S. (1901–85), outstanding George Eliot scholar of the mid-20th century and after. He published his *Mrs Sigourney: The Sweet Singer of Hartford* (1930) before beginning to saturate himself in George Eliot in 1933, the year in which he received his doctorate from Yale and in which the University Library acquired hundreds of George Eliot letters. He devoted himself to their editing, acquiring facts and developing insights which led to the image-changing *George Eliot and John Chapman, with Chapman's Diaries* (1940). *The Letters of George Eliot* (7 vols., 1954–5; 2 vols. of supplementary letters being issued in 1978) record a lifetime's achievement. His articles on Eliot over the years are evidence of his deep study, his sustained enthusiasm, his scholarly dedication, and his individual critical appraisals of her life, her work, and most impressively, of the backgrounds and foregrounds of Victorian literature. *George Eliot* (1968) is a scrupulously documented biography, conservative in tone though with some radical revelations, providing the humane and informed base from which contemporary evaluations begin. The sheer detail is impressive but never dull, the appraisal graceful, discriminating, and persuasive, so that we know what the subject was doing at particular times, with the medium in which she moved (her phrase) fully contextualized in terms of friends, places, even ambiences and associations. The objectivity is rarely marred: there is a tendency to accept the clichéd 'she was not fitted to stand alone', some hints that a lifetime's dedication is not without possessiveness, and a critical failure occasionally to integrate more fully the life with the works. Set against this is the admirable eschewing of the sensational and salacious (a determination not to debase the biographical currency), a sustained sympathetic identification which never degenerates into sentiment, an overview which relates each part to the whole. The ex-pansion of the admirable introduction in the first volume of the *Letters*, effectively mini-biographies of those in the Eliot circle, enhances the historical sense, amplifies our knowledge, and reflects both the width and depth of Haight's own, seen in his essays on Victorian literature, Renaissance studies, and American writing which span some 50 years, and his devotion to George Eliot which culminated in his vision, now fact, of the Clarendon Edition of her works. This was suitably inaugurated by the issue on the centenary of her death of the first volume, his exemplary text of *The Mill on the Floss*. Haight's other services to George Eliot include the redressing of John Walter *Cross, whose editing, cutting, and conflating he reveals without rancour. The supplementary volumes of the *Letters*, few by Eliot but those by Thornton Lewes (see LEWES FAMILY) and extracts from Edith *Simcox's *Autobiography of a Shirtmaker* for example, provide valuable information and insights. His biography, built on the truth of fact which cannot be superseded by the psychobiographer, opportunist, or sensationalist, underlines his dedication to George Eliot, to scholars, critics, and general readers. See also BIOGRAPHIES.   GRH

Haight (1968).

—— (ed.), *The George Eliot Letters*, 9 vols. (1954–78) (abbreviated as *L*).

—— *George Eliot's Originals and Contemporaries: Essays in Victorian Literary History and Biography*, ed. Hugh Witemeyer (1992).

Hamley, Edward Bruce (1824–93), distinguished soldier and author who became friendly with G. H. *Lewes and George Eliot. He served in the Crimea, wrote a history of the campaign, became Professor of Military History at Sandhurst, was knighted in 1880, and entered Parliament in 1886. He wrote a major book called *The Operations of War* (1866) while his literary talents are displayed in his novel *Lady Lee's Widowhood* (1853). He edited the first series of *Tales from Blackwood* (1858). His parodic skit 'The Last French Hero: Being Some Chapters of a Very French Novel Not Yet Published—by Alexandre Sue-Sand Fils' (*Blackwood's Edinburgh Magazine*, 87 (1860), 45–62) was enjoyed by Lewes, who shrewdly guessed Hamley's authorship. Styled 'The Gunner' by Eliot and Lewes, Hamley met them through John *Blackwood. He dined with the Leweses at Greenwich in June 1861. Scarcely a month passed before there was a pleasant visit from Hamley to Mrs Lewes (*L* iii. 441). That they continued friendly is shown by her receiving *The Operations of War Explained and Illustrated* (1866) and feeling that Hamley was in some ways one of the ablest men of her acquaintance. When he called in April 1868 she recorded that he was looking handsomer than ever (*L* iv. 431). In January 1871 she wrote praising him for his letter to *The Times* in which he condemned German ruthlessness in the *Franco-Prussian war against French villages and property (*L* v. 134). Hamley visited her in December 1879 a year after Lewes's death, though to her regret their talk was interrupted. A fringe friend, perhaps, but their shared love of animals is seen in his praise of Eliot's presentation of Vixen in *Adam Bede* and the ape Annibal in *The Spanish Gypsy*. His review of John Walter *Cross's *Life* stresses Eliot's having the good fortune to be the daughter of an upwardly mobile working man and thus able to present the life of the working classes from a fresh perspective. Hamley's tone is not dissimilar from Eliot's: it is at once conservative and radical, the tone of the Victorian humanist reared in the Christian tradition. His own writing is ironic, realistic, and entertaining, the humane current forever flowing and reflecting his wide and informed interests.   GRH

Handel, George Frideric (1685–1759), naturalized English composer of German birth. When George Eliot—or Mary Ann Evans—was 19, she announced that she wished never to hear another oratorio, and would be contented 'if the only music heard in our land were that of strict worship' (*L* i. 13). Two years later, however, she could write, 'I heard the Messiah on Thursday morning at Birmingham and some beautiful selections from other oratorios of Handel and Haydn on Friday' (*L* i. 68). Her enthusiasm for Handel's choral music was to remain undiminished, and always brought her a 'revival' (*L* iv. 134). When she was 39 she told Sara *Hennell—who also appreciated Handel—that there were few things she cared for more 'in the way of music than his choruses performed by a grand orchestra' (*L* iii. 71). In *Middlemarch*, Caleb Garth—who is reminded by Dorothea's voice of bits in *Messiah*, 'and when he could afford it went to hear an oratorio that came within his reach, returning from it with a profound reverence for this mighty structure of tones' (*MM* 56)—is to share this enthusiasm.

On 25 May 1859 at St James's Hall, she and G. H. *Lewes heard Handel's *Acis and Galatea* (*c*.1718; libretto principally by John Gay), described by Jane Glover as 'one of the few immortal accidents of truly English opera'. One week later, George Eliot was in the middle of writing the fight scene between Tom Tulliver and Bob Jakin in *The Mill on the Floss* (*MF* 1.6), which takes place three chapters before Maggie is in disgrace for dropping her cake when she is beguiled by Uncle Pullet's musical snuffbox playing 'the fairy tune' (*MF* 1.9), 'Hush, ye pretty warbling quire', from the first act of Handel's work. In 'Wheat and Tares', Philip sings to Maggie the shepherd-lover Acis' aria,

'Love in her eyes sits playing' (*MF* 5.3). See also MUSIC.   BG

> Glover, Jane, sleeve notes to *Handel: Acis and Galatea*, ed. Jane Glover (recorded 1978).

Hardy, Thomas (1840–1928), English novelist often compared with George Eliot and certainly influenced by her, though his development takes on an increasingly pessimistic direction until he largely abandons fiction for poetry after the criticism of *Jude the Obscure* (1895). The second subtitle of *Under the Greenwood Tree* (1872) is 'A Rural Painting of the Dutch School', perhaps a conscious echo of 'It is for this rare, precious quality of truthfulness that I delight in many Dutch paintings' (*AB* 17). The novel was also compared to *Silas Marner*. When *Far from the Madding Crowd* began publication in the *Cornhill* anonymously (January 1874) it recalled George Eliot for at least one reviewer, and its similarities with *Adam Bede* were duly noted later. Disconcerted at being suspected of imitating, Hardy wrote *The Hand of Ethelberta* (1876). He called it a somewhat frivolous narrative, and it was certainly unlike Eliot's novels; moreover an already conceived plot was shelved until *The Woodlanders* (1887).

But Eliot's influence is present in the main body of his fiction. *Under the Greenwood Tree* evokes memories of the Shepperton Church sequence at the very beginning of 'The Sad Fortunes of the Reverend Amos Barton' (complete with musical references though not with Hardy's developed particularity), while the celebrated Rainbow Inn sequence (*SM* 6) has the seminal rustic chorus which Hardy was to adapt and extend, and arguably that chorus is present in *Scenes of Clerical Life*, *Adam Bede*, and *The Mill on the Floss* as well, though it is more familial or parishional than rustic. The New Year's Eve party in *Silas Marner* (*SM* 11) has singing and dancing led by the fiddler Solomon Macey who is a pre-Hardy type. Even the urban *Middlemarch* (published in the year that *Under the Greenwood Tree* appeared) has lower-order commentators from Dagley to Mrs Dollop whose index is public events. *Felix Holt, the Radical* (1866) can also be seen as directly influencing Hardy's concerns. First, it has a marked element of Greek *tragedy about it (two chapter mottoes from *Sophocles, one from *Aeschylus underline this), the Mrs Transome story has all the burden of concealment, deception, suffering, and reappearance which are the staple situations of Hardy's fiction, as in *The Mayor of Casterbridge* (1880), *Tess of the D'Urbervilles* (1891), and *Jude the Obscure* (1896). Arguably the embittered Miss Aldclyffe in the earlier *Desperate Remedies* (1871) has a more direct connection with Mrs Transome. *Felix Holt* has other points of association with Hardy's practice, for instance the loving dwelling on the past and the far from the madding crowd motif which feature in the Introduction.

Country celebrations like a harvest supper, a coming of age, or a marriage are shared by *Adam Bede* and *Far from the Madding Crowd*, but the individual stamp of each writer is apparent rather than derivative. Adam is not dissimilar from Gabriel Oak in terms of reliability, Arthur Donnithorne is psychologically fuller as seducer and egoist than the predatory Troy, and Hetty is more lived with than Fanny Robin, though their journeys in anguish are comparable. Storms are forecast in *Adam Bede*, the storm is immediate in Hardy, with Gabriel (and Bathsheba) saving the ricks. But the humour of the Rainbow Inn sequence in *Silas Marner* with the omniscient irony uncondescendingly playing over ignorance, repetition, arrogance, and the whole gamut of commentary which contains its own comedy, is expanded and developed by Hardy right through to *Tess*. The timing of the scene, the convincing interaction in the interior, is wonderfully worked by Eliot, whose narrator observes of the shepherd in the Introduction to *Felix Holt* that his solar system was the parish, a remark definitively appropriate to Hardy's rustics (say in the Warren's malthouse gatherings in *Far from the Madding Crowd*) or in the nocturnal exchanges at Rollivers in *Tess*. Both novelists give their rustics a Shakespearean universality, though they are rooted in a localized foreground and provide a sense of continuity, tradition, and authenticity. They comment on the main action, but in Hardy are more signally developed, their ignorance sometimes encompassing a sly forecasting. Hardy's overall humour is more relaxed, his range of dialect tied to the truth of place but heard accurately, conveying dimensions of character and social personality. Hardy's rustics constitute a fuller chorus than Eliot's, but the spectrum from the sly to the simple is certainly present in her novels through to *Felix Holt*. There is the also the ultra-simple example, both comic and menacing, of Brother Jacob.

Other points of correspondence are the ill-fated impulsive characters like Mr Tulliver and Michael Henchard, the latter tracing a tragic arc beyond the reach (and perhaps beyond the realism) of the warmly obstinate miller; Tess's seduction, or rape, in the originally omitted 'Saturday Night in Arcady' chapter of the novel calls to mind 'the girl-tragedies that are going on in the world, hidden, unheeded, as if they were but tragedies of the copse or hedgerow, where the helpless drag wounded wings forsakenly' (*DD* 17). And one can go from the particular to the general. That both were greatly influenced by Auguste *Comte and *positivism after their early religious affiliations

(Hardy was originally destined for a career in the Church) is self-evident. Eliot's altruistic idealism is evident in her later novels, though it is muted by social conformity in *Felix Holt*, reduced in Dorothea (foundress of nothing but doing localized good), or vaguely Judaistic (Daniel goes to the promised land). The contrast with Hardy's later novels is marked, for his deepening pessimism allows of no compromise, admits no alleviation of the tragic process. Though Eliot and Hardy absorbed new knowledge and scientific advance, they moved in different directions in their final phase. Eliot's last work, *Impressions of Theophrastus Such*, breaks new if complex ground beyond the novel, while Hardy explored the past on the historical and personal level in *The Dynasts* and in the lyrical poetry of his later years.   GRH

Beer (1983).
Cox, R. G. (ed.), *Thomas Hardy: The Critical Heritage* (1970).
Harris, Nicola, 'Hardy and Eliot: The Eye of Narcissus' Looking-Glass', *George Eliot Review*, 28 (1997).

Harrison, Frederic (1821–1923), barrister, reformer, and follower of Auguste *Comte, important to George Eliot for his collaboration with her on *Felix Holt, the Radical* and *Daniel Deronda*, for their mutual interest in Comte, and for his response to her work. After their first meeting in 1860, Eliot began to notice Harrison's articles on religion in the *Westminster Review* and on labour unions in the *Fortnightly Review* which G. H. Lewes edited.

Harrison, who, in addition to being a lawyer and writer, had taught workers at the Working Men's College and Cleveland Hall, became a valuable consultant to Eliot as she struggled with the legal details of *Felix Holt* in January 1866. The episode helps to illuminate several aspects of Eliot's working methods and reveals Harrison's qualities as a jurist and a friend. Eliot's usual appetite for research failed her when faced with weighty legal tomes, which caused 'agonies of doubt' (*L* iv. 215–16). Harrison assured her that 'points of law are so little connected even remotely with the happiness of mankind that I fall with a will upon one which I hope will be' (*L* iv. 216). His suggestions, a settlement and a base fee, are incorporated into chapter 29 of *Felix Holt*.

Harrison's sympathy led Eliot to lend him the manuscript, making him the only person, apart from Lewes and her publishers, to read a work in progress. Encouraged by his advice and appreciation, Eliot extended his brief: 'if anything strikes you as untrue . . . where my drama has a bearing on momentous questions, especially of a public nature . . . tell me of your doubts' (*L* iv. 221). Harrison began to take almost the interest of a co-author, suggesting complicated variations of plot. Eliot thanked him politely, making it clear that help of this nature was inappropriate. When she consulted him again in April and May, Harrison read the manuscript and proofs, correcting minor points but limiting his advice to technicalities. He composed the Attorney-General's opinion in chapter 35 and later joked that he 'had written at least a sentence which was embodied in English literature' ('George Eliot's Place in Literature', 74).

At the end of 1874, Eliot diffidently sought Harrison's advice about legal matters in *Deronda*, writing, 'I hope when you learn the pettiness of my difficulties you will not be indignant, like a great doctor called in to the favourite cat' (*L* vi. 148). The consultation, the importance of which has been widely misunderstood, even by Harrison himself, continued through letters and meetings for six months. The implications of his advice on *Deronda* went beyond the legal technicalities of *Felix Holt*. His suggestion that Sir Hugo might wish to purchase a house from Grandcourt to leave his widow caused Eliot, as the manuscript shows, to rewrite a substantial portion of chapter 15. The negotiations to purchase Diplow, in which Deronda becomes an agent, are a central unifying device in the novel from chapter 28 (the point Eliot had reached when she received Harrison's suggestion) to the end, and offer numerous opportunities for plot ramifications and revelations of character.

While generous with his time and expertise, Harrison had an ulterior motive in placing Eliot in his debt. In July 1866, he outlined at length a proposal that Eliot should write a positivist novel. In her discouraging reply, Eliot promised to keep 'the great possibility (or impossibility) perpetually in my mind, as something towards which I must strive, though it may be . . . only in a fragmentary way' (*L* iv. 301). In May 1868, Harrison raised again the subject of his 'craving' for a fictional 'idealization of the Positive vision of society' (*L* iv. 448). Eliot advised him 'to encourage the growth . . . in your own mind rather than trust to transplantation' (*L* iv. 448). A request in 1877 for something 'by way of collect, hymn, or litany' for the positivists again had no result (*L* ix. 194).

Harrison's disappointment in Eliot's reluctance directly to promote the positivist cause influenced his final judgement of her and her writing. While recognizing her nobility and rare distinction, he held that all her best works were written by 1863 ('George Eliot's Place in Literature', 68). He could not extend to *The Spanish Gypsy* the enthusiasm he felt for earlier works, and wrote to Eliot with some embarrassment, praising its conception, but comparing himself to 'Thomas fingering the very nail-prints and yet striving to believe' (*L* iv. 485).

Privately, he described it as a 'fiasco' (Ashton 1996: 293). *Middlemarch* was 'the interminable meanderings of tedious men and women', while *Deronda* 'presented unpleasant characters who are neither beautiful nor interesting'. Eliot was 'more of a thinker than an artist', he concluded ('George Eliot's Place in Literature', 73–4, 77). He deplored her lack of spontaneity, and wished that Lewes 'could have inspired her with a dose of the rattling devil within him' (*Autobiographic Memoirs*, 109). See also LAW; POSITIVISM.   BSM

Harrison, Frederic, 'George Eliot's Place in Literature', *The Forum* (Sept. 1895).

—— *The Choice of Books* (1903).

—— *Autobiographic Memoirs* (1911).

Vogeler, Martha S., *Frederic Harrison: The Vocations of a Positivist* (1984).

Hawthorne, Nathaniel (1804–64), American novelist whom George Eliot, seeing reviews of his *Blithedale Romance* (1852) in August 1852, pronounced a grand favourite (*L* ii. 52). She read *Blithedale* that September but left no verdict upon it. Comments in the October 1852 *Westminster Review*, once attributed to George Eliot, were probably by R. W. Griswold (*Essays*, 457–8). In March 1857 she read *The Scarlet Letter* (1850) aloud with Lewes; at Florence in May 1860 she tried to find a copy of *The Marble Faun* (1860), just published; and as late as January 1873 she praised Hawthorne's treatment in the latter novel of Hilda's decision to be a copyist for the value it assigns to that order of work which is called subordinate, but becomes ennobling by being finely done (*L* ii. 311; iii. 300; v. 367). Contemporary critics struck comparisons and contrasts between George Eliot and Hawthorne (*Edinburgh Review*, 110 (1859), 223–46; *North British Review*, 33 (1860), 165–85), a practice which has continued. His influence has been traced in her plots, settings, characters, and moral vision, with particular emphasis upon *The Marble Faun* and *Romola* and upon *The Scarlet Letter* and *Adam Bede* and *Silas Marner*. Hawthorne's writing career was virtually finished by the time George Eliot's began; he probably read *Adam Bede*, but it does not seem to have influenced *The Marble Faun*, his last completed romance. Although Hawthorne was US Consul at Liverpool 1853–7, he and George Eliot never met. See also AMERICA.   KKC

Dahl, Curtis, 'When the Deity Returns: The Marble Faun and Romola', *Papers on Language and Literature*, 5 (1969).

Mills, Nicolaus, *American and English Fiction in the Nineteenth Century: An Antigenre Critique and Comparison* (1973).

Quick, Jonathan R., 'Silas Marner as Romance: The Example of Hawthorne', *Nineteenth-Century Fiction*, 29 (1974).

Stokes, Edward, *Hawthorne's Influence on Dickens and George Eliot* (1985).

Haydn, Joseph (1732–1809), Austrian composer. Writing from London on 30 March 1852, George Eliot told Cara *Bray that she had had two offers of music that she found irresistible. One offer, from Herbert Spencer, was to see Rossini's *William Tell*; the other was from Bessie *Parkes, who wanted Marian to go with her to hear Haydn's *Creation* (1798), which was to be performed at Exeter Hall on 2 April. 'I have had so little music this quarter and these two things are so exactly what I should like that I have determined to put off, for the sake of them, my other pleasure of seeing you,' she confessed (*L* ii. 16–17).

George Eliot seems to have little to say about Haydn's chamber music or symphonies, although in July 1866 G. H. *Lewes reported to Charles from Schwalbach that, in the mornings, he and 'Mutter' would 'lounge in the sun listening to the tolerable band performing overtures, movements from Beethoven, and Haydn's symphonies, pot-pourris and waltzes' (*L* iv. 282). *The Creation*, however, she clearly knew intimately. Set in the Garden of Eden, its text is based on an English libretto, which Gottfried van Swieten—who furnished Haydn with the German version—claimed was culled largely from John *Milton's *Paradise Lost*. The oratorio features significantly in 'A Duet in Paradise', the first chapter of Book 6, 'The Great Temptation', in *The Mill on the Floss*. With Lucy as piano accompanist, Stephen (as Adam) and Lucy (as Eve) sing the duet 'Graceful Consort', after which Stephen sings Raphael's aria, 'Now heaven in fullest glory shone'. BG

Robbins Landon, H. C., *Haydn: Chronicle and Works*, iv. *Haydn: The Years of 'The Creation' 1796–1800* (1977).

health. George Eliot appears to have had a generally sound constitution: she walked for exercise most days, though little can be deduced about her dietary regime. Yet she was subject to frequent indispositions, and it is difficult to escape the conclusion that at least some of her ailments were psychosomatic.

Headaches plagued her always. Cara *Bray wrote to her sister Sara *Hennell in 1846, when the work of translation was making George Eliot 'Strauss-sick', that 'I do pity her sometimes with her pale sickly face and dreadful headaches, and anxiety too about her father' (*L* i. 206), though within a couple of weeks George Eliot herself was writing to Sara, 'I have nothing on earth to complain of but subjective maladies' (*L* i. 207). An American medical man, George M. Gould, documented her symptoms from Cross's *Life*, and concluded that the headache, insomnia, biliousness,

and nervousness which afflicted her were effectively 'a simple and typical case of oldfashioned sick headache, due . . . to eyestrain' (*Biographic Clinics*, 6 vols. (1903–9), ii. 82). She does not seem to have had trouble with her eyes until the early 1870s, however, when her long-sightedness caused her to take 'to writing on my knees, throwing myself backward in my chair' (*L* v. 451). She had spectacles prescribed in 1875.

She suffered with her teeth, with occasional gastrointestinal problems, and with respiratory infections, mainly colds. Her lack of self-confidence and depression, always most in evidence when working on a novel, may sometimes have had a specific physical basis: for example, she was apparently menopausal while she was working on *Romola*.

During her last years she was often laid low by the kidney condition that declared itself in February 1874. She had a particularly incapacitating attack in the summer of 1879, of which she wrote to Charles Lewes on 7 July: 'Fancy! I am ordered to drink Champagne and am wasting my substance in riotous living at the rate of a pint bottle daily. Meanwhile my bodily substance in the shape of flesh is wasting also' (*L* vii. 179)—she noted 'Weight July 1st. 7 st. 5 1/2 lbs.' (*Journals*, 154). Progressive renal failure made her vulnerable to other infections like the laryngitis which led to her death on 22 December 1880. See also MEDICINE AND HEALTH. MAH

Hegel, Georg Wilhelm Friedrich (1770–1831). Both George Eliot and G. H. *Lewes had firsthand knowledge of Hegel even before John *Sibree's influential book *The Secret of Hegel* (1865) made the German philosopher's work widely known in Britain. Lewes in particular discusses Hegel repeatedly. His 1842 article in the *British and Foreign Review* entitled 'Hegel's Aesthetics' is, in fact, the first comment to appear in Britain on Hegel's *Ästhetik*, published by G. Hotho in 1835.

Especially in Lewes's case, a lifelong preoccupation with Hegel is evident. However, early appreciation of, for example, Hegel's distinction between poesy and modern prosaic science is soon overshadowed by an emphatic rejection of German idealistic speculation in the manner of Hegel ('a system in which Thought is the same as the Thing, and the Thing is the same as the Thought', *A Biographical History of Philosophy* (1894), 621). Similarly, in 'The *Future of German Philosophy' George Eliot praises Otto Friedrich Gruppe for his antimetaphysical, anti-Hegelian stance (*Essays*, 150).

Although Eliot's empiricism seems at first glance incompatible with Hegel's idealism there are a number of unmistakable parallels. For both, *history is a process and contemporary society consequently saturated with history. Yet in her concept of history she is closer to Charles *Darwin than to Hegel since history is not conceived of as a manifestation of the absolute nor does it exemplify the harmonious synthesis of opposites (*Versöhnung*). Just like Hegel in his *Phenomenology of the Spirit* Eliot believes that moral ideas must be mediated through work in the arena of society. Finally, Eliot's notion of the tragic is directly influenced by Hegel when she speaks, in 'The *Antigone* and its Moral' (1856), of a dramatic collision which is a conflict of two principles, both having their validity (*Essays*, 263). See also DARWINISM; PHILOSOPHY; TRAGEDY.   HUS

Ashton (1980).
McCobb (1982).
Putzell-Korab, Sara M., *The Evolving Conciousness: A Hegelian Reading of the Novels of George Eliot* (1982).

Heine, Heinrich (1797–1856), German poet whose work George Eliot admired, frequently cited, and discussed in her journalism. She wrote four articles on him in 1855–6 after her first visit to *Germany with G. H. *Lewes, the longest and most important of which is *'German Wit: Heinrich Heine', published in the *Westminster Review* in January 1856. In *Berlin in the winter of 1854–5 she and Lewes had met Karl August *Varnhagen von Ense, who was a source of information about Heine since the poet had attended his wife Rahel's salon in the early 1820s. Similarly, their acquaintances Adolf Stahr and Fanny Lewald, soon to be married, had visited Heine in exile, while Fanny's brother August had published his recollections of the writer. During their stay in Berlin Eliot and Lewes read several of Heine's works, including his *Geständnisse* (*Confessions*), whose wit she found initially amusing but wearisome after the first fifty pages on account of its lack of principle and purpose (*Journals*, 39–40). The fruit of this reading and discussion in Berlin were the four articles written in the year after their return. In the first of these, a review of a new American translation of his *Reisebilder* (*Pictures of Travel*) in the *Leader* in September 1855, she describes Heine as 'a master of a German prose as light and subtle and needle-pointed as Voltaire's French, and of a poetical style as crystalline, as graceful, and as musical as that of Goethe's best lyrics', although he lacks *Voltaire's moral conviction and *Goethe's profound wisdom (6: 843). This view of Heine's qualities as a writer of prose and poetry is developed and extensively illustrated in 'German Wit', which gives an account of his life and demonstrates a wide knowledge of his works, quoting them at length in her own translation. The reservations she had about his wit on reading *Geständnisse* appear again in her

criticism of the occasional coarseness and scurrility she finds in his writing; and in general she seems to be uncomfortable with Heine's self-conscious irony and more inclined to celebrate him as the creator of tender lyrics than to appreciate the complex divided self that he reveals in his poetry. Nevertheless she demonstrates the comic power and subtlety of his wit, including his mockery of England and the English, which she regards dispassionately: 'his ridicule of English awkwardness is as merciless as—English ridicule of German awkwardness' (*Essays*, 234). She also acknowledges his political commitment to freedom and democracy and, at the same time, the essential antagonism of wit and fanaticism which prevents him from ever becoming a thoroughgoing partisan—a stance with which she is evidently sympathetic for it is one that she shares in political matters (see POLITICS).

In the *Saturday Review* in April 1856 she criticizes a translation of Heine's *Book of Songs* in ways that reveal her own sensitivity to the subtlety and nuances of his poetry. Too often the living song becomes in English mechanical verse, and she discriminates between poor and passable translations with the sure eye of an experienced translator from German (see TRANSLATIONS BY GEORGE ELIOT). The fourth article, in the *Leader* in August 1856, is a review of a memoir of Heine which describes his marriage and private life, and she cites his refusal to align himself with any party, whether republicans or patriots, Christians or Jews. However, when she returned to Heine later in life, in 1869 and the early 1870s, it was precisely his Jewishness that seems to have interested her (see JUDAISM), and she drew on his work, particularly the 'Hebrew Melodies' from *Romanzero*, in writing *Daniel Deronda*. It was probably Heine's poem on Jehuda ben Halevy that introduced her to that medieval Jewish poet who inspires Mordecai's Hebrew verses (*DD* 38); and when the Jewish musician Klesmer reveals his love for Catherine Arrowpoint he softly plays the melody of his own setting of Heine's poem from *Lyrisches Intermezzo*: 'Ich hab' dich geliebet und liebe dich noch' ('I have loved you and love you still': *DD* 22). The epigraphs to three chapters (*DD* 34, 62, 63) are also drawn from Heine, two of them having specifically Jewish themes. As a Jew who converted to Christianity and then regretted it, Heine has an obvious relevance to the direction that Deronda's life takes from English society to Judaism.

In her early essays on Heine George Eliot responded to the mastery of language, to the wit and sarcasm as well as the lyricism, of a writer whose moral insouciance was alien to her. In her later years he stood as a representative of an alien culture to which, in her last novel, she displayed the same exemplary openness. It was his lyric poetry that seems to have appealed to her most, and after Lewes's death one of his poems was copied into her journal together with lines by *Shakespeare, *Chaucer, *Tennyson, and Goethe in a collection of verse about bereavement (*Journal*, 155). JMR

Ashton (1980).

Baker (1975).

Lauster, Martina, 'A Cultural Revolutionary: George Eliot's and Matthew Arnold's Appreciation of Heinrich Heine', in Martina Lauster and Günter Oesterle (edd.), *Vormärzliteratur in europäischer Perspektive II* (1998).

McCobb (1982).

Helps, Arthur (1813–75), writer, clerk of the privy council. George Eliot first met him at the home of Sir James Clark in 1853, describing him as 'sleek' with 'a quiet, humorous way of talking' (*L* ii. 135–6). G. H. *Lewes was a regular guest at his property Vernon Hill from the 1840s. Helps called on them at *Weimar. While his sympathy comforted Eliot, it did not extend to inviting her to Vernon Hill, and she spent the Christmases of 1855 to 1859 without Lewes, who enjoyed the 'high jinks' (*Letters of Lewes*, i. 258). In 1861 Lewes told Helps there was no one they both saw with such pleasure.

Helps reported that Queen *Victoria admired *The Mill on the Floss*, and Theodore Martin believed *Romola* to be 'the finest thing I have done' (*Journals*, p. 115). From the mid-1860s they saw less of him although he and Lewes corresponded about their writing. Created KCB in 1872, he died suddenly in 1875. Queen Victoria reportedly requested the joint signatures of Lewes and Eliot on their letter of condolence for her autograph collection (*L* vi. 129). JJ

The Letters of George Henry Lewes, ed. William Baker (1995).

Hennell, Charles Christian (1809–50), younger brother of Sara *Hennell and biblical scholar who influenced George Eliot's radical revaluation of *Christianity. Born in Manchester, he was the fifth of eight children in a Unitarian family. His father died in 1816 and they moved to Hackney. Charles entered business at 15 but studied deeply and, following the marriage of Charles *Bray to his sister Caroline (1836), examined the New Testament in order to refute, on behalf of himself and Cara, the sceptical rationalism of Bray. In fact his investigations achieved the opposite. The publication of *An Inquiry concerning the Origin of Christianity* (1838) was drawn to the attention of D. F. *Strauss, the German biblical scholar, who wrote a eulogistic preface to the German translation (1839). Hennell married Dr *Brabant's daughter Rufa *Brabant in 1843: she relinquished her translation of Strauss's *Das Leben Jesu* to Marian Evans in January 1844. Hennell's health and financial circumstances declined and he died in 1850.

He is perhaps the major influence of Eliot's early maturity. On 13 November 1841 she wrote to her mentor Maria Lewis that she was absorbed in the most interesting of all enquiries and that her conclusions might startle her friend (*L* i. 103). Six years later, shortly after the publication of her translation of *Das Leben Jesu*, she wrote to her close friend, Hennell's sister Sara, that her two readings of the *Inquiry* five years previous had been far surpassed by her present one: 'there is nothing in its whole tone from beginning to end that jars on my moral sense . . . the reasoning is so close, the induction so clever, the style so clear, vigorous, and pointed' (Cross, i. 164). She adds that it exemplifies the utmost that can be done towards obtaining a real view of the life and character of Jesus (165). The first reading undoubtedly contributed towards her crisis of faith, seen in her refusal to accompany her father to church (January 1842). Hennell's 'searching out the truth' changed her life, and his belief that his investigation would 'widen the scope of Christianity' and that as a result there would be 'a purer moral spirit'—phrases from his preface to the first edition—are concomitant with her development.

Hennell probed with uncompromising dedication the texts of the Apostles, subjecting them to close and critical scrutiny and placing them tellingly in their historical and political contexts. His concern, like George Eliot's later concern, is largely with the motives and motivations of character. His structure is a narrative structure, and he concludes that Jesus came to believe the delusion that he was the Messiah (ch. 1). The unequivocal force of this phrase cannot undermine the humane tolerance and enlightened comprehension with which it is used. Hennell's own narrative art possesses the excitements and climaxes of fiction, to which he often refers, as he examines the novel by various hands about the greatest character of all. Vivid characterizations punctuate the narrative, like those of Titus and Josephus, for example, from the death of Jesus to the end of the 1st century. Hennell excels at particularized stringent analysis, as did George Eliot, and the 'narrators' of the Gospels are accorded it. Matthew's representations of Christ gathered fiction: he relates miraculous incidents at the time of the Crucifixion which are not mentioned by other Apostles; the birth of Jesus resembles 'a wild eastern tale' (ch. 3); there is much of the 'rude poetry of warm and unrestrained imagination' and a yielding to 'the fascination of every fiction' which confirmed 'Jesus as an invisible protector'. Hennell suggests that the idea of the Resurrection suited Apostles and authorities alike: it was good propaganda for the emergent faith, it did no positive harm. He shows that there are contradictions in the accounts of the Resurrection and the Ascension. In a superb passage which would have delighted Marian Evans, he analyses the psychological necessities in the disciples and their followers which arose because of the feelings Jesus had awakened in them, and which could not be expected to subside:

Fictions proceeding from such feelings, and also connected, as they were, with the real interests of life, must be of a different character from those thrown out in the mere wantonness of imagination. Hence the appearance of simplicity, earnestness, and reality, which in the midst of palpable inconsistencies, pervade even the evangelic histories, and make even their fiction unique. (ch. 7)

Logical, consistent, probing, never less than reverent, his integrity reflected in his style, Hennell had an inspiring effect on Marian Evans. The most fascinating, and moving, section of *An Inquiry* interrogates the character of Christ. He is at once enthusiast, political activist, and prophet to his contemporaries; a moral teacher, a national deliverer, and comprehensively benevolent, embodying the highest level of human virtue. Hennell demolishes miracles but urges people not to throw away cherished associations because of this. He promotes the practical Christianity which Christ displayed, believing in reason and piety, his transcendent faith telling him that the 'enigma of our own and the world's existence' will one day be resolved (ch. 18).

His clear narrative wears learning lightly, but the dedication is exemplary, the humanity and humility obvious. His work is informed with perspective and wisdom, remarkable in view of his age: his cogent and crisp analyses of historical fact and their by-productive fiction were congenial to the character and temperament of Marian Evans. His emphasis on the abiding value of truth as distinct from the unquestioning acceptance of dogma became one of her cherished and immutable beliefs. His seeing Christianity in its practical manifestations as the moral life we should follow impregnates her fiction. They share too the sublime concern of writing for the good, for the enlightenment of mankind through the revealed truths of practical idealism and human interaction. Hennell died before George Eliot came into being, but in a sense he lives on through her as one of the most humane and liberal influences who helped to shape her artistic destiny. See also ATHEISM; BIBLE; MORAL VALUES; RELIGION OF HUMANITY. GRH

Hennell, C. C., *An Inquiry concerning the Origin of Christianity* (1838, 2nd edn. 1841).
—— *Christian Theism* (1839).
Hennell, S. S., *A Memoir of Charles Christian Hennell* (1899).
Willey, Basil, 'George Eliot: Hennell, Strauss and Feuerbach', in *Nineteenth-Century Studies* (1949).

Hennell, Sara Sophia (1812–99), close friend of George Eliot, the seventh child born into a strict Unitarian family. Her father was a successful merchant who died when Sara was 4, and the children were brought up with a deep and lasting sense of their religion and a dedication to the Christian ideal. From about the age of 20 Sara was a governess, for a time in the family of John Bonham Carter, MP, and she first met Marian Evans at the *Brays' house Rosehill in July 1842 where she stayed regularly. Her sister Caroline (Cara), two years her junior, had married Bray in 1836. Intellectual by nature and, like her brother Charles Christian *Hennell, interested in contemporary biblical scholarship, Sara was cultured, with musical and artistic talents, and she soon engaged Marian's affection and stimulated her interests. The first letters reflect their growing intimacy. Sara is initially 'my friend of the dark eye' but by March 1843 she is her 'dearest friend', an endearment which precedes the more equivocal 'Dearly beloved spouse' of September 1846 (*L* i. 223). But by this date Marian had completed her translation of D. F. *Strauss's *Das Leben Jesu*, which she took over from Rufa Hennell (née *Brabant) in January 1844. Sara had declined the translation herself and supported its allocation to Marian, though not without a little condescension. Marian consulted Sara frequently about the accuracy and the style of the translation and, despite occasional disagreements of emphasis, acknowledged Sara's practical corrections, suggestions, and supportive sympathy, admitting in April 1845 that without Sara's help she would have been in despair. Throughout their lifetime correspondence, which falls away to occasional and birthday letters, Marian and then George Eliot confides in Sara about Dr *Brabant, her eulogy on Ralph Waldo *Emerson, her praise for *An Inquiry concerning the Origin of Christianity* on rereading it, her appreciation of Mrs *Gaskell's *Life of Charlotte Brontë*. There is the remarkable letter of October 1859 in which Eliot gives details of her aunt Elizabeth Evans (see EVANS, MRS SAMUEL) and twelve years later Sara is one of the three exceptional people 'to whom we order "Middlemarch" to be sent' (*L* vi. 214). Occasionally G. H. *Lewes writes to her. In July 1860 he finds *Thoughts in Aid of Faith* both remarkable and interesting and then proceeds to demolish it on grounds of obscure passages. On another occasion when Sara writes to George Eliot with some

A daguerreotype of Sara Hennell (1812–99) taken in the 1840s when she and George Eliot were close friends.

criticism Lewes abstracts the letter and loses it, writing Sara a reprimand.

Of course, Sara is coupled with the Brays in the note which announces Marian's departure for *Germany (July 1854) and signals her liaison with Lewes. Sara's initial silence gives way after Marian's 'I love Cara and you with unchanged and unchangeable affection' (L ii. 182). With Marian's move to London in 1851 her letters to Sara tended to record her doings—meetings, journalism for John *Chapman, the expanding world which included Herbert *Spencer—though by January 1854 Sara was reading and criticizing (by invitation) the translation of Ludwig *Feuerbach which Marian felt was a positive help. Despite this she is tetchy about Sara's failure to comprehend certain passages, later reprimanding her for her praise of the translation in the *Coventry Herald and Observer. Sara's supposed coolness over Lewes must be modified in view of a recently discovered letter from her to Marian of 20 October 1854 which says that she and Cara wrote to Marian, disapproved of her action, but stressed that their affection for her would not change. In any case she responds to Marian's reiteration of love: 'I have a strange sort of feeling that I am writing to some one in a book, and not to the Marian we have known and loved so many years' (L ii. 186). The Coventry chrysalis soon developed into George Eliot all unbeknown to Sara and the Brays, and even in Eliot's letters there is the conscious hypocrisy of concealment when she tells Sara in April 1859 that 'Lewes has read Adam Bede and is as dithyrambic about it as others appear to be so I must refresh my soul with it now' (L iii. 46). It is not until June that Eliot reveals that she is the author to her closest friends.

Throughout all this and beyond Sara continued her theological investigations. Her prize essay 'Christianity and Fidelity' (1857) was reviewed by Lewes in the *Leader (28 February 1857), perhaps more sympathetically than he felt though he was able to condemn its prescribed form. Her Thoughts in Aid of Faith (1860) has for its subtitle Gathered Chiefly from Recent Works in Theology and Philosophy. Interestingly she refers to her brother's work and also undertakes some evaluation of Feuerbach and Spencer in her appraisal, which is impressive in terms of its contemporary range as well as the biblical bedrock on which she rests. Her mind is investigative and analytical, the power of argument and succinct expression of it deftly managed. Eliot and Lewes in their different ways disliked it and said so. But in Present Religion as a Faith Owning Fellowship with Thought (1865, 1873, 1887) her writing is both diffuse and opaque. Her A Memoir of Charles Christian Hennell (published in 1899) reflects her idolization of her brother. Her letters to Eliot contain snippets of

critical directness, and she accused her of making Romola a goddess rather than a woman. Her dedication to members of her family in adversity, her generosity in sending gifts, and her sensitive response to imagined and real offence, these things round Sara and reflect the sympathetic chords between the two women. But Sara's 'The sole thoughts that I can bear to attend to, are God's own truth, and justice to the authors who have tried to expound it' (L iii. 96) sufficiently underline her limitations. Marian had changed significantly, while Sara remained rooted in the studies she cherished and the faith she bore. In their lives they were divided, but the early habits of love and affinity, though changed by time, reflect more than the durability of duty.   GRH

Higher Criticism, The, name commonly given to German historical criticism of the *Bible, which George Eliot knew well, particularly from her work as a translator. See FEUERBACH, LUDWIG; HENNELL, CHARLES CHRISTIAN; STRAUSS, D. F.; and TRANSLATIONS BY GEORGE ELIOT.

Hill, Octavia (1838–1912), 'philanthropist' known to George Eliot, who approved of and supported her social work. She was a sister-in-law of Charles Lee Lewes (see LEWES FAMILY) and carried forward the interest in public health of her maternal grandfather Dr Thomas Southwood Smith. She was already active in Christian Socialist work with underprivileged children in London when she met John *Ruskin in 1853. Both his intellectual influence and practical support were to be significant, as he enabled her to further her artistic training, and later to purchase London property to be converted to public housing. Octavia personally managed the housing stock on a business footing, with such success that she attracted other contracts including one with the Ecclesiastical Commissioners who in 1884 employed her to handle Church property in Southwark. She had a strong interest also in preserving open spaces for the use of the people, and was one of the founders in 1895 of the National Trust.

George Eliot saw Octavia Hill frequently on a social basis, and maintained a close interest in her work, providing regular small donations, and in 1874 contributing with G. H. *Lewes £200 to a fund to make Octavia financially independent. She strongly approved the principles on which Octavia operated: she wrote on 2 December 1870 of 'a plan which is being energetically carried out for helping a considerable group of people without almsgiving, and solely by inducing them to work' (L v. 124); and more specifically, on 24 January 1873, of Octavia's scheme—not in this case successful—'of buying a public house to have it under good control' (L v. 373). The housing reforms of Octavia

Hill, along with those of Harriet *Martineau, may be reflected in Dorothea Brooke's plans. Florence *Nightingale observed that 'close at hand, in actual life . . . a connection of the author's . . . has managed to make her ideal very real indeed' (Ashton 1996: 327).   MAH

Ashton (1996).

history, George Eliot's view of. George Eliot's interest in history was early and abiding and her work is informed throughout by a rich historical consciousness. As a young woman she started to draw up a chronological chart of ecclesiastical history for publication, and her earliest surviving attempt at fiction is a fragment of an historical story, *'Edward Neville', heavily indebted to Walter *Scott, a favourite writer of her early years. In her mature work she continues to see individual and social life in historical terms, usually setting her fiction back several decades from the time of writing, like Scott in *Waverley*, and reflecting in her narrative commentary on the differences, and similarities, between past and present. In her review essay on the work of the German historian Riehl, 'The *Natural History of German Life', which appeared in 1856 just before she began to write fiction, she refers approvingly to his view of European society as 'incarnate history' and to social change as an organic evolutionary process in which 'what has grown up historically can only die out historically, by the gradual operation of necessary laws' (*Essays*, 287). Her own view of history is likewise evolutionary rather than revolutionary, and she holds broadly to a belief in *progress without ever succumbing to the complacency associated with Whig versions of history in the 19th century. She may write in the Finale of *Middlemarch* of 'the growing good of the world', but history as it appears in the novels is a complex and uneven process, and one that is examined by a critical and self-critical mind fully aware both of darker possibilities and of the problems involved in historical representation.

Those darker possibilities are visible in the narrator's meditation on history in *The Mill on the Floss*, which juxtaposes two visions of the historical process epitomized by the contrasting landscapes of the Rhine and the Rhône (*MF* 4.1). With its romantic ruined castles the Rhine suggests the 'grand historic life of humanity' and implies that history is continuous and meaningful, while the ruined villages along the banks of the Rhône tell the opposite story of 'a narrow, ugly, grovelling existence' beset by senseless catastrophes. This bleak vision of history as a series of disasters that allows no progress and sweeps away lives into oblivion, sundering past and present, challenges optimistic assumptions about 'the onward

tendency of human things' that appear later in the chapter. It is a glimpse of what the German writer Walter Benjamin (1892–1940), in his 'Theses on the Philosophy of History', was later to term the catastrophic continuum of history.

Post-structuralist criticism has argued that Eliot questions not only the idea of historical progress but also the process of historical representation itself. Thus J. Hillis Miller reads *Middlemarch* as deconstructing the dominant Western idea of history, with its premises of continuity and teleology, and undermining its own ground in history by showing that ground to be a fiction (see CRITICISM, MODERN: DECONSTRUCTION). Similarly, Jim Reilly points out that both *Middlemarch* and *Romola* are ambitious attempts at historical reconstruction that seem to unpick themselves by reflecting ironically on such reconstruction in the doomed projects of Casaubon and Bardo (Reilly, 114). Dino's vision in *Romola* of written parchment unrolling itself everywhere in a desert landscape, where the only human figures are men of bronze and marble who can offer no refreshment (*RO* 15), could also be taken as a nightmare vision of the aridity of the very historical writing that Eliot herself is engaged in. If deconstruction is inclined to make her work sound too radically relativist and self-cancelling, ignoring the firm ethical foundation of her humanist vision, its emphasis on the sceptical, ironic, self-questioning intelligence involved in her treatment of history is more illuminating than any attempt to show how her novels reproduce the historical schemes of, for instance, Auguste *Comte or G. W. F. *Hegel.

That scepticism is foregrounded by her focus on women in relation to history. In *Middlemarch* Dorothea, armed only with 'that toy-box history of the world' (*MM* 10) that has been the chief part of her education as a woman, is overwhelmed and oppressed by the weight of the past and the unintelligible residue of history in the 'ruins and basilicas, palaces and colossi' that she finds in Rome (*MM* 20). As she sits sobbing in 'the city of visible history', unable to respond to the funeral procession of the past with its 'strange ancestral images and trophies gathered from afar', she presents a graphic and moving image of woman's exclusion from a history made and written by men. In writing her own fictional history of provincial England in the 1830s, Eliot concludes by eloquently insisting on the vital, invisible contribution to historical progress made by the 'unhistoric acts' of women like Dorothea, members of that excluded half of humanity who lead hidden lives and 'rest in unvisited tombs' (*MM* Finale). And in placing a woman at the centre of her historical fiction in *Romola*, she takes the historical novel as established by Walter *Scott in a new direction. Like

Dorothea, Romola too is oppressed by the relics of the past as she sits amongst her father's collection of antiquities, looking 'with a sad dreariness in her young face at the lifeless objects around her—the parchment backs, the unchanging mutilated marble, the bits of obsolete bronze and clay' (*RO* 5); and the direction of her life is not only away from such hoarding of the past into a nurturing role in the present, it takes her out of history altogether into a realm of symbolic action in the plague village. As Dorothea Barrett has suggested, 'the symbolic implication is that woman cannot realize herself while trapped in the net of history' (introduction to Penguin edition (1996), p. xvi).

When Eliot comes to deal with near contemporary history in *Daniel Deronda*, a woman's life is again tellingly juxtaposed to historical action. Gwendolen's preoccupations with Grandcourt and his offer of marriage are contrasted at one stage with the historical drama of the *American civil war, which throws into relief the pettiness of her concerns; and at the end of the novel, when she learns of Deronda's historic mission to work for a Jewish homeland, she is dwarfed by 'these widestretching purposes in which she felt herself to be reduced to a mere speck' (*DD* 69). These juxtapositions are not simply a means of humbling Gwendolen, for they throw light on women's relationship to history in general, on the way their lives are lived on the margins of that masculine domain. When Hans Meyrick is working on paintings depicting the story of the Roman Emperor Titus and the Jewish Berenice, he observes that no one knows what became of Berenice in the end: 'The story is chipped off, so to speak, and passes with a ragged edge into nothing' (*DD* 37). Her life, unlike Titus', is not fully woven into the fabric of recorded history, and its ragged edge is typical of the lives of women in general, and of the female characters in *Daniel Deronda* in particular.

Women may live on the margins of a history dominated and written by men but they, like men too, cannot escape its determining power. Deronda's mother tries to cast off her Jewish inheritance both for herself and for him, only to see it reassert its influence when he commits himself to Judaism and the service of the Jewish people. In *Felix Holt, the Radical* Harold Transome's attempts to introduce political change are flawed by his ignorance of the past, and in his personal life it returns to thwart his career when he discovers the history of his family and his true parentage. As the epigraph to chapter 21 states, 'a man can never separate himself from his past history'. It is a truth confirmed by the example of Lydgate in *Middlemarch*, whose failure is due in part to his refusal to acknowledge his past: he does not learn from his impulsive proposal to the actress Laure in Paris, and repeats that behaviour with Rosamond, at the same time failing to see that he is attracted by precisely that aristocratic family history he wishes to repudiate. As Karen Chase has put it, he enacts George Eliot's version of Karl *Marx's dictum that those who ignore the past are condemned to repeat it (1991: 7–8).

History is a determining condition of human life in Eliot's world, but that does not amount to a grim historical *determinism. Describing the movement of the crowd in the moments leading up to the riot in *Felix Holt*, the narrator offers a pertinent observation: 'It was that mixture of pushing forward and being pushed forward, which is a brief history of most human things' (*FH* 33). History is made by human actions, but within conditions set by the actions of the past; or as the narrator of *Adam Bede* puts it, 'our deeds determine us as much as we determine our deeds' (*AB* 29). The image of the crowd struggling forward but not in full control of where it is going epitomizes the uneven, uncertain process of history as it emerges in the novels, implying something like another dictum of Marx, that men make history but not as they please. The forward movement, 'the onward tendency of human things', cannot be taken for granted, and it is constrained by the historical past whose inheritance has to be respected in any attempts at change, as is spelt out in the *'Address to Working Men, by Felix Holt'. Human history, too, has its unchanging features: the same sort of movement and mixture that characterizes the history of old provincial society in *Middlemarch* is to be found in older Herodotus, the Greek historian of the 5th century BC (*MM* 11); while the Angel of the Dawn's grand panorama of the Mediterranean landscape in the Proem to *Romola* relates the unchanging courses of the great rivers to 'the broad sameness of the human lot, which never alters in the main headings of its history—hunger and labour, seed-time and harvest, love and death'. George Eliot's understanding of history includes an awareness of such continuities as well as difference and development. See also CRITICISM, MODERN: NEW HISTORICIST APPROACHES; PROGRESS; SOCIETY; VICO; WOMAN QUESTION.   JMR

Chase (1991).

Miller, J. Hillis, 'Narrative and History', *ELH* 41 (1974).

Reilly, Jim, *Shadowtime: History and Representation in Hardy, Conrad and George Eliot* (1993).

Semmel (1994).

Hoffmann, E. T. A. (1776–1822), German Romantic writer to whose novel *Kater Murr* George Eliot refers in *Middlemarch* (*MM* 4). Hoffmann's fiction was very popular in England, many of his stories having been translated by Carlyle. His writing incorporates powerful elements of fantasy and grotesque. Hoffmann's first love was music, and musical scenes and characters populate his work. *Kater Murr* and numerous stories portray the misfortunes of the brilliant and eccentric composer Kapellmeister Johannes Kreisler. With her own keen interest in music likely to make her alive to its importance in Hoffmann's fiction, it is possible that Eliot incorporated a degree of Kreisler's grotesque characterization into her portrayal of the chimingly named Klesmer in *Daniel Deronda*. An otherwise lofty representative of serious Germanic culture, the composer Klesmer also has Kreisleresque aspects. Like the Kapellmeister, Klesmer suffers the incomprehension and prejudice of the bourgeoisie. He also shares a somewhat absurd appearance and disconcerting magician-like powers. He is a 'musical Magus' with uncanny mesmerizing power over the novel's heroine (*DD* 6). In this respect, Klesmer is reminiscent of not only Johannes Kreisler, but of the host of magnetic characters and effects which pervade Hoffmann's work.   DdSC

da Sousa Correa, Delia, 'George Eliot and the Germanic "Musical Magus"', in Rignall (1997).

Homer (*c.*8th century BC), Greek epic poet whose *Iliad* and *Odyssey* George Eliot knew well, reading them in the original, inscribing passages from them into her *notebooks, and referring to them in her *letters and fiction. Homer was her favourite Greek author after *Sophocles (see CLASSICAL LITERATURE). In the early 1870s she became interested in the question of the authorship of the Homeric poems and studied the literature on the subject in English and German ('*Daniel Deronda*' *Notebooks*, ed. Irwin, 3–12, 254–6). She inclined to the view of the German classical scholar Friedrich August Wolf (1759–1824) in his *Prolegomena ad Homerum* (1795) that the poems were composed orally by more than one author and that their artistic unity was imposed later. This emerged in a discussion in November 1873 with an American visitor, the historian and philosopher John Fiske (1842–1901), who left a vivid account of the occasion in a letter to his wife. He found George Eliot thoroughly acquainted with the whole literature of the Homeric question and was impressed by her amazing knowledge of the subject and by the way she 'talked of Homer as simply as she would of flat-irons' (*L* v. 464). He did not think that he converted her to his opposing view of the unity of the poems—a view shared by her friend Benjamin *Jowett, the master of Balliol, who wrote to her on the subject in 1879 (*L* ix. 285).

The most substantial reference to Homer in the fiction is in *The Mill on the Floss*, where the *Iliad* serves to define the different opportunities open to Maggie and Tom Tulliver in the aftermath of their father's bankruptcy by pointing to a distinction of *gender that stretches back to 'the days of Hecuba and Hector, Tamer of Horses' (*MF* 5.2). Inside the gates the women are confined to praying and watching the world's combat from afar, while outside the gates the men are engaged in a fierce struggle with things divine and human. However, the ending of the novel challenges this immemorial gender difference by reversing the epic roles when Maggie rows through the flood to rescue Tom trapped in the mill. See also GENRES.   JMR

George Eliot's 'Daniel Deronda' Notebooks, ed. Jane Irwin (1996).

Jenkyns, Richard, *The Victorians and Ancient Greece* (1980), ch. 6.

homes of George Eliot. George Eliot's childhood home was *Griff House, a red-brick farmhouse with extensive outbuildings situated outside *Nuneaton on the road to *Coventry. The Evans family moved there shortly after her birth in 1819, and it was there that she grew up. After her father Robert *Evans retired, she moved with him in March 1841 to Bird Grove, a substantial semi-detached villa at Foleshill on the outskirts of Coventry. In this house she laboured for two years on her translation of D. F. *Strauss's *Life of Jesus* (see TRANSLATIONS BY GEORGE ELIOT) and nursed her father through his last illness. After his death in May 1849, her effective home, when she returned from wintering in *Geneva in the spring of 1850, was not with any of her family but with her friends Charles and Cara *Bray at Rosehill, their large detached house in Coventry. This was her base during her first attempts at living in *London at John *Chapman's, until she moved there definitively, taking up residence in his house at 142 Strand on 29 September 1851. She stayed working on the *Westminster Review* for two years, moving to lodgings at 21 Cambridge Street on 17 October 1853, where her relationship with G. H. *Lewes began and from where she left with him for *Germany on 20 July 1854, shortly after the publication of her translation of Ludwig *Feuerbach's *The Essence of Christianity*. On their return in the following spring, the couple lived for a few months at 7 Clarence Row, East Sheen, until 3 October 1855 when they moved to lodgings at 8 Park Shot, Richmond, where they lived for three and a half years. *Scenes of Clerical Life* and much of *Adam Bede* were written there in the small sitting room where the scratching of Lewes's pen would drive her nearly wild (Haight 1968: 192). After enjoying more spacious quarters during their visit to Germany in 1858, they decided to rent a house, Holly Lodge at Southfields, Wandsworth, to which they moved

The Heights, George Eliot's country house at Witley in Surrey, purchased in December 1876, where she spent the summer months from 1877 to 1880.

on 11 February 1859. *The Mill on the Floss*, 'The Lifted Veil', and 'Brother Jacob' were written at Holly Lodge, although Eliot soon became dissatisfied with the house and its overlooked location (*L* iii. 118). Needing to move into central London so that Lewes's son Charles (see LEWES FAMILY) could be nearer to his work, they took most of an unattractive furnished house at 10 Hanover Square for three months from 24 September 1860, moving on 17 December to a house of their own at 16 Blandford Square. In the three years they spent there she completed *Silas Marner* and wrote *Romola*. When the lease was about to expire, they bought The *Priory, the handsome detached house at 21 North Bank, Regent's Park, which they moved into on 5 November 1863 and which was to be the novelist's principal home until the last months of her life. Developing a habit of renting houses in the country during the summer in order to write in quiet seclusion, she and Lewes later began to look for a country house of their own, and in December 1876 they bought a large red-brick house, The Heights at Witley in Surrey, standing in eight or nine acres of its own ground (Haight 1968: 500). There they would spend the summer months, and it was from there, after Lewes's death and her marriage to John Walter *Cross, that George Eliot moved to her last home, 4 Cheyne Walk, Chelsea, on 3 December 1880, three weeks before her death. See also LIFE OF GEORGE ELIOT.   JMR

Horace (Quintus Horatius Flaccus) (65–8 BC), Roman poet who is the Latin author George Eliot refers to most frequently in her writing. She shows a knowledge of his *Satires* as early as March 1841, and she adopts as her motto an adapted phrase from his *Epistles* (1. ii. 56)—'certum pete finem', which she translates as 'seek a sure end'—and uses it for her seal on her letters from 5 December 1840 (*L* i. 73). She quotes from him throughout her life, citing his 'non omnis moriar' (I shall not die completely) from his 30th Ode in 1859 when *Adam Bede* is proving to be a success (see RECEPTION). The same phrase recurs rather poignantly in a letter of April 1878 to John Walter *Cross, when she states that she values the thought of being remembered by him, 'Yet I like to be loved in this faulty, frail (yet venerable) flesh' (*L* ix. 236).

In her fiction half-forgotten tags from Horace are what remain of the classical education of undisciplined gentlemen like Arthur Donnithorne (*AB* 16) and Mr Brooke (*MM* 34, 38), while references to the poet abound in the discourse of the scholars in *Romola*, illustrating the renewed interest in classical antiquity of Renaissance culture. She uses the famous 'in medias res' from the *Ars Poetica* in her reflections on the make-believe of a

beginning in the epigraph to the first chapter of *Daniel Deronda*.

In March 1860 she wrote to Theodore Martin about his new translation of the *Odes*, expressing both her admiration and her reservations about ever achieving a successful translation of poetry (see 'TRANSLATIONS AND TRANSLATORS'), ending with a back-handed compliment that 'whenever my remembrance of the original is dim, you seem proportionately to excel' (*L* viii. 258). From the evidence of her writing, her ability to remember lines of her favourite Latin author remained generally undimmed. See also CLASSICAL LITERATURE.
                              JMR

Rendell, Vernon, 'George Eliot and the Classics', *Notes and Queries*, 193 (1948).

Houghton, Lord. See MILNES, RICHARD MONCKTON.

'How I came to write Fiction' appears in George Eliot's 1854–61 journal, following her 'Recollections' of the Scilly Isles and Jersey, and dated 'Dec. 6. 57', that is, at a point when the anonymous serialization of *Scenes of Clerical Life* in *Blackwood's Edinburgh Magazine* was almost at an end, and their publication in two volumes 'By George Eliot' in January 1858 imminent (see PSEUDONYM). Following the essay are notes concerning the publication and reception of *Scenes*, 'History of "Adam Bede"', and entries about the reception of the latter, with brief reference to the *Liggins affair: Harris and Johnston propose that this sequence of material has a particular integrity and describes 'the making of George Eliot' (*Journals*, 286). In this essay, she gives an account of her decision to embark on a career in fiction as the crystallization of a long-held ambition during the time she spent with G. H. *Lewes at *Tenby in 1856 on the second stage of the expedition described in 'Recollections of Ilfracombe'.

The narrative depends on Lewes as her audience, providing doubts and resistance which she overcomes. Similarly, her work overcomes doubts of her readers. Early on, she identifies deficiency in dramatic power as a potential difficulty for her ambition, which she systematically sets about addressing. Romantic inspiration is also at work. She is lying in bed in a reverie when the revelation of the title 'The Sad Fortunes of the Reverend Amos Barton' flashes into her mind. Her commitments as a journalist have to be fulfilled before she can proceed to fiction, so she completes *'Silly Novels by Lady Novelists' and 'Contemporary Literature' (part of the 'Belles Lettres' section) for the October 1856 issue of the *Westminster Review*. Only when these tasks are despatched can she turn from the discussion of other people's fiction to the production of her own. Elsewhere, her journal for 23

September 1856 records, 'Began to write "The Sad Fortunes of the Reverend Amos Barton", which I hope to make one of a series called "Scenes of Clerical Life"' (*Journals*, 63).

George Eliot's account of the submission of the *Scenes* to John *Blackwood provides a model for numerous interactions over the next twenty-odd years in which the sometimes querulous sensitivities of the author and of Lewes acting as her agent are assuaged by the astute and generous Scot. What is most striking in the essay, however, is her gleeful recording of the successful maintenance of anonymity: 'There was clearly no suspicion that I was a woman', with many assuming that the author was a clergyman. Praise of the serialized *Scenes*, especially 'Mr Gilfil's Love-Story', by prominent figures like Albert Smith, Arthur *Helps, Edward Bruce *Hamley, Aytoun, and William Makepeace *Thackeray, is itemized almost boastfully. The essay ends in anticipation of public reaction to the book.

'How I came to write Fiction' was first published by John Walter *Cross, in a disjointed abridged version (Cross, i. 414–29).   MAH

Hugo, Victor (1802–85), French poet, novelist, and dramatist about whose work George Eliot was never very enthusiastic, although she copied passages from some of the novels into her notebooks and used one excerpt as a chapter *epigraph in *Middlemarch*. G. H. *Lewes engaged with Hugo's writing more fully, but although he praised him in an early article in the *Westminster Review* in 1840 as the finest French Romantic playwright, he later criticized the plays for their lack of realism (Knapp, 191). While acknowledging Hugo's talents, Lewes found his writing generally shallow and insincere, and, as he wrote to John *Blackwood when offering to review *Les Misérables* for *Blackwood's Edinburgh Magazine* in 1862, 'too intensely French for my taste' (*L* iv. 27). It is likely that Eliot shared his view. She reviewed Hugo's collection of poems *Les Contemplations* (1856) in the *Westminster Review* in July 1856, but singled out for praise the simple, moving poems he had written on the death of his daughter rather than the loftier vein more typical of Hugo, in which he writes in the grand manner about God and the universe. Of his novels she seems to have known at least *Notre Dame de Paris* (1831), *Les Misérables* (1862), and *L'Homme qui rit* (1869), and uses a passage from the last as the epigraph to chapter 86 of *Middlemarch*. It is a meditation on the preserving power of love which makes for the constancy of those who love each other from early life to old age, like Fred Vincy and Mary Garth, who are shown to be on the verge of marriage in that chapter and are seen growing happily old together in

'white-haired placidity' in the Finale. There is nothing very distinctively Hugolian about the passage cited, but it indicates how Eliot could find something congenial even in a writer who was not to her taste; and there are a few other thematic parallels between her fiction and his (Knapp, 202–3). There is one other significant connection: when Lewes suggested to John Blackwood that *Middlemarch* be published in separate parts he had Hugo in mind, for he referred to the way that *Les Misérables* had appeared in five separate volumes over a period of months (*L* v. 145–6). A similar scheme was adopted for *Middlemarch*.   JMR

Knapp, Shoshana Milgram, '"Too intensely French for my taste": Victor Hugo as read by George Eliot and George Henry Lewes', in Rignall (1997).

humour. The range of George Eliot's humour reflects the social range of her fictional concerns, from the churchy ladies in 'The Sad Fortunes of the Reverend Amos Barton' and 'Janet's Repentance' to the idiosyncratic and mannered pronouncements of *Impressions of Theophrastus Such*—exercises in intellectual ventriloquism. The essays and reviews are notable for a balanced control of expression which is sometimes witty, occasionally epigrammatic, often ironic, pithy, and funny, like the description of the 'mind-and-millinery' species of novel in *'Silly Novels by Lady Novelists' (*Essays*, 301–2). In her essay on *'German Wit: Heinrich Heine' she gives her own acute definition of wit and humour.

In the early fiction there is a striking combination of narrative humour (admittedly somewhat heavy-handed) and aural accuracy. John, having spilled the gravy on Milly Barton's dress, tells the cook she should have wetted 'the *duree* a bit, to hold it from slippin': "Wet your granny!" returned the cook; a retort which she probably regarded in the light of a *reductio ad absurdum,* and which in fact reduced John to silence' (*SC* 1.3). The incongruity of the Latin tag reflects Eliot's early lack of discrimination. The progression from this self-conscious mode to the naturalness of Mrs Poyser ('it's ill livin' in a hen-roost for them as doesn't like fleas', *AB* 14), often without benefit of comment, is a considerable one: her put-down of the Squire, her economic motives emerging as verbal acid, is superb. Then there is the humorous commentary which appraises the locals as they await Dinah's preaching, its focus for instance on Joshua Rann, village shoemaker and more: 'the thrusting out of his chin and stomach, and the twirling of his thumbs, are more subtle indications, intended to prepare unwary strangers for the discovery that they are in the presence of the parish clerk' (*AB* 2).

In *The Mill on the Floss* the Hall Farm interiors are replaced by variegated Dodson ones, from Mrs

Pullet's medicated profuseness through Aunt Glegg's corrosive repertoire to Mrs Deane's obsessive cleanliness, the ear wonderfully accurate in recording actuality and innuendo. Here is Mrs Glegg reprimanding her sister Pullet for showing too great an interest in Mrs Sutton's dropsy: 'You couldn't fret no more than this, if we'd heared as our cousin Abbott had died sudden without making his will' (*MF* 1.7). Ironic commentary frequently subserves the effects of the dialogue: the result is sophistication with tolerance and warmth. Another facet of *irony, to be fully developed in the later novels, is seen in the presentation of Mr Stelling, that indolent non-educationist conditioned for preferment.

The humour in *Silas Marner* blends what is heard with what is implied with an adhesive of understanding and innuendo. The opening of chapter 6, the Rainbow Inn sequence, is a notation of narrative sophistication: men smoke their pipes 'in a silence which had an air of severity . . . staring at each other as if a bet were depending on the first man who winked . . . as if their draughts of beer were a funereal duty attended with embarrassing sadness'. The pace of the conversation reflects bucolic slowness, deliberation, ignorance, obstinacy, complacency; and the gamut of human reaction is seen and heard ironically and tolerantly, funnily and without condescension. The analogy with Shakespearean rustics (or Hardy's rustics) is apt because the particular naturalistically embraces the general.

This is all the more remarkable when one considers that Eliot broke off from her Italian story (*Romola*) in order to write *Silas Marner*. The humour in *Romola* is strained, the artificiality of the idiom in translation or approximation underpinning the sombre atmosphere but failing to alleviate it. *Brother Jacob* has the black comedy of Jacob, and *Felix Holt, the Radical* certain pathetic/comic sequences involving Job Tudge. But it is not until *Middlemarch* that we come to the full expression of Eliot's humour, the narrative irony in its various nuances which embraces Dorothea and Casaubon, a kind of subdued black marital comedy, in part reflected in the relationship of Lydgate and Rosamond. There is Mr Brooke in casually social or, on one occasion, sherry-riddled public delivery: 'We must look all over the globe:—"Observation with extensive view," must look everywhere, "from China to Peru", as somebody says—Johnson, I think, "The Rambler", you know' (*MM* 51). The overall mode is ironic across the social spectrum from the epigrammatic and gossipy verve of Mrs Cadwallader to the lower libels of Mrs Dollop.

In *Daniel Deronda* the humour is occasionally more caustically ironic: Mr Gascoigne 'had once been Captain Gaskin, having taken orders and a diphthong but shortly before his engagement to Miss Armyn' (*DD* 3). But if Klesmer's idiosyncratic whimsy and eccentric transitions are delightfully recorded, the verbal flights of Hans Meyrick are strained. *Impressions of Theophrastus Such* marks a movement into in-jokes and satirical objects. If pedantry and obsessions require humour to reconcile us to them, then the humour here seems to be more than tinctured with the nature of the subject. It is esoteric and formal, lacking the natural ease which marks the early fiction and the fluent sophistication which marks the late. Eliot's humour is the foil for the sometimes sombre effects of her narratives and is an essential component of her *realism.   GRH

Hutton, R. H., 'The Humour of *Middlemarch*', in *A Victorian Spectator: Uncollected Writings of R. H. Hutton* (1989).

Hunt, Thornton Leigh (1810–73), journalist and editor, eldest son of Leigh Hunt (1784–1859). In 1850, in partnership with G. H. *Lewes, he founded the *Leader, a weekly newspaper which covered politics and general news, and to which George Eliot later contributed several short articles. A fortnight after the first issue, which appeared in March, Lewes's wife Agnes gave birth to a son, Edmund Alfred Lewes. Hunt was the father, as he was of Rose Agnes Lewes, born in October 1851. Two more daughters followed in 1853 and 1857. By giving them his name Lewes had effectively condoned his wife's adultery and could not therefore get a divorce. As early as February 1852, before her commitment to Lewes, George Eliot reported to Charles Bray that a letter from George *Combe enquired about the reckless behaviour of Thornton Hunt: Combe was probably picking up on rumours of his relationship with Agnes Lewes (*L* ii. 12). A year earlier she had deplored the fact that Thornton called at the Strand but that John *Chapman had not introduced her to him. She did meet him at Rosehill, home of the *Brays, where he was staying for the weekend, in May. Eliot recorded her liking for Mrs Hunt in the wake of this visit, and in a letter to Chapman of 15 June 1851 (*L* i. 352) she noted Hunt's *mot* that 'Politics are as dull as boiled mutton chops'. He inserted her review of W. R. Greg's *The Creed of Christendom* in the *Leader* for 20 September 1851.

Writing to Combe, Eliot initially defended Hunt against charges of irresponsible behaviour by citing his willingness to work for the *Leader* without payment (*L* viii. 36). Thomas Woolner's letter to William Bell Scott in October 1854 associates Thornton with Lewes ('two blackguard literary fellows', *L* ii. 175–6) who hold their wives in common. In the same month Eliot wrote to John

Chapman that Lewes had decided to separate from his wife, insisting, however, that she was not involved (*L* viii. 124). At about this time Hunt ceased to be the publisher of the *Leader*.

With the return of Eliot and Lewes from Germany in March 1855 the vexing question of Hunt's non-payment of Agnes's bills arose, and Thornton, increasingly angered by the mutual sniping, challenged Lewes to a duel (December 1856) basically for calling him a liar. Lewes refused to withdraw, but a small 'Court of Honour' ruled that a duel would not take place. By the middle of 1857 Lewes was effectively paying money to Agnes for the upkeep of the children, and thereafter Eliot made gifts to Agnes's children by Hunt. In that year she condemned his review of Mrs *Gaskell's *The Life of Charlotte Brontë* in the *Leader* (*L* ii. 330). Hunt died virtually unnoticed, aged 62, in 1873 at the height of Eliot's reputation. He had made some provision for Agnes via an insurance policy, though Lewes continued payments to her. An eloquent defence of Hunt and castigation of Lewes occurs in Eliza Lynn *Linton's *My Literary Life* (1899) which, however, reads as if she had no knowledge of any relationship between Hunt and Agnes Lewes. See also LEWES FAMILY.   GRH

Hutton, R. H. (1826–97), essayist and journalist, joint editor of the *Spectator* from 1861 until his death, and one of the finest contemporary critics of George Eliot's fiction. From a Unitarian family, he studied at University College London and at universities in Germany, and although his intellectual background gave him something in common with George Eliot, unlike her (see ATHEISM) he remained a committed Christian. His writing was divided evenly between theology, literature, and politics, and as a literary reviewer he concentrated on contemporary works. He considered George Eliot the major Victorian realist and treated her as a thinker as well as a novelist, showing himself aware of the philosophical implications of her novels and in particular her debt to Ludwig *Feuerbach. He entered into a brief correspondence with her over *Romola*. Enquiring whether his *Spectator* review read too much into the book,

he received her assurance that there was nothing fanciful in his interpretation and her praise for the fullness with which he understood what she was attempting with Bardo and Baldassare (*L* iv. 96–7). Although he could be critical of her agnosticism, finding it unnatural, for instance, that Dorothea in her darkest trial (*MM* 80) never thinks of God (*CH* 313), he defended her against an attack in the *Church Quarterly* in 1877, arguing that her ethics, while not Christian, had all the inwardness of Christian ethics (Woodfield, 178).   JMR

Woodfield, Malcolm, *R. H. Hutton: Critic and Theologian* (1986).

Huxley, T. H. (1825–95), biologist and chief public supporter of Charles *Darwin in the controversy that followed the publication of *On the Origin of Species* in 1859. In 1854, when the future George Eliot was working on the *Westminster Review*, he upset her by submitting a hostile review of G. H. *Lewes's *Comte's Philosophy of the Sciences* (1853) for the January number of the journal. He accused Lewes of being an amateur with only a book knowledge of scientific subjects. George Eliot, by this time intimate with Lewes, tried in vain to have the article altered or omitted. Lewes was stung by the criticism, but a reconciliation with Huxley was later effected, probably through Herbert *Spencer, and he became a friend of the couple. In 1861 Huxley was embroiled in a public controversy with another of their scientific friends, Richard *Owen, in which he came out best. In 1869 he coined the term 'agnostic' to define his own position in relation to *religion, which closely corresponded to George Eliot's (see ATHEISM). When Lewes died Huxley was appointed one of the trustees of the George Henry Lewes Studentship at Cambridge established in his honour. When George Eliot died Huxley was opposed to the idea that she should be buried in Westminster Abbey, since she was not only a great writer but also 'a person whose life and opinions were in notorious antagonism to Christian practice in regard to marriage, and Christian theory in regard to dogma' (Haight 1968: 549). See also SCIENCE; TYNDALL, JOHN.   JMR

Ashton, Rosemary, *G. H. Lewes: A Life* (1991).

I

Ilfracombe, watering place on the coast of North Devon where George Eliot and G. H. *Lewes stayed 8 May–26 June 1856, the extent of their marine activities, walks, reading, writing, interaction with friends recorded in the 'Recollections of Ilfracombe' (*L* ii. 238–52). They found it enchanting, Eliot thought it 'the loveliest sea-place I ever saw, from the combination of fine, rocky coast with exquisite inland scenery' though it was 'all hill and no valley' (*L* ii. 252). At the same time she felt it unsuitable for 'delicate people' since the air was 'very harsh and trying' (*L* ii. 254).   GRH

illnesses. See HEALTH.

illustrations. Only one of George Eliot's novels was originally published with a full set of illustrations: *Romola*, which appeared in the *Cornhill Magazine* from July 1862 to August 1863 with plates and vignettes by Frederic *Leighton. Her short story 'Brother Jacob', also published in the *Cornhill*, in July 1864, was also illustrated by a well-known artist, Charles Keene (1823–91), who contributed one plate, *Mother's Guineas* and one initial letter.

In 1862 John *Blackwood proposed a Stereotyped Edition with illustrations, and George Eliot, putting aside a general dislike of illustrations, agreed to an apparently promising project.

Five of the novels were eventually published in this form, *Scenes of Clerical Life* (1868), *Adam Bede* (1867), *The Mill on the Floss* (1867), *Silas Marner* (1868), and *Felix Holt, the Radical* (1869). Each was engraved by James D. Cooper (1823–1904), and Edmund Morison Wimperis (1835–1900) contributed vignettes, each showing a scene of importance for the novel in question, to the title-pages of the volumes.

George Eliot admired the vignettes, but not the illustrations. The six woodcuts for *Adam Bede*, the first novel to appear, were by William Small

(1843–1929). Although they are fine examples of the illustration of the period, George Eliot objected to them. Three of the five illustrations to *Scenes* are by Robert Barnes (1840–95), a prolific illustrator then at the beginning of his career. In 1886 he was the first illustrator for *The Mayor of Casterbridge* by Thomas *Hardy. The same draughtsman was responsible for the three illustrations to *Silas Marner*.

The second illustrator of *Scenes of Clerical Life* was the painter and illustrator Francis Wilfred Lawson (fl. 1867–1913), who, like Barnes, worked as an illustrator for the *Graphic* magazine. There were six rather conventional illustrations for *The Mill on the Floss*, one at least by the genre painter and illustrator Walter James Allen (1859–91). Of the six illustrations for *Felix Holt*, one is by John F. Jellicoe (fl. 1865–1903), and two are signed with two crossed arrows, the other three are unsigned.

The first one-volume editions of *Romola* (1865), *Middlemarch* (1874), and *Daniel Deronda* (1877) all have vignettes on the title-page, that to *Romola* of the tower to the Palazzo della Signoria in Florence, that to *Middlemarch* an idealized townscape of a country town by Myles Birket Foster (1825–99), who was probably also the artist for the *Romola* vignette. The vignette for *Deronda* was engraved by Charles Jeens (1827–79). George Eliot had suggested Helen Allingham (1848–1926) as illustrator for the *Romola* cheap edition, and John Blackwood was prepared to agree to two illustrations and a title-page vignette, but Allingham declined the commission. See also VISUAL ARTS.   LO

Impressions of Theophrastus Such (*see page 166*)

industrialism. There are no gritty images of industrialism in George Eliot's fiction as there are in the novels of, say, Elizabeth *Gaskell or *Charles *Dickens. Eliot's novels are usually set in places far removed from the hustle and bustle of cotton mills or other kinds of heavy machinery. In *Felix Holt, the Radical*, manufacturing towns, scenes of various kinds of industrial discontent, are only briefly alluded to by the narrator (Introduction); and in *Silas Marner*, the great manufacturing town where Silas grew up before coming to Raveloe, is hardly described. Even Lantern Yard, tucked away in that town, is only briefly sketched. It had 'whitewashed walls' and 'little pews' (*SM* 2) and stood in the vicinity of Prison Street and Shoe Lane before it was knocked down and replaced by a 'big factory' (*SM* 21). The towns in *Felix Holt* and *Middlemarch* are based on *Nuneaton and *Coventry: the former was a market town and the latter had a ribbon-making industry, which is not mentioned in either novel. Sproxton miners are referred to in

(*cont. on page 170*)

NOVELS

OF

GEORGE ELIOT

VOL. I.

ADAM BEDE

WITH ILLUSTRATIONS

THE HALL FARM

WILLIAM BLACKWOOD AND SONS
EDINBURGH AND LONDON

The title-page and vignette of the bound volume of the Stereotyped Edition of *Adam Bede* (1867). George Eliot found the vignette, by Edmund Morison Wimperis, 'perfect—almost exactly as I saw the Hall Farm eight years ago in my mind's eye'.

G EORGE ELIOT's last published work and her experimental departure from the genre of the novel. It consists of eighteen chapters narrated by a 19th-century English bachelor who shares some characteristics with Eliot: he was raised in the Midlands and writes with nostalgia about his rural childhood from the perspective of a citizen of the 'nation of London'. But there the similarities end, for Theophrastus is a failed author, an irascible middle-aged man who reveals his own weaknesses in a series of sketches of people he meets—all with comic or allegorical names, like Merman, Mixtus, Ganymede, and Vorticella, suggestive of their personalities as well as literary, mythological, scientific, and historical figures.

Impressions is Eliot's contribution to a tradition initiated by Theophrastus (*c.*372–287 BC), the ancient Greek philosopher and student of *Aristotle whose *Characters* were translated into Latin by Isaac Casaubon (1592). Casaubon's translation was influential in sparking an English-language tradition of character writing, including works by Joseph Hall (1608) and Sir Thomas Overbury (1614); in French, the best-known example is La Bruyère's *Les 'Caractères' de Théophraste* (1688). By implicitly invoking this genealogy in the title and structure of the work, Eliot calls attention generally to cultural transmission through translation (see 'TRANSLATIONS AND TRANSLATORS'; TRANSLATIONS BY GEORGE ELIOT), and specifically to the incorporation of classical languages and sources into English literary tradition. The Greek presence begins with the title, which she originally proposed as 'Characters and Characteristics, or Impressions of Theophrastus Such, Edited by George Eliot'. The meaning of Theophrastus 'Such' recalls a Greek formula used by the original Theophrastus in his *Characters*, in which the chapters begin with the phrase *toiontos tis, hoios*, or 'such a type who'. Eliot's 'such' represents the translation of ancient Theophrastus into a modern context. The epigraph to the book is an untranslated Latin passage from Phaedrus' *Fabulae*, suggesting that the author has no intention of branding individual men, but rather truly to show life itself and the habits of men ('Verum ipsam vitam et mores hominum ostendere'). Furthermore, some of the characters have Greek and Latin names, such as Glycera, Minutius Felix, Lentulus, and Euphorion.

Eliot goes further than previous character writers by translating not only the form but the author into contemporary English culture. Translation is not merely across linguistic divides but across time. By making Theophrastus into both author and character and by the names she gives her characters, Eliot constantly acknowledges her literary antecedents and makes their work her own, a particularly appropriate emphasis because several chapters explicitly address the themes of literary property, borrowing, and plagiarism. But *Impressions* does not draw a straight Hellenic line of descent for English literature. European, American, and various colonial cultures are also invoked. Theophrastus has written a novel 'much tasted in a Cherokee translation' (*TS* 1) and he refers to the *Bible, the Koran, and to Chinese poetry. Most prominently and in continuity with *Daniel Deronda*, he argues that Christianity derives from Jewish tradition and the Hebrew language, chastising his contemporaries as too ignorant and provincial-minded to recognize the connection, and in this way pointing to the hypocrisy of many 19th-century anti-Jewish attitudes (see ANTI-SEMITISM; JUDAISM; COLONIALISM).

It is typical of the self-consciousness of *Impressions* (the word itself a pun for images impressed on the mind and words impressed on the page) that Eliot chose the tradition of English character writing; the unifying theme of the work as a whole is English tradition and English moral character, considered both individually and nationally (see NATIONALISM). While Eliot distinguishes Theophrastus from herself, she also expresses through him a variety of opinions about the state of contemporary authorship and culture. The chapters address and sometimes satirize various forms of writing: autobiographical, anthropological, economic, fictional. Most of the characters are minor authors whose egos are served by their insignificant publications. Taken together, the chapters represent an indictment of print culture, suggesting that the character flaws of authors are made public in their writings. These writings then fill the English cultural archive with inferior texts, causing Eliot, through Theophrastus, to worry about the legacy that the current generation will leave to the next. The sketchy characters and fragmented form are crucial to her project. Theophrastus exposes the myths of *history, the teleological narratives that retrospectively order the scattered and conflicting accounts of historical events. *Impressions* demands that readers impose coherence on the disordered information Theophrastus supplies about himself. The work suggests that the identity of individual subjects, like that of nations, is constructed through a process of selection and exclusion that resembles the process of making art.

Composition

The exact dates of composition are uncertain. Eliot made few references to *Impressions* in her correspondence prior to its completion. G. H. *Lewes records in his diary for 16 April 1878 that 'Polly read her ms.' (*L* vii. 21), and when he mailed the completed manuscript to John Blackwood on 21 November 1878, one of his last acts before his own death, he referred to it as 'the work of the last few months' (*L* vii. 78). Much of the book must have been written at The Heights, Witley, the newly furnished country home in which the Leweses stayed from 21 June to 11 November 1878 (see HOMES OF GEORGE ELIOT). Because her letters in 1878 are preoccupied with domestic concerns, and focus more on her own and Lewes's bad health than on their work, 1878 is not usually considered a period of productivity for Eliot. Yet, her intimacy with Lewes during the final year of his life and her silence to others about what she was writing are reflected in the cryptic playfulness of *Impressions*. The characters themselves, if not based on real people, nonetheless represent literary and society types that Eliot and Lewes would have joked about, such as Hinze, the compulsive flatterer, or Vorticella, a silly lady author.

Furthermore, though her daily progress on *Impressions* is not recorded, her letters indicate the genesis of some of the chapters as well as the overall conception of the book. On 17 January 1878, Eliot wrote to Barbara *Bodichon that she had been to see a pantomime for children and found it 'a melancholy business' (*L* vii. 6). 'Debasing the Moral Currency' (*TS* 10) explores the implications of pantomime and burlesque as demeaning presentations of the classics to children. On 26 January 1878, Eliot wrote to Blackwood in praise of La Bruyère's *Caractères*, lamenting that La Bruyère 'cannot be done justice to by any merely English presentation' (*L* vii. 11). Rough drafts for two chapters in *Impressions* (7, 16) are among the undated manuscript notes that were eventually published (without these two chapters) as *Essays and Leaves from a Notebook* (1884). These manuscript pages are now at the Huntington Library and are our only material clue to Eliot's process of writing *Impressions*. They contain other essays on topics central to *Impressions*, such as 'Authorship' and 'Imagination'. The bound manuscript of *Impressions* is in the British Library (Add. MS 34043).

Publication

Although the manuscript of *Impressions* was set in December of 1878 and Eliot corrected the page proofs in January and February of 1879, she refused to allow it to appear until a suitable time had passed after Lewes's death. She was anxious that her public not suspect her of working while he was dying. The book was published on 19 May 1879 in one volume octavo, bound in grey cloth with gilt centre and priced at 10s. 6d. It appeared with a publisher's note, a thin strip of paper inserted to lie across the title-page: 'The Manuscript of this Work was put into our hands towards the close of last year, but the publication has been delayed owing to the domestic affliction of the Author'. *Impressions* ran through four printings and was slightly revised for the 1880 Cabinet Edition. The Cabinet Edition text was used in subsequent reprints until 1994. The most significant variation between the manuscript and the published text is the reversal of order of the last two chapters: 'Shadows of the Coming Race' (18 in the manuscript and 17 in the first edition) and 'The Modern Hep! Hep! Hep!'. No evidence has yet been found for when the decision to make this change was made. The final order was set in the page proofs. At the proof stage, Eliot eliminated one long passage in response to Blackwood's criticism of her characterization of George III (*L* vii. 119, 22 March 1879). No significant changes were made to the 1880 Cabinet Edition. The proofs are now at the Harry Ransom Humanities Research Center at the University of Texas at Austin.

Reception

Few reviews of *Impressions* were positive. Repeated complaints were made of its intellectual density, scientific content, and its preoccupation with Jewish culture in the last and longest chapter, 'The Modern Hep! Hep! Hep!'. Many compared it unfavourably with Eliot's early novels and noted the increasing inaccessibility of her work. One exception was the review in *The Times* (5 June 1879), which praised the work highly. But even *The Times* concurred with other reviews that the book was too erudite to ever be popular. Subsequently, *Impressions* faded from the Eliot canon, often ignored or dismissed in criticism. The silence about *Impressions* throughout 20th-century criticism is an interesting case in reception studies. Rather than recapitulating the 19th-century critique that the work was too difficult, the standard interpretation became that the work was a disappointing falling-off, a lapse in Eliot's previous creative powers. Any sense of the work's complexity was lost. The explanation for this neglect lies in the experimentality of the work and the blinkering effect of conventional literary categories. *Impressions* has always defied critical or market categorization. It is neither a novel nor short story, yet it is a fictional work. It is not, as is usually assumed, a collection of essays in Eliot's voice. When individual chapters have been quoted out of context, the importance of narrative voice is overlooked and the views of Eliot's character are mistaken for her own. Eliot wrote *essays (mostly reviews), short stories, *poetry, and novels. *Impressions* is unique among her works, and even when situated in the character-writing tradition, goes so far beyond that genre in its attempt to show the gradual emergence of an author/character who is known only through his own words, that critics still rarely know what to do with it.

Plot

Impressions has no plot. It is unified chapter to chapter by the voice and character of Theophrastus. The chapters do, however, develop in complexity and in scope from autobiography (1–2), to individual character description (3–9), to a broader consideration of English culture (10–17), and finally to an assessment of modern nationalisms (18).

'Looking Inward' is Theophrastus' introspective analysis of his own character and a reflection on the genre of autobiography. He suggests that even in autobiography, an author reveals much about himself that he never intended, thereby alerting the reader to the unintentional exposures that will inevitably result in the chapters that follow. 'Looking Backward' is Theophrastus' reminiscence of his Midlands childhood and a fond look at his father, a conservative country parson of democratic social habits. He ends with a reflection of his life as a 'town bird', living a cosmopolitan life in *London with a constant sense of himself as a 'voluntary exile' whose identity is sustained by memories of the land and people of provincial England. 'How We Encourage Research' is a parable involving Proteus Merman, the upstart amateur scholar who dared to challenge the anthropological theories of Grampus and other big fish who rule the waters of orientalist discourse. It is a tragicomic account of academic hegemony and the sad fate of well-intentioned but self-absorbed aspirants to intellectual greatness. It is in this chapter that Eliot first introduces the language of evolutionary and other scientific theories that recurs throughout the text (see DARWINISM; SCIENCE). 'A Man Surprised at his Originality' tells the story of Lentulus, the harsh critic of other people's writing who hints at his own superiority, yet never manages to produce anything. 'The Too Deferential Man' describes Hinze, the cloying flatterer whose deferential behaviour is mere habit without motive. 'Only Temper' finds Touchwood the kindest of friends until 'temper' kicks in and makes him the most vicious of enemies. 'A Political Molecule' describes Spike, the most complacent of liberal manufacturers who is happy to embrace a cause as long as it happens to benefit him. 'The Watchdog of Knowledge' seems to reverse Theophrastus's judgement of Touchwood by excusing the bad temper of Mordax, which is actually a self-justification for Theophrastus' own bad treatment of his factotum Pummel. 'A Half-Breed' laments the lapsed values of Mixtus, who compromises a once-principled intellectual life for the self-satisfaction of economic and social success. 'Debasing the Moral Currency' marks a transition, for here Theophrastus begins to take on larger cultural issues, such as the fad for foreign languages and the treatment of great texts in the popular form of burlesque. 'The Wasp Credited with the Honeycomb' takes the form of a fable to comment on the notion of intellectual property. 'So Young!' takes a humorous look at the vanity of Ganymede, the middle-aged civil servant/author who cannot relinquish an image of himself as a youth. 'How We Give Ourselves False Testimonials and Believe in Them' deals with the value of realistic description in literature (see REALISM) and the dangers of confusing imagination with falsification and also with the notion of self-deception or 'traditions about ourselves'. 'The Too Ready Writer' juxtaposes the backward-looking genre of historical romance with the most immediate form of writing, journalism, and finds its two representatives, Pepin and Adrastus, equally lacking in integrity. 'Diseases of Small Authorship' looks at the microscopic world of Vorticella, a small author whose insipid influence has attracted other animalcules such as Volvox and Monas. 'Moral Swindlers' considers the devaluation of the word 'moral' and the relationship between public and private morality (see MORAL VALUES). 'Shadows of the Coming Race' considers the future, combining the discourses of Darwinian theory and science fiction to predict a world in which machines have adapted to supersede human beings (see PROGRESS). 'The Modern Hep! Hep! Hep!' is the most substantive and autonomous chapter; at the same time it is a logical culmination of the previous examinations of the relationship between a community and its individual members. In it Theophrastus views modern *nationalism (Greek, Italian, German) as the resurrection of a national past. He deplores English Christian prejudice against Jews and other peoples, and he supports the idea of a modern Jewish nation, reflecting implicitly on English nationality. Ultimately, Theophrastus concludes that traditions bind us, thereby retroactively investing his previous seventeen chapters about the uses and abuses of texts with new significance and completing the portrait of himself.

Critical Approaches

There is no tradition of critical debate about *Impressions*, merely an occasionally articulated consensus that there is not much to say about it. As early critics noted, the work is intellectually and verbally dense. In retrospect, it can be usefully viewed as a stylistic and thematic precursor of modernism, foreshadowing the elaborate sentence structure of Henry *James, the coded references of Gertrude Stein, the cultural allusions of T. S. *Eliot and James Joyce, and the fragmented consciousness of Virginia *Woolf. It poses a challenge to its readers; its difficulty is integral to its explicit critique of a 'debased' literary culture for which opportunistic authors and complacent readers are responsible. While Eliot seems to distance herself from her readers by loading *Impressions* with erudite references as well as by engaging in dialogue with Lewes, in no other work does she so explicitly concern herself with the ethics of writing and authorship. In this respect the work remains Victorian, firmly within the moral tradition of her novels. But it is important to keep in mind the crucial, experimental detaching of character from narrative context. In Eliot's novels, we learn about characters through narrated actions: about Daniel Deronda when he rescues Mirah or befriends Mordecai, about Rosamond and Lydgate as their marriage disintegrates, about Maggie when she loves Philip and then Stephen. Eliot's readers learned about St Ogg's or Middlemarch or Wessex as fictional communities where things happened that might reflect their lives in 1860, 1872, or 1876. *Impressions* is different because readers in 1879 had no way of knowing Theophrastus except through the words he uses to describe others and by knowing their own present culture, by knowing themselves. In *Impressions*, Eliot held out to her readers, not the Egyptian sorcerer's drop of ink, but a textual mirror to see themselves, as Theophrastus puts it, 'holding the mirror and the scourge for our own pettiness as well as our neighbours' (*TS* 1). *Impressions* sold because 'George Eliot' wrote it, but the experiment, from the point of view of critical reception and direct influence, was a failure. It is only with hindsight that we can see how extraordinarily much Eliot told us in her last book about her culture and about herself. NEH

Henry, Nancy, 'Ante-Anti-Semitism: George Eliot's *Impressions of Theophrastus Such*', in Ruth Robbins and Julian Wolfreys (edd.), *Victorian Identities* (1996).
—— 'George Eliot, George Henry Lewes, and Comparative Anatomy', in Rignall (1997).
Stange, Robert, 'The Voices of the Essayist', *Nineteenth-Century Fiction*, 35 (1980).

Felix Holt, but here and elsewhere industrialism is not of primary concern or interest.

Eliot's awareness of Britain's growing industrialism can be felt, however, in her deep political concerns (see POLITICS). *Felix Holt*, *Middlemarch*, and the *'Address to Working Men, by Felix Holt' variously reflect changing times brought about, in part, by manufacturing growth throughout the 19th century. Increased prosperity for many meant that more and more men were eligible to vote; and how to exercise the right to vote was of great concern to her. *Felix Holt* was written with at least one eye on the pending Second *Reform Act of 1867. When that Act added nearly a million extra voters to the electoral lists, Eliot wrote 'Address to Working Men, by Felix Holt' (1868) to reiterate what she saw were the obligations of the new, potential 'future masters': to respect the traditions she considered worth preserving. The 'Address' is aimed at a 'mixed assembly of workmen', namely 'artisans, and factory hands, and miners, and labourers of all sorts'. A reference to what Eliot considered the potential dangers of too much reform too soon is also heard in *Middlemarch* when Ladislaw and Mr Brooke discuss the implications of the reform movement led by industrial, not the landed, classes (*MM* 46). See also PROGRESS; TECHNOLOGY; URBANIZATION. AvdB

> Gallagher, Catherine, *The Industrial Reformation of English Fiction 1832–1867* (1985).
> Williams, Raymond, *The Country and the City* (1973).

influence of George Eliot on other writers.

The exact nature and extent of influence is always difficult to determine, but it is possible to identify the writers for whom George Eliot was important, and more detailed discussion of most of the figures mentioned here can be found under their individual entries. Thomas *Hardy claimed to consider Eliot more a thinker than a novelist, but when *Far from the Madding Crowd* began to appear anonymously in 1874 it was mistaken for her work, and her novels of provincial life certainly prepared the way for his, despite the distinctiveness of his vision. Henry *James engaged in an uneasy dialogue with her work throughout his career, from his reviews of her works as they appeared to the prefaces to the New York Edition of his novels in the first decade of the 20th century; and his *Portrait of a Lady* (1881) is clearly indebted to *Middlemarch* and *Daniel Deronda*. His fellow American novelist Edith *Wharton, in one of whose novels he discerned some 'George Eliotizing', was another admirer for whom *Deronda* was an important model. Emily *Dickinson famously pronounced on the glory of *Middlemarch* and responded to Eliot's life and fiction in her own poetry, while the American Jewish writer Emma *Lazarus, whose most famous lines are inscribed on the pedestal of the Statue of Liberty, found the example of her philo-Semitism inspiring. Contemporary English women writers, on the other hand, tended to find her example troubling and even demoralizing (Showalter 1977: 108). Margaret *Oliphant was inspired to write her autobiography by reading Cross's *Life* and wondered whether she was envious; and, as she was also a writer for William *Blackwood and Sons, she had to work in George Eliot's shadow, dropping the idea of a biography of Girolamo *Savonarola because it was too close to *Romola*. Eliza Lynn *Linton reacted with the bitterness of a less successful rival, criticizing in a spiteful memoir the superior

figure that George Eliot became. Mrs Humphry *Ward disclaimed any influence and, like Mary Elizabeth *Braddon, professed greater admiration for Charlotte *Brontë, but was dubbed the new George Eliot when her own novels appeared.

Although modernism was generally dismissive of high Victorian culture and George Eliot's *reputation was at a low ebb in the early decades of the 20th century, some of the greatest modernist novelists, such as Marcel *Proust and Virginia *Woolf, read her with insight and appreciation; and D. H. *Lawrence, another admirer, acknowledged her pioneering role as a psychological novelist who started putting all the action inside. For all three she was an important predecessor whose work left traces in their own. In the same period Katherine *Mansfield defended her against her detractors, while for another novelist of the same generation as Woolf and Lawrence, Ivy Compton-Burnett (1884–1969), she was a major formative influence. For the young Simone de *Beauvoir reading George Eliot was a decisive experience. More recently, following the revival of her reputation, a younger generation of women writers such as Margaret Drabble and Joyce Carol Oates have found in George Eliot's fiction a stimulus to their own (see Showalter 1980). JMR

> Bellringer (1993).
> Chase (1991).
> Showalter (1977).
> —— 'The Greening of Sister George', *Nineteenth-Century Fiction*, 35 (1980).

influence of other writers on George Eliot.

George Eliot's intellectual life and imaginative creations were nourished by a lifetime of extraordinarily wide and deep reading and rereading, and although it is possible to identify the writers who were most important in her development, it is necessary to be circumspect about claiming influence. She differs crucially from all the sources she drew upon, making them part of her own mental life rather than simply reproducing the views and attitudes of others. As she explained in a letter of 1849, the writers who had most profoundly influenced her, like Jean-Jacques *Rousseau and George *Sand, were not ones whose views she treated as gospel: 'It is possible that I may not embrace one of their opinions, that I may wish my life to be shaped quite differently from theirs' (*L* i. 277). The effect of reading Rousseau was thus to quicken her perceptions rather than teach her any beliefs. Hers was an intellect too powerful and original to be reduced to the sum of a determinate number of influences. The more important writers for whom some degree of influence may be, or has been, claimed are mentioned here, and their individual entries should be consulted for more detail.

Among earlier novelists Walter *Scott, the great favourite of her early years, was a formative influence in showing the possibility of a realist fiction that engages with a wide range of social life and the process of historical change. Samuel *Richardson was another important figure, and she may also have learned something from Henry *Fielding and Jane *Austen. She acknowledged the animating and bracing effect of reading Thomas *Carlyle (*Essays*, 213), and *Wordsworth's poetry was much loved and left its mark on her early work in particular, while a case can be made for the importance of *Byron, *Coleridge, and *Shelley. Among her contemporaries John *Ruskin was an inspiration with his insistence on the value of *realism in art, while Nathaniel *Hawthorne, whose work she admired, has also been cited as an influence, and the example of Elizabeth Barrett *Browning can be seen behind George Eliot's poem 'Armgart' (see POETRY). *Shakespeare's work she knew intimately and drew on deeply, while of the Greek tragedians *Sophocles was the one she claimed had most influenced her. Her knowledge of *languages meant that she was familiar with the work of the great European writers like *Dante, who was a great favourite, and *Cervantes, while *Goethe was a central figure in her creative life. Her reading of Heinrich *Heine, G. E. *Lessing, E. T. A. *Hoffmann, and Gottfried *Keller also left traces in her fiction. The biblical criticism of Charles Christian *Hennell and D. F. *Strauss helped shape her understanding of *myth and *religion, while the ethics of Baruch *Spinoza and the humanism of Ludwig *Feuerbach were crucial influences on her moral vision. How deeply she was indebted to Auguste *Comte has long been a matter of debate. Her friendship with Herbert *Spencer was intellectually important, and, of course, her partner G. H. *Lewes, whose encouragement was so central in her writing, played a crucial role in her intellectual as well as her emotional life. Her views were not identical with his, but constant contact with his lively mind and wide interests was a vital stimulus to her own development. The huge scope of her reading and the wide range of further possible influences can be seen from the many other writers who have entries in this volume. See also PHILOSOPHY.

JMR

'Influence of Rationalism, The', George Eliot's review of W. E. H. Lecky's *History of the Rise and Influence of the Spirit of Rationalism in Europe*, 2 vols. (1865), appeared in the first number of the *Fortnightly Review*, 15 May 1865 (repr. in *Essays*). A major element in the policy of the new

journal, of which G. H. *Lewes was editor, was that contributions should be signed, not anonymous: Eliot's brief notice of Owen Jones's 'The Grammar of Ornament', in the same issue of the *Fortnightly*, and *'Address to Working Men, by Felix Holt' (*Blackwood's Edinburgh Magazine*, January 1868), are the only other of her journal articles to be signed.

This and the *Blackwood's* piece are George Eliot's last periodical contributions: both represent her mature intellectual and moral position, with all the authority of her status as a novelist. They have in common a preoccupation with human irrationality: William Myers observes that at this time 'The gap between her humanist hopes and convictions and the actual conditions of life around her appears to have greatly depressed her' (109). Hence while Lecky is praised for his 'clever, fair-minded' work in preparing 'infusions of history and science' for the general reader (*Essays*, 398–9), he is criticized for his failure sometimes to make significant distinctions such as that 'between objective complexity and subjective confusion' (413). She concentrates her discussion on his chapters on the history of magic and witchcraft, and on persecution. She gives less attention to other sections of which she is more overtly critical, largely because she finds Lecky's definition of rationalism inadequate, and maintains that he has given too little attention to the development of physical science. Yet she is reluctant to concur in his dismissal of superstition, which may represent traditions that have affective value: 'Our sentiments may be called organised traditions; and a large part of our actions gather all their justification, all their attraction and aroma, from the memory of the life lived, of the actions done, before we were born' (409).

The review, with slight emendations and omitting the last paragraph (which criticized Lecky for his suggestion that the motivation to sacrifice self for an ideal has been compromised by the decline of religious belief, contrary to her own view that imaginative sympathy does not require the support and justification of any metaphysical system), was included in *Essays and Leaves from a Note-Book* (1884). MAH

Myers (1984).

intellectual history. See DARWINISM; PHILOSOPHY; SCIENCE.

irony is a central feature of George Eliot's fiction and its astringent presence challenges views of her as a solemn and ponderous moralist. More marked in the later novels, it disturbed some of the early reviewers of *Middlemarch*, who took exception to what one of them termed disagreeable sarcasms that were at odds with the broadly sympathetic treatment of life and character in her fiction (*CH* 289). The irony of the narrator's discourse often, indeed, seems designed to unsettle the reader into self-scrutiny: 'Let any lady who is hard on Mrs Cadwallader inquire into the comprehensiveness of her own beautiful views, and be quite sure that they afford accommodation for all the lives which have the honour to co-exist with hers' (*MM* 6). And a particular target of the narrator's irony is any complacent assumption of superiority the contemporary reader might harbour in relation to the past in which the action of the novel is set (see PROGRESS). Thus we are told that the period of *The Mill on the Floss* 'was a time when ignorance was much more comfortable than at present, and was received with all the honours in very good society, without being obliged to dress itself in an elaborate costume of knowledge' (*MF* 1.12). The apparent compliment to the present on its enlightenment turns into a jibe at its pretentious masquerade of learning. Eliot's prose is rich in such ironic shifts, which involve the reader in an active process of discrimination rather than unstrenuous consumption. The presentation of Dorothea in the opening chapters of *Middlemarch*, for instance, oscillates intriguingly between wryly critical distance and sympathetic approval:

A young lady of some birth and fortune, who knelt suddenly down on a brick floor by the side of a sick labourer and prayed fervidly as if she thought herself living in the time of the Apostles—who had strange whims of fasting like a Papist, and of sitting up at night to read old theological books! Such a wife might awaken you some fine morning with a new scheme for the application of her income which would interfere with political economy and the keeping of saddle-horses: a man would naturally think twice before he risked himself in such fellowship. (*MM* 1)

The ironic use of free indirect style here presents Dorothea through the eyes of a conventional Middlemarch man of means and, after registering the slightly absurd idealism of her behaviour, the passage starts to undermine that masculine perspective by exposing the banality of its material premisses and the timidity of its prejudices. The even-handed irony succeeds in placing both Dorothea's extremism and the narrow provincial outlook against which she is reacting. The critique of social convention conveyed here by indirection is expressed on other occasions by the more militant irony of the satirical shaft, like that aimed at Rosamond Vincy's schooling at Mrs Lemon's, 'where the teaching included all that was demanded in the accomplished female—even to extras, such as the getting in and out of a carriage' (*MM* 11). The range and variety of the ironic discourse in

Middlemarch help constitute that play of voices that recent post-structuralist criticism has drawn attention to in George Eliot's work (see CRITICISM, MODERN).

As well as verbal irony, her fiction also exploits the irony of circumstance, as alluded to in the narrative commentary on Lydgate's and Dorothea's initial reactions to each other: 'But any one watching keenly the stealthy convergence of human lots, sees a slow preparation of effects from one life on another, which tells like a calculated irony on the indifference or the frozen stare with which we look at our unintroduced neighbour' (*MM* 11). Thus the woman Lydgate does not at first warm to turns out to be his most fervent supporter at the crisis of his career. Such ironies are pervasive: in *Daniel Deronda* Gwendolen is at first impressed by Grandcourt's impassiveness, only to discover that it is the mark of a callousness which makes her marriage a miserable enslavement to his will.

Both verbal irony and the irony of circumstance contribute to the novels' power to question and unsettle, making them something other than the easily consumable fiction that Rosamond Vincy refers to when she claims that her brother's studies are not very deep because 'he is only reading a novel' (*MM* 11). Reading a novel by George Eliot involves exposure to this kind of self-conscious irony, which can strike at the conventional assumptions of character and reader alike.   JMR
Dentith (1986).
Wright (1991).

Italy and its culture were of particular significance to George Eliot in ways that she explicitly recognized in 'The Modern Hep! Hep! Hep!', the final chapter in her last published work, *Impressions of Theophrastus Such*. In the course of this essay, she dismisses stereotypes of Italy and Italians as she celebrates the cultural and political revival of the 19th century, which she sees as generated by commitment to 'a majestic past that wrought itself into a majestic future':

Half a century ago, what was Italy? An idling-place of dilettanteism or of itinerant motiveless wealth, a territory parcelled out for papal sustenance, dynastic convenience, and the profit of an alien Government. What were the Italians? No people, no voice in European counsels, no massive power in European affairs: a race thought of in English and French society as chiefly adapted to the operatic stage, or to serve as models for painters; disposed to smile gratefully at the reception of halfpence; and by the more historical remembered to be rather polite than truthful . . . Thanks chiefly to the divine gift of a memory which inspires the moments with a past, a present, and a future, and gives the sense of corporate existence that raises man above the otherwise more respectable and innocent brute, all that, or most of it, is changed. (*TS* 18)

It was her work on *Romola* in the early 1860s that brought such abstract ideas into focus, but her interest in Italy was of long standing. As Andrew Thompson argues, she 'kept returning to Italy and to its literature, both for renovation and for new inspiration' (1998: 5).

She began to learn Italian as early as 1840 (see LANGUAGES), requesting her friend Maria Lewis to buy her books on a visit to London 'that I might have something containing familiar Italian' (*L* i. 53); and kept up her reading in Italian throughout her life, especially during her research for *Romola*, and in her later years with the intensification of her devotion to *Dante. The extension of social and intellectual horizons consequent on her move to *London in 1851 heightened her appreciation of Italian culture, particularly the *visual arts, *music, and opera. Moreover, her career as a *journalist in the 1850s brought her into contact with Italian issues and personalities. In addition to writing on Italian topics herself, she commissioned the revolutionary Giuseppe *Mazzini to write on 'Europe: Its Condition and Prospects' for the *Westminster Review* of April 1852. This article expounded the principles of the *Risorgimento movement which George Eliot was otherwise encountering among her circle of acquaintance, G. H. Lewes not least. Her sympathies with Italy were reinforced as she became better informed about Italian politics. In general, she opposed tyranny and supported an ideal of national identity, but kept her distance from radical action (see NATIONALISM). So on 18 April 1864, she noted 'We went to the Crystal Palace to see Garibaldi', who was by then an almost legendary hero (*Journals*, 120); but in 1865 she explained at some length to Clementia *Taylor why she could not contribute to a fund in Mazzini's name, for fear that she would in fact be supporting conspiracy (*L* iv. 199–200).

George Eliot's first visit to Italy was brief, during her trip to Europe with the *Brays after her father's death in 1849, when they spent a week in Genoa before proceeding via Milan to Lake Como and Lake Maggiore and then over the Simplon Pass to Switzerland. Following her union with Lewes the desire to go again, for a more extended tour, was frequently expressed, almost as a goal to sustain her through hard times: she wrote to Cara Bray on 5 June 1857, 'we like our wandering life at present; it is fructifying and brings us material in many ways; but we keep in perspective the idea of a cottage among green fields and cows, where we mean to settle down (after we have once been to Italy) and buy pots and kettles and keep a dog' (*L*

ii. 339). This trip to Italy eventuated in 1860 as a reward for finishing *The Mill on the Floss* (Lewes too had just completed a book, *The Physiology of Common Life*). As she despatched the last sections of her novel, George Eliot was writing that she hoped to 'absorb some new life and gather fresh ideas' (*L* iii. 279) in Italy: on their return, she declared, 'We have had an unspeakably delightful journey—one of those journies that seem to divide one's life in two by the new ideas they suggest and the new veins of interest they open' (*L* iii. 311). She seems already to have had in mind the idea of writing an Italian novel, so that she 'at once caught . . . with enthusiasm' Lewes's suggestion, made in *Florence, that Girolamo *Savonarola's 'life and times afforded fine material for an historical romance' (*L* iii. 295). In addition to the major shift in her fiction represented by her turning away from pastoral English settings to 15th-century Florence, Eliot experienced changes to their domestic arrangements after their return to England. The financial success of *The Mill*, following that of *Adam Bede* the previous year (see EARNINGS; RECEPTION), made possible a less frugal lifestyle: and the acceptance that Marian Evans Lewes was 'George Eliot' enabled even so sensitive an author to live less obscurely.

Eliot and Lewes had travelled a good deal, both in the British Isles and on the Continent, since they set off together for *Weimar in 1854 (see TRAVELS). The three months of the Italian journey of 1860 was their first extended tour undertaken in relative affluence, though Lewes in particular continued mindful of expense. George Eliot wrote a full account of the trip in 'Recollections of Italy. 1860', which differs from her earlier travel journals in that it appears to have been written up on her return to England, rather than as they travelled. The account of Italy opens with a dramatic description of crossing the Alps, but subsequently her account of their own version of the Grand Tour concentrates less on the sublime and picturesque landscape, and more on artefacts like paintings, statues, and buildings. They went across Mont Cenis to Genoa, thence to *Rome, where they spent a month, and on to *Naples and as far as Sorrento, before returning to Naples to take the boat to Leghorn, and thence to Florence for a fortnight, and to Bologna and Padua en route to *Venice. Their homeward journey took them from Milan to the Italian lakes, then by the Splügen Pass across the Alps again to Switzerland. The journal does not display the avid concern of Eliot's letters about the fortunes of her newly published novel. From Florence she wrote eagerly to John *Blackwood, who had sent news of sales and reviews, 'now I am anxious to know whether Mudie has actually taken the 3d thousand' (*L* iii. 293).

Later in the same letter, she turns from Lewes's improving health to current affairs:

This news is naturally more important to us than the politics of Sicily, and so I am apt to write of it to our friends, rather than of Garibaldi and Tuscan filibusters; but things really look so threatening in the Neapolitan kingdom that we began to think ourselves fortunate in having got our visit done . . . we are selfishly careless about dynasties just now, caring more for the doings of Giotto and Brunelleschi, than for those of Count Cavour. (*L* iii. 294)

They had actually encountered Cavour in Turin, of which Eliot remarked that 'it is the centre of a widening life which may at last become the life of Resuscitated Italy', and described how 'we had a sight of the man whose name will always be connected with the story of that widening life—Count Cavour . . . A man pleasant to look upon; with a smile half kind half caustic; giving you altogether the impression that he thinks of "many matters", but thanks heaven and makes no boast of them' (*Journals*, 337).

In 1861 they made a briefer second visit, mainly to Florence, for work on *Romola*; and in 1864, on the spur of the moment they went to Venice with Frederic *Burton, specifically to study early Venetian art. Eliot and Lewes undertook a fourth journey in 1869, 'renewing old memories and recording new' (*Journals*, 135), because, as Lewes put it, 'Polly wants to see Arezzo and Perugia' (*L* viii. 445). On honeymoon with John Walter *Cross in 1880, George Eliot again went to Italy. Much of their itinerary took them to places where she had been with Lewes, who had a kind of presence en route: 'I had but one regret in seeing the sublime beauty of the Grande Chartreuse', she wrote to Charles Lewes. 'It was, that the Pater had not seen it' (*L* viii. 283). They proceeded over Mont Cenis (as in 1860) to Turin and thence to Milan for some days. Next, they went via Verona and Padua to Venice, where, on 16 June, Cross's apparent suicide attempt abruptly terminated their itinerary.

Though her journals and letters concentrate on Italian culture, at times George Eliot wryly weighed reminders of the frailties of the flesh against more intellectual and aesthetic considerations. Thus on 24 December 1879 she wrote to Elma *Stuart, then in Florence:

We were one spring at the Victoria Hotel on the Arno, so that I can imagine your view—just as I can imagine your beds and pillows. The pillows were the worse torture. They always produced a neck-ache, which remains a part of Italian travel for me along with glorious campanili and awful apses with Christ sitting in judgment. (*L* vii. 232)

George Eliot's engagement with Italy pervades her fiction from beginning to end. Caterina Sarti, in 'Mr Gilfil's Love-Story' (1857), is the orphaned daughter of an Italian singer brought up in England by childless Sir Christopher and Lady Cheverel. Her beautiful singing voice is part of the heritage of her Latin temperament, but so is her liability to ungovernable passion: both undesirable (female) tendencies that must be silenced by the English patriarchy. Andrew Thompson's account of this work is especially helpful in demonstrating its resonance for the 1850s Italian question. More complex connotations of 'Italy' develop in *Romola* and the novels following it. The prodigious erudition of *Romola* is directed towards establishing an analogy between present-day Europe and Savonarola's Florence. George Eliot proposes that the 19th century may be a turning point in Western civilization as momentous as that from medieval to Renaissance. Particular analogies emerge in questions about national identity and freedom from political coercion, appropriate forms of government, and the relation of Church and State.

Of all George Eliot's work, *Felix Holt, the Radical* most fully displays her immersion in Dante, in allusions to the *Divine Comedy*, especially, and in the Dantesque inflection of the theme of growth through suffering. Parts of the action of both *Middlemarch* and *Daniel Deronda* are set in Italy. The important sequence of the Casaubon honeymoon, and Dorothea's disorientation in Rome, draws in some measure on George Eliot's initial experience of Rome in 1860, but she is drawing also on Dante, especially *La vita nuova*, for an analogy between Dorothea and Beatrice. While the definition of 'provincial life' in *Middlemarch* proceeds against metropolitan and cosmopolitan contexts, *Daniel Deronda* has explicit international concerns. Again an Italian setting is used to present desolation in a marriage that culminates in the drowning of Grandcourt off Genoa. More pervasively, in the Jewish strand of the novel George Eliot mediates an alien culture and its nationalist aspirations for her English readership by sustained reference to Italian painting and music, as well as analogies with the Risorgimento. See also BROWNING, ELIZABETH BARRETT AND ROBERT; MEREDITH, GEORGE; STAËL, MME DE. MAH

Thompson (1998).

J

Jackson, Martha (Patty) (dates unknown), George Eliot's friend at the Misses Franklin's school in Coventry from 1832 to 1835. Afterwards they continued their self-education at home: they corresponded for several years, recommending and discussing books, Mary Ann's style mannered and moralizing but sometimes spirited. She encouraged her 'merry little Martha' to choose topics for their letters, adding, 'You will polish and sharpen me' (*L* i. 37, 48). In summer 1840 Martha's discovery of a floral dictionary, *The Language of Flowers*, inspired her to call herself Ivy (constancy) and her friend Clematis (mental beauty), an affectation that coloured their correspondence until December 1841. Martha, a devout evangelical, attributed her friend's apostasy to intellectual pride and Rosehill (see BRAY, CHARLES AND CAROLINE) influences but kept in touch against her mother's wishes. She wanted to know in 1859 if *her* Marian Evans had written *Adam Bede*. After her marriage to Henry Barclay, Marian's dentist, she emigrated to South Africa and later refused John Walter *Cross's request to include extracts from the friends' letters in his *Life* because he did not share her Christian beliefs. Regrettably, she never fulfilled her plan to publish the whole correspondence herself. Extracts appeared in *The Bookman*, 3 (1892–3) and *Poet-Lore*, 6 (1894), but the originals have been lost.   RMH

James, Henry (1843–1916), American novelist who reviewed George Eliot's work extensively and was indebted to it in some of his writing. When George Eliot and G. H. *Lewes eloped in 1854 to *Weimar to begin their life together, Henry James was an 11-year-old child. When James first called on them at their London home, The *Priory, in 1869, he was 26. As Gordon S. *Haight summarizes it, 'Amelia ushered into the drawing-room Miss Grace Norton and Miss Sara Sedgwick, introduc-

ing a stammering American youth named Henry James, who was about to experience his "unsurpassably prized admission to the presence of the great George Eliot" on whose work he had written three long articles' (1968: 416).

When James called on them again in April of 1878, nearly a decade later, she had just published *Daniel Deronda* (1876), the last of her novels; James was 35 and still to write most of his novels and all his important work. He had published *Roderick Hudson* (1876) and *The American* (1877); it would be another three years before *The Portrait of a Lady* (1881), a novel with substantial debts to George Eliot's last novel, and it would be another quarter of a century before his greatest novels, *The Wings of the Dove* (1902), *The Ambassadors* (1903), and *The Golden Bowl* (1904).

James and the Leweses did not meet often and his few personal contacts with the Leweses seemed usually to be unscheduled and to occur at moments of domestic tragedy in the Lewes household: moments furthermore which James tended to fictionalize with himself at the centre. The first meeting, described above by her biographer, took place on the day when Lewes's dying son, Thornie, arrived home for the last time (see LEWES FAMILY). The last took place ten years later on 1 November when Lewes was near death.

In the first instance James, who rushed away for the doctor and who entirely misunderstood the nature of Thornie's illness, came away with a sense of his importance in having aided a great author. In the second instance, he arrived unexpectedly in the company of the Leweses' nuisance neighbour, Mrs Greville, who had sent a copy of James's just-finished novel, *The Europeans*, and who arrived with James in tow at a time when neither Marian nor George was expecting him and when both were suffering from serious and, in Lewes's case, fatal illness. Thus preoccupied and not expecting their guests, the Leweses did not feel obliged to rustle up a tea and at the end of a short visit Lewes conveyed James's book back to its owner in such a way as to disappoint James of the praise he evidently expected. James seems to have departed full of his own annoyance, and without any sense of his hosts' own sorrow. Lewes died just over two weeks later.

James's report on an intermediate visit, paid to The Priory just months before his final visit, suggests the way in which his admiration for George Eliot was tempered with self-absorption:

The Leweses were very urbane and friendly, and I think that I shall have the right *dorénavant* [hereafter] to consider myself a Sunday *habitué*. The great G.E. herself is both sweet and superior, and has a delightful expression in her large, long, pale equine face. I had my turn at sitting beside her and being conversed with in a low, but most harmonious tone; and bating a tendency to *aborder* [broach] only the highest themes I have no fault to find with her. (*Letters of Henry James*, i. 61)

His expression suggests that he experienced some disappointment at not being able to find fault. Given the benefit he had from Eliot's and Lewes's hospitality and notice, and given the degree to which he borrowed from her work, James showed himself somewhat less appreciative than might have been expected in his reviews of her work and private comments in letters.

James regarded Eliot's novels as major, even 'glorious' achievements and similar in impetus to his own. There is no evidence to suggest that Eliot felt a similar affinity, although she did read his reviews and early novels, and did recognize their mutual interest in the degree to which events belong to psychic life, and not to a world of matter and motion of the kind suggested by earlier, more picaresque narrative traditions. For Eliot events always embody intention and motivation, and complex psychic preparations always constitute 'events' in ways too complex for the narrative strategies of 18th-century novels to handle. James goes still further along that path, in the sense that he consigns the reading consciousness more and more completely to the processes of language.

The differences between Eliot's writing and James's mark the uniqueness of each. What James consigns to language is not the collected consciousness of a community, but an *individual* consciousness, and one so focalized that it becomes the central condition of the book, even a problematically transparent condition. In doing this he pushes to the limit that consensus apparatus of realistic *narration*—the mechanism that produces an objectifiable order of things. Eliot, on the other hand, maintains the social interest and universality of the realist (historical) narrative conventions that she, like the rest of Europe, inherited from Sir Walter *Scott, and that she developed so profoundly (see REALISM). She provides above all a medium for social exchange and common cause. In James it is precisely these things that are the centres of strain and difficulty.

It is amusing, in hindsight, to read Henry James's thorough and yet, somehow, qualified praise of George Eliot. He reviewed *Middlemarch* as the finest example of the 'old-fashioned English novel' (Haight 1968: 444), something that seems especially strained considering Eliot's contribution to what was most forward looking in his own work. James's *The Portrait of a Lady* (1881)—the book that can be considered his turning-point novel, the one that showed him the way forward

towards his great later books—has often been considered a direct descendant of George Eliot's *Daniel Deronda*. Finally, and for a novelist with Henry James's flamboyantly digressive style, it seems positively perverse of him to characterize *Middlemarch* as 'a treasure-house of details' but 'an indifferent whole' (Haight 1968: 444).

The standards appropriate to appreciating James's novels were used retrospectively to misread George Eliot's achievement for over half of the 20th century, this thanks in part to the way in which the Jamesian critic Percy Lubbock universalized and disseminated the peculiar Jamesian narrative values contained in the unfortunate collection of prefaces to his novels which James wrote late in his career (see REPUTATION, CRITICAL). It was only after 1959 that this Jamesian influence began to be dispelled by criticism which explored the complex strategies of George Eliot's texts.

EDE

Letters of Henry James, ed. Percy Lubbock, 2 vols. (1920).
Ermarth, Elizabeth, 'The Example of Henry James', in *Realism and Consensus in the English Novel: Time, Space and Narrative*, 2nd edn. (1998).
Freadman, Richard, *Eliot, James and the Fictional Self* (1986).
Harvey (1961).

Jameson, Anna (1794–1860), writer, art critic, and feminist, whose *Winter Studies and Summer Rambles in Canada* (1838) George Eliot read in 1840, calling Jameson 'clever' and the book 'lively' but noting 'no fixed religious principles' (*L* i. 36). They met in 1852 through Bessie *Parkes, who introduced Eliot to Barbara *Bodichon at Jameson's home (*L* viii. 96). Eliot dined with Jameson in February 1854, but they never met again after Eliot's liaison with G. H. *Lewes. Jameson nevertheless praises Eliot as 'first-rate in point of intellect and science' although considered 'very free in all her opinions as to morals and religion' (*L* ii. 231). Eliot believed Jameson to have heart and soul (*L* ii. 341) and discovered in her art criticism inspiration for the St Ogg legend in *The Mill on the Floss* (1.12), calling her 'my private hagiographer' (Wiesenfarth 1977: 106). She took copious notes from Jameson's *Sacred and Legendary Art* (1848) while writing *Romola*, and invoked Jameson's description of St Barbara to describe Dorothea in *Middlemarch* (*Writer's Notebook*, ed. Wiesenfarth, 186). JJ

George Eliot: A Writer's Notebook 1854–1879 and Uncollected Writings, ed. Joseph Wiesenfarth (1981).
Johnston, Judith, *Anna Jameson: Victorian, Feminist, Woman of Letters* (1997).
Wiesenfarth (1977).

'Janet's Repentance'. See SCENES OF CLERICAL LIFE.

Jewsbury, Geraldine (1812–80), a prominent woman of letters who was particularly influential as a regular and prolific reviewer for the *Athenaeum* where she reviewed George Eliot's *Adam Bede*, and as reader of fiction for Bentley's publishing house. Jewsbury was the daughter of a Manchester cotton merchant and the younger sister of Maria Jane Jewsbury, who became a local celebrity for her poetry and fiction; Maria's *Letters to the Young* (1828) were based on letters written to Geraldine at school. Following Maria's marriage, Jewsbury kept house for her father and brother while embarking upon her own literary career as a novelist and journalist. Like George Eliot, Jewsbury was profoundly impressed as a young woman by the work of Thomas *Carlyle, and her correspondence with Carlyle led to a lifelong friendship with his wife, Jane Welsh *Carlyle. Jane Carlyle's delight in *Adam Bede* as a beautiful and human book was endorsed in Geraldine Jewsbury's review of the novel in the *Athenaeum* in 1859 where she praised it as a novel of the highest class (Holstrom and Lerner, 21).

Jewsbury's letters to Jane Welsh Carlyle are perhaps her most lasting literary legacy: passionate and self-mocking, moving across the whole spectrum of women's domestic, emotional and intellectual experience, the letters are informed by a strong sense of the two friends as 'indications of a development of womanhood which as yet is not recognised' (Ireland, 348). Jewsbury's novels are propelled by a similar concern with the frustrations and dilemmas of strong women pushing against Victorian orthodoxy and in this respect they have some affinity with George Eliot's work (see WOMAN QUESTION). Her first novel *Zoe: The History of Two Lives* (1845), which depicts a love affair between a married woman and a Roman Catholic priest, created something of a literary scandal and established Jewsbury's reputation as a proponent of 'George-Sandism' (see SAND, GEORGE). Jewsbury's second and most successful novel *The Half-Sisters* (1848) reworks the plot of Mme de *Staël's *Corinne*, tracing the fortunes of Bianca, the exuberant half-Italian 'woman of genius', and Alice, her docile and domesticated English half-sister.

George Eliot praised *The Half-Sisters* in her *Westminster Review* essay on Jewsbury's *Constance Herbert* (1855), which she found disappointing by comparison. In this essay Eliot meditates on questions close to her heart—duty, *renunciation, and the representation of morality in fiction—and she sees *Constance Herbert* as a misrepresentation of the nature of moral action, oversimplifying 'this tangled wilderness of life' and giving us instead 'a plan as easy to trace as that of a Dutch garden' (*Essays*, 135). Constance's renunciation of marriage because of the family history of insanity proves to be a lucky escape, since the object of her renunciation turns out to be worthless. It is the conflation of moral impulse and prudent calculation which disturbs Eliot: 'duty looks stern, but all the while has her hand full of sugar-plums, with which she will reward us by and by' (121).   GF

Selections from the Letters of Geraldine Endsor Jewsbury to Jane Welsh Carlyle, ed. Mrs Alexander Ireland (1892).

Clarke, Norma, *Ambitious Heights: Writing, Friendship, Love—The Jewsbury Sisters, Felicia Hemans, and Jane Welsh Carlyle* (1990).

Holmstrom and Lerner (1966).

Howe, Susanne, *Geraldine Jewsbury: Her Life and Errors* (1935).

Joachim, Joseph (1831–1907), Hungarian violinist. At 18 *Liszt's leading violin at *Weimar, he publicly abandoned the 'New Music' in 1860. In Berlin in 1869 he founded the renowned Joachim Quartet. His playing was greatly appreciated by George Eliot who, with G. H. *Lewes, heard him often in London where he became a member of their social circle. George Eliot commemorates his playing in her poem 'Stradivarius'. See also MUSIC; VIOLIN.   BG

Johnson, Samuel (1709–84), English author, critic, lexicographer, and talker; an early influence on George Eliot's *style, probably via her mentor Maria *Lewis. She quotes from him often, as for instance where she says of her incapacity for worldly enjoyment, 'I find, as Dr Johnson said respecting his wine, total abstinence much easier than moderation' (*L* i. 6). She mocks her own style later with regard to the overuse of 'I do', a phrase which Johnson described as 'a vitious mode of speech'. In June 1840 she told Maria Lewis about her visit to Lichfield where she saw the monument erected to Johnson in the market place. Her review of Brougham in the *Leader* (7 July 1855) contains a parody of a famous line from Johnson's *The Vanity of Human Wishes* (1749) which becomes 'To blunt a moral and to spoil a tale'. The essay on Heinrich *Heine in the *Westminster Review* (January 1856) recounts Johnson's advice to Hannah More (according to Mrs Piozzi) 'to consider what her flattery was worth before she choked him with it'. There are a number of references to *The Lives of the Poets* in the essay on Edward *Young in the *Westminster Review* (January 1857).

That Eliot read him with warmth throughout her life there is no doubt, and certainly she was stimulated by G. H. *Lewes, who once described Dempster as 'Dr Johnson turned rascal' (*L* ii. 351), parodied a favourite line of them both from *The Vanity of Human Wishes* ('Survey mankind from Pimlico to Kew', *L* iii. 349), and of course encouraged Alexander *Main to retell Johnson's Life, asserting, 'Mrs Lewes and I both hope that you will find this an agreeable and profitable piece of work' (*L* v. 397). Her article for the *Pall Mall Gazette* of 7 March 1865 contains a reference to Johnson's disproving Bishop Berkeley's theory of the non-existence of matter by kicking a stone.

Eliot and Lewes reread part of *The Lives of the English Poets* in 1872, Eliot feeling 'a delicious renewal of girlish impressions' (*L* v. 238). *Rasselas* is a constant point of reference: she expresses her delight in it to John *Blackwood, telling him it was 'one of my best-loved companions' in childhood (*L* vi. 123). It is mentioned in *Scenes of Clerical Life*, *The Mill on the Floss*, and *Middlemarch*, the latter also having Mr Brooke's misidentification of the second line of *The Vanity of Human Wishes* as 'The Rambler, you know' (*MM* 51). Chapter 61 has its epigraph from *Rasselas*. It is mentioned too in *Impressions of Theophrastus Such*, which also has a reference to Johnson observing that Isaac Newton could have done anything because he was a genius (*TS* 8). Three months before his death Lewes reports to Alexander Macmillan that Leslie Stephen's monograph on *Johnson* in the 'English Men of Letters' series 'gave her great pleasure' (*L* vii. 65).   GRH

journalist, George Eliot as. George Eliot was in some measure engaged with the world of Victorian journalism throughout her working life, though her most intense involvement was during her first career as an editor, critic, and translator in the 1850s. Her work as a journalist centred on the *Westminster Review*, and fell into two phases. During the first, from 1851 to 1854, she was the unpaid and unacknowledged editor of the *Westminster* (John *Chapman nominally held the position and provided her with board and lodging); during the second, which began with her elopement to Germany with G. H. Lewes in 1854 and ran to the beginning of her career in fiction in 1857, she produced a host of reviews and a set of major *essays, which include some of her most important theoretical pronouncements and document significant aspects of her intellectual development. Though she had an annuity under her father's will, she now needed to supplement it by her *earnings as a journalist, and wrote for her living.

Even before she embarked on her career as a journalist, George Eliot's work had appeared in various periodicals. Her first publication was a poem, 'Farewell', in the *Christian Observer* for January 1840; and during 1846 and 1847 some reviews, and her first original prose publications, *'Poetry and Prose from the Notebook of an Eccentric', appeared in the *Coventry *Herald and Observer*, owned and edited by her mentor Charles

*Bray (despite the title, the five sketches include no poetry). Later, she reviewed J. A. *Froude's novel *The Nemesis of Faith*, also for the Coventry paper (March 1849). Bray's connections enabled him to provide further encouragement of her literary ambitions, through introductions in October 1850 to John Chapman, then a publisher, and R. W. Mackay, whose *The Progress of the Intellect* he had just published, when they visited Rosehill. As a consequence, George Eliot was commissioned to review Mackay's book for the *Westminster Review* (January 1851). Chapman's negotiations to buy this important quarterly were completed by September 1851, by which time George Eliot, after a false start early in the year, had been established as a resident of Chapman's house at 142 Strand, and in effect as editor of the *Westminster Review*. She wrote to Chapman: 'With regard to the secret of the Editorship, it will perhaps be the best plan for you to state, that for the present *you* are to be regarded as the responsible person, but that you employ an Editor in whose literary and general ability you confide' (*L* viii. 23).

The Prospectus for the new regime, largely written by her, set out to effect a revival of the great radical tradition of the *Westminster*'s founding editors, Jeremy Bentham and James Mill. The *Westminster* is conceived 'as an instrument for the development and guidance of earnest thought on Politics, Social Philosophy, Religion, and General Literature' (*Selected Essays*, ed. Byatt and Warren, 4), committed to 'the deliberate advocacy of organic changes' but not flinching from printing contributions that diverge from the beliefs of the management. The Prospectus appeared in the issue for January 1852, the first for which she was responsible, which also included her review of Thomas *Carlyle's *Life of John Sterling* at the beginning of the 'Contemporary Literature of England' section. Subsequently she appears to have been so fully occupied by the constant negotiations required in commissioning articles, editing submissions, and coaxing contributors, and by her translation of Ludwig *Feuerbach's *Das Wesen des Christenthums*, that she did not write for the journal herself. In her editorial capacity, she was doing work for which she was well fitted by virtue of her years of study, her formidable intellect, and her business-like habits. She was at the centre of London's intellectual and cultural activity, and met such leading figures as Charles *Dickens, Herbert *Spencer, T. H. *Huxley, Richard *Owen, Wilkie *Collins, Francis Newman, Giuseppe *Mazzini, John Stuart *Mill, W. R. Greg, and W. E. Forster. Not all this new acquaintance was male: George Eliot was introduced to *Eliza Lynn (later *Linton) and Harriet *Martineau, for instance, and to two women who were to become her close friends,

Bessie *Parkes and Barbara Leigh Smith *Bodichon. Constantly benchmarking the *Westminster* against other journals, she developed an astute sense of topical issues, and of the niceties of aligning writers with subjects. That she was an asset to the enterprise was quickly recognized by the phrenologist George *Combe, who wrote to John Chapman on 7 December 1851: 'I would again very respectfully recommend to you to use Miss Evans's tact and judgment as an aid to your own' (*L* viii. 33).

She grumbled intermittently, declaring herself 'bothered to death with article-reading and scrapwork of all sorts' (*L* ii. 31). While she was able to assert, rightly, that 'the Review would be a great deal worse if I were not here' (*L* ii. 88), her frustration with Chapman's methods intensified to the point at which she could complain in a particular matter, 'If I were sole editor of the Westminster, I would take the responsibility on myself, . . . but being a woman and something less than half an editor, I do not see how the step you propose could be taken' (25 November 1853, *L* viii. 90). By this time she was committed to Lewes, and had moved from 142 Strand to lodgings in Cambridge Street. Her resignation from the *Westminster Review* came with her departure for *Germany with Lewes in July 1854, just as the Feuerbach translation was published. Once she was no longer editor, Chapman quickly enlisted her as a contributor, and almost immediately on arrival in Weimar she began the first of her full-scale essays, *'Woman in France: Madame de Sablé' (October 1854). This piece lacks the pungency of its successors, but it may express some personal concerns they do not: 'Heaven forbid that we should enter on a defence of French morals, most of all in relation to marriage! But it is undeniable, that unions formed in the maturity of thought and feeling, and grounded only on inherent fitness and mutual attraction, tended to bring women into more intelligent sympathy with men' (*Essays*, 56).

Through 1855 and 1856, she published a steady stream of essays and reviews (all of course anonymous, her productivity assisted by the contemporary practice of generous quotation from the work being discussed), mainly in the *Westminster Review* and the weekly *Leader*. Her first contribution to the *Leader*, of which Lewes had been a founder, was a review of W. R. Greg's *The Creed of Christendom* (20 September 1851), which was succeeded by thirty or so more in 1855–6. She also had two essays based on her German experiences in *Fraser's Magazine* in June and July 1855, and four reviews in the new weekly *Saturday Review* in the period from April to September 1856. Her reviewing involved considerable labour. As well as one-off reviews, she was solely responsible for the

'Belles Lettres' section in the *Westminster Review* for seven issues from July 1855 to January 1857. This section often ran to twenty pages in length, including at least one substantial review and sometimes shorter notices of twenty-odd further titles. Her range embraced history, art history and criticism, and works dealing with classical literature and English literature of earlier periods. The emphasis though was on contemporary poetry and fiction in English (including the *Brownings, *Tennyson, Charles *Reade—and also work by American authors notably Harriet Beecher *Stowe). Sometimes she economized by reviewing the same book in both the *Leader* and the *Westminster Review*, though of course in different terms: Charles *Kingsley's *Westward Ho!* is a case in point (*Leader*, 19 May 1855; *Westminster Review*, July 1855). She was not exclusively Anglophone, and wrote on other European literatures (sometimes in translation), especially *German literature: she produced notable pieces on *Goethe, and above all Heinrich *Heine. The major review essay, *'German Wit: Heinrich Heine' (*Westminster Review*, January 1856), reinforced the effect of her earlier pieces in making him known in England.

This essay is evidence of her intellectual range and influence. Her calibre is seen in a different register in *'Evangelical Teaching: Dr Cumming' (*Westminster Review*, October 1855), where she is in full flight against the *evangelicalism of her youth. And in a set of essays produced in the spring and summer of 1856, she articulated her principles of artistic creation. Her review of Ruskin's *Modern Painters*, iii (*Westminster Review*, April 1856) includes significant comments on *realism in art, but it is her article on Riehl, 'The Natural *History of German Life' (*Westminster Review*, July 1856), that most fully sets out the basis of her own artistic practice. Her reflections on the moral dimensions of *art, on *society, *history, and *language in this essay are complemented in lighter vein by *'Silly Novels by Lady Novelists' (*Westminster Review*, October 1856), which tartly fulfils her suggestion to John Chapman: 'I think an article on "Silly Women's Novels" might be made the vehicle of some wholesome truth as well as of some amusement' (*L* ii. 258).

George Eliot's career as journalist gave way to her career as a *novelist in January 1857, when her last 'Belles Lettres' and 'Worldliness and Other-Worldliness: The Poet Young' both appeared in the *Westminster Review* as *Scenes of Clerical Life* began serialization in *Blackwood's Edinburgh Magazine*. The essay re-evaluates an earlier favourite in the light of her mature ideas about what literature should be: she now maintains that Young offends against truth of feeling, and while her denunciation is vigorous, it displays also a salutary wit.

From this time, she contributed to journals infrequently, despite various solicitations. In 1858 she declined Bessie Parkes's invitation to write for the *English Woman's Journal*. As her reputation as a novelist developed, especially after the publication of *Adam Bede*, there were more approaches from journal editors: she resisted both Dickens, wooing her for *All the Year Round,* and Samuel Lucas, the editor of *Once a Week*, though later she famously succumbed to George *Smith's offer to serialize *Romola* in the *Cornhill Magazine*.

Some of her poems (see POETRY) were first published in journals, but most of George Eliot's periodical contributions after 1857 were in effect favours for journals with which Lewes was associated. To the *Pall Mall Gazette*, for which he was an adviser from 1865 to 1868, she contributed 'A *Word for the Germans', *'Servants' Logic', 'Futile Falsehoods', and 'Modern Housekeeping' (March–May 1865). He took on the editorship of the *Fortnightly Review* in 1865, and its first number, which came out on 15 May, carried two contributions from George Eliot, both signed, in accordance with *Fortnightly* principles: 'The *Influence of Rationalism', a substantial review of W. E. H. Lecky's *History of the Rise and Influence of the Spirit of Rationalism in Europe*, and 'The Grammar of Ornament', a shorter review of a new edition of the book of that name by their friend Owen Jones, who had redecorated The *Priory.

Her last major essay was written at the request of John *Blackwood, who after hearing Disraeli speak on the Reform Bill in Edinburgh in October 1867, wrote ingratiatingly, 'It strikes me that you could do a first rate address to the Working Men on their new responsibilities' (*L* iv. 395). She eventually obliged with *'Address to Working Men, by Felix Holt' (*Blackwood's*, January 1868), slipping easily into the congenial persona of the hero of her most recent novel to give full rein to her 'conservative rather than destructive' bent (*L* iv. 472). Blackwood, complimenting her, described it as 'noble', adding 'I wish the poor fellows were capable of appreciating it' (*L* iv. 402).

Throughout her life George Eliot continued to read current journals with attention, especially the quarterlies. She frequently recommended articles to friends and offered occasional evaluative remarks. In February 1879, still grieving intensely for Lewes, she noted in her diary: 'Headache still. Mr. John Cross came. Head worse, sending me to bed, and obliging me to lie still. Read J. S. Mill on Socialism [Mill's essays in the *Fortnightly*]' (*Journals*, 164, 168); and she was reading the *Cornhill* not long before her death. See also ESSAYS. MAH

George Eliot: Selected Critical Writings, ed. Rosemary Ashton (1992).
George Eliot: Selected Essays, Poems and Other Writings, ed. A. S. Byatt and Nicholas Warren (1990).

journals of George Eliot. George Eliot kept a journal at least from 1849 to within days of her death, a discontinuous narrative recorded in six notebooks. Five of these are in the Beinecke Rare Book and Manuscript Library, Yale University (diaries covering 1854–61, 1861–77, and 1880, and travel journals for tours in *Germany in 1858 and *Italy in 1860, and for Italy in 1864 and Normandy and Brittany in 1865); the sixth, her diary for 1879, is in the Berg Collection, New York Public Library. This narrative, though it covers such a long time-span, including the whole of her creative life, 'is not the sample of an even web' (*MM* Finale). Some of the daily entries are quite brief, a few words or a single sentence, but generally at least a few lines and often a couple of paragraphs. In addition, there are longer, more formal compositions for which she favoured the Wordsworthian title 'Recollections', mostly of travels abroad and at home.

There are some gaps in the sequence of journals. A journal dealing with the travels in *Spain undertaken by George Eliot and G. H. *Lewes in 1866–7 appears to have been dispersed; and her diary for 1878 is missing. Moreover, the portion of the diary covering 1849 to mid-1854 has been excised: Haight conjectures that while George Eliot may have removed these pages herself, more likely John Walter *Cross was responsible (*L*, vol. i, p. xv). In any case, this intervention means that the extant journals open dramatically on the scene aboard the cross-Channel ferry on which Marian Evans and George Henry Lewes embarked on their lives together on 20 July 1854:

I said a last farewell to Cambridge street this morning and found myself on board the Ravensbourne, bound for Antwerp about ½ an hour earlier than a sensible person would have been aboard, and in consequence I had 20 minutes of terrible fear lest something should have delayed G. But before long I saw his welcome face looking for me over the porter's shoulder and all was well. (*Journals*, 14)

There is a dramatic quality also in the last, unfinished entry in the 1880 diary (4 December 1880, *Journals*, 214):

J. to city in morning. Home to lunch.
Went to our first Pop. Concert and heard Norman Neruda, Piatti etc. Miss Zimmermann playing the piano. After

It is notable that the 1854–61 book, including both diary entries and longer essays, contains almost half the total of her extant journals. After the publication of *Adam Bede*, and particularly after *Romola*, the diary contracts markedly: there is an important way in which through the middle 1850s, when Marian Evans was a working *journalist, producing reviews and articles for her living, it was to her journal that she turned to do her own writing. At the end which opens on the deck of the *Ravensbourne*, this diary contains daily entries of varying lengths. At the other end are essays, most of which write up diary entries: so 'Recollections of Weimar 1854' is a version of the diary from 20 July to 3 November 1854 (see WEIMAR), and there are similar parallels between the diary and the 'Recollections' of *Berlin, *Ilfracombe, and Scilly and Jersey. These 'Recollections' include the only sections of the journals published in George Eliot's lifetime, two articles which appeared in *Fraser's Magazine* ('Three Months in Weimar' in June and *'Liszt, Wagner and Weimar' in July 1855—she revised these essays further for *Essays and Leaves from a Note-book* (1884): see *Essays*, 82–95 and 96–122) and, curiously, several paragraphs of 'Recollections of Ilfracombe, 1856' that appear also in Lewes's *Sea-Side Studies* (*Journals*, 261).

The remaining section of the 1854–61 diary is called 'The Making of George Eliot' by Harris and Johnston: it opens with her account of *'How I came to write Fiction', finished in early December 1857, and continues through memoranda recording sales and reception of the first publication using her *pseudonym, the two volumes of *Scenes of Clerical Life*, which came out in January 1858. Then comes 'History of "Adam Bede"', followed by notes on the fortunes of this novel on publication in February 1859. Here the activities of the writing self, 'George Eliot', are separated from the everyday activities of the woman who was otherwise calling herself Mrs Lewes. As the secret of the identity of 'George Eliot' was breached, the separation was not so carefully maintained when 'by mistake' she used the wrong end of the book.

While 'The Making of George Eliot' illuminates an aspect of George Eliot's anxiety of authorship, it also highlights the extent to which these journals chart the growth of the novelist. While her writing is one among the various matters noted in the diary, it is the dominant consideration, especially when she turned to fiction—as is nowhere more fully seen than in the agonized charting of the conception and production of *Romola*, the most complete account of the writing of one of her novels offered by the journals. In the reflective summaries which often conclude a year—that for 1870 is characteristic—it is notable that she accounts both for her 'private lot' and her writing life:

Here is the last day of 1870. I have written only 100 pages—good printed pages—of a story which I began about the opening of November, and at present mean to call 'Miss Brooke'. Poetry halts just now.
In my private lot I am unspeakably happy, loving and beloved. But I am doing little for others. (*Journals*, 142)

When Eliot farewells the 1854–61 and the 1861–77 diaries, both of which she thriftily used till they were full, it is striking that her writing life is the focus of her elegiac words. In the former, success as a writer is equated with 'some good purpose' (*Journals*, 90) in her life, and in the latter she is conscious of waning powers: 'Many conceptions of works to be carried out present themselves, but confidence in my own fitness to complete them worthily is all the more wanting because it is reasonable to argue that I must have already done my best' (*Journals*, 148).

None the less, the journals give the fullest documentation of George Eliot's private life there is—though for all that they are as close as she came to autobiography, they are not in any conventional sense confessional or revelatory. Always the thoroughly professional writer, even in these private writings George Eliot is addressing an audience, usually implied, at one point whimsically characterized: 'The chat was agreeable enough, but the sight of the gliding ships darkening against the dying sunlight made me feel chat rather importunate. I think, when I give a white bait dinner I will invite no one but my second self, and we will agree not to talk audibly' (*Journals*, 90). With some frequency, she turned to her journals for reassurance: for instance, concerned about her progress with *Daniel Deronda*, 'I see on looking back this morning—Christmas Day [1875]—that I really was in worse health and suffered equal depression about *Romola*—and so far as I have recorded, the same thing seems to be true of *Middlemarch*' (*Journals*, 145).

The narrative developed by the journals is of a woman deeply devoted to her partner, unsparing of herself in her ambition as a writer; liable to self-doubt yet with a capacity for fun; deeply curious and alive to sense impressions; and with considerable practical skills. The development of her mind is plotted, as she imbibes ideas about literature and language, art and architecture, science and religion. Her intellectual energies are formidable; her physical strength more sporadic. Many of the journals recount *travels, at home and abroad, while the daily routine of the Leweses is also chronicled: reading, writing, walks. After 1860, when they moved to central *London, visits paid and received become more frequent, and there are more excursions to *theatre, opera, concerts, and galleries (see MUSIC; VISUAL ARTS). By this time, the stigma of the common law union was in significant measure offset by the success of 'George Eliot'. Sometimes the narrative of George Eliot's journals can be extended by reference to her letters and working *notebooks, and to Lewes's journals and letters. Since Lewes was more consistent in his 'journalising' (his word) than his consort, some details of their activities, such as the guest list at a particular dinner, are more fully recorded by him.

The extent to which George Eliot's 'private lot' was entwined with Lewes's is evident from the outset of the journals. Every aspect of their lives was shared, not only family responsibilities and concern for each other's health, but intellectual and professional activities as well. At Ilfracombe in 1856 Eliot was an enthusiastic participant in the research which resulted in Lewes's *Sea-Side Studies* (1858): she relates, 'We had a glorious hunt this afternoon on the rocks and found two specimens of the Anthea Cereus and a red and blue spotted anemone—treasures to us' (*Journals*, 60). Likewise Lewes helped in her work, not only by taking on the role of her manager and agent, but by providing research assistance especially during the preparation of *Romola*, thus reciprocating the work on translations she did for his study of *Goethe.

Often, the journals record George Eliot's current reading, a good deal of it preparation for her own writing. Sometimes, they show her testing her field observations against booklearning, most famously in her initial disappointment with *Rome in 1860, 'Not one iota had I seen that corresponded with my preconceptions' (*Journals*, 341)—a disappointment she was to share with Dorothea Casaubon in *Middlemarch* in one of the few instances where journal material is obviously transposed into the fiction. Soon, George Eliot effected a reconciliation of her studies of art and of life: she described St Peter's, 'the supreme wonder', commenting that

some of the monuments are worth looking at more than once, the chief glory of that kind being Canova's lions. I was pleased one day to watch a group of poor people looking with an admiration that had a half childish terror in it at the sleeping lion, and with a sort of daring air, thrusting their fingers against the teeth of the waking mane-bearer. (*Journals*, 344)

This passage was singled out for censure by Lord Acton in his review of Cross's *Life* in *Nineteenth Century* in March 1885 (17: 464–85): 'She surveys the grand array of tombs in St Peter's, and remarks nothing but some peasants feeling the teeth of Canova's lion'. Other readers are more likely to savour the imaginative precision of this and com-

parable vignettes—take the rhapsodic account of Nuremberg in 1858:

How often I had thought I should like to see Nürnberg [Nuremberg], and had pictured to myself narrow streets with quaint dark gables! The reality was not at all like my picture, but it was ten times better. No sombre colouring, except the old churches: all was bright and varied, each façade having a different colour—delicate green, or buff, or pink, or lilac— every now and then set off by the neighbourhood of a rich reddish brown. And the roofs always gave warmth of colour with their bright red or rich purple tiles. Every house differed from its neighbour, and had a physiognomy of its own, though a beautiful family likeness ran through them all, as if the burghers of that old city were of one heart and one soul, loving the same delightful outlines and cherishing the same daily habits of simple ease and enjoyment in their balcony windows when the day's work was done. (*Journals*, 306)

After Lewes's death, George Eliot's consciousness of mortality was ever present: her journal for 1879 opens with an anthology of morbid verse, and on the anniversary of his death, she mournfully noted, 'I read his letters and packed them together, to be buried with me. Perhaps that will happen before next November' (*Journals*, 187). She had ample opportunity to make a comparable disposition of her own personal writings. Yet John Cross was charged, at least tacitly, with the task of writing her life story; and the journals survived to assist in his endeavours.

Material from the journals was first published by Cross in *George Eliot's Life*. His selections were heavily edited and sometimes intercalated with letters. Gordon S. Haight demonstrated the shortcomings of Cross's scholarship in his great edition of *The George Eliot Letters*, and included fuller and more accurate texts of some sections in the body of his edition, as well as brief quotations in his explanatory notes. He incorporated further journal material into his 1968 biography. However, it was not until *The Journals of George Eliot*, edited by Margaret Harris and Judith Johnston (1998), that the complete text of the journals was published, in a form which represented George Eliot's arrangement of them.   MAH and JJ

The Journals of George Eliot, ed. Margaret Harris and Judith Johnston (1998).

Jowett, Benjamin (1817–93), English classical scholar, theologian, and educationist, elected Master of Balliol College, *Oxford, in 1870. George Eliot met him there in that year. They became friends and after that she and G. H. *Lewes paid him weekend visits in the 1870s. He was at the supper party which celebrated the publication of the first book of *Middlemarch* (30 November 1871), at Weybridge with the *Cross family on New Year's Day 1871, and sent Eliot a present of game from the friends he was staying with in August 1872. He congratulated her on the outstanding nature of *Middlemarch*, suggesting that it provided discussion and friendship everywhere, and urged her to rest after her intellectual labours. His letters reflect his admiration for her: 'she has the cleverest head I have ever known, and is the gentlest, kindest, and best of women' (quoted in Abbott and Campbell, *Benjamin Jowett*, 2 vols. (1897), 3rd edn., i. 144). He said that she 'wanted to have an ethical system founded upon altruism'.

He stressed her feminine qualities always, and was among those who called on her a year after Lewes's death. In November 1879 Eliot was reading his *Thucydides*. That their friendship was deep, trusting, and mutual there is no doubt. He wrote to her on 30 December 1879 urging her to continue to write, telling her that she must not abandon what was a precious trust: after her decision to marry John Walter Cross he told her, 'You know that you are a very celebrated person' and that therefore she must expect people to talk about what she has done, adding wisely, 'but they will not talk long and what they say does not much signify. It would be foolish to give up actual affection for the sake of what people say' (*L* vii. 289). Again he urges her to continue to write.

Jowett never married. In his life he was surrounded by controversy, just as Eliot was. He represented for some years the symbol of liberal thought in the Church of England, rejecting the beliefs in eternal punishment and urging the use of critical reason in biblical studies. After 1860 he ceased to write on religious topics. In 1871 he produced his great edition of Plato and continued to be recognized for the strength and integrity of his personality and his outstanding qualities as a teacher. This meant an elevation of Balliol and extensive influence outside Oxford. His private charities, some only recently known, were extensive on behalf of poor families: he found in Eliot's writings a creed he could accept and extend, and she found in his intellect and genuine sympathy the kind of support which she most valued.

GRH

Judaism. George Eliot's preoccupation with Judaism has its origins in her childhood when she was subject to daily Bible readings and hymns. Her early teachers, Maria *Lewis and Rebecca and Mary Franklin, were baptist evangelicals who placed a strong emphasis upon readings in the Old Testament, the biblical history of the Jews and the prophecies relating to their dispersion and return. At Eliot's home, John *Bunyan's *The Pilgrim's*

Progress, Defoe's *The Political History of the Devil*—the eleventh chapter of which has a lengthy disquisition on biblical Jewish history—and Jeremy *Taylor's *Holy Living and Holy Dying*, were among the few books allowed.

At the age of 19 in August 1839 she made her first visit to *London. Instead of going with her brother to the theatre, she 'spent all her evenings alone reading . . . the chief thing she wanted to buy was Josephus' "History of the Jews"' (Cross, i. 39). The move to Foleshill in March 1841 further strengthened her interest in Judaism. Her neighbours, the wealthy Unitarians Charles and Caroline *Bray, Sara *Hennell, and the family of the independent minister John *Sibree, were aware of the latest developments in comparative religion and investigations into the historical origins of the Scriptures. The kind of ideas to which she was introduced are found in Charles Christian *Hennell's *An Inquiry concerning the Origin of Christianity* (1838) which she read in 1841. Hennell summarized rabbinical interpretations of the fifty-third chapter of Isaiah: Christian commentators perceived this chapter as heralding the coming of Jesus, the Messiah. Through Hennell's work Eliot was introduced to the ideas of the great Talmudic and post-Talmudic rabbinic thinkers: David Kimchi, Aben Ezra, Rabbi Jochanan ben Eliezer, and Maimonides; and to the Talmud, the Mishna, the Gemara, and the Zohar. In other words, to mystical and non-mystical Jewish writings.

During the Foleshill period Eliot and her friends began reading and translating the German Higher Criticism of the Bible with its questioning of biblical events and its reinterpretation of them as representing symbolic and mythological truths. She read and translated D. F. *Strauss's *The Life of Jesus*, Ludwig *Feuerbach's *The Essence of Christianity*, and Baruch *Spinoza's *Tractatus Politicus* and his *Ethics*. In 1848, when reading Benjamin *Disraeli's *Tancred*, she reacted with revulsion to its 'assumption of superiority in the Jews' (*L* i. 246). By the time she reached London in the early 1850s she knew much biblical history and interpretation, and was familiar with rabbinic ideas. She knew less about contemporary Jewish life. Her relationship with the philo-Semitic G. H. *Lewes, and their 1854 German visit, marked a turning point in her knowledge of Judaism. Lewes admired the freethinking radical Spinoza, and chose for his first major theatrical part to play Shylock. During the 1854 visit she met prominent Jews. Her 'heart swelled' and 'tears came' to her eyes during a performance of G. E. *Lessing's *Nathan der Weise* (Cross, i. 363–4). She met members of fashionable salon circles, read Heinrich *Heine, and met his friends. Heine had a profound impact upon her. She read his autobiographical confessions, *Geständnisse*. On her return home she wrote four essays about him. A Heine epigram—'Judea always seemed to me like a piece of the Occident lost in the Orient'—haunted her and found its way nearly two decades later into her notebooks. Eliot drew upon Heine three times for chapter epigraphs in *Daniel Deronda* (34, 62, 63). She read in his poem 'Prinzessin Sabbath' of the significance of the Sabbath for Judaism. She encountered the medieval poet and mystic Rabbi Jehuda Halevi in Heine's poem in his 'Hebräische Melodien' found in his *Romanzero*.

During her July 1858 trip with Lewes to *Prague they visited the Synagogue and the old Jewish burial ground (*L* ii. 469). She utilized the visit in the Prague passage in 'The Lifted Veil'. She met a Moldavian Jew in *Munich who told her about his mission of national redemption for his people. On subsequent trips with Lewes to the Continent she visited synagogues, Jewish areas of cities, and met assimilated and non-assimilated, religious and non-religious Jews. During an August 1866 visit to Amsterdam they 'looked about for the very Portuguese Synagogue where Spinoza was nearly assassinated as he came from worship. But it no longer exists. There are no less than three Portuguese Synagogues now—very large and handsome. And in the evening we went to see the worship there' (*L* iv. 298). Seven years later whilst in Frankfurt they 'stayed 5 days in order that we might attend service at the Synagogue (for Mutter's purposes)'. Lewes 'bought books—books on *Jewish subjects* for Polly's novel' (*L* v. 425).

Eliot's interest in and knowledge of Judaism gained in strength through personal friendships with Jewish intellectuals. She and Lewes met James Joseph Sylvester (1814–97), the distinguished mathematician debarred from taking his *Cambridge degree until the Test Acts were passed in 1872. She was close to the Talmud scholar and writer on Jewish subjects Emanuel *Deutsch who gave her Hebrew lessons. She read his work, heard his lectures, corresponded with him, knew his personal problems and his desire to travel to the Holy Land where Jewish agricultural settlements had begun to develop.

Eliot's notebooks from the 1860s onwards reveal lists of books on Jewish subjects and notes from them. Diary and journal entries, and items in her and Lewes's libraries, provide evidence of her extensive readings in Judaica. She read works in English, German, French, and Italian recommended to her by Deutsch, including extensive articles on Judaica, the 19th-century historians of Jewry, Zunz, Geiger, Steinschneider, and especially the eleven volumes of Heinrich Graetz, *Geschichte der Juden* (Leipzig, 1863–75) as they were published. She took notes from Charles Christian David Ginsburg's *The Kabbalah, its Doctrines, Development and Literature* (1863), and read Jehuda Halevi's mystic work *The Kusari* in Cassell's 1853 German version.

Elements of a fossilized frozen Judaism appear through the frenetic vision of Latimer in the early short story 'The Lifted Veil'. There are references in *Felix Holt, the Radical* to Jewish assimilation in the English Midlands: 'Hebrew names "ran" in the best Saxon families; the Bible accounted for them; and no one among the uplands and hedgerows of that district was suspected of having an Oriental origin unless he carried a pedlar's jewel box' (*FH* 20). The most sustained creative transformations of Judaism appear in *The Spanish Gypsy* and in *Daniel Deronda*. Eliot's poem is set in Andalusian Spain just before the 1492 expulsion of the Jews. In the poem, the young King Don Silva confides his secrets to his Jewish teacher: 'Kings of Spain | Like me have found their refuge in a Jew | and trusted in his counsel' (*SG* 196). The teacher Salomo Sephardo refuses to become a Catholic convert, and is a practising Jew dressed 'In skullcap bordered close with crisp grey curls' (*SG* 177). In her poem Eliot reveals her awareness of the social, political, and religious dilemmas faced by ethnic and religious minorities.

In *Gypsy* Eliot uses the writings of Rabbi Abraham Aben-Ezra (*c*.1092–*c*.1167), who questioned the authenticity of biblical revelations. The perception of a distinct national or ethnic group to which an individual must be associated runs as a crucial link through Eliot's writings. In *Gypsy*, Sephardo rejects Aben-Ezra's scepticism and affirms memory and tradition—the two elements which play a key role in Eliot's most sustained exploration of Jews and Judaism, *Daniel Deronda*. The novel's narration, characterization, and dialogical discourse are saturated with Judaism, Jews, and Jewish ideology. Its visionary, Mordecai, praises the ideas of 'a spiritual store' from his 'Masters' (*DD* 42), the great rabbinic tradition embodied in Hillel, Ben Azai, Chananja, Halevi, the Spanish Hebrew-Arabic poets, and others. He refers to other elements in Judaism, to a practical leader such as Moses and to the prophet Ezra. Mordecai's arguments for the restoration of Israel are not only based upon divine revelations and promises, but upon practical feasibility and the ideology of a national consciousness (see COLONIALISM; NATIONALISM).

Eliot's readings in the Kabbalah and in Jehuda Halevi, as well as the *Bible, the Midrash (the reworking of biblical stories and themes), and 19th-century Jewish historians, experience creative transformation in *Deronda*. Her plot depends upon secrets and their eventual revelation. Daniel Deronda and Mordecai are interpreters of dreams and visions. Gwendolen seeks out Daniel's assistance to interpret her dreams and disturbed visions. On the river, Daniel encounters Mirah, whom he saves, and her brother Mordecai. The meeting between Daniel and Mordecai is placed within a topography of revelation and allusion. Deronda looks up and sees Mordecai's face 'brought out by the western light into startling distinctness and brilliancy—an illuminated type of bodily emaciation and spiritual eagerness' (*DD* 40). Mordecai believes in the mystical doctrine of the transmigration of souls. He tells Daniel, 'You will take up my life where it was broken. . . . I shall live in you.' Mordecai is yearning for a 'second soul . . . to help out the insufficient first—who would be a blooming human life' (*DD* 43). This has its Kabbalistic counterparts in doctrines of the banishment of the soul, its exile to strange forms of existence, and the possibility of the soul's return from exile through the special relationship between souls.

Many diverse complicated strands of Judaism are found in *Deronda*, including the 19th-century historical plight of the Jew, and Jewish attempts to assimilate into the wider society in which they live. Deronda's mother attempts to throw off what she regards as the entrapping shackles of her inheritance. The musician Klesmer marries into the English aristocracy. At the end of the novel Deronda and Mirah set off for Jerusalem to restore in some way the ancestral Jewish homeland. These concerns are also found in an essay written after *Deronda*, 'The Modern Hep! Hep! Hep!', published in *Impressions of Theophrastus Such*, where Eliot draws upon Jewish history and the situation of the Jew in contemporary society (*TS* 18). Her interests echo those in her novel: moral concerns about English culture; sympathy for the oppressed; the necessity to preserve culture and tradition.

Eliot's absorption in Judaism may be attributed to three factors: her evangelical upbringing; her knowledge of German Higher Criticism of the Bible; personal friendships. Her treatment of Jews and Judaism has been controversial, creating partisan responses. These are found for instance in two contemporary reactions: Henry James's hostile 'Daniel Deronda: A Conversation', *Atlantic Review*, 38 (1877) and Rabbi David Kaufmann's defence of the novel and its ideas in his *George Eliot and Judaism* (1877). More than a century later much critical ink was spilt on the question of whether Daniel Deronda was circumcised or not. Some critics have perceived an over-indulgent idealism in Eliot's portrait of Jews and Judaism in her novel. Critics have found the Jewish plotting too utopian, and others have found Eliot too sympathetic to the Jews, so that they become spokespersons for a cause rather than complex characters. The Jewish elements of the novel and Daniel and Mirah's journey to Jerusalem, have been related to colonial and gender hierarchies (see CRITICISM, MODERN: POST-COLONIAL APPROACHES and GENDER STUDIES). There is little doubt that Eliot's use of Judaism in *Deronda* is complex and many features still remain to be elucidated and understood. Eliot's *Deronda*, and her creative transformation of Judaism, are a litmus test for subsequent criticism, and reader responses. These reveal readers' own perceptions of Jews and Judaism—a product of the social, political, economic climate in which they live. See also CHRISTIANITY; RACE; RELIGION.   WB

Some George Eliot Notebooks, ed. William Baker (4 vols., 1976–85).
Anderson, Amanda, 'George Eliot and the Jewish Question', *Yale Journal of Criticism*, 10 (1997).
Baker (1975).

Kant, Immanuel (1724–1804), German Philosopher. There is evidence that George Eliot had first-hand knowledge of his works (*L* iv. 328). Her most detailed commentaries on Kant from the point of view of the English empirical tradition and of the German philosopher Gruppe (who claimed that Kant's 'abstract notions' originate in concrete, sensuous experience) are to be found in 'The *Future of German Philosophy' (1855; repr. in *Essays*). Her article 'A *Word for the Germans' (1865) characteristically deconstructs English stereotypes concerning German idealism: 'The recipe for understanding *Kant* is first to get brains capable of following his argument, and next to master his terminology. Observing this recipe, the *Critique of Pure Reason* is not indeed easy reading, but it is not in the least cloudy. It is not fit for the club table' (*Essays*, 387–8).

Eliot does not confuse, as was usual then, the categories *transzendent* (beyond experience) and *transzendental*. The word *transzendental* refers to those categories of the mind such as space, time, and causality which, according to Kant, are the preconditions of any experience. Eliot, however, believes that a priori forms are not timeless but the product of evolutionary processes and therefore ultimately relative. In this sense Eliot's early aim was 'to reconcile the philosophy of Locke and Kant' (Dodd 1990: 97). After all Kant also believed that there was no knowledge without experience. Eliot shares with Kant the belief in meliorism (see PROGRESS) and the conviction that the realization of morality is strictly subject to the law of causality. An obvious reference to Kant's *Critique of Pure Reason* can be found in the following sentence taken from the story 'The Sad Fortunes of the Reverend Amos Barton': 'for in bucolic society five-and-twenty years ago, . . . "something to drink" was as necessary a "condition of thought" as Time and Space.' See also PHILOSOPHY.　　　HUS

Dodd (1990).

Keats, John (1795–1821). There are passing mentions of the poet by George Eliot, the first in a letter to Sara *Hennell (18 April 1849), when she quotes virtually the last six lines of 'On First Looking into Chapman's Homer' as defining her own enthusiastic reaction to J. A. *Froude's *The Nemesis of Faith* (1849). In August 1854 in *Weimar Eliot read Keats aloud to G. H. *Lewes as they picnicked on a delightful August day. Twenty-five years later she writes to John *Blackwood asking if her forthcoming edition of *The Legend of Jubal, and Other Poems* (1874) could be in the form of the 'delightful duodecimo edition of Keats's poems (without the *Endymion*) published during his life' (*L* vi. 26), a reference to the first edition of *Lamia, Isabella, The Eve of St Agnes, and Other Poems* (1820) owned

by herself and Lewes, though later she regretted having advocated it 'as a model' (*L* vi. 57). Eliot's continuing interest is shown by her reading aloud in June 1877 the *Life, Letters, and Literary Remains of John Keats* (1848), Richard Monckton *Milnes's important contribution to early Keats' studies. In 1860 (*L* iii. 288) she had mentioned 'Poor Keats's tombstone, with that despairing bitter inscription' ('Here lies one whose name was writ in water'). Writing to his son Charles in 1861 Lewes quotes, 'A thing of beauty is a joy for ever', the opening line of *Endymion*, and also writes to Elma Stuart (*L* vi. 293) mentioning his autograph letter of Shelley to Keats (July 1820), the former generous in its praise of his dying contemporary. Lydgate calls Rosamond his basil plant in the Finale of *Middlemarch*, a composite Keats–Boccaccio reference. Gwendolen's 'sort of Lamia beauty' is in the first chapter of *Daniel Deronda*, while the motto to chapter 43 has lines 1–5 of Keats's sonnet 'On Seeing the Elgin Marbles' (1817). See also ROMANTICISM.

　　　　　　　　　　　　　　　　　　　GRH

Pace, Timothy, 'Who killed Gwendolen Harleth? *Daniel Deronda* and Keats's "Lamia"', *Journal Of English and Germanic Philology*, 87 (1988).

Keller, Gottfried (1819–90), Swiss-German novelist and poet whose fiction has some affinities with George Eliot's, which have led to discussions of him as a possible influence. Like her he rejected the Christian faith and was influenced by Ludwig *Feuerbach, whose lectures he attended in Heidelberg. He was living in *Berlin when she spent the winter of 1854–5 there with G. H. *Lewes, and they both knew Karl August *Varnhagen von Ense and frequented the same salons, although there is no record of them ever having met. In July 1858 in *Dresden she read the first volume of his collection of stories, *Die Leute von Seldwyla* (1856), to assist Lewes in the preparation of his article on

'Realism in Art: Modern German Fiction', which was published in the *Westminster Review* in October 1858. The story, or *Novelle*, that bears the closest relationship to her own work is *Romeo und Julia auf dem Dorfe* (*A Village Romeo and Juliet*), whose theme she had anticipated in her 1856 essay on 'The *Natural History of German Life' when discussing the historical feuds between villages on the Rhine (*Essays*, 271). The story has parallels with *The Mill on the Floss*: the hero and heroine, offspring of peasant neighbours engaged in a bitter dispute over land, run away together by climbing on to a hay-barge making its way down the river, and, after a night of love, commit suicide together by drowning. There are other more detailed similarities of action and motif (McCobb 1979–80: 189–208), although the epic breadth of Eliot's novel is very different from the economy and compactness of Keller's *Novelle*, and his frank representation of sexual rapture, which Lewes objected to in his *Westminster* article, has no counterpart in *The Mill*. Keller's realism in *Die Leute von Seldwyla* leans towards satire and the grotesque in exposing the kind of rigidities of bourgeois behaviour that characterize the Dodsons and Tullivers in *The Mill*, whereas Eliot's criticisms are leavened by *sympathy. There are grounds for seeing the atypical 'Brother Jacob', which has been described as an experiment in the *Novelle* form, as closer to the mode of Keller's fiction (Diedrick, 461–8). JMR

Diedrick, James, 'George Eliot's Experiments in Fiction: "Brother Jacob" and the German Novelle', *Studies in Short Fiction*, 22 (1985).

Klieneberger, H. R., 'Gottfried Keller and George Eliot', *New German Studies*, 5 (1977).

McCobb, E. A., 'Keller's Influence on *The Mill on the Floss*: A Reassessment', *German Life and Letters*, 33 (1979–80).

Kempis, Thomas à (1379–1471), German Augustinian monk, religious writer, and mystic, named from his birthplace, Kempen. His real name was Hammerlein or Hammerken, and he is thought to be the author of *De Imitatione Christi* (*Of The Imitation of Christ*). In February 1849 (*L* i. 278) George Eliot wrote to Sara *Hennell that she had obtained a 'delightful' copy, adding, 'One breathes a cool air as of cloisters in the book—it makes one long to be a saint for a few months. Verily its piety has its foundations in the depth of the divine human-soul'. Eliot gave this copy to Sara two years later (she may even have loaned it to John *Chapman, who enters an extract into his diary), but undoubtedly translated from it for the epiphany in *The Mill on the Floss* (4.3), though later she recommended the Challoner translation (1706) to her friend Mrs Richard Congreve since it 'is as good as any you are likely to get among cur-

rent editions' (*L* iii. 440). She reread *De Imitatione Christi* in November 1859. Eliot's translation in *The Mill* is warm with self-identification, recognition, and sympathy: though the experience is Maggie's, the narrative voice is tremulous with felt associations, and the omniscience which begins with 'I suppose' suggests the sustenance which Eliot received from *De Imitatione Christi* throughout her life: 'And so it remains to all time a lasting record of human needs and human consolations'. See also CHRISTIANITY. GRH

Kingsley, Charles (1819–75), English author whose particular attitudes and much of his practice irritated George Eliot, evidenced by her review of his *Westward Ho!* (1855) in the *Westminster Review* (July 1855; repr. in *Essays*) and her article in the *Leader* (May 1855). Her irritation pre-dates these. She read his *Phaeton: Or, Loose Thoughts for Loose Thinkers* (1852) and longed to cut it up because it was so provoking (*L* ii. 66), later admitting that Kingsley 'riled' her. Yet she responded to his descriptions, writing to Sara *Hennell from Dover that the hills beyond looked 'as Kingsley says, like the soft limbs of mother Hertha lying down to rest'. But before she wrote about him she told John *Chapman that she hoped to get Kingsley's books when they arrived in *Berlin, 'without which an article on him might be like themselves, more imaginative than solid' (*L* viii. 116).

The review of *Westward Ho!* underlines her views on Kingsley as writer, and she apportions praise and criticism with discriminating clarity. Kingsley the man is poet, scholar, social reformer, familiar with country life, but the writer produces stereotypic situations. He over-preaches instead of letting the reader appreciate what is presented, and operates in extremes of goodness and badness, praise and dislike: his fierce antagonisms undermine the effects of his works. Moreover 'he sees, feels, and paints vividly, but he theorizes illogically and moralizes absurdly'. In *Westward Ho!* she finds 'all the writer's faults and merits in full blow'. Amyas Leigh would be more loveable if he were less exemplary, Kingsley's superb scene painting is balanced by his 'low gifts as a philosophizer', he divides the sheep and the goats too easily, but 'our dominant feeling towards his works is that of high admiration'.

That was to be qualified, one suspects, because of G. H. *Lewes's over-awareness of Kingsley's commercial success. She had a presentation copy of *Adam Bede* sent to Kingsley (John *Blackwood was extremely annoyed that a reviewer of the book considered Eliot a Kingsley follower), and towards the end of 1862 Kingsley was among those men who, like Lewes, as she told Sara Hennell, cared 'to know and speak the truth as well as they can'. They were bent on forming a club for men of science but the idea fell through. Later she became exasperated by Kingsley's dispute with John Henry *Newman, referring to his 'mixture of arrogance, coarse impertinence and unscrupulousness with real intellectual *in*competence' (*L* iv. 158–9). The result was her complete identification with Newman's reply, *Apologia pro Vita Sua*, in 1864.   GRH

L

landscape in George Eliot's fiction is typically the landscape of the English Midlands, described at length in the Introduction to *Felix Holt, the Radical* as the stagecoach traverses it, and more succinctly in *Middlemarch* when Fred and Rosamond Vincy ride to Stone Court through 'a pretty bit of midland landscape, almost all meadows and pastures, with hedgerows still allowed to grow in bushy beauty and spread out coral fruit for the birds' (*MM* 12). However picturesque this scene may appear, with 'the great oak shadowing a bare place in mid-pasture ... the huddled roofs and ricks of the homestead ... the grey gate and fences against the depths of the bordering wood', landscape is never simply decorative but always bears a meaning in relation to individual and social life. In Eliot's last work, *Impressions of Theophrastus Such*, the figure of Theophrastus looks back nostalgically on the Midland plains that were the scene of his, and his creator's, early years and points out how this familiar landscape bears the imprint of human activity, how 'some sign of world-wide change, some new direction of human labour has wrought itself into what one may call the speech of the landscape—in contrast with those grander and vaster regions of the earth which keep an indifferent aspect in the presence of men's toil and devices' (*TS* 2). The observation throws light on the function of landscape in Eliot's fiction, where it is always eloquent of some human significance. The contrasting landscapes of Rhine and Rhône in *The Mill on the Floss* speak of two different views of human *history (*MF* 4.1); the landscape Dorothea looks out on at Lowick when she returns from her honeymoon, with 'the long avenue of limes lifting their trunks from a white earth, and spreading white branches against the dun and motionless sky' (*MM* 28), speaks of her desolation of spirit; later in that novel the picturesque scene of Freeman's End, whose chimneys are choked with ivy

and about whose worm-eaten shutters the jasmine boughs grow in wild luxuriance, is eloquent testimony to Mr Brooke's negligence as a landlord (*MM* 39).

The Midland landscape in the Introduction to *Felix Holt* is polyphonic, speaking both of rural prosperity and rural poverty, of nature's beauty and human energy as the vista alternates between the slow-moving life of the countryside and the busy world of advancing *industrialism. The coach journey here passes rapidly from one phase of English life to another, while in *Adam Bede* two distinct kinds of life are epitomized by the contrasting landscapes of Stonyshire, with its bare hills and cotton-mills, and Loamshire with its rich, undulating agricultural land. When Adam, Dinah, and Seth discuss their preferred landscapes (*AB* 11), Dinah's preference for the bleak hills where life is hard reveals her puritan temperament and fund of compassion for the poor and suffering. But later in that novel the narrator's reflections on the crucifix set amidst a smiling foreign landscape stress the way that landscape may conceal as well as reveal, and that the pleasing prospect may hide a heart beating in anguish, as it does when Hetty Sorrel makes her journey in despair through the benign countryside of the English Midlands. Such a landscape may bear the imprint of human activity but, as Hetty's experience indicates, nature itself remains entirely indifferent to human emotion and human endeavour. See also NATURAL WORLD.   JMR

Rignall, John, 'History and the Speech of the Landscape in Eliot's Depiction of Midlands Life', *George Eliot–George Henry Lewes Studies*, 24–5 (1993).
Witemeyer (1979).

language in the work of George Eliot involves a number of related issues: for example, language as a system of communication, as a means of understanding the self and world, and as literary *style. Linguistically Eliot was very gifted. She was able to use at least seven languages (see LANGUAGES, GEORGE ELIOT'S KNOWLEDGE OF), read several literatures in the original, and translated D. F. *Strauss and Ludwig *Feuerbach from German (see TRANSLATIONS BY GEORGE ELIOT). As late as the early 1870s, she was learning Hebrew when doing research for *Daniel Deronda*. The language of her fictional works is characterized by a variety of dialects, accents, and registers and she had, according to John Walter *Cross, a most impressive sensitivity to language and its rhythms (Cross, iii. 420). Yet she was more than just a practical linguist: she read and made notes from a significant number of books on language, including Friedrich Max *Müller's 'great and delightful' *Lectures on the Science of Language* (*L* iv. 8), Ernest *Renan's

Histoire générale et système comparé des langues sémitiques, and Archibald Henry Sayce's *Introduction to the Science of Language.* She was able to develop her own theoretical views on language and on the related problems of interpretation, and contributed significantly to the mid-19th-century debate on language and *society. Her literary style became the very medium through which she consciously explored the dynamic nature and creative potential of language. As a novelist and thinker, she benefited from the unique view of the world opened up by her inward understanding of language, an understanding as much artistically mediated as philosophically grounded.

She was particularly interested in the historical dimension of language. In this she was influenced by 19th-century evolutionary theories of language and society. Yet her views come much closer to the conception as exemplified in thinkers such as Giambattista *Vico, Herder, and Humboldt, which is also shared by her contemporary countryman R. C. Trench in his *On the Study of Words* (1851). Unlike the evolutionists or propounders of the divine origin of human language, these thinkers held that language, precisely because it is a human and social institution, constitutes the unique site of human history and thus validates the possibility of moral knowledge and truth. Like Herder and Trench, Eliot sees a whole living world of tradition and *history dwelling in a language and emphasizes what she calls 'the subtle ramifications of historical language' (*Essays,* 288) and its continuing shaping power. She is most outspoken about this in her 1856 review essay 'The *Natural History of German Life'.

Such a position also explains why Eliot does not believe in any scheme of 'universal language'. For all her interest in comparative philology, she differs on this point from philologists such as Müller who conceive of the study of language as a synchronic science of permanent and universal properties. She finds that 'a universal language on a rational basis' has 'no uncertainty, no whims of idiom, no cumbrous forms, no fitful shimmer of many-hued significance, no hoary archaisms "familiar with forgotten years"' and will 'never express *life,* which is a great deal more than science' (*Essays,* 287–8). She is therefore deeply committed to presenting English rural life faithfully and convincingly by not giving in to the expectation of her 'genteel' middle-class urban readers (see READERSHIP). In her novels, she often consciously highlights local characteristics of speech forms against the norm of an assumed standardized language. In *Adam Bede, Silas Marner,* and *Middlemarch,* the varied colourfulness of the characters emerges from their wide range of colloquialisms and regionalisms, best suited to their positions and occasions (Mrs Poyser, Dolly Winthrop, Mr Brooke). 'She prefers to make her characters speak for themselves', as one contemporary reviewer of *The Mill on the Floss* aptly observed (*CH* 133). Parting with 'the anomalies and inconveniences of historical language', argues Eliot, 'you will have parted with its music and its passion, with its vital qualities as an expression of individual character' (*Essays,* 288). In *Romola,* such vital qualities are brought into focus through her use of Italian, which helps to revivify the dynamics of 15th-century Florentine town life and make its otherness audibly and tangibly dramatic and accessible.

Eliot is interested in language as a principle of survival and transformation, and in how language develops concurrently with social formation. The vocabulary of natural phenomena in *Bede,* for example, embodies communal ways of life as 'incarnate history'. The syntactical movements in her characters' speeches tend to reveal how the rhythmic patterns of their mental and psychological development are affected by social interactions. In this, Eliot comes close to the American philologist W. D. Whitney, who in his *Language and the Study of Language* (1868) sees language as the repository of the collective mind and community as ultimately responsible for changes in language. She constantly explores the capacity of words for acquiring new meanings by infusing into her fictional language a vocabulary from contemporary scientific discoveries and theories (see SCIENCE). She is particularly good at pushing beyond the normal senses of words by choosing those that are in common circulation but have increasingly acquired new scientific overtones. The common senses of words such as 'web', 'tree', or 'environment' are compounded with the Darwinian connotations of affinity or random transformation or the evolutionary senses of organic growth (see DARWINISM). For her, language remains a sustained historical development precisely because of its capacity for renewal.

Eliot's conception of the intellectual and affective functions of language has a direct bearing on her literary style. Her fictional language is for the most part analytical, poised, and as subtle as it is ironic. She is, however, often taken to task by critics for the didactic if not pedantic tone of her *narration, characterized by an abundant use of antitheses, clauses, and, according to W. J. Harvey, the 'Jamesian labyrinth of convoluted qualification' (1961: 208). Nevertheless, this 'grand' style 'burdened' with intellectual concerns is more than what it seems to be. In such concerns, as in those of her time, 'emotion and intellect are not kept apart but most completely imply each other' (Beer 1983: 150). She wrote at a time when scientific thinking or, for that matter, scientific language was not pitted against literary imagination. It is in this context that we may best understand why instead of subsuming everyday language into a language of history and moral philosophy, she often manages to recover historical and moral significances from modes of speech and language indigenous and organic to given cultural moments. The word 'radical', for instance, which at the time of the First Reform Bill referred primarily to the extreme section of the Liberal party, is used in *Felix Holt, the Radical* to mean 'going to the root' (*OED*) of the moral problems which defined the nature of electoral reform of the time. For the same reason, she likes to use 'slight' and concrete words as they are 'part of the soul's language' (*AB* 50) and mix them with synonyms of different registers, a practice which often results in the colloquial unexpectedly elevated into the formal. For the narrator to describe the profile of Gwendolen's 'neck' as the curve of her 'cervical vertebrae' projects her subconscious animality on to an aesthetic observation (*DD* 7). Eliot has a remarkable ability to revive, by means of words, aural, visual, and other sensory experiences; her sharp insight into the relations between the verbal and the sensual also helps to expand her range of *metaphors. Our moral stupidity may, as she famously puts it, prevent us from appreciating the beauty of 'ordinary human life' which becomes the 'roar' that 'lies on the other side of silence' (*MM* 20). The double nature of her perspective is also apparent in her frequent use of free indirect speech, which merges the point of view of the characters with that of the narrator, speech with meditation, and description with comments, so that both the private and the public, the moment and history, are addressed.

Her understanding of the evolutionary nature of language may be attributed to some of the most powerful intellectual influences on her such as Feuerbach, Auguste *Comte, Charles *Darwin, G. H. *Lewes, and Herbert *Spencer. Like them, she is concerned with the individual's relation to the social whole. Yet she equally recognizes the importance of the individual's expression of desires and his or her transformation of social and collective values. Language is to her not just the product but also the agent of social and historical formation. This view is sustained by her belief in the inherently ambiguous nature of language and its implications for interpretation. She is interested in the creative function of both the speaker and the listener and in the use of pun and wordplay. In *Romola*, the Florentine barber Nello knows well that 'we poor mortals can pack two or three meanings into one sentence' and 'it is not the less true that every revelation, whether by visions, dreams, portents, or the written word, has many

meanings, which it is given to the illuminated only to unfold' (*RO* 1). The narrator in *Middlemarch* again aptly reminds us, 'to all fine expression there goes somewhere an originating activity, if it be only that of an interpreter' (*MM* 16). Such an emphasis on interpretation, however, does not mean that for Eliot language cannot serve as a medium through which meaning and value may be ascertained. In her view, the inherent workings of ambiguities in language constitute the very process through which moral truth can be arrived at. Her adroit handling, as in *Middlemarch*, of the circulation of views, assumptions, and misreadings intimates the charting out of such an intricate route to the validation of moral meaning.

Her awareness of the creative potential of language is deeply rooted in her sophisticated understanding of the political nature of language. In dialects, for example, reside the gravity and weight of communal authority and the possibility of recovering the voice of ordinary people who are central to English rural life (see REALISM). Her radical speculations on the sedimented ethical and moral meanings in language also throw into relief how the hierarchical class status of her characters may be distinguished, as in *Felix Holt*, by different speech registers. Eliot's women can be remarkably direct in expression as they command rather than negotiate their own familiar circles. Mrs Cadwallader's 'prospective taunts' may force Mr Brooke to think twice before he speaks, as '[it] was of no use', the narrator concludes, 'protesting against Mrs Cadwallader's way of putting things' (*MM* 6). Eliot's other women characters such as Rosamond Vincy often betray a preoccupation with linguistic propriety symptomatic of social snobbery. In *Deronda*, there is a clear awareness that, when English becomes the mother tongue of Jewish characters, it adds an extra dimension to the issue of the revival of Jewish national consciousness (see JUDAISM).

Eliot is particularly sensitive to the workings of dominant ideas and doctrines as embedded in language. She finds that people are 'in bondage to terms and conceptions' representing forms of thinking that supported and defended 'the passions and the interests of dominant classes' in the past (*Essays*, 28–9). These forms of thinking will 'perpetually' resist any enlightened critique of existing values and conventions (*Essays*, 28). There is therefore the constant need for a process of critique and rectification in the social interchange of speech: 'A single word is sometimes enough to give an entirely new mould to our thoughts' (*L* i. 30). She consciously draws upon political and biblical discourses to explore the implications of contemporary debates (see BIBLE). In *Felix Holt*, entrenched memories such as are embodied in the 'sectarian phraseology' (*FH* 5) of the Dissenting community call for a corrective of amnesia to make its tradition more balanced. The failure of reform in that novel, on the other hand, can be taken as a failure to recognize the limits of the renovating power of a new vocabulary. Forms of language are thus valuable for both diagnostic and transformative purposes. For the writing of *Deronda*, Eliot studied ways of interpreting Hebrew scriptures and the function of Jewish transmitters and interpreters. She successfully highlights the extent to which hermeneutical gaps in interpreting Jewish canonical doctrines may influence the general sentiments of a community, particularly through the characterization of Mordecai, who wants to 'use the records as a seed' and to interpret according to the specific context of the present (*DD* 42). In all these ways, Eliot consciously explores how historically sedimented social and collective meanings in language may both constitute the identities of individuals and in turn be transformed by them. See also IRONY; NAMES IN GEORGE ELIOT'S FICTION; STYLE.   HL

Beer (1983).
Ermarth, Elizabeth Deeds, 'George Eliot and the World as Language', in Rignall (1997).
Harvey (1961).
Mugglestone, Lynda, '"Grammatical Fair Ones": Women, Men, and Attitudes to Language in the Novels of George Eliot', *Review of English Studies*, NS 46 (1995).

languages, George Eliot's knowledge of.

George Eliot was a fine linguist, acquiring a good reading knowledge of seven languages besides English in the course of her life: French, Italian, German, Latin (including medieval Latin), Greek, Spanish, and Hebrew. She began learning French at the Misses Franklin's school in Coventry in 1832, winning a prize after the first year. Italian followed and then German in 1840, both taught by Joseph Brezzi, a local language teacher. At the same time she was studying Latin with some help from a local clergyman, and by 1843 she was applying herself to Greek. She read widely in both classical languages, particularly during the period of her social ostracism in the 1850s after she started to live with G. H. *Lewes, and she attained a deeper knowledge of the classics than most university-educated men (Haight 1968: 195). In 1864 she learned Spanish, studying the grammar and translating passages from *Don Quixote* as Lewes read them out loud (Haight 1968: 378–9); and in 1867 the couple practised Spanish from a grammar and a conversation book on their way to *Spain (*L* iv. 334). In 1866 she met Emanuel *Deutsch and began taking Hebrew lessons from him (see JUDAISM), and in 1876 she was proficient enough to give Lewes lessons in the

language whilst they were on holiday in Switzerland (*L* vi. 274).

German and French were probably the modern languages she knew best, her knowledge of German in particular honed and deepened by her fine *translations. There is no precise record of how well she spoke it. When she first went to *Germany with Lewes in 1854 she claimed that her spoken German was not good enough to converse properly with D. F. *Strauss, whom they met on their outward journey (*L* ii. 171); but in the course of their lengthy visits to Germany she and Lewes led an active social life and made many friends, suggesting that she achieved a competent fluency in the language. In French, too, she was able to converse comfortably enough with the writers and intellectuals, such as Ernest *Renan, whom she and Lewes occasionally met in *Paris. John Walter *Cross, who travelled with her through Europe on their honeymoon, claimed that, while she was highly sensitive to language and its rhythms, she actually spoke all four modern languages 'with difficulty, though accurately and grammatically: but the mimetic power of catching intonation and accent was wanting' (Cross, iii. 423). How well equipped Cross was to pass judgement on fluency, accuracy, and accent in foreign languages remains uncertain.

Her knowledge of other languages was a central feature of her intellectual life, providing her with a sense of both the richness and relativity of *language and with a conviction of the value of cultural difference. As she put it in her 1865 essay 'A *Word for the Germans', 'it is precisely that partition of mankind into races and nations, resulting in various national points of view or varieties of national genius, which has been the means of enriching and rendering more and more complete man's knowledge of the inner and outer world' (*Essays*, 388). See also FRANCE; ITALY; NATIONALISM.   JMR

Ermarth, Elizabeth Deeds, 'George Eliot and the World as Language', in Rignall (1997).

Laurence, Samuel

(1812–84), portrait painter, who with his wife had lived with the Thornton Leigh *Hunts in Bayswater in the 1840s. He lunched with G. H. *Lewes and George Eliot in March 1860, having expressed a wish to paint Eliot's portrait (see PORTRAITS). This was done in August and September over nine sittings, in the style of his chalk head of William Makepeace *Thackeray (1852). The sittings were described to John *Blackwood and Barbara *Bodichon. Lewes expressed dissatisfaction with the portrait, and Blackwood showed every wish to acquire it. On 8 April 1861 Eliot wrote to Laurence that, having learned that he wished to exhibit the portrait at the

Royal Academy, and having discussed the matter with Lewes, she declined to give her consent for him to display it 'anywhere beyond the doors of your own atelier' (*L* iii. 401). It was sold to Blackwood in June 1861, and hung in the back parlour of his office in George Street, Edinburgh. According to Laurence, Lewes pressed him for the drawing, but he refused. A preliminary study, misdated 1857, is at Girton College, Cambridge. It captures her depressed mood at the time, but also the sensual, sardonic element in her nature.   GRH

law. George Eliot's letters, notebooks, and novels reveal her lifelong interest in the operation of the legal system and in broader ideas of justice. She became familiar with legal issues through her association with professional lawyers and her own extensive programme of reading. Some of her earliest legal research seems to have been undertaken for the purposes of her critical writings and editorial responsibilities. For example, in early 1854 she edited a lengthy article by the phrenologist George *Combe entitled 'Criminal Legislation and Penal Reform' for the *Westminster Review* (*L* viii. 75–111). When she turned to the production of fiction, Eliot took great pains to ensure the accuracy of any specifically legal material that was to be incorporated into the plot of a novel. In November 1859, G. H. *Lewes and Eliot instructed the solicitor Henry Sheard to draw up their wills (*L* iii. 205, 212). In the same month, Lewes consulted Sheard about the consequences of T. C. Newby's attempts to publish a sequel to *Adam Bede*, but there were no legal remedies for such exploitation (*L* iii. 208–9, 212–13). In subsequent months, Eliot consulted Sheard again with respect to the lawsuit which ruins the Tullivers in the second book of *The Mill on the Floss*. He read portions of her manuscript at the proof stage in order to confirm that her representation of the case brought by Wakem on behalf of Tulliver's adversary Pivart was legally correct and that the date for the sale of the Tullivers' property under the decree of Chancery was plausible (*L* iii. 246, 262–7).

In January 1866 she sought advice from the renowned positivist Frederic *Harrison of Lincoln's Inn to ensure the accuracy of the narrative sequence by which Esther could receive the Bycliffe inheritance in *Felix Holt, the Radical*. Her letters record detailed exchanges with Harrison on such topics as the statute of limitations, the difference between a settlement and the effects of heirship, and details of criminal trial procedure prior to the enactment of the Prisoners' Counsel Act in 1836 (*L* iv. 214–62). Harrison read the legal material at proof stage and confirmed its accuracy; he also contributed the advice of the Attorney-General in chapter 35 of the novel (*L* iv. 259–62;

also Harrison, *Memories and Thoughts* (1906), 146–50). Eliot consulted Harrison again in January 1875 with respect to questions of heirship and legitimacy as she formulated the plot of *Daniel Deronda* (*George Eliot's 'Daniel Deronda' Notebooks*, ed. J. Irwin (1996), 327–8). Eliot also knew the criminal jurist James Fitzjames Stephen; by 1865 he was included in the lists of their many callers in Lewes's journal. Later in life, she also knew the famous Professor of Jurisprudence Sir Henry Maine.

Eliot's notebooks reveal the extent of her reading on current and historical legal matters. For example, *A Writer's Notebook 1854–1879* (ed. J. Wiesenfarth, 1981) includes descriptions of the work of Wesleyans in prisons and madhouses and a summary of the legal implications of the extension of religious tolerance (24–5, 53–4). The four-volume *Some George Eliot Notebooks* (ed. W. Baker, 1976–85) also contain a number of legal entries. Volume i (MS 707) includes notes on continental conceptions of evidence, which were drawn from her reading of the sixth edition of William Best's *Principles of the Law of Evidence* (1875). Several legal maxims from the writings of John Austin, Jeremy Bentham, and Best are copied into this notebook, together with some information on military law from Charles Clode's *Military Forces of the Crown* (1869) (see *Some Notebooks*, ed. Baker, i, 193–207). *George Eliot's 'Middlemarch' Notebooks* (ed. J. Pratt and V. Neufeldt (1979), 202–7, 259–64) contain entries on Roman law, testamentary succession, and the position of women taken from her reading of Sir Henry Maine's *Ancient Law* (1861). She browsed in the seventh edition of Joshua Williams's *Principles of the Law of Real Property* (1865) in 1874–5 in preparation for the composition of *Daniel Deronda* (*George Eliot's 'Daniel Deronda' Notebooks*, ed. Irwin, 327; also *L* vi. 110). She also shared the Victorian taste for newspaper reports of crimes and trials (Altick, *The Presence of the Present* (1991), 515); in January 1872 she attended a day of the Tichborne trial and heard Justice Coleridge speak (*L* v. 237, 243).

Despite the irregularity of her union with Lewes, Eliot did not actively promote the reform of the laws regulating the position of married women. However, she did sign Barbara Leigh Smith *Bodichon's petition on the property rights of married women, which was presented to parliament in March 1856 (*L* ii. 225, Haight 1968: 204).

In her fictional narratives, Eliot uses this legal material to explore the relationship between evidence and just judgement. Trial scenes feature prominently in *Adam Bede* and *Felix Holt*. In *Adam Bede*, Eliot assesses the reliability of eyewitness testimony and circumstantial evidence, and in her representation of Hetty's trial, she is aware of the risk that legal hermeneutics may not uncover truth. *Felix Holt* is Eliot's most legally complex work; in addition to the treatment of the law of entail discussed in her letters to Harrison, Eliot also recreates accurately the rules of evidentiary procedure which governed trials for felony at the time of the First *Reform Act. Eliot's fiction is peopled with lawyers who are skilled in the manipulation of information and the lives of those around them, such as Dempster in 'Janet's Repentance', Wakem in *The Mill on the Floss*, and the blackmailing attorneys Jermyn and Johnstone in *Felix Holt*. She is also interested in alternative quasi-legal forms of judgement, as can be seen in the drawing of the lots in *Silas Marner* and Romola's interpretation of the confessions of Savonarola in *Romola*, and in *Middlemarch* and *Daniel Deronda* she explores the confession of guilty intentions which fall short of legal culpability. See also COMPOSITION; CRIME.   JMS

Welsh (1985).

—— *Strong Representations* (1992).

Lawrence, D. H. (1885–1930), English writer who admired the early fiction of George Eliot, especially *Adam Bede*, *The Mill on the Floss*, *Silas Marner*, and *Romola*. His first novel, *The White Peacock* (1911), used her model of the 'two couples' (E.T. (Jessie Chambers), 103) although his characters experienced a more modern alienation. He also saw her as the first to place the action inside the psyches of the characters (E.T. (Jessie Chambers), 105). Authors who engaged him most were objects of creative argument and this occurs with Eliot, if less overtly than with Thomas Hardy.

Early Eliot represented a formative literary and social world from which Lawrence had to escape. He accused Blanche Jennings, like George Eliot and Charlotte Brontë, of being in thrall to a female idea of male strength: 'The little cripple in *Mill on the Floss* was strong—but a woman despised his frailty' (*Letters of D. H. Lawrence*, i. 88), although Lawrence was seeking motherly support from Jennings as he struggled both with his teaching job and with 'Laetitia', an early version of *The White Peacock*, from which he was trying to remove the 'sentimentality'. He requested copies of '*Adam Bede* or *Mill on the Floss*' in November 1913 (*Letters of D. H. Lawrence*, ii. 101) when *Women in Love* (1920) was already gestating. In *Women in Love*, conventional male strength is exposed in Gerald Crich whom Gudrun Brangwen refuses to mother, seeing him as crying 'in the night' like Hetty Sorrel's infant by Arthur Donnithorne (ch. 31). Gudrun wants to 'stifle' the Arthur/Gerald figure as if acting in retrospect for the helpless Hetty. Lawrence is far from identified with Gudrun, yet the reversal of the George Eliot situation typifies his

relation to previous authors. He does not so much impose a new reading as see other immanent implications in their stories.

The Mill on the Floss reveals the effective fault-line in his relation to Eliot: 'Lawrence adored *The Mill on the Floss*, but always declared that George Eliot "had gone and spoilt it half way through". He could not forgive the marriage of the vital Maggie Tulliver to the cripple Philip' (E.T. (Jessie Chambers), 97–8). Despite someone's misremembering of the plot, since Maggie does not marry, the drift is clear: Eliot could recognize the force of passion but not its rights. Her ethical concern leads her to obfuscate passional demands by providing two impossible objects in Philip Wakem and Stephen Guest. By contrast, Lawrence's Ursula Brangwen would outgrow both Maggie's soulfulness and her intense relation with her father, which is one of the most powerful man/woman relations in Victorian fiction. And Lawrence's cripple in *Lady Chatterley's Lover* (1928) is an even starker reversal of conventional ethical sympathies. What is at stake is not whether Maggie finds passional fulfilment but how such a possibility is valued in Eliot's ethic of abnegation. Although Gillian Beer sees the drowning in *Women in Love* as a reversal of *The Mill on the Floss* and returning blame to the woman (Beer 1986: 102–3), the episode analyses the process of will in Gerald which is damaging but beyond ethical blame.

If the later George Eliot developed in the direction of Henry *James as the tragic historian of fine moral consciences, even the early Eliot had, for Lawrence, a Victorian predilection for 'padding and moral and reflection' such that, although 'very fond of her', he wished 'she'd take her specs off, and come down off the public platform' (*Letters of D. H. Lawrence*, i. 98, 101). Lawrence's suspicion of moral idealism, shared by others of his generation, saw in her an object lesson made only the more telling by her real power. George Eliot took up Charles *Dickens's idealizing of the woman 'and it became confirmed. The noble woman, the pure spouse, the devoted mother took the field, and was simply worked to death' (*Phoenix II*, 535).

Yet while sharing the modernist diagnosis of Victorian idealism and sentimentalism, Lawrence never merely debunked it like some of his contemporaries. He had no excessive fear of sentimentality and his quarrel with Eliot was from the inside. The difference emerges in a 1928 comment on a young Italian who had spoken slightingly of Giovanni Verga: 'They find Tolstoi ridiculous, George Eliot ridiculous, everybody ridiculous who is not "disillusioned." ... The *Story of a Blackcap* is sentimental and overloaded. But so is Dickens's *Christmas Carol*, or *Silas Marner*. They do not therefore become ridiculous' (*Phoenix II*, 280).

Even at the end of Lawrence's life, Eliot remained a touchstone. MB

Lawrence, D. H., *The Letters of D. H. Lawrence*, vols. i–ii, ed. James T. Boulton (1979–81).

—— *Phoenix II: Uncollected, Unpublished and Other Prose Works* (1968).

Beer (1986).

E.T. (Jessie Chambers), *A Personal Record* (1935).

Hirai, Masako, *Sisters in Literature* (1998).

Lazarus, Emma (1849–88), American Jewish poet and admirer of George Eliot. Lazarus is most famous for her sonnet 'The New Colossus', inscribed on the pedestal of New York Harbor's Statue of Liberty, welcoming immigrants to the United States: 'Give me your tired, your poor, | Your huddled masses yearning to breathe free'. Lazarus became an advocate of the idea of Jewish repatriation to Palestine, and was first guided to her romantic Zionism through reading Eliot's *Daniel Deronda*. First schooled in the poetic milieu of the American transcendentalists, Emma Lazarus became interested in the situation of the Jews in Russia by way of the British response to the pogroms of 1880. She saw Britain as an oasis of religious toleration, and Eliot's philo-Semitism stirred her desire to be recognized as a Jewish poet. She cited Eliot as an inspiration for Zionism: 'The idea formulated by George Eliot has already sunk into the minds of many Jewish enthusiasts, and it germinates with a miraculous rapidity' ('The Jewish Problem, *Century*, 34 (1886), 338). Lazarus dedicated her play *The Dance of Death* (1882) to Eliot, naming her as the writer 'who did the most amongst the artists of our day towards elevating and ennobling the spirit of Jewish Nationality'. Lazarus, like many wealthy women of her generation, found a vehicle for personal and social transformation by entering public life. Involved in the scheme to develop a Jewish Colony in Vineland New Jersey, she suggested that the colony be named after George Eliot: 'Why not, if a name must be found, select that of some friend to the jewish cause—such as Eliot, after George Eliot who has had such a noble and eloquent sympathy with us' (letter to Philip Cowen). Lazarus's Zionism came to her, not through her experience as an American Jew, but as a reader of Eliot's philo-Semitism. See also JUDAISM. AJ

Leader, The, weekly periodical of politics and culture to which George Eliot regularly contributed between 1854 and 1857. Founded in 1850 by Thornton Hunt, G. H. *Lewes and others, the *Leader* was an important organ for radicalism and advanced thinking, particularly around the politics of socialism. George Eliot wrote reviews frequently, and Lewes gave her the opportunity to develop her critical writing in the periodical.

Among her most interesting critical writings in the *Leader* are 'The *Future of German Philosophy' (28 July 1855) and 'The *Morality of *Wilhelm Meister*' (21 July 1855), in which George Eliot defends *Goethe's morality and suggests her own view of *realism and art reflecting life, later developed in her fiction. Lewes (who published under the pseudonym 'Vivian') was literary editor and drama critic, and his articles and reviews addressing realism are important in the history of literary criticism. By the late 1850s, the influence of the *Leader* was in decline, partly owing to increased competition in the weekly market after the founding of the *Saturday Review*. See also ESSAYS; JOURNALIST, GEORGE ELIOT AS. MWT

Leavis, F. R. (1895–1978), Cambridge literary critic who placed a fresh appreciation of George Eliot at the centre of his influential conception of the English novel. Apart from introductions to *Adam Bede* and *Daniel Deronda*, Leavis's major treatment of George Eliot occurs in *The Great Tradition* (1948) where his view of literature as a form of emotional and moral understanding found in her a primary exemplar.

Leavis does not typically offer original interpretation so much as an unusually intense, demonstrative reading whereby any falsity of feeling is exposed and true power is recognized. He reads as if participating in the creative struggle of the author so that even his negative criticism, rather than merely disparaging relative failure, brings out the difficulty and significance of the positive achievement. He challenged a then common view that her early works have a characteristic 'charm' which is lost as her later work becomes overburdened with moral reflection. Leavis acknowledged the 'charm' but insisted that it is a limiting term as against her mature achievement as he sought to define it. He argued persuasively that her characteristic weakness lies not in intellectual reflection, but in emotionally indulging the soulfulness of heroines such as Maggie Tulliver and Dorothea Brooke; an indulgence which readers have been too ready to follow. In contrast, he brought out the exemplary emotional understanding, conveyed dramatically, in the treatments of the Mrs Transome story in *Felix Holt, the Radical* and the Bulstrode story in *Middlemarch*.

Most attention is given to *Daniel Deronda* in which Leavis's sense of the relative quality of the Gwendolen Harleth and Deronda stories led him seriously to contemplate a separate edition of the Gwendolen story. He focused his appreciation of the Gwendolen narrative by comparison with Henry *James's reworking of it in *A Portrait of a Lady* (1881). Whereas James sought to make it more artistically intense, Leavis showed Eliot's apparently looser form to be artistically richer because of her greater grasp of her subject. James's achievement, however extraordinary, constitutes a slighter knowledge and dramatic presentation. Above all, Leavis saw the male author crucially indulging his heroine in a way that Eliot, in this case, does not; and it is relevant that Leavis's whole interest in the novel as a genre followed the lead of his wife, Queenie Leavis, a feminist who did not sentimentalize women.

By arguing his case largely through quotation from Eliot herself, Leavis made it seem self-evident, and his direct appeal to a fullness of understood life as constituting Eliot's specifically artistic achievement indicates the subtlety of his own aesthetic which is often mistaken for simple moralism. He prized her moral intelligence, not her moralizing. By an irony that might not entirely have displeased him, Leavis's apparently transparent reading of Eliot changed the common perception of her while allowing his own critical sophistication to remain as invisible as he showed her artistic achievement to be. See also REPUTA-TION, CRITICAL. MB

Leavis, F. R., 'Adam Bede', in Anna Karenina and Other Essays (1973).
—— (1948).
Bell, Michael, F. R. Leavis (1988).

'Legend of Jubal, The', a long poem published in 1874 which takes up the Old Testament legend of Jubal who was supposed to have invented the lyre and, by extension, the art of poetry. See POETRY OF GEORGE ELIOT. MR

Lehmann, Frederick (1826–91) and **Nina** (1830–1903), wealthy and cultured friends of George Eliot, whom she met on 25 April 1864 when she sat next to them at Covent Garden (though G. H. *Lewes knew them before). Frederick, born in Hamburg, was a partner in a steel firm, collected paintings, and played the violin well (Haight 1968: 389). His brother Rudolf was a portrait-painter who drew a portrait of Lewes in 1867. According to Frederick, he and George Eliot played together all the sonatas for violin and piano by Mozart and Beethoven, with Lewes as the only audience (see MUSIC). In 1866 he purchased his brother Emil Lehmann the rights to translate Felix Holt, the Radical into German (see TRANSLATIONS OF GEORGE ELIOT'S WORKS). Nina, née Chambers of the Edinburgh publishing family, was visited by Eliot and Lewes when she was staying in Pau for her health and they were on their way to *Spain in January 1867. In two days together Nina felt that she got to know the novelist far better than she could have done in years in London and wrote admiringly of her elevating presence and her modesty and humility (L iv. 336–7). George Eliot made

her tell her the whole story of her courtship and marriage, which seemed to interest her intensely. Friendship with the Lehmanns and their circle of friends was a mark of the social acceptance that eventually came to George Eliot from her success as a novelist. The Lehmanns were the grandparents of the writers John and Rosamond Lehmann. JMR

Lehmann, R. C., Memories of Half a Century (1908).
Mooney, Bel, 'The Lehmanns and George Eliot', George Eliot Fellowship Review, 15 (1984).

Leighton, Frederic (1830–96), English artist. George Eliot apparently met Leighton in May 1862, after he had been commissioned by George *Smith to illustrate Romola for the *Cornhill Magazine. Leighton already had an established reputation as a painter of subjects from the Florentine Renaissance. His first Royal Academy work, Cimabue's Madonna carried in triumph through the streets of Florence (Royal Collection, on loan to the National Gallery), had been bought by Queen *Victoria in 1855. G. H. *Lewes was delighted that Leighton was to illustrate Romola and both G. H. Lewes and George Eliot were anxious to see more of the artist's work. Leighton accordingly escorted them to the Academy exhibition of 1862, where they saw another painting with a Renaissance subject, Michelangelo nursing his dying servant (Leighton House).

Leighton was commissioned to provide two illustrations for each monthly number of Romola, together with an initial letter and a tailpiece to the Proem. He was paid £40 a number. The original plan was for twelve instalments, and when the novel was extended to fourteen Smith did not extend Leighton's contract. As a result there is only one full-page illustration in each of the last two numbers. The illustrations did not appear in the first book edition of 1863, but four were included in the one-volume edition of 1865. The two-volume 1863 illustrated edition reproduced all the illustrations together with a new decorated title-page.

Leighton's illustrations were woodcuts, inked on to the woodblocks from the original black and white chalk drawings on blue paper. Leighton complained to Smith about the quality of the engraving, carried out by Joseph Swain and W. J. Linton, and Smith responded by having the woodblocks photographed by W. Jeffrey in order to prove that the designs were accurately rendered. At least two sets of these photographs were in existence until comparatively recently. One is at the Houghton Library, Harvard, and the other, known to have been in the Victoria and Albert Museum, is at present missing. The original drawings (or the woodcuts) hung on George Eliot's drawing-room wall at The *Priory. The drawings descended through the family of G. H. Lewes and were purchased in the 1950s by an American collector.

Leighton worked from number to number, and explained, in answer to a question put in the 1880s, that he had no knowledge of the plot or of his subject for more than one or two numbers ahead. George Eliot gave him no directions about the appearance of the characters (L ix. 349). In fact, the novelist was at times dismayed by Leighton's interpretation of her scenes and characters, particularly in the early part of their collaboration. She criticized the first illustration, The Blind Scholar and his Daughter, telling Leighton that 'Her [Romola's] face and hair, though deliciously beautiful, are not just the thing—how could they be?' (L iv. 40). Leighton insisted upon the right of the artist to make his own decisions, and George Eliot eventually accepted the position, 'the exigencies of your art must forbid perfect correspondence between the text and the illustration' (L iv. 41). Novelist and artist met frequently during the publication period, and discussed the selection of episodes, but it appears that the choice of these ultimately remained with Leighton.

Leighton had comparatively little experience as an illustrator when he accepted the Romola commission, although his early training at the Stadel Institute in Frankfurt had developed him into a talented draughtsman. On the whole, he is less successful with the group scenes for Romola like A Florentine Joke, where there is often a suggestion of caricature. He excelled in the woodcuts of the more intimate episodes. There is much in Romola which is pictorial, and Leighton's gift for rendering the folds of drapery often lends a statuesque quality to the figures. The Visible Madonna, which shows Romola with the poor children of Florence, is related to a traditional Renaissance figure of Charity, and in At the Well she holds a child in the pose of *Raphael's Sistine Madonna (Picture Gallery, Dresden). In The Dying Message, where Romola kneels before her brother, her cloak spread out around her, the iconography of a saint's death is invoked. George Eliot herself particularly liked Leighton's treatment of Tessa and her child in You didn't think it was so pretty, did you?, where Tessa shows the baby to Baldassare, and Escaped where the cloaked Romola stands against a background of the towers and roofs of Florence. 'I see the love and care with which the drawings are done' (L iv. 41) she told him after seeing Nello in his illustration for Suppose you let me look at myself.

From the beginning of their collaboration, Leighton offered George Eliot advice about the Italian language and about aspects of the Italian Renaissance. When he told her that 'Che che' was not in period, George Eliot ignored him, but she was grateful for later suggestions. Leighton visited *Florence in the summer of 1862 and George Eliot asked him to look at certain details in paintings by Domenico Ghirlandaio (c.1448–94) for her, and suggested that he study the portraits of some of the real-life characters who appear in Romola.

A friendly relationship between Leighton and George Eliot developed as a result of their work on Romola. Leighton was an occasional guest at The Priory, and Lewes and George Eliot visited his studio to see the paintings he was about to send to the Academy exhibitions. They also attended Leighton's famous musical entertainments at 2 Holland Park, Kensington. On 16 March 1877 and 16 April 1878 she heard the violinist Joseph *Joachim (1831–1907) play there.

Leighton became president of the Royal Academy and was knighted in 1878, was created baronet in 1885, and became Baron Leighton of Stretton in 1896, shortly before his death. See also ILLUSTRATIONS; VISUAL ARTS.   LO

Ormond, Leonee and Richard, Lord Leighton (1975).
Turner, Mark, 'George Eliot v. Frederic Leighton', in Levine and Turner (1998).
Witemeyer (1979).

Lessing, Gotthold Ephraim (1729–81), German dramatist and critic whom George Eliot admired for the acuteness of his critical insight, the un-German lucidity of his prose, and the tolerant broadmindedness of his views. Her admiration was shared by G. H. *Lewes, who had published an article on Lessing in the Edinburgh Review in October 1845, seeing him as the father of German literature although possessed of a mind more British than German (Ashton 1980: 123). In *Berlin in 1854 she read much of his critical writing, including Laokoon (1766), which draws a masterly distinction between poetry and the plastic arts and which she declared to be the most un-German of all the German books she had ever read, with its clear and lively style and acute and pregnant thoughts (Journals, 34–5). She was later to give an appreciative account of the work in the 'Belles Lettres' section of the *Westminster Review in October 1856 (66: 566); and its argument informs the debate about poetry and painting between Ladislaw and Naumann in Middlemarch (MM 19). In Berlin she and Lewes also saw two of Lessing's plays: his bourgeois tragedy Emilia Galotti (1772) she judged to be a wretched mistake, but was moved to tears by 'the noble words of dear Lessing' in his 'crowning work' Nathan der Weise (1779), with its appeal for religious tolerance and for understanding between Jews, Christians, and Moslems (Journals, 249). She was later to follow his example in Daniel Deronda, where she makes a

similar appeal for tolerance and understanding in her sympathetic vision of Jews and Judaism. See also JUDAISM; RELIGION. JMR
Ashton (1980).

letters of George Eliot. These were published in nine volumes (1954–78), a monument to the scholarship, industry, and knowledge of the period of Gordon S. *Haight. The first seven volumes also contain letters by G. H. *Lewes, while about one-third of the total are from other correspondents. Haight restored passages pruned by John Walter *Cross (see BIOGRAPHIES), established correct sequences, discovered and printed letters for the first time, investigated the cultural background, and established the intimate foreground. The footnotes are an extension of the texts, often irradiating Victorian cultural and social history: as Eliot the novelist emerges, the letters themselves provide a commentary on writer, publisher, and reader relations and conventions in the mid-19th century. The last two volumes are accurately designated 'supplementary', with family letters from Lewes and his sons, a few important ones from Eliot herself, and passages from the autobiography of Edith *Simcox. George Eliot's letters provide the most complete inner biography of her in her various phases that we have, or indeed are likely to have, when they are read in conjunction with her *journals and *notebooks. They register her development from the provincial, spiritual, and intellectual young woman to the more widely intellectual professional writer whose dedication and integrity elevate that profession. They provide insights into her friendships, information about contemporary literary and social life, and reveal her own views about her writing, its aims and concerns.

Her early letters cover the period of fervent faith on the evangelical wing of the Church of England up to her refusal to accompany her father to church. Letters to her old teacher Maria *Lewis are redolent of religious enthusiasm, with their constant citings of Scripture and reiterative wishes to be useful, her love of words already evident. Although her ideas are narrow, there is an indication of wide reading in theology and literature as well as practical concern for unemployed weavers in her locality and for the poor in general. Intellectual engagement is seen in the projected ecclesiastical chart (L i. 44), her first verses (L i. 27–8), and in her signature use of the delightful language of flowers, where she is Clematis to Lewis's Veronica and Martha *Jackson's Ivy (L i. 60–1, 74–82, for example). New friends and influences signal change: she seeks 'the truth, my only fear to cling to error' (L i. 120–1). The major influence of Charles Christian *Hennell is shown in her statement that the

Scriptures are 'histories consisting of mingled truth and fiction' (L i. 128–30) in the decisive but touchingly responsive and responsible letter to her father (see EVANS, ROBERT) in February 1842.

The period from 1842 to 1849 is marked by the radical influence of the *Brays and Hennells, seen practically in Eliot's exchanges with Sara *Hennell during the translation of *Das Leben Jesu* which reflect their deepening relationship. Sara's help cannot offset oppression, depression, *Strauss-sickness (L i. 206). Before this there is the promise, soon shattered, of her stay with Dr *Brabant confided to Cara in November 1843 (L i. 163–8). Three letters indicative of her mixed personality stand out. The first is to Bray, self-mocking, about her (fictitious) experience with the wife-hunting translator-seeking Dr Bücherwurm (L viii. 12–15, October 1846); the second the discussion with John *Sibree which reflects the range of her intellectual interests and views (L i. 250–6, February–March 1848); finally there is the *cri de cœur* to the Brays as Robert Evans is dying: 'What shall I be without my Father?' (L i. 284, 30 May 1849).

The letters in the period 1849–54, beginning with the Swiss experience, are sometimes anticipatory of the future novelist through their witty, insightful comments on acquaintances. The London phase in the Strand is recorded from 18 November 1850. Details of her life punctuate letters to the Brays in 1851—literary, social gossip, practical work on John *Chapman's catalogue and her editing for the *Westminster* Review screening her private life. Her correspondence with Chapman reflects editorial efficiency, practicality, incisive critical capacity (see for example L ii. 47–50, July 1852). The impassioned letter to Herbert *Spencer was written in the same month (L viii. 56–7). Her introduction to Lewes had occurred in the previous October ('a sort of miniature Mirabeau in appearance', L i. 367), but it is not until the early months of 1854 that mentions of him increase, culminating in the confidingly terse note of 19 July 1854 to the Brays and Sara Hennell (L ii. 166) which omits him by name but announces the decisive action of leaving for *Germany.

From 1854 until the publication of *Adam Bede* marks the dual arrival of the successful professional writer and the privately fulfilled woman despite the pressures of maintaining anonymity and pseudonymity in uneasy tandem. The first admission over Lewes comes to Charles Bray in October 1854 (L ii. 178–9); a fuller, deeper, integral statement of love and faith to Cara almost a year later (L ii. 213–15). Eliot is touchy, pondering why she hasn't heard from Spencer (November 1855, L ii. 221), reprimanding Bessie Rayner *Parkes in March 1856 (L ii. 232) for addressing her as Miss Evans. From Tenby in July she suggests her article on 'Silly Women's Novels' to Chapman (*L* ii. 258), while from November onwards the correspondence initiated by Lewes with John *Blackwood begins over *Scenes of Clerical Life* (*L* ii. 269). Her first letter as 'George Eliot' is on 4 February 1857 (*L* ii. 291–2) to Major William *Blackwood, and by 11 June she is defending 'Janet's Repentance' to his brother John, a generous publisher who becomes a friend and generally tactful critic of her work (*L* ii. 347–8). Interspersed with this absorption in her writing is the private notification to Isaac of her 'marriage' (*L* ii. 331–2), and with the autumn comes the first mention of *Adam Bede* with 'My new story haunts me a good deal . . . It will be a country story—full of the breath of cows and scent of hay' (*L* ii. 387). By January 1858 she can record that it 'goes on with a pleasing andante movement' (*L* ii. 419). But with the novel's publication Eliot responds to the reviews, noting the praise of E. S. *Dallas in *The Times* (*L* iii. 24), jokily but apprehensively records the emergence of Joseph *Liggins (*L* iii. 44), and deliberately misleads Sara by telling her that Lewes is 'dithyrambic' about *Adam Bede* 'so I must refresh my soul with it now' (*L* iii. 46). Most significant of all is Eliot's delight at receiving Barbara *Bodichon's letter of praise and recognition of *Adam Bede* (*L* iii. 63–4). She later tells her that she works best 'in my remotest past' (*L* iii. 129). Letters throughout the rest of 1859 reflect her doing so as she prepares for, then begins, *The Mill on the Floss*, and acknowledges Mrs *Gaskell's generous letter to her in November (*L* iii. 198). The novel brought a letter from Edward *Bulwer-Lytton, her response to which is an important and determined underlining of her artistic integrity in 'the truthful presentation of a character essentially noble but liable to great error' beyond any narrow conception of the ethics of art (*L* iii. 318).

The early years of acceptance and fame are reflected in the letters both of a personal and a professional nature. There is her warm response to Bray about the strike of ribbon employers in Coventry in July 1860, followed by a letter offering him a loan of £100 to meet the costs of a libel case against him (*L* iii. 323–5). In August there is her delight in Charles Lewes's getting into the Post Office (*L* iii. 332), her letter full of news to François *D'Albert Durade (*L* iii. 346–8), and then her first mention of her 'historical romance' to John Blackwood in the same year (*L* iii. 339). Six months later she tells him that *Silas Marner* 'would have lent itself best to metrical rather than prose fiction' (*L* iii. 382). The 1860s reflect the intensity of her involvement with her writing but the *sympathy which is one of her most endearing qualities repeatedly surfaces. A letter to Bodichon in February 1862 (*L* iv. 13) expresses her sympathy for Queen

*Victoria (Prince Albert had died in the previous December) and her abhorrence of the *American civil war and the need for *education 'through the affections and sentiments'. Balancing this is the tetchy letter to Sara (April 1862, *L* iv. 25) reprimanding her for thinking the unthinkable ('I am NOT the author of the Chronicles of Carlingford'). Her positive identity is underlined in a letter to John Blackwood in May when she tells him that she has accepted George *Smith's offer for *Romola* (*L* iv. 34–5). Following the publication and reviews there is the warm if defensive letter to R. H. *Hutton in which she tells him that she always tries to convey 'as full a vision of the medium in which a character moves as of the character itself' and that 'great, great facts have struggled to find a voice through me' (*L* iv. 97). The Sunday afternoon receptions are made possible following the move to The *Priory (*L* iv. 111–13), while her major familial concern at the time is that Thornie (see LEWES FAMILY) wants to fight for the Poles against the Russians (*L* iv. 117), an aberration balanced by Charles's engagement (*L* iv. 156, June 1864). A long warm letter to Cara over the death of Nelly Bray (*L* iv. 183, March 1865) shows the continuing strength of old ties, but new ones begin with the long correspondence with Frederic *Harrison over the legal minutiae of *Felix Holt, the Radical* (*L* iv. 214, January 1866 onwards). In September she tells Blackwood that she is 'swimming in Spanish history and literature' (*L* iv. 305), and the necessary Spanish trip of early 1867 (see SPAIN) is recorded for Charles and Mrs *Congreve (*L* iv. 331–49). Her interest in Emily *Davies's 'desirable project of founding a College for women' is roused in November (*L* iv. 399), but her morbid tendency, so often expressed, is seen in a letter to Sara at the end of the year which reflects her oppression at the threat of general war in Europe and 'the starvation of multitudes' (*L* iv. 411).

Following *The Spanish Gypsy* and before the fusion which becomes *Middlemarch* there is the crisis of Thornie's illness and death: that it ate into her deeply is shown in letters to Bodichon (*L* v. 35–6, May 1869), then to Mrs Congreve (*L* v. 40–1), to Cara (*L* v. 44), and to Mrs Mark *Pattison in August referring to her own 'unused stock of motherly tenderness' (*L* v. 52). His death moves her to confide to Bodichon that she has 'a deep sense of change within' (*L* v. 70). Although in March 1870 she could write 'My novel . . . creeps on' the oppression and worry over Lewes continues (*L* v. 83), giving way to a wider oppression in August when the *Franco-Prussian war erupts and finds her initially anti-French (*L* v. 113). Although her views change, letters in the period January–April 1871 reflect her obsession with the degradation of war (*L* v. 131–42). In July practical arrangements for the part publication of *Middlemarch* are discussed (*L* v. 164–9). In October her sometimes obsessive concern for her *health is seen in her telling Cara, 'I am as thin as a medieval Christ' (*L* v. 197), while in December Sara is advised to look out for Charles *Dickens's *Life* (by John *Forster) for its important information about his childhood, though much of the rest 'would be better in limbo' (*L* v. 226). The warm letters to Mrs *Stowe continue (*L* v. 279, June 1872), the friendship with Elma *Stuart having begun four months earlier (*L* v. 244). There is an important letter to Mrs Cross in September from Homburg (*L* v. 312) which describes Eliot's revulsion at the 'Hell' of the gaming-tables, its substance later incorporated into *Daniel Deronda*, while in December there is one to 'My dear Nephew' (John Walter *Cross) about buying land in Surrey (*L* v. 340). Always she feels the responsibility of the writer, as she tells Elizabeth Stuart *Phelps in March 1873 (*L* v. 388). She writes to Mrs Congreve of their visit to *Cambridge in May (*L* v. 412), and late in that year she confides to Blackwood that she is 'simmering towards another big book' (*L* v. 454), delightedly telling Cara in December that the first volume of Lewes's *Problems of Life and Mind* has already sold 800 copies (*L* v. 472). The following year finds her consulting Blackwood about issuing a volume of her poems (March, *L* vi. 25–6), in June she is still 'brewing my future big book' (*L* vi. 58), and her friendships with women continue intimately affectionate (Dear Figliuolina for Mrs Mark Pattison, Dearest Georgie for Mrs *Burne-Jones, and Dearest Elma for Elma Stuart). Cross is elevated to 'My Dearest Nephew' (March 1875, *L* vi. 134) and becomes the recipient of some soul-searching about the wisdom of sending Bertie (Lewes) out to South Africa some ten years previously (*L* vi. 165). Bertie died on 29 June 1875. With *Daniel Deronda* now absorbing her attention, she tells Blackwood that Gwendolen is 'spiritually saved' (*L* vi. 188) and later, with regard to Mordecai, 'I was not born to paint Sidonia' (February 1876, *L* vi. 223). Delighted by praise but defensive about the Jewish parts of the novel, she wrote to Elizabeth Stuart Phelps at the end of 1876, 'there has been no change in the point of view from which I regard our life since I wrote my first fiction' (*L* vi. 318). There is one letter which has curiously ironic personal anticipations: this is to Bodichon, who has had a stroke, Eliot telling her of the marriage of Anne *Thackeray to Richmond Ritchie who was seventeen years her junior, this being 'one of several instances that I have known of lately, showing that young men with even brilliant advantages will often choose as their life's companion a woman whose attractions are wholly of the spiritual order'

(*L* vi. 398, August 1877). Early 1878 finds her intent upon the move to Witley (*L* vii. 5), writing affectionately as ever to Georgie Burne-Jones and Elma Stuart (*L* vii. 17–19). By June her letters are headed from The Heights (see HOMES), and in the following month there is a significant one in which she defines her function as an artist as being that of the aesthetic teacher who rouses 'the nobler emotions, which make mankind desire the social right' but without prescribing the only course (*L* vii. 44).

By now the last phase of Lewes's life is upon her. After his death she is silent until 7 January 1879 when she writes to Bodichon, signing herself 'Your loving but half dead Marian' (*L* vii. 93). The movement towards dependence on Cross is seen in letters and notes in January and February and her urgent need for his advice in April (*L* vii. 138). However, by July she can report to Charles that she weighs a mere 7 stones (*L* vii. 180), and it is not until October that she writes the life-affirming letter to Cross which begins 'Best loved and loving one' and is signed 'Beatrice' (*L* vii. 211–12). It is almost superfluous to add that they had been reading *Dante together for some time. She writes to her closest friends about her forthcoming marriage on 5 May 1880, the letter to Bodichon unposted in error and not forwarded until later (*L* vii. 268–70). There follows the generous reconciliatory letter to her brother Isaac (see EVANS, ISAAC) on 26 May (*L* vii. 287) in response to his brotherly recognition, forgiveness, and acceptance of her overdue respectable status. Thereafter her concern is with Cross's health, as in the letter to Elma Stuart of 27 June (*L* vii. 301–2) signed 'M. A. Cross'. But her old friends Cara and Sara are remembered in November and December (*L* vii. 340–1, 343–4) under the old signatures of 'Marian' and 'Pollian' before her sudden illness and death. Geoffrey Tillotson, in a discerning comment on Eliot's letters, wrote that they 'are unusual in that they resemble a novel', later adding that 'The novel that exists proverbially in all our lives is realized in these letters' (1965: 28, 32). See also LIFE OF GEORGE ELIOT.   GRH

The George Eliot Letters, ed. Gordon S. Haight, 9 vols. (1954–78) (abbreviated as *L*).
Selections from George Eliot's Letters, ed. Gordon S. Haight (1985).
Tillotson, Geoffrey and Kathleen, 'Novelists and Near-Novelists', in *Mid-Victorian Studies* (1965).

Lewes, Agnes. See LEWES FAMILY.

Lewes, Charles Lee. See LEWES FAMILY.

Lewes, George Henry (1817–78), writer and critic, who lived with George Eliot from 1854 until his death in 1878. George Eliot took his name, calling herself Marian Evans Lewes, though they were unable to marry because he could not divorce his wife Agnes.

Lewes was born in London on 18 April 1817, the third and youngest son of John Lee Lewes and Elizabeth Ashweek, and grandson of the celebrated comic actor Charles Lee Lewes, famous for playing the part of Bobadil in Ben Jonson's *Every Man in his Humour*. John Lee Lewes was a shadowy figure, a minor poet who lived in Liverpool and married Elizabeth Pownell, by whom he had four children between 1803 and 1808. By 1811, he had left his wife and set up home with Elizabeth Ashweek, a young woman born in 1787 of a Devonshire family. Together they had three sons: Edgar James, Edward Charles, and George Henry. John Lee Lewes disappeared out of his sons' lives when G. H. Lewes was about 2 years old, emigrating to Bermuda to join a brother of his who was a customs officer there. He returned, ill, to his native Liverpool, where he died in 1831. There is no evidence that G. H. Lewes knew about his own illegitimacy or about the existence of his father's legitimate family in Liverpool. He seems to have been told that John Lee Lewes died in 1819 (Ashton 1991: 9–10).

Lewes and his two brothers were brought up by their mother and a much disliked stepfather, John Gurens Willim, a retired captain in the army of the East India Company. Willim, who was ten years older than Elizabeth Ashweek, married her in St Pancras Old Church in 1823. Lewes attended several schools in London, France, and Jersey, and the family moved frequently, possibly because of money troubles. As Anthony *Trollope remarked in his obituary of Lewes in the *Fortnightly Review* in January 1879, 'his education was desultory, but wonderfully efficacious for the purposes of his life'. Trollope was here referring in particular to Lewes's expert knowledge of French language and literature, and to his early career as a young journalist trying to make a living in literary London without the usual benefits of a university education and family financial support.

Not much is known about Lewes's youth. He may have studied medicine briefly; his brother Edward was a doctor who travelled the world as a ship's medical officer until his death at sea in 1855. G. H. Lewes may have been a clerk with pretensions to authorship, like the hero of his first novel, *Ranthorpe* (1847). He remembered in an article on Baruch *Spinoza in the *Fortnightly Review* (1866) that he had belonged 30 years before to 'a small club of students' who met in a tavern in Red Lion Square, Holborn, to discuss philosophy. The group consisted of several self-educated men, including one who ran a second-hand bookstall, a journeyman watchmaker, and a bootmaker.

Lewes's first literary venture was a proposed life of *Shelley, in connection with which he approached Leigh Hunt, friend in his youth of Shelley and *Byron, and now a useful contact between Lewes and Shelley's widow Mary. Hunt was now middle-aged, living in Chelsea with his young family, but still inclined, as he had been as a young man, to attach himself to, and borrow from, others. His near neighbour Thomas *Carlyle described him as 'one of the ancient Mendicant Minstrels, strangely washed ashore into a century he should not have belonged to', and Charles *Dickens, more cruelly, caricatured him as the irresponsible eternal youth Harold Skimpole in *Bleak House* (1853).

Nothing came of the Shelley biography, because of Mary Shelley's opposition, but Lewes became friendly with the Bohemian Hunt family; Leigh Hunt published his early articles, and Lewes formed a firm—and fateful—friendship with Hunt's eldest son, Thornton Leigh Hunt. Lewes also got to know, through the Hunts, Carlyle and John Stuart *Mill, who helped him with introductions to journals. Carlyle also gave him letters of introduction to the German man of letters Karl August *Varnhagen von Ense when Lewes visited Berlin for an extended stay in 1838–9. During this trip Lewes began his research for the biography of *Goethe which he finally published in 1855.

In 1840 Lewes wrote the first of several long literary articles for the radical quarterly journal, the *Westminster Review*, edited at that time by John Stuart Mill. Over the years he was to write about French drama, Shelley, Spinoza, Goethe, Charlotte *Brontë, and to cover topics as diverse as drama, fiction, history, philosophy, and science in the *Review*. When he first met Marian Evans in 1851, both were important contributors to the *Westminster*, which John *Chapman was in the process of buying.

On 18 February 1841 Lewes married Agnes, eldest daughter of Swynfen Jervis, at St Margaret's Church, Westminster. Swynfen Jervis was a Radical MP with literary leanings, who had educated his daughter Agnes, aged 18 at the time of her marriage, to a high enough standard to enable her to help her ambitious young husband with his literary contributions to a number of periodicals.

Agnes bore Lewes five children: a girl, who died two days after her birth in December 1841; Charles Lee Lewes, born in November 1842; Thornton Arnott Lewes (Thornie), born in April 1844; Herbert Arthur Lewes (Bertie), born in July 1846; and St Vincent Arthy (1848–50) (see LEWES FAMILY). Lewes was busy writing on a wide range of subjects for the *Westminster Review*, the *British and Foreign Review*, the *Foreign Quarterly Review*, *Fraser's Magazine*, and the *Morning Chronicle*. His reviews

G. H. Lewes's sons Charles (1842–91), Thornton (1844–69), and Bertie (1846–75), for whom George Eliot was 'Mutter'. Top: Charles (*c.* 1864). Centre: Thornton (*c.* 1861). Bottom: Bertie (*c.* 1857).

of works by Dickens, William Makepeace *Thackeray, and Charlotte Brontë led to correspondences with all three authors, and to interesting relationships with each of them. It was fitting that Lewes, who was to become the encourager of George Eliot's fictional genius, should be such an accomplished critic of the fiction of her most famous predecessors and contemporaries in the genre.

One of Lewes's earliest articles was an appreciative review of Dickens's *Pickwick Papers, Oliver Twist*, and *Sketches by Boz*, in the *National Magazine and Monthly Critic* (1837). The two men met, and when Dickens formed his company of amateur actors in 1847, he asked Lewes to join them. Lewes spent the summer months touring provincial cities with Dickens and his friends Douglas Jerrold, John *Forster, Mark Lemon, John Leech, and others, acting comic roles in *The Merry Wives of Windsor* and—in the footsteps of his grandfather—*Every Man in his Humour* (though it was Dickens himself, not Lewes, who took his grandfather's part of Bobadil).

The group was formed again the following year for a similar tour, and Lewes was so enamoured of the acting life that he made a brief attempt to act professionally in 1849, as the hero of his own pseudo-Jacobean play, *The Noble Heart*, and as Shylock in *The Merchant of Venice*. Partly through the rivalry of his fellow actors, and partly because reviewers suggested that his voice and physique were not large enough to carry conviction on the stage, Lewes gave up thoughts of making the stage his career. However, as in every sphere of his multifarious activities, he put his knowledge of the stage to good use in subsequent years, taking on the persona of 'Vivian', the sharp-tongued theatre critic of the *Leader, a weekly newspaper founded and edited by Lewes and Thornton Hunt in 1850.

Lewes's relationship with Charlotte Brontë was a brief but interesting one. His review of *Jane Eyre* in *Fraser's Magazine* in December 1847 was the most friendly of the reviews the novel received. Charlotte Brontë wrote to thank the author, and a correspondence ensued, in which he advised her to read and learn verisimilitude from the novels of Jane *Austen, to which she replied in doughty defence of her own wilder imaginings. Piqued by his interest and opinion, she not only read Jane Austen's novels and commented critically on them in her replies to Lewes, but she also got hold of copies of Lewes's own two novels, *Ranthorpe* (1847) and *Rose, Blanche, and Violet* (1848). Neither is very good, the first being a semi-autobiographical account of the struggles in love and literature of a young man of no means, and the second a confused tale of three sisters and their various vicissitudes in love. Jane Carlyle pronounced *Rose, Blanche, and Violet* 'execrable', and Carlyle annotated his copy with hilarious comments about its 'folly' (Ashton 1991: 73–4).

Charlotte Brontë, in her distant vicarage at Haworth in Yorkshire, was fascinated by her correspondent's metropolitan existence, and by his amazing versatility. On hearing that, in addition to writing novels and regular articles, he was in Manchester in the spring of 1849 acting in *The Merchant of Venice* and *The Noble Heart* and giving lectures on the history of philosophy at the Manchester Athenaeum (he was also drumming up financial support for the planned newspaper, the *Leader*), Charlotte wrote admiringly to a friend: 'How sanguine, versatile, and self-confident must that man be who can with ease exchange the quiet sphere of the author for the bustling one of the actor!' (*Versatile Victorian: Selected Critical Writings*, ed. Ashton, 17–18).

By the time he met Marian Evans in 1851, Lewes, then aged 34, had, in addition to his acting and lecturing activities, written hundreds of articles and published several books. These included a hugely successful guide to philosophy from the Greeks to Immanuel *Kant, G. W. F. *Hegel, and Auguste *Comte, *A Biographical History of Philosophy* (four volumes in two, 1845–6), which sold nearly 10,000 copies in a year; *The Spanish Drama: Lope de Vega and Calderon* (1846); his two novels; his tragedy; *The Life of Maximilien Robespierre* (1849); and *The Game of Speculation*, an English adaptation of Honoré de *Balzac's *Mercadet* which had a successful run at the Lyceum Theatre in 1851. He had also successfully co-founded the *Leader*, a weekly newspaper of radical views.

Professionally, Lewes was therefore, as Charlotte Brontë observed with astonishment, widely active and successful. Personally, however, he was despondent. His close friendship with Thornton Hunt had not only led to their joint founding of the *Leader* in 1850, with Hunt as political editor and Lewes as literary editor. So close were the two men that Lewes, who embraced the Shelleyan ideals of freethinking in religion and free living in sexual matters, condoned—perhaps even encouraged—Hunt's adultery with Agnes. On 16 April 1850, two weeks after the launching of the *Leader*, Agnes gave birth to Edmund, the first of four children she was to have by Hunt, not Lewes. Lewes registered the child as his, thereby making it impossible for himself ever to sue for divorce on grounds of adultery. Relations with Hunt continued to be warm; Agnes had a second child by Hunt—Rose—in October 1851, the very month in which Lewes was introduced to Marian Evans by John Chapman, the radical publisher and prospective owner and editor of the *Westminster Review*.

By the summer of 1852, however, Lewes had grown disillusioned with the domestic experiment

(Ashton 1991: 119–22). Having registered the births of Edmund and Rose, he did not register those of Ethel, born in October 1853, or Mildred, born in May 1857. Despite his continuing literary activities, and in particular the spectacular success of *The Game of Speculation* in 1851, this time in the early 1850s was, he later recalled, 'a very dreary *wasted* period of my life' (Ashton 1991: 119–20).

It was not initially the meeting with Marian Evans which changed things for him. In 1852 she was in love with Herbert *Spencer, writing impassioned letters to him that summer from Broadstairs; Lewes to her was a stimulating colleague on the *Westminster*, one of many radical men of literature and politics with whom she consorted on her arrival in London in 1851 as a lodger at Chapman's house, 142 Strand, and as editorial assistant to Chapman on the *Westminster*.

Herbert Spencer was the person whose friendship helped Lewes in his time of trouble. Lewes wrote in his journal in January 1859 that he owed Spencer a debt of gratitude for helping him out of the despair he had felt about his marriage (though he did not confide his unhappiness to Spencer at that time):

I had given up all ambition whatever, lived from hand to mouth, & thought the evil of each day sufficient. The stimulus of his intellect, especially during our long walks, roused my energy once more, and revived my dormant love of science. His intense theorizing was contagious, & it was only the stimulus of a *theory* which could then have induced me to work. (Ashton 1991: 120)

Lewes and Spencer shared an interest in science, and in Comte's *positivism, a philosophical system which rejected dogmatic Christianity in favour of the *'religion of humanity', offering a view of society as held together not by common religious beliefs but by social interaction between classes and professions. During 1852 Lewes published in the *Leader* a series of explanatory articles on Comte's system, which appeared as a book, *Comte's Philosophy of the Sciences*, in 1853. It was Spencer who provided the important link between Lewes and Marian Evans. By early 1853 Spencer was taking Lewes with him when he went to visit her. He recalled later that on one occasion, 'when I rose to leave, he said he should stay'. Spencer continued, 'From that time he commenced to go alone, and so the relation began—(his estrangement from his wife being then of long standing).' To Spencer, who had been obliged to reject Marian's advances and make it clear that he was interested in friendship, not marriage, the new turn of affairs was 'an immense relief' (Ashton 1991: 133).

It is probable that Marian Evans and Lewes became lovers sometime in 1853. She helped him with his articles for the *Leader* when he became ill in the spring of 1854. He had been planning for some months to go to *Germany to finish his research for the biography of Goethe; Marian, who completed her translation of Ludwig *Feuerbach's contribution to the 'religion of humanity', *Das Wesen des Christenthums (The Essence of Christianity)*, for publication by Chapman in 1854, agreed to go with him. In Germany she could help him with *The Life of Goethe*, and they could live together openly despite not being legally married.

Having told only John Chapman and Marian's old Coventry friend Charles *Bray (but not his wife Cara and her sister Sara *Hennell, with both of whom Marian had a close friendship), Lewes and Marian set off in July 1854 for an extended stay in *Weimar and *Berlin. In Weimar Lewes met people who had known Goethe; translated, with Marian's help, various passages from Goethe's works for inclusion in the biography; and continued to send regular articles to the *Leader*. The £20 a month he earned was given to Agnes to support her and the children.

The couple's great happiness in Weimar, where they were accepted socially, and where they met the composer *Liszt, who was also living with a woman to whom he was not married, was tempered by news from England about the unpleasant rumours and responses at home to their relationship. Carlyle, who was at first supportive, accepting that Marian had not been the cause of the breakdown of the Lewes marriage, ceased to correspond with Lewes, while others, including Cara Bray and at first Sara Hennell, stopped writing to Marian.

They spent the cold winter months in Berlin, where Lewes found Varnhagen von Ense once more helpful with materials for the biography of Goethe. In March 1855 they returned to England to face an uncertain future living in rented rooms and coping with the shock and displeasure of their friends and acquaintances. Only Spencer, Chapman, Bray, and a few other friends—including two brave female friends, Bessie Rayner *Parkes and Barbara Leigh Smith *Bodichon—continued to visit and consort with Lewes and Marian as they had done before the liaison became public.

The *Life of Goethe* was published in November 1855, and was well received and highly successful, selling over 1,000 copies in the first three months, and going through several reprints over the years until long after Lewes's death. It is a wonderfully fresh and fair account of Goethe's complicated and sexually rather scandalous life and of his extraordinarily wide range of writings. Lewes's interest in science made him an excellent appreciator of Goethe's scientific efforts, as his expertise in literary criticism and in European languages and culture qualified him to write authoritatively on the poetry, novels, drama, and essays.

Moreover, with his own marital history to draw on, Lewes was able to be sympathetic towards Goethe's mistakes, without completely condoning them. He appreciated Goethe's breadth of experience and what Marian was to characterize in an essay on Goethe ('The *Morality of Wilhelm Meister*', which appeared in the *Leader* in November 1855) as Goethe's 'large tolerance' in his works towards 'mixed and erring humanity' (*Essays*, 146–7).

Not only was Marian justly proud of this work in which she had supported Lewes during his research and writing; she also associated its production with the fulfilment of her personal happiness with him. When she sent a copy to Charles Bray in late November 1855, she wrote: 'I can't tell you how I value it, as the best product of a mind which I have every day more reason to admire and love' (*L* ii. 221).

Lewes and Marian continued to write articles for the *Leader* and the *Westminster Review*. Lewes took up scientific studies in earnest. The summer of 1856 was spent away from London (partly to get away from prying eyes and scandalous tongues) in a series of coastal resorts in England and Wales, where Lewes, with Marian as his companion, undertook a study of marine life which bore fruit first in two series of articles in *Blackwood's Edinburgh Magazine* in 1856 and 1857, then in a popular illustrated book, *Sea-Side Studies*, in 1858.

In late August 1856 Lewes set off with his two older sons, Charles and Thornie, to Switzerland, where he settled them in a progressive boarding school near Berne. They knew nothing about either their father's relationship with Marian or their mother's with Thornton Hunt; one of the reasons for moving them to Switzerland may have been to protect them from London gossip as they grew up. Charles was nearly 14 and Thornie 12.

On his return, Lewes encouraged his brilliant but diffident companion to fulfil an ambition she had long harboured but never quite dared to put to the test: the writing of fiction. During 1855–6 she had written a number of astonishingly wide-ranging, knowledgeable, and, above all, witty review articles in the *Westminster Review*, including her trenchant attack on religious intolerance in *'Evangelical Teaching: Dr Cumming'* (October 1855) and her hilarious account of *'Silly Novels by Lady Novelists'* (October 1856).

Emboldened by Lewes's praise of her wit and narrative verve in these essays, as well as in a fictional sketch she had shown him in Germany, Marian began writing 'The Sad Fortunes of the Reverend Amos Barton', the first of three stories which would make up *Scenes of Clerical Life* (1858). Lewes sent the story to his publisher John *Blackwood, saying it was by a friend of his who was shy of revealing 'his' identity.

This was the first of Lewes's acts of generosity towards his partner's career. From then until his death, he would act unswervingly and energetically as her literary agent and encourager, the go-between between George Eliot and her publishers, her critics, and her readers. His very last letter before his death in 1878 was to be one to Blackwood negotiating for the publication of her *Impressions of Theophrastus Such*.

There were those who commented adversely at the time, and after, on Lewes's excessive defending of Marian from the outside world: he was known to hide bad reviews from her, and he frequently asked Blackwood and kind but frank friends like Barbara Leigh Smith Bodichon to temper their expressions of criticism in their letters. The novelist Margaret *Oliphant wrote about his keeping Marian in a 'mental greenhouse', suggesting that he was in some way doing her a disservice and that her novels show the strains of her unnatural social situation (Ashton 1991: 197).

Whatever one's views on the latter point, there is little doubt that his patience, optimism, and sheer energetic delight in her genius created the enabling conditions for her writing. Marian herself was certain of the importance of the role Lewes played. In March 1859 she dedicated the manuscript of her first full novel, *Adam Bede*, to 'my dear husband, George Henry Lewes', adding that the work 'would never have been written but for the happiness which his love has conferred on my life' (Ashton 1991: 197–8).

He in turn was in no doubt about what their happy relationship had done for him. It was at this time, in January 1859, that he confided in his journal the remarks about Spencer's friendship having helped him at a dreary, wasted time in his life, adding that Spencer had been the means of his getting to know Marian: 'To know her was to love her. To her I owe all my prosperity & all my happiness' (Ashton 1991: 194).

Her tremendous success as a novelist was to bring him great pleasure, as well as rendering them both, in due course, not only free from the financial anxiety which accompanied their early years together, but by 1863 very comfortably situated. To him she owed not only endless encouragement in the face of her deep depression about her own work and worth but a companionable partnership in all her intellectual interests and a lively source of fun and wit. He found in her a devoted wife, an intellectually stimulating companion, an equal, a woman whose genius he saw and admired as well as one whom he loved. And he had the rare generosity and freedom from rivalry and jealousy to put her career interests above his own.

In the excitement which followed publication in February 1859 of *Adam Bede*, which was an immediate critical and financial success, George Eliot—the mysterious new author who had suddenly appeared as a serious rival to Dickens and Thackeray—had much need of Lewes's qualities of mind and temperament. All England was gossiping about the identity of the author. Joseph *Liggins of Warwickshire was suspected; he omitted to deny the rumour, which rapidly got out of hand, with Marian's friends in Coventry and her now estranged brother Isaac *Evans joining in the speculation.

Marian was at first determined not to divulge the secret of authorship, but by the summer of 1859, with Liggins stories still appearing in *The Times* and other papers, and with London clubs buzzing, thanks to indiscretions by Spencer and Chapman, with rumours about the strong-minded woman of the *Westminster Review*, she bowed at last to *force majeure* and let it be known that she was the author.

Lewes chose this time also to tell his sons about the breakdown of his marriage and his partnership with Marian. Charles, now nearly 17, would be leaving school soon, and Lewes intended him to live not with Agnes and the younger children (fathered by Hunt), but with himself and Marian. He visited the boys—Bertie had now joined them—at their Swiss school at Hofwyl in July 1859 and, helped by the fact that the fame of *Adam Bede* had reached even that remote corner, told them the whole story. Though they continued to write to their mother, they now began, in their awkward, boyish ways, to write letters to Marian too. While Agnes remained 'Mamma', Marian was addressed as 'Mother' and later 'Mutter'.

In November 1859 Lewes renewed his old friendship with Dickens, which had faded after 1853, when Lewes had, in several articles in the *Leader*, attacked Dickens's poor science in handling the spontaneous combustion of Mr Krook in *Bleak House*. Dickens now came to visit and to meet Marian, on whom he had his eye as a possible contributor of fiction to his journal *All the Year Round*. He also commissioned some natural history articles from Lewes. Blackwood published Lewes's *Physiology of Common Life* in 1859–60, a work which was translated into several languages and was to stimulate the great Russian scientist Pavlov to abandon a theological career for one in physiology (Ashton 1991: 6).

George *Smith, the publisher who was about to set up the *Cornhill Magazine*, also came to call, hoping to persuade both George Eliot and Lewes

to contribute to his new journal, of which Thackeray was the editor. Lewes, glad also to revive his old acquaintance with Thackeray, wrote a series of 'Studies in Animal Life' in 1860, in which he was an early supporter of Charles *Darwin's ground-breaking hypothesis of natural selection in *On the Origin of Species*, published in November 1859.

Another literary friend at this time was Anthony Trollope, also a contributor to the *Cornhill*. When Charles came home from Hofwyl in the summer of 1860, Trollope gave useful advice on how to get him a job at the Post Office, where Trollope worked. Lewes and Marian moved from Wandsworth to central London to make it easier for Charles to get to work. They also began to entertain and accept invitations more than they had done since their return from Germany in 1855, when Marian had been excluded from many invitations and was too shy and proud to issue any of her own except to a few very close female friends and her old male friends Spencer, Bray, and Chapman.

The success of *Adam Bede* and *The Mill on the Floss*, and the perception that she and Lewes were living in a faithful marriage in all but the legal sense, moved several acquaintances—as well as the wider reading public—to accept the situation which they had at first deplored.

Lewes continued to write articles and reviews, mainly but not exclusively on scientific subjects; he also fitted in with Marian's needs, which included the desire to flee the country every time a new novel was about to be published. They established a pattern of going abroad for a few months when each work was finished, partly for her to recuperate from the exhaustion of completing her work, partly to escape the immediate critical response in England. Lewes's health began to deteriorate at this time, with headaches and nausea taking on the nature of a chronic complaint.

When Thackeray gave up the editorship of the *Cornhill Magazine* in March 1862, George Smith persuaded Lewes, despite the latter's increasingly poor health, to take over at the princely salary of £600 a year. In 1863 the Leweses felt financially secure enough to buy a large house of their own, The *Priory near Regent's Park, which they arranged to have furnished in lavish style by Lewes's friend the designer Owen Jones, and where they began to entertain friends at a weekly salon. Lewes's second son, Thornie, who had finished his schooling at Edinburgh and sat and failed the Civil Service examinations, went off to farm in Africa late in 1863. He was to be joined in Natal by his younger brother Bertie in 1866.

In January 1865 Lewes was asked by Trollope to be the editor of a new liberal periodical, the *Fortnightly Review*. Lewes agreed, though reluctantly because of his health. The periodical became a distinguished organ of liberal, but not party-political, thought, devoted to literature, science, and culture as well as to airing the political concerns in the months of agitation leading to the passing of the Second *Reform Act in 1867. Trollope, T. H. *Huxley, Spencer, George Eliot, and George *Meredith were among the distinguished writers who contributed. Lewes himself wrote an influential series of essays, 'The Principles of Success in Literature', in which he called for literary realism of an imaginative, rather than a 'coat-and-waistcoat' kind. He also wrote long articles on Spinoza and Comte.

Lewes's health was so precarious that by the end of 1866 he had resigned the editorship, which was taken over by John *Morley. Astonishingly, he and Marian, who also suffered from disabling headaches and a recurrent kidney complaint, set off in the winter of 1866–7 for *Spain, undertaking long uncomfortable coach journeys on bad roads for the sake of seeing the Alhambra near Granada and other famous sights of southern Spain.

For the rest of his life, Lewes worked tirelessly at his great project, 'Problems of Life and Mind', which after the publication of *Middlemarch* in 1871–2 he took to calling, self-mockingly, 'The Key to all Psychologies', in an echo of poor Mr Casaubon's unfinished work of scholarship, the 'Key to all Mythologies', in the novel.

Life did in the end imitate art, for though three volumes of the work were published between 1873 and 1877, the final two volumes had to be completed and seen through the press by a distraught George Eliot in the months after Lewes's death in November 1878. Lewes was disappointed that the scientific community received his ambitious work of physiology-cum-psychology more politely than enthusiastically.

Thornie and Bertie had little luck in Natal, either financially or in terms of their health. Poor Thornie came home early in 1869, while George Eliot was writing *Middlemarch*, fatally ill with spinal tuberculosis. After months of excruciating pain, during which Lewes and Marian nursed him, he died in October 1869, aged 25. Bertie stayed on in Natal, where he married a local girl, but in 1875 he too died young—aged 29—leaving behind a widow and two small children.

In 1877 the Leweses, through their new friend John Walter *Cross, found a house in the country at Witley, near Godalming in Surrey (see HOMES). They spent only two summers there, during which Lewes got increasingly weaker from enteritis. On 21 November 1878 he wrote to Blackwood sending part of George Eliot's *Impressions of Theophrastus Such*, and on 30 November he died. He was buried in Highgate Cemetery.

Friends paid handsome tribute to this man of many parts in obituaries which gave résumés of his career. His versatility, his verve, his wit, the breadth of his knowledge, and the generosity of his spirit were alluded to in article upon article. Trollope wrote a fine obituary of him in the *Fortnightly Review* which he had edited so expertly, and another friend, Robert Lytton, wrote that Lewes 'had the most omnivorous appetite of any man I knew; a rare freedom from prejudice; soundness of judgment in criticism, and a singularly wide and quick sympathy in all departments of science and literature' (Ashton 1991: 278–9). These qualities made him both one of the most interesting men of letters of his time and, as she well knew and deeply valued, the perfect companion for George Eliot.

RA

The Letters of George Henry Lewes, ed. William Baker, 2 vols. (1995).
Versatile Victorian: Selected Critical Writings of George Henry Lewes, ed. Rosemary Ashton (1992).
Ashton, Rosemary, *G. H. Lewes: A Life* (1991).

Lewes, Herbert Arthur. See LEWES FAMILY.

Lewes, Thornton Arnot. See LEWES FAMILY.

Lewes family. When George Eliot began living with G. H. *Lewes as his wife in 1854, he was already married, indissolubly, to Agnes Jervis (1822–1902), by whom he had three children who survived infancy (the first child, a daughter, having died two days after her birth in December 1841, and another, St Vincent Arthy, dying in 1850 two months before his second birthday). The three children were Charles Lee Lewes (1842–91), named after his great-grandfather, a celebrated comic actor; Thornton Arnott Lewes (1844–69), named after two of G. H. Lewes's friends, Thornton Hunt and the sanitary reformer Neil Arnott; and Herbert Arthur Lewes (1846–75).

Agnes Jervis was 18 when she married Lewes in St Margaret's church, Westminster, on 18 February 1841. Her father was Swynfen Jervis, Radical MP for Bridport, Dorset, who had a London home in Whitehall Place and a country seat, Darlaston Hall, near Stone in Staffordshire. Lewes met Agnes, the Jervis's eldest daughter, either in London, where he moved in Radical circles which included Arnott and the reforming doctor Thomas Southwood Smith, or in Staffordshire, where he may have been employed as a tutor to Agnes's younger brothers and sisters (Ashton 1991: 34).

Swynfen Jervis was an amateur *littérateur* as well as a campaigning politician. Thomas *Carlyle described him rudely as 'a dirty little atheistic radical, living seemingly in a mere element of pretentious twaddle'; Lewes's irrepressible second son Thornie called him 'Pantaloon'; and Lewes himself seems

G. H. Lewes (1817–78) with Pug, 1859. An American visitor somewhat later described Lewes as 'like an old-fashioned French barber or dancing master, very ugly, very vivacious, very entertaining'.

to have had his father-in-law in mind when describing Mr Meredith Vyner, the father of the three girls in his novel *Rose, Blanche, and Violet* (1848), who is laughed at 'for his dirty nails and his love of Horace' (Ashton 1991: 35).

Agnes herself was a pretty, well-educated young woman, apparently happy in her marriage to Lewes and well liked in his circle of Radical politicians and Bohemian men of letters. Lewes's chief mentor as a young man was Leigh Hunt, whose eldest son, Thornton (see HUNT, THORNTON LEIGH), not only collaborated with Lewes on journalistic ventures, but also became, at some point, the lover of Agnes. The two young men embraced free-loving ideals, and Thornton and his wife Kate Gliddon were living in what was rumoured to be a 'phalanstery', or sexually open community. They shared a house in Bayswater with Kate's brother John Gliddon, who was married to Thornton's sister Mary, and also with the painter Samuel *Laurence and his wife, another Gliddon. Lewes and Agnes appear never to have lived in the house, but they visited it frequently (Ashton 1991: 56–7).

The Leweses' marriage was perfectly happy for several years. Agnes helped Lewes with some of his journalism as well as bearing him five children between 1841 and 1848. By 1849, when Lewes and Hunt were raising subscriptions for their new radical weekly newspaper, the *Leader*, Agnes was having a sexual relationship with Thornton Hunt. Her last child by Lewes, St Vincent Arthy, was born in May 1848, and her first by Hunt, Edmund, in April 1850, just after the opening number of the *Leader* appeared. At this time, judging from Lewes's extremely friendly letters to Hunt and from the fact that Lewes registered Edmund's birth with himself named as the father, the arrangement was mutually acceptable (Ashton 1991: 55–7).

Agnes, who remains a shadowy figure, quietly living her unorthodox domestic life in Kensington, bore three more children to Hunt, who seems never to have left his wife or moved in with Agnes. In October 1851—the same month in which Lewes was first introduced to Marian Evans—Rose was born, and Lewes once more registered the birth. Ethel followed in October 1853, by which time Lewes was no longer living with Agnes in Kensington (indeed he may already have been intimate with Marian Evans, see Ashton 1991: 132–47). Mildred was born in May 1857, long after Lewes had set up home with Marian Evans. Because he had registered two of the births as his own children, he was unable in law to sue for divorce on the grounds of Agnes's adultery.

Lewes continued to make provision for Agnes and her children, sending them his regular earnings from the *Leader* and taking an interest in his own three children's schooling. The boys attended a day school in Bayswater until they were in their early teens, when Lewes considered hiring a tutor or sending them to boarding school. He told a friend in 1856 that Charles and Thornie were 'clever, and eager to get on', being already 'tolerably grounded in Latin, and French' and having begun to learn German. The youngest, Bertie, aged not quite 10, was being educated at home, being '*very* backward, because for some years his health was delicate, and I did not like his being at school' (*L* viii. 152).

Through Marian's Coventry friend Sara *Hennell, Lewes heard about a liberal, multinational boarding school in Hofwyl, near Berne, to which he took Charles and Thornie, aged nearly 14 and 12 respectively, in 1856. Bertie joined his brothers the following year, and Lewes visited them every summer, finally introducing them to Marian in 1860, by which time she was famous for *Adam Bede* and *The Mill on the Floss*.

Though Lewes kept his relations with Agnes cordial, he got annoyed with her inability to manage the money he sent her, and, more particularly, with the irresponsibility of his former friend Thornton Hunt, who was unable, or unwilling, to keep up his financial responsibilities towards the children he had fathered by Agnes. In December 1856 Lewes remonstrated with Agnes on account of her being '£150 in debt mainly owing to T[hornton]'s defalcations'. An 'angry correspondence & much discussion' followed, as Lewes noted in his journal (Ashton 1991: 178).

Although the Hunt–Lewes marriage arrangements were the talk of literary London, both before and after Lewes began living with Marian Evans, the younger children appear not to have known that Lewes was not their father. Ethel wrote in extreme old age (in 1938) that she remembered Lewes regularly coming to visit and reading to her and her siblings. 'It was a most wicked thing to ever connect my Mother's and Mr Thornton Hunt's names together', she wrote (Ashton 1991: 180).

Lewes's own sons were told the whole story when he visited them at Hofwyl in July 1859. Henceforth they continued to write to 'Mamma' (Agnes), whom they scarcely ever saw, but began to correspond also with Marian, whom they called 'Mother' or 'Mutter'. Charles came home with Lewes and Marian in 1860, took the Civil Service examinations, and with Anthony *Trollope's help was found a clerkship in the Post Office. He continued to live with the Leweses, an amiable and industrious member of the household, until he married, in March 1865, Gertrude Hill, granddaughter of Lewes's old friend Dr Southwood Smith.

After Lewes's death in November 1878, Charles was Marian's chief comforter. He undertook much of her correspondence, as his father had done, and, generous like his father, was delighted for her when she decided, after much doubt, to marry John Walter *Cross in 1880. Charles continued to work steadily at the Post Office; he translated works from German; in the 1880s he campaigned with his sister-in-law Octavia *Hill (one of the founders of the National Trust) to save Parliament Hill Fields from the developers. He also became one of the first members of the Greater London Council. But his health was delicate. In 1891 he died in Egypt, where he had gone, on doctor's orders, to escape the British climate. He was under 50 years old.

Lewes's other two sons died even younger. Thornie, the irreverent, cheerful, charming, rebellious one, left Hofwyl soon after Charles, and was sent to Edinburgh to complete his education. George Eliot's publisher John *Blackwood was hospitable to him, and watched his exploits with amusement. In 1863 Thornie failed his final Civil Service examination and refused to resit, having taken it into his head that he would like to go to Poland to fight the Russians. He was dissuaded from this, and his thirst for adventure appeased by the arrangement to send him out to Natal in October 1863 to try his hand at farming (Ashton 1991: 217–19).

Bertie learned farming in Scotland for several months, then set off to join Thornie in Natal. Together they had various adventures and mishaps with the farming experiment and with some attempts at trading with local African chiefs. In January 1869 Lewes received a heartbreaking letter from his delightful, difficult son. Thornie gave a lively account of a failed speculation which was to have made his fortune, then described his state of health. Suffering agonies from kidney stone, 'wasting away', eating almost nothing, unable to work, to sit, or to sleep, he was in need of medical attention which he could only get in England. He asked his father for money for the passage home.

Thornie arrived, shockingly emaciated and in extreme pain, in May 1869. Lewes and Marian nursed him through a dreadful summer until his death in October, aged 25, of tuberculosis of the spine.

In Natal, Bertie soldiered on alone. In 1871 he married Eliza Harrison, daughter of an English settler. They had two children, touchingly named Marian and George after Bertie's father and his famous partner. In 1875, aged 29, Bertie died of bronchitis while visiting Durban.

Agnes Lewes, who had seen her sons only infrequently since they had gone to school in Switzerland—though she came to visit Thornie during his

last illness—outlived her sons, her husband, and George Eliot. She died in 1902 at the ripe age of 80. See also WILL.   RA

Ashton, Rosemary, *G. H. Lewes: A Life* (1991).

Lewis, Maria (1800?–87), teacher, friend, and correspondent of George Eliot. In her ninth year Mary Ann Evans joined Mrs Wallington's school in *Nuneaton where the Irish-born Maria Lewis, an evangelical Anglican aged 28, was the principal governess. She was kind to an unhappy child who sought a friend in her teacher, whose squint perhaps reassured a girl distrustful of her own appearance. A frequent visitor at *Griff House, Miss Lewis soon won the Evans's approval.

After Mary Ann had transferred to her Coventry school in 1832, she maintained her friendship with Miss Lewis who became governess for the family of the Revd Latimer Harper in Northamptonshire until 1841. Her influence is evident in Mary Ann's correspondence. After her mother's death (1836) she begged her former teacher to visit her although 'I have no society but my own to offer' (*L* i. 4). Her need for approval expressed itself in frequent apologies for self-centredness and in a ponderous piety that condemned the tittering of choirboys in St Paul's and the blasphemy of a religious oratorio in *Coventry.

However strained its religiosity, the correspondence eased her loneliness, gave her an emotional outlet, and enabled her to share her reading and reflections with an intelligent, sympathetic friend: 'I generally let my feelings flow to the end of my pen as soon as I begin to write to you' (*L* i. 57). She sent Maria an early poem, the first to appear in print, and outlined a formidable plan for a chart of ecclesiastical history. Although stilted in style, the heavy Johnsonian English she learned from Miss Lewis had its value for a future writer drawn to antithesis and the wisdom of weighing one argument against another. Moreover, *evangelicanism was to leave her with an acute sense of both personal responsibility and the consequences of moral decision that would later pervade her fiction (Purkis 1985: 29–30).

Undoubtedly there were signs of strain. In October 1840, she gave Maria the flower name of Veronica (meaning Fidelity in Friendship), but in 1841 she requested the abandonment of such artificiality. Her friendship with the *Brays created a deeper breach. Her refusal to attend church on 2 January 1842 was observed by her guest, Miss Lewis, who lingered at Bird Grove in a painful atmosphere until 14 January when she left to take over her new school in Nuneaton. Their correspondence had petered out by 1849. Although hurt, Maria had complied when Mary Ann requested the return of her letters.

In 1874 George Eliot learned of Maria's address and wrote to her, enclosing £10. She responded with pleasure and George Eliot sent her a letter and money at least once a year until her death. Miss Lewis retired to Leamington, read her former pupil's novels with eager pride, and told John Walter *Cross that no one had known George Eliot as intimately as she had known her.   RMH

Bodenheimer (1994).
Purkis (1985).
Redinger (1975).

library of George Eliot. It is difficult to distinguish George Eliot's library from G. H. *Lewes's. The main sources for the analysis of their library are the books Charles Lee Lewes (see LEWES FAMILY) gave in 1882 to Dr Williams's Library, London; the list of books made by Mrs Elinor Southwood Lewes Ouvry (1877–1974), the daughter of Charles Lee Lewes and Gertrude (née Hill), of books in her mother's house; the Foster auction Sale Catalogue of 15 May 1923 and the Sotheby auction Sale Catalogue of 27 June 1923.

Charles Lee Lewes presented to Dr Williams's Library his 'Father's valuable library of philosophical and scientific works'. In July 1882 he wrote to Dr Sadler, a trustee of the Library: 'what I contemplate giving is not the whole of my Father's books, but what I should term his scientific library'. There are at least 2,405 Eliot and Lewes items at Dr Williams's, some consisting of more than a single volume. Many items are books, some are offprints. Some have Eliot's signature, some have Lewes's signature, some are signed by both, and some are not signed at all; many books are annotated by Eliot or Lewes or both of them. Nine hundred and sixty-five titles, 40 per cent of the books given to Dr Williams's, were scientific, and 251 titles, 10.4 per cent, involved philosophy. Absent in significant quantity were literary works. Critical works, histories of various dialects, and philology, constitute the fourth largest number of subject-categorized items.

A subject analysis of works listed by Mrs Ouvry reveals that there are 461 English Literature items, 44.4 per cent of the total, the largest proportion of the subjects represented. Many are primary texts and collections of authors favoured by Eliot and Lewes. According to Foster's Sale Catalogue 'about 1200 volumes of Books, being Portions of the Libraries of George Eliot and G. H. Lewes' were for sale. There is some duplication as some, but by no means all, of Eliot's and Lewes's books sold at Sotheby's, are also present in Mrs Ouvry's listing. The total number of items at Dr Williams's, on Mrs Ouvry's list, at Foster's auction, and Sotheby's sale, amounts to well in excess of the 10,000 volumes contained in Anthony *Trollope's

libraries, the upward of 10,000 volumes contained in Macaulay's library, and the 4,000 volumes from the William and Elizabeth *Gaskell Sale Catalogue. Even taking into consideration duplication, upwards of 10,000 volumes is probably a conservative estimate of the size of the library left to Charles Lee Lewes. It is hardly surprising that avid bibliomaniacs and book users such as Eliot and Lewes would have built up a large collection.

WB

Baker, William, *The George Eliot–George Henry Lewes Library: An Annotated Catalogue of Their Books at Dr. Williams's Library* (1977).
—— *The Libraries of George Eliot and George Henry Lewes* (1981).
Collins, K. K., 'Sources of Some Unidentified Serial Offprints in The George Eliot–George Henry Lewes Library', *Papers of the Bibliographical Society of America*, 73 (1979).
—— 'Sources of Remaining Unidentified Serial Offprints in The George Eliot–George Henry Lewes Library', *Papers of the Bibliographical Society of America*, 77 (1983).

life of George Eliot. When the subject of this *Companion* began writing 'The Sad Fortunes of the Reverend Amos Barton', her first work of fiction, in September 1856, she had not yet fixed on the famous *pseudonym. She had, however, good reasons for wishing to remain anonymous as she made a bid for fame as a novelist. Socially she liked to be known as Marian Evans Lewes, though she was not legally married to her partner G. H. *Lewes; nor was she ever able to marry him. Almost 37 when she turned to writing novels, she not only had before her years of astonishing success, but she had already lived through an unusual number of excitements and upheavals in her personal life, as well as having acquired a reputation as a translator, essayist, and reviewer of formidable range and power (see JOURNALIST, GEORGE ELIOT AS; TRANSLATIONS BY GEORGE ELIOT).

When Marian Lewes invented the name 'George Eliot' to give to her publisher John *Blackwood, it was one of a number of name changes she made as she embraced, or adjusted to, the various vicissitudes of her life. She was at different times Mary Anne (with an *e*) Evans, Mary Ann Evans, Marian Evans, Marian Evans Lewes, and finally Mary Ann Cross. Even if she had not added 'George Eliot' to these, she would have had a claim to fame as one of the most interesting writers and thinkers of the Victorian period. Born in 1819, the same year as Queen *Victoria, she died in 1880 the most famous woman of the age and, since the death of Charles *Dickens in 1870, indisputably the greatest living English novelist.

George Eliot lived in a time of fast and complex change. Politically, the two great *Reform Acts of

1832 and 1867 enfranchised the middle classes and parts of the working class—though not women—and did away with the worst abuses of pocket and rotten boroughs, giving proper representation to growing industrial cities like Birmingham and Manchester. Socially and economically, ordinary people experienced revolutionary changes in their lives through the coming of the railways, the determined programme of sanitary reforms carried out by Edwin Chadwick and others, and such important advances in medicine as the introduction of anaesthetics and antiseptic conditions in surgery in the mid-19th century by men like James Simpson and Joseph Lister. Intellectually, the doctrine of evolution (see DARWINISM), the progress of knowledge in geology and biology, and the increase in historical criticism of the *Bible caused many Victorians to question the inherited assumptions of their religious faith. T. H. *Huxley coined the term agnostic in 1869 to describe his stance towards religion; because he could not prove the existence of God, and because the burden of the scientific evidence seemed to him to make the idea of God an illusory one, he declined to believe in a transcendent creator.

George Eliot adopted the same position. In throwing off her early beliefs she came into conflict with her orthodox family, as she did also when she embarked on her liaison with Lewes. She was a rebel, but in some ways a reluctant one. The pains, clashes, and excitements of her own life made a living background to the sympathetic representation in her novels of the contradictions and bewilderments of her characters, caught up in similar changes. Two of her novels, *Felix Holt, the Radical* (1866) and *Middlemarch* (1871–2), are set at the time of the First Reform Bill and capture the responses to, and effects of, reform agitation among the provincial communities she creates with such imagination and sureness of touch. The subtitle of *Middlemarch*, 'A Study of Provincial Life', provides an appropriate description of most of her novels; her inwardness with the subject springs from the rich experiences of the first 30 years of her own life.

Mary Anne Evans was born on 22 November 1819 at South Farm in Arbury, Warwickshire. She was the third child of the second marriage of Robert *Evans, manager of the large estates of the *Newdigate family. Robert Evans's work on the estate was wide-ranging. He surveyed land and buildings, managed relations with the tenant farmers on the estate, collected rents, oversaw repairs, arranged the buying and selling of land, and was involved in negotiations with road-builders and coal-mining businesses in the area. His journals and the letters between him and his boss, Francis Newdigate, show him to have been an in-

ventive and inconsistent speller but a man of integrity and determination, and one in whom his employer invested a great deal of trust and authority.

His first wife, Harriet, by whom he had a son (Robert, born in 1802) and a daughter (Fanny, born in 1805), died in 1809. In 1813 he married Christiana Pearson, the daughter of a local farmer. The children of this marriage were Christiana, known as Chrissey (born in 1814), Isaac (born in 1816), and Mary Anne, the youngest, born in 1819. (Twin sons were born in March 1821, but survived only a few days.)

In the spring of 1820, when Mary Anne was only a few months old, the family moved from South Farm to a large house known as *Griff House, situated just off the main road between *Nuneaton and *Coventry. This was her home until she was 21. It had stables and outbuildings, a dairy and farmyard, and an orchard. In her semi-autobiographical sketch, 'Looking Backward', in her last published work, *Impressions of Theophrastus Such* (1879), George Eliot describes her native country as 'fat central England' with its elms, buttercups, and tree-studded hedgerows, but she remembers also the coal mining, the building of roads and railways, the cutting of canals to carry the coal from the mines. It was not all lush, rural, idyllic; many of the local villagers worked in the pits and lived in poor cottages on the Newdigate Estate, and some of the tenant farmers lived in conditions of poverty rather than plenty.

When George Eliot drew her fictional pictures of middle England, she called on her memories of her childhood, as she rode round the estate with her father, visiting tenants and observing the contrast between their lives and that of the landed family at the magnificent Arbury Hall, where she was allowed, as a clever schoolgirl, to browse in the family library.

In 1828, at the age of 9, Mary Anne boarded with her older sister Chrissey at Mrs Wallington's school in Nuneaton where she came under the religious influence of an evangelical teacher, Maria *Lewis, to whom most of her earliest extant letters—earnest, pious, sometimes self-righteous—are addressed. From 13 to 16 she attended a school in Coventry run by two daughters of a Baptist minister, Mary and Rebecca Franklin. Religious Dissent of all varieties was strong in the Midlands. Not only was evangelical *Anglicanism well represented; there were also chapels of all kinds of Dissent: Baptist, Wesleyan, Unitarian, Quaker, Congregationalist. Though her own family belonged to the regular, middle-of-the-road Anglican community, Mary Anne came into contact, and sometimes into close friendship, with people from all these sects. As a teenager she worried her brother Isaac by taking her severe piety to extremes, frowning on theatregoing and neglecting her dress and appearance—going about 'like an owl', as she said, 'to the great disgust of my brother' (Cross, i. 157).

At the Misses Franklin's school she won prizes in French and in English composition, and was known for her fine piano-playing. Schoolmates later remembered her as a serious, clever girl, but a shy and sensitive one, who used to hate performing in public, and who often ran out of the room in tears. At Christmas 1835, when she was just 16, Mary Anne came home to domestic crisis. Her mother, who had been in poor health since the death of the twins, was dying painfully of breast cancer, and her father had an attack of kidney pain while away from home on estate business.

After her mother's death in February 1836, Mary Anne stayed at home to help her sister Chrissey keep house. Isaac was now helping his father with the estate business, and would eventually take over from him, working for the next generation of the Newdigate family. In May 1837 Chrissey married Edward *Clarke, a doctor in nearby Meriden. Mary Anne was bridesmaid, and when signing the register after the wedding, she dropped the *e* from her Christian name. She now became the housekeeper for her father and her brother Isaac until Isaac, too, got married in 1841. It was decided that he and his wife should live at Griff; Robert Evans would retire as agent to the Newdigates, and he and Mary Ann would look for another house. In March 1841 they moved to Foleshill, on the outskirts of Coventry. Perhaps Robert Evans hoped that his youngest daughter would find a suitable husband in Coventry despite her plain looks and serious demeanour. Instead, she made a new set of friends who would have an important influence on her future life.

Though her formal education had ended in 1836 with the death of her mother and the assumption of domestic duties, she had continued to read widely and had lessons at home in Italian and German. She also had read, under Maria Lewis's guidance, improving works such as the life of Wilberforce.

Mary Ann's piety at the age of 20 was remarkable even in an age of pious *evangelicalism among the provincial middle and lower classes. She and Maria Lewis carried on a spiritual correspondence laced with sentimentality which sounds almost parodic when read today. Thus she christened Miss Lewis 'Veronica', signifying 'Fidelity in Friendship', and was in turn given the name 'Clematis', which meant, appropriately enough, 'Mental Beauty'. In their correspondence they discussed their reading, mostly of religious and morally edifying works. One such letter, written by Mary Ann in March 1841, ends with a paragraph full of quotations from the Bible to bolster her spiritual aspirations:

I have a very short allowance of time for preparation this morning, and must therefore content myself with assuring you of my continued love, and with asking your prayers that my spirit may not become warped by intercourse with earthly trifles and considerations of worldly interest, but may rather be urged to cling closely to heavenly hopes. (*L* i. 82)

Such pious fervour did not—perhaps could not—last. As with Maggie Tulliver, heroine of *The Mill on the Floss*, there was a reaction from extreme piety and saintliness. Mary Ann was soon reading widely in non-religious literature: *Shakespeare, Walter *Scott, *Cervantes, *Schiller, Thomas *Carlyle. After the move in 1841 to Foleshill she also came under the influence of the attractive *Bray family of Coventry.

Charles Bray was a wealthy ribbon manufacturer, a progressive in politics and a philanthropist who used his wealth to set up schools and support hospitals in order to improve the social conditions of the poor. He was a freethinker in religion, a robust and original man, who did not care what his neighbours thought of him. In his autobiography, *Phases of Opinion and Experience during a Long Life* (1884), Bray remembered with pride how his large house, Rosehill, was a Mecca for radicals and intellectuals who enjoyed the 'free-and-easy mental atmosphere' and 'the absence of all pretension and conventionality' which prevailed there. According to him, 'Every one who came to Coventry with a queer mission, or a crotchet, or was supposed to be "a little cracked", was sent up to Rosehill' (*Phases of Opinion*, 69–70).

With his quiet wife Cara, herself inclined to piety but not an orthodox Christian, and Cara's sister and brother, Sara and Charles Christian *Hennell, Bray offered Mary Ann an intellectually challenging milieu. Already bookish and well read in several languages, she became interested in historical accounts of the Bible—one by Charles Hennell and several by German biblical historians—which threw doubt on the accounts of miracles and on the supernatural elements in the Gospel stories of the life of Christ.

By the end of 1841, at the age of 22, after reading, among other works of historical scholarship, Charles Hennell's *Inquiry concerning the Origin of Christianity* (1838), Mary Ann had come to the view that Christianity was based on 'mingled truth and fiction' (*L* i. 28). On 2 January 1842 she refused to accompany her father to church. The result was anger and silence, a kind of domestic excommunication which lasted for some months. Her brother Isaac told her she was jeopardizing the family's good name by associating with Coventry radicals

Watercolour of George Eliot as a young woman, painted by her friend Cara Bray in 1842.

and infidels. He despaired of her ever finding a husband, now that she was adding 'modern' opinions to her plain appearance. Mary Ann was almost turned out of the house by her father, but eventually he relented. She agreed to attend church with him as before, while he tacitly accepted that she could think what she liked about Christianity, and from then on an uneasy truce existed between them. She continued to keep house for him until he died in 1849, trying to be a dutiful daughter, but reserving the right to hold her own opinions on the subject of religion and to continue her friendship with the Brays.

At Rosehill she met and had discussions with many liberal thinkers, including the social experimentalist Robert Owen, the social philosophers Herbert *Spencer and Harriet *Martineau, the radical publisher John *Chapman, and Ralph Waldo *Emerson on his visits from America. At the end of 1843, when Charles Hennell married Rufa *Brabant, it was arranged that Mary Ann should take over from Rufa the translation of D. F. *Strauss's *Das Leben Jesu, kritisch bearbeitet* (*The Life of Jesus, critically examined*, 1835–6). Mary Ann was well qualified for the task, knowing German, being the most learned member of the Bray–Hennell circle, and having studied the Bible closely, first as ardent evangelical, then as historical critic. In 1846 John Chapman published, in three volumes, her anonymous translation of this work, which painstakingly investigated the events of Christ's life as told in all four Gospels and found them to be not historical, but mythological—the wished-for fulfilment of Old Testament prophecies. Mary Ann received £20 for her labours. In 1854 Chapman published—this time with her name, Marian Evans, on the title-page—her second translation of a German work demystifying Scripture, Ludwig *Feuerbach's *Das Wesen des Christenthums* (*The Essence of Christianity*, 1841). Strauss, and more particularly Feuerbach, had an influence on her own position, illustrated widely in her novels, as a humanist for whom relations between man and man, and man and woman, have all the sanctity reserved in orthodox religion for the relationship between man and God.

Though still a serious young woman, inclined to depression and self-doubt and painfully conscious of her plain appearance, Mary Ann began to show that she was not just formidably intelligent and knowledgeable, but also sharp-witted and imaginatively gifted. On 21 October 1846 she wrote Charles Bray a spoof letter which gives notice that this woman has all the qualities required of a novelist: wit, wisdom, imagination, and an ability to turn her own experience to good account fictionally. She exploits with playful ease the hard intellectual labour, not without its *longueurs*, of translating Strauss's work in her description to Bray of a fictitious visit from a Professor Bücherwurm of Moderig University (Professor Bookworm of Musty University):

Down I came, not a little elated at the idea that a live professor was in the house, and, as you know I have quite the average quantity of that valuable endowment which spiteful people call assurance, but which I dignify with the name of self possession, you will believe that I neither blushed nor made a nervous giggle in attempting to smile, as is the lot of some unfortunate young ladies who are immersed in youthful bashfulness. (*L* viii. 13)

She goes on to describe this personage and to give a sample of his conversation. He is, by his own account, 'a voluminous author—indeed my works already amount to some 20 vols.—my last publication in 5 vols. was a commentary on the book of Tobit'. He has come to England in search of a wife who will double as the translator of his scholarly works, and he is peculiar enough to desire, 'besides ability to translate, a very decided ugliness of person and a sufficient fortune to supply a poor professor with coffee and tobacco, and an occasional draft of schwarzbier, as well as to contribute to the expenses of publication'. He expresses himself satisfied that Mary Ann fulfils these criteria, though he is sorry that she has no beard, 'an attribute which I have ever regarded as the most unfailing indication of a strong-minded woman'.

Mary Ann tells Bray how delighted she was by this proposal, since she is desperate to be saved from the 'horrific disgrace of spinster-hood' and to be taken away from England. The whole letter is a delightful *jeu-d'esprit*, turning her learning to light-hearted and witty account, and making a brave joke about her plain looks and her anxiety that, at the age of nearly 27, she will not find a husband. Her shrewd portrait of the learned and egotistical professor looks to us now like a preparatory sketch for Mr Casaubon in *Middlemarch*, whose proposal to Dorothea Brooke shows that he, too, wants a secretary and adoring admirer as a wife. Moreover, her ability here to illustrate her story by means of allusions, analogies, and *metaphors drawn from literature, *science, *religion, and *history gives a foretaste of the distinctiveness of her gifts as a novelist with a quite remarkable range of reference.

She needed her wit during the next few years. It was a lonely and painful time since she had to nurse her father through his long illness, during which he was demanding and ungrateful. She was exhausted, physically and emotionally, when he died at the end of May 1849.

Robert Evans was buried in Chilvers Coton churchyard, next to his wife. His property was divided between his sons Robert and Isaac; Fanny and Chrissey, who had been given £1,000 each when they married, received another £1,000 in his will, as well as household items. Mary Ann was left £2,000 in trust, a sum which, when invested, would yield about £90 a year in interest—enough to allow her to consider living independently, but not enough to live on without supplementary earnings.

What was an unmarried woman of nearly 30 with an inheritance of less than £90 a year to do? She refused to do the conventional thing: to go and live with her married brother Isaac, resigning herself to a life of plain sewing, playing the piano, and reading to her nephews and nieces in a household of conventional religious and social observance which was to her stiflingly narrow. She knew that she and Isaac disagreed about everything: *politics, religion, and the duties of younger sisters to obey their older brothers.

In characteristically generous fashion, the Brays stepped in. They took her with them on a trip to Switzerland and *Italy. After six weeks of travelling, the Brays returned to England, leaving Mary Ann in *Geneva, where she bravely took lodgings and spent a winter trying out her new-found independence, and taking stock. She was lucky to find a sympathetic family, the *D'Albert Durades, to take her in as a paying guest. The husband, François D'Albert Durade, was an artist who painted her portrait in February 1850, representing her as modest, pensive, long-faced, but pleasant-looking (see PORTRAITS).

By the time she returned to England in March 1850, Mary Ann had more or less made up her mind to move to *London and pursue a career in journalism. A short stay with Isaac and his family at Griff, followed by a rather less painful visit to Chrissey at Meriden, convinced her that she could not make her home among them. The decision to move to London was a momentous one, and was accompanied by a change of name. She now called herself, as befitted an independent, grown-up woman, Marian Evans, and in January 1851 she took up lodgings in the Strand.

London in 1851 was a thriving city of culture and contrasts. The largest metropolis in the world was preparing for the Great Exhibition to be held in the Crystal Palace which was even then being built in Hyde Park. The brainchild of Prince Albert, the Exhibition was the largest ever held; visitors from all over the world came to admire the latest inventions in every branch of industry. Those who came from Europe, particularly members of governments and royal families, also marvelled at, and envied, the political stability of Britain which allowed the bringing together of such large crowds only three years after the *revolutions of 1848 had

broken out in almost every capital city of Europe except London.

London also resembled a vast building site at this time. Euston Station had opened in 1837 and Waterloo in 1848, and when Marian Evans arrived in London, King's Cross was under construction. Not far from the Strand were some notorious slums, including 'The Rookery', on which Dickens based his Chancery slum Tom-All-Alone's in *Bleak House*, which he began writing in 1851. Sanitation was still minimal, though following an outbreak of cholera in London in 1849 Edwin Chadwick of the General Board of Health had begun to plan a system of sewerage which would stop the sewage from passing into the Thames, as it still did when Marian Evans arrived.

Through Charles Bray, Marian Evans had an immediate entrée into the world of radical politics and journalism, of freethinking and, in the case of some of the friends she now made, free living as well. The Chapman household at 142 Strand was itself a most unconventional one. The three-storey building, looking over Somerset House and the Thames at the back, was both the workplace and the home of the publisher John Chapman.

Chapman specialized in publishing works of a left-wing or sceptical tendency. He had been impressed by Marian's intellect and by her stamina in completing the translation of Strauss. He came to value these qualities even more when in 1851 he bought the great radical periodical, the *Westminster Review*, first set up in the 1820s to further the cause of political and social reform in the long run-up to the Reform Act of 1832. Marian Evans became, in effect, the editor of the *Review*, as well as one of its best and most widely admired reviewers. Chapman came to rely heavily on her judgement in everything to do with the *Review*.

The upper floors of 142 Strand were occupied by Chapman's family and a succession of lodgers—literary people whose books he published or who wrote for the *Westminster Review*. Chapman held Friday night parties, when writers gathered to talk about literature and politics of a mainly radical kind. It was through Chapman that Marian Evans met Herbert *Spencer and his friend, the critic G. H. Lewes, with both of whom she was to fall in love.

But first she succumbed to the charms of Chapman himself. He was handsome, worldly, successful, and his admiration for her abilities flattered Marian. Chapman lived with his wife Susanna, a woman fourteen years older than he was (Chapman was 30 in 1851), their two children, and the children's governess, Elisabeth Tilley, who was also Chapman's mistress.

Into this metropolitan ménage was thrust the provincial young woman of plain and earnest appearance but of strong will and strong passion. A comedy was played out over the next few months, with Chapman arousing the jealousy of his wife (who apparently accepted the governess's role in their lives) and, more especially, his mistress by the attention he gave to the new paying guest. He visited Miss Evans's room, where she played the piano for him and taught him German. They were caught holding hands. Mrs Chapman and Elisabeth joined forces to expel the interloper. Marian fled in tears to the Brays in Coventry, her ears ringing with Chapman's assurances that he admired her *mental beauty* (Clematis again), but found her lacking in physical beauty.

To Marian Evans these events were, of course, far from funny. But she sensibly abandoned all hopes of Chapman as a lover and—setting a pattern which she was to follow with Herbert Spencer too—settled down to a friendly, professional relationship with him. The women at 142 Strand relented, and in the autumn of 1851 Chapman brought Marian back to London, where she began to guide him in the editorial department of the *Westminster Review*. He was the nominal editor. She, from a mixture of diffidence, modesty, and fear of playing a public role, was happy to remain behind the scenes, doing the work and letting Chapman put his name to it.

During 1851 Marian, sometimes accompanied by Chapman, attended lectures in geometry at the new Ladies' College in Regent's Park, later renamed Bedford College. She also frequently stepped across the Strand with Chapman to see plays put on at the Lyceum Theatre in Catherine St (now Aldwych).

Marian worked closely with Chapman on the *Westminster* until 1854. What he gained from the partnership was the help of her sharp brain, wide knowledge, willing labour, and an ability to deal tactfully yet firmly with touchy contributors. Chapman himself lacked all these qualities, as one of the chief contributors, George *Combe, somewhat brutally pointed out to him. Combe was a well-known phrenologist, a practitioner of that 'science' by which character was to be read by feeling the contours of the head. In 1851 he felt Marian Evans's bumps at Bray's house, and concluded, 'she appeared to me the ablest woman I have seen', having 'a very large brain' and large bumps of 'concentrativeness' and 'love of approbation' (*L* viii. 27–8). To Chapman he wrote bluntly in December 1851:

I would very respectfully recommend to you to use Miss Evans's tact and judgment as an aid to your own. She has certain organs large in her brain which are not so fully developed in yours, and she will judge more correctly of the influence upon other persons of what you write and do, than you will do yourself. (*L* viii. 33)

Combe was to be shattered by the news, three years later, that Marian had 'run off' to the Continent with a married man. He wrote to Bray in November 1854: 'I should like to know whether there is insanity in Miss Evans's family; for her conduct, with *her* brain, seems to me like morbid mental aberration' (*L* viii. 129).

As for Marian, she gained from the partnership with Chapman a widened social circle, the experience of running a review, the freedom to take decisions, and the chance to review works for the *Westminster* ranging from science, to *philosophy, to evangelical sermons, to literature English, French, and German. In her work for the *Westminster Review* from 1851 to 1856, she found her voice as a writer. The essayist, increasingly confident, wide-ranging, witty, and rhetorically complex, paved the way, we may say with the aid of hindsight, for the future novelist George Eliot (see ESSAYS).

It would be hard to exaggerate the unusualness of Marian Evans's social position as a single working woman in London in the early 1850s. Along with a very few other brave females—the idiosyncratic social reformer Harriet *Martineau comes to mind—she was pursuing an unconventional path. Women of no fortune either married (whereupon their income promptly became their husbands' property under the law) or took jobs as governesses or live-in companions to rich relations or acquaintances. Such positions were unenviable—witness not only *Jane Eyre* but also George Eliot's own portraits of young women forced into such situations. There is, for example, Mary Garth in *Middlemarch*, who keeps house for her rich relative, Mr Featherstone, and is treated abominably by him. In *The Mill on the Floss* Maggie Tulliver becomes a schoolteacher after her father's ruin and death, and though George Eliot does not show her in this role, she has Maggie talk about this period of her life as a time of 'joyless days of distasteful occupation' as opposed to 'the intense and varied life she yearned for' (*MF* 6.2).

Marian Evans herself avoided such a dismal fate (though she had thought of becoming a teacher in Leamington when her father threatened to make her leave the house in 1842). But there was a risk attached to cutting loose in the way she did. Her brother disapproved of the move to London, and made her feel that she would no longer be welcome in his home, even for visits. She was now in a society composed entirely of men, and though it was stimulating to associate with them freely and unchaperoned, she was risking her reputation in doing so. She must often, too, have missed the

Sketch of George Eliot in 1860 (misdated 1857) by Samuel Laurence (1812–84).

companionship of a female friend in London, though she still had Cara Bray and Sara Hennell in Coventry to write to. She told them of all her doings in her letters.

In one letter of May 1852 she reported to her friends a great occasion at 142 Strand. It bears eloquent witness to the excitement of her life and the unusualness of her position. Chapman held a meeting of publishers, writers, and booksellers to protest against the Booksellers' Association, a cartel of larger publishers which fixed the price of books, prohibiting small publishers like Chapman from offering discounts. Dickens took the chair, 'preserving', according to Marian, 'a courteous neutrality of eyebrow, and speaking with clearness and decision' (L ii. 23).

Everyone from the liberal and radical wing of London literary life was there: Herbert Spencer, Lewes, the scientist (and discoverer of dinosaurs) Richard *Owen, Wilkie *Collins, and many more distinguished men. Marian Evans was also there—the only woman.

We also have a pen portrait of Marian Evans at this time from a fellow journalist and fellow lodger at 142 Strand. In 1885 William Hale *White read John Walter *Cross's Life of George Eliot (Cross having married her in 1880)—a work which W. E. *Gladstone famously described as 'a Reticence in three volumes'. White felt moved to write his recollection of Marian Evans, his fellow lodger in the Strand in the early 1850s:

She was really one of the most sceptical, unusual creatures I ever knew, and it was this side of her character which was to me the most attractive . . . I can see her now, with her hair over her shoulders, the easy chair half sideways to the fire, her feet over the arms, and a proof in her hands, in that dark room at the back of No. 142, and I confess I hardly recognize her in the pages of Mr Cross's—on many accounts—most interesting volumes. I do hope that in some future edition, or in some future work, the salt and spice will be restored to the records of George Eliot's entirely unconventional life. (*Athenaeum*, 28 November 1885)

White was undoubtedly right to try to redress the balance. Cross took absurd liberties with his wife's letters, as Gordon S. *Haight pointed out in his unexpurgated text of George Eliot's *letters. Haight gives some examples of this: when George Eliot wrote 'It is raining horribly here—raining blue devils', Cross omitted the last three words; when she bemoaned the loss of some proofs, saying 'I would rather have lost one of my toes', he changed 'toes' to 'fingers' (L, vol. i, p. xiii).

What would Cross have made of a letter from George Eliot to Chapman in February 1856, one which has only recently come to light (published with five other new letters to Chapman in the *Huntington Library Quarterly* in 1991)? In it she vigorously urges him not to print in the *Westminster* an article by a 'Miss H' on the French woman writer George *Sand:

Before I had read the article I supposed her to be a woman of talent; I now think her one of the numerous class of female scribblers who undertake to edify the public before they know the proper use of their own language. The whole of the introduction, & every passage where Miss H. launches into more than a connecting sentence or two, is feminine rant of the worst kind, which it will be simply fatal to the Review to admit. (Ashton, 'New George Eliot Letters', 121–2)

Further, 'I would not trust the most ordinary subject, still less the most delicate, to a woman who writes such trash'; and 'Everything she says about George Sand is undiscriminating Bosh'. Her letters to Chapman about the conduct of the *Westminster* are all like this, confident, wide-ranging, managerial, even magisterial towards her boss, attractive, desirable, but intellectually inferior man of the world.

This unconventional young woman, who had attended lectures, theatre, and opera during 1851 with Chapman, was soon going to the theatre and opera with Herbert Spencer. By June 1852 Marian was reporting to the Brays that she and Spencer were seen so often in one another's company that 'all the world is setting us down as engaged' (L ii. 35). Marian would have liked nothing better, but Spencer began to back down. In July Marian went off to Broadstairs for a lonely holiday; from there she fired off several managing letters to Chapman about the *Westminster Review*, careful letters to Combe, whom Chapman was pressing for money to help the *Westminster* out of a financial crisis, and, at the same time, love letters to Spencer. She wrote begging him to visit her at Broadstairs. All her passion and pride and humour are on display, as well as her loneliness and uncertainty:

Dear Friend

No credit to me for my virtues as a refrigerent. I owe them all to a few lumps of ice which I carried away with me from that tremendous glacier of yours. I am glad that Nemesis, lame as she is, has already made you feel a little uneasy in my absence, whether from the state of the thermometer [a reference to the very high temperatures that July] or aught else. We will not inquire too curiously whether you long most for my society or for the sea-breezes. If you decided that I was not worth coming to see, it would only be of a piece with that generally exasperating perspicacity of yours which will not allow one to humbug you. (An agreeable quality, let me tell you, that capacity of being humbugged. Don't pique yourself on not possessing it.) (*L* viii. 50–1)

Spencer visited her briefly and obviously discouraged her, for a week later she wrote again, almost proposing marriage to him:

I want to know if you can assure me that you will not forsake me, that you will always be with me as much as you can, and share your thoughts and feelings with me. If you become attached to some one else, then I must die, but until then I could gather courage to work and make life valuable, if only I had you near me. . . . Those who have known me best have always said, that if ever I loved any one thoroughly my whole life must turn upon that feeling, and I find they say truly. You curse the destiny which has made the feeling concentrate itself on you—but if you will only have patience with me you shall not curse it long. You will find that I can be satisfied with very little, if I am delivered from the dread of losing it. (*L* viii. 56–7)

She ends this remarkable letter with the comment:

I suppose no woman ever before wrote such a letter as this—but I am not ashamed of it, for I am conscious that in the light of reason and true refinement I am worthy of your respect and tenderness, whatever gross men or vulgar-minded women might think of me.

These letters give some insight into how, when she came to write fiction, George Eliot could be so penetrating in her analyses of the complex relations between men and women, both those who marry and those—like Maggie with Stephen and Philip, or like Gwendolen with Daniel Deronda—who have intimate relationships which do *not* end in marriage.

By the following year, 1853, G. H. Lewes had replaced Spencer in Marian Evans's affections, and fortunately he returned them. He, too, was a regular contributor to the *Westminster Review*, as well as theatre critic for the **Leader*, the weekly paper which he co-edited with his friend Thornton Hunt. Lewes, two years older than Marian, had had a busy and varied career. From an insecure background, brought up by his mother and a hated stepfather, with a miscellaneous schooling, he had worked his way to prominence in literary London by means of prodigious talent, versatility, and hard work.

When he met Marian Evans through Chapman in 1851 he had written a popular history of philosophy; two novels; several plays and adaptations of French farces, some of which Marian saw at the Lyceum with Chapman or Spencer; a biography of Robespierre; and hundreds of articles and reviews. He was planning a life of **Goethe*. Apart from

editing the *Leader*, he had also acted successfully with Dickens's amateur theatre company, and had even toyed with the idea of going on the stage professionally. Like Marian he was fluent in French and German, and widely read in literature, philosophy, and science. He was an atheist. He was also, irrevocably, married.

Lewes had married in 1841 Agnes Jervis, the beautiful daughter of a Radical MP. They had agreed to have an open marriage, the result of which was that in addition to having three surviving sons by Lewes, Agnes had by 1851 borne two more children whose father was not Lewes, but his friend Thornton Hunt. She was to have two more children by Hunt in 1853 and 1857. Lewes, having entered on this open marriage, duly registered the first two of these children as his own. When he subsequently met and fell in love with Marian Evans, he could not sue for divorce, since under the terms of the law he had condoned his wife's adultery by registering the births of her children by Hunt in his own name. Though he was by 1853 disillusioned with his domestic arrangements—and notably did *not* register the birth of Agnes's daughter, Ethel, born in October 1853—he had disqualified himself from ever seeking a divorce.

He had, however, left Agnes, probably in 1852, though he visited her and his children frequently, supported them financially, and was generous to Agnes for the rest of his life, as was George Eliot after his death (see LEWES FAMILY). (Agnes outlived them both by many years, living on until 1902.)

Lewes and Marian became lovers. He came and went at Chapman's, and in October 1853 she moved to new lodgings at 21 Cambridge St, Hyde Park Square, where she could receive Lewes less publicly. It has been assumed by most of her biographers that their liaison dated from this move of hers, but it can be shown that they were probably intimate by the end of 1852 or beginning of 1853. In fact, it seems that Marian was already attracted to Lewes while she was still 'in love' with Spencer (Ashton, *G. H. Lewes*, 132–43). The heroines of her novels are often in a state of doubt about their feelings. Maggie Tulliver, the most obviously autobiographical of them, certainly loves two men at once—or three, when one considers that her deepest feelings are those for her brother Tom. George Eliot knew from her own experience that it is possible to be confused in one's emotional life. We can detect a certain amount of this kind of confusion in some of her letters to the Brays during 1852–3.

The Brays did not much like Lewes. Unorthodox though they were, they thought him bohemian, flippant, metropolitan, not quite respectable. Marian's own reaction to him on meeting him with Chapman in October 1851 was to describe him to Bray as 'a sort of miniature Mirabeau', a reference to his famed ugliness (*L* i. 367). But soon she was meeting him regularly in the company of Spencer, with whom Lewes was friendly, and her letters to the Brays during the 'romance' with Spencer often mention Lewes in the next breath, as it were. In June 1852 the Brays were obviously trying to bring Spencer to the brink of a proposal to Marian. They invited Spencer to visit them in Coventry later that summer, when Marian would also be there. (They were her substitute family to escape to, now that her own family had disowned her.) Marian connived at the matchmaking. For some reason, the invitation to Spencer went via Lewes, who was also invited to visit, though not at the same time as Spencer. Marian's response was a rather excited and contradictory one:

Entre nous, if Mr Lewes should not accept your invitation now, pray don't ask him when I am with you—not that I don't like him—*au contraire*—but I want nothing so Londonish when I go to enjoy the fields and hedgerows and yet more, friends of ten years' growth. (*L* ii. 37)

In the end, Marian visited the Brays alone at the end of October, having bravely clarified her position with Spencer in Broadstairs in July.

Meanwhile, she had been reading on this holiday Lewes's not very good novel *Rose, Blanche and Violet* (1848), and her letters from now on are peppered with references to his articles for the *Westminster* and his doings as theatre critic of his own weekly newspaper, the *Leader*. Soon she was visiting the *theatre with Lewes, not Spencer. On her thirty-third birthday, 22 November 1852, she wrote to the Brays describing her day. After lunch she had just got down to work when, 'with two clear hours before dinner, rap at the door—Mr Lewes—who of course sits talking till the second bell rings' (*L* ii. 68).

In December 1853 she wrote one of her strong letters to Chapman, trying to get him to refuse an article by the new star on the scientific horizon, T. H. Huxley, in which Huxley attacks Lewes's book *Comte's Philosophy of the Sciences*, praising Harriet Martineau's rival book, an abridged translation of Comte's work. Lewes's book had been published by Bohn, Martineau's by Chapman himself. Marian pulls no punches in advising Chapman to 'expunge' Huxley's review from the *Westminster*:

I think I ought to have a voice in the matter, in virtue of the share in the management of the W[estminster] R[eview] which I have had hitherto . . . My opinion is, that the editors of the Review will disgrace themselves by inserting an utterly worthless & unworthy notice of a work by one of their own writers—a man of much longer & higher standing than Mr. Huxley, & whom Mr. H's seniors in science & superiors both in intellect & fame treat with respect. (Ashton, 'New George Eliot Letters', 120)

In another letter written probably on the same day, she added, 'Do you really think that if you had been the publisher of Mr. Lewes's book and Bohn the publisher of Miss Martineau's, Mr. Huxley would have written just so? "Tell that to the Marines"' (*L* ii. 133).

It seems very likely that she and Lewes became lovers about this time. Sometime in 1853 they reached a momentous decision—more significant for her than for him—the decision to live together openly as man and wife. Once more Marian Evans changed her name, though not legally. From now on she called herself 'Mrs Lewes'.

Though it was not uncommon for Victorian men to have mistresses in addition to, or in place of, their wives—Bray, Chapman, Wilkie *Collins, Dickens, for example—such arrangements were usually kept quiet. This was different. Marian and Lewes made no secret of their liaison, which they considered a true marriage. It was Marian's reputation which suffered most. As she wrote in September 1855 to her old friend Cara Bray, who at first could not bring herself to see Marian: 'Light and easily broken ties are what I neither desire theoretically nor could live for practically. Women who are satisfied with such ties do not act as I have done—they obtain what they desire and are still invited to dinner' (*L* ii. 214).

In her novels George Eliot often puts her heroines in difficult—even dangerous—emotional situations in which they attract criticism from society for breaking, or appearing to break, its social rules. Dorothea begins to love Will Ladislaw even while she is dutifully married to Mr Casaubon; it is a tribute to George Eliot's power as a writer, and her knowledge of human nature, that she persuades us that Dorothea herself is unaware of her feelings for Ladislaw. She shows, of course, that Mr Casaubon himself is all too aware of the chemistry between his young wife and his young cousin.

In *The Mill on the Floss*, in which George Eliot sails closest to the wind in terms of describing prohibited relationships, she has Maggie fall in love with Stephen Guest against all her wishes and her sense of prior duties. They elope together, then Maggie returns without consummating the affair but to all appearances the fallen woman. George Eliot permits herself a pungent attack on society's way of thinking the worst in relations between the sexes. She fairly excoriates the gossips, pointing out how much harder public opinion is on the *woman* in such situations than on the *man*:

Maggie had returned without a trousseau, without a husband—in that degraded and outcast condition to which error is well known to lead; and the world's wife, with that fine instinct which is given her for the preservation of society, saw at once that Miss Tulliver's conduct had been of the most aggravated kind. . . . As for poor Mr Stephen Guest, he was rather pitiable than otherwise: a young man of five and twenty is not to be too severely judged in these cases—he is really very much at the mercy of a designing bold girl. And it was clear that he had given way in spite of himself—he had shaken her off as soon as he could: indeed, their having parted so soon looked very black indeed—for her. (*MF* 7.2)

In 1854 Lewes and Marian signalled their intention only to their closest friends. As he needed to visit Weimar and Berlin to research his life of Goethe, it was to Weimar that they went together in July 1854, Marian sending her famous telegram to Charles and Cara Bray and Sara Hennell:

Dear Friends—all three
I have only time to say good bye and God bless you. Poste Restante, Weimar for the next six weeks, and afterwards Berlin. (*L* ii. 166)

While the rumour mill worked energetically at home (with Chapman and Bray joining in the head-shaking and moralizing), Marian and Lewes settled down to hard work and social pleasure at *Weimar. There they met the composer *Liszt, who was living with a married woman without raising eyebrows.

Marian and Lewes, too, were accepted without fuss. But on their return to England in March 1855, Marian found that she was no longer accepted in mixed society. She and Lewes found lodgings first at Clarence Row, East Sheen, then at 8 Park Shot, Richmond, where they remained until February 1859, by which time 'George Eliot' had sprung upon the world with the publication of *Scenes of Clerical Life* in 1858 and the immediately successful *Adam Bede* in February 1859. Their male friends from the *Westminster Review* circle visited, of course, as before, but none brought their wives. Marian had to tell her enthusiastic feminist friend Bessie *Parkes to address letters to 'Mrs Lewes', not 'Miss Evans', so as not to arouse the suspicion of the landlady. Lewes was invited out to dinner, but not Marian.

It was in 1856 that Marian, encouraged by Lewes, first tried her hand at fiction. She was already well known in literary circles as the author of several trenchant articles and reviews in the *Westminster Review* on subjects ranging from science to history to biblical criticism to literature. One of the last long articles she wrote for Chapman before

beginning 'The Sad Fortunes of the Reverend Amos Barton', the first of the three stories which made up *Scenes of Clerical Life*, was a sparklingly witty attack on the 'left-handed imbecility' of certain minor female novelists. Called *'Silly Novels by Lady Novelists', and published in the *Westminster Review* in October 1856, it divides the novels according to certain classes: 'the *mind-and-millinery* species', 'the *oracular* species', and 'the *white neck-cloth* species'. This last type represents evangelicalism, a subject Marian knew much about from her early life as well as from her wide reading. She criticizes those contemporary novelists who mix evangelical religion with high society. 'The real drama of evangelicalism', she writes, 'for any one who has genius enough to discern and reproduce it—lies among the middle and lower classes' (*Essays*, 318). Whereupon she set about showing how it could, and should, be done.

Because of her anomalous social position she chose to write under a pseudonym. In November 1856 Lewes sent the manuscript of 'Amos Barton' to the Edinburgh publisher John Blackwood, saying it was by a 'shy, ambitious' friend of his (*L* ii. 269, 276). No name was given for this unknown author, and Blackwood actually began corresponding, via Lewes, with 'My Dear Amos'. He knew he was dealing with a potentially great writer, telling his mysterious correspondent in January 1857 that he had recently confided to Thackeray that he had 'lighted upon a new Author who is uncommonly like a first class passenger' (*L* ii. 291). Marian replied to this praise on 4 February 1857, signing herself for the first time 'George Eliot' (see PSEUDONYM).

It was not unusual for Victorian women to publish under male pseudonyms: most famously, the Brontë sisters had published their works in the 1840s under the names Currer, Ellis, and Acton Bell. But it would be wrong to think that women found it necessary to hide behind a masculine name to get published and appreciated. Novel writing had long been recognized as a genre suitable for women to write—particularly the novel of social manners, a subject which they could be expected to know about. Hence Fanny Burney and Maria *Edgeworth had written under their own names at the beginning of the century, and Mrs *Gaskell was happy to write her novels without recourse to a pseudonym.

But Marian's case was different. She was known as the freethinking radical of the *Westminster Review* (the 'strong-minded woman', as Carlyle called her, *L* ii. 176 n.) and the woman who was living with a married man. She needed the protection of a pseudonym. It also suited her constitutional diffidence and fear of failure to conceal her identity, as it had suited her to be the unnamed though independent and managing editor of Chapman's *Westminster Review*.

The *Scenes of Clerical Life* were published serially, in *Blackwood's *Edinburgh Magazine* from January to November 1857, often appearing on facing pages with Lewes's lively work of popularizing marine biology, 'Sea-side Studies', which was being serialized at the same time. Publication in book form followed early in 1858. Meanwhile, Marian had taken the brave decision to tell her family in Warwickshire of her new life with Lewes. She wrote to Isaac, who, when he ascertained that her marriage was not a legal one, instructed his solicitor to inform his sister that he wished to have no more contact with her. He prevailed on their sister Chrissey and half-sister Fanny to stop corresponding too. It was a blow to Marian's feelings, though she was not surprised at Isaac's disapproval, having encountered it at the time of losing her faith and again when she made the move to London.

Marian was encouraged by the success of her stories to set about writing her first full-length novel, *Adam Bede*, which brought her instant fame on its publication early in 1859. Dickens admired it (and guessed the author was a woman); Mrs Gaskell was flattered to be asked if she had written it.

Inevitably, however, gossip got to work, both in London's literary circles, where Herbert Spencer let out the secret of the authorship, and in Warwickshire, where readers, including members of Marian Evans's estranged family, recognized characters and settings in both *Scenes of Clerical Life* and *Adam Bede*. Authorship was claimed for a Midlands man called Joseph *Liggins, who, although he never went into print on the subject, allowed others to do so without refuting the claim. The 'Liggins business' dragged on for two years, with letters being written in *The Times* and the pro-Liggins faction refusing to accept Blackwood's public statements denying that Liggins was the author. The business of keeping her identity secret, though important to the sensitive Marian, caused her anguish, and the persistence of the Liggins myth, combined with the rumours of literary London, led her at last to admit defeat and allow it to be known, in June 1859, that 'George Eliot' was Marian Evans, alias 'Mrs Lewes' or the 'strong-minded woman' of the *Westminster Review*.

Her friends were, on the whole, pleased, though Sara Hennell felt jealous and suddenly left behind by a friend now departed into 'glory', and Herbert Spencer also showed jealousy and resentment at his friend's tremendous success (*L* iii. 49 n., 95–6). But Cara Bray, who had taken a long time to accept the liaison with Lewes, wrote warmly congratulating her friend, and robust feminist friends like Bessie Parkes and Barbara *Bodichon were

jubilant both at her success and at the discomfort of those who disapproved of her life.

For readers and critics were stunned to find that the novelist they had welcomed for her humanity, her humour, her tolerance, and the strongly moral—though neither moralistic nor religious—ethos of her work was none other than the free-thinking, free-loving (as the caricature of her relationship with Lewes went) Marian Evans.

In due course society adjusted to the shock of finding that one of its greatest writers was an unbeliever and a woman in a compromising social position. By the time George Eliot had written her sixth novel, *Middlemarch*, in 1871–2, her status as England's finest living novelist was assured. With fame and success her social position altered too. She and Lewes were able to exchange a succession of cramped lodgings in Sheen, Richmond, Wandsworth, and Marylebone for a grand house, The *Priory, in Regent's Park, to which they moved in 1863.

But at the time of *Adam Bede* itself, Marian found that her enjoyment of its complete success—with accolades in all the journals and sales of more than 10,000 copies in the first year, well beyond her, or Blackwood's, wildest dreams—was soured by the Liggins problem and the uproar in some quarters which followed on the lifting of the veil of anonymity. Only Lewes's encouragement and cheerfulness and Blackwood's firm and friendly support—he paid her an extra £400 for *Adam Bede* to give her a fair share in its unexpected success—kept her from giving up fiction and even, according to Lewes in September 1859, leaving England altogether to get away from the 'fools' who 'obtrude themselves upon her' (*L* viii. 245). Marian's debt to Lewes is eloquently expressed on the manuscript of the novel (now in the British Library), which she dedicated to him: 'To my dear husband, George Henry Lewes, I give this M.S. of a work which would never have been written but for the happiness which his love has conferred on my life.'

'The Lifted Veil' is the title of an uncharacteristically gloomy, even morbid, tale of second sight and hatred which Marian wrote early in 1859, as *Adam Bede* was being published and work on her next novel, *The Mill on the Floss*, had begun. Both the short story and the new novel bear witness to the distress and depression against which Marian was struggling, despite her domestic happiness with Lewes and her success as a novelist. The miracle is that *The Mill on the Floss*, with its tragic plot based on the loving yet mutually thwarting relationship between a brother and sister, Tom and Maggie Tulliver, and its bold approach to the difficulties of sexual attraction, should also be such a humorous work. It is evidence of Marian's

Portrait of George Eliot in 1865 by Frederic Burton (1816–1900), which Lewes had hanging in his study in The Priory.

ability to turn painful personal experience to comic, as well as tragic, account.

As she wrote this novel, she learned that her sister Chrissey was dying of consumption. In February 1859 Chrissey wrote, regretting the break in their relations. She died in March. No wonder Marian's bitter feelings towards Isaac find expression in some harsh authorial remarks about Tom Tulliver in *The Mill on the Floss*. What is more remarkable is the warmth she is also able to put into the portrait.

Marian's second novel was published in April 1860, and within four days had sold 4,600 copies (Haight 1968: 327); but Marian and Lewes had gone abroad on an extended trip to *Italy late in March to avoid the inevitable comments on the identity of the author. They visited all the major Italian cities; in *Florence Lewes drew Marian's attention to the history of the city in the late 15th century, particularly the role in public life played by the Dominican monk Girolamo *Savonarola, who led a religious revival after the fall of the Medici family but was tried and executed as a heretic in 1498. George Eliot was to base her novel *Romola* (1863) on his story.

In June they travelled to Hofwyl in Switzerland, where Lewes's three sons, Charles, aged nearly 18, Thornie, aged 16, and Herbert, aged 14, were at school. They brought Charles back to London with them; he studied for the Civil Service exams and took up a job as clerk in the Post Office. Because of the inconvenience for Charles of travelling to work daily from the Leweses' home in Wandsworth, they moved into London, first to a house in Harewood Square, near Regent's Park, then round the corner to Blandford Square. Gradually, Marian began to go out to concerts, theatre, and dinner parties, finding that she was becoming more welcome in general society than she had been on her return from Germany with Lewes in 1855. Samuel *Laurence painted her portrait, completing it in September 1860. Lewes did not like it, but Blackwood, recognizing the 'sad pensive look' which had struck him when he first met her, bought it to hang in his office in Edinburgh (*L* iii. 343).

In November she began her short novel *Silas Marner*, which she finished in March 1861. With its happy ending, its legendary—even symbolic—plot of the miser who turns into a philanthropist and finds happiness in adopting a child, it is different from her other novels, while sharing their humour and breadth of understanding. Though contemporary readers were, on the whole, fondest of *Adam Bede* among her novels, the response to *Silas Marner* was gratifyingly warm.

This was not to be the case with her next novel, the one on which she laboured for longest and not to altogether happy effect. *Romola* was thoroughly researched for (too much so, according to Lewes and to many readers and critics), both in Italy and in the Reading Room of the British Museum, but the writing went slowly and by fits and starts. The resulting novel, though full of fine things, is too crowded and laborious to come to life imaginatively.

Relations with Blackwood had suffered a strain when Marian was writing *The Mill on the Floss*; she felt he had not done enough to dispel the Liggins myth and feared, not without justification, that he was nervous about the public response to that novel now that the identity of George Eliot was widely known. When George *Smith, a London publisher with money to spare and a new journal, the *Cornhill Magazine*, to launch, offered Lewes the editorship of the journal and George Eliot an unprecedented £10,000 to publish *Romola* in twelve monthly parts in the *Cornhill*, beginning in July 1862, she accepted, though with a bad conscience. Trying to keep up with the relentless pace of part publication proved a nightmare for her; the novel fell rather flat with critics and the public; Smith lost money on it; she felt badly towards him for his loss and towards Blackwood for having deserted him.

During 1863 the Leweses, now rather well off thanks to Marian's earnings, searched for a larger house. They found The Priory near Regent's Park. Lewes's friend, the designer Owen Jones (chief designer of the Crystal Palace), was commissioned to decorate the living rooms at considerable expense, and in November 1863 the Leweses moved in and entered on a splendid style of living. Here at The Priory they soon began to hold regular Sunday afternoon parties for friends and visitors, including Charles *Darwin, Huxley, Spencer, Henry *James, and the artist Frederic *Leighton, who illustrated *Romola*.

They were also increasingly invited out together by literary friends and admirers. In 1877 George Eliot was even introduced to royalty in the person of Queen Victoria's daughter Princess Louise. Queen Victoria herself had read the novels, admiring *Adam Bede* so much that in 1861 she had commissioned Edward Henry Corbould to paint two scenes from the novel—one of Dinah Morris preaching, the other of Hetty Sorrel making butter in the dairy.

In 1865 Frederic *Burton drew her portrait, which he gave to the National Portrait Gallery in 1883. Friends reckoned that this was the best likeness of the few she allowed to be taken. Like Laurence's, it shows a melancholy long-faced woman with abundant brown hair and intelligent but sad eyes. Contemporaries who saw her agreed with her own estimate of her appearance as plain (and many enjoyed noticing that Lewes, too, was ugly);

Henry James summed it up best, perhaps, when he wrote to his brother William in 1878: 'The great G.E. herself is both sweet and superior, and has a delightful expression in her large, long, pale equine face' (Ashton 1996: 275).

As agitation in Parliament led up to the passing of the Second Great Reform Act of 1867, George Eliot returned to England and to the familiar Midlands countryside of her early novels with her novel about the upheavals of society at the time of the First Reform Act of 1832, *Felix Holt, the Radical* (1866). For this she approached her old publisher John Blackwood, who responded with warmth to her return. He appreciated, as did her readers, the richly observed social scene, but the election riot on which the plot turns, based in part on a polling-day riot which occurred in her native Nuneaton in 1832, is a rather tame affair, and Felix Holt himself is unconvincing both as a radical and as a hero. There is also an over-elaborate mystery about exchanged identities and legal arrangements of estates, not unlike that in Dickens's most recent novel, *Our Mutual Friend* (1865) and in Wilkie Collins's works.

In December 1866 Marian and Lewes visited *Spain. Lewes's health was poor, and the journey was gruelling, but both had long wished to see Granada and the Alhambra. While on this visit, Marian got the idea of writing about the expulsion from Spain of the Moors and the gypsies in the 1490s, and the result was *The Spanish Gypsy* (1868). The gypsy of the title, Fedalma, has to choose between duty to her race and love of a Catholic duke. As with *Romola*, the conception and execution are less than successful, the more so as, after some deliberation, she cast this story in the form of a dramatic poem in blank verse. One of her most sympathetic and astute critics, R. H. *Hutton, noticed that 'verse to her is a fetter, and not a stimulus'; Henry James asked readers to imagine what it would be like if, say, Tennyson had written a novel, or George Sand a tragedy in French alexandrines (Ashton 1996: 294).

Polite though the response had been to *Romola*, *Felix Holt*, and *The Spanish Gypsy*, George Eliot was aware of a drop in her popularity. She could not know that her next work, an amalgam of two stories begun and abandoned, would be acclaimed her masterpiece. *Middlemarch* was written while Marian battled against self-doubt and illness. It was the result of a brilliant idea to knit together her story about the arrival of a young doctor in a Midlands town shortly before the Reform Act of 1832 and a second story, 'Miss Brooke', about the marriage choice of an idealistic young woman of the landed gentry.

Not only did Marian suffer from the usual agonies of composition; she and Lewes spent the summer of 1869 nursing Lewes's second son Thornie through the excruciatingly painful illness of tuberculosis of the spine, of which he finally died, aged 25, in October 1869. The irrepressible Thornie had failed his Civil Service examinations and had gone out to Africa to farm. The venture, undertaken with his younger brother Herbert, was not wholly successful financially, and Thornie had contracted his fatal illness. Lewes sent him money to take the passage home, in the hope that he might be cured in England. Instead, he came home to die.

By May 1871 it was clear to George Eliot and Lewes that *Middlemarch* was becoming too long to fit the usual three-volume format. Lewes suggested to Blackwood that, on the model of Victor *Hugo's *Les Misérables*, it should be brought out in eight parts at two-monthly intervals, then published in four volumes. This mode of publishing was duly adopted, and the novel appeared to public delight and astonishment from December 1871 to December 1872. About 5,000 copies of these 5s. parts were sold. By 1879 nearly 30,000 copies had been sold in one edition or another, earning George Eliot about £9,000 (Haight 1968: 443). This amazingly fully realized 'Study of Provincial Life' brought the author admiring reviews and letters from friends and strangers enthusing about her understanding of human life, male and female, rich and poor, professional and domestic, married and unmarried, happy and unhappy.

On a visit to Germany in the summer of 1873 the Leweses visited the spa town of Bad Homburg. There they witnessed a scene of international gambling at the casino which was to provide material for the striking opening of George Eliot's next and last novel, *Daniel Deronda*. Like *Middlemarch*, it appeared in eight parts, this time monthly during 1876. While creating once more a panorama of social classes and opinion and showing how individuals interact at times of social change, this novel spreads its net even wider than its predecessor, taking in the English aristocracy at one end of the scale and poor London Jews at the other end. George Eliot's ambitious plot brings the two extremes into close contact through the figure of Deronda himself; her comic treatment of the ludicrous hunting and shooting county set is daringly offset by her respectful description of the Jewish religion and culture embodied in the ailing scholar Mordecai.

George Eliot was nervous, confessing in April 1876 that 'the Jewish element' would be 'likely to satisfy nobody' (L vi. 238). She was right. Though the novel sold well, and though Blackwood, while not keen on the parts exclusively concerned with Mordecai's philosophy and vision of a Jewish homeland, saw that the work was full of brilliance, critics were puzzled, praising the 'English' parts for the familiar humour and insight, while they felt awkward about the 'Jewish element'.

As usual, Marian was exhausted at the end of writing another long novel. In November 1876 she and Lewes found a country house in Witley, near Haslemere in Surrey, which they bought with a view to spending the summers there. They were to enjoy only two idyllic summers, and even those were overshadowed by anxiety about Lewes's failing health. He died of enteritis and cancer on 30 November 1878, aged 61. Marian was plunged into loneliness, unable to decide whether to publish her rather subdued set of ironic character sketches, *Impressions of Theophrastus Such*, which Blackwood eventually brought out in 1879. For months she could bear to be visited only by Lewes's one remaining son Charles and by the friend who had found the house at Witley for them, the banker John Walter *Cross.

Cross's mother had died within a few days of Lewes. He, a bachelor of 40 who had lived with his mother and sisters, needed consolation too. Several months later he asked Marian, nearly twenty years his senior, to marry him. She hesitated, still devastated by the loss of Lewes and acutely aware of the great age difference, but in the spring of 1880 she agreed to marry Cross. Despite her lack of religious belief, and presumably in deference to the Cross family, they were married in St George's, Hanover Square, on 6 May 1880. Charles Lewes gave her away.

She and Cross went on their honeymoon to Italy, leaving behind a startled public and some disapproving friends. George Eliot, who now reverted to her childhood Christian name, calling herself Mary Ann Cross, seemed destined to shock in the great decisions of her life. If the orthodox had shaken their heads at the 'elopement' with Lewes, both they and the non-orthodox found it hard to adjust to her sudden marriage to a man much younger than herself. One positive—if meagre—result was a brief letter of congratulations from her estranged brother Isaac, content that she was now legally married.

Her happiness was short-lived. Cross became depressed on the honeymoon and fell, or threw himself, from the balcony of their Venice hotel into the Grand Canal. Though little is known about the details of his illness, it fuelled gossip at home, with many a club-going acquaintance of Cross's commenting on both the age gap and the intelligence gap between husband and wife (Ashton 1996: 377). For the principals, it was a nightmare.

Back home by the end of July, George Eliot and Cross went to Witley to recuperate. She suffered from recurring kidney trouble. On 3 December

1880 they moved into their splendid new house, No. 4, Cheyne Walk, by the Thames at Chelsea. Less than three weeks later, on 22 December, George Eliot died of kidney disease exacerbated by a throat infection.

Cross enquired about the possibility of burial in Westminster Abbey, where Dickens and other great writers had been buried. Some friends, including Herbert Spencer, thought that she, too, should have her place in Poets' Corner. But others felt that her denial of Christian faith, as well as her 'irregular' life with Lewes, ruled this out. Cross dropped the idea, and she was buried instead alongside Lewes in the Dissenters' part of Highgate Cemetery. It was fitting that she should be laid to rest beside the man who had cherished her and encouraged her genius, overriding her tendency to paralysing self-doubt and despondency. But it was also fitting that in 1980, 100 years after her death, a memorial stone was finally established in Poets' Corner, so that this great writer should be seen to be honoured in the same way as others who have enriched, as she undoubtedly did, the national literature.   RA

Ashton (1996).

—— *G. H. Lewes: A Life* (1991).

—— 'New George Eliot Letters at the Huntington', *Huntington Library Quarterly*, 54 (1991).

The Letters of George Henry Lewes, ed. William Baker, 2 vols. (1995).

Life of Jesus, The. George Eliot's translation of D. F. *Strauss's *Das Leben Jesu* (1835–6) published anonymously by John Chapman in 1846.

'Lifted Veil, The' (*see page 230*)

Liggins, Joseph (1800–72), alleged author of George Eliot's early fiction. In June 1857, her half-sister Fanny told her that some stories in *Blackwood's Edinburgh Magazine*, set in Chilvers Coton and Arbury, had been written by Mr Liggins of Attleborough, an assertion Marian understandably denied. The circulation of 'keys' to characters in *Scenes of Clerical Life* intensified speculation about the author's identity. The chief contender was Joseph Liggins, the son of a prosperous Nuneaton baker who sent him to Cambridge, with a view to a career in the Church. He fell into bad company, was rusticated from the university in 1824 and never returned there (*L* iii. 21). He did some tutoring, was temporarily resident in the Isle of Man, and was at one time on the staff of a Liverpool newspaper. In July 1857, a claim in the *Manx Sun* that 'Liggers' (*sic*) had written *Scenes* initially amused Marian who remembered Liggins in Nuneaton as 'a tall black coated clergyman in embryo' (*L* iii. 46), but she became increasingly irritated when others championed him: Quirk and

(*cont. on page 232*)

Caricature of Liggins writing *Adam Bede*, by Anne Leigh Smith, the sister of George Eliot's close friend Barbara Leigh Smith Bodichon, 1859.

NOVELLA by George Eliot in two chapters, with supernatural elements; narrated in the first person. (Apart from its use in her early essays, 'From the Notebook of an Eccentric', and the opening chapter of *The Mill on the Floss*, the only other work for which George Eliot used the first-person mode is her last: *Impressions of Theophrastus Such*.)

Composition and Publication

Begun while George Eliot was living at Park Shot, Richmond, and completed at Holly Lodge, Wandsworth, 'The Lifted Veil' was originally published in *Blackwood's Edinburgh Magazine* (July 1859) five months after the appearance on 1 February of her first full-length novel, *Adam Bede*. She had started work on *The Mill on the Floss* in January, but was for a while unable to progress with it after learning in March of the death of her estranged, but much-loved, sister Chrissey (see EVANS, CHRISTIANA). Instead, she rapidly completed this 'slight story of an outré kind—not a *jeu d'esprit*, but a *jeu de melancolie*' (*L* iii. 41), as she initially described it—begun when her 'head was too stupid for more important work' (*L* iii. 60 n.). Purporting to think little of the tale, while nevertheless citing G. H. *Lewes's opinion that it was 'very striking and original' (*L* iii. 41), she offered it to John *Blackwood to publish or not, as he chose.

Though he could hardly reject it, Blackwood was taken aback by its nature and advised deleting the revivifying experiment that provides the denouement, and which he particularly disliked. His advice was not taken, but he successfully resisted Lewes's suggestion that George Eliot should append her name to the story. Lewes's argument was that such a move would put paid to the rumour that Liggins was the author of *Scenes of Clerical Life* and *Adam Bede*, since he was obviously unlikely to produce anything of this kind; but, anxious to protect from tarnish the prestige won by *Adam Bede*, Blackwood preferred to publish the new story, for which he paid £37 10s., anonymously. Continuing to recoil from the idea of allowing George Eliot to be identified as its author, in 1866 he chose to exclude both it and her only other short story, 'Brother Jacob', from the recognized series of her works, offering as his reason 'their painful want of light' (*L* iv. 322). In 1873, however, he acknowledged an increased admiration for 'The Lifted Veil', and proposed including it in a new series of *Tales from Blackwood*; but George Eliot rejected the idea. She wrote on 28 February 1875:

I think it will not be judicious to reprint it at present. I care for the idea which it embodies and which justifies its painfulness. . . . But it will be well to put the story in harness with some other productions of mine, and not send it forth in its dismal loneliness. There are many things in it which I would willingly say over again, and I shall never put them in any other form. (*L* v. 380)

At this point she composed the motto which was prefixed to it when, duly recognized, it was eventually reprinted in the Cabinet Edition of her works in 1878. According to her wish, it was placed in harness with *Silas Marner* and 'Brother Jacob', although Blackwood would rather have made the two stories a separate slim volume. The manuscript has disappeared.

Reception

Reflecting Blackwood's response, for many decades the story met with little enthusiasm. Henry James, for example, found it 'woefully sombre . . . the *jeu d'esprit* of a mind that is not often—perhaps not often enough—found at play' (*Nation*, 25 Apr. 1878), though he at least recognized its power, and found it a 'fine piece of writing'. By 1906, Theodore Watts-Dunton (in his introduction to the World's Classics Edition of the story), on the other hand, was able to admire only a few 'gems of thought and reflection' (p. xvi) in it, asserting that it manifests 'a very serious artistic infirmity' (p. xvi). The general tendency was either to overlook 'The Lifted Veil', or to regard it as an aberration or failure.

Plot

Latimer begins his narrative as the time of his foreseen death—from *angina pectoris*—approaches. He hopes his story will win him posthumously the fellow feeling denied him in life.

Deprived of love after his mother's death, as a sensitive child Latimer had been subjected to an uncongenial scientific education. Nourishing his 'poet's sensibility' by reading Plutarch, Shakespeare, and Cervantes 'by the sly', but incapable of creative expression, he had become increasingly isolated. Sent to *Geneva ostensibly to complete his education, he is drawn to another social outcast, the gifted but ugly and impoverished Meunier. This interlude of companionship is terminated when Latimer, convalescing from a severe illness, is visited by his father and told that he is to be taken on a homeward journey by way of *Prague. Left alone, he has a vision of an unknown city lying under the relentless glare of the midday sun. Exulting in what he hopes is a manifestation of his 'newly-liberated genius', Latimer tries to generate another vision, but the next—of his father accompanied by a neighbour and a disturbingly 'fatal-eyed' young woman, Bertha Grant—is as spontaneous as the first. It leaves him cold and trembling. This vision is immediately succeeded by the actual appearance of the group: that which Latimer had at first welcomed as a power turns out to be the 'disease' of clairvoyance.

From this point Latimer is subjected to involuntary mind-reading, and only Bertha's mind remains unexposed to him. He is intoxicated by her mystery, and filled with jealous hatred of his brother Alfred, to whom she is betrothed. When Latimer reaches Prague his prescience is confirmed: it is the city of his first vision.

Alfred is fortuitously killed, and Latimer marries Bertha. After some months, 'the veil which had shrouded Bertha's soul' is lifted, revealing her contemptuous cruelty. Utterly alienated, Latimer's preternatural insight fades. Soullessly awaiting death, his condition is briefly alleviated by a visit from the now successful Meunier, during which Bertha's maid, Mrs Archer, dies. Meunier conducts a revivification experiment on the woman, who had had some strange hold over her mistress. She returns to life just long enough maliciously to reveal Bertha's intention of murdering Latimer. Afflicted anew with preternatural insight, he becomes a wanderer until disease forces him to rest. The last words of the story record the onset of his death throes on the predicted date of 20 September 1850.

Critical Approaches

Despite U. C. Knoepflmacher's perspicacious study of the story (1968), and his recognition of its importance 'to our grasp of George Eliot's development as a philosophical novelist' (160), on the whole a dismissive attitude to 'The Lifted Veil' subsisted until the late 1970s. It is given cursory attention by Gordon S. Haight in his 1968 *Biography*, for example, and condemned by Marghanita Laski in 1973 as 'sadly poor' (*George Eliot and her World*, 1973: 71). Along with 'Brother Jacob', it was altogether omitted from the

Chronology of George Eliot's Life and Works in the important British Library centenary exhibition (11 December 1980–26 April 1981), while—also in 1980—Christopher Ricks was able to summarize it as simply 'the weirdest fiction she ever wrote' (786). However, the serious attention exemplified by Knoepflmacher had begun to gain ground in the mid-1970s, with commentators such as Gillian Beer intensively exploring the concerns of the story in the light of George Eliot's other works. Beer claims that 'By studying *The Lifted Veil* alongside *Middlemarch* we can come to a fuller knowledge of the ways George Eliot sought out beyond the "desolate loneliness" of single consciousness' (1975: 94). Suggesting that 'Latimer's dilemma, in its mixture of determinism, solipsism, and hyper-aesthesia corresponds to the perils latent in George Eliot's situation as a novelist' (101), Beer points to the contrast between Latimer's 'receptive hypersensitivity' and the 'out-going creativity' (103) in Ladislaw's definition of the poet in *Middlemarch*.

A growing body of work focuses on the scientific background to 'The Lifted Veil', with Kate Flint, for example, exploring a connection between it and the kind of contemporary medical experimentation of which George Eliot would have been aware. But, for the supernatural elements in her story, she undoubtedly drew on the then widely debated, often conflicting evidence offered by phrenologists and mesmerists (see MESMERISM; PHRENOLOGY). Mesmerized subjects frequently claimed to become clairvoyant while in an induced trance, with the nature of their reported visions and mind-reading corresponding in many ways to Latimer's. But the key to George Eliot's intensified 'care for the idea' represented in 'The Lifted Veil' lies in the moral philosophy implicit in her shaping of Latimer's destiny. Unlike Maggie Tulliver, whose quest for enlightenment and fulfilment must acknowledge the claims of others, Latimer strives only for self-gratification. Failing to recognize that the aridity of his first vision is a reflection of an ungenerative sensibility, his attempts to achieve by efforts of will the creativity that has been denied him, are answered by a revealed spiritual wasteland. BG

Beer, Gillian, 'Myth and the Single Consciousness: *Middlemarch* and *The Lifted Veil*', in Adam (1975).

Eagleton, Terry, 'Power and Knowledge in "The Lifted Veil"', *Literature and History*, 9 (1983).

Flint, Kate, 'Blood, Bodies, and *The Lifted Veil*', *Nineteenth-Century Literature*, 51 (1997).

Gray, Beryl, Afterword to 'The Lifted Veil' (1985).

Knoepflmacher (1968).

Ricks, Christopher, 'It was her books to which she gave birth', *Listener*, 11 Dec. 1980.

Swann, Charles, 'Déjà Vu, Déjà, Déjà Lu: "The Lifted Veil" as an Experiment in Art', *Literature and History*, 5 (1979).

Anders (clergymen), Bracebridge (an Atherstone magistrate), and Newdegate of Arbury (see NEW-DIGATE FAMILY) supported his claims. Letters appeared in *The Times* and elsewhere while a poverty-stricken Liggins complained he had never been paid for *Adam Bede*. Two years of troubling gossip precipitated Marian's final revelation of the truth. Her experience is reflected in *The Lifted Veil*, in her references in her fiction to rumour, scandal, and hidden identity, and in her chapter in *Impressions of Theophrastus Such* on origination, 'The Wasp Credited with the Honeycomb' (*TS* 11). Liggins appears not finally to have escaped from poverty. At the end of his life he was found desti-

tute and taken into Chilvers Coton workhouse, where he died in 1872. RMH

Lind, Jenny (1820–87), coloratura soprano known as 'the Swedish nightingale'. In 1849 she abandoned opera to perform in concerts and oratorios. In 1852 she married the conductor Otto Goldschmidt, who in 1875 founded the London Bach Choir, which she reputedly organized and in which she sang.

In April 1871, George Eliot and G. H. *Lewes met Jenny Lind at a matinée. Lewes reported that 'She sang four songs—not to our delight by any means' (*L* v. 144), recording four years later that he had 'always felt an instinctive antipathy towards her' (*L* vi. 155 n.). Gwendolen Harleth in *Daniel Deronda* has a 'moderately powerful soprano' which someone had said 'was like Jenny Lind's' (*DD* 5).   BG

Linton, Eliza Lynn (1822–98), journalist and novelist. Her career as a woman writer making an independent living by her pen brought her into contact and rivalry with George Eliot, whose far greater success she envied. Like George Eliot she upset her father when she was a girl by renouncing *Christianity, and then went to London as a young woman to make a literary career, becoming the first woman journalist to draw a regular salary from a newspaper when she was taken on by the *Morning Chronicle* in 1848. She moved in some of the same circles as George Eliot, knowing John *Chapman and Dr *Brabant and enjoying the friendship of Sara *Hennell and the *Brays, whom she visited at Rosehill, their house in Coventry. The two writers first met at John Chapman's house in the Strand when George Eliot was staying there in November 1850, and they left very different accounts of that meeting. George Eliot wrote to Sara Hennell the next day that Eliza had been effusive in her admiration, declaring she had never been so attracted to a woman before as to George Eliot, who was 'such a loveable person'(*L* i. 337). Lynn Linton, in the highly critical memoir of George Eliot which first appeared in the journal *The Woman at Home* (1895) and forms part of her posthumously published *My Literary Life* (1899), insisted that she was distinctly unimpressed by the tone of superiority adopted by a woman who appeared 'underbred and provincial', was badly dressed, and 'had an unwashed, unbrushed, unkempt look altogether' (*My Literary Life*, 95).

The two women had some contact in the 1850s, George Eliot referring to Eliza Lynn sympathetically in her letters, particularly before her marriage to the engraver W. J. Linton in 1858, when she praised her large-hearted energy in taking on his seven children (*L* ii. 340). After that marriage ended in separation in 1866 they were in contact again, but Lynn Linton seems to have dropped out of the Eliot–Lewes circle in later years. It is about that later phase of George Eliot's career that her memoir is most memorably spiteful, castigating the sibylline figure Eliot became in the wake of her success: 'she grew to be artificial, *posée*, pretentious, unreal' (*My Literary Life*, 97). 'She was always the goddess on her pedestal', surrounded by worshippers at her Sunday receptions, and 'so interpenetrated head and heel, inside and out, with the sense of her importance as the great novelist and profound thinker of her generation, as to make her society a little overwhelming, leaving on

baser creatures the impression of having been rolled very flat indeed' (*My Literary Life*, 98, 99). In reality, Lynn Linton claims, she was jealous and exacting in her relationship with G. H. *Lewes and so weak that she had to be protected from anything that might upset her. The 'crowning act of weakness in her life' (*My Literary Life*, 102) was her marriage to John Walter *Cross, which degraded her own past; and in an anonymous review in *Temple Bar* (April 1885) Lynn Linton condemned Cross's *Life* as an attempt to 'embalm the image of the Ideal George Eliot' (Anderson, 181). The unflattering portrait painted by Lynn Linton reveals her envy and resentment at what she saw to be the inequitable treatment of the two women writers: her own novels were far less successful and her separation from her much older husband met with criticism, while George Eliot's novels were widely acclaimed and her unorthodox relationship with Lewes was ultimately condoned.

A complex and contradictory figure, Eliza Lynn Linton led an independent and emancipated life while achieving her greatest impact not as a novelist but as a campaigner against women's emancipation in the conservative *Saturday Review* in the 1860s and 1870s. When she came to write about George Eliot's novels in *Women Novelists of Queen Victoria's Reign* (1897), she was unable to put aside her personal hostility for long. While acknowledging the greatness of the work, she set out to determine its weaknessess, finding fault with the air of pedantry and preaching in the too frequent philosophic passages, the anachronism of some novels, the inartistic features of others, and even the clumsiness of the sentences and the grammatical errors. Shuttling uncomfortably between praise and censure, the criticism repeatedly comes back to the falsely respectable relationship with Lewes which pretended to be the marriage that it was not: for 'all her teaching went to the side of self-sacrifice for the general good, of conformity with established moral standards, while her life was in direct opposition to her words' (*Women Novelists*, 88). That final phrase may more aptly describe the emancipated anti-feminist herself than George Eliot. See also WOMAN QUESTION.   JMR

Anderson, Nancy Fix, *Woman against Women in Victorian England: A Life of Eliza Lynn Linton* (1987).

Layard, George Somes, *Mrs. Lynn Linton: Her Life, Letters and Opinions* (1901).

Sanders, Valerie, *Eve's Renegades: Victorian Anti-Feminist Women Novelists* (1996).

Liszt, Franz (1811–86), Hungarian composer and virtuoso pianist to whom G. H. *Lewes introduced George Eliot in 1854 at *Weimar where Liszt was Kapellmeister and Director of the Court Theatre. They enjoyed very friendly terms. Liszt's personal situation had something in common with

Eliza Lynn Linton (1822–98) in her later years when she produced her spiteful memoir of George Eliot.

that of Eliot and Lewes. He was openly living with the Princess Sayn-Wittgenstein, who was seeking a divorce from her husband. Liszt invited Eliot and Lewes to breakfast and Eliot recorded her impression of his appearance and piano-playing in her journal:

Then came the thing I had longed for—Liszt's playing ... For the first time in my life I beheld real inspiration—for the first time I heard the true tones of the piano. He played one of his own compositions—one of a series of religious *fantaisies*. There was nothing strange or excessive about his manner. His manipulation of the instrument was quiet and easy, and his face was simply grand. (*L* ii. 170)

There is an element of homage to Liszt in Eliot's portrayal of the composer Klesmer in *Daniel Deronda*. Klesmer, described as 'not yet a Liszt', also excites the admiration of his more receptive listeners by playing one of his own compositions. The title of Klesmer's fantasia *Freudvoll, Leidvoll, Gedankenvoll* is derived from Liszt's setting of a poem from Goethe's *Egmont* (*DD* 5). Klesmer's lofty pronouncements on the role of the artist may also echo views which Eliot heard Liszt express. In his study of Liszt, Alan Walker concludes that Klesmer's 'ideas on talent, genius, musicality, and priest-like devotion to work are basically the ideas of Liszt ... it is not impossible that George Eliot took them down from Liszt *verbatim*' (*Franz Liszt* (1989), ii. 250).

Liszt introduced Eliot and Lewes to the music of Wagner and Eliot undertook the translation of an article on Wagner and Meyerbeer recently published by Liszt in the *Neue Zeitschrift für Musik*. 'The Romantic School of Music' appeared in Lewes's **Leader* for 28 October 1854. This is a condensed form of Liszt's original article which discusses the importance of Meyerbeer for Wagner's operatic development. Some original introductory comment by Lewes on Meyerbeer's empty straining after musical effect qualifies Liszt's view of Meyerbeer's operas as representing a necessary stage preceding the full integration of musical and dramatic elements in Wagner's operatic writing. Eliot was to refer disparagingly to Meyerbeer in *Daniel Deronda* where he is associated with Lush, the amateur of luxury and music (*DD* 11, 25). Liszt's article also provided Eliot with material for her 1855 essay on **'Liszt, Wagner, and Weimar'*. See also MUSIC.   DdSC

'Liszt, Wagner, and Weimar'. George Eliot's essay, published in *Fraser's Magazine* in July 1855 (repr. in *Essays*), is essentially concerned with Wagner and represents one of the first favourable critiques of Wagner in English. The article was written following Wagner's first visit to England to conduct a series of concerts for the New Philharmonic Society. Despite a disclaimer to the effect that she was not writing as a music critic (*Essays*, 100), Eliot was in a unique position in 1855 in being able to base her judgements on actual experience of Wagner's music and on Liszt's expert elucidation of his ideas. She provides a direct transfer of recent German music criticism to the English press at a time when what was known of Wagner's theories provoked general hostility. Her defence of Wagner is largely based on material which appeared both in Adolf Stahr's 1852 *Weimar und Jena* and in an 1854 article by Liszt which Eliot had translated as 'The Romantic School of Music' for the **Leader* in 1854 (5: 1027–8). In 'Liszt, Wagner, and Weimar', Eliot reproduced selected passages from this material with qualifications and emphases which throw light on her own aesthetic preoccupations.

Eliot describes the conflict between Wagner and his critics as being the same, on a far more significant scale, as 'the old controversy between **Gluck and Piccini, between the declamatory and melodic schools of music'—the controversy later to be embodied in Klesmer's condemnation of **Bellini in *Daniel Deronda* (*Essays*, 100; *DD* 23). The general importance of evolutionary thought (see DARWINISM) for Eliot's work makes it particularly significant that Wagner's account of opera's past and his plans for its future satisfied criteria of organicism and evolutionary development. Eliot's discussion of the 'organic unity' of Wagner's music, which is derived from the evolution of action out of character, shows her repeatedly linking notions of artistic and biological organicism, affirming that the same organicism which was to be fundamental to the novels underlay her sense of dramatic and musical structure:

An opera must be no mosaic of melodies stuck together with no other method than is supplied by accidental contrast, no mere succession of ill-prepared crises, but an organic whole, which grows up like a palm, its earliest portion containing the germ and prevision of all the rest. (*Essays*, 101–2)

Eliot pays careful attention to the musical composition of Wagner's operas, distinguishing between **Meyerbeer's employment of melodic repetition and Wagner's far more complex and integral development of motif into

The artifice ... of making certain contrasted strains of melody run like coloured threads through the woof of an opera, and also the other dramatic device of using a particular melody or musical phrase as a sort of Ahnung or prognostication of the approach of action of a particular character. (104)

Such adverse criticism as Eliot directs towards Wagner's musical writing in *Tannhäuser* arises not because she perceives in it any failure to fulfil his declared aesthetic goals but because she personally finds it lacking in melody. Nevertheless, her critical assessment is ultimately informed by the criteria of evolutionary progress. Speculating as to the form the music of the future might take, Eliot draws an analogy between musical, literary, and biological evolution:

who knows? It is just possible that melody, as we conceive it, is only a transitory phase of music, and that the musicians of the future may read the airs of Mozart and Beethoven and Rossini as scholars read the *Stabreim* and assonance of early poetry. We are but in 'the morning of the times,' and must learn to think of ourselves as tadpoles unprescient of the future frog. (102–3)

Eliot thus appeals explicitly to the concept of evolution to explain the 'tadpole' stage of her own musical taste. Wagner's music is not yet an entirely comprehensible language to her, and a *Beethoven quartet offers a *Wordsworthian return to the 'pregnant speech of men after a sojourn among glums and gowries' (*Essays*, 103). However, whilst in terms of individual taste she found herself 'accidentally in agreement with ... anti Wagner critics', Eliot's enthusiasm for Wagner's ideas as representing 'the direction in which the lyric drama must develop itself' makes her essay an important defence of his art and an illumination of her own aesthetic ideals (*Essays*, 103, 100). See also MUSIC.   DdSC

London and its immediate surroundings were where George Eliot made her home from late September 1851, when she moved into John *Chapman's house in the Strand to become the effective editor of the *Westminster Review*, until her death in Cheyne Walk, Chelsea, in December 1880 (see HOMES). It was London that provided the stimulating intellectual and cultural milieu in which her talents as a writer were able to flower; and the man who did most to encourage and foster her career as a novelist, her partner G. H. *Lewes, was significantly described by her early in their relationship as 'Londonish' in a letter to her friends the *Brays in Coventry (*L* ii. 37). His restless, enquiring mind, wide-ranging interests, and cosmopolitan knowledge of the world marked him out as a man of the metropolis. Like Theophrastus in her last work *Impressions of Theophrastus Such*, whose 'consciousness is chiefly of the busy, anxious metropolitan sort', she, too, came to belong to the 'Nation of London' and to care for its life, 'half sleepless with eager thought and strife' (*TS* 2). But although she profited from the dynamic intellectual culture of the capital and always appreciated its rich offerings in *music, the *visual arts, and *theatre, she clearly found the urban environment oppressive. When she and Lewes moved into central London from Wandsworth in the autumn of 1860, she sank into a depression which she attributed to the loss of the country that she had formerly enjoyed in walks on Wimbledon Common and, before that, in Richmond Park (*L* iii. 360). Her letters and journals frequently allude to the restorative effect of escaping from the capital into the country. As she put it to Barbara *Bodichon in August 1863: 'The wide sky, the *not*-London, makes a new creature of me in half an hour. I wonder then why I am ever depressed—why I am so shaken by agitation. I come back to London, and again the air is full of demons' (*L* iv. 102). When, in *Middlemarch*, Dorothea announces her intention of marrying Ladislaw and moving to London, her sister Celia's baffled response, 'How can you always live in a street?' (*MM* 84), is a comic expression of Eliot's own kind of antipathy. It is only in her last novel *Daniel Deronda* that London features as a setting and even there it is not rendered with any solidity of specification. She makes no attempt to emulate Charles *Dickens by dramatizing the press and pace of metropolitan life, or the physical appearance of the urban landscape. The Meyrick's narrow, shabby house in Chelsea is one of 'many such grim-walled slices of space in our foggy London' (*DD* 18), but the narrator proceeds to dwell on the vital intellectual life and warm domesticity behind that bleak exterior. The outdoor London scenes in the novel are confined to the river, on which Deronda rows to enjoy the still seclusion it offers (*DD* 17) and where he rescues Mirah in a solitary spot by Kew Gardens. When the Thames is described in the centre of the city by Blackfriars Bridge, the working river is transfigured by a sunset sky into a backdrop for the visionary encounter of Deronda and Mordecai, with 'the alternate flash of ripples or currents, the sudden glow of the brown sail, the passage of laden barges from blackness into colour, making an active response to that brooding glory' (*DD* 40). London is never brought to life as a peopled world like the rural settings of the earlier novels (see LANDSCAPE). See also LIFE OF GEORGE ELIOT.   JMR

'Lord Brougham's Literature', George Eliot's review of Lord Brougham's *Lives of Men of Letters and Science, Who Flourished in the Time of George III* (6 vols., 1845–6; repr. in 2 vols., 1855), appeared anonymously in the *Leader* on 7 July 1855 (repr. in *Essays*). It is a typically forthright Victorian unsigned review, showing George Eliot in full professional flight as a journalist. The thrust of her commentary is that while the Scottish statesman and lawyer Henry Peter Brougham, first Baron of Brougham and Vaux, may have been distinguished in public life (as defender of Queen Caroline in 1820, as Lord Privy Chancellor from 1830 to 1835, and as a founder of London University and proponent of other educational initiatives), he has offended 'by writing third-rate biographies in the style of a literary hack!' (*Essays*, 138). She spends about a quarter of the review attacking Brougham's slovenly style and inaccurate quotation (the latter a failing from which George Eliot was not entirely free). Moreover, she accuses him of adopting a *faux naïf* stance in relation to well-known facts of the lives of *Voltaire, Hume, and others. What might be excused in someone writing under pressure, for his living, is not to be excused in a member of the '"privileged classes"' (137) for whom writing is an idiosyncratic hobby in which he is to be humoured. This last criticism was not altogether fair to Brougham, who had been one of the founders of the *Edinburgh Review* in 1802, though his excitable temperament and carelessness in writing were notorious.

The swingeing denunciation drew comment from George Eliot's Coventry friend Charles *Bray, to whom she defended herself at some length in a letter of 16 July 1855, effectively providing an explication of her argument in the review. She protests that

The article on Lord Brougham was written conscientiously . . . I consider it criminal in a man to prostitute Literature for the purposes of his own vanity and this is what Lord Brougham has done . . . Literature is Fine Art, and the man who writes mere literature with insolent slovenliness is as inexcusable as a man who gets up in a full drawing-room to sing Rossini's music in a cracked voice and out of tune . . . I consider the 'Lives' *bad* and *injurious*. (*L* ii. 210)

(The analogy between the writing of literature and the performance of the singer does not seem exact: perhaps a deadline was pressing?) The position so vigorously developed here is consistent with the ideas about *art being worked out in her other *essays and reviews at this time.   MAH

Lytton, Edward George Bulwer-. See BULWER-LYTTON, EDWARD GEORGE.

M

'Maga'. See BLACKWOOD'S EDINBURGH MAGA-
ZINE.

Main, Alexander (1841–1918), editor of two anthologies of excerpts from George Eliot's work. A
sycophantic Scotsman with frustrated journalistic
ambitions, Main introduced himself to Eliot in a
letter of August 1871 which praised her novels extravagantly on the excuse of asking how to pronounce 'Romola'. George Eliot answered that
Main's appreciation made her cry for joy, and
G. H. *Lewes encouraged their correspondence as
a way to bolster her flagging confidence (*L* v. 184).
Later that year, Main proposed to compile an anthology of *Wise, Witty, and Tender Sayings in Prose
and Verse, Selected from the Work of George Eliot*,
which Eliot authorized and Lewes persuaded John
*Blackwood to publish by Christmas 1871. Main's
preface compared Eliot with *Shakespeare and
asserted that she had 'for ever sanctified the novel
by making it the vehicle of the grandest and most
uncompromising moral truth'. New editions followed in 1873, 1878, and 1880, adding supplementary quotations from each new novel as they
appeared. By 1896 the *Sayings* had gone through
ten British editions.

At Christmas 1878, Main assembled a different
series of quotations for the *George Eliot Birthday
Book* (priced at 5s.), a diary decorated with one or
two inspirational aphorisms from George Eliot for
every day of the year. Its 'gaudy' binding, designed
to appeal to girls and to 'a colonial class', made
Lewes and Eliot worry about catering to a 'vulgar'
taste (*L* vi. 423; vii. 44, 58). Lewes tried to distract
Main from his now-embarrassing obsession with
George Eliot by setting him to work on an abridg-
ment of Boswell's *Life of Johnson*, which Main insisted on prefacing with an epigraph from *The
Spanish Gypsy*, as if unable to stop quoting George
Eliot even when commissioned to excerpt some-

one else. Despite a preface by Lewes, Main's *Conversations of Doctor Johnson* (1874) was ridiculed
by reviewers. John Blackwood (who nicknamed
Main 'the Gusher') showed no interest in his proposal of a larger anthology of 'English lyrics, from
Shakespeare to George Eliot'.

Although she described birthday books as 'the
vulgarest things in the book stalls', George Eliot
took the trouble to suggest particular quotations
for the *Birthday Book*, insisting that Main include
a disproportionate number of chapter epigraphs
and excerpts from the poems (*L* vi. 423, 431). But
Lewes cautioned Main that 'it would not do for the
public to suppose she had had any share in the
books, beyond that of giving permission to its
being executed' (*L* v. 211). The concern was not
simply that Eliot's self-promotion would appear
immodest. More fundamentally, Eliot's correspondence suggests that Main's anthologies made
her worry about the tension between abstract generalizations and narrative particulars in her work.
Main's proposed preface to the second edition of
the *Sayings* provoked her to protest:

Unless my readers are more moved towards the
ends I seek by my works as wholes than by an assemblage of extracts, my writings are a mistake. I
have always exercised a severe watch against anything that could be called preaching. . . . Unless I
am condemned by my own principles, my books are
not properly separable into 'direct' and 'indirect'
teaching. My chief doubt as to the desirability of the
'Sayings' has always turned on the possibility that
the volume might encourage such a view of my
writings. (*L* v. 459)

By isolating sententious passages from her work,
both anthologies left George Eliot vulnerable to
the attacks on her didactic ambitions and narra-
torial intrusions that began to proliferate after her
death. See REPUTATION, CRITICAL.   LP

Carroll, David, 'The Sibyl of Mercia', *Studies in the
Novel*, 15 (1983).
Price, Leah, 'George Eliot and the Production of
Consumers', *Novel*, 30 (1997).

Mansfield, Katherine (1888–1923), New
Zealand-born writer of incisive stories and critical
reviews, pioneer New Woman. Her most notable
reference to George Eliot occurs in the letter she
wrote to Middleton Murry on 25 November 1919,
from Ospedaletti where she was convalescing, after
reading her cousin Sydney Waterlow's centenary
review in that week's *Athenaeum*, the journal taken
over by Murry earlier that year. Waterlow's interpretation was based on his sense that Eliot's organizing principle was an emotional apprehension
of the universe, but that it failed her, frequently
leading to characters and relationships that were

reflections of preconceived ideas and of her will to improve the world, rather than beings made vital by an objective creative vision. Mansfield's response was indignant: 'He never gets under way. The cartwheels want oiling. I think, too, he is ungenerous.' She goes on to outline how much she feels Waterlow, with his blinkered criteria, has missed. She culminates her remarks, 'Oh, I think he ought really to have been more generous. And why drag Hardy in? . . . I feel I must stand up for my SEX'. Mansfield is alive to Eliot's profound feel for the materiality of being and the textures of experience: 'Her English, warm, ruddy quality . . . think of some of her pictures of country life—the sense of sun lying on warm barns—great warm kitchens at twilight when the men come home from the fields—the feeling of *beasts* horses and cows—the peculiar passion she has for horses' (*Letters of Katherine Mansfield*, iii. 118). Here Mansfield warms to her subject, chooses an example, and points to a dynamic rereading of what might be taken to be set-piece pastoral. What Mansfield gleans is a far cry from Waterlow's identification of improving schemata. She exposes Eliot's passionate yet subtly coded eroticism and her finely tuned sense of a woman's awakening: 'when Maggie Tulliver's lover walks with her up & down the lane & asks her to marry [*MF* 6.11], he leads his great red horse and the beast is foaming—it has been hard ridden and there are dark streaks of sweat on its flanks—*the beast is the man* one feels SHE feels in some queer inarticulate way'. Mansfield's own best stories, acute observations, are similarly evocative and resonant with powerful, subversive atmospheres and subliminal suggestions.

Katherine Mansfield's first husband George Bowden, singer and civil servant, responding to a letter from one of her biographers, Anthony Alpers, about the vacillations over their divorce (it had been a marriage of convenience for her), wrote in 1950, 'she was less averse to her way of life with Murry—with its suggestion of the romantic literary tradition of George Eliot and George Sand—than to the stigma of being the guilty party in an undefended suit in London as it was then'. Rather like George Eliot's fiction, Mansfield's stories continue to affect the work and insights of new generations of women writers. Many of her contemporaries including Elizabeth Bowen, Katherine Ann Porter, and Eudora Welty addressed her work directly; Alpers's biography of Mansfield (1980) devotes a chapter to the links, personal and writerly, between 'Katherine and Virginia' (*Woolf). See also CRITICISM, MODERN: FEMINIST APPROACHES. AE

The Critical Writings of Katherine Mansfield, ed. Clare Hanson (1987).
The Collected Letters of Katherine Mansfield, vol. iii, ed. Vincent Sullivan and Margaret Scott (1993).
Myers, Jeffrey, *Katherine Mansfield: A Biography* (1978).
Tomalin, Claire, *Katherine Mansfield: A Secret Life* (1987).

manuscript collections. The most important collections of George Eliot's manuscripts are in the Beinecke Rare Book and Manuscript Library, Yale University, and the British Library. The British Library collection is distinguished by its holdings of the manuscripts of all her novels and poems as published, except for *Scenes of Clerical Life* which is in the Pierpont Morgan Library, New York (bought from William *Blackwood and Sons in 1911), and the short story 'Brother Jacob' and the poem 'A College Breakfast Party', bound together, which are at Yale. From *Adam Bede* on, her practice was to present the handsomely bound manuscript of each work, feelingly inscribed, to G. H. *Lewes after publication; Gertrude Lewes, the widow of Lewes's son Charles (see LEWES FAMILY), presented these 24 volumes to the British Museum in 1891. The British Library also holds a *Romola* notebook, and letters.

The Yale collection includes well over 1,000 of George Eliot's *letters (about half the known total), all but one of her *journals and diaries, manuscript *notebooks, and the manuscript of her translation of Baruch *Spinoza's *Ethics*, together with an important collection of Lewes's papers, including letters, and all but one of his extant diaries and journals. Professor Chauncey Brewster Tinker instigated the purchases of the nucleus of these holdings when John Walter *Cross's niece, Miss Elsie Druce, put letters, journals, and other material which had remained in Cross's possession after completion of *George Eliot's Life* into several sales at Sotheby's in the 1930s. Subsequently Gordon S. *Haight was instrumental in many acquisitions. Related material in Beinecke includes a collection of extracts from correspondence among the *Bray and *Hennell families, and John *Chapman's 1851 diary.

The next most significant collection is the Blackwood archive in the National Library of Scotland, which includes many letters to and from the publishers and George Eliot and G. H. Lewes. Blackwood's archive of corrected proofs, with manuscript additions by George Eliot, is at the University of Texas.

Other libraries in the United States which have George Eliot manuscripts include the Research Libraries of the New York Public Library (her diary for 1879 is in the Henry W. and Albert A. Berg Collection, as is a notebook, while the Carl H. Pforzheimer Shelley and his Circle Collection

Chapter I.

Men can do nothing without the make-believe of a beginning. Even Science, the strict measurer, is obliged to start with a make-believe unit, & must fix on a point in the stars' unceasing journey when his sidereal clock shall pretend that time is at Nought. His less accurate Grandmother Poetry has always been understood to start in the middle; but on reflexion it appears that her proceeding is not very different from his; since Science too reckons backwards as well as forwards, divides his unit into billions, & with his clock-finger at Nought really sets off in medias res. No retrospect will take us to the true beginning; & whether our prologue be in heaven or on Earth, it is but a fraction of that all-presupposing fact with which our story sets out.

Was she beautiful or not beautiful? and what was the secret of form or expression which gave the dynamic quality to her glance & made it an epoch? Was the good or the evil genius dominant in those beams? Probably the evil; else why was the effect that of unrest rather than of undisturbed charm? Why was the wish to look again felt as coercion & not as a longing in which the whole being consents?

She who raised these questions in Daniel Deronda's mind was occupied in gambling: not in the open air under a Southern sky, tossing coppers on a ruined wall with rags about her limbs; but in one of those splendid resorts which the enlightenment of ages has prepared for the same species of pleasure at a heavy cost of gilt mouldings, dark-toned colour & chubby nudities, all correspondingly heavy — forming a suitable condenser for human breath, belonging in great part to the highest fashion & not easily procurable to be breathed in elsewhere in the like proportion, at least by persons of little fashion. —

It was near four o'clock on a September day, so that the atmosphere was well-brewed to a visible haze. There was deep stillness only broken only by a light rattle, a light chink, a small sweeping sound, & an

---

Opening page of the manuscript of *Daniel Deronda* (1876), bound in four volumes, in the British Library (Add. MSS 34039–42).

holds notebooks used for *Daniel Deronda*); Princeton University Library (notebooks and letters); Harvard University Library (notebook and letters); the Folger Shakespeare Library (notebooks); and the Huntington Library (notebook and letters). In Britain, there are letters and a notebook in the Bodleian Library in Oxford; a notebook, letters, and Evans family material in the Nuneaton Public Library. Smaller holdings are widely dispersed.   MAH

> Haight, Gordon S., 'The George Eliot and George Henry Lewes Collection', *Yale University Library Gazette*, 46 (1971).
> Rosenbaum, Barbara, and White, Pamela (edd.), *Index of English Literary Manuscripts*, vol. iv. *1800–1900*, pt I. *Arnold–Gissing* (1982).
> Sutton, David C. (ed.), *Location Register of English Literary Manuscripts and Letters: Eighteenth and Nineteenth Centuries*, i. A–J (1995).

Manzoni, Alessandro (1785–1873), acclaimed Italian novelist, whose best-known work *I Promessi Sposi* (*The Betrothed*) was described by Giuseppe *Verdi (who composed a Requiem Mass for the first anniversary of Manzoni's death) as 'one of the greatest books ever to emerge from the human brain . . . a consolation for mankind', and which George Eliot read at least twice in her life, in 1869 and again in 1880. *I Promessi Sposi* underwent a series of revisions between its first publication in 1825–7 and 1840–2, particularly with regard to language (pre-Unification Italy had not one common language but several regional dialects), the final version, after much research in Florence, being written in the language of cultured Florentines which Manzoni subsequently advocated as the common language of united Italy. The first English translation was in 1828.

I Promessi Sposi deals with Lombardy under Spanish rule in the 17th century, concentrating on the fortunes of the lovers Renzo and Lucia who endure famine, war, and plague as well as corruption in Church and State before they are finally united. Analogies with the situation of Italy in the 19th century were readily apparent. Manzoni admired Walter *Scott's historical fiction for its use of period setting as a means of analysing contemporary moral and political issues: George Eliot may have kept the examples of both Scott and Manzoni in mind during her work on *Romola*. She certainly emulated Manzoni's technique of interspersing chapters of historical context among more purely fictional ones.

In December 1842 George Eliot was reading a translation of part of his *Osservazioni sulla morale cattolica* (Observations on Catholic Morality, 1819) along with much of Friedrich *Schiller's work when she wrote to Cara *Bray, 'I have skimmed Manzoni, who has suffered sadly in being poured out of silver into pewter' (*L* i. 153). She read *I Promessi Sposi* aloud to G. H. *Lewes in January 1869, and to John Walter *Cross in August 1880.

MAH

> Manzoni, Alessandro, *The Betrothed*, trans. Bruce Penman (1972).

'Margaret Fuller and Mary Wollstonecraft'. George Eliot's essay on the work of these two pioneering feminists was published in the *Leader* on 13 October 1855 (repr. in *Essays*). She establishes 'several points of resemblance', despite the difference of dates, between Margaret *Fuller's *Woman in the Nineteenth Century* (1845) and Mary *Wollstonecraft's *Vindication of the Rights of Woman* (1792). Her review also acknowledges the striking differences between the imaginations and literary styles of the two writers. 'Margaret Fuller's mind was like some regions of her own American continent', Eliot writes, 'where you are constantly stepping from the sunny "clearings" into the mysterious twilight of the tangled forest—she often passes in one breath from forcible reasoning to dreamy vagueness' whereas Wollstonecraft is 'nothing if not rational' (*Essays*, 201).

Eliot highlights how both Fuller and Wollstonecraft stress that whilst men are afraid that an improved education will make the opposite sex their equals, 'they are really in a state of subjection to ignorant and feeble-minded women' (200). 'Men pay a heavy price for their reluctance to encourage self-help and independent resources in women', Eliot writes; 'The precious meridian years of many a man of genius have to be spent in the toil of routine, that an "establishment" may be kept up for a woman who can understand none of his secret yearnings, who is fit for nothing but to sit in her drawing-room like a doll-Madonna in her shrine' (204–5). This and other issues which Eliot emphasizes through her selection of extracts from Fuller's *Woman in the Nineteenth Century* can later be seen dramatized in her portrayal of Rosamond in *Middlemarch*.

It would be wrong to suggest that Eliot, writing in the masculine voice of the periodical reviewer, was making concern for the welfare of men paramount over any concern for the welfare of women themselves. She mocks the attitudes which underlie resistance to women's *education: 'Anything is more endurable than to change our established formulae about women, or to run the risk of looking up to our wives instead of looking down on them'. However, Eliot is equally scathing about views of women's 'actual equality' or 'moral superiority' to men, pointing out the logical consequence that, if this were true, 'then there would be a case in which slavery and ignorance nourished virtue, and so far we should have an argument for the continuance of bondage' (*Essays*, 205).

Rejecting arguments that women themselves must improve before their position can be bettered, she insists that, as with all social improvement, there is 'a perpetual action and reaction between individuals and institutions; we must try and mend both by little and little' (205). The passages which Eliot selects from Fuller and Wollstonecraft highlight how excruciating are the constraints imposed by narrow conceptions of woman's role. Central to Eliot's essay is her criticism of the 'folly of absolute definitions of woman's nature and absolute demarcations of woman's mission'. She quotes with approval Fuller's assertion that, far from there being any obvious role 'natural' to women, ' "Nature ... seems to delight in varying the arrangements, as if to show that she will be fettered by no rule" ' (203). See also WOMAN QUESTION.   DdSC

marriage, portrayal of. George Eliot took marriage seriously and treated her own irregular but deeply fulfilling relationship with G. H. *Lewes as though it were a marriage properly solemnized by the Church and recognized in law. In translating Ludwig *Feuerbach she had encountered his celebration of marriage as 'the free bond of love' (Haight 1968: 137) and it was on this principle that she acted. From her first work of fiction to her last, marriage occupies a central position, not so much as the goal to which the trials of courtship eventually lead, but rather as the state of matrimony in its various forms. 'Marriage, which has been the bourne of so many narratives', as she puts it in the Finale to *Middlemarch*, 'is also a great beginning', and it is on the 'home epic' which it initiates that much of her fiction concentrates. When, in *Middlemarch*, Mr Brooke informs Dorothea that Casaubon has asked his permission to propose to her, he does his best to curb her eagerness to accept the proposal by pointing out the disadvantages of marriage: 'It *is* a noose you know. Temper, now. There is temper. And a husband likes to be master' (*MM* 4). In reply Dorothea loftily proclaims that 'Marriage is a state of higher duties'. George Eliot's portrayal encompasses both these contrasting possibilities, from Milly Barton's saintly commitment to husband and family in the first of the *Scenes of Clerical Life* to Gwendolen Harleth's experience of subjection to her husband's tyrannical will in *Daniel Deronda*.

That marriage can be the key to emotional fulfilment is affirmed by the passage of solemnly liturgical asseveration celebrating the betrothal of Adam and Dinah in *Adam Bede*: 'What greater thing is there for two human souls than to feel that they are joined for life—to strengthen each other

in all labour, to rest on each other in all sorrow, to minister to each other in all pain ... ?' (*AB* 54). That it can serve as the basis of a harmonious social order is suggested by the glimpse of Adam and Dinah's family life in the Epilogue, by the exemplary domestic felicity of the Garths in *Middlemarch*, and by the solid mutual happiness of Fred Vincy and Mary Garth in the Finale to that novel. But the main emphasis falls on the pitfalls and deceptive promises of marriage, and the suffering that results from a mistaken choice of partner. It is women who are most susceptible to romantic illusions about marriage and for whom the 'pilulous smallness' of 'the cobweb of pre-matrimonial acquaintanceship' (*MM* 2) is usually most dangerous. Rosamond Vincy finds Lydgate, with his 'careless politeness of conscious superiority', almost perfect (*MM* 27), while Dorothea not only invests Casaubon with a superiority of mind that he does not possess, but also suffers from the delusion that 'the really delightful marriage must be that where your husband was a sort of father' (*MM* 12). It is on women, too, that economic necessity bears most heavily: Both Janet in 'Janet's Repentance' and Gwendolen in *Daniel Deronda* contract their miserable marriages to tyrannical husbands in order to avoid another form of subservience, the impecunious life of the governess. If marriage so often turns out to be a noose in George Eliot's fiction, the ideological and material pressures that lead women in particular into that noose are clearly presented.

The burden of an unhappy marriage is not borne exclusively by women, however, as the example of Lydgate shows. Rosamond's misplaced conviction that his gentlemanly superiority makes him a perfect partner is matched by his assumption of her innate submissiveness as a woman, and it is he who proves to be the greater victim of the mistake. The process by which he comes to be shaped after the average is largely determined by his marriage, which, instead of bringing him the 'sweet furtherance of satisfying affection—beauty—repose' (*MM* 36) that he had ingenuously expected, turns into a battle of wills in which he is perpetually thwarted and finally defeated. Rosamond's imperious egoism is nevertheless an exception among the married women of Middlemarch and it throws into relief the unselfish support given to their husbands by the dependable Mrs Garth, and Mrs Bulstrode, movingly loyal to Bulstrode in his hour of disgrace (*MM* 74). In these figures the role of wife involves an exemplary selflessness which affirms the moral value of marriage.

Those female characters who reject marriage for a career, like the heroine of the poem 'Armgart' (see POETRY), or use it simply to further a career, like Daniel Deronda's mother, are seen in a more ambiguous light: the one finally reduced to the role of a solitary singing teacher, and the other, lonely and dying, seeing her son embracing the Judaism that she had gone to such lengths to reject. The search for a *vocation outside marriage is always problematic for women in George Eliot's world. When Dorothea marries Ladislaw at the end of *Middlemarch* and is 'absorbed into the life of another' to be 'only known in a certain circle as a wife and a mother', the narrator concedes the grounds for regret but at the same time points out the absence of obvious alternatives: 'But no one stated what else that was in her power she ought rather to have done' (*MM* Finale). Mr Gascoigne's pompous assertion in *Daniel Deronda* that 'Marriage is the only true and satisfactory sphere of a woman' (*DD* 13), seems to be borne out by much of the fiction, although its function is highly ironic in context. It is a statement of unexamined convention that is one of the pressures persuading Gwendolen to accept Grandcourt's proposal against the promptings of her conscience.

The marriage of Gwendolen and Grandcourt is Eliot's most powerful portrayal of marital misery. It is also a profound study of psychological cruelty, which shows Gwendolen, trapped in her painted, gilded prison, tormented by the sadistic will and frozen silences of her reptilian husband (Dowling, 322–36). Here the terrible intimacy of marriage is used to explore the potential for cruelty and murderous violence in the human psyche, while the combination of outward respectability and inner corruption in the Grandcourts' union serves as an indictment of a sphere of English social life. See also FAMILY LIFE; SOCIETY; WOMAN QUESTION.

JMR

Dowling, Andrew, ' "The Other Side of Silence": Matrimonial Conflict and the Divorce Court In George Eliot's Fiction', *Nineteenth-Century Literature*, 50 (1995).

Foster, Shirley, *Victorian Women's Fiction: Marriage, Freedom and the Individual* (1985).

Martineau, Harriet (1802–76), woman of letters, who first met George Eliot through the *Brays' Unitarian connections in 1845. The two women were on intimate terms in the early 1850s, when Eliot was living at 142 Strand and assisting John *Chapman in the editorship of the *Westminster Review*, to which Martineau was a regular contributor. When Chapman was threatened with bankruptcy in 1854, Martineau helped to frustrate the attempt of her estranged brother James to take over the *Westminster Review* by lending Chapman £500.

Born in Norwich into a Unitarian manufacturing family of Huguenot descent, Martineau was disabled by increasing deafness from childhood.

Following the collapse of the family finances, she supported herself through her writing from an early age. Martineau was described by George Eliot as 'the only English woman who possesses thoroughly the art of writing' (*L* ii. 32). She was a prolific producer across a versatile range, including political economy, travel, history, philosophy, autobiography, fiction for children and adults, and a translation of Auguste *Comte; she was, at various times, an advocate of abolition, philosophical radicalism, reform of the marriage laws, and *mesmerism. Her most lasting work is probably *Deerbrook* (1839): the influence of this novel upon Victorian women writers is comparable to that of Mme de *Staël's *Corinne*.

Deerbrook deals with the factions, rivalries, and prejudices within an English rural community: it is a compelling, exhausting, and profoundly didactic novel, but it touched a chord for its Victorian female readers because it turned the bourgeois Englishwoman's 'mission' into high drama, representing her personal struggle between strength and weakness as a matter of urgent social importance, vital to the stability and harmony of the community within which she lives. When George Eliot read *Deerbrook* in 1852 she was 'surprized at the depths of feeling it reveals' (*L* viii. 51). Martineau's novel is most likely to be read now as a precursor of *Middlemarch*, and it is notable that while Martineau heartily disliked *Felix Holt, the Radical*, *Adam Bede*, and *The Mill on the Floss*, she described *Middlemarch* as a novel of genius, almost unbearably moving.

Although Eliot and Martineau were in frequent professional and social contact, their relationship was an uneasy one. The roots of their differences—between Martineau's commitment to showing the world as it *could be* and Eliot's to showing the world as *it is*—may be demonstrated in an anecdote recounted by Martineau to Henry Reeve: 'Miss Evans insists (or did formerly) that, in all the arts, true delineation is good art. This was before a disagreeable picture of a stork killing a toad. Being asked whether men on a raft eating a comrade would be good in art, she was silent' (*Selected Letters*, 190; Webb, 39). Gallagher places this anecdote in the context of debates within the developing realist tradition: both writers were committed to forms of literary representation which would interconnect facts and values. But Martineau favours a 'deductive' and didactic narrative which demonstrates the connection between facts and values, Eliot an 'inductive' method in which the sympathetic imagination of the reader is expanded and transformed through the narrative process itself (Gallagher, 219–21).

Martineau and G. H. *Lewes were literary adversaries; Lewes's review of Martineau's *Letters on* *the Laws of Man's Nature and Development* (1851) was severe, and there was a rivalry over their books on Comte, which were published in close proximity. Following George Eliot's liaison with Lewes, a rift developed between Eliot and Martineau, and the two women had little contact after 1854, but they maintained a continuing interest in each other's lives and work. In a letter to John Chapman in 1856, Eliot made what she called an 'odd request': 'When Harriet Martineau dies—if I outlive her—and her memoirs are published, I should like to write an article upon her. I need hardly say that mine would be an admiring appreciation of her' (*L* ii. 258). See also UNITARIANISM; WOMAN QUESTION.   GF

Harriet Martineau: Selected Letters, ed. Valerie Sanders (1990).

David, Deirdre, *Intellectual Women and Victorian Patriarchy: Harriet Martineau, Elizabeth Barrett Browning, George Eliot* (1987).

Gallagher, Catherine, *The Industrial Reformation of English Fiction: Social Discourse and Narrative Form, 1832–1867* (1985).

Webb, R. K., *Harriet Martineau: A Radical Victorian* (1960).

Marx, Karl (1818–83), German political philosopher. Expelled from Prussia in 1842, he met Friedrich Engels in Paris, settling in England after the revolutions of 1848. The first volume of *Das Kapital* was published in 1867, the second, completed by Engels, after Marx's death. Marx proposed writing for the **Westminster Review* while George Eliot was its editor, but nothing came of this—possibly because she disliked Marx's intermediary, Andrew Johnson. They never met, and she seems to have been unaware of his work. Nor was there much chance of her sympathizing with it. Marx was only moderately impressed with her—Felix Holt he thought a knowledgeable hero, but affected, and his family preferred the Brontës (S. S. Prawer, *Karl Marx and World Literature* (1978), 377–8).

She and Marx are none the less connected through Ludwig *Feuerbach. Marx's 'Theses on Feuerbach' (*On Religion*, 69–72), written in 1845, apply also to George Eliot and thinkers like Auguste *Comte who emphasize the distinction between theory and practice. According to Marx, this distinction assumes theory to be 'the only genuinely human attitude'. He prefers what he calls 'practical-critical' thought, which has 'reality and power' because it arises from the experience of working people. Feuerbach represents religion as disguised self-knowledge—people think they are worshipping God, but in fact are worshipping the best in human nature. But such alienated thinking has a cause in the divisions in family and social relations generated by capitalist production. This,

not religion, 'must be criticized in theory and revolutionized in practice'. The 'human essence', Marx argues, cannot be understood in terms of an abstract individual, but is to be found in 'the ensemble of human relations'. Feuerbach's manner of thinking privileges the theorist and so divides 'society into two parts, one of which is superior to society (in Robert Owen, for example)'—or in Felix Holt, Daniel Deronda, or the 'landholder, the clergyman, the mill-owner, the mining agent' who, George Eliot suggests in 'The *Natural History of German Life', are unbiased observers of their work-people (*Essays*, 272). In the early fiction, the reliable observer is typically a clergyman, Mr Cleves in 'Amos Barton', Mr Irwine in *Adam Bede*, Dr Kenn in *The Mill on the Floss*. A more abstract embodiment of this figure is the horseman who observes Dinah preaching in *Adam Bede*. It may or may not be significant that he is the Governor of a prison.

From Marx's point of view, there is another, more pervasive 'Feuerbachian' tendency in George Eliot's writing. 'Feuerbach,' Marx notes, 'not satisfied with *abstract thinking*, appeals to *sensuous contemplation*.' The pervasive combination in George Eliot's writing of (implicit) theoretical self-assurance and an uncontentiously 'human' capacity for discernment and sympathy, which the simplest reader can share with the humblest character as well as the author herself, may account for Marx's lack of enthusiasm for her work. However, her engagement with contradiction at the level of 'sensuous contemplation', especially in the mature fiction, should at least partially rehabilitate her among Marxist critics. See also CLASS; CRITICISM, MODERN; POLITICS; SOCIETY.   WM

Marx, K., 'Theses on Feuerbach', in K. Marx and F. Engels, *On Religion* (n.d.).

Eagleton, T., *Criticism and Ideology* (1976).

Myers (1984).

Maurice, F. D. (1805–72), theologian and Christian socialist, appointed professor at King's College (1840) and professor of moral philosophy, *Cambridge (1866). His *Theological Essays* (1853) caused his removal from King's, essays George Eliot dismissed as 'muddy rather than "profound"' (*L* ii. 125). Maurice's books were reviewed in the **Westminster Review* during Eliot's editorship, Charles *Kingsley denouncing her to him as 'the woman who used to insult you', and as 'G. H. Lewes's concubine' (*Essays*, 124). Nevertheless Maurice's letter praising *Romola* she records as 'the greatest, most generous tribute ever given to me in my life' (*Journals*, 118). Lewes too was ecstatic, calling it 'noble' for an 'old man, and a celebrated man to write to a woman frowned on by the world, precisely on the grounds of morality!' (Ashton 1991: 217). Eliot and Maurice first met at a rally for Giuseppe *Garibaldi in 1864 (Haight 1968: 395) but there is little to suggest subsequent meetings. Eliot occasionally attended his sermons and exchanged letters and books with him. Charles Lewes's sister-in-law Emily married Maurice's son in 1872.   JJ

Ashton, Rosemary, *G. H. Lewes: A Life* (1991).

Mazzini, Giuseppe (1805–72), Italian patriotic leader in the van of the *Risorgimento, under perpetual banishment from 1831 onwards. He wrote fervidly, tirelessly, and worked largely from London and for his poorer compatriots there. George Eliot found him suitable as a contributor to the *Westminster Review*, admiring his devotion to Italian unity and the establishment of a republican government. But she underwent something of a change in attitudes later: by the mid-1860s her caution was evident, and is seen in her refusal to contribute to the Mazzini Fund despite having 'a real reverence for Mazzini' and asserting 'Mr Lewes and I would have liked to subscribe to a tribute to Mazzini, or to a fund for his use, of which the application was defined and guaranteed by his own word' (*L* iv. 199–200). But she fears that it will be used for conspiracy, and deplores the corruption and suffering that could ensue. See also GARIBALDI; NATIONALISM.   GRH

medicine and health. *Middlemarch* is preeminently the work in which George Eliot's interest in medicine and health is foregrounded. Historical developments such as the professionalization of the practice of medicine, and advances in such disciplines as anatomy and physiology, are depicted particularly in the strand of the narrative concerned with the fortunes of Tertius Lydgate. But his preferred treatments, using new instruments like the stethoscope, and in some cases declining to prescribe medicines, are too radical for many Middlemarchers. (Silas Marner, who has learned medicinal uses of herbs from his mother, is similarly estranged from his neighbours by his methods of treatment.) The most bizarre medical experiment in George Eliot's fiction, however, is the brief resuscitation of a dead woman by blood transfusion in 'The Lifted Veil'. The threat of epidemics of infectious diseases like cholera, ever present to the Victorians, is addressed in *Middlemarch* by the planned New Fever Hospital, and figures in the plague-stricken village which proves Romola's salvation.

Unlike George Eliot herself, her characters generally enjoy robust *health. But throughout her work, medical conditions and their treatment variously provide significant elements of plot and characterization. In the first of the *Scenes of Clerical Life*, Milly Barton's exhaustion from frequent childbearing is evident, while the third, 'Janet's Repentance', takes a hard look at the heroine's alcoholism (Janet is helped by a consumptive though charismatic clergyman, Edgar Tryan). In *Adam Bede*, Mrs Poyser's illness keeps her in bed for crucial weeks of Hetty's pregnancy. The Dodson clan are essentially hale, though Uncle Pullet proudly stores all Mrs Pullet's empty physic bottles. In 'Brother Jacob', the central character is 'a very healthy and well-developed idiot', one of seven brothers: there is no implication of degeneracy as with Durfey Transome, senior and junior, in *Felix Holt, the Radical*. An early indication of the ostentatious integrity of Felix Holt himself is provided by his refusal to continue to purvey his father's Cathartic Lozenges and Restorative Elixir. See also CRITICISM, MODERN: NEW HISTORICIST APPROACHES.   MAH

melodrama. Like many 19th-century novelists, George Eliot has recourse to moments of melodrama in her fiction, and, as Peter Brooks (1995) has suggested, such moments are important for leading us beneath the surface of things to the underlying spiritual and psychological reality of the action. This process is illustrated in emblematic fashion by the scene in which Gwendolen Harleth appears in a *tableau vivant* as Hermione in *The Winter's Tale* (*DD* 6). As she stands with her arm on a pillar showing off her pretty foot and instep, the musician Klesmer strikes a loud chord on the piano which causes a wooden panel to fly open, revealing the picture of the dead face and fleeing figure. Gwendolen utters a piercing cry, a terrifying expression of terror on her face, and falls trembling to her knees. Here music and drama, the twin components of melodrama in its original sense, combine to reveal the hysterical fears and existential insecurity that lie behind Gwendolen's poised exterior as a fashionable society lady, and this vulnerability is later to be exposed in her miserable marriage to the tyrannical Grandcourt and in his dramatic death, which is obliquely prefigured in this scene. Such moments, like the later occasion when she receives Grandcourt's diamonds from Lydia Glasher on her wedding night and is found by Grandcourt shrieking with terror (*DD* 31), are one of the ways in which this novel conducts its exploration of the psyche and casts light on the 'unmapped country within us' (*DD* 24).

There are melodramatic incidents in other works—Caterina Sarti bent on killing Captain Wybrow with a dagger and finding him already dead from a heart attack (*SC* 2.13); the blood transfusion scene in 'The Lifted Veil'; and Godfrey Cass's secret opium-addicted wife Molly dying in the snow on her way to confront him on New

Year's Eve (*SM* 12)—and they reveal a dark under-side of Gothic romance that troubles and compli-cates a predominantly realistic representation of life (see REALISM). However, the polarized simpli-fications of good and evil that are typical of melo-drama have no place in Eliot's moral vision (see MORAL VALUES), with its finely discriminating scrutiny of what she once referred to as 'mixed and erring' humanity (*Essays*, 146). Significantly, the melodramatic episode in *Middlemarch* when the actress Laure, with whom the student Lydgate is infatuated, stabs her husband on stage in an actual melodrama, takes place in *Paris, and is thus bracketed off from the life of the English provinces as explicitly foreign territory. Melodrama, as this may suggest, is not fundamental to George Eliot's fiction in the way that it clearly is in the case of Charles *Dickens. JMR

> Brooks, Peter, *The Melodramatic Imagination: Bal-zac, Henry James, Melodrama, and the Mode of Excess* (rev. edn. 1995).
> Carroll (1992).
> Vicinus, Martha, 'Helpless and Unfriended: Nine-teenth-Century Domestic Melodrama', *New Literary History*, 13 (1981).

Mendelssohn (-Bartholdy), Felix (1809–47), German composer and conductor. When at the age of 19 Mary Ann Evans, the future George Eliot, piously announced that she had no soul for music, and that she wished never to hear another ora-torio, she had recently attended a performance of music that had included several items from Mendelssohn's *St Paul* (1836). Afterwards, she was moved to ask herself, 'can it be desirable, and would it be consistent with millenial holiness for a human being to devote the time and energies that are barely sufficient for real exigencies on acquir-ing expertness in trills, cadences, etc.?' However, once her innate pleasure in music had been al-lowed to re-establish itself, she developed great enthusiasm for Mendelssohn. She told Sara *Hen-nell that, after seeing the composer himself con-duct *Elijah* (1846) at Exeter Hall on 28 April 1847, she had longed to see her 'just to exchange an ex-clamation of delight' (*L* i. 233). Later, her most positive reference to his music is to Clara *Schu-mann's fine playing of one of his piano quintets (*Journals*, 134).

In February 1869, George Eliot and G. H. *Lewes met Mendelssohn at a dinner party, and on 17 June 1870 began reading his letters aloud. George Eliot wrote that they give a sense 'of com-munion with an eminently pure, refined nature, with the most rigorous conscience in art' (*L* v. 107). See also MUSIC. BG

Meredith, George (1828–1909), novelist and poet. As an aspiring writer, he was acquainted with

G. H. *Lewes in the *Leader* circle, and the two men maintained a wary but not quite antipathetic relationship: Meredith once described Lewes as the 'mercurial little showman', and after a visit from Meredith in 1859 Lewes commented that he produced 'an impression of considerable weari-ness on both' (*L* viii. 234 n.). There was social con-tact during 1859 when Meredith sometimes joined George Eliot and Lewes walking on Wimbledon Common, once accompanied by his son Arthur (1853–90), who was to follow the Lewes boys to Hofwyl School. Meredith and Lewes continued occasional professional dealings, especially after the inception of the *Fortnightly Review* where Meredith's novel *Vittoria* was serialized in 1866.

Both George Eliot and Lewes reviewed Mere-dith's first work of fiction with enthusiasm. George Eliot described it as 'a work of genius, and of poetical genius' (*Leader*, 5 Jan. 1856, 15–17), and urged Sara *Hennell, 'If you want some idle read-ing, get "The Shaving of Shagpat," which I think you will say deserves all the praise I gave it' (*L* ii. 226). However, she was distinctly critical of Meredith's performance when he succeeded her in writing the 'Belles Lettres' section for the *West-minster Review* in the four issues from April 1857 to January 1858. Her complaint that 'the tone is so flippant and journalistic' (*L* ii. 421) is a version of a criticism of Meredith that was to be recurrent throughout his career. He was an inveterate ex-perimentalist, with a notoriously—even ostenta-tiously—dense prose style, who achieved his greatest following after the publication of *Diana of the Crossways* (1885) but never enjoyed the respect accorded George Eliot.

Their first three-volume novels came out al-most simultaneously. Lewes notes reading 'To myself "The Ordeal of Richard Feverel" ' (*L* viii. 234 n.), but whereas the success of *Adam Bede* was registered by the important *Mudie's Library taking extra copies, after protests from subscribers about its sexual candour Meredith's novel was dropped from its list. A couple of years later, Meredith, chronically short of funds, expressed envy of the offer made for *Romola* by George *Smith. This entirely intelligible reaction did not colour his respect for George Eliot's achievement, at least as a 'female writer'. In his capacity as pub-lisher's reader for Chapman and Hall, late in 1864 he advised a budding author to avoid an 'ex-clamatory . . . feminine' style: 'If you will look at the works of the writer of *Adam Bede*, you will see that she, the greatest of female writers, manifests nothing of the sort' (*Letters of Meredith*, ii. 296).

Though Meredith is at least ostensibly more radical than Eliot, his novels, like 'the works of the writer of *Adam Bede*', engage critically with their intellectual, social, and political contexts. A good example is provided by *Beauchamp's Career* (1876), whose serial publication in the *Fortnightly* overlapped the part publication of *Daniel Deronda*: both engage in analysis of near contemporary English society and its problems, with some reference to international contexts (the election sequence in *Beauchamp's Career* is sometimes compared with *Felix Holt, the Radical*). There are other analogies: *Rhoda Fleming* (1865) is a Meredithian version of the 'milkmaid seduced by the squire' plot of *Adam Bede*; while in *Emilia in England* (1864; republished as *Sandra Belloni*) and its sequel, *Vittoria* (1866), Meredith develops his response to the *Risorgimento, less intellectualized than George Eliot's in *Romola* though he too centres his novel on a heroine who takes on symbolic significance. It is in the analysis of sexual politics that Eliot and Meredith are most akin. His most famous novel, *The Egoist* (1878), has striking affinities both with the Dorothea plot of *Middlemarch* and the presentation of Gwendolen in *Daniel Deronda*—and also with the situation of Isabel Archer in Henry *James's *The Portrait of a Lady* (1881). MAH

The Letters of George Meredith, ed. C. L. Cline, 3 vols. (1970).

Roberts, Neil, *Meredith and the Novel* (1997).

mesmerism, named after Franz Anton Mesmer (1734–1815), the Austrian physician whose interest in animal magnetism evolved into a mode of treatment through hypnosis. Mesmerism, which was often associated with *phrenology, was widely demonstrated in Britain from the late 1830s, and George Eliot had experience of it, which she drew on in her fiction. Experiments—in which the patient or subject fell into a (sometimes allegedly clairvoyant) trance induced by an operator who would use a system of passes, or would gaze into the subject's eyes—were frequently conducted publicly, and attracted large audiences.

Many Victorians were fascinated by the phenomenon, which was promoted both as a science, and as 'a power sacred to higher purposes' (Harriet Martineau, *Letters on Mesmerism* (1845), 51). George Eliot's friend Herbert *Spencer contributed three articles in 1844 to *The Zoist* which described itself as 'A Journal of Cerebral Physiology and Mesmerism and their Application to Human Welfare'. The founder of the journal was John Elliotson, whose use of mesmerism in his treatment of patients had in 1838 cost him the Chair in Medicine at the University of London.

When in March 1852 the phrenologist George *Combe complained to George Eliot that the *Westminster Review*—of which she was effectively the editor—reputedly ignored mesmerism and phrenology as topics of scientific investigation, she could reasonably reply

that the great majority of 'investigators' of mesmerism are anything but 'scientific'. The reason for excluding that or any other subject of moment from the Review, would be the difficulty of getting it adequately treated. An ordinary pilot will do for plain sailing, but we want clear vision and long experience when we set out on voyages of discovery. (*L* viii. 41)

Sensationalism and charlatanism had clouded intellectual and moral perspectives, encouraging scepticism, and George Eliot's distinction between subject and treatment is a useful indication both of the status of mesmerism in the mid-19th century, and of her own attitude to it. When she met Elliotson nineteen months later, she was able to sympathize with the physician's indignation about an article by the physiologist William Benjamin Carpenter, 'Electro-Biology and Mesmerism' (*Quarterly Review*, September 1853), which, she acknowledged, 'blinks all the facts of mesmerism' (*L* ii. 126). Her knowledge of the 'facts' was based partly on experience, since in July 1844, when she was 24, William Ballantyne Hodgson had succeeded in influencing her 'to the degree that she could not open her eyes, and begged him most piteously to do it for her, which he did immediately by passes' (*L* i. 180).

Several of George Eliot's male protagonists are endowed with magnetic power, and can compel or subdue with their eyes. In *The Mill on the Floss*, for example, from his very first encounter with Maggie, Stephen Guest's objective—which develops into an obsession—is to make her look at him and receive his look in turn. The influence of his gaze and the influence of his voice combine as the irresistible (though ultimately resisted) power of his will over hers. In the opening chapter of *Daniel Deronda*, Gwendolen—winning at gambling—becomes uncomfortably aware that her own eyes are arrested by Deronda's scrutinizing gaze, while the reptilian Grandcourt's gaze transfixes like a cobra's. See also SCIENCE; SPIRITUALISM. BG

metaphor is a resource which George Eliot uses with her characteristic sensitivity to linguistic complexity, exploiting it both as a means of making connections and for its power to suggest, rather than specify, meaning. Modern criticism first focused on metaphor as a structuring device, particularly in the later novels like *Middlemarch*, where running metaphors like those of the web and the mirror can be seen to unify the different strands of a complex and wide-ranging narrative, thus offering a means of rebutting Henry James's well-known criticism that '*Middlemarch* is a treasure-house of details, but it is an indifferent whole' (*CH* 353). Mark Schorer shows how expressive and systematic metaphor is in *Middlemarch*, and how groups of metaphors work to define it as 'a novel of religious yearning without religious object' (556). Metaphors of large vistas associated with Dorothea and her aspirations are juxtaposed to the ante-rooms and winding passages of Casaubon's life which restrict her, while later the image of the burden links Dorothea's moral predicament with Lydgate's: her view from the window of 'a man with a bundle on his back and a woman carrying her baby' (*MM* 80) as she comes to her crucial moral decision, is echoed at the end of the next chapter when Lydgate sees himself as having taken up the 'burthen' of Rosamond's life and resigns himself to 'carrying that burthen pitifully' (*MM* 81). Examples such as these, or the metaphor of the journey in the same novel, support Schorer's contention that 'George Eliot's metaphors tend always to be, or become, explicit symbols of psychological or moral conditions' (550), even though such a definition does not cover the full range of metaphorical language in her work. Metaphors of webs and tissues, seeds and organisms, for instance, belong to the scientific discourse that helps shape her understanding of the world (see SCIENCE). On the other hand a deftly ironic metaphor may serve simply to define a social type, as when a pompous politician with strong opinions about the British Empire and world politics is summed up by an appropriately geographical image: 'Mr Bult . . . had the general solidity and suffusive pinkness of a healthy Briton on the central table-land of life' (*DD* 22).

Where critics like Schorer and Barbara Hardy see metaphor as an instrument of formal and thematic unity, later post-structuralist criticism draws attention to its power to undermine and deconstruct the very unity it appears designed to promote (see CRITICISM, MODERN: DECONSTRUCTION). J. Hillis Miller concedes that in *Middlemarch* there are all-encompassing metaphors that seek to present a comprehensive image of society, but argues that they interfere with each other, so that the text becomes a 'battleground of conflicting metaphors' (144). Thus the famous image of the candle on the pier glass (*MM* 27), which proposes that all seeing is distorted by the ego of the seer, questions the narrator's claim to insight in such phrases as concentrating 'all the light I can command' (*MM* 15), with its implied image of the microscope and its mirror (see NARRATION). As a result the web of interpretative metaphors becomes a net in which the narrator, too, is entangled and trapped (Miller, 144). The metaphorical nature of language defeats any attempt to create a complete picture of life.

That George Eliot was fully aware of the slippery nature of figurative language is clear from the passage which Miller alludes to: 'for we all of us, grave

or light, get our thoughts entangled in metaphors, and act fatally on the strength of them' (*MM* 10). That awareness is not confined to her late work. In the context of Tom Tulliver's education in *The Mill on the Floss* she reflects on how a change of metaphor can change one's perspective on an issue, and how *Aristotle's praise of metaphorical speech as a sign of high intelligence might have been accompanied by a 'lamentation that intelligence so rarely shows itself in speech without metaphor,—that we can so seldom declare what a thing is, except by saying it is something else' (*MF* 2.1). In her understanding here of the problematic relationship of language to reality she anticipates post-structuralism and, more specifically, Friedrich *Nietzsche's view of the intrinsically metaphorical nature of language on which it draws. George Eliot, whose moral stance Nietzsche despised, may not go so far as his radical vision of truth as simply 'a mobile army of metaphors, metonymies, anthropomorphisms' (Nietzsche, 46–7), but she does reveal a degree of epistemological scepticism when she writes in the same novel of 'that complex, fragmentary, doubt-provoking knowledge which we call truth' (*MF* 6.12); and her use of metaphor reflects this epistemological premiss. Suspicious of dogmatic precepts and didactic formulas, on the grounds that 'the mysterious complexity of our life is not to be embraced by maxims' (*MF* 7.12), she exploits the metaphorical resources of language to allow meaning to emerge without becoming fixed and final. As Ladislaw claims in *Middlemarch*, 'language is a finer medium' than painting because 'it gives a fuller image, which is all the better for being vague' (*MM* 19). The use of metaphors of light and dark, death and life, water and space to describe the relationship of Dorothea and Casaubon can be seen as a means of exploiting this vagueness, as evidence of Eliot's refusal to simplify the characters and their courtship so that the illusion of their privacy is preserved despite the presence of a wise and knowing narrator (Gezari, 98–9). Metaphors thus engage us as readers in the process of exploring and discovering relationships. The recurrent metaphors of webs and tissues in *Middlemarch* are images of connectedness that invite us to make connections in our interpretation of the text, but without imposing a specific interpretation upon us. See also LANGUAGE; SYMBOLISM.   JMR

Gezari, Janet K., 'The Metaphorical Imagination of George Eliot', *ELH* 45 (1978).

Miller, J. Hillis, 'Optic and Semiotic in *Middlemarch*', in Jerome H. Buckley (ed.), *The Worlds of Victorian Fiction* (1975).

Nietzsche, Friedrich, 'On Truth and Lies in a Nonmoral Sense', in *The Portable Nietzsche*, trans. Walter Kaufman (1971).

Schorer, Mark, 'Fiction and the Matrix of Analogy', *Kenyon Review*, 11 (1949).

Wright (1991).

Methodism was the set of evangelical Christian churches and sects which began in the 18th century when some Oxford undergraduates (Anglicans as all Oxford students were), including most famously the brothers Charles and John Wesley, set out to live pious lives on 'methodical' religious principles. 'Methodist' was their nickname. The movement was biblicist, pietistic, conversionist, sometimes Calvinist, but in the case of the Wesleys' followers, Arminian (see EVANGELICALISM), and it spread rapidly. It became known as the Evangelical Revival and comprised what in the 18th century was known as Enthusiasm. The Wesleys remained Anglican clergymen all their lives but their close followers soon insisted on forming a separated denomination, the Methodist Church. And already by the 1790s breakaway groups from this formation were occurring. The parent body then became known as Wesleyan Methodism. The most important splinter group from Wesleyanism, the one calling itself Primitive Methodists, began in 1812. They were dubbed 'ranters' for singing through the streets of Belper in Derbyshire. George Eliot's Derbyshire Aunt Samuel (see EVANS, MRS SAMUEL) was a Methodist preacher. She and her husband were first of all Wesleyan Methodists but went over to the Primitives when the Wesleyan Conference suppressed the preaching of women which it had formerly condoned. Later the Evanses joined the new Derbyshire Arminian Methodist group known as the Derby Faith Folk, formed in 1832. The couple founded the Derby Faith chapel in Wirksworth.

The young evangelical Anglican George Eliot was in great religious sympathy with her evangelical Methodist preaching aunt. They exchanged confessional, evangelically charged letters, and in long conversations with her aunt George Eliot heard the story of how she tended Mary Voce, a child-murderer in Nottingham gaol, which became the germ of *Adam Bede* (*L* ii. 502–5). Dinah Morris was easily recognized as a version of her aunt (see CHARACTERS, ORIGINALS OF), and Seth Bede, 'the Methody', as a version of her uncle. George Eliot filled out the personal story with much research—in Robert Southey's *Life of Wesley* (1820), for example—and was at great pains to get right the detail of Methodist spirit and practice. And Dinah Morris is one of the most sympathetically portrayed Christians in all of George Eliot, even though her Christian sympathy for Lisbeth Bede and the child-murderer Hetty Sorrel gets reread as having in truth a mere Feuerbachian human kindness to recommend it. In her post-evangelical essay *'Evangelical Teaching: Dr Cumming'* George Eliot used her aunt's Methodist recollections as an example of the way evangelicals sophisticate the truth for their religious ends: 'the more enthusiastic Methodists ... regard as a symptom of sinful scepticism an inquiry into the evidence of a story which they think unquestionably tends to the glory of God' (*Essays*, 166). It is not uninteresting that two contemporary broadsheets about the Mary Voce incident contradict several details in the Methodist broadsheet which support's her aunt's narrative (see appendix 2 to the World's Classics Edition of *Adam Bede*, ed. Valentine Cunningham). Perhaps the scepticism of the Cumming article had some foundation, even though her aunt's story was the foundation of an unarguably great novel. See also ANGLICANISM; RELIGION; RELIGION OF HUMANITY. VC

Cunningham (1975).

Meyerbeer, Giacomo (1791–1864), German opera composer. In *Daniel Deronda*, Herr Klesmer contemptuously characterizes Grandcourt's companion, the amateur cellist Lush, as 'too fond of Meyerbeer and Scribe—too fond of the mechanical-dramatic' (*DD* 11). This judgement echoes G. H. *Lewes's, expressed in prefatory comments to George Eliot's translation and condensation of an article by *Liszt, published by Lewes as 'The Romantic School of Music. Liszt on Meyerbeer-Wagner', *Leader* (28 Oct. 1854). George Eliot saw *Les Huguenots* (1836) in May 1852 and in June 1862; *L'Étoile du Nord* (1854) in May 1858; and *Le Prophète* (1849) in April 1861. See also MUSIC.

BG

Middlemarch: A Study of Provincial Life (*see page 250*)

Mill, John Stuart (1806–73), Victorian logician, utilitarian philosopher, writer on economics and politics, and champion of women's enfranchisement, whose work was of help to George Eliot. She relied on his *System of Logic* (1843) and his *Principles of Political Economy* (1848) as works of 'reference' (*L* i. 310, 363). She took a sympathetic, but level-headed, view of his brief career as MP for Westminster (1865–8). Reminiscing for Elizabeth Stuart *Phelps, 13 August 1875 (*L* vi. 163), she denied 'any personal acquaintance with J. S. Mill—never saw him, to my knowledge, except in the House of Commons'. She added that 'his books, especially his Logic and Political Economy', had been of 'much benefit' to her; but felt they had not 'made any marked epoch' in her mental life.

In Mill, Eliot found factual information or corroboration of her own principles rather than any radical restructuring or awakening of her con-

(*cont. on page 258*)

GENERALLY considered to be George Eliot's greatest novel, published in eight parts between December 1871 and December 1872.

Composition

The novel had a long and complex gestation. As early as March 1867 Eliot mentioned to her publisher John *Blackwood a project for an English novel (*L* iv. 355), but for the next year she was preoccupied with her verse drama *The Spanish Gypsy*. Then on 1 January 1869 her journal includes among the tasks to be accomplished in the coming year a 'novel called "Middlemarch" ' (*Journals*, 134). On 19 July she noted that she was writing an introduction to the novel, and on 2 August 'Began Middlemarch (the Vincy and Featherstone parts' (Cross, iii. 95, 97). By 11 September she had written three chapters, but at that point the novel seems to have been put aside while she and G. H. *Lewes coped with his son Thornton's fatal illness (see LEWES FAMILY). For the next twelve months she wrote little— mainly poetry—and at one point confessed to being in despair about future work (*L* v. 119–20), until on 2 December 1870 her journal reveals her experimenting with a story. On 31 December she records that she has written 100 pages of a story called 'Miss Brooke'. At some moment early in 1871 she must have decided to incorporate this story into the stalled novel, for by 19 March she could record in her journal that she had written about 236 pages of her novel and wanted to finish it by November, though feared she had 'too much matter, too many "momente" ' (*Journals*, 142). On 5 April Lewes was able to announce to an American publisher, 'It is a story of English provincial life—time 1830— and will be in three volumes' (*L* v. 139).

As work progressed the three-volume format began to seem too constricting. Writing to John Blackwood on 7 May 1871 Lewes mentioned that four volumes would be required and proposed publishing the novel in eight half-volume parts over a period of months— a proposal which Blackwood, keen to break the stranglehold of the circulating libraries with their preference for three-volume novels, accepted (see SERIALIZATION). By the end of October, delayed by illness, Eliot had completed three of the eight books and, as she continued, the need to keep a balance in each book between the different elements of the multiple plot became an important consideration. On 1 December 1871 the first book was published with less than half of the novel completed. By 8 May 1872 she had written five books but found the prospect of the remaining three a daunting one. Anxious for seclusion, she and Lewes rented a house at Redhill in Surrey for three months, leaving The *Priory on 24 May. The move proved beneficial. The sixth book was written in two months and the seventh in less than six weeks, with Eliot's confidence growing as the published parts won general admiration. The last chapters of Book 8 were sent off on 13 September and, after correcting proofs, Eliot and Lewes left for a holiday at Bad Homburg in *Germany with only the Finale still to write. This was completed on 2 October.

The manuscript is in the British Library, Add. MSS 34034–7, in four volumes bound in red leather and dedicated 'To my dear Husband George Henry Lewes, in this nineteenth year of our blessed union December 1872'.

Publication

The novel was published in eight parts—each part consisting of one book, bound in light green wrappers and priced 5s.—according to the scheme proposed by Lewes on 7 May, with one modification. The first six books were published at two-monthly intervals starting on 1 December 1871, but on 13 July Lewes suggested that the last two books should be published at monthly intervals, so that the final part would appear at the beginning of December 1872 in time for Christmas. Blackwood agreed and the plan was adopted. Concurrently with William *Blackwood and Sons' British publication the novel appeared in New York in weekly instalments in *Harper's Weekly* from 16 December 1871 to 15 February 1873. In December 1872 the remaining copies of the eight books (366 according to Blackwood's records) were bound up into four volumes in blue cloth with gold lettering and priced 42s. (two guineas). On 8 March 1873 a 'new edition'—in reality a new impression from the same plates—was published in four volumes octavo bound in green cloth and priced 21s. (one guinea). In May 1874 a second (cheap) edition was published in one volume priced 7s., 6d., and in December 1878 the *Cabinet Edition appeared in three volumes.

George Eliot's habitual use of -*ize* endings was changed to -*ise* to conform to Blackwood's house style. For the 1874 cheap edition she carried out a thorough correction of the text and made important changes to the penultimate paragraph of the Finale in particular, deleting the criticism of Middlemarch society for having 'smiled on propositions of marriage from a sickly man to a girl less than half his own age' which had appeared in both the manuscript and the first edition. Here she was responding to criticism, since reviewers had pointed out that Middlemarch society had not in fact smiled on Dorothea's marriage. Also deleted was the observation that society had similarly smiled 'on modes of education which make a woman's knowledge another name for motley ignorance', which had appeared in the first edition but not in the manuscript. For these and other variants, and a full publishing history, see the Clarendon Edition, ed. David Carroll (1986).

Illustrations

The eight individual parts bore a circular vignette of a country scene on the wrapper, drawn by Birket Foster and engraved by C. Jeens. Another vignette by Foster of an idealized townscape appeared on the title-page of the cheap edition of 1874.

Reception

From the appearance of the first instalment *Middlemarch* met with general acclaim, although not quite with the enthusiasm that *Adam Bede* had aroused. It seized and held the attention of the reading public, selling 6,000 copies of Book 1 and about 5,000 copies of each of the subsequent parts. Although this was not as much as Lewes had hoped for— he was counting on 10,000—the popularity of the novel became clear on publication of the cheap edition in May 1874, which sold 10,000 copies in the first six months and almost 31,000 copies by the end of 1878 (*CH* 28).

Several newspapers and journals reviewed the separate instalments as they appeared. R. H. *Hutton's series of reviews in the *Spectator* show him responding with delight to minor characters like Mrs Cadwallader and Mr Brooke; recoiling critically from the unnaturalness of Dorothea's decision to marry Casaubon; criticizing the narrator's sarcasms and the hostility shown to attractive, limited young women like Rosamond; reflecting on the melancholy of a novel in which 'George Eliot never makes the world worse than it is, but she makes it a shade darker' (*CH* 298); and gradually coming to the view that '*Middlemarch* bids more than fair to be one of the great books of the world' (*CH* 302). Like other early reviewers he noted the centrality of the *woman question, which was not to be taken up again until the appearance of feminist criticism in the 1970s (see CRITICISM, MODERN: FEMINIST APPROACHES). In his final review of the whole novel he affirmed the value of having lived with it over the space of the year as it appeared in instalments, growing slowly familiar with its characters and seeing the human elements combine into plot; and he concluded by asserting that it was a great book and that George Eliot would now stand with Henry *Fielding and Walter *Scott in the second rank of writers below *Shakespeare.

The melancholy which Hutton discussed was noted by many reviewers and readers. After reading the first instalment Eliot's close friend Barbara *Bodichon likened Dorothea to a 'child dancing into a quick sand on a summer morning' and was fearful of the horrible tragedy that seemed to be coming (*L* ix. 33–4), while Lord Houghton (see MILNES, RICHARD MONCKTON) in the *Edinburgh Review* in January 1873 described the author as 'the sad chronicler of the weakness of our race'. Even her ardent admirer Edith *Simcox's review in the *Academy* could write of her large theory of the universe 'which is at once so charitable and so melancholy' (*CH* 325). Simcox was unequivocal in pronouncing *Middlemarch* Eliot's greatest work, with few equals in English fiction, and her critical acuteness enabled her to see that it was doing something new in concentrating on the inner life and making the material circumstances of the outer world subordinate to mental experience. In a striking phrase she claimed that 'the effect is as new as if we could suppose a *Wilhelm Meister* written by Balzac' (*CH* 323). In another important review in the *Fortnightly Review* Sidney Colvin praised the novel as the 'chief English book of the immediate present' (*CH* 331) and defined the contrast between the old world that was its subject matter and the new manner in which it was treated. On the life of the English provinces before the Reform Bill George Eliot brought to bear the many-sided culture and sophisticated analytical intelligence of the modern world, so that whereas 'the matter is antiquated in our recollection, the manner seems to anticipate the future of our thoughts' (*CH* 332). Like most of the reviewers of the complete novel in the early months of 1873 Colvin had criticisms to make. He found the author lacking in impartiality in the treatment of characters and, like many critics, was puzzled as to the general lesson of the novel, seeing a contradiction between the emphasis in the Prelude and Finale on the way in which society frustrates the noble aspirations of women and the fact that Dorothea's mistaken choice of Casaubon is her own delusion not society's. To this ambiguity in the novel's moral and intellectual point of view he attributed the sense of sadness and flatness created by the ending, in particular Dorothea's subdued and restricted role as Ladislaw's wife.

Henry *James in an unsigned review in *Galaxy* in March 1873 also combined praise with criticism, declaring that *Middlemarch* was 'at once one of the strongest and one of the weakest of English novels'. Its weakness lay in its diffusiveness, so that, as he famously pronounced, '*Middlemarch* is a treasure-house of details, but it is an indifferent whole' (*CH* 353)—the reviewer in the *Nation* in January had made a similar point. While James found nothing more real and intelligent in English fiction than the painful scenes between Lydgate and Rosamond, he saw Ladislaw as an artistic failure, remaining vague and impalpable and never overcoming the impression of being a mere dilettante (*CH* 356). Nevertheless, with all its faults *Middlemarch* was a splendid performance that marked the end of the development of the old-fashioned English novel and raised the question of where fiction could go next: 'If we write novels so, how shall we write History?' (*CH* 359).

Plot

Set in a Midlands town just before the Reform Bill of 1832 and subtitled 'A Study of Provincial Life', *Middlemarch* traces the web of intersecting lives that constitutes a provincial community. There are four main strands to the narrative. The first involves the wealthy and idealistic Dorothea Brooke, who, eager to do something out of the ordinary with her life, mistakenly marries the desiccated, pedantic scholar and clergyman Edward Casaubon. Released from an unhappy marriage by the death of her much older husband, she finds herself in love with his cousin Will Ladislaw, a young man of wide interests but unfocused ambition. She finally marries him, moving to London to support him in a career in politics. A misguided marriage and unrealized aspirations are also at the centre of the second story: Tertius Lydgate, an ambitious young doctor with plans to do good work for Middlemarch and great work for the world, falls for the charms of Rosamond Vincy, the attractive but self-centred daughter of a local manufacturer. Hampered by circumstances in Middlemarch, by an obstructive wife, and by mounting debt, he fails to realize his high ambitions and has to settle for the conventional life desired by Rosamond, becoming a fashionable doctor in London and on the Continent treating wealthy patients for gout. The third story provides an ultimately idyllic contrast of modest achievement and fulfilled love. Fred Vincy, Rosamond's brother, unsuited to a career in the Church which is all that his university education has prepared him for, and disappointed in his expectation of a large inheritance from his uncle Peter Featherstone, is saved from a life of fecklessness by his love for his childhood sweetheart Mary Garth. He finds sensible employment in estate management with her father Caleb and settles down to a happy marriage, assisted by the quietly heroic self-denial of the Revd Camden Farebrother, who renounces his own interest in Mary and urges Fred to be worthy of her. The fourth strand of the narrative concerns the prosperous and sanctimonious banker Bulstrode who is brought down by the revelation of his disreputable past. Driven to crime by his desire to conceal it, he brings about the death of the blackmailer Raffles while he is tending him in an illness. Although his wife remains touchingly loyal to him in his disgrace—while remaining ignorant of the fact that he is really guilty of murder—he can no longer hold his head up in Middlemarch and leaves the town to go where he is not known. Of the principal characters only Mary and Fred remain in Middlemarch at the end, but the novel, with its large cast of secondary characters, such as Dorothea's amiably meandering uncle Mr Brooke and the sharp-tongued rector's wife Mrs Cadwallader, has created a strong sense of the continuing life of a provincial community.

Critical Approaches

Although George Eliot's critical *reputation went into a decline after her death, *Middlemarch* could still be singled out for praise in the years of her unpopularity. Virginia *Woolf famously described it in 1919 as 'the magnificent book which with all its imperfections is one of the few English novels written for grown-up people' (*Times Literary Supplement*, 20 November 1919). When her reputation revived, critics like Barbara Hardy (1959) and W. J. Harvey (1961) with their attention to the form of her fiction, countered Henry James's criticism of *Middlemarch*'s diffusiveness by demonstrating the formal coherence and control Eliot achieves in the novel, in particular by the use of running images like the web and the labyrinth (see METAPHOR). More recent post-structuralist criticism has come to challenge such control by bringing out the ambiguities and contradictions in the text, and showing that its continuing vitality lies in the inexhaustible variety and complexity of the readings it allows. As the narrator puts it early in the novel, 'Signs are small measurable things, but interpretations are illimitable' (*MM* 3). From this point of view even the title 'Middlemarch' appears intriguingly unstable, yoking together opposing notions of centre and borderland and creating uncertainty as to whether it suggests the march of progress or the triumph of middling mediocrity (Wright 1991: p. xiv).

The Prelude introduces two of the novel's central and related concerns by alluding in its opening sentence to 'the history of man' and proceeding to comment on the 'blundering lives' of women and the question of women's nature. *Middlemarch* is, indeed, a novel about *history: it seeks to recreate the conditions of English provincial life in the early 1830s with careful attention both to the details of social history and to the larger historical events of the time, such as the Reform Bill, the building of the railways, and the death of King George IV. At the same time the problems of reform relate to the period in which Eliot was writing—the Second Reform Bill had recently been passed in 1867 (see REFORM ACTS)—and the novel conveys some of the anxieties of that time. As Gillian Beer has pointed out, one of the anxious questions it raises in relation to the position of women is whether any real emancipation has been achieved in the years between 1830 and 1870 (Beer 1986: 170). Moreover, when Dorothea finds herself oppressed by the weight of the historical past in Rome, the novel reflects on the problematic relationship of women to a history from which they have been largely excluded.

The question of women's nature addressed in the Prelude was a topic of discussion in the women's movement at the time Eliot was writing, and the 'indefiniteness' she ascribes to it is clearly seen in the novel not as an innate characteristic but as a social construct. The abstract quality is given concrete form in the particular predicament of Dorothea Brooke in the opening chapters, as she broods with a misplaced sense of gratitude on the possibility that Casaubon might wish to marry her: 'For a long while she had been oppressed by the indefiniteness which hung in her mind, like a thick summer haze, over all her desire to make her life greatly effective' (*MM* 3). The only escape from such indefiniteness, even for a privileged young woman like Dorothea, is into the definition offered by *marriage and the role of wife. To be defined as Mrs Casaubon turns out to be a stifling imprisonment in which her emotional and sexual energy is painfully repressed. And even though she is released by Casaubon's early death into a life where her sexuality and passionate longings can be acknowledged and expressed, the problem of definition remains. To the disappointment of many women readers from Florence *Nightingale on, Eliot does not have Dorothea define herself by making her way in the world as an independent woman but commits her to another marriage that looks to many like a sad compromise. Even in its ending the novel insists upon the constraints of a woman's lot. Nevertheless in the final paragraph of the novel, which makes an eloquent and moving claim for the significance of those unhistoric lives that end in unvisited tombs, Dorothea's original and persistent predicament is again alluded to, but with an important change of emphasis: '. . . but the effect of her being was incalculably diffusive'. Indefiniteness is now charged with a positive meaning: a state of frustrating indeterminacy has been transformed into quietly creative, diffusive action whose effects may not be measurable but are real enough for succeeding generations.

Although the claim made for Dorothea's achievement at the end is modest and muted, her life is presented in terms of a progress from hazy fantasy to moral enlightenment—a progress which is defined by scenes of seeing: Dorothea before her engagement, with her bright full eyes, looking before her as she walks, 'not consciously seeing, but absorbing into the intensity of her mood, the solemn glory of the afternoon' (*MM* 3); then, after her marriage, overwhelmed by the accumulated history of Rome and by the vastness of St Peter's in particular, whose red drapery affects her like 'a disease of the retina' (*MM* 20); and later returning from this unhappy honeymoon to gaze blankly out upon the winter landscape at Lowick, which reflects back to her the desolation of her own emotional state (*MM* 28). The culmination of these moments of seeing is the famous moral climax where she opens her curtains and looks out upon a world of labour and endurance, in which she resolves to play her part by doing what she can to help her friends (*MM* 80). This scene at the window is a dramatic enactment of the transcendence of self, a moral opening out to the needs of others, and in Eliot's moral scheme it stands in contrast to the kind of seeing associated with the demanding ego. In a celebrated passage the narrowly self-interested Rosamond is defined by the parable of the candle on the pier glass, which creates the optical illusion that all the scratches on the surface of the mirror are arranged in concentric circles around the central flame (*MM* 27). The mirror is the appropriate emblem for the narcissistic Rosamond as the window is for the open-hearted Dorothea. However, although Eliot's moral scheme is a simple one it is never schematic but always subject to enlivening variations. Thus even Rosamond has her moment of selflessness when, moved by Dorothea's example, she 'involuntarily' puts her lips to Dorothea's forehead and reveals to her Ladislaw's true feelings. The involuntary gesture is redeemingly out of character for a woman whose behaviour is otherwise governed by her imperious will. In this novel the will is the agent of the demanding ego, and the legal wills of Featherstone and Casaubon are shown to be the pernicious attempts of their overbearing egos to control events and subordinate other people even from beyond the grave.

These wills are a striking instance of one life impinging upon another—Featherstone depriving Fred of his expected inheritance and Casaubon seeking to prevent Dorothea marrying Will Ladislaw—and they take up the sinister implications of the image of the web, which the narrator uses to suggest the way in which lives are 'woven and interwoven' (*MM* 15) in the multiple narratives of the novel (see SOCIETY). If neither Fred nor Dorothea is ultimately trapped in the web of another's will, Lydgate is less fortunate, falling victim to Rosamond's inflexible ego. But, in another fateful intersection of lives, his downfall contributes to the making of his brother-in-law Fred. When Fred catches sight of Lydgate playing billiards for money in the Green Dragon, he stifles his own impulse to revert to his former life of gambling and self-indulgence (*MM* 66); and the chapter ends with Farebrother renouncing his own interest in Mary Garth and urging Fred to be worthy of her. A decisive step in the young man's redemption is thus brought about by his witnessing the depths to which Lydgate has sunk—the medical scientist, in an ironically appropriate simile, has seemingly slipped back down the evolutionary tree and is 'acting, watching, speaking with that excited narrow consciousness which reminds one of an animal with fierce eyes and retractile claws' (*MM* 66).

The interweaving of different lives, the connecting commentary of the narrator, and the widespread use of images of connection like the web do not make for the straightforward unity that some critics like to claim for the novel. Lives are often discontinuous—Lydgate's early promise and subsequent decline, Bulstrode's shameful past and apparently respectable present—and the novel dwells as much on difference and disparity as on relatedness. At Featherstone's funeral Dorothea and other members of her circle observe the event from an upper window of Casaubon's house, which defines the social position of the gentry, 'dotted apart on their stations up the mountain' from where 'they looked down with imperfect discrimination on the belts of thicker life below' (*MM* 34). And the difference in social status is compounded by the very different responses to the event of the individual onlookers. The famous moment at the beginning of chapter 29 when the narrator self-consciously switches attention from Dorothea to Casaubon—'but why always Dorothea? Was her point of view the only possible one with regard to this marriage?'—underlines the difficulty of making connections, of bringing Casaubon into the orbit of the sympathetic understanding that is so readily granted to Dorothea. The reader is challenged to make, and to reflect upon, the extension of sympathy that Eliot, in her essay 'The *Natural History of German Life', takes to be the moral function of art; and the laboured transition from easy identification with the attractive heroine to inwardness with her husband's shrivelled soul reproduces in the process of reading the pattern of Dorothea's own moral development, her replacement of the self-centred vision by insight into the needs of others. Since 'the quickest of us walk about well wadded with stupidity' (*MM* 20), such sympathetic connections are hard to achieve, but they are the source of whatever unity the novel has. As Karen Chase has put it, '*Middlemarch* is not held together by some overarching moral perspective; it is held together by *our* learning to perform many and diverse acts of sympathy' (1991: 44). Unity in this novel has to be worked for by the reader, just as community in the fictional world is only achieved through the active sympathy of such figures as Dorothea.

Although it provides a moral perspective on the characters and their actions, the narrative voice in *Middlemarch* (see NARRATION) is also varied rather than unified, shifting very obviously between sarcasm and sympathy in a manner which the earliest readers and reviewers found puzzling, and using *irony in more subtle and complex ways. Sometimes it ironically adopts the values of conventional Middlemarch in order to discredit them; at others it combines mockery and sympathetic understanding in its two-edged presentation of characters, of Dorothea in particular. It can appeal solemnly to the reader in the first person plural, soliciting assent—'we are all of us born in moral stupidity, taking the world as an udder to feed our supreme selves' (*MM* 20)—but it can also mock any sense of historical superiority (see PROGRESS) the reader of the 1870s, and later, might feel in looking back at an age 'innocent of future goldfields, and of that gorgeous plutocracy which has so nobly exalted the necessities of genteel life' (*MM* 1). This richly varied voice with its shifting tones and registers establishes the narrator as a dominant presence and source of interest in the novel. The comparison with Fielding at the beginning of chapter 15 is highly pertinent, for, despite the distinctions that are made between them, the narrators of *Tom Jones* and *Middlemarch* occupy a similarly commanding position. But there is one central difference: where Fielding's narrator is unambiguously masculine, the narrative voice of *Middlemarch* seems to transcend *gender. In equal command of the 'masculine' discourse of *science and the 'feminine' discourse of feeling, it resists gender categorization and remains elusively androgynous. The ambiguity of an author with a man's name who is known to be a woman extends here to the narrative voice and signals a challenge to gender distinctions that is taken up in the narrative. When Dorothea looks at the miniature of Aunt Julia, Ladislaw's grandmother, and sees her features turning into his, there is a deliberate blurring of the distinctions between the sexes, and this carries over into Ladislaw's character. Sensitive, intuitive, with 'transparent skin' (*MM* 21) and 'delicate throat', caring 'little for what are called the solid things of life and greatly for its subtle influences' (*MM* 47), he has many characteristics conventionally associated with women, without forfeiting his role as the principal man in Dorothea's later life—although whether such a man is a suitable partner for Dorothea remains a matter of dispute (Barrett 1989: 134). For her part she, too, challenges what is usually considered appropriate for her sex in her ardent desire to play an active role in the world, 'to lead a grand life, here—now—in England' (*MM* 3); while the links and parallels between her life and Lydgate's—his 'intellectual ardour' (*MM* 15) and her ardent if unfocused aspirations, the impulsiveness that leads both of them into miserable marriages—underline the fact that the principal difference between men and women is not one of nature but of the opportunities open to them in society at a particular historical juncture.

The allusions in the opening sentence of the novel to the 'history of man' and the 'experiments of Time' point to the larger context of Eliot's scrutiny of individual lives in a provincial community, and indicate an aspiration to comprehensiveness and an allegiance with science that are characteristic of 19th-century *realism. The subtitle, 'A Study of Provincial Life', carries an echo of the subdivisions of that other grandly encompassing realist project, Honoré de *Balzac's *Comédie humaine*, which similarly proposes an affinity between the novelist and the scientist. The narrator's commentary, which draws heavily on scientific discourse, seeks to persuade us of the general truth implied in the experience of the characters, while the chapter *epigraphs relate that experience to the wider context of world literature. Drawing on the authority of the *Bible and John *Bunyan, Shakespeare and *Cervantes, *Wordsworth and *Goethe, the epigraphs seem designed to endorse the truth of the local particulars and to suggest that this study of English provincial life is a valid account of human life in any place and at any time. This implicit claim to enduring and encompassing truth has led to *Middlemarch* being criticized as a 'classic realist text' which deceptively conceals its own premises and partiality in presenting itself as an objective, transparent window on the world. However, the realism of *Middlemarch* is more complex, sophisticated, and self-conscious than the already subtle realism of ordinary lives found in *Adam Bede* and the early works, and George Eliot is as fully aware of the problems of epistemology, *language, and representation as any post-structuralist critic. The parable of the pier glass draws on science to suggest the inescapable subjectivity of vision, and this qualifies the perceptions of the narrator as much as those of the characters; language is acknowledged as slippery and figurative (see METAPHOR; CRITICISM, MODERN: DECONSTRUCTION); and even character may be simply a construct of the perceiving mind (see CHARACTERIZATION). The comprehensiveness of *Middlemarch*, properly understood, involves not just the creation of an encompassing, richly detailed, various, and spacious fictional world, but also a self-reflexive awareness of the problems and processes of fictional creation itself. See also ENDINGS OF NOVELS.

JMR

Adam (1975).
Barrett (1989).
Beaty, Jerome, '*Middlemarch*' From Notebook to Novel (1960).
Beer (1986).
Blake, Kathleen, 'Middlemarch and the Woman Question', *Nineteenth-Century Fiction*, 31 (1976–7).
Chase (1991).
Hardy (1959).
—— (1982).
Karlin, Daniel, 'Having the Whip-hand in Middlemarch', *George Eliot Review*, 28 (1997).
Peck (1992).
Wright (1991).

sciousness. G. H. *Lewes knew Mill from the early 1830s and Eliot shared his sense that Mill's high-minded version of the utilitarian philosophy of the 'greatest happiness of the greatest number' placed him 'amongst the world's vanguard' (*L* ii. 49). She endorsed Mill's empirical, inductive system of logic, insofar as it sought moral and spiritual truths through experience, rather than taking them blindly from preconceived ideas. Retaining his mother's evangelical optimism (without her theology), Mill combined a radical approach with high concepts of human virtue, once freed from illogical man-made rules. Eliot warmed early to this approach, and her approval of Mill's sincerity was confirmed by reading his *Three Essays on Religion* (1874), a copy of which she borrowed from Herbert Spencer.

Like Lewes, Eliot respected Mill's economic views, which were those of laissez-faire capitalism moderated by government action on behalf of certain beneficial interests. This 'inauthoritative' role of government was developed in his *Considerations on Representative Government* (1861), which Eliot borrowed from the London Library in January 1866, while completing *Felix Holt, the Radical*. Admiring Mill's grasp on political ideas, Eliot was not anxious, in July 1865, 'that he should be in Parliament: thinkers can do more outside than inside the House' (*L* iv. 196). Nevertheless, on Mill's election later that month, she took an interest in his efforts to allow women to vote in certain cases. Questions of enfranchisement remained for her, however, a matter of moral force rather than political contrivance. Writing to John *Morley, 14 May 1867, she added, 'I would certainly not oppose any plan . . . to establish . . . an equivalence of advantages for two sexes, as to education and the possibilities of free development', but felt men did not sufficiently recognize that 'as a matter of mere zoological evolution, woman seems to me to have the worse share in existence', a fact no Act of Parliament could correct (*L* iv. 364). Of Mill's *On the Subjection of Women* (1869) she confided to Barbara *Bodichon (2 July 1869) that she found 'the second chapter excellent' but 'the third and fourth not so strong and well argued as they ought to have been' (*L* viii. 458). Mill sought governmental experiments in 'the utmost legislative and social equality that can be attained' (Hardman, 110) in order to assess scientifically the true relations between classes and sexes: an approach that made his political arguments in favour of equalizing those relations somewhat circular, to the disapproval of the conservative (and logical) Eliot. She preferred a human detail to any theory baldly stated. Thus to Barbara Bodichon (7 Nov. 1880), she praised Mill (*Principles of Political Economy* (1848), ii. 355–7) for writing about the Parisian

house-painter Leclaire, 'who initiated an excellent plan for co-operative sharing for his workmen', and regretted that this 'had not been otherwise taken much notice of' (*L* vii. 333).

Eliot's judicious approach to Mill was of use in June 1851, when the publisher John *Chapman, with her considerable help, was drawing up a new prospectus for the *Westminster Review*, which he had recently purchased. Proofs were sent for approval to J. S. Mill, as a former owner and editor. His 'animadversions' were less than helpful, and Chapman drafted an irate reply. Eliot intervened with brisk and effective guidance for the tactful handling of the philosopher, and disaster was averted (*L* i. 351; viii. 23–4). There was, however, a tiresome fuss (*L* ii. 47, 63–4) about Mill's article on 'Whewell's Moral Philosophy', which appeared in the *Westminster Review* in 1852.

Coping with Mill seems to have given Eliot insight into his *Autobiography* (1873), with its account of his relationship with Mrs Harriet Taylor (1807–58), whom he married in 1851, and who has points of resemblance with Eliot herself. Theirs was an intellectual partnership rising, in the case of *On Liberty* (1859), into actual collaboration (Hardman, 73–87). But it also involved, on the part of Mill (emotionally damaged by his father's severe upbringing), a dependence that was not quite adult. Eliot and Lewes had visited Harriet's tomb at Avignon in April 1861, and been 'much affected' by the 'tender praises' with which Mill had adorned it (*L* iii. 408). She intuited the personal complexities of the relationship. But she also recognized its significance for the future of intellectual partnerships between the sexes. It deserved to be handled with tact. Unfortunately, Mill produced an account that drove Eliot to prophesy (with her usual accuracy) in a letter to Barbara Bodichon, December 1873 (*L* v. 467), 'that the exaggerated expressions in which he conveys his feeling about his wife would neutralize all the good that might have come from the beautiful fact of his devotion to her'.   MH

Mill, John Stuart, *The Collected Edition*, ed. J. M. Robson, 33 vols. (1963–91).

—— and Bentham, Jeremy, *Utilitarianism and Other Essays*, ed. Alan Ryan (1987).

Hardman, Malcolm, *Six Victorian Thinkers* (1991).

Kamm, Josephine, *John Stuart Mill in Love* (1977).

Mill on the Floss, The (see opposite page)

Millais, John Everett (1829–96), English painter. George Eliot greatly admired Millais's *A Huguenot on St Bartholemew's Day* (private collection) when she saw it in the Royal Academy exhibition of 1852. The painting's subject is a Catholic woman trying to save her Protestant lover from

(cont. on page 267)

GEORGE ELIOT's second novel, published in 1860, and the one that is closest to her own life in its portrayal of an intense and painful brother–sister relationship. It is also the only one of her novels to have a tragic ending. As a novel about childhood and adolescence with a strong autobiographical dimension it has prompted comparisons with Charlotte *Brontë's *Jane Eyre* (1847) and Charles *Dickens's *David Copperfield* (1849–50).

Composition

The first indication of work on the novel is a diary entry of 12 January 1859 which records going into London to check the Annual Register for 'cases of *inundation*' (*Journals*, 76). The concluding flood thus appears to have been in her plans from the beginning, while for the childhood scenes in particular she drew heavily on her own experience and her relationship with her brother Isaac. Composition proceeded very slowly at first, not helped by moving house on 5 February from Richmond to Wandsworth (see HOMES), by excitement at the success of *Adam Bede* published on 1 February, and by the death of her sister Chrissey on 15 March (see EVANS, CHRISTIANA). Immediately after that death she broke off work on the novel to write 'The Lifted Veil' and did not resume until the story had been completed on 26 April. By the middle of June she was able to hand the first 110 pages to John *Blackwood, who responded warmly. Finding it difficult to work at Wandsworth she travelled extensively with G. H. *Lewes that summer: to Switzerland for two weeks via Paris on 9 July; to North Wales on 26 August and then Weymouth from 31 August to 16 September, where she visited a mill and looked in vain for a river that might provide the final flood; and then on 26 September to Lincolnshire to see the Trent, finding in that river and its tributary the Idle the appropriate setting for the Mill and the flood, and in *Gainsborough a model for St Ogg's. Writing then began to proceed more rapidly. The first volume was completed by 16 October, the second by 16 January, and the third at great speed by 21 March. The final pages were sent to William *Blackwood and Sons in Edinburgh the same day and proofs were returned two days later, to be read and corrected before George Eliot and Lewes left for *Italy on 24 March. During composition the novel was referred to by various titles, including 'The Tulliver Family', 'St Ogg's on the Floss', 'Maggie', and 'Sister Maggie'. It was John Blackwood who suggested the eventual title, although George Eliot, in accepting it, observed that, strictly speaking, the Mill was situated not on the Floss but on its tributary (*L* iii. 244–5).

Publication

At first John Blackwood was keen to publish the novel serially in *Blackwood's Edinburgh Magazine*, but the success of *Adam Bede* made George Eliot and Lewes doubt whether this would be as profitable as publication in book form, which would take immediate advantage of the author's popularity. After a period of strained relations and misunderstandings with Blackwood agreement was reached for an edition of 4,000 copies for which George Eliot would receive £2,000. The novel was published on 4 April 1860 in three volumes octavo, bound in orange-brown cloth, priced 31s. 6d. A second edition followed on 1 December 1860 in two volumes, priced 12s., and a third on 1 December 1862 in one volume, priced 6s. The plates of the third edition were used for an illustrated edition in one volume published on 1 November 1867, priced 3s. 6d. The fourth or Cabinet Edition in two volumes (vols. viii and ix) appeared in August and September 1878, priced

5s. The first American edition was published in April 1860 in one volume duodecimo by Harper & Brothers and W. I. Pooley & Co., New York; and the first continental reprint was the Copyright Edition of 1860 in two volumes octavo, published by Christian Bernhard *Tauchnitz in Leipzig. The manuscript is in the British Library (Add. MSS 34023–5), bound in maroon leather and dedicated to 'my beloved Husband, George Henry Lewes'.

George Eliot corrected page proofs of the first edition and corrected a copy of the second edition as a basis for the third. She did not see proofs of the Cabinet Edition, which was produced during Lewes's final illness. There are some divergences between the manuscript and the first and later editions: words ending in -*ize*, Eliot's normal spelling, were changed to -*ise* to conform to Blackwood's house style; the manuscript also contained a lot of colourful dialect in the characters' speech which she toned down in proof, having tried it out on Lewes for intelligibility (*L* ii. 500). For details of textual variants and a full publishing history see the Clarendon Edition, ed. Gordon S. Haight (1980).

Illustrations

The third Stereotyped Edition of 1 November 1867 contains seven illustrations drawn by W. J. Allen, except for the vignette of Dorlcote Mill on the title-page which is signed EMW, and engraved by James Cooper.

Reception

The novel was soon a commercial success, selling 6,000 copies in the first two months. The early reviewers considered it at least the equal of *Adam Bede*, although likely to be less popular. The rendering of childhood was widely praised, as were the convincingly realistic characters. An unsigned review in the *Spectator* claimed that 'in very few works of fiction has the interior of the mind been so keenly analysed' (*CH* 111), comparing the novel to *Jane Eyre* in this respect, with the difference that Maggie is an ordinary rather than an exceptional young woman. The *Saturday Review* also saw George Eliot as not inferior to Brontë and Jane *Austen, while primly criticizing Brontë's and Eliot's portrayal of passionate love: 'There are emotions over which we ought to throw a veil' (*CH* 119). In a sympathetic and perceptive review in *The Times* E. S. *Dallas maintained that George Eliot had attempted a more difficult task than the Brontës in portraying characters 'in all their intrinsic littleness' (*CH* 134). He also identified the struggle for survival that the novel presents, noting 'how everybody in this tale is repelling everybody, and life is in the strictest sense a battle' (*CH* 133); and he perceived the tragic nature of the work: 'the riddle of life as it is here expounded is more like a Greek tragedy than a modern novel' (*CH* 135). Where Dallas argued that George Eliot's genius had transformed the unpromising material of mean and prosaic lives into truthful art, the novel's most hostile review in the *Dublin University Magazine* found it simply 'a series of photographic sketches, of which a good deal is provokingly commonplace, and a good deal more is tiresomely repellant' (*CH* 148). The childhood scenes were superfluous and the moral vision of the novel defective in its bleak determinism, 'showing fate triumphant not only against human happiness, but still more against human virtue' (*CH* 151). Twenty years later, after George Eliot's death, John *Ruskin allowed himself a splenetic outburst along similar lines, declaring that only lofty characters were worth describing at all, that Maggie and Tom were merely commonplace, 'while the rest of the characters are simply the sweepings out of a Pentonville omnibus' (*CH* 167).

For the early reviewers the last third of the novel was the most frequent target of criticism. To many the final volume seemed to be at odds with the first two: 'There is a clear dislocation in the story, between Maggie's girlhood and Maggie's great temptation' as the *Guardian* put it (*CH* 129). Edward *Bulwer-Lytton in a letter to John Blackwood also found the tragedy not adequately prepared, a criticism George Eliot conceded had some foundation (*L* iii. 317). He, like many others, found fault with Maggie's feelings for Stephen Guest as out of character and demeaning, a view most violently expressed much later by Algernon *Swinburne, who apoplectically dismissed Stephen as a 'thing' and a 'cur' (*CH* 164–5). Dinah Mulock in a sympathetic review in *Macmillan's Magazine*, while also finding Maggie's love for Stephen hard to believe in, anticipated the concerns of later criticism by focusing on the problem of the ending, finding it ambiguous as to whether the death of Tom and Maggie was a translation to something higher or simply an escape (*CH* 158–9).

Plot

The novel opens with a description of the river Floss and its landscape, and of Dorlcote Mill, where a small girl is standing by the water watching the mill-wheel as dusk falls. This vividly realized scene is then revealed to be a reverie on the part of the narrator, sitting in an armchair and dreaming of a February afternoon many years ago. That remembered past becomes the fictional present in which the life of the Tulliver family is presented. The small girl by the water is the imaginative and emotionally intense Maggie, who is devoted to her elder brother Tom but the frequent object of his anger.

Mr Tulliver sends Tom away to be educated by a clergyman, Mr Stelling, where the boy makes slow progress. On a visit to her brother Maggie makes friends with his fellow-pupil Philip, the sensitive, intelligent, but crippled son of the lawyer Wakem, an old adversary of Mr Tulliver who is acting for his opponent Pivart in a lawsuit about an irrigation scheme upstream of the Mill which is reducing the flow of water. Mr Tulliver eventually loses the case and is financially ruined. The news that Wakem has taken over the mortgage on the Mill prostrates him with a stroke. When he recovers, he learns that he is bankrupt and that Wakem plans to keep him on at the Mill as manager. He accepts the humiliating position but swears, and gets Tom to swear, that he will not forgive or forget what Wakem has done. Maggie continues to meet Philip in secret at the Red Deeps. He is in love with her and she goes as far as saying that she wants never to be parted from him. However, Tom finds out about their meetings and forbids further contact. He himself finds employment in St Ogg's through his uncle Deane and works hard to save enough money to pay off his father's debts. He finally succeeds and, after a dinner at which the creditors are paid off, Mr Tulliver meets Wakem on his way home and gives him a thrashing with his whip. Wakem is not seriously hurt but Mr Tulliver dies the same night.

At her cousin Lucy's Maggie, now a young woman, meets Lucy's good-looking suitor Stephen Guest, heir to the largest business in St Ogg's for which Tom is working, and she also renews contact with Philip. Philip tells his father of his love for Maggie, and Wakem reacts with fury. Stephen is increasingly attracted to Maggie, arousing Philip's jealousy. When he declares his love for her, she reminds him of his commitment to Lucy and hers to Philip. Then Stephen turns up in place of the expected Philip to take her for a row on the river and, despite protesting, she allows herself to be helped into the boat. Rowing and drifting with the current in an enchanted haze, they go far past their destination without her realizing it and have to be picked up by a Dutch vessel in the estuary. They pass the night on deck while the ship makes its way to Mudport. Stephen implores Maggie to marry him and proposes that they should return to St Ogg's as man and wife. She refuses and returns alone to face her disgrace. Tom will not allow her into the house, but Mrs Tulliver will not abandon her, leaving home with Maggie to take lodgings with Bob Jakin and his family. The society of St Ogg's condemns her, and the only people who take her side are the rector Dr Kenn and her aunt Glegg, for whom family solidarity is paramount. Lucy also contrives to see her and assure her that she understands, while Philip writes to express his unchanging love. A letter from Stephen again tempts her with an offer of marriage, but she does not succumb. Then St Ogg's is flooded; Maggie escapes in a boat and rows to the Mill to rescue Tom. Together again, their boat is overturned by a mass of debris and they drown in a last embrace. In a brief conclusion five years have passed, the Mill has been rebuilt, and Tom and Maggie lie buried together in the church-yard, their grave visited by the two men who loved her.

Critical Approaches

The dislocation that early reviewers saw between the first two volumes and the third, between Maggie's childhood and her temptation, is only one instance of discontinuity in a novel marked by division, conflict, and contradiction. The most closely autobiographical of George Eliot's works, *The Mill* both dwells with *Wordsworthian piety on the positive shaping power of the past and at the same time reveals its crippling constraints. It presents a story of personal development (see BILDUNGSROMAN) that is explicitly related to the general 'onward tendency of human things' (*MF* 4.1), but it also shows that development to be tragically cut short and human history to display no sure signs of *progress. It dramatizes the oppressive effects of patriarchal conventions on a young woman's life and nevertheless ends by uniting oppressor and oppressed in a reconciling embrace. 'In writing the history of unfashionable families' (*MF* 4.3), it is committed, like *Adam Bede* before it, to the mode of social *realism, but boldly departs from it at the beginning and at the end, and pauses to reflect upon the problematic relationship of *language to reality in the context of Tom's education (see METAPHOR). Such features as these have been the spur to critical discussion, opening up different possibilities of interpretation by offering not certainty but, to use George Eliot's own words, 'that complex, fragmentary, doubt-provoking knowledge which we call truth' (*MF* 6.12).

The opening chapter elides the distinction between reverie and reality, associates river and tide with the idea of a loving, 'impetuous embrace', and links both narrator and Maggie with a watery other-world of 'dreamy deafness' outside time. The metaphorical association of the river with the strong current of Maggie's emotional life is thus suggested from the outset, and it is taken up later in the name of the location for her secret meetings with Philip Wakem, the Red Deeps, and in the fateful rowing trip with Stephen Guest in the chapter entitled 'Borne Along by the Tide' (*MF* 6.13), as well as in the concluding flood. But in adopting the final title of the novel instead of one identifying Maggie as the central figure, George Eliot signalled the importance of that social context of which the river is a crucial part (see SOCIETY). The Floss is thus also related to *history and social change, to the past and the working present of St Ogg's. The name of the town derives from the sainted ferryman of the legendary past, while its prosperity comes from its role as a port linking the locality with the wider world. The waters that turn Mr Tulliver's mill may have done so for generations but they, too, are caught up in the process of change, and it is their use in a modern irrigation scheme that brings about his

George Eliot's brother Isaac Evans (1816–90) in later years. *The Mill on the Floss* draws on her memories of him and their childhood companionship.

downfall. The river is also the current of history that bears the Tullivers along. When the narrator pauses to reflect on the course of that history at the beginning of Book 4, it is, appropriately, in terms of two rivers, the Rhine and the Rhône, that two contrasting visions of the historical process are defined. The Rhine with its romantic ruins of castles suggests the 'grand historic life of humanity' (*MF* 4.1), a history that links past to present in a meaningful continuity, while the ruined villages of the Rhône convey the opposite sense of life as 'a narrow, ugly, grovelling existence', of history as devoid of any positive pattern or meaning. Although the same chapter goes on to talk of the 'historical advance of mankind', the bleak vision of history and human possibility prompted by the Rhône landscape sounds a note of pessimism which is never silenced and which rings out most loudly in the tragic conclusion.

History in this novel includes natural history, and the contrasting visions of Rhine and Rhône raise questions about the nature of evolution and its implications (see DARWIN-ISM). Although George Eliot had written over a third of the novel by the time she read Charles *Darwin's *On the Origin of Species* in November 1859, *The Mill* alludes throughout to the evolutionary science with which she was thoroughly familiar from her collaboration with Lewes, and to the evolutionary theories that she knew from Auguste *Comte and Herbert *Spencer. Natural history informs both the language of the characters—as when Mr Tulliver talks of his children's characteristics in terms of 'crossing o' breeds' (*MF* 1.2)—and the observations of the narrator. Tom and Maggie, more articulate and accomplished than their parents, are presented as examples of young natures 'that in the onward tendency of human things have risen above the mental level of the generation before them' (*MF* 4.1); but that evolution is neither secure nor benign. In the end it seems that the Tulliver family represents a community unable to adapt to changing circumstances and too riven by inner conflict to survive, so that its younger members, wrecked by the debris of the modern mechanical world, perish as victims of an evolutionary process that favours the fittest rather than the best. In this novel the drama of evolution turns out to be a tragedy.

Commenting on the narrowness of the lives of the Dodsons and Tullivers, the narrator claims that 'you could not live among such people', and that 'I share with you this sense of oppressive narrowness' (*MF* 4.1). It is possible to read this as an authorial confession that *she* could not live among such people and is sharing her experience of their narrowness in writing the fiction. In Maggie's struggles with her confining conditions and her much-loved but oppressive brother, George Eliot is clearly confronting the world of her upbringing which she had rejected and which, after her liaison with Lewes had become known, had rejected her (see LIFE). Her contradictory feelings about that past are visible in the contrast between the specific representation of Maggie's childhood and the narrator's Wordsworthian reflections on childhood in general (see NATURAL WORLD). What is experienced largely as unhappiness at the hands of an overbearing and unforgiving brother is celebrated by the narrator as a time of benignly formative influences: 'We could never have loved the earth so well if we had had no childhood in it' (*MF* 1.5). Nevertheless, it would be reductive to read the novel merely as disguised autobiography, and George Eliot is clearly addressing the general issue of women's position in the world in the story of Maggie (see WOMAN QUESTION). Tom's domineering treatment of her, and even his affection for her, involve an inability to imagine her in anything but a subservient role: 'he was very fond of his sister, and meant always to take care of her, make her his housekeeper, and punish her when she did wrong' (*MF* 1.5). This is simply one

manifestation of a larger system of oppressive patriarchal authority, most crudely expressed in Wakem's outburst to his son: 'We don't ask what a woman does—we ask
whom she belongs to' (*MF* 6.8). Too intelligent and spirited to follow her mother's example of placid housekeeping and denied the education offered to her brother, Maggie
suffers the frustration of energies and abilities that have no adequate field of action. It is
a frustration which, even as a child, she acutely senses in other women when she observes
that 'all women are crosser than men' (*MF* 2.1). When taunted by her brother that she,
too, would be a woman one day, she retorts, 'But I shall be a clever woman.' In her case
cleverness provides no alternative to the repression of energy and ambition that leads to
crossness, but it does make for more subtle forms of sublimation, like her adoption of
the doctrine of *renunciation she finds in Thomas à *Kempis. That she should find comfort in willingly embracing the submission of self conventionally demanded of women
defines the intensity of her predicament. Like the witch she reads of as a child in Defoe
she is caught in a double bind; damned if she conforms to her gender role and damned
if she tries to transcend it, as she does when she asserts her independence by freely associating with Philip Wakem in the Red Deeps.

It is Philip who persuasively criticizes her renunciation as 'a narrow self-delusive
fanaticism which is only a way of escaping pain by starving into dulness all the highest
powers of your nature' (*MF* 5.3); but he himself can only offer intellectual companionship rather than the deeper fulfilment of sexual love. That Stephen Guest should present
to Maggie the possibility of such a love is not as implausible as many critics have maintained if he is seen in the context of her repressed and reduced emotional state, and in
comparison to the other two men in her life, the crippled Philip and the domineering
Tom. Stephen combines the physical presence that the former lacks and the courteous respect for Maggie as an adult and an equal that the latter has never shown her. Ironically,
however, the effect of his attentions is to impose upon her another form of dependence.
In their disastrous outing on the river, in which he acts as a 'stronger presence that
seemed to bear her along without any act of her own will', she finds 'an unspeakable
charm in being told what to do, and having everything decided for her'. In surrendering
to the current of her desire she is also playing the part of a conventionally submissive
woman; and both are out of character, involving a suspension of thought and memory
for the pleasure of the moment: 'thought did not belong to that enchanted haze in which
they were enveloped—it belonged to the past and the future that lay outside the haze'
(*MF* 6.13). The act of renunciation she then performs in leaving Stephen can be seen in
this context not as an escape from pain but as a painful reassertion of her moral character. But whether she is acting out of strength or out of weakness remains a matter of critical dispute. Is her rhetorical question, 'If the past is not to bind us, where can duty lie?'
(*MF* 6.14), the mark of a fully developed moral awareness (see MORAL VALUES), or a
means of rationalizing her capitulation to the oppressive past? In rejecting Stephen is she
heroically preserving the unity of her life and the sense of her own moral identity, or is
she performing an act of perverse self-denial that is tantamount to suicide?

Critics have sought to illuminate this episode by relating it to George Eliot's elopement
with Lewes, finding parallels between the life and the fiction in the combination of moral
heroism and undeserved shame and social ostracism (Bodenheimer 1994: 102). Barbara
Hardy reads it as implying George Eliot's claim that if any real commitment to another
person had been threatened, she would never have embarked upon the relationship with
Lewes (1970: 51). For the fictional character the moral choice leads simply into an impasse

from which she is only rescued by the fortuitous flood and an untimely death. It is this ending that has attracted most criticism and provoked most debate. Henry *James in 1866 saw it as the chief defect of the novel because nothing has prepared the reader for it: 'the story does not move towards it; it casts no shadow before it' (*Atlantic Monthly*, 18: 490). Many influential later critics have agreed with him, including F. R. *Leavis in *The Great Tradition* (1948) and W. J. Harvey in *The Art of George Eliot* (1961). James was clearly wrong in one respect, since the ending is prepared for in a formal sense by various allusions and foreshadowings, but a problem remains at the level of action, as Barbara Hardy has argued in her extended critique of the conclusion. A novel that has stressed the need to live without the opium of fantasy ends with a fantasy of reconciliation and vindication (Hardy 1970: 50). Seen in this light the ending is a dream of wish-fulfilment that uncritically replicates Maggie's childhood habit of 'refashioning her little world into just what she would like it to be' (*MF* 1.6). The final embrace of brother and sister, supposedly recapturing a childhood of loving companionship that has never been seen in the novel, obliterates the reality of unhappiness and discord so powerfully established. The epitaph that concludes the novel, 'In their death they were not divided', simply points up the extent to which in life they were.

However, as recent feminist criticism has proposed, this dreamlike resolution may be read, not as a failure to maintain the realistic texture of the narrative, but as a deliberately provocative break with realism to demonstrate 'the inadequacy both of the social choices available to Maggie and of the novelistic forms available to her creator' (Shuttleworth 1991: 492). Thus in the rescue scene Maggie is shown breaking out of the age-old gender roles that reach back to *Homer—'inside the gates, the women with streaming hair and uplifted hands offering prayers ... outside the men in fierce struggle with things divine and human' (*MF* 5.2). Outside on the flood waters Maggie rows energetically to rescue Tom trapped inside the Mill, reversing their usual positions, overthrowing Victorian notions of separate spheres, and casting off the passivity and dependence that marked her in the earlier episode on the river with Stephen. Provocative, too, are the erotic overtones of the reunion of brother and sister in a final orgasmic embrace, a form of incestuous *Liebestod*. From this perspective the ending can be understood as 'an imaginative reaching beyond analytic and realistic modes to the metaphors of unbounded female desire' (Jacobus, 222). It is an example of women's writing challenging both the conventions of Victorian culture and the conventions of realist fiction.

The Mill remains nevertheless a predominantly realist novel, vividly evoking middle-class provincial life in the 1820s and 1830s and relating the experience of individuals to the wider context of social development. The decline of Mr Tulliver's fortunes and the rise of the trading firm of Guest & Co. mark the transition from a pre-industrial to a mercantile economy implicitly connected to industrialization. This realism, particularly with respect to the Dodson sisters, is often comic and ironic in its portrayal of middle-class manners and prejudices. The prosperous Pullets' obsession with tidiness and security, for instance, is characterized by their barred and chained front door, 'kept always in this fortified condition from fear of tramps who might be supposed to know of the glass-case of stuffed birds in the hall and to contemplate running in and carrying it away on their heads' (*MF* 1.9). George Eliot was at pains to deny that her irony implied contempt and protested against the view of many critics that the Dodsons were mean and uninteresting (*L* iii. 299); but the novel itself is more ambivalent. On the one hand, when the narrator's irony turns against 'good society' with 'its claret and velvet carpets', it is clear that this novel, like *Scenes of Clerical Life* and *Adam Bede*, is making a claim for commonplace lives and 'unfashionable families' (*MF* 4.3) as a proper subject of fiction; but on the other, the Dodsons and their values are an important element in the stifling conditions that oppress Maggie. It is in the figure of Mr Tulliver that the ordinary life most clearly escapes condescending *irony, not so much in the narrator's rather defensive claims that 'the pride and obstinacy of millers and other insignificant people . . . have their tragedy too' (*MF* 3.1), but in the dramatic rendering of that tragic downfall, which shows how a generous and warm-hearted man is ruined by his own impulsive and stubborn behaviour (see TRAGEDY).

The juxtaposition of comic and tragic elements in the same set of characters is one illustration of the 'mysterious complexity of our life' that the novel insists upon in criticizing the 'men of maxims' who judge actions like Maggie's according to rigid general rules rather than 'the special circumstances that mark the individual lot'. Individuals here have the capacity to surprise, as when Mrs Glegg shows unwonted flexibility and Mrs Tulliver uncharacteristic strength of character in taking Maggie's side after her return without Stephen. There is 'no master key that will fit all cases' (*MF* 7.2), and even the narrator (see NARRATION) may seem not 'to know what to make of the issues raised by the story' (Martin, 43). Rich in ambiguity, conflict, and contradiction, this novel offers knowledge that is indeed 'complex, fragmentary, doubt-provoking', and also leaves open the question of whether we can always call it truth. JMR

Ashton (1990).

Auerbach, Nina, 'The Power of Hunger: Demonism and Maggie Tulliver', *Nineteenth-Century Fiction*, 30 (1975).

Beer (1986).

Bodenheimer (1994).

Ermarth, Elizabeth Deeds, 'Maggie Tulliver's Long Suicide', *Studies in English Literature*, 14 (1974).

Hardy, Barbara, 'The Mill on the Floss', in Hardy (1970).

Jacobus, Mary, 'The Question of Language: Men of Maxims and *The Mill on the Floss*', *Critical Inquiry*, 8 (1981–2).

Martin, Graham, '*The Mill on the Floss* and the Unreliable Narrator', in Anne Smith (ed.), *George Eliot: Centenary Essays and an Unpublished Fragment* (1980).

Shuttleworth, Sally (ed.), *The Mill on the Floss* (1991).

the Massacre of St Bartholomew's Day 1572 during the French Wars of Religion. 'The face of the woman is never to be forgotten' (*L* ii. 38), George Eliot told Cara *Bray. With G. H. *Lewes she came to know Millais socially, and they visited his studio when his Academy pictures were on display before the annual exhibition. They were there in April 1877, when Lewes particularly asked that there should be no other visitors, and George Eliot was there again in March 1880.

Millais's late painting *The Girlhood of St Theresa* of 1893 (private collection) shows the saint and her brother setting out on their crusade, and is said to have been inspired by the Prelude to *Middlemarch*. Millais was a founder member of the *Pre-Raphaelite Brotherhood in 1848 and became President of the Royal Academy in 1896 and Baronet in 1885. See also VISUAL ARTS. LO

Milnes, Richard Monckton (1809–85), politician, man of letters, traveller, patron of young writers, and friend of George Eliot and G. H. *Lewes. According to Gordon S. *Haight, he was 'the most conspicuous lion-hunter of his day' (1968: 388). He held extraordinary parties at Upper Brook Street in London which brought together a wide range of artists, writers, and intellectuals from Britain and abroad. On 20 June 1864 he brought George Eliot a copy of his poems. Thereafter he came to The *Priory regularly, and G. H. Lewes and Eliot often dined with him.

Eliot sent Sara *Hennell the autograph of 'our good Richard' in June 1852 (*L* ii. 38). He became a peer in 1863. According to Lewes he spoke of *Romola* with great admiration, generally corresponded with Lewes not Eliot, though she appealed to him for help to get their friend Edward Pigott elected as secretary to the Royal Academy. Once she chastised him for inflicting an importunate visitor on her (*L* vii. 19). He reviewed *Middlemarch* for the *Edinburgh Review* (January 1873): in May 1876 he invited her to meet the King of the Belgians but the completion of *Daniel Deronda* took precedence (Lewes went alone). He wrote her an extraordinary letter on receiving the news of her forthcoming marriage to John Walter *Cross: 'I have condoled with you so sincerely that I can congratulate you, in the deep consciousness of the wonderful weft of pain and pleasure that makes up our emotional existence' (*L* ix. 308–9). This perhaps sums up a man whose *Life, Letters and Literary Remains of John Keats* (1848) ensures that he will be remembered despite the 'weft' of verbal and social excesses which made up his life.   GRH

Milton, John (1608–74), English poet, who is a constant point of reference for George Eliot. Her early letters are speckled with quotations from *Paradise Lost* like Satan's 'Evil be thou my good' (iv. 110), his 'What matter where if I be still the same' (i. 256), and 'The unaccomplished works of Nature's hand | Abortive, monstrous or unkindly mixed' (iii. 455–6). There are references to *Il Penseroso*, and even the occasional adaptation from it (Eliot's 'sober-suited morn' where Milton has 'civil-suited'). Eliot writes to Cara *Bray of her husband Charles as 'your Adam "who with serene front governs" ' (*Paradise Lost*, vii. 509; *L* i. 154). A friend ambitious of undertaking German and French translation is castigated for thinking she could work at it 'from morn to noon, from noon till dewy eve' (*Paradise Lost*, vii. 742–3; *L* i. 214). Eliot writes of Milton's *Ode on the Morning of Christ's Nativity* as 'that beautiful Ode' of which she has just committed a fragment to memory (*L* i. 36), and two years later she quotes *L'Allegro* in a letter to Mrs Pears about the bird 'That comes in spite of sorrow | And at my window bids good morrow' (*L* i. 125). The same poem is echoed in a letter to the Brays in 1846, while in 1852 she alludes to *Lycidas* in writing to Herbert *Spencer 'I mean to live laborious days' (*L* viii. 52). Even in *Recollections of Weimar* in 1854 she can happily (if feebly) parody the last line of *Lycidas* as she and Lewes leave 'To seek new streets and faces new!'. There is a delightful self-mockery to Sara *Hennell in 1855 (*L* ii. 211): 'I have just been reading that Milton suffered from indigestion and flatulence—quite an affecting fact to me'. In August 1855 she writes a review of a book on Milton for the *Leader (repr. in Essays)*. Sensitive about *The Spanish Gypsy* she responds to William MacIlwaine who had written to her with discriminating praise by praising Milton in turn for his subtleties in verse, asserting that he 'is very daring, and often shocks the weaklings

who think that verse is sing-song' (*L* iv. 469). An 1872 letter to her close friend Maria *Congreve refers to 'my demigod Milton' (*L* v. 238), and in the same year she and G. H. *Lewes were reading Samuel *Johnson's *Life of Milton*. Two years earlier they had reread *Paradise Lost*, Eliot observing, 'What novices in wickedness were Milton's devils!' (*L* v. 118). *Comus* is occasionally mentioned, Satan's 'the mind is its own place' is quoted more than once.

Eliot's fiction reflects her saturation in Milton. In 'Amos Barton' there is a mention of *Paradise Lost* (*SC* 1.3), in *Adam Bede* (*AB* 2) there is the 'spotty globe' of *Paradise Lost* (i. 291), while in 'The Lifted Veil' Latimer's prevision is compared to the certainty with which 'Milton saw the earthward flight of the Tempter'. *Felix Holt, the Radical* compares Rufus Lyon and Milton as seen through fashionably mocking eyes (*FH* 6), in *Middlemarch* Casaubon is the supposedly 'affable archangel' (*MM* 3), echoing the epigraph from *Paradise Lost* (vii. 40–1, 50–3). *Daniel Deronda* has mentions of *Areopagitica* (*DD* 37), *Paradise Regained* (*DD* 41), Mirah's anger is compared to that of Ithuriel (*DD* 61), the epigraph to chapter 65 is from *Comus*, while the novel ends expressively and inspirationally with a salute to the demigod by quoting *Samson Agonistes*. *Impressions of Theophrastus Such* appropriately has a salutary note from *Areopagitica* in chapter 15, 'Diseases of Small Authorship'.   GRH

money and debt are prominent issues in George Eliot's writing. Emily *Davies reported in 1869 that 'She spoke very strongly about the wickedness of not paying one's debts. She thinks it worse than drunkenness, not in its consequences, but in the character itself' (*L* viii. 466). Her own punctiliousness in money matters, Haight suggests, was 'bred deep in her nature by generations of Garths and Dodsons and Poysers' (*L*, vol. i, p. xlviii), and certainly the evidence of her *letters and *journals is that the personal economies that were necessary in her early years never yielded to wanton extravagance in her later affluence (see EARNINGS). The responsibilities represented by money were evident in her life as in her work: she used her wealth for the support of a range of Evans and Lewes relatives (see WILL), and enjoyed making appropriate gifts.

The moral dimension of debt is poignantly acknowledged by Godfrey Cass, realizing that he must 'pass for childless' because 'there's debts we can't pay like money debts, by paying extra for the years that have slipped by' (*SM* 20). Godfrey and his brother Dunstan are among a number of young men in George Eliot's fiction in whom the compounding difficulties of getting into debt are depicted. Many of them, like the Casses, are financially embarrassed when they trade on their expectations: other instances are Fred Vincy, Will Ladislaw, and Tertius Lydgate in *Middlemarch*. Some are simply poor and dependent, or with dependants: clergymen like Amos Barton, Camden Farebrother in *Middlemarch*, and Gwendolen Harleth's uncle, Henry Gascoigne, come to mind.

Debt incurred through failure of investments or business arrangements drives plot elements most obviously in *The Mill on the Floss* (where Mr Tulliver's troubles are compounded by the loan to his brother-in-law Moss for which he has been guarantor, though Tom Tulliver, with Bob Jakin's aid, repays the creditors). But such failures occur also in the web of financial interactions in *Middlemarch*, not only in the operations of Bulstrode the banker; and in *Daniel Deronda*, where the loss of Mrs Davilow's fortune precipitates the disastrous marriage of her daughter Gwendolen to Henleigh Grandcourt.

The presentation of women and money is particularly interesting in George Eliot's work. The importance of prudent housekeeping is frequently shown, and Mrs Poyser's dairy is more than a tribute to her cleanliness: her butter and eggs are an integral part of the economy of the Hall Farm, and a tangible contribution to its revenues. In *Felix Holt, the Radical* Esther Lyon renounces her inheritance for love, while in the absence of a competent male, the redoubtable Mrs Transome undertakes major responsibilities in the management of the family estates—a task Dorothea Casaubon, for all her interest in plans, entrusts to Caleb Garth. Women's ability to earn money is limited by the range of occupations open to them (see WOMAN QUESTION), as Maggie Tulliver, Mary Garth, and Gwendolen Harleth variously recognize. See also POVERTY AND WEALTH.   MAH

monuments to George Eliot are comparatively recent apart from that on her grave in Highgate Cemetery, London, and the obelisk which was moved from Arbury to the George Eliot Memorial Garden, Nuneaton, in 1951.

A memorial stone, sculpted by John Skelton, was unveiled in Poets' Corner, Westminster Abbey, in 1980.

A bronze statue, created by John Letts, a Warwickshire sculptor, was unveiled in 1986 in Newdegate Square, Nuneaton. A glass-fibre model from the clay original stands outside the George Eliot Hospital, Nuneaton, and in the Cheverel Wing there stands a bronze bust by John Letts.

Plaques exist in various places.   KA

moral values. George Eliot's moral vision is clear and simple in its basic principles, yet subtle and discriminating in the treatment of individual cases. Hers is a humanist ethic which owes something to the *Christianity she rejected, but it is not simply Christian morality without the sanction of faith, as Friedrich *Nietzsche charged. She was influenced by Baruch *Spinoza's ethics and his emphasis on the importance of tempering self-interest by fellow feeling; and like another humanist who was similarly influenced, Auguste *Comte, she saw the principal moral challenge of human life to lie in the subordination of egoism to altruism. Her insistence on the supreme value of *sympathy for others and the curtailment of personal desire can be seen in her first work of fiction, *Scenes of Clerical Life*. When Janet Dempster tends her dying husband, the narrator comments on how in such situations 'the moral relation of man to man is reduced to its utmost clearness and simplicity': 'As we bend over the sick-bed, all the forces of our nature rush towards the channels of pity, of patience, and of love, and sweep down the miserable choking drift of our quarrels, our debates, our would-be wisdom, and our clamorous selfish desires' (*SC* 3.24). Romola's ministrations to the inhabitants of the plague village are a later instance of this kind of exemplary sympathy and selflessness. However, human life and relations are not often reduced to such clearness and simplicity. The value of self-abnegation has its limits, for Eliot's fiction shows how the ego, too, has its legitimate claims. The moral stature of a figure like Dorothea in *Middlemarch* derives from her passionate, aspiring selfhood, not simply from her capacity for *renunciation. Moreover, moral distinctions are rarely clear-cut: as Eliot declares in her early essay on 'The *Morality of *Wilhelm Meister*', 'the line between the virtuous and vicious, so far from being a necessary safeguard to morality, is itself an immoral fiction' (*Essays*, 147). Her own characters, rather like Goethe's, are examples of mixed and erring humanity, and even the most self-centred may be partly redeemed by 'some noble impulse, some disinterested effort, some beam of good nature' (*Essays*, 146), as when Rosamond Vincy in *Middlemarch* momentarily sets aside her habitual egoism and, in an involuntary impulse of sympathy, tells Dorothea the truth about her relations with Ladislaw. In her effort to prevent her fiction lapsing from the picture to the diagram (*L* iv. 300), Eliot is always attentive to the view expressed by the narrator of *The Mill on the Floss* 'that moral judgements must remain false and hollow, unless they are checked and enlightened by a perpetual reference to the special circumstances that mark the individual lot' (*MF* 7.2). Thus even a morally unattractive character like Bulstrode, who has descended as far as murder, can be brought within the orbit of sympathetic understanding as an object of compassion as well as moral censure (*MM* 74).

The figure of Bulstrode illustrates another aspect of Eliot's moral scheme: the importance of acknowledging the past, with all its errors and obligations, as a necessary condition of the fully developed moral life. 'If the past is not to bind us, where can duty lie?', as Maggie Tulliver asks rhetorically in explaining to Stephen Guest why she will not seek happiness with him at the expense of Lucy's and Philip's (*MF* 6.14). George Eliot's insistence on the value of continuity with others and continuity with one's own past shows her urgently seeking a rational basis for a morality that can no longer rest on religious faith. See also DETERMINISM; NATURAL WORLD; RELIGION.

JMR

Myers (1984).
Hardy (1959).

'Morality of *Wilhelm Meister*, The', an article by George Eliot published in the *Leader* in July 1855 (repr. in *Essays*), ostensibly occasioned by a new translation of *Goethe's novel *Wilhelm Meister's Apprenticeship* by R. Dillon Boylan. It also served to advertise in advance G. H. *Lewes's *Life of Goethe*, which was due to appear later that year. The short essay is the fruit of Eliot's extensive engagement with Goethe's work whilst she was helping Lewes with his biography, and she takes a similar line to his in defending Goethe's novel against the widely held view in Britain that it was an immoral book. Acknowledging that Goethe reveals no moral bias, neither showing hatred of bad actions nor sympathy with good, she maintains that overt moralizing is not an effective way for a novelist to have a moral influence, since it creates an impression of cold contrivance instead of engaging the sympathy of the reader. She is also sarcastically dismissive of supposedly moral denouements that distribute rewards and punishments 'according to those notions of justice on which the novel-writer would have recommended that the world should be governed if he had been consulted at the creation' (*Essays*, 145). She concedes that not everything is a fit subject for art, and that a writer like Honoré de *Balzac often oversteps the limit of what is acceptable, but argues that Goethe's portrayal of irregular relationships, like that between Wilhelm and the actress Marianne, remains within the legitimate limits of art. The terms in which she conducts her defence of Goethe anticipate the direction her own fiction will take and the central importance of *sympathy: 'the novelist may place before us every aspect of human life where there is some trait of love, or endurance, or helplessness to call forth our best sympathies'. Goethe's presentation of 'mixed and

erring' humanity does just this, for in his characters there is always some redeeming quality, 'some noble impulse, some disinterested effort, some beam of good nature' (146). But it is also a question of form, and the critical understanding of the future novelist can be seen in George Eliot's insight into the way that a mode of narration can have a moral effect. What is really moral in Goethe's novel is, for her, his unhurried mode of treatment, without exaggeration or *melodrama: 'he quietly follows the stream of fact and of life; and waits patiently for the moral processes of nature as we all do for her material processes' (146–7). The mark of his moral superiority is thus his large tolerance; and in defending Goethe in these terms she is taking a stand against a narrowly moralistic view of life and of fiction that is commonly found in her own culture. When she concludes 'that the line between the virtuous and the vicious, so far from being a necessary safeguard to morality, is itself an immoral fiction' (147), she is defining a view of human nature that will govern her own practice as a novelist. See also BILDUNGS-ROMAN; MORAL VALUES.

JMR

Morley, John (1838–1923). Morley was a rising man of letters when he reviewed *Felix Holt, the Radical* for *Macmillan's Magazine* in August 1866 (repr. in *CH*); he also reviewed *The Spanish Gypsy* for *Macmillan's*, and possibly others. George Eliot, exercised about the reception and sales of the novel, wrote to John *Blackwood that 'one or two things . . . did satisfy me' in this review (*L* iv. 309). On Morley's being identified as the author, an introduction followed, and he became an occasional guest at The *Priory. G. H. *Lewes and Morley were already acquainted in journalistic circles, maintaining a relationship of mutual respect with no particular liking. The younger man succeeded Lewes as editor of the *Fortnightly Review* in 1867, a position he filled until 1882, taking on the editorship of the *Pall Mall Gazette* also from 1880 to 1883. The inspiration for the 'English Men of Letters' series was his, and he edited the first series, contributing the volume on Burke (1879), who had also been the subject of his first book (1867). Biography was his forte: his most notable work in this genre is his *Life of Gladstone* (1903), for which his second career, as a Radical politician, particularly equipped him. He was elected as Liberal member for Newcastle in 1882, and went on to positions as Chief Secretary for Ireland (1886 and 1892–5), and Secretary of State for India (1905–10), being created Viscount Morley of Blackburn in 1908.

Morley's review of *Felix Holt* welcomed George Eliot's return after the aberration of *Romola* to her characteristic 'studies of English life, so humorous, so picturesque, and so philosophical, which at once raised her into the very first rank among English novelists' (*CH* 252). He saw it as 'essentially a novel of character', with unfortunately contrived plot elements, which demonstrated the delicacy of George Eliot's methods of bringing out her view of life (*CH* 257). Along with its humour and the suggestiveness of her style, he praised its treatment of 'the curse which a man can be to a woman' (*CH* 255, though Morley was to encounter qualifications in George Eliot's support for women's issues such as the suffrage when in 1867 he identified with John Stuart *Mill's amendment to Gladstone's Reform Bill). Just as Morley's review of *Felix Holt* intelligently articulated the basis of George Eliot's reputation in the middle 1860s, so his review of John Walter *Cross's *Life* skilfully captured the shift that had occurred by 1885, in his observations about the attenuation of her work due to 'her reserved fashion of daily life', and her existing (largely due to Lewes's ministrations) in a 'moral and intellectual hothouse' (*Critical Miscellanies*, 3 vols. (1886), iii. 106, 108). MAH

mottoes. See EPIGRAPHS.

Mozart, Wolfgang Amadeus (1756–91). In January 1851, when George Eliot first took up residence at John *Chapman's establishment in the Strand, she immediately hired a piano for herself. The following day Chapman sat in her room while she played one of Mozart's masses. However, although by 1859 she had collected 'about eighteen sonatas and symphonies of Beethoven' (*L* iii. 177), at least until July of that year she had none of Mozart's symphonies, and invited the musical Charles Lee Lewes (see LEWES FAMILY), with whom she often played duets, to be guided in his choice of them by his own tastes (*L* iii. 125).

Perhaps in response to Charles's enthusiasm, Mozart became an important part of George Eliot's repertoire. In the winter of 1866, she and Frederick *Lehmann played together every piano and violin sonata of Mozart and *Beethoven (*L* viii. 385 n.), and among her opera collection were Mozart's *Le nozze di Figaro* (1786), *Don Giovanni* (1787), and *Die Zauberflöte* (1791).

She and G. H. *Lewes clung delightedly together when, in Salzburg in 1858, they heard 'the striking up of the chimes, playing a tune of Mozart's' (*Journals*, 320–1), and in Paris in 1865 were very disappointed to see Verdi's *Rigoletto* instead of the expected *Die Zauberflöte* (*Journals*, 390).

Mozart is one of the composers Lewes said he and George Eliot were 'made to respond to' (*L* v. 85). See also MUSIC. BG

'Mr Gilfil's Love-Story'. See SCENES OF CLERICAL LIFE.

Mudie's Library, leading circulating library owned by Charles Mudie. Mudie's was the 'leviathan' of Victorian lending libraries, charging readers only a guinea a year for borrowing privileges, well under the rates of other circulating libraries. Mudie's advertised a 'Select' list, which guaranteed morally sound literature already approved by Mr Mudie himself. It was important, for the sake of promotion if nothing else, to appear on Mudie's Select list, and George Eliot found it odd that *Scenes of Clerical Life* was left off. Mudie's exercised tremendous power in the publishing industry because of the huge volume of his purchases, often in the thousands for the works of popular novelists like George Eliot, which he bought at discount. Mudie's eventually took 3,000 copies of *The Mill on the Floss*, for example. There were many reservations about the towering presence of Mudie's in the literary market place, and George Eliot worried that Mudie would 'strangle' good fiction because of his insistence on particular kinds of middle-class literature. Authors and publishers often tried to devise innovative publishing forms, largely through serialized part-issue, to get round the libraries, as George Eliot and John *Blackwood did with *Middlemarch* (see SERIALIZATION). The buying power of the circulating libraries kept the three-volume-novel system alive until the 1890s, when new forms of literature toppled the triple-decker once and for all. See also READERSHIP; RECEPTION. MWT

Griest, Guinivere, *Mudie's Circulating Library and the Victorian Novel* (1970).

Müller, Friedrich Max (1823–1900), German-born orientalist, mythographer, and language scholar, who settled in Oxford in 1849 and held various positions in the University, culminating in his appointment to a chair of comparative philology in 1868. George Eliot knew his work well, writing to Sara *Hennell on 14 January 1862 of 'Max Müller's great and delightful book', *Lectures on the Science of Language* (1861), which 'tempts me away from other things' including Anthony *Trollope's *Orley Farm*, then appearing serially (*L* iv. 8). She was equally stimulated by the second series of *Lectures* (1864), 'with which I was consoling myself under a sore throat' (*L* iv. 160). Eliot and G. H. *Lewes continued to read Müller's work as it came out, and met him and his wife in *Oxford in June 1873. On her 61st birthday, 22 November 1880, George Eliot recorded progress in the education of John Walter *Cross: 'Having finished Spencer's Sociology we began Max Müller's Lectures on the Science of Language' (*Journals*, 213).

Müller's fascination for George Eliot derived from his search for a common origin of *language, in which his work has significant analogies both with Charles *Darwin's quest for the origin of species, and with the endeavours of the various seekers after a 'Key to all Mythologies' in *Middlemarch*, where Müller's conviction of the centrality of solar mythology is reflected in the characterization of Will Ladislaw and in the scientific imagery of the novel. He further held that metaphor and myth corrupt language by modifying the original meanings of words. See also DARWINISM; SCIENCE.

MAH

Beer (1983).

Munich, the Bavarian capital, where George Eliot and G. H. *Lewes spent three months in 1858 when she was writing *Adam Bede*. They reached Munich on 7 April and took rooms at 15 Luitpoldstrasse. Although she complained about the capricious climate and about the impossibility of dining at any other hour than one o'clock, and was often ill with colds and headaches, Munich proved to be a hospitable place. They met academics and intellectuals, the writers Heyse, Geibel, and Bodenstedt, and scientists, including the famous chemist von Liebig and the anatomist von Seebold, with both of whom they enjoyed friendly relations. The only drawback to associating with the professors with whom the city was swarming, she told Sara *Hennell, was that she was obliged to sit on the sofa with her hostess while the men on the other side of the table discussed all the subjects she was interested in (*L* ii. 454). She and Lewes also went to the theatre and attended concerts, at one of which she heard Prince Radziwill's music to *Goethe's *Faust*, a work in which Gretchen's fate has parallels with that of Hetty Sorrel in the novel she was writing. The art galleries, particularly the Alte Pinakothek with its Dürers and Flemish paintings, were another source of pleasure (see VISUAL ARTS), and it was in Munich that she wrote the celebrated passage on *realism in *Adam Bede*, praising the truthfulness of Dutch paintings of ordinary life (*AB* 17). What meant more to her even than the art was the sight of the distant snow-covered Alps from the Theresienwiese (*Journals*, 311). Nevertheless, the languor and depression produced by the Munich air and way of life were such that, despite the kindness of the friends they had made there and the city's cultural attractions, she was glad to leave on 7 July when they set off for *Dresden (*Journals*, 319). This was her only extended stay in Munich, although she visited it briefly on her later travels, the last occasion being with her husband John Walter *Cross in the last year of her life. It does not figure in her fiction. See also GERMANY; TRAVELS.

JMR

music. Six years after George Eliot's death, the violinist and musicologist Frederick Niecks wrote in the *Monthly Musical Record* (1 October 1886),

'Unless my memory plays me false—which, I think, it does not—I may say of George Eliot that she very rarely alludes in her works to music, and still more rarely discusses matters musical'. Although Niecks goes on to acknowledge that, whenever George Eliot does discuss music, she 'proves that she had a right to speak on the subject' (219), his memory does play him false. Throughout her writings—fiction, non-fiction, personal—George Eliot makes extensive use of musical allusion and musical analogy, for music was essential to her life and to her thinking. For her, 'music that stirs all one's devout emotions blends everything into harmony—makes one feel part of one whole, which one loves all alike, losing the sense of a separate self' (*Journals*, 308). This sense of music-engendered unity is conveyed to her novels and poems as an organizing principle.

It has been claimed that Ludwig *Feuerbach's conception of music is central in understanding its significance in George Eliot (Cirillo, 219). But six years before the publication in 1854 of her translation of Feuerbach's *Das Wesen des Christenthums* (1841), she had already declared that 'painting and sculpture are but an idealizing of our actual existence. Music arches over this existence with another and a diviner' (*L* i. 247). Mary Ann Evans was 28 when she made those statements, though her attitude to music had changed radically from that of her piously evangelical, earlier self. At 19, having attended a performance of an oratorio, the future author of *Daniel Deronda* had claimed to have 'no soul for music', telling her former teacher, Maria *Lewis, that she deemed 'it little less than blasphemy for such words as "Now then we are ambassadors for Christ" to be taken on the lips of such a man as [John] Braham [1774–1856] (a Jew too!). . . . it would not cost me any regrets if the only music heard in our land were that of strict worship' (*L* i. 13). George Eliot's specific reference is to the duettino from *Mendelssohn's *St Paul* (1836), which takes its text from 2 Corinthians 5: 20. Two years later, however, she was able to tell the same correspondent that she had heard *Messiah* at Birmingham, and on the following day 'some beautiful selections from other oratorios of Handel and Haydn' (*L* i. 68).

Once her liberating friendship with Charles and Cara *Bray was established, her delight in music extended to glees and duets. By the time she was 27 she had succumbed to Italian opera, finding no difficulty in reconciling the 'perfect treat' (*L* i. 233) of *Bellini's *I puritani* (1835) with the excitement induced the previous day by the Sacred Harmonic Society's rendition—conducted by the composer—of Mendelssohn's 'new' oratorio, *Elijah* (1846): 'It is a glorious production and altogether I look upon it as a kind of sacramental purification of Exeter Hall, and a proclamation of indulgence for all that is to be perpetrated there during this month of May' (*L* i. 234).

With the widening of her social and intellectual milieu, Mary Ann's musical taste had developed as rapidly as her piety had receded. With this development, her allusions to music shed their earlier sententiousness and became aurally keener and more telling. 'I find it teazes and disturbs me to read any other person's translation', she wrote when applying herself to her own translation of D. F. *Strauss's *Das Leben Jesu, kritisch bearbeitet* (1835–6; see TRANSLATIONS). 'It is like hearing another piano going just a note before you in the same tune you are playing' (*L* i. 194). The specificity of this reveals her as the musician she unequivocally was, for to make—or to participate in the making of—music, had become as crucial to her as it was to listen to the performances of others.

Her musical enthusiasm and talent as a pianist revealed themselves early. A younger schoolfellow at the Misses Franklin's school in *Coventry in later life told her own children how Miss Evans's 'music master, a much-tried man, suffering from the irritability incident to his profession, reckoned on his hour with her as a refreshment to his wearied nerves, and soon had to confess that he had no more to teach her'. As the most proficient musician in the school, she would sometimes be required to play to visitors, but was known afterwards often 'to rush to her room and throw herself on the floor in an agony of tears' (Cross, i. 21). At Rosehill, the Brays' home, however, she was to prove to be a willing accompanist, and, as she sought to shape her life after her father's death in 1849, to have a piano at her disposal became a priority. In Switzerland, where she chose to remain alone after accompanying the Brays on a European tour, the bereaved Mary Ann initially felt isolated and dull. But after she had moved from Plongeon on Lake Geneva to the home—in *Geneva itself—of the hospitable *D'Albert Durades, her spirits lifted. Finding herself among people of 'breadth of culture' (*L* i. 314), she was comfortable and pampered—and musically fulfilled. There were two pianos, one of which she had hired for her own use. M. D'Albert played and sang, and there were regular gatherings to perform masses or operatic music, with the future George Eliot characteristically reporting after one such occasion her delighted response to the 'splendid bass voice' of one guest, and the 'fine tenor voice' (*L* i. 317) of another.

Having decided to earn her bread by her pen, Marian (as she was about to become) returned to England and took lodgings at the Strand, London establishment of the publisher-bookseller John

*Chapman, who divided his attentions between his wife and his children's governess, Elisabeth Tilley. Music had had no part in the domestic scheme of things until the arrival of Miss Evans, who quickly set about hiring a piano for her own room. The day after its delivery, and with Chapman her solitary audience, 'she played one of Mosart's [*sic*] Masses with much expression' (as he recorded in his diary for 12 January 1851; Haight, 1969: 131). Such intimate recitals were not to be countenanced, and so within days another piano was purchased for the Strand drawing room, where Miss Evans was able to entertain the whole family with 'a profusion of excellent music' (Haight 1969: 138).

As Mrs Lewes she continued in her domestic and social life to fulfil the role of pianist with enthusiasm. The acquisition on 3 October 1861 of a new grand piano encouraged her 'to play more than I have done for years before' (*L* iii. 460). Musical evenings were a household regularity. In the winter of 1866, for example—and wishing she could herself play the violin, because it 'gives that *keen edge* of tone which the piano wants' (*L* iii. 126)—she and the gifted amateur violinist Frederick *Lehmann performed 'every piano and violin sonata, of Mozart and Beethoven'. Lehmann—who considered George Eliot to be 'a very fair pianist, not gifted, but enthusiastic, and extremely painstaking'—reported that G. H. *Lewes, their only audience, would 'groan with delight whenever we were rather successful in playing some beautiful passage' (R. C. Lehmann, *Memories of Half a Century* (1908), 132). The most poignant record—Cross's—of her musical role concerns the last summer of Lewes's life, when she accompanied his rendition—given between bouts of cramping pain—of most of Count Almaviva's part in *Rossini's *Barber of Seville*. The ailing Lewes sang 'with great *brio*, though without much voice' (Cross, iii. 295).

With perhaps a predilection for the late Classical and Romantic composers, George Eliot's taste in music became increasingly eclectic rather than progressive, though she continued throughout her career assiduously to extend her knowledge of it. With Chapman she had often attended the monthly concerts given by the singing teacher and music historian John Pyke Hullah (1812–84) in St Martin's Hall in London, which had been built for his work, while her already acknowledged pleasure in opera was intensively indulged after she had been introduced to Herbert *Spencer at one of Chapman's soirées. As sub-editor of *The Economist*, Spencer had free admission to Covent Garden opera house, and between the beginning of April and the end of May 1852 had escorted Marian to performances there of *Donizetti's *Les*

Martyrs (1839; a revised version of his banned *Poli-uto*, 1838), *Meyerbeer's *Les Huguenots* (1836), Halévy's *La Juive* (1835), Bellini's *Norma* (1831), and Rossini's *William Tell* (1829). This last opera George Eliot was to see several times more, but with Lewes. It was during a performance of it at *Munich on 30 May 1858 that the fight in the woods between Adam and Arthur (*AB* 28) came to her 'as a *necessity*' after Lewes had 'expressed his fear that Adam's part was too passive throughout the drama' (*L* ii. 504).

George Eliot was a great admirer of *Liszt (especially as a pianist), whom she met in *Weimar in 1854. But she was never able to respond with full enthusiasm to *Wagner, despite Liszt's championship of him, frankly confessing her inability to enjoy his music as much as she enjoyed *Mozart, *Beethoven, or Mendelssohn. However, it is not always acknowledged that she was less inclined to be merely dismissive of his music than many of her contemporaries—including Lewes, though his expressed views, such as that Wagner's music 'remains to us a language we do not understand' (*L* v. 317), do appear to subsume hers, and are usually taken to do so. That statement of Lewes's was made on 10 October 1872; but in an essay George Eliot had contributed seventeen years earlier to *Fraser's Magazine* in July 1855, *'Liszt, Wagner, and Weimar', she had made an impressive attempt to diagnose the problems presented not only by the composer, but by the expectations or preconceptions of the British audience: as Thomas Pinney has pointed out, 'George Eliot's article is certainly one of the earliest friendly comments on Wagner in the English press' (*Essays*, 96). Although she drew for historical information on a long article by Liszt which had appeared in the *Neue Zeitschrift für Musik* (16 June 1854)—and which she had herself translated and compressed for Lewes to print in the *Leader* as one of his 'Vivian' letters—the views proffered in her *Fraser's* article do not masquerade as those of a music critic, but as those of someone merely 'with an ear and a mind susceptible to the direct and indirect influences of music'. Such acknowledgements, however, serve to underscore her counterbalanced difficulty in understanding 'how any one who finds deficiencies in the opera as it has existed hitherto, can give fair attention to Wagner's theory, and his exemplification of it in his operas, without admitting that he has pointed out the direction in which the lyric drama must develop itself, if it is to be developed at all' (*Essays*, 100). For Wagner, the 'true musical drama' must be 'an organic whole', while 'those who sing his operas must be content with the degree of prominence which falls to them in strict consonance with true dramatic development and ordonnance'

(*Essays*, 102). George Eliot's objection is to what she perceives as the increasing 'exclusion of melody to the degree at which he has arrived in *Lohengrin* [1850]'. She and Lewes had attended a performance of this opera in Weimar on 22 October 1854, and—while she acknowledges in 'Recollections of Weimar' that she, too, was weary by the end of the second act—it was Lewes who did not have the patience to sit it through (*Journals*, 233). To them both, it must be said, it had 'seemed something like the whistling of the wind through the keyholes of a cathedral, which has a dreamy charm for a little while, but by and bye you long for the sound even of a street organ to rush in and break the monotony' (*Essays*, 102). She speaks only for herself, however, when registering delight with *Der Fliegende Holländer* (1843), declaring that the poem and the music were alike charming, while *Tannhäuser* (1845) she found thrilling, apart from the third act (*Journals*, 26). Both operas left in her a real desire to hear them again. *Lohengrin*, on the other hand, not only abandons melody, by which, she asserts, emotions are swayed, but 'fails in one great requisite of art, based on an unchangeable element in human nature—the need for contrast' (*Journals*, 233).

Soon after hearing *Lohengrin*, contrast—and musical gratification—were providentially provided for the Leweses when they came across a group of musicians exquisitely performing a Beethoven quartet: 'it was like returning to the pregnant speech of men after a sojourn among glums and gowries' (*Essays*, 103). The idea of music as 'pregnant speech' is crucial to an understanding of its significance to George Eliot. A consciously susceptible listener, what she had come to understand was that musical receptivity is rooted in the sounds that are associated with the growth of awareness, and with things loved. Even when her attitude to the art of music was at its loftiest, she made instinctive references to the sounds and rhythms of nature and everyday life. 'I hear the swirl of the scythe as I watch the delicate grasses trembling under the eager and restless alighting of the humming insects' (*L* i. 86), the 21-year-old Mary Ann wrote. In less poetically elevated form, this fancy is transmitted both to chapter 2 of *Adam Bede*, when 'the sound of the scythe being whetted makes us cast more lingering looks at the flower-sprinkled tresses of the meadows', and to chapter 16, when the purposeful swirling sound of the scythe enhances Arthur Donnithorne's own satisfied sense of purpose as he rides along.

References to such influences permeate George Eliot's writings, in which the capacity for human sympathy is often measured by degrees of sensitivity to qualities of voice and natural sound, to domestic harmonies, and to music of many kinds. A

16.th March/79 —
St. James Hall

George Eliot attending a concert, drawn by Princess Louise on her programme, 1877.

telling example appears in one of her review essays for the *Westminster*, where she develops an analogy from a much-quoted line in *Wordsworth's 'Tintern Abbey' (1798) in order to define a particular kind of achievement. Of Ashford Owen's now virtually forgotten novel *A Lost Love* (1855), she writes: 'The story is a melancholy one, but without any exaggerated sorrows; the tragic notes in it belong to that "still, sad music of humanity", which seems to make hardly a perceptible element in the great world symphony. But every tender and watchful nature has an ear for such notes' (*Selected Essays*, ed. Byatt and Warren, 330).

Throughout her fiction and poetry, George Eliot uses the faculty—or lack of it—of that kind of musical responsiveness to define the capacity for human responsiveness. In 'Mr Gilfil's Love-Story' in *Scenes of Clerical Life*, for example, the clue to Caterina Sarti's redeemableness lies less with her own exquisite, heart-rending singing than with her response to the deep bass note of a harpsichord. It is this sound that reawakens her from her guilt-induced torpor after Anthony Wybrow's death, and makes it possible for her to make Mr Gilfil supremely happy for a little while: 'The soul that was born anew to music was born anew to love'. Adam Bede listens for Dinah's mellow, modulated tones 'as for a recurrent music' (*AB* 50) before fully realizing that he loves her, while the 'intense thrill' with which Dinah is shaken a few pages later when she hears his powerful deep voice indicates that reconciliation between her faith and her passion is both imminent and appropriate. When Silas Marner sits beside his recovered gold (which he thinks has been restored for Eppie's sake), his features are illuminated by a sense of wonder: it is 'as if a new fineness of ear for all spiritual voices had sent wonder-working vibrations through the heavy mortal frame—as if "beauty born of murmuring sound" had passed into the face of the listener' (*SM* 19; the narrator's quotation is from Wordsworth's 'Three years she grew'). In *Middlemarch*, Dorothea—who sobs when she hears the great organ at Freiberg, but whose premarital contempt for domestic 'small tinkling' recalls the superior intolerance of the young Mary Ann Evans—herself possesses a voice that reveals her innate musicality, her innate passion, and her largeness of spirit. To Will Ladislaw it is 'like the voice of a soul that had once lived in an Aeolian harp' (*MM* 9); to Lydgate it is the 'voice of deep-souled womanhood' (*MM* 58); while to Caleb Garth it is simply 'like music' (*MM* 56): it reminds him of a recitative from one of George Eliot's favourite oratorios, *Handel's Messiah*. Its qualities are evidence of Dorothea's kinship to her author, whose own tones—variously described as 'soft', 'singularly musical', 'harmonious', and even

(by Cross) 'organ-like'—impressed many who met her (see VOICE OF GEORGE ELIOT).

Acknowledging that she 'owed so many thoughts and inspirations of feeling' (*L* iii. 71) to the stimulus of music, with Lewes George Eliot regularly attended recitals of the kind she associated with 'pregnant speech' (essentially quartets, quintets, sonatas, and song). They often went to the Popular Concerts at St James's Hall, hearing from their cheap (shilling) seats some of the favourite artists of the day. These included the violinist Joseph *Joachim (who became a friend), the cellist Alfredo Carlo *Piatti, the pianists Clara *Schumann and Arabella Goddard, and the tenor John Sims Reeves. Despite complaining about the gas and bad air, the Leweses continued to attend public concerts right through the 1860s and 1870s, though they seemed increasingly to prefer private music parties, where Lewes in particular could enjoy the society of other distinguished guests: a characteristic late 1870s entry in his diary reads, 'We went to a music party at [Lord] Leighton's: Joachim, Piatti, Hallé, ... Mad[ame] Joachim sang. Talked to the Chief Justice, the Percy Wyndhams, ... Millais, Mrs [soon to be Lady] Ponsonby etc.' (*L* vii. 21).

Undoubtedly, though, they derived one of their chief shared pleasures from their own musical gatherings for family and friends such as George Redford, who had a fine baritone and played the cello, and Edward F. S. Pigott, who (according to George Eliot) possessed a 'delicious tenor' voice. At The *Priory house-warming party on 24 November 1863 (which also celebrated Charles Lee Lewes's 21st birthday), Leopold Jansa played the violin. Anxious to develop her skills as an accompanist, George Eliot decided to take lessons from him. Almost inevitably, the works she chose to study were Beethoven's sonatas for piano and violin, for Beethoven was certainly one of the composers she most profoundly appreciated, and most frequently referred to. By 1859 she had already amassed a collection of 'about eighteen' of his sonatas and symphonies, and—with Herbert Spencer and George Redford as the guests—the acquisition in October 1861 of her new piano was celebrated with a Beethoven night. She loved *Schubert too, delighting especially in his 'difficult' songs. In the manuscript of *Daniel Deronda* (*DD* 32), what Deronda first hears Mirah Cohen (inappropriately) sing—'filling out its long notes' —is 'Adieu', once thought to be by Schubert; but, after consulting the musically compatible Charles, George Eliot substituted Beethoven's 'Per pietà non dirmi addio' ('Ah, perfido!'). She described this as an early love of hers: 'I picked it out with delight in Knight's collection when I had no one else's taste as a finger-post' (*L* vi. 184). Sixteen years earlier, she had told Charles that she particularly wished him to learn 'Adelaide', 'that exquisite song of Beethoven's' (*L* iii. 178); 'that ne plus ultra of passionate song' (*L* iii. 365).

From her two great opera singers—the dedicated, marriage-sacrificing heroine of her poetic drama 'Armgart', and the egoistic Princess Halm-Eberstein in *Deronda*—to the untalented but enthusiastic amateur flautist Fred Vincy in *Middlemarch*, George Eliot's fictive societies include many musicians. Whether professional or amateur, singer or instrumentalist, the sympathetic capability of each performer is measured according to sensibility or disposition, not proficiency. Rosamond Vincy, for example, is a startlingly impressive pianist. Her performance takes possession of Lydgate the first time he hears her; but while he is persuaded that her apparently 'large rendering of noble music' (*MM* 16) indicates an exceptional nature, the reader is made aware that it is merely imitative. Conversely, *Deronda*'s Catherine Arrowpoint, whose mastery of the instrument is equal to Rosamond's, is a true artist. According to George Eliot's arch-musician, Herr Klesmer, she has 'a soul with more ears to it than you will often get in a musician', and is thus a worthy bride for him. Gwendolen Harleth's complacency concerning her own potential as a singer is extinguished by Klesmer, but she reveals both her innate musicality, and the magnanimity that is one of her saving graces, when she openly acknowledges Mirah's superior artistry.

George Eliot took extraordinary care with the selection of music for *Deronda*, and its application. Every aspect of how and by whom it is performed, and how it is responded to, is supremely important. Its most significant function is perhaps to indicate the kinship (and thus the possibility of future reconciliation) between Hebrew and Christian—between all religious promptings—when the effect on Deronda of the chanted liturgy in the Rabbinical Synagogue in Frankfurt (*DD* 32) is elaborately associated with the effect of the more accessible compositions (for many of her contemporary readers) of Allegri and *Palestrina. Nowhere in George Eliot's works is auditory sympathy—between characters, and between reader and character—more suggestive of human sympathy.

George Eliot made copious music-related preparations for this novel, taking extensive notes or paraphrases—mainly from the sections on music before 1600—from Hullah's *History of Modern Music: A Course of Lectures* (1862), and copying long passages from the Belgian music historian F. J. Fétis's essay on Palestrina in his *Biographie universelle des musiciens et bibliographie générale de la musique* (1835–44). It is *The Mill on the Floss*,

however, that offers George Eliot's most directly personal revelation of her own musicality. In this novel, the influence of sound—rhythmic, sensuous, or liquid—is paramount, while what is sung—from, for example, Handel's *Acis and Galatea*, *Haydn's *Creation*, Bellini's *La Sonnambula*, or *Auber's *La Muette de Portici*—comments textually as well as musically on plot, situation, and internal drama. Above all her protagonists, it is with Maggie Tulliver that George Eliot most fully and directly shares her responsiveness to all kinds of music, whether searching, passionate, or exuberant. See also PIANO; VIOLIN; VOCATION.

BG

Eliot, George, 'Ashford Owen's A Lost Love and C. W. S. Brooks's Aspen Court', in *George Eliot: Selected Essays, Poems and Other Writings*, ed. A. S. Byatt and Nicholas Warren (1990).

'The Romantic School of Music: Liszt on Meyerbeer–Wagner', trans. George Eliot, *Leader*, 28 October 1854.

Cirillo, Albert R., 'Salvation *in Daniel Deronda*: The Fortunate Overthrow of Gwendolen Harleth', *Literary Monographs*, 1 (1967).

Gray (1989).

Haight (1969).

New Grove Dictionary of Music and Musicians (1980).

Scholes, Percy A., *The Oxford Companion to Music*, 10th edn., ed. John Owen Ward (1970).

Myers, F. W. H. (1843–1901), school inspector and essayist, introduced to George Eliot and G. H. *Lewes at The *Priory in February 1872 by Henry *Sidgwick, a fellow lecturer at Trinity College, *Cambridge (*L* v. 409). Myers became a regular visitor often dining at The Priory. Eliot told John Walter *Cross they often spoke of Myers with 'regard and admiration' (*L* vi. 6). In December 1872 Myers wrote to Eliot in praise of *Middlemarch* saying 'you seem now to be the only person who can make life appear potentially noble and interesting' (Haight 1968: 451). At his invitation Eliot and Lewes paid their first visit to Cambridge to see the boat races from 19 to 21 May 1873 (*L* ix. 90) but as Eliot declared, 'the real pleasure of the visit consisted in talking with a hopeful group of Trinity young men' (*L* v. 412).

This visit is celebrated by Myers in his reminiscences of Eliot published in November 1881. The two stroll together in a rapidly darkening garden where she, 'taking as her text the three words which have been used so often as the inspiring trumpet-calls of men,—the words *God, Immortality, Duty,*—pronounced, with terrible earnestness, how inconceivable was the *first*, how unbelievable the *second*, and yet how peremptory and absolute the *third*'. They part 'beneath the last twilight of starless skies', the devastated young man left to gaze 'on vacant seats and empty halls ... and heaven left lonely of a God' (Myers, 62). Gordon S. *Haight suggests this account is 'over-dramatized' (1968: 465) while Carroll reads it as a distillation constructing Eliot as 'the stern and sombre sage, deprived of Christian hope, teaching her substitute religion' (*CH* 36). See also ATHEISM; CHRISTIANITY; RELIGION OF HUMANITY; REPUTATION, CRITICAL.   JJ

Myers, F. W. H., 'George Eliot', *Century Magazine*, 23 (1881).

myth. Comical as his enterprise seems, Casaubon's 'Key to all Mythologies' holds the key to George Eliot's own understanding and use of myths. Although she never defined the term, it seems clear she thinks of a myth as a religious narrative whose meaning has been detached from its creed. As such it is the very embodiment of those universal ideas that, although they have not lost their eternal human significance, can no longer be conceived in their old theological forms. The fact that *Higher Criticism of the Bible, to which Eliot had herself made a significant contribution through her translations of D. F. *Strauss and Ludwig *Feuerbach, had subsumed Christianity into the category of myth rendered not only ancient religions but modern ones capable of being incorporated into what she describes in *Middlemarch* as one boundless 'harvest of truth' (*MM* 3). The key, thus, for Eliot to mythology was to recognize that myths were products not of divine inspiration but of the human imagination. Casaubon, whose work in other respects foreshadows Frazer's *The Golden Bough*, fails because, pursuing his research in the archives of the Vatican (*MM* 10), he thinks of myths theologically. It remains for Ladislaw to grasp the mythic truth of religion. An embodiment of Dionysus and so a mythic figure himself, Ladislaw knows that he must keep 'his memorials in his head' (*MM* 54).

While figures like the Indian 'Bouddha' (*DD* 37) and the (probably) Phrygian 'Cabeiri' (*MM* 20) appear occasionally in her work, most of the myths in Eliot's fiction are Roman, Greek, and Judaeo-Christian. Sometimes, in a comparative spirit, these are layered to remind us of the structural parallels. Nearly every event in *Romola* occurs on a date that is significant in important analogous ways on both the Christian and pagan calendars. In *Silas Marner* myths are blended: Silas himself represents a Lar and his stone cottage reproduces the national Roman shrine of Vesta, but Eppie, a Christ child, recreates a Garden of Eden beside his house.

Not infrequently, however, different myths serve different purposes. In many cases, classical myths are distinguishing marks of secularism. The Revd Irwine and his family, even to his dog named Juno, are, ironically but not pejoratively, associated with the Roman pantheon (*AB* 5) and Gwendolen in *Daniel Deronda* is identified with Diana. In others, they epitomize philosophical, psychological, or historical universals. Tito Melema's Benthamite hedonism—the 'end' of life is 'to extract the utmost sum of pleasure' he holds (*RO* 11)—is shown to be but a modern instance of an eternal principle of which Bacchus, whom he embodies, is taken, as the god of joy, to stand as the eternal type. Moral truths are commonly carried in Judaeo-Christian mythology. In the same novel, Girolamo *Savonarola, articulating Christian tenets which Eliot reads as mythic truths, offers what in effect becomes, and is so practised by Romola, a mythological religion.

Giambattista *Vico and Herder, whose work she knew well, had seen in myths historical evidence for the life and character of the peoples who had conceived them and Eliot, in her historical narratives, often uses them in this way. The invocation in *Romola* of Christian, Roman, and Greek mythologies embeds, in one historical moment which acts as their point of intersection, the past of the three most important cultures that came to shape the modern world. In *Daniel Deronda*, *Judaism, translated into a mythology—by rejecting 'superstition', Mordecai strips it of its creed (*DD* 42)—becomes the novel's means of exploring the life and character of the Jews.

It is always implicit in Eliot, and occasionally explicit, that, as human fabrications, myths have their natural home in art rather than in Holy Scripture (see VISUAL ARTS), and the mythic paradigms in which she often anchors her tales, many times in ways that anticipate the same techniques in D. H. *Lawrence and James Joyce, constitute the most important symbolic element of her art (see SYMBOLISM).

Eliot's use of mythology is not without its humorous edge, for she is acutely sensitive to the occasionally ironic disparity between the ideal or universal significance of her mythological models and the factual realities of her characters and actions. Tom, thus, in *The Mill on the Floss*, injures his foot and so would seem to become the Philoctetes to whom Philip Wakem compares him (*MF* 2.6). Empiricist, materialist, and even Mammonist that he is, however, Tom has obviously the wound but not his archetype's magic bow. See also BIBLE; CLASSICAL LITERATURE; RELIGION.   FB

Bonaparte (1979).

Swann, Brian, '*Silas Marner* and the New Mythus', *Criticism*, 18 (1976).

Wiesenfarth (1977).

names in George Eliot's fiction are important, usually in symbolic ways that fasten pivotal
points in her themes. Hingeing sometimes on
plays of sound (thoroughly secular, Godfrey Cass
in *Silas Marner* is 'free of God'), sometimes on a
play of meanings (in Raveloe, Marner's religion
ravels in both senses of the word, unwinding as a
literal creed but winding again as it is translated
into a humanistic religion), generally Eliot's
names are grounded in popular or traditional images, etymologies, or allusions. Thus, the common
association of gypsies with unbridled passion suggests that, sober as he seems, Adam Bede, with a
dog named Gyp, hides a wild, rebellious heart. A
popular *metaphor, the river of time, provides the
name of the Brookes in *Middlemarch* and illustrates the complex uses to which Eliot can put her
names, from the satiric characterization of Mr
Brooke as 'leaky-minded' (*MM* 63) to Dorothea's
role in the novel, developed by further water references, as a brook seeking a channel through which
to flow into the stream of *progress. The titular
name of the town in this novel invokes an image
habitually used in condition-of-England fiction,
of civilization on the march, and implies that England stands, at the moment of the Reform Bill (see
REFORM ACTS), the heart of its historical plot, still
in the middle of its march.

Names that have roots in *myth or *religion
usually carry universal, historical, or transcendent
meaning and biblical names customarily bring
biblical chronicles into the narratives (see BIBLE).
Romola, from the founder of *Rome, is rendered
an image of Western *history by embodying
the city Eliot held to be the 'visible' incarnation
of the 'hemisphere' (*MM* 20); Adam Bede and
Arthur Donnithorne, the latter alluding in his surname to the thorn that is Adam's sin, both re-
enact the biblical fall; and speaking spiritual truths
to a materialistic age, Daniel, like his biblical
namesake, deciphers the handwriting on the wall
(*DD*).

Frequently Eliot plays with names and the
paradigms they invoke. The title figure in 'Brother
Jacob' is neither clever nor resourceful. Nevertheless, he outwits his brother, not to establish the
tribes of Israel but to restore a moral right. Works
of literature too are commonly incorporated into
the narratives through the agency of names. Tertius Lydgate's name in *Middlemarch*, by remind-
ing us that in the third—the *tertius*—book of his
Fall of Princes the poet John Lydgate condemns
physicians for their excessive materialism, brings a
medieval allegory into a Victorian text. In many
cases, the key to a name lies in its etymology: Maggie, from the Greek for pearl, despised for her
virtues in St Ogg's, functions in *The Mill on the
Floss* as the pearl cast before swine and Rosamond

and Dorothea, the rose of the world and the gift of
God, are allegorical opposites in the structure of
Middlemarch. Even nicknames are significant.
Dorothea's efforts to find a meaning in modern
life through theology, for Eliot an obsolete point
of view, makes her a Dodo, an extinct bird. See
also LANGUAGE; SYMBOLISM.   FB

Hamilton, Lynn, 'Nicknames in the Novels of
George Eliot', *Literary Onomastics Studies*, 13 (1986).

Naples beguiled George Eliot and G. H. *Lewes
on their Italian tour of 1860: 'Once at Naples in delicious weather, the temptation to spend an additional week there for the sake of seeing at our
leisure Salerno, Paestum, Amalfi, and Sorrento
was made all the stronger because we both needed
that more quiet pleasure for our health's sake,
after the excitement of Rome' (*L* iii. 301). They
were based in Naples from 30 April to 15 May 1860,
enjoying the natural beauty of the scenery as well
as antiquities. Pompeii was undoubtedly the highlight, and they went twice, the first time in company with some uncongenial Russians, and later
on their return from Sorrento: 'we visited the
silent Pompeii again. That place had such a peculiar influence over me that I could not even look
towards the point where it lay on the plain below
Vesuvius, without a certain thrill' (*Journals*, 353).
She was profoundly moved by the artefacts from
Pompeii on display in the Museo Borbonico, 'endless objects that tell of our close kinship with those
old Pompeians' (*Journals*, 351).

They were in Naples again from 26 March to 4
April 1869, arriving, as Lewes put it, 'in the romantic belief that sunlight and warmth will be
something more than mythical *there*' (*L* viii. 448).
Alas, the weather in Naples proved no exception to
the cold and rain experienced throughout that
Italian journey.   MAH

Thompson (1998).

Napoleon III (Louis Napoleon Bonaparte)

(1808–73), emperor of France. He ill-advisedly declared war against Prussia on a pretext on 15 July 1870. He was crushingly defeated at Sedan on 1 September, capitulated, and lived in exile at Chislehurst, Kent, from 1871 until his death. George Eliot condemned his policy against Prussia, but with the Prussian atrocities daily evident and the Siege of *Paris endemic of the suffering of war, she shifted her allegiance. In 1879, according to Edith *Simcox, she looked back on his 'one bad action as a means', feeling that he intended to do good things (*L* ix. 282). See also FRANCE; FRANCO-PRUSSIAN WAR.   GRH

narration. Among critics who are not well disposed to George Eliot, the narrator in her novels is regarded as a serious artistic defect. In the earlier decades of this century the belief that 'telling' was a less artistic method than 'showing', a view associated particularly with Gustave *Flaubert and Henry *James, was strongly prevalent (see REPUTATION, CRITICAL). Novelists, it was argued, should adopt an impersonal approach to narration and write in 'dramatic' terms; as Percy Lubbock, a critic much influenced by James, put it in a book first published in 1921: 'Everything in the novel, not only the scenic episodes but all the rest, is to be in some sense dramatized' (*The Craft of Fiction* (1966), 123).

These ideas were reinforced by modernist concepts of artistic impersonality as in Stephen Dedalus's praise, in James Joyce's *A Portrait of the Artist as a Young Man* (1916), for the kind of literary art in which 'The personality of the artist passes into narration itself . . . The personality of the artist . . . finally refines itself out of existence, impersonalizes itself, so to speak' (ch. 5). In the context of such views George Eliot's approach to narration became problematic. Even in the mid-1950s George Steiner could write in one of his early essays: 'By interfering constantly in the narration George Eliot attempts to persuade us of what should be artistically evident' ('A Preface to *Middlemarch*', *Nineteenth-Century Fiction*, 9 (1954–5), 271).

The publication of Barbara Hardy's *The Novels of George Eliot: A Study in Form* (1959) and W. J. Harvey's *The Art of George Eliot* (1961) marked something of a turning point in George Eliot criticism. Both these critics were sympathetic to New Critical formalism and both attempted to justify George Eliot's narration in formalist terms though Harvey still had some doubts: he took it as 'axiomatic' that the narrator 'becomes objectionable when the author intrudes directly into her fiction either by way of stage directions or of moral commentary' (1961: 69). J. Hillis Miller, at this time a critic strongly influenced by phenomenology, defended 'omniscient' narration in George Eliot and other Victorian writers in the following terms: 'The narrator is an all-embracing consciousness which surrounds the minds of the characters, knows them from the inside, but also sees them in terms of their relations to one another and in terms of the universal facts of human nature which they exemplify' (*The Form of Victorian Fiction* (1968), 83). Elizabeth Deeds Ermarth takes a similar view, the narrator being seen as 'a Feuerbachian species-consciousness, not solely individual yet not transcendental but incarnate in the works of collective human minds and hands, past and present' (1985: 139). A different defence is to argue that even if the narration seems more devoted to 'telling' than 'showing', 'telling' becomes dramatic if the narrator is exposed as a 'far less secure and constant presence' than most critics and readers have thought. This is the view taken by Dorothea Barrett in *Vocation and Desire: George Eliot's Heroines* (1989: 29–30): 'Irritation with the narrator is rooted in the conviction that she is in complete control: once we detect cracks in what was the apparently smooth surface of her narrative, she becomes more interesting and less easily defined'.

George Eliot's *letters and *essays testify to the fact that she was a self-conscious artist who was interested in formal questions, as her short essay 'Notes on Form in Art' indicates. She thought of her novels in structural terms and though she did not oppose Alexander *Main's compilation of passages from her writing under the title *Wise, Witty, and Tender Sayings in Prose and Verse* (1871), she was worried that these passages might make it appear that her works were not artistic wholes:

If it were true I should be quite stultified as an artist. Unless my readers are moved towards the ends I seek by my works as wholes than by an assemblage of extracts, my writings are a mistake. I have always exercised a severe watch against anything that could be called preaching, and if I have ever allowed myself in dissertation or in dialogue [anything] which is not part of the structure of my books, I have sinned against my own laws. (*L* v. 458–9)

It seems clear then that she regards the narrator as a structural part of her novels and not as a vehicle for moralizing comments that have a separate and independent existence.

Narration whether it is omniscient or impersonal implies form since any narrative will give shape and structure to its material. A question concerns George Eliot is where form comes from. In *'Notes on Form in Art' she argues that form 'refers to structure or composition . . . And what is structure but a set of relations selected and combined in accordance with the sequence of mental states in the constructor, or with the pre-conception of a whole which he has inwardly evolved?' (*Essays*, 434). Form therefore is produced by the subject and not immanent in the object. This suggests she would object to impersonal narration on philosophical grounds because it did not acknowledge the role of the subject in the creation of form. Even when narration seems neutral in her fiction one can detect the constructive influence of the subject, as in the opening of the first chapter of *Middlemarch*:

Miss Brooke had that kind of beauty which seems to be thrown into relief by poor dress. Her hand and wrist were so finely formed that she could wear sleeves not less bare of style than those in which the Blessed Virgin appeared to Italian painters.

This is not 'objective' description but the narrator's interpretation of Miss Brooke. It is the narrator who both perceives that she looks good in clothes that would not normally enhance a woman's beauty and introduces the parallel with the representation of the Virgin Mary by Renaissance painters. Someone else perceiving Miss Brooke would almost certainly not see her in such terms. The narrator goes on to suggest that there is an element of role-playing in her plainness of dress. There is therefore an implied separation between Miss Brooke as a 'cluster of signs'—a phrase used later in the novel (*MM* 15)—and how these signs are interpreted by the narrator.

In *Middlemarch* it is especially emphasized that the narrator is an interpreter of signs with a particular viewpoint. Creating a contrast with Henry *Fielding's more discursive approach to the novel, the narrator writes:

I at least have so much to do in unravelling certain human lots, and seeing how they were woven and interwoven, that all the light I can command must be concentrated on this particular web, and not dispersed over that tempting range of relevancies called the universe. (*MM* 15)

The light imagery in the above passage links it with the opening paragraph of chapter 27 in which the ego is compared to a candle light imposing form on the scratches on a pier glass:

It is demonstrable that the scratches are going everywhere impartially, and it is only your candle which produces the flattering illusion of a concentric arrangement, its light falling with an exclusive optical selection. The scratches are events, and the candle is the egoism of any person now absent—of Miss Vincy, for example.

Clearly this must apply also to the narrator's structuring of the events that make up the novel as

much as to any character's ego. The reader is also reminded that the narrator has designs in writing this novel: 'whatever has been or is to be narrated by me about low people, may be ennobled by being considered a parable' (*MM* 35).

It is unlikely that George Eliot, because of her rejection of metaphysical ideas, would have been happy with the term 'omniscient narrator' with its implication that the narrator has godlike powers to penetrate the minds of the characters as well as being able to range with superhuman knowledge over past, present, and future. In all of the novels the narrator is kept separate from George Eliot as author. Indeed, in her early fiction, *Scenes of Clerical Life* and *Adam Bede*, the narrator is male. In the rest of her novels, written after her real identity had been revealed, she avoids indicating whether the narrator is male or female, and in her last work, *Impressions of Theophrastus Such*, the narrator is again male. All of her novels present the narrator as someone who is writing a novel about events and characters that the narrator regards as real, with the narrator being generally referred to as a historian and the novel as a history. Thus in *Adam Bede* the narrator writes: 'But I gathered from Adam Bede, to whom I talked of these matters in his old age . . .' (*AB* 17), and in *The Mill on the Floss* the narrator remembers the scene at Dorlcote Mill as if it had a historical existence: 'I have been pressing my elbows on the arm of my chair, and dreaming that I was standing on the bridge in front of Dorlcote Mill, as it looked one afternoon many years ago' (*MF* 1.1). In *Middlemarch* Caleb Garth is referred to as someone the narrator knew as a real person: '(pardon these details for once—you would have learned to love them if you had known Caleb Garth)' (*MM* 23). This approach obviously has difficulties with *Romola*, a novel set in the late 15th century, for how could the narrator then be convincingly characterized as a historical novelist writing about people the narrator had known? George Eliot still avoids orthodox omniscient narration, however, by creating the spirit of a dead Florentine who visits scenes that are real for him. The narrator follows the Florentine's gaze and interprets it from a modern point of view.

The advantage of this approach to narration is that it does not suggest that the narrator has godlike powers. If the narrator is a historical novelist writing about real people and real events and is thus part of the fiction, then the narrator's knowledge of the inner minds of the characters derives not from a metaphysical penetration of their consciousnesses but rather from the historical novelist's reconstruction and interpretation of their intentions, desires, motivations. And the emphasis on the narrator as a constructor and interpreter of the narrative makes it clear to the reader that other viewpoints and interpretations are possible. Barbara Hardy in a chapter entitled 'Plot and Form' in her study of George Eliot discusses 'coincidence' as a formal device and calls the deaths of Casaubon and Featherstone 'the most interesting coincidence in *Middlemarch*' (1959: 120). But this is no coincidence. It is the narrator who organizes the narrative in such a way that these two deaths are juxtaposed. In narratological terms, the link between the deaths belongs to 'discourse' and not 'story'.

It is probably the intrusions of the narrator that George Eliot's critics have regarded as most objectionable. But such an apparent anti-dramatic device can create quite powerful artistic effects, and this is particularly clear in *Middlemarch*. For example, the reader is pulled up sharp at the opening of chapter 29:

One morning, some weeks after her arrival at Lowick, Dorothea—but why always Dorothea? Was her point of view the only possible one with regard to this marriage? I protest against all our interest, all our effort at understanding being given to young skins that look blooming in spite of trouble.

This is disingenuous on the part of the narrator as the reader's sympathy for Dorothea has been influenced by the narrative's concentration on her viewpoint and by the presentation of Casaubon as a somewhat absurd pedant whose marriage to Dorothea is against nature. But the effect of this shift in focus, together with the subsequent psychological analysis of Casaubon, is to make the reader powerfully aware that points of view—and the narrator's should also be included—are relative and shaped by interests and often prejudices, and to recognize Casaubon's human otherness, his 'equivalent centre of self' (*MM* 21). See also IRONY; REALISM; STYLE.   KMN

Barrett (1989).
Ermarth (1985).
—— *Realism and Consensus in the English Novel: Time, Space and Narrative*, 2nd edn. (1998).
Hardy (1959).
Harvey (1961).
Newton, K. M., 'The Role of the Narrator in George Eliot's Novels', *Journal of Narrative Technique*, 3 (1973).

nationalism. George Eliot participated to a degree in a vagueness common in her time surrounding the definition of nationhood, and consequently also in an uncertainty over the validity and parameters of nationalism. Terms such as 'nation', 'race', 'people' were frequently conflated in the 19th century as can be seen in this quotation from her last novel, *Daniel Deronda*, as Daniel tries to explain his nationalist vocation to Gwendolen:

I am going to the East to become better acquainted with the condition of my race in various countries there . . . The idea that I am possessed with is that of restoring a political existence to my people, making them a nation again, giving them a national centre, such as the English have, though they too are scattered over the face of the globe. (*DD* 69)

The idea of a 'political existence' is important here to the definition of a nation, and to Daniel's idealistic nationalism. In earlier definitions, *race, *language, culture, and territory were some of the factors which could define an aggregation of persons as a nation. To an extent those factors still hold true today in our conception of nationhood, but Daniel's emphasis on 'political existence' and a 'national centre' are in line with more recent definitions of the nation, and the goals of nationalism.

Eliot was highly aware of the debates over the various nationalist struggles in Europe in her lifetime. In the early 1850s she moved to London and began editing with John *Chapman the *Westminster Review*. Chapman's house on the Strand, where she lodged, was often a meeting place for the numerous political refugees from the revolutions and nationalist uprisings of 1848, who were attracted to this hub of radical intellectual activity. Here George Eliot met Giuseppe *Mazzini, exiled leader of the underground struggle for a united republican Italy, and the principal theorist of nationalist movements in Europe.

Repeatedly in her own writing George Eliot criticizes the complacency of England's own nationalist consciousness—a narrow 'provincial nationalism' as Patrick Brantlinger has described it (268), which blinds itself through a jingoistic sense of national superiority to those struggles for freedom and national definition among other peoples. To combat this narrowness, this 'national disgrace', Eliot contends, 'There is nothing I should care more to do, if it were possible, than to rouse the imagination of men and women to a vision of human claims in those races of their fellow-men who most differ from them in customs and beliefs' (*L* vi. 301–2). This universality or sense of connection to 'fellow-men', however, is best nurtured in a 'local habitation', a theme which runs through her writing, as in the well-known passage 'A human life, I think, should be well rooted in some spot of a native land, where it may get the love of a tender kinship for the face of the earth . . . The best introduction to astronomy is to think of the nightly heavens as a little lot of stars belonging to one's own homestead' (*DD* 3).

Like Gwendolen, Deronda's upbringing has been rootless in that he is uncertain of his parentage. Eliot's description of Daniel's star-gazing later in the novel makes it clear that he looks upon the universe so impartially, so detachedly, that he can find no specific focus, no 'little lot of stars', to give his feelings of universal philanthropy the urgency necessary for decisive action. It is not until he sees the star of the East, so to speak, in his dawning vocation to bring a national existence to the Jewish people that Deronda finds a catalyst for his undefined desire to do good in the world.

One recent critic has referred to Deronda as a Mazzini figure (Brantlinger, 272), and insofar as he represents Eliot's view that country or 'local habitation' is the fulcrum which supports a growth into universal brotherhood, this is true. But Mazzini wondered in 1847 whether it was 'sufficient merely to proclaim these sacred truths' of universal brotherhood in order to triumph over despotism: 'Our work is one of *realisation*; we have to *organize* . . . not thought, but action' ('Nationality and Cosmopolitanism', *People's Journal*, 3 (1847), 258). Action, and the realization of a nationalist dream, is of course missing from *Daniel Deronda*. Instead Daniel may be likened to Dorothea Brooke in the manner in which he influences the lives of others; no matter how universally ambitious Dorothea may be, her effect upon others is 'incalculably diffusive' and consists of 'unhistoric acts'. One of the principal differences that Deronda's life has made by the end of the novel is his influence upon Gwendolen Harleth: as she writes to him, 'it shall be better with me because I have known you'. Like Dorothea's influence, Daniel's is unhistoric here and not that of a nationalist revolutionary like Mazzini. This may be due in part to the fact that by the time Eliot wrote this last novel she had for some time been distanced from her early radical associations. When asked to contribute to the Mazzini fund in 1865, Eliot refused, explaining that although she and Lewes had 'a real reverence for Mazzini' they could not contribute because the money might support nationalist 'conspiracy'. Conspiracy, she felt, although sometimes 'sacred' and 'necessary', could lead to 'acts which are more unsocial in their character than the very wrong they are directed to extinguish' (*L* iv. 199–200). And in 1863 George Eliot and Lewes were anxious to dissuade Lewes's son Thornie from leaving England to fight alongside Polish nationalists against the Russians. George Eliot wrote in a letter that 'his father felt that it would be a sin to allow a boy of nineteen to incur the demoralization of joining coarse men engaged in guerilla warfare' (*L* iv. 117). Understandable though these reservations may be, they are a far cry from her quasi-religious expression of idealistic nationalism in *Impressions of Theophrastus Such*: 'not only the nobleness of a nation depends on the presence of national consciousness, but also the nobleness

of each individual citizen'. We lose our selfish egoism in 'our sense of relationship with something great' and 'worthy of sacrifice' (*TS* 18).

George Eliot keenly delineated national character—whether English or European—in her writing, and often in the form of caricature; there is the unimaginative, gentlemanly stolidity of Sir James Chettam with his dimpled hands and well-groomed chestnut, and the 'odious German staccato endings' which Klesmer falls into when in a temper. Eliot was also aware of the possibilities for the creation of a national community of readers. Homi Bhabha has written in *Nation and Narration* (1990) that 'narrative performance interpellates a growing circle of national subjects' and George Eliot seems to have registered the possibility of this in the reception of her novels: after the success of *Adam Bede* she wrote in 1859 to an old friend from *Geneva, François *D'Albert Durade, that 'I have written a novel which people say has stirred them very deeply—and *not* a *few* people, but almost all reading England' (*L* iii. 186–7). But *Middlemarch*, like many of her novels, is 'a study of provincial life' rather than national life. Finally, it is difficult to draw the line between provincial, regional, and national in Eliot's work. 'Local habitation', 'some spot of native land' is extremely important in the development of the human life into one which can embrace universal fellowship. But it is not always clear that this 'local habitation' is envisioned by Eliot as the nation. On the one hand she quotes Drayton's lines as epigraph to *Felix Holt, the Radical*, 'Upon the midlands now the industrious muse doth fall | The shires which we the heart of England well may call', but Dorothea Brooke's epiphanic moment occurs at dawn when she opens her curtain to see labourers outside her entrance gate beginning their day; she feels part of 'the largeness of the world and the manifold wakings of men to labour and endurance' (*MM* 80). That they are fellow beings is more important than whether or not they are English.

Fascinated by the study of national character, both European and English, and by the nationalist movements of her day, George Eliot nevertheless seems to have been far more in sympathy with the effects of 'unhistoric acts' than with revolutionary nationalist struggle (see HISTORY; POLITICS). Perhaps this is why she added, probably at proof stage, Daniel's final sentence in his explanation to Gwendolen of his nationalist vocation: 'At the least, I may awaken a movement in other minds, such as has been awakened in my own' (*DD* 69). The actions and realization of nationalist struggle that Mazzini called for are quietly put to one side here in favour of an intellectual influence which may be 'incalculably diffusive' and therefore much more in line with the interests and sympathies she expresses across her writings. See also COLONIAL-ISM; SOCIETY.   SAG

Brantlinger, Patrick, 'Nations and Novels: Disraeli, George Eliot and Orientalism', *Victorian Studies*, 35 (1992).

Cohen, Monica F., *Professional Domesticity in the Victorian Novel* (1998).

Fleishman, Avrom, 'Daniel Charisi', in *Fiction and the Ways of Knowing* (1978).

nationhood. See NATIONALISM.

'Natural History of German Life, The', one of George Eliot's most important essays, which sets out the aesthetic principles and organic understanding of social life that were later to inform her fiction. Written at Tenby and Ilfracombe from 13 May to 5 June 1856 when she was helping G. H. *Lewes with his work for *Sea-Side Studies*, the essay was published in the *Westminster Review* in July 1856 (repr. in *Essays*). The basis of the essay is a review of the third editions of two works by the German social historian Wilhelm Heinrich von Riehl, *Die Bürgerliche Gesellschaft* (1851) and *Land und Leute* (1853), which form the first two parts of his *Naturgeschichte des Volks*, a pioneering 'natural history' of German society. As an admirer of Riehl's work, George Eliot sets out to make it more widely known in Britain, not only for its intrinsic merits but also 'as a model for some future or actual student of our own people' (*Essays*, 273), a role which she herself was later to fill in her own way as a writer of fiction.

Starting from the assumption that the real characteristics of the working classes are scarcely known to anyone outside them, she begins the essay by discussing the representation of working people, 'the masses', in art and literature and criticizing the idyllic unreality of their portrayal, particularly in social novels. Stigmatizing this as a grave evil, she sets out that view of the artist's function that is to be the basis of her own creative life: 'The greatest benefit we owe to the artist, whether painter, poet, or novelist, is the extension of our sympathies' (270). *Scott and *Wordsworth, two writers she particularly admired, are cited as exemplary in the way that they portray peasant life realistically, thus doing more to link the higher classes with the lower than any number of sermons or philosophical dissertations. The assumption is that neither writers nor readers are members of the lower classes, but that the interests of social harmony and understanding can be served by truthful representation. The function of art is thus both moral and social, as she makes clear in her famous declaration: 'Art is the nearest thing to life; it is a mode of amplifying experience and extending our contact with our fellow-men beyond the bounds of our personal lot'. The moral

end of art is not served by sentimental misrepresentation, and what mankind needs to know are the real, not the imagined, motives and influences that act on the labourer or artisan. She wants art to be sympathetic towards ordinary people, but combines that demand with a harsh view of the intended objects of such sympathy: 'the peasant in all his coarse apathy, and the artisan in all his suspicious selfishness' (271). There is one contemporary novelist who has come near to achieving this end: Charles *Dickens, she maintains, has succeeded in representing the external aspect of the urban population and would make the greatest contribution to the extension of social sympathies if he could render their inner, emotional lives as truthfully as he does their manners and idiom.

This introductory discussion defines in advance the direction which her own early fiction is to take, particularly in *Adam Bede*. And when she goes on to describe Riehl's portrayal of the German peasantry, she imagines it to be similar in its mental culture and habits to English farmers and labourers of 50 years ago, the period that she is to focus on in that novel. Moreover, in the German peasant's adherence to tradition and custom and his inveterate habit of litigation there are affinities with the mental habits of the Dodsons and the Tullivers that she is to examine in her second novel, *The Mill on the Floss*, which could be described as a natural history of English life. Riehl's study is sociological but it appeals to the future novelist's imagination, and she illustrates some of his observations by drawing parallels with characters and incidents in the novels of Scott. She clearly finds his social and political conservatism congenial and approves of his view of European society as 'incarnate history', with its conservative implication that revolutionary change is not to be attempted: 'What has grown up historically can only die out historically, by the gradual operation of necessary laws' (*Essays*, 287).

This organic view of the human world is supported by a comparison with *language, which is similarly resistant, she argues, to rational intervention and imposed change. The music, subtlety, wit, and imaginative power of language are dependent on its historical evolution, with all the uncertainties and anomalies that that entails. A rationally constructed universal language 'which has no uncertainty, no whims of idiom, no cumbrous forms, no fitful shimmer of many-hued significance, no hoary archaisms' (287) would be deodorized and dead, able to express science but unable to express life. The argument here is cleverly conservative and has been criticized as an attempt 'to limit political discussion by locating analysis and decision, science and action, understanding and will, morally below language and life' (Myers 1984: 155–6). Certainly an implied disapproval of revolutionary action can be sensed throughout the essay. The failed attempts at revolutionary change in Germany are ascribed to the abstract nature of the democratic and socialistic theories that inspired them; and it is the tendency towards universalizing abstraction that she criticizes in the socialists. While they are commended for studying closely at least one social group, the factory workers, they are censured for taking that one social fragment to stand for the whole of society. She cites with approval Riehl's dictum that 'a universal social policy has no validity except on paper', and what she shares with him is a commitment to detailed and differentiated understanding as opposed to generalization and dogma: 'we have no master key that will fit all cases' (*MF* 7.3), as she is later to put it. What she omits from her discussion of his work is any mention of his deep prejudices, in particular his *anti-Semitism (Semmel 1994: 53).

Most of her discussion of Riehl is concerned with his thorough and unsentimental survey of the peasantry. Although she has to pass over his treatment of the bourgeoisie, she notes his definition of the social philistine as one who is governed by selfish and private interests alone—a type that she was to reproduce in her novels. Altogether the essay reveals the artistic, political, moral, and philosophical views that were to shape her fiction, and in summing up Riehl as a clear-eyed, practical, large-minded, and sometimes caustic conservative (*Essays*, 299), she defines an outlook very like her own. See also HISTORY; JOURNALIST; PHILOSOPHY; POLITICS; REALISM; SCIENCE; SOCIETY.　　JMR

Graver (1984).
Myers (1984).
Semmel (1994).

natural world. In George Eliot's fiction nature is not a source of meaning but derives its significance from human activity and human consciousness. The delight experienced by the narrator of *The Mill on the Floss* when walking through a wood on a mild May day, stems from the childhood memories that make the natural world so familiar that it becomes 'the mother tongue of our imagination' (*MF* 1.6); whilst the river Floss itself is not only important as a working river that brings trade to St Ogg's, but its powerful current and rushing tide also take on a metaphorical significance in relation to the strong and turbulent stream of Maggie Tulliver's emotional life. The interrelationship of the human and the natural world in this novel is so insistent, colouring the discourse of the characters and the narrator through *metaphor and simile—such as Mr

Tulliver's 'an over 'cute woman's no better nor a long-tailed sheep' (*MF* 1.2)—that it gives the history of the 'emmet-like Dodsons and Tullivers' (*MF* 4.1) the semblance of natural history. It shows how Eliot has something of a natural scientist's understanding of nature, partly acquired from assisting G. H. *Lewes in his researches, in particular his investigation into marine life for *Sea-Side Studies*. That understanding is used to illuminate human life by analogy with the life of plants and *animals. In a manuscript passage Maggie's powerful potential is conveyed by a suggestive image drawn from the natural world: 'A girl of no startling appearance ... may still hold forces within her as the living plant-seed does, which will make a way for themselves, often in a shattering, violent manner' (*MF* 3.5). This type of analogy is used later in *Middlemarch*, although to more ironic effect as the natural scientist Lydgate is likened to a jellyfish in his relation to Rosamond, or 'an animal with fierce eyes and retractile claws' when his financial straits drive him to gambling at billiards (*MM* 66).

In the early novels the natural world is often presented in terms of a nostalgic pastoral that dwells on its beauty and abundance, as in the description of Hayslope and its surroundings in *Adam Bede*: 'the level sunlight lying like transparent gold among the gently-curving stems of the feathered grass and the tall red sorrel, and the white umbels of the hemlocks lining the bushy hedgerows' (*AB* 2). But this benign beauty depends on the mind of the perceiver, and nature can provide no solace or refuge to a mind in misery, as Hetty Sorrel finds in her journey in despair. The same Midland fields and hedgerows present only a prospect of 'cold, and darkness, and solitude' that fills her with horror (*AB* 37). Nature's indifference to human suffering is spelt out by the narrator's recollection of a wayside crucifix in a smiling European landscape, an 'image of agony ... strangely out of place in the midst of this joyous nature' (*AB* 35).

Nature may be indifferent, and 'the selfish instincts are not subdued by the sight of buttercups', as she sardonically remarks in her essay on 'The *Natural History of Human Life' (*Essays*, 270); nevertheless men and women's openness to nature tends to be an index of moral worth in Eliot's world. When Silas Marner is locked into a life of solitary weaving and hoarding, 'his steps never wandered to the hedge-banks and the lane-side in search of the once familiar herbs' (*SM* 2); his shrinking from nature is one with his shrinking from human contact. In *Middlemarch* there is an echo of the pastoral mode of the early novels in the family life of the morally admirable Garths, who are typically shown in orchard or garden (*MM* 57,

86); and in *Daniel Deronda* Gwendolen's recovery from the satanic masquerade of her life in fashionable society is indicated by her vision of Offendene and the natural world around it as 'a restful escape, a station where she found the breath of the morning and the unreproaching voice of birds' (*DD* 64). The natural world is less prominent in the later novels, but it is still used at strategic moments to throw light on human behaviour. See also DARWINISM; DETERMINISM; LANDSCAPE; MORAL VALUES; SCIENCE. JMR

> Eliot, George, 'The Natural History of German Life', in *Essays.*
> Ashton (1990).
> Ermarth (1985).
> Knoepflmacher, U. C., and Tennyson, G. B. (edd.), *Nature and the Victorian Imagination* (1977).

Nazarene movement. George Eliot encountered the work of the Nazarene school of painters during her visits to *Germany in 1854 and 1858 and to *Rome in 1860. The name Nazarene had been mockingly applied to a group of young German artists, two of whom, Friedrich Overbeck (1789–1869) and Franz Pforr (1788–1812), founded the Brotherhood of St Luke in 1809. They settled in Rome in 1810, and were joined by other artists, including Carl Philipp Fohr (1795–1818), Peter Cornelius (1783–1867), and Julius Schnorr von Carolsfeld (1794–1872). The initial Nazarene style was deeply influenced by the work of Italian artists of the early Renaissance, and in particular that of Pietro Perugino (*c*.1445/50–1523) and of his pupil, the young *Raphael. German artists of the 15th and 16th centuries were further sources for Nazarene painting.

Pforr and Fohr both died young, and Overbeck was the only member of the group to remain in Rome, where George Eliot met him in 1860. She drew upon his long hair and his picturesque costume, with a maroon velvet cap, for her description of Adolf Naumann, one of those 'long-haired German artists at Rome' whom the narrator of *Middlemarch* sees as survivors of the Romantic movements (*MM* 19). Naumann's dialogue with Will Ladislaw stresses the Catholic aspects of Nazarene painting, frequently referred to in Britain as 'Christian Art', aspects which were unlikely to appeal to George Eliot (see CHRISTIANITY). She treats Naumann's projected painting, 'Saints drawing the Car of the Church', with some *irony. Entirely in the Nazarene style, the fictional work has some parallels with Overbeck's *The Triumph of Religion in the Arts* (1833–40, Stadel Institute, Frankfurt). Both Dorothea and Edward Casaubon in *Middlemarch* are models for figures in Naumann's painting, Dorothea for St Clara and Casaubon for St Thomas Aquinas. Naumann has

also been associated with Josef von Furich (1800–76), a Nazarene artist of a later generation, whose *Triumph of Christ* (1840, Museum Narodwe, Poznan) provides a closer parallel with the fictional painting.

Cornelius and Schnorr von Carolsfeld both returned to Germany where they undertook sequences of frescos in public buildings, most notably in *Munich. In an article of 1856 in the *Westminster Review* (65: 308–9) George Eliot quoted with approval a parody of Cornelius by the French writer Edmond About (1828–85) and she reacted sharply in 1858 against the Cornelius frescos of classical subjects (now destroyed) in the Munich Glyptothek.

George Eliot showed even less enthusiasm for the work of Cornelius's pupil, Wilhelm Kaulbach (1805–74), whose paintings she saw in *Berlin in 1854 and in Munich in 1858. His huge *Destruction of Jerusalem* in the Neue Pinakothek seemed to her to be 'a regular child's puzzle of symbolism' (Cross, ii. 37). She visited Kaulbach's studio in 1858, and expressed some admiration for his earlier work. He had, she believed, been led astray by the demands of German public art. Kaulbach's use of *symbolism in a large-scale historical painting alienated George Eliot who had little liking for such grand 'machines'. For her, Kaulbach's departure from *realism, characteristic of late Nazarene art, vitiated the whole project. See also VISUAL ARTS. LO

> Witemeyer, Hugh, 'George Eliot, Naumann and the Nazarenes', *Victorian Studies*, 18 (1974).

Netherlands. George Eliot visited the Netherlands with G. H. *Lewes in June 1866 on a two-month tour of *Belgium, Holland, and the Rhine provinces of *Germany. They found Rotterdam a wonderful place, and Lewes gives a lively description of it in a letter—large ships moored right up to the streets, and 'rows of trees mingling their green effects with the crowds of masts . . . women in wooden shoes carrying huge brass vessels that shine like gold—sailors in red and blue shirts—fruit stalls scattered about' (*L* iv. 273). However, the noise of drunken sailors in the narrow streets made their night in an indifferent hotel hideous, and they moved on to a luxurious hotel in The Hague, where they visited museums and the picture gallery. Dutch paintings (see VISUAL ARTS) were the most important feature of the culture of the Netherlands for George Eliot, and she praised their 'rare, precious quality of truthfulness' as a model of realistic art in a celebrated passage of *Adam Bede* (*AB* 17). See also TRAVELS. JMR

new historicist approaches. See CRITICISM, MODERN: NEW HISTORICIST APPROACHES.

Newdigate family. George Eliot was born at South Farm on the estate of Arbury Hall near *Nuneaton, the home of the Newdigate family. Both house and hall still stand today, and Arbury is still owned by the Newdigates. Eliot's father had been an agent in Staffordshire to Francis Parker who in 1806 had succeeded to Arbury and taken the additional name of Newdigate. He brought his agent with him. As a child Eliot was allowed the run of Arbury and heard stories of Francis's cousin and predecessor, Sir Roger Newdigate. Sir Roger and his wife Hester appear almost undisguised as Sir Christopher and Lady Cheverel in 'Mr Gilfil's Love-Story' in *Scenes of Clerical Life*. Arbury, which remains unspoilt today, can also be easily recognized in the same tale. Attempts to find a Newdigate to match up to Captain Wybrow are, however, doomed to fail.

The succession to Arbury Hall was complicated. Upon Francis Parker Newdigate's death in 1835 the estate passed not to his son, also called Francis, with whom Robert Evans maintained a friendly correspondence, but to his nephew called rather confusingly Charles Newdigate Newdegate. It was this man's mother who allowed Eliot to use the library at Arbury. Charles Newdegate was a Member of Parliament and by all accounts a genial personality. It was he who, not surprisingly, was sure that *Scenes of Clerical Life* was based on real events in the neighbourhood of Nuneaton, although he did not guess that Eliot was the author. In *Scenes of Clerical Life* the Newdigate family appears not only in the guise of the Cheverels but also as a different family the Oldinports. The change of name is not very subtle. The Oldinports are mentioned neutrally in 'Amos Barton', but with some hostility because of their meanness in 'Mr Gilfil's Love-Story'. Francis Parker Newdigate is supposed to have been mercenary in contrast to his son, the younger Francis, and some have seen in the relationship between these two and their agent Robert Evans the germs of the story of *Adam Bede* where Adam finds Arthur Donnithorne generous and his grandfather grasping. There is of course no Hetty Sorrel to complete the equation. Alternatively the complicated legal questions involved in the Newdigate succession may find an echo in the complex pattern of matters dealing with inheritance in a number of novels, notably *Felix Holt, the Radical* (see LAW). TJW

Newman, John Henry (1801–90), Christian apologist, prime initiator and supporter of the Oxford movement who defected to *Roman Catholicism in 1845. George Eliot was initially drawn towards his brother Francis William Newman (1805–97), whose *Unitarianism, embracing piety and rationalism, she found sympathetic. She was very enthusiastic about John Henry's *Apologia pro Vita Sua* (1864), welcoming his castigation of Charles *Kingsley's 'mixture of arrogance, coarse impertinence and unscrupulousness with real intellectual incompetence' and responding warmly to his own revelation of a life which she recognized as being deeply different from her own but with 'how close a fellowship in its needs and burthens—I mean spiritual needs and burthens' (*L* iv. 158–9). A few weeks later she continues to praise it, telling Sara *Hennell that she envies her opportunity of seeing and hearing Newman (*L* iv. 160). In May 1870 her friend Mrs Pattison took her to see Newman's small conventual dwellings at Littlemore (*L* v. 44). GRH

Nietzsche, Friedrich (1844–1900), German philosopher who relentlessly insisted on the implications of his declaration in *Also Sprach Zarathustra* (*Thus Spoke Zarathustra*, 1883–92), 'that *God is dead!*' (*Portable Nietzsche*, 124). George Eliot's alleged unwillingness to accept these perceived implications led Nietzsche to attack her in *Götzen-Dämmerung* (*Twilight of the Idols*, 1889):

G. Eliot. They are rid of the Christian God and now believe all the more firmly that they must cling to Christian morality. That is an English consistency; we do not wish to hold it against little moralistic females à la Eliot. In England one must rehabilitate oneself after every little emancipation from theology by showing in a veritably awe-inspiring manner what a moral fanatic one is. That is the penance they pay there.

We others hold otherwise. When one gives up the Christian faith, one pulls the right to Christian morality out from under one's feet . . . Christianity is a system . . . By breaking one main concept out of it, the faith in God, one breaks the whole . . .

When the English actually believe that they know 'intuitively' what is good and evil . . . we merely witness the effects of the dominion of the Christian value judgment and expression of the strength and depth of this dominion . . . For the English, morality is not yet a problem. (*Portable Nietzsche*, trans. Kaufmann, 515–16).

This ignores the influence on George Eliot of German and French atheists such as D. F. *Strauss, Ludwig *Feuerbach, and Auguste *Comte. However, George Eliot *was* associated with G. H. *Lewes, Herbert *Spencer, and Bain, i.e. the 'English' psychologists whom Nietzsche attacked in *Zur Genealogie der Moral* (*On the Genealogy of Morals*, 1877) for

pushing into the foreground the nasty part of the psyche, looking for the effective motor forces of human development in the very last place we would wish to have found them, e.g., in the inertia of habit, in forgetfulness, in the blind and fortuitous association of ideas: always in something that is purely passive, automatic, reflexive, molecular, and moreover, profoundly stupid. (158)

W. B. Yeats criticized George Eliot on very similar grounds *before* he himself came under Nietzsche's influence.

Dinah Morris's much-emphasized lack of self-consciousness, Romola's somnambulistic second flight from Florence, and even Dorothea Brooke's awakening to a new life after her night of anguish after finding Ladislaw in compromising intimacy with Rosamond Lydgate might be cited as examples of the kind of forgetfulness, passivity, or reflexiveness Nietzsche seems to have in mind. More seriously, perhaps, his diagnosis of a pathological cruelty and self-abasement in *Judaism and *Christianity may be reflected in the images of tortured flesh common in George Eliot, and particularly prominent in Dinah Morris's vision of Hetty Sorrel as a torn and bleeding lamb, the Inquisitor in *The Spanish Gypsy*, and much of the imagery associated with Gwendolen Harleth and the Jewish characters in *Daniel Deronda*. See also ATHEISM; METAPHOR; MORAL VALUES; ROMANTICISM. WM

Nietzsche, F., *The Portable Nietzsche*, trans. W. Kauffmann (1954).
—— *The Genealogy of Morals*, trans F. Goffing (1956).
Myers (1984).

Nightingale, Florence (1820–1910), nursing reformer with whom George Eliot was acquainted, and who admired her fiction, though expressed criticism of the course of Dorothea's life in *Middlemarch*. They first met in June 1852 when Florence Nightingale and her aunt visited the future novelist at 142 Strand (see HOMES). George Eliot claimed to have liked them both and to have been much pleased with Florence: 'There is a loftiness of mind about her which is well expressed by her form and manners' (*L* ii. 45). The famous exploits at Scutari during the Crimean War later in that decade she referred to as Florence Nightingale's 'blessed labours' (*L* iii. 15). It was no doubt her success as a social reformer that made Nightingale critical of *Middlemarch*, complaining in 'A Note of Interrogation' in *Fraser's Magazine* (May 1873), that the author could find no better outlet for her heroine than marriage to two inferior men, while she had close at hand the example of a woman (Octavia *Hill) who had realized her ideal in practical social work (see WOMAN QUESTION). There were, however, limits to what Nightingale considered appropriate practical activity for a woman, and she remained unsympathetic to organized efforts at female emancipation like those

of George Eliot's friend, and her own first cousin, Barbara Leigh Smith *Bodichon, with whom she had very little contact since the Leigh Smiths were ostracized by their relatives on account of their illegitimacy. Her attitude to the women's movement had some affinities with George Eliot's, while her work presented an inspiring example of what women could achieve in a life of service; and it is echoed in the figure of Romola tending to the inhabitants of the plague village. JMR

notebooks of George Eliot. A considerable number of George Eliot's notebooks have been preserved, giving insight into her working methods, and providing evidence of her industry and erudition (see also JOURNALS; MANUSCRIPT COLLECTIONS). Some of them are substantial, others slight; some relate to particular works, others are broader in scope. The notebook edited by Joseph Wiesenfarth as *George Eliot: A Writer's Notebook, 1854–1879, and Uncollected Writings* (1981) is unique because it was used for such a long period. When it was acquired by the Yale University Library in 1931, it was thought to be a commonplace book, but Wiesenfarth demonstrates that it is in fact a working notebook which constitutes the sole manuscript record of George Eliot's research for *Adam Bede* and *The Mill on the Floss*, and which includes also material related to *Romola*, *Felix Holt, the Radical*, *The Spanish Gypsy*, *Middlemarch*, and *Daniel Deronda*, and to poems, reviews, and *essays. In this notebook, there are entries not only in English, but in French, German, Greek, Hebrew, Italian, Latin, and Spanish: while other notebooks also have non-English entries, this one, in use for more than 25 years, has the most comprehensive demonstration of George Eliot's proficiency in *languages. At some stage, George Eliot alphabetized pages of the book, but did not maintain consistency in arranging entries alphabetically; similarly, her index to the contents is not complete.

The School Notebook (at Yale) is the earliest extant. In a careful copperplate hand, the 14-year-old 'Marianne Evans' (as her flourishing signature designates herself) did some arithmetic, transcribed favourite poems, and drew a couple of sketches. She included some original writing as well, an essay on 'Affectation and Conceit', and her earliest surviving fiction, the opening of *'Edward Neville', a historical tale set in the English Civil War of the mid-17th century, which are printed as appendices to Gordon S. *Haight's *George Eliot* (1968).

The composition of *Romola* cost George Eliot endless pain. John *Blackwood observed in December 1861 that 'She seems to be studying her subject as subject never was studied before' (*L* iii.

474), and the evidence of that study is documented in five notebooks (in addition to *Writer's Notebook*). She called one of them 'Quarry for *Romola*' (Parrish Collection, Princeton University Library), a name she favoured for notebooks given over to later works also. It contains information from many sources on the social and political history of 15th-century *Italy. Another notebook entitled 'Florentine Notes' (British Library), used exclusively for *Romola*, has similar material on the history of *Florence and local detail. The notebook held in the Bodleian Library, Oxford, has a large amount of *Romola* material, mainly quotations from classical and Italian authors, and lists of Italian proverbs and sayings (the balance is preparation for *The Spanish Gypsy*); similar material appears in a notebook in the New York Public Library Research Collections (published in *Some George Eliot Notebooks*, vol. ii, ed. William Baker (1984)).

Another of the Yale notebooks contains material relevant both to *Felix Holt* and *The Spanish Gypsy*. It includes notes of her reading in such sources as House of Commons Select Committee Reports on Agriculture (1833) and on bribery at elections (1835), *The Times* and *Annual Register* for 1832, and Samuel Bamford's *Passages from the Life of a Radical* (1840), which inform the political context of *Felix Holt*. Further fragments of preparation for *The Spanish Gypsy* (reading in Spanish history and the like) are to be found in a notebook at Texas, and another at Yale.

The 'Quarry for "Middlemarch" ' is at Harvard (it was initially published as a supplement to *Nineteenth-Century Fiction* (1950), ed. Anna T. Kitchel, and has since been reprinted in whole or in part, for instance in the Norton Critical Edition of *Middlemarch*, ed. Bert G. Hornback (1977)). It contains such items as notes from *The Lancet* on medical matters, and outlines of chapters. John Clark Pratt and Victor A. Neufeldt edited the notebook entitled 'Miscellaneous Quotations' (in the Folger Library, Washington), and part of a notebook in the Henry W. and Albert A. Berg collection, New York Public Library, labelled 'Miscellanies' and 'Quotations, Latin, English & Greek—and Hebrew matters' in *George Eliot's 'Middlemarch' Notebooks: A Transcription* (1979). These notebooks document, for example, her interest in ancient *myth and customs (Casaubon's research), and medical studies of fever (Lydgate's research).

A notebook in the Nuneaton Public Library, entitled 'Greek Philosophy & Locke & Comte', to be dated later than 1872, contains notes on classical texts, including *Aristotle's *Ethics* and the English translation of Auguste *Comte's *Politique positive*, together with miscellaneous notes on astronomy and geology. The Huntington Library holds a book labelled 'Miscellaneous Notes/George Eliot', which contains a page of quotations from various authors, and 33 entries ranging in length from a few lines to seven and a half pages, two of which (in revised form) appear in *Impressions of Theophrastus Such* (1879); a further fifteen were included by Charles Lewes (see LEWES FAMILY) in *Essays and Leaves from a Note-Book* (1884).

Jane Irwin's edition of *George Eliot's 'Daniel Deronda' Notebooks* (1996) transcribes, with commentary and annotation, three notebooks and part of a fourth, all housed in the New York Public Library. A section of the Berg notebook, in use from the late 1860s and used also for *Middlemarch*, contains notes on *Homer, Pindar, and physical science, and on a number of Jewish figures and documents, history, and religious practices. The three notebooks in the Pforzheimer collection contain similar material recorded probably from late 1871 to the composition of *Daniel Deronda*: Irwin has traced the interconnections of these memoranda, and their relation to the Berg notebook.

At times, *letters complement the notebooks (for instance, when George Eliot discusses a book she is reading); similarly, her journals and diaries at times parallel the memoranda of particular notebooks.   MAH

Rosenbaum, Barbara, and White, Pamela (edd.), *Index of English Literary Manuscripts*, vol. iv. 1800–1900, pt. I. *Arnold–Gissing* (1982).

'Notes on Form in Art' (1868) was first published by Thomas Pinney in *Essays of George Eliot* (1963), from a manuscript notebook at Yale which includes also an essay entitled 'Versification'. Dated the year after the publication of *The Spanish Gypsy*, the essay arises out of a period of experiment in different *genres by George Eliot, who was writing a good deal of *poetry in the late 1860s and early 1870s, and deals particularly with poetic form. Her adherence to the Romantic tradition of *Wordsworth, *Coleridge, and their German counterparts is evident throughout in the assumption that lyric poetry is normative, and especially in the notion of organic form common to all the arts which is developed: 'The highest Form, then, is the highest organism, that is to say, the most varied group of relations bound together in a wholeness which again has the most varied relations with all other phenomena' (*Essays*, 433).

'Notes on Form in Art' qualifies such earlier pronouncements on realism as that which opens chapter 17 of *Adam Bede* by its concentration on formal properties of the work of art. A. S. Byatt puts this shift of emphasis in the context of Eliot's thinking through ideas of 'the ideal and the real, the particular and the universal, and incarnation' going back at least to the translation of Ludwig *Feuerbach in the early 1850s (*George Eliot: Selected Essays, Poems and Other Writings*, ed. Byatt and Warren (1990), p. xxxi): Rosemary Ashton relevantly insists on the influence of Baruch *Spinoza on both Feuerbach and Eliot (*George Eliot: Selected Critical Writings* (1992), p. xix). It is notable that Eliot's interrogation of concepts of *realism proceeds in language and analogies drawn from various areas of scientific enquiry (see SCIENCE), and anticipates the thoroughgoing commitment of *Middlemarch* to awareness of the determinants of knowledge in such demands as 'Even taken in its derivative meaning of outline, what is form but the limit of that difference by which we discriminate one object from another?—a limit determined partly by the intrinsic relation or composition of the object, & partly by the extrinsic action of other bodies upon it' (*Essays*, 434). See also CRITICISM, MODERN: DECONSTRUCTION. MAH

Novalis (1772–1801), German Romantic writer. George Eliot owned a collected edition of his works including the novel *Heinrich von Ofterdingen* (1802) in which Novalis invented the Romantic symbol of 'die blaue Blume' (the blue flower) (McCobb 1982: 229). Eliot quoted from Novalis's novel in her account of 'Three Months in Weimar' remarking that water is, 'as Novalis says, "an eye to the landscape" ' (*Essays*, 85). In *The Mill on the Floss* an allusion to Novalis forms part of an important narrative comment on the relation of inner character and outward circumstance. Eliot qualifies Novalis's dictum that 'character is destiny'. For Maggie's 'history', she asserts,

is a thing hardly to be predicted even from the completest knowledge of characteristics. For the tragedy of our lives is not created entirely from within. 'Character' says Novalis, in one of his questionable aphorisms—'character is destiny.' But not the whole of our destiny. (*MF* 6.6)

Eliot refers to Novalis in 'The Lifted Veil' where her narrator comments, 'Did not Novalis feel his inspiration intensified under the progress of consumption?' (LV 1). This suggests that Eliot may have had some of the hallucinatory aspects of Novalis's writing, as well as his biography, in mind when portraying Latimer's exaggerated sensibility. See also ROMANTICISM; TRAGEDY. DdSC
McCobb (1982).

novelist, George Eliot as. It is as a novelist that George Eliot came into being (see PSEUDONYM) and achieved a position in English literature which merits this *Companion* and which Marian Evans the journalist and translator, brilliantly gifted though she was, could never have attained.

In an age which saw the great flowering of the English novel she was one of its finest practitioners. Born in the same decade as Mrs *Gaskell, William Makepeace *Thackeray, Charles *Dickens, Anthony *Trollope, and the *Brontë sisters, she belonged to the great generation of mid-Victorian novelists. Starting to write fiction relatively late in life at the age of 36 and outliving all those writers except Trollope, she was, following the death of Dickens in 1870, indisputably the greatest living English novelist for the last ten years of her life, the decade in which she produced *Middlemarch* and *Daniel Deronda*.

Of all that generation of novelists she was the most formidably erudite, and her powerful intellect, armed with a knowledge of seven *languages besides English, ranged across cultures and across disciplines—*history, *philosophy, *science, the *visual arts, *music, as well as literatures ancient and modern—in a lifetime of intensive reading and rereading, as can be seen from her *journals, *letters, and *notebooks. She participated intensely in the intellectual life of Europe and her early reviewers found it quite natural to compare her fiction with that of a great European writer like *Goethe. At the same time her profound knowledge of European literature and culture was brought to bear, in all her novels except *Romola* and *Daniel Deronda*, on the regional, provincial life of the English Midlands.

In 1876, when she was engaged on her last novel, she described all her writing as a set of experiments in life (*L* vi. 216); but they were also experiments in the art of fiction, for she was always trying something new. With the first of the *Scenes of Clerical Life* in 1857 she committed herself to a *realism of the ordinary life, centred on a commonplace individual, and in all three of those early stories she drew on the characters and the settings that she recalled from her early years in *Warwickshire. In *Adam Bede* (1859) she defines and defends that kind of realism in a celebrated passage (*AB* 17), but also develops it in exploring in the fuller form of the novel the lives of carpenters and farming people in a richly imagined pastoral setting. The popular success of *Adam Bede*, which established her as a novelist (see RECEPTION), did not induce her to repeat the formula—to the regret of some of her reviewers—and in *The Mill on the Floss* (1860) she continued to write about unfashionable families but with a more intense focus on the turbulent emotional life of the central character Maggie Tulliver in a drama of *family life and social pressures that is brought to a problematic and tragic conclusion (see ENDINGS; TRAGEDY). *Silas Marner: The Weaver of Raveloe* (1861) focuses like *Adam Bede* on a rural community in a pastoral setting but takes the form of a short, fable-like narrative with fairy-tale motifs, and its double plot of contrasting yet connected stories, together with its alien and alienated central figure, anticipate the later fiction. With *Romola* (1862–3) she tried her hand at a painstakingly researched historical novel in the tradition of Walter *Scott, though one that shows a sophisticated awareness of the problems of such historical writing. And here for the first time she tried serial publication, to be repeated in her last two novels (see SERIALIZATION). In *Felix Holt, the Radical* (1866) she extended the range of her English provincial fiction to include Radical politics as well as Dissenting religion, and, with the tragic figure of Mrs Transome, to raise questions about the relations between the sexes. The *woman question touched on here, and addressed earlier in *The Mill*, becomes a central issue in *Middlemarch* (1871–2), the great novel of her maturity in which her realistic representation of *society appears in its most subtle, searching, and self-conscious form. Here, and in her last novel *Daniel Deronda* (1876), her subject is not the life of ordinary working people as in the early fiction, but rather the drama of exceptional individuals confronting problems of *marriage and *vocation; and in presenting that drama she shows herself to be the great psychological novelist who impressed later writers like Henry *James and D. H. *Lawrence. *Deronda* marks a new departure in dealing with near-contemporary life, whereas all the other novels were set back several decades from the time of writing; and in aspects of its form it tests the limits of realist practice and anticipates the developments of modernist fiction. Her final published work, *Impressions of Theophrastus Such* (1879), is another experiment, this time not a novel at all but a self-conscious addition to the Theophrastan tradition of character writing that reflects upon writing and culture in general.

Her aim in *Daniel Deronda* 'to widen the English vision a little' (*L* vi. 304) with her sympathetic representation of Jewish life illustrates a central feature of her fiction. She saw her novels as interventions, as a way of reaching across divisions of *class and culture and of strengthening social ties through the extension of *sympathy: 'If art does not enlarge men's sympathies, it does nothing morally', she maintained, arguing that the effect she wanted to produce was to make people imagine and feel the experience of those who were different from them in everything but 'the fact of being struggling, erring human creatures' (*L* iii.

111). This didactic dimension to her writing does not, however, make her the ponderous moralist she was often dismissed as being in the decades following her death (see REPUTATION, CRITICAL). As the first great agnostic English novelist she was certainly concerned to establish a secular basis for morality, but her moral scrutiny of her characters' lives is subtle and discriminating and always attentive to the particular circumstances of the individual case (see MORAL VALUES). She was consciously on guard against preaching in her novels (*L* v. 458–9), and her typical narrator may be authoritative but is also sceptical, undogmatic, ironic, and even elusive, whilst the narrative viewpoint is relativized in ways that make 'omniscient' an inappropriate term to describe it (see NARRATION).

Where she was once depreciated as a didactic moralist or admired for expressing timeless truths about human nature, modern *criticism has come to see George Eliot as a more turbulent and contradictory figure, and one whose fiction is not so much solemnly assertive as challengingly interrogative in its sustained complexity. Critically engaged with the most advanced thinking of her day, fully aware of problems of *language and representation, vibrant with tension and conflict, *irony and acerbic wit, her novels have an enduring appeal that derives in great measure from their invigorating power to question and unsettle rather than to console.   JMR

Barrett (1989).
Beer (1986).
Ermarth (1985).
Hardy (1959).
McDonagh (1997).

Nuneaton, the model for Milby in *Scenes of Clerical Life*, has changed considerably since George Eliot lived there (1819–41). Her birthplace, South Farm, is inaccessible unless permission to visit is granted by the Arbury Estate. Her childhood home, *Griff House, is now a Beefeater Restaurant.

Her schools—the Dame School, Miss Lathom's in Attleborough, and The Elms in Vicarage Street—no longer exist but The Elms, close to the parish church, gave her a close view of the town's happenings.

Nuneaton Library, Church Street, houses a collection of books, papers, etc. and Nuneaton Museum, Riversley Park, has a George Eliot Gallery and a collection of memorabilia.   KA

'O may I join the choir invisible'. See POETRY
OF GEORGE ELIOT.

obituaries of George Eliot were principally the
occasion for appraisal of her achievement as a
novelist. Leslie *Stephen in the February *Cornhill
Magazine* sonorously declared: 'In losing George
Eliot we have probably lost the greatest woman
who ever won literary fame, and one of the very
few writers of our day to whom the name "great"
could be conceded with any plausibility' (*CH*
464–5). Stephen's opinions were to gain particular
authority, and the subversive implications of his
gendered discrimination of her greatness to
emerge more forcefully, with his later accounts of
her in the *Dictionary of National Biography* entry
(1888) and the 'English Men of Letters' volume
(1902). His obituary enunciated the distinction between her inspired realistic early novels and the
studied, over-intellectualized later works which
held sway as critical orthodoxy for more than half
a century (see REPUTATION, CRITICAL).

Obituaries also permitted more open discussion of George Eliot's life than previously. Beyond
acknowledgement at G. H. *Lewes's death of their
long relationship, and the announcement of her
marriage to John Walter *Cross, little biographical
information about George Eliot entered the public
domain in her lifetime. The point is made explicitly in one of the earliest obituaries, in the *Academy*
(8 January 1881): 'She chose to keep her public and
her private life apart'. This piece stressed the advantage to Lewes of the union (contrary to the prevailing view that the advantage was mainly on her
side), and also confronted her apostasy while allowing her lofty morality. The obituary in another
weekly, the *Athenaeum* (1 January 1881), concentrated on her work, anticipating the issues to be
taken up repeatedly as the monthlies and quarterlies brought out their tributes: categorization of

her fiction, particularly in terms of its moral and
intellectual aspects, and the implications of her
gender for appreciation of her achievement. The
writer commented of *Romola, The Spanish Gypsy*,
and *Daniel Deronda* that 'They are romances of
the historic imagination, consciously creative instead of being, as in the other novels, unconsciously reproductive', maintaining moreover that
'she herself was her greatest work'—because of her
erudition, in *languages, *science and *philosophy, *history, and *music and painting (see
VISUAL ARTS). So positive a valuation of the later
novels was rare: the preference was overwhelmingly for the early works, where the artist keeps the
philosopher at bay, and questions of the author's
religious orthodoxy are contained. There were few
obituaries as strenuously engaged with critical
issues as James *Sully's in *Mind*. Sully's obituary of
Lewes had gratified George Eliot because of its
high estimate of Lewes's philosophical work: now
he argued that proper understanding of her art
must acknowledge the scientific strength of her
psychological observations.

Tributes prepared by close associates naturally
offered personal reminiscences, and in some cases
quoted from letters and other documentary
sources. Appropriately, the most substantial
obituaries were in the two journals with which
George Eliot had the closest association, the
Westminster Review and *Blackwood's Edinburgh
Magazine* ('Maga'). Her old friend Mark Call (see
BRABANT, ELIZABETH REBECCA) was particularly
well placed to write for the *Westminster Review*.
'George Eliot: Her Life and Writings' runs to more
than forty pages, and provides reliable information for instance about her contributions to the
Westminster Review (concerning which some less
well-informed statements were made elsewhere),
and even the year of her birth (it was given as 1820
on her coffin, and the error frequently repeated).
For all that Call's tone verges on veneration, his
George Eliot is not completely idealized ('Her
scholarship . . . was sufficient for all literary purposes'). He shirks none of the potentially con-
tentious issues, providing analysis of her religious
position (a qualified *positivism) and of her *politics (evasive conservative), together with a stout
defence of her union with Lewes ('The marriage of
true hearts').

The obituary in the February *Blackwood's*
was prepared by the young novelist Alexander Al-
lardyce, with input from William (Willie) Blackwood, Joseph Langford, and Sir Edward Bruce
*Hamley. Its celebration of the achievement of the
pre-eminent Blackwood's author goes beyond formal eulogy, and particularly acknowledges her
special relationship with John Blackwood 'whose
proudest literary success was the recognition and

promotion of her genius' (see BLACKWOOD, WIL-
LIAM AND SONS). The explicit concern of this 'affectionate tribute to her memory' is with the
writings and not the woman. None the less, Al-
lardyce sketches her early life by analogy with
Maggie Tulliver's, implying that the true source of
George Eliot's genius was her Midlands childhood, rather than later 'metaphysical study or scientific research'. The emergence of 'George Eliot',
following Lewes's approach to 'Maga' on her behalf in 1856, is traced with copious quotation from
the firm's archives, giving insider information
such as John Blackwood's suggestion of the title of
The Mill on the Floss. George Eliot is praised as 'the
most careful and accurate among authors', providing her publisher with 'beautifully written
manuscript'. Moreover, 'her grasp of business was
not less striking than her literary power'. Praise of
her personal charm and capacity for *sympathy
modulates into the claim, supported by quotation
from 'O may I join the choir invisible' (see POETRY
OF GEORGE ELIOT), that her greatest love was for
Humanity.

In the May issue of *Nineteenth Century*, Edith
*Simcox declares and demonstrates her privileged
position as an intimate of George Eliot. To personal reminiscences Simcox added first-hand research in *Coventry and its environs, and her own
distinctive interpretations. She lays stress on the
significance of the 'perfect union' with Lewes, to
whom 'we owe . . . the complete works of George
Eliot', and who presided over a cult of worship.
But her comments on Eliot as idol are acute: 'does
not so much incense end by becoming in some
sort a necessity to its recipient?' Simcox avows that
she is concentrating on the woman more than the
artist, though she is interested in biographical parallels and projections in the fiction. Moreover, she
offers some illuminating readings, especially of
moral quandary in the novels, and of the influence
of one character on another. She gives a measured
account of 'her views with regard to women' (in
principle support of 'the most "advanced" opinions', which must in practice be implemented
conservatively), and closes with almost rhapsodic
praise of 'the sweetness and power of all she was'.

Among the many other obituaries, that in the
Century Magazine (November 1881), by F. W. H.
*Myers (whose *Wordsworth* was one of the last
books George Eliot read: *Journals*, 214), has a particular status. The theme of Myers's eulogy is that
'The story of George Eliot's life . . . is merely the
record of the steady development of a strong and
serious mind', and that her wisdom should continue to inspire those able to bring 'the same per-
vading air of strenuous seriousness' to their
reading as she displayed. While his account of her
pronouncement on 'the words *God*, *Immortality*,

Duty' in the Fellows' Garden of Trinity College,
*Cambridge, has become one of the most fre-
quently cited illustrations of her moral position, it
is only part of a judiciously inflected sketch which
shows also 'her intense mental vitality', and her
sensitivity, manifested both as gentleness and consideration for others and as morbid self-reproach.

Another substantial obituary by Charles Kegan
Paul in *Harper's New Monthly Magazine* (May
1881) was illustrated by engravings of places associated with George Eliot, and portraits of her and
Lewes. He follows the standard model, recapitulating for an American audience parallels between
characters and locations in Eliot's work and their
real life prototypes, introducing his own reminiscence of receptions at The *Priory, and reinforc-
ing the analysis in other obituaries of the paradox
represented by Eliot's combination of a delicate
and retiring demeanour with great intellectual
strength.

Tributes in verse include Algernon *Swin-
burne's sentimental sonnet 'The Deaths of
Thomas Carlyle and George Eliot' (*Athenaeum*, 30
April 1881). Some of the poems (for example those
by Elizabeth Stuart *Phelps) made out that George
Eliot was of God's party without knowing it; while
Emily Jane Pfeiffer's pair of sonnets 'The Lost
Light' (dated 29 December 1880, the day of the
funeral), enlisted her, 'Lost queen and captain,
Pallas of our band', under 'The banner of insur-
gent womanhood'. See also BIOGRAPHIES; RECEP-
TION.   MAH

Oliphant, Margaret (née Wilson, 1828–97),
Scottish-born novelist and woman of letters,
author of 98 novels, more than 50 short stories, 25
works of non-fiction, and over 300 periodical articles. She was, like George Eliot, very much a
Blackwood's author (see BLACKWOOD, WILLIAM
AND SONS) though the two women never met. She
described herself as 'a fat, little, commonplace
woman, rather tongue-tied' (*Autobiography*, 17), a
self-image which belies her professionalism and
her considerable business acumen. Recent studies
qualify the conventional view that she sacrificed
the possibility of producing work of high quality
because of the need to publish prolifically to support her extended family.

When *Scenes of Clerical Life* came out in book
form in January 1858, Oliphant, who already had a
reputation in the literary world, was reported to be
confident that they were not written by a woman
(*Journals*, 295). By the time *The Rector and the
Doctor's Family*, the first of the *Chronicles of Carlingford* series for which Oliphant is now best
known, began anonymous publication in *Blackwood's Edinburgh Magazine* in 1861, George Eliot
was a dominant figure who smartly rejected the

attribution of the work to her, while writing with some admiration of Mrs Oliphant and her capacity to do 'a perfectly stupendous amount of work of all sorts' (*L* iv. 25–6). Though George Eliot may not have realized it, because the work was unsigned, she was reading Mrs Oliphant's 'My Faithful Johnny' in the *Cornhill* just before her death (*Journals*, 214). In such writings as *The Victorian Age in English Literature* (1892), or her review of John Walter *Cross's *Life*, Oliphant accorded a high place to George Eliot's work, especially 'Amos Barton' and *Adam Bede*. It was reading Cross that determined her to write her own autobiography, in which she confessed to some envy: 'Should I have done better if I had been kept, like her, in a mental greenhouse and taken care of?' (*Autobiography*, 15)—looked after by 'a caretaker and worshipper unrivalled—little nasty body though he looked' (*Autobiography*, 17). MAH

Oliphant, Margaret, review of Cross's *Life*, *Edinburgh Review*, 161 (Apr. 1885), 514–53.

—— *The Autobiography of Margaret Oliphant*, ed. Elisabeth Jay (1990).

Jay, Elisabeth, *Mrs Oliphant: 'A Fiction to Herself' A Literary Life* (1995).

opera. See MUSIC.

Owen, Richard (1804–92), anatomist and palaeontologist, Hunterian Professor of Physiology at the Royal College of Surgeons, founder of the Natural History Museum, and a friend of George Eliot and G. H. *Lewes. She first saw him when she was working on the *Westminster Review* at John *Chapman's house in the Strand, where he attended a meeting on 4 May 1852, chaired by Charles *Dickens, to protest against the fixing of book prices by the Booksellers' Association. She wrote to *Bray that 'Owen has a tremendous head and looked, as he was, the greatest celebrity of the meeting' (*L* ii. 24). She got to know him in 1855 when they were neighbours in East Sheen and

Lewes used to consult him on scientific questions in relation to his work on Goethe. As the leading scientist of the day, he was of great assistance to Lewes, who dedicated his *Sea-Side Studies* to him. He was also an early admirer of George Eliot's fiction, thinking highly of 'Amos Barton' and declaring *Adam Bede*, of which he received a presentation copy, to be the finest work since Scott (Haight 1968: 275). In 1861 he was embroiled in a public controversy with another member of the Eliot–Lewes circle, T. H. *Huxley, about whether the human brain was anatomically distinct from that of the higher apes. As a Christian he argued that it was, citing the presence of a small bone, the 'hippocampus minor', as evidence; but Huxley the agnostic had the better of the argument, showing that the same bone could also be found in other primates (Ashton 1991: 214–15). JMR

Ashton, Rosemary, *G. H. Lewes: A Life* (1991).

Oxford, university town visited regularly by George Eliot and G. H. *Lewes in the 1870s. They became friends with Benjamin *Jowett at Balliol and the *Pattisons at Lincoln. First impressions were disappointing, but then they 'turned through Christ Church into the Meadows and walked along by the river. This was beautiful to my heart's content' (*Journals*, 25 May 1870). On this visit they had a fine view of the Oxford towers, went to the Ashmolean Museum, saw the gardens of New College surrounded by the old City wall, admired the cloisters at Magdalen, went to the Bodleian and the Sheldonian theatre, where they heard Emanuel *Deutsch speak on the Moabite stone, saw a boat race from the Oriel barge, and wandered through the lovely gardens of Merton. Eliot's notes express a warm love for the places and the culturally stimulating experiences attendant upon them. See also BROWNING, OSCAR. GRH

Oxford movement. See TRACTARIAN MOVEMENT.

painting. See VISUAL ARTS.

Palestrina, Giovanni (*c*.1525–94), Italian composer, to whom George Eliot most notably refers when describing Daniel Deronda's sense of transcendent communion during the Hebrew litany as he 'gave himself up to that strongest effect of chanted liturgies which is independent of detailed verbal meaning—like the effect of an Allegri's *Miserere* or a Palestrina's *Magnificat*' (*DD* 32).

In notes from an essay on Palestrina by the musicologist Fétis, Eliot transcribes his assessment of Palestrina's music as 'une des plus belles inspirations de l'esprit humain' (*George Eliot's 'Daniel Deronda' Notebooks*, ed. Jane Irwin (1996), 443). The rich contrapuntal textures of Palestrina's choral music provide an expression of the individual's potential to participate in a spiritual communion: 'a self oblivious lifting up of gladness' (*DD* 32). Palestrina's music, its effect 'independent of . . . verbal meaning', conveys the significance for Deronda of the Hebrew service when he does not yet know about his Jewish inheritance nor understand the liturgy (*DD* 32). Deronda subsequently insists that 'the service impressed me just as much as if I had followed the words—perhaps more' (*DD* 32). Eliot's reference to Palestrina thus establishes an analogy with the greatest composer of unaccompanied church music to evoke the effect of the Hebrew liturgy for her non-Jewish readership. See also MUSIC.   DdSC

Pall Mall Gazette, The, innovative evening newspaper founded by George *Smith in 1865. George Eliot contributed four articles in the newspaper's inaugural year: 'A *Word for the Germans' (7 March); *'Servants' Logic' (17 March); 'Futile Falsehoods' (3 April); and 'Modern Housekeeping' (13 May). G. H. *Lewes was both a frequent contributor and an editorial adviser after he left the *Cornhill Magazine*. Taking its lead from a newspaper in William Makepeace *Thackeray's novel *Pendennis*, the *Pall Mall* was to be 'written by gentlemen for gentlemen' and it became an important organ of broadly liberal opinion. As noted in the Prospectus, it aimed 'to bring into Daily Journalism that full measure of thought and culture which is now found only in the Reviews'. See also JOURNALIST, GEORGE ELIOT AS.
                                              MWT

parents of George Eliot. Her father Robert *Evans (1773–1849) trained as a carpenter but rose by his exceptional abilities to be a land agent, managing estates for the landed gentry. Her mother Christiana (1788?–1836), Robert's second wife, was the youngest daughter of Isaac Pearson, a prosperous farmer of Astley in Warwickshire. There is little mention of her in Eliot's *letters and

P

*journals and it is clear that her father was the more important figure in her development.
                                              JMR

Paris. George Eliot visited the French capital for the first time in June 1849, when she was taken on a European tour by her friends *Charles and Cara *Bray after the death of her father. She returned to the city on many occasions right up to the last year of her life, usually stopping only briefly when travelling to or from other places on the Continent. She appears at first to have disliked Paris, which may help account for the short visits; but in January 1865 she and G. H. *Lewes went there expressly for a ten-day holiday, after which she was able to write: 'I have lost my old dislike of Paris—but, it must be confessed that the Paris of today is another Paris than the one I used to detest' (*L* viii. 333). Paris at the height of the Second Empire, undergoing transformation by Haussman, had changed radically from 1849 and it provided the couple with rich entertainment: they went to the theatre or the opera nearly every night and spent the days sightseeing. The most interesting sight was the apartment where Auguste *Comte had lived: 'Such places, that knew the great dead, always move me deeply', she wrote to Maria *Congreve (*L* iv. 176). Nearly two years later, in December 1866, they spent three days there on their way to *Spain and breakfasted with a number of politicians and intellectuals, including the historian Ernest *Renan.

It is these later experiences of Parisian theatres and Parisian intellectual life that are reflected in the brief appearance of Paris in *Middlemarch*, in the retrospective account of Lydgate's experience as a medical student in the city (*MM* 15). Paris is both a seat of learning, where the study of medicine is far more advanced than anywhere in Britain, and at the same time a place of melodramatic theatricality quite alien to Middlemarch, which steps off the stage into ordinary life when the actress Laure fatally stabs her husband. As the scene of this melodramatic murder and of Lydgate's wild infatuation, Eliot's fictional Paris borrows some of the lurid qualities of French novels of metropolitan life like Honoré de *Balzac's and may owe as much to her reading as to her experience as a visitor.

She and Lewes visited Paris shortly after the completion of Middlemarch in the autumn of 1872 and found it changed again, this time for the worse after the *Franco-Prussian war; and they compared it unfavourably to the *Germany they had just left. Lewes was able to buy a kind of waistcoat he had been seeking for years, but apart from satisfying that consumer desire, Paris was a place of sad ruins, rain, and trashy bookshops that had them quickly fleeing to Boulogne (L v. 318). Later visits were happier, especially in June 1876, when Eliot corrected proofs of Daniel Deronda in the Tuileries gardens, went to the Russian church with Lewes to hear the exquisite singing, and saw Sarah *Bernhardt act. That was the last visit shared with Lewes. In May 1880 she visited Paris for a final time with her new husband John Walter *Cross, and relived old memories by returning to the Russian church. See also FRANCE; MUSIC; RELIGION; THEATRE.   JMR

Parkes, Bessie (Elizabeth) Rayner (Mme Louis Belloc) (1829–1924), campaigner for women's education, employment, and suffrage, who formed a close friendship with George Eliot in 1851. Bessie Parkes came from a reforming family. She was the daughter of the radical Dissenting reformer Joseph *Parkes, and great-granddaughter, on her mother's side, of Joseph Priestley. 'Miss Parkes is a dear, ardent, honest creature, and I hope we shall be good friends', enthused Eliot in a letter to the Brays (L ii. 9). Bessie Parkes's record of her first impressions is less wholeheartedly confident. 'I know you will *like* her for her large unprejudiced mind', she wrote to Barbara Leigh Smith *Bodichon who also became a close friend (L ii. 9). However, Parkes is uncertain whether Eliot will develop the 'high moral purpose' necessary to real friendship (L ii. 9). A little later, Parkes wrote again to give an account of her pleasure at her growing friendship with Eliot commenting that 'As I know her better, the harsh heavy look of her face softens to a very beautiful tender expression' (L ii. 16). She came to value what she described as Eliot's 'odd mixture of truth and fondness . . . She never spares, but expresses every opinion, good and bad, with the most unflinching plainness, and yet she seems able to see faults without losing tenderness' (L ii. 87).

Parkes wrote poetry, frequently reflecting her feminist concerns, about which she obtained Eliot's advice and encouragement: 'Publish the poems with all my heart, but don't stop there', wrote Eliot during the summer of 1852; 'Work on and on and do better things still' (L ii. 45). Parkes's first collection of Poems was published by John *Chapman in 1852. G. H. *Lewes described these in the Leader (8 January 1853) as displaying more learning than emotion but the book received a more sympathetic notice, probably written by Eliot, in the *Westminster Review (where, apart from Tennyson's Ode on the Death of the Duke of Wellington, it was the only poetry reviewed that quarter). The review describes the book as 'containing some genuine poetry . . . characterised by a spiritual vein of sentiment which seeks to penetrate the symbolisms of nature, and to interpret its living voice, in language graceful and melodious'; 'She belongs to the contemplative school', it concluded, 'and in some of her pieces reminds us of Emerson' (Westminster Review, 59: 287). Eliot continued to read Parkes's poetry and whilst selective in the poems she praised as poetry was generally appreciative of the quality of thought which they contained (L ii. 129).

Bessie Parkes later composed a detailed account of Eliot's manner and *appearance in an article for the Contemporary Review in 1894 entitled 'Dorothea Casaubon and George Eliot':

In daily life the brow, the blue eyes, and the upper part of the face had a great charm. The lower half was disproportionately long. Abundant brown hair framed a countenance which was certainly not in any sense unpleasing, noble in its generous outline, and very sweet and kind in expression. Her height was good, her figure remarkably supple; at moments it had an almost serpentine grace. Her characteristic bearing suggested fatigue; perhaps, even as a girl, she would hardly have been animated; but when she was amused her eyes filled with laughter. She did not look young when I first saw her, and I have no recollection of her ever looking much older. (213)

Parkes asserts, on the strength of her own background, that despite her lack of religious belief, Eliot was in character the 'living incarnation of English Dissent' in her 'horror of a lie, her unflinching industry, and sedulous use of all her talents, her extraordinary courage—even her dress, which spend as she might and ultimately did, could never be lifted into fashion' (208). Eliot was invited frequently to dinner with Joseph Parkes and his guests. She nevertheless sensed that she was regarded as a dubious influence on Bessie, and in a half-playful letter admonished her not to 'be playing pranks and shocking people because I am

A sketch of George Eliot's feminist friend Bessie Rayner Parkes, later Belloc (1829–1924), 'a dear, ardent, honest creature', who was particularly close to her in the the early 1850s.

told they lay it all to me and my bad influence over you' (*L* ii. 44).

In 'Dorothea Casaubon and George Eliot', Bessie Parkes recalled Eliot as she descended the stairs on Joseph Parkes's arm, dressed in black velvet, usually worn only by married women at the time, 'the only lady, except my mother, among a group of remarkable men, politicians, and authors of the first literary rank' (213). 'A real, deep thought and quiet wit' are what Parkes recalls in Eliot's conversation, which was interesting rather than charming with always a want of brightness: 'Her nature smouldered deeply' but never 'burst into a quick flame' (214). The overall effect of Eliot's presence, Parkes asserts, was peculiarly impressive for her great weight of intellect told in all circles (213). She suggests that but for the deliberate casting away of her social chances when she left for Germany with Lewes, Eliot would have been a great success independently of her novels (213–14).

Parkes says little about Lewes himself, but implies a sense of puzzlement that Eliot should have been so devoted to him (215–16). When speaking of Eliot's later life, Parkes (herself a Catholic convert) suggests that Eliot should not be judged by the moral tenets of a *Christianity which she had repudiated. Parkes claims to have been made privy to Eliot's plans to accompany Lewes to the Continent in 1854. Despite her father's horrified fury at the news of Eliot's elopement, Bessie nevertheless wrote in secret and received warm appreciation in reply (*L* ii. 173–4). 'If you knew everything,' wrote Eliot in a subsequent letter, 'we should probably be much nearer agreement even as to the details of conduct than you suppose. In the mean time, believe no one's representations about me' (*L* ii. 196). Parkes paid a visit on Eliot's return to London at which Eliot expressed much pleasure, although Parkes took some time to conform to her wish to be addressed as 'Mrs Lewes' rather than 'Miss Evans' (*L* ii. 200, 232, 384).

Bessie Parkes edited a number of radical women's magazines, beginning with the *Waverly Journal* in 1857. Eliot advised Parkes to concentrate on articles about philanthropy, rather than literary contributions: 'Not because I like philanthropy and hate literature, but because I want to *know* about philanthropy and don't care for second-rate literature' (*L* ii. 379). Parkes was one of a group of feminists who centred on Langham Place in London in the late 1850s. They set up a reading room for women and in 1858, together with Barbara Bodichon, Parkes established the *English Woman's Journal* which she edited and for which Emily *Davies also worked for a time. The journal was designed to be a serious and avowedly feminist publication in which the need for middle-class women to gain access to meaningful employment

was a key issue. Although she was subsequently to lament the low quality of contributions to the magazine, Eliot declared herself much moved by Parkes's article for the opening number, which attacked the narrow range of employment opportunities currently open to women, and she offered advice on the review content of the journal (*L* ii. 436–7). The *English Woman's Journal* failed to attract a sufficient readership and subsequently collapsed.

The radical feminism of Bessie Parkes, Barbara Bodichon, and Emily Davies forms a contrast to Eliot's own highly ambivalent attitude to issues such as the female franchise and professional life (see WOMAN QUESTION). Writing to Parkes from *Weimar, Eliot had combined a wish that she would soon receive a copy of Parkes's polemical work *Remarks on the Education of Girls* with an unapologetic assertion of her own differing views on matters relating to women: 'If I happen to write anything you don't like about women, you must tolerate me, since in all things I am obliged to say with old Luther "That is my belief—I cannot speak otherwise" ' (*L* ii. 174). Nevertheless, after Parkes's book was misrepresented by a reviewer for the *National*, who maintained that she recommended young women to read indecent literature, Eliot had vigorously defended the purity and seriousness of Parkes's work and character, whatever mistakes she may have made in style or ideas (*L* ii. 486).

As a feminist, Bessie Parkes rejected the notion that women should be content to restrict their social function to the relatively passive realm of influence and advocated that they be allowed free entry into the professions. In 'Dorothea Casaubon and George Eliot', she regretted that in *Middlemarch* Dorothea should have been given what Parkes took to be the contemplative St Theresa as a model rather than a more active example appropriate to the time of the novel's setting. Parkes laments Dorothea's misuse of her life, outlining its historical context to emphasize that the novel is set in a time of vibrant activity for women (209). She comments on the ironic disparity, troubling to later critics also, between Dorothea's passivity and the life of Eliot herself, born only ten years later, and who proved to be 'one of the most really efficient workers of modern times' (210).

Parkes also laments that 'Women seem to have held aloof with a sort of fear from any attempt to measure the achievements of that extraordinary mind', suggesting that the lack of female critics of Eliot's writing is particularly poor given her own status as a role model for other women, for

neither her ponderous weight of learning, nor the full flow of her thought, nor the extraordinary wealth of illustration with which she wrought out her meaning should have hindered women from discussing the utterances of one who was in her own person essentially womanly, and who bore down upon the younger members of her own sex with what seemed at the time to be an almost irresistible impact. (207)

In 1868 Parkes married Louis Belloc (becoming the mother of Hilaire Belloc). From the mid-1850s, she and Eliot rarely saw each other. Eliot's letters to Barbara Bodichon during the time of the *English Woman's Journal* show some impatience at what they both regarded as Parkes's lack of judgement, but later letters stress that she valued the memories of their close friendship. In 1863 Parkes sent Eliot a copy of her latest poetry collection *Ballads and Songs*. Eliot responded warmly to the poems as 'giving me glimpses of the history of your mind in the years during which we have seen so little of each other' (*L* iv. 85). One of the last letters Eliot wrote before her death in 1880 was to invite Bessie to lunch (*L* vii. 347–8). In a birthday letter to Parkes in June 1852, Eliot had predicted that her friend would live to contribute to the future progress for which Eliot hoped: 'you, who will touch more closely on the Millenium than I, will both get a glimpse and give an example of better things' (*L* ii. 36). In the event, Bessie Parkes outlived Eliot by more than four decades.   DdSC

Parkes, Bessie, 'Dorothea Casaubon and George Eliot', *Contemporary Review*, 65 (1894).

Parkes, Joseph (1796–1865), lawyer and reforming politician, founder of the Reform Club, and father of George Eliot's friend Bessie *Parkes, later Mme Belloc. Originally from Birmingham, he was working in London from 1833, and it is in his house in Savile Row that his daughter recalls Marian Evans in her early London years attending his dinner parties. Parkes was a Unitarian and he subsidized the young Mary Ann Evans's translation of D. F. *Strauss's *Das Leben Jesu* (see TRANSLATIONS), seeing biblical criticism as part of a political campaign against the Anglican establishment. When the future novelist went off to Germany to live with G. H. *Lewes in 1854, Parkes was outraged, writing of her folly and vice, warning his daughter against associating with her, and declaring Lewes to be a morally bad man (Ashton 1996: 124–5).   JMR

Ashton (1996).

Pascal, Blaise (1623–62), French scientist and Christian apologist, whose *Pensées* were given to George Eliot as a school prize when she was 14; in 1878, recalling this event, she adds that she continually returned to them for their 'deep though broken wisdom' (*L* vii. 11). Her early letters testify

to the impact the work had made on her, referring to Pascal's evocations of radical uncertainty and the existential isolation of humanity, and to his assertion that man's claim to grandeur lies exclusively in his consciousness of his fallen state (*L* i. 7, 25, 56). A reference in an essay on Mme de Sablé in the *Westminster Review* (October, 1854) shows that George Eliot was aware that the manuscripts of the *Pensées* had undergone a major reassessment in France in the 1840s, highlighting the fragmentary and unfinished nature of Pascal's project (*Essays*, 74–5). This may be important for *Middlemarch*. The young Dorothea 'knew many passages of Pascal's *Pensées* by heart' (*MM* 1); she thought that marrying Casaubon might be like marrying Pascal (*MM* 3); and at his death, Casaubon—like Pascal—leaves notes for an unfinished project. Such references increase the pathos of Casaubon's destiny as well as of Dorothea's. Among other analogies between Pascal's thought and George Eliot's fictional imagination is the juxtaposition of a possible allusion to Pascal's concept of the 'two infinities' in the epigraph to *Daniel Deronda* (*DD* 1) with the gambling theme which emerges in that chapter: the 'wager' fragment is among Pascal's best-known metaphysical paradoxes (Shaffer 1975: 282).   TCC

Cave, Terence, 'A "deep though broken wisdom": George Eliot, Pascal, and *Middlemarch*', *Rivista di letteratura moderne e comparate*, 51 (1998).

Shaffer (1975).

Pater, Walter (1839–94), writer whom George Eliot met in May 1870 at a supper party in *Oxford, where he was a fellow of Brasenose College (*Journals*, 140). When his *Studies in the History of the Renaissance* (1873) appeared, she agreed with Margaret *Oliphant's criticisms in a review in *Blackwood's Edinburgh Magazine* in November 1873, adding that 'Mr Pater's book . . . seems to me quite poisonous in its false principles of criticism and false conception of life' (*L* v. 455). Despite her dislike of Pater's aestheticism her own historical novel *Romola* has been cited as an important influence on his *Studies* and his novel *Marius the Epicurean* (1885), a claim which has subsequently been contested. See also VISUAL ARTS.   JMR

Delaura, David J., '*Romola* and the Origin of the Paterian View of Life', *Nineteenth-Century Fiction*, 21 (1966–7).

Hill, Donald L., 'Pater's Debt to *Romola*', *Nineteenth-Century Fiction*, 22 (1967–8).

Pattison, Mark (1813–84), rector of Lincoln College, *Oxford, and, like George Eliot whom he knew, a powerful figure in the intellectual world of the Victorians. He did much to shake British universities in general and Oxford in particular out of their 18th-century torpor into becoming proper places for scholarship. In 1861 he married Emilia Frances Strong who was 27 years his junior. The marriage was clearly an unhappy one. After Pattison's death his widow married the controversial Liberal politician Sir Charles Dilke.

There are some parallels here with the story of Dorothea Brooke, who was also twenty-seven years younger than Casaubon. Pattison wrote a book on the scholar Isaac Casaubon. The *Dictionary of National Biography*, following a number of 19th-century sources, suggests an equation, but modern opinion led by Gordon S. *Haight is generally contemptuous of the idea that Eliot used the story of the Pattisons in *Middlemarch*.

Mrs Pattison is first mentioned by George Eliot in correspondence of January 1869, and there are frequent references to both Pattisons in the next three years during which *Middlemarch* was composed. G. H. *Lewes and Eliot stayed at Lincoln in May 1870, and there are a number of letters between Mrs Pattison and Eliot in the crucial years. But both Pattisons continued to be friendly with Lewes and Eliot after the publication of *Middlemarch* which does not seem to have caused any resentment. Pattison does seem to have resented any caricature of himself in Rhoda Broughton's *Belinda*. But Casaubon is too distant from Pattison to be a caricature. Pattison was ahead of his times, admiring the work of Germans. Lewes and Eliot read and approved of his writings. In contrast Casaubon's scholarship is out of date and despised. Likewise Mrs Pattison's piety appears to be High Church, while Dorothea is more of an evangelical.

Finally, and perhaps most tellingly, although the subject is a difficult one, marital difficulties between the Pattisons appear to have been very different from those between the Casaubons. Whereas Casaubon is not virile enough, Pattison appears to have been too virile for his wife's taste. In his declining years Pattison caused scandal in Oxford by his association with Meta Bradley, the niece of a fellow head of college. We cannot imagine Casaubon engaged in an affair with a cousin of Mr Cadwallader.   TJW

Haight, Gordon S., Review of J. Sparrow, *Mark Pattison and the Idea of a University*, *Notes and Queries*, 213 (May 1968).

pets owned by George Eliot. George Eliot's fondness for *animals, very likely developed in her country childhood, attracted comment throughout her life. Her greatest affection was for dogs, certainly as pets.

It appears that her household was first supplied with a dog by John *Blackwood, who at the considerable cost of 30 guineas made her an inspired gift during the troublesome *Liggins affair: her

journal for 29 July 1859 reads '*Pug came!*' (*Journals*, 79). Described by Lewes as 'a great beauty, though not wise' (*L* iii. 124 n.), Pug ingratiated himself thoroughly, accompanying his owners to Christmas dinner at the *Congreves. On New Year's Day 1862, the thoughtful and forbearing Blackwood sent George Eliot 'a china *pug* as a memorial of my flesh and blood Pug, lost about a year ago'—and her journal entry continues, '*I began my Novel of Romola*' (*Journals*, 107).

Pug's flesh-and-blood successor was Ben the 'lovely bull terrier, . . . who is fast becoming the pet and tyrant of our household' (Journal of G. H. Lewes, 8 February 1864, in Haight 1968: 374), and who by 1871 had 'gone where the good bulldogs go' (*L* ix. 15). Dash, a dark-brown spaniel, with 'all Ben's virtues, with more intelligence, and a begging attitude of irresistible charm' (*L* v. 238), was lost within a month early in 1872, and appears not to have been replaced.

Dogs are considerably more significant as characters and in imagery in George Eliot's writing than any other species of animal: Adam Bede's dog Gyp and Grandcourt's Fetch and Fluff are among the striking canine presences.   MAH

Phelps, Elizabeth Stuart (1844–1911), American novelist best known for *The Story of Avis* (1877) and *The Gates Ajar* (1868). She wrote to George Eliot on 26 February 1873 extravagantly praising *Middlemarch* ('as pure as a lily . . . the novel of the Century' (*L* v. 388 n. 8) and began a correspondence in which Eliot revealed her gratitude and uncertainties. Phelps, who suffered from ill health, lectured on Eliot, who provided her with biographical details. She told Eliot how well Harriet Beecher *Stowe spoke of her: Eliot was flattered and responsive, saying how she felt sympathetic and respectful herself towards Miss Phelps (later Mrs H. D. Ward). Eliot's letter of 16 December 1876 is revealing: here she asserts her consistency of viewpoint in her writings and that her principles have been unchanged throughout. She also records her sensitivity to reading anything about herself, and considers *America as 'the seed-ground and nursery of new ideals' (*L* vi. 317–18). In November 1877 she states that she is reading *Avis*, a novel which may reveal her own influence in that it rewrites the opening of *Daniel Deronda* by showing a woman musing on another woman. On 10 April 1879 she responds to Miss Phelps's kindness by telling Eliot that she is busy working on G. H. Lewes's papers.   GRH

philosophy. As her reviewers have often noted with half-disguised perplexity, George Eliot read everything, usually in the original language. Her letters and essays are full of references to Parmenides, *Plato, *Aristotle, Immanuel *Kant, David

Hume, G. W. F. *Hegel; to social theorists like Jean-Jacques *Rousseau, Jeremy Bentham, James and John Stuart *Mill, Auguste *Comte, and Herbert *Spencer; to the Kabbalah; to Baruch *Spinoza and Ludwig *Feuerbach and the new German *Higher Criticism of the *Bible. Such lists, however, only scratch the surface of a wide, disciplined, and generous habit of reading that always took her well beyond English national borders and that put her in touch with the movements and with the leading philosophers of her time.

Her reading of philosophy, in other words, was an integrated result: not an exclusive devotion to philosophy mainly, but the thorough knowledge of an original intelligence alert to the seismic shifts already shaking the epistemological foundations of her world. She read widely in science, she read obscure churchmen, she read feminists, politicians, historians, novelists, and poets from different national traditions. She took regular doses of mathematics and logic. She knew many of the key figures of her age both in England and abroad in European capitals; they included politicians, political theorists, theologians, philosophers, composers and musicians, feminists, scientists, novelists, and painters.

In this lifelong experimental education she had the constant and long-term advantage of sharing interests and reading, often aloud, with her equally gifted partner, G. H. *Lewes. Like him, George Eliot interested herself in a wide range of material because she saw the philosophical bearing of practical problems and the practical implications of philosophical dispute. Critics innocent of philosophical intelligence themselves—David Cecil comes to mind—often have presented to her readers very distorted impressions of her work and its philosophical dimension, assuming that because she read philosophy, it probably determined her books.

But George Eliot's wide acquaintance with various philosophers was as limited in its influence on her as it was powerful, a point not always fully taken by her interpreters. She was certainly influenced by German philosophy; she also commented that 'Germany yields more intellectual produce than it can use and pay for' (Essays, 298). Herbert Spencer's ideas, which she knew well, appealed to her but his universal systematizing did not. She had thorough understanding of *utilitarianism and *positivism, two major 19th-century philosophical movements with English gravitational centres; but she also expresses in her essays and letters clear and pronounced reservations about them, especially about positivism. Her investment in those movements has generally been overrated in direct proportion to the degree to which her other reading has been ignored—a

reading that did not particularly favour English sources and thus did not focus as interpreters have done on utilitarianism and positivism.

She shared the positivist scepticism about metaphysics and admired the influential French positivist Comte; his thoroughgoing English disciples the *Congreves and Frederic *Harrison were her lifelong friends; but she disagreed openly with them about positivist views and she saw Comte's limitations. He was a great enough thinker to be 'treated with reverence by all smaller fry', but to her was also decidedly 'one sided' (L iii. 439). Again, she shared utilitarianism's emphasis on consequences and on collective responsibility, and she admired John Stuart Mill's work and was a close friend of Herbert Spencer, but she was not a utilitarian and found problems with some of its political positions. She edited the *Westminster Review which had been earlier edited by John Stuart Mill and which she later helped revive with great success.

But while her reading and personal associations engaged her with the thought of positivism and utilitarianism, her ideas about social identity and individual freedom were even more influenced by philosophers who had considerably less attention in English than Comte and Mill: philosophers like Spinoza, whose Ethics she translated into English; like D. F. *Strauss and Feuerbach whose interventions in German theology known as the Higher Criticism radically historicized Christian texts and traditions (see TRANSLATIONS BY GEORGE ELIOT).

Feuerbach's text especially, which she translated and published by choice, not by assignment, remains the single most important external source for understanding George Eliot's writing. The radical historicizing of dogmatic truth to be found there is an impulse to be found everywhere in George Eliot's work. Spinoza and Feuerbach suited more closely than Hegel or Comte her scepticism about universal systematizers. She had been one such systematizer herself when little more than a child, and she left that behind with other childhood things.

Whether or not she informed herself about it or sympathized with its exponents, what ultimately she objected to in any belief system—whether positivism, or Catholicism, or utilitarianism, or Zionism—was its elevation of finite principles into universal dogma. In the mixed and entangled affairs of human culture, never to resist the inevitable, but instead to work wholeheartedly for some possible better: this, she said, was the only 'brief heading that need never be changed' (L iv. 499).

Because George Eliot's philosophical intelligence was integrated with her artist's intelligence, and because of the breadth of her knowledge, she anticipated philosophical problems that reached their full formulation long after her day. She looks forward to various 20th-century philosophers most particularly in her insistence on the indissoluble bond between ideas and things. This insistence permeates her novels, and is summarized succinctly in a review on 'The *Future of German Philosophy' (1855), where she comments on an argument she is reviewing in terms that invoke a critique of the entire tradition of Western philosophy: the severing of *ideas* from *things* is the fundamental error of philosophy, and, from Parmenides downwards, has issued in nothing but the bewilderment of the human intellect. She particularly mentions Kant's elaborations of this fundamental error. 'These abstract terms on which speculation has built its huge fabrics are simply the *x* and *y* by which we mark the boundary of our knowledge; they have no value except in connexion with the concrete. The abstract is derived from the concrete: what, then, can we expect from a philosophy the essence of which is the derivation of the concrete from the abstract (*Essays*, 150–1)?' The spirit of this passage exists everywhere in her fiction, where she explores in various ways the importance of recognizing that ideas only exist incarnate, worked by human intention into some material or other.

Because of this intimacy between object and intention, there is no such thing, humanly speaking, as a dissociated world of objects because all objects appear to us in terms of one language or another. What they may be, apart from those measurements, remains impenetrably mysterious. In short, she criticizes Western philosophy from Parmenides to Kant for fostering objectifications that result in giving opportunity to dogmatists.

The inseparability of ideas and things for George Eliot has nothing to do with the thought that everything is subjective. The 'hard, unaccommodating Actual' (*DD* 33) is actual enough; but that actuality is, to use 20th-century phenomenology's much later phrase, intentional. Eliot turned from writing essays to writing novels precisely because she believed that there are no such things as ideas without concrete expression. Ideas do not exist in a Platonic Elsewhere but instead in expression—in language, in wood and stone, in cultural traditions and institutions, in individual personalities and lives. This implies, and her novels reveal, a very radical view of the possibilities for the objectified world of empirical science and philosophy. For her, objects only exist in human formulation; to notice them at all is to incorporate them into a linguistic universe, what she called 'the realm of light and speech'. The inseparability of ideas and things, in short, means that ideas are incarnate, and objects are intentional.

The other forward-looking philosophical formulation that resonates through George Eliot's work comes from her translation of Feuerbach, *The Essence of Christianity*: doubtless the essence of man is *one*, but this essence is infinite; its real existence is therefore an infinite, reciprocally compensating variety, which reveals the riches of this essence. Unity in essence is multiplicity in existence (*Essence*, pt. 1, ch. 16). The language and the issues are not far from those found in Jean-Paul Sartre, Albert Camus, and the existentialist philosophers of a century later. Such thinking permeates Feuerbach's text, and George Eliot's English resolves them in a way particularly suggestive of future directions in philosophy. The same could be said of her insistence on the reduction of dualistic separations between ideas and things, mind and matter, subject and object. But without pursuing the deconstructive valences of these insights, it can be said that George Eliot has substantial responsibility for dissemination in English of a philosophical ferment that was already alive in her day and that is in many ways still under way.

Her work especially anticipates the emphasis on *language, characteristic of 20th-century poststructuralism where language becomes a model for all systems of usage, whether it be fashion, politics, or interpersonal relationships. Inspired in part by Ferdinand de Saussure these ideas have been developed by philosophers such as Jacques Derrida, whose work demonstrates how language as a model for coded practice has invaded 'the universal problematic', and Jean-François Lyotard who has christened the intractable difference between such coded systems as 'the differend'. It is precisely this emphasis on language that enables George Eliot to formulate in a similar way the problems of social and cultural relationship. Certainly Eliot's lifelong interest in language—in addition to her beloved English she read and used Italian, German, Latin, French, Hebrew, and Greek (see LANGUAGES)—is fundamental to her understanding of the world.

As a thoroughly modern philologist, George Eliot is able to show in her work how languages, and the coded systems of belief and value that operate like language, create the conditions of intelligibility, the foundational preparations for expression, that determine possible perception and speech. Her emphasis on the empowering but discrete ways that such systems operate has affinities with Lyotard's concept of 'the differend': the intractable difference requiring negotiation that lies at the heart of our contemporary politics. What is at stake between them is whether the constructed world is one or many: whether the grammatical differences between systems can be mediated, perhaps according to a common grammar of some kind, or whether their differences are absolute and unmediatable and thus require some other form of negotiation.

But while George Eliot can formulate the post-modern problem, and while she self-consciously pushes cultural relativism close to its limits, she finally insists in her work that all limited languages share a common world. Mediation of a kind that sustains a common world may be difficult; it may be hampered by traditional usage and prejudice; but mediation is possible. These philosophical problems materialize in her narratives, where she continually forces her readers from one value system to another, one private centre of interest to another, in a highly achieved narrative medium that provides an outside to every inside, a contextualizing margin to every system. See also LANGUAGE.   EDE

Ermarth, Elizabeth Deeds, 'George Eliot and the World as Language', in Rignall (1997).
Feuerbach, Ludwig Andreas, *The Essence of Christianity*, trans. Mary Ann Evans (George Eliot) (1854).
Lyotard, Jean-François, *The Differend: Phrases in Dispute*, trans. Georges van den Abbeele (1988).
Spinoza, Benedict de, *Ethics* (*Opera Posthuma*, 1677), trans. George Eliot (1854–6); 1st pub. edn. by Thomas Deegan (1981).

phrenology. Developed by the Viennese physician Franz Joseph Gall (1757–1828), the science of phrenology was introduced to Britain at the turn of the century, and became popular in the ensuing decades through public lectures and publications by practitioners, notably J. G. Spurzheim (1776–1832) and George *Combe, with whom George Eliot was acquainted. Phrenology held that, rather than a homogeneous organ, the brain was the composite of mental organs, each one controlling a different aspect of a person's physical, moral, and intellectual being. Organized topographically, and discernible from the contours of the skull, the relative size of each component was an index of its power, so that a reading of character was possible from the shape of the head and face. Phrenology has an important place in the development of a modern understanding of psychology, principally in its identification of the brain as the organ of the mind, refuting previous explanations which emphasized the influence of an immaterial and external principle (such as God) in the causation of mental effects. Moreover, as Cooter points out, in the mid-19th century, phrenology was 'an important vehicle of liberal ideology, helping to effect major reforms in penology, education, and the treatment of the insane' (5).

George Eliot's first recorded interest in phrenology is found in her correspondence with Maria *Lewis in 1838. Later, through Charles *Bray, who had lectured on phrenology in Coventry in 1836,

Eliot met leading phrenologists of the time: Cornelius Donovan (1820–72), who gave her instruction in February 1844, and James Deville (1777–1846), who, also in 1844, made a cast of her head. Through Bray, she met Combe who wrote of her phrenological profile:

She has a very large brain, the anterior lobe is remarkable for length . . . ; the base is broad at Destruc[tiveness]; but moderate at Aliment[iveness], and the portion behind the ear is rather small in the regions of Comb[ativeness] Amat[iveness] and Philopro[genitiveness]. Love of approb[ation], and Concentrativeness are large. (*L* viii. 27)

Phrenological readings of Eliot by her contemporaries have been used in the 20th century as a source of biographical information—surprisingly, given current scepticism regarding such methods. A case in point is Gordon S. *Haight's use of Bray's tendentious phrenological interpretation, that she always 'requir[ed] some one to lean upon', preferring . . . the stronger sex to the other' and that 'she was not fitted to stand alone' (1968: 51), as the organizing principle of his biography.

In her novels, Eliot often uses phrenological descriptions of facial features to convey character. In *Adam Bede*, for instance, a phrenological vocabulary is adopted to describe Seth's 'coronal arch' (*AB* 5), and Dinah's 'low perpendicular brow' (*AB* 30). Latterly, however, Eliot distanced herself from the claims of phrenology to a scientific assessment of character—what G. H. *Lewes scathingly calls the 'art of cranioscopy'(*L* ii. 210). For Eliot, as for Lewes, the importance of phrenology was its underlining of the material basis of mind. This insight is central to Eliot's realist technique in presenting complex psychological states through material *metaphors or analogues, and is explored most extensively in *Daniel Deronda*. See also REALISM; SCIENCE.   JM

Cooter, Roger, *The Cultural Meaning of Popular Science: Phrenology and the Organisation of Consent in Nineteenth-Century Britain* (1984).
Feltes, N. N., 'Phrenology from Lewes to George Eliot', *Studies in the Literary Imagination*, 1 (1968).
Postlethwaite, D., *Making it Whole: A Victorian Circle and the Shape of their World* (1984).
Witemeyer (1979).

Physiology of Common Life, The (1859–60). This work by G. H. *Lewes extended his investigation of the natural world begun in *Sea-Side Studies*, while its focus on the human body and mind foreshadowed his later work. The *Physiology* was popular with students for its liveliness and accessibility and attained an international reputation, as illustrated by the reference to it in Dostoevsky's *Crime and Punishment* (ch. 2).

NEH

piano. George Eliot's first piano lessons were from William McEwan (1840?–65), the organist of Hinckley parish church. She was considered to be the most outstanding pianist among the pupils at the Misses Franklin's school in Coventry, although playing to visitors tormented her. Throughout her adult life, however, she played willingly for G. H. *Lewes, for his family, and for friends, and was a ready accompanist.

For George Eliot, to have a piano was a necessity. She hired one for her own use while staying with the *D'Albert Durades in *Geneva, and, upon arriving at John *Chapman's establishment in the Strand in January 1851, immediately hired one for her room. After she had incensed both Chapman's wife and mistress by giving him a private Mozart recital, a second, household piano was hired. A new grand piano which George Eliot had chosen with care in 1861 was initially enjoyed after its delivery on 3 October as 'a great, great pleasure' (*L* iii. 456). Later George Eliot became dissatisfied with its 'touch', and complained to Charles Lee Lewes (see LEWES FAMILY)—with whom she often played duets—that it was 'a piano on which it is impossible to play delicately' (*L* iv. 30). Charles's own talent was nurtured with the 'privilege' (*L* iii. 404) of lessons from the pianist and composer Henry Brindley Richards (1819–85).

George Eliot greatly admired *Liszt's manner of playing. 'For the first time in my life I beheld real inspiration—for the first time in my life I heard the true tones of the piano', she wrote in 1854 after watching and hearing him in *Weimar (*Journals*, 21). She also admired Clara *Schumann. Her fictive pianists include Maggie Tulliver and Lucy Deane in *The Mill on the Floss*; Rosamond Vincy in *Middlemarch*; and Herr Klesmer, Catherine Arrowpoint, and Gwendolen Harleth in *Daniel Deronda*.

George Eliot's Broadwood grand piano, on which recitals are still occasionally given, is on permanent display in the Museum and Art Gallery, *Nuneaton. BG

Piatti, Alfredo Carlo (1822–1901), celebrated Italian virtuoso cellist and composer of cello music, and associate of Joseph *Joachim. George Eliot and G. H. *Lewes, who often heard him in London, admired him, and were particularly disappointed by his absence from a concert of chamber music in February 1869 (*Journals*, 134). See also MUSIC. BG

Plato (*c*.429–347 BC), Greek philosopher whose work formed part of George Eliot's extensive reading, though it appears not to have appealed to her strongly. When staying with George *Combe in Edinburgh in 1852, she remarked rather acidly that, although there were many visitors and much conversation at the Combes', her host's interlocutors had little to do but 'shape elegant modes of negation and affirmation like the people who are talked to by Socrates in Plato's dialogues' (*L* ii. 59). The following year she observed in a letter to Combe that the idea of Plato and others that immortality was the destiny of the worthy was very fascinating, but it seemed to her rather 'the hallucination of an intense personality' than an idea with any foundation in reason (*L* viii. 70). In 1861 she discussed Plato and *Aristotle with G. H. *Lewes while walking on Primrose Hill (*Journals*, 98), and in 1869 and 1879 she was reading the *Republic*. JMR

poetry of George Eliot. Most people who have read George Eliot's novels have also read her poetry, albeit without realizing. Many of the epigraphs which serve as chapter headings in her novels *Felix Holt, the Radical*, *Middlemarch*, and *Daniel Deronda* are poetic fragments composed by George Eliot herself. It is a curious strategy. The *epigraphs serve both as a clue to what will follow in each chapter, and as an alternative, often ironic, commentary on what has gone before—depending on whether you read them before, or after, or even refer to them during, the reading of a chapter. The mixture of 'real' quotations borrowed from *Shakespeare, *Wordsworth, and the *Bible, as well as many other sources, put alongside the 'made up' quotations which are George Eliot's own, means that Eliot makes herself into one of the sages whose word is a form of law, a yardstick for moral reading and thinking. In a similar way George Eliot's poetry functions as a parallel text to the novels; many of the same concerns and themes are taken up there, and quite often a poetic text, composed at about the same time as a novel, will reflect and enlarge upon the prose. This is nowhere more obvious than in the case of the verse drama 'Armgart' which was written while George Eliot was working on *Middlemarch*, but there are other cases too.

Eliot published only two volumes of verse in her lifetime. *The Spanish Gypsy* in 1868, and *The Legend of Jubal and Other Poems* in 1874 (reissued with some additional poems under the title of *The Legend of Jubal and Other Poems, Old and New* in 1878). Otherwise her poetry was published in magazines such as *Blackwood's Edinburgh Magazine* or *Macmillan's*. Some fragments were left unpublished, and are to be found in extant letters or jotted down in her working notebooks. Angela Leighton has described the poetry as 'essentially the work of a novelist on leave' (Leighton and Reynolds, 221) and though this may be true, George Eliot does use her holiday in order to play very seriously.

The earliest of George Eliot's poems that we have today were written in *letters to friends, and date from the late 1830s to 1840s. They are largely derivative in sentiment and style and borrow, as one might expect, from her predecessors such as *Keats and Wordsworth. That said, there are elements which connect the character of these poems to those of her contemporaries: the 'Sonnet; Oft, when a child, while wand'ring far alone' sounds like the expressions of a desired freedom from social constriction to be found in the work of Elizabeth Barrett *Browning or Charlotte *Brontë; and her poem 'Question and Answer' uses the form of the catechism in much the same playful way as Christina Rossetti. Not that there is any question of debt or influence. Rather, this suggests a shared set of formulas and themes which were learned by all the Victorian women poets from their reading, especially, of the many annuals and album books designed for a female readership—an audience which certainly included George Eliot given her close knowledge of *The Keepsake* for 1832 which she discusses in *Middlemarch* chapter 27, even if she did complain in 'The *Natural History of German Life' (1856) about 'the effeminate feebleness of the "Keepsake" style' (*Essays*, 268). As far as one can tell—and many notebooks and letters for this period may have been destroyed—George Eliot did not start writing poetry again until the 1860s. When she does, her tone and subjects are all her own. By this time she was an established writer of fiction, able to command large advances and a sizeable audience. In a curious poem 'A Minor Prophet' which also happens to be very funny, Eliot relates the story of a 'friend', a 'vegetarian seer, I By name Elias Baptist Butterworth, I A harmless, bland, disinterested man, I Whose ancestors in Cromwell's day believed I The second Advent certain in five years . . .'. Her account of Butterworth's belief in an interventionist amelioration of the world includes some amusing passages which imagine a nature purged of all carnivorous animals, as well as some intriguing defences of all the 'cheerful queernesses' of creation. The deformities and uglinesses of the world speak to her of toil and achievement, and are to be valued above ideals of beauty and utopian plans for their promise of gradual improvement: 'Presentiment of better things on earth I Sweeps in with every force that stirs our souls I To admiration, self-renouncing love, I Or thoughts, like light, that bind the world in one'. The progressist notions of development that inform George Eliot's earlier fictions are here in the contemporaneous poems too, in 'A Minor Prophet', 'Ex Oriente Lux', and, especially in 'O may I join the choir invisible' which construes a vision of a sceptic's heaven made out of separate souls striving individually and collectively toward harmony; 'So to live is heaven: I To make undying music in the world, I Breathing as beauteous order that controls I With growing sway the growing life of man'.

The connected web of images in this poem to do with poetry, *music, singing, breath, and self-expressiveness is a recurring theme which is particularly notable in George Eliot's poetry. Of course it is there in the fiction too, in Eliot's numerous pictures of singers (Caterina, Rosamond, Gwendolen) and performers (Dinah, Alcharisi), but even a rapid glance through Eliot's poetry titles shows how fertile a theme this was for her: 'The Legend of Jubal' tells the myth of how Jubal invented the lyre, in 'How Lisa Loved the King' she asks a minstrel to set a poem about her love in order to bring it to the king's attention, the heroine of 'Armgart' is an opera singer, 'Stradivarius' is about the power of the master-craftsman's violins, 'Arion' and 'Erinna' both tell stories of classical poet-singers, and in *The Spanish Gypsy* her heroine is admired and praised by the poet Juan. As so often in George Eliot's poetry, it is as if she sets herself the hard questions here, and if she sometimes allows herself the pleasure of an optimistic fantasy in her poetry ('the novelist on leave') she often also comes to more severe, more despairing conclusions. Her Romantic insistence upon the power of 'singing' reads it as a contribution to a shared cultural life which connects rich and poor ('How Lisa Loved the King' and *The Spanish Gypsy*), which civilizes barbarian robbers ('Arion'), which unites whole nations ('The Legend of Jubal'), and which improves man's nature: 'That is your way of singing, Agatha; I Just as the nightingales pour forth sad songs, I And when they reach men's ears they make men's hearts I Feel the more kindly' ('Agatha'). Isobel Armstrong has suggested that George Eliot's poetry, and George Eliot's idea of poetry, proposes a new humanist myth of how self and society are constructed, and one, moreover, which privileges the 'expressive' literary mode which is frequently associated with the feminine, and often derogated as such (372). But if her poetry, 'singing', can promote a collective unity, typically in George Eliot the individual life still is subject to pressures which deny personal cohesion and fulfilment. In 'The Legend of Jubal', for instance, Jubal invents the lyre and a range of songs which are taken up and sung by all the people. Tired of hearing these repetitions of himself, Jubal leaves his country to seek new inspiration. After aeons he returns, to find that his name is worshipped as the god and father of singing, and he is celebrated with festival and ritual. Looking for an ecstatic welcome, he announces himself as Jubal; but the people attack him for profanation, beat him, and leave him for dead. His 'Past' appears before him: 'This was thy lot, to feel, create, bestow, I And that immeasureable life to know I From which the fleshly self falls shrivelled, dead, I A seed primeval that has forests bred.'

The double pull of George Eliot's poetry, toward optimistic resolution and harsh scepticism, is nowhere so apparent as in her handling of 'the *woman question'. In the early days of modern feminist criticism (see CRITICISM, MODERN: FEMINIST APPROACHES) George Eliot was often seen as an anomaly whose ambivalent political positioning meant that she could not be paraded as a worthy proto-feminist. The fact that she lived out, in private, the radical existence of an independent woman both sexually and intellectually, could not be squared with the fact that, in her novels, women's lives are often given conventional 19th-century conclusions; Dorothea dwindles into a wife and mother; Dinah gives up preaching. It is in her poetry, however, once again a form where she seems to have felt herself freer and where she could be more experimental, that George Eliot most fully works out her thinking on sexual politics. Questions to do with the construction of *gender and the conventions of contemporary sexual difference dominate in the poetry to be closely followed with related questions of *race and identity.

The sonnet sequence 'Brother and Sister' is one of the texts which deals with these issues. This is a series of poems which is often read very simply as a parallel text to *The Mill on the Floss*, or else as a parable about Eliot's own relationship with her brother Isaac (see EVANS, ISAAC). It is both of these of course, but much more too. The very fact that it is a sonnet sequence positions it interestingly for it invokes the tradition of courtly love where the male poet speaks in praise of his beloved—a tradition which had memorably been revised only lately by one of Eliot's contemporaries, Elizabeth Barrett Browning in 'Sonnets from the Portuguese' (1850), and which was soon to be challenged again in Christina Rossetti's 'Monna Innominata' (1881). Eliot's 'Brother and Sister' similarly perverts the model. It is a love poem spoken by a woman to a man and it complains. While the landscape of this childhood world is another Eden, events here are transmuted and translated: brother takes the role of God or Adam who knows and names the 'snakes and birds', whose 'knowledge marked the boundary I Where men grew blind', who plucked 'The fruit that hung on high beyond my reach'. Under the rule of her conventional mother and her conventional brother, the 'little sister' in this poem must 'keep the trodden ways', while he must 'employ I A measuring glance to guide my tiny shoe'. And yet, all the time, the sister-narrator here disturbs the untroubled surface of her poem by reading beyond this idyllic

landscape, by seeing the copse 'where wild things rushed', by knowing about the 'abode I Of mystic gypsies, who still lurked between I Me and the hidden distance of the road', by watching the barges which come from 'some Unknown beyond it, whither flew I The parting cuckoo toward a fresh spring time'. In the end, the sister herself is the 'cuckoo' who flies from the nest to which she does not belong. But not before she has taken from this restrictive world a punning 'text' ('Those long days measured by my little feet I Had chronicles which yield me many a text') which stands her in good stead—and which literally does so, if one thinks of *The Mill on the Floss* as that textual result—and a 'silver perch', the fish which she manages to catch while doing what she should not have been doing, daydreaming, as any writer of fiction must always dream. Even the pious end of the sequence has its subversive side. 'But were another childhood-world my share, I I would be born a little sister there.' Does it mean that she would actively like to play the role of the little sister? or does it mean that, unfortunately, she will inevitably be treated as the little sister because that is indeed 'the woman's lot'?

Social conditioning and cultural expectations are the themes of George Eliot's two most ambitious and wide-ranging poems, *The Spanish Gypsy* and 'Armgart'. *The Spanish Gypsy* is an epic narrative drama set in 15th-century Spain. Eliot originally began this work in the winter of 1864 and 1865. She took it very seriously and spent much effort in researching the background, as she had done when creating her novel *Romola* (set in Girolamo *Savonarola's *Florence) some four years earlier. The exotic and far-off setting of *The Spanish Gypsy* links it with the work of her predecessors and contemporaries among the women poets who regularly used foreign settings to explore oppositions of gendered stereotypes in terms of a 'masculine' north and a 'feminine' south. Letitia Elizabeth Landon's *The Improvisatrice* (1842) and *The Venetian Bracelet* (1829) are two such works, as is Elizabeth Barrett Browning's *Aurora Leigh* (1857), a work which George Eliot read at least three times and which she admired greatly. In 1868 after a visit to *Spain Eliot revised and enlarged *The Spanish Gypsy* for publication.

Fedalma is, or might be, the Spanish Gypsy of the title. She is a foundling who has been brought up by the noble mother of Don Silva. Silva is fighting a holy war against the Moors at the instigation of the Inquisition represented at Silva's court by the intolerant Father Isidor. The scene begins in a tavern where the common people are discussing the news that the war is to cease for a brief while so that Silva can marry Fedalma. The priests are against this marriage because she is a foundling, but also because there is an unaccountable strangeness and independence about her. The poet Juan defends her. Fedalma loves Don Silva but she craves a look at the world before she has to perform the great lady as Silva's wife and descends into the city square where she is irresistibly drawn to the music, and she dances before all the people. This dance, like Jubal's lyre, like Armgart's singing, represents a race-memory which goes back to Miriam, to Troy, to Eden: 'a soft undertone I And resonance exquisite from the grand chord I Of her harmoniously bodied soul'. At this moment Fedalma is recognized by Zarca, the outlawed gypsy leader who is led across the square in chains. He reveals himself to Fedalma as her father, and demands that she gives up her happy ordinary woman's fate of marriage and become the leader, the mother to her oppressed people. Which is, eventually, what she does, leading the gypsies into Africa to found a new race allied with the Moors, the enemy of Spain, the country that had raised her.

Fedalma struggles throughout to establish an identity when outside pressures consistently undercut or thwart her. The overlap between the concerns of the poems and Eliot's novels is clear; she uses two passages from an early draft of *The Spanish Gypsy* as chapter epigraphs in *Felix Holt* (*FH* 44, 45) while the epigraph to the Epilogue of that novel consists of lines that appear in her poem 'A Minor Prophet'. Fedalma also has a 'jewel scene' which is reminiscent of Dorothea's in *Middlemarch*, chapter 1. But the paradox is that Fedalma's apparently externalized social pressures are actually inside; they are to do with her race, her inheritance, her birth, much as Daniel Deronda is shaped by his unknown heritage. George Eliot's preoccupations with foundlings or adopted children suggest how, increasingly in her later work, she came to question any consoling humanist theory of a fully integrated and consistent identity. In *The Spanish Gypsy* everything is in flux; the title is a paradox, for there can be no such thing as an outcast gypsy who is also pure Spanish; and Zarca, in any case, has as much right to the title (or as little) as Fedalma herself.

In 'Armgart' Eliot takes up a similar theme. The title is Armgart's name, just the surname, and means, therefore, her working name, the single name which expresses her role as a great opera singer. In fact of course, by the end of the poem, Armgart is Armgart no more because she has lost her voice and been forced to retire. Actually, Armgart always had been someone else. As the first scene of the verse drama opens, the directions state that the room is dominated by two pillars bearing busts of *Gluck and *Beethoven. Armgart, we learn, is performing in Gluck's opera *Or-pheus and Eurydice* that night, and she triumphs. Toward the end of the verse drama we hear Armgart regret that the singer Paulina will take over Armgart's role in Beethoven's *Fidelio*. George Eliot was a keen musician (see MUSIC) and knew her opera, and Armgart's roles seem to have been carefully chosen. Both of them, Orpheus and Fidelio, are cross-dressing roles though in different senses, since Orpheus is a male role while Fidelio is a woman masquerading as a man. Because of her great gift, Armgart is privileged to be different from other women: 'I need not crush myself within a mould I Of theory called Nature: I have room I To breathe and grow unstunted'. Like Barrett Browning's Aurora Leigh (on whom she was certainly modelled) Armgart refuses marriage to a man who would have her give up her singing. Then she becomes ill; the doctor succeeds in saving her life, but fails to save her voice. Armgart is miserably full of self-pity until her cousin Walpurga, who is, interestingly, lame, and who had selflessly looked after Armgart, takes her to task. Armgart complains because now she is nothing: 'I read my lot I As soberly as if it were a tale I Writ by a creeping feuilletonist and called I "The Woman's Lot: a Tale of Everyday:" I A middling woman's, to impress the world I With high superfluousness . . .'. But Walpurga points out that Armgart has no right to difference: 'Where is the rebel's right for you alone? I Noble rebellion lifts a common load; I And what is he that lifts his own load off I And leaves his fellows toiling? Rebel's right? I Say rather, the deserter's.' In a very modern avowal of sisterhood, Armgart resolves to move back to the provincial town Walpurga had left for her sake, and to hand on her gift by teaching singing. Set beside *Middlemarch* it is an interesting commentary on the novel.

George Eliot's always ambivalent attitude to poetry, indeed to writing, is summed up in two contrasting poems from a notebook now at Yale. One is a sceptic's poem: 'I grant you ample leave I To use the hoary formula "I am" I Naming the emptiness where thought is not. . . .' and which concludes that any amount of self-naming will not make the Ego into any more than a 'Being looking from the dark, I . . . That notes your bubble-world: sense, pleasure, pain, I What are they but a shifting otherness, I Phantasmal flux of moments?' The other is a poem called 'Erinna' and prefaced by the story of the classical poetess who went on singing though chained to her spinning wheel: 'Hark the passion in her eyes I Changes to melodic cries I Long she pours her lonely pain. I Song unheard is not in vain . . .'. Her poetry may provide a place for play, but George Eliot's story is still the same: not the singer, but the song. See also VOCATION.

MR

'Poetry and Prose from the Notebook of an Eccentric'

George Eliot: Collected Poems, ed. Lucien Jenkins (1989).

Leighton, Angela, and Reynolds, Margaret (edd.), Victorian Women Poets: An Anthology (1995).

—— (ed.) Victorian Women Poets: A Critical Reader (1996).

Armstrong, Isobel, Victorian Poetry: Poetry, Poetics and Politics (1993).

Beer (1986).

Blake, Kathleen, 'Armgart—George Eliot on the Woman Artist', Victorian Poetry, 18 (1980).

Bodenheimer, Rosmarie, 'Ambition and its Audiences: George Eliot's Performing Figures', Victorian Studies, 34 (1990).

Brown, Susan, 'Determined Heroines: George Eliot, Augusta Webster, and Closet Drama by Victorian Women', Victorian Poetry, 33 (1995).

'Poetry and Prose from the Notebook of an Eccentric' consists of five prose sketches, George Eliot's first published original writing except for the poem 'Farewell' in the Christian Observer (January 1840). They appeared in Charles *Bray's Coventry Herald and Observer at irregular intervals between 4 December 1846 and 19 February 1847 (repr. in Essays). The sketches test out different styles, and while the wisdom of hindsight shows in them motifs that were to be recurrent in George Eliot's work, they can hardly be said to give promise of a brilliant literary career. In her last published work, Impressions of Theophrastus Such (1879), she returned to the form of the moral essay delivered by a persona, in a symmetry that was presumably inadvertent.

The 'Introductory' essay gives the reflections of a mourner by the grave of his friend Macarthy, who has died in his early forties with his talents unrecognized. The standpoint is broadly humanist, and there is significant use of scientific imagery. The narrator has agreed to publish selections from the large trunk of manuscripts left by Macarthy. 'How to avoid disappointment' is an anecdote about an artist who devotes himself to the ideal of art and the production of works which embody the good, the true, and the beautiful. 'The Wisdom of the Child' argues that the simplicity and purity attributed to the child since Jean-Jacques *Rousseau are fully comprehended only by the philosopher who has profound understanding of the child's trust and self-renunciation. 'A little fable with a great moral' is a version of the myth of Narcissus, prefiguring in the tale of two Hamadryads characters such as Hetty Sorrel who are dangerously infatuated with their reflected image. 'Hints on Snubbing' is a satiric piece in Thackerayan vein. See also JOURNALIST, GEORGE ELIOT AS. MAH

politics. Towards the end of George Eliot's Life as Related in her Letters and Journals, John Walter

*Cross dwells on what he calls the catholicity of his wife's judgement and concludes that her wide sympathy and understanding of so many points of view made it difficult to ascertain what her exact relation was to any religious creed or to any political party. She did not consider any religious formula sufficient nor any known political system likely to be final. Instead, she 'had great hope, for the future, in the improvement of human nature by the gradual development of the affections and the sympathic emotions, and "by the slow stupendous teaching of the world's events"—rather than by means of legislative enactments' (Cross, new edn. 1886, 623–4).

Gordon S. *Haight's biography and edition of the *letters suggest otherwise. In his biography, Haight remarks on how Eliot's conservatism increased with age. For example, he notes her refusal in August 1865 to contribute to a fund for the Italian revolutionary Giuseppe *Mazzini. Although she had long admired Mazzini and would have been glad to help him personally, she was worried that the fund might be used to finance some form of conspiracy (see NATIONALISM). Haight also recalls a letter of 19 December 1868, in which Eliot congratulated Charles *Bray for his opposition to the introduction of secret ballots in elections, something the Chartists had called for as early as 1839 (Haight 1968: 99, 395). When secret ballots were eventually introduced in the 1874 election and William Gladstone's Liberals were defeated by Benjamin Disraeli's Conservatives, she wrote to Barbara *Bodichon, 'Do you mind about the Conservative majority? I don't'; and to John *Blackwood, 'I who am no believer in Salvation by Ballot, am rather tickled that the first experiment with it has turned against its adherents' (L vi. 14, 21–3). The entry for 26 December 1879 in Edith *Simcox's Autobiography offers still further evidence of Eliot's conservative thinking: 'She defended Disraeli vigorously—was "disgusted with the venom of the Liberal speeches from Gladstone downwards"; Dizzy was ambitious and no fool, "and so he must care for a place in history, and how could he expect to win by doing harm?" ' (Haight 1968: 533).

In fact, Cross and Haight are not very far apart in their assessments. Eliot's writing frequently argues that a strong sense of moral duty, based on feelings of sympathy and understanding, will lead towards a better future—and that doing one's moral duty more often than not involves subscribing to conservative measures. In that respect, she shared in some of the philosophical thinking of her age. Auguste *Comte for instance, whose writing she knew well, taught that the chief focus of a future positivist society would be on men's moral, not intellectual, natures. Eliot rejected his utopian and authoritarian philosophy but approved of his emphasis on the importance of the historical past shaping the nation state (see HISTORY).

The Second *Reform Act of 1867 added almost a million names to the voting lists, and in 'The *Address to Working Men, by Felix Holt', Eliot felt in duty bound to teach the newcomers their civic duties. Early on in the 'Address', Felix says that a better, radical future can only be achieved by conserving the old social order and ways of doing things—by exercising what critics sometimes call Eliot's radical conservatism.

Now the only safe way by which society can be steadily improved and our worst evils reduced, is not by any attempt to do away directly with the actual existing class distinctions and advantages, as if everybody could have the same sort of work, or lead the same sort of life (which none of my hearers are stupid enough to suppose), but by the turning of Class Interests into Class Functions or duties. (*Essays* 421)

If all do their duty, Felix adds, there should be no impunity for foolish or faithless conduct. If history teaches us anything, however, it is that not everyone will do his duty, and so we can safely rule out any utopian future. The best way forward, therefore, is to approach all political issues in 'the right temper, without vain expectation, and with a resolution which is mixed with temperance'.

A similar attitude informs Eliot's sexual politics (see WOMAN QUESTION). Eliot told John *Morley that mere zoological evolution has resulted in women having 'the worse share in existence'. We can and should do something about that by controlling our moral evolution, by exercising love in the largest sense. However,

The one conviction on the matter which I hold with some tenacity is, that through all transactions of goal towards which we are proceeding is a clear discerned distinction of function (allowing always for exceptional cases of individual organization) with as near an approach to equivalence of good for woman and for man as can be secured by the effort of growing moral force to lighten the pressure of hard non-moral outward conditions. (14 May 1867, L iv. 364–5)

In the words of the 'Address', the lot of women can be steadily improved, not by any attempt to do away with existing gender distinctions and advantages, but by turning such distinctions and advantages into gender functions or duties. However, the implications of her fiction are often more radical and questioning than the views she expressed in her letters and the 'Address' (see CRITICISM, MODERN: FEMINIST APPROACHES). See also CHARTISM; PROGRESS; REVOLUTIONS OF 1848; RADICALISM. AvdB

Eagleton, Mary, and Pierce, David, *Attitudes to Class in the English Novel* (1979).
Hindley, Charles Edward, '*Middlemarch*: Some Problems of Social and Political Focus', in Anita Weston and John McRae (edd.), *Middlemarch: Il romanzo* (1987).
Semmel (1994).

Pope, Alexander (1688–1744), English poet, not widely referred to by George Eliot. The first mention is in a letter to Maria *Lewis in 1839 where Eliot says that she is not writing on poor paper 'as the poet Pope would have done' (L i. 24), picking up on Jonathan *Swift's sneer at 'paper-sparing Pope'. A year later she defines the nature of contentment and the 'calm sunshine it sheds on the soul', which is loosely from the *Essay on Man* (1733, iv. 168). In 1852 she refers to John *Chapman's skill in 'the art of sinking', not in poetry, but in letter-writing (L ii. 51), a reference to Pope's 'Peri Bathous, or the Art of Sinking in Poetry'. In 'Mr Gilfil's Love-Story' she parodies 'The feast of reason and the flow of soul' (from *Satires, Epistles and Odes of Horace*) as 'the feast of gossip and the flow of grog'. In reference to a bad painter, she quotes, 'So vast is art, so narrow human wit' (from the *Essay in Criticism*), and there are two echoes of the *Essay on Man* in *Middlemarch* (MM 18, 43). GRH

portraits of George Eliot. There are a number of portrait drawings and one oil portrait from life of George Eliot. Among the earliest known portraits is a half-length watercolour of 1842 by Caroline *Bray, showing the novelist seated, and now in the National Portrait Gallery. A pencil drawing by the same artist and of the same date is in a private collection. There is a slightly later (c.1847) drawing of George Eliot in a hat by Sara *Hennell (1812–99) in a private collection. (A later hatless drawing by the same artist is dated to c.1867.) The one known oil is another half-length portrait, by the Swiss artist François *D'Albert Durade. Painted at the artist's request in 1849, it dates from the time George Eliot spent with his family in *Geneva. The original painting is in Coventry Library, and a replica of the same date is in the National Portrait Gallery.

Samuel *Laurence, an artist with a particular reputation for his chalk and crayon drawings of Victorian writers, asked permission to draw a head and shoulders' portrait in June 1860. George Eliot initially put him off, because she was about to travel abroad, but G. H. *Lewes promised that she would sit on her return. Reporting that her last sitting (Laurence had asked for six) was on 28 August, George Eliot declared that she would not go through the process again. When Laurence wanted to exhibit the portrait at the Royal Academy in 1861, George Eliot, on the advice of Lewes, refused permission for it to be shown outside Laurence's studio. Rejected by Lewes, the drawing was bought by John *Blackwood and is now in the British Museum. Another drawing, also showing the novelist full face, is at Girton College, Cambridge.

George Eliot's friend Frederic *Burton also asked to draw her, and his head and shoulder portrait of 1865 in the National Portrait Gallery is perhaps the best-known image. George Eliot began sitting on 29 June 1864 and a portrait drawing (presumably the same one) was completed on 22 July 1865. George Eliot liked the Burton portrait and gave permission for it to be exhibited at the Royal Academy and for reproductions to be made, although this did not apparently happen until after her death. A second version of the Burton portrait is in the Birmingham City Art Gallery and a third drawing is in a private collection. There is another drawing attributed to Burton in the British Museum, but it seems unlikely that George Eliot was the sitter.

Three drawings of George Eliot in later life are in the National Portrait Gallery. Laura Alma Tadema (1852–1909) made two pencil sketches of the novelist's head in profile, one in 1877 and the other at about the same date, and Lowes Cato Dickinson (1819–1908) is the artist of a strong profile drawing made at a concert in 1872. A similar sketch of 1877 (private collection) by Princess Louise (1849–1939) was also drawn at a concert. The *Punch* artist George Du Maurier (1834–96) made at least two pencil sketches of the older George Eliot on visits to The *Priory. It seems probable that most of these sketches were made without the sitter's knowledge.

George Eliot declared that she disliked photography, but there are a number of images of her. One of the earliest was taken by Sophus Williams at the Kunstverlag, *Berlin, presumably in 1855. John Edwin Mayall (1810–1901) at the London Stereoscopic Company took photographs of both George Eliot and G. H. Lewes in February 1858, and his image of George Eliot became the basis for an etching of 1884 by Paul Rajon (1843–88). Another photograph, taken in profile, is in the collection of Coventry City Libraries. See also AP-PEARANCE, PERSONAL.   LO

positivism, a philosophy of science and society, developed by Auguste *Comte, and a formative, much-debated influence on George Eliot's thinking and her work.

Comte's original system, published in the six-volume *Cours de philosophie positive* (1830–42), is relatively unproblematic. Comte divided history into three phases. The first—Theological—period was initially dominated by animist beliefs—

'Fetichism'—then by Polytheism, and finally by Monotheism, culminating in Catholicism. The Reformation initiated a Negative or Metaphysical period, in which supernatural agency was replaced by abstractions—'cause' in philosophy, phlogiston in chemistry, 'rights' in politics. This culminated in the French Revolution and the worship of Reason. The failure of the Revolution initiated the final—Positive—period: all aspects of reality, including society, would be scrutinized according to measurable and regular sequences rather than 'causes'; the principle of 'rights' would yield to that of duties, and Submission—to scientific and political authority and a new spiritual power—would be universal.

Each period was associated with corresponding developments in the moral and political spheres. As Reason replaced Feeling in thought, so Altruism replaced Egoism in action, the whole process being reproduced in the development of the individual—'the phases of the mind of a man correspond to the epochs of the mind of the race' (*Positive Philosophy*, trans. Martineau, i. 3). Simultaneously, social and gender relations reproduce the organization of the mind. So just as there are three mental powers, Feeling, Intellect, and Will, so there are three social classes, Workers, 'the Spiritual Power' (the intellectual and religious class), and Practical or governing Class. In ancient and feudal societies, the Practical Class was principally engaged in hunting and war; in modern society in industry and commerce. A practically minded boy, like Tom Tulliver, would typically be fascinated by hunting and war when passing through the personal equivalent of Polytheism and Monotheism, but would then turn his attention to business. However, the practical, masculine life stimulates Egotism, and needs to be subjected to the influence of the emotional and moral Altruism developed by women. As the bearers of spiritual and family values, women properly submit to male authority in practical matters, but exercise a decisive moral influence over their brothers, husbands, and sons. A typical girl also passes through 'the epochs of the mind of the race'. Again *The Mill on the Floss* illustrates the general picture. As a little girl Maggie has 'a fetish' in the form of her doll; later she reads the *Imitation of Christ*—Comte called Catholicism 'the religion of our adolescence' (*System*, iv. 20); in adulthood her religious feelings are absorbed into her aesthetic and particularly her musical life, though she still submits to the authority of 'the spiritual power' in the person of Dr Kenn. Comte, however, would have had doubts about Maggie, since he believed that women were 'constitutionally in a state of perpetual infancy', their 'more lively moral and physical sensibility' being 'hostile to scientific abstraction and concentration' (*Positive Philosophy*, trans. Martineau, ii. 135).

George Eliot seems to have respected the scientific principles of early positivism in all her prose writings except possibly 'The Lifted Veil' and *Daniel Deronda*, both of which treat of prevision and second sight. In the former, however, Latimer's mental state, particularly his mind-reading, suggests clinical paranoia, and there is disagreement about whether Mordecai's prevision in *Daniel Deronda* violates scientific principles, Knoepflmacher arguing that it does (*Religious Humanism and the Victorian Novel* (1965), 116–48), Myers that it is consistent with the evolutionary and associationist psychologies of Herbert *Spencer, Bain, and G. H. *Lewes (*The Teaching of George Eliot* (1984), 215–20).

More controversial is the influence of positivism as a formally constituted religious system—George Eliot and Lewes were hardly in a position to respect Comte's ban on second marriages—but the religious, moral, and even political ethos of the fiction and the poems is strongly if only implicitly positivist. Wishing to replace worship of God with that of Humanity, Comte decided that Humanity was best represented in the great images of the Virgin Mary, and it is as a visible madonna that Romola functions among the plague-stricken villagers after her flight from Florence. At another level, Felix Holt (both in the novel and in his 'Address to Working Men') seems implicitly to accept Comte's view that gradual extensions of the franchise were politically unsettling, that 'demogogues and sophists . . . alienated the working class from their natural industrial leaders' (the employers), while the latter were improperly coercing their workers (*Positive Philosophy*, trans. Martineau, ii. 454). Like Comte, Felix seems happy to leave government to conservatives—the party, according to Comte, 'endeavouring to reconcile order and progress' (*Appeal to Conservatives* (1889), 5)—confident in the efficacy of public opinion, as represented by a working class properly guided by leaders like himself, in effect the modern 'spiritual power', the spontaneous emergence of which Comte believed to be imminent.

Against this must be set Frederic *Harrison's judgement, as a positivist, that *The Spanish Gypsy* was 'treason to human life' (*L* iv. 485). Richard *Congreve, on the other hand, called it 'a mass of Positivism' (Haight 1968: 405). It certainly does not deny positivist insights and values, even if it does embody them in a marginalized, vulnerable people. George Eliot's interest in *race in later life may have modified or obscured the positivist orientation of her thinking: the *Judaism of *Daniel Deronda* is certainly not consistent with the Comtist religious system, but it *is* a *religion of

Humanity. An early anonymous commentator wrote of the ideas of Comte, Charles *Darwin, Lewes, and Spencer passing 'through the alembic of her mind' (*George Eliot Moralist and Thinker* (1884), 3), and it is perhaps most useful to see her positivism in such telling details as Silas Marner's 'fetichistic' affection for his companionable old pot, or Lydgate's failure to take up with the Saint-Simonians in Paris—Comte had been Saint-Simon's secretary, and could have saved Lydgate much fruitless research. See also PHILOSOPHY.

WM

Comte, A., *The Positive Philosophy of Auguste Comte* freely trans. and condensed by Harriet Martineau, 2 vols. (1853).
—— *System of Positive Polity*, 4 vols. (1875–7).
—— *Appeal to Conservatives* (1889).
Wright, T. R., 'George Eliot and Positivism: A Reassessment', *Modern Language Review*, 76 (1981).
—— *The Religion of Humanity: The Impact of Comtean Positivism on Victorian Britain* (1986).

postcolonial approaches. See CRITICISM, MODERN: POST-COLONIAL APPROACHES.

poverty and wealth. Portrayals of real poverty are rare, arguably absent, in George Eliot's fiction. Occasionally, she offers glimpses of significant financial hardships. For example, in *Adam Bede*, the 'rich undulating district of Loamshire to which Hayslope belonged' is compared with the 'grim outskirt of Stonyshire' where life is hard (*AB* 2); in *The Mill on the Floss*, the poor district of Basset is noted as are Mr and Mrs Moss hopelessly struggling to make ends meet (*MF* 1.8); and in *Middlemarch*, Dorothea draws attention to 'Kit Downes . . . who lives with his wife and seven children in a house with one sitting room and one bedroom hardly larger than this table!—and those poor Dagleys, in their tumble-down farmhouse, where they live in the back kitchen and leave the other rooms to the rats!' (*MM* 39). Often, however, Eliot's characters tend to misuse or otherwise exaggerate the meaning of poverty. Mr Tulliver accuses himself of bringing his wife and family to poverty when he loses ownership of the mill and its land, although he and his family are allowed to stay on (*MF* 3.8); Felix Holt looks forward to a life of poverty, which he expects will bring him great satisfaction (*FH* 27); and Dorothea turns her back on financial independence for genuine happiness with Ladislaw, crying, ' "I don't mind about poverty—I hate my wealth" ' (*MM* 83). The harrowing images of urban and agricultural poverty found in the novels of Charles *Dickens, Elizabeth *Gaskell, Charles *Kingsley, and Thomas *Hardy are not found in Eliot's. Eliot's poverty amounts to financial stress, not absolute horror, the sort experienced by, say, Jo the crossing-sweeper in

Dickens's *Bleak House*: 'Jo lives—that is to say, Jo has not yet died—in a ruinous place, known to the like of him by the name of Tom-all-alone's' (ch. 16).

The same is true of, Eliot's representations of wealth. In *Adam Bede*, Arthur Donnithorne is comfortably off, but not very rich; in *Felix Holt, the Radical*, Harold Transome's supposed fortune of £500,000 is, in fact, £150,000, with most of that tied up in mortgages; and in *Daniel Deronda* Grandcourt, who is potentially wealthy, is, in fact, heavily in debt. There are no fabulously wealthy people in Eliot's fiction like Dickens's Mr Merdle who is thought to be 'immensely rich; a man of prodigious enterprise; a Midas without the ears, who turned all he touched to gold. He was in everything good, from banking to building. He was in Parliament, of course. He was in the City, necessarily. He was Chairman of this, Trustee of that, President of the other' (*Little Dorrit*, ch. 21).

Eliot's instances of poverty and wealth remain largely in the backgrounds of her novels. They are not really used to shock readers into an awareness that the comfort of some is often paid for by the suffering of others. However, her deep concern with political reform in *Felix Holt, Middlemarch*, and the *'Address to Working Men, by Felix Holt' can be traced, in part, to Britain's growing wealth throughout the 19th century. Increased prosperity for many meant that more and more men were eligible to vote; and how to exercise the right to vote was of great concern to Eliot. *Felix Holt* was written with at least one eye on the pending Second *Reform Act of 1867. When that Act added nearly a million extra voters to the electoral lists, she wrote 'Address to Working Men, by Felix Holt' (1868) to reiterate what she saw were the obligations of the new, potential 'future masters': to respect the traditions she considered worth preserving. A reference to what she considered the potential dangers of too much reform too soon is also heard in *Middlemarch* when Ladislaw so impresses Mr Brooke with his thundering avalanche metaphor. ' "I don't want to change the balance of the constitution" ', says Mr Brooke, to which Ladislaw answers

'But that is what the country wants . . . Else there would be no meaning in political unions or any other movement that knows what it's about. It wants to have a House of Commons which is not weighted with nominees of the landed class, but with representatives of the other interests. And as to contending for a reform short of that, it is like asking for a bit of an avalanche which has already begun to thunder.' (*MM* 46)

The 'other interests' he has in mind are those who have benefited from the growing, industrial economy. See also CLASS; EARNINGS; MONEY AND DEBT; POLITICS; SOCIETY. AvdB

Prague, capital city of Bohemia in the Austro-Hungarian empire which George Eliot and G. H. *Lewes visited in July 1858 on their way from *Munich to *Dresden. She found it a grand old city and was particularly impressed by the Jewish cemetery, the Alter Friedhof, with its 'multitude of quaint tombs in all sort of positions looking like the fragments of a great building', and by the old synagogue 'with its blackened groins, and lamp for ever burning', where their Jewish guide read them some Hebrew out of the old book of the law (*Journals*, 324). They drove across the famous Nepomuk bridge with its avenue of statues and up to the castle, from where the view was, she declared, one of the most impressive in the world. Her account of the visit in her journals focuses mainly on buildings and the visible grandeur and antiquity of the city, and it is these features of Prague that figure in the fictional precipitate of the visit to be found in 'The Lifted Veil'. In Latimer's premonitory vision, triggered by his father's mention of the word Prague, the city appears in its 'dusty, weary, time-eaten grandeur' as a place arrested in the past, and one where the buildings and statues are more real than the present inhabitants. The tourist's impressions are recast in a dark and melancholy form:

The city looked so thirsty that the broad river seemed to me a sheet of metal; and the blackened statues, as I passed under their blank gaze, along the unending bridge, with their ancient garments and their saintly crowns, seemed to me the real inhabitants and owners of this place, while the busy, trivial men and women, hurrying to and fro, were a swarm of ephemeral visitants infesting it for a day. (LV 1)

And when Latimer eventually arrives in Prague and stands under 'the blackened, groined arches of that old synagogue' and listens to a Jewish guide reading Hebrew, he repeats his creator's experience but evaluates it with scathing negativity. This 'surviving withered remnant of medieval Judaism' represents 'a more shrivelled death-in-life' even than the statues of Christian saints. Prague, reworked by George Eliot's imagination in its darkest vein after the death of her sister Chrissey (see EVANS, CHRISTIANA), is not a grand old city but an arid wasteland where oppressive forms of outworn life linger on. JMR

Pre-Raphaelite Brotherhood. Founded in 1848 by a group of young artists and writers, the Pre-Raphaelite Brotherhood was the most forward-looking body in British art in the earlier part of George Eliot's career. Championed by John *Ruskin in 1851 for their pursuit of truth and accuracy in their painting, the Pre-Raphaelite painters had an immediate appeal for George Eliot. In 1852 she expressed regret that no one on the staff of the *Westminster Review was able to write a general article on the literature and art of the group and, in a review of Ruskin's *Lectures on Architecture and Painting* of 1854, Eliot praised the Pre-Raphaelites for beginning their careers with a precise transcription of nature. She became personally acquainted with two of the founder members, Dante Gabriel *Rossetti (whom she advised on Hamlet's phrenology) and Thomas Woolner (1825–92). She knew another member, William Holman Hunt (1827–1910), by 1864, but there are indications that the painter disapproved of her relationship with G. H. *Lewes and had previously refused to meet her.

Of the Pre-Raphaelite group, George Eliot was most impressed by the work of Hunt, although she had reservations about a number of his works and was unable to come to an overall conclusion about him. Although she spoke of him in terms of the highest praise, she seems not to have liked those individual paintings which she discussed. When she saw *The Hireling Shepherd* (Manchester City Art Galleries) in the Royal Academy of 1852, she was impressed by the truthfulness of the landscape background, but the representation of the shepherd and shepherdess annoyed her. To her eyes they were artistic rather than real peasants. She misread the painting, a satire on the distraction of the clergy through the religious controversies of the day, but it is improbable that she would have warmed to *The Hireling Shepherd* even had she been aware of its true subject. She was even more critical of Hunt's most famous work, *The Light of the World* (1854, Keble College, Oxford) and Ruskin's defence of the painting failed to remove her distaste for its Christian symbolism. She was again uneasy when, in 1864, she saw a very different Hunt painting, *The Afterglow in Egypt* (Southampton Art Gallery). Here the hard work and the accurate rendering of certain details were commended, but she concluded that the painting lacked either inspiration or overall coherence. *Isabella and the Pot of Basil* (1868, Laing Art Gallery, Newcastle-upon-Tyne) struck her favourably, but in this case she gives no details of her reactions.

George Eliot apparently found the work of another of the founding Pre-Raphaelites, John Everett *Millais, easier to enjoy than that of Hunt. In 1852, she expressed considerable enthusiasm for Millais's *A Huguenot on Bartholomew's Day* (private collection), which she saw in the Royal Academy exhibition. It may be significant that this was a painting in which many felt that Millais was abandoning his Pre-Raphaelite principles.

From 1861 she was friendly with Edward *Burne-Jones, one of the second wave of Pre-Raphaelite painters. She regarded Burne-Jones as a great painter, and the letter which she wrote to him in 1873, after a visit to his studio, speaks of his work with the warmest praise. She thanked him for his gift, not only to herself, but to humanity as a whole. Noting the sadness of much of his work, she declared that she found an innate sense of sweetness and beauty in his paintings. These things, she told Burne-Jones, were the outward signs of a noble mind (*L* v. 390–1).

George Eliot's statements on the work of the Pre-Raphaelite group are entirely appropriate to the history of the movement. She began by writing of them as part of an exciting new trend, and by concentrating on the work of Hunt, arguably the member who most closely obeyed the rules of the brotherhood. Very shortly, however, she began to think of the painters separately, and to judge Pre-Raphaelite works on an individual basis. Her response to the work of Burne-Jones suggests that she had, at least by 1873, become less concerned with realism and more open to concepts of symbolism and mood creation. See also VISUAL ARTS.

LO

Murdoch, John, 'George Eliot and the Pre-Raphaelites', *Journal of the Warburg and Courtauld Institutes*, 37 (1974).
Witemeyer (1979).

Priory, The. This was the name of the house at 21 North Bank, Regent's Park, which George Eliot and G. H. *Lewes purchased on 21 August 1863, paying £2,000 for a 49-year lease. After the house had been modernized and decorated at considerable expense by the interior designer Owen Jones, the couple moved in on 5 November 1863. It was to be the novelist's principal home until the last months of her life, and it was here that she and Lewes held their Sunday afternoon receptions for friends and admirers. One friend, Charles *Dickens, referred facetiously to attending service at The Priory in a letter to Lewes, and Henry *James recalled 'a kind of sanctity in the place, an atmosphere of stillness and concentration, something that suggested a literary temple' (*CH* 502). However, another American visitor, Charles Eliot Norton, while finding the drawing rooms pleasant and cheerful, criticized nearly all the works of art in the house as revealing a lack of artistic feeling (Haight 1968: 410).

JMR

Problems of Life and Mind (1874–9), G. H. *Lewes's ambitious attempt to reconcile metaphysics and the positive sciences by delimiting the formal fields of physiology and psychology, is important to George Eliot's life and writing because of her own interest in 19th-century science, and also because it was she who sorted through

An engraving in Cross's *Life* of the drawing room at The Priory, where George Eliot and G. H. Lewes received guests and admirers at their Sunday receptions from 1863 to 1878.

Lewes's notes and unfinished manuscripts to complete the last two volumes after his death.

Problems contains three series in five volumes: *The Foundations of a Creed* (vols. i–ii, 1874–5), *The Physical Basis of Mind* (vol. iii, 1877), and *The Study of Psychology* (vols. iv–v, 1879). It represents Lewes's attempt to break from his role as a popularizer of the philosophic and scientific ideas of others, and to make his own original contribution to science. As a whole, the work is prescient in its attempt to show the inextricability of mind and body and the importance of the social 'medium' or 'General Mind', in shaping both. Throughout the 1870s, Lewes incorporated, responded to, and elaborated on the scientific theories of his contemporaries, including Herbert *Spencer and Charles *Darwin. Lewes had several disadvantages compared to many of those whose work he engaged and whose respect he sought: he had no university education, no laboratory of his own, and his health was declining. Eliot showed great concern for the reception of his work and for his reputation as she revised the final volumes, and indeed, *Problems* never received the recognition she and Lewes thought it deserved as a contribution to contemporary science. Opinion is divided on its value now, and the argument has yet to be made for its role as an original contribution in the history of science. See also DARWINISM; SCIENCE.   NEH

Collins, K. K., 'George Henry Lewes Revised: George Eliot and the Moral Sense', *Victorian Studies*, 21 (1978).

—— 'Reading George Eliot Reading Lewes's Obituaries', *Modern Philology*, 85 (1987).

Voegler, Martha, 'George Eliot as Literary Widow', *Huntington Library Quarterly*, 51 (1988).

progress, idea of. George Eliot held broadly to a belief in progress, in 'the onward tendency of human things' (*MF* 4.1) and 'the growing good of the world' (*MM* Finale). In 1877 she described herself as a 'meliorist' (*L* vi. 333–4), one who believes in the possibility of improving the world through properly directed human effort. She thought that she had coined the term herself, though the *OED* lists an earlier usage. But her belief in progress is always a qualified one, and from her earliest fiction she turns her *irony against complacent assumptions that the present is necessarily superior to the past, sardonically claiming in 'Janet's Repentance' that 'Milby is now a refined, moral, and enlightened town', whilst describing signs of progress that are merely material and superficial (*SC* 3.2). The values and customs of the past are often presented with nostalgic affection, as in the celebration of the leisured pace of life in *Adam Bede*: 'Leisure is gone—gone where the spinning-wheels are gone . . . Ingenious philosophers tell you, perhaps, that the great work of the steam-engine is to

create leisure for mankind. Do not believe them: it only creates a vacuum for eager thought to rush in' (*AB* 52). There is loss as well as gain in the 'historical advance of mankind' (*MF* 4.1).

Her faith in progress was shaken by the brutality of the *Franco-Prussian war and increasing doubts are registered in the later works. In *Middlemarch* there is an awareness of how little has changed since the early 1830s and ironic asides aimed at the developments that have occurred since those days 'innocent of future goldfields, and the gorgeous plutocracy which has so nobly exalted the necessities of genteel life' (*MM* 1). And although Dorothea is said at the end to be making her modest contribution to the growing good of the world, the novel has shown in the story of Lydgate's frustrated ambitions how difficult it is for progressive ideas to succeed. In *Daniel Deronda* established society is the object of unsparing criticism and appears to have little potential for progress, so that hope for the future is directed abroad to an undefined East where Deronda is to undertake his vague Messianic mission to serve the Jewish people. Eliot's last work *Impressions of Theophrastus Such* presents a debate about progress in 'Shadows of the Coming Race', in which an automated future is envisaged. Theophrastus expresses the fear that, with these technological developments, 'our race will have diminished with the diminishing call on their energies', while his interlocutor argues that technological progress can only be liberating (*TS* 17). Although Eliot generally believes that advances in science and human knowledge contribute to social progress, she is here subjecting that belief to the play of a sceptical intelligence. As a meliorist she is neither optimistic nor pessimistic, but even the ways in which the world may be improved are open to question. See also DARWINISM; HISTORY; SOCIETY; SCIENCE; TECHNOLOGY.   JMR

McDonagh (1997).

'Progress of the Intellect, The'. This review of R. W. Mackay's *The Progress of the Intellect, as Exemplified in the Religious Development of the Greeks and Hebrews*, 2 vols. (1850), was George Eliot's first contribution to the *Westminster Review*, where it appeared anonymously in January 1851 (repr. in *Essays*). John *Chapman, editor of the *Westminster* and publisher of the book, invited her to review it following their first meeting when, in company with Mackay, he visited the Brays in October 1850.

She slipped readily into the pompous persona of an experienced male reviewer, giving the customary generous space to paraphrase and extended quotation. Already, however, her commanding intellect, supported by her wide reading in Auguste

*Comte and in German Higher Criticism, is apparent in this critical analysis. The review is essentially sympathetic to Mackay's enterprise, which parallels and so legitimates George Eliot's own position following her break with orthodox Christianity.

Eliot maintains that Mackay's study is unique of its kind because while it follows the Germans' work on mythology and biblical criticism, 'the greater solidity and directness of the English mind ensure a superiority of treatment' (*Essays*, 30). His analysis establishes that it is necessary to recognize 'the presence of undeviating law in the material and moral world' as well as 'of that invariability of sequence which is acknowledged to be the basis of physical science' (31), so that religion and science are seen to be inseparable. Mackay's book is 'the nearest approach in our language to a satisfactory natural history of religion' (35). She outlines his case for believing that examination of the records of many cultures shows that the basis of all mythology is nature worship, both in the pagan Greek and the Hebrew traditions, commenting, however, that 'Some of his pages read like extracts from his common-place book, . . . rather than like a digested result of study' (35). As Pinney observes, 'Readers of *Middlemarch* will recognize more than one hint of Casaubon's history' (*Essays*, 36 n.). See also JOURNALIST, GEORGE ELIOT AS. MAH

projected works. At various times in her life, George Eliot projected works which never eventuated. The earliest of consequence was an original work advertised in the **Leader* in June 1853, *The Idea of a Future Life*, by 'the Translator of Strauss's Life of Jesus' (*L* ii. 90 n.). During her career as a journalist, she speculated for example about such possible companion pieces to ***'Woman in France: Madame de Sablé' as 'Ideals of Womanhood' and 'Woman in Germany' for the **Westminster Review*, and a piece on Sir Walter ***Scott for **Fraser's Magazine* (*L* ii. 190, 200).

In ***'How I came to write Fiction', George Eliot relates her intention to add to *Scenes of Clerical Life*: 'especially I longed to tell the story of the Clerical Tutor, but my annoyance at Blackwood's want of sympathy in the first two parts of Janet (although he came round to admiration at the third part) determined me to close the series and republish them in two volumes' (*Journals*, 291). She moved promptly to work on *Adam Bede*, however, making considerable progress during the journey to **Germany in 1858, in the course of which Lewes wrote to **Blackwood of 'our rapture' in Nuremberg: 'Who knows but some day we may have a Nürnberg novel, as the product?' (*L* ii. 449). Lewes quite often proposed possible subjects to her, most famously *Romola*: during their first visit to **Flor-

ence, he suggested 'an historical romance' based on Savonarola and 'Polly at once caught at the idea with enthusiasm' (21 May 1860, *L* iii. 295). A work set in **Italy seems already to have been in prospect, since during 1858 there were references in correspondence with Blackwood to 'the Italian story you have in view' (*L* ii. 463; also 510). Not all of Lewes's hints were followed up: his tantalizing birthday gift to George Eliot in 1870 was 'a Lockup book for her Autobiog' (*L* v. 123).

During the time of experiment that followed the publication of *Romola*, there were plans for poetic works that seem not to have been carried out, though at times poems changed their names in the process of composition. One of the more persistent possibilities was a poem on Timoleon, the Corinthian liberator of Syracuse in the 4th century BC, which was in George Eliot's mind in late 1868 and 1869. More than once, in a vote of confidence not easy to justify given *The Spanish Gypsy*, Lewes urged her to try a play: in 1864, serious thought was given to her writing a play for the actress Helen **Faucit; and again in 1873 ideas about a piece for the stage were floated (*L* v. 425 n.).

At times, projected works were transmuted into a different form from that originally envisaged: the best documented is the merging of the two separate conceptions 'Miss Brooke' and 'Middlemarch'. Generally George Eliot seems to have nurtured her ideas, and there is little evidence of notions for novels which failed to germinate beyond fragments of a novel set during the Napoleonic wars (Baker 1980: 9–20). MAH

Baker, William, 'A New George Eliot Manuscript', in Anne Smith (ed.), *George Eliot: Centenary Essays and an Unpublished Fragment* (1980).

Proust, Marcel (1871–1922), French novelist, essayist, and critic, who was an enthusiastic admirer of George Eliot's fiction. He seems to have read her work in translation, and from references in his letters and writings it is clear that he had a good knowledge of at least *Scenes of Clerical Life*, *Adam Bede*, *The Mill on the Floss*, *Silas Marner*, and *Middlemarch*. George Eliot's novels were, he later claimed, the cult of his adolescence (*Correspondance*, xix (1991), 124), but he continued to refer to them throughout his life. In 1899 when he was labouring on *Jean Santeuil*, a novel he was never to complete, he wondered whether he was not simply heaping up ruins like Dorothea's husband in *Middlemarch*; but a more revealing affinity with his own work can be seen in his affection for *The Mill on the Floss*, the book he once said that he had loved the most. In a letter of 1910, during the composition of his great novel *A la recherche du temps perdu* (1913–27)—translated as *Remembrance of Things Past* (1922–31)—he remarked on the power that English and American literature had had on him, mentioning George Eliot, Thomas *Hardy, and Stevenson in particular, and claiming that two pages of *The Mill on the Floss* could reduce him to tears (*Correspondance*, x (1983), 55). The appeal of the *Mill* lay no doubt in its proximity to his own concerns, in the way that it draws on the deep springs of memory in its evocation of childhood and dwells on the determining power of early experience. The narrator's reflections on how memories of childhood invest the natural world with meaning—'We could never have loved the earth so well if we had had no childhood in it' (*MF* 1.5)—anticipate Proust's meditation at the end of the Combray section in the first volume of *A la recherche*. Just as the details of a woodland walk on a mild May morning 'thrill such deep and delicate fibres' in Eliot's narrator because they are familiar from the past, so the cornflowers, hawthorns, and apple trees that Proust's narrator encounters in his walks immediately establish contact with his heart because they are situated on the same deep level as his own past life. The two passages of fond retrospect have affinities of tone and cadence as well as a similar pattern of thought, while the childhood sections of both novels focus on the experience of a dreamy, sensitive, and imaginative child. There are parallels, too, between the opening chapters of the two novels. The richly realized scene of the Floss and Dorlcote Mill dissolves into the reverie of the narrator seated in an armchair in a move that is recalled by the transitions between sleep and waking, dream and reality, past and present, that mark the opening pages of *A la recherche*.

Proust's most extensive comments on George Eliot's work are to be found in two pages of brief notes of uncertain date—probably written between 1896 and 1904 (Couch 1967: 151)—and published as part of the *Nouveaux mélanges* in *Contre Sainte-Beuve* (*Against Sainte Beuve*, trans. John Sturrock (1988), 324–5). The notes focus exclusively on *Adam Bede* and *Silas Marner* and are warm in their praise of George Eliot's poetic and sympathetic rendering of rural working life; her sensitive feeling for nature; her fresh, unjaded way of looking at things; and the exact and eloquent way in which caricatural characters are made to speak without caricature. Many of the features Proust singles out are ones that will be later found in his own work, particularly her sense of the mysterious grandeur of human life and the life of nature, and her feeling for the changes that take place in us and in things during the course of our life. Proust also reveals some of his own preoccupations—with evil and with the weakness of the will—in describing George Eliot's moral vision. Her work brings out the difference between the evil that we do to others—the real evil—and the evil that befalls us, which may turn out, like Silas Marner's betrayal, to be the condition of a greater good that is to be bestowed upon us. And she shows the progressive capitulation of will-power in, for instance, Arthur Donnithorne's resolve not to see Hetty Sorrel and his continuing to do so. Such failures of resolution, and the way that they spread their fatal repercussions in every direction, reveal the interdependence of human lives and the slow corrosive effects of time that Proust's novel was to explore so fully. Appropriately enough that novel contains one character, the young woman Andrée in *A l'ombre des jeunes filles en fleur*, who is said to be translating one of George Eliot's works.

Proust writes approvingly in these notes of George Eliot's conservative spirit, which must have chimed with the nostalgic dimension of his own sensibility, but in her later works she prefigures him as a radical explorer of the psyche. The slow disintegration of Lydgate in *Middlemarch* is the kind of process that Proust himself was to explore, while in *Daniel Deronda*, a novel which there is no record of him having read, Eliot traces the hidden pathways of feeling and the 'unmapped country within us' in ways which challenge straightforward notions of character. In the enigmatic Grandcourt she creates a figure who is as mysterious and opaque as the characters in *A la recherche* with their capacity for startling transformations. The affinities between the two writers may be more far reaching than Proust's own critical comments suggest, but it is doubtful whether they provide grounds for claiming influence. What is certain is that George Eliot was an important predecessor for Proust as a writer who engaged with, in the words of the Prelude to *Middlemarch*, 'the history of man, and how that mysterious mixture behaves under the varying experiments of Time'.   JMR

Proust, *Correspondance*, 21 vols., ed. Philip Kolb (1970–93).
Couch (1967).
Gary, Franklin, 'In Search of George Eliot: An Approach through Marcel Proust', *Symposium*, 4 (1933).
McKenzie, P., 'George Eliot's Nightmare, Proust's Realism', *Modern Language Review*, 79 (1984).
Mein, Margaret, *A Foretaste of Proust* (1974).

pseudonym, choice of. The adoption of a male pseudonym by a woman writer is conventionally held to be a safeguard against accusations of unfeminine exposure in the market place, and certainly sensitivity about her extramarital union was a real consideration for the woman who went by the name Marian Evans Lewes at the time she embarked on writing fiction. The name 'George Eliot' appeared in print on the title-page of the two-volume *Scenes of Clerical Life* in January 1858, though the signature 'George Eliot' had been used as early as 4 February 1857, in a letter to John *Blackwood, as the anonymous serialization of *Scenes* was getting under way: 'it will be well to give you my prospective name, as a tub to throw to the whale in case of curious enquiries' (*L* ii. 292). For a time the newly fledged novelist tried strenuously to distance her personal self from the public persona designated by the nom de plume, an attempt documented in her journals where she recorded matters to do with 'George Eliot' separately from her daily doings, but the controversy generated by the claims of Joseph *Liggins that he was the author of *Adam Bede* eroded her secrecy (*Journals*, 285–8).

She gave an explanation of her choice of pseudonym to John Walter *Cross: 'my wife told me the reason she fixed on this name was that George was Mr Lewes's Christian name, and Eliot was a good mouth-filling, easily-pronounced word' (Cross, i. 430–1). Blanche Colton Williams in her *George Eliot* (1936) appears to have been the first to offer an elaboration, suggesting that ' "To L—I owe it" gave her "Eliot" ' (132). Another speculation is that she may have had in mind Jane Eyre's adoption of the name 'Elliott' during her wanderings. See also GENDER; 'HOW I CAME TO WRITE FICTION'; SAND, GEORGE. MAH

psychoanalytic approaches. See CRITICISM, MODERN: PSYCHOANALYTIC APPROACHES.

psychology. See SCIENCE.

publishers. The publisher most identified with George Eliot's career was the Edinburgh-based house of William *Blackwood and Sons, who published all of her work that appeared in book form under the name 'George Eliot', with the sole exception of *Romola*. George *Smith, of *Smith, Elder & Co., tempted her away from Blackwood for that novel, which was serialized in his journal, the *Cornhill Magazine*, from July 1862 to August 1863, with publication in three volumes in July 1863.

Her first book, the translation of D. F. *Strauss's *Das Leben Jesu* as *The Life of Jesus Critically Examined*, was published anonymously in 1846 by Chapman Brothers. The same publisher, under the name of John *Chapman, also brought out *The Essence of Christianity*, her translation of Ludwig *Feuerbach's *Das Wesen des Christenthums* in 1854, the only one of her books to appear with a version of her given name on the title-page ('Marian Evans').

Her career in journalism was substantially with the *Westminster Review*, at the time owned and nominally edited by Chapman. During 1857, *Scenes of Clerical Life* was serialized anonymously in *Blackwood's Edinburgh Magazine*, to which she subsequently contributed 'The Lifted Veil' (anonymously published July 1859) and 'Address to Working Men, by Felix Holt' (January 1868) and poems; other poems appeared in *Macmillan's Magazine*. Publications such as reviews and essays tended to be in journals with which Lewes had an association, such as the *Leader*, which he ran with Thornton Hunt in the early 1850s, Chapman and Hall's *Fortnightly Review*, of which he was the first editor (1865–6), and George Smith's evening newspaper the *Pall Mall Gazette*, which he also edited (1865–8). See also PUBLISHERS, NEGOTIATIONS WITH. MAH

publishers, negotiations with. The circumstances attending George Eliot's first publication in the *Christian Observer* are not known; her next publications were in the Coventry *Herald*, purchased by her friend and mentor Charles *Bray in 1846. There is no record of negotiation with him, nor with John *Chapman who published her translations of D. F. *Strauss (*The Life of Jesus, Critically Examined*, 1846) and Ludwig *Feuerbach (*The Essence of Christianity*, 1854), and who was nominally editor of the *Westminster Review* during the period from 1852 to 1854 when George Eliot was in fact doing the editorial work. In 1855 she completed a further translation, of Baruch *Spinoza's *Ethics*, which G. H. Lewes had originally undertaken for Bohn. Despite acrimonious correspondence conducted by Lewes, this translation was not published. Lewes's role as George Eliot's literary agent evolved from his overtures to John Parker in 1855, which resulted in the placement of two essays in *Fraser's Magazine*. The decisive step was taken in November 1856 when Lewes (whose *'Sea-side Studies' were then appearing in *Blackwood's Edinburgh Magazine*) wrote to John Blackwood, head of the Edinburgh-based publishing house of William *Blackwood and Sons: 'I trouble you with a m.s. of "Sketches of Clerical Life" which was submitted to me by a friend who desired my good offices with you' (*L* ii. 269). Blackwood's reply, 'I am happy to say that I think your friend's reminiscences of Clerical Life will do' (*L* ii. 272), inaugurated a professional and personal relationship that was of utmost importance to Eliot's career.

Even before the identity of Lewes's friend was revealed to him, John Blackwood came to appreciate the need to tread warily with the author writing as 'George Eliot'. He brought good literary and business judgement, together with diplomatic skills, generosity, and personal dignity, to the negotiations, which are well documented in Haight's edition of the letters. From the beginning, he increased payment beyond that contracted for when sales warranted, and then recognized her success in higher offers for subsequent works.

After the publication of *Adam Bede* (and more particularly, after the surrender of the secret of her authorship), George Eliot was approached by a number of editors of journals, but she refused both Charles *Dickens, seeking to publish her in *All the Year Round*, and Samuel Lucas, hoping to attract her to *Once a Week*. She stayed with Blackwood, though at times cool with him, until George *Smith of *Smith, Elder & Co. lured her away for *Romola*. Lewes and Smith had a long-standing acquaintance, revived when in 1860 Smith recruited Lewes to write for his new journal, the *Cornhill Magazine*. Lewes's journal for 27 February 1862 records a visit from Smith:

In the course of our chat he made a proposal to purchase Polly's new work for £10,000. This of course includes the entire copyright. It is the most magnificent offer ever yet made for a novel; and Polly, as usual was disinclined to accept it on the ground that her work would not be worth the sum! (*L* iv. 17–18)

A deal was struck at £7,000, with the copyright to revert to George Eliot after six years. She found it hard to fulfil her contract, and had to renegotiate the number of serial instalments. Writing was slow and monthly publication uncongenial, especially for the difficult experiment of *Romola*, which though much admired in some quarters was not generally popular. Blackwood, with whom correspondence about an Italian novel had been ongoing since 1860, behaved with considerable restraint in the face of this defection; and was rewarded by George Eliot's returning to him with her next novel, never to stray again. It is unclear whether she first offered *Felix Holt, the Radical* to Smith, although Smith himself claimed that she did (Haight 1968: 384): certainly she felt conscious that *Romola* had not fulfilled his commercial expectations, making a gift to him of the story 'Brother Jacob' for which he once offered £250 (it was published in the *Cornhill* for July 1864). As late as 1880, she demurred about accepting an honorarium from Smith when he brought out a two-volume De Luxe edition of *Romola* (*L* vii. 247, 328).

Throughout her long association with Blackwood, George Eliot—or Lewes on her behalf—paid close attention to market forces, and to strategies for bringing out cheap and collected editions at opportune times. Possibilities for serialization in one form or another were frequently contemplated but abandoned (Lewes went so far as to get costings for publication of *The Mill on the Floss* in monthly parts for instance), until Blackwood was persuaded to try the experiment of publishing *Middlemarch*, and later *Daniel Deronda*, in half-volume parts. Blackwood's investment in the George Eliot industry was extended by publication in December 1871 of *Wise, Witty, and Tender Sayings in Prose and Verse, selected from the works of George Eliot* by a young Scottish devotee, Alexander *Main, who also compiled *The George Eliot Birthday Book*, published in 1878. The last major edition was the *Cabinet Edition, of which the first volumes came out late in 1877: it eventually ran to 24 volumes including *Essays and Leaves from a Note-book* and Cross's *Life*. George Eliot paid particular attention to the design, suggesting that it might be octavo, like a set of Fielding she owned (*L* vi. 351), and specifying 'a rich olive green for the colour—a hue which sets off well both the gold and the black' of the cover design (*L* vi. 422–3).

Lewes usually made the running in any negotiations, and people in Blackwood's regarded him as avaricious. But George Eliot did not distance herself from publishing negotiations. Margaret Oliphant was well placed to judge that George Eliot was herself 'an admirable woman of business, alert and observant of every fluctuation of the book-market, and determined that in every way her works should have the fullest justice done to them' (*Annals of a Publishing House: William Blackwood and his Sons, Their Magazine and Friends*, 2 vols (1897), ii. 446). Certainly after Lewes's death when Eliot took over all the correspondence with Blackwood, together with other matters of business, she proved to be thoroughly up to the mark, concluding among other negotiations final arrangements with Nicholas Trübner for publication of the fourth and fifth volumes of Lewes's *Problems of Life and Mind*. A full publishing history of each novel is given in the respective Clarendon Edition. See also EARNINGS.

MAH

Anderson, R. F., 'Negotiating for *The Mill on the Floss*', *Publishing History*, 2 (1977).
—— ' "Things wisely ordered": John Blackwood, George Eliot, and the Publication of *Romola*', *Publishing History*, 11 (1982).
Sutherland (1976).

Purcell, Henry (1658/9–95), English composer, whose music entrances Maggie Tulliver in *The Mill on the Floss* and marks the beginning of her awakening into physical passion. In Book 6 of the novel, 'Purcell's music with its wild passion and fancy', sung earlier in the evening by Stephen Guest, remains 'vibrating in her still' as she becomes 'conscious of having been looked at a great deal . . . with a glance that seemed somehow to have caught the vibratory influence of the voice' (*MF* 6.3). Purcell continues to be implicated in the musical seduction of Maggie Tulliver by Stephen Guest. References to his music suggest a contrast with *Haydn's *The Creation* to which George Eliot alludes in her satirical portrait of Stephen's courtship of Maggie's cousin Lucy, and which Philip Wakem condemns as having a sort of 'sugared complacency and flattering make-believe' (*MF* 6.1). Lucy asks Stephen to bring a volume of Purcell scores, and whilst she and Philip are occupied in singing from this, Stephen takes the opportunity seductively to place a footstool for Maggie before adding the force of his rich bass to the music (*MF* 6.7). They are singing from Purcell's music for the Dryden–Davenant adaptation of *The Tempest*. This setting was familiar to Eliot from Coventry days and clearly remained an important musical memory. In 1862 she wrote to Sara *Hennell asking to borrow her copy of the music for her friends to sing (*L* iv. 12; ix. 348). See also MUSIC. DdSC

race. George Eliot's writing career spans the period during which British social relations came to be understood not in terms of caste but through the more mobile category of *class, a movement that was accompanied by a parallel, if reversed, shift in the meaning of the category of 'race': from a synonym for 'a people' (the German *Volk*) to a 'scientific' concept based on a fixed hierarchy of relatively unchanging racial groups defined by inherited characteristics. George Eliot's work reflects both of these great conceptual and social transitions; her notion of race, in particular, deploys both a 'romantic' element of a people joined by ties of blood and collective memory (see NATION-ALISM), and a 'scientific' element of empiricist description and classification that (despite its self-conscious 'modern-ness') harks back to an older, aristocratic, model based on heredity and caste.

This ambiguity can be seen in her most explicit comment on race—her dismissal of Benjamin *Disraeli's theory of races in her letter of 11 February 1848 to John *Sibree: 'Extermination up to a certain point seems to be the law for the inferior races—for the rest, fusion both for physical and moral ends. It appears to me that the law by which privileged classes degenerate from continual intermarriage must act on a larger scale in deteriorating whole races' (*L* i. 246). Again, in her review of Riehl's work in 'The *Natural History of German Life', she employs the classificatory mode of mid-Victorian science to describe the German peasantry in terms of race—'The peasants may still be distinguished into groups by their physical peculiarities. In one part of the country we find a longer-legged, in another a broader-shouldered race'—and then goes on to describe these rural folk as the last links to an earlier nobility: 'These same features ['high foreheads, long straight noses, and small eyes'] can be found on noblemen's faces in sculptures in the church of St. Elizabeth at Marburg' (*Essays*, 274). The 'conflict of races' that George Eliot sees in Harriet Beecher *Stowe's work is 'the great source of *romantic* interest—witness "Ivanhoe"' (*Essays*, 326; emphasis added).

By the time of *Daniel Deronda* (1876), when anthropology was emerging as a legitimate scientific discipline, George Eliot's conception of race appears to have undergone a shift: Daniel's blood inheritance is explicitly racial, and it determines his identity in the last instance, despite his mother's vain attempt to deny her (and therefore Daniel's) Jewishness. We can trace, therefore, in George Eliot's work the transition to modern categories of 'race', although she never entirely leaves behind the world of Walter *Scott. Her scattered remarks point both backward and forward simultaneously. On the one hand, she can unthinkingly use the

language of Victorian racism, as when she talks of the extermination of 'inferior races', or describes G. H. *Lewes's son Charles 'work[ing] like a nigger at his music' (*L* iii. 404) or says that 'my idle brain wants lashing to work like a negro' (*L* ii. 318); on the other hand, she can embrace both racial diversity and human similarity at the same time: 'The human race has not been educated on a plan of uniformity, and it is precisely that partition of mankind into races and nations ... which has been the means of enriching and rendering more and more complete man's knowledge of the inner and outer world' (*Essays*, 388). See also ANTI-SEMITISM; COLONIALISM; JUDAISM.   TW

Rachel (1821–58), French actress, Rachel Félix, daughter of a Jewish peddler, who came to be known throughout the world as simply 'Rachel'. In Paris her brilliance was first extolled by Jules Janin; in London, in the 1840s and 1850s, G. H. *Lewes played a significant part in consolidating her reputation and George Eliot later used her as an important point of reference in *Daniel Deronda*. Taken up by Joseph Isidore Samson, a famous teacher at the Conservatoire, Rachel had been inducted into the Comédie-Française at the age of 17; but as a result of incessant international touring between 1841 and 1856 she became universally recognized as the greatest *tragédienne* of the age. This was all the more remarkable since she specialized in the neoclassical plays of Corneille and Racine which had fallen out of fashion even in France. Part of her secret was to invest stiff and unyielding roles with modern Romantic feeling. For Lewes, who first wrote about her in the *Atlas* in 1846 employing phrases that he was to repeat in notices of her many subsequent visits, she was always to be 'the panther of the stage', above all when she embodied Phèdre. 'There always seemed something not human about her,' he wrote, 'she had little tenderness, no womanly caressing softness, no gaiety, no heartiness.' This element of feral danger was reinforced by Rachel's reputation as an exceptionally strong-willed woman and by her well-known series of lovers, many of whom were men of substance. Charlotte *Brontë was to put all these Rachelesque qualities into her fictional actress, the terrifying Vashti, in *Villette* published in 1853. However, when Eliot accompanied Lewes to see Rachel that same year she declared herself disappointed: the real-life actress didn't live up to the fictional approximation (*L* iii. 98).

That early sense of anticlimax colours the clearly signalled presence of Rachel in *Daniel Deronda*. When Gwendolen Harleth plans a theatrical entertainment it is the great French actress whom she initially hopes to emulate, even though the performance turns out to be the transformation scene from *The Winter's Tale*. In the event, Gwendolen's amateur rendering, and the unforeseen moment of expressiveness when she is confronted by a concealed picture, both expose her vulnerability and hint at certain, as yet unrealized, strengths. Tragic representation, if it is to have value, must reach below surface theatricality and tap a bedrock of actual experience: Gwendolen still has much to learn. Even so, it is Deronda's mother, the Princess, who most resembles Rachel in her abuse of her own acting abilities. Eliot's ambivalence towards the world of the stage allows her to explore the full range and complexity of the histrionic temperament. By the 1870s Rachel lived on mainly in memories of old playgoers, her celebrants including Benjamin *Disraeli and Matthew *Arnold. The theatrical sections of *Deronda* are a corrective to this myth-making, a critique of past glories that manages, nevertheless, to respect their lasting influence. See also THEATRE; TRAGEDY.

JS

Litvak, Joseph, *Caught in the Act: Theatricality in the Nineteenth-Century Novel* (1992).
Marshall, Gail, *Actresses on the Victorian Stage* (1998).
Stokes, John, 'Rachel's "Terrible Beauty": An Actress among the Novelists', *ELH* 51 (1984).

radicalism. The electoral and related issues in *Middlemarch* and especially *Felix Holt, the Radical*, and the *'Address to Working Men, by Felix Holt' are largely shaped by radicalism: a British working- and middle-class action and reaction to what was seen by reformers as political intransigence, especially during the reform periods of the late 18th to the late 19th centuries.

Most British radicals were less concerned with ideologies or abstractions than specific demands to alleviate human suffering, which varied in intensity from region to region owing to fluctuating economic, social, and political conditions. Among the poor, hunger and starvation were common, as were appalling working and living conditions; subsequent demonstrations, calls, and petitions by workers and their sympathizers for either social and economic changes, or political reform, or improved educational opportunities comprised radical demands. Among the middle classes, agitation was primarily aimed at extending the voting franchise.

Since radicalism (derived from the Latin *radix* meaning 'root') challenged the status quo, it was generally condemned by Parliament, the authorities, and the conservatively minded as dangerous provocation, if not outright sedition. And demonstrations often threatened to, and sometimes did, erupt into violence: riots flared up in the Midlands over wheat prices in 1811–12; skirmishes with troops occurred over unemployment and 'combination' or labour unionizing in and around Glasgow in the early 1820s; and incidents of machine breaking, rick burning, and large-scale rioting took place throughout towns and districts in England during the Reform Bill crisis of 1829–32. Some radical demands culminated in reform measures, however, most notably The Great *Reform Act of 1832, which was eventually carried when the middle classes were championed by influential, reform-minded people from across the social, political, and religious spectra, including at one point King William IV. Still other radical demands, those of *Chartism for example, failed to move Parliament until decades later.

In *Felix Holt* and *Middlemarch*, Eliot looks back to the early 1830s when radicalism was very much part of England's political agenda. But, as Barbara Hardy has suggested, in *Felix Holt* where radicalism is of central concern, the term is 'used with caution, irony, an invisible question mark and redefinition' (*Particularities: Readings on George Eliot* (1982), 166). Calls for reform in the early part of the century were of special interest to Eliot because the Second Reform Bill of 1867 lay just over the horizon. It was being shaped at the time of writing *Felix Holt* by the continued radicalism that had grumbled along in various forms after 1832. In *Felix Holt* and to a lesser extent *Middlemarch*, radicalism is carefully sifted in an attempt to separate its kernels from the chaff. Eliot demonstrates that the term means different things to different people. Mrs Transome, for instance, recalls the Radical politician Sir Francis Burdett (1770–1844). When her son, Harold, tells her he plans to stand as a Radical MP, the narrator says, 'There were rich Radicals, she was aware, as there were rich Jews and Dissenters, but she had never thought of them as county people. Sir Francis Burdett had been generally regarded as a madman' (*FH* 1). Others share Mrs Transome's bewilderment: in chapter 3 the narrator explains that most Treby Magnians were only dimly aware of the differences between Tories, Whigs, and Radicals, although most lumped Radicals with 'Dissenters, Deists, Socinians, [and] Papists' as well as 'hypocrites . . . and atheism generally'. Meanwhile, Harold Transome's surprising radicalism appears to be only an expression of his iconoclastic attitude towards family and tradition, while Felix Holt's is part of his earnest desire to help workers. He tells Rufus Lyon that his radicalism is indeed political, 'but I want to go to some roots a good deal lower down than the franchise' (*FR* 27). But what happens if the workers are not interested in those rather vague, though no doubt noble, roots? Among other things, the Treby Magna riot shows him how easily the feeding hand can be bitten.

Thus, Eliot's point is, radicalism, a term easily bandied about, has no hard and fast definition that all can agree on; and yet it is the driving force for various kinds of reform. And what sort of reform awaits us? The abolition of what is good and worthwhile and the introduction of chaos? Radicalism has its place, Eliot implies, so long as it promotes the general well-being of everyone; but that requires a careful consideration of values and not an adherence to inflamed rhetoric—a point she made the subject of her 'Address to Working Men, by Felix Holt'. See also HISTORY; POLITICS; PROGRESS.   AvdB

Raphael (Raffaello Sanzio, 1483–1520), Italian painter of the High Renaissance. For George Eliot Raphael was first and foremost the painter of her favourite work of art, the *Sistine Madonna* of 1512. She first saw the painting in 1858, in a special section of the Picture Gallery at *Dresden and professed herself overwhelmed. She would already have known the painting from reproductions and it was, in any case, an object of veneration for the positivist group who followed in the footsteps of Auguste *Comte. There is an oblique reference to the *Sistine Madonna* in *Adam Bede* where the narrator compares Seth Bede's sight of Dinah Morris to the vision of a supreme painting of the Madonna after it has been temporarily obscured by a woman's head (*AB* 26). In *The Mill on the Floss*, Philip Wakem tells Maggie Tulliver, in whom he wants to instil a sense of the mysterious, of the *Sistine Madonna* (*MF* 5.1)

For many Victorian art lovers Raphael was the greatest of painters, often placed with *Shakespeare in a pantheon of immortals. George Eliot's response to his work was more equivocal. In 1845 she declared her admiration for Raphael's *St Catherine*, recently purchased by the National Gallery, but, when her view of art began to be influenced by that of John *Ruskin, she became aware of his doubts about Raphael's true quality. That she did not blindly follow Ruskin, however, is evident from her statement, made in *Munich in 1858, that she preferred *Rubens to any other painter, but that, when she had seen more of his work, she would probably favour Raphael. Shortly afterwards she saw the *Sistine Madonna*, but this was not conclusive: a few years later the narrator of *The Mill on the Floss* compares the foolish Mrs Tulliver to one of Raphael's early Madonnas, and wryly notes that such weak women soon lose control when their children grow older (*MF* 1.2)

George Eliot's first journey to *Rome in 1860 gave her the opportunity to see a number of Raphael's most famous later works, including those in the Stanze of the Vatican Palace and in the Vatican Museum. For George Eliot the *School of Athens* (*c*.1510–12) in the Stanza della Segnatura in the Vatican and the *Triumph of Galatea* (*c*.1512) in the Villa Farnesina were almost the finest frescos in Rome, only surpassed by the Michelangelo ceiling in the Sistine Chapel. Edward Casaubon in *Middlemarch* offers to accompany Dorothea on a visit to the Farnesina, but in so lukewarm a tone that she refuses (*MM* 20). It is implied that the joyous eroticism of the *Triumph of Galatea* would not provide the right setting for so cool a bridegroom. Dorothea does, however, see and discuss with Will Ladislaw the *Madonna del Foligno* in the Vatican Museum, another of George Eliot's own favourite works by Raphael (*MM* 22).

Raphael's *Coronation of the Virgin* supplied George Eliot with another passage for *Middlemarch*. In the opening paragraph of chapter 19 the narrator comments on a mistake made by William Hazlitt in his *Notes of a Journey through France and Italy* (1826). Hazlitt believed that the grave from which Raphael shows the Virgin rising was a flower vase, rather than a miraculous bursting forth of roses and lilies. For the narrator this error, by a leading critic, becomes an instance of the prevailing ignorance among travellers to Rome in the 1820s. See also VISUAL ARTS.   LO

Witemeyer (1979).

Reade, Charles (1814–84), English novelist and playwright, who calls out George Eliot's wrath as early as 17 January 1858 when she tells Sara *Hennell, 'How could you waste your pretty eyes in reading "White Lies"' (Reade's novel published in 1857). She castigates Reade's work as 'the inflated plagiarisms of a man gone mad with restless vanity and unveracity' (*L* ii. 422). There is perhaps some envy over Reade's initial success, for Mudie took 1,000 copies of *It's Never Too Late to Mend* (1856). Things can't have been helped by E. S. *Dallas in *The Times* suggesting that the trial scene in chapter 46 of *Felix Holt, the Radical* probably derived from a 'similar situation which Mr Charles Reade has introduced into his last novel'. The reference here is to *Griffth Gaunt, or Jealousy* (1866) which Eliot had not read. Doubtless she and Lewes registered Reade's falling out with their friend Anthony *Trollope in 1871 when he 'borrowed' the plot of Trollope's *Ralph the Heir* for his play *Shilly Shally*. Nevertheless when Eliot and Lewes visited Benjamin *Jowett in June 1873 in Oxford they probably had tea with Reade at Magdalen. They read *A Woman Hater* in June 1877 which Lewes found jarring. GRH

readership. When writing for the *Westminster Review* before she became a novelist, George Eliot was addressing a readership of liberal intellectuals, and although she broadened the range of her readers when she began to write fiction, she still sought to appeal to an intellectual elite as well as to a popular audience. After the publication of *The Mill on the Floss* in 1860 she was severely irritated to learn from François *D'Albert Durade in *Geneva that a French critic had referred to her as a rival of Dinah Mulock, the author of *John Halifax, Gentleman* (1856), whom she loftily dismissed as 'a writer who is read only by novel readers, pure and simple, never by people of high culture' (*L* iii. 302). With *Romola*, as she told Sara *Hennell after the first instalment of the novel had appeared in July 1862, she realized that people of high culture were the only ones she was likely to appeal to, since 'of necessity, the book is addressed to fewer readers than my previous works, and I myself have never expected—I might rather say *intended*—that the book shall be as "popular" in the same sense as the others' (*L* iv. 49). Her expectations were fulfilled for the novel did not prove to be a popular success. The rest of her fiction, however, was more inclusive in its appeal and seems to presuppose a readership that ranges from the relatively naive to the sophisticated while remaining broadly middle class.

Blackwood's Edinburgh Magazine, in which her first stories, *Scenes of Clerical Life*, appeared, catered for a conservative middle-class audience, and George Eliot's awareness of the sensibilities of such a readership is registered in the narrator's ironic allusions to 'my refined lady-readers', whose interest in the story of Mr Gilfil's love might be annihilated by the description of him drinking gin and water (*SC* 2.1). This kind of deference to a genteel readership is a feature of the early novels in particular, where that readership has to be brought to interest itself in humble people and ordinary working lives; but the deference is always laced with *irony that turns against narrow prejudice and assumptions of superiority. In her later career, in 1867, she claimed that young men were the class

of readers she most wanted to influence with her fiction—a measure of her didactic aspirations as a novelist (*L* iv. 397). With the success of *Adam Bede* (see RECEPTION) she won a readership that extended far beyond that of *Blackwood's*, reaching from an admiring Queen *Victoria to workers like the future Labour leader Thomas Burt who discovered her novels in the Blyth Mechanics' Institute in the 1860s (Altick, 200). *Mudie's circulating library bought 3,000 copies of her next novel *The Mill on the Floss*, while American editions, Christian Bernhard *Tauchnitz's English reprints on the European continent, and translations into foreign languages secured an international readership. However, that readership was never as large as Dickens's—sales of the instalments of *Middlemarch* averaged about 5,000 compared with 28,000 for *Our Mutual Friend* (1864)—or that achieved by a runaway best-seller like Harriet Beecher *Stowe's *Uncle Tom's Cabin* (1852), which sold over 300,000 in its first year compared with *Adam Bede*'s 15,000. Nevertheless, her readership was substantial and remained loyal, so that even her less successful novels like *Felix Holt, the Radical* achieved sales that other novelists would have been delighted with (Sutherland 1976: 189). The bold attempt to widen the English vision a little with the sympathetic treatment of *Judaism in *Daniel Deronda* won her new readers in the Jewish community in Britain and abroad without apparently alienating her regular readership, while a difficult new venture like her last work *Impressions of Theophrastus Such* had as many readers, or at least purchasers, as the novels, despite hostile reviews. See also EARNINGS; PUBLISHERS; REPUTATION, CRITICAL. JMR

Altick, Richard D., *The English Common Reader* (1957).

Flint, Kate, *The Woman Reader 1837–1914* (1993).

Sutherland (1976).

realism was seen by George Eliot as the proper goal of art before she began to write novels, and it subsequently became a central feature of her fiction, and one that has been the focus of much critical discussion in recent years. In April 1856, reviewing the third volume of John *Ruskin's *Modern Painters*, she maintained that his achievement as a critic lay in the emphasis he placed on truth to nature:

The truth of infinite value that he teaches is *realism*—the doctrine that all truth and beauty are to be attained by a humble and faithful study of nature, and not by substituting vague forms, bred by imagination on the mists of feeling, in place of definite, substantial reality. (*Westminster Review*, 66: 626)

In July 1856, in her essay on 'The *Natural History of German Life', she applied Ruskin's teaching to the representation of ordinary people in literature, praising *Scott and *Wordsworth, and criticizing social novels for their unreality (*Essays*, 270). 'We want to be taught to feel,' she argued, 'not for the heroic artisan or the sentimental peasant, but for the peasant in all his coarse apathy, and the artisan in all his suspicious selfishness' (271). She saw Charles *Dickens as powerfully realistic in 'rendering the external traits of our town population' but as 'transcendent in his unreality' as soon as he tried to depict their inner life.

When she began to write her first story a few weeks later, she clearly set out to avoid such unreality, as well as the feebler forms of unfaithfulness to the 'working-day business of the world' she wittily castigates in her essay on *'Silly Novels by Lady Novelists' (*Essays*, 302). Seeking 'to represent to you the humble experience of ordinary fellowmortals' (*SC* 1.7), she focuses with Amos Barton on a man who is 'palpably and unmistakably commonplace' (*SC* 1.5), thus taking a stand against the assumption that fashionable society was the proper subject of fiction. The realist aesthetic she suggests here, and which she sets out more fully in chapter 17 of her first novel *Adam Bede*, has a strong moral as well as a democratic dimension. Her determination 'to tell my simple story without trying to make things seem better than they were' is defined as a commitment to difficult truth as opposed to easy falsehood (*AB* 17)—a commitment that chimes with G. H. *Lewes's view in his 1858 article 'Realism in Art: Recent German Fiction' that the antithesis of realism is 'Falsism' (*Westminster Review*, 70: 493). The Dutch painting that is held up by the narrator as a model of artistic truthfulness for its 'pictures of a monotonous homely existence' is important for the delicious sympathy it generates for ordinary lives. Realism in art is for George Eliot an instrument of human solidarity, strengthening social bonds and sympathetic ties between people of different types and classes on the principle proclaimed in the famous passage from 'The Natural History of German Life': 'Art is the nearest thing to life; it is a mode of amplifying experience and extending our contact with our fellow-men beyond the bounds of our personal lot' (*Essays*, 271).

Her early works are realist fictions of the ordinary life as defined and defended in *Adam Bede*, concentrating on 'the common working-day world' (*SC* 1.9) of the Midlands, 'writing the history of unfashionable families' (*MF* 4.3). Individual characters with complex psychologies are set in a material and social world that is represented in circumstantial detail, down to the tablecloths, spoons, and china that Mrs Tulliver sits weeping over in *The Mill on the Floss* when bankruptcy threatens. Private experience, like Maggie Tulliver's turbulent emotional life, is always connected to the wider public world of law and custom, prejudice and gossip, on the premiss that, as the narrator of *Felix Holt, the Radical* puts it, 'there is no private life which has not been determined by a wider public life' (*FH* 3). Walter Scott, whose novels George Eliot knew from childhood, was an influential predecessor in this respect, and although *Romola* was her only conventional historical novel, her fiction is normally set back in time and rendered with historical specificity.

The embedding of individual characters in a larger social and historical reality is most fully developed in *Middlemarch*, where her realism appears in a more sophisticated form. There is the same insistence on the law of consequences—'Consequences are unpitying' (*AB* 16)—which is spelt out as clearly in the lives of Bulstrode and Lydgate as it had been in those of Arthur Donnithorne and Hetty Sorrel; but the multiplication of plots and perspectives, as in the different views of Featherstone's funeral in chapter 34, creates a more complex and differentiated representation of social reality (Ermarth 1998: 240). There is also a rich abundance of material details that creates a vivid sense of life, and, while appearing trivial, takes its place within a larger pattern (Karlin, 34–5). Of all her novels, *Middlemarch* most clearly demonstrates the realist's typical ambition to present a comprehensive account, an encompassing image of society. It is an ambition she shares with that other great realist Honoré de *Balzac: the subtitle of *Middlemarch*, 'A Study of Provincial Life', recalls the terminology he uses in subdividing his vast *Comédie humaine*, and like him George Eliot draws an analogy between the practice of the novelist and that of the scientist. And like Balzac in France, George Eliot has been seen by modern criticism, sometimes dismissively, as the exemplary English realist, with *Middlemarch* often cited as the classic realist text.

The best-known criticism of the novel along those lines is Colin MacCabe's in *James Joyce and the Revolution of the Word* (1979), who sees the classic realist text as one that refuses to acknowledge its own status as writing and establishes a hierarchy of discourses with that of the narrator at the top, claiming unqualified access to, and knowledge of, the world beyond the text. The discourse of the *Middlemarch* narrator thus serves as a metalanguage to which all the other forms of discourse in the novel are subordinate and which functions simply as a window on reality. This dismissive view of 19th-century realism in general, and George Eliot's in particular, was a feature of British poststructuralist criticism in this period (Newton 1991: 5–7). Catherine Belsey in *Critical Practice* (1980) is similarly critical of *Middlemarch*'s claim to offer a truthful representation of the world and sees its kind of realism as presenting a reassuring confirmation of reality as it is conventionally understood. From this perspective realism simply reproduces received notions of reality and naively assumes that language can be transparent and that the world can be made sense of by a unified and self-determining human subject. It is ideologically conservative and intellectually undemanding.

Such criticism has not gone unchallenged. David Lodge has shown how the use of free indirect style (see IRONY; STYLE) in *Middlemarch* makes the narrator's discourse something more complex and elusive than MacCabe's monolithic metalanguage, and argues that its ambiguity and indeterminacy are a source of the novel's enduring vitality (Newton 1991: 184). American poststructuralist criticism like that of J. Hillis Miller reads *Middlemarch* not as naively realist but, on the contrary, as a sophisticated deconstruction of classic realism, fully aware of the slippery, figurative nature of language (see METAPHOR) and of the text as construct (see CRITICISM, MODERN: DECONSTRUCTION). If such deconstruction may go too far in pressing its claim that the novel is self-cancelling—ignoring, for instance, the firm moral foundation of Eliot's vision—its emphasis on the subtlety and self-consciousness of her realism is entirely justified. Even in *Adam Bede* where the narrator had claimed to be faithfully representing 'men and things as they have mirrored themselves in my mind', the characteristic realist image of mirroring had been employed with the qualifying awareness that 'the mirror is doubtless defective' (*AB* 17), and in *Middlemarch* that kind of awareness is more subtly and pervasively present. The novel draws attention not only to the problematic nature of language, but also, with its strategically placed chapter *epigraphs, to its own intertextuality, and to the partial nature of all vision, including that of the narrator (see NARRATION). At the same time its confident handling of character includes an insight into the possibility that character may be merely a construct of other minds: a man like Lydgate may be a centre of social attention 'and yet remain virtually unknown—known merely as a cluster of signs for his neighbours' false suppositions' (*MM* 15). Terence R. Wright's study of the novel (1991) does justice to the sophisticated nature of its realism by showing how poststructuralist critical perspectives can open up a rich variety of meanings that rebut the reductive notion of the classic realist text.

George Eliot's last novel *Daniel Deronda* shows how her use of the realist mode was constantly evolving. Opening with a reflection on 'the make-believe of a beginning', ranging from the mundane to the mythical, and exploring the hidden depths of the psyche in ways that question the unity and transparency of character (see CHARACTERIZATION), *Deronda* displays a degree of creative self-consciousness that anticipates the practice of modernism in pressing the conventions of realism to their limits.

George Eliot's commitment to realism was a constant and crucial feature of her fiction (even the fantastic elements of 'The Lifted Veil' can be seen as a means of examining the premises of her realist art). Human life is always seen under the pressure of the 'hard unaccommodating Actual' (*DD* 33), and subject to a rigorous law of cause and effect, action and consequence. Her narrators are not credited with a transcendent omniscience but appeal to, and seek to promote through the extension of sympathy, a shared understanding of the world that bridges differences of class and culture. This aspiration to consensus does not involve reproducing uncritically the prevailing forms and values of the social world; it is, rather, the mark of a realism that is alert to conflict and contradiction and subjects the represented reality to the questioning scrutiny of a sceptical and self-critical intelligence. See also SOCIETY; SYMBOLISM.   JMR

Chase (1991).
Ermarth, Elizabeth, *Realism and Consensus in the English Novel* (1983, 1998).
Karlin, Daniel, 'Having the Whip-hand in *Middlemarch*', *George Eliot Review*, 28 (1997).
Newton (1991).
Peck (1992).
Wright (1991).

reception. The story of George Eliot's reception is one of early triumphant success with *Adam Bede* in 1859, which established a lasting readership and ensured critical attention for the rest of her career, even though the later novels never aroused quite the same degree of enthusiasm amongst reviewers as the first one. Before *Adam Bede*, the three stories that comprised *Scenes of Clerical Life* were respectfully received by the few reviewers who noticed them when they were published in book form in January 1858, but they caused little stir. Charles *Dickens, after receiving a presentation copy, praised them for their truth and delicacy in a letter to the author, and the handful of short notices commended the pathos and *humour with which homely, everyday life was represented. While there was a general suspicion that 'George Eliot' was a *pseudonym, the subject of the stories encouraged the view that the author was probably a clergyman, a misapprehension that was to be beneficial to *Adam Bede*. That novel was published on 1 February 1859 and, after a brief dismissive review in the *Spectator* on 12 February, it began to evoke a chorus of approval, with favourable reviews in the *Athenaeum*, the *Saturday Review*, and the

Westminster Review. On 12 April E. S. *Dallas began his unsigned review in *The Times* with a forthright declaration: 'There can be no mistake about *Adam Bede*. It is a first-rate novel, and its author takes rank at once among the masters of the art' (*CH* 77). Dallas's judgement was widely endorsed: Dickens wrote another letter of generous praise, as did Jane Welsh *Carlyle, while Queen *Victoria's admiration was such that she commissioned paintings of two scenes from the novel. George Eliot's reputation was established for her lifetime. *Adam Bede* sold over 15,000 copies in 1859, and although this did not match the sales achieved by Dickens (see READERSHIP), it was a great success by any standards. By March 1860 G. H. *Lewes could proclaim that it had been translated into Dutch, French, German, and Hungarian; and it continued to sell steadily at home as William *Blackwood and Sons skilfully marketed it in cheaper editions.

The early reviewers were unaware of the true identity of the author and found nothing to disturb them in the novel's moral vision and treatment of *religion. Dallas responded to the warm human sympathy he found in the book by describing it as 'but a secular rendering of the deepest sentiment of Christianity' (*CH* 78). When it became known in the summer of 1859 that George Eliot was really Marian Evans, the translator of D. F. *Strauss and Ludwig *Feuerbach (see TRANSLATIONS BY GEORGE ELIOT) and the partner of the already married Lewes, her standing as a novelist was too well founded to be undermined. As the critic Richard Simpson, himself a committed Christian, was to put it in 1863, 'George Eliot was already accepted as a great artist; her teaching had been dubbed clerical, and it was too late in the day to turn upon her and call her an atheist' (*CH* 225). Nevertheless some reviewers did make sneering comments about her as a woman writer (Showalter 1977: 95).

When her next novel *The Mill on the Floss* appeared in April 1860, it profited from the success of its predecessor, selling 6,000 copies in the first seven weeks, but the critical response was less enthusiastic. The third volume of the novel became the focus of the strongest and most sustained criticism that Eliot's work ever provoked (*CH* 13), with critics finding fault with the disjunction between the slow-moving representation of childhood and the brief, turbulent life of Maggie Tulliver as a young woman, and vehemently condemning her relationship with Stephen Guest as either artistically offensive or psychologically unconvincing. After the strong initial sales, the later editions sold only slowly. A year later *Silas Marner* was welcomed with relief as a return to the manner of *Adam Bede* and its bucolic world. It sold 8,000

copies in the first year, and its symmetrical fable-like structure, pastoral charm, and benign conclusion concealed its unorthodox vision and ensured its continuing popularity. It was the last of her novels that could be so easily assimilated, for with the *serialization of *Romola* in 1862–3 George Eliot broke new and difficult ground. The studious reconstruction of 15th-century Florence marked a turning point in her career, as David Carroll has argued, dividing her readers into those prepared to accept, and curious to follow, each new development of her talent, and those who continued to hark back nostalgically to the world of the early fiction (*CH* 19). *Romola* thus won respect from a minority who appreciated the power of an intellect now openly displayed, but it never achieved popular success.

Felix Holt, the Radical in 1866 sold well initially but the reviews found the novel lacking in unity and were particularly critical of the figure of Felix himself, and sales fell away. In publishing terms the novel was a failure, but having sold nearly 5,000 copies in its first edition, that failure would have been considered a considerable success by most novelists (Sutherland 1976: 189). It is a measure of George Eliot's standing with her readership that, when she turned to *poetry with *The Spanish Gypsy* in 1868, she was more successful than might have been expected given the limited nature of her poetic gifts. The verse drama was politely received and went into three small editions, earning the author £1,000 in the next ten years and selling particularly well in the United States (Haight 1968: 405–6).

When *Middlemarch* appeared in instalments in 1871–2 it proved a popular success. George Eliot herself thought that not even *Adam Bede* had met with such enthusiasm (*L* v. 357), and the popularity of the novel was demonstrated by the sales of the cheap edition that came out in May 1874 and amounted to 10,000 in the first six months and 31,000 by the end of 1878. Nevertheless the reviewers had reservations, criticizing its fragmentary structure and finding it a melancholy work by comparison with the early fiction. There was respect for the intellectual power of the novel and the scale of its achievement but a widespread sense that its *realism, unsustained by Christian faith, created a bleak vision of human life.

With her last novel *Daniel Deronda* George Eliot was at the height of her fame, generally regarded as the greatest living English novelist. The eight monthly instalments that appeared in 1876 sold even better than those of *Middlemarch*, though most readers and reviewers only responded enthusiastically to the Gwendolen story, while Deronda's discovery of his Jewish origins and his mission tended to find sympathy only with Jewish readers, who were delighted at the treatment of Judaism and the avoidance of racial stereotypes. Only the most perceptive critics refrained from cutting the book into halves and saw that George Eliot was attempting a new and challenging kind of fiction (*CH* 35). Nevertheless, the positive response to the more familiar element in the novel showed her ability to retain and delight the readership that she had won with *Adam Bede*, while continuing to pursue her own pioneering course. Even her last work, *Impressions of Theophrastus Such*, sold well when it appeared in 1879, although the reviews were almost all hostile, taking exception to its intellectualism and its preoccupation with the Jews in its last chapter. In this respect *Theophrastus* confirmed the critical view that there was a growing predominance of strenuous intellect over creative imagination in George Eliot's late work, and it was this view that played an important part in the swift decline of her reputation after her death (see REPUTATION, CRITICAL). See also EARNINGS.   JMR

Carroll, David, introduction to *CH*.
Perkin (1990).
Showalter (1977).
Sutherland (1976).

Reform Acts (1832 and 1867). These provide the important political background against which *Felix Holt, the Radical*, *Middlemarch*, and the *'Address to Working Men, by Felix Holt'* should be read. The two Acts redistributed parliamentary seats and extended the male, middle-class franchise. The First Reform Act of 1832, also known as the Great Reform Bill, added 143 to Parliament's 658 seats and about 300,000 voters to the electoral lists; the Second Reform Act of 1867 a further 53 seats and 938,000 voters. The public duties entailed in that enlarged access to power were of great concern to Eliot.

Prior to 1832 only men with freeholds worth an annual rent of 40 shillings could vote for MPs representing large, mainly agricultural areas known as 'counties', or villages and market towns called 'boroughs'. The distribution of seats throughout England, Scotland, Wales, and Ireland, however, was such that comparatively few people actually voted. Worse, bribery, intimidation, or other forms of corruption often predetermined the outcome of elections, since rich landowners could easily control how tenants would vote—in extreme cases by threatening eviction, the withdrawal of custom, or physical violence. In many borough elections a ridiculously small number of voters returned Members. For instance, only 33 votes sent Edinburgh's one MP to Parliament; seven votes Old Sarum's two MPs; and a single vote the Member for Bossiney in Cornwall. Old

Sarum and Bossiney were known as 'rotten' boroughs, for obvious reasons, and there were also 'nomination', 'close', or 'pocket' boroughs, so called because their seats were only open to relatives of the men who owned the seats or others rich and ambitious enough to buy them. Immediately before 1832, there were 470 borough as opposed to 188 county seats, but the already large and fast-growing industrial towns (Manchester, Birmingham, Sheffield, and Leeds) had no direct representation, being considered parts of county seats. The Whig-led coalition ministry under Lord Grey introduced the Great Reform Bill in March 1831. It was principally designed to eliminate expensive elections, disenfranchise corrupt boroughs, enfranchise large commercial towns, and, most significantly, extend the vote to men owning or renting property worth £10 per year, known as £10 householders. The Bill narrowly passed the House, ran into difficulty in Committee, and was defeated by the Lords. Following considerable civil unrest, much political wrangling, and a threat by King William IV to fill the House of Lords with reform-minded peers, the Bill was reintroduced and became law in June 1832.

Political anomalies persisted after 1832: few boroughs had more than 7,000 electorates, some still returned two MPs with less than 200 votes, and a number of borough seats were specially created by the Whigs bowing to mercantile or other party interests. Landowners were still able to pressure qualified tenants to vote for their chosen candidates. Eliot's father, Robert *Evans, an estate manager, 'arranged' to have Lord Aylesford's tenants vote for the Conservative incumbent in the election immediately after the 1832 Bill (Haight 1968: 33). *Chartism took up some of the reform issues denied in 1832, but its last grand demonstration was in 1848. In 1851, however, further political reform once more became a pressing issue. Reform bills were mooted in 1852, 1854, and 1860 but were soon dropped in the face of apathy and opposition; a further two were defeated in the House in 1859 and 1866. Nevertheless, political pressure from the Reform League, which organized enormous rallies sometimes referred to as the Hyde Park riots of 1866 and 1867, as well as pressure from the more moderate Reform Union and the provincial press, who variously represented articulate, skilled workers' unions, gradually helped to persuade Parliament that further reform was inevitable. Eventually, in August 1867, the Conservative government under Prime Minister Benjamin *Disraeli carried the Second Reform Act. In addition to extending the franchise to all rate-paying, borough householders in England, Wales, and Scotland, whether owners or not, and redistributing seats, the Act also limited the number of times electorates could vote for MPs in multi-member constituencies, a measure designed to give representation to minority parties. Ireland, however, was virtually left unaffected by the Act. There the franchise remained narrower than it had been prior to 1829.

Eliot's 'Address to Working Men, by Felix Holt' is deliberately aimed at these newly enfranchised workers and urges them to think carefully about various traditions worth preserving before insisting on still further reform. In both *Felix Holt* and *Middlemarch*, the action centres on or around the 1832 Reform Act. And in both novels the retrospects are there, in part at least, to remind readers of the successes and failures surrounding that milestone in British history. See also POLITICS; PROGRESS.   AvdB

religion was always an object of respect for George Eliot, even though she lost her own religious faith in early adult life (see CHRISTIANITY; LIFE OF GEORGE ELIOT) and remained an agnostic (see ATHEISM). Taking her cue from D. F. *Strauss and Ludwig *Feuerbach, she saw the idea of God as the projection of a human ideal. In a letter to her friend Barbara *Bodichon in November 1862 she insisted that she never tried to undermine anyone's religious belief in her writing and that she had lost all antagonism to religious doctrine: 'I care only to know, if possible, the lasting meaning that lives in all religious doctrine from the beginning till now' (*L* iv. 64–5). In her fiction there is no sign of antagonism towards religion, whose lasting meaning for her lay in the basic human feelings that it expressed. There was an intensity to her own humanism that made her sympathetic to Auguste *Comte's positivist *religion of humanity.

In 1873 when the ideas for *Daniel Deronda* were beginning to germinate, she wrote to John Walter *Cross about how she considered all the great religions of the world to be 'rightly the objects of deep reverence and sympathy—they are the record of spiritual struggles which are the types of our own' (*L* v. 447–8). This was particularly true of *Judaism and *Christianity, on which her own youth had been nourished. She found religious assemblies particularly appealing in that they represented a community coming together to worship the highest Good and were informed by a binding belief or spiritual law which lifted human beings above the slavery of personal passion or impulse (*L* v. 448). She was deeply moved by a visit to a synagogue in Amsterdam in 1866, and she and G. H. *Lewes used to attend the Russian church on their visits to Paris for the beauty of the music and the ritual. This respect for religion is manifested in the sympathetic treatment of Jewish life and customs in *Daniel Deronda*. And when commenting

on modern civilization after visiting hideous industrial towns in Yorkshire, she was able to remark that 'Egypt and her big calm gods seems quite as good' (*L* iv. 362).   JMR

religion of humanity refers in the first place to Auguste *Comte's systematic attempt to found a humanist religion on a scientific basis, with its own creed and code of conduct. George Eliot was sympathetic to Comte's ideas (see POSITIVISM) but suspicious of dogma, and she was not a follower of his religion of humanity, differing from the strict form which he had given it, as the positivist Frederic *Harrison admitted (Haight 1968: 506). Her own humanism could be described as a religion of humanity of a more informal kind, owing much to Baruch *Spinoza and Ludwig *Feuerbach. See also RELIGION.   JMR

Paris, Bernard J., 'George Eliot's Religion of Humanity', *ELH* 29 (1962).

Wright, T. R., *The Religion of Humanity: The Impact of Comtean Positivism on Victorian Britain* (1986).

Rembrandt (Rembrandt Harmensz Van Rijn, 1606–69), Dutch painter. George Eliot's experience of Rembrandt's paintings presumably began in the National Gallery in London where an important collection was already on display by the date of her arrival in *London. It is probable that George Eliot had the Gallery's *Head of a Rabbi* (1653–7) in mind when Hans Meyrick declares that Mordecai, in *Daniel Deronda*, is a 'better model than Rembrandt had for his Rabbi' (*DD* 52).

In 1858, George Eliot saw two other important groups of Rembrandts, in *Berlin and in *Dresden. It has been suggested that she had his *Ganymede carried off by an Eagle* (1635) in mind when she described Totty Poyser, lifted into the air by Adam Bede: 'I don't believe Ganymede cried when the eagle carried him away, and perhaps deposited him on Jove's shoulder' (*AB* 30). George Eliot thought the Rembrandt painting, in which Ganymede is crying and urinating in fright, an 'offence' (Cross, ii. 60).

George Eliot responded warmly to Rembrandt's portraits, not only for their *realism, but also for a nobility which she attributed to the painter's 'virile selective sensibility' (*TS* 13). She was less enthusiastic, however, about Rembrandt's large subject pictures, which she regarded as overblown and out of touch with human reality. As a result, Rembrandt was not ranked as highly with her as other favourite old masters.   LO

Witemeyer (1979).

Renan, Ernest (1823–92), French historian and philologist whose study of Semitic languages led him to question the divine authority of the *Bible. George Eliot read his works extensively, starting with the *Essais de morale et de critique* (1859) when

renunciation

G. H. *Lewes was writing an article on Renan to be published in *Blackwood's Edinburgh Magazine* in December 1859, and continuing with his *Études d'histoire religieuse* (1861). In July 1863 she claimed that he was a favourite with her and that she felt more kinship with his mind than with that of any other living French author (*L* iv. 95). However, his most famous work which had appeared that year, *La Vie de Jésus*, which treated Christ as human rather than divine, was of little interest to her, offering nothing new to the translator of D. F. *Strauss's *Life of Jesus* (see TRANSLATIONS BY GEORGE ELIOT). The attempt to construct a life out of materials of biographical significance seemed to her to be misplaced: 'We can never have a satisfactory basis for the history of the man Jesus, but that negation does not affect the Idea of the Christ either in its historical influence or its great symbolic meanings' (*L* iv. 95). She did later concede that Renan's book had so much artistic merit that it would have a beneficial effect on ordinary minds 'by giving them a sense of unity between that far-off past and our present' (*L* iv. 123). Nevertheless it lowered him in her estimation and she no longer saw him as one of the finest minds of the time. In December 1866 on their way to *Spain she and Lewes met Renan in *Paris at a breakfast given by Mme Mohl and the meeting reinforced her revised view. He was, she wrote, 'very much like a Belgian priest in aspect—broad, coarse, suave, agreeable, commonplace; he talked just as the thousand and one Frenchmen talk—inconsiderately, superficially' (*L* iv. 328). Although his conversation was pleasant enough, it was intellectually undistinguished: he talked the usual nonsense about Auguste *Comte, she maintained, and only knew Immanuel *Kant at second hand, and that inaccurately.   JMR

renunciation is a persistent problem in George Eliot's fiction. Insofar as it involves the overcoming of selfish desire, it represents a positive moral achievement, a 'moral heroism' (*Essays*, 134), but one that lies dangerously close to perverse self-denial and wilful martyrdom. George Eliot always insists on the arduous and painful nature of renunciation, and in an early review is exasperated by Geraldine *Jewsbury's *Constance Herbert* for suggesting that what is renounced will invariably prove not worth the keeping. For Eliot 'it is this very perception that the thing we renounce is precious, is something never to be compensated for, which constitutes the beauty and heroism of renunciation' (*Essays*, 134–5). This is the lesson that Maggie Tulliver learns in *The Mill on the Floss*, where the problem of renunciation is explored most fully. She first finds renunciation extolled in Thomas à Kempis and embraces it without know-

ing 'the inmost truth of the old monk's outpourings, that renunciation remains sorrow, though a sorrow borne willingly' (*MF* 4.3). Her too ready resignation to a restricted and unfulfilling life is sharply criticized by Philip Wakem as a 'narrow self-delusive fanaticism which is only a way of escaping pain by starving into dulness all the highest powers of your nature' (*MF* 5.3). Such a betrayal of life's potential is a particular temptation for a woman, since it amounts to acquiescence in the restricted role offered to her in a patriarchal society. Maggie later comes to realize the justice of Philip's charge when she is faced with the painful reality of renouncing Stephen Guest rather than betraying her own conscience. She now experiences the true meaning of renunciation, but with that insight the novel's exploration ends, for the question of what kind of life can be made on the basis of this renunciation is left unanswered by the dispensation of the tragic ending.

Romola takes the issue a stage further. The renunciation that Savonarola offers Romola is a clue for threading a new life, a call to action to which she responds with 'all the energy of her will' (*RO* 41). It gives her a role and a purpose, first as a visible and secular Madonna tending the inhabitants of the plague village, and then as celibate mother to Tessa and Tito's children. Nevertheless, despite the fact that Romola thus frees herself from the domination of men, the idealizing affirmations of the last part of the novel cannot entirely dispel doubts about the narrowness of the life beyond passion that her renunciation has brought her.

The possibility advanced in *Romola* that renunciation may constitute a formative step is taken up in the later novels. Like Maggie Tulliver, Dorothea in *Middlemarch* first indulges in renunciation of an unexacting kind—she likes giving up, as Celia points out, when her sister talks of giving up riding (*MM* 2)—and then comes to experience the true cost of it at the moral crisis of her life, when she stifles her own pain at the apparent loss of Ladislaw and determines to act to help others (*MM* 80). There is an affinity here with *Goethe's notion of renunciation, or *Entsagung*, which Eliot knew from his *Wilhelm Meister*, a novel she reread in 1870: for Goethe it is a voluntary restriction of the self that serves the full development of the individual and the social group to which he or she belongs. Not only Dorothea's self-conquest but also Deronda's renunciation of Gwendolen in George Eliot's last novel can be seen in this way, and the open-ended future of both the main characters in *Deronda* suggests that renunciation may be enabling rather than simply a painful limitation. See also MORAL VALUES; WOMAN QUESTION.
                                          JMR

Beer (1986).

reputation, critical. When George Eliot died in December 1880 she was generally considered to be the greatest English novelist of her day. 'Had we been asked a few weeks ago, to name the greatest living writer of English fiction', Leslie *Stephen wrote in his commemorative article in the *Cornhill Magazine* in February 1881, 'the answer would have been unanimous. No one . . . would have refused that title to George Eliot' (*CH* 464). That high reputation was soon to suffer an apparent decline from which it only began clearly to recover in the middle of the 20th century. Nevertheless, despite this general pattern of decline and recovery in her reputation, her work remained the object of continuing attention and appreciation even during the early decades of the 20th century, when those who wrote about it tended to insist that it had fallen into neglect. How far the rhetoric of decline and neglect corresponded to actuality may be open to question, but it was a recurrent feature of critical writing about George Eliot from the 1890s to the 1940s.

Stephen's own appraisal was not uncritical, taking up some of the reservations that had appeared in the reviews of the later novels (see RECEPTION). He omitted *Felix Holt, the Radical* and *Daniel Deronda* altogether from the list of works representing the highest level of the author's capacity, and considered that the early works up to *Silas Marner* were the ones that bore the unmistakable mark of genius. Seeing George Eliot as preeminently the novelist of the quiet English country life that she knew in her youth, he stressed the charm of the early work as opposed to the later tendency 'to substitute elaborate analysis for direct presentation' (*CH* 478). That view was often endorsed and the decline towards abstraction was related by some critics to what they perceived to be the growing *atheism evident in the later works. As David Carroll has shown, such distinctions between the early work and the late, between presentation and analysis, between lapsed Christian and militant atheist, were a common feature of criticism in the 1880s (*CH* 38).

There were, however, more discerning critics who did more than deal in these procrustean antitheses and valued George Eliot as something other than the creator of charming idylls. In a penetrating article in *Mind* in July 1881, James *Sully preferred sober analysis to evaluation, and sought to define the distinguishing features of the modern art of fiction as it appeared in her work. Taking modern tragedy to involve not divine necessity but an internal psychological necessity, he stressed the organic complexity of Eliot's characters and her powers of psychological analysis, which he acutely defines as 'the unfolding of inner germs of action, the spreading out before the eye of the compli-

cated activities of imagination and desire, impulse and counter-impulse, which are conduct in process of becoming' (*Mind*, 6: 388). He argued that the moral influence of the fiction came not from any didactic effort on the author's part but from the subtle sympathetic contact of the reader's mind with her own, and he emphasized the satisfying intellectual activity that this contact entailed. This was an appraisal of George Eliot's fiction for a serious intellectual readership, and while not concerned with ranking her as a novelist, Sully presented a powerful case for her importance, concluding that 'her fine sense of the determinateness of human events, of the continuity of our experience, and of the gradations by which character develops, mark her off as the writer of stories who has moved furthest onward in the direction of contemporary ideas' (393).

Her death did, indeed, provoke very different reactions. John *Ruskin felt free to indulge in a broadside against *The Mill on the Floss* in the *Nineteeenth Century* in October 1881, castigating George Eliot as the consummation of the English Cockney school of fiction, in which the personages are picked up from behind the counter or out of the gutter. On the other hand F. W. H. *Myers's reminiscences in the *Century Magazine* in November 1881, which famously described her pronouncing on God, Immortality, and Duty in the Fellows' Garden of Trinity College, Cambridge, created a highly misleading image of her as a solemn and lofty sybil that was to cast a long shadow. It was reinforced by the publication of John Walter *Cross's *Life* in 1885 (see BIOGRAPHIES), which, while it undermined the idea of her development from orthodox faith to atheism as a key to the novels by showing the consistency of her intellectual position, presented her as a sombre and remote figure by editing out evidence of her humour, vivacity, and irreverent wit—what William Hale *White, who had known her in her early London years, called the savour and spice of her personality (see LIFE). White's letter of protest at Cross's biography was of no avail, and the image of her as a gloomy Victorian sage coloured her reputation into the next century, often serving as a lens through which the novels were viewed and denigrated.

In his sympathetic review of Cross's *Life* in the *Atlantic Monthly* in May 1885, Henry *James was warm in his admiration for George Eliot's magnificent mind and the 'rich, deep, masterly pictures of the manifold life of man' (*CH* 504) that she created, but he expressed reservations about the work that were affected by the image of the writer projected in the biography. Claiming that she was unable to be sufficiently superficial about her irregular union with Lewes but brooded on it with an intensity close to the morbid, he proceeded to find the fault of her fiction to be a related excess of reflection and absence of spontaneity. That move from discussion of the life to disparaging reflections on the fiction became a common feature of criticism in the following decades. James attached particular importance to the criticism in her journal of Honoré de *Balzac's *Le Père Goriot* as a hateful book, a remark which for him demonstrated that she took the novel to be not primarily a picture of life but a moralized fable. There was in his view an absence of free aesthetic life in her work: 'We feel in her, always, that she proceeds from the abstract to the concrete; that her figures and situations are evolved, as the phrase is, from her moral consciousness, and are only indirectly the products of observation' (*CH* 498). The criticism, however ill-founded, was often to be endorsed in the following decades. Although James saw reflection getting the better of perception particularly in the later novels, it did not prevent him from admiring *Middlemarch* and Gwendolen and Grandcourt in *Daniel Deronda*, and judging *Romola* to be 'on the whole the finest thing she wrote' despite the fact that it did not seem positively to live except in the person of Tito Melema (*CH* 500).

James's respectful reservations were soon to be superseded by more irreverent criticism. By 1890 W. E. Henley in his *Views and Reviews* could have fun at George Eliot's expense with a series of epigrams: of her books, he wrote, 'it is doubtful whether they are novels disguised as treatises, or treatises disguised as novels'; while she is 'George Sand *plus* Science and *minus* Sex' (Hutchinson 1996: i. 546). George Saintsbury in *Corrected Impressions* (1895) returned to the distinction between the early works and those that followed *Silas Marner*, pronouncing *Felix Holt* and *Middlemarch* to be studies of immense effort and erudition but 'on the whole dead', while *Daniel Deronda* was 'a kind of nightmare'. Even the success of the extremely clever *Adam Bede* could be explained by the absence of serious rivals at the time of its publication; and Saintsbury concluded by writing an obituary of the novelist's reputation: 'for some years past George Eliot, though she may still be read, has more or less passed out of contemporary critical appreciation' (Haight 1965: 167–8). Her fame, once so great, has now, he can confidently claim, almost utterly vanished away. Arnold *Bennett, dipping into *Adam Bede* in the following year, shared this sceptical revision of her standing, feeling sure that she would never be among the classical writers, and writing dismissively in his journal of her transparently feminine, wordy, and undisciplined style.

Leslie Stephen's sympathetic full-length study, *George Eliot* (1902), did something to rescue her

from what Edith *Wharton referred to, in her review of his book in the *Bookman* in May 1902, as the momentary neglect into which the novelist had fallen, but he still held to some of the reservations expressed in his obituary article. *Middlemarch*, for example, lacks the peculiar charm of the earlier work and, for all its power, falls short of the great masterpieces by owing too much to speculative doctrines and not maintaining a close enough contact with the world of realities. Edith Wharton in her review judiciously qualifies this criticism of the later works by arguing that what they lost in structural unity they gained in penetration, irony, and poignancy of emotion. But while demonstrating how George Eliot's handling of dialogue and characterization grew sharper and stronger in the course of her career, she did concede that the novels became narrower as they grew deeper, and attributed that development to her withdrawal from ordinary contact with life after embarking on her relationship with G. H. *Lewes (a view that echoes Henry James's in his review of Cross's *Life*). The consequent loss of perspective was the central defect of the later books.

There were other lengthy critical studies around the turn of the century: W. C. Brownell, *Victorian Prose Masters* (1901), and Henry H. Bonnell, *Charlotte Brontë, George Eliot, Jane Austen: Studies in their Works* (1902). These testify to a continuing current of academic interest, and both are favourable, though Brownell's contention that George Eliot has no *style is at odds with Bonnell's sensitive stylistic analysis. Brownell, too, could write of the neglect into which the novelist had fallen, and neither work seems to have been able to counteract it. The intellectual climate of the early 20th century, with its challenges to the forms and values of high Victorian culture, was unsympathetic to her work. Ford Madox *Ford in his *Critical Attitude* (1911) dismissed her from a modernist standpoint for her solemn moralizing and for seeking to be a preacher rather than an artist, while Edmund *Gosse made the common move from supercilious comments about her appearance, as he recalled it from his youth, to condescending criticism of the pedantry and lack of charm that marred her writing. He declared that she had been ridiculously overpraised, citing Lord Acton's (see DALBERG-ACTON, JOHN) equation of her with *Shakespeare, *Sophocles, *Cervantes, and *Dante, and maintaining that her current neglect was the revenge of time for the excessive praise she had enjoyed in her lifetime. His criticisms repeat the usual charges that the bright vitality of the early work gives way to the strenuous application of an earnest intellect that cannot be content with pleasing but must explain and teach. This depreciation of her as a solemn teacher or preacher is a refrain of criticism in this period, running from Gosse and Ford, through E. M. *Forster and Elton, to Cecil in the 1930s, and it was only the finer responses of great modernist writers like Virginia *Woolf and Marcel *Proust that anticipated modern criticism by registering the richness and complexity of her work.

When Virginia Woolf honoured the centenary of George Eliot's birth with her tribute in the *Times Literary Supplement* on 20 November 1919, she could admit to having accepted the late Victorian version of the novelist as 'a deluded woman who held phantom sway over subjects even more deluded than herself' (Haight 1965: 183), and as the embodiment of a seriousness that a younger generation could only laugh at and dismiss. Her own article was a challenge to that orthodoxy, although the perspectives it opened up were not to be properly appreciated and developed until the emergence of academic feminist criticism in the 1970s (see CRITICISM, MODERN: FEMINIST APPROACHES). Whereas her father Leslie Stephen had seen George Eliot's work to have been determined, but also implicitly limited, by her being a woman, Virginia Woolf took the woman's experience as presented in Eliot's heroines to be the vital, though problematic, centre of the work. Far from being a solemn sage, the novelist was a troubled spirit, questioning and baffled, who took on and tried to reach beyond 'the burden and complexity of womanhood' (Haight 1965: 189). Moreover, while acknowledging the appealing warmth of the early work, Woolf did not accept the by now conventional view that the later work marked a decline, but argued that Eliot's power was at its highest in the mature *Middlemarch*, which she famously pronounced to be a magnificent book and 'one of the few English novels to be written for grown-up people' (Haight 1965: 187).

In spite of Virginia Woolf's insights George Eliot's reputation continued to languish. In his *A Survey of English Literature, 1830–1880* (1920) Oliver Elton maintained that in exhaustively describing life she missed the spirit of life itself. The modernist emphasis on impersonality also ran counter to her form of *narration, and Percy Lubbock's *The Craft of Fiction* (1921), which, under the influence of Henry James, elevated 'showing' above 'telling', helped establish a critical orthodoxy which was unsympathetic to her achievement and encouraged a misreading of her work. Thus E. M. Forster in his *Aspects of Fiction* (1927) could dismiss her novels as shapeless and stylistically ponderous by comparison with the work of French and Russian novelists. Her reputation probably reached its lowest ebb in the early 1930s. In an article in *Symposium* in 1933, 'In Search of George Eliot: An Approach through Marcel

Proust', Franklin Gary maintained that of all the great Victorian novelists none had fewer readers and less critical notice than she did; and he had recourse to a comparison with a writer who was highly regarded in an attempt to rehabilitate her, hoping that it might be through Proust that she would be read again. Proust was one modernist who had admired her, and her reputation in *France (and the same was true in *Germany) had not undergone such a steep decline as in Britain: there were two full-length critical studies and a biography published in the 1920s and 1930s (see Couch 1967: 164–5), as well as a substantial discussion in Madeleine Cazamian's *Le Roman et les idées en Angleterre* (1923).

Lord David Cecil's treatment of her in his *Early Victorian Novelists* (1934) confirmed the situation Gary had described and did nothing to alter it. While acknowledging the sharpness and subtlety of her moral scrutiny and intellectual understanding of her characters and conceding that she is the only novelist of her time who writes on the scale of the great continental novelists, Cecil accounts for the catastrophic slump in her reputation by referring to the bleakness of her exclusively moral point of view and the drabness of the virtues which she upholds. With aristocratic disdain he dubs these schoolteachers' virtues, sees her as a philistine in her view of art, inferior in her creative imagination to Dickens, and petty and provincial by comparison with *Tolstoy. Monumental and profoundly impressive though she is, she never produced a wholly satisfactory work of art, since the driving force of her intellect was too powerful for her imagination.

It was not until the next decade that the tide of her critical reputation clearly began to turn, with F. R. *Leavis's articles in *Scrutiny* in 1945–6, later to form part of his *The Great Tradition* (1948), starting the process of revaluation. He was the first to question the Jamesian criticism that her novels were moralized fables with an absence of free aesthetic life, arguing that a novelist's preoccupation with form was inseparable from the matter of moral vision and discrimination. He also challenged some of the commonplaces of Eliot criticism, particularly the distinction between the charm of the early work and the strenuous intellectualism of the later. Charm for him was overrated in comparison with maturity and it is in the mature fiction, especially *Middlemarch* and the Gwendolen story in *Daniel Deronda*, that he sees a fully developed moral and artistic intelligence magnificently at work. The moral seriousness that Cecil had sneered at is valued as a central aspect of that maturity. Where there are weaknesses, they are seen as symptoms of immaturity, and he singles out the tendency of the author to identify too closely with heroines such as Maggie Tulliver, leading to idealization and sentimentality. But such lapses do not detract from the overall achievement, which he ranks with the greatest of novelists. Dismissing as breathtaking in its absurdity Elton's criticism of her as inferior to George *Meredith and Thomas *Hardy, he indicates her true place and quality by invoking Tolstoy: she may not be as transcendently great as the Russian, but she is great in the same kind of way, achieving a depth and reality that can be described as Tolstoyan.

Some of Leavis's critical pronouncements may be questionable or even absurd, like his famous proposal that the Gwendolen story should be separated from *Daniel Deronda* and published as a separate novel, but his combative advocacy did much to rescue George Eliot from critical neglect and condescension. As a central figure in the tradition of the English novel she was owed serious attention, and from the late 1940s she began to receive it. Joan Bennett's *George Eliot: Her Mind and Art* (1948) presents a sensitive reading of the fiction which, like Leavis, stresses the strengths of the later novels, arguing, for instance, for the unity of *Middlemarch*, where every element has a function in the whole design. Critical attention is focused on formal coherence and moral vision, and Bennett aims to show how mind and art combine, how the author's wide knowledge and strenuous thinking contribute to the vision of the world in the novels, even though the rift between thinker and artist manifests itself as an occasional weakness. The appearance around this time, too, of Gerald Bullett's study of the life and works, *George Eliot: Her Life and Books* (1947), and Basil Willey's discussion of the importance for the novelist of Hennell, Strauss, and Feuerbach in his *Nineteenth-Century Studies* (1949), indicate how George Eliot's reputation was beginning to recover.

Ten years later three fine studies, Jerome Thale's *The Novels of George Eliot* (1959), Reva Stump's *Movement and Vision in George Eliot's Novels* (1959), and Barbara Hardy's *The Novels of George Eliot: A Study in Form* (1959), soon followed by W. J. Harvey's *The Art of George Eliot* (1961), secured that recovery. As their titles suggest Hardy and Harvey both focus on the aesthetic and formal properties of the novels, Harvey defending the use of what he calls the omniscient narrator against Jamesian criticisms, and Hardy bringing out the complicated artifice of the fiction that is disguised by the quiet normality of George Eliot's world. Hardy's important and influential work examines the detailed workings of the novels with illuminating sensitivity, noting particularly how we are made subtly aware of the alternative courses that the lives of the characters might have taken. In

demonstrating the formal sophistication of George Eliot's practice, she puts her firmly in the company of the great modernists, arguing that the organization of her fiction is as subtle and complex as that of Henry James, or Proust, or Joyce. Greatness is now proclaimed without the condescending qualifications so common in earlier criticism.

The New Critical approach of Hardy and Harvey, which sought to demonstrate the formal and thematic coherence of the novels, found a congenial subject in George Eliot's work, and it dominated critical discussion in the following decade when emphasis was commonly placed, as in David Daiches's 1963 study of *Middlemarch*, on the author's firm control over her material. When critical practice began to change after 1970 under the impact of structuralist and post-structuralist theory and the emergence of modern feminism, she remained a central though often contested figure, for her work is rich and complex enough to offer abundant scope to readers alert to cultural codes and ideological construction, to tension and contradiction, discontinuity and *différance*. For these developments after 1970 see CRITICISM, MODERN. JMR

Bellringer (1993).
Carroll, David, introduction to *CH*.
Couch (1967).
Haight (1965).
Hutchinson (1996).

reviewer, George Eliot as. See JOURNALIST, GEORGE ELIOT AS.

revolutions of 1848. Living in *Coventry with her father and as yet untravelled on the Continent, George Eliot observed the events of the revolutionary year in Europe from afar. She responded to news of the February Revolution in *Paris with excitement. In a letter of 8 March to John *Sibree which sparkles with wit and vivacity, she expresses her delight at his enthusiasm, finding him 'just as sansculottish and rash as I would have you' (*L* i. 253). She herself is radical enough to wish to see the Italians chase the 'odious Austrians out of beautiful Lombardy' (*L* i. 255) and to cast a mocking eye on monarchy, impatient with those who pity the deposed king Louis Philippe: 'Certainly our decayed monarchs should be pensioned off: we should have a hospital for them, or a sort of Zoological Garden, where those worn-out humbugs may be preserved'. Even the young *Victoria is referred to in similar terms as 'our little humbug of a queen'. Nevertheless her radical fervour has its limits and she is at pains to keep the idea of revolution at a safe distance, arguing that any similar movement at home would be simply destructive, given the inferiority of the British working classes to the French: 'Here there is so much larger a proportion of selfish radicalism and unsatisfied, brute sensuality (in the agricultural and mining districts especially) than of perception or desire of justice' (*L* i. 254). The future for Britain lies in 'the slow progress of political reform' since there is nothing in the constitution to obstruct it. This preference for evolutionary change became a central feature of her essentially conservative social outlook in later years, as can be seen in her 1856 essay 'The *Natural History of German Life' and the *'Address to Working Men by, Felix Holt' in 1868. See also SOCIETY; POLITICS; PROGRESS; RADICALISM.   JMR

Butwin, Joseph, 'The Pacification of the Crowd: From "Janet's Repentance" to *Felix Holt*', *Nineteenth-Century Fiction*, 35 (1980–1).

Richardson, Samuel (1689–1761), English novelist who was a long-standing influence on George Eliot. After she had corrected the proofs of *The *Life of Jesus* she read *Sir Charles Grandison* (1753–4), exclaiming that 'I had no idea that Richardson was worth so much', and adding 'The morality is perfect—there is nothing for the new lights to correct' (*L* i. 240). She wrote to Bessie Rayner *Parkes in October 1852, 'Like Sir Charles Grandison? I should be sorry to be the heathen that did not like that book', though she didn't warm to Harriet Byron, suggesting that Sir Charles's sister 'is the gem, with her marmoset' (*L* ii. 65). In her essay on *'Woman in France: Madame de Sablé' Eliot observes 'Few English women have written so much like a woman as Richardson's Lady G.': half a lifetime later she wrote to Cara *Bray remembering the latter's loaning her the novel for a visit to the Isle of Wight in 1847, 'where I read it at every interval when my father did not want me, and was sorry that the novel was not longer. It is a solace to hear of anyone's reading and enjoying Richardson. We have fallen on an evil generation who would not read "Clarissa" even in an abridged form' (*L* vi. 320). As late as August 1877 Eliot and G. H. Lewes were rereading *Sir Charles Grandison*.

One other connection which she probably appreciated was the fact the *Burne-Joneses, Edward and Georgiana, who became regular visitors and friends of Eliot and Lewes from February 1868 onwards, had moved into the Grange, the large house in North End Lane, Fulham, where Richardson had written his novels. There is one humorous observation in *The Mill on the Floss* (*MF* 1.4) where Maggie stands 'on a chair to look at a remarkable series of pictures representing the Prodigal Son, in the costume of Sir Charles Grandison, except that . . . he had not like that accomplished hero, the taste and strength of mind to dispense with a wig'. The incident may have wider implications, for the

Mill has been seen by Margaret Anne Doody (1980–1) as, among many other things, an answer to *Grandison*. She examines the brother/sister parallels and differences in the two novels, noting the centrality of the women characters for both writers and their development through some experience of pain. There are connections, too, between Richardson's novel and *Daniel Deronda*, which alludes to it and similarly takes a virtuous man as its hero, while creating more dramatic interest in its female characters, like Gwendolen and Alcharisi. Gwendolen's sisters feel that her advancement is 'as interesting as "Sir Charles Grandison"' (*DD* 28), and later make her post-marital visit comparable to Harriet Byron reappearing out of her 'happiness ever after' (*DD* 44), a distinct irony in view of Gwendolen's suffering. The parallel between Deronda and Grandison is also ironically qualified by another comparison with Richardson, when Sir Hugo tells him 'You are a dangerous young fellow—a kind of Lovelace who will make the Clarissas run after you instead of your running after them' (*DD* 32). The remark is jocular but, as Gillian Beer (1986) has suggested, there is a sense in which Deronda does play the part of a Lovelace, violating Gwendolen by abandoning her.

Richardson's morality, carried beyond realism, his psychology of character, essentially true, his style, finely weighted, his narrative verve involving expectation and crises, were undoubtedly congenial to Eliot. She, too, was adept at the epistolary mode (witness Casaubon's letter of proposal to Dorothea), and in general Richardson's responsible and dedicated concern for fiction was very close indeed to her own.   GRH

Beer (1986).

Doody, Margaret Anne, 'George Eliot and the Eighteenth-Century Novel', *Nineteenth-Century Fiction*, 35 (1980–1).

Riehl, Wilhelm Heinrich. See 'NATURAL HISTORY OF GERMAN LIFE, THE'.

Risorgimento (lit. 'Resurgence'), term used for the movement towards Italian unification achieved in 1860, towards which George Eliot was ambivalent. In 1848 she expressed a wish to see the Italians chase the 'odious Austrians out of Lombardy' (*L* i. 255), but by 1865 she was writing that she was not very interested in the doings of Garibaldi or Cavour as she was more concerned with G. H. *Lewes's health and with Giotto and Brunelleschi.

Such a complaint may seem rather like the tetchy English tourist complaining that the politics of natives were getting in the way of the sightseeing. But this would be a too hasty judgement. As *Romola* and *Felix Holt, the Radical* show, Eliot was not really hostile to *radicalism, and she was fully aware of the abuses of the old order whether in 15th-century *Florence or 19th-century England or Italy. But she did see, and history has proved her right, that revolutions can cause as many problems as they cure, and that truth in politics has an ephemeral quality in relation to the eternal verities of literature, morality, and art. See also ITALY; MAZZINI; GARIBALDI; NATIONALISM; POLITICS; REVOLUTIONS OF 1848. TJW

> Goode, John, '"The Affections Clad with Knowledge": Woman's Duty and the Public Life', *Literature and History*, 9 (1983).

Roman Catholicism. The unreformed, Roman Catholic Christian Church of Western Europe was in Victorian England the religion of genteel old English families, of immigrants from Catholic countries (especially Ireland), and of converts (particularly from the Church of England—those significant numbers of men, often clergymen, and women, who moved on from the Anglo-Catholic party in the Church of England right into the Church of Rome). Extreme Protestants, most of them evangelicals of some sort (see EVANGELICALISM), were often extremely antagonistic to what they saw as an unwarranted granting of civil liberties to Catholics and to the allowing of papal missions to Reformed England. The former Anglican priest Cardinal John Henry *Newman and the Irish Archbishop of Westminster, Cardinal Nicholas Wiseman, were special focuses of Protestant fear and aggression. In her early evangelical phase, George Eliot was notably open to the beauties of early Anglo-Catholic holiness (she greatly valued the verses of John Keble's *The Christian Year*, 1827), but she was as fierce as any strict Protestant at the much more Catholic-minded *Tracts for the Times*, associated with Newman's creeping Romanism: they were attempts 'to fraternize with the members of a church carrying on her brow the prophetical epithets applied by St John to the Scarlet beast, the Mystery of iniquity' (letter of 20 May 1839, to George Eliot's evangelical schoolteacher Maria *Lewis: *L* i. 26). As post-Christian critic and novelist she expressed much satirical dismay at the anti-popery she had once endorsed (Dr Cumming's violent views about Catholics being puppets of Satan in her *'Evangelical Teaching: Dr Cumming', *Westminster Review*, October 1855; gentle Miss Pratt's affection for the anti-Catholic novel *Father Clement* (1823) by Grace Kennedy, in 'Janet's Repentance'). As part of her long fictional engagement with the varieties of *Christianity, George Eliot naturally turned to the Roman Catholic subject—though, unusually for her, in historical costume dramas. Her long poetic drama *The Spanish Gypsy* is set in the 1490s, when Catholic Spain was viciously expelling the Moors and exiling gypsies. The ponderously researched (and very Browningesque) Florentine novel *Romola*, set in the same period, looks closely at the character, beliefs, and career of the Italian Dominican mystic and social reformer Girolamo *Savonarola, as a key part of her fictionalization of the greatest period of Florentine humanism. George Eliot's strong view was that entering the great cultural tradition of Catholic Europe was necessary for the truly educated and enlightened English self. Dorothea Brooke's Roman honeymoon in *Middlemarch* is a main stage in her long education out of Protestant narrowness. The shock of Rome—the Scarlet Woman of apocalyptic Protestant nightmare, the home of all the fearful red-hatted cardinals, its religious inflammatoriness brought home by the city's red Christmas draperies—spreads across her hurt Protestant gaze 'like a disease of the retina' (*MM* 20). But the pain is therapeutic. Not dissimilarly—though less dramatically—it's the reading of *The Imitation of Christ*, the classic of Catholic spirituality by Thomas à *Kempis (translated into English in 1440), which raises Maggie Tulliver in *The Mill on the Floss* from her slough of despond and the uncultured Protestant narrowness of her family and her neighbourhood—that 'Variation of Protestantism Unknown to Bossuet' as the title of a chapter has it (*MF* 4.1). (Bossuet was the great Catholic author of *L'Histoire des Variations des Églises protestantes*, 1688.) But for all the way that Catholic and Catholic-European broadening is shown as vital for the moral health of narrowly Protestant English female souls, George Eliot never allowed Catholic spirituality and morality a final say. Maggie Tulliver's transformation by the Kempisian 'Voice From the Past' preaching renunciation to her (*MF* 4.3) is, as ever with George Eliot, a conversion into true humanity (helped on, incidentally, by *The Christian Year*). And Romola has to grow through her devotion to the charismatic Savonarola, with his alluring bonfires of female 'vanities'—much as the devoted evangelical Dorothea grows out of her infatuated admiration for the Protestant Revd Mr Casaubon—into a sharing of the 'common life' that is much more merely humanist than devotional and doctrinal ('God's Kingdom is something wider—else, let me stand outside it with the beings that I love', *RO* 59). The reformist Catholic spirituality of Savonarola, like the *Methodism of Dinah Morris in *Adam Bede*, only has meaning when it has been thoroughly demythologized and humanized. See also ANGLICANISM; RELIGION OF HUMANITY. VC

Romanticism. George Eliot, like many of the major Victorian writers—*Tennyson, Robert

*Browning, Thomas *Carlyle, Charles *Dickens, the *Brontës—was born before 1820, in what is normally considered to be the Romantic period, and it may be more useful in some respects to characterize these writers as 'later Romantics' rather than Victorians.

There is ample evidence in George Eliot's letters and essays that she was well read in Romantic writing in English but what perhaps separates her from many of her contemporaries is that her knowledge of European Romantic writing was also extensive. The fact that she accompanied G. H. *Lewes to *Germany while he was researching his biography of *Goethe was a particularly significant experience as this gave her first-hand contact with a German intellectual life that had its roots in Romanticism.

If one takes an overview of George Eliot's writing it seems clear that her strongest affiliations are with those writers whom one can call 'positive' Romantics: writers who aspired to a vision of the world that could unite humanity and provide the individual life with meaning. She can be included in a Romantic tradition that would include *Wordsworth, *Coleridge, *Shelley, Schelling, and Schleiermacher among others. But most of these figures based their positive vision on the acceptance of metaphysical beliefs of one sort or another, such as Wordsworth's nature philosophy. Though George Eliot accepted the underlying humanist philosophy of the positive Romantics she did not accept the metaphysical ideas that often underlay that humanist philosophy. This raised the issue whether such a humanist philosophy was sustainable without its metaphysical underpinnings. One can see a parallel here with her relationship to *Christianity in that she valued Christian morality and ethics but rejected Christian metaphysics.

George Eliot was famously attacked by Friedrich *Nietzsche in *Twilight of the Idols* (1888) for believing that Christian morality could be preserved if belief in God were discarded and the German philosopher can be seen as the culmination of a Romantic tradition alternative to that which George Eliot favoured. A relationship can be seen between the Byronic tradition of Romanticism with its elevation of the ego, its *irony, its scepticism, and the writings of Nietzsche. Nietzsche provides a philosophical justification for ideas that can be found in Romantic writers such as *Byron, the early Friedrich Schlegel, and Chateaubriand. George Eliot's significance as a later Romantic writer is that at the level of ideas she shares the anti-metaphysical philosophy of the Byronic Romantic tradition but she does not accept its rejection of Christian moral values in favour of various egotistic and ironical alternatives. Her writings can be seen as having a double aim: to present a critique of the egotism, irony, and scepticism of the Byronic Romantic tradition without resorting to metaphysics and to justify the humanist vision of the positive Romantics in non-metaphysical terms.

Egotism is a recurrent theme in George Eliot's writings and it clearly has a Romantic aspect (see MORAL VALUES). This is seen most obviously in her poetry, particularly 'Armgart' and *The Spanish Gypsy* (see POETRY OF GEORGE ELIOT) in which she is not constrained by the requirements of realism in her representation of the egotist. Thus in 'Armgart', the eponymous heroine is said to bear

> Caesar's ambition in her delicate breast,
> And nought to still it with but quivering song!

But this opera singer who believes nothing should stand in the way of her self-realization and who embodies such Byronic attitudes as defiance, assertion of the will, and adherence to a set of self-created values, loses her singing voice through illness yet she still reacts in Byronic fashion:

> An inborn passion gives a rebel's right:
> I would rebel and die in twenty worlds
> Sooner than bear the yoke of thwarted life,
> Each keenest sense turned into keen distaste,
> Hunger not satisfied but kept alive
> Breathing in languor half a century.

Armgart is finally moved to repudiate this Byronic philosophy, partly in response to her servant Walpurga's attack on her:

> For what is it to you that women, men,
> Plod, faint, are weary, and espouse despair
> Of aught but fellowship? Save that you spurn
> To be among them?

Armgart clearly influenced the characterization of the Princess Halm-Eberstein in *Daniel Deronda*, another opera singer who places egotistic self-realization above all other considerations, and Byronic influence is apparent in such characters in her novels as Mrs Transome in *Felix Holt, the Radical* and Gwendolen Harleth in *Daniel Deronda*, and even Lydgate in *Middlemarch* has some Byronic characteristics. Also prominent in the novels are nihilistic egotists who represent the more sceptical and nihilistic aspect of Romantic egotism, notably Tito Melema in *Romola*, Christian in *Felix Holt* and Grandcourt and Lapidoth in *Daniel Deronda*. George Eliot's general critique of egotism as a philosophy in her characterization of such figures as Tito is that the individual consciousness is a social product: it could not exist without language and social influences. This means that the individual can never authentically separate him or herself off from social life and the moral considerations that are intrinsic to it. Even the egotistic and sceptical arguments used by Byronic and nihilistic characters to justify their devotion to the self have emerged from a social context. Thus for George Eliot moral and social responsibility are products of social life and do not require external validation from religious or metaphysical sources.

Another fundamental Romantic aspect of her writing is the emphasis placed on feeling as an organ of knowledge. It clearly has priority over reason and rationality. But George Eliot is different from the earlier Romantics in being also concerned with philosophical and theoretical justifications of this idea. Feeling is fundamental to Ludwig *Feuerbach's philosophy in his *Essence of Christianity*, which she translated. It is also crucial to the thinking of Herbert *Spencer and G. H. Lewes with which she was well acquainted. Lewes believed evolutionary theory did not undermine ethics and argued that human beings inherit animal feelings which constitute the basis of a moral sense which 'the social life has developed into devoted affection, passionate sympathy, and self-denying forethought' (*The Study of Psychology* (1879), 144–5). These words may actually be George Eliot's as she completed this book from Lewes's notes after his death.

Yet like the Romantics, George Eliot was aware that though feeling could be a direct means of knowledge, it could also take the form of almost uncontrollable impulses that could be destructive in their effects. Thus Maggie Tulliver is subject to rebellious feelings which 'would flow out over her affections and conscience like a lava stream, and frighten her with a sense that it was not difficult for her to become a demon' (*MF* 4.3). Yet for George Eliot impulsive and rebellious feeling should not be suppressed by adopting some rigid system, as both Maggie Tulliver and Romola try to do by accepting external controls derived from Thomas à *Kempis and Girolamo *Savonarola respectively; rather feeling itself can control and sublimate impulse if feeling is related to one's whole self and thus takes account of both past and present. When Romola in despair finds herself in the plague-ridden village feeling requires no rational justification for her to act 'with so energetic an impulse to share the life around her, to answer the call of need and do the work which cried aloud to be done, that the reasons for living, enduring, labouring, never took the form of argument' (*RO* 29). The power of impulse is controlled and directed because it is in continuity with her sense of whole self.

The idea of a whole self reveals another aspect of George Eliot's thinking, namely the importance she attaches to memory. To lose touch with memory threatens human identity. The narrator in *Silas Marner* writes regarding Marner's sense of

alienation that 'Minds that have been unhinged from their old faith and love, have perhaps sought this Lethean influence of exile, in which the past becomes dreamy because its symbols have all vanished, and the present too is dreamy because it is linked with no memories'. This leaves Marner with only 'a mechanical relation to the objects of his life' (*SM* 2). One of the dangers of impulse is to lead to acts that destroy the continuity of self that memory makes possible. In 'Janet's Repentance' from *Scenes of Clerical Life* the narrator writes: 'There are moments when by some strange impulse we contradict our past selves—fatal moments, when a fit of passion, like a lava stream lays low the work of half our lives' (*SC* 3.14). Individuals who act wilfully in contradiction to their sense of continuity of self sustained through memory risk severe psychological damage. This is clearly exemplified in such characters as Tito in *Romola* and Gwendolen Harleth in *Deronda*.

Though the ending of *The Mill on the Floss* continues to be seen as problematic by many critics, the choice Maggie Tulliver makes to leave Stephen Guest and return to St Ogg's is based on her need to act in accordance with her whole self and the memories that sustain it: 'the sense of contradiction with her past life in her moments of strength and clearness, came upon her like a pang of degradation' (*MF* 7.5). Memory interacts with feeling to provide the guidance she seeks: 'It came with the memories that no passion could long quench; the long past came back to her, and with it the fountains of self-renouncing pity and affection, of faithfulness and resolve' (*MF* 7.5). Yet this is a tragic choice since it involves a rejection of the passionate feeling aroused in her by Stephen Guest, and returning to her former life cannot repair the damage that has been done by appearing to have eloped with him.

Many Romantics favoured an organicist social philosophy and this is another significant aspect of George Eliot's fiction. As human beings need a sense of continuity of self with its basis in memory, *society likewise needs an analogous sense of identity (see HISTORY). Her last book, *Impressions of Theophrastus Such*, is very concerned with how to achieve social cohesion in a society that seems in danger of becoming fragmented. The narrator writes of 'the divine gift of a memory which inspires the moments with a past, a present, and a future, and gives the sense of corporate existence that raises man above the otherwise more respectable and innocent brute' (*TS* 18). Without such a sense of corporate existence the world seems spiritually dead. In early novels such as *Adam Bede* and *Silas Marner* George Eliot had depicted societies which belonged to the past and that were organic in certain respects in that they had shared traditions, symbols, and implicit values which served to sustain a sense of community consciousness. Significantly in *Deronda*, the novel set closest to her own time, English society is depicted in pessimistic terms as having little sense of corporate existence. The organicist ideal is proclaimed by the proto-Zionist Mordecai—the Romantic as visionary—and Daniel Deronda—a Shelleyan Romantic who longs to devote his life to a higher ideal—forsakes England in order to further Mordecai's organicist goal.   KMN

Newton, K. M., *George Eliot: Romantic Humanist* (1981).

Stone, Donald D., *The Romantic Impulse in Victorian Fiction* (1980).

Rome was visited by George Eliot on two occasions. It was the principal destination of the Italian journey of 1860: she and G. H. *Lewes concentrated on getting there by Palm Sunday, 1 April, and left for *Naples on 29 April. As was customary when they travelled, they supplemented guidebooks with other reading, such as H. G. Liddell's *A History of Rome from the earliest times to the establishment of the Empire* (1855), as Lewes said, 'to repair the breaches in our historical knowledge' (*Journals*, 328). But their preparation did not equip them for what they encountered, to the extent that on arrival George Eliot declared, 'Not one iota had I seen that corresponded with my preconceptions' (*Journals*, 341). She soon aligned her expectations with what she saw, however, 'gradually rising from the depth of disappointment to an intoxication of delight' (*L* iii. 286). The disappointment, and a more protracted phase of disorientation, together with particular experiences such as a visit to the studio of the painter Overbeck, were later to be shared with Dorothea Casaubon in *Middlemarch*.

George Eliot recorded in enthusiastic yet discriminating detail her pleasure both in classical antiquities and 'Christian Rome' (*Journals*, 344). For instance, she found the Easter ceremonies on the whole 'a melancholy, hollow business', except for 'the wonderful spectacle of the illumination of St. Peter's [on Easter Sunday]. That really is a thing so wondrous, so magically beautiful, that one can't find it in one's heart to say, it is not worth doing ... the grand illumination flashed out and turned the outline of stars into a palace of gold. Venus looked on palely' (*Journals*, 345).

On their second visit to Rome, 4–21 April 1869, the Leweses consciously avoided Holy Week, but found themselves caught in celebrations of the jubilee of ordination to the priesthood of Pope Pius IX on 11 April. However, they enjoyed better weather and better health in Rome than in other parts of their itinerary. Though they expressed a 'desire not to be disturbed in our visit to this city of tombs' (*L* v. 25), they inevitably encountered acquaintances, including members of the Cross family, whom Lewes already knew. At the time, George Eliot did not remark her introduction to John Walter *Cross. Ironically, it was Lewes who noted in his diary for 18 April: 'Mrs Cross with son and daughter came for an hour. *My Fifty Second Birthday*. Both Polly and I had entirely forgotten it' (*Journals*, 94). See also ITALY.   MAH

Thompson (1998).

Romola (*see page 340*)

Rossetti, Dante Gabriel (1828–82), English poet, painter, translator. In July 1862 George *Smith sent George Eliot a copy of Rossetti's *The Early Italian Poets from Ciullo D'Alcamo to Dante Alighieri* (1861). She noted Guido Guinicelli's *canzone* 'Of the Gentle Heart' in Rossetti's translation, and later inserted it as epigraph to chapter 61 of *Daniel Deronda*. On 9 January 1870 Rossetti lunched at The *Priory, and four days later Eliot and G. H. *Lewes went to see his pictures (of Pandora, Beatrice, Cassandra, Mrs Morris, for example): he was present when they dined with Barbara *Bodichon on 7 February (from time to time Bodichon assisted Rossetti materially). Ten days later he sent Eliot his sonnets on Mary Magdalene and Pandora, suggesting they might enhance appreciation of the drawings, together with photographs of them and of the *Rosa Triplex* and *Hamlet*. Eliot's letter (*L* v. 78–9) expresses her gratitude for 'the head marked June 1861—it is exquisite'—and her interest in the Magdalene, which Rossetti had suggested he would revise. She says, 'I hope you will keep in the picture an equally passionate type for her' and hopes too that they may talk about his modifications. She has reservations about the *Hamlet*, feeling, with ironic pedantry, that 'Hamlet had a square anterior lobe'.

In May Rossetti sent Eliot an inscribed copy of his *Poems* (1870). She told him that 'The sonnets towards "The House of Life" attract me peculiarly' (*L* v. 93, 8 May 1870). He was at Lord Houghton's (see MILNES, RICHARD MONCKTON) when they dined there a week later. Eliot was obviously sympathetic towards him and, at the least, found his poetry stimulating and moving. There are two interesting postscripts. The first follows R. W. Buchanan's attack on Rossetti in 'The Fleshly School of Poetry' (*Contemporary Review*, October 1871). Buchanan was estranged from Eliot and Lewes as a result, though he wrote Eliot a very sympathetic letter after Lewes's death. The second is drawn attention to by Jan Marsh in her *Christina Rossetti: A Literary Biography* (1994) where she says that as Gabriel lay dying his sister, the poet Christina, was

(*cont. on page 350*)

Romola

PUBLISHED serially in 1862–3, a novel much concerned with turning points and transition, and marking a turning point in George Eliot's writing life. John Walter *Cross recounts that 'The writing of "Romola" ploughed into her more than any of her other books. She told me she could put her finger on it as marking a well-defined transition in her life. In her own words, "I began it a young woman,—I finished it an old woman"' (Cross, ii. 352). Her career was at the halfway mark, and this historical novel is a radical experiment, in which she shifted her ground from the English Midlands world she had recreated in her earlier fiction to a scene distant both in time and place, *Florence at the end of the 15th century, constructed on the basis of prodigious research. At the time she was writing, in the early 1860s, the definition of this period as 'the Renaissance' was being consolidated by historians such as Michelet and Burckhardt, who interpreted the interaction between humanist development of the pagan classical tradition and a vitalized *Christianity, centred in Florence, as a turning point for Western Europe. George Eliot's text develops individual case histories in the reworked context of historical events, to produce—in the sober estimation of Andrew Sanders—'a masterpiece integral to the entire cultural achievement of the nineteenth century' (196).

Composition

Writing in his journal for 21 May 1860 in Florence, G. H. *Lewes claimed credit for the conception of *Romola*:

This morning while reading about Savonarola it occurred to me that his life and times afford fine material for an historical romance. Polly at once caught at the idea with enthusiasm. It is a subject which will fall in with much of her studies and sympathies; and it will give fresh interest to our stay in Florence. (*L* iii. 295)

Immediately their activities took focus from this idea. They visited the Dominican convent of San Marco, the site most closely associated with Girolamo *Savonarola: Lewes went through the building, taking notes, while Eliot remained in the chapter house where in chapter 15 of the novel Romola visits her dying brother and meets Savonarola, 'no woman being allowed admission beyond this precinct'. They bought a copy of Savonarola's poems, and a recent French biography of him, thus initiating an extraordinary process of study that was to extend more than a year before she began to write in earnest, and more than two years before the commencement of the novel's serial publication (see SERIALIZATION).

On their return to England, domestic matters—including a move to central London—took precedence; and the 'sudden inspiration' (*L* iii. 371) of *Silas Marner* 'thrust itself between me and the other book I was meditating' (*L* iii. 360). That work completed, the Leweses set off again for *Italy on 19 April 1861, with the express purpose of researching *Romola*. They spent a month in Florence consulting books on costume, topography, and history in the Magliabecchian Library, and acquainting themselves so thoroughly with the city that Margaret *Oliphant was to declare *Romola* a guidebook to Florence 'not to be equalled by any Murray known to man' (*Blackwood's Edinburgh Magazine*, 116 (1874), 82).

George Eliot was already subject to doubts about her ability to execute the project, but back in England energetically embarked on further reading and note-taking. She consulted scores of works in Italian, Latin, French, and German as well as English in the course of her endeavours, drawing most heavily on Marco Lastri's *Osservatore fiorentino*

(1776–8) and Pasquale Villari's *Storia di Fra Girolamo Savonarola e de' suoi tempi* (1859–61), as her extensive working *notebooks show.

She made many plans and false starts in the latter part of 1861; then on New Year's Day 1862 '*I began my Novel of Romola*' (*Journals*, 107). Her anxieties and wretched health made the process of composition anything but smooth, and in February her concentration was shaken by an approach from the entrepreneurial publisher George *Smith, who offered £10,000 for the book, including the entire copyright (*L* iv. 17–18). She had reservations, but Smith was not deterred: he soon enlisted Lewes as consulting editor for the *Cornhill Magazine*, and in May struck acceptable terms with George Eliot: £7,000 for the serialization in twelve monthly parts of 32 pages to begin in July, with exclusive rights to book publication for seven years (see PUBLISHERS, NEGOTIATIONS WITH).

This defection took John *Blackwood, her regular publisher, unawares. He kept up dignified communication, to his eventual advantage, even accepting for the June issue of *Blackwood's Edinburgh Magazine* an advertisement announcing the new novel as forthcoming in the *Cornhill*.

When George Eliot settled terms with Smith, she had only eight chapters of *Romola* written. Her recurrent physical and psychological malaise painfully protracted work on the novel. She battled to meet her deadline each month, and was at once pleased by and suspicious of compliments on the serial version as it came out. In January 1863, she realized that she could not finish the novel in the twelve parts for which she had contracted, so Smith agreed that she could have another two episodes. The end was in sight when on 16 May she triumphantly recorded, 'Killed Tito in great excitement!' (*Journals*, 117). It was, however, 9 June before she could exclaim, 'Put the last stroke to Romola. Ebenezer!' (118).

The manuscript of *Romola* is in the British Library, Add. MSS 34027–9, inscribed, 'To the Husband whose perfect Love has been the best source of her insight & strength, this manuscript is given by his devoted Wife, the writer'.

Publication

Romola was first published in fourteen monthly parts in the *Cornhill Magazine* from July 1862 to August 1863, with 24 *illustrations by Frederic *Leighton. The first edition, published by *Smith, Elder & Co., appeared in three volumes octavo in July 1863, bound in dark green cloth, at the customary price of one-and-a-half guineas; though a second issue followed immediately, there was a first-edition remainder issue in 1864, the three volumes bound as one and sold for 6s. This was in anticipation of the one-volume Illustrated Edition, published at 6s. in September 1865, which included four illustrations from the *Cornhill* and a title-page vignette newly drawn by Leighton. Smith Elder produced a 'new edition' in June 1869 at 2s. and 6d. just before their exclusive rights expired in August.

Though George Eliot had returned to Blackwood in 1866 for the publication of *Felix Holt, the Radical*, it was not until 1877 that a Blackwood's edition of *Romola* appeared, but then it had a place of honour as the lead title in the *Cabinet Edition. George Eliot made some minor changes for this edition, in addition to the numerous changes, none of major textual significance, which she had made first in proofing the *Cornhill* version and then in preparing it for book publication, and in reading proof of the 1865 one-volume edition. Many variants were the result of printers applying house style especially in punctuation. In the definitive Clarendon Edition of *Romola* (1993), Andrew Brown provides full collations of textual variants. It is notable that for all the trauma of writing *Romola*, George Eliot made no essential modification to it once it appeared in print.

Illustrations

George Smith commissioned Frederic Leighton to produce 24 illustrations for the *Cornhill* serialization. The particular recommendation of this rising young artist was that he had studied in Florence, and specialized in Florentine Renaissance subjects. Lewes recorded that they visited the Royal Academy exhibition on 20 May 1862, specifically to look at the six paintings by Leighton.

Originally each of the twelve episodes was to have two illustrations, for which Leighton was to receive £40 per number. In the event, in addition to the full-page illustrations, Leighton provided illustrated vignettes framing the capital letters at the start of each serial part and a tailpiece to the Proem. But when the number of episodes was increased to fourteen, Smith did not commission additional illustrations, so that Parts 10, 12, 13, and 14 have only one each.

Author and artist developed an effective working relationship. George Eliot's suggestions for modifications to the first illustration, *The Blind Scholar and His Daughter*, reveal both her powers of observation ('I should have wished Bardo's head to be raised with the chin thrust forward a little—the usual attitude of the blind, I think'), and something of her mental image of her characters (Romola's 'face and hair, though deliciously beautiful, are not just the thing', *L* iv. 40). There was, however, no time to make changes to Leighton's design. By contrast, she was thrilled with the other illustration for the opening episode, *Suppose you let me look at myself*: 'Unmitigated delight! Nello is better than my Nello' (*L* iv. 41). Leighton worked from page proofs of each instalment, with such indication of the design of the whole novel as its author may have vouchsafed, her occasional suggestions of subjects for illustration, and frequent detailed instructions.

In part the interaction depended on George Eliot's accommodating to the demands of the partnership. She found Leighton invaluable because he knew Florence by heart, and they had deep discussions on matters like details of costume and the appearance of historical characters such as Piero di Cosimo. She was alive to difficulties in the mode of production, commenting on 'the misrepresentation—(it is almost that) which the engravers have made of these two first drawings' (*L* iv. 49). As the serialization proceeded, this consummate professional articulated a distinction between the respective roles of author and artist:

I am quite convinced that illustrations can only form a sort of overture to the text. The artist who uses the pencil must otherwise be tormented to misery by the deficiencies or requirements of the one who uses the pen, and the writer, on the other hand, must die of impossible expectations. (*L* iv. 55–6)

In effect, George Eliot recognized that the text is only one contributing factor in the production and interpretation of literary illustrations. Hugh Witemeyer (1979) elaborates this position. He considers the iconography of Leighton's images, the relations among the illustrations and other works by Leighton, and the repetition and variation within the *Romola* series. Mark W. Turner takes the issue further (Levine and Turner 1998: 17–35), insisting on the ideological context represented by publication in the *Cornhill*.

Leighton initially sketched the illustrations in black and white chalk on grey paper, then reworked in pen and ink on woodblocks to be handed over to the engravers (both men employed, Joseph Swain and W. J. Linton, were highly regarded exponents of their craft). Before the engravers took over the blocks, Smith had photographs made, which were hung in The *Priory.

Reception

While *Romola* was being serialized, G. H. Lewes boasted of 'the wonderful eulogies which have reached her from learned Florentines, and Englishmen of high culture' (*L* iv. 58). In 1876, he referred to its being 'received with a universal howl of discontent' (*L* vi. 312). The two statements are not altogether incompatible. When the book version appeared, Lewes observed that it 'has been flatly received by the general public though it has excited a deep enthusiasm in almost all the élite' (*L* iv. 102). In fact, there was hardly a review that did not express, however diplomatically, serious reservations about the novel. For some readers, George Eliot's change of tack away from the version of pastoral represented by her earlier fiction was intolerable; and even those who were impressed by the erudition of *Romola* could not always get a purchase on the nature of her fictional experiment.

Contemporary responses to *Romola* marked out the parameters of critical discussion of the novel for a century and more. A basic, and typical, ambivalence was summed up by the **Saturday Review*: 'No reader of *Romola* will lay it down without admiration, and few without regret' (*CH* 207). The essence of both admiration and regret is encapsulated in Anthony **Trollope's congratulations after the first number, praising the descriptions of Florence, 'wonderful in their energy and in their accuracy', and the 'artistically beautiful' characterization of Romola, but issuing a prescient warning: 'Do not fire too much over the heads of your readers. You have to write to tens of thousands, and not to single thousands' (*L* viii. 303–4). What the *Saturday* reviewer aptly described as 'instructive antiquarianism' (*CH* 208) was to be a stumbling block for many on account both of its relentless detail, and the seeming irrelevance of the exotic locale. *The Times* regarded the period setting as a device to give a sense of magnitude and elevation to the work (5 September 1863, 11), while the **Westminster Review* took the recourse to a foreign background as a sign of weakness and exhaustion: it enabled a bold delineation of intellectual and ethical concerns, but the exploration of moral questions failed to convince (*CH* 213). A similar view emerged from the discussion in the *Saturday Review*, which discerned that George Eliot was pursuing her recurrent concerns in a new guise: 'Stripped of their Florentine covering, . . . several of the characters of *Romola*, and some of the chief events, are old . . . the authoress seems to be haunted with the consequences that flow from the weakness of men' (*CH* 209–10).

Had the central characters been perceived to be more engaging, *Romola* might have had a better press. The *Athenaeum* recognized a coherent structure in the book version that had not emerged in serial reading; 'but neither the politics nor the people are really alive—they are only well dried, preserved and coloured', and for this reviewer, Savonarola is 'the gem of the book' (*CH* 197; on the whole, reviewers made no categorical distinctions between the presentation of historical personages and invented characters). R. H. **Hutton in the *Spectator* provided the most potent account of *Romola*, but had little enthusiasm for Romola, especially by comparison with the wonderful development of Tito's character and the portrait of Savonarola. Of the titular heroine, Hutton complains it is 'difficult to say whether we know her intimately, or whether we have only a very artistic idea of what she is *not*, and what she *is* only by inference and contrast . . . We do not say the character is not natural—we only say it is half-revealed and more suggested than fully painted' (*CH* 202–3).

Hutton's review is particularly distinguished by its identification of the relation of the Florentine setting with contemporary England: 'The great artistic purpose of the story is to trace out the conflict between liberal culture and the more passionate form of the Christian faith in that strange era, which has so many points of resemblance with the present' (*CH* 200). Impressed by his understanding of her intentions, George Eliot took the unusual step of engaging in correspondence with him, in the course of which she offered an important formulation of her narrative method: 'It is the habit of my imagination to strive after as full a vision of the medium in which a character moves as of the character itself' (*L* iv. 97).

The publication of *Romola* occasioned a major retrospect of 'George Eliot's Novels' by Richard Simpson, in the *Home and Foreign Review* (October 1863). The essay works from the premiss that George Eliot lacks inspiration, and is hostile to her as an unbeliever, yet develops its argument through illuminating analysis of her narrative technique. It is one piece of evidence among many that, by the time *Romola* appeared, George Eliot was convincingly established as a novelist who counted.

Plot

After a Proem (prelude) in which the spirit of a 15th-century Florentine is imagined comparing mid-19th-century Florence with the city as he knew it, the novel proper begins in 1492, with the death of Lorenzo de' Medici. The tension between the ruling Medici and the popular party influenced by the ascetic Prior of San Marco, Fra Girolamo Savonarola, is central to the political action, in which the Medici are expelled from Florence, and an expedition led by Charles VIII of France enters the city in triumph. Other historical personages figure in the novel, including Piero di Cosimo, Leonardo da Vinci, and Machiavelli; a cast of Florentines including Nello the poet barber, and Bratti, a peddlar, form a chorus.

The titular heroine Romola de' Bardi acts as amanuensis for her blind scholar father Bardo. Her brother Dino has become a monk and a devotee of Savonarola. When the brilliant young Greek Tito appears, like many others she succumbs to his charms, and they are married. Tito also goes through a mock marriage with a simple milkmaid Tessa, by whom he has two children. He is ambitious but weak-willed and treacherous: he betrays his foster father Baldassarre Calvo, and gets embroiled in devious and duplicitous political intrigue. On Bardo's death Tito arranges to sell both his library and his jewels without Romola's consent, to the detriment of their relationship. Romola, disguised as a nun, leaves Florence, but is persuaded to return by a chance encounter with Savonarola into whose orbit of influence she comes for a time.

Baldassarre returns to Florence as a prisoner of Charles VIII. As Savonarola's political fortunes come to their climax, Romola learns both of Baldassarre's association with Tito, and of Tito's relationship with Tessa. She pleads with Savonarola to spare the life of her godfather, the Medicean Bernardo del Nero, in vain. After the execution of Bernardo, she leaves Florence by boat, and finds herself in a plague-stricken village: taken for the Virgin Mary, she tends the sick and dying. Meanwhile Baldassarre eventually has his vengeance on Tito, and on her return to Florence Romola learns of their deaths. Savonarola, having been excommunicated, is executed by burning. Romola sets up house with Tessa and the children, and her cousin Monna Brigida.

Critical Approaches

George Eliot was nothing if not a self-conscious writer. She told Sara Hennell when *Romola* had just begun serial publication:

Frederic Leighton's (1830–96) illustration of 'The Blind Scholar and his Daughter' for *Romola*.

Of necessity, the book is addressed to fewer readers than my previous works, and I myself have never expected—I might rather say *intended*—that the book should be as 'popular' in the same sense as the others. If one is to have freedom to write out one's own varying unfolding self, and not be a machine always grinding out the same material or spinning the same sort of web, one cannot always write for the same public. (*L* iv. 49)

She had now secured release from material pressures, with the success of *Adam Bede* confirmed by the favourable reception of *The Mill on the Floss* and *Silas Marner*. Moreover, the reputation of the novelist 'George Eliot' gave some countenance to the woman so sensitive to the scandal of her common-law union with G. H. Lewes, as she began to go more into London society. The artistic freedom she claims in *Romola* is to be located particularly in her decision to write a historical novel, so emulating more directly than in her earlier fiction the novelist who exercised the greatest fascination on her as a young reader. The practice of Walter *Scott, inaugurated in *Waverley* (1814), of setting the moral development of a fictional protagonist in the context of recorded historical events, was taken up with intensity by George Eliot in this book. The settings in time and place of Eliot's previous works had all been at a little distance from the mid-19th-century metropolitan London of her main reading public, but like many provincial novels, they focused on the impact of change in closed rural communities. Not only does *Romola* draw on more specific historical events than do the earlier works in their depiction of the extension within England of new modes of belief, and of industry and commerce, its late 15th-century Florentine setting throws into sharper relief the nature and extent of change between that far-off time and the reader's brave new world.

George Eliot's immediate reactions to her Italian journey of 1860, during which the seed of *Romola* was planted, concentrated on understanding the classical past. The influence of Christianity in art and architecture (see VISUAL ARTS), as well as in the daily lives of the Roman Catholic population (see ROMAN CATHOLICISM), also impressed her, but she consciously kept at bay the contemporary politics of the *Risorgimento that were bringing the nation of Italy into being. *Romola* casts her reflections on the significance of the interaction over time of spiritual, cultural, and political forces as structural and thematic parallels between individual histories of progress towards self-realization, and the master narrative of Western civilization (see HISTORY; POLITICS; PROGRESS). It is a hugely ambitious undertaking, and any critical approach to the novel, as the responses of Eliot's contemporaries show, has to wrestle with the relentless plotting and patterning of such parallels. Two dominant critical approaches have been through character (study of the individual's progress), and through intellectual contexts (study of the historical processes presented in the novel).

It is axiomatic that from the beginning *Romola* was named for its heroine—the only one of George Eliot's novels so distinguished. And that heroine is resonantly named (see NAMES). Gordon S. *Haight reports that 'Romola is not a Christian but a place name', of a hill outside Florence (1968: 351). But in responding to Alexander *Main's enquiry about the pronunciation of the name, George Eliot incidentally gave an important clue: 'You have been rightly inspired in pronouncing Romŏla, and in conceiving Romŏlo as the Italian equivalent of Romulus' (*L* v. 174). In other words, she bears the feminine version of the name of the mythological founder of *Rome. When a later George Eliot heroine initially experiences Rome as a 'stupendous fragmentariness', the narrator of *Middlemarch* observes that Rome is still 'the spiritual centre and interpreter' of the world (*MM* 20). Felicia Bonaparte (1979) drives the point home: 'it was in Rome that Greece survived and Christianity flourished, and it was from Rome, in one way or another therefore, that the Western world inherited its consciousness' (20). Here is the burden of the tale of *Romola*.

Orthodox mid-19th-century Anglican morality provided the terms in which critics initially traced Romola's moral development (see ANGLICANISM; MORAL VALUES). Raised as a humanist by her father, she encounters the power of faith in the supernatural in Savonarola, but only emerges into altruism from the constraints of her egotism as she learns the true *sympathy of fellow feeling through the painful experiences of Tito's infidelities and her work with the poor and suffering. Such a reading is unexceptionable but unsatisfactory in ways that have been made explicit by feminist criticism taking off from the feisty discussion of 'George Eliot as the Angel of Darkness' by Sandra Gilbert and Susan Gubar in *The Madwoman in the Attic* (1979).

There are, of course, feminist critics who follow Kate Millett in *Sexual Politics* (1969) in accusing George Eliot of failing to write the revolution and remaining fixated on 'the pervasive Victorian fantasy of the good woman who goes down into Samaria and rescues the fallen man—nurse, guide, mother, adjunct of the race' (139)—a fantasy arguably exemplified in *Romola*. At the least, it is allowed to be a work representing the difficulties faced by women in finding fulfilment and vocation; but some have seen an unfortunate irony in the fact that George Eliot's gift of £50 for Girton College was entered as from 'the author of Romola' (*L* viii. 414)—a work that had earned the author thousands of pounds.

The case for the potency with which George Eliot frames the *woman question is made by Gillian Beer. Her account of *Romola* brings out the painful affect of 'the unflinching analysis' in the novel, showing that it is the 'mixture of cumbersome detail and of excoriating insight which makes *Romola* hard to cope with for any willing reader' (1986: 113–14). A central concern of the novel is with a woman's responsibility and duty to her father, and to father figures: images of the father are treated with 'extraordinary violence' (121). The blind scholar Bardo, abandoned by his natural son who has become a zealous disciple of Savonarola, is repudiated also by his son-in-law. Tito sells off Bardo's library and his gems—as he has already robbed his foster father, another scholar, Baldassarre—and Tito effectively abandons his children by Tessa. Savonarola, by virtue of his holy orders, is called 'Father', and acts as an authoritarian father in the city until he too is denounced and burned at the stake. The secular leaders similarly fail to act paternally; Romola's godfather Bernardo is one of them, and his execution has the dire personal consequence of depriving her of his protection and counsel. In the wake of these paternal derelictions, Romola assumes all kinds of authority, initially through her ministry in the plague-stricken village, and then as head of her household. Beer proposes that the use of the word 'madonna' as a term of address throughout the novel 'allows George Eliot to ease the transition between the divine and the ordinary and to keep the whole upon the plane of human affairs' when Romola is imaged as the Virgin Mary during the plague sequence (124).

In an argument complementary to Beer's, Margaret Homans discusses *Romola* in terms of ideologies of motherhood, and introduces a further set of issues: 'what is the relation between Romola's lot with respect to language and Eliot's own?' (216). Her answer essentially is that while Romola begins by transmitting male texts, in her role as secretary to her father for example, in her apotheosis as the Virgin she incarnates the Word, and 'disconcerts the opposition and even the difference between literal and figurative' (221).

The new feminist Romola is more robust, and *Romola* more assertive, than in previous readings either of character or novel. Yet the ending is far from an unequivocal endorsement of female authority, as Romola interprets her story to a scholar in the making under her tutelage, Lillo, the son of Tito and Tessa. His sister is not so privileged.

None the less, it must be acknowledged that from the first some commentators have (very intelligibly) given the novel to Tito. Henry *James pronounced that 'perception and reflection, at the outset, divided George Eliot's great talent between them' (*CH* 498), and for him, Tito is an exceptional product of her perception, in a novel that otherwise 'smells of the lamp' (*CH* 500). The historical figure of Savonarola is an important point of reference, because other accounts and interpretations of his career as hero and martyr are latent in *Romola*. The most rewarding of readings that concentrate on character trace shifting likenesses and differences.

Research into the historical and intellectual contexts of *Romola* has also illuminated the text. The Florentine history of the Medici, Savonarola, the artists, and churchmen depicted, is unlikely to be immediately familiar to a present-day reader. It would have been relatively unfamiliar to many Victorian readers also, even among the caste to whom George Eliot thought of herself as writing (see READERSHIP). In essence, the Medici party is conservative, oligarchic, accustomed to rule by control of family alliances: Romola's godfather Bernardo del Nero is one of its leaders. The appeal of Savonarola's populist Piagnoni party is that it is republican, basing a call for reform on the invocation of Christian principles in public as well as personal life. The third major group is the oligarchical Arrabbiati party of Dolfo Spini, which looks to alliances with the Sforzas in Milan and the Borgias in Rome. This remote and exotic history permits a freedom of analogy in exploring the idea of renascence, in terms of rebirth for individuals, and in terms of the interpretation of the period of the Renaissance.

J. B. Bullen shows that in the early 1860s the term 'Renaissance' still had an unstable and highly ambiguous status in English writing, and relevantly insists that George Eliot does not represent a period which appears coherent (209). In this respect she is writing within the context of historiographical discourses, but she is also a confident exponent of philosophical discourse, notably the *positivism of Auguste *Comte which, as Bullen convincingly demonstrates, pervades *Romola*. Comte interprets the history of the West in terms of the evolution of religious awareness, through Theological, Metaphysical, and Positive phases, and requires an understanding of the past for comprehension of his *religion of humanity. An individual's development is analogous; here is an important conceptual hinge, and a significant modification of readings of the novel in terms of Christian moral orthodoxy.

Only from the 1970s, with the work of Felicia Bonaparte and Joseph Wiesenfarth, as well as Bullen, did the significance of the mythologies and belief systems in play in *Romola* become apparent. A key image is Piero di Cosimo's painting of the three masks: 'a drunken laughing Satyr, another a sorrowing Magdalen, and the third, which lay between them, the rigid cold face of a Stoic' (*RO* 3). Bullen reads the painting in positivist terms (1994: 236), while Bonaparte interprets it in terms of character: the Bacchic Tito, Stoic Bardo, suffering Savonarola—or Romola (1979: 36)? The richness of classical mythology—Bacchus and Ariadne, Creon and Antigone—as well as of Christian allusion is explored by characters in the novel, as well as providing explicatory challenges for critics (see MYTH). Another significant intertext is *Dante. The implications of interpretation have been teased out by David Carroll in his important study *George Eliot and* the *Conflict of Interpretations* (1992). His account of '*Romola*: duplicity, doubleness and sacred rebellion' not only canvasses interpretation as a subject of the novel (he quotes Nello's caution: 'everybody has his own interpretation of that picture', *RO* 3), but proposes that the Victorian view of myth as the embodiment of irreducible contradictions is inherent in the novel.

Henry James's dictum that George Eliot 'proceeds from the abstract to the concrete' (*CH* 498) implies some of the considerations addressed in approaches to *Romola* through genre. Robert *Browning, reading the three-volume version in 1863, described it as 'the noblest and most heroic prose-poem that I have ever read' (*L* iv. 96). Poetry is valorized as inherently more abstract, more wrought, than prose. Thus Felicia Bonaparte, in her comprehensive groundbreaking study of *Romola*, argues that 'it is precisely because *Romola* is a poem that it has always displeased us most' (1979: 5); but she goes further, to propose that it is an epic conception (see GENRES). Bonaparte brings a wealth of scholarship to her explication of Romola's personal story as a synthesis of pagan and Christian in parallel with Renaissance history.

Accordingly, *Romola* has been particularly well served by approaches through narratology and poetics. Attention has been drawn to George Eliot's skill in manipulating narrative sequence, as in the following example of symmetry of characters' rise and fall. In chapter 61, 'Drifting Away', Romola sets off in her boat, to reappear when she makes the landfall in chapter 68, 'Romola's Waking'. Meanwhile, in chapters 62 to 67 (the whole of the serialized Part 13), Savonarola, once all-powerful, is discredited, and Tito and Baldassarre have their fatal confrontation. Similarly, there are striking, and subtle, effects of repetition and resonance: the alternation of interior, enclosed spaces, with more accessible spaces like the barber's shop; and other spaces which are open or public, for example.

George Levine, whose account of the traditional application of notions of *realism to George Eliot's fiction has been so influential, takes up in a different way the charge that the novel is researched rather than realized. He argues that the character of Tito is built out of a tradition of realism, and that of Romola, in tension with his, out of a tradition of romance (1970: 81), and uses the term 'fable' to explain the symbolic elements of Romola's story. More recently, Caroline Levine, in 'The Prophetic Fallacy: Realism, Foreshadowing and Narrative Knowledge in *Romola*' (Levine and Turner 1998: 135–63), has interrogated the assumptions of realism in the light of deconstructionist and poststructuralist narrative theory (see NARRATION; CRITICISM, MODERN: DECONSTRUCTION). Like Carroll, she makes much of the novel's concern with signs, reading, translation, interpretation, in her stimulating account of how *Romola* thematizes the quest for origins and intelligibility.

Finally, there are approaches through biography, which read this massively studied novel about a woman who is debarred from the vocation of scholar, but who is able to transcend a number of cultural and other divisions and proscriptions, as a self-projection that curiously justifies George Eliot's own claim about writing out her unfolding self. F. R. *Leavis in *The Great Tradition* (Peregrine edition 1962) barely touched on *Romola*, which he sees as so overwhelmed by the abstraction of her research as to be deficient in 'felt life', except where 'the closeness of relation between heroine and author' (62) mars the work as it had done *The Mill on the Floss*. There is some relevance in this observation, but not in the way Leavis means: and this is not only because George Eliot drew Romola from her close friend Barbara *Bodichon.

Bessie *Parkes maintained in *A Passing World* (1897) that 'it was an open secret' that Barbara Bodichon had 'suggested the conception of *Romola* to George Eliot'

(21). Barbara was a political activist from her early years, waging campaigns about the Married Women's Property Laws, and about women's work and professional standing. She underwrote the *English Woman's Journal*, set up in 1858, and by 1862 she was already considering the cause of higher education for women which she took up in earnest later in the decade. She figures in *Romola* as an embodiment of an activism which Marian Evans would not share (see WOMAN QUESTION), and for which Romola strives.

But more immediate motifs from Eliot's life are figured in the novel, and perceptively elucidated by Rosemarie Bodenheimer (1994). *Romola* was written while Eliot was in her early forties, moving past the possibility of childbearing: Romola's finding children—the lost Lillo in chapter 56 and then Benedotto, the survivor in the stricken village, in chapter 68—poignantly inflect conventional meanings of young life. At this time, as mother to Lewes's sons, she found a surrogate maternal role. Beyond such possible transpositions, Bodenheimer discerns shared patterns of turning back and moral revaluation in George Eliot and her heroine (83, 276).

Barbara Hardy memorably observed, '*Romola* is undoubtedly a book which it is more interesting to analyse than simply to read' (1959: 175). From the beginning, readers have had difficulty in 'simply' reading *Romola*, but generations of analysis have enriched formal 'readings' of the novel. And as in the 1860s, readers have been drawn to this extraordinary book with a kind of unwilling compulsion. George Eliot accorded it a particular place among her works, writing to Blackwood in 1877: 'I think it must be nearly ten years since I read the book before, but there is no book of mine about which I more thoroughly feel that I could swear by every sentence as having been written with my best blood, such as it is' (*L* vi. 335–6). Histrionic, certainly—but *Romola* provokes extreme responses, and any approach finds it uniquely testing.   MAH

Beer (1996).

Bonaparte (1979).

Booth, Alison, 'Trespassing in Cultural History: The Heroines of *Romola* and *Orlando*', in *Greatness Engendered: George Eliot and Virginia Woolf* (1992).

Brown, Andrew, Introduction to Clarendon Edition (1993).

Bullen, J. B., *The Myth of the Renaissance in Nineteenth-Century Writing* (1994).

Fraser, Hilary, *The Victorians and Renaissance Italy* (1992).

Hardy (1959).

Homans, Margaret, 'Figuring the Mother: Madonna Romola's Incarnation', in *Bearing the Word: Language and Female Experience in Nineteenth-Century Women's Writing* (1986).

Levine and Turner (1998).

Levine, George, '*Romola* as Fable', in Hardy (1970).

Sanders, Andrew, *The Victorian Historical Novel 1840–1880* (1978).

Thompson (1998).

Wiesenfarth (1977).

Witemeyer (1979).

invited to contribute to the 'Eminent Women' series. George Eliot was among the subjects offered: Christina declined. See also POETRY OF GEORGE ELIOT.   GRH

Rossini, Gioachino (1792–1868), Italian composer whose opera *Guillaume Tell* (1829) features significantly in George Eliot's life. On 1 April 1852, she went with Herbert *Spencer to hear it at the Royal Italian Opera, Covent Garden. Almost exactly one year later, she saw it again—this time with G. H. *Lewes, whom she had begun to find 'especially . . . kind and attentive' (*L* ii. 98). The Leweses heard it again the following year. On 30 March 1858, when they were at *Munich, the scene depicting the fight between Adam and Arthur in chapter 27 of *Adam Bede* came to George Eliot 'as a *necessity*' (*L* ii. 504) when she was listening to yet another performance.

Having put the last stroke to *Romola* on 9 June 1863, George Eliot celebrated by going to hear *La gazza ladra* (1817). Not long before he died, the ailing Lewes 'with great *brio*' sang 'the greater portion' (Cross, iii. 295) of Count Almaviva's part in *Il barbiere di Siviglia* (1816). George Eliot played the accompaniment. See also MUSIC. BG

Rousseau, Jean-Jacques (1712–78), Swiss-French philosopher, novelist, and man of letters whose work was an early inspiration to George Eliot. When Ralph Waldo *Emerson met her at her friends the *Brays' house in *Coventry and asked her what had first wakened her to deep reflection, she replied that it was Rousseau's autobiographical *Confessions* (*L* i. 27); and in the early 1850s she told William Hale *White that all the labour of learning French was worth while if it resulted in nothing more than reading that same book (*L*, vol. i., p. xv). She first read Rousseau— his *Émile* (1762), and *Julie, ou la nouvelle Héloïse* (1761), as well as the *Confessions* (1781–8)—in 1846 after finishing the labour of translating D. F. *Strauss (see TRANSLATIONS), and her encounter with this new and intense sensibility was a liberating experience. Her earliest published comment on Rousseau, in an article in the *Coventry *Herald and Observer* on 5 February 1847, stresses the importance of perception, citing him looking at a plant as an example of a mind restored through intellectual cultivation 'to that state of wonder and interest with which it looks on everything in childhood' (*Essays*, 19–20). The significance of his work, like that of George *Sand which she was reading in the same period, lies, indeed, in the way that it helped quicken her own perceptions. In a letter of 9 February 1849 to Sara *Hennell she maintains forcefully that the influence of both writers on her did not stem from their opinions, which she did not necessarily share, nor from their lives, which in Rousseau's case contained much that was reprehensible: it was simply that 'Rousseau's genius has sent that electric thrill through my intellectual and moral frame which has made man and nature a fresh world of thought and feeling to me—and this not by teaching me any new belief'. She continues by declaring that 'the rushing mighty wind of his inspiration has so quickened my faculties that I have been able to shape more definitely for myself ideas which had previously dwelt as dim "ahnungen" in my soul—the fire of his genius has so fused together old thoughts and prejudices that I have been ready to make new combinations' (*L* i. 277). It was in this state of heightened receptivity to the new that she

was able to respond excitedly to news of the 1848 revolution in Paris (see REVOLUTIONS OF 1848).

She remained loyal to this early enthusiasm for Rousseau, even though references to him in the fiction are not always positive. In 1876 she and G. H. *Lewes spent some weeks of their summer holiday in France and Switzerland rereading Rousseau, and travelled to Chambéry just to make a pilgrimage to Les Charmettes, where they visited the rooms he had lived in with Mme de Warens in 1736. Eliot made a point of returning to Les Charmettes in the last year of her life with her new husband John Walter *Cross, and wrote in a letter of gathering roses in Jean-Jacques's garden, a fitting act of homage to a writer whose 'deep sense of external nature' (*Essays*, 55) she particularly admired (see NATURAL WORLD).

There are traces of Rousseau's sense of nature in her fiction, as Hugh Witemeyer has shown. His experience at Lake Bienne in the *Confessions* and *Les Reveries du promeneur solitaire* (*Reveries of a Solitary Walker*) are alluded to in 'The Lifted Veil' during the narrator Latimer's happy schooldays in *Geneva: 'I used to do as Jean-Jacques did—lie down in my boat and let it glide where it would' (*LV* 1). And for both figures the experience of solitary happiness in the presence of nature is a temporary recovery of a state of innocence. There are affinities, too, between Latimer, George Eliot's oddest narrator, and the narrator of the *Confessions*: both men are introspective and egocentric, suspicious and highly sensitive, self-dramatizing and frank about moral failings, and both withdraw from a society whose hypocrisies they criticize and end in a state of isolation (Witemeyer, 'George Eliot and Jean-Jacques Rousseau', 125–6). Eliot's comment in *Impressions of Theophrastus Such* that half our impressions of Rousseau's character in the *Confessions* come from what he unconsciously reveals (*TS* 1), may also be pertinent to her use of a first-person narrator in Latimer. Another echo of Rousseau's experience on the lake occurs in *Daniel Deronda* in relation to a very different figure, Deronda himself, who first sees Mirah when he is lying back in his boat in a solitary spot on the Thames. However, from this moment on, the direction of his life is not towards nature and solitude in the manner of Rousseau but towards the community he is to find in Judaism and the service of his people. A positive connection between the three works of Rousseau she read in 1846 and *Deronda* has been seen to lie in their common exploration of beneficence, while the hostile reference to Rousseau in relation to Mrs Arrowpoint (*DD* 22) has been attributed to the anxiety of influence (Still, 62, 72). JMR

Peck (1992).
Redinger (1975).

Still, Judith, 'Rousseau in *Daniel Deronda*', *Revue de littérature comparée*, 56 (1982).

Witemeyer, Hugh, 'George Eliot and Jean-Jacques Rousseau', *Comparative Literature*, 16 (1979).

Rubens, Peter Paul (1577–1640), Flemish painter. George Eliot's enthusiasm for the paintings of Rubens reflects her belief that he was a realist artist, rather than a painter of the ideal. Some of her British contemporaries found Rubens's secular work meretriciously sensuous, but George Eliot's warm response is more in line with European and late 19th-century standards of taste.

George Eliot and G. H. *Lewes, like many cultivated Victorian travellers, made a point of seeing Rubens's *Descent from the Cross* (1612–14) in Antwerp Cathedral on their European journey in 1854. For them the painting lived up to its reputation, and confirmed George Eliot's belief that 19th-century artists were less imaginative and expansive than old masters like Rubens.

Four years later, in *Munich, George Eliot was a regular visitor to the Rubens room in the Alte Pinakothek. She was deeply impressed by the living force of Rubens's representation of human beings, in contrast to the more stylized, and to her mind unconvincing, men and women of other artists. *Samson taken by the Philistines* (*c*.1612–15) delighted her, both for its rendering of character and for its painterly qualities, and she was deeply moved by the *Crucifixion* (*c*.1612). At that time, she declared that Rubens was the artist whose work gave her most pleasure.

George Eliot had further opportunities to study important collections of Rubens paintings. The National Gallery in London had a fine group of works, and George Eliot saw at least three more important collections: in *Dresden and *Vienna later in 1858 and in Madrid in 1867.   LO

Witemeyer (1979).

Rubinstein, Anton (1829–94), Russian composer and pianist introduced to George Eliot by *Liszt in 1854. Gordon S. *Haight proposes Rubinstein rather than Liszt as the model for Klesmer in *Daniel Deronda*, citing a letter from G. H. *Lewes, written in 1876, whilst Eliot was finishing the novel (Haight 1968: 490). At the prospect of their dining with Anton Rubinstein Lewes writes: 'We shall so like to renew our acquaintance with Klesmer—whom we met at Weimar in'54!' (*L* ix. 176–7). After dinner, they heard Rubinstein play *Beethoven, Chopin, Schumann, and (like Klesmer) his own compositions. 'Stupendous playing' was Lewes's response (*L* vi. 251). Haight points out that Rubinstein's appearance matched Eliot's description of Klesmer's 'massive features' and 'thick mane of hair' (Haight 1968: 490; see also Haight, 'George Eliot's Klesmer', 214). Rubinstein's origins, a

German-Jewish mother and a Russian father, match Klesmer's combination of 'the German, the Sclave, and the Semite' (*DD* 5). He studied in Russia and Germany and toured Europe extensively. Liszt was an important influence and the only virtuoso pianist whose fame Rubinstein did not eventually eclipse. He might well have been characterized, as Eliot terms Klesmer, as 'not yet a Liszt' (*DD* 22). Rubinstein represents cosmopolitan and German elements within the development of Russian music, in contrast to more nationalistic composers. In *Daniel Deronda*, Klesmer is the 'Wandering Jew' (*DD* 22), disseminating a cosmopolitan fusion of European and Judaic tradition, in contrast to Mordecai's mission to revivify the 'centre' of Judaism (*DD* 42). See also MUSIC.

DdSC

Haight, Gordon S., 'George Eliot's Klesmer', in Maynard Mack and Ian Gregor (edd.), *Imagined Worlds* (1968).

Ruskin, John (1819–1900), Victorian critic whose writings on art were an inspiration for George Eliot, though she was less enthusiastic about his political opinions. In June 1854, she reviewed his Edinburgh *Lectures on Architecture and Painting* in the *Leader* (*Writer's Notebook*, ed. Wiesenfarth, 238–43). With an acuity that puts her in a class of her own among contemporary critics of Ruskin, she affirms the principles that mark her creative response to his ideas: 'He may be called the great Protestant of Modern Art; he first exhorted us to think for ourselves'. Art is no mere dilettantism, since its influence permeates public and private life, and 'no one has a *right* to be indifferent'. Ruskin has liberated the mind from false deference to the past, since only that which 'is true in its own time is classical'.

Ruskin's influence on Eliot went deeper than any mere opinions about art; though it is symptomatic that she shared his sense of the falseness of the revival implied by the mawkish neo-medievalism of the German *Nazarene movement, for instance. These painters were fashionable in England by the early Victorian period, and the publisher John Murray urged Ruskin to produce a volume praising them. His refusal to do so, and his preference for J. M. W. *Turner, led him to write the first volume of *Modern Painters* (1843). Eliot's analysis (*MM* 19–22) of the cultural implications of the Nazarenes—under the satirical designation of 'certain long-haired German artists at Rome'—indicates she shared much that was positive, as well as negative, in Ruskin's outlook. In March 1850 she was making contact with Ruskin's friend, B. Godfrey Windus, the retired Tottenham coachmaker who showed his Turner drawings to strangers bringing letters of introduction (*L* i. 332).

A reading of her comments, and Ruskin's, about their *Pre-Raphaelite contemporaries suggests a measure of agreement: respect for seriousness and pleasure in detail is offset by worries about their contemporary relevance and their failure to convey living expression.

During February 1856 Eliot was relishing the third volume of *Modern Painters*, which she would 'read . . . aloud for an hour or so after dinner'. She reviewed this volume the following April (Ashton 1992: 247–59), praising Ruskin's advocacy of 'definite, substantial reality' at the expense of 'vague forms, bred by imagination on the mists of feeling'. She considered the 'thorough acceptance of this doctrine would remould our life; and he who teaches its application . . . is a prophet for his generation'. Acknowledging the 'vigour and splendour' of Ruskin's style, she found it yet more remarkable for 'its precision'. Her *Ilfracombe journal (see JOURNALS OF GEORGE ELIOT) of May–June 1856 shows her developing her personal version of a 'Ruskinian' style of precise evocation of colour and form, based on a sense of geology and of the functional meaning of natural phenomena. At this time, she was pleased to hear from Barbara Leigh Smith (later *Bodichon) 'of the success your pictures have, and especially of Ruskin's encouragement'. Having now also read volume iv of *Modern Painters*, she felt moved to add: 'What books his two last are! I think he is the finest writer living' (*L* ii. 228, 245, 255). Reviewing volume iv in July 1856 (*Westminster Review*, 66: 274–8), she quoted at length from 'Of Mountain Beauty', taking especial interest in Ruskin's reading of *Shakespeare's native *landscape and her own, including such characteristic Warwickshire details as 'clumps of pine on little sandstone mounds, as at the place of execution of Piers Gaveston' (*Works* vi. 451).

Sharing with G. H. *Lewes the Victorian preference for fact over fancy, she adopted Ruskin's definition of the 'pathetic fallacy' as a criticism of the Romantic tendency to see nature as a mere mirror of the observer's feelings (see NATURAL WORLD). This theme—the realignment of the inner moral intelligence through patient observation of the outer world—would be a major inspiration for *Middlemarch*. Equally significant, as Eliot saw, was Ruskin's accompanying insight: that 'imaginative art includes the historical faculties . . . but . . . subservient to a poetic purpose' (*Westminster Review*, 65: 629, 633). She also endorsed the Ruskinian corollary that, despite the dislocations and interruptions that often pass for conventional *history, in the true history of European consciousness 'all is continuous' (*Westminster Review*, 66: 70). These communitarian and psychological perceptions into the meaning of history would

help to engender the philosophic ambitions of *Daniel Deronda*.

On the appearance of *Scenes of Clerical Life* in January 1858, Ruskin was one of nine persons to whom a copy was sent, by request of the author, as a testimony of regard. That same month, however, Eliot expressed reservations about his *Political Economy of Art* (1857) in a letter to Sara *Hennell (*L* ii. 418, 422). Ruskin was out of step with conventional Victorian political economy, as understood by John Stuart *Mill, Herbert *Spencer, and G. H. Lewes. Like Karl *Marx, he held a labour theory of value, regarding labour as the source of capital, and not vice versa. While sharing his sympathy with the workman, Eliot dismissed this assumption behind Ruskin's economics, and its mildly socialist inferences, as 'arrogant absurdity'. Her own capacity for absorption, however, and her respect for the principle of 'eternal progress', which was the motto of the *Leader*, allowed her to see this aspect of Ruskin's work, partly in parody, and partly in celebration, as 'the inspiration of a Hebrew prophet' which 'must be stirring up young minds in a promising way'.

The Mill on the Floss appeared in April 1860, just as Ruskin was moving beyond narrower artistic concerns to contemplate the series of essays on economics (issued later that year in *Cornhill Magazine* under the title 'Unto This Last') which would mark a new departure in his career and which would be almost universally condemned. Given Eliot's inner dialogue with Ruskin's ideas, it is interesting to find her, immediately after completing what was for her the comparably pivotal and traumatic labour of writing *The Mill*, turning for comfort to passages of Ruskin's art criticism (from *The Stones of Venice* and the fifth volume of *Modern Painters*) which addressed the vulnerability they shared (*Writer's Notebook*, ed. Wiesenfarth, 43). While relevant, at the objective level, to her forthcoming visit to *Italy with Lewes (begun March 1860), the subjectivity of the selection suggests a deeper need. She copies a passage on ways in which 'Society always has a destructive influence on an artist'; and another on the monastic seclusion of Fra Angelico (Ruskin, *Works*, xi. 53; viii. 370–1). This period marks a point of divergence for Ruskin and Eliot. In writing *Romola* (which began to appear in *Cornhill Magazine* in July 1862), Eliot was plunging deep into the Victorian obsession with antique Italy from which Ruskin was simultaneously striving to emancipate himself. When, after her death, Ruskin was given a salacious misrepresentation of *The Mill* by an acquaintance, he made mention of it, after a hasty reading, among fictions to be condemned as 'foul' in an article of October 1881 for the magazine *Nineteenth Century* (*CH* 166–7). Maggie Tulliver, he opined, typified 'the modern heroine' as a mass of 'hesitating and self-reproachful impulses'. In an 'Epilogue' of 1881 to *The Stones of Venice*, he linked the novel with the grisly drawings of Gustave Doré as examples of the irresponsible power of modern art (*Works*, xi. 234; xxxiv, 286). His strictures have been outdone by some recent psychological critics (Peggy F. Johnstone, *The Transformation of Rage* (1994), 67). From his viewpoint, Eliot had allowed her own subjective needs to spoil her art; but from Eliot's viewpoint he had allowed his 'excessive contempt' for everything that fell below his standard of 'the noble and beautiful' to warp his critical balance. Precisely this latter tendency in Ruskin she had predicted in reviewing *Modern Painters* (*Westminster Review*, 66: 274). Responsive as she was to 'a certain rough flavour of humour' in Ruskin's manner, however (Ashton 1992: 251), she might have enjoyed his confession that it was only 'now George Eliot was in Heaven . . . without any chance of [his] meeting her afterwards', that he had dared criticize her, since he maintained the principle of never writing in discouragement of the living. On a more serious note, he wrote warmly of his admiration for her, and bracketed *Silas Marner* with the immortal Aesop's Fables (*Works*, xxvii. 425; xxxiv. 558; xxxvii. 372). Visiting *Venice with John Walter *Cross, in the summer of 1880, Eliot had written to Charles Lee Lewes (see LEWES FAMILY), 'We edify ourselves with what Ruskin has written about Venice in an agreeable pamphlet shape [*St. Mark's Rest*, issued 1877–84], using his knowledge gratefully and shutting our ears to his wrathful innuendos against the whole modern world'. Always more interested (despite *Romola*) in contemporary character than ancient art, she became fascinated on this occasion with J. W. Bunney, 'an excellent painter and an interesting man', currently employed by Ruskin to make records of Venetian buildings threatened with destructive restoration at the hands of profiteering builders (*L* vii. 294–7).

Rejecting Ruskin's economic theories, Eliot nevertheless endorsed his sense of the challenge presented by the march of profiteering capitalism and its harmful impact on the natural and built environment, and on the life of the craftsman. A review of Owen Jones's *The Grammar of Ornament* for the *Fortnightly Review* of 15 May 1865 echoes many ideas from the 'Nature of Gothic' chapter of *The Stones of Venice*, of 1853, while stopping short of the socialistic inferences William Morris would draw from it. In creating Adam Bede, from October 1857, it seems likely Eliot was

actively concerned to do honour to the sort of organic dignity of life and work whose significance Ruskin also had emphasized.

The divergence between Ruskin and Eliot was perhaps more theoretical than real. Both abandoned evangelical doctrine, yet maintained in practice evangelical convictions about the moral stewardship of talent. Both incurred scandal and agony, and a deepening of sympathetic power, as a result of Victorian marriage laws. Eliot was more attracted to the 19th-century creed of *positivism than Ruskin was; yet, like him, she resisted the persuasions of Frederic *Harrison to make any formal commitment, preferring to give moral and financial support for practical projects of amelioration, such as that represented by the life and work of Octavia *Hill, the housing reformer, Ruskin's drawing pupil and protégée, and sister-in-law to Charles Lee Lewes (*L* v. 161). A pioneer of a different kind whom they both befriended was William R. Shedden-Ralston, the compiler of Russian songs and folklore and early translator of *Turgenev. It was in his company that Ruskin made his only recorded visit to The *Priory, on Sunday, 8 February 1874. George Eliot and G. H. Lewes first met Ruskin at the exhibition of the Royal Society of Painters in Water-Colours, 11 December 1869. Ruskin clearly formed a high opinion of her capacities, since in May 1873 he approached her through Shedden-Ralston with a request for help. G. H. Lewes made a tentative response: 'Mrs. Lewes is naturally much gratified by Mr. Ruskin's opinion, which however is too flattering to her, she having little experience of practical organization'. What scheme Ruskin had in mind is unknown. It could have been some aspect of his work with Octavia Hill, or maybe he saw Eliot as editor of Shedden-Ralston's project on Russian history, currently (like some of his own schemes) collapsing for want of that quality which, to her advantage, can still be seen to distinguish her work from his: 'organization' (*L* vi. 13–14; ix. 95). See also VISUAL ARTS.   MH

The Works of John Ruskin, ed. E. T. Cook and Alexander Wedderburn, 39 vols. (1903–12).
Unto this Last and Other Writings by John Ruskin, ed. Clive Wilmer (1985).
George Eliot: Selected Critical Writings, ed. Rosemary Ashton (1992).
George Eliot: A Writer's Notebook 1854–1879, and Uncollected Writings, ed. Joseph Wiesenfarth (1981).
Dodd (1990).
Witemeyer (1979).

'Rutherford, Mark'. See WHITE, WILLIAM HALE.

'Sad Fortunes of the Reverend Amos Barton, The', see SCENES OF CLERICAL LIFE.

Sand, George, pen-name of Aurore Dudevant (1804–76), most prominent French woman writer of George Eliot's day, whose life and works much influenced her. Eliot was particularly affected by reading Sand during the late 1840s, after she had emerged from her religious crisis, but was experiencing a harrowing and lonely period nursing her dying father. At this time she read (at least) the novels *Indiana* (1832), *Lélia* (1833), *Jacques* (1834), *Spiridion* (1838–9), *Consuelo* (1842–3), and *Le Meunier d'Angibault* (1845), plus the travel narrative *Lettres d'un voyageur* (1834–7).

Several aspects of these texts would have struck Eliot. They explore spiritual and psychological malaise, and how this might be combated: Eliot characteristically grasps at a stoical passage from *Lettres d'un voyageur* about accepting both good and bad fortune (*L* i. 250–1). They also deal with such varied interests of Eliot's as marital relationships, foreign travel (see TRAVEL), French political developments (see FRANCE), the relationship between personality and physiognomy, the power of *music, and the character of the great artist.

Eliot was none the less aware of Sand's controversial reputation, deriving from her marital separation and freewheeling sexual life, her cross-dressing and cigar-smoking, and her radical political and social views. Hence she assures her main confidante of this period, Sara *Hennell, that she by no means endorses Sand's ideas. But in a claim which foreshadows her own aims as a novelist, she declares that Sand can in six pages 'delineate human passion and its results—some of the moral instincts and their tendencies—with such truthfulness such nicety of discrimination such tragic power and withal such loving gentle humour that one might live a century with nothing but one's own dull faculties and not know so much as those six pages will suggest' (9 February 1849, *L* i. 278). Eliot also found in Sand the conviction, later important to her own novels, that literature does not work morally through crudely advocating moral maxims: defending *Lélia*, Sand had argued that a novel best communicated with its readers through representing human experience in ways they could empathize with (*L* i. 243). Meanwhile *Lettres d'un voyageur* would have shown Eliot how Sand experimented with a variety of male narrators.

Sand's championing of 'human passion' possibly helped Eliot to commit herself to her unorthodox union with Lewes, while her own *pseudonym 'George' was arguably a tribute to Sand as well as to him. (Lewes himself had long been a Sand enthusiast.) When the pair travelled to

*Weimar in 1854 and met Sand's friend *Liszt, the meeting both recalled to Eliot the celebration of Liszt's musical genius in *Lettres d'un voyageur*, and brought home to her how much her own life had changed since she had read it (*L* ii. 171). She went on to discuss Sand in her 1854 essay, *'Woman in France: Madame de Sablé', as one instance of women's 'vital influence' on France's literary development.

In Eliot's own fiction, Caterina Sarti ('Mr Gilfil's Love-Story') and Maggie Tulliver (*The Mill on the Floss*)—particularly in their passionate natures and their susceptibility to music—owe something to Sand's singer heroine of *Consuelo*. Similarly, the love triangle Stephen–Maggie–Philip in *Mill* echoes *Consuelo*'s Anzoleto–Consuelo–Albert. Eliot's concern with idealistic, high-minded figures, and equally with easygoing but selfish natures who deteriorate through yielding to temptation, is characteristic of Sand as well. Sand's virtuous artisan figures (in *Le Meunier d'Angibault*, and *Le Compagnon du Tour de France*, 1840), look forward to Eliot's Adam Bede and Felix Holt, while *Silas Marner*'s depiction of the transforming power of love recalls Sand's rural novels such as *La Mare au Diable* (1845–6), *François le champi* (1847–8), and *La Petite Fadette* (1848–9). And although the unsuccessful marriages in *Indiana* and *Jacques* do not foreshadow Eliot's novels in specific terms, they do highlight the suffering caused by premarital delusions, especially those resulting from inadequate female *education.

As contemporaries noted in increasingly frequent comparisons between the two writers, Sand and Eliot also differed: Eliot was an exponent of *realism, while Sand was more given to idealization; Eliot was analytical and cerebral whereas Sand was poetic and emotional; Sand espoused the rightness of the heart's instincts, while Eliot emphasized duty and facing the consequences of one's acts. Hence, while Eliot probably drew for Maggie Tulliver's spiritual experience on Sand's autobiographical account in her *Histoire de ma vie* (1855), she is more positive about Thomas à *Kempis's The Imitation of Christ* than Sand, who rejects its creed of self-renunciation (see RENUNCIATION). In 1872, F. W. H. *Myers both aligned and distinguished the two writers. Eliot is able, he tells her, to 'make life appear potentially noble and interesting without starting from any assumptions', and although Sand comes close, she needs 'some fixed point to lean against', whereas Eliot has avoided despair, despite knowing 'the worst' (*L* ix. 68). See also WOMAN QUESTION.   JW

> Thomson, Patricia, *George Sand and the Victorians: Her Influence and Reputation in Nineteenth-century England* (1977).

Saturday Review, The, weekly periodical of 'Politics, Literature, Science and Art' to which George Eliot contributed several reviews, and which, despite its nickname of the 'Saturday Reviler', generally reviewed her fiction favourably. Founded in 1855, the *Saturday Review* quickly established itself as a significant organ of conservative thought. Competing with other weeklies such as the *Athenaeum*, *Spectator*, and **Leader*, the *Saturday Review* addressed itself primarily, and often haughtily, to the middle and upper classes. G. H. *Lewes was also an early contributor. See also JOURNALIST, GEORGE ELIOT AS.   MWT

Savonarola, Girolamo (1452–98), eloquent and charismatic Italian Dominican spiritual reformer. In *Florence with George Eliot in May 1860, G. H. *Lewes was reading about Savonarola when the idea occurred to him that 'Polly' should write 'an historical romance' (*L* iii. 295) about the life and times of the denunciatory, influential Dominican preacher who made an enemy of Pope Alexander VI, and whose downfall culminated in excommunication, torture, and execution. George Eliot was inspired by the idea, and the next several days were spent by the Leweses absorbing as much as possible of whatever related to Savonarola. They went to the Accademia della Bella Arte and studied Fra Bartolommeo's portrait of him. They visited San Marco, the convent of which he had become prior in 1491—where, since women were forbidden entrance, George Eliot stayed in the chapter house admiring Fra Angelico's *Crucifixion* while Lewes toured the interior taking notes for her. They bought a copy of Savonarola's poems (edited by Audin de Rian, 1847), a copy of F. T. Perrens's biography, *Jérôme Savonarola, sa vie, ses prédications, ses écrits* (1859), and examined a manuscript volume of Savonarola's in the Magliabecchian Library. They visited both the Great Hall in the Palazzo Vecchio 'built under Savonarola's direc

tion', and the Palazzo Corsini to see the painting depicting Savonarola's death. This work is now understood to be by an unknown artist. However, Lewes's attribution of it in his journal to one Pollaiuolo (Haight 1968: 326) has generally gone unchallenged. Lewes presumably had Antonio Pollaiuolo (1429?–98) in mind, though the index to Haight gives Simone Pollaiuolo (1457–1508), who was an architect. Before the Leweses left Florence, the foundation for the 'great project' (*L* iii. 307) that was to be *Romola* had been laid.

George Eliot's extensive reading for *Romola* included several accounts of Savonarola's life, including the biographies by Pacifico Burlamacchi and Pasquale Villari. She also read Savonarola's treatise on the government of Florence (which is included with Audin de Rian's edition of the poems), many of his sermons, his *De veritate Profetica* (1497), and his *Compendio di Revelatione* (1498).

The 'deep personal sympathies with the old reforming priest' (*L* iii. 420) she developed in the course of this reading are manifested in the treatment she accords his character in the novel.   BG

Scenes of Clerical Life (*see opposite page*)

Schiller, Friedrich (1759–1805), German poet and dramatist who was George Eliot's favourite German author when she first began to read the language and its literature. After starting to learn German in March 1840 she was reading his *Maria Stuart* by October, and with her friend Cara *Bray she went on in the early 1840s to read all of his plays, much of his poetry, his history of the Thirty Years War, and Thomas *Carlyle's *Life of Schiller* (McCobb 1982: 11). Schiller's idealism and portrayals of heroic humanity appealed to the young Mary Ann Evans, and her friend Mary *Sibree records her enthusiasm for the heroic Marquis de Posa in *Don Carlos* (1787), and how once, placing the works of Schiller together, she exclaimed: 'Oh, if *I* had given those to the world, how happy I should be' (Cross, new edn. 1886, 53). She often refers to him in her early letters, calling him on one occasion 'our divine Schiller' (*L* viii. 13). This early enthusiasm receded as she grew older, and *Goethe became the most important German writer for her in her maturity, a development that was reinforced by her relationship with G. H. *Lewes, who always ranked what he saw as Goethe's objectivity far higher than Schiller's subjectivity (Ashton 1980: 125). Nevertheless, she was thrilled to see the house where Schiller had lived in *Weimar (*Journals*, 234). A recent study has argued that *The Mill on the Floss*, with its impulse to heroism and truth to self, owes much to Eliot's early love for Schiller (Guth, 22). It is, however, in

(*cont. on page 364*)

G EORGE ELIOT's first work of fiction, consisting of three stories, 'The Sad Fortunes of the Reverend Amos Barton', 'Mr Gilfil's Love-Story', and 'Janet's Repentance', was published anonymously in *Blackwood's Edinburgh Magazine* from January to November 1857. The correspondence which preceded the series was masterminded by G. H. *Lewes, who archly referred to 'my clerical friend', stressed the latter's diffidence, courted John *Blackwood's encouragement, indicated the nature of the tales, and defined the human rather than the theological concerns of the author.

Composition

Inspiration in the present as well as creative recollection and derivations from the past are the starting points. By the summer of 1856 Lewes and Eliot had been living together for two years. He was intent upon his scientific investigations of the seashore, in which he was practically, and with contiguous interest, assisted by her. She was clarifying her thoughts, already present or taking shape in her articles for the *Westminster Review*, stressing the closeness of art to life and regretting that there were no representations of religious life in English fiction equivalent to Harriet Beecher *Stowe's of the negroes. The visits to *Ilfracombe, *Tenby, the Scilly Isles, and Jersey in 1856 and 1857 sharpened her direction: she was happy and secure in the loving mutuality of shared interests and unquestioned support and faith. She was intent on knowing the names of things, she wished 'to escape from all vagueness and inaccuracy into the daylight of distinctive ideas' (*L* ii. 251). Lewes noted in his *'Sea-side Studies', the published result of their investigations, that 'the study of Life must of all studies best nourish the mind with true philosophy'. It is a statement that Eliot would endorse and exemplify throughout her fiction. 'Sea-side Studies' was published in *Blackwood's* from August to October 1856 (first series) and June to October 1857 (second series), the first paralleling the writing of 'The Sad Fortunes of the Reverend Amos Barton', the second the publication of 'Janet's Repentance'. Their shared lives had produced this simultaneous achievement.

'The Sad Fortunes of the Reverend Amos Barton' was written from 23 September to 5 November 1856. Eliot's journal entry for 6 December 1857 (*L* ii. 406–10) is a self-conscious, hindsight-informed account headed *'How I came to write Fiction'. It describes her 'dreamy doze' one morning when they were at Tenby (26 June to 9 August 1856) with 'G's' enthusiastic response to her reverie title for the first scene. She was anxious to begin writing, and after they returned to Richmond discussed her story with Lewes during a walk in Kew Park on 18 August. First she had to complete her work for the *Westminster Review*. It was on 6 November that Lewes sent the manuscript to John Blackwood saying that the series would be about the country clergy some twenty-five years ago.

'Mr Gilfil's Love-Story' was begun on 25 December 1856, six weeks after Blackwood had assured Lewes that 'your friend's reminiscences of Clerical Life will do' (*L* ii. 272). The signature 'George Eliot' was first used in a letter from the author to William Blackwood on 4 February 1857. The first three parts had been sent by 1 March, and it was finished in the Scilly Isles on 8 April. Blackwood was worried by Caterina's taking the dagger and also by the huddling up of the endings of the stories (*L* ii. 323). Eliot rejected the first objection, but wrote an epilogue to meet the second in May.

'Janet's Repentance' was begun towards the end of May, the first part being sent on the 30th, shortly after Eliot had written to her brother Isaac saying that she was married. The Leweses were in Jersey, from where she wrote to Mrs John Cash (see SIBREE, MARY) that her sufferings had been 'a preparation for some special work that I may do before I die' (*L* ii. 343). Eliot responded to Blackwood's criticism of the harsh colours of 'Janet's Repentance' by offering to close the series, but Blackwood backed off, and after the Leweses' return to Richmond on 26 July her writing gathered momentum. In September publication of the three stories in volume form was agreed, and the last part of 'Janet's Repentance' was sent to Blackwood on 10 October 1857.

Publication
Scenes of Clerical Life was published in two volumes on 5 January 1858 ('By George Eliot' on the title-page), the price being 21*s*. It was bound in purple cloth. A second edition followed in July 1859, priced at 12*s*., a third in April 1860. The manuscript is in the Pierpont Morgan Library, MA 722.

Illustrations
The single-volume Stereotyped Edition of 1868 (the sixpenny number's edition of 1863) has a title-page vignette of Shepperton Church and five illustrations.

Reception
Eliot had the inestimable support of John Blackwood, effectively her first critic. His praise of the pathos and humour in 'Amos Barton' was balanced by a comment on her tendency to over-analyse: her response through Lewes indicated her hypersensitivity, and his later praise was only occasionally tempered by strictures, as in his reaction to parts of the other two stories. He disliked the harshness in the presentation of Milby and of Dempster's and Janet's recourse to alcohol. Eliot's response was to assert her artistic freedom and the studied *realism of her people and their place. Presentation copies of the first edition went to Charles *Dickens and Thomas *Carlyle. Dickens was quick to recognize the hand of the woman in the fiction, and Jane Carlyle's fulsome praise distinguished the uncloying sincerity of the work. The few reviews were generally favourable. Samuel Lucas in *The Times* (2 Jan. 1858) praised the realism and the charm, noting the humour, pathos, clarity, and simple descriptive power. The *Saturday Review* (29 May 1858) registered the 'quiet truth' of the central characters, picking out Mr Gilfil in particular. The first phase of a triumphant career was over (see RECEPTION).

Plot
'The Sad Fortunes of the Reverend Amos Barton' is set back in time to the author's young womanhood, with Shepperton parish providing an authentic sense of place. The line is direct, the story of a commonplace, earnest clergyman, middle-aged and striving to support his wife and six children on an income of £80 per annum. He is in debt, his devoted wife Milly is expecting another child, and he alienates his parishioners by a want of tact. Milly is loved and Amos largely tolerated because of her, but when he takes into their home the dubious Countess Czerlaski, widow of a Polish dancing master, who has fallen out with her half-brother Mr Bridmain, gossip in the small community becomes increasingly directed against Amos, who is innocent in giving hospitality but susceptible to the Countess's flattery. He is blind to Milly's suffering. She is overworked, uncomplaining, generous in her acceptance of the Countess. The servant Nanny, however, rounds on the Countess, who leaves with some grace but, before Milly can feel fully relieved, she herself becomes ill, weakened by overwork and the birth of her seventh child. She dies, and the community which had criticized Amos now moves back towards him in

sympathetic recognition of his sufferings. It is too late. His loss is compounded by having to move to a distant curacy with his children. Some years later, in a brief epilogue, he returns to Shepperton with his eldest daughter Patty to visit Milly's grave.

'Mr Gilfil's Love-Story' has its main action at Cheverel Manor, home of Sir Christopher Cheverel and his wife. The year is 1788, though there is retrospect to 1773. The household consists of themselves, the young Italian girl Caterina Sarti, whom they have adopted, and Sir Christopher's ward, the chaplain Maynard Gilfil. In addition there is Captain Wybrow, Sir Christopher's nephew and heir, who has trifled with Caterina and continues to do so though he is paying court to an heiress, Beatrice Assher, in accordance with Sir Christopher's wishes. Gilfil silently loves Caterina, who is passionately in love with Wybrow. Miss Assher comes to stay at Cheverel Manor, Wybrow continues to flirt with Caterina: Miss Assher becomes suspicious, but Wybrow persuades her that Caterina has thrown herself at him, and she reproaches Caterina, who is in turn humiliated and enraged. She takes a dagger and sets off for an assignation with Wybrow in the shrubbery: her intention to kill him for his treachery is forestalled by finding him dead from a heart attack. She flees Cheverel Manor, is traced and found by Gilfil, lies dangerously ill for some time, and then marries him. She dies within a year and Gilfil, Vicar of Shepperton, lives on for 40 years, an eccentric but loved man, the locked room in his house symbolizing the all-too-brief happiness in the past.

'Janet's Repentance' is set in Milby in the early 1830s. Robert Dempster, an alcoholic lawyer, who has brutalized his wife over the years and driven her to drink, represents Church orthodoxy in the town and is strongly resistant to the arrival of the evangelical preacher Edgar Tryan, who proposes among other reforms to institute a Sunday evening lecture. Janet Dempster is conditioned to support her brutal husband and does so, but after her meeting with Tryan whose health is deteriorating from overwork, she begins to see spiritual salvation for herself in working for others. She is turned out by her drunken husband in a rage one night, shelters with a neighbour, but returns to him when he is dying of delirium tremens. After his death she resists the temptation to return to drink herself, nurses the dying Tryan, and devotes herself to good works for others as a result of the selfless example he has shown her.

Each scene derives from factual place, and some of the characters from people known to Marian Evans, or known of by her, in her girlhood. Shepperton is *Chilvers Coton, Cheverel Manor is Arbury Hall (the Cheverels are the *Newdigates, who employed Robert *Evans), Milby is *Nuneaton. Amos Barton derives from the Revd John Gwyther, Maynard Gilfil from the Revd Bernard Gilpin Ebdell, who baptized Mary Anne Evans on 29 November 1819 and was Vicar of Chilvers Coton from 1786 until 1828, Edgar Tryan from the Revd J. E. Jones. The Dempsters derive from Mr and Mrs J. W. Buchanan, with George Eliot acknowledging 'the real Dempster was far more disgusting than mine' (L ii. 347).

Critical Approaches

The definiteness of place and association is seen in the opening description of Shepperton Church, a personified and intimate identification which immediately establishes the warmth and particularity of the narrative to come. The place and space of individuals in their known community is the adhesive. Incident and pathos are deftly combined, witness the spilling of the gravy on Milly's much-turned dress (*SC* 1.3), or the heart-rending sequence of the children and near-bereft husband saying goodbye to the dying Milly (*SC* 1.8). Amos's parishioners provide a chorus to the events and the conduct of their minister, the devotion of Milly is seen when the domestic situation gives way to the public one as Amos visits the 'College' of the poor. The sympathetic ambience is underpinned by a low-key realism, the dialogue, often dialect, providing the index to character and situation. Contrast is used effectively in the interiors from Cross Farm to the Vicarage to Camp Villa, supplemented by a clear psychological notation of character which sees Amos and Milly in interaction, the Countess and Nanny, and the tellingly uncaricatured presentation of the children and the individuals of the clerical meeting. These plus the choric functions of Mrs Hackit and Mr Pilgrim provide a convincing exposition of community and individual. Milly is the first of George Eliot's idealizations of selfless womanhood, with her self-abnegation and lovingness, her absorption in her husband and children, the economic deprivation she endures, the incessant childbearing which finally kills her. Place beside this the Countess's egoistic and shallow stance, her simulated social position and reflex flattery, and you have the essential psychological areas which George Eliot is to expose again and again in her fiction. Yet Milly is not cloying, and the Countess is not entirely devoid of feeling, as we see when after that signal confrontation with Nanny she makes her own decision to leave and tells the white lies necessary to reassure Milly as a consequence. Already there is a subtlety and economy in analysis of character and situation.

The local context is reinforced by an ironic mode which has words, in the shape of gossip, or words, in the shape of the clerical meeting (also with gossip) seen in contradistinction to the reality of Amos's life. Both have the edge of satire and the stamp of truth, with individuals speaking across a spectrum of verbal kindliness to verbal malice. The *irony consists of exposing the difference between those who talk and the reality of those talked about, here the Bartons in their sad and saddening situation. After the clerical meeting events prove the inefficacy of talk. The Countess leaves (admittedly hastened by downstairs gossip), Milly's premature baby is born, and three short chapters are sufficient to close the sad fortunes. This brevity has its counterpart in the sudden changes which occur in life, the events which subdue talk by the omnipresence of their impact. Structurally too there is the dramatic immediacy of this as compared with the leisurely historical span with which the story opens. If the narrative voice (see NARRATION) is occasionally given to the unusual or pompous word or phrase, like 'supererogatory' and 'unmitigated bohea', or pretentious quotation (one in Greek from Sophocles' *Philoctetes*), it is more commonly employed in conveying authentic historical period detail, in describing the humorous or petty or sad interaction of ordinary lives, and in diffusing a wise and tolerant perspective on life without condescension. There is a rather self-conscious use of the first person: 'I fear', 'I recall', and 'I was so crude a member' (of the congregation). Milly's deathbed scene (*SC* 1.8) has a sparseness of narrative balancing the physical sparseness (and an emotional fullness too felt for words), and there is an unobtrusive realism and wisdom of perspective which ring true. The children 'cried because Mamma was ill and papa looked so unhappy; but they thought, perhaps next week things would be as they used to be again'.

'Mr Gilfil's Love-Story' employs retrospect, an integral part of Eliot's mature art, witness those on Lydgate and Gwendolen later. Until the major crisis of the action this is only loosely a clerical 'scene', since Gilfil is often peripheral to the main drama, which is dominated by the somewhat desiccated society ethos of Cheverel Manor. The visiting Beatrice Assher and her mother, the former the desirable object of Wybrow's prescribed matrimonial aims, spark the dramatic action. Beneath the façade is the concealed but felt love of Gilfil for Caterina, the impassioned love of Caterina for Wybrow (her fiery Italian temperament is not merely operatic), a subtly ironic portrayal of the indolent Wybrow, and a superb focus on the egoistic but far from blind Beatrice Assher. Sir Christopher, however, is blind to these emotional contexts. The stately costume parade is displaced by an incisive psychological focus which has Sir Christopher suggesting to Gilfil that he marry Tina (the diminutive by which he styles Caterina, the 'little singing bird') at the same time as Wybrow marries Beatrice. This was suggested by Wybrow, who had been pressurized in his turn by Beatrice. This insensitivity (Gilfil is aware of the relationship between Caterina and Wybrow) is complemented by Wybrow's, with his tendency to do nothing and just let things take their course, plus the increasing anguish of Caterina, who feels her betrayal and suddenly develops murderous intentions. The moral synthesis of guilt and innocence, which is to be repeated notably in Eliot's final novel *Daniel Deronda*, where Gwendolen wishes Grandcourt to drown though trying ineffectually to save him, is seen here in Caterina's anguish before and after her discovery. But there are moving moments before this: Sir Christopher's kindness to the Widow Hartopp, to whom he is supposedly hard while contingently providing for her, or the pathos of the Cheverels' childlessness, which makes Caterina a surrogate daughter (but not quite in terms of birth and status) and Wybrow an unworthy heir-presumptive. There are moments too of rare tranquillity, as when Gilfil takes the evening service in the small chapel and brings family and servants together in an illusory and supposedly unchanging communion before momentous changes. Then there is the inward suffering of Gilfil, controlled, chaplainly, contrasted with the volatile outbursts of Tina—who is often given animal or bird imagery to characterize her febrile moods—and the casual egoism and opportunism (hardly animation) of Wybrow—who finds it convenient to accept the love of 'a little, graceful, dark-eyed, sweet-singing woman, whom no one need despise' (*SC* 2.4). Her tremulous suffering as she sees Wybrow making up to Beatrice is movingly registered: Caterina is vulnerable because she lives for emotion alone, some of which has hitherto been subsumed by her singing. The physical and social contrasts with Beatrice are also emphasized, and omniscient commentary, here somewhat crudely interjected, establishes the widest of perspectives: 'While this poor little heart was being bruised with a weight too heavy for it, Nature was holding on her calm inexorable way, in unmoved and terrible beauty' (*SC* 2.5). But Caterina's exchanges with Beatrice as well as Wybrow are finely done, bringing out all her emotionalism (and insights) as well as the inherited condescension of the lady. Wybrow's lies have all the languor of a man whose poor energies are given up almost exclusively to self-contemplation. Nevertheless they provoke the crisis and then the catastrophe and Gilfil, whose story this is, can only watch in virtually silent contemplation the drama which is being played out before him. Through a deft plot detail Eliot brings him centre stage by having Wybrow, confronted by Sir Christopher, insinuatingly suggest that he, Gilfil, should marry Caterina, thus freeing him, Wybrow, from his own importunities, though of course he puts it in such a way that Sir Christopher ceases to suspect him and finds him nobly appropriate as his heir. Gilfil's goodness is appreciated by the anguished Caterina, who wishes she could have loved him, an early instance of the alternative life which bulks so large in Eliot's fiction. It is a further tragic irony that Gilfil is unaware of Caterina's casual meeting with Beatrice which provokes her to take the dagger. The masterstroke is her finding him dead: her passionate passing desire has become fact. From now on Gilfil moves much more centrally into the action, taking the dagger from her pocket while she is in a collapsed swoon, but such is George Eliot's identification with her character that we know that he cannot remove her guilt, and that the breakdown which leads to her death has already begun. Caterina's confession to Gilfil, so like Gwendolen's confession to Daniel when she describes Grandcourt's drowning and her own crisis, is redolent of guilt, psychologically convincing, immediate, searing to speaker, reader, listener alike: 'But when I meant to do it,' was the next thing she whispered, 'it was as bad as if I had done it' (*SC* 2.19). Responsibility, motivation, wish, will, all are present, character and reader confronted with the dilemma of judgement.

'Janet's Repentance' is an advance even on the positives of the first two scenes: it is longer, allowing for a more complete artistic presentation, a deeper investigation of character with a more fully integrated psychology, together with a sustained social emphasis. John Blackwood was disturbed, since the tone is intent on conveying the unacceptable reality of alcoholism, wife-beating, dishonesty, and layerings of hypocrisy. The graphic narrative begins in the bar of the Red Lion in Milby (*SC* 3.1), unfamiliar territory for a female author but done with (masculine) assurance and accuracy, as later in *Silas Marner* (*SM* 6). The conversation reflects local religious controversy at a time of national religious divisions, epitomized by the Anglican tradition on the one hand and the Dissenting movements towards change on the other, but it is dominated by the irascible and arrogant lawyer Dempster, already drinking himself towards the delirium tremens of his last days. The story unfolds in significant social settings, with a finely ironic balance struck between the male world of pub bar, here directed towards punitive action, and the feminine world of comment and commentary epitomized by the conversation in Mrs Linnet's parlour (*SC* 3.3). The advance in structural coherence in 'Janet's Repentance' complements the other advances: by the end of that chapter the reader has met the already overtaxed Edgar Tryan and can weigh him against Dempster in the moral (and Christian) scales. These early chapters effectively establish the private and public action and interaction, with an ironic force which is proleptic in its effects. For instance, Dempster's public verbal bullying is translated into the physical (private) fact of his brutalizing his wife Janet. There is the public (and peaceful) preparation for the confirmation ceremony, with a (temporarily) happy glance at the Dempster home and of Janet's visit to her mother. The surface of life appears to be secure, tranquil, but the next picture in the Dempster home is that of the lawyer preparing, with the aid of his anxious-to-please wife, the public humiliation of Edgar Tryan over his Sunday evening lectures. By a superb structural effect, however, it is Dempster who is later to be publicly humiliated by his violence and drunkenness, while Tryan survives the battering satirical shafts (some of which are Janet's) and the threats of physical violence with the courage of principle and faith. And to compound the contrast, Janet comes through her terrible domestic ordeals and finds a new life which is made possible for her by the practice and example of Tryan, the man she was earlier helping to degrade. The public scene of Tryan supported by his adherents, and in particular the frail and aged Mr Jerome, is in fact central and proleptic, with its linking of the past religious tradition, the present manifestations of change, and the future results of change on the public and private level. Casual conversation has already suggested that Dempster will kill himself one day by overturning his gig: he does, but more than this, he and the obdurate attitudes for which he stood are overturned too. The cruel parody of the playbills penetrates Tryan's sensitive nature, but the narrative voice registers that he will pass again up Orchard Street in death, having given life. Janet looks on, her eyes are 'worn with grief and watching, and she was following her beloved friend and pastor to the grave' (*SC* 3.9). Here the phrase 'grief and watching' has associative weight. It looks forward to Janet's exhausting care for her dying husband, a triumph of the spirit of love, of true Christianity over abuse and pettiness. The retrospect on Tryan earlier, his desertion of Lucy, and his finding her dying in the street, is a kind of flimsy moral didacticism which balances the title of the story by explaining Tryan's repentance.

Janet's own repentance really begins during her first meeting with Tryan, when a muted sympathetic rapport is struck. Janet's factual haven with Mrs Pettifer is the beginning of her reintegration into positive life. Mrs Pettifer is the catalyst who makes Janet's movement towards human reclamation possible. Here the omniscient commentary is both particular and generalized without any loss of truth. It is an index to Janet's continuing depression and initial indecision, but her seeing Tryan again reorientates her on a deeper level of which she has been unaware. With him she experiences a mystical and wordless recognition of a love beyond definable love, and her early dependence on him is as natural as her earlier dependence on alcohol, the difference being that nullity is replaced by the possibility of salvation. There is a superbly ironic integration here, for the beginning of Janet's reclamation occurs contemporaneously with Dempster's last degradation. After his brutal treatment of the groom, his alcoholic frenzy causes the accident. Janet is ignorant of what has happened and Tryan, sensitively cognizant of her state, suggests that she is not told until later. The truth will out, Janet cannot be long protected, and inadvertently learning of her husband's severe injuries, she takes her decision. She nurses him and strives to interpret his disordered subconscious fears, the meshes of guilt in his delirium: the sequence is convincing psychological realism: 'she's cold—she's dead . . . she'll strangle me with her black hair . . . her hair is all serpents . . . they're black serpents . . . they hiss . . . let me go . . . she wants to drag me with her cold arms' (*SC* 3.23). Janet's selfless devotion, her refusal to leave the man who has degraded her, emphasizes the penetrating repentance of the title. Janet does not know, cannot know, whether her husband's incoherent lip movements signal his repentance or not. Her loyalty to Dempster despite the trampled past is not just personal: it is a type of simple, practical, unswerving Christian giving seen in Tryan and absorbed by her as the love which transcends self-suffering and self-need. Janet has one terrible last temptation after the loss of her mentor, but is saved by his example. She begins to live for others. Eliot here has two death scenes which symbolize Janet's positive progression. When Janet kisses her husband she kisses a corpse, symbolic of the past which has been a living death to her for so long. But when she kisses Tryan there is life in death: he says to her, ' "Let us kiss each other before we part." She lifted up her face to his, and the full life-breathing lips met the wasted dying ones in a sacred kiss of promise' (*SC* 3.27). Tryan's bequest to Janet is devotion to the life of others. This theme is to be fully orchestrated throughout Eliot's ensuing work.

Scenes is already mature in terms of its appraisal of life, its authentication of period (one of Eliot's greatest strengths), its range of humanitarian concern, its wisdom without condescension or arrogance, the feeling presence of a narrative persona whose moral ambience is firm without being stern or narrowly judgmental. The detailed particularities include a sense of structure—which places character in community but encompasses private conscience and consciousness—humour in commentary and dialogue with the ear of truth, an appraisal of individual interaction with unobtrusive, even unwritten but deductive, evaluation, intellectual stringency, and aesthetic, artistic awareness. The realism which characterizes the above is sustained by a psychological assurance which is both social and individual: the elevation of the commonplace is one of the central motifs of a fiction which was breaking new ground. The *language of characters is faithfully recorded. The *humour is unforced, the sadness evolves naturally from individual situations. Eliot is an interpreter of the time she knew through hindsight (see HISTORY), but she conveys timeless and universal truths about human nature to her readers. Her artistic development and the range of her sympathetic interrogation were to expand, but each story registers her command of narrative and her knowledge of life. Collectively they mark her arrival: substantively they guarantee her future.

Even as late as 1948 there was qualified doubt, so that Joan Bennett, in her *George Eliot: Her Mind and her Art*, could argue that the parade of the children into the room where Milly Barton is dying (see DEATH) is more literary than naturalistic, that the pathos is overdone, and that Milly's tortured words to her husband praising his goodness to her when they both know the truth is itself an offence against truth. But from Barbara Hardy onwards (*The Novels of George Eliot: A Study in Form*, 1959) critics have argued the formal excellence of *Scenes* as well as their realism. Barbara Hardy's first chapter, with its unequivocal title of 'The Unheroic Tragedy' and its functional focus on how 'the collective personality of the community acts as a causal agent' (21) is a groundbreaking investigation of the many qualities of *Scenes* in its own right. Thomas Noble's full-scale study *George Eliot's 'Scenes of Clerical Life'* (1965) pays special attention to Eliot's 'Doctrine of Sympathy' and examines the distinctive areas of humour, pathos, romance, and melodrama, as well as 'the real drama of Evangelicalism'. Jenny Uglow has demonstrated in her *George Eliot* (1987) that 'Tryan's rescue of Janet from despair is supported by a mass of "secondary helpers", the love of her mother, and her women friends' (90). Women are not merely passive, but have a communal strength of their own. Five years later, Karen Brady in *George Eliot* (1992), brings a persuasive feminist perspective to her consideration of 'Mr Gilfil'. She records that some critics have suggested that Tina is undermined because of her foreignness, but feels that it is rather that 'the exclusion and abuse that she suffers' derives from a combination of 'her gender, class and nationality' (73). David Carroll applies the biblical term hermeneutics (interpretation) to his examination of the works and is particularly insightful on *Scenes*. The three stories, for they are little more than that, have a simple but convincing, not to be underrated, authenticity; the great novels which follow are reared on these tracings of truth.   GRH

Carroll (1992).
Knoepflmacher (1968).
Noble, Thomas A., *George Eliot's 'Scenes of Clerical Life'* (1965).
Uglow (1987).

Daniel Deronda that Schiller is an explicit point of reference: Mab Meyrick, moved by the reading of a novel, alludes to the 'Ode to Joy' in claiming that she feels like Schiller and wants to embrace the world (*DD* 18); Mirah says that she learned evil and good from reading Schiller and Shakespeare (*DD* 19); and in her suspicion of Gwendolen she likens her to the treacherous Princess Eboli in *Don Carlos* (*DD* 52). The references are incidental, but it is consonant with the visionary idealism of her last novel that George Eliot should be re-minded of her early enthusiasm for the idealistic Schiller.   JMR

Ashton (1980).
Guth, Deborah, 'George Eliot and Schiller: The Case of The Mill on the Floss', *George Eliot–George Henry Lewes Studies*, 34–5 (1998).
McCobb (1982).
Wiesenfarth, Joseph, 'The Greeks, the Germans and George Eliot', *Browning Institute Studies*, 10 (1982).

Schopenhauer, Arthur (1788–1860), German philosopher whose work George Eliot knew from

1852, when the *Westminster Review, which she was effectively editing, published a pioneering essay about him by John Oxenford. She was warm in her praise of Oxenford's article, which was responsible for bringing Schopenhauer to public attention both in Britain and in Germany, where the philosopher had hitherto been largely ignored. She did not comment directly on Schopenhauer's philosophy, though its pessimism was unlikely to have appealed to her. Early in 1873, when she was beginning to plan *Daniel Deronda*, she read his principal work, *Die Welt als Wille und Vorstellung* (*The World as Will and Idea*, 1819), where he sees all life as subject to the Will, a blind and irrational life-force to which human beings are enslaved by their own desires and which has no purpose beyond perpetuating itself and the suffering that it causes. Schopenhaurian ideas have been detected in *Deronda*: in Eliot's increasing pessimism about social life and her elevation of *music, which Schopenhauer took to be the highest art form (McCobb, 321–30); while Grandcourt has been read allegorically as the embodiment of the Schopenhaurian Will, whose nihilism Eliot decisively rejects (Raina, 371–82). See also PHILOSOPHY.

JMR

McCobb, E. A., 'The Morality of Musical Genius: Schopenhaurian Ideas in *Daniel Deronda*', *Forum for Modern Language Studies*, 19 (1983).

Raina, Badri, '*Daniel Deronda*: A View of Grandcourt', *Studies in the Novel*, 17 (1985).

Schubert, Franz (1797–1828). George Eliot was deeply appreciative of the Austrian composer Schubert, in whose songs, she told G. H. *Lewes's son Charles (see LEWES FAMILY) in October 1859, she especially delighted (*L* iii. 178). Schubert's 'Erlkönig', sung by Gustave Hippolyte Roger (1815–79), was included in the only concert she and Lewes had attended during their 1854–5 visit to *Berlin. This had been 'a treat not to be forgotten'. Roger 'gave the full effect to Schubert's beautiful and dramatic music, and his way of falling from melody into awestruck speech in the final words, "*war todt*" ['was dead'], abides with one. I never felt so thoroughly the beauty of that divine ballad before' (*Journals*, 251). In 1858, during their visit to *Munich, the Leweses spent a pleasant evening at the home of comparative anatomist and zoologist Professor Karl von Siebold and his wife, when, accompanied by her husband, Frau von Siebold sang Schubert's songs 'with much taste and feeling' (*L* ii. 454). In chapter 32 of *Daniel Deronda*, Mirah was initially intended to sing 'Adieu', once thought to be by Schubert; but after consulting Charles Lewes, George Eliot replaced this with *Beethoven's contextually more suitable 'Per pietà non dirmi addio' ('Ah, perfido!').

The Leweses were also responsive to Schubert's instrumental music. They heard his Octet on 8 March 1868, and a 'glorious concert' (*Journals*, 135) they attended on 20 February 1869 wound up with his Trio. On both occasions, Joseph *Joachim and Alfredo Carlo *Piatti were performing

Schubert was included in George Eliot's own repertoire. In the summer of 1869, she would sometimes play either his music, or Beethoven's, to Lewes's son Thornie as he lay, mortally ill, on the drawing-room sofa.

George Eliot's diary entry for 8 September 1879 is confined to the two words 'Darwin. Schubert' (*Journals*, 180). See also MUSIC.

BG

Schumann, Clara Josephine (Wieck) (1819–96), renowned concert pianist, and composer. Married to the composer Robert Schumann (1810–56), Clara was the principal exponent of her husband's works. George Eliot and G. H. *Lewes first saw her in October 1854, at a musical party at *Liszt's in *Weimar. George Eliot described her as 'a melancholy, interesting looking creature' (*Journals*, 29), but later recalled her piano playing as 'great', though Liszt's was 'the greatest' (*L* iii. 15). Ten years later George Eliot praised Clara Schumann's playing of *Mendelssohn and *Beethoven (*L* v. 12), and heard her again in March 1877 (*L* ix. 190). See also MUSIC.

BG

science. George Eliot embarked on her novelistic career well versed in the intertwined developments in scientific and social thought of her era. Indeed, one impetus behind her turn to fiction was the desire to show, with real emotional force, how the moral and social world are fully integrated and ruled by the same laws of causal sequence that govern the *natural world. In her early essay 'The *Progress of the Intellect', published in the *Westminster Review* in January 1851 (repr. in *Essays*), Eliot draws attention to the 'revelation' contained in the 'recognition of the presence of undeviating law in the material and moral world—of that invariability of sequence which is acknowledged to be the basis of physical science, but which is still perversely ignored in our social organization, our ethics, and our religion' (*Essays*, 31). In Eliot's secular world-view, science was to offer the moral framework (see MORAL VALUES) once supplied by *religion. What she here defines as 'that inexorable law of consequences' becomes the key both to the plotting of her fiction, and her representations of psychological life. Science, for Eliot, brings a new way of looking at *history:

every past phase of human development is part of that education of the race in which we are sharing; every mistake, every absurdity into which poor human nature has fallen, may be looked on as an experiment of which we may reap the benefit. A correct generalization gives significance to the smallest detail, just as the great inductions of geology demonstrate in every pebble the working of laws by which the earth has become adapted for the habitation of man. (*Essays*, 31)

Eliot is drawing here on the work of the geologist Charles Lyell, whose *Principles of Geology* (1830–3) laid the foundations for uniformitarianism in geology, the belief that the earth's surface has been gradually transformed by the operation of uniform causes still in operation, and who also created the extended timescale which made Charles *Darwin's theories possible (see DARWINISM).

Eliot's novels can be seen as similar forms of 'experiment' in history, offering a moral education to both characters and readers by showing the uniform workings of law in human history (see DETERMINISM). In *Adam Bede* Mr Irwine points out to Arthur the moral implications of 'that inexorable law of consequences': 'consequences are unpitying. Our deeds carry their terrible consequences, quite apart from any fluctuations that went before—consequences are hardly ever confined to ourselves' (*AB* 16). Eliot, like her friends and contemporaries G. H. *Lewes and Herbert *Spencer and the French philosopher Auguste *Comte, subscribed to the view that society not only followed the same laws of natural science, but was actually formed like a natural organism, where all elements were interconnected, and movement in one part necessarily affects the whole. This belief in the interconnection of part and whole underpins the whole range of historical sciences that emerged in the 19th century, from geology and physiology to philology, palaeontology, and evolutionary biology. In her *essays, *notebooks, and novels Eliot draws on a diverse range of reading across these fields to sustain her social arguments. Behind *Adam Bede* lies the theory articulated in her essay 'The *Natural History of German Life' (1856) that society is '*incarnate history*': 'The external conditions which society has inherited from the past are but the manifestation of inherited internal conditions in the human beings who compose it; the internal conditions and the external are related to each other as the organism and its medium, and development can take place only by the gradual consentaneous development of both' (*Essays*, 287). Eliot's later painstaking efforts to recreate the historical texture of Renaissance *Florence in *Romola* are guided by the same principle. As Eliot observes in a letter,

It is the habit of my imagination to strive after as full a vision of the medium in which a character moves as of the character itself. The psychological causes

which prompted me to give such details of Florentine life and history as I have given, are precisely the same as those which determined me in giving the details of English village life in *Silas Marner* or the 'Dodson' life, out of which were developed the destinies of poor Tom and Maggie. (*L* iv. 96–7)

In *Adam Bede* Eliot largely adopted the position outlined in her essay of a 'natural historian', depicting the lives of her chosen specimens. Her subsequent fiction is more experimental in form, drawing on detailed work by Herbert Spencer and G. H. Lewes in the field of physiological psychology to show at a deeper level the ways in which history shapes the individual workings of the mind. Spencer had offered in *The Principles of Psychology* (1855) an evolutionary theory of the development of mind, and in *The *Physiology of Common Life* (1859–60) which Lewes was working on whilst Eliot wrote 'The Lifted Veil' and *The Mill on the Floss*, Lewes attempts to offer a physiological account of all the movements of the mind, both conscious and unconscious. Eliot's fiction directly engages with this material: we enter *The Mill* in a state of dream, while the seemingly Gothic elements of 'The Lifted Veil' where the narrator, Latimer, is paralysed by visions of the future, are referred directly to the contemporary theory of double consciousness (a theory recently developed by Eliot and Lewes's friend, the medic Henry Holland, in *Chapters on Mental Physiology*, 1852). Latimer demands of his readers: 'Are you unable to give me your sympathy—you who read this? Are you unable to imagine this double consciousness at work within me, flowing on like two parallel streams which never mingle their waters and blend into a common hue?' (*LV* 1).

Physiological psychology traced the flow of impulses in the mind as that of streams or currents, and in *The Mill* one finds this language operating both literally in psychological description, and symbolically through the overarching role of the river Floss. Mr Tulliver's beating of Wakem, or Maggie's leaving of Stephen, can be referred to Lewes's theory of 'Automatic Actions' whereby sensation follows the established channels of mind. Significantly, Lewes uses the example of a mill wheel to demonstrate his theory of different levels of consciousness in the mind (*Physiology of Common Life*, ii. 59). This sense of the multilayered nature of the mind is also applied by Eliot to history, so that St Ogg's 'inherited a long past without thinking of it, and had no eyes for the spirits that walk the streets'. St Ogg's is depicted in Darwinian terms as an 'outgrowth of nature' (*MF* 1.12), but also, like Maggie, as possessing a complexly layered psychological history, where the 'shadows' of the past can rise up, unbidden and uncontrollable. Eliot is still adhering to 'that inexorable law of consequences', only now it operates in a more complex, multi-layered model of history. The ending of the novel, with its dramatic flood, also poses a challenge to uniformitarian ideas of history, suggesting in its place earlier 'catastrophic' notions of geological development.

It would be difficult to overestimate the influence of scientific thought and culture on George Eliot's fiction. From the very start her life with Lewes revolved around the twin spheres of literature and science. Their circle of friends, and their ambitious programmes of evening reading, move seamlessly between the two. Eliot's diary entry for 16 October 1855, for example, records that 'We are reading Gall's *Anatomie et Physiologie du Cerveau* in the evening, with, occasionally, Carpenter's Comparative Physiology. "The Newcomes" [Thackeray] as light fare after dinner.' (Gall was the originator of the science of *phrenology, which features in a minor way in Eliot's fiction, and, more importantly, was the first scientist to argue that the brain is the organ of the mind. W. B. Carpenter was one of the leading figures in physiological psychology.) Eliot first started writing fiction when actively involved with Lewes on an extended natural history trip which was to provide the basis of his *Sea-Side Studies* (1858). Her interest in the minute processes of life revealed to the engaged observer, either by microscope or by training of the eye, is one that expands and develops with her fiction. In *Felix Holt, the Radical*, one can hear echoes of Eliot's own initiation into seaside study as Mrs Transome's failure to notice Mr Lyon is judged to stem not from 'studied haughtiness, but from sheer mental inability to consider him—as a person ignorant of natural history is unable to consider a fresh-water polype otherwise than as a sort of animated weed, certainly not fit for table' (*FH* 30). Although the observation is humorous in tone it points to the ways in which Eliot finds in science the extension of vision she wishes to offer her readers.

Science and its relations to vision are crucial to Eliot's most overtly scientific work, *Middlemarch*. The novel is defined in the Prelude as an 'examination of the history of man' under the 'varying experiments of Time'. In the long discussions of the experimental methodology of the pioneering doctor Lydgate, one can trace Eliot's meditations on her own fictional practice. Lydgate dismisses the rather static natural history of Farebrother, with his rows and rows of dead specimens, in favour of an experimental science which studies the interactive processes of a dynamic structure. His method is not merely that of observation, but the exercise of disciplined imagination: 'the imagination that reveals subtle actions inaccessible by

any sort of lens, but tracked in that outer darkness through long pathways of necessary sequence by the inward light which is the last refinement of Energy, capable of bathing even the ethereal atoms in its ideally illuminated space' (*MM* 16). Following Lewes, and his mentor the eminent French physiologist Claude Bernard, Eliot now defines science as the reaching out of imagination, extending vision even beyond the realms of telescope or microscope. Science, Lewes argued, in the first volume of *Problems of Life and Mind* (which he was working on whilst George Eliot wrote *Middlemarch*) is an 'Ideal Construction'. Like Eliot he believes science can offer the moral guidance necessary for Victorian culture: 'It is the greatness of Science that while satisfying the spiritual thirst for knowledge, it satisfies the pressing desire for guidance in action: not only painting a picture of the wondrous labyrinth of Nature, but placing in our hands the Ariadne thread to lead us through the labyrinth' (*Problems of Life and Mind*, i. 26). The image of the labyrinth is central to *Middlemarch*. Like that of the river Floss in *The Mill*, it creates an overarching symbolic unity in the text, operating simultaneously at multiple levels, from accurate physiology to mythic resonance. Science in this novel does not merely offer a model of imaginative practice, but is in turn integrated into the imaginative processes of symbolic and creative construction.

The image of the labyrinth first occurs to describe the ways in which Dorothea's energies are trapped and impeded by the constrictions of Middlemarch society, 'hemmed in by a social life which seemed nothing but a labyrinth of petty courses, a walled-in maze of small paths' (*MM* 3). The question for Dorothea, as for Lydgate, is whether the 'retarding friction'(*MM* 15) of society will cause their energies to be 'dispersed among hindrances' (*MM* Prelude), or whether it will, in the words of the Finale, achieve 'fine issues' or channels of positive social effect. The language, as in *The Mill*, is that of physiological psychology, drawing on contemporary physical theories of force and motion. Dorothea's entrapment in marriage, and the workings of Casaubon's mind, are equally figured in labyrinthine imagery. The large vistas she had hoped to find in his mind are replaced by 'anterooms and winding passages which seemed to lead nowither' (*MM* 20). To Will Ladislaw, Dorothea appears as if imprisoned, entrapped by a minotaur (*MM* 22). She proves herself to be, however, the true spirit of Science, or Ariadne, showing us the way out of the labyrinth. Following her night of sorrow she awakes to see the far-off figures on the road and field, and realizes that she is 'a part of that involuntary, palpitating life' (*MM* 80). Her moral revelation is simultaneously a scientific one: a recognition of the organic, interconnected nature of social life.

Victorian critics of Eliot's fiction frequently complained of her use of science and scientific language. A reviewer of *Romola* commented with distaste on the 'psychologico-medical study of Baldassarre', and blamed Lewes for this 'lapse in artistry' (*CH* 235), while Henry *James grumbled that *Middlemarch* was 'too often an echo of Messrs Darwin and Huxley' (*CH* 359). Much of the overt scientism of Eliot's language has been lost for us over time as startling usages have become part of our common currency. One can see, however, repeated instances in *Middlemarch* where the principles of the persistence of force are used, albeit in a light-hearted manner, to describe psychological responses. Of Mr Casaubon's disappointment in marriage, Eliot observes: 'It is true that he knew all the classical passages implying the contrary; but knowing classical passages, we find, is a mode of motion, which explains why they leave so little extra force for their personal application' (*MM* 10). Matter and force, or motion and feeling, Lewes argued, were all identical. Eliot creatively deploys this principle to range between artistic levels, from the physiology of psychological experience, to the symbolic structures of *myth.

The most famous examples of scientific imagery in *Middlemarch* all concern the field of vision. The vexing problem of how to interpret Mrs Cadwallader's matchmaking activities is compared to that of analysing a drop of water with a microscope: with each new strength of lens, and the revelation of further minute causes in play, a different picture is unfolded (*MM* 6). Eliot is fascinated by perspective, and the potentiality for transformed vision offered by science. As the image suggests, however, knowledge can never be absolute, since a stronger lens would always reveal a more complex picture. The radical subjectivity of vision is also captured in the image of the pier glass, drawn from 'an eminent philosopher among my friends' (Herbert Spencer): place a candle against a pier glass and the random spread of scratches 'will seem to arrange themselves in concentric circles round that little sun' (*MM* 27). Science furnishes a parable concerning the subjective basis of perception, but the implications, like the concentric circles of scratches, extend outwards to encompass Eliot's own methodology. *Middlemarch* inaugurates a more dynamic, self-reflexive methodology for George Eliot, grounded in the revelations of science (see NARRATION; REALISM). As narrator she is constantly shifting stance, aware of the changing interpretations to be created by changing perspectives. Taking his image from the beating heart, Lydgate insisted that there must be a 'systole and diastole in all inquiry' and that 'a man's mind

must be continually expanding and shrinking between the whole human horizon and the horizon of an object glass' (*MM* 63). Unlike Lydgate, who lamentably fails to follow his own methodology, Eliot strives to establish this shifting perspective, moving constantly between part and whole.

Eliot also foregrounds in this novel the moral dangers of vision. T. H. *Huxley, in an essay 'The Physical Basis of Life', published in the *Fortnightly Review,* had observed that the apparent silence of a tropical forest was due to the dullness of our hearing: 'could our ears catch the murmur of those tiny Maelstroms, as they whirl in the innumerable myriads of living cells which constitute each tree, we should be stunned, as with the roar of a great city' (Ian Adam, 'A Huxley Echo in *Middlemarch*', *Notes and Queries* (June 1964), 227). In Eliot's work that roar becomes a test of moral sensitivity: could we bear to know all the tragedy of our fellow human beings' lives?: 'If we had a keen vision and feeling of all ordinary human life, it would be like hearing the grass grow and the squirrel's heart beat, and we should die of that roar which lies on the other side of silence. As it is the quickest of us walk about well wadded with stupidity' (*MM* 20). Although Eliot's aim in writing fiction is still to extend her readers' sympathies, she recognizes that the intensification of vision can paralyse.

Daniel Deronda opens with a radical declaration of the fictionality of all beginnings, supported by the practice of astronomy which too must construct 'the make-believe of a beginning'. Science in this novel is aligned with the wide sweep of the heavens, and prophetic visionary practice. Mordecai, on seeing Deronda row towards him as he had so often envisaged, feels an exultation, 'not widely different from that of the experimenter, bending over the first stirrings of change that correspond to what in the fervour of concentrated prevision his thought has foreshadowed' (*DD* 40). Far from being a dry practice of recording and measuring, science here is figured as ardour and creativity, the breaking of the mould of established thought. It offers a fitting model for Eliot's artistic practice in this, her most experimental novel. In counterpoint to Mordecai's vision, however, we have the terrified premonitions of Gwendolen which are also fulfilled. Scientific creativity, it seems, is shadowed by neurosis. Interpretation trembles in the balance.

Daniel Deronda develops two of the dominant scientific strands in Lewes and Eliot's recent work and reading: evolutionary psychology and psychiatry. Mordecai, with his vision of the Hebrew culture as an 'inheritance which has never ceased to quiver in millions of human frames' (*DD* 42), offers a positive vision, based on the work of Spencer and Lewes, of an integrated process of psychological and cultural evolution. The finely drawn portrait of Gwendolen, however, with her 'fits of terror' and ultimate breakdown is grounded more on the pessimistic psychiatry of Henry Maudsley, and others, who traced a growing pattern of mental disease, of inherited and manufactured weaknesses and sensitivities, which would lead to social degeneration. Science, in its creative and progressive guise, is finely balanced by pathology. One of the strengths of *Daniel Deronda* lies in the delicate tension between these two strands.

It is fitting that Eliot's final major work should be one of science: the preparation for publication, after Lewes's death, of the last two volumes of *Problems of Life and Mind,* entitled *The Study of Psychology.* Eliot not only rewrote, but also added sections, intensifying Lewes's vision of a progressive, cultural inheritance, embedded in an evolving psychology. Art is transformed into science as Eliot's vision of the 'finely-touched spirit' of Dorothea, spreading out into social channels of effect, is given scientific embodiment. Developing Lewes's argument that consciousness of social interdependence will create social sympathy, Eliot concludes that in 'highly wrought natures' we will see 'a complete submergence . . . of egoistic desire, and an habitual outrush of the emotional force in sympathetic channels' (the text of Eliot's major additions are given in K. K. Collins, 'G. H. Lewes Revised: George Eliot and the Moral Sense', *Victorian Studies*, 21 (1978), 491). In this final, loving tribute to her partner, Eliot once more finds in science the basis of a moral vision.   SAS

Beer, Gillian, *Arguing with the Past: Essays in Narrative from Woolf to Sidney* (1989).

Levine, George, 'George Eliot's Hypothesis of Reality', *Nineteenth-Century Fiction*, 35 (1980).

Shuttleworth (1984).

Scott, Walter (1771–1832), Scottish novelist and poet, created baronet in 1820, whose Waverley novels were one of the great formative influences on George Eliot. She first encountered them as a child and her references to, and quotations from, them throughout her life show her intimate and detailed knowledge of the texts. Scott became for her, as G. H. *Lewes put it, an almost sacred name (*L* vii. 65); she would write of him in her maturity as 'dearly-beloved Scott' (*L* iii. 378), and maintain that she worshipped him devoutly. In 1871 she accounted for this veneration in a letter to a young Scottish admirer, Alexander *Main:

I like to tell you that my worship for Scott is peculiar. I began to read him when I was seven years old, and afterwards when I was grown up and living alone with my Father, I was able to make the evenings cheerful for him during the last five or six

years of his life by reading aloud to him Scott's novels. No other writer would serve as a substitute for Scott, and my life at that time would have been much more difficult without him. It is a personal grief, a heart-wound to me when I hear a depreciating or slighting word about Scott. (*L* v. 175)

One time that she took a less respectful view of him was during her pious evangelical phase, when she found it hard to justify the reading of novels and romances, and, writing to Maria *Lewis in 1839, could even utter a slighting word about Scott's character on reading Lockhart's *Life*: 'The spiritual sleep of that man was awful: he does not at least betray if he felt any thing like a pang of conscience . . . He sacrificed almost his integrity for the sake of acting out the character of the Scottish Laird, which he had so often depicted' (*L* i. 24). This condescending dismissal was an exception—though in later life she did criticize him for putting himself under 'the pressure of money-need' (*Essays*, 441)—and it was possibly prompted by a desire to impress her correspondent with her strict principles. Twenty years later she and Lewes were reading Lockhart's biography again and were moved to admiration by Scott's character, by 'his energy and steady work, his grand fortitude under calamity, and the spirit of strict honour to which he sacrificed his declining life' (*L* iii. 16). On the following New Year's Day Lewes presented her with a set of the Waverley novels, which his inscription describes as 'these works of her longest-venerated and best-loved Romancist' (Haight 1968: 319).

When she began to write fiction the example of Scott's anonymity encouraged her to try to preserve her own, and many years earlier it was Scott who had inspired one of her first attempts to write a narrative. According to Edith *Simcox, when she was a child of about 7 she was reading a copy of *Waverley* (1814) which a neighbour had lent to her sister, and she had still not finished it when the book had to be returned; so she set about writing out the story as far as she had read it, beginning with Waverley's adventures at Tully Veolan and continuing until the book was retrieved for her (Cross, new edn. 1886, 11). The episode is described in the sonnet she used as the *epigraph to chapter 57 of *Middlemarch*, while the use of such epigraphs can also be seen as a legacy of Scott:

They numbered scarce eight summers when a name
 Rose on their souls and stirred such motion there
As thrill the buds and shape their hidden frame
 At penetration of the quickening air:
His name who told of loyal Evan Dhu,

Of quaint Bradwardine, and Vich Ian Vor,
Making the little world their childhood knew
    Large with a land of mountain, lake, and scaur,
And larger yet with wonder, love, belief
    Toward Walter Scott, who living far away
Sent them this wealth of joy and noble grief.
    The book and they must part, but day by day,
In lines that thwart like portly spiders ran,
    They wrote the tale, from Tully Veolan.

A few years later her first surviving attempt at fiction, inscribed in a school notebook and dated 16 March 1834, is a fragment of a historical story known as *'Edward Neville', and it shows her following the example of Scott rather than simply writing him out from memory. The choice of historical subject (the English civil war), the youthful hero, and the combination of fictional and historical characters all owe a clear debt to the Waverley novels.

The legacy of Scott in her mature fiction is more subtle but pervasive: it can be seen in her sense of the determining power of *history; in her representation of provincial communities, which show how 'there is no private life which has not been determined by a wider public life' (FH 3); in her sense of place and grasp of the processes of change; and in her mastery of colloquial dialogue. She once named Scott, together with Henry *Fielding and *Shakespeare, as a writer who dared to be colloquial when representing popular life (L iii. 374), and she matched him with the vividly idiosyncratic speech of characters like Mrs Poyser in Adam Bede or the rustics in the Rainbow Inn in Silas Marner. Some of these general affinities are anticipated in the references she makes to Scott in her essay on 'The *Natural History of German Life', which she wrote just before she began to write the first of the Scenes of Clerical Life and which sets out some of the premisses of her fiction. Writing approvingly of the German historian Riehl's view of European society as 'incarnate history', she uses examples from the Waverley novels to illustrate and support his characterization of German peasant life; and, more significantly, she sees The Antiquary (1816) and 'The Two Drovers' as containing exemplary representations of humble life which succeed in extending the reader's sympathy and linking the higher classes with the lower (Essays, 270). These references to Scott are not surprising, for the understanding of *society in historical and organic terms which emerges in this essay, together with the power of fiction to give a realistic account of social life across the different classes, were already familiar to her from the Waverley novels. Her own fiction was to follow Scott's lead, but in ways which often adapt, develop, or interrogate his practice.

Most of her novels adopt Scott's device in Waverley of setting the action back several decades from the time of writing, to a period either within her own early memory or that of her parents' generation. For Scott 1745 represented the distant, but not too remote, point from which his readers could measure how far modern Scotland had developed. George Eliot extends and develops this measuring perspective in her practice as a narrator, drawing attention to the historical distance of the action and the characters from time to time, but with an added irony which strikes at any sense of complacent superiority her readers might feel in looking back, as in The Mill on the Floss, to 'those dark ages when there were no Schools of Design, before schoolmasters were invariably men of scrupulous integrity, and before the clergy were all men of enlarged minds and varied culture' (MF 2.4); or in Middlemarch to a time 'innocent of future goldfields, and of that gorgeous plutocracy which has so nobly exalted the necessities of genteel life' (MM 1). Her choice of period and focus on moments of historical transition, like that of the First Reform Bill (see REFORM ACTS) in Felix Holt, the Radical and Middlemarch, may owe something to Scott, with his view that, as he puts it in the introduction to The Fortunes of Nigel (1822), 'the strong contrast produced by the opposition of ancient manners to those which are gradually subduing them afford the lights and shadows necessary to give effect to a fictitious narrative'. Yet the contrasts between ancient and modern in her fiction are less stark and dramatic than in Scott's romances, while her examination of the complex mechanisms of social change goes beyond manners and mores to involve *science and knowledge, as well as economics and *politics. Like Scott she is opposed to revolutionary change and holds to a broad belief in evolutionary *progress, while showing signs in her later work of an increasing scepticism about the way society is developing.

In The Mill on the Floss there is a more specific engagement with Scott's work, which plays as important a part in Maggie's development as it had in her creator's. The Waverley novels are her childhood reading and an interest she shares with Philip Wakem, who entertains Tom with fighting stories taken from Scott (MF 2.4). When she is miserable in adolescence she fantasizes about how 'she would go to some great man—Walter Scott, perhaps, and tell him how wretched and how clever she was, and he would surely do something for her' (MF 4.3). But her reading of Scott is, in fact, bound up with her unhappiness and serves to confirm it. When Philip offers her a copy of The Pirate (1821) Maggie describes how she once began it but could not get beyond the scene where Minna is walking with Cleveland. Continuing the story in her head, she composed several endings, but all of them were unhappy: 'I could never make a happy ending out of that beginning' (*MF* 5.1). And in a spirit of lacerating self-denial she refuses the book on the grounds that it would make her long for a full life. Scott's fiction represents a rich world of the imagination but, at the same time, it endorses her painful sense of otherness and hopelessness by its stereotyped division of heroines into fair and dark, of whom the dark woman, like Minna in *The Pirate*, is doomed to suffer. That pattern is repeated in *The Mill* in the juxtaposition of Maggie and her fair-haired cousin Lucy, but it is used with ironical and critical detachment. Maggie's wish to reverse the fates of Scott's dark heroines in her own life, 'to avenge Rebecca and Flora Mac-Ivor, and Minna and all the rest of the dark unhappy ones' (*MF* 5.4), challenges the pattern of Scott's romance; and although she fails to achieve it in the end, her failure is not a triumph for the blonde-haired woman, while the grounds for it have to be sought, not in the conventions of romance, but in the constricting conditions of social and family life (see FAMILY LIFE, PORTRAYAL OF). The course of the heroine's life in this novel is plotted against the patterns of Scott's fiction that she is so familiar with.

The contrast between two visions of history that is presented in the narrator's meditation at the beginning of Book 4 of *The Mill on the Floss* also draws on Scott, though less overtly. The grim landscape of the Rhône, with its suggestions of a historical process without pattern or meaning, is juxtaposed to the romantic prospect of the 'castled Rhine' whose ruins 'have crumbled and mellowed into such harmony with the green and rocky steeps, that they seem to have a natural fitness, like the mountain pine' (*MF* 4.1); and this organic landscape, which implies a vital continuity between past and present and a meaningful history, leads the narrator to evoke a past age of romance in terms directly reminiscent of Scott. The 'robber barons', 'the wandering minstrel, the soft-lipped princess, the pious recluse and the timid Israelite', in that 'time of colour when the sunlight fell on glancing steel and floating banners', resemble the cast and setting of a novel like *Ivanhoe* (1819). Scott is honoured here in affectionately ironic pastiche. In celebrating 'the grand historic life of humanity' Eliot indulges in a flight of the romantic historical imagination associated with her 'best-loved Romancist', and this excursus stands out from the rest of the novel, which is concerned with more prosaic forms of life.

Her view of the Waverley novels implied in this passage is a partial one, singling out the romance to the exclusion of the *realism, and it has been read by one critic as an illustration of the negative influence of Scott, of George Eliot's misreading of him as a writer in the heroic, symbolic mode (Shaw, 393–402). That influence is discernible in the much-debated conclusion. The final symbolic embrace of Maggie and Tom is seen from this point of view as a mistaken attempt to raise them from their narrow, prosaic existence to the level of the 'grand historic life of humanity' by placing them centre stage as heroic figures. Succumbing thus to the lure of the symbolic, Eliot is tempted away from her, and Scott's, true strength, which is the grasp of the particular and unheroic. That may be to overestimate the power of Scott's example; but it is also possible to see the ending in relation to Maggie's earlier reaction to his novels, as her attempt at making good her desire to avenge the dark heroines by abandoning resigned passivity for action and self-assertion (Wilt, 475).

Romola is the only one of George Eliot's works that is a historical novel in the same sense as Scott's, combining fictional and historical figures in a drama located at a moment of historical crisis; and her learned but laborious reconstruction of Renaissance *Florence opens itself to the same kind of criticism as his medieval romances do in contrast to his novels about 17th- and 18th-century Scotland. Just as he is at his best when working closer to home, so too might *Middlemarch* be described as a more successful historical novel than *Romola*. At the same time *Romola* shows Eliot adapting Scott's model by juxtaposing to the historical figure of Savonarola not a young man like the typical hero of the Waverley novels, but a woman. Although Romola shares with Scott's male protagonists like Edward Waverley, or Henry Morton in *Old Mortality*, a distaste for fanaticism, reacting angrily to the seer Camilla Rucellai and her wild visions (*RO* 52), her position as a woman takes the novel in a different direction: towards a realm of symbolic action in the plague village and towards a conclusion that is more private than public, with Baldassare acting out her revenge on Tito as well as his own, and with her assumption of responsibility for Tito's illicit family (Welsh 1985: 193). As a highly self-conscious successor to Scott, *Romola* is also a novel that reflects on the writing of history and on the attempt at historical reconstruction that it itself presents.

In *Middlemarch* the presence of Scott's novels is an appropriate period detail of English provincial life in the early 1830s: Mr Brooke has read them and refers to them; Mr Trumbull the auctioneer claims to have bought a copy of *Ivanhoe*, pronouncing it 'a very nice thing, a very superior publication' (*MM* 32); and Mary Garth, whose copy of what would have been the latest Scott novel, *Anne of Geierstein* (1829), has prompted Trumbull's observation, is a great admirer of the Waverley novels and knows them in detail. It is a measure of the good sense and happy domesticity of the Garths that, in a scene which illustrates their exemplary family life, Mary's brother Jim is reading aloud from *Ivanhoe* to the rest of the family under the great apple tree in the orchard (*MM* 57). That chapter has as its epigraph the sonnet about *Waverley* cited above.

There is also an echo of Scott in the figure of Will Ladislaw, whose life traces a course from the drifting of a dilettante to decisive commitment that resembles the typical Waverley hero's 'famous wavering path from privacy to purpose, from destiny inside the gates to history outside the gates' (Wilt, 476). And this pattern is more marked, and more central, in *Daniel Deronda*, where Deronda himself may owe as much to Scott as to *Goethe in his privileged apprenticeship to life and eventual discovery of a vocation. Like Scott's Ivanhoe he is a disinherited one who is finally restored to his inheritance, while in his emotional life he precisely reverses the pattern of Ivanhoe (Semmel 1994: 122–3). Where Scott's hero chooses the Saxon Rowena in preference to the Jewish Rebecca, Deronda abandons the English Gwendolen for the Jewish Mirah. In her last novel George Eliot finally fulfils Maggie Tulliver's desire to avenge Rebecca and all Scott's dark, unhappy heroines.

In a review of 1856 she had compared Harriet Beecher *Stowe's *Dred* (1856) to Scott in its depiction of a people for whom Hebraic Christianity was still a reality and who applied the Old Testament to their daily life (*Essays*, 327), and she praised Scott's portrayal of Balfour of Burley and the Covenanters in *Old Mortality*. In writing *Daniel Deronda* she drew on her knowledge of this novel in her creation of the visionary Mordecai, for whom the Old Testament is similarly still alive, maintaining that she was aiming for 'an outline as strong as that of Balfour of Burley for a much more complex character and a higher strain of ideas' (*L* vi. 223). But if in this case Scott provides the model for a kind of fanatic, his more general importance for her, particularly visible in this last novel and in *The Spanish Gypsy*, lies in the tolerant breadth and generosity of his imagination, which sympathetically encompasses marginalized and oppressed minorities like the Jews in *Ivanhoe* and the gypsies, with Meg Merrilies, in *Guy Mannering* (1815). It is in this sense that Scott was a central figure in her creative life, offering the example of a wise, generous, and undogmatic form of fiction that entered sympathetically into different forms and conditions of life. JMR

Baker, William, ' "Her Longest-Venerated and Best-Loved Romancist": George Eliot and Sir Walter Scott', in J. H. Alexander and David Hewitt (edd.), *Scott in Carnival* (1993).

Semmel (1994).

Shaw, Harry E., 'Scott and George Eliot: The Lure of the Symbolic', in J. H. Alexander and David Hewitt (edd.), *Scott and his Influence* (1983).

Welsh (1985).

Wilt, Judith, 'Steamboat Surfacing: Scott and the English Novelists', *Nineteenth-Century Fiction*, 35 (1981).

sculpture. See VISUAL ARTS.

'Sea-side Studies' (subsequently *Sea-Side Studies*). These studies by G. H. *Lewes were published in *Blackwood's Edinburgh Magazine*, August–October 1856 and June–October 1857, and as a book, *Sea-Side Studies*, in February 1858. They were the first result of his scientific investigations of marine biology—basically molluscs, sea anemones, and the like—undertaken at *Ilfracombe, *Tenby, the Scilly Isles, and Jersey in 1856–7 in the company of George Eliot. The second series appeared at the same time as 'Janet's Repentance'. Lewes's researches were facilitated by the use of the microscope. The essays are lively and stimulating, and expressive of enthusiasm and the shared love and support of Eliot. GRH

secrecy is a common motif in George Eliot's fiction, and it represents a problem whose moral and psychological implications are explored in all her novels from *Adam Bede* onwards. When, in *The Mill on the Floss*, Philip Wakem asks Maggie to continue to meet him in the Red Deeps, she is disturbed by the fact that 'such interviews implied secrecy, implied doing something that she would dread to be discovered . . . and that the admission of anything so near doubleness would act as a spiritual blight' (*MF* 5.1). Her fine sensibility defines the problem: secrecy sunders the private life from the public, creates doubleness and division within the self, and casts a spiritual blight from which it may be impossible to recover. Arthur Donnithorne's secret relationship with Hetty Sorrel in *Adam Bede* ruins both their lives, and in *Silas Marner* Godfrey Cass's secret marriage and unacknowledged fatherhood are paid for in remorse, childlessness, and the loss of Eppie to Silas. In the earlier fiction secrets tend to be, like these, concerned with sexual relationships—Mrs Transome's past affair with Jermyn in *Felix Holt, the Radical* and Tito's bogus marriage to Tessa in *Romola* are other examples—but in *Middlemarch* and *Daniel Deronda* secrecy has a wider reach: Bulstrode's disreputable past of receiving stolen goods and cheating Ladislaw's mother out of her inheritance, and Gwendolen's knowledge of Lydia Glasher's claim on Grandcourt and her own feelings of guilt at his death. Whatever its object, secrecy is a moral disorder which dissociates thought from action (Ermarth 1985: 109) and introduces division and discontinuity into individual lives. Bulstrode, for instance, in his past 'found himself carrying on two distinct lives; his religious activity could not be incompatible with his business as soon as he had argued himself into not feeling it incompatible' (*MM* 61). Such doubleness involves him keeping secrets even from himself in a deliberate act of repression; and in Eliot's world the repressed past always returns, in Bulstrode's case threatening him with disgrace and exposing him to blackmail.

Alexander Welsh has located the origins of this concern with buried pasts and discontinuous lives at the point where George Eliot's true identity became known and the discontinuity between her own past and present apparent (1985: 149). *Silas Marner* is the first novel to deal with such discontinuity and it sets out the problem and its resolution with almost schematic clarity, as Silas first loses and then recovers 'a consciousness of unity between his past and present' (*SM* 16). That recovery crucially involves confessing his past to his neighbour. From Hetty in the condemned cell with Dinah Morris, to Gwendolen Harleth in her relations to Deronda, confession is seen as the antidote to the blight of secrecy. Admitting the secrets of the past to another person is a healing act of self-recognition, and in *Daniel Deronda*, where such confession is not an isolated incident but a lengthy process, George Eliot seems to anticipate the insights of psychoanalysis and its talking cure as Gwendolen unburdens herself of her worst secrets. See also CRIME; FREUD; MORAL VALUES.

JMR

Ermarth (1985).
Welsh (1985).

serialization was a primary method of publishing novels in the 19th century, either in magazines or in separate part-issue instalments. While George Eliot is not usually considered to be one of the jobbing serial novelists of the Victorian period, half of her novels were published in some serial form. She began her career as a writer of fiction by publishing the stories in *Scenes of Clerical Life*—'The Sad Fortunes of the Reverend Amos Barton', 'Mr Gilfil's Love-Story', and 'Janet's Repentance'—as a series in **Blackwood's Edinburgh Magazine* between January and November 1857. Initially, this story series was planned to be longer, but George Eliot was discouraged by some of the publisher John *Blackwood's comments, and moved on to write her first novel, *Adam Bede*. *Romola* appeared, illustrated by a young Frederic *Leighton, in the immensely popular monthly **Cornhill Magazine* in 1862–3; *Middlemarch* was published in the innovative form of six bi-monthly part-issue instalments and two monthly

instalments in 1871–2; and *Daniel Deronda* in eight monthly instalments in 1876. *Adam Bede* was planned as a serial but was published in three volumes, the publisher feeling that the subject matter was not suited to magazine serialization. Although serial fiction had been around since the 18th century, it was Charles *Dickens who largely revived the practice with his phenomenally successful *Pickwick Papers* in the late 1830s. Increasingly, serial fiction became a staple of periodical literature, especially with the shilling monthly magazine boom in the 1860s, led by magazines such as *Cornhill*. Publishers used serials to sell magazines, advertise writers on their publishing lists, and increase their profits. It is sometimes suggested that George Eliot's fiction did not lend itself to the fragmentation and pace of the serial method, with the requisite demands of creating narrative suspense at the end of each instalment, and the pressure of writing to strict deadlines. Reviewers and readers were less than enthralled at first by *Romola*, for example, the Italian Renaissance subject of which was a departure from her other fiction about the Midlands. Writing to a business associate, John Blackwood (whom George Eliot left to publish in *Cornhill*) said of *Romola* that 'no doubt it will be a fine thing but it was doubtful in my mind how far it would bear being given in fragments in the Magazine and certainly it would not suit the readers of the Cornhill' (*L* iv. 38). But the gradual unfolding of her plots and her focus on character development over time are in many ways suited to the extended time frame of reading a novel in serial form. Furthermore, by the time she wrote *Daniel Deronda*, she had become skilful in handling the serial composition, and, arguably, that last novel is her finest achievement in the serial form. Serialization continued to be a dominant form of publication—and virtually all Victorian novelists were serial novelists—until the collapse of the three-volume novel in the 1890s. See also COMPOSITION; PUBLISHERS, NEGOTIATIONS WITH.

MWT

Hughes, Linda K., and Lund, Michael, *The Victorian Serial* (1991).
Martin, Carol A., *George Eliot's Serial Fiction* (1994).

servants, domestic. On 1 January 1874 George Eliot made her customary retrospect of the 'happy old year', mentioning among its blessings that 'in our own home we have had that finish to domestic comfort which only faithful, kind servants can give' (*Journals*, 144). She was very conscious of the importance of domestic servants, and mindful that 'it is difficult for us masters and mistresses to allow enough for the difference between our drawing-room point of view and that of the kitchen' (*L* v. 197). She prided herself on her skills

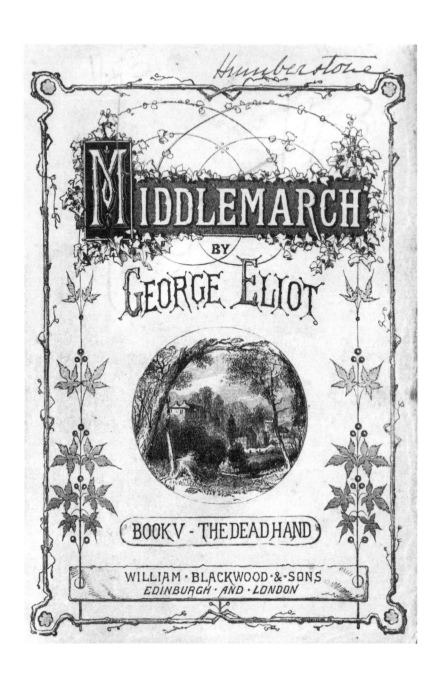

Wrapper for the fifth instalment of *Middlemarch*, published in August 1872.

of household management, and having been accustomed to dealing with servants from her early years, continued to provide close supervision of them throughout her life (documented, for instance, in a detailed list of the housemaid's accountabilities at The *Priory, which extends to scheduling the frequency of polishing the front door handle: Haight 1968: 440 n.). Her *letters and *journals refer to the difficulties of securing suitable servants, both for herself and others, from early 1859 when she and G. H. *Lewes were setting up at Wandsworth (see HOMES), through various domestic crises, including the bombshell in 1871 when the long-serving sisters Grace and Amelia Lee gave notice. Their successors were Mrs Mary Dowling, the cook, who told neighbours of George Eliot's 'breaking down entirely—her screams heard throughout the house' after Lewes's death (Haight 1968: 516)—and Elizabeth and Charlotte, one of whom was probably the 'watch-dog of a servant who knew uncommonly well how to dispose of' such unwanted visitors as 'Interviewers and strangers of every description' (Clifford, 112). Edith *Simcox reported that during her first meeting with George Eliot after Lewes's death, 'She spoke of the servants, of the comfort of human kindness without companionship when any nearer sympathy would be intolerable' (*L* ix. 262). The comment nicely indicates her abiding belief that servants should know their place—a belief manifested with customary complexity in such characterizations as Mrs Transome's Denner in *Felix Holt, the Radical* and Dorothea's Tantripp in *Middlemarch*. See also 'SERVANTS' LOGIC'. MAH

Clifford, Lucy, 'A Remembrance of George Eliot', *Nineteenth Century*, 74 (1913).

'Servants' Logic' is the second of four essays George Eliot contributed under the pen-name 'Saccharissa' to George *Smith's new evening newspaper, the *Pall Mall Gazette*, for which Lewes was editorial adviser. The conceit of the essay, published on 17 March 1865 (repr. in *Essays*), is that servants, like all lower order animals, are impervious to rational argument: reason and education may gradually prevail, but in the meantime 'A mild yet firm authority which rigorously demands that certain things be done, without urging motives or entering into explanations' (*Essays*, 395) is recommended. Gordon S. *Haight's description, 'An entertaining account of the psychology of cooks' (*L* iv. 184 n.), now seems inept against William *Myers's discussion of its disturbing condescension in helpful comparison with depictions of the working class in her fiction (1984: 116). See also JOURNALIST, GEORGE ELIOT AS; SERVANTS, DOMESTIC. MAH

Myers (1984).

settings, original basis of. What is popularly known as the George Eliot Country is largely based in and around *Nuneaton in North *Warwickshire. The town itself was the model for Milby in *Scenes of Clerical Life* but it has now changed considerably; bombing in the Second World War and later redevelopment have removed some of the buildings and streets George Eliot knew as a girl. 'Orchard Street', Lawyer Dempster's House, 'Shepperton Vicarage', and 'The College of the Poor' have all disappeared.

*Chilvers Coton, half a mile from the centre of Nuneaton, is the basis of Shepperton in *Scenes*, the church Shepperton Church with its 'intelligent eye, the clock' in the 'substantial tower'. The tower is all that remains of the original church which was bombed in 1941 and was later rebuilt. In the churchyard is the tomb of Emma Gwyther who is considered to be the original of Milly Barton in 'The Sad Fortunes of the Reverend Amos Barton'. Opposite the church is Chilvers Coton Heritage Centre, once the Free School briefly mentioned in 'Amos Barton'. Nuneaton parish church, dedicated to St Nicolas, is Milby Church in 'Janet's Repentance'. Not far away, in Market Place, is the George Eliot Hotel, once The Bull, and the original of the Red Lion in 'Janet's Repentance'. Paddiford Common in the same story is set in Stockingford, another district on the edge of the town. The second story in *Scenes*, 'Mr Gilfil's Love-Story', is set at Arbury Hall, fictionalized as Cheverel Manor. Its splendid Gothic decoration in various rooms in the Hall are clearly described. Near the Arbury estate is the village of Astley whose church is clearly identified as Knebley Church in 'Mr Gilfil'. Next to the church is Astley Castle (Knebley Abbey) now a ruin. Between the town and Griff House is Griff Hollows, a still fairly rural area known even to local people as Red Deeps, as in *The Mill on the Floss*. While Griff House is not Dorlcote Mill, its attics, once the playground of Mary Ann Evans and her brother, undoubtedly inspired those where Maggie and Tom play. Opposite Griff House is Gipsy Lane where Mary Ann would have seen gypsies encamped as they were to do in *Mill*. A quarry still exists in the same area as described in the 'Brother and Sister' Sonnets (see POETRY), but the Brown Canal no longer runs through Griff Hollows.

Silas Marner is set in North Warwickshire but with no identifiable buildings or places. A Rainbow Inn, however, still exists in Allesley, near Coventry, which George Eliot would have seen on her frequent visits to her sister at Meriden.

Events in *Middlemarch* are similar to those in Coventry while George Eliot lived there—the coming of the railway and the urgent need for a fever hospital—but there are no identifiable buildings. It is more the spirit of the city than its topography, although there was a Green Dragon (now transplanted) and still is a Hearsall (Helsall) Common. In *Adam Bede* George Eliot set Hetty Sorrel's trial in the city's medieval Guildhall of St Mary.

Adam Bede is set in the Derbyshire/Staffordshire borders of her father's youth. Loamshire is Staffordshire, Stonyshire is Derbyshire, Stoniton is Derby, Hayslope is Ellastone, Norbourne is Norbury, Eagledale is Dovedale, Stonefield is Wirksworth, Oakbourne is Ashbourne, and Rosseter is Rocester. Bartle Massey in the novel was a real teacher and his cottage still exists at Roston Common.

St Ogg's in *The Mill on the Floss* is largely based on *Gainsborough since George Eliot needed a tidal river for the climax of the novel, which the Trent provides with its Eagre of Bore. Gainsborough's Old Hall is the setting for the bazaar at which Maggie and Lucy help.

In the Introduction to *Felix Holt, the Radical* the coach journey from Treby Magna through Little Treby to Transome Court can be compared to a journey from Coventry through Stoneleigh to Stoneleigh Abbey some three miles from the city.

Romola is set in 15th-century Florence with its buildings clearly identified and not fictionalized.

Various settings appear in *Daniel Deronda* but one identifiable building is Lacock Abbey in Wiltshire which was the model for Sir Hugo Mallinger's Topping Abbey. See also CHARACTERS, ORIGINALS OF.   KA

Shakespeare, William (1564–1616), English actor, dramatist, and poet, whose works George Eliot began studying as a 13-year-old pupil at the Misses Franklin's school in Coventry in 1832 and continued reading until her death in 1880, and which significantly influenced her own fiction. Her detailed readings of his drama and poetry resulted in numerous Shakespearean *epigraphs (or mottoes, as she preferred to call them), allusions, references, and extracts in the novels, *letters, *notebooks, and *journals. In *The George Eliot Letters*, Gordon S. *Haight identified well over a hundred allusions to, or brief quotations from, 28 of Shakespeare's 37 plays. Sometimes, these are playfully intended, as is, for instance, the allusion to *Hamlet* (I ii. 129) in a letter to G. H. *Lewes's oldest son, Charles, dated 19 September 1880, where Eliot refers to his complaint of putting on too much weight: 'Johnnie [Cross] sympathises with your disgust at the too too solid flesh that will not melt, but at present we are rejoicing that he is laying on a little flesh' (*L* vii. 325–6). At other times, however, the allusions show glimpses of Eliot's very close and thoughtful readings. Refer-

ring to the same line from Hamlet's soliloquy in a letter to Charles Ritter, dated 11 August 1878, when commenting on his French translation of her poem 'O may I join the choir invisible' (in particular the line 'Poor anxious penitence, is quick dissolved'), she wrote, 'The word "dissolved" has no such fixed, narrow associations in English as in French. Hamlet uses even the word "melt" without exciting ridicule or offence in this connection' (*L* vii. 56).

Eliot's contemporaries quickly saw strong parallels between her novels and Shakespeare's plays. Within months of the publication of *Adam Bede*, Theodore Martin (1816–1909) spoke for many when he told John *Blackwood, Eliot's publisher, the story and characters are 'so large, so Shakespearean in their breadth of sympathy' (*L* iii. 42). By the time *Middlemarch* was published, Eliot was routinely seen as a latter-day Shakespeare. Herbert *Spencer (1820–1903) reportedly called her 'the female Shakespeare' (*L* v. 463), and in 1883, three years after her death, the critic P. Bayne published 'Shakespeare and George Eliot' in which he more or less considered the two to have equal stature (*Blackwood's Edinburgh Magazine*, 133 (1883), 165–85).

As a teenager, while still influenced by one of her evangelical teachers, Maria *Lewis, Eliot showed only a grudging respect for Shakespeare's work. In a letter dated 16 March 1839, she spoke about the 'malign influences' of fiction generally and warned that although Shakespeare has a 'higher claim ... on our attention ... we have need of as nice a power of distillation as a bee to suck nothing but honey from his pages' (*L* i. 21–4). Her admiration steadily grew, however, once she abandoned her religious faith and especially when she met Lewes, who was a playwright and a literary and drama critic, frequently commenting on Shakespeare and things Shakespearean. Such was his reputation that the Hungarian tragedian Neville Moritz sought him out while visiting England in 1878 to see whether or not he 'approved of his conception and execution' of Othello before his public performance of the part (*L* ix. 218–19). Eliot's reputation as a Shakespeare scholar was also recognized: in the same year, Alexander Macmillan, of *Macmillan's Magazine*, tried, but failed, to persuade her to write a life of Shakespeare for John *Morley's 'English Men of Letters' series (Haight 1968: 507).

In 1875 Lewes published *On Actors and the Art of Acting*, based on articles and reviews selected from the many already published in the *Westminster Review* and other journals. One of Eliot's many notebooks, the Pforzheimer Holograph 3 (see *Some George Eliot Notebooks*, ed. William Baker, 4 vols. (1976–85)), points to the strong probability that she helped Lewes with the research for his book. In the chapter 'Shakspeare [sic] as Actor and Critic', Lewes suggests that for all his sensitivity and genius, Shakespeare was probably a bad actor. Eliot's notebook contains a telling entry based on her reading of Henry Chettle's edition of Robert Greene's *Groat's Worth of Wit* (1592) and, probably, Alexander Dyce's edition of Shakespeare's works (1857, 1864–7). The entry notes Shakespeare's excellent qualities, adding that the rest of the evidence rather implied that his acting was indifferent. Eliot's entries are often difficult to date, but it is reasonable to suppose that these were made when she was helping Lewes.

Both Eliot and Lewes enjoyed reading aloud to each other and her journals show that Shakespeare was one of their favourite authors. For instance, during their first trip to *Germany from July 1854 to March 1855, they read, and she occasionally commented on, *Measure for Measure, Romeo and Juliet, Julius Caesar* ('very much struck with the masculine style of this play, and its vigorous moderation, compared with "Romeo and Juliet"' (*Journals*, 36)), *Antony and Cleopatra, Henry IV, Othello, As You Like It, King Lear* ('sublimely powerful'), *The Taming of the Shrew, Coriolanus, Twelfth Night, The Merchant of Venice, A Midsummer Night's Dream, The Winter's Tale, Richard III,* and *Hamlet*. Such readings evidently lead to critical discussions: Lewes considered a good play to be a perfect fusion of poetry and drama; Shakespeare, he said, had this ability; most 19th-century playwrights in England, Germany, and France did not (see 'The Drama: Authors and Managers', 1842; 'The Rise and Fall of the European Drama', 1845; 'Shakspeare [sic] in France', 1865). In *'How I came to write Fiction' Eliot explains that the desire to write a novel had long been with her, but 'I always thought I was deficient in dramatic power, both of construction and dialogue. . . . My "introductory chapter" was pure description though there were good materials in it for dramatic presentation'. Lewes encouraged her to continue writing what became 'The Sad Fortunes of the Reverend Amos Barton', despite the fact that he 'distrusted—indeed disbelieved in, my possession of any dramatic power' (*L* ii. 406–10). That she had Shakespeare principally in mind when thinking about dramatic power may be seen in a letter she wrote to Sara Hennell shortly after the publication of *Scenes of Clerical Life*:

In opposition to most people, who love to *read* Shakspeare [sic], I like to see his plays acted better than any others: his great tragedies thrill me, let them be acted how they may. I think it is something like what I used to experience in old days listening to uncultured preachers—the emotions lay hold of

one too strongly for one to care about the medium. (*L* iii. 228–9)

There are a number of Shakespearean allusions in *Scenes of Clerical Life*, indicating that she turned to him from the beginning of her creative writing career not only as model for learning how to fuse drama with poetry but also as a means for creating moral and thematic resonances. The allusions in *Scenes of Clerical Life* are to Shakespearean characters and are primarily designed, through association, to encourage readers to view Eliot's ordinary people and their situations with added sympathy and understanding. Thus, in 'The Sad Fortunes of the Reverend Amos Barton' the hero is mentioned in the same breath as Macbeth and Hotspur, not because Barton resembles them in heroic stature but because, in his own small way, he too is a complex individual charged with ideas, beliefs, and feelings that are often chaotic and irrational, yet deeply held. *Adam Bede* also depicts 'low life' and 'ordinary heroes' with the help of some Shakespearean allusions; but additional allusions to the 'working-day' and 'golden' worlds of Hayslope encourage the view that one of the novel's unifying principles, its moral vision, is loosely based on *As You Like It*, insofar as Eliot's characters, like Shakespeare's, are variously taught to recognize the need for moral discrimination and right moral conduct.

As Eliot's art matured, her Shakespearean associations became more various, potent, subtle, and suggestive. As *realism, the style of writing she strongly advocated in 'The *Natural History of German Life' (*Westminster Review*, July 1856) gave way to more complex, experimental styles, she selected not just Shakespearean characters and settings but also themes, motifs, and ideas to help her explore and develop plot structures as well as complex social, political, and moral issues. The plot and treatment of lost and rekindled love in *Silas Marner*, for instance, mirror *The Winter's Tale*. Critics have suggested that *Wordsworth's poetry, Charles *Dickens's *A Tale of Two Cities* (1859), the fairy tale 'Prince Darling', or perhaps the Polish story *Jermola the Potter* by Jósef Ignacy Kraszewski (1812–87) may have inspired Eliot to write *Silas Marner*. Wordsworth is most often seen as the likeliest influence because *Silas Marner*'s epigraph is taken from 'Michael' (1800) and because Eliot also told Blackwood, 'I should not have believed that any one would have been interested in it but myself (since William Wordsworth is dead)' (*L* iii. 382–3). Nevertheless, Eliot's readings of *The Winter's Tale* when in Germany and elsewhere, and her close analyses of other Shakespearean characters, plots and themes at the time of writing *Silas Marner* add weight to David Carroll's observation in 'Reversing the Oracles of Religion' that there are 'significant similarities of detail' between novel and play.

Carroll points out that Eppie's biblical name, Hepzibah, refers to Isaiah 62: 4, adding, 'This quotation from Isaiah ("Thou shalt no more be termed forsaken") brings to mind a similarly abandoned and significantly named child, Perdita.' He notes a number of common details: both works have themes of regeneration; Eppie and Perdita are abandoned in winter following the breakdown of their parents' marriages; they are 'miraculously rescued by rustic characters and brought up in a frugal, pastoral world'; and their moments of rescue are a 'foretaste of regeneration to follow', coinciding with deaths of Antigonus and Molly Farren. Silas confuses Eppie's golden hair for his stolen gold, and Perdita's discovery by the Shepherd prompts the Clown to say, 'You're a made old man; if sins of your youth are forgiven you, you're well to live.—Gold, all gold!' (*The Winter's Tale*, III. iii. 112–21). Carroll concludes:

In the course of each work, after the discovery of the child, there occurs a gap of sixteen years, we are re-introduced to the heroines in the pastoral setting—Perdita and Flora of the spring feast, and Eppie intent on planning the garden for Silas's cottage (ch. 16)—as they are each seeking ways of marrying their lovers, Florizel and Aaron. Finally, of course, reconciliation and regeneration are achieved by the influence of this second generation upon the first, and achieved in each case by means of natural 'miracles'. (1977: 215–16 n.)

Having combined psychological realism with romance elements, both novel and play show how a series of uncontrollable events are put into operation once people upset what amounts to the moral order of things. However, novel and play also suggest that the dangers posed by nature's indifference to human suffering can be either avoided or made bearable through the agency of human love. Leontes's jealousy results in the unexpected deaths of Mamillius and Antigonus as well as the strange 'death' of Hermione. Therein lie causes for lasting grief. Yet Antigonus's kindness, the Bohemian rustics' generosity, and Florizel's love, variously help Perdita to survive, flourish, and be restored to her rightful position in life. Similarly, the deep, abiding love between Eppie and Silas overcomes the far-reaching damage done by William Dane's treachery, Dunstan Cass's theft, and Godfrey Cass's betrayal of his daughter. Each work demonstrates that love, in its largest sense, is 'an art | Which does mend nature—change it rather' (*The Winter's Tale* IV. iv. 95–6). Eliot strongly believed in the truth of this idea, as can be seen in the fact that she used the same allusion in a letter to John

Morley about what could be done to alleviate the unfair lot of women (*L* iv. 364–5).

In the later notebooks, Eliot recorded numerous lines and passages from a variety of Shakespeare's plays and sonnets, subsequently using 31 as chapter epigraphs for *Felix Holt, the Radical*, *Middlemarch*, and *Daniel Deronda*, making Shakespeare her most frequently quoted source (Wordsworth came next, providing her with nine). Eliot's epigraphs serve a variety of purposes and are integrally related to the chapters in which they appear, even though some were not included in drafts until after the manuscripts were completed. David Leon Higdon has shown that by alluding to other texts, characters, or allegorical figures (Love, Mischief, Rumour), the epigraphs establish themes, identify the genesis of a character, root abstractions in particularities, create *irony through discrepancies, or metaphorically sketch in ideas or characters subsequently fleshed out in chapters (1970: 127–51).

The Shakespearean epigraphs work with other allusions to instruct, entertain, and build dramatic structures within the novels. For instance, in *Middlemarch*, described by Barbara Hardy as Eliot's most Shakespearean novel (*Middlemarch: Critical Approaches to the Novel* (1967), 10), structure and humour are very Shakespearean. The epigraph to chapter 60, ' "Good phrases are surely, and ever were, very commendable"—*Justice Shallow*' (cf. *2 Henry IV*, III. ii. 73) recalls Shallow's respect for vogue words, like Bardolph's 'accommodated'. Mr Borthrop Trumbull, Middlemarch's auctioneer, also has a deep reverence for the English language. As Shallow does in Shakespeare's play, Eliot's 'amateur of superior phrases' (*MM* 32) not only brings comic relief but, with other minor characters, adds to the novel's subplots that lie behind what the narrator calls the world's 'huge whispering gallery' (*MM* 41), the otherwise undistinguished Middlemarchers tirelessly commenting on the main action. The supposed culpabilities of Lydgate and Bulstrode are freely discussed in the Green Dragon and the Tankard, and the epigraph introducing chapter 71 reads

CLOWN. ... 'Twas in the Bunch of Grapes, where, indeed, you have a delight to sit, have you not?
FROTH. I have so; because it is an open room, and good for winter.
CLOWN. Why, very well then: I hope here be truths.

(*Measure for Measure*, II. i. 127–32)

The Clown's lines are, in fact, Pompey's, spoken when he stands before Escalus accused as a bawd and pimp. During his defence, he calls on the aptly named Froth as an alibi. Though amusing, the scene parallels Claudio's serious plight: he is arrested on similar charges and then condemned to death by Angelo. The 'truth' that Pompey refers to can be summarized this way: if Escalus punishes him for sinful behaviour, he will have to punish most of Vienna; and if that happens, in ten years there will be no one left to punish (cf. II. i. 227–40). In this case, common sense prevails and he is let off. In *Middlemarch*, the 'truths' arrived at by Bambridge, Hawley, Mrs Dollop, and others are based on pure speculation concerning Raffles's death. Eliot's minor characters are just as silly as the *habitués* of Shakespeare's Bunch of Grapes, and she presents them with a similar sense of humour. But as in *Measure for Measure*, they also serve a serious purpose, recalling the sanitation committee meeting where Bulstrode is forced to resign. In the play, Escalus shows mercy; in the novel even educated people follow the lead of the town's Froths. Lydgate does escort Bulstrode away from the meeting but does so grudgingly; and even the Revd Farebrother maintains an embarrassed silence, suspecting Lydgate of ulterior motives when coming to Bulstrode's aid. Only Dorothea listens to the evidence and stands by Lydgate.

The complex and subtle way in which Eliot used Shakespeare is seen when, say, a particular play resurfaces at different stages in a novel. *Measure for Measure*, with its strong interest in the need for mercy and forgiveness, crops up throughout *Middlemarch*, including the Finale when Dorothea's fate is recalled: 'Her finely-touched spirit had still its fine issues, though they were not widely visible'. Duke Vincentio tells Angelo 'if our virtues | Did not go forth of us, 'twere all alike | As if we had them not. Spirits are not finely touch'd | But to fine issues . . .' (*Measure for Measure*, I. i. 33–6). To forgive Casaubon, marry Ladislaw, and have his children are Dorothea's fine issues, as Shakespeare's Isabella's are to forgive Angelo, abandon the idea of becoming a nun, and marry the Duke. Dorothea, we are told, thus finds peace of mind and happiness. Critics, however, argue over the question of whether or not Eliot condemns her to yet another subordinate role.

Other types of Shakespearean entries in various notebooks include comments on the strengths and weaknesses of Shakespeare's verse, particularly the sonnets, the transmissions of his texts through the ages, and his portrayals of women. Many of these found their way into the later novels. The sonnets provided Eliot with epigraphs for *Felix Holt, the Radical* (*FH* 27) and *Middlemarch* (*MM* 24, 58, 82). She read all of Shakespeare's poetry at different times of her life but made a detailed study of the sonnets in July 1869, recording lines and observations in what are now known as the Berg and

Folger notebooks. The Folger entries come under the headings of 'Fine Pauses' and 'Evidence of Shakespeare's Genius', although she also noted ' "We acknowledge great power, but we experience great weariness", says [Walter Savage] Landor [1775–1864] of Shakespeare's sonnets' (*Middlemarch' Notebooks*, ed. Pratt and Neufeldt, 78). The entries in the Berg notebook are more extensive. They comprise an analysis of 24 sonnets, focusing on Shakespeare's 'Confidence in his poetic immortality', his pauses, trivial conceits, use of language, frequently feeble couplets, and 'exquisite utterances of love'. It is from this group of sonnets, nos. 22–108, that the epigraphs for *Middlemarch* are chosen. She completed her 1869 study of the sonnets with the following observation, adding the last two sentences at a later date:

Here are only 24, & some of these one lingers over rather for the music of a few verses in them than for their values as wholes. I am convinced that the greater number of the sonnets are artificial products, governed by the fashion of sentiment which had probably grown out of the imitation of the Italian poets. These 'sugared sonnets among private friends' have owed much of their mysteriousness to the imaginations of writers who set out with the notion that Shakespeare was in all things exceptional, & so never think of comparison with contemporaries even when the occasion is thrust upon them. 1872. Nevertheless, I love the Sonnets better & better whenever I return to them. They are tunes that for some undefinable reason suit my frame. (*Middlemarch' Notebooks*, ed. Pratt and Neufeldt, 209–13, 265–6)

See also THEATRE.   AvdB

George Eliot's 'Middlemarch' Notebooks: A Transcription, ed. John Clark Pratt and Victor A. Neufeldt (1979).

Carroll, David, 'Reversing the Oracles of Religion', in R. P. Draper (ed.), *George Eliot: The Mill on the Floss and Silas Marner* (1977).

Higdon, David Leon, 'George Eliot and the Art of the Epigraph', *Nineteenth-Century Fiction*, 25 (1970).

Novy, Marianne, *Engaging with Shakespeare: Responses of George Eliot and Other Women Novelists* (1994).

Sircy, Otice C., ' "The Fashion of Sentiment": Allusive Technique and the Sonnets of *Middlemarch*', *Studies in Philology*, 84 (1987).

van den Broek, A. G., 'Shakespeare at the Heart of George Eliot's England', *George Eliot–George Henry Lewes Studies*, 24–5 (1993).

Shelley, Percy Bysshe (1792–1822), Romantic poet. In *Middlemarch* Ladislaw is twice compared, by Mr Brooke, to Shelley: 'he has the same sort of enthusiasm for liberty, freedom, emancipation' (*MM* 37). It is generally thought that Ladislaw is partly modelled on G. H. *Lewes, George Eliot's partner, who was an ardent Shelleyan when he was a young man and who had tried to write a biography of the poet. However, Ladislaw is not the only character in *Middlemarch* who has associations with Shelley. Dorothea Brooke is perhaps a more deeply Shelleyan figure. Shelley is distinctive among the Romantics for combining utopian social idealism derived from the Enlightenment with Romantic ardour and enthusiasm. The words 'ardour' and 'ardent' are continually associated with Dorothea. For her as for Shelley feeling is a form of knowledge. Ladislaw asserts that a poet's soul is one 'in which knowledge passes instantaneously into feeling, and feeling flashes back as a new organ of knowledge', to which Dorothea responds: 'I understand what you mean about knowledge passing into feeling, for that seems to be just what I experience' (*MM* 22). Naumann's description of her—'sensuous force controlled by spiritual passion' (*MM* 19)—also calls to mind Shelley. But though she is an idealist who wishes to make the world correspond with her ideal, at first she distrusts her feelings and believes she must acquire a form of knowledge that is independent of feeling, thus her disastrous marriage to Casaubon: 'She was humiliated to find herself a mere victim of feeling, as if she could know nothing except through that medium' (*MM* 20). Her development in the novel is towards the realization that feeling can be trusted as a form of knowledge.

In *Daniel Deronda*, a novel dominated by Romantic concerns, Shelley is also a significant influence. Like Dorothea, Deronda—who is linked with 'the poet who writes a Queen Mab at nineteen' (*DD* 16)—combines social idealism with intensity of feeling: 'I have always longed for some ideal task, in which I might feel myself the heart and brain of a multitude' (*DD* 63). But Deronda's feelings, before he meets Mirah and Mordecai, tend to become cut off from his sense of self because of scepticism and extreme self-consciousness. This is shown by his experience after rowing on the Thames: 'He was forgetting everything else in a half-speculative, half-involuntary identification of himself with the objects he was looking at, thinking how far it might be possible habitually to shift his centre till his own personality would be no less outside him than the landscape' (*DD* 17). George Eliot had shown in her story 'The Lifted Veil' that she was aware of the darker side of Shelley's thought, as the title is derived from his poem 'On Death': 'Who lifteth the veil of what is to come?' It is likely that she drew on the scepticism and narcissistic subjectivism characteristic of *Alastor* and other poems written around the same time in her characterization of Deronda. See also ROMANTICISM. KMN

Sibree, John (1823–1909), Coventry friend and correspondent of George Eliot. When she moved to Foleshill in 1841, among her first acquaintances were the Revd John Sibree (Independent minister) and his family. Personal and intellectual interests drew her to his 18-year-old son John who in 1842–3 studied Theology in Germany and later at Spring Hill College, Birmingham. Their friendship ripened as he gave her lessons in Greek. In 1847 after reading her translation of D. F. *Strauss, he initiated a correspondence that encouraged her to express lively, radical, even vehement views on *race, revolution, royalty, and the arts. When she challenged him to explain his religious faith, his inability to do so influenced him to abandon the ministry, a decision that pleased her but not his parents. Later she kept in touch, in 1856 seeking him (unsuccessfully) as tutor for G. H. *Lewes's boys at his home in Stroud, and in 1858 sending him assurance that his translation of G. W. F. *Hegel was 'acceptable'. Teasingly, she described him as 'the reticent John Sibree—terribly chary of praise that could commit himself' (*L* iii. 15), but she valued his intellect and character. In the 1880s he published some minor poetry and *Human Anatomy Simplified*. See also REVOLUTIONS OF 1848. RMH

Sibree, Mary (1824–95), Coventry friend, pupil, and correspondent of George Eliot, who first met the 16-year-old daughter of Revd John Sibree when she moved to Foleshill in 1841. Later Mary told John Walter *Cross that her five years of friendship with George Eliot had formed 'the most important epoch in my life' (Cross, i. 158). She also supplied him with valuable memories of George Eliot's life in Foleshill, including the only firsthand account we have of her friend's loss of faith: 'I vividly remember how deeply Miss Evans was moved' (Cross, new edn. 1886, i. 397). Mrs Sibree feared for her daughter's faith, but since Mary Ann avoided controversy the weekly tutorials in German, begun in 1844, were allowed to continue. Nevertheless in 1849 Mary asked for her friend's letters to be directed to Rosehill because she feared her father's objections. Disappointed, George Eliot acknowledged Mary's 'sweet good' nature but regretted the 'egotism' of 'Sibreeanism' (*L* i. 315). Later she expressed pleasure in a renewal of correspondence, and in Mary's move (as Mrs John Cash) to Rosehill, her publication of *The Credentials of Conscience* (1868), and her visit in 1873 when Mary found George Eliot's memory of Coventry friends undimmed. RMH

Sidgwick, Henry (1838–1900), lecturer in classics, later philosopher of Trinity College, *Cambridge. He is named by George Eliot in 1873 as 'a chief favourite of mine', adding that his

Cambridge friends 'always expect him to act according to a higher standard than they think of attributing to any other chief man' (*L* v. 445). They probably met through G. H. *Lewes in the late 1860s. Sidgwick exchanged his classical lectureship for one in moral philosophy in 1869, and joined the scholarly circle around Eliot and Lewes in the 1870s. Involved in women's education, he provided rent to house female students at Cambridge, was on the council of the women's college at Girton, but fell out with Emily *Davies over his opposition to women sitting the Little-Go and Pass examinations. Eliot and Lewes stayed with him on a visit to Trinity College in 1877. When Eliot established the George Henry Lewes Studentship in Physiology at Cambridge in memory of Lewes, she consulted Michael Foster, Henry Sidgwick, and T. H. *Huxley. Sidgwick became one of five Trustees appointed to administer the Studentship.   JJ

Caine, Barbara, *Victorian Feminists* (1992).
McWilliams-Tullberg, Rita, *Women at Cambridge: A Men's University—Though of a Mixed Type* (1975).

Silas Marner: The Weaver of Raveloe (*see page 382*)

'Silly Novels by Lady Novelists' was written by 12 September 1856 and published in the *Westminster Review* in October (repr. in *Essays*). Eliot had 'this odious article to write in a hurry', having asked Chapman 'to get a substitute' since she had greatly suffered over the pain and removal of a wisdom tooth (*L* ii. 261). The mood shows. This indictment of fatuous and false writing, sentimentality, artificiality, romance, is written with a cutting edge. It is an exposure of the 'girls' of the period who pour into print escapist indulgences which bear no relation to life. The essay is wittily organized into species of novel, the first being the mind-and-millinery one with its beautiful, learned, pious, paragon know-all heiress heroine (or fetching, perfect non-heiress), the cynosure of male attention, 'the ideal woman in feelings, faculties, and flounces' (*Essays*, 302) who survives all adversities and of course moves in the best society. Stereotypes enact the improbable and the impossible, a heroine is 'a polking polyglott' (305), affectations of learning are pretentious, sententious, dull. There are romantic plots, tinsel dialogue, nib-tipped melodrama. It is a blessing if there is 'frank ignorance, and no pedantry' instead of 'rhetorical solutions of the mysteries of the universe' or clever nothings like 'Vice can too often borrow the language of virtue' (309). The oracular species expounds religious, moral, and philosophical theories (or rather doesn't), resenting those 'who have thought it quite a sufficient task to exhibit men and things as they are' (310), an early underlining of the writer's concern for *realism.

Telling examples are given of edifying periphrasis (312), the quotations are a delight throughout, with the rider that literary feminine silliness only confirms 'the popular prejudice against the more solid education of women' (316). The really cultured woman, by contrast to these verbal exhibitionists, 'does not give you information, which is the raw material of culture,—she gives you sympathy, which is its subtlest essence' (317). The white neckcloth species (evangelical) is vulgar, ignorant, and provokes Eliot to define what is to become her creed: 'The real drama of Evangelicalism . . . lies among the middle and lower classes . . . Why can we not have pictures of religious life among the industrial classes in England, as interesting as Mrs Stowe's pictures of religious life among the negroes?' (318–19). Interestingly, Eliot's review of Harriet Beecher *Stowe's underrated but profound *Dred* was published in the same number of the *Westminster*: eleven days after completing this essay she began the first of her *Scenes of Clerical Life*. Finally she castigates the modern-antique species, 'a leaden kind of fatuity' (320), deploring its grandiloquence, attacking critics for fickleness in praising these false productions, asserting sadly that literary women often lack 'an appreciation of the sacredness of the writer's art' (323). Vanity is all too often the motivation, but women writers can equal men in fiction, provided that the right elements are present—'genuine observation, humour, and passion' (324). George Eliot was to provide them, and this essay signals the emergent novelist already secure in her knowledge, responsibility, and practical and theoretical stance. See also JOURNALIST, GEORGE ELIOT AS; WOMAN QUESTION.   GRH

Simcox, Edith (1844–1901), philosopher, trade-unionist, social activist, and would-be lover of George Eliot in the last years of Eliot's life.

In one sense Edith Simcox appears always as the loser in her relations with George Eliot. Simcox wished to be George Eliot's biographer, but John Walter *Cross as husband claimed the task. Simcox would dearly have liked also to be George Eliot's lover, but Cross achieved that too. With the helpless insight of the rival, Edith Simcox foresaw the marriage. Cross and Simcox, both twenty years younger than George Eliot, seem like contending siblings in the meta-family that G. H. *Lewes constructed around her in the 1870s, a family that changed its nature very soon after his death. Nevertheless, both Simcox and George Eliot drew much from their difficult friendship. Simcox wrote what remains some of the finest criticism of George Eliot's work in her essay on *Middlemarch* (*Academy*, January 1873) and her memorial essay

(*cont. on page 389*)

G EORGE ELIOT's third, shortest, and—as a form of moral fable with a resemblance to fairy tale—most accessible novel. It was published on 2 April 1861.

Composition

On 28 August 1860 Eliot told her publisher John *Blackwood of her plan to write a historical novel about Girolamo *Savonarola set in *Florence—a plan that was to be realized with the writing of *Romola*—but she also indicated that she first wanted to write another English story (*L* iii. 339). In September she wrote one short story, 'Brother Jacob', though that ironic allegorical tale is too short and spare to be seen as a representation of specifically English life. At the end of September she and G. H. *Lewes moved from Wandsworth to a furnished rented house at 10 Harewood Square near Regent's Park (see HOMES), and on 28 November she noted in her journal that she was engaged in writing a story 'the idea of which came to me after our arrival in this house, and which has thrust itself between me and the other book I was meditating. It is "Silas Marner, the Weaver of Raveloe" ' (*Journals*, 87). Writing was initially slow and interrupted by another move, to 16 Blandford Square, in the middle of December. On 12 January 1861 she mentioned the new work to Blackwood for the first time and underlined again how the story suddenly imposed itself upon her: 'I am writing a story which came *across* my other plans by a sudden inspiration . . . It is a story of old-fashioned village life, which has unfolded itself from the merest millet-seed of thought' (*L* iii. 371). In the new house the story began to proceed more rapidly, and on 15 February 1861 the first thirteen chapters were sent to Blackwood. He responded with his usual encouragement and praise, despite finding these first hundred pages 'very sad, almost oppressive' (*L* iii. 379). In her reply she did not wonder at his reaction: 'indeed, I should not have believed that any one would have been interested in it but myself (since William Wordsworth is dead)', had not Lewes been strongly impressed. But she was able to hope that Blackwood would not find the complete story sad at all, since it would show 'in a strong light the remedial influence of pure, natural human relations' (*L* iii. 382–3). The mention of *Wordsworth suggests an important source of inspiration, which is honoured in the lines from his poem *Michael* that serve as the epigraph to the novel: 'A child, more than all other gifts | That earth can offer to declining man, | Brings hope with it, and forward-looking thoughts.' Indeed she felt that the story would have been more suitable for metrical treatment than prose, except for the fact that verse would not have allowed 'an equal play of humour'. In this same letter she also describes how the subject came to her 'first of all, quite suddenly, as a sort of legendary tale, suggested by my recollection of having once, in early childhood, seen a linen-weaver with a bag on his back; but, as my mind dwelt on the subject, I became inclined to a more realistic treatment' (*L* iii. 383). The remainder of the novel was written quickly. The next five chapters were sent to Blackwood on 4 March, and the final three together with the conclusion on 10 March 1861. The manuscript is in the British Library (Add. MS 34026).

Publication

The novel was short enough to be contained in one volume, and Blackwood's proposal that it should sell at 12*s.* was accepted. The printers worked at great speed. By 18 March the proofs had been read and a week later George Eliot received a bound copy of the novel. The first edition was published on 2 April 1861 in one volume octavo, bound in orange-brown cloth, price 12s. The first American edition was published by Harper & Brothers in New York in 1861. In November Eliot made corrections to the first edition for a second, which appeared in 1863. The third Stereotyped Edition was published in 1868, and in 1878 *Silas Marner* appeared in the *Cabinet Edition in the same volume as 'The Lifted Veil' and 'Brother Jacob'.

Words ending in *-ize* in the manuscript were changed to *-ise* to conform to Blackwood's house style, and the lighter punctuation of the manuscript was made heavier and more formal. There were a number of printer's errors in the first edition which were corrected for the second. For the Cabinet Edition Eliot lightened some of the punctuation. For a selected list of textual variants see the World's Classics Edition, ed. Terence Cave (1996).

Illustrations
The third Stereotyped Edition carried a title-page vignette of Raveloe village and two full-page illustrations, of Eppie as a child on Silas's hearth, and of her choosing to stay with him when the Casses offer to take her into their home as their daughter (see ILLUSTRATIONS).

Reception
After the problematic ending of *The Mill on the Floss*, *Silas Marner* was greeted with relief by many critics, and their common response was to see it as a return to the mode of *Adam Bede*. The *Saturday Review* in April 1861 claimed that it was as good as *Adam Bede*, only shorter, and maintained that George Eliot was without rival in her depiction of the poor and the lower middle class (*CH* 170–1). The most searching of the first appreciations was R. H. *Hutton's unsigned review in *The Economist* in the same month. The new novel did not have the tragic power of *Adam Bede* but it was a more perfect whole, and one of its most striking features was the way it gave a strong intellectual stamp to a story of unintellectual life: even the conversation of the rustics in the Rainbow Inn touched humorously on topics that occupied more cultivated minds, such as the relationship between objective and subjective, or substance and form. The intellectual character of the work could be seen in the contrast between the narrowing effect of the innocent love of gold and the way in which Silas's life and contact with others were widened and deepened by his love for the child who replaced the gold. Intellectual subtlety was also evident in George Eliot's use of poetic justice: avoiding the condign punishment that novelists usually mete out, she allowed Godfrey Cass a run of good fortune and then showed how his comfortable life was embittered by his earlier weakness and cowardice (*CH* 175–8).

E. S. *Dallas in an unsigned review in *The Times* praised the truthfulness of the presentation of everyday life, which raised a mean existence into dignity by endowing it with conscience and kindliness. However, he considered the 'half-witted' Silas as inappropriate for a central character and identified a structural imbalance in the novel, which devoted two-thirds of its length to Silas's hopeless estrangement from his fellow men and then presented only the result of his reformation through his love for Eppie rather than its process. He concluded that the novel was not what its author originally intended but was 'huddled up at the end' (*CH* 179–85). The *Westminster Review* in July 1861, on the other hand, dwelt on the complete correlation of the characters and their circumstances, which made Raveloe an organic whole and the novel itself a unity whose symmetrical structure contained no excess or impurity (*CH* 186–7). The most hostile review—'a duller book it has seldom been our lot to read through'—came in April 1862 from the *Dublin University Magazine*, which had also been highly critical of *The Mill on the Floss*. The abuse was sustained, singling out the boorish characters and the 'twaddle' of the Rainbow scene, the 'half-dazed, weak-bodied, passive-minded hero', and the author's philosophy, which 'seldom deep or original before, seems here to roam delighted over a dead level of the tritest commonplace'. Altogether the novel amounted to a libel on English country life (*CH* 189–94). By contrast, Henry *James, writing in the *Atlantic Monthly* in October 1866, praised it for possessing the rounded simplicity and absence of loose ends that mark a classical work.

These early reviewers saw the novel as practising the same kind of *realism as *Adam Bede*, faithfully representing the ordinary lives of humble people, and they praised or condemned it according to their beliefs. Only Hutton penetrated deeper, and even he did not see anything unorthodox in its view of life and religion. Two years later in October 1863, in an unsigned article in the *Home and Foreign Review* on 'George Eliot's Novels', Richard Simpson acutely observed an underlying ideology that was not conventionally Christian, reading the novel as 'an apology for the special doctrines of Feuerbach's humanitarianism worked up with the utmost dialectic and psychological ability' (*CH* 229). Much modern criticism has followed his lead.

Plot

At the beginning of the 19th century Silas Marner has been working as a self-employed weaver in the village of Raveloe in the fertile Midlands for fifteen years. Previously he had worked in a Northern industrial town and had been a member of the Dissenting community of Lantern Yard. Falsely accused of theft from a dying man by his friend William Dane, who took advantage of one of Silas's cataleptic trances to commit the theft himself and plant incriminating evidence on Silas, the weaver had left the community in bitterness and despair when it pronounced him guilty after a drawing of lots, and had travelled South to find refuge in Raveloe. There he leads a solitary life, hoarding the money he earns and gaining the reputation of being a miser. When Dunstan Cass, the wastrel younger son of the Squire, secretly steals this hoard of money and disappears, the horrified Silas seeks help from the other villagers by going to the Rainbow public house; he receives sympathy from the good-hearted Dolly Winthrop, and begins to take more part in the life of the community. On New Year's Eve Molly, the unacknowledged and laudanum-addicted wife of the Squire's eldest son Godfrey, tries to reach Raveloe to confront him with their child and expose his secret marriage, but she succumbs to her addiction and dies in the snow, while the 2-year-old child wanders in through Silas's open door while he is in another trance. Godfrey keeps his secret and Silas keeps the child, names her Eppie (short for Hephzibah) after his mother and little sister, and brings her up as his daughter. Godfrey marries the beautiful Nancy Lammeter but their marriage remains childless, while Silas with his adopted daughter becomes an accepted member of the village community. Sixteen years later the Stone-pit near Silas's cottage is drained and the skeleton of Dunstan Cass discovered with the stolen money. The shock of the discovery prompts Godfrey to confess to Nancy his earlier marriage and the true identity of Eppie. The Casses go to Silas and offer to take Eppie into their home as their daughter, but she prefers to stay with Silas, even when she learns that Godfrey is her real father. With Eppie, Silas visits the Northern town of his early life in the hope of establishing his innocence of the crime he was once accused of, but Lantern Yard has disappeared, replaced by a factory, and there is no one left who knew him. The story concludes with Eppie marrying Dolly Winthrop's son Aaron.

Critical Approaches

Combining elements of the legendary tale and the realistic treatment that George Eliot mentioned to Blackwood in her letter of 24 February, *Silas Marner* has often been read as a straightforward moral fable with fairy-tale motifs and coincidences, which, together with its relative brevity, make it a suitable text for the schoolroom. Despite its surface simplicity and reassuringly positive ending, however, it displays Eliot's characteristic seriousness of purpose, her readiness to explore complex issues—of *history, psychology, morality, religious belief—in subtle and searching ways. It may be a short work but it is a profound one.

The last of her early fictions of life in the English Midlands before she broke new ground with *Romola*, it presents an initial description of Raveloe, as 'a village where many of the old echoes lingered, undrowned by new voices' (*SM* 1), which might appear nostalgic. Certainly in the early stages of writing she admitted in her journal to mental depression, which she attributed to the loss of the country entailed by the move into central *London (*Journals*, 86–7). But the social and historical contrast that the opening chapter draws between the traditional community of Raveloe and the narrow religious sect in the Northern industrial town which Silas has left behind him, is not all in the former's favour. 'The movement, the mental activity, and the close fellowship' which marked his life as an artisan in a Dissenting religious community, indicate a more dynamic existence than that of the village, with its bad farming, its suspicions and superstitions, and its accepted hierarchy of class. His flight to the village seems to be in one sense a step backwards in time, but Eliot makes it plain that, although Raveloe may be 'aloof from the currents of industrial energy and Puritan earnestness' (*SM* 3), it is not outside the current of history, for even its present prosperity is shown to have a specific historical cause. The war with France has kept agricultural prices high and allowed the wealthier villagers to 'farm badly quite at their ease, drawing enough money from their bad farming, in those war-times, to live in a rollicking fashion, and keep a jolly Christmas, Whitsun, and Easter tide' (*SM* 1). The apparently time-honoured, warmly communal festivals of 'Merry England' are the product of historical conditions which, with the hindsight available to narrator and reader, can be seen to be all too temporary: 'the fall of prices had not yet come to carry the race of small squires and yeomen down that road to ruin for which extravagant habits and bad husbandry were plentifully anointing their wheels' (*SM* 3).

Raveloe and Lantern Yard are linked not only by history but also by the primitive nature of their beliefs: the superstitions and 'lingering echoes of the old demon-worship' (*SM* 1) to be found in the village are matched by the faith the religious sect places in the drawing of lots to decide whether Silas is guilty of theft. The novel examines different forms of belief with a kind of anthropological curiosity, seeing their roots to lie in the emotional need of human beings for some means of understanding their world. When Silas's fondness for his brown pot and his brick hearth are described in terms of fetishism (*SM* 16), it is evident that Eliot is interpreting his behaviour in the light of Auguste *Comte's theory of the evolution of religious consciousness (see POSITIVISM), in which a fetishistic attachment to objects marks the earliest stage. But the narrator's plea, 'let all new faith be tolerant of that fetishism', is sympathetic rather than dismissive, for Eliot understands the psychological demands that such attachment satisfies. Similarly Silas's miserly obsession with his gold coins is shown to be a means of filling the void left by his loss of faith in God and man. The emphasis placed on the 'bright faces' of the coins, which become so familiar to him that he would not exchange them for others 'with unknown faces' (*SM* 2), defines them as substitutes for the human beings they replace, and will eventually be replaced by in their turn. Miserly hoarding is here a compensatory activity, innocent and understandable, not the succumbing to the demonic power of *money that it is in the work of novelists like Charles *Dickens and Honoré de *Balzac.

The course of Silas's development is clearly traced with the aid of the symbolic motif of gold (see SYMBOLISM). Losing his trust in God and man, he withdraws into his solitary weaving and hoarding; after the loss of the gold and its replacement by the golden-haired child who restores his capacity for love, he regains trust in his fellow men and is left with a dim sense of beneficent higher powers: 'but the child was sent to me: there's dealings with us—there's dealings' (*SM* 16). This renewed faith, brought about by the coming of a child in the Christmas season, is close enough to a conventional religious one to have left most contemporary readers undisturbed (see ATHEISM); but the faith the novel is affirming is secular rather than religious. Silas's belief that 'there's good i' this world' is a belief in a goodness whose origin, as the story has indicated, is human not divine. The philosophical doctrine which lies behind this view of human sympathy as the fundamental moral power in the world is that of Ludwig *Feuerbach, whose *Essence of Christianity* George Eliot had translated in 1854 and whom she echoed in a later letter when she wrote that 'the idea of God . . . is the Ideal of a goodness entirely human (i.e. an exaltation of the human)' (*L* vi. 98). David Carroll has shown how closely she is working from Feuerbach in this novel and has persuasively argued that she follows Feuerbach in asking the reader to assess the various religious beliefs in the novel by measuring their human content (1967: 154). Judged in this way the evangelical community of Lantern Yard emerges as badly as the evangelical preacher George Eliot castigated in her 1855 essay *'Evangelical Teaching: Dr Cumming' (see EVANGELICALISM). Behind the piety and the prayers lies the unpleasant human reality of William Dane's jealousy and unscrupulous self-interest, to which Silas falls victim.

The wrong-headed faith in chance exhibited by the Lantern Yard community in deciding Silas's fate by the drawing of lots is one of the threads that links his story to that of the Casses. Godfrey, too, worships at the altar of 'Favourable Chance . . . the god of all men who follow their own devices instead of obeying a law they believe in'. When faced by difficulty, he flees to 'his usual refuge, that of hoping for some unforeseen turn of fortune, some favourable chance which would save him from unpleasant consequences' (*SM* 9). The moral failure implied in such a flight is illuminated by a letter George Eliot wrote to her friend Barbara *Bodichon when she was writing the novel. Discussing the comfort that may be afforded to some by the forms and ceremonies of the Catholic Church, she declared her own belief that 'the "highest calling and election" is to *do without opium* and live through all our pain with conscious, clear-eyed endurance' (*L* iii. 366). Opium, literally present in the novel in Molly's laudanum, is metaphorically implied in Godfrey's eagerness to close his eyes to his past and evade its consequences; and it is the inexorable law of consequences that asserts itself in the end to punish him.

Silas, although bearing the lesser responsibility of a victim, suffers a similar temptation in seeking the 'Lethean influence of exile, in which the past becomes dreamy because its symbols have all vanished, and the present too is dreamy because it is linked with no memories' (*SM* 1). His life is made discontinuous by the rupture of accusation and exile and, as he loses sight of the past—always a symptom of moral decline in Eliot's world—his mechanical alienated labour at the loom and miserly hoarding become another form of opium. His myopia is moral as well as physical, and his eventual restoration to wholeness is marked by a return to clear-eyed consciousness: after the sixteen years of his life with Eppie 'his large brown eyes seem to have gathered a longer vision . . . and they have a less vague, a more answering look' (*SM* 16). What he regains, too, is the 'sense of unity between his past and present life' (*SM* 2) which had briefly flickered in him when the sight of the sick cobbler's wife reminded him of his dying mother and moved him to apply his knowledge of herbal remedies. The continuity of Godfrey's life is also restored when he acknowledges his past and his paternity and is made to endure, clear-eyed and chastened, the childlessness that is his appropriate penance. Nevertheless, even though the stories of Silas and Godfrey can be read as demonstrations of 'the orderly sequence by which the seed brings forth a crop after its kind' (*SM* 9), the novel stops short of an unambiguous affirmation of the organic wholeness and orderliness of life, as modern critical studies have stressed. Sally Shuttleworth has shown how the narrator's allegiance to theories of orderly sequence and morally responsible action is undermined by the decisive role played in the novel by chance and the loss of rational control involved in Silas's cataleptic trances (1984: 83). Susan Cohen has pointed out the antithetical nature of the terms the narrator uses in describing Silas's life as 'a history and a metamorphosis' (*SM* 1)—the one implying continuity and the other radical physical change—and has argued that the novel 'simultaneously constructs and deconstructs its own continuity' (425). The most signal instance of such deconstruction is the failure of Silas's attempt to set right the wrongs of the past by returning to Lantern Yard. Seeking a clear-eyed confrontation with the past, he finds that all its traces have been obliterated. The injustice he has suffered cannot be redressed and the world he knew has no knowledge of him, with a factory now standing on the site of Lantern Yard. The advance of the industrial world shows social history following its own laws, which have little to do with the orderly organic sequence of seed and crop. Discontinuity here is permanent and it challenges the vision of an organically unified world that much of the novel seems to aspire to. Rather like *The Mill on the Floss, Silas Marner* juxtaposes contrasting views of the historical process.

The story of Silas's redemption through fatherhood has also been sceptically examined by feminist criticism. Sandra Gilbert has argued that the connection established between Silas's gold and golden-haired Eppie defines the daughter as a treasure, a gift the father is given so that he can then give to others, thus weaving himself back into the structure of society (Gilbert, 361). His rehabilitation is achieved through possession of a daughter who functions in anthropological terms as a currency, the exchange of which constitutes society. Thus this benign tale of redeeming love ultimately affirms the patriarchal structure of society and the Law of the Father. The lesson the daughter has to learn is to bury her mother—whose story the novel more or less suppresses—and give herself to her father, and the emotional disturbance that this causes is faintly registered in the sad gentle gravity that occasionally comes across Eppie's playfulness and in her preoccupation with her mother's wedding ring.

It is, however, a measure of the subtlety of this apparently simple novel that it can sustain almost the opposite reading, as a text which challenges both patriarchy and conventional notions of *gender. Silas's weaving is work traditionally associated with women and his role in raising Eppie is as much maternal as paternal, blurring the distinction between the sexes and suggesting that the nurturing role of the mother is not biologically determined nor confined to women alone (see FAMILY LIFE, PORTRAYAL OF). And when Eppie rejects her 'lawful father', as Godfrey Cass's wife Nancy dubs him (*SM* 19), her rejection carries wider implications (see CLASS). Refusing to be tempted by social status and material prosperity, she declares her loyalty to the class she has been brought up in: 'I wasn't brought up to be a lady, and I can't turn my mind to it. I like the working-folks, and their victuals and their ways' (*SM* 19). This dignified rejection of a man who is not just her biological father but who, as squire, stands at the head of the rural community, implies a criticism of the inherited patriarchal structure of English society as a whole (Uglow 1987: 157).

There is a radical dimension to *Silas Marner*, apparent both in its unsparing treatment of the squirearchy and in its questioning of social conventions. Even though the novel concludes with the conventional happy marriage of romantic comedy in the wedding of Eppie and Aaron, this has to be seen against the unidealized marriages of Godfrey Cass, and Priscilla Lammeter's comically caustic insistence on the value of the single life to which her looks are likely to confine her: 'As I say, Mr Have-your-own way is the best husband, and the only one I'd ever promise to obey' (*SM* 11). Here, as in its central focus on the marginalized Marner and his unorthodox family, this novel explores and honours the unconventional, extending sympathetic understanding to lives that are more ordinary, unprepossessing, and often inarticulate than the conventional subjects of fiction.

These simple lives are, as Hutton noted in his contemporary review, presented with great intellectual sophistication. Like her central character, the writer, too, is a kind of weaver, creating a tissue of intertextual allusions and motifs, as she may have hinted in naming the village Raveloe. The epigraph points to Silas as a Wordsworthian rustic and solitary, while his surname carries an echo of another Romantic archetype, *Coleridge's Ancient Mariner. The series of afflictions that he suffers recall those of Job, whose days are 'swifter than a weaver's shuttle, and are spent without hope' (Job 7: 6); and like Lot he is led out of 'the city of destruction' (*SM* 14), if not by an angel then by an angelic child. Eppie herself, her pastoral upbringing, and her regenerative role are reminiscent of Perdita in *Shakespeare's *A Winter's Tale*, and the discovery of both children is linked miraculously with gold in the minds of rustic characters (Carroll 1967: 200). And of course the redemptive appearance of a child in midwinter has obvious echoes of the Christmas story. Nevertheless, although these literary, legendary, and mythical motifs are woven into the text, they are not seamlessly assimilated but exist in tension with each other and with the whole, for this novel is only obliquely related to the works on which it draws. Silas's story has a different issue from Wordsworth's Michael's, and nature here has no Wordsworthian educative, restorative power but is closer to the uncanny world of Coleridge's poem. Silas's afflictions are the work of men not God, and he is similarly saved by human rather than divine intervention. And despite its happy resolution the novel remains more unsettling than a Shakespearean romance. George Eliot's intertextuality is ironic and interrogative, and in a work which shows how myths and superstitions are the questionable ways in which people make sense of their lives, none of the inherited patterns of myth or literature quite fits or provides a master key to interpretation. A residue of the mysterious and enigmatic remains.

David Carroll has shown how this is partly due to the structure of the novel, which presents two stories of widely different lives that nevertheless turn out to be linked in strange and unpredictable ways, creating an area of mystery between them. That mystery is also apparent in the unfathomable workings of consciousness manifested in Silas's cataleptic trances (which takes up in a different way a subject first dealt with in 'The Lifted Veil'), and in the grim process of alienation to which he succumbs while working at his loom: 'Strangely Marner's face and figure shrank and bent themselves into a constant mechanical relation to the objects of his life, so that he produced the same sort of impression as a handle or crooked tube, which has no meaning standing apart' (*SM* 2). Quietly Eliot points to the grotesque reification produced by mechanical labour and conveys a vivid insight into the strange psychological and physiological effects of work that illuminates more than the personal peculiarity of a solitary eccentric. The mystery of this metamorphosis at the loom is distantly related to the process of industrial development that creates the final area of mystery in the novel, by obliterating Lantern Yard and leaving Silas for ever in the dark about whether the truth of the robbery, and of his own innocence, ever emerged. Dolly Winthrop fatalistically concludes that 'It is the will o' Them above as a many things should be dark to us' (*SM* 21); but the novel makes clear that this darkness has no transcendental origin but is immanent in human existence. That Silas finds a light to live by is reassuring, but his redemption through love and trust in his fellow beings does not dispel all the darkness in the text, and this residue of mystery challenges the reader into interpretation.

The last of George Eliot's early novels of ordinary working life in the English Midlands, *Silas Marner* is less a nostalgic farewell than a new departure which anticipates the novels to come. The drama of problematic paternity is taken up again in *Romola* and *Felix Holt, the Radical*, while the latter novel engages more fully with the industrial development glimpsed at the end of *Marner*. The double plot, involving lives that are only related by chance, looks forward to the complex structures of *Middlemarch* and *Daniel Deronda*, where in a more encompassing exploration of *society George Eliot traces the 'stealthy convergence of human lots' and the 'slow preparation of effects from one life on another' (*MM* 11). Out of the millet-seed of thought from which *Silas Marner* unfolded there were to grow eventually the great novels of her last decade.   JMR

Carroll, David, 'Reversing the Oracles of Religion', *Literary Monographs*, 1 (1967).

Cohen, Susan R., 'A History and a Metamorphosis: Continuity and Discontinuity in *Silas Marner*', *Texas Studies in Literature and Language*, 25 (1983).

Gilbert, Sandra M., 'Life's Empty Pack: Notes toward a Literary Daughteronomy', *Critical Inquiry*, 3 (1985).

Nunokawa, Jeff, 'The Miser's Two Bodies: *Silas Marner* and the Sexual Possibility of the Commodity', *Victorian Studies*, 36 (1993).

Shuttleworth (1984).

Swann, Brian, '*Silas Marner* and the New Mythus', *Criticism*, 18 (1976).

Uglow (1987).

'George Eliot, a Valedictory Article' (*Nineteenth Century*, May 1881). She also wrote a secret diary that she later entitled 'Autobiography of a Shirt Maker' in which she recorded the twists and turns of her relations with George Eliot and with ardent self-awareness tries to find a language that will make tolerable to herself the strength of her feelings. That awareness allows her also to ask questions about wider social assumptions of the day. The diary, after remaining for many years in manuscript only, has been newly published, edited by Constance M. Fulmer and Margaret E. Barfield under the title *A Monument to the Memory of George Eliot*.

The tendency, looking back, is to interpret Edith Simcox solely through her place in the life of George Eliot. Gordon S. *Haight's edition of the letters emphasized Simcox's devotion through his chosen extracts from the 'Autobiography' to the degree that she seemed to have no life of her own and to exist as a rather unwieldy lapdog in the Leweses' drawing room. The many letters between the two women (Haight thought around 200) do not survive. It is to misconstrue the friendship, quite apart from demeaning Simcox, if the strength of Simcox's own achievements is lost sight of. George Eliot respected and honoured Edith Simcox and she did so because Simcox was a formidable presence in so many intellectual and active fields. Indeed, of all her later women friends Edith Simcox is the only one who could offer equal intellectual engagement.

Edith Simcox was known in the 1870s as a writer capable of reviewing philosophy, literature, and history in three European languages. She wrote for the most highbrow neo-Hegelian journal the *Academy* from its first issue on (at first under the name H. Lawrenny). She contributed also to other liberal journals like the *Fortnightly Review* and the *Nineteenth Century*. In 1877 she published *Natural Law: An Essay in Ethics* of which *Mind* wrote: 'This thoughtful and able work is in many respects the most important contribution yet made to the Ethics of the Evolution-theory' (*Mind*, 8, 1877). She translated from German philosophers for the language-theorist Friedrich Max *Müller and, over a period of nearly twenty years, she worked at her major study of property rights in ancient cultures as they bore on women's roles and identity. That study was published, somewhat belatedly in the anthropological debates of the time, as *Primitive Civilizations or the Outlines of the History of Ownership in Archaic Communities*, 2 vols (1894).

The reason why her *Primitive Civilizations* took so long was mainly because of Edith Simcox's activism. She was an important figure in the early Socialist and Trade Union Movement. She was one of the first two women to be admitted as a delegate at a Trade Union Congress, representing the Shirt and Collar Makers in 1875. She composed the constitution for the Second Socialist International. She sat on the London Education Board and founded the Lodgers' League. She travelled in Europe on Socialist delegations. And, with Mary Hamilton, she founded and organized for eight years a co-operative of women shirt-makers. Here her commitment was not simply to committees and to like-minded peers but also to the working women alongside whom she daily laboured to make the co-operative prosper. In her account of those years, 'Eight Years of Co-operative Shirt-making' (*Nineteenth Century*, June 1884) she offers a trenchant analysis of the problems between social classes and the blindness of the bourgeoisie.

Among the wry and affectionate anecdotes about her fellow workers she includes the account of her difficulties in finding a workshop for the company:

we found that we might have been accepted had we wanted a studio, or a school, or even a milliner's shop, but as shirtmakers we must betake ourselves

to humbler and more expensive quarters ... As working shirtmakers ... we were fortunate in securing half as house for 90L., under a landlord whose exceptional amenity explained itself afterwards when we learned he was an admirer of George Eliot's works. (*Nineteenth-Century*, 15: 1041)

So George Eliot has her place in the economics of activism (though the house is still expensive). The unillusioned figuring of the relations between Liberals and Radicals in this article raises a question about the friendship between Simcox and Eliot and its effects in George Eliot's late work. Certainly, *Daniel Deronda* takes seriously the intellectual aspirations and achievements of working men and it may well be that conversation with Edith gave George Eliot closer insight into the intellectual life of London craftsmen. But Simcox works with women, breaking open the stereotype of the 'intelligent working-man' to include the intelligent working woman. Perhaps the resistant friendship with Simcox entered *Daniel Deronda* more profoundly in another way.

Repeatedly in that work the question is raised: how far must a person go to fulfil the desires of others dependent on them? Daniel resists Gwendolen's desires; Daniel's mother reveals herself to him in order to restore his ethnic heritage as a Jew but refuses his hopes that she will be a mother to him and asserts her right to lead her own life apart from the cultural expectations of motherhood. George Eliot, likewise, had withdrawn from the mother–daughter relationship that Simcox sought as one way of channelling her precipitous desires: 'her feeling for me', Edith reports her as having made plain, 'was *not* at all a mother's' (Haight 1968: 533).   GB

A Monument to the Memory of George Eliot: Edith Simcox's Autobiography of a Shirtmaker, ed. Constance M. Fulmer and Margaret E. Barfield (1998).

Beer, Gillian, 'A Troubled Friendship', *George Eliot Review*, 29 (1998).

—— 'Edith Simcox: Philosophy, Passion, Politics', *Women: A Cultural Review*, 6 (1995).

McKenzie, K. A., *Edith Simcox and George Eliot* (1961).

Smith, Barbara Leigh. See BODICHON, BARBARA LEIGH SMITH.

Smith, Elder & Co., one of the most significant publishers of fiction in the Victorian period, and publisher of George Eliot's *Romola*. Founded as a stationery shop in 1816, the firm became notable as a publisher of fiction after George *Smith took charge upon his father's death. Smith was known as a generous publisher, as suggested by the £7,000 he paid for *Romola*, serialized in his *Cornhill Magazine*, which temporarily lured the author away from William *Blackwood and Sons. It was the highest amount Smith ever paid for a novel, and it was not financially remunerative; *Romola* never captured the public's imagination like Maggie Tulliver or Hetty Sorrel. Smith, Elder also published the *Pall Mall Gazette* (which published four articles by George Eliot) and the huge multi-volume project of the *Dictionary of National Biography*. Other important novelists on Smith, Elder's list include William Makepeace *Thackeray, Anthony *Trollope, Charlotte *Brontë, and Elizabeth *Gaskell. George Smith, known as the 'Prince of Publishers', was a sharp businessman, and in the decade between the 1850s and 1860s, he increased the firm's takings tenfold to establish Smith, Elder as the most important Victorian publishing house, particularly of fiction. See also PUB-LISHERS. MWT

Smith, George (1824–1901), publisher who lured George Eliot from William *Blackwood and Sons for the publication of *Romola*. He was born in Fenchurch Street over the premises of *Smith, Elder & Co., booksellers and publishers, which moved to 65 Cornhill shortly after his birth. His father died in 1846 and the weight of the firm now devolved upon George: he was bold, sagacious, surprisingly mature at 22, and soon appointed W. S. Williams as reader and literary adviser. The early failure of *Rose, Blanche and Violet* (1848) by G. H. *Lewes was soon abundantly compensated for by the success of *Jane Eyre* (1848). Unaffectedly chivalrous to *Charlotte and Anne *Brontë ('the most spirited and vigilant of publishers', said Charlotte) he courted William Makepeace *Thackeray and secured Mrs *Gaskell, though her libel on Mrs Robinson caused him to withdraw the first edition of *The Life of Charlotte Brontë* (1857) from publication. In 1859 he laid the foundations for the *Cornhill Magazine*, printing 120,000 copies for the launch on 1 January 1860 with Thackeray as editor and Anthony *Trollope's *Framley Parsonage* as the star serial. Thackeray resigned in March 1862. Smith founded the *Pall Mall Gazette* (1865) with which Trollope and G. H. Lewes were associated, his business ever diversifying (he imported Apollinaris water in 1873). His greatest venture was the plan, soon operational under Leslie Stephen, for the *Dictionary of National Biography* in 1882. He was greatly liked: Millais called him 'the kindest man and the best gentleman I have had to deal with'. His dealings with George Eliot concern *Romola*. His 'magnificent offer' for the copyright was £10,000, with the additional bonus that he would print 'Brother Jacob' to tide over the three months she needed before *Romola* could begin appearing in the *Cornhill*. Lewes was made consultant editor of the *Cornhill* (salary £600 per annum). John Black-wood was told on 19 May 1862 of her acceptance of Smith's offer. Ultimately she took £7,000 instead of the contracted £10,000 and gave Smith 'Brother Jacob' as a gift (*Cornhill*, July 1864). According to Smith, when Eliot finished the second volume of *Felix Holt, the Radical* Lewes sent it to him, but he rejected it (Haight 1968: 384). As a result she returned to Blackwood. Smith, ever kind and generous, produced (to her delight) the de luxe edition of *Romola* (1880). She and Smith were always on good terms. He gave her stalls for the opera, a copy of *Henry Esmond*, illustrations of *Romola*, and presents ranging from bonbons to a travelling bag. See also PUBLISHERS, NEGOTIATIONS WITH.

GRH

Glynn, Jennifer, *Prince of Publishers: A Biography of George Smith* (1986).

society is generally understood by George Eliot in organic terms, so that when she considers its present condition in 1868 in the *'Address to Working Men, by Felix Holt', she can liken it to 'that wonderful piece of life, the human body, with all its various parts depending on one another, and with a terrible liability to get wrong because of that delicate dependence' (*Essays*, 420). This view of society as a delicate organism is essentially conservative, but it is as hostile to ruthless individualism as it is to attempts at radical change by any group or class. The intricate network of society, in which both individuals and classes are enmeshed, is the product of a long process of evolution, and, as she puts it in her early essay on 'The *Natural History of German Life', 'what has grown up historically can only die out historically, by the gradual operation of necessary laws'. The sense of society as 'incarnate history' (*Essays*, 287), as a constantly evolving organism of interdependent parts which act on one another in subtle and unexpected ways, is succinctly captured in the description of old provincial society in *Middlemarch*:

Old provincial society had its share of this subtle movement: had not only its striking downfalls, its brilliant young professional dandies who ended up living up an entry with a drab and six children for their establishment, but also those less marked vicissitudes which are constantly shifting the boundaries of social intercourse, and begetting new consciousness of interdependence. Some slipped a little downward, some got higher footing: people denied aspirates, gained wealth, and fastidious gentlemen stood for boroughs; some were caught in political currents, some in ecclesiastical, and perhaps found themselves surprisingly grouped in consequence; while a few personages or families that stood with rocky firmness amid all this fluctuation, were slowly presenting new aspects in spite of solidity, and altering with the double change of self and beholder. (*MM* 11)

It is this kind of movement that *Middlemarch* brings dramatically to life in tracing the fortunes of the principal characters and showing how, for instance, the talented Lydgate comes to be shaped after the average whilst his brother-in-law Fred Vincy overcomes his initial fecklessness and attains social responsibility; the decline of the one playing a part in the rise of the other.

Middlemarch is Eliot's fullest representation of the organism of society and its complex interdependencies, but the same organic understanding informs the other novels, though with differences of emphasis. The early novels *Adam Bede* and *Silas Marner* present a more positive sense of community and a greater confidence in the capacity of ordinary working people like Adam and Silas to promote the common good. There are, of course, strains and tensions that stem from the hierarchical social structure of village life, and in both novels the squirearchy's assumptions of superiority are challenged at dramatic moments by the artisan heroes (see CLASS), but the values of the traditional community, or *Gemeinschaft* to use the term given currency by the German sociologist Tönnies (Graver 1984: 94–102), remain largely intact. Hayslope and Raveloe with their customary celebrations and rituals provide the settled conditions in which Adam can flourish and Silas can be restored to faith in humanity and the sustaining power of love, even though in the latter novel the process of social change is visible both in the industrialization that transforms the northern town from which Silas comes and in the decline of the patriarchal authority of the Casses, whose title of squire dies away.

In *The Mill on the Floss* that process of change is more central, and modern society, or *Gesellschaft*, can be seen encroaching on a traditional community as Mr Tulliver falls foul of new technology and unsuccessful litigation. While the community of the family is characterized by its oppressive narrowness, society is exposed to scornful irony as that 'good society' that 'has its claret and its velvet carpets, its dinner-engagements six weeks deep, its opera and its faëry ballrooms' (*MF* 4.3). The narrator's reflections here take on an unusually radical edge in defending the novel's focus on the history of unfashionable families and taking the side of the marginalized Maggie Tulliver, suffering from the deprivations of her lot:

But good society, floated on gossamer wings of light irony, is of very expensive production; requiring nothing less than a wide and arduous national life condensed in unfragrant deafening factories, cramping itself in mines, sweating at furnaces, grinding, hammering, weaving under more or less oppression of carbonic acid—or else, spread over sheepwalks, and scattered in lonely houses and huts on the clayey or chalky cornlands, where the rainy days look dreary. (*MF* 4.3)

Despite the polemical vigour of this passage, it is not so much making a political point about economic exploitation in the manner of Karl *Marx, as insisting on the interdependence of classes and soliciting sympathy for those whose lives are marked by 'the emphasis of want', who have to endure collectively the narrowness of opportunity that afflicts Maggie as an individual. It is the absence of sympathetic understanding and the sway of prejudice that mark society's reaction to Maggie's return from her fateful boat trip without Stephen Guest, when she becomes the object of censure by public opinion and the world's wife. Public opinion may be of the feminine gender, as the narrator sardonically remarks (*MF* 7.2), but the conventions and prejudices of society bear particularly heavily on women of independent spirit and ardent aspiration like Maggie and George Eliot's later heroines (see WOMAN QUESTION).

This more critical view of society is taken up in *Felix Holt, the Radical* which is marked by fears of anarchy and class conflict typical of the 1860s. In the years leading up to the time of the novel's action in the early 1830s, the respectable market town of Treby Magna is said to have taken on the more complex life brought by the mines and manufactures of industrialism, developing from a quietly traditional community tolerant of minority views into a society divided by competing religious denominations and political factions. These social changes provide the public context for the private lives of the principal characters, for, as the narrator famously insists,

there is no private life that has not been determined by a wider public life, from the time when the primeval milkmaid had to wander with the wanderings of her clan, because the cow she milked was one of a herd which had made the pastures bare. (*FH* 3)

Nevertheless, although the novel initially engages with the wider life of class and politics, after the election-day riot it retreats from the intractable conflicts of the public arena to the more manageable problems of personal relationships. As the riot makes clear, there is diminished confidence in the ordinary popular life that had seemed to provide society with its secure foundation and its future potential in *Adam Bede* and *Silas Marner* (Dentith 1986: 64–5). If there is any hope of progress, it lies with exceptional, even eccentric, individuals like Felix Holt, who is singularly remote from the workers whose interests he seeks to serve.

The same is true of all the novels from *Romola* onwards: the 'growing good of the world' is dependent on high-minded individuals like Romola herself, or Dorothea, or Daniel Deronda, whose noble aspirations have to contend with the resistance and inertia of society at large. The image of the web that is so obviously central to *Middlemarch* suggests not only the network of dependencies and interrelations that constitute social life, but also its power to trap and frustrate the energies of the individual, as the fate of Lydgate demonstrates. His exceptional talents and noble intentions are thwarted by the pressures of Middlemarch society and by his own 'spots of commonness', by the fact that he shares the values and prejudices 'found in ordinary men of the world' (*MM* 15). The common and the ordinary no longer command respect but have become obstacles to progress and enlightenment.

What is most radical about Felix Holt is his blunt dismissal of material ambition and acquisitive individualism, his refusal to join in 'the push and scramble for money and position' (*FH* 27); and in the later novels in general there is a closer and more critical focus on the mercenary and materialist aspects of social life. The criticism is sharpest in *Daniel Deronda*, the one novel that deals with near-contemporary society and its affluent upper class. The opening scene of 'dull, gas-poisoned absorption' around the gaming tables at Leubronn presents a range of European types and social classes all reduced to a 'uniform negativeness of expression' by the alienating power of money (*DD* 1). It is the lack of money caused by a bank failure that drives Gwendolen into her disastrous marriage with Grandcourt, and it is money and the capital value of his land that provide him with the power to exercise his tyrannical will. This is a recognizably modern and commercial society, where fortunes are won and lost through speculation and land is traded as a commodity or a capital asset.

Although the landowning aristocracy has a human face in the amiable figure of Sir Hugo Mallinger, the vision of the English ruling class is a damning one, and the power it wields is shown to extend to Britain's imperial possessions abroad (see COLONIALISM). Deronda himself has been raised with all the privileges of that class, his leisured apprenticeship to life 'sustained by three or five per cent on capital which somebody else has battled for' (*DD* 17), but he registers the alienated condition of English social life by looking to his Jewish roots for a sense of identity and belonging (see JUDAISM). The examination of society in this novel extends to questions of *race and *nationalism. Although Jewish life seems to offer the attractions of an organic community in contrast to

the alienating modernity of English society in which figures like Gwendolen lead explicitly rootless lives (*DD* 3), Eliot's sceptical vision qualifies this simple contrast by showing how the oppressively patriarchal aspect of Judaism has driven Deronda's mother to forsake it. In this last novel George Eliot breaks new ground in her scrutiny of society, which can no longer be fully understood in the organic terms she has previously used, and she even raises questions about the nature of the ethnic community to which her central character commits himself. The sceptical note is characteristic, for she is always inclined to question utopian attempts to reform society, like Girolamo *Savonarola's in Florence, which, as *Romola* shows, are ultimately inimical to individual freedom and happiness (Semmel 1994: 68–75). Society as 'incarnate history' resists revolutionary efforts to redesign it according to abstract theories, however noble their intentions. See also FAMILY LIFE, PORTRAYAL OF; HISTORY; MONEY AND DEBT; POLITICS; POVERTY AND WEALTH; PROGRESS.   JMR

Dentith (1986).

Ermarth, Elizabeth Deeds, 'Is There Such a Thing as Society', in *The English Novel in History 1840–1895* (1997).

Graver (1984).

McDonagh (1997).

Semmel (1994).

Sophocles (*c*.496–406 BC), Greek tragic dramatist, George Eliot's favourite classical author, 'the single dramatic poet who can be said to stand on a level with Shakespeare', as she wrote in her 1856 essay 'The *Antigone* and its Moral'. In 'The Sad Fortunes of the Reverend Amos Barton', the first of the *Scenes of Clerical Life*, she quotes two lines from Sophocles' *Philoctetes* in Greek, adding, 'The Countess did not quote Sophocles, but . . .' (*SC* 1.4). In 'Janet's Repentance', the last of the *Scenes*, she quotes from *Electra*, again in Greek, with the comment that Sophocles speaks to us 'across the ages, finding, as usual, the simplest words for the sublimest fact' (*SC* 3.13). The purpose of these somewhat clumsy allusions—she was later to refer ruefully to her 'bit of pedantry' (*L* iii. 356)—is to give a tragic resonance to her stories of everyday life and dignify commonplace courage or unhappiness. Similarly, in *The Mill on the Floss*, we are told that 'Mr Tulliver had a destiny as well as Oedipus' (*MF* 1.13). The theme is more subtly treated in *Middlemarch*. Dorothea in Rome is compared by an onlooker to a fusion of ancient and modern, 'a sort of Christian Antigone—sensuous force controlled by spiritual passion' (*MM* 19). This motif returns in the book's last paragraphs, which both contrast Antigone's 'heroic piety' with the less conspicuous heroisms required in modern circumstances and liken her sacrifice to those still

Spain

forced on ordinary people by the actions of others in their society. See also CLASSICAL LITERATURE; TRAGEDY. RHAJ

Spain. George Eliot's interest in Spain, unusual among her contemporaries, probably began with her reading of Spanish literature of the Golden Age, c.1500–c.1681, and developed into a broader concern with Spanish cultural history and religion. In girlhood, her imagination was engaged by *Don Quixote*. Later, G. H. *Lewes, who had written *The Spanish Drama: Lope de Vega and Calderon* in 1846 and had a continuing enthusiasm for Spain, nurtured and shared her interest. Spain's history, with its unique combination of Christian, Moorish, Jewish, and gypsy culture, fascinated Eliot in her quest for a deeper understanding of human nature.

Eliot's only sustained treatment of a Spanish subject is her dramatic poem *The Spanish Gypsy* (see POETRY). She learned Spanish in 1864 and, as was her practice when dealing with a subject far removed from her personal experience, she researched extensively into the history and literature of Spain. Her notebook for 1854–79 contains passages from her reading on gypsies in German, French, and English, including extracts from George Borrow's *The Zincali; or An Account of the Gipsies of Spain* (1843). She also read widely in Spanish history, with particular emphasis on the reign of Ferdinand and Isabella and the Inquisition.

The composition of *The Spanish Gypsy* was a struggle, and was temporarily abandoned for *Felix Holt, the Radical*. When Eliot returned to her dramatic poem, she and Lewes began seriously to consider visiting Spain. Such an undertaking required both commitment and a sense of adventure, as Spain was largely unvisited by British travellers at this time, although such a visit had just been made easier by the opening of a railway across Spain in 1864. Guidebooks, such as Henry Blackburn's *Travelling in Spain in the Present Day* (1866), which Eliot consulted, were more of a deterrent than an incentive to would-be travellers, warning of a harsh climate, filthy accommodation, indigestible food, boorish natives, obstructive officials, and primitive, not to say dangerous, modes of transport. While visiting *France in December and January 1866–7, the Leweses decided to continue to Spain, and sailed to San Sebastian at the end of January. They then proceeded by rail across northern Spain to Barcelona, stopping briefly en route in Saragossa and Lerida. From Barcelona, they went by steamboat to Alicante and Malaga, and then travelled by stagecoach to Granada, where they stayed for a week. They also visited Cordoba and Seville before proceeding to Madrid,

and then home via France. Their tour lasted forty days, making, in Eliot's words, 'a great loop all round the east and through the centre of Spain' (*L* iv. 349). None of their misgivings about the journey, the longest they ever made, were justified. Lewes's health improved, and Eliot's worst mishap was a cold caught by spending too long looking at pictures in the Prado, where, allegedly, corrupt officials had pocketed the money allocated for heating.

The Leweses were encouraged in their journey by the appreciative letters about Spain written by their friend, Barbara *Bodichon, whose artist's eye prepared them for Spain's particular aesthetic qualities. Their own letters record their delight in the people, landscape, art and architecture, and warmth of the sun. Eliot noted regional differences and the dress and behaviour of the people, commenting on their courtesy in not staring. The non-European spirit of Spain reminded Eliot of her reading about the East. 'I could have fancied myself in Arabia', she wrote (*L* iv. 351). Her highest praise went to Spain's most spectacular treasures, however. Granada was a place of 'transcendent beauty' (*L* iv. 347). The cathedral of Seville, the world's largest Gothic cathedral, built on the foundations of a Moorish mosque, and the paintings in Madrid she declared 'enough to justify Western civilization, with all its faults' (*L* iv. 351).

The Spanish Gypsy, Eliot's most atypical work, reflects her reading about Spain, but shows little evidence of her first-hand knowledge. The Spanish Christians, Moors, Jews, and gypsies could be Victorians in fancy dress. In spite of Eliot's real engagement with the Spanish landscape, she seldom succeeded in making the background to *The Spanish Gypsy* more than a cardboard stage setting. While Spain undeniably had a powerful hold over Eliot's mind and imagination, she did not bring this enthusiasm to its most effective outcome in works dealing directly with Spain and its people.

After her Spanish experiment, Eliot returned to an English setting in *Middlemarch*, but her preoccupation with Spain is demonstrated by her use, in the first paragraph, of the example of St Theresa's attempted childhood martyrdom to suggest the kind of heroic life that was impossible for a Victorian Englishwoman. The reference amounts to more than a passing allusion. Her novelist's imagination cannot resist dramatizing the incident, and Theresa and her small brother are described as they 'toddled from rugged Avila, wide-eyed and helpless-looking as two fawns' (*MM* Prelude). In spite of its brevity, this deftly summoned image of little children against an inhospitable landscape captures more of the atmosphere of Spain than many laboured passages of *The Spanish Gypsy*.

In *Daniel Deronda*, George Eliot married her concerns with *race, *religion, and *nationalism, all central to *The Spanish Gypsy*, with an English setting. Nevertheless, as the title and hero's name suggest (Ronda is a Spanish town), Spain and what its history represented to Eliot pervade the book. Like Fedalma, Deronda only learns of his family background and ethnic origins as an adult, and the discovery that he is descended from a proud line of exiled Spanish Jews leads him to his *vocation in the quest for a national homeland for his people. The most spacious of Eliot's novels, *Deronda* carries its main characters and the reader beyond the fully realized, but limited, English setting, reflecting the deep impression made on Eliot by the vastness and grandeur of the Spanish landscape. In its cultural vision, likewise, the novel projects a future where the best strains of eastern and western tradition will work together, as they once did in a multi-ethnic, multi-confessional Spain.   BSM

McMullen, Bonnie, ' "The Interest of Spanish Sights": From Ronda to *Daniel Deronda*', in Rignall (1997).

Spanish Gypsy, The, a long poem published in 1860 after a visit to *Spain. George Eliot's concerns here are questions to do with racial purity (see RACE) and the role of women in society (see WOMAN QUESTION), which were to be taken up more fully in the later novels *Middlemarch* and *Daniel Deronda*. See POETRY OF GEORGE ELIOT; SPAIN.   MR

Spencer, Herbert (1820–1903), philosopher and close friend of George Eliot, whom she first met in 1851 whilst she was editing the *Westminster Review*. Spencer was sub-editor of *The Economist* and occupied rooms above their offices opposite Eliot's lodgings in The Strand. He and Eliot frequently attended the opera and theatre together and were constantly in each other's company. This gave rise to speculation that they were engaged but Eliot informed her friends the Brays that 'We have decided that we are not in love with each other and that there is no reason why we should not have as much of each other's society as we like' (*L* ii. 22). She also assured Spencer himself 'how remote it is from my habitual state of mind to imagine that any one is falling in love with me' (*L* viii. 42). However, according to Spencer's later account, 'Her feelings became involved and mine did not' (*L* viii. 43). 'It was a most painful affair,' Spencer recorded, 'continuing throughout the Summer of 52 . . . into the beginning of 53' (*L* viii. 43). During this summer, they visited the *Brays together in Coventry, and Spencer appears to have been a visitor at Eliot's holiday retreat at Broadstairs. One of her surviving letters to him (amongst several which were deposited in the British Museum with

instructions for them to remain sealed up until 1985) is a bold, if poignant, plea for Spencer's love. Eliot requests 'to know if you can assure me that you will not forsake me, that you will always be with me as much as you can and share your thoughts and feelings with me' (*L* viii. 56). Declaring, 'I find it impossible to contemplate life under any other conditions', she adds the assurance that 'you will find that I can be satisfied with very little'. She concludes: 'I suppose no woman ever before wrote such a letter as this—but I am not ashamed of it, for I am conscious that in the light of reason and true refinement I am worthy of your respect and tenderness, whatever gross men or vulgar-minded women might think of me' (*L* viii. 57).

Spencer described Eliot as 'The most admirable woman, mentally, I ever met' (*Autobiography*, i. 397). He maintained that he was deterred from marrying her because of her lack of physical beauty: 'The lack of physical attraction was fatal. Strongly as my judgement prompted, my instincts would not respond' (*L* viii. 43). In 1854, Spencer wrote two articles for the *Leader* on 'Personal Beauty' which insisted on a correlation between physical beauty and intellect. Eliot's disparagement of physiognomy in novels such as *Adam Bede* has been read as a specific rebuttal of Spencer's association of outer appearance with inner qualities of character and mind (Paxton, 47–8).

Spencer introduced G. H. *Lewes to Eliot and claimed to have felt 'an immense relief' once their growing attachment to one another became apparent (*L* viii. 43). He remained a mutual friend despite a period of coolness in 1859, brought about, according to Lewes, by his jealousy of Lewes and Eliot's professional success (Haight 1968: 292). Spencer had also divulged the secret of Eliot's authorship to John *Chapman. Reconciliation followed when Spencer wrote in warm appreciation of *Adam Bede* (*L* viii. 245–7). He subsequently wrote also in high praise of *Middlemarch* and of *Romola* (*L* viii. 305). He was a regular visitor and a frequent participant in musical evenings at The *Priory. Spencer was amongst the mourners at George Eliot's funeral and kept a photograph of her until the end of his life. This, possibly because of his extreme solicitude for his own health, was considerably later than most of his scientific and philosophical contemporaries.

Spencer was a major proponent of the view that laws of evolution governed every sphere of existence. He wrote a number of articles during the 1850s which promoted the theory of evolution, then more commonly known as 'the development theory'. Spencer became the main popularizer of a number of concepts subsequently regarded as 'Darwinian' (see DARWINISM), including the application of evolutionary theory to society,

Photograph of Herbert Spencer (1820–1903), the philosopher and friend of George Eliot, in 1858. When she asked him why he had such a smooth forehead, he replied, 'because I am never puzzled'.

psychology, and the arts. It was Spencer who coined the phrase 'survival of the fittest' and declared that evolution necessarily involved progress.

In 'The Development Hypothesis', published in the *Leader* in March 1852, Spencer mounted a defence of the 'Theory of Evolution' in which he proclaimed its universal applicability: 'the development of every faculty, bodily, moral, or intellectual' being 'all explicable on this same principle' (Spencer, *Essays*, i. 391–2). Spencer was thus formulating his ideas about evolution at the time when Eliot was most closely associated with him. They discussed his *Principles of Psychology* during the summer of 1852 (Haight 1968: 116). Spencer was never particularly given to acknowledging intellectual debt, but we may suppose that Eliot's involvement in his work was in many ways invaluable. She and Lewes continued to read Spencer's work, sometimes in draft form, in later years. Well before Spencer's publication of his 'Development Hypothesis' article, Eliot had incorporated the idea that the theory of evolution was applicable to every area of human life into her first essay for the *Westminster* in 1851. In her review of Mackay's *Progress of the Intellect*, she recognizes 'the presence of undeviating law in the material and moral world—of that invariability of sequence which is acknowledged to be the basis of physical science, but which is still perversely ignored in our social organization, our ethics and our religion' (*Essays*, 30–1).

Spencer explained that he had developed his theories by taking laws of organic development identified by German embryologists and applying them more universally, so constructing his scientific, social, and aesthetic theories as interdependent aspects of evolutionary organicism (Spencer, *Essays*, i. 2). His 1857 articles on 'Progress, Its Law and Cause' and on 'The Origin and Function of Music' detailed the application of his theory to the arts in general and to music in particular (Spencer, *Essays*, i. 1–30, 359–84). Spencer's development theory was clearly significant in providing some of the philosophical background for Eliot's comments on the arts, as it did for her writing in general. Eliot's evolutionary interest in the arts was already apparent in her 1854 article on '*Liszt, Wagner, and Weimar*', an appreciation, in organicist and evolutionary terms, of *Wagner's views on the historical and future development of opera.

Eliot confronts Spencer's thought in ways which frequently expose both the consequences and limitations of his theories. Her amused scepticism about whether Spencer's systematic theories provided adequate explanation for all the phenomena to which they were applied is already apparent from her description of botanical ex-

peditions to Kew with Spencer in June 1852 where, if the flowers failed to fit the theories, it was '*tant pis pour les fleurs*' ('too bad for the flowers') (*L* ii. 40). A response to Spencer's work forms a significant part of Eliot's engagement with contemporary *science in her fiction. Her emphasis on the conflict and the cost to the individual of *progress is in contrast to Spencer's optimistic faith, throughout his long career, on evolution as a process bringing outer and inner circumstances into the closer adjustment necessary to individual happiness. In *The Mill on the Floss*, for example, Eliot's portrayal of the tragic fate of an individual caught in the conflict between 'older' and 'higher' culture destabilizes the idea of history as inevitable progress to which Spencer's social evolutionism laid claim (*L* viii. 465–6).

Eliot portrays her characters as subject not only to external conflict with their environment, but more crucially, to internal conflict fuelled by their susceptibility to the involuntary, and potentially dissonant, forces of the physiology which formed the basis of Spencer's psychological theory. Spencer viewed the processes of the mind and body as organically linked, implying the potential for an irreducible conflict of subjective states to coexist within the individual. This effectively undermines the possibility of an independent controlling conscience which could resolve the clash between duty and passion such as that portrayed by Eliot in *The Mill on the Floss*. In his chapter on 'The Feelings' in *The Principles of Psychology*, Spencer argued against the apparent autonomy of emotional and intellectual processes:

to say that there is really no line of demarcation between reason, and sentiment or passion, will, by most, be thought a contradiction of direct internal perceptions. Nevertheless . . . if all mental phenomena are incidents of the correspondence between the organism and its environment . . . then, we may be certain, *à priori*, that the Feelings are not, scientifically considered, divisible from other phenomena of consciousness. (*Psychology*, 584)

In *The Mill on the Floss*, both the admonishing voice which Maggie hears as she reads Thomas à *Kempis and the opposing influence of Stephen Guest's seductive singing, are shown to have an involuntary physical effect on her which is consistent with Spencer's account of physiological response as the basis for emotion and which emphasizes that part of Maggie's tragedy lies in her susceptibility to psychological forces beyond her control, including the shifting constitution of the individual subject. Biologically, the mind and body are shown as being as inextricably linked as the individual and society. On a psychological level, arbitrary physical responses undermine the possibility of a coherent individual identity or controlling conscience. Spencer blithely pointed out the implication of his physiological psychology for conceptions of the unified individual. He denied that the subject possessed any continuity apart from its changing mental states, stating that it is an 'illusion' to suppose 'that at each moment the *ego* is something more than the composite state of consciousness which then exists' (*Psychology*, 617–18). Eliot's dramatizations of the conflicting psychological processes within the organically connected subject query the feasibility of what Spencer called 'that grand progression which is now bearing Humanity onwards to perfection' (*Psychology*, 620).

Eliot was not alone in regarding Spencer as peculiarly deaf to the personal tragedies consequent upon his view of psychology. The scientist T. H. *Huxley, also a friend, commented that 'Spencer's definition of a tragedy was the spectacle of a deduction killed by a fact' (*DNB 1901–1911*: 366). Spencer seemed untroubled by the paradox entailed in his optimism about evolutionary progress as ultimately beneficial to the individual. He cheerfully combined his conviction that free will was incompatible with progress, and a view of the historical process as given to increasing interdependence, with a laissez-faire individualistic morality. Despite the contradictions inherent in his system, Spencer evinced undiminished optimism about evolutionary progress as an unassailable given which would guarantee ultimate harmony. Beyond its serious intellectual engagement with Spencer's thought, Eliot's writing stands as a passionate rejection of the reductive certainties of Herbert Spencer's Synthetic Philosophy and of the lack of puzzlement which, as he records explaining to her, left Spencer's brow unfurrowed. When Eliot asked him why he had such a smooth forehead, his reply was 'because I am never puzzled', an explanation which she declared 'the most arrogant thing I ever heard uttered' (*Autobiography*, i. 399). See also DETERMINISM.

DdSC

Spencer, Herbert, *The Principles of Psychology* (1855).
—— *Essays: Scientific, Political, and Speculative*, i. (1858).
—— *An Autobiography*, 2 vols. (1904).
Ashton (1983).
Burrow, J. W., *Evolution and Society: A Study in Victorian Social Theory* (1966).
Paxton, Nancy, *George Eliot and Herbert Spencer* (1991).
Shuttleworth (1984).

Spinoza, Baruch (Benedict de) (1632–77),

Jewish-Dutch philosopher. George Eliot was involved with Spinoza's work as early as 1849, when she wrote to one of her Coventry friends that she

was translating his *Tractatus Theologico-politicus*, and while this project was not completed, she did complete in 1856 a translation of his *Ethics* (see TRANSLATIONS BY GEORGE ELIOT). As an author she had previously published her translations of D. F. *Strauss's *Das Leben Jesu* (1836; trans. 1846) and Ludwig *Feuerbach's *Das Wesen des Christenthums* (1841; trans. 1854) and the first in a series of brilliant *essays for the *Westminster Review*. When her new companion, G. H. *Lewes, failed through impolitic negotiations to secure publication of her completed Spinoza translation, Marian Evans's disappointment was intense.

Her interest in Spinoza was part of the general admiration for his work among English and German Romantics. To them Spinoza appears as the philosopher of freedom because of his allowance for what he called 'intuition' beyond the scope of reason. Despite the difficulty of Spinoza's style, which in addition to being in medieval Latin is also in an almost geometrical form of logic, his arguments concerning the relation of finitude and freedom struck a chord with a generation looking beyond rationalism as did his emphasis on intuition, and his insistence on going both beyond the relatively mechanical Cartesian models of consciousness and beyond Lockian (what Feuerbach called 'vulgar') empiricism. Instead of a world of continuities and rationalization of the kinds found in Descartes and Locke and based on humanist models current since at least 1500, Spinoza contemplates a world composed of multiple systems, and systems within systems, in what we might in the late 20th century call field equilibrium.

For Spinoza, the fullest truths lie outside every system or representation, and the model of knowledge must allow for the ragged edges which human limitation will always impose upon any perception or understanding. It is not at all hard to see how this philosopher inspired the future George Eliot, whose one watchword throughout her career was the thought that 'finality is another name for bewilderment and defeat'.

Spinoza was particularly against the grain of the Enlightenment in his depreciation of human 'purpose'. Purpose is a sign of human limitation, not a high expression of its unlimited power. To have a purpose is to work against the Divine Substance and thus to waste energy and to spoil what would otherwise be balanced and harmonious. As a basis for all social and political dealings among people, this thought required more sophistication than most commentators could muster in response to Spinoza. But George Eliot was able to find in his work a justification for moral activity that went far beyond conventional religious pieties and was far more liberating. The influence of this Spinoza can be seen in her treatment of rural life in all her novels, and in all her essays, especially 'The *Natural History of German Life', *'Worldliness and Other-Worldliness: The Poet Young', and *'Evangelical Teaching: Dr Cumming', which are among the wittiest treatments of moral hubris in the language.

Spinoza's limited human existence ('modal' existence), however, is not only completely finite and limited in its grip on truth, it is also entirely a predicate of God (or 'Substance'), which means that all finite existence is by definition included in a common divinity. Factionalism of whatever kind—religious, social, moral, political—is an expression of confusion on the part of finite beings in full denial of their finitude. To acknowledge one's limits, however, is to go beyond them and thus to make possible linkage between separate persons and systems. Feuerbach makes a similar case in his anthropological treatise translated by Marian Evans as *The Essence of Christianity* (1854).

So we can hear the voices of Spinoza and Feuerbach in many of George Eliot's most characteristic phrases: for example, when she writes that 'a *universal social policy has no validity except on paper*' ('The Natural History of German Life', repr. in *Essays*, 289); or that her character the Revd Stelling in *The Mill on the Floss* taught 'the right way, indeed, he knew no other' (*MF* 2.1). Her large tolerance has stimulated irritated responses from some critics over the years, but in 'The *Morality of *Wilhelm Meister*' she insisted with *Goethe that the distinction between right and wrong, 'the line between the virtuous and the vicious, so far from being a necessary safeguard to morality, is itself an immoral fiction' (*Essays*, 147). Some of her most forward-looking qualities are traceable to values found in Spinoza, for example, her emphasis on difference as the basis of unities, her sense of the world as a complex of systems, her faith in the efficacy of knowledge, her sense that knowledge is emotional as well as intellectual, and her emphasis on the importance of action.

George Eliot differs from Spinoza in important ways, however, as she differs from all the varied sources which influenced her writing. She does not accept Spinoza's assumption of a single common basis for natural and cultural life; on the contrary, she distinguishes culture as a realm of freedom quite separate from the 'calm determinism' of nature. Both realms operate according to laws, but the definition of law in each differs absolutely (see DETERMINISM). It was precisely her respect for scientific method (see SCIENCE), with its patient watching and its experimental departure from dogma, that suggests the key difference between natural determinism and cultural determinism. Furthermore she believes that within the horizon of *history and *language, human

purpose has efficacy and, quite unlike Spinoza, she emphasizes the power of a guiding idea for shaping activity beyond immediate wants.

Having experienced in her own life the evils of prejudice and factional smugness, George Eliot seems to have felt a personal affinity with the philosopher who lived in Holland doubly estranged: first as a Jewish refugee from the Spanish Inquisition, and then as a freethinker at odds with Jewish orthodoxy. His influence on her work is to be found in these large issues, and not in particular equivalences. See also MORAL VALUES; PHILOSOPHY.   EDE

Spinoza, Benedict de, *Ethics* (*Ethica Ordine Geometrico Demonstrata*, in *Opera Posthuma*, 1677), trans. George Eliot, ed. Thomas Deegan, *Salzburg Studies in English Literature*, 102 (1981).

Ermarth (1985).

Lewes, G. H., 'Spinoza's Life and Works', *Westminster Review*, 39 (1843).

spiritualism. In contrast with numerous of her contemporaries, George Eliot retained a predominantly sceptical attitude towards the popular interest in spiritualism. Literary figures who expressed a more serious interest included Harriet *Martineau, Erasmus Darwin (brother of Charles), William Makepeace *Thackeray, Anthony *Trollope, John *Ruskin, Elizabeth Barrett *Browning, and Margaret *Oliphant.

Eliot's reservations about spiritualism are evident from her exchange of letters with Harriet Beecher *Stowe, an enthusiastic adherent of spiritualist beliefs. In an 1869 letter, Eliot distinguishes between a valid interest in psychological experience and 'spiritualism' in the sense of 'spirit communications by rapping, guidance of the pencil etc.' which appears to her 'either as degrading folly, imbecile in the estimate of evidence, or else as impudent imposture' (*L* v. 48–9). Spiritualism, she feared, offered a distraction from the 'more assured methods of studying the open secret of the universe': as an object of scientific investigation, the 'alleged manifestations' of spiritualism suffered from their dependence on 'individual testimonies as to phenomena witnessed, which testimonies are no more true objectively because they are honest subjectively' (*L* v. 49). In 1872, after Stowe described receiving communication from the spirit of Charlotte *Brontë, Eliot confessed to 'but a feeble interest in these doings, feeling my life very short for the supreme and awful revelations of a more orderly and intelligible kind which I shall die with an imperfect knowledge of' (*L* v. 280–1). However, she continues, 'Others, who feel differently, and are attracted towards this study, are making an experiment for us to see whether anything better than bewilderment can come of it' (*L* v. 281).

Amongst these 'others' was the philosopher F. W. H. *Myers. In 1874, Eliot and G. H. *Lewes were persuaded to attend a seance hosted by Darwin's brother at which Myers, Charles *Darwin, and T. H. *Huxley were among those present. Such an occasion serves as a reminder of how far from a 'fringe' interest spiritualism was at the time. Darwin had become troubled about spiritualism after the involvement of his cousin Francis Galton. He suspected that the claims of mediums were false, but nonetheless requested Huxley further to investigate the activities of Williams, the medium. (Meanwhile his co-discoverer of natural selection, Alfred Russel Wallace, was prepared to revise his theory of evolution in the light of his firm belief in the truth of spiritualism.) During the seance in question, a bell is reputed to have rung, candlesticks leaped, and a rushing sound of wind was heard. Darwin had retired to bed with a headache. Eliot and Lewes later left 'in disgust' when Williams refused to allow lights during his performance, Lewes having already been unable to resist cracking jokes whilst others were silent (*L* vi. 6; Desmond and Moore, 607–8).

In Eliot's letters to Stowe, criticism is always tempered by assertions that 'I would not willingly place any barrier between my mind and any possible channel of truth affecting the human lot (*L* v. 253). Such assertions represent more than politeness towards her correspondent. Whatever her reservations about spirit manifestations, Eliot undoubtedly did evince a strong interest in what might be termed the 'other side' of *science: 'indications of claire-voyance witnessed by a competent observer are of thrilling interest and give me a restless desire to get at more extensive and satisfactory evidence', she commented in 1852 (*L* viii. 45). By the time of *Daniel Deronda*'s publication, a systematic study such as she advocated was about to take place. Myers was preparing to investigate the phenomena he christened 'telepathy'—a term which largely came to replace what Eliot's contemporaries knew as 'sympathetic clairvoyance'— becoming a founding member of the Society for Psychical Research (1882). Whilst Myers and his colleagues had begun their work by investigating spiritualism, they soon encountered the problems of trickery and reliance on individual testimony, which Eliot herself had identified (*L* v. 49). They transferred their major research interest to psychic phenomena such as thought-transference and hypnotism. Eliot knew most of those who were to become leading members of the SPR, including Edmund *Gurney, a possible model for the hero of *Daniel Deronda*, a work which parallels the 'visionary excitability' and 'forecasting ardour' of scientist and prophet (*DD* 41). The novel portrays extremes of sympathetic communication which

verge on the clairvoyant. A gentle mockery of popular spiritualism ('It must be the spirits') is compatible with Eliot's account of the composer Klesmer's genuinely uncanny power to mesmerize Gwendolen and to function as the 'medium' of her 'spiritual dread' (*DD* 6).

Eliot's interest in what lies beyond the boundaries of perception is most memorably expressed in her account in *Middlemarch* of 'that roar on the other side of silence' which would become audible to more sensitive organs of hearing (*MM* 20). It is a concern obviously central to 'The Lifted Veil' in which Eliot elaborates a nightmare account of the impact of preternaturally enhanced perception. Her interest in the limits of science and of psychology also permeates the rest of Eliot's work, most intensively *Daniel Deronda* where 'The driest argument has its hallucinations' (*DD* 41) and where 'second sight' and unspoken 'communication' like 'two chords whose quick vibrations lie outside our hearing' (*DD* 38, 61) suggest that 'the other side of silence' might become palpable. Describing Eliot herself in his memoirs, the psychologist James *Sully explicitly linked her capacity for *sympathy with somewhat uncanny powers of perception: 'George Eliot enfolded her auditors in an atmosphere of discriminative sympathy', Sully wrote; 'She had a clairvoyant insight into mind and character, which enabled her to get at once into spiritual touch with a stranger, fitting her talk to his special tastes and needs, and drawing out what was best in him' (Sully, *My Life and Friends: A Psychologist's Memories* (1918), 263–4). See also MESMERISM.   DdSC

Desmond, Adrian, and Moore, James, *Darwin* (1991).
Proceedings of the Society for Psychical Research, 5 vols. (1882–9).
Royle, Nicholas, *Telepathy and Literature* (1991).

Staël, Mme (Germaine) de (née Necker, 1766–1817), writer, much admired by George Eliot, who said in her 1854 *Westminster Review* essay *'Woman in France: Madame de Sablé': 'Madame de Staël's name still rises first to the lips when we are asked to mention a woman of great intellectual power' (*Essays*, 55). De Staël is perhaps best known now for infuriating Napoleon with her outspoken opposition to his policies and for the punitive treatment she received as a result, but in her day she was celebrated for her fiction—especially *Delphine* (1802) and *Corinne* (1807)—for her writings on politics, nations, ideas, and literature, and for the brilliance of her salon. The influence of *Corinne*, which George Eliot first read as a young woman, cannot be overestimated.

Corinne is, ostensibly, an affirmation of national diversity, which is located in the novel in the eponymous heroine and her English lover, Oswald Nelvil. Nelvil represents the 'best of Britishness': courage, honour, moral principle, restraint. Corinne is the embodiment of Italy: passion, beauty, spontaneity, culture. The narrative is propelled by the desire to bring the two together: by the desire for, and the impossibility of, union between the qualities—the collective imaginations—of the two nations. But this meeting and merging of nations and genders is destabilized when Corinne's previously obscure origins are revealed: she proves to be only half-Italian, the daughter of an English aristocrat. She has a half-sister, Lucille, who is positioned as Corinne's opposite, the exemplar of English bourgeois femininity: blonde, reserved, silent, insipid, childlike, domesticated. Nelvil returns to England and marries Lucille. Up to this point, the narrative has dwelt upon Corinne's ravishing amplitude, but after Nelvil's departure, Corinne's physique shrinks: she becomes pale, thin, and dishevelled, prone to fainting and tears. Finally, she orchestrates her own death and is reunited with Oswald Nelvil, only to deliver him back to Lucille, telling her, 'May he live with you in happiness' (418).

Corinne is, famously, the novel which Maggie Tulliver failed to finish, but, as Ellen Moers has demonstrated, *The Mill on the Floss* has clear allegiances to *Corinne*. Moers perceives Eliot's novel as a revenge fantasy which interrogates *Corinne*'s plot by validating the unruly brunette, but George Eliot, unlike Maggie, had read to the end of de Staël's novel, and she would have seen that the 'blond-haired woman' does not actually carry away all the happiness, as Maggie suggests. In *The Mill on the Floss*, as in *Corinne*, Maggie delivers Stephen back to Lucy. The primary structural difference between the two texts is that Maggie's amplitude is not diminished during the course of the narrative; she remains robust and healthy until taken by the flood. The difference may be attributed to the fact that Maggie's transgressiveness is rooted within the English landscape which has nurtured her, and, also, to the imagined potential elasticity of her community. *The Mill on the Floss* draws on codes and motifs taken from *Corinne*, but reinflects them to extricate them from their association with foreignness and to locate them within English kinship structures. The novel is propelled by a sequence of moves in which the censoring of Maggie's body is paralleled by its validation, a complicated process of robing and disrobing in which the women of the community are complicitous and through which Maggie's 'queenly' qualities are recognized. Eliot inflects what she calls in the novel 'the mother tongue of our imagination' with the potential for a new meaning: one which will allow its mute inglorious

Corinnes, its disbonneted Maggies, a sense of home. GF

Staël, Germaine de, *Corinne, or Italy*, trans. and ed. Avriel H. Goldberger (1987).
Frith, Gill, 'Playing with Shawls: George Eliot's Use of *Corinne* in *The Mill on the Floss*', in Rignall (1997).
Gutwirth, Madelyn, *Madame de Staël, Novelist: The Emergence of the Artist as Woman* (1978).
Moers, Ellen, *Literary Women* (1977).
Winegarten, Renee, *Mme de Staël* (1985).

Stephen, Leslie (1832–1904), described as 'man of letters and philosopher' in the *Dictionary of National Biography*, of which he was the first editor (1882–91) and principal contributor, writing nearly 400 entries including that on George Eliot (1888). His obituary of her appeared in the February 1881 issue of the **Cornhill Magazine*, of which he was the editor (1871–82); and he provided the George Eliot volume for the second series of 'English Men of Letters' (1902). He had written on Johnson, Pope, and Swift in the first series, the 18th century being his particular period interest.

The obituary opens with the assertion that 'In losing George Eliot we have probably lost the greatest woman who ever won literary fame', and proceeds to the judgement that 'The works of George Eliot may hereafter appear as marking the termination of the great period of English fiction which began with Scott' (*CH* 464–5). While Stephen's conviction of her greatness is unwavering, his essays develop classic formulations of a preference for her earlier realistic works over the later philosophic and didactic ones, and significant discriminations beautifully epitomized by the observation in the 'English Men of Letters' volume 'that George Eliot's talent scarcely included the rare gift of a just appreciation of her own limitations' (147). He attributed these limitations to her 'eminently feminine' intellect, where the necessary aggression of the true philosopher is undercut by valorization of feeling (200).

Delicate as a boy, Stephen's physical stamina developed during his time at *Cambridge, first as an undergraduate, and then as a tutor and Fellow of Trinity Hall. Because of his Cambridge connection, George Eliot consulted him about aspects of university life when she was working on *Daniel Deronda*. He took to many sports, including rowing, but mountaineering and long country walks were particular passions—transferred by his friend George *Meredith to the character of Vernon Whitford in his novel *The Egoist* (1879). Stephen's younger daughter, Virginia *Woolf, represented other aspects of his 'reserved and melancholy' manner (*DNB*) in the character of Mr Ramsay in *To the Lighthouse* (1927). See also REPUTATION, CRITICAL. MAH

Sterne, Laurence (1713–68), Irish novelist, whose *Tristram Shandy* (1759–67) and *A Sentimental Journey* (1768) George Eliot was certainly familiar with. She and G. H. *Lewes read the latter aloud to each other in the autumn of 1875, and an epigraph is taken from it for chapter 19 of *Daniel Deronda*. *Tristram Shandy* was always a favourite. Eliot read it aloud in May 1859 and again through January and February 1873. Prior to that, Lewes had written to John *Blackwood (in May 1871) using Sterne's novel as a rough model for the publication of the forthcoming *Middlemarch*: '*Tristram Shandy* was published ... at irregular intervals and great was the desire for the continuation' (*L* v. 146). In a letter to John Blackwood in 1858 Eliot had quoted briefly from *Tristram Shandy*. Despite the scant references in the novels, there is little doubt of her love for Sterne. In her early essay *'German Wit: Heinrich Heine', where she distinguishes between wit and humour, Sterne provides an inevitable point of comparison with Heine's travel writing, and she refers to the raciness of his humour. However, in her later 'Leaves from a Note-book', she concedes that there are objections to his 'wild way' of telling the story in *Tristram Shandy*, which lie more 'in the quality of the interrupting rather than in the fact of interruption' (*Essays*, 446).   GRH

Stowe, Harriet Beecher (1811–96), America's foremost 19th-century woman novelist, important to George Eliot as an example, as a reader, and as a personal friend. Internationally acclaimed for *Uncle Tom's Cabin; or, Life Among the Lowly* (1852), Stowe was also the author of *Dred: A Tale of the Great Dismal Swamp* (1856), *Oldtown Folks* (1869), and numerous other novels, stories, pamphlets, and articles. Although they never met, Stowe and Eliot, through reading each other's work and a ten-year correspondence, developed close bonds.

Eliot read *Uncle Tom's Cabin* shortly after its publication, but her response to Stowe's slavery novels is expressed most vividly in her review of *Dred* for the *Westminster Review* in October 1856 (repr. in *Essays*). Defining 'genius' as a 'writer who thoroughly possesses you by his creation', Eliot applies the term to Stowe throughout. Praising Stowe's emotional intensity and range and her comprehensive treatment of her subject, Eliot proclaims that *Dred* and *Uncle Tom* will assure Stowe 'a place in that highest rank of novelists who can give us a national life in all its phases'. Moreover, 'she attains her finest dramatic effects by means of her energetic sympathy, and not by conscious artifice' (*Essays*, 326, 329).

The terms in which Eliot praises Stowe require particular attention when it is noted that only four days after writing the review her own career in fiction began with 'The Sad Fortunes of the Reverend Amos Barton'. In terms of dramatic expressiveness and breadth of subject matter, Eliot learned much from a woman whose source of creative energy was closely linked to the mass popular mentality of her day, and whose sympathies were formed by a background of *evangelicalism. Many specific examples could be cited to demonstrate the care with which Eliot studied Stowe's work. Stowe offered proof to Eliot, who, as a *journalist and editor, had long been concerned with questions of major national importance, that serious issues could also be treated effectively in fiction by a woman. No longer need Eliot be inhibited by the negative examples she outlined for the same number of the *Westminster Review* in *'Silly Novels by Lady Novelists'. Stowe had directly confronted questions of politics, religion, economics, race, and gender. What was done by one woman might be done by another.

Stowe's *Agnes of Sorrento* appeared in the *Cornhill Magazine* in 1862 immediately before *Romola*. Stowe alludes to *Romola* in her controversial article of September 1869, 'The True Story of Lady Byron's Life', where she compares the conflict between the Byrons to that between Romola and Tito. This article, and the book that followed in 1870, *Lady Byron Vindicated*, gravely damaged Stowe's reputation. Eliot regretted that Stowe felt impelled 'to publish what is only worthy to die and rot' (*L* v. 54), but she trusted Stowe's motives and sympathized with her under the weight of 'harsh and unfair judgments' (*L* v. 71).

Shortly before this debacle, Stowe had initiated a correspondence with Eliot (15 April 1869) which developed into an intimate epistolary friendship. Stowe could hardly have imagined how Eliot would welcome her generous overture. A letter in 1853 from Stowe to another correspondent, which Eliot had seen, had caused her to exclaim: 'The proceeds of her first writings she devoted to buying her first feather bed! The whole letter is most fascinating and makes one love her' (*L* ii. 92). Eliot's replies echo Stowe's tone of sisterly warmth. Here was a correspondent with whom she had no fear of being misunderstood: 'dear friend and fellow-labourer ... you have had longer experience as a writer, and fuller experience as a woman' (*L* v. 31). Sharing domestic details and their innermost hopes and fears, they formed an affectionate bond in which each could speak frankly and with complete intellectual independence. The friendship helped to sustain both women through severe personal trials for the next ten years.

Daniel Deronda (1876) most strikingly demonstrates the impact of Stowe. Pointedly set during the period of the *American civil war, which some blamed Stowe for causing, Eliot dramatizes issues of *race, *religion, *politics, and *gender against the largest historical and geographical backdrop she ever attempted. Indeed, the novel can be read as a coded letter to her American exemplar. Seven years earlier, Stowe had sent her *Oldtown Folks*, which, like Eliot's early work, deals with rural community life in the recent past. Eliot had told Stowe, who worried about the British reception, that an important work's influence grows from 'its reception by a few appreciative natures, and is the slow result of radiation from that narrow circle' (*L* v. 30). *Deronda* was the practical demonstration. The point was not lost on Stowe, who, while reading the monthly parts, wrote to Eliot, 'I feel with you in some little, fine points,—they stare at me as making an amusing exhibition' (Calvin Ellis Stowe, *Life of Harriet Beecher Stowe* (1889), 475). See also AMERICA.   BSM

Hedrick, Joan, *Harriet Beecher Stowe: A Life* (1994).
Moers, Ellen, *Literary Women* (1977).
Wolstenholme, Susan, *Gothic (Re) Visions: Writing Women as Readers* (1993).

Strauss, David Friedrich (1808–74), German theologian and biblical critic whose *Das Leben Jesu, kritisch bearbeitet* (1835–6) was translated by Mary Ann Evans, the future George Eliot, as *The Life of Jesus, Critically Examined* (1846). She was later to meet him briefly on two occasions, in 1854 and 1858.

Strauss's book was a landmark of 19th-century religious thought and the subject of considerable controversy. In his exhaustive examination of the Four Gospels he seeks to distinguish between the historical and the unhistorical in the different accounts of Christ's life, interpreting the unhistorical or fictional elements as myths that stem from themes and motifs deeply embedded in Jewish history and culture. Thus, after scrupulously weighing the evidence, he sees the accounts of the arrival of the Magi and the Massacre of the Innocents as products of the mythological imagination: the first myth emanating from Jewish Messianic beliefs—the prophecy of Balaam about the star that would come out of Jacob—and the second from Jewish history—Pharaoh's order for the slaying of the first-born. The Resurrection receives similar treatment: the story of the empty tomb is the product of legend, while the appearances of the risen Christ to the disciples are interpreted psychologically as visions or hallucinations created by the intense enthusiasm of the early Christians. Strauss was not an atheist but was unable to believe in a transcendent personal God intervening supernaturally in the course of history; and his aim was to dispense with the myths and symbols of Christianity and

base faith on conceptual thinking alone. The hostile reaction to his work destroyed his university career as a theologian. He was relieved of a teaching post in the theological seminary at Tübingen and, when he was appointed to a chair of theology at Zurich in 1839, the public outcry was so great that, after a referendum which went in favour of his opponents, he was not allowed to take up his appointment and had to be given a pension for life. In his later years the criticism he had received turned him against Christianity and he embraced materialism.

His translator was sympathetic to his general approach in *Das Leben Jesu*, having arrived herself in 1842 at a view of the Scriptures as 'consisting of mingled truth and fiction' (*L* i. 128). Her friend Charles Christian *Hennell had investigated the historical truth of the Gospels in his *Inquiry concerning the Origin of Christianity* (1838), the 1841 second edition of which she possessed and had read by 1842. (Strauss arranged for the German translation of Hennell's book, which had been written in ignorance of his own study, and wrote a complimentary preface.) However, Strauss's exhaustive method of investigating every episode in the Gospels in the same methodical way, setting out traditional religious interpretations, followed by historical explanations, and finally his own mythical reading of the event, proved exhausting to translate. According to her friend Cara *Bray his dry dissection of the beautiful story of the Crucifixion made George Eliot ill, 'Strauss-sick' (*L* i. 206), and she often complained of being sick of her task. By the time she reached the last 100 pages of the 1,500 she found it totally uninteresting, since Strauss had already anticipated all the principles and many of the details of his criticism. In her view, he inevitably went wrong on occasions in 'working out into detail an idea which has general truth, but is only one element in a perfect theory, not a perfect theory in itself' (*L* i. 203). Her impatience here with Strauss's systematic attempt to apply an all-embracing theory may be echoed in her portrayal of Casaubon's vain effort to find a 'Key to all Mythologies' in *Middlemarch*; and it is certainly reflected in her enduring belief, expressed in *The Mill on the Floss*, that 'we have no master key that will fit all cases' (*MF* 7.2). A more positive residue of her work on Strauss was her understanding of *myth, her lasting respect for religious myths as the embodiment of human needs and emotions (see RELIGION), and her use of a securalized version of myth in *Silas Marner*, where Silas's stolen gold is replaced by the gift of the golden-haired child who enters his life in the Christmas season.

In July 1854, when she was on her way to *Weimar with G. H. *Lewes at the beginning of their life together, a chance meeting with Dr R. H. *Brabant in the train led to a meeting with Strauss in Cologne, which Brabant was able to arrange. It was a melancholy occasion: Strauss looked strange and cast down, and Eliot's spoken German was not good enough to permit any real communication between them (*L* ii. 171). Their second meeting in July 1858, at the end of her three-month stay in Munich with Lewes, was happier: by this time she was capable of conversing in German and she declared herself very favourably impressed by him (*L* ii. 472). His work was important for providing her first extended contact with the German scholarship that she praised in 1851 for having introduced 'a truly philosophic spirit into the study of mythology' (*Essays*, 36). See also ATHEISM; CHRISTIANITY; TRANSLATIONS BY GEORGE ELIOT.

JMR

Strauss, David Friedrich, *The Life of Jesus, Critically Examined*, trans. George Eliot, ed. Peter C. Hodgson (1972).
Ashton (1980).
Paris, Bernard J., 'George Eliot and the Higher Criticism', *Anglia*, 84 (1966).
Willey, Basil, 'George Eliot: Hennell, Strauss and Feuerbach', in *Nineteenth-Century Studies* (1949).

Stuart, Elma (1837?–1903), one of George Eliot's most devoted admirers in her last years, who memorialized her role as 'spiritual daughter' (the term first used by George Eliot in a letter of 8 March 1874, *L* vi. 27) when she was buried next to George Eliot in Highgate Cemetery. The inscription on her tombstone begins: 'Elma Stuart, née Fraser, of Ladhope, Roxburghshire, whom for 8½ blessed years George Eliot called by the sweet name of "Daughter" '. The widow of a lieutenant in the Black Watch and mother of Roland, she lived mainly in France with her cousin and 'guardian angel', Mrs Menzies.

Elma introduced herself in 1872 with a letter praising *Middlemarch*, and the gift of an oak bookslide which she had carved herself. A relentless giver, she improved the acquaintance by sending more carved items including toys for Blanche Lewes, a shawl, photographs, flowers. The correspondence gives some engagingly intimate glimpses of George Eliot, who in 1875 reported her invention 'of braces to hold up my flannel and calico drawers', a 'return for all the thoughts and stitches you have given me' (*L* vi. 133), and in 1878 treated Elma's son Roland, declaring, 'He ought to know what a Pantomime is' (*L* vii. 4). At other times, her epistolary vein is the one of high sententiousness so well discussed by Rosemarie Bodenheimer, who analyses George Eliot's 'strongly maternal and sometimes disciplinary voice' (1994: 251), and conjectures that 'her letters to Elma do suggest the release of a maternal passion blocked not only by her childlessness but by the truncated relationship with her own mother' (252). MAH

Letters from George Eliot to Elma Stuart, ed. Ronald Stuart (1909).
Bodenheimer (1994).

style. An early writer on George Eliot, W. C. Brownell in *Victorian Prose Masters* (1902), declared bluntly that 'she has no style' (120). However obtuse that observation, it does point to the difficulty of definition. What Brownell saw as the absence of style could be better described as a range and flexibility of discourse that cannot be reduced to a single set of stylistic characteristics. Even the voice of the third-person narrator, whose authoritative and knowing presence could be seen as one of the most distinctive features of her fiction (see NARRATION), is shifting and often elusive, moving between different registers and employing *irony and indirection, as well as offering direct moral commentary and philosophical reflection. The solemn and sententious pronouncements that seem so typical of her narrator—'We are all of us born in moral stupidity, taking the world as an udder to feed our supreme selves' (*MM* 21)—have to be set against similarly epigrammatic observations that are made enigmatic by the lurking presence of irony: 'the woman dictates before marriage in order that she may have an appetite for submission afterwards' (*MM* 9). Eliot has frequent recourse, as here, to free indirect style, which blurs the distinction between the voice of the narrator and that of the characters, and may serve to mimic conventional attitudes and opinions to ironic effect. The narrative discourse encompasses both lofty generalization and vivid particularity, using, for instance, the sharp detail of a striking simile to illustrate a point: 'Mr Cadwallader was a large man . . . with that solid imperturbable ease and good-humour which is infectious, and like great grassy hills in the sunshine, quiets even an irritated egoism, and makes it rather ashamed of itself' (*MM* 8). It also exploits the resources of *metaphor and *symbolism and draws on the discourse of *science, while the use of chapter *epigraphs in the later novels supplies a further level of implied commentary and adds to the variety of voices at work in the text (see POETRY).

Dialogue extends the stylistic range and variety of the fiction, from Mrs Poyser's homespun, pointed epigrams in *Adam Bede* to the brilliantly acid exchanges between Grandcourt and Gwendolen in *Daniel Deronda*. Virginia *Woolf was wrong to maintain that George Eliot's mind was too slow and cumbersome to lend itself to comedy, for the wit and *humour of the early *essays is carried over into the fiction to create various forms of comic effect through dialogue: from the broad comedy of Mrs Poyser, or the Dodson sisters in *The Mill on the Floss*, to the dramatic scene, both comic and moving, in which Catherine Arrowpoint tells her parents of her determination to marry the musician Klesmer (*DD* 22).

The speech of the characters and the voice of the narrator can also draw on the language and cadences of the *Bible, as in the case of the preacher Dinah Morris in *Adam Bede* and in the visionary discourse of Mordecai in *Daniel Deronda*. George Eliot's thorough knowledge of the King James Version of the Old and New Testaments is altogether an important resource that contributes to the stylistic richness and variety of her writing.

The syntactical complexity of her sentences and the learned nature of her diction—sometimes described as Johnsonian—have led to accusations of stylistic ponderousness and pedantry, but complexity is usually deployed in the service of careful discrimination (Harvey 1961: 210), while there is an ironic self-consciousness about the level of language she is using and a lightness of touch to offset any solemnity. Weightiness is only one component of a style that is more varied and versatile than is sometimes assumed. See also GENRES; LANGUAGE; NAMES; 'NOTES ON FORM IN ART'. JMR

Harvey (1961).

Kroeber, Karl, *Styles in Fictional Structure: The Art of Jane Austen, Charlotte Brontë, George Eliot* (1971).

Sully, James (1842–1923), psychologist, who recalls in his memoirs George Eliot's 'captivating' smile, the 'charm' of her 'low-pitched voice', and her almost preternatural levels of sympathy with others (260). He first saw the Leweses at St James's Hall and noted their response to the music (259). Sully shared Eliot's love of *music and became a frequent participant in musical evenings at The *Priory.

Sully records Eliot advocating the 'Meliorism' (see PROGRESS) by which she mediated between optimism and pessimism (264). He helped Eliot revise the final volumes of G. H. *Lewes's *Problems of Life and Mind* after his death. An important influence on Sigmund *Freud amongst others, he stressed the debt which the study of psychology owed to biological science and elaborated the psychological theories of scientists such as Herbert *Spencer and Lewes. Sully's work, including his perceptive accounts of dream and memory, suggests some significant affinities with Eliot's writing. See also OBITUARIES; REPUTATION, CRITICAL. DdSC

Sully, James, *My Life and Friends: A Psychologist's Memories* (1918).

Swift, Jonathan (1667–1745), Anglo-Irish writer of poetry and prose, satirist, clergyman. George

Eliot first mentions him obliquely in 1839 (*L* i. 24) where she quotes his remark on 'paper-sparing Pope'. Nearly twenty-one years later she compares *Keats's bitter inscription on his tombstone to Swift's epitaph on his monument in St Patrick's Cathedral, Dublin (a Latin sentence which means 'Where fierce indignation can no longer tear his heart', *L* iii. 288). Later, while recommending Charles Lee Lewes (see LEWES FAMILY) to read William Makepeace *Thackeray's *Lectures on the English Humourists*, she notes that his portrait of Swift is more exaggerated than in *Esmond* (*L* iv. 91): Swift's much-quoted phrase 'sweetness and light' from *The Battle of the Books* (1704) occurs in a letter to Mrs Mark Pattison in 1873 following the wide currency it obtained from Matthew *Arnold's *Culture and Anarchy* (1859). There are mentions of *Gulliver's Travels* (1726) in *Middlemarch* (*MM* 15, 32), Laputa being specifically cited in 'A *Word for the Germans' (*Pall Mall Gazette*, 7 March 1865) and *Impressions of Theophrastus Such* (*TS* 3). GRH

Swinburne, Algernon Charles (1837–1909). English poet who compared George Eliot unfavourably with Charlotte Brontë, seeing her as belonging to the first order of intellect but not, like Brontë, to the first order of genius. Eliot makes no mention of his poetry in her *letters and *journals, but G. H. *Lewes refers to him in passing, complaining to John *Blackwood that *The Times* had not noticed the first two parts of *Middlemarch*, 'though if Swinburne has a cold' it would certainly have been reported (*L* v. 247). Lewes considered him a minor poet, though he persuaded Lord Houghton (see MILNES, RICHARD MONCKTON) to review 'Chastelard' in the *Fortnightly Review* in April 1866. In July 1913 Mrs Clifford, writing in the *Nineteenth Century*, reported that George Eliot 'considered *Bothwell* the finest of his long poems, and its second act a wonderful thing'. Eliot also spoke of Swinburne's attack on her in *A Note on Charlotte Brontë* (1877), being angered by his suggestion that she had borrowed from Elizabeth *Gaskell's *The Moorland Cottage* for *The Mill on the Floss*. Eliot probably saw this after Lewes's death. This determined attempt to undermine her reputation includes such rhetorical vituperation as 'Having no taste for the dissection of dolls, I shall leave Daniel Deronda in his natural place above the ragshop door; and having no ear for the melodies of a Jew's harp, I shall leave the Spanish Gypsy to perform on that instrument to such audience as she may collect' (*Note on Brontë*, 21–2). GRH

Barrett, Dorothea, 'The Politics of Sado-Masochism: Swinburne and George Eliot', in Rikky Rooksby and Nicholas Shrimpton (edd.), *The Whole Music of Passion: New Essays on Swinburne* (1993).

Switzerland

Switzerland was the first country on the European continent in which George Eliot made an extended stay. After her father's death she spent the winter of 1849–50 lodging with the *D'Albert Durades in *Geneva. In 1856 she and G. H. *Lewes decided to send Lewes's sons (see LEWES FAMILY) to a Swiss school at Hofwyl near Berne, and the couple paid visits to Switzerland in the summers of 1859 and 1860 in connection with that schooling. In 1868 and 1876 she and Lewes enjoyed summer holidays in the Swiss mountains. See also KELLER, GOTTFRIED; ROUSSEAU, JEAN-JACQUES; TRAVELS.   JMR

symbolism. George Eliot's most revealing comments on the subject of symbolism occur in a few brief exchanges in *Middlemarch*: when Dorothea, on learning that Ladislaw plans to paint Tamburlane as a symbol of the world's physical progress, exclaims 'What a difficult kind of shorthand!'; when Adolf Naumann speaks of searching, towards his own symbolic ends, for the 'idealistic in the real' (*MM* 22); when, describing Naumann's portrait of Casaubon as Aquinas, Mr Brooke calls it 'symbolical' and therefore 'the higher style of art'; and when he adds that in such art Casaubon must be completely 'at home' (*MM* 34). Closer to the German Romantics (see ROMANTICISM) than to the *symbolistes* in France and probably influenced by Thomas *Carlyle's chapter 'Symbols' in *Sartor Resartus*, Eliot clearly thinks of symbolism as a means of effecting a synthesis between *philosophy and literature—between the concepts in which are grounded the themes and structures of her novels and the characters and actions that instantiate and explore them—and of embedding, in concrete narratives concerned with individual lives, levels of universal truth. Casaubon is not at home in such 'higher' art (the 'higher' style of art in the sense of 'Higher' Criticism) but Brooke believes he ought to be because the ideas it frequently carries are those religious, transcendent verities which, dissociated from their creeds and placed in the human imagination, Eliot still (and increasingly so as her fictional thought matured) invoked to counter what she saw as the empiricism, the secularism, the materialism of her age.

Eliot is not unaware of the difficulty symbolism presents to a reader: the 'lines and lights of the human countenance', she writes ironically in *The Mill on the Floss*, 'are like other symbols—not always easy to read without a key' (*MF* 3.7). 'Signs', she writes again in *Middlemarch*, 'are small measurable things' while 'interpretations are illimitable' (*MM* 3). But so essential does she consider the ability to perceive the world in this symbolic manner that it is often in her fiction the distinctive mark of the visionary, as in the case of Mordecai in

Daniel Deronda who invariably thinks in symbols. Its absence, as in Tom Tulliver who is described as wholly 'deficient' in the 'power of apprehending signs' (*MF* 1.4), is always seen as a deadly flaw.

If *realism is implicitly a repudiation of paradigms, Eliot's symbolism qualifies hers, framing her mimetic narratives—intended to offer 'a faithful account of men and things' as she has observed them (*AB* 17)—with a poetic scaffolding which gives formal and substantive coherence to her fiction, while at the same time serving to explicate reality or guide it to an ideal end. See also MYTH.   FB

Bonaparte, Felicia, '*Middlemarch*: The Genesis of Myth in the English Novel', *Religion and Literature*, 8 (1981).

Dale, Peter, 'Symbolic Representation and the Means of Revolution in *Daniel Deronda*', *Victorian Newsletter*, 59 (1981).

Swann, Brian, '*Middlemarch*: Realism and Symbolic Form', *ELH* 39 (1972).

sympathy. In her last essay for the *Westminster Review*, *'Worldliness and Other-Worldliness: The Poet Young' (January 1857; repr. in *Essays*) George Eliot stated that 'in proportion as morality is emotional, i.e., has affinity with Art, it will exhibit itself in direct sympathetic feeling and action, and not as the recognition of a rule' (*Essays*, 379). This concept informs George Eliot's entire canon and, with variations, is repeatedly expressed. 'If Art does not enlarge men's sympathies, it does nothing morally', she wrote in 1859 (*L* iii. 111).

Before she had finished 'Mr Gilfil's Love-Story', the second story in *Scenes of Clerical Life*, her first published fiction, John *Blackwood suggested to her that Mr Gilfil showed signs of becoming too abject as a lover, while the heroine, Caterina, should be given 'a little more dignity to her character' (*L* ii. 297). Replying that her stories always grew out of her 'psychological conception of the dramatis personae', George Eliot added: 'My artistic bent is directed not at all to the presentation of eminently irreproachable characters, but to the presentation of mixed human beings in such a way as to call forth tolerant judgment, pity, and sympathy' (*L* ii. 299). This association of tolerance, pity, and fellow feeling characterizes her presentation of individuals throughout her works.

Sympathy is 'the one poor word which includes all our best insight and our best love', says the narrator in *Adam Bede* (*AB* 50), and it is indeed a word that occurs frequently in George Eliot's writings. The degree to which her protagonists are endowed with the capacity for human sympathy is invariably the key to how the reader is meant to judge them. It is George Eliot's most cherished moral virtue, and is bestowed, for example, abundantly on Dinah Morris in *Adam Bede*, but withheld from Hetty Sorrel's nature. Maggie Tulliver in *The Mill on the Floss*, Romola, and Dorothea Brooke and Lydgate in *Middlemarch*, all share this capacity, which perhaps exhibits its most ideal embodiment in Daniel Deronda, whose 'early-awakened sensibility and reflectiveness had developed into a many-sided' and 'plenteous, flexible sympathy' (*DD* 32).

George Eliot's doctrine or principle of sympathy springs from her own 'plenteous, flexible sympathy'. Sympathy, Forest Pyle suggests, is what George Eliot employs as 'the means by which the Romantic wound opened by the imagination is to be sutured, the break closed'. Pointing out that imagination and sympathy are 'terms with close genealogies in British literary and philosophical texts of the eighteenth and nineteenth centuries', and that 'the close cultural affiliations between sympathy and the imagination can make the two concepts difficult to distinguish', Pyle claims that, in George Eliot, there is a divergence between the two. 'While Eliot presents both sympathy and imagination as the effects of a Romantic desire to extend consciousness, . . . sympathy, unlike the imagination, is the medium of resolution' (149–50). See also ART; MORAL VALUES.   BG

Noble, Thomas A., 'The Doctrine of Sympathy', in *George Eliot's 'Scenes of Clerical Life'* (1965).

Pyle, Forest, *The Ideology of Imagination* (1995).

T

Tauchnitz, Christian Bernhard (1816–95), German publisher in Leipzig well known for his paperback reprints of English novels. He secured the rights for the continental reprint of all George Eliot's novels except *Middlemarch*, where G. H. *Lewes negotiated better terms from his rival Asher in Berlin. Asher paid £327 compared with the £100 Tauchnitz had paid for *The Mill on the Floss*, although that was already more than Tauchnitz paid for most novelists except Charles *Dickens. The competition forced Tauchnitz to pay even more, £250, for *Daniel Deronda*. George Eliot met him in Leipzig in 1858 on her second visit to *Germany with Lewes, and in December 1859 he paid a visit to her at Holly Lodge (see HOMES), when she described him as 'a tall fresh-complexioned, small-featured, smiling man, in a wig' (*Journals*, 83). See also EARNINGS; PUBLISHERS, NEGOTIATIONS WITH.   JMR

Nowell-Smith, Simon, 'Firma Tauchnitz 1837–1900', *Book Collector*, 15 (1966).

Taylor, Jeremy (1613–67), English divine. George Eliot admiringly paraphrases a passage from Taylor in a letter of 4 June 1841 (*L* i. 95); *Holy Living* and *Holy Dying* are among the devotional works read by Adam Bede (*AB* 19) and Mr Tulliver (*MF* 1.3); and Dorothea Brooke 'knew many passages of . . . Jeremy Taylor by heart' (*MM* 1). George Eliot was attracted not only by Taylor's richly imaginative style and by the fervour of his moral writings but also by his syncretic theology, which draws on Neoplatonist thought and the Kabbala, connecting ordinary human experience with transcendental insights. A striking instance is the chapter epigraph in *Daniel Deronda* (*DD* 60), taken from a sermon in which Taylor, citing the prophet Daniel as an example, reflects on the special gift required to understand the 'secret' truth of Scripture.   TCC

Taylor, Peter Alfred (1819–91) and **Clementia** (d. 1908), friends of George Eliot from her earliest days in London, when she met Clementia (née Doughty) at 142 Strand. The Taylors, both political Radicals, had married in 1842. Peter, a grandson of Samuel Courtauld, founder of the great silk firm, was involved in Italian freedom movements when Eliot made his acquaintance, being a friend and supporter of Giuseppe *Mazzini. He served as Liberal MP for Leicester 1862–84.

Clementia, at one time governess to Peter's sisters, identified particularly with women's issues, the suffrage most of all, though she was unable to carry George Eliot with her (see WOMAN QUESTION). Her support for women was individual as well as abstract. She made a point of visiting in the early 1860s despite George Eliot's variously motivated protestations that 'I have found it a necessity of my London life to make the rule of *never* paying visits' (*L* iii. 397–8). Given her staunchness, she might well have been pained to be informed of Eliot's marriage by proxy: George Eliot wrote in semi-apology on 2 August 1880, 'Do not reproach me . . . I value you as one of the purest-minded, gentlest-hearted women I have ever known' (*L* vii. 308–9).   MAH

technology. George Eliot's interest in technology and its impact is memorably dramatized, for instance, in the perturbation occasioned by the advance of the railway in *Middlemarch*. While she did not live to experience the internal combustion engine, towards the end of her life she encountered some of the inventions which revolutionized communications technology. Oscar *Browning in his *Life of George Eliot* (1890) tells of her interest in the operation of an American typewriter which had been given to him (125). She wrote to Barbara *Bodichon on 17 January 1878, 'What do you say to the Phonograph, which can report gentlemen's bad speeches with all their stammering?' (*L* vii. 7). A little later she attended a demonstration of the telephone with G. H. *Lewes, commenting, 'It is very wonderful, very useful' (*L* vii. 16 n.). She noted receipt and despatch of telegrams in her journal for 1879 (*Journals*, 179, 186). See also PROGRESS.   MAH

television adaptations of George Eliot's works have been fewer than radio dramatizations (which have most often been of *Adam Bede* and *The Mill on the Floss*, least often if at all of *Scenes of Clerical Life*, *Romola*, and *Felix Holt, the Radical*) and fewer also than film or theatrical treatments. Television versions of novels by any of Jane *Austen, the *Brontës, Charles *Dickens, and Anthony *Trollope far outnumber adaptations of George Eliot's works. This entry includes only television versions shown in serial episodes: for full-length films 'made for television', see FILM.

There were television serials of *Silas Marner* in 1964, *The Mill on the Floss* in 1965, *Middlemarch* in 1968. The most important adaptations have been those of George Eliot's last two novels, both of which were originally published in half-volume parts and hence may lend themselves particularly to serialization. In 1970 there was a memorable early colour serial, in six episodes, of *Daniel Deronda*, dramatized by Alexander Baron, produced by David Conroy, and directed by Martin Craft, with Robert Hardy as Grandcourt, John Nolan as Deronda, and Martha Henry as Gwendolen. Robert Hardy also appeared, splendidly, as Mr Brooke, in the 1994 *Middlemarch*, possibly the most popular adaptation of any of George Eliot's works in any medium. Other members of the cast were Juliet Aubrey (Dorothea), Patrick Malahide (Casaubon), and Rufus Sewell (Ladislaw). The co-production of the British Broadcasting Corporation and the Boston, Mass., Public Broadcasting System, with script by Andrew Davies, Anthony Page as director, and Louis Marks as producer, had a budget of over £6 million for its six episodes (about six and a half hours' viewing). Its ratings in the United Kingdom were high, and in one week the novel topped the paperback bestseller list. Andrew Davies proclaimed to the London *Evening Standard* 'a private and arrogant conviction that, in some ways, a dramatic adaptation might actually enhance the story', and while there were inevitably dissenting voices, most admirers of George Eliot appeared to find this television version an authentic reading of *Middlemarch*. See also THEATRICAL ADAPTATIONS. MAH

Tenby, focal point of Eliot's early happiness when she stayed there 14–24 July 1843 with the *Brays, *Hennells, and Rufa *Brabant. She returned with G. H. *Lewes thirteen years later, leaving *Ilfracombe 26 June 1856 intent on their seaside studies at Tenby, particularly of molluscs and medusae (see 'SEA-SIDE STUDIES'). On 29 July she told Sara that their visit had been of zoological value, but the place was dull and vulgar in comparison with Ilfracombe. Nevertheless it was at Tenby that Lewes suggested to her that she write fiction and she 'dreamed' the title of her first story (*L* ii. 407). See 'HOW I CAME TO WRITE FICTION'. GRH

Tennyson, Alfred (1809–92), poet, to whom George Eliot was introduced by Mrs Blackwood in 1858, and with whom she later developed a cordial friendship. At Shottermill in 1871, and later at Witley (see HOMES), Eliot and G. H. *Lewes found themselves neighbours to the Tennysons, and the acquaintance was continued in London through a series of visits, dinners, and readings. From the poet's wife, Emily, we have a memorable impression of George Eliot's 'soft soprano voice, which almost sounds like a fine falsetto' (see VOICE OF GEORGE ELIOT) and 'her strong, masculine face' (*Memoir*, ii. 107); and Eliot provides an equally vivid impression of Tennyson after reading to an appreciative audience: 'I saw an expression in his face that always reminds me of a large dog laying down its ears and wagging its tail on being stroked and patted' (*L* ix. 237). In 1878 Eliot and Lewes attended the wedding in Westminster Abbey of Tennyson's younger son Lionel, who later represented his father at George Eliot's funeral.

As a literary celebrity, Tennyson (who had been appointed Poet Laureate in 1850, and would be created baron in 1883) was a significant reference point in Eliot's professional self-awareness. In praise of *Felix Holt, the Radical* Frederic *Harrison told her that he knew of families where 'the volumes have been read chapter by chapter and line by line and reread and cited as are the stanzas of *In Memoriam*' (*L* iv. 285); and Tennyson had been one of several writers to whom Eliot sent a copy of *Scenes of Clerical Life* in 1858. When John *Blackwood proposed a cheap edition of *The Spanish Gypsy* in 1868, the 6 shilling edition of Tennyson's *Idylls of the King* suggested itself as an obvious model (*L* iv. 480), just as the Library Edition of his works (which Eliot rushed out to buy the day before he was due to read at The *Priory in 1877) was an equally obvious model for the complete edition of her works that she and Blackwood were pondering (*L* vi. 358). (Both precedents were rejected on aesthetic grounds.) That Eliot's linguistic consciousness was steeped in Tennyson's poetry is suggested by the casual familiarity with which she quotes it throughout her letters; the quotation is invariably continuous with her own syntax. His poetry was also part of her emotional life: several accounts of Tennyson reading 'Guinevere' in 1871 have George Eliot in tears; and after Lewes's death she took to intensive reading of *In Memoriam* (1850), parts of which she copied into her journal. But her admiration was qualified, and the poetry of Tennyson's that Eliot liked best was the poetry that was least like her own (see POETRY). Her harsh, anonymous review of *Maud* in the *Westminster Review* (October 1855), written before she had met Tennyson, is prefaced by generous praise of 'Ulysses', 'Locksley Hall', 'Morte d'Arthur' (all published in 1842), of the 'lyrical gems' in *The Princess* (1847), and of *In Memoriam* for its 'sanctification of human love as religion'. She held to this judgement, telling John Walter *Cross in 1877 that she regarded *In Memoriam* as 'the chief of the larger works', but that she considered 'some smaller wholes among the lyrics as the works most decisive of Tennyson's high place among the immortals' (*L* vi. 416). Her critique of *Maud* is driven by her novelist's awareness, for her review of the poem supplies the narrative which is so dispersed through the poem's complicated structure; but it is also that of a poet drawn to dramatic forms, and her central insight (which must have stung Tennyson) is that that poem's dramatic mask of madness fails to disguise the poet's identification with his hero's morbidity. Nevertheless, Tennyson's opinion always counted with her, and in 1874, when *Middlemarch* was selling splendidly, his thoughtless remark, 'Everybody writes so well now', seriously disconcerted her (*L* vi. 76).

Most of Eliot's novels are set before Tennyson's first significant publications in 1830 and 1832, and his poetry is not quoted in the novels. However, the portrait of Arthur Donnithorne in *Adam Bede* may owe something to the 'great broad-shouldered genial Englishman' Sir Walter Vivian of *The Princess* (1847) as the ideal English squire to whom the flawed Arthur will never measure up (*AB* 5); and the 'bad practices' of which Felix Holt complains in his **'Address to Working Men'*— 'commercial lying', 'adulteration of goods', 'political bribery'—are the core of Tennyson's social criticism in *Maud*. When Eliot began heading chapters with *epigraphs she turned to Tennyson as rarely as she did to other living authors, and then with mixed success. In the first edition of *Daniel Deronda*, ll. 75–6 of 'Locksley Hall' (a poem which Eliot had said in 1855 was 'so familiar that we dare not quote it') were misquoted, mislineated, and attributed to *In Memoriam* (*DD* 17). But in *Felix Holt* eight lines of *In Memoriam* (one stanza from each of sections 85 and 129) are beautifully proleptic of Esther's developing feelings (*FH* 43).

In December 1871 an article in the *Spectator*, 'The Idealism of George Eliot and Mr Tennyson', compares and contrasts *Middlemarch* with Tennyson's most recent Arthurian poem 'The Last Tournament'. Tennyson's faith in divine purpose swings the comparison in his favour, and while the title acknowledges Eliot as Tennyson's literary comrade, it is natural that he should have loomed larger in her imagination than she did in his. He considered *Scenes*, *Adam Bede*, and *Silas Marner* as her best novels, and he told his wife that with *Romola* Eliot got 'somewhat out of her depth' (*Memoir*, ii. 107). Nevertheless, Robert *Browning found him reading it in bed (*L* iv. 96), and Eliot records him speaking of it 'with unbounded admiration' (*L* iv. 102). His opinion of the later novels, or of her poetry, is not known, which suggests that he did not consider her a rival; and, ever obsessive about reviewers, he can never have known of Eliot's authorship of the *Westminster*

notice of *Maud*. Their friendship was always warm and good-natured because they genuinely liked each other, and because they each knew how to treat difficult topics. The closest they came to discussing 'her want of belief in an after-life' was at one of their partings when Tennyson, a self-professed believer, pressed her hand and wished her well with her molecules. She replied that she got on very well with them (*Memoir*, ii. 226).   SP

Tennyson, Hallam, Alfred, *Lord Tennyson: A Memoir by his Son*, 2 vols. (1897).

Thackeray, Anne Isabella (1837–1919), William Makepeace *Thackeray's eldest daughter, generally called Anny. She was her father's amanuensis, breaking into fiction herself with *The Story of Elizabeth*, derived from her youthful period in Paris (serialized in the **Cornhill Magazine* September 1862–January 1863, coinciding with parts 3–7 of *Romola*). On 5 September 1862 G. H. *Lewes worried that she hadn't sent the finale of the story before going abroad. Her best-known works are *The Village on the Cliff* (1867), *Old Kensington* (1873), *Miss Angel* (1875), and *Mrs Dymond* (1885). She contributed to the *DNB*, and wrote introductions to the Biographical Edition of her father's novels (1903). On 4 December 1865 George Eliot sent Mrs *Congreve *The Story of Elizabeth*, saying it was charmingly written. Anny was invited to The Heights after her marriage to Richmond Ritchie (later knighted) on 2 August 1877, an event welcomed by Eliot, who noted the age difference (he was seventeen years younger), ingenuously remarking that she knew several instances of young men who 'will often choose as their life's companion a woman whose attractions are wholly of the spiritual order' (*L* vi. 398). Anny responded with sensitivity and understanding to news of Eliot's marriage to John Walter *Cross (*L* vii. 284).

GRH

Thackeray, William Makepeace (1811–63), novelist. He was a great friend of John *Blackwood's, had appreciated G. H. *Lewes's review of *Vanity Fair* (1847–8), and, at the time of George Eliot's emergence, stood high in reputation and influence, hence George *Smith's invitation to him to edit the **Cornhill Magazine* which was launched in January 1860. In fact he was waning both in health and ability. He stayed with the *Brays when he lectured in Coventry 23 April 1855, and sent Lewes a letter (28 April) containing his reminiscences of *Weimar (the Pumpernickel of *Vanity Fair*) which was printed in 'The Closing Scenes' finale of *The Life of Goethe* (1855). In October 1854 in Weimar Eliot read *The Great Hoggarty Diamond* (1841) and in 1855 *The Newcomes* (1853–5). In the previous year in a letter to Cara Bray Eliot rejected Harriet *Martineau's put-down of

Vanity Fair in comparison with *The History of Henry Esmond* (1852) by stressing the similarities, saying 'Lady C is Amelia, Esmond is Dobbin, Trix is Becky' (*L* ii. 157). By 11 June 1857 she was somewhat flattered to be thought a disciple of Thackeray's: she rejects the idea but observes that most people of 'any intellect' would consider him to be on the whole 'the most powerful of living novelists' (*L* ii. 349).

She was anxious to know Thackeray's reaction to *Scenes of Clerical Life* and had a presentation copy sent to him in January 1858. When she revealed her identity to John Blackwood (28 February 1858) he reported to her that Thackeray had spoken highly of *Scenes*, but had unequivocally asserted that they were not written by a woman. Intrigued as she was, she and Lewes were aware of the decline in Thackeray's own writing: Eliot told Sara *Hennell shortly after the final instalment of 'Janet's Repentance' was issued, that they were disappointed with the first number of *The Virginians* (1857–9) with its 'recurrence of the everlasting type—the old lady courted for her money and fond of champagne' (*L* ii. 401). Although George Smith could report that Thackeray spoke warmly of 'The Sad Fortunes of the Reverend Amos Barton', he later admitted that though he admired Eliot he couldn't read her books. A typical Thackerayan snippet of humour caused him to refer to Lewes as 'Mr Bede'. Blackwood drew a comparison between Eliot and Thackeray in respect of 'Janet's Repentance', writing on 8 June 1857 that the third clerical scene, in which he found the alcoholism and wife-beating unpalatable, or feared that readers of 'Maga' would, was 'written in the harsher Thackerayan view of human nature' (*L* ii. 344).

Lewes was initially flattered by Thackeray's invitation to him to contribute to the *Cornhill*, proudly telling his sons about it, but by May 1860, five months after the launch, Eliot is wondering whether Thackeray has 'gathered up his slack reins' in the magazine (*L* iii. 300). By July 1861, eighteen months before Thackeray's death, Lewes is commenting on Thackeray's bitterness over the failure of his own recent work and his jealousy (even of his friend *Trollope) of those who are successful, though he acknowledges the admirable work that Thackeray has done (*L* iii. 434). Eight months later Thackeray resigned from the *Cornhill*. He died on 24 December 1863, Lewes attending the funeral (1 January 1864) at Kensal Green with 'a very large gathering—between 1000 and 1500 people; among them most of the artistic and literary celebrities' (*L* iv. 126).

Although Eliot greatly admired the Thackeray of *Vanity Fair* and *Esmond* (she considered the latter a fine book but also thought it a disturbingly uncomfortable one, recognizing the sweep, the power, the omnipresent morality of his work), there is little suggestion that she was directly influenced either by his methods or his content in her own work. She recommended Charles Lee Lewes (see LEWES FAMILY) to read the lectures on the English humourists, though she found the estimate of Jonathan *Swift and Joseph *Addison more distorted than in *Esmond*. She criticized Thackeray's praising of the second rate in terms of personality and work in the lectures as having a vitiating effect on them, though she found them admirable in other respects and a pleasure to read. When George Smith sent her a copy of *Esmond* in March 1863 she found her wish to reread it quickened while acknowledging that a ten-year gap meant that 'one gets a different person and finds new qualities in everything' (*L* iv. 79). Thackeray's parodic prodigality, his looseness of structure in the later works, the tone which can run the gamut from satire to sentiment, could hardly be found sympathetic by a writer intent on studied but certainly not overplayed *realism. Eliot's humour is based on provincial observation and a naturally ironic perspective, Thackeray's on cosmopolitan experience incorporated into a sardonically ironic stance. Eliot wrote to the Brays in November 1852 of *Esmond*: 'The hero is in love with the daughter all through the book, and marries the mother at the end' (*L* ii. 67). This comment comes before she had expressed her own theories of fiction in her *Westminster Review* articles and reviews and then put them into practice. The epilogues in *Scenes*, *Adam Bede*, *The Mill on the Floss*, and *Middlemarch* are a summary continuation (see ENDINGS), just as Thackeray at the end of *Vanity Fair* (in chapter 67) finishes his novel but practically concludes with a section on what happened afterwards. Eliot responded to Thackeray's varied and generally stimulating output, but her great provincial novels are far from the cosmopolitan ethos which marks the Thackerayan oeuvre, with her historical sense (except in *Romola*) enhanced by a realism derived from direct experience and association.   GRH

theatre. While George Eliot's love of music was nurtured in her early years and flourished always, her interest in theatre came later as she experienced it in a range of modes, from pantomime to classical drama. When she went to a pantomime in 1862, she wrote to Sara *Hennell, 'Ah, what I should have felt in my real child-days, to have been let into the further history of Mother Hubbard and her Dog!' (*L* iv. 10) She took care to ensure that younger generations did not lack such opportunities, treating Georgiana *Burne-Jones and her son Philip, rising 5 years old, to a pantomime in

January 1869. By the time she took Roland Stuart in 1878, the thrill had waned: 'It was a wild delight to him and a dreariness to us' (L vii. 13).

During her youthful evangelical phase, however, she found the idea of theatrical performance offensive to the extent that on her first visit to *London in 1838, she refused to accompany her brother Isaac to the theatre. Her principles modified, in 1845 she went to Birmingham with the *Brays 'to see Macready act Brutus! I was not disappointed on the whole, and it was a real treat, notwithstanding a ranting Cassius and a fat, stumpy Caesar and a screeching Calpurnia' (L i. 195–6). When she went to live in *London in the 1850s, she began to go often to the theatre, frequently seeing both high- and lowbrow productions. She was often in company with Herbert *Spencer, with whom she saw 'a French piece (done by Mr. G. H. Lewes)', The Chain of Events, at the Lyceum in April 1852. In a characteristically pungent comment, she remarked: 'It is a very long chain and drags rather heavily. No sparkle, but a sort of Dickens-like sentimentality all through . . . As a series of tableaux I never saw anything equal to it. But to my mind it is execrable moral taste to have a storm and shipwreck with all its horrors on the stage. I could only scream and cover my eyes' (L ii. 18). In June 1853 she went with G. H. *Lewes 'to see Rachel again' in Adrienne Lecouvreur, observing that 'I have not yet seen the "Vashti" of Currer Bell in Rachel' (L ii. 104) (see RACHEL). Over the years, George Eliot was to see many of the major actors of her time perform: she first saw Ristori in Medea in London in 1857, and saw later performances in other plays in London and Rome; she saw Fechter, Salvini, Coquelin, Sarah *Bernhardt, Henry Irving.

Lewes's involvement in the theatre as playwright, drama critic, and sometime actor, was influential on George Eliot. Their honeymoon in *Germany in 1854 set the pattern for their life together in various ways, not least attendance at the theatre in *Weimar where they saw plays by Freytag, Kotzebue, and Ploetz, as well as farces and vaudevilles. When they moved on to *Berlin, they again saw a number of popular pieces along with G. E. *Lessing's Nathan der Weise and Emilia Galotti. They saw a good deal of the actor Ludwig Dessoir, both on stage and socially. He sought them out, and visited on a number of evenings, when there was discussion and declamation of *Shakespeare. At this time, in addition to extensive study of *Goethe (including his plays) for Lewes's study of him, Eliot and Lewes embarked on a steady diet of Shakespeare in their regular programme of reading aloud to each other.

Back in England, their theatregoing was curtailed, for economy, perhaps, and because they chose to set up house out of central London, distancing themselves from old haunts and potential scandal about their liaison. In September 1856 George Eliot reported her first expedition to the theatre since their return from Germany early in 1855. It was not until 1860 when they moved back to central London and Charles Lewes (see LEWES FAMILY) returned from Hofwyl to live with them that their theatregoing became frequent once more. Living close to the Marylebone Theatre, and with a young man in the house, such pieces as 'the Pirate of the Savannah!' (3 August 1861, Journals, 99) made a break from research for Romola. Late in 1860, John *Blackwood at Lewes's instigation proposed 'a Theatrical Article from you at Christmas', suggesting 'you might do a first-rate thing about London theatres and audiences and the process of acquiring the requisite experience would be a diversion' (L iii. 355), but George Eliot declined.

Lewes extravagantly declared in 1869 'because we never go to the theatre in London, we hugely enjoy it abroad' (L viii. 445). Though the first part of his claim must be qualified, there can be little doubt of their enjoyment of theatre abroad. In *Paris early in 1865 they went to the theatre six nights out of ten, a record eclipsed on a later visit, in 1874, when Lewes claimed 'We went every night to the theatre' (L vi. 86). On their travels they were catholic but not uncritical in their attendance at theatrical performances from *Munich to St Malo, Berlin to Barcelona.

There were times when George Eliot considered writing for the theatre, usually at Lewes's suggestion. The possibility of her writing a play for Helen *Faucit was discussed in early 1864: Eliot noted 'G. went to see Helen Faucit on business of mine' (Journals, 119), and they went to Glasgow expressly to see her act (they saw her also in London at different times). A fragmentary outline of three acts of 'Savello' appears to have been drafted by Lewes (L iv. 132), but the scheme did not come to anything. However, at this period Eliot was particularly interested in dramatic form, and by September 1864 she was 'trying a drama on a subject that has fascinated me' (Journals, 120), a work which after much labour and many transmutations became The Spanish Gypsy.

In the end, the theatre killed her. She told Edith Simcox that she had taken a chill during a performance of Agamemnon, given in Greek by Oxford undergraduates at St George's Hall, Langham Place, on 17 December 1880 (though John Walter *Cross blamed a draught at the Saturday Popular Concert the following day). To the last, George Eliot's intellectual powers were on the stretch: 'The representation was a great enjoyment—an exciting stimulus—and my wife proposed that during the winter we should read together some of

the great Greek dramas' (Cross, iii. 437). See also
MUSIC; THEATRICAL ADAPTATIONS.   MAH

theatrical adaptations. George Eliot was emphatic in her refusal to countenance theatrical
adaptations of her writings: 'I can have nothing
whatever to do with the adaptation of my work to
the stage, and I must decline to have my name
connected with any such adaptation', she wrote to
quash hopes of performing *Daniel Deronda* (1 February 1880, *L* ix. 288), though G. H. *Lewes had
played with the idea in April 1879: 'Sketched a
scene and characters for stage version of Deronda'
(*L* vii. 13 n.). There was a moderately successful
Daniel Deronda at the Q Theatre, London, in 1927.
   In Eliot's lifetime there were unauthorized
adaptations, however, such as J. E. Carpenter's
Adam Bede for the Surrey Theatre in 1862, which
dilutes George Eliot's focus on the aspirations of
women as different as Dinah Morris and Hetty
Sorrel: Dinah is reduced to the role of Hetty's
confidante, and the question of Hetty's guilt and
repentance defused. Hetty turns out 'to be guilty
of nothing—the dead child was not hers at all, but
belonged to gypsies, and Arthur Donnithorne, as
the audience learns just before the final curtain,
was married to her all along!'—but felt constrained to conceal his marriage to conserve his inheritance (Kerry Powell, *Women and Victorian
Theatre* (1997), 108–9). It was easier to produce
unauthorized adaptations in the USA, where such
unlikely items as Mary L. Cobb, *Poetical Dramas
for Home and School. The Spanish Gypsy arranged
from George Eliot* (1873) appeared.
   On 27 September 1876, Lewes noted in his journal: 'In the evening private box at the Haymarket
to see *Dan'l Druce*, a piece partly founded on "Silas
Marner." Wretched stuff, poorly acted' (*L* viii.
303). This was Sir William Gilbert's *Dan'l Druce,
Blacksmith* in which the motif of redemption
through a lost child echoes *Silas Marner* though
the play is in no sense an adaptation of the novel.
An anonymous version of *Silas Marner* under the
title *Effie's Angel* was produced at Sheffield in 1871.
A libretto (Rachel Trickett) and score (John
Joubert, opus 31, dated March 1959–August 1960)
for *Silas Marner: an opera in three acts after the
novel by George Eliot* are at the Nuneaton Central
Library.
   A version of *The Mill on the Floss* was produced
in *Nuneaton in 1919 for the centenary of George
Eliot's birth. Other adaptations this century seem
mainly to have been for amateur performances.
However, a new approach to adapting George
Eliot emerged in the 1990s. In his adaptation of
Adam Bede (1990) Geoffrey Beevers tackled the
problem of representing the narrator's voice by
sharing it among the cast, attributing a passage of

omniscient *narration to an appropriate character, who delivered that speech directly to the audience so as to offer immediate insights on the
action. Beevers has also adapted *Silas Marner*
(1998). In 1994, Helen Edmundson made a much-
acclaimed *The Mill on the Floss* for the Ipswich-
based Shared Experience Theatre Company, in
which at some points the whole cast appears as a
crowd or chorus wordlessly externalizing the
tensions George Eliot presents in the narrator's
commentary. Edmundson also used the device of
having Maggie played by three actors to project
the character's struggles and self-doubt. In both
Beevers's and Edmundson's adaptations, actors
double roles, in part for economy, but to telling effect: thus Maggie's father and the father figure of
Dr Kenn are played by the same actor, as are her
champions Bob Jakin and Philip Wakem (this
actor also does the kindly but ineffectual Uncle
Pullet). See also FILMS; TELEVISION ADAPTATIONS;
THEATRE.   MAH

Thoreau, Henry David (1817–62), American
writer and naturalist, whose *Walden* (1854) George
Eliot praised in January 1856 for its author's union
of a deep poetic sensibility with a keen eye in observing nature. To readers who might question the
utility of living alone in a cabin by a pond, she
promised 'plenty of sturdy sense' (*Westminster Review*, 65: 302) in Thoreau's unworldliness and supplied key excerpts in illustration, italicizing several
epigrammatic passages (as Haight notes, 1968: 183)
like those found in her own novels. An example:
'Philanthropy is almost the only virtue which is
sufficiently appreciated by mankind. Nay, it is
greatly overrated; *and it is our selfishness which
overrates it*' (*Westminster Review*, 65: 303). This review (one of several favourable notices of *Walden*
written by women) also served George Eliot as an
occasion to take aim at 'people—very wise in their
own eyes—who would have every man's life
ordered according to a particular pattern' (302).
In chapter 15 of *Middlemarch* she used a related
image to introduce Lydgate, who never meant to
be one of 'the multitude of middle-aged men who
go about their vocations in a daily course determined for them much in the same way as the tie of
their cravats'. See also AMERICA; MORAL VALUES.
          KKC

Titian (Tiziano Vecellio, *c.*1487–1576), Venetian
painter. Titian was well represented from the early
days of the National Gallery in London, and
George Eliot would have known his work, including the famous *Bacchus and Ariadne* (1523), there.
   In 1858, she and G. H. *Lewes greatly admired
Titian's sumptuous Danae (*c.*1554) in *Vienna,
and in the *Dresden Picture Gallery they praised
what they believed to be a painting by Titian,

Venus (1508–10). To them the work was 'fit for its purity and sacred loveliness to hang in a temple with Madonnas' (Cross, ii. 59). Today this recumbent nude is attributed to Giorgione (1475–1510), with the proviso that Titian may have painted some areas left unfinished at Giorgione's death.

During their time in Dresden, Eliot and Lewes made daily visits to look at Titian's *Tribute Money* (*c*.1516), a painting which they liked so much that they hung up a print at The *Priory. George Eliot introduces the painting into *Daniel Deronda*, comparing Titian's skill in characterization to her own difficulties in describing the faces of Daniel and Mordecai: 'I wish I could perpetuate those two faces, as Titian's "Tribute Money" has perpetuated two types presenting another kind of contrast' (*DD* 40).

Earlier in the novel, Daniel is compared to the subject of another painting by Titian, almost certainly *The Man with a Glove* (*c*.1523) in the Louvre in *Paris. Daniel's hands, we are told, are 'long, flexible, firmly-grasping hands, such as Titian has painted in a picture where he wished to show the combination of refinement with force. And there is something of likeness, too, between the faces belonging to the hands—in both the uniform pale-brown skin, the perpendicular brow, the calmly penetrating eyes' (*DD* 17).

George Eliot and Lewes saw many works by Titian in *Venice in 1860. Two of his most famous paintings, *St Peter Martyr* (1530, now destroyed) and the *Assumption of the Virgin* (1516–18, now once more hanging in the Church of the Frari, but seen by George Eliot in the Accademia) particularly attracted them. Writing of the *Assumption*, George Eliot praised the expression of ecstasy on the Madonna's face, contrasting its healthiness with the pallor and sense of strain which she often found in such paintings. The figures of the Apostles at the foot of the painting, and of God the Father above, seemed to her inferior, but she believed that the central figure, the Virgin herself, ranked only slightly below that in *Raphael's *Sistine Madonna*. The Titian *Assumption* is probably the work to which George Eliot refers when, in chapter 17 of *Adam Bede*, she contrasts an ideal work of art to the paintings of the rustic Dutch school: 'a Madonna, turning her mild face upward and opening her arms to welcome the divine glory'.

George Eliot returned to Venice in 1864, and it was on this occasion that the *Annunciation* (1540) by Titian in the Scuola di San Rocco was pointed out to her. She was struck by this representation of a young woman facing a momentous destiny, and was inspired by it to write *The Spanish Gypsy*. It is also possible that the painting influenced the vocation theme of *Daniel Deronda*.

With the exception of the *Danae* and the misattributed *Venus*, George Eliot followed the taste of her day in admiring Titian's religious, rather than his mythical, works. Many Victorians found the latter excessively sensuous. An exception was made for certain of his portraits (although Lewes rated them lower than the religious works). In addition to the *Man with a Glove*, George Eliot is known to have admired *Titian's Daughter* (*c*.1850, *Girl with a Bowl of Fruit*) in the Picture Gallery in *Berlin. Titian has always been famous as a painter of colour, but it was apparently as a painter of profound feeling that George Eliot most valued him. See also VISUAL ARTS.   LO

Witemeyer (1979)

Tolstoy, Count Lev Nikolaevich (1828–1910), Russian novelist who read George Eliot's novels and included her amongst the authors who made a great impression on him between the ages of 35 and 50 (*Tolstoy's Letters*, ed. Christian, ii. 486), the period in which he wrote his greatest novels, *War and Peace* (1863–9) and *Anna Karenina* (1873–7). Since none of his writing was available in translation in George Eliot's lifetime—and Russian was one European language she did not know (see LANGUAGES)—his knowledge and respect were not reciprocated (as they were, for instance, in the case of his compatriot *Turgenev). In his letters Tolstoy singles out *Scenes of Clerical Life* and *Felix Holt, the Radical* for particular praise, although it is *Middlemarch* that seems to have the closest affinity with his own work, inviting comparison with *Anna Karenina* as a great multi-plotted novel in the tradition of European *realism. An American reviewer of *Anna Karenina* in the *Critic* in 1886 saw Tolstoy as a sort of double of George Eliot, maintaining that his novel had all the breadth and complexity, insight and profound analysis, power of generalization and lifelikeness, that were to be found in *Middlemarch*. Many later critics have followed this lead, some sensitively, like Barbara Hardy with her illuminating comparisons in *The Appropriate Form* (1964); others tendentiously, like Lord David Cecil in *Early Victorian Novelists* (1934), who finds *Middlemarch* drab, petty, and provincial by comparison with Tolstoy.

The suggestion that the English novel Anna is reading on the train from Moscow to St Petersburg is *Middlemarch* has no real evidence to support it—indeed, Tolstoy makes no mention of the work in his letters or journals—but it would be an appropriate pointer to the echoes of Eliot's novel in Tolstoy's. Like Dorothea, Anna is a passionate woman married to a passionless and pedantic man, but Tolstoy goes beyond the quiet misery of Dorothea to work out the tragic potential of the woman's predicament, showing how Anna's wholehearted commitment to a passionate love for another man, in defiance of her own conscience as well as social convention, culminates in suicidal despair. (In admiring *Felix Holt* Tolstoy may have been responding to the tragic figure of Mrs Transome and the way that she suffers the bitter consequences of an adulterous affair.) Karenin is as stifling in his effect on his wife as Casaubon but is more sympathetically and less ironically presented, while Levin's wife Kitty resembles the practical Celia, who is sometimes called by the same name. Like *Middlemarch* Tolstoy's novel traces the 'stealthy convergence of human lots' (*MM* 11), though that process may be even stealthier in that his characters' lives are not marked by those crises of moral decision, like Dorothea's (*MM* 80), that are so typical of George Eliot. Comparison between the two writers may tend to bring out the greater scope of Tolstoy's fiction, ranging as it does from intensely realized physical sensation to metaphysical speculation on the meaning of existence, but, as F. R. *Leavis (1948) maintained, it is in such company that George Eliot properly belongs, for at its best her work has a Tolstoyan depth and reality.   JMR

Tolstoy's Letters, ed. R. F. Christian, 2 vols. (1978).

Blumberg, Edwina J., 'Tolstoy and the English Novel: A Note on *Middlemarch* and *Anna Karenina*', *Slavic Review*, 30 (1971).

Hardy, Barbara, *The Appropriate Form* (1964).

Knapp, Shoshana, 'Tolstoy's Reading of George Eliot: Visions and Revision', *Slavic and East European Journal*, 27 (1983).

Leavis (1948).

Tractarian movement. This strictly begins with John Keble's (1792–1866) assize sermon in 1833, and George Eliot writes about it in letters to Maria *Lewis. The first mention is in May 1839 when the *Tracts for the Times* had reached a peak of popularity: according to John Walter *Cross's *Life* (i. 32) Isaac Evans had now taken up a High Church position and disliked his sister's evangelical fervour. Eliot is unable to stabilize her views but regards the religious controversy as being 'full of interest to me' as she seeks to discover 'the nature of the *visible* church' (*L* i. 25). She refers to 'the authors of the Oxford Tracts' paying 'their compliments to Rome, as a dear though erring Sister' (*L* i. 26), almost an anticipation of the later exodus. But she dislikes the fact that they ignore 'pious non-conformists'. Eliot was influenced by Isaac Taylor's *Ancient Christianity, and the Doctrines of the Oxford Tracts for The Times*, published in 1839–40, which asserted that the 4th-century Church 'upon which the Tractarians sought to graft the institutions of the English church was already corrupted with superstition' (*L* i. 63–4). In 'The Sad Fortunes of the Reverend Amos Barton'

Amos himself feels 'the effect of the Tractarian agitation' which was 'beginning to tell even on those who disavowed or resisted Tractarian doctrines' (*SC* 1.2).   GRH

trade unions and labour relations. None of George Eliot's novels depict the working conditions of people involved in manufacturing industries or the relationships and negotiations between trades unions and employers. None use the term 'labour relations', and only *Felix Holt, the Radical* mentions 'trades-unions'. In the novel's Introduction the narrator refers to Mr Sampson's coach rattling through the manufacturing towns, 'the scene of riots and trades-union meetings', and suggests that most 'rural Englishmen' saw Reform as 'a confused combination of rick-burners, trades-unions, Nottingham riots, and in general whatever required the calling-out of the yeomanry'. In chapter 20, a young farmer named Joyce considers Radicals and 'delegates from the trades-unions' to be one and the same; and in chapter 30, which describes the Nomination Day rally in Duffield, Felix's look of 'habitual meditative abstraction' is favourably compared with the 'rather hard-lipped antagonism of the trades-union man'.

These recollections and observations could be seen to indicate Eliot's disapproval of unions, an idea apparently supported elsewhere in *Felix Holt*. In chapter 3, for instance, the narrator notes the decline of tolerance and the concomitant rise of political agitation among Treby Magnians since the town 'took on the more complex life brought by mines and manufactures, which belong more directly to the great circulating system of the nation than to the local system'. And, again, in chapter 33, which describes Treby Magna's riot, Felix uneasily discerns among the crowd 'men of that keener aspect which is only common in manufacturing towns'. However, in her *'Address to Working Men, by Felix Holt', Eliot, in fact, promoted the idea of unions, although she argues that their main aim should be to work towards the good of society as well as the individual.

The rise of trade unions began in the early part of the 19th century and was immediately opposed by the Establishment. In 1815, unions were deemed illegal 'combinations', and only 'friendly societies', such as Benefit Clubs (mutual insurance societies protecting members against illness or the effects of old age) were condoned. By 1824–5, unions were tolerated, although as late as 1867 a court again ruled them illegal for falling outside the scope of the Friendly Societies Act of 1855. Trade-union activity tended to be stronger outside industrial towns and was for a time linked with *Chartism. Some Chartists belonged to the Utopian Grand National Consolidated Trades Union, which saw

tragedy

life for a few months in 1834 and tried to create a life of virtue and cooperation.

During the period 1850–68, plans for Grand National unions gave way to smaller unions made up of skilled men. The Amalgamated Society of Engineers was founded in 1851 and others soon followed. Though interested in general politics, these unions primarily asked for specific improvements in working conditions as well as the relaxation of the often unfair Master and Servant Act (the latter discriminated against workers and was eventually replaced by the Employers and Workmen Act of 1875). However, from 1866 onwards many unions once again urged each other to join ranks. The growing strength of the so-called 'labour aristocracy' culminated in the formation of the Trades Union Congress in 1868. What concerned Eliot, though, was the increased tendency of unions to join radical Liberals in demanding parliamentary reform without a due regard for political stability. See also INDUSTRIALISM; POLITICS; PROGRESS.

AvdB

tragedy, one of the many *genres George Eliot embedded in her narratives, was not for her a literary form as much as a philosophic idea. The essence of what she considered to be the tragedy of human existence never altered radically. It was, as she says in *Felix Holt, the Radical,* the collision of will and destiny (Introduction), an 'irreparable' conflict, as she further elaborates in her 'Notes on "The Spanish Gypsy" and Tragedy in General', 'between the individual and the general', between 'our individual needs' and the social or natural circumstances that make 'the dire necessities of our lot'. Our sympathies, she proceeds to say, always lie with the individual but it is of 'the general' that 'we recognize the irresistible power' (Cross, iii. 31–7).

Such sympathy for the individual echoes Aristotelian pity just as the power granted the general recalls Aristotelian terror. But, without repudiating these traditional tragic elements, Eliot reinvents the genre and redefines it for her time. When, for example, in describing Casaubon's futile efforts at scholarship, she speaks of his lot as one 'in which everything is below the level of tragedy except the passionate egoism of the sufferer' (*MM* 42), the key to our sympathy, it is evident, as well as to his tragedy, is not so much Aristotelian as Eliot's acceptance of the notion, grounded in the subjectivity of the empiricist point of view, that each individual not only stands at the centre of his own world but is entitled to do so, even when—as in Hetty Sorrel, for whom the narrator of *Adam Bede* often expresses sympathy—we are presented with a character whose moral sense is profoundly deficient.

Such a concept of tragedy overlaps to an extent the Hegelian definition of the conflict between two rights, and Eliot's discussion of *Antigone*, which is G. W. F. *Hegel's prime example, in 'The *Antigone and its Moral', does not reject this principle. But Eliot's reading of *Sophocles' play and of what constitutes its tragedy is closer to the Marxist view—not because Karl *Marx had influenced her but because they shared a century—in that she conceives Antigone as a moral pioneer, one whose vision seeks to take the world onward in its *progress but who, having come too early in the evolution of things, is destroyed in the attempt. Maggie in *The Mill on the Floss* is created in this mould, a figure whose moral imagination has reached a level of understanding far beyond the norm of St Ogg's.

One of the most remarkable elements in Eliot's idea of tragedy anticipates Arthur Miller's attempt, in *Death of a Salesman* and its companion 'Tragedy and the Common Man', to reinterpret *The Poetics* so as to make it applicable to ordinary human existence. In some sense, for Eliot as for Miller, every life is a tragedy. 'Looking at individual lots', she writes in her 'Notes on "The Spanish Gypsy"', 'I seemed to see in each the same story, wrought out with more or less of tragedy.' Answering, in *The Mill on the Floss*, the Aristotelian requirement that a certain magnitude exist in characters and action—a 'ti mevgeqo', she writes, quoting *The Poetics* (vii. 2) in Greek (*MF* 1.10)— Eliot insists that the 'pride and obstinacy' of people like Mr Tulliver, 'insignificant' though they seem, 'have their tragedy too' (*MF* 3.1). It is only, she comments in *Middlemarch*, because we are unable to hear the 'roar . . . on the other side of silence' that we do not feel the 'tragedy which lies in the very fact of frequency' (*MM* 20). See also ARISTOTLE; CLASSICAL LITERATURE; THEATRE.

FB

Bonaparte, Felicia, *Will and Destiny* (1975).
Easterling, P. E., 'George Eliot and Greek Tragedy', *George Eliot Review*, 25 (1994).
Guth, Barbara. 'Philip: The Tragedy of *The Mill on the Floss*', *Studies in the Novel*, 15/4 (1983).

'Translations and Translators' is an article by George Eliot, which was originally published in the *Leader* on 20 October 1855 (repr. in *Essays*). This essay is a review of J. M. D. Meiklejohn's translation of Immanuel *Kant's *Critique of Pure Reason,* as well as the second edition of Mary Anne Burt's English rendering of German poetry entitled *Specimens of the Choicest Lyrical Productions of the Most Celebrated German Poets.* Both these works appeared in 1855. Whilst Eliot expressed a great deal of praise for Meiklejohn's English version of Kant's treatise, which she considered to be 'the very hardest nut . . . for a translator to crack', she criticized Burt's attempt to make German poetry accessible to English readers (*Essays*, 208–9). In Eliot's view, Burt's misrepresentations were so serious that she deemed it to be her duty as a reviewer to alert especially those readers without a first-hand knowledge of the original texts to the inadequacy of poetic translations. In this context Eliot also questioned the opinion that the Germans are better at translating foreign poetry than their English colleagues and came to the conclusion that even accomplished translators like Schlegel and Tieck, whose German renditions of *Shakespeare were sometimes successful, could be found guilty of serious inaccuracies (*Essays*, 210–11).

What is more, Eliot's 1855 essay in the *Leader* is the most comprehensive theoretical statement she published on the topic of translation. It reflects her own mixed feelings about the subject in question and is complemented by earlier similar observations in her letters (*L* i. 191; ii. 156; Stark 1997: 136–7). On the one hand, Eliot still believed in the importance of translation and argued firmly that solid professional training was an indispensable prerequisite for carrying out this task (*Essays*, 208; *L* i. 212–13). Though 'infinitely below the man who produces *good* original works', she considered the translator to be 'infinitely above the man who produces *feeble* original works' (*Essays*, 211). On the other hand, Eliot stated that 'translation does not often demand genius' (208). In the last two sentences of her review she also disclosed to her readers that she had intended to discuss the moral qualities, such as patience and fidelity, as well as the sense of responsibility required in the translator. Eventually, however, she decided not to explore the topic because she felt she had 'gossiped on this subject long enough' (211).

It is significant that the article in the *Leader* was written when George Eliot was on the verge of abandoning her own efforts to render German and Latin texts into English. Her essay constitutes a sensitive and subtle, but surprisingly short and to a certain extent dismissive, tribute to an occupation which had taken up a considerable amount of her time and energy for over a decade and had served as a useful form of literary apprenticeship in her life. The desultory nature of the *Leader* review can at least in part be explained by the fact that in 1855 Eliot had arrived at a turning point in her personal development and started to direct her attention to the production of '*good* original works' of her own. See also LANGUAGES; TRANSLATIONS BY GEORGE ELIOT; TRANSLATIONS OF GEORGE ELIOT'S WORKS. SS

Stark, Susanne, 'Women and Translation in the Nineteenth Century', *New Comparison*, 15 (1993).

—— 'Marian Evans, the Translator', in Susan Bassnett (ed.), *Translating Literature* (1997).

translations by George Eliot. George Eliot carried out her major translations of theological works from the German and Latin between 1843 and 1856. Her wide-ranging linguistic competence also covered a comprehensive literary and scholarly knowledge of French, Italian, and Spanish, as well as a sound grasp of Greek and Hebrew (see LANGUAGES), which was required for her English rendering of German biblical criticism (Cross, iii. 423).

An English version of D. F. *Strauss, *Das Leben Jesu* (1835–6) was propagated by Eliot's freethinking and rationalist Coventry friends, the *Brays, the *Hennells, and the *Brabants. Strauss made use of philological scholarship in order to establish the true story of the life of Jesus and thus questioned the credibility of the New Testament. His ruthless method of dissecting biblical sources was frequently perceived as a threat to orthodox religiosity and led to his dismissal from the theological seminary at the University of Tübingen. After having considered translating *Mémoire en faveur de la liberté des Cultes* (1826) by the Swiss theologian Alexandre Rodolphe Vinet from the French in 1842, Eliot took over the translation of *Das Leben Jesu* from Rufa Brabant one year later. By 1843 Rufa had rendered a considerable amount of the first volume of the work's fourth edition into English, but she withdrew from the project when she married Charles Hennell, one of the ardent defenders of Strauss's radical ideas in Britain (*L* i. 135, 171; Haight 1968: 52–3). It took Eliot over two years to complete *The Life of Jesus*. Her swift progress at the beginning of the project reflects her sympathy for the revolutionary traits of Strauss's work and coincided with the spiritual departure from her own evangelical upbringing (*L* i. 176; Ashton 1996: 36–8). Especially towards the end of her translation, however, Eliot questioned the author's method and disapproved of his erudite fragmentations, which made her feel 'Strauss-sick' (*L* i. 206). Despite these objections she remained faithful to the German original 'word for word, thought for thought and sentence for sentence', and her English was considered to be stylistically pleasing (Anon., 'Strauss' Life of Jesus', *Prospective Review*, 2 (1846), 479). With a view to making the work more attractive for a larger readership, she advocated its abridgement, but her suggestion was not pursued (*L* i. 354).

The second, equally controversial, German theological treatise George Eliot rendered into English in 1853–4 was Ludwig *Feuerbach's *Das Wesen des Christenthums* (1841). Feuerbach's theology sought to anthropomorphize religious doctrine, attempted to detach sacraments from their ecclesiastical context, and thus made the supernatural elements of religion part of a historically traceable world centred on human needs. Eliot's decision to translate Feuerbach was self-initiated, and her enthusiasm for his ideas is likely to have been responsible for her wish to make his philosophy palatable for English readers (*L* ii. 153). As a result, she edited Feuerbach's text and exercised more freedom in her translation than she dared to employ in rendering Strauss's work into English (*L* ii. 140–2, 154). Despite these efforts, *The Essence of Christianity* received less attention in the British periodical press than *The Life of Jesus*. It is significant, however, that Feuerbach's treatise is the only work in which her real name Marian Evans appeared in print, while the translator remained anonymous in the case of Strauss and at first did not even wish to see her gender revealed to the author.

From 1854 to 1856 George Eliot was engaged in her last substantial translation project: an English rendering of Baruch *Spinoza's *Ethics* (1677) from the Latin (*L* ii. 186, 233). Her choice of this text can, in many ways, be perceived as a continuation of her previous preoccupation with theological works. G. H. *Lewes, for example, argued that Spinoza's criticism of the Bible and his attacks on the institution of priesthood as injurious to the general welfare anticipated the rationalism of 19th-century German philosophical thinking ('Spinoza's Life and Works', *Westminster Review*, 39 (1843), 380). In addition, it is known that in 1849, and probably already in 1843, Eliot spent time rendering Spinoza's *Tractatus Theologico-Politicus* (1670) from Latin into English (*L* i. 158). This translation remained unpublished, while her version of the *Ethics* was eventually printed in 1981. Tensions between Lewes and the publisher Henry George Bohn had impeded the publication of the work during Eliot's lifetime. In the context of her co-operation with Lewes it also deserves to be mentioned that Eliot supported his *Life of Goethe* (1855) by providing translations from the German (see GOETHE).

It is significant that the period in her life in which George Eliot engaged in translation preceded and was distinct from the phase in which she wrote fiction. At a time when she still shrank back from the novel as a morally questionable genre, she considered anonymous periodical reviews as well as the translation of complex philosophical treatises to be a suitable literary occupation (*L* i. 23; Cross, i. 51). The English versions of these works were ironically often attributed to a mediator of male intellect and learning (Anon., *Prospective Review*, 2 (1846), 479; Lindsay Alexander, *British Quarterly Review*, 5 (1847), 206). Eliot, on the other hand, turned to translation at the beginning of her career, because she felt attracted by the mute, ancillary nature of the task. It allowed

her to voice ideas close to her heart without having to face the public exposure incurred by independent authorship. Her involvement in translation projects, which contributed to her linguistic, scholarly, and spiritual development, as well as her ability to deal with the commercial aspects of the London publishing scene, can be perceived as part of a literary apprenticeship. As noted above, Eliot's assertiveness grew during what Leslie Stephen described as her 'Pythagorean probation of silence' (*CH* 466). What is more, the creative writing under a male pseudonym, for which George Eliot became famous after 1857, was shaped substantially by the abilities she gained and the web of ideas she wove during the 'translation phase' in the first half of her life. See also 'TRANSLATIONS AND TRANSLATORS'.   SS

Ashton (1980).
—— (1996).
Stark, Susanne, 'Marian Evans, the Translator', in Susan Bassnett (ed.), *Translating Literature* (1997).
Willey, Basil, 'George Eliot: Hennell, Strauss, and Feuerbach' in *Nineteenth Century Studies* (1949).

translations of George Eliot's works during her lifetime appeared mostly in French, German, and Dutch, but also in Hungarian and Italian. George Eliot, although an accomplished translator herself (see TRANSLATIONS BY GEORGE ELIOT), was ambivalent about translation of her own work, writing in 1858, 'I shudder at the idea of my books being turned into hideous German by an incompetent translator' (*L* ii. 499). Her anxiety arose from 'the dread of having one's sentences metamorphosed into an expression of somebody else's meaning instead of one's own' (*L* iii. 231). Some twenty years later she is still expressing the same doubts, complaining in 1879, 'I have no faith in the translation of my books, and yet cannot forbid it' (*L* vii. 119). The financial returns for translations were also very small, mostly in the £25 range (see EARNINGS).

François *D'Albert Durade translated Eliot's early novels, *Adam Bede, The Mill on the Floss,* and *Silas Marner,* into French with her blessing. They corresponded regularly discussing particular issues, for instance a suitable title for *Mill,* Eliot objecting strongly to 'Amour et Devoir' and instructing Durade to 'resist to the death' any title of that kind (*L* iv. 69). She comments on his charming translation of the tavern scene in *Silas* but notes that here and there 'it was inevitable that, for want of the knowledge which only a native of England can have, you should mistake the meaning of a phrase' (*L* iv. 67). Her support lessens from 1865, Eliot complaining that his publishers are failing because the public generally seems unaware of the existing French translations (*L* iv. 211). Durade also translated *Scenes of Clerical Life* and *Romola.*

Eliot, however, had no power to offer *Romola* to Durade because Smith, Elder & Co. owned the copyright and his translation did not finally appear until 1878. Eliot, mourning for G. H. *Lewes, told Durade she had not looked at the translation, 'finding no interest in my own work at present' because 'my appetite for life is gone' (*L* vii. 115). In 1880 she responds quite testily to an enquiry from him regarding *Felix Holt, the Radical,* 'I know nothing of any translation, and if I *have* known, I have forgotten' (*L* vii. 257).

German translations of Eliot's early work were arranged with the publisher Duncker who had commissioned Julius Frese, described by Lewes as 'very competent' (*L* viii. 147), to translate Lewes's *Goethe* published in 1856. Duncker was offered *Adam Bede,* and subsequently *The Mill* and *Silas,* with Frese as translator (Ashton 1991: 168). In 1866 Frederick *Lehmann purchased for his brother Dr Emil Lehmann translation rights to *Felix Holt,* which appeared in 1867. He also translated *Middlemarch* (1872–3). Adolf Strodtmann translated *Daniel Deronda* (1876). In 1879 Eliot told John Blackwood she had heard that 'Strodtmann's translation of D.D. is better than those of Middlemarch and Felix Holt', adding, 'I feel that it is treason to Literature to encourage incompetence. . . . For my part, I should not care if my books never were turned into other words than those in which I wrote them' (*L* vii. 119–20). See also FRANCE; GERMANY; 'TRANSLATIONS AND TRANSLATORS'.

JJ

Ashton, Rosemary, *G. H. Lewes: A Life* (1991).

travels. George Eliot was introduced to travel abroad by her Coventry friends and mentors, Charles and Cara *Bray, who bore her off to Europe in June 1849, within days of her father's funeral. Their itinerary took them south through *France to Nice, thence to Genoa, Milan, and the Italian Lakes, and across the Alps to *Geneva, where she decided to spend the winter of 1849–50. Prior to this, she had travelled in the British Isles, sometimes with the Brays, with whom she went to Wales and Scotland, and sometimes with members of her family: for example in his last years, she more than once accompanied her father to seaside resorts. The practice of travelling within Britain continued throughout her life, with sorties ranging from a few days to months, to country or coastal locations.

Her life with G. H. *Lewes began with travel, as they set off for *Germany together in July 1854. Their months in *Weimar and *Berlin were justified by Lewes's research for his *Life of Goethe,* and recorded in a detailed journal as George Eliot was often to do in subsequent travels (though Lewes kept up the practice more systematically). Simi-

larly, their major excursions to *Ilfracombe in 1856, and to Scilly and Jersey in 1857, were motivated by Lewes's work on marine biology, and their next journey abroad, to Germany in 1858, by his scientific research.

As the success of George Eliot's fiction improved their financial situation, economy in travelling became less a matter of concern, as was evident first during a brief break in *Switzerland in July 1859 when Lewes visited his sons at Hofwyl, and then during the journey to *Italy in 1860 which was such a watershed in their lives. This trip was undertaken without a specific work agenda, and inaugurated their custom of setting off on their travels after George Eliot completed a book, in this case, *The Mill on the Floss* (also Lewes had completed *The *Physiology of Common Life*). The return to Italy in 1861, principally to *Florence to prepare for *Romola,* was a reversion to the notion of a study tour; while the third Italian journey, in 1864, taken in company with Frederic *Burton, had a focus on early Italian art. By the mid-1860s, each spring or summer the Leweses habitually crossed the Channel for a tour lasting a couple of months to Germany, or Italy, or France; and took shorter trips also at other seasons. More adventurously, in the winter of 1866–7 they went to *Spain. In the 1870s, they developed the practice of spending summer in a country location out of London, usually in Surrey, but continued to travel abroad until 1876, when they went to France and Switzerland in what was to be their last tour together.

As early as 1860, George Eliot expressed a preference for privacy during travel: 'My philanthropy rises several degrees as soon as we are alone. Mr. Lewes is more sociable than I am, but finds travelling society rather too strongly American in its flavour to be quite desirable, and so we concur in the disposition to know nobody' (*L* iii. 295). To this end they were at pains to have accommodation with a private sitting room, but Eliot's increasing fame made privacy more difficult. In 1867, Lewes wrote to his son Charles from Granada: 'You know I never write my name legibly or in full in the hotel books, wishing to preserve the obscurity of nobodies', and recounted the consequences of a variation in practice: 'It was whispered round at once who we were, and the attention of the guests was flattering but boring' (*L* iv. 346).

The last major tour undertaken by George Eliot was her honeymoon with John Walter *Cross in 1880, when their itinerary took them to many places in France, Italy, Switzerland, and Germany already familiar to her. Though Cross was well travelled, George Eliot clearly took a tutelary role on this journey. Into the bargain, it was Cross, the younger and fitter of the couple, who fell ill: he later commented, as others had done, on the physical invigoration of George Eliot abroad (see HEALTH). MAH

Trollope, Anthony (1815–82), novelist, close friend of G. H. *Lewes and then of George Eliot. Lewes consulted Trollope about the placing of his son Charles in the Post Office, where Trollope was himself employed, and by 20 July 1860 this was done, though later (May 1862) Trollope reported that Charley was not doing well. As early as December 1860 Eliot spoke of Trollope as their friend, and thereafter he dined or lunched with them regularly. She records reading *Orley Farm* during its monthly issue 1861–2, being particularly interested in Lady Mason. Trollope attended the house-warming party on 24 November 1863 at The *Priory and in celebration of Charles's (now upwardly mobile in the Post Office) coming of age. On a professional level Lewes was worried about offending Trollope over his own reservations about the *Fortnightly Review* editorship, while on the personal one Eliot was intrigued by Trollope's improvement under the Banting regime: 'thinner by means of it . . . the better for the self-denial' (*L* iv. 170). Trollope's resignation from the Post Office (October 1867) is noted, and in January 1873 he confided to Lewes that his son Harry wanted 'to marry a woman of the town' (*L* v. 357). He was also present when the Leweses met the Crown Prince and Princess of Germany in January 1878.

That they both valued him warmly is shown by Eliot's telling François *D'Albert Durade in 1862 that he was 'one of the heartiest, most genuine, moral and generous men we know' (*L* iv. 59), and that Trollope reciprocated fully is seen in his obituary tribute to Lewes in the *Fortnightly*. He wrote to Mary Holmes in May 1876 that he loved and admired Eliot and considered her a close and valued friend. Eliot confessed that she was forced to abstain from reading contemporary fiction unless it was by Miss Anne *Thackeray or Trollope, and even with the latter she had to abandon *The Prime Minister* (1876) after he had sent her the first number. Trollope ranked her second among contemporary novelists in *An Autobiography* (1883), above Charles *Dickens, below William Makepeace *Thackeray, and it is their interaction as critics of each other's work which provides interest for us today. While editor of *St Paul's* Trollope published a review of *The Spanish Gypsy* which heartened Eliot, who was already aware of his critical predilection for what she wrote: his warm letter about *Romola* (28 June 1862) included praise for characters, descriptions of *Florence, and the 'artistically beautiful' conception of Romola herself, but advised Eliot not to 'fire too much over the heads' of her readers while assuring her, 'I shall

never envy your success, or the great appreciation of what you have done that will certainly come' (*L* i. 186–7).

As well as offering Lewes an unlimited number of the 8,000 cigars he had imported from Cuba he offered her the private testimony she cherished: to others he sometimes qualified his praise, telling Mary Holmes that she could be heavy, abstruse, 'sometimes almost dull,—but always like an egg, full of meat' (*L* ii. 627, September 1874). Trollope waxed humorous to John *Blackwood, saying, 'Mr & Mrs Felix Holt have returned blooming like two garden peonies' (*Letters of Trollope*, i. 349, August 1866), but he praised *Felix Holt, the Radical* to Eliot, writing of the 'more elaborated thought' in it, singling out Mrs Transome, and struggling to approve Felix by cunningly calling him 'the result of an admirably conceived plan of a character', though he still asserted his preference for *Adam Bede* and *Romola* (*L* i. 346, August 1866). His reservations about *The Spanish Gypsy* as poetry are conveyed in a letter to Lewes (*L* i. 449, October 1868) though he finds that 'Fedalma, Zarca & Juan are perfect'. Thereafter his occasional comments (but not to her) become more censorious: *Daniel Deronda* is 'trying' and artistically flawed, smelling too much of oil and exhibiting a striving after effects which are unsuccessful. Even Gwendolen is censured for being disgusting but not interesting, though he adds, 'Homer was allowed to nod once or twice, & why not the author of Adam Bede and Romola?' (*Letters of Trollope*, ii. 689, May 1876).

In *An Autobiography*, published after his death and hers, he observes that her real strength is in analysis, that in her later period she is more the philosopher than the novelist, that her teaching survives, and that the last three novels exhibit her lack of ease: this does not register a deterioration in her so much as a switch of direction away from her known ground, typified by Mrs Poyser, to higher things. Trollope is profoundly moved by her death, telling the inquisitive Kate Field that her private life should remain private like that of anyone else who becomes famous through literary talent. The mutuality of supportive appreciation is felt in Eliot's appraisals of *The Small House at Allington* (1864) and, particularly, *Rachel Ray* (1863). She tells him it is 'natty and complete as a nut on its stem', his novels make people the better for reading them: 'They are like pleasant public gardens, where people go for amusement and, whether they think of it or not, get health as well' (*L* iv. 110, October 1863). But her reading and writing itinerary allowed her later only 'bits of Mr Trollope, for affection's sake' (*L* vi. 123, February 1875). That affection was abundantly returned and on one occasion in an obliquely complimentary way. 'Josephine de Montmorenci', one of

Trollope's stories collected in *An Editor's Tales* (1870), has an ambitious but disabled novelist who adopts the pseudonym of the story title. She is really Maryanne Puffle, is philosophical, serious, intriguing, and has her pretty sister negotiate with the editor before revealing herself. Details in the narration indicate a private joke with the Leweses, as R. H. Super has suggested (*The Chronicler of Barsetshire* (1988), 271). In a letter after Eliot's death he wrote 'I did love her very dearly' (*L* ii. 887, 24 December 1880). His writing to her about her work is consciously tempered by that love.

GRH

The Letters of Anthony Trollope, ed. N. John Hall (1983).

Trollope, Thomas Adolphus (1810–92), younger brother of Anthony and friend of George Eliot. He was educated at Harrow, Winchester, and *Oxford, and settled in *Florence in 1843 where he and his first wife Theodosia (d. 1865) established the Villino Trollope. There they entertained cultural celebrities, had one child Beatrice (Bice), and were sympathetic to Italian nationalistic aspirations. In 1866 he married Frances Eleanor Ternan (1835–1913), governess in his family, sister of Ellen Ternan, mistress of Charles *Dickens: she became the biographer of her mother-in-law and a successful novelist. Thomas wrote prolifically, travel, novels, stories, histories. When Eliot and G. H. *Lewes were in Florence in May 1861 Tom persuaded them to extend their stay. He took them to Camadoli (they slept comfortably in the cowhouse), they visited monasteries, and Lewes described Trollope as 'a most loveable creature'. In June Eliot wrote thanking him for advice on detail for *Romola*, in July she read his *La Beata* (1861). Some of the heroine's characteristics anticipate Tessa's. Eliot valued Trollope greatly, he dined with them in August 1865 after his first wife's death, and brought his second wife to them in July 1867. The Leweses stayed with the Trollopes 20–5 March 1869, and Eliot's appreciative thank-you (1 April), apparently after an argument on religion, called him 'a friend who is among the best of men with the worst of theories' (*L* v. 22). His new house, she told John *Blackwood, had a magnificent view of Florence. They stayed again 23–7 April. Trollope and Bice lunched at The *Priory 10 May 1874 (Eliot loved hearing Bice sing). In August 1878 the Trollopes stayed at The Heights, Witley (see HOMES), and were taken to see *Tennyson. Trollope's memorable account of George Eliot and Lewes is found in his *What I Remember* (1887). GRH

Turgenev, Ivan (1818–83), Russian novelist who admired the work of both George Eliot and G. H.

*Lewes and was on friendly terms with them. He first visited them at The *Priory on 8 January 1871, after which he sent George Eliot a French translation of his *A Sportsman's Sketches* (1847–51). She seems to have read a number of his works, including *Rudin* (1856), and although there is no record of what she thought of them, she may have found in his treatment of peasant life in the *Sketches* and of the country gentry some affinity with her own work. French critics certainly praised them both as novelists of an ideal objectivity (Waddington, 751), and Lord David Cecil in *Early Victorian Novelists* (1934) found grounds for comparing Elena in *On the Eve* with Dorothea in *Middlemarch*. Turgenev was a frequent visitor to The Priory and corresponded occasionally, sometimes writing in English but more often in French. He became a close friend of John Walter *Cross's brother-in-law W. H. Bullock Hall, and it was at Hall's country house at Six Mile Bottom outside Cambridge that the best-documented meeting of the two novelists took place in October 1878. Oscar *Browning, who was also present, left an account of the house party from 21 to 24 October in his *Life of George Eliot* (1890; see BIOGRAPHIES). Lewes acclaimed Turgenev as the greatest living novelist, whereupon Turgenev rose to toast George Eliot as the one who truly deserved that title. He and Eliot discussed literature, and to Lewes he stated his preference for *The Mill on the Floss* as the most natural and artistic of her works. After the visit he wrote to Lewes, now mortally ill, offering some painkilling pills and expressing again his admiration for George Eliot. After Lewes's death on 30 November he wrote a sensitive letter of condolence. In May 1880 he wrote to her again inviting her to attend the inauguration of a statue to Pushkin that summer in Moscow, but she was already away in Italy on her honeymoon with Cross. JMR

Waddington, Patrick, 'Turgenev and George Eliot: A Literary Friendship', *Modern Language Review*, 66 (1971).

Turner, J. M. W. (1775–1851), English painter. Brief references to Turner's paintings in several of George Eliot's novels and stories make it clear that she knew his work well, and was fully aware of the changes in style which marked the stages of his career. In a letter of 1868 she speaks of the late afternoon light on Regent's Park, 'exalting it into something that the young Turner would have wanted to paint' (*L* iv. 476). By contrast, she writes in 'Brother Jacob' of the brightly coloured contents of a pastry-cook's window 'which to the eyes of a bilious person might easily have blended into a faery landscape in Turner's latest style' (BJ 2). The passage in *Daniel Deronda* where Mordecai stands on Blackfriars Bridge (*DD* 40) has also been associated with the later work of Turner, as George Eliot describes the evening light effects on the Thames, a subject popular with the painter.

There is little information about George Eliot's actual experience of Turner paintings. One which is recorded is her 1851 visit, with John *Chapman, to the large collection of Turner watercolour and oil paintings which belonged to the Tottenham coachbuilder B. G. Windus.   LO

Witemeyer (1979).

Tyndall, John (1820–93), physicist, Professor of Natural Philosophy at the Royal Institution from 1853, and one of the eminent scientists, like Richard *Owen and T. H. *Huxley, who belonged to George Eliot's and G. H. *Lewes's circle of friends and acquaintances. Having made a particular study of light—demonstrating how diffusion of the sun's rays causes the sky to appear blue—and having explained optical illusions in his 1870 lectures on *The Use and Limit of Imagination in Science*, he may be the friend who provided the example of the candle on the pier glass which serves as a parable of the distorting effect of egoism in chapter 27 of *Middlemarch* (the other candidate is Herbert *Spencer). When George Eliot died, Tyndall wrote to the Dean of Westminster in support of the proposal that she should be buried in Westminster Abbey, claiming that if he were to give his permission 'the verdict of the future will be that Dean Stanley has enshrined a woman whose achievements were without parallel in the previous history of womankind' (Haight 1968: 548–9). See also SCIENCE.   JMR

Unitarianism was an early and continuing experience for George Eliot. The *Brays were Unitarians: Gordon S. *Haight describes Mr and Mrs Hennell, parents of her friends the *Hennells, as 'staunch Unitarians of the Priestley school' (*L*, vol. i, p. lvi), and Bessie Rayner *Parkes 'inherited a strong Unitarian tradition' (*L* i. 1). After the move to Coventry and her increasing intimacy with the Brays and Hennells, Robert *Evans feared that his daughter had found a new allegiance: in her poignant letter to him of 28 February 1842 she specifically denies 'that I have any affinity in opinion with Unitarians more than with other classes of believers' (*L* i. 128). Yet she had observed to Cara Bray 'What a beautiful *refined* Christianity your Unitarianism is!' (*L* i. 116). Eliot's close friend Barbara *Bodichon was a Unitarian. Eliot wrote to Sara Hennell that she and Lewes would be attending the christening of Charles and Gertrude's baby (see LEWES FAMILY) 'in a free Unitarian fashion' (*L* v. 347). After a visit to Rosslyn Hill Unitarian Chapel, Hampstead, they went to Thornton Lewes's grave (25 December 1869); G. H. Lewes's funeral service was conducted by the Unitarian minister Dr Sadler in the chapel at Highgate Cemetery (4 December 1878). Sadler officiated at Rosslyn Hill at Eliot's own funeral on 29 December 1880 and, as Haight notes, changed Eliot's 'immortal dead who live again' to those 'who still live on' (*L* ix. 324). Eliot's feeling for the freedom, integrity, and sincerity of Unitarian practice is another underlining of her need to explore and experience the spirituality so essential to her fulfilment. See also ATHEISM; CHRISTIANITY; RELIGION. GRH

urbanization is a feature of 19th-century social life that barely features in George Eliot's fiction. The course of her own life took her from rural *Warwickshire to *London, and she often remarked on how she found the urban environment oppressive; but in setting most of her works back several decades from the time of writing to the Midland villages and towns that she had known in childhood, she did not have to confront one of the major social developments of her own lifetime. Urbanization is alluded to in *Silas Marner*: when Silas returns after thirty years in Raveloe to the Northern town which he left after he was expelled from the religious community of Lantern Yard, it has become 'a great manufacturing town' which is unrecognizable to him, and the site of Lantern Yard is occupied by a modern factory (*SM* 21). In the coach journey which forms the Introduction to *Felix Holt, the Radical* the new manufacturing towns and mining villages do not yet impinge

directly on the slow-moving life of the rural Midlands, but their future encroachment is indicated by the handlooms which 'made a far-reaching straggling fringe about the great centres of manufacture' and by the 'breath of the manufacturing town, which made a cloudy day and a red gloom by night on the horizon' and 'diffused itself over all the surrounding country, filling the air with eager unrest'. But as yet these busy centres of urban life 'seemed to make but crowded nests in the midst of the large-spaced, slow-moving life of homesteads and far-away cottages and oak-sheltered parks'. It is the predominance of this rural life that is suggested in *Middlemarch* when Celia reacts to the news that her sister Dorothea is to move to London by asking in disbelief, 'How can you always live in a street' (*MM* 84). See also INDUSTRIALISM; PROGRESS; TECHNOLOGY. JMR

utilitarianism holds that happiness is the end of life and that actions which promote it are right, those which do not are wrong. Jeremy Bentham was its founding advocate, with John Stuart *Mill its greatest follower. George Eliot was of course in early contact with another of its supporters, Harriet *Martineau. Her most direct statement on the subject would appear to be that reported by Edith *Simcox in her *Autobiography* (*L* ix. 217): 'She thought the weak point of Utilitarianism, in Sidgwick and others, lay not in their taking human welfare as the standard of right but in their trying to find in it the *moral* motive.' Utilitarianism in her view failed to provide an adequate basis for a moral view of the world. See also PHILOSOPHY.

GRH

Collins, K. K., 'G. H. Lewes Revised: George Eliot and the Moral Sense', *Victorian Studies*, 21 (1977–8). Myers (1984).

V

Varnhagen von Ense, Karl August (1785–1858), German diplomat and author of many critical and biographical works, including one on *Goethe. He met George Eliot by chance on her first Sunday in *Berlin as she and G. H. *Lewes were strolling in the Linden on 5 November 1854. In her 'Recollections of Berlin' Eliot writes, 'we met a nice-looking old gentleman with an order round his neck and a gold headed cane in his hand, who exclaimed on seeing G. "Ist's möglich"' (*Journals*, 243). Lewes must have emphasized Eliot's literary qualifications to Varnhagen, as his diary records that Mr Lewes's 'companion is an Englishwoman, a Miss Evans, editor of the *Westminster Review* and translator of Strauss's *Life of Jesus* and Feuerbach's *Essence of Christianity*' (Ashton 1991: 159). Eliot writes of being received 'very kindly' by Varnhagen and Fraulein v. Solmar, noting that 'as they are in the best society of Berlin, this is no slight advantage' (*L* ii. 184). The social tolerance of the Germans in general struck Eliot as 'free from the bigotry and exclusiveness of their more refined cousins' (*Journals*, p. xx).

Lewes first met Varnhagen in Berlin in 1838 through an introduction from Thomas *Carlyle. Varnhagen was a key literary figure and Lewes maintained an often importunate correspondence with him, contacting him again in 1853 when planning to visit Berlin. Varnhagen proved to be of invaluable assistance to Lewes, as he and Marian laboured over Lewes's study of Goethe, by lending books and reading articles. When Lewes's *Life and Works of Goethe* was published in 1855 after their return to England, he noted particularly that 'Varnhagen has written to me in the highest terms about it. He has recommended its translation' (*L* viii. 147). The German translation proved an embarrassment, as footnotes acknowledging assistance from German scholars were omitted, tarnishing the work's reception in Germany.

Varnhagen, while condemning some superficiality, appears to have maintained the work's general quality and it is possible that the correspondence dwindled due to divergent interests, or Varnhagen's increasing ill health to which Lewes refers in 1857, rather than from rancour on Varnhagen's part. The last existing letter from Eliot to Varnhagen's niece Ludmilla Assing expresses her gladness 'to see myself remembered in his letters' (*Letters of Lewes*, ed. Baker, i. 267). See also GERMANY.   JJ

Ashton (1996).
—— *G. H. Lewes: A Life* (1991).
The Letters of George Henry Lewes, ed. William Baker (1995).

Venice. Of all the Italian cities, Venice has perhaps the most powerful mythology for Anglo-Saxon travellers. George Eliot and G. H. *Lewes fully experienced its spell when they spent eight days there on their first Italian tour of 1860, attended by a courier named Domenico. They arrived at night: 'Soon we were in a gondola on the Grand Canal, looking out at the moonlit buildings and water. What stillness! What beauty! . . . Venice was more beautiful than romances had feigned' (*Journals*, 362).

They returned in 1864, particularly to study early Venetian art, and George Eliot found 'everything more beautiful than it was to us four years ago' (*L* iv. 149). On this occasion, they were in company with the artist Frederic *Burton, whose expertise heightened the pleasure of both, though Lewes at times struck out on his own, to take in 'the incessant variety of pictures [Venice] presents. I don't mean painted pictures only, though they are superb, but animated pictures which are to be seen at almost every step' (*L* iv. 150). He also did some serious shopping, purchasing among other things an alethoscope, a kind of stereoscope.

George Eliot visited Venice once more, on her honeymoon with John Walter *Cross in 1880. 'Our days here are passed quite deliciously', she wrote (*L* vii. 294), though she also enquired importunately about letters which appeared to have miscarried. They had been there a fortnight when the calamity of Cross's throwing himself into the Grand Canal from their hotel balcony on 16 June caused them to turn homewards as soon as he was fit to travel. See also ITALY.   MAH

Buzard, James, *The Beaten Track: European Tourism, Literature, and the Ways to 'Culture' 1800–1918* (1993).
Thompson (1998).

Verdi, Giuseppe (1813–1901), Italian opera composer. The attitude of both George Eliot and G. H. *Lewes towards Verdi seems to have been somewhat ambiguous. Confessing to his son Charles that 'the Music of the future' was not for him and the 'Mutter', Lewes continued, 'Schubert, Beethoven, Mozart, Gluck or even Verdi—but not Wagner—is what we are made to respond to' (*L* v. 85). Bearing in mind that Verdi was Lewes's almost exact contemporary, that 'or even' somewhat compromises the composer's status in Lewes's musical pantheon. He and George Eliot knew several of Verdi's operas well. In *Weimar in 1854, they had heard *Ernani* (1844), conducted by *Liszt; and seem to have enjoyed hearing *Attila* (1846) and *Il trovatore* (1853) 'bawled' (*L* iii. 412, 414) during their visit to *Italy in 1861. The following year, they accepted George *Smith's stalls at the Royal Italian Opera, Covent Garden, to see *Rigoletto* (1851): 'music poor', reported Lewes (*L* iv. 37). While George Eliot found this opera 'unpleasant', she also thought it 'a superlatively fine tragedy in the Nemesis—I think I don't know a finer' (*L* iv. 93).

On the whole, the evidence suggests that Lewes's relish for Verdi seems to have been greater than George Eliot's. On 13 October 1868, she asked Charles (see LEWES FAMILY) to procure 'an arrangement of Verdi's best operas for the Piano. Pater likes hearing those things' (*L* iv. 478). See also MUSIC.   BG

Vico, Giambattista (1688–1744), Italian philosopher of history, copies of whose *Scienza Nuova* (in the original and in French) George Eliot and G. H. *Lewes owned. Their marginal notes and underlinings suggest that what interested them in this volume were especially Vico's notions of *history, customs, *language, and *myth. In some ways Vico's ideas confirmed rather than influenced Eliot's thought. In others the two reached like conclusions but for very different reasons. Conscious as she was, for instance, that there was 'no creature . . . so strong' it could fail to be, in part, 'determined by what lies outside it' (*MM* Finale), Eliot completely agreed with Vico that human beings could be understood only in a historical context, although for Vico this was true because he believed the human mind could only grasp what it had created, the institutions it had made. But in a number of critical areas they held premises in common. Vico's insistence that history was not the activities of the state but the very life of the people and could therefore be resurrected only as an organic whole accorded well with Eliot's efforts to write history through fiction. Vico believed that early peoples apprehended the world poetically and that their myths were literal transcripts of what they felt they had perceived. Furthermore, their apprehensions were encoded in their language, so that an etymological study of the meanings of their words would go far to reproduce their comprehension of the world. Eliot,

more broadly, held that myths expressed, not only in early times, the characters of diverse peoples, and she saw, as in *Romola*, that she could recreate an age, and even many layers of history, by embodying mythic *symbolism in her characters and events. And, as in the case of Ladislaw who is described as 'enthusiastic' (*MM* 19) to suggest that he has internalized the idea of the divine, Eliot often uses words for their etymological meanings (see LANGUAGE). Sacred rites were, in addition, as important to her as to Vico (see RELIGION). In her only marginal note, Eliot remarks that Vico always considered marriage and burial sacred, suggesting perhaps that *death and *marriage must be, if only metaphorically, seen as sacred in her own work.   FB

Bonaparte, Felicia, 'George Henry Lewes, George Eliot, and Vico', *New Vico Studies*, 2 (1984).

Victoria, Queen (1819–1901, reigned 1837–1901). George Eliot's views of the Queen changed with her own success and her sympathetic recognitions after the death of the Prince Consort in 1861. In March 1848, in the year of European *revolutions, she wrote to John *Sibree that there was no hope of revolution in England, asserting, 'Our little humbug of a queen is more endurable than the rest of her race because she calls forth a chivalrous feeling, and there is nothing in our constitution to obstruct the slow *progress* of political reform' (*L* i. 254). But when Sir Arthur *Helps told her in November 1860 that the Queen had been speaking admiringly of her books (especially *The Mill on the Floss*) she recorded, 'It is interesting to know that Royalty can be touched by that sort of writing', adding that she was grateful to Helps 'for his wish to tell me of the sympathy given to me in that quarter' (*Journals*, 87). The sympathetic chord was strengthened when Helps gave her Victoria's *Leaves from the Journal of Our Life in the Highlands* (1869), which he had edited. Eliot wrote to thank him, saying that she felt an affinity with it 'because I am a woman of about the same age, and also have my personal happiness bound up in a dear husband whose loss would render my life simply a series of social duties and private memories' (*L* iv. 417).

The Queen's admiration for Eliot's early fiction was pronounced. She read *Adam Bede* aloud to the Prince Consort in the autumn of 1859—she liked it and he was impressed—later rereading it and recommending it to the Princess Royal. She ordered two watercolours of scenes from the novel by Edward Henry Corbould, one of Dinah preaching, the other of Hetty butter-making. Theodore Martin, who was writing a biography of the Prince Consort, asked John *Blackwood to tell Eliot how devoted the Queen was to her works, especially

Painting of a scene from *Adam Bede*, 'Dinah Morris preaching on Hayslope Green', commissioned by Queen Victoria from E. H. Corbould in 1861.

Adam Bede (*L* vi. 137). She was also much moved by 'Mr Gilfil's Love-Story'. The Queen and George Eliot shared the same birth year (1819) and, in different ways, they have both suffered the vicissitudes of reputation, the novelist standing as a representative figure of the age to which the Queen gave her name.   GRH

Vienna, the Austrian capital, was visited by George Eliot and G. H. *Lewes in 1858 and 1870. In July 1858 they spent some days there on their way from *Munich to *Dresden. Eliot found the aspect of the city to be that of an inferior *Paris, the shops having an elegance not to be found in *Germany and the houses tall and stately. The exquisite tower of St Stephen's cathedral, 'that glorious building', was worth going to Vienna to see (*Journals*, 322–3), though the interior was cruelly marred by excessive ornamentation (324). She was also impressed by the art galleries, particularly paintings by *Titian and Giorgione at the Belvedere and by *Rubens in the Liechtenstein collection (see VISUAL ARTS). She and Lewes visited the anatomist Hyrtl, who showed them his work on the vascular and nervous systems of animals and fascinated them with an account of how he had lost his fortune in the *revolution of 1848. Their second visit in April 1870 was affected by illness: Eliot had a severe cold and ulcerated throat, and Lewes in his diaries states that they were glad enough to leave the city, which had completely changed its character since their first visit and lost all its charm (*L* v. 87–91). Vienna features in *Daniel Deronda* as one of the scenes of Mirah's unhappy life with her father, though her account of her acting career there and her father's attempt to prostitute her contains no particularized description of the city (*DD* 20).   JMR

violin. An enthusiastic pianist, George Eliot told Charles Lee Lewes (see LEWES FAMILY) that she wished she could also play the violin because it 'gives that *keen edge* of tone which the piano wants' (*L* iii. 126). In 1863 she took lessons from the violinist Leopold Jansa in order to improve her skills as an accompanist, and during the winter of 1866 Frederick *Lehmann took his violin to her house every Monday evening until together they had played every one of *Mozart's and *Beethoven's piano and violin sonatas. George Eliot greatly admired the violinist Joseph *Joachim, whose playing she and G. H. *Lewes frequently heard during the 1860s and 1870s.   BG

Virgil (Publius Vergilius Maro) (70–19 BC), Latin poet whose work George Eliot knew well. In the first chapter of her first story the narrator self-consciously breaks into the narrative to remark that an accomplished writer would take the

opportunity to quote Virgil in relation to calumny (*SC* 1.1), but claims to be unable to do so. The narrator here is not to be identified with the author, whose *letters, *essays, and *journals show her readily able to quote from the *Aeneid* and *Georgics* in particular. Nevertheless, references to Virgil in the fiction are infrequent. In *Romola*, which can been seen as an attempt at a modern epic like the *Aeneid* (see GENRES), the barber Nello refers to the debate about whether he should be spelt Virgil or Vergil (*RO* 3), while in the Introduction to *Felix Holt, the Radical* the coachman is likened to the figure of Virgil who acts as *Dante's guide in the *Inferno*. The infernal dimension of the Transomes' life is underlined by a reference to the poets Dante (*Inferno*, xiii) and Virgil (*Aeneid*, iii), who 'have told us of a dolorous enchanted forest in the under world'. When George Eliot died, her husband John Walter *Cross had lines from Dante which are addressed to Virgil inscribed on her coffin. See also CLASSICAL LITERATURE.   JMR

Rendell, Vernon, 'George Eliot and the Classics', *Notes and Queries*, 193 (1948).

visual arts. George Eliot's taste in the visual arts was in no sense an unusual one for an educated Victorian. Like many of her contemporaries she greatly admired the sculpture of the classical period and paintings by Italian masters of the middle and late Renaissance. Even her celebrated liking for the Dutch genre works of the 17th century was not as unexpected as has sometimes been suggested, and, when reacting to contemporary art, George Eliot selected for particular praise works which were generally popular.

George Eliot's earliest first-hand experience of the fine arts probably came at Arbury Hall and at Packington Hall, both country houses where her father was agent (see EVANS, ROBERT). We know from *Scenes of Clerical Life* that she was alert to the interior decoration of Arbury and aware of the collections of family portraits which hung there, including works by Sir Peter Lely (1618–80) and George Romney (1734–1802), although in 'Mr Gilfil's Love-Story' she gives the Romney portraits to Sir Joshua Reynolds (1723–92). In the same story she presents a family picture gallery as a symbol of continuity, a foil for the vulnerability of the outsider, Caterina Sarti. George Eliot employed a similar strategy in *Daniel Deronda* where she juxtaposes Daniel against the Mallinger portraits, and where they are also introduced to represent a family line from which the character is excluded. By that time, George Eliot had mastered the tradition of English portraiture. In May 1867 she went to the second of three famous exhibitions of historical portraits at the South Kensington Museum (now the Victoria & Albert Museum), this one devoted to the 18th century. She had other opportunities of seeing grand manner portraits, notably at the Dulwich Picture Gallery in 1859 and at the National Gallery. Her response is shown when, in *Deronda*, she contrasts the aristocratic style of portraiture of Anthony Van Dyck (1599–1641) and Joshua Reynolds, with the more realist portrait style of *Rembrandt. In the novel, the former is associated with Gwendolen Harleth, the latter with Mordecai Cohen.

When she settled in *London in 1851 George Eliot took the opportunity to become familiar with the British Museum, with its great collections of classical sculpture, and the National Gallery, then a far smaller collection than it is today but already strong in Italian high Renaissance works, Rembrandt, and French 17th-century landscapes. George Eliot was also a regular attender at the annual Royal Academy exhibitions of contemporary paintings.

George Eliot's appreciation of the fine arts took on a new aspect when she left England with G. H. *Lewes in 1854. Their first port of call was Antwerp where they looked at the paintings of *Rubens and at the *Descent from the Cross* in particular. This was an iconic work with British travellers on their way to the Low Countries and *Germany. In the picture gallery at *Berlin in 1854 and later in those of *Munich and *Dresden, which she visited in 1858, George Eliot became familiar with three of the greatest collections of European art, each strong in Dutch 17th-century painting, in Italian Renaissance art, and in classical sculpture.

George Eliot reviewed the third and fourth volumes of *Modern Painters* by John *Ruskin in 1856, and she found herself broadly in sympathy with his demand for *realism and truth in art. Ruskin himself would not, however, have shared her liking for the small Dutch genre works which she so much admired in Berlin, Munich, and Dresden, even though his writing had helped to inspire her own vision of art. Ruskin having confirmed her own belief that art must truthfully reflect life, George Eliot then applied this standard to the Dutch School. She states her position with much force in chapter 17 of *Adam Bede*, 'In which the story pauses a little'. George Eliot's demand there that the fine arts, and, by implication, literature, should deal with the humble and unattractive as well as with the idealized and beautiful, also finds expression in her 1856 essay on the work of Wilhelm von Riehl, 'The *Natural History of German Life', where she criticizes those painters who represent rustic figures in an inaccurate and trivializing manner.

The Dutch 17th-century paintings which George Eliot praised are small in scale, unidealized, and predominently concerned with humble

activities, women peeling vegetables or gutting fish. It was in Munich that she saw a work by Gerrit Dou of an old woman saying grace, which seems to have inspired her comment in *Adam Bede* that she could turn, 'without shrinking' from paintings of celestial and heroic scenes: 'to an old woman bending over her flower-pot, or eating her solitary dinner, while the noonday light, softened perhaps by a screen of leaves, falls on her mob-cap, and just touches the rim of her spinning-wheel, and her stone-jug, and those cheap common things which are the precious necessaries of life to her' (*AB* 17).

George Eliot's liking for the work of Rubens which she saw in Antwerp and Munich, can also be interpreted as a reaction to the strong humanity of his paintings. Many British travellers complained of the fleshly quality of Rubens's paintings, but George Eliot was delighted by what she saw of him in Munich, as she was by several forceful works by Albrecht Dürer (1471–1528) in the same collection.

The novelist was, however, equally, if not more, attracted by the ideal in art, and this was a taste which was to develop as she grew older. In 1858 she saw *Raphael's *Sistine Madonna* in Dresden, and declared it to be the greatest painting in the world. The human touch of the representation of mother and child particularly delighted her, but this is not a painting of the humble and commonplace. Indeed it was often regarded in the 19th century as a supreme, even visionary, work of Christian faith.

A journey to *Italy in 1860 took George Eliot and Lewes to *Paris, where she saw the Louvre, and then on to *Rome, *Naples, *Florence, and *Venice. The paintings in Florence particularly attracted her, and this enthusiasm found her in step with her more enlightened contemporaries. When George Eliot made the decision to write *Romola* she embarked upon a process of educating herself in Florentine Renaissance art. Among other relevant works, she read *The Lives of the Painters* by Giorgio Vasari (1511–74) and the *Autobiography* of Benvenuto Cellini (1500–71), *The Poetry of Sacred and Legendary Art* (1848) by Anna *Jameson, Jean Coindet's *Histoire de la Peinture en Italie* (1849), and Franz Kugler's *A Handbook of the History of Painting* (1837, trans. 1842).

The frescos of Domenico Ghirlandaio (c.1448–94), in Santa Maria Novella and Santa Trinità in Florence, provided George Eliot with detailed information about the appearance of costumes and domestic interiors during the period of her novel, and she introduced a number of known art works into *Romola*. Among these are the doors of the Florentine baptistery by Lorenzo Ghiberti (1378–1455), the statue of *Judith and Holofernes* by Donatello (1386–1466), Fra Angelico's (1387–1455)

Crucifixion in the cloister of San Marco, and *The Vision of St Bernard* by Filippino Lippi (*c*.1457–1504). At times even George Eliot's scrupulous research failed her, however. She places the Filippino Lippi painting in the church of the Badia, to which it was removed only in 1529, and she has Girolamo *Savonarola praying in front of a *Madonna* by Fra Bartolommeo (1472 or 1475–1517), which was not in fact painted until after his death.

A number of painters appear as characters in *Romola*, some like Fra Bartolommeo or Mariotto Albertinelli (1474–1515) in fleeting roles, but Piero di Cosimo (*c.* 1462–1521?) plays a major part in the plot. Only one genuine work by Piero is introduced into *Romola*: the *Venus, Mars, and Cupid* now in the Picture Gallery in Berlin. The rest of the paintings attributed to him in the novel are invented: the *Bacchus and Ariadne* triptych, the *Allegory* with three masks, *Sinon deceiving Priam*, and *Oedipus and Antigone*. Each of these invented paintings is introduced in order to reflect Piero's gift for understanding human nature, a quality which seems to associate him with the novelist.

At the time of George Eliot's first visit to Italy, painters before Giotto (*c*.1267–1337) were beginning to attract attention. Robert *Browning's painter poems were an indicator of a change in taste, pre-dating much, if not all, scholarly interest in so-called 'primitive' artists. George Eliot and G. H. Lewes made a point of seeing a number of works by early or pre-Renaissance painters. They looked at the frescos by Giotto in the Arena chapel in Padua in 1860 and at the 15th-century frescos by various artists in the Campo Santo in Pisa in 1861.

In front of a painting then attributed to Cimabue (*c*.1240–1302) in the Uffizi Gallery in Florence (now thought to be by Duccio, active 1278–1319), they commented on Cimabue's superiority to his predecessors, but rated his *Madonna* far below Giotto's, which stood beside it. They preferred the *Madonna* of an even earlier painter, Guido da Siena (active during the 13th century), which they saw in the church of San Domenico in Florence, to any Cimabue, and studied the Sienese paintings in the Accademia gallery with great interest. Eventually, however, they placed Guido da Siena below Giotto as an artistic genius.

George Eliot saw many sculptures and paintings during her Italian journeys and her responses were noted in a journal which reflects clearly her likes and dislikes (see JOURNALS). Several works which are now among the most famous in the world are not mentioned there. *Primavera* (*Spring*) and *The Birth of Venus* by Sandro Botticelli (1447–1510) were still ignored by almost all British visitors to the Uffizi Gallery in Florence and George Eliot was no exception. The later fame of Botticelli was stimulated by the rise of aestheticism in the 1860s and 1870s and Walter *Pater was among those who recognized the quality of the artist. Pater's *Studies in the History of the Renaissance* of 1873 contains essays on Botticelli and on the Venetian painter Giorgione (1478–1511). Giorgione's *La Tempesta*, in the Accademia in Venice, is another work which draws crowds of 20th-century admirers, but which George Eliot apparently passed without notice. She did, however, introduce a painting by Giorgione, then sometimes called *Lucrezia Borgia* (*Laura*, 1506, Kunsthistoriches Museum, Vienna), into 'The Lifted Veil' where it provides a parallel for the evil of Bertha. Latimer 'stood long alone before it, fascinated by the terrible reality of that cunning, relentless face, till I felt a strange poisoned sensation, as if I had long been inhaling a fatal odour' (LV 1).

George Eliot also reflects the tenets of aestheticism in her emphatic rejection of the paintings of the Bolognese 17th-century painters, including Ludovico (1555–1619) and Annibale Carracci (1560–1609), Guercino (1591–1666) and Guido Reni (1575–1640). Commended by Joshua Reynolds in his *Discourses* of 1768–89, the Bolognese masters, pre-eminent with an earlier age of tourists, were now losing their appeal. George Eliot professed herself bored, and even dismayed, by their work in Genoa and in Bologna. Of Reni's heads of Christ she had already spoken disparagingly during her time in Dresden, and a *Supper at Emmaus* attributed to him even appears, as an object of some derision, at the auction in chapter 60 of *Middlemarch*.

The last major city in George Eliot and G. H. Lewes's exploration of Italy was Venice. George Eliot already knew the work of *Titian well from Berlin and Dresden, and she was delighted by what she saw of him in Venice. She admired certain works by Giovanni Bellini (*c*.1430–1516) and Paolo Veronese (*c*.1528–88), but not those of Jacopo Tintoretto (1518–94), so much admired by Ruskin. George Eliot was particularly struck by *St Barbara* by Palma Vecchio (1480–1528) in the church of Santa Maria Formosa, 'an almost unique presentation of a hero-woman' (Cross, ii. 244).

George Eliot's experience of European art inevitably affected her response to the work of her contemporaries. Visiting the studio of the sculptor John Gibson (1790–1866) in Rome in 1860, she dismissed him as a weak imitator of the ancient Greek masters. She was rather more enthusiastic about the work of another veteran of the Roman art world, the pioneer painter of the *Nazarene movement, Friedrich Overbeck (1789–1869), and incorporated aspects of his appearance and his work into the figure of Adolf Naumann in *Middlemarch*. George Eliot's comment on the Nazarenes, 'certain long-haired German artists at Rome' (*MM* 19), is among her most original observations on the fine arts, a successful element in establishing an authentic Roman background for the early 1830s. George Eliot already knew the work of the Nazarenes from Berlin and Munich. In Munich she had particularly disliked the frescos on classical subjects painted in the Glyptothek by Peter Cornelius (1783–1867), another Nazarene painter. Her distaste for the work of Cornelius's pupil, Wilhelm Kaulbach (1805–74), was even stronger. The highly charged symbolism of his giant canvases on ancient and religious history seemed to her pretentious and unrealistic.

In the earlier part of her career George Eliot was much impressed by the work of the English equivalent of the Nazarenes, the *Pre-Raphaelite Brotherhood. Like the Nazarenes, the Pre-Raphaelites looked back to early Renaissance art for inspiration, but George Eliot was more impressed by their credo of truth to nature, and by the pursuit of accuracy which won the respect of the Pre-Raphaelites' early champion, John Ruskin. The young George Eliot's enthusiasm for Ruskinian scientific accuracy and precision inclined her to favour the paintings of William Holman Hunt (1827–1910) over those of the other Pre-Raphaelite brothers. Even Hunt irritated her, however, with what she believed to be unreal peasants in *The Hireling Shepherd* (1852, Manchester City Art Galleries). As a novelist of the rural world, George Eliot was particularly concerned that representations of rustic life should be truthful, not idealized.

Significantly, George Eliot excepted Hunt's rendering of fields and woodlands in *The Hireling Shepherd* from her strictures on the painting's subject matter. Like her contemporaries, she had a particular affection for landscape painting, a genre which recalled the countryside for so many recent city dwellers. In 1848 George Eliot wrote of her enthusiasm for the work of William Clarkson Stanfield (1793–1867), David Roberts (1796–1864), and Thomas Creswick (1811–69): 'to me even the works of our own Stanfield and Roberts and Creswick bring a whole world of thought and bliss—"a sense of something far more deeply interfused". The ocean and the enclosing hills are spirit to me, and they will never be robbed of their sublimity' (*L* i. 248). Of the three painters whom George Eliot names, Creswick, with his Midland landscape scenes, must have reminded her of her early years. Stanfield is best known for his dramatic seascapes and mountain landscapes and Roberts for his paintings of Scotland and the Middle East.

At the Royal Academy summer exhibition of 1872, having by then seen most of the great galleries of Europe, George Eliot singled out two quiet rural scenes for praise from an exhibition which

she found largely disappointing. These were *The Harbour of Refuge* (Tate Gallery), set in the garden of a group of almshouses and by the young Frederick Walker (1840–75), and *Harvest Moon* (Tate Gallery), a near visionary landscape by an older artist, George Hemming Mason (1818–72), who had died earlier in the year. George Eliot's elegy for the landscape of the past in the 'Looking Back' chapter of *Impressions of Theophrastus Such* in 1879 (*TS* 2) makes it clear that she continued to recall the Midland scenes of her early years with deep emotion (see LANDSCAPE). Her early novels, and in particular *Adam Bede*, evoke a lost world of harvest fields, flowers, and farm cottages. Even so, and perhaps with a touch of hypocrisy, George Eliot objected, as she makes clear in chapter 39 of *Middlemarch*, to those artists who saw only an opportunity for a picturesque sketch in a tumbledown and insanitary country dwelling. 'It is true that an observer, under that softening influence of the fine arts which makes other people's hardships picturesque, might have been delighted with the homestead called Freeman's End'.

One might expect to find George Eliot admiring the work of John Constable (1776–1837) whose landscape paintings influenced those of artists whom she admired, but she seems not to have been aware of him. Among the earlier generation of landscapists, she singles out J. M. W. *Turner, championed by Ruskin in *Modern Painters*. She visited the large collection of Turner watercolours amassed by B. G. Windus in 1851 and refers briefly to his work in novels and stories, references that make clear her awareness of the shift towards abstraction in Turner's later style.

If George Eliot could respond to landscape painting, she was often unenthusiastic about other aspects of contemporary British art. The Royal Academy exhibitions sometimes depressed her and in 1854 she came home 'in a miserably uninspired state—which is rarely the case with me after seeing the pictures' (*L* ii. 155). The one work which she found to admire was by a Dutch artist living in France, Ary Scheffer (1795–1858), whose *Francesca da Rimini* (Wallace Collection) shows Dante's condemned lovers whirled round in the Inferno. Two years before, at the 1852 exhibition, she had picked out *A Huguenot* (private collection) by John Everett *Millais.

Both paintings were very popular, and George Eliot's liking for them was by no means original or remarkable. It does, however, give a clue to what she liked in contemporary subject pictures. Both provoke thoughts of love and tenderness. Scheffer's picture of Paolo and Francesca da Rimini is the more obviously tragic, but Millais's study of a Catholic girl trying to save her protestant lover from the Massacre of St Bartholemew has its own message of loss and destruction. In both cases, George Eliot was particularly struck by the rendering of the expression on the young woman's face. A painting of a similar subject caught her attention ten years later in 1864 when she saw *The Meeting on the Turret Stairs* (National Gallery of Ireland) by her friend Frederic *Burton at the Old Watercolour Society exhibition. Here Hillelil and Hildebrand, lovers from Norse legend, snatch a kiss on the staircase. 'The subject might have been made the most vulgar thing in the world—the artist has raised it to the highest pitch of refined emotion' (*L* iv. 147).

George Eliot was acquainted with several contemporary artists, among them members of the Pre-Raphaelite group. She particularly admired the near symbolist work of Edward *Burne-Jones, who became a good friend, and she also knew Holman Hunt, John Millais, Dante Gabriel *Rossetti, and the sculptor Thomas Woolner (1825–92). Among other well-known artists of the period, she came to know Frederic *Leighton when he was illustrating *Romola* and, in 1870, she finally met his close friend, George Frederic Watts (1817–1904), whose serious and often allegorical work she had always admired. Watts made her a gift of a version of his bust of *Clytie* (1868, Watts Gallery, Compton) in 1870, in tribute to her work as a novelist. The cartoonist and illustrator, George Du Maurier (1834–96), was a regular guest at The *Priory, often coming with his friend the painter Thomas Armstrong (1835–1911), later director of Art at the South Kensington Museum.

The closest artist friend of George Eliot and G. H. Lewes was the Irish painter Frederic Burton, whom they first met in Munich in 1858. Burton, who later became director of the National Gallery, made portrait drawings of George Eliot in 1864 and 1865 (see PORTRAITS). In May and June 1864 George Eliot and Lewes travelled in Italy with Burton, whose knowledge of art made their journey particularly enjoyable. They spent three weeks in Venice, and then visited other north Italian cities, looking extensively at painting and sculpture.

In comparison with certain other novelists, Thomas *Hardy and Marcel *Proust among them, George Eliot makes comparatively little use of ecphrasis, the introduction of a specific work of art into her narratives. *Romola* is something of an exception, but even here, as noted above, there are as many invented paintings as there are actual works of art. George Eliot herself declared that *The Spanish Gypsy* was inspired by a Titian *Annunciation* in the Scuola of San Rocco in Venice, but the painting does not actually appear in the poem. Raphael's *Sistine Madonna* in Dresden, which was for George Eliot the greatest painting in the world, is mentioned specifically (but not described) in

The Mill where Philip Wakem tells Maggie Tulliver that many things in human nature are inexplicable: 'The greatest of painters only once painted a mysteriously divine child; he couldn't have told how he did it, and we can't tell why we feel it to be divine' (*MF* 5.1) Raphael also provides George Eliot with two points of focus in the Roman chapters of *Middlemarch*, the first in chapter 19 where she establishes the ignorance of British tourists in the 1820s and 1830s through reference to a mistake made by William Hazlitt (1778–1830) in his *Notes of a Journey through France and Italy* where Hazlitt described the sacred flowers, springing from the tomb of the ascended virgin in Raphael's *Coronation of the Virgin* (*c*.1503, Vatican Museum) as 'an ornamental vase due to the painter's fancy'. The second reference comes in the next chapter where Edward Casaubon suggests to Dorothea that they view the Raphael frescos in the Villa Farnesina. His tone is so chilling that she inevitably desists: 'He is the painter who has been held to combine the most complete grace of form with sublimity of expression. Such at least I have gathered to be the opinion of cognoscenti.' The frescos of *Cupid and Psyche*, by Raphael and others (*c*.1517–18) to which Casaubon refers and the *Triumph of Galatea* (*c*.1512), also in the Farnesina, are among the most sensual of Raphael's works, surely chosen here as a striking contrast to the coldness of the Casaubons' marriage.

Recollections of a few paintings and sculptures lie behind George Eliot's descriptions of certain faces in her novels. Both Dinah Morris in *Adam Bede* and Romola are compared to St Catherine of Alexandria, and it is probable that George Eliot had in mind a painting on the same subject by Raphael (*c*.1507) in the National Gallery. In *The Mill* Lucy Deane has 'a face breathing playful joy, like one of Correggio's cherubs' (*MF* 6.9). There are four great altarpieces by Correggio in Dresden, all of them with cherubs, the most famous being the *Holy Night* or *Notte* (1522–30), where the fair-haired angels in the sky could suggest the 'triumphant revelation' with which the narrator invests Lucy. George Eliot, however, admired a particular cherub with legs and arms wide apart from the *Madonna with St Sebastian* (1523–4).

Almost all such references come in the narrator's commentary and not in the words or thoughts of the characters. One exception is the reference to Giorgione in 'The Lifted Veil' mentioned above. A more characteristic example is the way in which the temperament of Mrs Tulliver is described in *The Mill* by means of a comparison with one of Raphael's early Madonnas. 'I have often wondered whether those early Madonnas of Raphael, with the blond faces and somewhat stupid expressions, kept their placidity undisturbed when their strong-limbed strong willed boys got a little too old to do without clothing' (*MF* 1.2). Tessa, in *Romola*, looks like 'one of Fra Lippo Lippi's round cheeked adoring angels' (*RO* 34). Bernardo Dovizi, in the same novel, is described through his own portrait by Raphael (*RO* 20). Mordecai in Deronda is compared to the so-called *Jewish Rabbi* by Rembrandt in the National Gallery (*DD* 52), and Daniel himself to two figures in paintings by Titian, Christ in *The Tribute Money* (*c*.1516; *DD* 40) and (almost certainly) to *The Man with a Glove* (*c*.1523; *DD* 17).

George Eliot makes some direct references to classical sculpture. Dorothea Brooke is placed next to the *Ariadne* in the Vatican gallery and George Eliot again displays her knowledge of earlier scholarship when she notes in chapter 19 of *Middlemarch* that the statue was then thought to be of Cleopatra. Ariadne is far more appropriate for the novelist's purposes, providing a clear parallel for Dorothea, abandoned on her honeymoon in favour of her husband's researches. The unhappy Hetty Sorrel in *Adam Bede* is said to be like 'that wonderful Medusa-face with the passionate passionless lips' (*AB* 37), the *Rondanini Medusa* in Munich (Glyptothek). The Transomes' entrance hall in *Felix Holt, the Radical* is dominated by copies of classical statues, and an amusing note is struck as Mrs Holt gazes at a *Silenus and Bacchus* (Glyptothek, Munich and Capitoline Museum, Rome) and decides that it must be a family portrait, with a strange-looking father who feels great affection for the baby in his arms. A parallel is clearly set up with old Mr Transome and his grandson, who are playing together nearby.

If anything, George Eliot is more at ease with classical reference than she is with reference to the work of the old masters. On their journeys, she and Lewes would always spend many hours in galleries of sculpture, and, from the tone of George Eliot's comments, they caused her less critical anxieties than old master paintings.

Some of these insecurities undoubtedly originated with George Eliot's unease with baroque and mannerist art. Her problems with Guido Reni and the Bolognese school not only reflect the date at which she was living, but also a personal dislike of what she regarded as strained and unnatural art. The baroque was generally unpopular with Victorian critics, and was often seen, through its association with the Roman Catholic Church, as opposed to the puritan values of the Protestant north.

George Eliot was frequently disappointed when she looked at the work of Michelangelo, a forerunner of the baroque style, although he was acknowledged in the 19th century as a great master. His statues of *Night* and *Day* on the tomb of

Lorenzo de Medici (1519–33) in the church of San Lorenzo in Florence, popular with art lovers now as they were in George Eliot's day, were rejected by Lewes and George Eliot as pretentious. *Moses* (1515–16) in the church of Sant Pietro in Vincoli in Rome did not live up to the novelist's expectations, nor did his painting of the *Holy Family* (1504–5) in the Uffizi. *Christ* (1514–21) in the church of Santa Maria sopra Minerva in Rome, by contrast with these strong works, struck her as 'namby-pamby' (Cross, ii. 185). *David* (1501–4, Accademia, Florence) is another work, immensely popular in the 20th century, which George Eliot never mentions. She occasionally expressed a liking for a sculpture or drawing by Michelangelo, including one of the figures in the *Deposition* (before 1552) belonging to the Duomo in Florence, whom she calls Joseph of Arimathea, but who is in fact Nicodemus, and the *Pietà* (1497–1500) in St Peter's in Rome. Somewhat unexpectedly, she declared the Sistine ceiling (1508–12) to be 'the most wonderful fresco in the world' (Cross ii. 183), but it is clear that George Eliot was, at best, equivocal about Michelangelo's work.

Michelangelo's *David* stood in the Loggia dei Lanzi in Florence, together with *Judith with Head of Holofernes* completed by Donatello (1388–1466) in the last part of his career and *Perseus* (completed 1554) by Benvenuto Cellini (1500–71). George Eliot introduced the Donatello statue briefly into *Romola*, but, when she first saw this celebrated row of Renaissance statues in 1860, she expressed distaste for them, dismissing *Perseus* in particular as a fantasy work rather than a reflection of humanity.

Later journeys took George Eliot to *Spain in 1867 and back to Italy in 1869 and 1880. Her Spanish journal is lost, and as a result there are no details of her response to the Prado in Madrid. There was little apparent change to her taste for Italian painting on the two later visits. Broadly, therefore, it would be fair to say that George Eliot's chief experience of art came in London, where she was able to visit galleries, exhibitions, and artists' studios, and on her earlier visits to European galleries, particularly those in Berlin, Munich, and Dresden, in 1854 and 1858, and in Italy during the formative journeys of 1860, 1861, and 1864.   LO

Ormond, Leonee, 'Angels and Archangels: Romola and the Paintings of Florence', in Levine and Turner (1998).

Witemeyer (1979).

vocation is a theme of paramount importance in George Eliot's work. In *Middlemarch*, Lydgate's scientific aspirations and Dorothea's longing to find a channel for her sense of vocation are central. Eliot also represents vocation as a more appropriate subject for the novel rather than a narrow preoccupation with romantic love. Whilst romantic love often spells the death of vocation, Eliot also shows the two as entangled and analogous by employing the language of romantic love to describe vocational passion such as Lydgate's intellectual 'ardour' (*MM* 15).

In *Daniel Deronda*, Eliot heads the chapter which presages the influence which Deronda will have over Gwendolen's struggling sense of vocation with a quotation from Walt Whitman's 'Vocalisation': 'Surely whoever speaks to me in the right voice, him or her I shall follow' (*DD* 29). Both Gwendolen and Deronda are in search of an inspired course of action and the issue of vocation is repeatedly given literal expression in images of *music and voice (see VOICE, REPRESENTATIONS OF) (as also in Dinah's preaching in *Adam Bede*). Gwendolen has had her hopes of a singing career dashed by the composer Klesmer's condemnation of her lack of true 'vocation' (*DD* 23). Deronda, working towards the discovery of his own Zionist vocation, reflects that a people's innate 'ancestral life', even if unrecognized, is 'like a cunningly-wrought musical instrument' which 'under the right touch, gives music' (*DD* 43). Much of the music which Mirah sings serves to distinguish her specific calling as a Jew. Mordecai, reborn into the heritage of the Jewish martyrs, declares that his soul 'sang with the cadence of their strain' (*DD* 40).

'Vocation' also stands directly for 'giving voice'. Gwendolen's failure to find a vocation is epitomized by the way in which she feels 'Throttled into silence' by Grandcourt (who refuses to allow her to take singing lessons) (*DD* 54, 48). Her fear of the murderous desires this repression breeds recalls the singer Armgart's pity for the voiceless woman in Eliot's 1870 poem of the same name (see POETRY):

> 'Poor wretch!' she says, of any murderess—
> 'The world was cruel, and she could not sing:
> I carry my revenges in my throat'.

Eliot explores numerous issues relating to female vocation through the women musicians portrayed in *Deronda*: Gwendolen, Catherine Arrowpoint, Mirah, and the prima donna Alcharisi. Alcharisi asserts her right to fulfil her musical gift despite the repressive wish of her father that she live the life of an ideal Jewish woman: 'My nature gave me a charter' (*DD* 53). In 'Armgart' Eliot had similarly had her singer reject the notion that there is anything unnatural in female artistic vocation:

> I am an artist by my birth—
> By the same warrant that I am a woman:
> Nay, in the added rarer gift I see
> Supreme vocation . . .

Armgart complains that narrow views of woman's nature force a choice between equally fundamental aspects of her being. Yet she is also criticized for her insensitivity to the lives of ordinary women. Eliot's prima donnas both make claims for women's vocational fulfilment and manifest anxieties about female ambition (see WOMAN QUESTION). Deronda's mother is led by her professional aspirations to abandon her son. In contrast, Mirah Cohen's entirely professional standing as a musician and her wish to use her training to earn a living, are tempered by her dislike of overtly public performance and an ultimately overriding 'vocation' as Deronda's wife. Her domesticated artistry exemplifies how Eliot seems equally troubled by the question of women achieving independence and fulfilment of their gifts and by issues of woman's true nature and the proper spheres for female activity. Armgart eventually resolves the apparently irreducible conflict between vocation and love, not through *marriage, but by remaining faithful to her art as a teacher. This compromise seems to offer the possibility of vocation free of egoism, but none of Eliot's female characters (and few of her men) are granted complete fulfilment of their vocational desires.

Armgart and Alcharisi also illustrate the real dangers of vocation for women—the singer's *is* a dubious hold on power. Both lose their voices. Once the singing voice is gone, the woman will not be heard: 'Song was my speech', says Armgart, left speechless by the loss of her singing voice. The prima donna's ambition and concomitant 'dread of sliding' suggest the published writer's wish to make her voice heard and her fears about her own vocation. Eliot herself made this connection, writing to John *Blackwood as she was finishing *Daniel Deronda*: 'As to confidence in the work to be done I am somewhat in the condition suggested to Armgart, "How will you bear the poise of eminence, With dread of falling?"' (*L* vi. 75).

The higher vocation of music therefore provides an analogy for other forms of artistic expression, most specifically for writing (*DD* 23). A vocation for singing represents a proper calling in itself, and, more broadly, stands for inspired expression. The composer Klesmer emphasizes 'the inward vocation and the hard-won achievement' of the committed professional artist (*DD* 23). Eliot's claim for the narrative importance of vocation is also an assertion of writing as a superior calling. The novel casts a stringent eye over the issue of authorial vocation and authorship. Deronda rejects both singing and authorship as a solution to his professional indecision, the latter as 'a vocation which is understood to turn foolish thinking into funds' (*DD* 17). Eliot has Rex

Gascoigne invoke musical and literary production to defend his study of law as more valuable than indulgence in dilettante artistic activity: '"Give me something to do with making the laws, and let who will make the songs" . . . I don't see that law-rubbish is worse than any other sort. It is not so bad as the rubbishy literature that people choke their minds with. It doesn't make one so dull' (*DD* 58). Eliot thus underpins her dramatization of the quest for a vocation with her conviction that 'the deepest disgrace is to insist on doing work for which we are unfit—to do work of any sort badly' (*L* iv. 425).   DdSC

voice, representation of. George Eliot was extremely sensitive to tones and qualities of voice, and pronounced it inexcusable to sing even to a drawing-room audience 'in a cracked voice and out of tune' (*L* ii. 210). She therefore gave careful consideration to the vocal timbre of her most important characters, whether they sang or not, using it as an indication of the capacity—or lack of it—for sympathy, tenderness, or persuasiveness. Authoritative men such as Adam Bede, Tertius Lydgate in *Middlemarch*, and Daniel Deronda, possess either expressly baritone voices, or—as in the case of Felix Holt, and Savonarola in *Romola*—speak in tones that are manifestly deep, powerful, or sonorous. Those who lack either authority or—like Mr Casaubon in *Middlemarch*—sexual charisma, correspondingly lack vocal resonance. Amos Barton's 'hoarse and feeble' oratory in *Scenes of Clerical Life*, for example, resembles 'a Belgian railway-horn, which shows praiseworthy intentions inadequately fulfilled' (*SC* 1.2). In *The Mill on the Floss*, Philip Wakem's tenor, which emotion makes higher and feebler, is indicative of his powerlessness as the rival of Stephen Guest, whose deep bass (he can sing a low F natural with ease) profoundly affects Maggie Tulliver. As the narrator in *Daniel Deronda* says, nature creates even a 'rare and ravishing tenor . . . at some sacrifice' (*DD* 17), and Philip's tenor is less than ravishing. Ideally, Grandcourt's handsome physique would suit Duke Alfonso in Donizetti's *Lucrezia Borgia*, who attempts to poison the man he believes to be his wife Lucrezia's lover—except that, as Hans Meyrick points out (*DD* 45), it could never produce the fine baritone: instead, a languorous drawl camouflages Grandcourt's brand of malevolence. *Romola*'s beguiling Tito Melema is endowed with a singular, essentially pleasing voice (which, however, Romola is ultimately to find repulsive), though its melting, honeyed, indefinite quality suggests his capacity for treachery.

George Eliot's women also reveal their natures by their voices. Noble, passionate, or influential women are often specifically contralto, or express themselves in tones of exceptional clarity. The voices of Caterina Sarti in 'Mr Gilfil's Love-Story', Dorothea, Mrs Garth, and Mary Garth in *Middlemarch*, and Mirah in *Deronda*—whose notes are 'like a bird's wooing' (*DD* 32)—all belong to the lower range. Dinah Morris masters her audience in an 'articulate thrilling treble' (*AB* 8), while Romola's pure, distinct utterance is compared to the lower notes of the flute (*RO* 5). Since the heroine of George Eliot's poetic drama 'Armgart' triumphs as Gluck's Orpheus, and aspires to sing Beethoven's Fidelio, she is probably a soprano, though this is never stated (in 1855 Eliot had heard the role of Orfeo sung by Johanna Wagner, the composer's niece, who was a soprano and who later lost her voice like Armgart). Presented as pre-eminently a true artist who reveres both her teacher and the composers whose works she interprets, her weakness is her craving for plaudits. Destined to suffer the loss of the singing voice that is 'channel to her soul', she ultimately triumphs over despair, resigns herself to her loss, and resolves to bequeath the gift of her musicianship through her own teaching. By contrast, the voice of *Middlemarch*'s Rosamond Vincy is a key to her spiritual negativity. Her singing is accomplished and well trained—'sweet to hear as a chime perfectly in tune' (*MM* 16)—and her silvery voice can effortlessly render anything her audience cares to hear; but, like her piano playing, it expresses no soul of her own. See also VOCATION.   BG

Gray (1989).
—— 'Power and Persuasion: Voices of Influence in *Romola*', in Levine and Turner (1998).

voice of George Eliot. Although there are some discrepancies in the various responses to George Eliot's voice, it undoubtedly had charm. Its most consistently recorded quality was that of softness, but it was also found 'singularly musical and impressive' (*L* ix. 182 n.), 'penetrating' (*L* iv. 337), and—by Henry James—'most harmonious' (*L* vii. 20 n.). It seems to have struck Tennyson as 'soprano . . . almost . . . like a fine falsetto' (*L* v. 169 n.), though John Walter *Cross establishes it as rich, deep, and flexible, with 'organ-like tones' (Cross, iii. 370). See also APPEARANCE, PERSONAL; VOICE, REPRESENTATION OF.   BG

Voltaire (1694–1778). François Marie Arouet Voltaire, French philosopher, poet, playwright, and writer of fiction, whose work George Eliot knew well but responded to with mixed feelings. When writing about Heinrich *Heine in the *Leader* in September 1855 she applauded Voltaire's moral conviction and his light, subtle, and needle-pointed French, but adopted a more critical stance in her 1856 essay *'German Wit: Heinrich Heine', where once again Voltaire provided a point of comparison. In her brilliant distinction between wit and humour she cites Voltaire as 'the intensest example of pure wit' who 'fails in most of his fictions from his lack of humour' (*Essays*, 220). His philosophical tale *Micromégas*, about a giant from a planet of Sirius visiting earth, is perfectly adapted to his wit and wisdom since it deals only with ideas, but *Candide*, which attempts to give pictures of life, fails for its lack of humour: 'The sense of the ludicrous is continually defeated by disgust, and the scenes, instead of presenting us with an amusing or agreeable picture, are only the frame for a witticism' (*Essays*, 220). Nevertheless she was interested enough to be reading *Candide* again after many years' interval in September 1879.

JMR

W

Wagner, Richard (1813–83), German composer to whose music George Eliot and G. H. *Lewes were introduced by *Liszt, who directed a number of Wagner's operas in *Weimar during 1854. They enjoyed *Der Fliegende Holländer* and *Tannhäuser* but found *Lohengrin* tedious (Haight 1968: 156).

Whilst in Weimar, Eliot undertook the translation of an article on Wagner by Liszt and wrote an article for *Fraser's Magazine* entitled *'Liszt, Wagner and Weimar' (repr. in *Essays*). She admits that she is not personally able fully to appreciate Wagner's music, but as a defence of his organic and progressive dramatic theories, her article constitutes possibly the first appreciation of Wagner published in England, where professional music critics were predominantly hostile to his work. She and Lewes continued to find Wagner's music difficult to enjoy. 'The Mutter and I have come to the conclusion that the Music of the future is not for us', wrote Lewes in 1870 after they had had further opportunity to hear *Tannhäuser* in Berlin (*L* v. 85).

Wagner is amongst the musicians implicitly referred to in the portrayal of the composer Klesmer in *Daniel Deronda*. Klesmer represents an advanced stage of musical culture in opposition to fashionable British society which enjoys *Bellini and *Meyerbeer. He condemns the heroine Gwendolen's choice of an aria by Bellini as representing a 'puerile' stage of civilization, so reiterating the correlation between states of musical and social evolution which is established in Eliot's 'Liszt, Wagner, and Weimar' essay (*DD* 5). Klesmer's criticism of Bellini may be read in the context of the battle 'between the declamatory and melodic schools of music' which Eliot had discussed in relation to Wagner's music (*Essays*, 100). Eliot caricatures her own confessed inability fully to enjoy Wagner's music of the future when an admirer of Gwendolen praises her censured singing

with: 'It is not addressed to the ears of the future, I suppose. I'm glad of that: it suits mine' (*DD* 10). He is, instead, an enthusiast for croquet, 'the game of the future' (*DD* 5).

Lewes also defended Wagner in his *Actors and the Art of Acting* (1875), where the growth of an audience for Wagner in Germany, the home of advanced artistic standards, is invoked to encourage a receptive attitude towards his art in Britain (229–34). Eliot and Lewes met Wagner and his wife Cosima (Liszt's daughter) numerous times during Wagner's visit to England for a series of concerts in 1877 (Haight 1968: 502). They attended rehearsals and concerts and dined together. Lewes records a party to 'hear Wagner read from his *Parzival*, which he did with great spirit and like a fine actor', a comment which confirms the dramatic importance for both Eliot and Lewes of Wagner's work despite their personal reservations about its musical qualities (*L* vi. 373). See also MUSIC. DdSC

Ward, Mrs Humphry (1851–1920), novelist who, as a young woman, met George Eliot and was later compared to her when she herself became a successful writer. She was born Mary Augusta Arnold, granddaughter of Dr Arnold of Rugby and daughter of Thomas, whose crises of faith took him in and out of Roman Catholicism with disturbing material consequences for his family. When Mary left school in 1867 she was already writing, mainly fiction. Her ability was recognized by Mark *Pattison, Rector of Lincoln College, Oxford, who set her to research Spanish history in the Bodleian and other Oxford libraries. The Pattisons included Mary Arnold among the guests at a party for George Eliot and G. H. *Lewes when they visited *Oxford for May Week 1870. Nearly fifty years later, Mary Ward, by then a significant novelist and social reformer, wrote of this occasion, declaring her 'prompt and active dislike' of Lewes, partly because of his domination of his partner. Her famous description of George Eliot's taking her aside to speak of the Leweses' Spanish journey of 1866–7 is admiring yet faintly equivocal: George Eliot 'was too self-conscious, too desperately reflective, too rich in second thoughts' to be a great talker, though

she could—in monologue . . .—produce on a listener exactly the impression of some of her best work. As the low clear voice flowed on, . . . I *saw* Saragossa, Granada, the Escorial, and that survival of the old Europe in the new, which one must go to Spain to find . . . I shut my eyes, and it all comes back:—the darkened room, the long, pallid face, set in black lace, the evident wish to be kind to a young girl. (*A Writer's Recollections*, 108–9)

Mary married Humphry Ward, a don and journalist, in 1872. When they moved from Oxford to

London with their three children in 1881, her literary career began in earnest. The huge success of her second novel *Robert Elsmere* in 1888 made the name of Mrs Humphry Ward. Reviews hailed her as the new George Eliot, on account both of the magnitude of her achievement and the nature of the spiritual and intellectual struggles depicted in the book. Though Ward herself resisted any attribution of influence, throughout her work appear heroines such as Marcella Boyce (in *Marcella*, 1894, and its sequel, *Sir George Tressady*, 1896), who like George Eliot's characters negotiate dilemmas of ethical and marital choice. In 1898 she declined William (Willie) *Blackwood's invitation to write a book on George Eliot, because 'I do not feel naturally drawn to it, great as my admiration for her is' (Peterson, 102). She found the poetry and passion of the *Brontës, especially Charlotte, more congenial than George Eliot's relative austerity, as her prefaces to *Smith Elder & Co.'s Haworth edition of the Brontës' work (1899–1900) demonstrate.

Mrs Humphry Ward worked energetically in other than literary arenas. She was instrumental in setting up education and welfare services in Bloomsbury; late in life she supported Britain's war effort through her writing. She was staunchly committed to improving women's educational opportunities and hence their prospects for involvement in public life, and took part in establishing Somerville, the first Oxford women's college. But she was a vehement anti-suffragist, as is evident in such novels as *Delia Blanchflower* (1915). In her qualified feminism, as in many other ways (including frequent ill health), Mary Ward had more in common with George Eliot than she discerned (see HEALTH; WOMAN QUESTION).   MAH

Ward, Mrs Humphry, *A Writer's Recollections* (1918).
Peterson, William, *Victorian Heretic: Mrs Humphry Ward's Robert Elsmere* (1976).
Sutherland, John, *Mrs Humphry Ward: Eminent Victorian, Pre-eminent Edwardian* (1990).

Warwickshire, the English Midland county of George Eliot's birth and upbringing (and *Shakespeare's, too), provides the setting of much of her fiction. The stories in *Scenes of Clerical Life* are set in and around *Nuneaton in the north-east of the county, and she returns to the same region in *Felix Holt, the Radical* where Loamshire is a fictional name for Warwickshire. On the other hand the Loamshire of *Adam Bede* is more the Derbyshire of her father's origins (see EVANS, ROBERT), although Hetty Sorrel in her wanderings also traverses the Warwickshire countryside around Stratford-upon-Avon. *The Mill on the Floss*, too, draws on places around Nuneaton as well as *Gainsborough in Lincolnshire. The village of Raveloe in the 'rich

central plain' of England (*SM* 1) where Silas Marner establishes himself, seems again to be a Warwickshire location, while *Middlemarch* is set in and around *Coventry. Mrs Lemon's school, where Rosamond Vincy receives her scanty education, is 'close to a county town with a memorable history in church and castle' (*MM* 16), a description which fits Warwick itself. See also CHARACTERS, ORIGINALS OF; SETTINGS, ORIGINAL BASIS OF.   JMR

Weimar, German town associated particularly with *Goethe, where George Eliot and G. H. *Lewes spent three months, from 2 August to 3 November 1854, when they first left England to live together. The professional purpose of their visit was research for Lewes's biography of Goethe, in which Eliot assisted him. She recorded their experience in an essay in her journal 'Recollections of Weimar 1854' (*Journals*, 215–40) which was recast into two articles published in *Fraser's Magazine* in June and July 1855, 'Three Months in Weimar' and *'Liszt, Wagner, and Weimar' (both repr. in *Essays*).

The town was the seat of the dukes of Weimar and the capital of their small principality, but it was still to the eyes of Londoners not much bigger than a village. William Makepeace *Thackeray had amiably satirized it as 'Pumpernickel' in *Vanity Fair* (1848). Eliot's first impression was not favourable: 'One's first feeling was—how could Goethe live here in this dull, lifeless village' (*Essays*, 84), with its dingy streets, shabby shops, and bovine inhabitants. But the beauty of the park around the river Ilm and the town's associations with Goethe and *Schiller redeemed it. The park became an emblem of the new happiness of her life with Lewes: 'Dear Park of Weimar! In 1854, two loving, happy human beings spent many a delicious hour under your shade and in your sunshine, and to one of them at least you will be a "joy for ever" through all the sorrows that are to come' (*Journals*, 220). She was also thrilled to find an inscription on a small house saying that Schiller had lived there, and was moved to tears by the simplicity of Goethe's study and dark little bedroom, contrasting it with the grandeur of Walter *Scott's house at Abbotsford. The couple visited several places in the vicinity connected with Goethe, including Ilmenau where they climbed up to the wooden hut that served as a hunting lodge for the Duke and found the poem 'Über allen Gipfeln' inscribed by Goethe's own hand near the window frame (Cross, i. 337). In 1867 they returned to Ilmenau, with its wooded walks and invigorating air, to spend a fortnight's holiday.

Condescending about the primitive simplicity of Weimar, the poor quality of German meat and beds, and the 'bovine bourgeoisie' (*Essays*, 94–5), she and Lewes nevertheless encountered real inspiration there in the piano playing of *Liszt, Kapellmeister at the court, with whom they made friends. Attendance at three of *Wagner's operas appealed to them less. Weimar was George Eliot's introduction to *Germany and she retained an affection for its kind of provincial life. Writing from Paris in 1872 and drawing the contrast with Germany, she maintained that 'we have an affinity for what the world calls "dull places" and always prosper best in them' (*L* v. 318). Weimar was just such a place.   JMR

Röder-Bolton, Gerlinde, 'George Eliot's Weimar', *George Eliot Review*, 25 (1994).

Wellington, Duke of (1769–1852), Irish soldier and statesman, whose supposed commands to a certain Mrs C interested George Eliot, as she reveals in writing to Charles *Bray (*L* i. 269), telling the same recipient seven years later that his letters rival Wellington's in terms of their curtness. Earlier she had remarked Benjamin *Disraeli's plagiarism in his tribute to the Duke in the House of Commons (noted by the *Morning Chronicle* and the *Leader*) of Thiers's funeral oration on Marshal Gouvion Saint-Cyr (*L* ii. 69).   GRH

Westminster Review, The, one of the great quarterly reviews of the 19th century to which George Eliot contributed. Founded by James Mill and Jeremy Bentham in 1824 as a Radical review, to compete with the Whig *Edinburgh Review* and the Tory *Quarterly Review*, the intellectually heavyweight *Westminster* was consistently committed to reform and addressed issues such as *education and women's rights in often radical ways. Its contributors and editors, including John Stuart *Mill, read like a catalogue of the most significant and progressive thinkers in 19th-century British liberalism. After John *Chapman purchased the title in 1852, George Eliot anonymously edited the *Westminster*, while Chapman remained the public face of the periodical. 'With regard to the secret Editorship,' she wrote to Chapman in 1851, 'it will perhaps be the best plan for you to state, that for the present *you* are to be regarded as the responsible person, but that you employ an Editor in whose literary and general ability you confide' (*L* viii. 23). She collaborated on the new prospectus and, in addition to editing numerous issues, contributed a number of very fine *essays. Her first long review was of R. W. Mackay's The *Progress of the Intellect* (January 1851) on the history of religion, an appropriate subject given her translations of D. F. *Strauss and Ludwig *Feuerbach (see TRANSLATIONS BY GEORGE ELIOT). Because of her editorial duties, her next major article did not appear until 1854. Other important articles include *'Evangel-

ical Thinking: Dr Cumming' (October 1855) which condemns the intolerance of evangelicalism, and *'Silly Novels by Lady Novelists' (October 1856) which chastises much popular women's literature for being vapid and uncritical of the real world. In a telling move, ten days after writing 'Silly Novels', George Eliot began writing her own fiction, which became *Scenes of Clerical Life*. In many of her articles, we see themes which would become developed arguments in her fiction. Through the intellectual circle of the *Westminster*, George Eliot came into contact with many of the most important intellectuals in Britain and Europe, in the fields of science, philosophy, and political economy, such as Mill, T. H. *Huxley, and Herbert *Spencer. The endorsement of Auguste *Comte's *positivism by a number of *Westminster* contributors was just one of the intellectual strands in the magazine which appealed to George Eliot's sensibilities and informs her fiction. Generally, the intellectually serious and radical magazine suited George Eliot's interests and talents, and provided her with a radical and lively circle of friends, including, crucially, G. H. *Lewes. See also JOURNALIST, GEORGE ELIOT AS.   MWT

Wharton, Edith (1862–1937), American novelist who knew George Eliot's work well and whose own fiction has some affinities with Eliot's later novels in particular. She was born into a superior New York family, seen as a disciple of Henry *James but distinctively a major novelist in *The House of Mirth* (1905), *The Custom of the Country* (1913), and *The Age of Innocence* (1920), as well as the short novel *Ethan Frome* (1911), a study of claustrophobic psychological intensity. Wharton's first novel *The Valley of Decision* (1902) is substantially different from any of her following fiction: it is in the *Romola* terrain, though she was in fact following James, Charles Eliot Norton, Howells, Nathaniel *Hawthorne, and Mme de *Staël as well as George Eliot. She read, researched, travelled in Italy, and her heroine, Fulvia Vivaldi—helpmeet to her father and unhappy in love—has derivations from Romola. In her review of Leslie *Stephen's *George Eliot* (1902) for the *Bookman* (May 1902), Wharton refers to Eliot's mastery of dialogue in the novels, praises her characterization, but calls in question her reflective passages, asserting that as an observer of life she is more successful than as a moralist. Wharton's own selective focus on illuminating incidents—she is the mistress of the novella, witness the four which span four decades in *Old New York* (1924)—none the less exposes morality, and false morality, throughout her concern with what Marilyn French has appropriately called the 'untitled aristocracy' of American society. Her ease of expression, the light

John Chapman (1821–94), the owner and editor of the *Westminster Review* when George Eliot worked on the journal; known to his friends when young as 'Byron' on account of his good looks, he is shown here in middle age (date of photograph unknown).

loaded irony with which she presents the nuances of conversational hypocrisy and power, owe something to *Middlemarch* and *Daniel Deronda* but much more to her own subtle recognitions of the society shark beneath the surface. Certainly the Archery Club sequence at Newport in *The Age of Innocence* serves as plot and moral pivot very like Gwendolen's triumph at Brackenshaw Park in *Daniel Deronda*. In November 1907 James wrote to Wharton about her novel *The Fruit of the Tree* (serialized in Scribner's in that year), praising the admirable writing but noting more open 'George Eliotizing' than usual. He further observed 'fine benevolent finger-marks' in her work, analogous to the wide reading evident in Eliot's fiction (*Henry James and Edith Wharton: Letters 1900–1915*, ed. Lyall Powers (1990), 78, 240). And just as Eliot probes the woman problem through her heroines, so does Wharton. Society sits in judgement on Ellen Olenska and Lily Bart, and arguably Undine Spragg is a transatlantic equivalent to the upwardly mobile Rosamond Vincy. But Wharton's essential genius is rooted in shorter fiction, Eliot's in the unfolding moral crises which change lives. Both realize—and recreate—the not so distant past with incisive historical and social accuracy. Wharton is the cosmopolitan writer, exposing diseased culture, desiccated indolence, and impotence, her pristine prose cleverly, ironically mirroring the false sheen of society. In a letter in July 1900 she praises a fellow writer's heroine by comparing her to 'Gwendolen Grandcourt', but she advises a friend in 1913 that although she is pleased that he is going to read George Eliot, 'Skip Silas Marner & Adam Bede' (*The Letters of Edith Wharton*, ed. R. W. B. and N. Lewis (1988), 41, 311).

GRH

Gilbert, Sandra M., 'Life's Empty Pack: Notes toward a Literary Daughteronomy', *Critical Inquiry*, 11 (1985).

Hutchinson, Stuart, 'From *Daniel Deronda* to *The House of Mirth*', *Essays in Criticism*, 47 (1997).

White, William Hale (1831–1913), writer who used the pen-name of 'Mark Rutherford' and who, in his fictionalized autobiography and memoirs, has left a vivid portrait of Marian Evans as she was in her early years in London before she became George Eliot. White worked with her on the *Westminster Review at John *Chapman's house in the Strand, where they both were boarders. He arrived a year after her in October 1852 and they were fellow boarders until she moved out a year later. In 'George Eliot as I knew Her', a chapter in his posthumously published *Last Pages from a Journal* (1915), he recalls how, as a shy and introverted young man, he first met her and was immediately struck by her remarkable qualities. She

won his gratitude by responding eagerly to a trifling remark of his, and he found this to be typical of her unresting 'search for the meaning and worth of people and things' (*Last Pages*, 133). He also found her personally attractive: 'Her hair was particularly beautiful, and in her grey eyes there was a curiously shifting light, generally soft and tender, but convertible into the keenest flash' (132).

Long after her death when he visited the widow of G. H. *Lewes's son Charles (see LEWES FAMILY), he could write of his love for George Eliot; and in his quasi-autobiographical fiction *The Autobiography of Mark Rutherford* (1881) Rutherford is shown to be deeply and reverentially in love with the figure of Theresa, who is clearly based on Marian Evans (in appearance, character, and such accomplishments as her musical ability). Both are working for the publisher Wollaston, closely modelled on Chapman, and when Rutherford makes an error in instructing the printer and collapses in tears, pouring out to Theresa his sense of failure and worthlessness, she comforts him tenderly and later rectifies and pays for the mistake. As a consequence he is overcome with love for her, while continuing to be in love with another woman. Rutherford's worship corresponds to White's own feelings as expressed in later letters and memoirs, and he always deeply regretted not maintaining contact with Marian Evans after he left Chapman's employment. In retrospect he was particularly upset by having refused her invitation to see the French actress *Rachel perform, possibly out of jealousy because the tickets had come via Lewes (Stone, 443). In 1876 he did write to her to solicit help for a friend and received a reply from Lewes saying that she remembered him well.

His account of the Marian Evans he knew at the *Westminster Review* stands in sharp contrast to the sibylline image of the novelist projected by John Walter *Cross's *Life*. White insisted that later views of her as eminently respectable were wide of the mark, since respectability implied mental compromise such as she would never make (*Last Pages*, 133). His letter to the *Athenaeum* in an attempt to correct Cross's portrait describes her as 'one of the most sceptical, unusual creatures I have ever known' and paints a vivid picture of her at 142 Strand, with her hair over her shoulders, her feet over the arms of an easy chair, and a proof in her hand (see LIFE).

White's novel *The Revolution in Tanner's Lane* (1887) shares similarities of subject and setting with *Felix Holt, the Radical*—Radical politics and Dissenting religion, mob scenes and a French connection—but it is more sympathetic to popular political action and more sceptical and radical in its political outlook (Swann, 75–97). JMR

Stone, Wilfred H., 'Hale White and George Eliot', *University of Toronto Quarterly*, 25 (1956).

Swann, Charles, 'Evolution and Revolution: Politics and Form in *Felix Holt* and *The Revolution in Tanner's Lane*', in Francis Barker et al. (edd.), *Literature, Society and the Sociology of Literature* (1976).

Whitman, Walt (1819–92), American poet, whose controversial *Leaves of Grass* George Eliot quoted in a review of April 1856, cautiously distancing herself from 'his contempt for the "prejudices" of decency' (*Westminster Review*, 65: 650). Whitman's indecency, however, became a repeated issue for George Eliot, one that extended even beyond her death. Around 1871 (or so he later told Whitman), H. Buxton Forman convinced her to read *Leaves of Grass*, where she found a 'message for her soul' (Traubel, ii. 434). In March 1876, however, the *Saturday Review*'s attack upon Whitman's 'shameless obscenity' and his 'small *coterie*' of English admirers (41: 360–1) led George Eliot to fear that the two lines from Whitman which formed the motto for chapter 29 of *Daniel Deronda* might indicate a special admiration which she was very far from feeling (*L* vi. 241). (The lines eventually survived.) In 1883 Mathilde *Blind retailed the Forman story, though now George Eliot was said to have confessed that she found in Whitman what was 'good for her soul' (*George Eliot* (1883), 210). From that moment Whitman's supporters enlisted George Eliot's name as 'a precious war-weapon' in their fight for his acceptance (Traubel, iii. 128). In a printed letter of 1894, W. B. Yeats, for example, cited her as one of the 'fit though few' who 'did [Whitman] honour and crowned him among the immortals' (*Collected Letters of W. B. Yeats*, ed. John Kelly, i. (1986), 416). According to Traubel, Whitman said that he and George Eliot 'stood for the same things up to a certain point but there parted company, she to look back, I to look ahead'; he concluded that living 'in the midst of crowding conventions' overcame her natural rebelliousness (Traubel, ii. 434, 439). Of George Eliot's fiction, Whitman seems to have preferred *Scenes of Clerical Life* (Traubel, ii. 553). He also admired her essays, which he discovered late in life, saying of the essay on Young, 'I never knew George Eliot could let herself out so' (Traubel, ii. 560). KKC

Traubel, Horace, *With Walt Whitman in Camden* (1906–92).

will. George Eliot's last will and testament was signed on 6 May 1880 directly after her marriage to John Walter *Cross. Her new husband was appointed a trustee of the will along with Charles Lee Lewes, G. H. *Lewes's eldest son (see LEWES FAMILY). Charles Lewes was also appointed the sole executor of the will and its residuary legatee. The

sum of £5,000 was bequeathed to her niece Emily Clarke (1844–1924), the daughter of her sister Chrissey (see EVANS, CHRISTIANA); and £1,000 to G. H. Lewes's nephew Vivian Byam Lewes (1852–1915). Her old friend Cara *Bray was left an annuity of £100 and her housekeeper Mrs Mary Dowling an annuity of £40. The trustees were also instructed to invest £12,500 as a trust fund to provide an income for Eliza Lewes, the widow of G. H. Lewes's youngest son Herbert Arthur Lewes. In the event of her death or remarriage, half of that sum was to be held in trust for her son George Herbert Lewes (b. 1875), which he would receive on reaching the age of 21, while the other half was to be used to provide an income for life for her daughter Marian Lewes (b. 1872). The residue of the estate went to Charles Lee Lewes.

The will was proved on 9 February 1881. The figure of £40,000 at the bottom of the document, after a note of George Eliot's death on 22 December 1880, may be taken to indicate the approximate value of the whole estate (roughly equivalent to £2 million today). It is noticeable that only one member of George Eliot's own family received a legacy, and, apart from her friend Cara Bray and her housekeeper, the beneficiaries of the will were all relatives or descendants of G. H. Lewes. JMR

Wise, Witty and Tender Sayings of George Eliot. See MAIN, ALEXANDER.

Witley, The Heights. See HOMES OF GEORGE ELIOT.

Wollstonecraft, Mary (1759–97), feminist and sympathizer with the French Revolution whose 1792 work *Vindication of the Rights of Woman* George Eliot reviewed posthumously in her 1855 *Leader essay on *'Margaret Fuller and Mary Wollstonecraft'. In this essay, Wollstonecraft provides a comparison with the work of the contemporary American feminist Margaret Fuller. Eliot counters the scandalous reputation enjoyed by Wollstonecraft's work during the 19th century, insisting that readers will actually find it 'eminently serious, severely moral, and withal rather heavy'. This may well be 'the true reason', Eliot speculates, for Wollstonecraft not having been republished since the 1790s. Mary Wollstonecraft, she imagines, 'wrote not at all for writing's sake, but from the pressure of other motives' (*Essays*, 201). Eliot chooses extracts from Wollstonecraft's work which are pertinent to debates of her own time, including Wollstonecraft's suggestion that women might be 'physicians as well as nurses' (*Essays*, 204). She particularly endorses Wollstonecraft's view that woman's current state of ignorance leaves her intellectually and morally debased (*Essays*, 205).

'Woman in France: Madame de Sablé'

Wollstonecraft's attempted suicide when, in despair over her lover's neglect, she wet her garments in rain to increase their weight and leaped into the Thames, may have influenced Eliot's depiction of Mirah wetting her cloak in preparation for drowning herself in *Daniel Deronda* (*DD* 17). Eliot had referred to Wollstonecraft's suicide attempt in an 1871 letter to Emanuel *Deutsch (*L* v. 160–1). See also WOMAN QUESTION.   DdSC

'Woman in France: Madame de Sablé', article by George Eliot published in the *Westminster Review* in October 1854 (repr. in *Essays*).

It was a review article on three books published in French, most particularly on Victor Cousin's *Madame de Sablé: Études sur les femmes illustres et la société du XVIIe siècle* (1854) and nominally on Sainte-Beuve's *Portraits de femmes* (1844) and Jules Michelet's *Les Femmes de la Révolution*. The review was commissioned by John *Chapman and written and delivered just after Marian Evans had left the editorship of the *Westminster* and had gone off to *Weimar with G. H. *Lewes. Chapman's invitation was thus a very welcome piece of continuity and recognition at a point of traumatic break with her previous life and, not least in their strained financial circumstances, a welcome paying job.

In this essay the writer who was soon to be George Eliot demonstrates some of her characteristic powers, especially including the fullness of her preparation and the tendency to rely on dramatic vignettes. The latter particularly shines in this essay, which makes the gatherings of 17th-century salons come alive, and which in the process demonstrates her emphasis on the profoundly *embodied* quality of social and cultural life.

The essay formulates issues about the situation of women in England that remain evident in her work through her career. The image sketched in one of her letters of George Eliot confined in a corner after dinner with ladies doing needlework is an image that captures the contradictoriness of the life led by a woman with her diversified abilities. George Eliot was deeply sympathetic to the plight of women. She can easily be counted as an important early feminist (see WOMAN QUESTION). She did not participate in rallies because of a personal life so continuously fraught by the courageous choices she made that her health nearly buckled under the strain; she simply had not the luxuries available to women who, as she said, get what they want by indirection so they can still be invited to dinner. But there is little question in her novels that the miserable limitations of women's lives occupied her continuously. Her portraits of young, badly educated women such as, for example, Rosamond Vincy in *Middlemarch* and Gwendolen Harleth in

Daniel Deronda, show exactly what happens to young girls who are prevented from developing their full capabilities and who are subjected by a so-called civilized society to the mental equivalent of foot-binding (see EDUCATION). The implications of Madame de Sablé's example for contemporary English society are summarized succinctly at the end of the essay, and the passage is worth quoting at length because of the number of themes it contains for her future work:

Such was Madame de Sablé, whose name is, perhaps, new to some of our readers, so far does it lie from the surface of literature and history. We have seen, too, that she was only one amongst a crowd— one in a firmament of feminine stars which, when once the biographical telescope is turned upon them, appear scarcely less remarkable and interesting. Now, if the reader recollects what was the position and average intellectual character of women in the high society of England during the reigns of James the First and the two Charleses—the period through which Madame de Sablé's career extends— we think he will admit our position as to the early superiority of womanly development in France: and this fact, with its causes, has not merely an historical interest, it has an important bearing on the culture of women in the present day. Women become superior [to their previous more ignorant condition] in France by being admitted to a common fund of ideas, to common objects of interest with men; and this must ever be the essential condition at once of true womanly culture and of true social well-being. (*Essays*, 80)

The Marquise de Sablé who was the friend and confidante of Blaise *Pascal among many others at the forefront of her day, was not required by her society to suffer and be still, and consequently her society moved to a state of cultural advancement far ahead of what was possible in England. For 17th-century France, needlework and its equivalents were not enough.

George Eliot demonstrates also an adept rhetorical management of a difficult topic for an English audience, so that it might slip past unconscious resistances. The unfavourable comparisons with English society framing her portrait of the French salons are put irresistibly: 'Those famous habitués of the Hôtel de Rambouillet [Richelieu, Corneille, the Great Condé, Balzac, and Bossuet] did not, apparently, first lay themselves out to entertain the ladies with grimacing "small talk", and then take each other by the sword-knot to discuss matters of real interest in a corner; they rather sought to present their best ideas in the guise most acceptable to intelligent and accomplished women' (*Essays*, 58). Such anecdotes were bound to raise consciousness in English society, and that remains clearly the purpose of her essay.

The essay's guiding thoughts are two ideas central to all George Eliot's work. The first thought is that society is a homeostatic condition: for better or worse, all parts affect all other parts. Where women are marginalized, ill-educated, and positively confined to a corner and to needlework, their whole culture feels the pang; and conversely, where women have among all citizens an equal opportunity to develop, their culture reaps the reward. The second thought is that every individual makes a difference but that individuals alone do not make conditions: it is an aggregate of women, not just a few exceptionally privileged ones, who make the critical mass that binds society to one course or another. English society in the mid-19th century supported social practices that excluded women by law from almost any exercise of social, political, and economic rights and responsibilities. George Eliot was by no means alone in her analysis. These themes link her particularly with John Stuart *Mill, who was the founding editor of the *Westminster Review* which she later took over and revived, and who was and perhaps still is a major, even the main, apologist for women's liberation; and these themes link her with George *Meredith, whose work she encouraged and who in novels, poetry, and essays focused on the self-destructive misogyny of English culture. And these in turn had taken over and disseminated the agendas articulated in an earlier generation by Mary *Wollstonecraft. George Eliot's work takes up and advances their work for women's social, political, and economic rights.

But George Eliot was not sentimental about women, and she demonstrates that in this essay. After one extract describing one Mme de Longueville's intellectual feebleness, Eliot comments as follows:

Surely, the most ardent admirer of feminine shallowness must have felt some irritation when he found himself arrested by this dead wall of stupidity, and have turned with relief to the larger intelligence of Madame de Sablé, who was not the less graceful, delicate, and feminine, because she could follow a train of reasoning, or interest herself in a question of science. In this combination consisted her pre-eminent charm: she was not a genius, not a heroine, but a woman whom men could more than love—whom they could make their friend, confidante, and counsellor; the sharer, not of their joys and sorrows only, but of their ideas and aims. (*Essays*, 80)

Eliot suggests here, as she does throughout her career, that to excuse stupidity in women is to reproduce it, and thus to reproduce the conditions

of servitude and limitation. To claim that women have special powers, solely because they are biologically women, is an argument from magic of the kind George Eliot has no patience with. Such claims trivialize women's real experience and actively deny them opportunity even to grow up. And this trivialization and this denial is not done only by men, but by women who reinforce the closed circuit of misogynist self-justification.

EDE

woman question, the. For George Eliot this was indeed a question in the richest meaning of the word, a long interrogation into the social fate of woman. Her origins as a novelist coincided with the origins of a modern feminism, and her reluctance to lend her energies to the new movement has been the cause of both suspicion and disappointment (see CRITICISM, MODERN: FEMINIST APPROACHES) in her time as in ours. Anything more than superficial consideration, however, shows that her writing was by no means a refusal to engage the question of woman (see, for instance, 'WOMAN IN FRANCE: MADAME DE SABLÉ'). The engagement occurs in her own terms and within the realm of her fictional project, and if it yields no brisk recommendations for public policy, it makes a persistent challenge to the work of narrative.

Throughout the 1850s, a group of increasingly active women and some sympathetic male legislators demanded change in the laws of divorce and married women's property. In a series of celebrated cases, among them the notorious case of Caroline Norton, the extent of women's vulnerability within marriage was dramatized before the public. The legal nullity of the wife, her inability to sign contracts or to possess property of her own, and the near impossibility of her successful suit for divorce, aroused enough public pressure to generate parliamentary attention in the middle years of the decade. As Lord Chancellor, Lord Cranworth introduced bitterly contested bills for divorce in 1854, 1856, and 1857. During the debates proposals were heard for the reform of married property, an issue that was decisive for the petitioning feminists, but when the bill finally passed in the summer of 1857, it left the property question to one side, and while the Divorce and Matrimonial Causes Act made divorce no longer the exclusive privilege of wealthy men, it codified the asymmetry between men and women. For a man the grounds for divorce could be a wife's adultery alone, while for a wife the required grounds were adultery compounded by cruelty, incest, bigamy, or bestiality. Not until 1870 was the first Married Woman's Property Act passed.

As the debates of the 1850s raged, George Eliot was beginning her literary career with *Scenes of*

Self-portrait of Barbara Leigh Smith Bodichon (1827–91), one of George Eliot's closest friends, who was active in the women's movement, campaigning for women's property rights and helping found Girton College, Cambridge.

Clerical Life, all three stories of which were set at least a quarter-century in the past. The historical distance would become a fundamental technical gesture, consistently repeated until her last novel, *Daniel Deronda*. Yet everywhere in the oeuvre, the contemporary debates leave traces in the narrative. As the parliamentarians pondered a legislative response to horrific tales of domestic brutality, 'Janet's Repentance', the third of the *Scenes*, narrated its heroine's endurance of her husband's relentless beatings, thus recording from its own removed perspective precisely the kind of scandalous incident that was making for public outcry. And as feminists worked toward the establishment of a woman's college, George Eliot in *The Mill on the Floss* was exposing the agony of Maggie Tulliver, whose intelligence had been so badly neglected.

Although the novels continually engage with the struggles of women, George Eliot was wary of more direct forms of political commitment. This was not for want of a forum. Her friendship with Barbara Leigh Smith (later *Bodichon), who published *A Brief Summary in Plain Language of the Most Important Laws Concerning Women* in 1854, and with Bessie Rayner *Parkes, who co-founded the *English Woman's Journal* in 1858, gave her the closest access to the prevailing arguments. The refusal to participate in such activism was partly a choice of commitments; when Bessie Parkes asked her to contribute to the *Journal*, George Eliot wrote that 'my vocation lies in other paths . . . I expect to be writing *books* for some time to come' (*L* ii. 431). She interprets her turn to fiction, which happened to coincide with the resurgence of feminism, as a withdrawal from the stresses of public controversy. After Frederic *Harrison asked her to write a novel in support of the teachings of Auguste *Comte, she famously rejoined that aesthetic teaching is 'the highest of all teaching', but 'if it ceases to be purely aesthetic—if it lapses anywhere from the picture to the diagram—it becomes the most offensive of all teaching' (*L* iv. 300). Art is necessarily an abstention from advocacy. At one moment of sharp controversy in late 1857, she wrote to Charles *Bray that she 'should be sorry to undertake any more specific enunciation of doctrine on a question so entangled as the "Woman Question"'. Expressing admiration for those 'who are struggling in the thick of the contest', she identifies her place as with the Epicurean gods who treasure the privileges of detachment (*L* ii. 396).

Perhaps more significantly, the carefully managed distance from the struggle reflects an abiding uncertainty about its aims. George Eliot often writes of her inability to reach firm judgements on the goals of feminism: 'I repeat that I do not trust

very confidently to my own impressions on this subject' (*L* iv. 365). She did sign the petition for reform in Married Woman's Property, though she hoped for 'proper provisos and safeguards' before such a bill passed, and her own contribution was to add a paragraph asserting the parallel need to protect husbands from their wives' debts (*L* ii. 227). Her greatest enthusiasm and conviction were for educational reform, supporting the establishment of Girton College, because 'the better Education of Women is one of the objects about which I have *no doubt*' (*L* iv. 395).

About other such 'objects' George Eliot had great and ongoing doubt. In 1852 she remarks that the '"Enfranchisement of women" only makes creeping progress; and that is best, for woman does not yet deserve a much better lot than man gives her' (*L* ii. 86). When in the late 1860s John Stuart *Mill enters parliament and presses the claims of enfranchisement, she writes to Sara *Hennell, 'I proceed to scold you a little for undertaking to canvass on the Women's Suffrage question. Why should you burthen yourself in that way, for an extremely doubtful good?' (*L* iv. 390). The recurrent note is that of hesitation in the face of complexities. In the rapidly changing social climate George Eliot regrets the tones of political certainty, preferring instead to insist that the problems are entrenched and the solutions obscure:

I feel too deeply the difficult complications that beset every measure likely to affect the position of women and also I feel too imperfect a sympathy with many women who have put themselves forward in connexion with such measures, to give any practical adhesion to them. There is no subject on which I am more inclined to hold my peace and learn, than on the 'Woman Question'. It seems to me to overhang abysses, of which even prostitution is not the worst. (*L* v. 58)

The quick pursuit of a new legal dispensation for women, the insistence on an immediate change in relations of property, the demand for an overturning of the conventions of 'separate spheres' for men and women—these hallmarks of a robust new politics struck George Eliot as too hasty and decided. Without putting herself in opposition to her feminist friends, she kept her distance from their political ardour, pondering the question slowly and placing it in contexts developed in her own writing.

Her mature thought depends on a conception of social life as a living organism that grows and changes only slowly; transformation cannot be willed in a moment; it must be prepared carefully over time. The *'Address to Working Men, by Felix Holt' (1868) was explicitly directed to the extension of male suffrage in the Second *Reform Act, but it equally reflects her judgements on the feminist campaigns of the past decade, revealing the extent to which the woman question coincides with the worker question. Faced with the prospect of a great social transformation, her Felix Holt asks not that the change be stopped, but that it proceed slowly, on the principle that 'general prosperity and well-being is a vast crop, that like the corn in Egypt can be come at, not at all by hurried snatching, but only by a well-judged patient process' (*Essays*, 417). Because society is a great body, all its parts are linked in the 'wonderful slow-growing system of things' (421); the necessity is to avoid 'a fatal shock' which comes from a 'too hasty wresting of measures which seem to promise a partial relief'. 'I am a Radical,' says Felix Holt, 'I expect great changes, and I desire them. But I don't expect them to come in a hurry, by mere inconsiderate sweeping' (424). The 'Address' concludes by defending the 'treasure of knowledge,' which must be valued far more than any immediate practical change.

George Eliot's eager support for women's *education, but not for female suffrage, should be seen in this light. Education appears to her as the alternative to elections. Not a hasty, hurried snatching, it is part of a long, organic process leading perhaps to radical change in the relations of the sexes, but not all at once, and not soon. On this one point, she identifies her 'strong conviction ... that women ought to have the same fund of truth placed within their reach as men have', and that the highest bonds between men and women 'can only be produced by their having each the same store of fundamental knowledge' (*L* v. 58). In the late 1860s, when she feels beset by the need to make judgements, she clings to education as a basis for modest reform, consistent with her caution.

Nevertheless, the vision of an educated civic culture rich with freely circulating knowledge does not imply a movement toward social equality. The other persistent thread in the complex of beliefs is George Eliot's persistent concern with difference in 'function'. The organic metaphors for *society suggest that just as parts of the body have their own separate purposes, so individuals and groups should expect to play widely different roles. Even after being liberated through education, women would still not assume the positions held by men; they would continue to have functions of their own, functions which would be more clearly discerned as knowledge spread: 'Let the whole field of reality be laid open to woman as well as to man, and then that which is peculiar to her mental modification, instead of being, as it is now, a source of discord and repulsion between the sexes, will be found to be a necessary complement to the truth and beauty of life' (*Essays*, 81). History will bring not an overcoming of sexually assigned differences, but a clarification of their necessity. George Eliot tenaciously affirms the 'spiritual wealth acquired for mankind by the difference of function', and writes that humanity simply cannot 'afford to part with that exquisite type of gentleness, tenderness, possible maternity suffusing a woman's being with affectionateness' (*L* iv. 467–8).

The judgements offered in *essays, *letters, and conversation are most often discreet refusals of the political ambitions developing through the strenuous efforts of the new feminists. Any evaluation of George Eliot's position, however, must do more than parse the scattered utterances that were her immediate reactions to quickly changing events, especially because her doubts were reflected in the vigorously unsettled character of the early feminist movement. Sharp divisions emerged, for instance, on the question of whether the reform of property law should be prior to a new divorce act, some women holding that if the property rights of married women were fully granted, there would be no need for a change in the law of divorce. Agreement on the need to improve the conditions of women dissolved when the question turned to political equality. Caroline Norton, one of the most effective campaigners for divorce legislation, wrote mockingly of the 'absurd claim of equality' advanced by some of her allies. Anna *Jameson, an important early partisan of reform, continued to hold to 'natural' distinctions between the public work of men and the domestic labour of women, and she bitterly criticized the political demands of American feminism, which she saw as much too extreme, bringing 'discredit and ridicule' on the cause (Anna Jameson, *Sisters of Charity: Catholic and Protestant, Abroad and At Home* (1855), 11).

Quite apart from the political conflicts and the legislative struggles, attention to the condition of women was provoked by new exemplary lives, especially that of Florence *Nightingale, whose experience in the Crimean War (1854–56) suddenly changed the terms in which many middle-class women thought about their lives. Where the dismal role of the governess had once seemed the only work consistent with ideals of gentility, now nursing became a widely attractive vocation; to many people it seemed to offer the answer to the question of woman. Yet Nightingale, who founded a nursing school at St Thomas's Hospital in 1861, sharply distinguished her goals from those of the feminists, writing in the immensely popular *Notes on Nursing* that her readers should keep clear from the 'jargon' of the 'rights of women, which urges women to do all that men do' (*Notes on Nursing: What it is, and what it is not* (1860),

76). The case of Nightingale suggests the complexity of the social currents, for despite her anti-feminist avowals, there can be no doubt that she opened possibilities for agency, vocation, and self-reflection that encouraged the political struggle.

George Eliot's relation to the woman question owes a great deal to the precedent of Florence Nightingale. First, this is because Nightingale provided an image of resolute commitment to the life of service that informed George Eliot's conceptions of her heroines, for example, Janet in 'Janet's Repentance', Dinah in *Adam Bede*, and perhaps most significantly the eponymous heroine of *Romola*, whose selfless, but also charismatic, devotion to the inhabitants of a plague-stricken village closely recalls the prevailing image of Nightingale's work in the Crimea. A second, more general, influence can be seen in the effort to think about the changing lives of modern women beyond the categories of politics and law. Nightingale's work and her fame, as well as her anti-feminism, suggested how it might be possible to imagine an inspiring grandeur for women without challenging the slower rhythms of organic social change.

George Eliot could not believe in the immediate widening of female *vocation. Although this separated her sharply from the ambitions of some of her closest friends, it remained the constraint within which she performed her grandest acts of imagination. Despite her own great public success, she declined to build her plots around narratives of women making their way in the public sphere, as doctors, as teachers, as nurses, as novelists. Even Nightingale bridled at the refusal of *Middlemarch* to find some concrete social endeavour for Dorothea—like the labour of Octavia *Hill with working-class housing—where she might give fuller play to her gifts. Perhaps George Eliot's most direct response to the demand for a broader sphere and richer possibilities for women comes in the Finale to *Middlemarch*, where the narrator reacts to the complaint that Dorothea's life, 'so substantive and rare', was 'absorbed into the life of another' and that she would be known only 'as a wife and mother'. The rejoinder is that 'no one stated exactly what else that was in her power she ought rather to have done'. This agnosticism seems to have been George Eliot's considered view toward the life of women in the 1850s, 1860s, and 1870s, as well as in the fictional historical past of her novels.

Yet, even her unaccommodating answer shows just how fully she has put the question of woman. If her work has provoked feminist challenge from her time to ours, this is because the novels, with their succession of large-souled heroines, suggest all the larger destinies that they sternly withhold. In emphasizing how female heroism of the past,

such as the heroism of Antigone or St Theresa, is unimaginable in the present, the fiction poses its challenge to modernity.

It also does so by dramatizing the weakness of men alongside the constrained women. On the one hand, the fiction consistently displays instances of male treachery, sexual immorality, and brutality. The cruelty of Tito Melema and Grandcourt mark one extreme of male degradation; the self-deception and moral feebleness of Arthur Donnithorne and Bulstrode mark another. Gilbert and Gubar have understood this in terms of the 'belief that men are more completely damned than women by precisely their license to act out impulses necessarily restricted in women' (1979: 514). On the other hand, George Eliot unsteadies the inherited image of masculine heroism; in such characters as Daniel Deronda and especially in Will Ladislaw, she makes 'feminine' responsiveness a central element of the male protagonist. If Henry James saw Ladislaw as a weakly drawn figure, a mere 'woman's man', other readers have recognized an effort to reconceive masculinity and to adjust the man in relation to the strength of the woman.

In keeping with her commitment to slow and deliberate change, George Eliot made her most determined engagement with the woman question at the end of her career. While others had settled their positions, she remained at once concerned and unsettled, and in her last two novels she dramatizes the reach of her uncertainty. The very refusal to imagine new vocations for women created stark and productive conflicts between the power of her last heroines and a social world unable to accommodate their gifts. In *Middlemarch* Dorothea appears as an incarnation of St Theresa fated to live out a modest destiny incommensurate with the grandeur of her type. In the poem 'Armgart', the title character takes up one of the few vocations allowed to George Eliot's women, that of singer, and speculates that without this outlet for her ardour she would have lost all self-possession: 'She often wonders what her life had been | Without that voice for channel to her soul. | She says, it must have leaped through all her limbs—Made her a Maenad—made her snatch a brand | And fire some forest . . .' (scene i).

In *Daniel Deronda*, Deronda's mother, the Princess Halm-Eberstein, the singer Alcharisi, is another figure whose first demands are fully and unsentimentally uttered: the demand to fulfil the promise of her gift, to avoid the imprisonments of home life, to be free of the burdens of womaliness, to be free of her son. Alcharisi, like Mrs Transome in *Felix Holt, the Radical*, fiercely displays the claims of women, but rather notoriously, the two characters are consigned to the interstices of the plot, which then goes on to make its peace with the claims of duty and responsibility.

Gwendolen Harleth, George Eliot's last heroine, is deprived of the gift that would justify her revolt. Her singing is not strong enough; she is condemned to ordinary life. At the end of *Daniel Deronda* she must turn home to her mother and accept the prospect of limitation and ongoing moral struggle. With no outlet for her visions of freedom, no field on which she can act her desires, Gwendolen is the heroine at a final impasse in the final novel. Her destiny, simply to live on without any certainty of vocation, even the vocation of happiness, makes the harshest possible formulation of the woman question. What life can there be for the unexceptional woman who refuses to coincide with womanliness? The novel projects no consoling future; it leaves the heroine's destiny both open and blank. If it refuses solidarity with modern proponents of social change, it also disturbs the certainty of those who would deny change. It asks all those who have put woman in question to think not quickly, but deeply. See also GENDER; HISTORY; POLITICS. KC

Barrett (1989).
Beer (1986).
Gilbert and Gubar (1979).

women, education of. See EDUCATION; WOMAN QUESTION.

Woolf, Virginia (1882–1941), critical essayist, innovative novelist, and enthusiastic admirer of George Eliot. At a time when her English contemporaries were variously dismissing Eliot as a dinosaur (see REPUTATION, CRITICAL), Woolf, in her centenary essay on George Eliot, offered her now celebrated reflection on *Middlemarch*: 'the magnificent book which with all its imperfections is one of the few English novels written for grown-up people' (*Times Literary Supplement*, 20 November 1919). This was a view evidently shared by Sigmund *Freud who observed of the same novel that it had illuminated important aspects of his relations with his wife. While it may have been F. R. *Leavis who restored Eliot to significant stature in his landmark intervention *The Great Tradition* (1948), Woolf was among the first of the modernists publicly to proclaim George Eliot's energizing and abiding relevance. Over and above noting the well-worked novelistic attributes, Woolf maintained that Eliot had reached 'beyond the sanctuary (of womanhood) ... to the strange bright fruits of art and knowledge', and lighted also on 'the difference of view' that Eliot exposed and explored, striking a chord with an emerging politicized feminine sensibility. Forthright young women were roused: Katherine *Mansfield, for instance, in her letter to J. M. Murry on 25 No-

vember 1919, rose to Eliot's defence on reading Sydney Waterlow's centenary article 'George Eliot, 1819–1880' in the *Athenaeum*, 21 November 1919. With Woolf in mind, Mansfield found Waterlow plodding and ungenerous. More recently, in her comprehensive parallel study *Greatness Engendered: George Eliot and Virginia Woolf* (1992), Alison Booth places the Two Grand Old Women of Letters squarely in the field of vying contemporary feminist discourses, problematizing greatness, and tracing between the paired precursors 'a paradigm of ambivalent affiliation' derived from Gilbert and Gubar (as opposed to a more adversarial approach along the lines of Bloom's 'anxiety of influence').

We know from her *Reading Notebooks* (ed. Silver, 200–2) and references in her letters and diary that Eliot was much on Woolf's mind during 1919, and that she was 'reading through the whole of George Eliot, in order to sum her up once and for all, upon her anniversary' (*Letters of Virginia Woolf*, ed. Nigel Nicolson, ii. (1976), 321). In this playful letter to Lady Eleanor Cecil in January, she has just read John Walter *Cross's *Life* and is delighted and intrigued by the George Eliot she discovers, appreciating the societal constraints within which she operated—Woolf's writing life was to be concerned with challenging such strictures. In August, Woolf is immersed in the novels of Henry *James, Thomas *Hardy, and Eliot. 'George Eliot fascinates me', she writes to Margaret Llewelyn Davies (*Letters of Virginia Woolf*, ii. 385), cumulating subversive insights—Woolf would proceed radically to rework normative methods of representation. Her attentive rereading of the novels at this time leaves indelible touches on her own work. There are instances like the single drop of ink that opens *Adam Bede* which reappears, somewhat transformed, to open *Jacob's Room* (1922) in the pen of tearful Betty Flanders. Whereas in Eliot the inkdrop declares itself secure in its power to mirror and reveal evoked worlds—*realism encapsulated—in Woolf drop turns to blot, figuring writing as more susceptive an illusionist, and suggesting the impressionistic fluency with which Woolf began to test convention and reorganize experience. There are direct references too. In *Jacob's Room*, while Miss Julia Hedge, the feminist, waits for books in the British Museum, she wets her pen and scans the names that ring the dome crowning the reading room; she is heard to muse, 'Oh damn, why didn't they leave room for an Eliot or a Brontë?'

In her reviews and critical essays, as one of the measures in her strategy to restore disappearing and lost women's voices to the reading public, Woolf regularly alluded to Jane *Austen, Emily *Brontë, Charlotte *Brontë, and George Eliot as rallying points—not necessarily always with un-alloyed admiration. *A Room of One's Own* (1929), an expanded reworking of papers on women and fiction that she presented at Newnham and Girton, Cambridge, in October 1928, spends several pages in its fourth section contextualizing and comparing 'the four famous names'. Here Woolf is trenchant in her view that Eliot's 'capacious mind' could, but for the limitations imposed by forces beyond her control, have applied itself and resonated far beyond the confines of the novel. At the stage where Woolf is proposing that women think back through their mothers, and that they trace a *woman's sentence*—some more adequate tool for woman's expression—one of her trump cards is to declare, 'George Eliot committed atrocities with [the man's sentence] that beggar description'. Over and above the *ad feminam* gestures in some of its arguments, Woolf's *A Room*, in title and sentiment, recalls Eliot's own wish to John *Sibree: 'O the bliss of having a very high attic in a romantic continental town, such as Geneva—far away from morning callers dinners and decencies; and then to pause . . . and think' (*L* i. 261)—something Eliot was able to experience herself a year later in 1849. That room in *Geneva marked a turning point for Mary Ann Evans; Virginia Woolf advocated such a room, together with an independent purse, for every [writing] woman: 'it is necessary to have five hundred a year and a room with a lock on the door . . . five hundred a year stands for the power to contemplate . . . a lock on the door means the power to think for oneself'.

Middlemarch itself flutters across the Woolf text, glimpsed, for example, when the free-spirited Minta Doyle in *To the Lighthouse* (1927) leaves the third volume on the train: in this intertextual gesture, the conversation turns to Eliot, and Minta, who does not know the outcome of the plot, indulges Mr Ramsay's patrician sense of her foolishness—Mr Ramsay being a version of Leslie *Stephen, Woolf's father, whose own *George Eliot* (1902) was a volume in the 'English Men of Letters' series. Ironic overlaps such as these foreground wider considerations, beyond the gendered vision. Gillian Beer in her essay 'Beyond Determinism: George Eliot and Virginia Woolf' discusses the ways in which the two authors understand, wrestle with, and respond to the deepening deterministic mindset that seemed to pervade the patterns of intelligibility provided by the 'strange bright fruits' of the dominant order: in particular the theories of Charles *Darwin, Karl *Marx, and Freud, vast teleological systems haunted by an underlying need for certitude. Both Eliot and Woolf challenge this all-embracing rationale, Eliot rather more organically, Woolf, deconstructively. They explore writerly methods of resisting, subverting, parody-ing, defamiliarizing the existential determinants available to them.

In the wake of her death, Woolf's reputation followed a trajectory not dissimilar to George Eliot's. Like Eliot's, Woolf's reputation, too, has had its satirical detractors. See also CRITICISM, MODERN: FEMINIST APPROACHES.   AE

Woolf, Virginia, 'George Eliot', *TLS*, 20 Nov. 1919, repub. in Woolf, *The Common Reader* (1925).

Virginia Woolf's Reading Notebooks, ed. Brenda R. Silver (1983).

Beer, Gillian, 'Beyond Determinism', in *Arguing with the Past* (1989).

Showalter, Elaine, 'The Greening of Sister George', *Nineteenth-Century Fiction*, 35 (1980–1).

'Word for the Germans, A', the first of four articles written by George Eliot in the spring of 1865 for volume 1 of the *Pall Mall Gazette*, launched by George *Smith, the publisher of *Romola*, and with the assistance of G. H. *Lewes as editorial adviser (repr. in *Essays*). The short essay was written on 1 March and published on 7 March. Addressing the question of national character, which was a matter of contemporary debate, she challenges the British stereotype of the German as a 'cloudy metaphysician', tartly observing that the most eminent metaphysician Immanuel *Kant is only cloudy in the sense that 'a mathematician is cloudy to one ignorant of mathematics' (*Essays*, 387). Mildly ironic about British notions of superiority, she sees differences of national culture and character as enriching our knowledge of the inner and outer world. The distinctive characteristics of the German mind, which she defines as 'largeness of theoretic conception, and thoroughness in the investigation of facts', have given it its pre-eminent position in contemporary scholarship. Maintaining that 'no one in this day really studies any subject without having recourse to German books' (389), she anticipates the criticism that Ladislaw in *Middlemarch* is to make of the scholar Casaubon for not knowing German. She concedes that German books are rarely well written and attributes this to their exhaustive treatment of a subject from every angle, as well as to the structure of the language itself, which 'lends itself to the formation of involved sentences, like coiled serpents, showing neither head nor tail' (390). Her experience as a translator from German seems to show here (see TRANSLATIONS BY GEORGE ELIOT); and in general the essay illustrates the importance she attaches to cultural diversity and her admiring, but not uncritical, familiarity with German intellectual life. See also GERMANY; LANGUAGES.   JMR

Wordsworth, William (1770–1850), English poet (Poet Laureate from 1843), read by George Eliot throughout her adult years with undimmed enthusiasm. To her he remained, as she phrased it shortly before her death, the 'incomparable Wordsworth' (L vi. 439). Allusions in *letters, reviews, and *essays throughout the late 1840s and the 1850s reflect how thoroughly she studied the poet who was to provide more *epigraphs for her novels than anyone except *Shakespeare. In January 1858 she and G. H. *Lewes were deep in Wordsworth, 'with fresh admiration for his beauties and tolerance for his faults' (L ii. 423), and a month later they had finished The Excursion, 'which repaid us for going to the end by an occasional fine passage even to the last' (L ii. 430). The poem was read again the following year. George Eliot knew Wordsworth's posthumously published autobiographical poem The Prelude equally well. In 1867 Lewes, who had not admired it when it was first published, was reading it aloud for the second time. Eliot read from the same volume (now in the Beinecke Library, Yale University) with John Walter *Cross over July to August 1880, just months before she died. In the last weeks of her life she read her friend F. W. H. *Myers's Wordsworth, just published in the 'English Men of Letters' series. As Thomas Pinney has observed, the record of her reading 'seems to confirm Cross's remark that George Eliot's early burst of enthusiasm for Wordsworth "entirely expresses the feeling she had to him up to the day of her death"' (21).

What was unusual about George Eliot's appreciation was that she had an appetite for Wordsworth, as she put it, 'at full length' (L i. 34). When she was 21 she acquired the six volumes of the 1836–7 Collected Wordsworth and passages copied into her notebooks from even the most forbiddingly dull poems testify to the thoroughness with which she combed them. Most Victorians agreed with Matthew *Arnold that Wordsworth's poetry was best appreciated in a selection, but George Eliot did not. 'Except for travelling and for popular distribution', she told Frederic *Harrison in 1880, 'I prefer Moxon's one-volumed edition of Wordsworth to any selection. No selection gives you the perfect gems to be found in single lines, which are to be found in the "dull" poems' (L vii. 261)

Eliot was drawn to Wordsworth through profound temperamental and artistic affinity. 'I have never before met with so many of my own feelings, expressed just as I could like' (L i. 34), she remarked in 1839. Both writers entertained the highest conception of the function of *art as an instrument for moral education. 'Art is the nearest thing to life; it is a mode of amplifying and extending our contact with our fellow-men beyond the bounds of our personal lot' (Essays, 271). This rightly famous statement of the humanist case for art (and similar ones throughout George Eliot's letters) can be paralleled by comparable affirmations in Wordsworth's Prefaces to Lyrical Ballads of 1800 and 1802, and in his letters, notably the manifesto letter to John Wilson, 7 June 1802.

The Prefaces and Lyrical Ballads also played a considerable part in determining the subject matter and tenor of George Eliot's early work. The importance of her review essay, 'The *Natural History of German Life' (Essays, 266–99), cannot be overstressed, but it might also be noted that her absorption in Wordsworth had in large measure prepared George Eliot for Riehl and that in the Wordsworth she reread while writing Adam Bede she found imaginative representation of much that she dwelt on in the essay—that 'peasant conservatism' stems from adherence to 'the old custom of the country'; that the peasant feels intense 'historical piety' to the familiar and what is immediately connected with himself; that manners and customs are 'determined' by physical geography; that 'men's affection, imagination, wit and humour' are bound in 'with the subtle ramifications of historical language'. Lyrical Ballads and The Excursion, Wordsworth's theoretical prefaces, and the notes to the poems on language, customs, and places, provided quite as much reinforcement as Riehl for George Eliot's reverence for the vitality that inheres in the local, the known, 'familiar with forgotten years' (Excursion, 2. 276), and for her conviction that it is the artist's duty to direct 'our sympathy with the perennial joys and struggles, the toil, the tragedy, and the humour in the life of our more heavily-laden fellow-men' towards a true object rather than a false one. It is appropriate that Adam Bede should signal its lineage by opening with an epigraph from Wordsworth, lines from The Excursion (6. 651–8) about the importance of lowly people, 'nature's unambitious underwood'.

In religious belief poet and novelist travelled in opposite directions: Wordsworth became increasingly devout and explicitly Christian whereas George Eliot left behind the evangelical fervour of her early years. Systematic formulations of belief, however, were anathema to both (see MORAL VALUES). What brought them together as artists was a shared apprehension of life as a profound mystery, 'too deep for tears' (Wordsworth, Ode: Intimations of Immortality). George Eliot acknowledged that it was perhaps rather too much her way 'to urge the human sanctities through tragedy' and in this she was at one with Wordsworth, whose greatest narrative poems, Michael for example, or The Ruined Cottage, dwell on the unchanging fundamentals of human suffering. But what she also admired in Wordsworth was his reverence for human greatness in adversity. Whereas most of her contemporaries valued Wordsworth's poetry for its Christian succour, George Eliot dwelt on whatever in it gave intimations of human grandeur. In the last year of her life she commended certain passages of Wordsworth to Frederic Harrison as possibly helpful in his endeavours for the *religion of humanity. One is *Prelude*, 11. 393–5, lines which inspired her own ode, 'O may I join the choir invisible' (see POETRY):

> There is
> One great society alone on Earth:
> The noble Living and the noble Dead.

The other is the last eight lines of what she called the 'magnificent sonnet on Toussaint l'Ouverture', which ends with a ringing tribute to 'man's unconquerable mind'. Of this passage Eliot wrote, 'I don't know where there is anything finer' (*L* vii. 262).

Traces of Wordsworth's presence are found all through George Eliot's work, but as an imaginatively shaping force it is at its strongest in *Adam Bede*, *The Mill on the Floss*, and *Silas Marner*, each of which might be seen as an exploration of a primary Wordsworthian theme. *Adam Bede* is most obviously linked to *Lyrical Ballads* and *The Excursion* by its rural setting, whose historical and ideological significance is expounded in the aesthetic manifesto of chapter 17. But the novel is also Wordsworthian in a fuller sense. In a note to *The Thorn* in 1800 Wordsworth emphasized feelings as the true province of poetry and in the Preface to *Lyrical Ballads* declared that in his own poems, 'the feeling therein developed gives importance to the action and situation, and not the action and situation to the feeling'. In *Adam Bede* the aged Adam pronounces on his experience of life with a similar emphasis, 'It isn't notions sets people doing the right thing—it's feelings' (*AB* 17), and his words sum up the primary movement of the narrative. Feeling most sensitively registers moral discrimination. That Arthur Donnithorne should dismiss Wordsworth's poems in *Lyrical Ballads* as 'twaddling stuff' (*AB* 5) is not in itself very damning, but it points to something undeveloped in his emotional make-up, whose far-reaching consequences the narrative unfolds. Hetty's weaknesses are depicted as deficiencies of feeling in relation to her own past, to the children of the Hall Farm, to other people, and she is truly 'saved' not by the reprieve but her eventual ability to reciprocate Dinah's compassionate embrace. Some readers, the narrator remarks, will judge the Rector, Mr Irwine, little better than a pagan, but he is clearly a wise shepherd of a flock that includes such as blacksmith Chad Cranage: 'If he had been in the habit of speaking theoretically, he would perhaps have said that the only healthy form religion could

take in such minds was that of certain dim but strong emotions suffusing themselves as a hallowing influence over family affections and neighbourly duties' (*AB* 5). These sentiments might have been uttered by the clergyman whose words stand as epigraph to the whole novel, the Pastor of *The Excursion*.

The Mill on the Floss has been termed George Eliot's 'most Wordsworthian novel' (Stone, 194) and it is not difficult to see why. It begins with an act of memory which, like the 'Spots of Time' in *The Prelude*, fuse past and present through recall of specific objects—'I remember those large and dripping willows. I remember the stone bridge'—and the narrative is studded with passages which further recall that poem as they dwell on childhood and the value of 'that sweet monotony where everything is known, and *loved* because it is known' (*MF* 1.5). Tom's return from school to the 'familiar hearth' prompts a further Wordsworthian meditation. Where would we be, 'if our affections had not a trick of twining round those old inferior things—if the loves and sanctities of our life had not deep immoveable roots in memory' (*MF* 2.2).

The language evokes *The Prelude* but *The Mill on the Floss* differs crucially from Wordsworth's self-revelation. Whereas the autobiographical poem is shaped to demonstrate how early loves and sanctities saved the poet in his life-crisis by maintaining a 'saving intercourse' with his 'true self' (*Prelude* 10. 914–15), *The Mill on the Floss* explores the power of the past to stifle as well as to nourish. Critics agree that Maggie's cry, 'If the past is not to bind us, where can duty lie' (*MF* 6.14), is the key to understanding how she handles her relationship with not only Stephen Guest but all the men in her life, but they differ vehemently about whether the narrative overall endorses it. Critical debate, which tends to focus on the ending of the novel, is still engaged with the question of whether Maggie is a strong figure, ultimately secure in an identity formed by 'days . . . | Bound each to each by natural piety' (Wordsworth, 'My Heart Leaps Up'), or whether on the contrary she is someone whose life is tragically stunted because of her misreading of the Wordsworthian myth of origins.

Silas Marner opens with a quotation from Wordsworth's *Michael*: 'A child, more than all other gifts | That earth can offer to declining man, | Brings hope with it, and forward-looking thoughts', and the novel recalls Wordsworth in local uses of language and in the trajectory of the story overall. Silas is rescued from trauma and alienation and integrated into domestic and community life through the unlooked-for gift of Eppie. His unconditional love, like Michael's for his son Luke, unblocks the silted channels of

'Worldliness and Other-Worldliness: The Poet Young'

Silas's feelings and restores 'a consciousness of unity between his past and present' (*SM* 16). Novel and poem differ essentially insofar as Wordsworth's shepherd loses his son and grieves alone among the mountains, whereas George Eliot's weaver enjoys a contented old age sitting in a garden created by Eppie and her husband. But *Michael* and *Silas Marner* both celebrate what Wordsworth called 'the strength, disinterestedness, and grandeur of love' (letter to John Wilson, 7 June 1802), and it is not surprising that George Eliot should have thought of Wordsworth as her ideal reader. Her tale, she wrote to John Blackwood in 1861, was not a story she 'believed that any one would have been interested in ... but myself (since William Wordsworth is dead)' (*L* iii. 382). See also NATURAL WORLD; ROMANTICISM.   SG

Gill, Stephen, *Wordsworth and the Victorians* (1998).
Homans, Margaret, *Bearing the Word: Language and Female Experience in Nineteenth-Century Women's Writing* (1986).
Pinney, Thomas, 'George Eliot's Reading of Wordsworth: The Record', *Victorian Newsletter*, 24 (1963).
Stone, Donald D., *The Romantic Impulse in Victorian Fiction* (1980).

'Worldliness and Other-Worldliness: The Poet Young'. In this essay on the 18th-century poet Edward *Young, published in the *Westminster Review* in January 1857 (repr. in *Essays*) George Eliot returned to a writer who had been among the favourites of her adolescence—but returned with a vengeance. The essay deconstructs with devastating wit the style and the life of a man whose characteristic gesture was a flight into religious abstraction. Quoting Young's lines, 'Far beneath | A soul immortal is a moral joy', George Eliot (then still Marian Evans) comments:

But Young could utter this falsity without detecting it, because, when he spoke of 'mortal joys', he rarely had in his mind any object to which he could attach sacredness. He was thinking of bishoprics and benefices, of smiling monarchs, patronizing prime ministers, and a 'much-indebted muse'. Of anything between these and eternal bliss, he was but rarely and moderately conscious. (*Essays*, 368)

George Eliot, the translator of *Spinoza and *Feuerbach, and the soon-to-be author of *Scenes of Clerical Life* (1857–8), pillories in Young the same inflated egotism, the same confusion of ambition and piety, the same carelessness of detail and lack of respect for difference, the same seedy desire for trivia that she was soon to explore in her novels. This passage, for example, etches one phase of his unflattering portrait:

after being a hanger-on of the profligate Duke of Wharton, after aiming in vain at a parliamentary

career, and angling for pensions and preferment with fulsome dedications and fustian odes, he is a little disgusted with his imperfect success, and has determined to retire from the general mendicancy business to a particular branch; in other words, he has determined on that renunciation of the world implied in 'taking orders', with the prospect of a good living and an advantageous matrimonial connection. (*Essays*, 337)

We can see in this the parochial snobberies and laughable ambitions of George Eliot's worst characters, given more savage treatment than they get in her novels where they have more than one side. And we see the ability of the writer to put into a single telling mental gesture, a whole world of value.

This essay is one of those which most demonstrates George Eliot's ability as a controversialist and commanding essayist; she has the novelist's comprehensive and the satirist's discriminating view. Young's suitability as a target for this pitiless attack is constituted by what she shows to be his immense, immodest pretension, especially in his self-ordained role as cultural teacher and guide. This puts him beyond the pale within which she allows even *Middlemarch*'s Edward Casaubon some protection. She especially pillories Young's so-called religion as little more 'than egotism turned heaven-ward. Religion, he tells us ... is "ambition, pleasure, and the love of gain" directed towards the joys of the future life instead of the present. And his ethics correspond to his religion' (*Essays*, 378).

With her thorough grounding in *philosophy and in *history Marian Evans could see through the style to the generic problems with Young it reflected, in particular his fondness for antitheses. These are not merely familiar 18th-century poetic devices, but part of a formulation of perception itself that goes back to the Greeks and which she characterized as the mistake of philosophy from Parmenides to Immanuel *Kant (*Essays*, 150). Deprive Young of his antitheses, and 'more than half of his eloquence would be shrivelled up. Place him on a breezy common, where the furze is in its golden bloom, where children are playing, and horses are standing in the sunshine with fondling necks, and he would have nothing to say.' As a guide Young trains attention away from what can be known and worked with and instead invites it to fly for motive to 'the remote, the vague, and the unknown' (368–9). But for George Eliot, such deflection and denial of specificity is a denial of those incarnate traditions (see DETERMINISM) which make up the alphabets of life.

Other-worldliness, then, is not the opposite of worldliness but, on the contrary, merely one of its faces. Other-worldliness certainly is not the basis for moral or religious principle that Young pretends it to be (she makes a similar, even wittier case in her essay *'Evangelical Teaching: Dr Cumming'). She reveals in the case of Young that other-worldliness is nothing more than worldliness in an acquisitive mood. What differs from them both is the spirit of respect for what is given that sees it as an essential basis for creating what is new. That respect for the material basis of every action—what she sometimes called resignation but which has nothing to do with passivity—inspires her exposé of the likes of the poet Young.

EDE

Y, Z

Young, Edward (1683–1765), English poet whose *Night Thoughts* (1742–5) are a favourite source of quotation for the young, fervent George Eliot. Letters to Maria *Lewis from 1838 to late 1841 include pedantic parody from Young (*L* i. 5), while Maria is urged to love certain lines 'for my sake' (*L* i. 7). Young's choice of unusual words is reflected in 'fuliginously', Eliot calls him 'the prophet of Selwyn' (she means 'Welwyn', where he was rector); in 1844 she quotes his theory about the key of life opening the gates of death, mentioning it again in 1866. A letter of May 1878 (L vii. 27) indicates a softening of the judgements expressed in *'Worldliness and Other-Worldliness: The Poet Young' where she subjects her early favourite to savage criticism.   GRH

Zionism. See JUDAISM.

MAPS

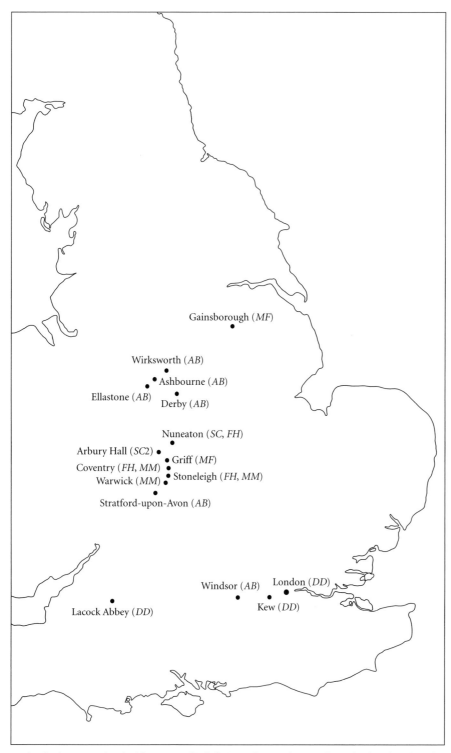

Gainsborough (*MF*)

Wirksworth (*AB*)

Ashbourne (*AB*)

Ellastone (*AB*)   Derby (*AB*)

Nuneaton (*SC, FH*)

Arbury Hall (*SC2*)   Griff (*MF*)

Coventry (*FH, MM*)

Warwick (*MM*)   Stoneleigh (*FH, MM*)

Stratford-upon-Avon (*AB*)

Windsor (*AB*)   London (*DD*)

Kew (*DD*)

Lacock Abbey (*DD*)

England: Places associated with George Eliot's fiction. The novels are indicated in brackets (see also the entry for settings).

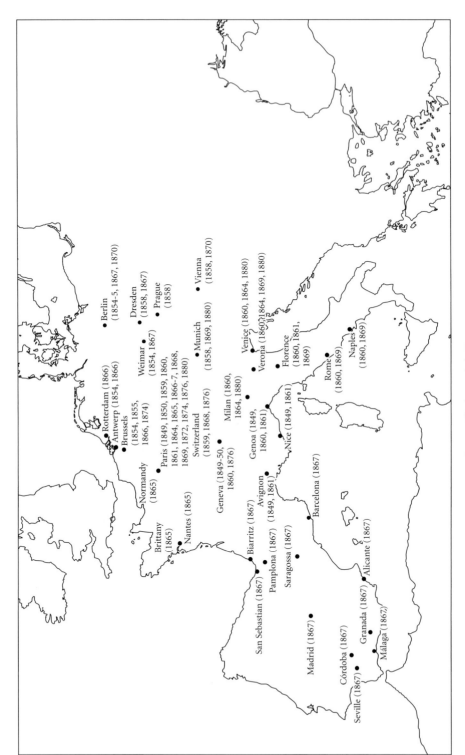

Berlin (1854-5, 1867, 1870)

Dresden (1858, 1867)

Prague (1858)

Vienna (1858, 1870)

Munich (1858, 1869, 1880)

Weimar (1854, 1867)

Rotterdam (1866)

Antwerp (1854, 1866)

Brussels (1854, 1855, 1866, 1874)

Normandy (1865)

Paris (1849, 1850, 1859, 1860, 1861, 1864, 1865, 1866-7, 1868, 1869, 1872, 1874, 1876, 1880)

Switzerland (1859, 1868, 1876)

Geneva (1849-50, 1860, 1876)

Milan (1860, 1864, 1880)

Venice (1860, 1864, 1880)

Verona (1860, 1864, 1869, 1880)

Florence (1860, 1861, 1869)

Rome (1860, 1869)

Naples (1860, 1869)

Genoa (1849, 1860, 1861)

Nice (1849, 1861)

Brittany (1865)

Nantes (1865)

Biarritz (1867)

Avignon (1849, 1861)

Barcelona (1867)

Pamplona (1867)

Saragossa (1867)

Alicante (1867)

San Sebastian (1867)

Madrid (1867)

Granada (1867)

Córdoba (1867)

Málaga (1867)

Seville (1867)

George Eliot's travels in Europe.

GENERAL BIBLIOGRAPHY

George Eliot's Published Writings

Novels
Adam Bede (1859)
The Mill on the Floss (1860)
Silas Marner: The Weaver of Raveloe (1861)
Romola (1862–3)
Felix Holt, the Radical (1866)
Middlemarch: A Study of Provincial Life (1871–2)
Daniel Deronda (1876)

Short Fiction
Scenes of Clerical Life (1858) (comprises 'The Sad
    Fortunes of the Reverend Amos Barton', 'Mr
    Gilfil's Love-Story', and 'Janet's Repentance',
    published serially in *Blackwood's Edinburgh
    Magazine*, 1857)
'The Lifted Veil' (1859)
'Brother Jacob' (1864)

Poetry
The Spanish Gypsy: A Poem (1868)
The Legend of Jubal and other Poems (1874)

Other Writing
Impressions of Theophrastus Such (1879)

The most authoritative collected edition of the
above works which was published in her own lifetime, and which she corrected, is The Cabinet
Edition, 20 vols. (1878–80). The Clarendon Edition
(1980–), most of which has now appeared, is
establishing the definitive critical text of the
novels.

Essays
Essays and Leaves from a Note-Book, ed. Charles Lee
    Lewes (1884).
Essays of George Eliot, ed. Thomas Pinney (1963).
*George Eliot: A Writer's Notebook 1854–1879, and
    Uncollected Writings*, ed. Joseph Wiesenfarth
    (1981).
*George Eliot: Selected Essays, Poems and Other
    Writings*, ed. A. S. Byatt and Nicholas Warren
    (1990).
George Eliot: Selected Critical Writings, ed.
    Rosemary Ashton (1992).

Translations
Strauss, David Friedrich, *The Life of Jesus, Critically
    Examined* (1846).
Feuerbach, Ludwig, *The Essence of Christianity*
    (1854).
Spinoza, Benedict de, *Ethics* (1981).

Letters and Journals
*George Eliot's Life as Related in her Letters and
    Journals*, ed. J. W. Cross, 3 vols. (1885; new edn.
    with additions, 1886) (unless otherwise stated,
    references are to the 1st edn. of 1885).
The George Eliot Letters, ed. Gordon S. Haight, 9
    vols. (1954–78).
The Journals of George Eliot, ed. Margaret Harris
    and Judith Johnston (1998).

Notebooks
Essays and Leaves from a Note-Book, ed. Charles Lee
    Lewes (1884).
Quarry for 'Middlemarch', ed. Anna T. Kitchel
    (1950).
*Some George Eliot Notebooks: An Edition of the Carl
    H. Pforzheimer Library's George Eliot Holograph
    Notebooks, MSS 707, 708, 709, 710, 711*, ed.
    William Baker, 4 vols. (1976–85).
*George Eliot's 'Middlemarch' Notebooks: A
    Transcription*, ed. John Clark Pratt and Victor A.
    Neufeldt (1979).
*George Eliot: A Writer's Notebook 1854–1879, and
    Uncollected Writings*, ed. Joseph Wiesenfarth
    (1981).
George Eliot's 'Daniel Deronda' Notebooks, ed. Jane
    Irwin (1996).

Bibliographies and Reference Works

Ashton, Rosemary, '"George Eliot" 1819–1880', in
    Joanne Shattock (ed.), *The Cambridge
    Bibliography of English Literature*, vol. iv (3rd
    edn., 1999).
Fulmer, Constance Marie, *George Eliot: A Reference
    Guide* (1977).
Hands, Timothy, *A George Eliot Chronology* (1989).
Hartnoll, Phyllis, *Who's Who in George Eliot* (1977).
Harvey, W. J., 'George Eliot', in Lionel Stevenson
    (ed.), *Victorian Fiction: A Guide to Research*
    (1964).
Knoepflmacher, U. C., 'George Eliot', in George H.
    Ford (ed.), *Victorian Fiction: A Second Guide to
    Research* (1978).
Lake, Brian, and Nassau, Janet, *George Eliot in
    Original Cloth: A Bibliographical Catalogue*
    (1988).
Levine, George, *An Annotated Critical Bibliography
    of George Eliot* (1988).
McDonagh, J., 'George Eliot', in *Annotated
    Bibliography for English Studies*, vol. iii (1997).
Mudge, I. G., and Sears, M. E., *A George Eliot
    Dictionary* (1924).

General Bibliography

Pinion, F. B., *A George Eliot Companion* (1981).

Purkis, John, *A Preface to George Eliot* (1985).

Slates, Lisa, and Glusman, Michelle, 'George Eliot Resources on the World Wide Web', *George Eliot–George Henry Lewes Studies*, 34–5 (1998).

Biographical Studies

These works are referred to by author and date in the entries.

Adams, Kathleen, *Those of Us Who Loved Her: The Men in George Eliot's Life* (1980).

Ashton, Rosemary, *George Eliot: A Life* (1996).

Bodenheimer, Rosemarie, *The Real Life of Mary Ann Evans: George Eliot, Her Letters and Fiction* (1994).

Haight, Gordon S., *George Eliot: A Biography* (1968).

—— *George Eliot and John Chapman: with Chapman's Diaries* (1940; 2nd edn. 1969).

Hughes, Kathryn, *George Eliot: The Last Victorian* (1998).

Karl, Frederick, *George Eliot* (1995).

Laski, Marghanita, *George Eliot and her World* (1973).

Redinger, Ruby, *George Eliot: The Emergent Self* (1975).

Taylor, Ina, *George Eliot: Woman of Contradictions* (1989).

Critical Studies

The works listed below are those which are frequently cited in the entries, where citation is usually by author or editor and date (with the exception of *George Eliot: The Critical Heritage*, which is abbreviated to *CH*). They represent only a part, but an important part, of the vast secondary literature on George Eliot. Numerous other references, particularly to articles, are given in the bibliographies to individual entries.

Adam, Ian, *This Particular Web: Essays on Middlemarch* (1975).

Ashton, Rosemary, *George Eliot* (1983).

—— *The German Idea: Four English Writers and the Reception of German Thought 1800–1860* (1980).

—— *The Mill on the Floss: A Natural History* (1990).

Baker, William, *George Eliot and Judaism* (1975).

Barrett, Dorothea, *Vocation and Desire: George Eliot's Heroines* (1989).

Beer, Gillian, *Darwin's Plots: Evolutionary Narratives in Darwin, George Eliot and Nineteenth-Century Fiction* (1983).

—— *George Eliot* (1986).

Bellringer, Alan W., *George Eliot* (1993).

Bennett, Joan, *George Eliot: Her Mind and Art* (1948).

Bonaparte, Felicia, *The Triptych and the Cross: The Central Myths of George Eliot's Poetic Imagination* (1979).

Brady, Kirstin, *George Eliot* (1992).

Carroll, David (ed.), *George Eliot: The Critical Heritage* (1971).

—— *George Eliot and the Conflict of Interpretations* (1992).

Chase, Karen, *George Eliot: Middlemarch* (1991).

Couch, John Philip, *George Eliot in France: A French Appraisal of George Eliot's Writings, 1858–1960* (1967).

Creeger, George (ed.), *George Eliot: A Collection of Critical Essays* (1970).

Cunningham, Valentine, *Everywhere Spoken Against: Dissent in the Victorian Novel* (1975).

Dentith, Simon, *George Eliot* (1986).

Dodd, Valerie A., *George Eliot: An Intellectual Life* (1990).

Ermarth, Elizabeth Deeds, *George Eliot* (1985).

Gilbert, Sandra, and Gubar, Susan, *The Madwoman in the Attic: The Woman Writer and the Nineteenth-Century Literary Imagination* (1979).

Graver, Suzanne, *George Eliot and Community: A Study in Social Theory and Literary Form* (1984).

Gray, Beryl, *George Eliot and Music* (1989).

Haight, Gordon S. (ed.), *A Century of George Eliot Criticism* (1965).

Handley, Graham, *State of the Art: George Eliot, a Guide through the Critical Maze* (1990).

Hardy, Barbara (ed.), *Critical Essays on George Eliot* (1970).

—— *The Novels of George Eliot: A Study in Form* (1959).

—— *Particularities: Readings in George Eliot* (1982).

Harvey, W. J., *The Art of George Eliot* (1961).

Holstrom, John, and Lerner, Laurence (edd.), *George Eliot and her Readers: A Selection of Contemporary Reviews* (1966).

Hutchinson, Stuart (ed.), *George Eliot: Critical Assessments*, 4 vols. (1996).

Knoepflmacher, U. C., *George Eliot's Early Novels: The Limits of Realism* (1968).

Leavis, F. R., *The Great Tradition: George Eliot, Henry James, Joseph Conrad* (1948).

Levine, Caroline, and Turner, Mark W. (edd.), *From Author to Text: Re-reading George Eliot's 'Romola'* (1998).

McCobb, Anthony, *George Eliot's Knowledge of German Life and Letters* (1982).

McDonagh, Josephine, *George Eliot* (1997).

Myers, William, *The Teaching of George Eliot* (1984).

Newton, K. M. (ed.), *George Eliot* (1991).

Paris, Bernard J., *Experiments in Life: George Eliot's Quest for Values* (1965).

Peck, John, *Middlemarch: George Eliot* (1992).

Perkin, J. Russell, *A Reception-History of George Eliot's Fiction* (1990).

Rignall, John (ed.), *George Eliot and Europe* (1997).

Semmel, Bernard, *George Eliot and the Politics of National Inheritance* (1994).

Shaffer, Elinor, *'Kubla Khan' and the 'Fall of Jerusalem': The Mythological School in Biblical Criticism and Secular Literature 1770–1880* (1975).

Showalter, Elaine, *A Literature of Their Own: British Women Novelists from Brontë to Lessing* (1977).

Shuttleworth, Sally, *George Eliot and Nineteenth-Century Science* (1984).

Spittles, Brian, *George Eliot* (1993).

Sutherland, John, *Victorian Novelists and Publishers* (1976).

Thompson, Andrew, *George Eliot and Italy: Literary, Cultural and Political Influences from Dante to the Risorgimento* (1998).

Uglow, Jenny, *George Eliot* (1987).

Welsh, Alexander, *George Eliot and Blackmail* (1985).

Wiesenfarth, Joseph, *George Eliot's Mythmaking* (1977).

Witemeyer, Hugh, *George Eliot and the Visual Arts* (1979).

Wright, T. R., *George Eliot's Middlemarch* (1991).

ALPHABETICAL LIST OF CHARACTERS

This list contains most of the named characters in the novels and short fiction, and in the poems 'Armgart' and *The Spanish Gypsy*. It also includes the names of the principal figures in *Impressions of Theophrastus Such*. The key to the abbreviations is to be found on p. xxii.

Abbott, Cousin	*MF*	Bardi, Romola de'	*RO*
Abel	*MM*	Bardo (Bardo de' Bardi)	*RO*
Abel, Mrs	*MM*	Barone, Ser Francesco di Ser (Ser Ceccone)	*RO*
Acciajoli, Dianora	*RO*	Bartolommeo, Fra (Buccio della Porta)	*RO*
Adam, Mrs	*DD*	Barton, Amos (The Revd Amos Barton)	*SC1*
Adrastus	*TS*	Barton, Chubby	*SC1*
Albani, Maestro	*SC2*	Barton, Dickey	*SC1*
Alcharisi (Halm-Eberstein, The Princess		Barton, Fred	*SC1*
Leonora)	*DD*	Barton, Mrs Milly	*SC1*
Alexander VI, Pope	*RO*	Barton, Patty	*SC1*
Alfred	*LV*	Barton, Sophy	*SC1*
Alice	*MF*	Barton, The Revd Amos	*SC1*
Alice	*SC1*	Barton, Walter	*SC1*
Alick	*AB*	Bass, Trapping	*MM*
Allen, Sister	*AB*	Bates, Mr	*SC2*
Alvar, Don	*SG*	Bazley	*DD*
Amador, Don	*SG*	Beale, Molly	*SC3*
Angus	*DD*	Beck, Mrs	*MM*
Ann	*SC3*	Becky	*SC2*
Antonio, Luca	*RO*	Bede, Adam	*AB*
Archer, Mrs	*LV*	Bede, Lisbeth	*AB*
Arias	*SG*	Bede, Seth	*AB*
Aritella, Lamberto dell'	*RO*	Bede, Thias (Matthias)	*AB*
Armgart	'Armgart'	Beevor, Mrs	*MM*
Armstrong, Mr	*SC3*	Bellamy, Mr and Mrs	*SC2*
Arrowpoint, Catherine	*DD*	Ben	*MF*
Arrowpoint, Mr and Mrs	*DD*	Benedetto	*RO*
Askern, Mr	*MF*	Benevieni, Girolamo	*RO*
Assher, Beatrice	*SC2*	Berta, Monna	*RO*
Assher, Lady	*SC2*	Best, Mrs	*AB*
Assher, Sir John	*SC2*	Bethell	*AB*
		Betty	*AB*
Baccio	*RO*	Betty	*SC1*
Bacon, Miss	*AB*	Betty	*SC3*
Bagshawe, The Revd Mr	*SC1*	Bincome	*MF*
Bagster	*MM*	Blarney, Lord	*SC1*
Baines, John	*AB*	Blasco	*SG*
Baird, The Revd Mr	*SC1*	Blick, Dr	*SM*
Baker, Will	*AB*	Blough, Lord	*DD*
Baldassare (Baldassare Calvo)	*RO*	Bodkin, Brother	*FH*
Bale, Kester	*AB*	Bond, Miss	*SC1*
Ballard, Mrs	*MM*	Bond, Mr	*SC1*
Bambridge, Mr	*MM*	Bond, Mrs	*SC1*
Banks, Mr	*DD*	Bond, Tommy	*SC2*
Banks, Mr	*FH*	Boni	*RO*
Bardi, Bardo de'	*RO*	Bonsi, Domenico	*RO*
Bardi, Dino de' (Fra Luca)	*RO*	Bowyer, Mr	*MM*

462

Braccio, Ser	*RO*	Carr, Mr	*MF*
Brackenshaw, Lady Beatrice	*DD*	Carroll	*AB*
Brackenshaw, Lady Maria	*DD*	Carter, Mrs	*MM*
Brackenshaw, Lord and Lady	*DD*	Casaubon, Dorothea (Dorothea Brooke)	*MM*
Brady	*SC3*	Casaubon, The Revd Edward	*MM*
Brand, Mr	*SC1*	Cass, Bob	*SM*
Bratti (Bratti Ferravecchi)	*RO*	Cass, Dunstan (Dunsey)	*SM*
Brecon, Young	*DD*	Cass, Godfrey	*SM*
Brendal, Harry	*DD*	Cass, Squire	*SM*
Brent	*FH*	Casson, Mr	*AB*
Bretton, Mrs	*MM*	Cecca	*RO*
Brewitt	*DD*	Cecco	*RO*
Brick, Mrs	*SC1*	Ceccone, Ser (Ser Francesco di Ser Barone)	*RO*
Bridget	*AB*	Cei, Francesco	*RO*
Bridmain, Edmund	*SC1*	Cennini, Bernardo	*RO*
Briggs	*MM*	Cennini, Domenico	*RO*
Brigida, Monna	*RO*	Cennini, Pietro	*RO*
Brimstone	*AB*	Chad's Bess (Bessy Cranage)	*AB*
Brindle, Mike (Michael Brincey)	*FH*	Chaloner, Mr and Mrs	*BJ*
Brinley, Mrs	*SC3*	Charisi, Daniel	*DD*
Britton, Luke	*AB*	Charisi, Ephraim	*DD*
Brooke, Mr	*MM*	Charles VIII of France	*RO*
Brooke, Celia (Kitty)	*MM*	Cherry, Mrs	*FH*
Brooke, Dorothea (Dodo)	*MM*	Chester	*AB*
Brooks	*SC2*	Chettam, Lady	*MM*
Brumby, Dick	*MF*	Chettam, Sir James	*MM*
Brumley	*MF*	Cheverel, Lady (Henrietta)	*SC2*
Bryce	*SM*	Cheverel, Sir Christopher	*SC2*
Buchan	*DD*	Chichely, Mr	*MM*
Bucks, Mrs	*MF*	Chowne, Mr	*AB*
Budd, Mr	*SC3*	Choyce	*AB*
Bugle	*DD*	Christian, Maurice (Henry Scaddon)	*FH*
Bulstrode, Ellen	*MM*	Chubb, Mr (William)	*FH*
Bulstrode, Kate	*MM*	Cioni, Ser	*RO*
Bulstrode, Mrs Harriet	*MM*	Clement, Sir James	*FH*
Bulstrode, Nicholas	*MM*	Clemmens	*MM*
Bult, Mr	*DD*	Cleves, The Revd Martin	*SC1*
Bunch	*MM*	Cliff, Mr	*SM*
Bunney, Master	*MM*	Clintock, Young	*DD*
Burge, Jonathan	*AB*	Clintup, Mr	*MM*
Burge, Mary	*AB*	Cohen, Addy	*DD*
Button, Peggy	*FH*	Cohen, Adelaide Rebekah	*DD*
Butts, Sally	*SC3*	Cohen, Eugenie Esther	*DD*
Bycliffe, Maurice Christian	*FH*	Cohen, Ezra	*DD*
Bygate, Mr	*AB*	Cohen, Ezra Mordecai	*DD*
Byles, Luke	*SC3*	Cohen, Jacob Alexander	*DD*
		Cohen, Mrs	*DD*
Cadwallader, Mrs Elinor	*MM*	Cohen, Sara	*DD*
Cadwallader, The Revd Humphrey	*MM*	Cook, Phib	*SC3*
Calcondila, Demetrio	*RO*	Cooper, Timothy	*MM*
Calibut, Mr	*FH*	Corsini, Luca	*RO*
Callum	*MM*	Cosimo, Piero di	*RO*
Calvo, Baldassarre (Jacopo di Nola)	*RO*	Coulter, Ann	*SM*
Cambini, Andrea	*RO*	Cox	*SM*
Caparra, Niccolò	*RO*	Crabbe, Mr	*MM*
Capponi, Piero	*RO*	Crackenthorpe, The Revd Mr	*SM*
Carp, Dr	*MM*	Cragstone, Lady	*DD*
Carpe, The Revd Mr	*SC1*	Craig, Mr	*AB*

Alphabetical List of Characters

Alphabetical List of Characters

Alphabetical List of Characters

Puglia, Fra Francesco di	RO	Salvestro, Fra (Fra Salvestro Maruffi)	RO
Puller, Mr	DD	Salviati, Marco	RO
Pullet, Mr	MF	Sampson, Mr	FH
Pullet, Mrs (Sophy)	MF	Samson, Dr	SC2
Pummel	TS	Sandeman, Squire	SC3
Putty, James	FH	Sandro	RO
Pym	AB	Sandy Jim (Jim Salt)	AB
		Sarah	DD
Quallon, Mr	DD	Sarah	SM
Quicksett	DD	Sargent, The Revd Mr	SC1
Quorlen	FH	Sarti	SC2
		Sarti, Caterina (Tina)	SC2
Rachel	SC1	Sasso, Meo di	RO
Radborough, The Dean of	SC1	Satchell	AB
Radley	SC3	Savonarola, Fra Girolamo	RO
Raffles, John	MM	Scaddon, Henry (Maurice Christian)	FH
Ralph	AB	Scala, Alessandra	RO
Ram, Mr	DD	Scala, Bartolommeo	RO
Ramble, Squire	SC2	Scales, Mr	FH
Rann, Joshua (Old Joshway)	AB	Schmidt	LV
Rann, Sally	AB	Sephardo	SG
Rappit, Mr	MF	Sforza, Ludovico	RO
Ratcliffe	SC3	Sharp, Mrs	SC2
Raymond, Mr and Mrs	DD	Sherlock, The Revd Theodore	FH
Raynor, Anna	SC3	Silly Caleb	SC3
Raynor, Mrs	SC3	Silly Jim	SC1
Renfrew, Mrs	MM	Silva, Don	SG
Richards, Patty	SC2	Simmons	MM
Ricketts, Dame	SC3	Sims, Mr	FH
Ridolfi, Giovan Battista	RO	Sinker, Mr	DD
Ridolfi, Niccolò	RO	Sircome, Mr	FH
Rigg, Joshua	MM	Sitwell, Sir Jasper and Lady	SC2
Riley, Mr	MF	Sloagan, Lord	DD
Robins, Clara	SC3	Smith, The Revd Mr	SC3
Robisson, Mr	MM	Snell, John	SM
Rodd, Mr	BJ	Soderini, Pagolantonio	RO
Rodney, Jem	SM	Sorrel, Hetty	AB
Roe, Mr	AB	Spanning, Dr	MM
Roldan	SG	Spence, Mr	MF
Romola (Romola de' Bardi)	RO	Spicer, Mr	MM
Rosamond (Rosamond Vincy)	MM	Spike	TS
Rose, The Revd Mr	SC3	Spilkins	FH
Rose, Timothy	FH	Spilkins, Mr	MM
Rucellai, Bernardo	RO	Spini, Dolfo	RO
Rucellai, Camilla	RO	Sprague, Dr	MM
Ryde, The Revd Mr	AB	Spratt, Mr	FH
		Spratt, Mr	SC1
Sadler	MM	Spray, The Revd Mr	MF
Saft, Tom (Tom Tholer)	AB	Standish, Mr	MM
Sally	MM	Stannery, Lord	DD
Sally	MF	Startin, Mrs	DD
Sally	SC2	Steene, Mr and Mrs	BJ
Sally	SC3	Steene, Widow	AB
Salt	MF	Stelling, Mrs Louisa	MF
Salt, Ben (Timothy's Bess's Ben)	AB	Stelling, The Revd Walter	MF
Salt, Bess (Timothy's Bess)	AB	Stickney, The Revd Mr	SC3
Salt, Jim (Sandy Jim)	AB	Stilfox	DD
Salt, Mr	FH	Stokes, Master Tom	SC2

Alphabetical List of Characters

TIME CHART

Showing George Eliot's life and career
in the wider historical and literary context of the period

	George Eliot's Life	Historical and Literary Context
1819	Born at South Farm, Arbury, near Nuneaton, Warwickshire (22 Nov.). Baptized Mary Anne Evans.	Births of Ruskin, the future Queen Victoria, Theodor Fontane, and Gottfried Keller. Peterloo Massacre. Scott's *Ivanhoe* and first two cantos of Byron's *Don Juan* published.
1820	Evans family move to Griff House.	Death of King George III; accession of George IV. Shelley's *Prometheus Unbound*, Keats's *Hyperion* published.
1821	Twin brothers born and live only ten days.	Death of Keats. Birth of Flaubert. Scott's *Kenilworth*, Shelley's *Adonais* published.
1822		Death of Shelley.
1823		Scott's *Quentin Durward* published.
1824	Starts at Miss Lathom's school in Attleborough.	Carlyle's translation of Goethe's *Wilhelm Meisters Lehrjahre*. Death of Byron.
1825		Opening of first passenger railway between Stockton and Darlington. Manzoni's *I promessi sposi* published.
1826	First journey away from home when she visits Derbyshire and Staffordshire with her parents.	
1827	When a borrowed copy of Scott's *Waverley* has to be returned, she writes out the story for herself.	Deaths of Beethoven and Blake. Heine's *Buch der Lieder* published.
1828	Starts at Mrs Wallington's boarding school in Nuneaton, where Maria Lewis is a teacher. Reads Bible intensively.	Wellington becomes Prime Minister. Corn Law Act.
1829		Catholic Emancipation Act. Peel establishes Metropolitan Police.
1830		Death of George IV; accession of William IV. July Revolution in France; accession of Louis Philippe. Stendhal's *Le rouge et le noir* and Tennyson's *Poems, Chiefly Lyrical* published.
1831		First Reform Bill introduced and rejected. Parliament dissolved.
1832	Starts at the Misses Franklin's school in Coventry. Witnesses two days of rioting in Nuneaton during election (Dec.).	First Reform Act. Goethe's *Faust Part II* and George Sand's *Indiana* published. Deaths of Goethe and Scott.
1833		Keble's Assize sermon marks beginning of Oxford movement. Slavery abolished in the British Empire. First Factory Act regulating

		child labour. Carlyle's *Sartor Resartus* and George Sand's *Lélia* published.
1834	Begins a school notebook (16 Mar.) which contains the opening of a story, 'Edward Neville'. Beginning of intense evangelical phase.	Death of Coleridge. Poor Law Amendment Act. Transportation of Tolpuddle Martyrs. Publication of Balzac's *Le Père Goriot* begins.
1835	Mother's health declines. Leaves the Misses Franklin's school (Dec.). Father suffers acute attack of kidney stone (31 Dec.).	Strauss's *Das Leben Jesu* published.
1836	Death of mother (3 Feb.). Receives Holy Communion for the first time (25 Dec.).	Beginning of Chartist movement. Lockhart's *Life of Scott* and Dickens's *Pickwick Papers* begin publication.
1837	Bridesmaid at wedding of sister Christiana (Chrissey) to Edward Clarke at Meriden, near Coventry. Signs register as Mary Ann. Takes over running of household at Griff.	Death of William IV and accession of Queen Victoria. Publication of Carlyle's *French Revolution*. Dickens's *Oliver Twist* serialized.
1838	Begins to gain reputation as a learned lady and is offered use of Arbury Hall library. First visit to London with brother Isaac; refuses to go to the theatre.	Anti-Corn Law League founded in Manchester. Serialization of Dickens's *Nicholas Nickleby* begins. Charles Hennell publishes *An Inquiry into the Origins of Christianity*.
1839	Visit to Griff of Methodist Aunt Samuel, from whom she derives the germ of *Adam Bede*. Begins to learn Italian. Early attempts at poetry. First journey by rail to London with her father. Reading Wordsworth with enthusiasm.	Chartist riots. Stendhal's *La Chartreuse de Parme* published.
1840	First published work, the poem 'As o'er the fields', appears in the *Christian Observer* (Jan.). Begins to learn German.	Marriage of Queen Victoria to Prince Albert. Penny Post established. Birth of Thomas Hardy.
1841	Moves to Coventry with father (Mar.). Marriage of brother Isaac. Makes friends with the Brays, reads Charles Hennell's *Inquiry*, and begins to entertain religious doubts.	Peel becomes Prime Minister. Carlyle's *On Heroes and Hero-Worship* published. Feuerbach publishes *Das Wesen des Christenthums* anonymously.
1842	Refusal to accompany her father to church (2 Jan.) signals her break with orthodox Christianity. Meets Cara Bray's sister Sara Hennell and begins a close friendship.	Tennyson's *Poems*, Browning's *Dramatic Lyrics*, and Wordsworth's *Poems, Chiefly of Early and Late Years* published. Balzac starts publication of his fiction as *La Comédie humaine*.
1843	Holiday in Wales with the Brays, Hennells, and Rufa Brabant (July). Lengthy stay with Dr Brabant at Devizes ends when his wife insists that she leave the house (Nov.–Dec.).	Carlyle's *Past and Present* and first volume of Ruskin's *Modern Painters* published. Wordsworth appointed Poet Laureate.
1844	Undertakes to complete Rufa Brabant's translation of Strauss's *Das Leben Jesu*.	Disraeli's *Coningsby* published.
1845	Meets Harriet Martineau. Accompanies the Brays on a holiday to Scotland (Oct.). Works on Strauss translation.	Engels publishes *The Condition of the Working-Class in England* in German. Disraeli's *Sybil* published. Newman received into the Roman Catholic Church.
1846	Translation of Strauss published anonymously by Chapman as *The Life of Jesus* (June). Publishes review of Quinet and Michelet in the Coventry *Herald* (Oct.), and then 'Poetry and Prose from the Notebook of an Eccentric'.	Famine in Ireland after failure of potato crop. Repeal of the Corn Laws. Marriage of Robert Browning and Elizabeth Barrett.

Time Chart

1847   Visits London with Charles Bray (Apr.) and Isle of Wight with father to improve his declining health (Sept.–Oct.).

Charlotte Brontë's *Jane Eyre* and Emily Brontë's *Wuthering Heights* published. Serialization of Thackeray's *Vanity Fair* begins. Factory Act restricts hours worked by women and children.

1848   Enthusiastic correspondence with John Sibree about the revolution in France. Meets Emerson, 'the first *man* I have ever seen' (July). Father's death seems imminent.

Revolutions in Europe. Publication of the *Communist Manifesto*. Demise of the Chartist movement. Pre-Raphaelite Brotherhood founded. Mrs Gaskell's *Mary Barton* published. Death of Emily Brontë.

1849   Begins to translate Spinoza. Death of father (May). Taken abroad for a holiday by the Brays and decides to stay on in Geneva alone. Spends the winter lodging with the D'Albert Durades.

Fall of Mazzini's Roman Republic. Serialization of Dickens's *David Copperfield* begins. Matthew Arnold's *The Strayed Reveller* and Charlotte Brontë's *Shirley* published.

1850   Returns to England in March, finding it dismal. Begins association with the *Westminster Review* with a review of Mackay's *Progress of the Intellect*. Stays two weeks at Chapman's in the Strand (Nov.). Decides to make writing her career.

Deaths of Balzac and Wordsworth. Tennyson made Poet Laureate. Publication of Wordsworth's *The Prelude*, Tennyson's *In Memoriam*, Hawthorne's *The Scarlet Letter*, Kingsley's *Alton Locke*, Turgenev's *A Month in the Country*, and Herbert Spencer's *Social Statics*.

1851   Takes up lodgings at Chapman's (Jan.). Difficult domestic situation forces her to leave and return to the Brays in Coventry (Mar.). Chapman buys *Westminster Review* and asks her to assist in editing. Returns to lodge with him and work on *Review* (Sept.). Friendly with Herbert Spencer through whom she meets G. H. Lewes (Oct.).

Great Exhibition opens in London (May). Serialization of Harriet Beecher Stowe's *Uncle Tom's Cabin* begins, and Melville's *Moby Dick* and first part of Ruskin's *Stones of Venice* published.

1852   Editing *Westminster Review*. Friendship with Bessie Parkes, through whom she meets Barbara Leigh Smith, later Bodichon. Close to Herbert Spencer, who rejects her love (July). Visits Harriet Martineau in Ambleside (Oct.).

Death of Wellington. Serialization of Dickens's *Bleak House* begins. Thackeray's *Henry Esmond* published.

1853   Moves out of Chapman's house (Oct.). Relationship with Lewes begins. Resigns editorship of the *Westminster* at end of year.

Harriet Martineau's translation of Comte appears as *Positive Philosophy*. Charlotte Brontë's *Villette* and Mrs Gaskell's *Cranford* published.

1854   Translates Feuerbach's *Wesen des Christenthums*. Translation published under her own name as *The Essence of Christianity* (July). Leaves with Lewes for Germany (20 July). They stay in Weimar and (from Nov.) Berlin. Writes 'Woman in France' for *Westminster Review*.

Crimean war begins (Mar.). Patmore's *The Angel in the House* and Tennyson's 'Charge of the Light Brigade' published.

1855   Returns to England (Mar.) and lives with Lewes as his wife. Writes and reviews intensively for the *Leader* and *Westminster Review*. Two articles on experiences in Weimar appear in *Fraser's Magazine*.

Florence Nightingale nursing in Crimea. Lewes's *Life of Goethe*, Mrs Gaskell's *North and South*, Trollope's *The Warden*, Browning's *Men and Women*, Kingsley's *Westward Ho!*, and Tennyson's *Maud* published. Serialization of Dickens's *Little Dorrit* begins. Death of Charlotte Brontë.

1856   Completes translation of Spinoza's *Ethics* but it is not published. 'The Natural History of German Life' appears in *Westminster*.

End of Crimean war. Petition on Married Women's Property Rights. Death of Heine. Flaubert's *Madame Bovary*, Gottfried Keller's

Summer (May–Aug.) in Devon and South Wales. Conceives idea of a story, 'Amos Barton', at Tenby (July). Begins writing it in Richmond (22 Sept.). Lewes sends it to John Blackwood (Nov.).

1857 'Amos Barton' appears in *Blackwood's Edinburgh Magazine* (Jan.), followed by 'Mr Gilfil's Love-Story' and 'Janet's Repentance'. Informs her brother Isaac that she is living with Lewes (May); he breaks off all communication. Begins writing a novel, *Adam Bede* (Oct.).

1858 The three stories published by Blackwood as *Scenes of Clerical Life* by George Eliot (Jan.). Meets John Blackwood at Richmond and reveals the identity of George Eliot (Feb.). Second visit to Germany—Munich and Dresden—with Lewes (Apr.–Aug.). Completes *Bede* (Nov.).

1859 *Adam Bede* published (Feb.) to general acclaim. Death of sister Chrissey. 'The Lifted Veil' appears in *Blackwood's* (July). Visited by Dickens who invites her to write a novel for *All the Year Round* (Nov.)

1860 Finishes second novel (Mar.) and leaves with Lewes for three months' holiday, mainly in Italy. *The Mill on the Floss* published (Apr.). Lewes's eldest son Charles comes to live with them.

1861 *Silas Marner* published. Leaves with Lewes for second visit to Italy (Apr.). Does research for *Romola* in Florence.

1862 Accepts £7,000 for *Romola*; serialization in *Cornhill Magazine* begins (July). First visit from Robert Browning.

1863 Labour of writing *Romola* completed (June); first edition published (July); serialization ends (Aug.). Purchases The Priory (Aug.) and moves in (Nov.). Thornton Lewes goes to Natal.

1864 Third visit to Italy with Lewes, accompanied by Frederic Burton. Conceives idea of *The Spanish Gypsy* in Venice and begins to work on it. 'Brother Jacob' published in *Cornhill*.

1865 Lewes makes her suspend work on *Gypsy* on account of her depression. Takes up journalism again, writing articles for the *Pall Mall Gazette* and the *Fortnightly*. Starts to compose *Felix Holt*. Holiday in Normandy and Brittany (Aug.)

1866 Accepts Blackwood's offer of £5,000 for *Felix Holt*, published in June. Leaves with

Die Leute von Seldwyla, and Meredith's *The Shaving of Shagpat* published. Freud and G. B. Shaw born.

Indian Mutiny. Baudelaire's *Les Fleurs du mal*, E. B. Browning's *Aurora Leigh*, Mrs Gaskell's *Life of Charlotte Brontë*, and Trollope's *Barchester Towers* published. Birth of Conrad.

Indian Mutiny suppressed. Government of India Act transfers British rule in India to the Crown. *English Woman's Journal* launched.

Darwin's *On the Origin of Species*, Smiles's *Self-Help*, and Tennyson's *Idylls of the King* published.

Unification of Italy. Source of the Nile discovered. Serialization of *Great Expectations* begins. Wilkie Collins's *The Woman in White* and Hawthorne's *The Marble Faun* published.

Outbreak of American civil war. Death of Prince Albert. Turgenev's *Fathers and Sons* published. Death of Elizabeth Barrett Browning.

Bismarck becomes Chancellor of Prussia. M. E. Braddon's *Lady Audley's Secret*, Wilkie Collins's *No Name*, Flaubert's *Salammbô*, Hugo's *Les Misérables*, Christina Rossetti's *Goblin Market*, and Ruskin's *Unto this Last* published.

Lincoln's Gettysburg Address. First underground railway opened in London. Death of Thackeray. Mrs Gaskell's *Sylvia's Lovers* published.

First Socialist International meets in London. Dickens's *Our Mutual Friend* and Tolstoy's *War and Peace* begin publication. Newman's *Apologia pro Vita Sua* and Trollope's *Can You Forgive Her?* published.

End of American civil war and assassination of Abraham Lincoln. Death of Mrs Gaskell. Matthew Arnold's *Essays in Criticism*, Lewis Carroll's *Alice in Wonderland*, and Swinburne's *Atalanta in Calydon* published.

Prussian victory over Austria at Sadowa. Dostoyevsky's *Crime and Punishment*, Mrs

Time Chart

Lewes for holiday in Holland, Belgium, and Germany (June). Takes up work on *Gypsy* again. Sets out with Lewes for France and Spain (Dec.).

1867 Journey to South-West France and tour of Spain (until Mar.). Continues work on *Gypsy*. She and Lewes return to Germany (Aug.–Sept.) to revisit 'scenes of cherished memories'. Writes 'Address to Working Men, by Felix Holt' for *Blackwood's* (Nov.)

1868 'Address' published (Jan.). Donates £50 to Emily Davies's scheme for Girton College, Cambridge. *The Spanish Gypsy* published (May). Two months' holiday with Lewes in Switzerland and the Black Forest (May–July). Visited by Darwin (Nov.).

1869 Begins work on *Middlemarch*. Fourth visit to Italy with Lewes (Mar.–Apr.). Meets John Walter Cross for first time in Rome. Begins correspondence with Harriet Beecher Stowe. Helps nurse Thornton Lewes, invalided home from Natal. First visit from Henry James. Death of Thornton (Oct.) leaves sense of 'a permanently closer relationship with death'.

1870 Last visit from Dickens (Mar.). Travels to Berlin and Vienna with Lewes where both are enthusiastically received (Mar.–May). Holiday on East Coast (June–July). Starts a story 'Miss Brooke', later to become part of *Middlemarch*.

1871 First visit from Turgenev. Takes cottage at Shottermill, Hampshire (Apr.–Aug.), where she meets Tennyson for first time and continues to work on *Middlemarch*. First instalment of *Middlemarch* published (Dec.).

1872 *Middlemarch* instalments well received. Three-month stay at Redhill, Surrey (May–July). Travels with Lewes to Germany for three weeks at Bad Homburg, where she writes Finale to *Middlemarch* (Sept.–Oct.). Final instalment of *Middlemarch* published (Dec.).

1873 Reading books on Judaism in preparation for a new novel, *Daniel Deronda*. Takes two months' holiday in France and Germany with Lewes (June–Aug.).

1874 First attack of kidney pain (Feb.). *The Legend of Jubal and Other Poems* and one-volume edition of *Middlemarch* published (May). Spends summer at Redhill, Surrey, working on *Deronda* (June–Sept.). Takes

Gaskell's *Wives and Daughters*, and Swinburne's *Poems and Ballads* published.

Second Reform Act. Dual Monarchy of Austria-Hungary established. Marx's *Das Kapital* (vol. i), Ibsen's *Peer Gynt*, Meredith's *Vittoria*, Trollope's *The Last Chronicle of Barset*, and Zola's *Thérèse Raquin* published.

Disraeli's first ministry followed by Gladstone's. Trade Union congress founded. Last public hangings in England. Browning's *The Ring and the Book*, Wilkie Collins's *The Moonstone*, Louisa May Alcott's *Little Women*, and Dostoyevsky's *The Idiot* published.

Girton College for Women founded at Cambridge. Opening of Suez Canal. Arnold's *Culture and Anarchy*, Blackmore's *Lorna Doone*, Flaubert's *L'Education sentimentale*, and John Stuart Mill's *On the Subjection of Women* published.

Franco-Prussian war. Prussian victory at Sedan. End of Second Empire and establishment of Third Republic in France. Siege of Paris. First Married Women's Property Act. Death of Dickens.

Proclamation of Second German Empire at Versailles. Paris Commune. Education Act introduces primary education for all. Hardy's *Desperate Remedies*, Meredith's *The Adventures of Harry Richmond*, and Zola's *La Fortune des Rougon* (first in *Les Rougon-Macquart* series) published. Birth of Proust.

Hardy's *Under the Greenwood Tree* and Nietzsche's *Birth of Tragedy* published.

Pater's *Studies in the History of the Renaissance* and Rimbaud's *Une saison en enfer* published. Tolstoy's *Anna Karenina* begins to appear.

Gladstone resigns; Disraeli's second administration begins. Hardy's *Far from the Madding Crowd* published. James Thomson's 'The City of Dreadful Night' appears.

two weeks' holiday with Lewes in Paris and Brussels (Oct.).

1875 Further kidney attacks. Spends summer at Rickmansworth, Hertfordshire, writing *Deronda* (June–Sept.). Receives news of death of Bertie Lewes in South Africa (July). Two weeks' holiday in Wales (Sept.–Oct.).

Disraeli buys controlling interest in Suez Canal for Britain. Uprising against Turkish rule in the Balkans. Henry James's *Roderick Hudson* and Trollope's *The Way We Live Now* published. Death of Kingsley.

1876 Publication of *Daniel Deronda* in eight monthly instalments begins (Feb.). Finishes writing *Deronda* and sets off with Lewes for holiday in France and Switzerland (June–Aug.). Cross finds them a country house, The Heights at Witley in Surrey, which they buy (Dec.).

Queen Victoria proclaimed Empress of India. Massacres of Christians in Turkish Bulgaria. Alexander Bell invents telephone. Meredith's *Beauchamp's Career* and Trollope's *The Prime Minister* published. Death of George Sand.

1877 Agreement with Blackwood for Cabinet Edition of her works. Meets Cosima and Richard Wagner, and sees much of Tennyson. Spends summer at Witley (June–Oct.). One-volume edition of *Deronda* published.

Russo-Turkish war. Henry James's *The American* and Zola's *L'Assommoir* published.

1878 Publication of Cabinet Edition begins with *Romola* (Jan.). Returns to Witley for the summer (June–Nov.). Lewes's health deteriorates. Four-day visit to the Bullock-Halls near Cambridge, where Turgenev is also a guest. Lewes, terminally ill, sends manuscript of first part of *Impressions of Theophrastus Such* to Blackwood. Death of Lewes at The Priory from cancer (30 Nov.). Death of Anna Cross, John Cross's mother (9 Dec.).

Congress of Berlin to settle the Eastern Question. Fontane's *Vor dem Sturm* and Hardy's *The Return of the Native* published.

1879 Intense and solitary mourning for Lewes. Prepares his *Problems of Life and Mind* for publication. Accepts visit from Cross (Mar.). *Impressions of Theophrastus Such* published (May). Founds a studentship at Cambridge as memorial to Lewes. Grows closer to Cross. Death of John Blackwood (Oct.).

Zulu war. Ibsen's *A Doll's House*, Henry James's *Daisy Miller*, Meredith's *The Egoist*, and Stevenson's *Travels with a Donkey in the Cevennes* published.

1880 Cross proposes marriage for third time and is accepted (Apr.). Marriage at St George's, Hanover Square (6 May). Honeymoon in France, Italy, and Germany (May–July). Reconciliation with brother Isaac. Move to 4 Cheyne Walk (3 Dec.). Attends concert and catches chill (18 Dec.). Rapidly declines with laryngitis and kidney pain and dies at Cheyne Walk (22 Dec.). Buried in Highgate Cemetery (29 Dec.).

Disraeli resigns. Parnell demands Home Rule for Ireland. First Anglo-Boer war. Death of Flaubert. Zola's *Le Roman expérimentale* and Hardy's *The Trumpet-Major* published.

PICTURE ACKNOWLEDGEMENTS